SPECIALIZED AREAS [SECTIONS 4100–4250]

Introduction to Accounting Recommendations that Apply only to Not-for-profit Organizations

NOT-FOR-PROFIT ORGANIZATIONS

Introduction to Accounting Guidelines

ACCOUNTING GUIDELINES

Intermediate Accounting

SEVENTH CANADIAN EDITION

Intermediate Accounting

Donald E. Kieso, PhD, CPA
KPMG Peat Marwick Emeritus Professor of Accounting
Northern Illinois University
DeKalb, Illinois

Jerry J. Weygandt, PhD, CPA
Arthur Andersen Alumni Professor of Accounting
University of Wisconsin
Madison, Wisconsin

Terry D. Warfield, PhD
PricewaterhouseCoopers Research Scholar
University of Wisconsin
Madison, Wisconsin

Nicola M. Young, MBA, FCA

Halifax, Nova Scotia

Irene M. Wiecek, CA
University of Toronto
Toronto, Ontario

John Wiley & Sons Canada, Ltd.

National Library of Canada Cataloguing in Publication Data

Intermediate accounting / Donald E. Kieso… [et al.]—7th Canadian ed.

Includes index.
ISBN 0-470-83372-6 (v. 1).—ISBN 0-470-83373-4 (v. 2)

1. Accounting. I. Kieso, Donald E.

HF5635.I573 2004   657'.044   C2003-905287-7

Production Credits
Editorial Manager: Karen Staudinger
Publishing Services Director: Karen Bryan
Sr. Marketing Manager: Janine Daoust
New Media Editor: Elsa Passera
Developmental Editors: Leanne Rancourt and Amanjeet Chauhan
Formatting: Quadratone Graphics Ltd. (Heidi Palfrey)
Cover Design: Interrobang Graphic Design
Cover Photo: Kitchin and Hurst/Firstlight
Printing & Binding: Tri-Graphic Printing Limited

Printed and bound in Canada
10 9 8 7 6 5 4 3 2 1

John Wiley & Sons Canada, Ltd.
6045 Freemont Blvd.
Mississauga, Ontario   L5R 4J3
Visit our website at: www.wiley.com/canada

Dedicated to our husbands

  John and George

and to our children

  Hilary

  Tim

  Megan

  Nicholas, and

  Katherine

*for their support, encouragement, and
tolerance throughout the writing of this book;
and to the many wonderful students who have
passed through our Intermediate Accounting
classrooms. We, too, have learned from you.*

About the Authors

Canadian Edition

Nicola M. Young, MBA, FCA is a Professor of Accounting in the Sobey School of Business at Saint Mary's University in Halifax, Nova Scotia where her teaching responsibilities have varied from the introductory offering to final year advanced financial courses to the survey course in the Executive MBA program. She is the recipient of teaching awards, and has contributed to the academic and administrative life of the university through chairing the Department of Accounting, membership on the Board of Governors, the Pension and other Committees. Professor Young has been associated with the Atlantic School of Chartered Accountancy for over twenty-five years in a variety of roles, including program and course development, teaching, and program reform. In addition to contributions to the accounting profession at the provincial level, Professor Young has served on national boards of the Canadian Institute of Chartered Accountants (CICA) dealing with licensure and education. For the last twelve years, she has worked with the CICA's Public Sector Accounting Board (PSAB) as an Associate, as a member and chair of the Board, and as chair and member of PSAB Task Forces.

Irene M. Wiecek, CA is a faculty member of the Joseph L. Rotman School of Management at the University of Toronto where she teaches accounting courses at all levels in various programs including the Commerce Program, the Master of Management & Professional Accounting Program (MMPA) and the MBA Program. The Associate Director of the MMPA Program for many years, she was recently appointed Co-Director of the ICAO/Rotman Centre for Innovation in Accounting Education. Irene is involved in professional accounting education both at the Institute of Chartered Accountants of Ontario and the CICA, teaching and developing case/program material in various programs including the ICAO School of Accountancy and the CICA In-depth GAAP course. In the area of standard setting, she is Chair of the Canadian Academic Accounting Association Financial Accounting Exposure Draft Response Committee. Irene is a member of the CICA Qualifications Committee which provides leadership, direction and standards for admission into the CA profession.

U.S. Edition

Donald E. Kieso, Ph.D., C.P.A., received his bachelor's degree from Aurora University and his doctorate in accounting from the University of Illinois. He has served as chairman of the Department of Accountancy and is currently the KPMG Peat Marwick Emeritus Professor of Accountancy at Northern Illinois University. He has done postdoctorate work as a Visiting Scholar at the University of California at Berkeley and is a recipient of NIU's Teaching Excellence Award and four Golden Apple Teaching Awards. Professor Kieso has served as a member of the Board of Directors of the Illinois CPA Society, the AACSB's Accounting Accreditation Committees, the State of Illinois Comptroller's Commission, as Secretary-Treasurer of the Federation of Schools of Accountancy, and as Secretary-Treasurer of the American Accounting Association. He served as a charter member of the national Accounting Education Change Commission. He received the Outstanding Accounting Educator Award from the Illinois CPA Society, in 1992 he received the FSA's Joseph A. Silvoso Award of Merit, and the NIU Foundation's Humanitarian Award for Service to Higher Education.

Jerry J. Weygandt, Ph.D., C.P.A., is Arthur Andersen Alumni Professor of Accounting at the University of Wisconsin-Madison. He holds a Ph.D. in accounting from the University of Illinois. Articles by Professor Weygandt have appeared in the *Accounting Review, Journal of Accounting Research, Accounting Horizons, Journal of Accountancy,* and other academic and professional journals. These articles have examined such financial reporting issues as accounting for price-level adjustments, pensions, convertible securities, stock option contracts, and interim reports. He has served on numerous committees of the American Accounting Association and as a member of the editorial board of the *Accounting Review*; he also has served as President and Secretary-Treasurer of the American Accounting Association. In addition, he has been actively involved with the American Institute of Certified Public Accountants and has been a member of the Accounting Standards Executive Committee (AcSEC) of that organization. He has served on the FASB task force that examined the reporting issues related to accounting for income taxes and is presently a trustee of the Financial Accounting Foundation. Professor Weygandt has received the Chancellor's Award for Excellence in Teaching and the Beta Gamma Sigma Dean's Teaching Award. He is on the board of directors of M & I Bank of Southern Wisconsin and the Dean Foundation. He is the recipient of the Wisconsin Institute of CPA's Outstanding Educator's Award and the Lifetime Achievement Award. In 2001, he received the American Accounting Association's Outstanding Accounting Educator Award.

Terry D. Warfield, Ph.D., is Associate Professor of Accounting at the University of Wisconsin-Madison. He received a B.S. and M.B.A. from Indiana University and a Ph.D. in accounting from the University of Iowa. Professor Warfield's area of expertise is financial reporting, and prior to his academic career, he worked for five years in the banking industry. He served as the Academic Accounting Fellow in the Office of the Chief Accountant at the U.S. Securities and Exchange Commission in Washington, D.C., from 1995-1996. While on the staff, he worked on projects related to financial instruments and financial institutions, and he helped coordinate a symposium on intangible asset financial reporting. Professor Warfield's primary research interests concern financial accounting standards and disclosure policies. He has published scholarly articles in *The Accounting Review, Journal of Accounting and Economics, Research in Accounting Regulation,* and *Accounting Horizons,* and he has served on the editorial boards of *The Accounting Review, Accounting Horizons,* and *Issues in Accounting Education.* He has served on the Financial Accounting Standards Committee of the American Accounting Association (Chair 1995-1996) and the AAA-FASB Research Conference Committee. Professor Warfield has received teaching awards at both the University of Iowa and the University of Wisconsin, and he was named to the Teaching Academy at the University of Wisconsin in 1995.

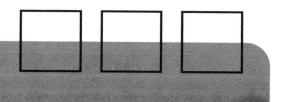

Preface

The first Canadian edition of *Intermediate Accounting* made its appearance over twenty years ago. Over the years it has changed, as have the many students who have used it. This edition represents another step in the metamorphosis of the textbook, with changes that reflect the way accounting is currently practised and the way in which students come to understand these concepts and procedures.

As always, we have aimed for a balanced discussion of the concepts and the procedures so that these elements reinforce one another. We have focused on the rationale behind transactions before discussing the accounting and reporting for those transactions. As with previous editions, we have thoroughly updated and revised every chapter to include coverage of all of the latest developments in the accounting profession and practice. In addition, we have included features to make all of this coverage even more understandable and relevant to today's accounting student. We have completely updated the look of the text, added new pedagogical features, enhanced the technology package that accompanies the text, and we continue to emphasize the use of company data and examples so that students easily relate what they are learning to the real world of business.

Based on extensive reviews and interactions with intermediate accounting instructors and students from across the country, we have introduced new features to help students learn and made content changes to ensure that Kieso, Weygandt, Warfield, Young, Wiecek, *Intermediate Accounting* sets the standard for currency, continuing to reflect the most up-to-date standards and reasons for their evolution.

NEW FEATURES

Student-friendly Design

We are pleased to present the concepts of intermediate accounting in an all-new four-colour design. We believe this student-friendly look will help to ease the transition into this more complex course. The use of colour also allows us to better highlight the pedagogical features and provide clear scans of the financial statements we use to illustrate the concepts presented thereby enhancing the realism even further and ensuring accuracy.

Enhanced Pedagogical Structure

Four new features have been introduced to the text's already solid pedagogical structure. We have enhanced our chapter openings even further with the introduction of new feature stories that introduce students to the concepts about to be discussed through real Canadian business situations. Throughout each chapter students are asked "What do the Numbers Mean?" and are presented with discussions applying accounting concepts to business contexts. These short breaks in the text will help students fully appreciate, from a business perspective, the impact of accounting on decision-making. In addition, a "Perspectives" section has been added to most chapters. This section discusses the effect on the financial statements of many of the accounting choices made by corporate management, alerting students to look behind the numbers. Finally, the accounting equation has been inserted in the margin next to key journal entries to help students understand the impact of each transaction on the financial position and cash flows of the company.

What do the Numbers Mean?

New Cases

New case material has been incorporated to reinforce the importance of in-context, applied decision-making. In addition to understanding the mechanics and theory of accounting, students also need to be sensitized to the fact that accounting decisions are not made in a vacuum. They involve businesses and people with biases, problems, and complexities. The cases feature both real companies and fictitious scenarios. The former allows us to expose students to reading and interpreting real financial statement excerpts. The latter allows us to develop the financial reporting environment scenario more fully, giving students insight into the thought processes that might occur behind the scenes in financial reporting. The "Integrative Cases" that appear in many of the chapters incorporate several issues in each case. These issues draw from material in other chapters in order to help students build issue identification skills. Finally, we have added a "Case Primer" on the Digital Tool which provides a framework for case analysis.

Integration of Ethics Coverage

Rather than featuring ethics coverage and problem material in isolation, we have introduced a new ethics icon to highlight ethical issues as they are discussed within each chapter. This icon also appears beside each exercise, problem, or case where ethical issues must be dealt with in relation to all kinds of accounting situations.

Increased Technology

Kieso continues to provide the most comprehensive and useful technology package available for the intermediate course. With this edition, there are three key components to the technology package.

Interactive Homework is available to all students at the text website. This new feature allows them to work the problems indicated in the text with the Interactive Homework icon on-line. They will be able to try the questions an unlimited number of times as the variables presented will change with each try. They will also get instant feedback so they know how they are doing.

Interactive Homework

eGrade is an expanded version of Interactive Homework that provides instructors with all of the end-of-chapter exercises and problems, allowing them to create the assignments they want. With this added instructor involvement, attempts at completing the assignments are recorded in a gradebook where the progress of each student can be tracked.

We have enhanced the *Digital Tool.* This collection of useful tools is now accessed from the text website using the password provided in the back of each text. New to this edition are interactive tutorials on the accounting cycle, interest capitalization, and more. Also featured are a case primer, demonstration problems, and expanded ethics coverage.

CONTINUING FEATURES

Many things have contributed to the success of Kieso over the last twenty years. Chief among these are its real-world emphasis and its currency and accuracy.

Real-World Emphasis

Since intermediate accounting is a course in which students must understand the application of accounting principles and techniques in practice, we strive to include as many real-world examples as possible.

Currency and Accuracy

Accounting changes at a rapid pace—a pace that has increased in recent years. An up-to-date book is more important than ever. As in past editions, we have endeavored to make this edition the most up-to-date and accurate text available.

The following list outlines the revision and improvements made in the chapters of this volume.

Chapter 1

- New *Handbook* material on GAAP hierarchy acknowledging the vastly expanded accounting body of knowledge.

- Coverage of the impact of SOX and new CSA draft requirements.

- Update on global harmonization of accounting standards.

Chapter 2

- New *Handbook*/Exposure Draft material on Comprehensive Income, Financial Instruments, MD&A Guidance on Preparation and Disclosure, and Consolidation of Variable Interest Entities (discussed under the economic entity concept).

- New focus on the historical cost principle as a valuation principle in transition. The new standards on Financial Instruments advocate fair value as a valuation method of choice.

- Introduction of sections on Making Accounting Choices and Issue Identification to help students with case analysis as well as real-life decision-making.

- Sections on Financial Engineering and Fraudulent Financial Reporting and the slippery slope that financial preparers find themselves on once they begin to let financial statement outcomes affect financial reporting decisions.

Chapter 3

- Former Appendix 3B (cash based versus accrual based accounting) moved to chapter 4 to allow a tie in with earnings from operations.

Chapter 4

- New *Handbook*/Exposure Draft material on Comprehensive Income and Disposal of Long-lived Assets and Discontinued Operations.

- Appendix 4A (accounting for discontinued operations) has been eliminated based on the new *Handbook* Section 3475 which simplifies the accounting.

- Inclusion of new material on understanding a company's business model. Transparent financial statements must present the underlying business of the company in an understandable way and therefore, students must understand how a company earns its income.

- Material on quality of earnings updated with a stronger link to the conceptual framework material in chapter 2.

Chapter 5

- New *Handbook*/Exposure Draft material on Financial Instruments and Comprehensive Income.

- Discussion of classifications in the balance sheet expanded to include discussions on monetary versus nonmonetary and financial versus non-financial assets and liabilities.

- Decreased emphasis on the mechanics of the preparation of cash flow statements since this is covered in a later chapter. Increased emphasis on interpretation of the cash flow statement.

- Expansion of Appendix 5A to tie back to business model established in chapter 4. This section links the business model with the cash flow statement, tying it into the operating, investing and financing activities framework. The discussion emphasizes business risks and the importance of full disclosure of risks. It also links the concepts of business model and risks to ratio analysis.

Chapter 6

- New *EIC Abstract* material on revenue recognition.

- Incorporation of more material on complex transactions such as bundled and barter sales and sales where the seller is acting as an agent as opposed to a principal.

Chapter 7

- New *Handbook*/Exposure Draft material on Financial Instruments (parts related to Trading Securities).

- Temporary investments transferred to chapter 7 from chapter 10.

- Long-term accounts and notes receivable, including notes with unrealistic interest rates and imputed interest, transferred to chapter 10.

- Calculator and spreadsheet methods of calculating present values moved to the Digital Tool.

- Reduced coverage on compensating balances

- Section on secured borrowing downplayed on basis that the accounting is the same as for any asset used as security.

- Section on securitization of receivables expanded, but kept at an elementary level—significantly increased use of this by business.

Chapter 8

- More emphasis on the steps needed to get to the inventory number reported on the balance sheet.

- Basket purchases transferred to this chapter from chapter 9 as it deals with a cost issue.

Chapter 9

- Disclosures added for companies using the retail method.

- Expanded discussion of inventory turnover and effect of choices in accounting for inventories.

Chapter 10

- New *Handbook*/Exposure Draft Material on Financial Instruments (recognition and measurement and comprehensive income) and Differential Reporting.

- Chapter restructured to cover only long-term investments, including long-term accounts and notes receivable previously covered in chapter 7.

- Coverage in chapter in line with the Exposure Draft on Financial Instruments. A summary of the existing standards for investments, with a description of the major upcoming changes now forms the appendix.

Chapter 11

- New *Handbook* material on Asset Retirement Obligations and Exposure Draft material on Nonmonetary Exchanges.

- Coverage of the cost of natural resource assets transferred here from Chapter 12.

- All calculations dealing with interest capitalization now in the appendix to the chapter. The emphasis in the chapter material is the choice available and the difference it could make to financial statements.

- New section on asset retirement costs included in the original cost of an asset with the details of calculation in chapter 14.

- The whole area of asset exchanges rewritten in order to condense it and make it clearer.

- Increased emphasis on the managing of income by capitalizing instead of expensing.

- The dispositions coverage is now in chapter 12.

Chapter 12

- New *Handbook* material on Impairment of Long-lived Assets and Disposal of long-lived Assets and Discontinued Operations.

- The capitalization of costs into the depletion base moved to chapter 11.

- Updated coverage of asset impairment standards and the rules for subsequent measurement.

- Disposals now covered in this chapter, rather than chapter 11.

Chapter 13

- New *Handbook* material on Impairment of Long-lived Assets, and EICs on Identification of Reporting Units, and Unit of accounting for testing impairment

- Structure of chapter changed to categorize intangibles by the classifications used in the Handbook.

- Improved discussion of what "indefinite life" means.

- Expansion of discussion of what factors should be considered in determining useful life.

- Discussion of technology-related intangibles provided.

- Discussion on the effect of companies' changing from old standards to new standards, especially with goodwill.

- Perspectives section on intellectual capital and knowledge assets plus warnings about financial statement analysis when comparing companies with significant intangibles.

ACKNOWLEDGMENTS

We thank the users of our sixth edition, including the many students who contributed to this revision through their comments and instructive criticism. Special thanks are extended to the reviewers of and contributors to our seventh edition manuscript and supplements.

Manuscript Reviewers for this seventh edition were:

Cécile Ashman
Algonquin College

Maria Belanger
Algonquin College

David T. Carter
University of Waterloo

Johan De Rooy
University of British Columbia

Esther Deutsch
Ryerson University

Carolyn Doni
Cambrian College

David Fleming
George Brown College

H.T. Hao
McMaster University

Mary A. Heisz
University of Western Ontario

Darrell Herauf
Carleton University

Johnny Jermias
Simon Fraser University

Dominique Lecocq
York University

Valorie Leonard
Laurentian University

Cameron Morrill
University of Manitoba

Clifton Philpott
Kwantlen University College

Joe Pidutti
Durham College

Wendy Roscoe
Concordia University

Jo-Anne Ryan
Nipissing University

David J. Sale
Kwantlen University College

Helen Vallee
Kwantlen University College

Betty Wong
Athabasca University

Appreciation is also extended to colleagues at the Rotman School of Management, University of Toronto and Saint Mary's University who provided input, suggestions and support, especially Joel Amernic and Dick Chesley—who have provided inspiration through many high-spirited debates on financial reporting theory and practice—and Peter Thomas, who has shared many teaching insights over the years!

Many thanks to the staff at John Wiley and Sons Canada, Ltd. who are superb: Publisher John Horne and Editorial Manager Karen Staudinger who have been so supportive throughout; Karen Bryan, Publishing Services Director, for her incredible efforts; Elsa Passera, New Media Editor who took on the Digital Tool; Carl Comeau and Darren Lalonde, Sales Managers; Janine Daoust, Sr. Marketing Manager; and of course all the sales representatives who introduce us and the text to the many talented instructors across the country. They are a committed group of capable people who feed back concerns, questions, and kudos to help us continually improve. The editorial contributions of Laurel Hyatt and Alan Johnstone were also appreciated. We are particularly grateful to Leanne Rancourt and Amanjeet Chauhan who dealt with us on an almost daily basis and kept everything on track.

Special thanks also to Margaret Forbes, Ann Bigelow, Sibongile Mukandi, and Sophie (Zhi Hua) He for their contributions to the Digital Tool and research services, as well as Cécile Ashman, Maria Belanger, Lynn deGrace, Brock Dykeman, Majidul Islam, Gabriela Schneider, Enola Stoyle, and Lisa White who contributed to the related supplements.

We appreciate the co-operation of the staff of the Accounting Standards Board of the Canadian Institute of Chartered Accountants, especially that of its Director, Ron Salole, as well as that of the CICA itself in allowing us to quote from their materials. We thank Intrawest Corporation for permitting us to use its 2003 Annual Report for our specimen financial statements.

Finally, we would like to thank Bruce Irvine and Harold Silvester who, through twenty years of association with and five editions of this text, provided such a strong foundation. Their enthusiasm for intermediate accounting and their sharing of this with so many students set a standard for the rest of us to follow.

If this book helps teachers instill in their students an appreciation of the challenges, value, and limitations of accounting, if it encourages students to evaluate critically and understand financial accounting theory and practice, and if it prepares students for advanced study, professional examinations, and the successful and ethical pursuit of their careers in accounting or business, then we will have attained our objective.

Suggestions and comments from users of this book are always appreciated. We have striven to produce an error-free text, but if anything has slipped through the variety of checks undertaken, please let us know so that corrections can be made to subsequent printings.

Irene M. Wiecek
TORONTO, ONTARIO

Nicola M. Young
HALIFAX, NOVA SCOTIA

February 2004

BRIEF CONTENTS

CONTENTS

CHAPTER 13
Goodwill and Other Intangible Assets, 667

TABLES

Increased Awareness

Recent corporate scandals and the subsequent regulatory fallout have changed the world of financial reporting. Canada's own energy giant, Enbridge Inc., has not been immune.

"The Enron fiasco, coupled with Worldcom and a number of others, has led to significant changes in regulatory practice, and all public companies are affected by that," says Scott Wilson, senior vice-president and controller at Enbridge.

As a foreign private issuer listed on the New York Stock Exchange, Calgary-based Enbridge is subject to the requirements of the U.S. Sarbanes-Oxley Act. But, as Wilson points out, the Canadian regulatory system is making changes in reporting and governance requirements as well.

Enbridge's financial reporting has always been transparent, he says. What has changed is managements' and investors' awareness and scrutiny of the financial information. Investment analysts are looking for more information than they used to, Wilson says.

In an effort to be fully transparent, Enbridge has an investor website that includes all its financial information. The company has also recently separated its quarterly news release information from the quarterly MD&A (management discussion and analysis) reports that go to the securities commission. The rules for the securities document are more stringent, requiring more technical information. "It's not a user-friendly document," Wilson says.

Coupled with the increased investor relations is the need to keep up with accounting standards. "The changes that are coming out of the accounting regulatory bodies, particularly in the U.S., are fast and furious," Wilson says. "We are a U.S. registrant, and we reconcile our financial statements to U.S. GAAP, so we have to comply with all of those U.S. requirements."

Staying abreast of these changes has heightened management's focus on accounting. Wilson says, "The president of this company and those of many public companies are much more knowledgeable of accounting standards and requirements than they would have been in the past."

CHAPTER 1

The Canadian Financial Reporting Environment

Learning Objectives

After studying this chapter, you should be able to:

1. Describe the essential characteristics of accounting.
2. Identify the major financial statements and other means of financial reporting.
3. Explain how accounting assists in the efficient use of scarce resources.
4. Explain the meaning of "stakeholder" and identify key stakeholders in financial reporting.
5. Identify the objective of financial reporting.
6. Explain the notion of management bias with respect to financial reporting.
7. Understand the importance of user needs in the financial reporting process.
8. Explain the need for accounting standards.
9. Identify the major entities that influence the standard-setting process and explain how they influence financial reporting.
10. Explain the meaning of generally accepted accounting principles (GAAP).
11. Explain the significance of professional judgement in applying GAAP.
12. Understand issues related to ethics and financial accounting.
13. Identify some of the challenges facing accounting.

North American financial reporting systems are among the best in the world. Our commitment to maintaining strong financial reporting systems is paramount because in this changing business world, relevant and reliable information must be provided so that our capital markets work efficiently. In the past several years, our financial reporting systems have been overhauled and significantly strengthened. The purpose of this chapter is to explain the environment of financial reporting and the many factors affecting it. The content and organization of the chapter are as follows:

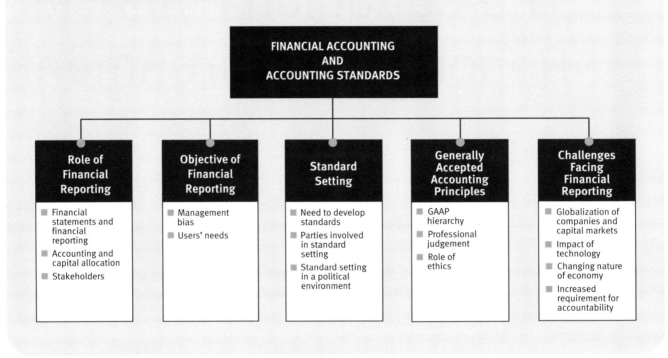

ROLE OF FINANCIAL REPORTING

Like other human activities and disciplines, accounting is largely a product of its environment. The environment of accounting consists of social, economic, political, legal conditions, restraints, and influences that vary from time to time. As a result, accounting objectives and practices are not the same today as they were in the past. **Accounting theory and practice have evolved and will continue to evolve to meet changing demands and influences.**

Over the past several years, the accounting landscape has changed dramatically, being shaped by such spectacular corporate failures such as WorldCom Inc., Enron, and Arthur Andersen. WorldCom, a telecom company, had pre-bankruptcy assets of over $100 billion (U.S.) and is the largest company to file for bankruptcy protection in U.S. history. Enron, an energy trader, formerly the seventh largest corporation in America, was at the time the second largest company to file for bankruptcy protection in the U.S. Both

WorldCom and Enron misrepresented the financial position and results of operations in their financial statements. Andersen was one of the five largest public accounting firms in the world. The firm ended up closing its doors in 2002 after being charged with obstruction of justice relating to Enron, then one of its largest clients. The accounting profession is still dealing with the fallout from these events.

Objective 1
Describe the essential characteristics of accounting.

Accounting may best be defined by describing its three essential characteristics: (1) **identification, measurement, and communication of financial information about** (2) **economic entities to** (3) **interested persons**. These characteristics have described accounting for hundreds of years. Yet, in the last 30 years, economic entities have increased so greatly in size and complexity, and the interested persons have increased so greatly in number and diversity, that the responsibility placed on the accounting profession is greater today than ever before.

Financial Statements and Financial Reporting

Financial accounting (financial reporting) is the process that culminates in the preparation of financial reports for the enterprise as a whole for use by both **internal and external** parties. Users of these financial reports include investors, creditors, and others. In contrast, **managerial accounting** is the process of identifying, measuring, analysing, and **communicating financial information** to **internal** decision-makers. This information may take varied forms, such as cost benefit analyses and forecasts needed by management to plan, evaluate, and control an organization's operations.

Objective 2
Identify the major financial statements and other means of financial reporting.

Financial statements are the principal means through which financial information is communicated to those outside an enterprise. These statements provide the firm's history, quantified in money terms. The financial statements most frequently provided are (1) the **balance sheet**, (2) the **income statement**, (3) the **statement of cash flows**, and (4) the **statement of owners' or shareholders' equity**. In addition, **note disclosures** are an integral part of each financial statement.

Some financial information is better provided or can only be provided through financial reporting other than financial statements. Examples include the president's letter or supplementary schedules in the corporate annual report, prospectuses, reports filed with government agencies, news releases, management's forecasts, and descriptions of an enterprise's social or environmental impact. Such information may be required by authoritative pronouncement, regulatory rule[1] or custom, or because management wishes to disclose it voluntarily. The primary focus of this textbook is the basic financial statements.

Accounting and Capital Allocation

Because **resources** are limited, people try to conserve them, use them effectively, and identify and encourage those who can make efficient use of them. Through an **efficient use of resources**, our standard of living increases.

Objective 3
Explain how accounting assists in the efficient use of scarce resources.

Markets, free enterprise, and competition determine whether a business will be successful and thrive. The accounting profession has the very significant responsibility of **measuring company performance** accurately and fairly on a timely basis. Accounting enables investors and creditors to **compare** the income and assets employed by companies. Investors can thus **assess the relative risks and returns** associated with investment

---

[1] All public companies must disclose certain information under provincial securities law. This information is captured by the provincial securities commissions under the Canadian umbrella organization, the Canadian Securities Administrators (CSA), and is available electronically at www.sedar.com.

opportunities and thereby channel resources (i.e., invest in these companies or lend them money) more effectively. This process of **capital allocation** works as follows:

Illustration 1-1

Capital Allocation Process

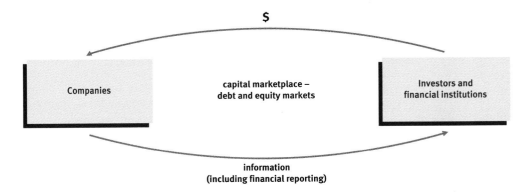

In Canada, the primary exchange mechanisms for allocating resources are **debt and equity markets**[2] as well as **financial institutions** such as banks.[3]

An effective process of capital allocation is critical to a healthy economy, which promotes productivity, encourages innovation, and provides an efficient and liquid market for buying and selling securities and obtaining and granting credit.[4] Unreliable and irrelevant information leads to **poor capital allocation**, which adversely affects the securities markets and economic growth. Reported accounting numbers affect the **transfer of resources** among companies and individuals. Consider the fact that stock prices generally rise when positive news (including financial information) is expected and/or released. **Credit rating agencies** use accounting and other information to rate companies' financial stability.[5] This gives investors and creditors **additional independent information** with which to make their decisions. A good rating can mean greater access to capital and at lower costs.

Stakeholders

Stakeholders are parties who have something at stake in the financial reporting environment, e.g., salary, job, investment, or reputation. Key stakeholders in the financial reporting environment include **traditional users** of financial information as well as **others**. In the stakeholder context, **users** may be more broadly defined to include not only parties who are directly relying on the financial information for resource allocation (such as investors and creditors) but also others who facilitate the efficient allocation of resources (such as financial analysts and regulators).

The broader definition of users includes anyone who **prepares, relies on, reviews, audits, or monitors financial information**. It includes investors, creditors, analysts, managers, employees, customers, suppliers, industry groups, unions, government departments

---

[2] The largest, most senior equity market in Canada is the Toronto Stock Exchange (TSX). The junior market—the TSX Venture Exchange (formerly the CDNX Stock Market)—was created in 2001 to handle startup companies. The Montreal Exchange, known as the Canadian Derivatives Exchange, is the prime market for derivatives and futures trading.

[3] According to a PricewaterhouseCoopers survey "Canadian Banks 2002," the six largest banks in Canada from largest to smallest are: Royal Bank of Canada, Bank of Nova Scotia, Toronto-Dominion Bank, Canadian Imperial Bank of Commerce, Bank of Montreal, and National Bank of Canada.

[4] AICPA Special Committee on Financial Reporting "Improving Business Reporting, A Customer Focus" (*Journal of Accountancy*, Supplement, October 1994).

[5] For example, institutions such as Dominion Bond Rating Service, Standard and Poor's, and Moody's rate issuers of bonds and preferred shares in the Canadian marketplace.

and ministers, the public in general (e.g., consumer groups), regulatory agencies, other companies, standard setters, as well as auditors, lawyers, and others. Illustration 1-2 shows the relationships among these stakeholders.

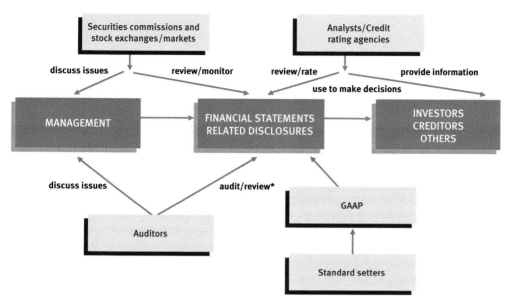

Selected Key Stakeholders in the Financial Reporting Environment

not all financial statements are required to be audited. In general, all companies whose shares or debt are **publicly traded or those whose assets/revenues exceed a certain size must have an audit and therefore comply with GAAP. Other companies may have their statements audited and/or comply with GAAP depending on **user needs.***

Company management **prepares** the financial statements. It has the best insight into the business and therefore knows what should be included in the financial statements. The statements are then **audited and reviewed** by auditors who may discuss with management how economic events and transactions have been communicated in the financial statements. The value added by the auditors lies in their independence. They act on behalf of the shareholders to ensure that management is properly accounting for the economic transactions. The auditors also **review** the information to ensure that it reflects sound accounting choices.

Investors and creditors **rely on** the financial statements to make decisions. It is up to these parties to scrutinize the information given. Standard setters **set generally accepted accounting principles (GAAP),** which are often used to prepare the financial statements. GAAP helps **reduce management bias** by providing direction as to how events should be accounted for. Securities commissions and stock exchanges **monitor** the financial statements to ensure full and plain disclosure of material information and to determine whether the companies may continue to list their shares on stock exchanges. Finally, the credit rating agencies and analysts **monitor and analyse** the information produced by the company, looking for signs of change, i.e., improved or deteriorated financial condition.

As noted above, the system provides **checks and balances** to ensure that the people with capital—the investors and creditors—have good information so that they can decide where best to invest or allocate their capital. The system does not always work, however. Because the system involves people, human behaviour is often a key unpredictable variable. People often act in their own **self-interest** rather than in the **best interest of the capital marketplace and hence the economy**.

Consider the much-publicized case of Enron. Enron was formed in 1985 through a merger, beginning life as a pipeline company. Its business changed over the years as energy wholesaling and trading overtook the pipeline operations. Revenues grew exponentially to more than $100 billion (U.S.) and the company reported profits of just under $1 billion (U.S.) by 2000. Enron's shares were trading at over $80 (U.S.). All this came to an abrupt

What do the Numbers Mean?

halt when the company declared bankruptcy in December 2001. Its shares were delisted by the New York Stock Exchange in January 2002. Since then, thousands of people have been affected by the fall of Enron, losing investments, jobs, and pensions.

Arthur Andersen, one of the top five **public accounting firms** in the world, was a direct casualty of the Enron bankruptcy, closing its offices later in 2002 after being convicted of obstructing justice in the ensuing government investigations. **Credit rating agencies** such as Moody's Investor Services and **analysts** also came under scrutiny, the government wanting to know why the rating agencies had not been able to determine much earlier that Enron was overextended.[6] **Investment banks** such as Citigroup and J.P. Morgan Chase were criticized for assisting Enron in setting up the very aggressive financing schemes that eventually led to its downfall.[7]

Why did the financial reporting system not function properly in this case? How did the capital marketplace allow so much capital to be channelled into a company that went bankrupt shortly thereafter? Where were the checks and balances? In hindsight, the fault rests with almost every player in the financial reporting system. **Self-interest** was a key factor.

Enron Management overstated the company's financial health, thus personally benefiting from bonuses and stock options. The **auditors** gave the company financial statements an unqualified audit report, indicating that the financial statements were fairly presented. During the time that they were doing the audit, they also earned millions of dollars in consulting fees. Were they truly independent? The **analysts** and **credit rating agencies** did not recognize and signal that the company was financially unsound (or recognized it but did not signal it in a timely manner to the marketplace). Here there was an independence issue also: many of the analysts worked for banks that were providing financing and selling other services to Enron. Could the analysts be objective in assessing Enron when they were working for institutions that were earning significant fees and other forms of income from them?

The **Securities and Exchange Commission**, although it collected the financial information from the company on a timely basis, failed to detect any problem. Finally, the **investors and creditors** invested their capital without really understanding what they were investing in. They did not really understand the significant risk that they were taking. Most of these stakeholders were overly keen on being involved with such a large, apparently successful company. They did not stop to ask whether Enron was just too good to be true. In hindsight, it was.

OBJECTIVE OF FINANCIAL REPORTING

Objective 5
Identify the objective of financial reporting.

To help establish a foundation for financial accounting and reporting, the accounting profession has articulated an overall objective of financial reporting by business enterprises. This is laid out in Illustration 1-3.

Note the emphasis on **resource (or capital) allocation** decisions and **assessment of management stewardship**.[8] In order to make resource allocation decisions, users look for information about **an enterprise's ability to earn income and generate future cash flows**, which will be used to meet obligations and generate a return on investment. In order to assess management stewardship, users traditionally look at **historical data** to **determine (in hindsight)** whether the decisions that management made regarding obtaining and using the company's resources are acceptable and **optimize shareholder**

---

[6] In January 2002, a U.S. Governmental Affairs Committee launched a broad investigation into the collapse. This committee studied the role of stakeholders, primarily the watchdogs in the capital marketplace, to determine what went wrong.

[7] U.S. Senate Permanent Subcommittee on Investigations Staff Report on Fishtail, Bacchus, Sundance and Slapshot: Four Enron Transactions Funded and Facilitated by U.S. Financial Institutions, (December 11, 2002).

[8] Management's duty to manage assets with care and trust is described as its fiduciary responsibility.

"The objective of financial statements is to communicate information that is useful to investors, members, contributors, creditors, and other users in making their resource allocation decisions and/or assessing management stewardship. Consequently, financial statements provide information about:

(a) an entity's economic resources, obligations, and equity/net assets;

(b) changes in an entity's economic resources, obligations, and equity/net assets; and

(c) the economic performance of the entity."

Source – *CICA Handbook*, Section 1000.15

Illustration 1-3

Objective of Financial Reporting

International Insight

The objectives of financial reporting differ across nations. Traditionally, the primary objective of accounting in many continental European nations and in Japan has been conformity with the law. In contrast, Canada, the U.S., the UK, the Netherlands, and many other nations hold the view that the primary objective is to provide information for investors. Insights into international standards and practices will be presented throughout the text.

wealth and value. Users may also attempt to **predict** the impact of current decisions made by management on the company's future financial health.

Management Bias

As previously mentioned, company **management** is responsible for preparing the financial statements and normally attests to this fact at the beginning of the financial statements. At Air Canada, M. Robert Peterson, Executive Vice-President and Chief Financial Officer, and Robert A. Milton, President and Chief Executive Officer, have both signed a statement to this effect for the Air Canada financial statements, which is shown in Illustration 1-4.

Management's Report

The consolidated financial statements have been prepared by management in accordance with generally accepted accounting principles and the integrity and objectivity of the data in these financial statements are management's responsibility. Management is also responsible for all other financial information and for ensuring that this information is consistent, where appropriate, with the information and data contained in the financial statements.

In support of its responsibility, management maintains a system of internal control to provide reasonable assurance as to the reliability of financial information and the safeguarding of assets. The Corporation has an internal audit department whose functions include reviewing internal controls and their application, on an ongoing basis.

The Board of Directors is responsible for ensuring that management fulfills its responsibilities for financial reporting and internal control and exercises this responsibility through the Audit Committee of the Board, which is composed of directors who are not employees of the Corporation. The Audit Committee meets with management, the internal auditors and the external auditors at least four times each year.

The external auditors, PricewaterhouseCoopers conduct an independent audit, in accordance with generally accepted auditing standards and express their opinion on the financial statements. Their audit includes a review and evaluation of the Corporation's system of internal control and appropriate tests and procedures to provide reasonable assurance that, in all material respects, the financial statements are presented fairly. The external auditors have full and free access to the Audit Committee of the Board and meet with it on a regular basis.

M. Robert Peterson
Executive Vice President
and Chief Financial Officer

Robert A. Milton
President and
Chief Executive Officer

Illustration 1-4

Air Canada's Management Report Acknowledging Responsibility for the Financial Statements

Companies have come increasingly under attack for preparing **biased information**, i.e., information that presents the company in its best light, as in the Enron case mentioned earlier. This is sometimes referred to as **aggressive financial reporting** (as compared with **conservative financial reporting**) and might take the form of overstated assets and/or net income, understated liabilities and/or expenses, or carefully selected note disclosures that emphasize only positive events.[9]

There are many reasons why financial statements might be the subject of management bias, including the fact that they give information to users about **management stewardship**, as previously mentioned. Managers' compensation is often based on net income or share value. There is also a strong desire to **meet financial analysts' expectations** and thus have continued access to capital markets. Financial analysts monitor earnings announcements carefully and compare them with their prior expectations. They post what they refer to as **"earnings surprises"** daily on their websites. Earnings surprises occur when a company reports net income figures that are different from what the market expects (prior expectations). The focus is on net income or earnings. If net income is lower than expected, this is a negative earnings surprise and the market will generally react in a negative manner, resulting in declining stock prices.[10]

Objective 6

Explain the notion of management bias with respect to financial reporting.

Another reason management might have a financial reporting bias is **to comply with contracts** entered into by the company. Many lending agreements and contracts require that certain benchmarks be met, often relating to financial stability or liquidity. These requirements often stipulate that the company maintain certain minimum financial ratios. The lenders then monitor compliance, requesting that the company submit periodic financial statements.

Users' Needs

Objective 7

Understand the importance of user needs in the financial reporting process.

The objective of financial reporting is to **provide useful information to users**. As noted in Illustration 1-2, investors and creditors are among the key users of financial information. Providing information that is useful to users is a challenging task given their **differing knowledge levels** and needs. **Institutional investors**[11] hold an increasing percentage of equity share holdings[12] and generally devote significant resources to managing their

---

[9] David Brown, Chairman of the Ontario Securities Commission (OSC), spoke at length on this topic in a speech entitled "Public Accounting at a Crossroads" in 1999. Arthur Levitt, Chair of the Securities and Exchange Commission (SEC), discussed his concerns over this issue in "Numbers Game," a major address to the New York University in 1998. Both the OSC and the SEC review financial statements and financial reporting practices in the course of ensuring that investors have "full and plain disclosure" of all material facts needed to make investment decisions. In their speeches, Mr. Brown and Mr. Levitt both cited specific cases where they felt that financial reporting practices were problematic.

[10] For instance, for quarterly earnings numbers released May 23, 2003, the Nasdaq website notes that there were 26 positive earnings surprises and 5 negative earnings surprises. Two companies met the expectations of analysts (no surprise). Positive earnings surprises included Electronic Boutique Holdings and GAP Inc. Selected negative earnings surprises noted for the same week included PSS World Medical Inc. and Quality Systems Inc.

[11] Institutional investors are corporate investors such as insurance companies, pension plans, mutual funds, and others. They are considered a separate class of investors due to their size, financial expertise, and the large size of the investments that they hold in other companies. In general, institutional investors have greater power than the average investor, for the above noted reasons.

[12] The Canadian Coalition for Good Governance (CCGG) is a group of institutional investors that controls over $350 billion in investments. Its members include many significant pension funds in Canada such as Alberta Teachers' Retirement Fund, Ontario Teachers' Pension Plan, OPSEU Pension Trust, as well as many significant mutual funds and financial institutions such as Mackenzie Financial Corp., RBC Global Investment Management, and TSL Global Asset Management. According to its website (www.ccgg.ca), CCGG was started in 2002 to "improve the performance of publicly traded corporations through the promotion of good governance practices across Canada." Pension funds, insurance companies, and mutual funds hold just under 50% of the total equity holdings for shares listed on the NYSE.

investment portfolios. Can preparers of financial information assume that the average individual investor has the same needs and knowledge level in terms of business and financial reporting as the institutional investor?

Meeting all user needs is made more challenging when coupled with the potential for management bias. If the financial statements are aggressively prepared, they might be misleading to potential investors, who may wish to see the company in the worst light **before** they invest (as opposed to after). Generally accepted accounting principles assume that users have a **reasonable knowledge** of business and accounting.

STANDARD SETTING

Need to Develop Standards

The main controversy in financial reporting is, "Whose rules should we play by, and what should they be?" The answer is not immediately clear because the users of financial statements have both **coinciding and conflicting needs** for information of various types. A **single set** of general-purpose financial statements is prepared with the **expectation** that the majority of these needs will be met. These statements are expected to present fairly the enterprise's financial operations.

As a result, accounting professions in various countries have attempted to develop a **set of standards** that are **generally accepted** and **universally practised**. Without these standards, each enterprise would have to develop its own standards, and readers of financial statements would have to familiarize themselves with every company's peculiar accounting and reporting practices. It would be almost impossible to prepare statements that could be compared.

This common set of standards and procedures is called generally accepted accounting principles (GAAP). The term "generally accepted" means either that an authoritative accounting rule-making body has established a reporting principle in a given area or that over time a given practice has been accepted as appropriate because of its universal application.[13] Although principles and practices have provoked both debate and criticism, most members of the financial community recognize them as the standards that over time have proven to be most useful. A more extensive discussion of what constitutes GAAP is presented later in this chapter.

8 Objective
Explain the need for accounting standards.

International Insight

Nations also differ in the degree to which they have developed national standards and consistent accounting practices. Professional accounting bodies were established in the Netherlands, the UK, Canada, and the U.S. in the nineteenth century. In contrast, public accountancy bodies were established in Hong Kong, Singapore, and Korea only in the last half-century.

Parties Involved in Standard Setting

Prior to 1900, single ownership was the predominant form of business organization in our economy. Financial reports emphasized **solvency and liquidity** and were limited to **internal use** and scrutiny by banks and other lending institutions. From 1900 to 1929, the growth of large corporations, with their absentee ownership, led to **increasing investment and speculation** in corporate stock. The stock market crashed in 1929 and contributed to the Great Depression. These events emphasized the need for **standardized and increased corporate disclosures** that would allow shareholders to make informed decisions.

A number of organizations are instrumental in developing financial reporting standards in Canada. The major organizations are:

1. Canadian Institute of Chartered Accountants (CICA) www.cica.ca

9 Objective
Identify the major entities that influence the standard-setting process and explain how they influence financial reporting.

---

[13] The terms "principles" and "standards" are used interchangeably in practice and throughout this textbook.

2. Provincial securities commissions such as the Ontario Securities Commission (OSC) www.osc.gov.on.ca

3. The Financial Accounting Standards Board (FASB) www.fasb.org and the Securities and Exchange Commission (SEC) www.sec.gov

4. International Accounting Standards Board (IASB) www.iasb.org

1. *Canadian Institute of Chartered Accountants (CICA)*

International Insight

The Canadian and U.S. legal systems are based on English common law, whereby the government generally allows professionals to make the rules. These rules (standards) are, therefore, developed in the private sector. Conversely, some countries follow codified law, which leads to government-run accounting systems.

The first official recommendations regarding standards of financial statement disclosure were not published until 1946. Today, the **Accounting Standards Board (AcSB)** of the **Canadian Institute of Chartered Accountants (CICA)** has primary responsibility for setting GAAP in Canada[14] and produces a variety of authoritative material, including the foremost source of GAAP, the *CICA Handbook*. The *CICA Handbook* was originally published in 1968 and now consists of five volumes of accounting and assurance guidance.[15]

The CICA AcSBs key objective is to ensure that the **framework for measurement and reporting facilitates the global flow of capital and serves the public interest** by enhancing relevance, quality, and credibility of information used for evaluating and improving organizational performance.[16] Note the emphasis on **global capital allocation** and **organizational performance**. Both aspects will be touched upon later in the chapter when emerging trends in the profession are discussed.

Two basic premises underlying the process of establishing financial accounting standards are: (1) the AcSB should be **responsive to the needs and viewpoints** of the **entire economic community**, not just the public accounting profession, and (2) it should **operate in full public view** through a "due process" system that gives interested persons ample opportunity to make their views known. The **Accounting Standards Oversight Council (AcSOC)** provides oversight to AcSB activities, setting the agenda and reporting to the public, among other things. Membership on the AcSB and the AcSOC draws from a wide range of groups interested or involved in the financial reporting process.[17]

The steps in Illustration 1-5 show the evolution of a typical addition or amendment to the *CICA Handbook*.

Due process, by definition, is a lengthy process. To react more quickly to current financial reporting issues, the AcSB established the **Emerging Issues Committee (EIC)**. The EIC is a standing committee, which meets several times each year. It studies issues presented to it by interested parties such as companies that need a ruling on an accounting issue that may not be dealt with in the *Handbook*. It also studies and clarifies *Handbook* wording and applicability. After careful consideration, the EIC produces **EIC Abstracts**, which are then incorporated into the *Handbook*. EIC Abstracts are considered a primary source of GAAP.

---

[14] The Canadian Business Corporations Act and Regulations (CBCA) Part XIV Financial Disclosure and Part 8 (paras. 70 and 71), as well as provincial corporations acts, require that most companies incorporated under these acts prepare financial statements in accordance with GAAP as prepared by the CICA.

[15] The *Handbook* is also available to students in CD format and to members on-line at www.cica.ca. With the rapid pace of change in standard setting, most members use the on-line source as their primary source of GAAP.

[16] "Leading change in the CA profession in Canada," (Toronto: CICA, 2000). In 1998, partially in response to the CICAs Inter-Institute Vision Task Force, the CICA Task Force on Standard Setting issued its final report. The report reaffirmed, among other things, the fact that standard setting should remain in the private sector, i.e., with the CICA.

[17] According to the CICA website, AcSOC membership consists of senior members from business, finance, government, academe, the accounting and legal professions, regulators, and the financial analyst communities. The members have a broad perspective of the complex issues facing standard setters. The goal is to achieve full representation across the spectrum of stakeholders.

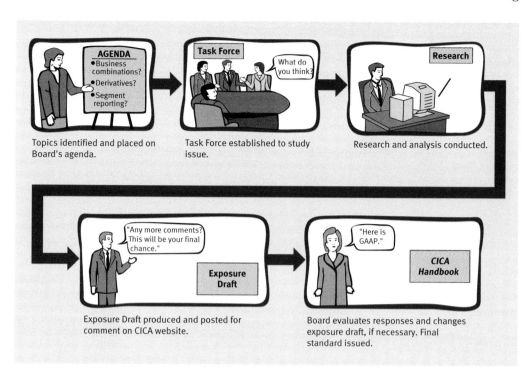

Illustration 1-5

Evolution of a New or Revised Standard

2. *Provincial Securities Commissions*

Provincial securities commissions[18] oversee and monitor the capital marketplace. They ensure that the participants in the capital markets (e.g., companies, auditors, brokers and dealers, and investors) adhere to securities law and legislation with the ultimate objective of ensuring that the marketplace is fair. For instance, the British Columbia Securities Commission acknowledges responsibility for the following:

- to ensure that investors have access to the information they need to make informed investment decisions

- to provide rules of fair play for the markets

- to establish qualifications and standards of conduct for people registered to advise investors and to trade on their behalf and

- to protect the integrity of the capital market and the confidence of investors.

As part of ensuring that investors have access to the information that they need to make informed decisions, securities law and legislation requires that companies that issue shares to the public and whose shares trade on a Canadian stock exchange or stock market produce GAAP financial statements.[19] The commissions generally rely on the CICA to develop GAAP and professional accountants to use sound judgement in its application.

International Insight

The International Organization of Securities Commissions (IOSCO) is a group of more than 100 securities regulatory agencies or securities exchanges from all over the world. IOSCO has existed since 1987. Collectively, its members represent a substantial proportion of the world's capital markets.

---

[18] In Canada, securities regulation is carried out on a provincial basis with the 10 provinces and three territories looking after the companies in their jurisdiction. Many feel that this is cumbersome and costly and are lobbying for a national securities commission. Some movement has been made in this direction. The provincial and territorial regulators have formed the Canadian Securities Administrators (CSA). The CSA is primarily responsible for developing a harmonized approach to securities regulation across the country (www.csa-acvm.ca). At present the CSA collects and archives all required filings under the respective securities regulations (www.sedar.com).

[19] For instance, Ontario Securities Act Sections 75 to 83.

Ontario is home to the largest stock exchange in Canada, the Toronto Stock Exchange (TSX), and therefore most large public companies are registered with the Ontario Securities Commission (OSC). In the past few years, the OSC has begun to review and monitor the financial statements of companies whose shares are publicly traded with the view to assessing whether the statements present fairly the financial position and results of operations.[20] Further, it has begun to issue its own disclosure requirements, signalling to companies how the OSC interprets GAAP.[21] Stock exchanges as well as securities commissions have the ability to fine the company and/or delist the company's shares from the stock exchange, denying the company access to capital markets.

3. Financial Accounting Standards Board and the SEC

In the U.S., the Financial Accounting Standards Board (FASB) is the major standard-setting body. The American Institute of Certified Public Accountants (AICPA) is the main professional accounting body for Certified Public Accountants. However, unlike Canada, the AICPA does not have primary responsibility for standard setting—the Securities and Exchange Commission (SEC) does. The SEC has affirmed its support for FASB by indicating that financial statements conforming to FASB standards will be presumed to have substantial authoritative support. The SEC has indicated in its reports to the U.S. government that it continues to believe that the initiative for establishing and improving accounting standards should remain in the private sector, subject to commission oversight. Like the Canadian securities commissions, it also signals its position on various financial reporting issues through what it refers to as Financial Reporting Releases.

FASB has a substantial impact on Canadian financial reporting. Firstly, since Canadian GAAP is based on principles and is fairly open to interpretation, **accounting professionals often look to the more rule-oriented, specific guidance** noted in the FASB pronouncements. Secondly, many Canadian companies also list on U.S. stock markets and exchanges such as NASDAQ (National Association of Securities Dealers Automated Quotation) and the NYSE (New York Stock Exchange). In order to list on a U.S. exchange, these companies **must follow U.S. GAAP** or at least provide a reconciliation between Canadian and U.S. GAAP in the financial statements. As we move toward international harmonization, the U.S. accounting standards will have an ever-increasing influence on Canadian and international standards due to the significant capital pool associated with these markets.[22]

4. International Accounting Standards Board (IASB)

Most countries recognize the need for more uniform standards. As a result, the International Accounting Standards Committee (IASC) was formed in 1973 to attempt to narrow the areas of divergence. The IASCs objective in terms of standard setting was to work generally to improve and harmonize regulations, accounting standards, and procedures relating to the presentation of financial statements. Eliminating differences is not easy because the financial reporting objectives in each country differ; the institutional structures are often not comparable, and strong national tendencies are pervasive.

International Insight

By the year 2005, some 7,000 companies in the European Union will adopt IASB standards.

[20] The OSC has a Continuous Disclosure Team that regularly reviews public companies' financial statements. The team plans to review each company at least every four years. For the year ended March 31, 2002, 517 companies were reviewed, comprising 29% of the active Ontario-based reporting issuers.

[21] For instance, in 2000, Rules 51-501 and 52-501 were issued dealing with disclosures for annual and interim financial statements. Staff Accounting Notice 52-303 on "Non-GAAP Earnings Measures" was issued in 2002.

[22] In the CICA Task Force on Standard Setting, the committee commented that international harmonization was not likely to happen without the SECs support. It further commented that failure to obtain that support would make FASB the *de facto* world standard setter. Since that report, harmonization initiatives have been progressing with startling speed. The CICA AcSB has stated that harmonization is a key objective. Therefore, all new and revised standards should take into consideration harmonization with U.S. GAAP.

Nevertheless, much headway has been made since IASCs inception, and international standards may gradually supplant national standards. In 2001, a new **International Accounting Standards Board (IASB)** was created (essentially becoming the main standard-setting body for international accounting standards). Its goal, according to the new chair, is to **increase the transparency of financial reporting by achieving a single, global method of accounting**.

The AcSB recently re-affirmed its commitment to international harmonization of accounting standards.[23] It was a long-standing member of the IASC and now also has representation on the IASB. Throughout this textbook, international considerations are presented to help you understand the international reporting environment.

Digital Tool

Expanded discussion of International Accounting.

www.wiley.com/canada/kieso

Standard Setting in a Political Environment

Possibly the most powerful force influencing the development of accounting standards is the stakeholders. Standard-setting stakeholders are the parties most interested in or affected by accounting standards, rules, and procedures. Like lobbyists in the provincial and national government arena, stakeholders play a significant role. **Accounting standards are as much a product of political action as they are of careful logic or empirical findings.** As part of its mandate, the AcSB includes as its members all stakeholders, allowing them a **formal voice** in the process. Furthermore, through due process, all interested parties may comment on the proposed changes or new standards.

Stakeholders may want particular economic events accounted for or reported in a particular way, and they fight hard to get what they want. They know that the most effective way to influence the standards that dictate accounting practice is to participate in formulating them or to try to influence or persuade the formulator.

Should there be politics in setting financial accounting and reporting standards? The AcSB does not exist in a vacuum. Standard setting is part of the real world, and it cannot escape politics and political pressures. That is not to say that politics in standard setting is bad. Considering the economic consequences[24] of many accounting standards, it is not surprising that special interest groups become vocal and critical (some supporting, some opposing) when standards are being formulated. The AcSB must be attentive to the economic consequences of its actions; however, it should not issue pronouncements that are primarily politically motivated. While paying attention to its constituencies, the AcSB should base its standards on sound research and a conceptual framework grounded in economic reality.

An illustration of an economic consequence issue is the turmoil caused by employee stock option plan (ESOP) accounting. Historically, stock options issued under ESOPs have been treated as **capital transactions** and therefore, the related accounting **did not affect net income**. More recently, however, the profession has supported treating options issued under these plans as **operating transactions** since they represent employee remuneration. In many cases, these plans provide benefits in lieu of salary, and since salary is

Underlying Concept

Options issued under ESOP are stock options in **legal form**; however, many argue that the **economic substance** is that they are operating costs. Therefore, they should be recorded as payroll expense.

---

[23] One of the CICA's long-term goals resulting from its Task Force on Standard Setting was to help create one set of internationally accepted standards in the private sector. The task force committed that Canada would play a significant role in establishing these standards while retaining the authority to set unique Canadian accounting standards where circumstances warrant.

[24] "Economic consequences" in this context means the impact of accounting reports on the wealth positions of issuers and users of financial information and the decision-making behaviour resulting from that impact. The resulting behaviour of these individuals and groups could have detrimental financial effects on the providers (enterprises) of the financial information. For a more detailed discussion of this phenomenon, see Stephen A. Zeff, "The Rise of Economic Consequences," *Journal of Accountancy*, (December 1978), pp. 56-63.

recorded as an **expense**, it is logical to record ESOPs as an expense.

Initially, when the AcSB issued the new *Handbook* Section 3870 on stock-based compensation, it allowed a **choice** in the way the options were accounted for—it **did not mandate treating the related costs as operating transactions**. This was due to the tremendous pressure put upon the AcSB by companies that felt that expensing these options would affect their net income and hence the cost of and ability to raise capital. Many felt that the related costs associated with the options were not operating costs and therefore should not flow through the income statement. The AcSB has since revised this section to **mandate expensing costs associated with stock options**. Given the current focus on transparency in financial reporting, many stakeholders are now more accepting of this position.

GENERALLY ACCEPTED ACCOUNTING PRINCIPLES

Objective 10

Explain the meaning of generally accepted accounting principles (GAAP).

GAAP as developed by the AcSB has substantial authoritative support through the Canadian and provincial business corporations acts and also through securities legislation. All companies whose shares or debt trade in a public market must follow GAAP. Most other incorporated companies also follow GAAP as it provides the most useful information.

GAAP Hierarchy

GAAP encompasses **not only specific rules, practices, and procedures** relating to particular circumstances but also **broad principles and conventions of general application**, including underlying concepts. GAAP is divided into either **primary sources** or **other sources**, referred to as the **GAAP hierarchy**. According to *Handbook* Section 1100, **primary** sources of GAAP (in descending order of authority) are listed below:

- *Handbook* **Sections** 1300-4460, including Appendices and Board Notices[25]

- **Accounting Guidelines**, including Appendices and Board Notices

- **Background Information** and **Basis for Conclusions** documents including Appendices

- Abstracts of Issues discussed by the Emerging Issues Committee (**EIC Abstracts**), including Appendices

- Illustrative Examples of those pronouncements noted above

- **Implementation Guides** authorized by the Board

Other sources noted in Section 1100 include:

- **Pronouncements** by accounting standard-setting bodies in other jurisdictions

- **Research Studies**

- Accounting **textbooks, journals, studies, and articles**

---

[25] Board Notices, Background Information, Basis for Conclusion, and Implementation Guide documents have not technically been part of the *Handbook* in the past. Since the *Handbook* is now available electronically, this opens the door for an expanded body of knowledge to be made available on CD or on the CICA website. By including these other sources as primary sources of GAAP, the body of knowledge has and will continue to expand significantly.

- Other

In general, primary sources must be looked to **first**. Where primary sources do not deal with the specific issue at hand, the entity should adopt accounting policies that are **consistent with the primary sources** as well as the concepts laid out in Section 1000 (the **conceptual framework**). Business is constantly changing and new business transactions and contracts are being entered into and therefore the other sources are important sources of GAAP.

Professional Judgement

Professional judgement plays an especially important role in Canada. This is due to the basic philosophy that Canadian accountants hold with respect to standard setting: that **there cannot be a rule for every situation**. Canadian standards are therefore based primarily on **general principles** rather than **specific rules**. The basic premise is that professional accountants with significant education and experience will be able to apply these principles appropriately to any situation as they see fit.

11 Objective
Explain the significance of professional judgement in applying GAAP.

Role of Ethics

In accounting, as in other areas of business, ethical dilemmas are encountered frequently. Some of these dilemmas are simple and easy to resolve. Many, however, are complex, and solutions are not obvious. Management biases—either internally prompted (e.g., to maximize bonuses) or externally prompted (e.g., to meet analysts' earnings expectations)—are at the root of many ethical dilemmas. These biases sometimes lead to an emphasis on short-term results over long-term results and place accountants (both internal and external) in an environment of conflict and pressure. Basic questions such as "Is this way of communicating financial information transparent?", "Does it provide useful information?", and "What should I do in this circumstance?" cannot always be answered by simply adhering to GAAP or following the rules of the profession. Technical competence is not enough when ethical decisions are encountered.

Doing the **right thing** and making the right decision is not always easy. Right is not always evident and the pressures to "bend the rules," "play the game," or "just ignore it" can be considerable. In these cases, self-interest must be balanced with the interests of others. The decision is more difficult because a public consensus has not emerged to formulate a comprehensive ethical system to provide guidelines.

This whole process of **ethical sensitivity** and selection among alternatives can be complicated by time pressures, job pressures, client pressures, personal pressures, and peer pressures. Throughout this textbook, ethical considerations are presented to sensitize you to the type of situations you may encounter when performing your professional responsibility.

12 Objective
Understand issues related to ethics and financial accounting.

Digital Tool

Expanded discussion of Ethical Issues in Financial Accounting.
www.wiley.com/canada/kieso

CHALLENGES FACING FINANCIAL REPORTING

In North America, we have the most liquid, deep, secure, and efficient public capital markets of any country at any time in history. One reason for this success is that our financial statements and related disclosures have captured and organized financial information in a useful and reliable fashion. However, much still needs to be done. During 2001 and 2002, the viability of the capital market system was challenged by several significant corporate

13 Objective
Identify some of the challenges facing accounting.

scandals as previously mentioned in this chapter. The resulting turmoil gave all stakeholders a chance to re-examine their roles in the capital marketplace and to revisit if and how they add value to the system.

In the United States, where the problems occurred, the end result was to increase government regulation in the capital marketplace. The **Sarbanes-Oxley Act (SOX)** was enacted in 2002, increasing resources for the SEC to combat fraud and curb poor reporting practices.[26] The SEC has **increased its policing efforts**, approving **new auditor independence rules** and **materiality guidelines** for financial reporting. In addition, the SOX introduces sweeping changes to the institutional structure of the accounting profession. The following are some of the legislation's key provisions:

- An accounting oversight board was established, having oversight and enforcement authority. It will establish auditing, quality control, and independence standards and rules (**Public Company Accounting Oversight Board** or **PCAOB**).

- Stronger **independence rules** for auditors. Audit partners, for example, will be required to rotate every five years.

- CEOs and CFOs must **forfeit bonuses and profits** where there is an accounting restatement.

- CEOs and CFOs are required to **certify** that the financial statements and company disclosures are appropriate and fairly presented.

- **Audit committees** will need independent members and members with financial expertise.

- **Codes of ethics** must be in place for senior financial officers.

Stakeholders in the capital marketplace were faced with the question of whether similar reforms should be put in place in Canada. Companies that issue shares in the United States are bound by the SOX[27] and therefore these companies have no choice. Many stakeholders feel that unless Canada matches the standard set by the SOX, Canadian capital markets will be seen to be inferior. As a result, many of the SOX requirements have been, or are in the process of being, put in place as follows:

- The **Canadian Public Accountability Board** (www.cpab-ccrc.ca) has been formed to look after similar issues as the PCAOB.

- The **OSC** has issued draft rules that, among other things, require company management to attest to the appropriateness and fairness of the financial statements, public companies to have independent audit commitees and public accounting firms to be subject to the Canadian Public Accountability Board.[28]

- The **CSA** has issued a harmonized draft statement that requires significantly increased disclosures, including ratings from rating agencies, payments by companies to stock promoters, legal proceedings, and details about directors, including their prior involvement with bankrupt companies.[29]

- The **Province of Ontario** has made amendments to the Securities Act.

- A **parliamentary committee of the federal government** recently issued a report that would see similar regulatory reforms introduced into federal legislation.

The impact of these reforms on the North American capital marketplace has been to

---

[26] Sarbanes-Oxley Act of 2002, H. R. Rep. No. 107-610 (2002).

[27] Sarbanes-Oxley Act of 2002, Section 106 (2002).

[28] OSC Multilateral Instrument 52-109, 52-110, and 52-108.

[29] CSA revised National Instrument 51-102, "Continuous Disclosure Obligations."

put **more emphasis on government regulation** and less on **self-regulation**.

Globalization of Companies and Capital Markets

Many companies list on foreign stock exchanges. Larger stock exchanges are cultivating these listings. On-line trading has made these markets (and through the markets, the companies) more accessible in terms of investing. Trading now happens around the clock. The move is toward global markets and global investors. The financial reporting environment is no longer constrained by Canadian borders nor only influenced by Canadian stakeholders.

As mentioned in the chapter, **U.S. and IASB accounting standards are becoming increasingly intertwined with Canadian standards**. All parties are committed to **convergence of standards;** however, there are many issues that standard setters must deal with. One key issue is the **principles versus rules** debate.

The **United States uses a rules-based approach**. In a rules-based approach—much like the Canadian tax system—there is a rule for most things. The result is that the body of knowledge is significantly larger. Also there is a tendency for companies to interpret the rules literally. Many companies take the view that if there is no rule dealing with a particular situation, they are free to choose whatever treatment they think is appropriate. Similarly, many believe that as long as they comply with a rule even in a narrow sense, they are in accordance with GAAP. Unfortunately, this does not always provide the best information for users. As the AcSB harmonizes current Canadian standards with U.S. standards, much of the U.S. wording is being imported into Canadian GAAP. Thus it would appear that **Canadian GAAP is gradually moving from a principles-based approach** toward a rules-based approach. This trend may be counteracted by the AcSB mandate for international convergence, since the **IASB standards are more principles-based**. Interestingly, while Canada is drifting toward a rules-based approach, FASB and the SEC have initiated a project to review the appropriateness of the principles-based approach in the U.S. environment (mandated by the SOX).

Impact of Technology

Accountants are **purveyors of information**. They **identify, measure, and communicate useful information to users**. Technology affects this process in many profound ways. The CICA, in its Report of the Inter-Institute Vision Task Force, concluded that we are presently in the third wave of computer technology. The first wave related to mainframes and the second wave related to personal computers. The third wave is driven by use of networks and convergence of computers and telecommunications technologies. Companies are now connected electronically to their banks, their suppliers, and regulatory agencies. The task force notes that in this third wave, automation focuses on stakeholders, distribution, and consumption. This gives stakeholders ready access to a significant amount of very timely company information.

As technology continues to advance at a dramatic pace, giving users **greater access to more and more information more and more rapidly**, the requirement for timely information beyond annual and quarterly financial statements will rise sharply. Will this lead to **on-line real-time and/or continuous reporting**? Will this decrease reliance on the annual financial statements due to their lack of timeliness and therefore relevance? Will this change the role of the public accountant?

The Internet's flexibility allows users to take advantage of tools such as search engines and hyperlinks and quickly find related information about the company. Financial reports are more relevant because the medium allows companies to disclose more detail, which the user can then aggregate and analyse. From the company's perspective, disseminating information over the Internet gives the company access to a significantly larger group of users. Information can be targeted to specific users. Costs are also greatly reduced.

Some of the main drawbacks are concerned with accessibility: will all users have the knowledge and capability to access the information? Equal access is certainly important for a level playing field. Another issue is quality and reliability of the information, especially given the fact that the information may not be audited. Would certain sites and content be more reliable than others? Finally, would the practice leave companies open to computer hackers?

A continuous reporting model is already incubating in the capital markets arena. Securities commissions and stock markets already require ongoing disclosures of public companies. These disclosures are being monitored by the securities commissions and stock markets. Companies can now file required disclosures electronically with securities commissions. Investors can log on to a website and tap in to conversations including earnings calls, briefings with analysts, and interviews with senior management and market regulators. These conversations were not previously accessible to the average investor. The CICA issued a research study in 1999 to assess the impact of technology on financial reporting.[30]

Changing Nature of the Economy

Much of North America is transforming from an economy based on traditional manufacturing and resource extraction to what has become known in the past decade as a **"knowledge-based" economy**.[31] In terms of market value of publicly traded shares, companies, such as **Microsoft, Cisco, Intel, Lucent, AT&T,** and **IBM** dominate the North American markets. What these companies all have in common is that a significant percentage of the value attributed to their shares is linked to factors such as their **relationships with customers and suppliers, knowledge base or intellectual assets, ability to adapt to a changing technological environment, and adept leadership**. This is different from the more traditional manufacturing and resource-based economy where value was more closely linked to physical and tangible assets and financing.

Most of the assets of these "new economy" companies are not reflected at all in the balance sheet, yet they drive the company value. As noted by the CICA Task Force:

> "In light of these shifts (i.e., in the economy), to maintain its relevancy, the (accounting) profession must move beyond interpreting the past. Increasingly what matters is the ability for organizational decision-makers to be positioned for the future. This ability to look forward is driven by one's ability to measure organizational performance along an increasingly broad spectrum of measures, both financial and non-financial... Chartered Accountants must provide decision-makers with the tools necessary to measure and report on organizational performance in all its aspects, not just the historical and financial." [32]

The knowledge-based companies that are beginning to dominate capital markets need **more relevant models for measuring and reporting value, creating assets that are currently not recognized on the balance sheet**. Not much progress has been made in this area due to the difficulty of objectively valuing these assets and their potential impact on future earnings. Having said this, underwriting firms such as **CIBC World Markets**

---

[30] The Impact of Technology on Financial and Business Reporting. (Toronto: CICA, 1999).

[31] R. McLean, The Canadian Performance Reporting Initiative, (Toronto: Ontario Premier's Council and the CICA, ongoing), Chapter 2.

[32] The Report of the Inter-Institute Vision Task Force, (Toronto: CICA, 1996), page 9.

value these companies every time one goes public. The market also values these assets and the companies that house these assets through the stock prices. How, if at all, can those values be reflected in the financial statements?

Increased Requirement for Accountability

There is a **growing number of institutional investors**, partially because more and more capital is being invested in pension plans and mutual funds. The impact is that investors have become **more sophisticated in terms of knowledge levels**. Institutional investors, because of their size, have **greater representation in corporate boardrooms** and are thus more involved in running the companies they invest in. Given this, companies are being prodded toward **increased accountability**.

Financial performance is rooted in a company's business model (i.e., the earnings process, how companies finance the process, and what resources companies invest in). This has historically not always been the focus of financial accounting. However, a company's ability to articulate its strategic vision and carry out that vision affects financial performance. The accounting information system is also part of a larger system of information management—a system that contains a significant amount of non-financial information.

Will investors move **beyond the financial reporting model** to a more **all-inclusive model of business reporting**—one that includes not only financial information but other key indicators and measurements that help predict value creation and monitor organizational performance? The CICA AcSB mandate includes a thrust to **develop and support frameworks for measuring and reporting information used for evaluating and improving organizational performance.**[33] Changes in these directions would broaden the focus from financial reporting to business reporting.

The CICA also has several other initiatives in this area:

- The CICA **Risk Management and Governance Board** (formerly the Criteria of Control Board) focuses on a practical, commercial approach to risk management and governance.

- With the TSX, the CICA is part of a **Committee for Corporate Governance**, which has called for public companies to report on **internal financial control and regulatory compliance**.

- The **Canadian Performance Reporting Board** of the CICA has issued standards on Management Discussion and Analysis disclosures.

All of these and other initiatives take a broader view toward an all-inclusive model of business reporting.

Related to this theme of "business reporting" is the development and fairly widespread use of a business strategy model called the **balanced scorecard**.[34] This model notes that **financial measures are merely one component of useful information that decision-makers need to make effective decisions about the company**. The model views the company from four differing perspectives: financial, customer, internal processes, and learning and growth. These four perspectives are linked to the company's strategic vision and objectives are developed within each of these perspectives. The objectives help the company achieve its strategic vision. Measures are developed to determine whether the objectives are being met.

---

[33] J. Waterhouse and A. Svendsen, Research Report entitled Strategic Performance Monitoring and Management: Using Non-Financial Measures to Improve Corporate Governance, (CICA,1998) and A. Willis and J. Desjardins, Environmental Performance: Measuring and Managing What Matters, (CICA, 2001).

[34] R. Kaplan and D. Norton, *The Balanced Scorecard*, (Boston: Harvard Business School Press, 1996).

Illustration 1-6

*The Balanced
Scorecard Model*

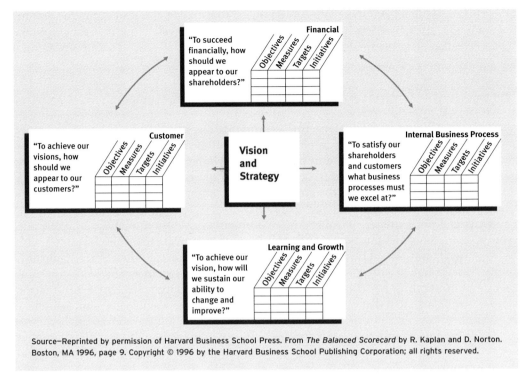

Source—Reprinted by permission of Harvard Business School Press. From *The Balanced Scorecard* by R. Kaplan and D. Norton. Boston, MA 1996, page 9. Copyright © 1996 by the Harvard Business School Publishing Corporation; all rights reserved.

Illustration 1-6 depicts a **balanced scorecard model**. This model is used to help focus a company's internal efforts more effectively to meet its strategic goals. The question is whether external users of financial statements also need to monitor these measures and whether companies should allow access to external parties to this information. If the information is important for company management to make decisions, is it not important for external users as well?

We believe that the challenges presented by these changes must be met in order for the accounting profession to continue to provide the type of information needed for an efficient capital allocation process.

Conclusion

Financial reporting is standing at the threshold of some significant changes. Is the accounting profession up to the challenge to deal with this? At present, we believe that the profession is reacting responsibly and effectively to remedy identified shortcomings and to move forward with a new vision. Because of its substantial resources and expertise, the profession should be able to develop and maintain high standards and meet its mandate. It is and will continue to be a difficult process requiring time, logic, and diplomacy. By a judicious mix of these three ingredients, and a measure of luck, the accounting profession will continue to be a leader on the global business stage.

Summary of Learning Objectives

1 Describe the essential characteristics of accounting.

The essential characteristics of accounting are: (1) identification, measurement, and communication of financial information about (2) economic entities to (3) interested persons.

2 Identify the major financial statements and other means of financial reporting.

The financial statements most frequently provided are (1) the balance sheet, (2) the income statement, (3) the statement of cash flows, and (4) the statement of owners' or shareholders' equity. Financial reporting other than financial statements may take various forms. Examples include the president's letter or supplementary schedules in the corporate annual report, prospectuses, reports filed with government agencies, news releases, management's forecasts, and descriptions of an enterprise's social or environmental impact.

3 Explain how accounting assists in the efficient use of scarce resources.

Accounting provides reliable, relevant, and timely information to managers, investors, and creditors so that resources are allocated to the most efficient enterprises. Accounting also provides measurements of efficiency (profitability) and financial soundness.

4 Explain the meaning of "stakeholder" and identify key stakeholders in financial reporting.

Stakeholders are parties that have something at stake in the financial reporting environment, e.g., salary, job, investment, and reputation. Key stakeholders are investors, creditors, analysts, managers, employees, customers, suppliers, industry groups, unions, government departments and ministers, the public in general (e.g., consumer groups), regulatory agencies, other companies, standard setters, auditors, lawyers, and others.

5 Identify the objective of financial reporting.

According to the *CICA Handbook*, the objective of financial statements is to communicate information that is useful to investors, members, contributors, creditors, and other users in making their resource allocation decisions and/or assessing management stewardship. Consequently, financial statements provide information about:

(a) an entity's economic resources, obligations, and equity/net assets

(b) changes in an entity's economic resources, obligation and equity/net assets and

(c) the entity's economic performance.

6 Explain the notion of management bias with respect to financial reporting.

Management bias implies that the financial statements are not neutral: that the preparers of the financial information are presenting the information in a manner that may overemphasize the positive and underemphasize the negative.

7 Understand the importance of user needs in the financial reporting process.

The financial reporting process is based on ensuring that users receive decision-relevant information. This is a challenge as different users have different knowledge levels and needs. Management bias may render financial information less useful.

8 Explain the need for accounting standards.

The accounting profession has attempted to develop a set of standards that is generally accepted and universally practised. Without this set of standards, each enterprise would have to develop its own standards, and readers of financial statements would have to familiarize themselves with every company's peculiar accounting and reporting practices. As a result, it would be almost impossible to prepare statements that could be compared.

9 Identify the major entities that influence the standard-setting process and explain how they influence financial reporting.

The CICA AcSB is the main standard-setting body in Canada. It derives its mandate from the CBCA as well as provincial acts of incorporation. Public companies are required to follow GAAP in order to access capital markets. This is monitored by provincial securities commissions. FASB and the IASB are also important as they influence Canadian standard setting. Canada is committed to international harmonization of GAAP.

Digital Tool

Glossary

www.wiley.com/canada/kieso

KEY TERMS

Accounting Standards Board (AcSB), 10

Accounting Standards Oversight Council (AcSOC), 10

American Institute of Certified Public Accountants (AICPA), 12

Canadian Institute of Chartered Accountants (CICA), 10

capital allocation, 4

CICA Handbook, 10

due process, 10

EIC Abstracts, 10

Emerging Issues Committee (EIC), 10

ethical dilemmas, 15

financial accounting, 3

Financial Accounting Standards Board (FASB), 12

financial reporting, 3

financial statements, 3

GAAP hierarchy, 14

generally accepted accounting principles (GAAP), 9

International Accounting Standards Board (IASB), 13

management bias, 8

management stewardship, 6

managerial accounting, 3

objective of financial reporting, 6

Ontario Securities Commission (OSC), 12

professional judgement, 15

provincial securities commissions, 11

Securities and Exchange Commission (SEC), 12

stakeholders, 4

Toronto Stock Exchange (TSX), 12

10 Explain the meaning of generally accepted accounting principles (GAAP).

Generally accepted accounting principles are either principles that have substantial authoritative support, such as the *CICA Handbook*, or given practices that have been accepted as appropriate over time because of universal application.

11 Explain the significance of professional judgement in applying GAAP.

Professional judgement plays an important role in Canadian GAAP since much of GAAP is based on general principles, which need to be interpreted.

12 Understand issues related to ethics and financial accounting.

Financial accountants, when performing their professional duties, are called on for moral discernment and ethical decision-making. The decision is more difficult because a public consensus has not emerged to formulate a comprehensive ethical system that provides guidelines in making ethical judgements.

13 Identify some of the challenges facing accounting.

Some of the challenges are globalization, leading to a requirement for international harmonization of standards; increased technology, resulting in the need for more timely information; the move to a new economy, resulting in a focus on measuring and reporting non-traditional assets that create value; and increased requirement for accountability, resulting in the creation of new measurement and reporting models that look at business reporting as a whole.

Brief Exercises

BE1-1 Differentiate broadly between financial accounting and managerial accounting.

BE1-2 Differentiate between "financial statements" and "financial reporting."

BE1-3 How does accounting help the capital allocation process?

BE1-4 What are some of the major challenges facing the accounting profession?

BE1-5 What are the major objectives of financial reporting?

BE1-6 Of what value is a common set of standards in financial accounting and reporting?

BE1-7 What is the likely limitation of "general-purpose financial statements"?

BE1-8 What are some of the developments or events that occurred between 1900 and 1930 that helped bring about changes in accounting theory or practice?

BE1-9 If you had to explain or define "generally accepted accounting principles," what essential characteristics would you include in your explanation?

BE1-10 Explain the difference between primary and other sources of GAAP.

BE1-11 The chairman of the FASB at one time noted that "the flow of standards can only be slowed if (1) producers focus less on quarterly earnings per share and tax benefits and more on quality products, and (2) accountants and lawyers rely less on rules and law and more on professional judgement and conduct." Explain his comment.

BE1-12 Explain the role of the Emerging Issues Committee in establishing generally accepted accounting principles.

BE1-13 What is the role of the Ontario Securities Commission in standard setting?

BE1-14 What are some possible reasons why another organization, such as the OSC and SEC, should not issue financial reporting standards?

BE1-15 What are the sources of pressure that change and influence the development of accounting principles and standards?

BE1-16 Some individuals have indicated that the AcSB must be cognizant of the economic consequences of its pronouncements. What is meant by "economic consequences"? What dangers exist if politics play too much of a role in the development of financial reporting standards?

BE1-17 If you were given complete authority in the matter, how would you propose that accounting principles or standards be developed and enforced?

BE1-18   One writer recently noted that 99.4% of all companies prepare statements that are in accordance with GAAP. Why then is there such concern about fraudulent financial reporting?

BE1-19   A number of foreign countries have reporting standards that differ from those in Canada. What are some of the main reasons why reporting standards are often different among countries?

BE1-20   How are financial accountants challenged in their work to make ethical decisions? Is technical mastery of GAAP not sufficient to the practice of financial accounting?

Writing Assignments

WA1-1   Some argue that having various organizations establish accounting principles is wasteful and inefficient. Rather than mandating accounting standards, each company could voluntarily disclose the type of information it considered important. In addition, if an investor wants additional information, the investor could contact the company and pay to receive the additional information desired.

Instructions

Comment on the appropriateness of this viewpoint.

WA1-2   Some accountants have said that politicization in the development and acceptance of generally accepted accounting principles (i.e., standard setting) is taking place. Some use the term "politicization" in a narrow sense to mean the influence by governmental agencies, particularly the securities commissions, on the development of generally accepted accounting principles. Others use it more broadly to mean the compromise that results when the bodies responsible for developing generally accepted accounting principles are pressured by interest groups (securities commissions, stock exchanges, businesses through their various organizations, financial analysts, bankers, lawyers, etc.).

Instructions

(a) What arguments can be raised to support the politicization of accounting standard setting?

(b) What arguments can be raised against the politicization of accounting standard setting?

(CMA adapted)

WA1-3   Presented below are three models for setting accounting standards.

1. The purely political approach, where national legislative action decrees accounting standards.

2. The private, professional approach, where financial accounting standards are set and enforced by private professional actions only.

3. The public/private mixed approach, where standards are set by private sector bodies that behave as though they were public agencies and whose standards to a great extent are enforced through governmental agencies.

Instructions

(a) Which of these three models best describes standard setting in Canada? Comment on your answer.

(b) Why do companies, financial analysts, labour unions, industry trade associations, and others take such an active interest in standard setting?

(c) Cite an example of a group other than the AcSB that attempts to establish accounting standards. Speculate as to why another group might wish to set its own standards.

WA1-4   Increased availability and accessibility of computers and Internet availability have had a significant impact on the process of financial reporting. Most companies have websites and make available to stakeholders a significant amount of financial information, including annual reports and other financial information. This has sparked the question of whether companies should move to a continuous reporting model versus the current discrete model where financial statements are generally issued only quarterly and annually. Under a continuous reporting model, the company would make more information available to users on a real time or perhaps a "delayed" real-time basis (e.g., weekly).

Instructions

What are the pros and cons of a continuous reporting model? Consider the various stakeholders in the capital marketplace.

WA1-5   The chapter makes reference to Enron and WorldCom. Both companies were accused of misstating their financial statements. The auditors signed audit reports on both companies attesting that the financial statements were fairly presented.

Instructions

How is it possible that a company can misrepresent its financial statements and still receive a "clean" audit opinion from the auditors?

WA1-6   The following information was drawn from Ontario Securities Commission (OSC) Statement of Allegation dated August 30, 2000 against **Philip Services Corp. (Philip)**. The allegation relates to the information contained in the company prospectus that included audited financial statements for the years ended December 31, 1995 and 1996.

The prospectus included an unqualified audit opinion, meaning that the auditors had concluded in the audit report that the financial statements presented the company's financial position and results of operations fairly in accordance with GAAP. At the time, the company was a leading integrated service provider of ferrous scrap processing, brokerage, and industrial outsourcing services. The OSC alleged that the company failed to provide full, true, and plain disclosure in the prospectus of material facts in respect of the restructuring and special charges.

Instructions

(a) Explain the meaning of the term "GAAP" as used in the audit report.

(b) Explain how you determine whether or not an accounting principle is generally accepted.

(c) Discuss the sources of evidence for determining whether an accounting principle has substantial authoritative support.

(d) Discuss how the auditors might have issued a clean audit opinion when the OSC is alleging that the company did not provide full disclosure of material facts.

WA1-7   As mentioned in the chapter, the capital marketplace reaction to recent corporate failures has been to increase government regulation.

Instructions

(a) Identify what steps Canada and the United States have taken to increase government regulation.

(b) What other options might have been available to stakeholders in terms of strengthening the capital marketplace?

(c) What are the strengths and weaknesses of government regulation?

Cases

Refer to the Case Primer on the Digital Tool to help you answer these cases.

CA1-1   When the AcSB issues new standards, the implementation date is usually 12 months from date of issuance, with early implementation encouraged. Paula Popovich, controller, discusses with her financial vice-president the need for early implementation of a standard that would result in a fairer presentation of the company's financial condition and earnings. When the financial vice-president determines that early implementation of the standard will adversely affect the reported net income for the year, he discourages Popovich from implementing the standard until it is required.

Digital Tool

www.wiley.com/
canada/kieso

Instructions

Discuss, including ethical issues.

(CMA adapted)

CA1-2   The **T. Eaton Company** (Eaton's) was a private Canadian company that experienced cash flow difficulties and hired new management to turn the company around. The company then went public and the shares sold at $15. Within months, the stock price plummeted and eventually, Sears bought out Eaton's when it was on the threshold of bankruptcy.

Instructions

Who are the stakeholders in this situation? Explain what is at stake and why and how they were affected when the stock price plummeted.

CA1-3   The University of Toronto *Bulletin*, a university newspaper, announced in its January 29, 2001 edition that **Moody's Canada Inc.** (a financial rating agency) gave the University of Toronto a rating of AA2 after reviewing the university's books. This is a strong rating and ranks on a level higher than the university's single largest funder, the Province of Ontario.

Instructions

(a) Who are the stakeholders in the university financial reporting environment?

(b) What financial information might Moody's have based its decision on?

(c) What is the impact to the university of obtaining this strong rating?

(d) How might this information affect how the stakeholders deal with the university in the future?

Research and Financial Analysis

RA1-1   Quebecor Media Inc.

In a *Financial Post* article dated September 17, 2002, it was reported that Standard and Poor's downgraded Quebecor Media Inc.'s credit ratings by two levels from BB to B+. The credit rating agency was concerned about the company's ability to refinance portions of its debt. Both BB and B+ are considered "junk" bonds and are below the BBB− category, which is the lowest grade that many pension and mutual funds may hold.

In the article, analysts were noted as saying the company's financial profile has weakened due to tight debt covenants and resulting cash flow restrictions.

Instructions

What is the downgrading's impact on Quebecor? Explain the impact of the sentence regarding "junk bond" status on the downgrading of the credit rating.

RA1-2   Ontario Securities Commission (1)

The Ontario Securities Commission (OSC) has suggested that:

1. Canadian companies be allowed to follow U.S. GAAP when they file documents with the OSC.

2. U.S. companies be allowed to file only U.S. GAAP statements to satisfy OSC requirements.

Instructions

Research and prepare an essay considering the following:

(a) Hypothesize why the OSC might have taken these stands.

(b) How might Canadian investors benefit if U.S. standards become Canadian GAAP? How might they be disadvantaged?

(c) How do Canadian and U.S. standards differ (in general)?

(d) Review the financial statements of large Canadian companies whose shares trade on the TSX as well as a U.S. exchange. (Hint: look at www.sedar.com under "Company Profile" then "View this company's documents" then "annual financial statements.") These companies generally include a note to the financial statements reconciling net income under Canadian GAAP to net income under U.S. GAAP. Select five companies and calculate the dollar and percentage difference between the two numbers. Discuss the implications of reporting two separate net income numbers.

RA1-3   Ontario Securities Commission (2)

The OSC performs annual reviews of companies that list on the TSX as part of its Continuous Review Process. In August 2002, the OSC issued a report on its activities for the previous year ended March 31, 2002. As part of its review, the OSC reviewed 137 Ontario-based TSX 300 companies looking at disclosure and reporting of Non-GAAP earnings measures.

Instructions

(a) Define what is meant by "Non-GAAP earnings measures."

(b) Summarize the OSC findings.

(c) Recap the reporting requirements in OSC Staff Notice 52-303 (www.osc.gov.on.ca).

(d) Why was this Staff Notice issued?

(e) Based on the report, is the reporting of "Non-GAAP earnings measures" a problem?

RA1-4   IASB

Michael Sharpe, then Deputy Chairman, International Accounting Standards Committee, made the following comments before the FEI's 63rd Annual Conference: "There is an irreversible movement toward the harmonization of financial reporting throughout the world. The international capital markets require an end to:

1. The confusion caused by international companies announcing different results depending on the set of accounting standards applied. Recent announcements by Daimler-Benz (now DaimlerChrysler) highlight the confusion that this causes.

2. Companies in some countries obtaining unfair commercial advantages from the use of particular national accounting standards.

3. The complications in negotiating commercial arrangements for international joint ventures caused by different accounting requirements.

4. The inefficiency of international companies having to understand and use myriad accounting standards depending on the countries in which they operate and the countries in which they raise capital and debt. Executive talent is wasted on keeping up to date with numerous sets of accounting standards and the never-ending changes to them.

5. The inefficiency of investment managers, bankers, and financial analysts as they seek to compare financial reporting drawn up in accordance with different sets of accounting standards.

6. Failure of many stock exchanges and regulators to require companies subject to their jurisdiction to provide comparable, comprehensive, and transparent financial reporting frameworks giving international comparability.

7. Difficulty for developing countries and countries entering the free market economy, such as China and Russia, in accessing foreign capital markets because of the complexity of and differences between national standards.

8. The restriction on the mobility of financial service providers across the world as a result of different accounting standards.

Clearly, eliminating these inefficiencies by having comparable high-quality financial reporting used across the world would benefit international businesses."

Instructions

Research the issue using the Internet and answer the following questions:

(a) What is the International Accounting Standards Board and what is its relationship with the International Accounting Standards Committee?

(b) What stakeholders might benefit from the use of international accounting standards?

(c) What do you believe are some of the major obstacles to harmonization?

RA1-5   Canadian Coalition for Good Governance

The Canadian Coalition for Good Governance was formed in 2002 and represents a significant number of institutional investors in Canada.

Instructions

(a) How does an institutional investor differ from other investors?

(b) In your opinion, what impact does the presence of a significant number of investors have on financial reporting decisions made by management?

(c) Go to the coalition's website www.ccgg.ca and identify the coalition's three largest members.

(d) Go to these companies' websites and identify their major investments.

RA1-6   SOX

During 2002, the Sarbanes-Oxley Act was issued in the United States to strengthen the capital marketplace. For the next year, there were many debates in Canada as to whether the securities commissions in Canada should adopt the same regulations.

Instructions

(a) Why was the Act issued and what are its key components?

(b) What do you expect will be the Act's impact on the U.S. capital marketplace?

(c) Do some research on the Internet and discuss the pros and cons of Canada adopting the same rules for companies listed on the TSX and TSX Venture Exchange. (Hint: look on the websites of the provincial securities commissions, the CICA, the TSX as well as the *Globe and Mail* and *Financial Post*. Key words might be SOX, corporate accountability, and "post Enron.")

RA1-7   Principles versus Rules

Canadian and U.S. accounting standards are based on differing philosophies. Canada uses a principles-based approach while the United States uses a rules-based approach. The United States is currently studying the merits of the principles-based approach.

Instructions

(a) Identify the main factor that motivated FASB to consider switching to the principles-based approach.

(b) Download and review the FASB Issues Proposal for a Principles-Based Approach to U.S. Accounting Standard Setting.

(c) Articulate the differences between a rules-based approach and a principles-based approach.

(d) Comment on which approach would be better for Canada.

RA1-8   Impact of Technology

The following is a quote taken from the Foreword to *The Impact of Technology on Financial and Business Reporting*, a research study published by the CICA in 1999:

> "Changes in technology have had, and are continuing to have, a profound effect on how information is captured, summarized, and communicated."

Instructions

Discuss, making reference to the research report and current real life examples.

Soaring Profits

WestJet Airlines may seem like a young upstart in the airline industry, but it is also a survivor. In July 2003, WestJet reported its 26th consecutive profitable quarter. The Calgary-based airline, which focuses on low fares and no frills, credits its success to sound business planning and financial management. "It is critical to have financial information on a timely basis," Senior Vice President and Chief Financial Officer Sandy Campbell says. "You can't manage what you can't measure."

The main users of WestJet's financial statements are its shareholders. "We're always looking at what the analysts and shareholders are asking, and often they are asking the same thing, so we incorporate it," Campbell says. In the management discussion and analysis (MD&A), WestJet will include, for example, information on the airline's fleet plan, the average cost for fuel, the number of employees, and an explanation of why the numbers are up or down.

What WestJet doesn't provide is projections for the future, unlike other public companies. "They fall onto a slippery slope of having to constantly revise their expectations," the Certified General Accountant says, pointing out that the future could include outside market influences, such as an outbreak of disease or incidents of terrorism, beyond the company's control.

Transparency has always been a priority for WestJet's financial reporting. From its 1996 startup, the airline has acted like a public company, providing quarterly and annual reports to its shareholders, Campbell says. In 1998, the company became a reporting issuer, coming under the jurisdiction of the Alberta Securities Commission. It was listed on the Toronto Stock Exchange in July 1999.

Now offering flights across Canada, WestJet has grown at an average of 50% a year, Campbell says. "We measured every step along the way: how well we were executing [the business plan] and whether we were indeed creating value for the travelling public and, more importantly, for our shareholders."

CHAPTER 2

Conceptual Framework Underlying Financial Reporting

Learning Objectives

After studying this chapter, you should be able to:

1. Describe the usefulness of a conceptual framework.
2. Describe the main components of the conceptual framework for financial reporting.
3. Understand the objective of financial reporting.
4. Identify the qualitative characteristics of accounting information.
5. Define the basic elements of financial statements.
6. Describe the basic assumptions of accounting.
7. Explain the application of the basic principles of accounting.
8. Describe the impact that constraints have on reporting accounting information.
9. Explain the factors that contribute to choice in financial reporting decisions.
10. Identify the four types of financial reporting issues and what makes certain issues more important than others.
11. Explain the practice of financial engineering.
12. Identify factors that contribute to fraudulent financial reporting.

Users of financial statements need relevant and reliable information. To help develop this type of financial information, accountants use a conceptual framework that guides financial accounting and reporting. This chapter discusses the basic concepts underlying this conceptual framework. The content and organization of this chapter are as follows:

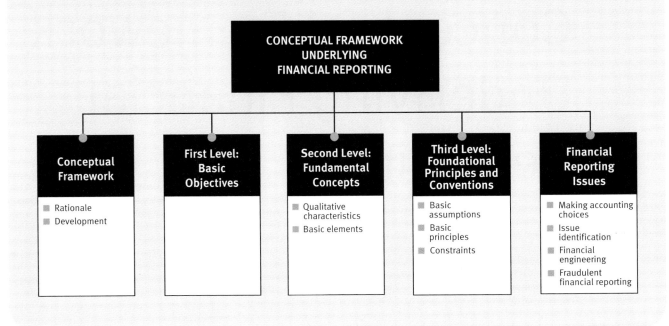

CONCEPTUAL FRAMEWORK

A **conceptual framework** is like a constitution: it is a "coherent system of interrelated objectives and fundamentals that can lead to consistent standards and that prescribes the nature, function, and limits of financial accounting and financial statements."[1] Many have considered the real contribution of Canadian and American standard-setting bodies, and even their continued existence, to depend on the quality and utility of the conceptual framework.

Rationale for Conceptual Framework

Objective 1
Describe the usefulness of a conceptual framework.

Why is a conceptual framework necessary? First, to be useful, **standard setting should build on and relate to an established body of concepts and objectives**. A soundly developed conceptual framework should enable the AcSB to issue more **useful and consistent** standards over time. A **coherent** set of standards and rules should result, because

---

[1] Conceptual Framework for Financial Accounting and Reporting: Elements of Financial Statements and Their Measurement, FASB Discussion Memorandum, (Stamford, Conn.: FASB, 1976), page 1 of the Scope and Implications of the Conceptual Framework Project section.

they would be built upon the same foundation. The framework should **increase** financial statement users' **understanding** of and **confidence in** financial reporting, and it should **enhance comparability** among companies' financial statements.

Second, **new and emerging practical problems** should be more quickly solved by referring to an existing framework of basic theory. It is difficult, if not impossible, for the AcSB to prescribe the proper accounting treatment quickly for highly complex situations. Practicing accountants, however, must resolve such problems on a day-to-day basis. Through the exercise of **good judgement** and with the help of a **universally accepted conceptual framework**, it is hoped that practitioners will be able to dismiss certain alternatives quickly and then focus upon a logical and acceptable treatment.

Development of Conceptual Framework

Over the years, numerous organizations, committees, and interested individuals have developed and published their own conceptual frameworks, but no single framework has been universally accepted and relied on in practice. Recognizing the need for a generally accepted framework, the FASB in 1976 issued a three-part discussion memorandum entitled "Conceptual Framework for Financial Accounting and Reporting: Elements of Financial Statements and Their Measurement." It set forth the major issues to be addressed in establishing a conceptual framework for setting accounting standards and resolving financial reporting controversies. From this arose six "Statements of Financial Accounting Concepts." A seventh on accounting measurement was added in 2000. The AcSB followed suit, issuing *CICA Handbook* Section 1000—Financial Statement Concepts.

Illustration 2-1 provides an overview of a conceptual framework.[2] At the first level, the objectives identify accounting's **goals and purposes** and are the conceptual framework's building blocks. At the second level are the **qualitative characteristics** that make accounting information useful and the **elements of financial statements** (assets, liabilities, equity, revenues, expenses, gains, losses, and other comprehensive income). At the third or final level are the **foundational principles and conventions** used in establishing and applying accounting standards. These include **assumptions**, **principles**, and **constraints** that describe the present reporting environment.

International Insight

The IASB has issued a conceptual framework that is broadly consistent with that of the United States and Canada.

2 Objective
Describe the main components of the conceptual framework for financial reporting.

FIRST LEVEL: BASIC OBJECTIVES

As we discussed in Chapter 1, the objective of financial reporting according to *CICA Handbook* Section 1000 is to communicate information that is **useful** to investors, creditors, and other users in making their **resource allocation** decisions and/or **assessing management stewardship**. Consequently, financial statements provide information about:

(a) an entity's economic resources, obligations, and equity/net assets;

(b) changes in an entity's economic resources, obligations, and equity/net assets; and

(c) the economic performance of the entity.[3]

In providing information to users of financial statements, the accounting profession uses **general-purpose financial statements**. These are basic financial statements that provide information that meets the needs of **key** users.[4] The intent of such statements is to provide the **most useful information possible at minimal cost** to various user groups.

3 Objective
Understand the objective of financial reporting.

---

[2] Adapted from William C. Norby, *The Financial Analysts Journal*, March/April 1982, p. 22.

[3] *CICA Handbook*, Section 1000.15.

[4] Normally investors and creditors, per *CICA Handbook*, Section 1000.11.

Illustration 2-1

*Conceptual Framework
for Financial Reporting*

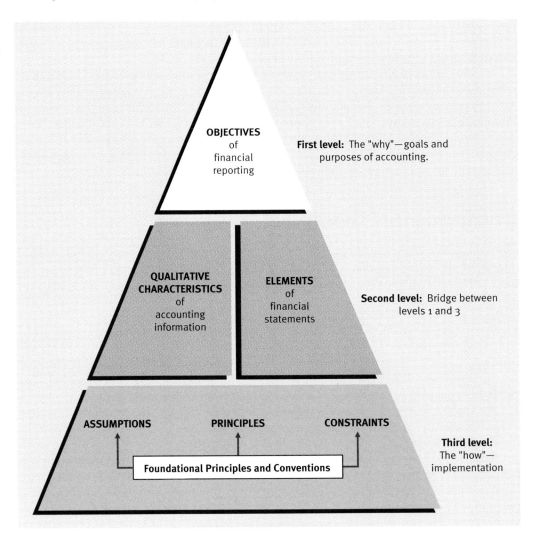

Underlying these objectives is the notion that users need **reasonable knowledge** of business and financial accounting matters to understand the information contained in financial statements. This point is important: it means that preparers of financial statements can assume users have a level of reasonable competence when it comes to reading, interpreting, and understanding the information presented. This impacts the way and extent to which information is reported.[5]

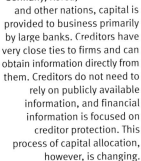

SECOND LEVEL: FUNDAMENTAL CONCEPTS

The objectives (first level) are concerned with accounting's **goals and purposes**. Later, we will discuss the ways these goals and purposes are **implemented** (third level). Between these two levels, it is necessary to provide certain **conceptual building blocks** that explain the **qualitative characteristics** of accounting information and define the **elements of financial statements**. These conceptual building blocks form a bridge

---

[5] Users are presumed to have a reasonable understanding of business and economic activities and accounting as well as a willingness to study the information with reasonable diligence according to the *CICA Handbook*, Section 1000.19.

between the why of accounting (the objectives) and the how of accounting (recognition and measurement).

Qualitative Characteristics of Accounting Information

Choosing an acceptable accounting method, the amount and types of information to be disclosed, and the format in which information should be presented involves determining **which alternative provides the most useful information for decision-making purposes** (**decision usefulness**). The conceptual framework has identified the **qualitative characteristics** of accounting information that distinguish better (more useful) information from inferior (less useful) information for decision-making purposes.

4 **Objective**

Identify the qualitative characteristics of accounting information.

Decision-Makers (Users) and Understandability

Decision-makers vary widely in the types of decisions they make, the methods of decision-making they employ, the information they already possess or can obtain from other sources, and their ability to process the information. For information to be useful, there must be a connection between these users and the decisions they make. This connection, **understandability**, is the information quality that permits reasonably informed users to perceive its significance. Fair presentation is achieved by applying GAAP including providing sufficient information in a manner that is clear and understandable.[6]

Relevance and Reliability

Relevance and **reliability** are qualities that make accounting information useful for decision-making.

Relevance.   To be relevant, accounting information must **make a difference in a decision**.[7] If certain information has no bearing on a decision, it is irrelevant to that decision. Relevant information helps users make predictions about the ultimate outcome of past, present, and future events; that is, it has **predictive value**. Relevant information also helps users confirm or correct prior expectations; it has **feedback value**.

For example, when a company issues an interim earnings announcement, this information is considered relevant because it provides a basis for forecasting **annual** earnings. It also gives feedback value as to how the company is performing to date. In February 2001, Nortel Networks Corp. announced that it would miss earlier projected financial targets for the year by 50%, a significant amount. Upon receipt of the information, users revised their expectation of annual earnings.

For information to be relevant, it must also be **available** to decision-makers before it loses its capacity to influence their decisions. Thus **timeliness** is a primary ingredient.

If Nortel did not report its interim results until six months after the end of the period, the information would be much less useful for decision-making purposes. In fact, when Nortel made the February announcements, there was some concern over whether the information could have been released even earlier. The announcement came two days after Nortel had finalized a deal to purchase a Zurich-based subsidiary from JDS Uniphase. As partial consideration for the deal, Nortel paid 65.7 million of its shares, which ended up being worth substantially less once the earnings announcement was made.

The following chart shows the rapid price fall of Nortel stock from mid-year 2000 to mid-year 2001. Note the significant decline in February 2001.

What do the Numbers Mean?

---

[6] *CICA Handbook*, Section 1400.04.

[7] Qualitative Characteristics of Accounting Information, Statement of Financial Accounting Concepts No. 2 (Stamford, Conn.: FASB, May 1980), par. .47.

For information to be relevant, it should have predictive or feedback value and it must be presented on a timely basis.

Reliability.   Accounting information is reliable to the extent that it is **verifiable**, is a **faithful representation** of the underlying economic reality, and is reasonably free of error and bias (**neutral**). Reliability is necessary for individuals who have neither the time nor the expertise to evaluate the information's factual content.

Verifiability is demonstrated when **independent** measurers, using the **same measurement methods**, obtain similar results. If outside parties arrive at different conclusions using the same measurement methods, then the statements are not verifiable. Auditors could not render an opinion on such statements. Some numbers are more easily verified than others, e.g., cash can be verified by confirming with the bank where the deposit is held. Other numbers, such as accruals for environmental cleanup costs, are more difficult (although not necessarily impossible) to verify as many assumptions are made to arrive at an estimate. Numbers that are easy to verify with a reasonable degree of accuracy are often referred to as "hard" numbers. Those that have more measurement uncertainty are referred to as "soft."

Representational faithfulness means that the numbers and descriptions **represent what really exists or happened**. The accounting numbers and descriptions agree with the resources or events that these numbers and descriptions purport to represent. Numbers and financial statements are thought to be representationally faithful when they are **transparent** and when they reflect the **economic substance** of an underlying event or arrangement **over the legal form**.

Below is an excerpt from the notes to the financial statements of Enron Corp. for the year ended December 31, 2000. The complexity of the business arrangements make it difficult to understand the nature of the underlying transactions. It contributes to a set of financial statements that lack transparency.

What do the Numbers Mean?

"In 2000 and 1999, Enron sold approximately $632 million and $192 million, respectively, of merchant investments and other assets to Whitewing. Enron recognized no gains or losses in connection with these transactions. Additionally, in 2000, ECT Merchant Investments Corp., a wholly-owned Enron subsidiary, contributed two pools of merchant investments to a limited partnership that is a subsidiary of Enron. Subsequent to the contributions, the partnership issued partnership interests representing 100% of the beneficial, economic interests in the two asset pools, and such interests were sold for a total of $545 million to a limited liability company that is a subsidiary of Whitewing. See Note 3. These entities are separate legal entities from Enron and have separate assets and liabilities. In 2000 and 1999, the Related Party, as described in Note 16, contributed $33 million and $15 million, respectively, of equity to Whitewing. In 2000,

Whitewing contributed $7.1 million to a partnership formed by Enron, Whitewing and a third party. Subsequently, Enron sold a portion of its interest in the partnership through a securitization. See Note 3."[8]

Neutrality means that information cannot be selected to **favour one set of stakeholders over another**. Factual, truthful, unbiased information must be the overriding consideration when preparing financial information.

Livent Inc. was a Canadian company that produced and presented large Broadway style musicals. In 1993, the company went public, listing its shares on the TSX. By 1998, it filed for bankruptcy protection amid allegations of accounting irregularities and was investigated by the Ontario Securities Commission in 2001. The following excerpt is from the OSC Notice of Hearing and Allegation concerning the issue of manipulation of the financial statements:

> "... at the end of each financial reporting period, Livent accounting staff circulated to the Respondents a management summary reflecting actual results (including net income, on a show-by-show basis, compared to budget), as well as any improper adjustments carried forward from a prior financial period in connection with each show. Having regard to the actual results, the Respondents then provided instructions, directly or indirectly, to the Livent accounting staff specifying changes to be made to the actual results reflected in the company's books and records. In order to give effect to the Respondents' instructions, Livent accounting staff manipulated Livent's books and records by various means which did not accord with GAAP. The effect of the manipulations was to improve the presentation of Livent's financial results for the reporting period. Draft financial statements would then be generated for the reporting period incorporating the manipulations. These draft financial statements were then distributed to the Livent audit committee and, thereafter the Livent board of directors, for their review and approval. The Respondents attended meetings of the audit committee and the board of directors where these draft financial statements were discussed and ultimately approved. The Respondents did not disclose to the audit committee or the board of directors that, to their knowledge, the financial statements were false or misleading."

Among other things, management was charged with deliberately and systematically biasing the information. This contributed to the company's eventual downfall.

In practice, many assumptions must be used by management in dealing with uncertainty in financial reporting. When choosing assumptions, management must use its best estimates (**management best estimate**). How does the concept of **neutrality** fit with the concept of **conservatism**?

Few conventions in accounting are as misunderstood as the concept of **conservatism**. In situations involving uncertainty and professional judgement, conservatism dictates that **net assets and net income not be overstated**. Does this represent a bias? Not necessarily. It's more a default guideline. It acknowledges a **pre-existing tendency** of companies to overstate net assets and net income. Therefore it acts as a feature to counterbalance this tendency. An example of conservatism in accounting is the use of the lower of cost and market approach in valuing inventories.

Users of financial statements are more tolerant of understated net assets and net income than overstated balances. Therefore, if the issue is in doubt, it is better to understate than overstate net income and net assets. Of course, if there is no doubt, there is no need to apply this constraint.

What do the Numbers Mean?

International Insight

In Japan, capital is also provided by very large banks. Assets are often undervalued and liabilities overvalued. These practices reduce the demand for dividends and protect creditors in event of a default.

---

[8] Consolidated financial statements of Enron Corp. for the year ended December 31, 2000

There is yet another aspect to neutrality: neutrality in standard setting. Some argue that standards should not be issued if they cause undesirable economic effects on an industry or company (the **economic consequences argument,** which was mentioned in Chapter 1). This has been the long-standing argument against full recognition of employee stock option costs. Standards must be free from bias, however, or we will no longer have **credible financial statements.** Without credible financial statements, individuals will no longer use this information.

Comparability and Consistency

Information about an enterprise is more useful if it can be compared with similar information about another enterprise (**comparability**) and with similar information about the same enterprise at other points in time (**consistency**).[9]

Comparability.   Information that has been measured and reported in a similar manner for different enterprises is considered comparable. Comparability enables users to **identify the real similarities and differences in economic phenomena** because they have not been obscured by incomparable accounting methods. For example, the accounting for pensions is different in North America and Japan. In Canada and the United States, pension cost is recorded as incurred, whereas in Japan there is little or no charge to income for these costs. As a result, it is difficult to compare and evaluate the financial results of General Motors or Ford with those of Nissan or Honda. **Resource allocation decisions involve evaluations of alternatives**; a valid evaluation can be made only if comparable information is available. Although not a substitute for comparable information, full disclosure of information sometimes allows users to deal with inconsistencies.

Consistency.   When an entity applies the **same accounting treatment to similar events, from period to period**, the entity is considered to be consistent in its use of accounting standards. It does not mean that companies cannot switch from one accounting method to another. Companies can change methods, but the changes are restricted to situations in which it can be demonstrated that the newly adopted method results in a **more appropriate presentation** of the underlying economic events.[10] In these cases, the accounting change's nature and effect, as well as justification, must be **disclosed** in the financial statements for the period in which the change is made.[11]

When there has been a change in **accounting principles**, the auditor refers to it in an explanatory paragraph of the audit report. This paragraph identifies the nature of the change and refers the reader to the note in the financial statements that discusses the change in detail.

Tradeoffs

It is not always possible for financial information to have all the qualities of useful information. Sometimes a choice must be made regarding which quality is more important.

Relevant information must have **feedback value, predictive value,** and be **timely. Reliable** information is **verifiable, representative of reality,** and **neutral.** Given that

---

[9] Since the accounting environment is continually changing, comparability and consistency are difficult to achieve in practice. Tax laws change, new industries appear, new financial instruments are created, and mergers and divestitures occur.

[10] The AICPA Special Committee on Financial Reporting noted that users highly value consistency. It notes that a change tends to destroy the comparability of data before and after the change. Some companies take the time to assist users to understand the pre- and post-change data. Generally, however, users say they lose the ability to analyse from period to period.

[11] *CICA Handbook,* Section 1506.16.

companies must issue annual financial statements, how long after the year-end date should they be issued? Financial statements are often released several weeks or months after year end. Earlier issuance meets the timeliness criteria but issuance at a later date allows time for management and auditors to check the statements to ensure reliability. At some point in time, however, the information becomes irrelevant due to lack of timeliness. Which is more important, timeliness or reliability? Each situation must be evaluated separately considering the facts and users.

The accounting profession is continually striving to produce financial information that meets all of the qualitative characteristics of useful information.

Basic Elements

An important aspect of developing any theoretical structure is the body of **basic elements** or definitions to be included in the structure. At present, accounting uses many terms that have specific meanings. These terms constitute the **language of accounting and business.** There are many elements that users expect to find on the financial statements, including **assets, liabilities, equity, revenues, gains, expenses, losses,** and **other comprehensive income**. In addition, within each of these categories are numerous subcategories such as **current** and **non-current** assets, cash, inventory, etc. The conceptual framework defines the basic elements so that users have a common understanding of the main items presented on the financial statements.

5 Objective
Define the basic elements of financial statements.

One such term is **asset**. Is an asset something we own? How do we define "own?" Is it based on **legal title** or **possession**? If ownership is based on legal title, can we assume that any leased asset would not be shown on the balance sheet? Is an asset something we have the **right to use**, or is it anything of value used by the enterprise to generate revenues? If the answer is the latter, then why should the enterprise's management not be considered an asset?

The elements of financial statements that are most directly related to measuring an enterprise's performance and financial status are listed below. Each of these elements will be explained and examined in more detail in subsequent chapters.

Elements of Financial Statements[12]

Assets are probable future economic benefits obtained or controlled by a particular entity as a result of past transactions or events. They have three essential characteristics:

1. they embody a **future benefit;**

2. the entity can **control access** to this benefit; and

3. the **transaction** or event giving the entity access to this benefit **has occurred**.

Generally, if a company has access to and control over substantially all of the **risks and rewards** of ownership, the asset should be recognized.

Liabilities are probable future sacrifices of economic benefits arising from present duty or responsibility to others, as a result of past transactions or events, where there is little or no discretion to avoid the obligation. Liabilities also have three essential characteristics:

1. they embody a **duty or responsibility;**

2. the entity has **little or no discretion to avoid** the duty; and

3. the **transaction** or event obligating the entity **has occurred.**

---

[12] Taken from *CICA Handbook*, Section 1000.29 to .40.

Equity/Net Assets is a **residual interest** in the assets of an entity that remains after deducting its liabilities. In a business enterprise, the equity is the **ownership** interest.

Revenues are increases in economic resources, either by inflows or other enhancements of an entity's assets or settlement of its liabilities resulting from an entity's **ordinary activities**.

Expenses are decreases in economic resources, either by outflows or reductions of assets or incurrence of liabilities resulting from an entity's **ordinary revenue-generating activities**.

Gains are increases in equity (net assets) from an entity's **peripheral or incidental transactions** and from all other transactions and other events and circumstances affecting the entity during a period, except those that result from revenues or investments by owners.

Losses are decreases in equity (net assets) from an entity's **peripheral or incidental transactions** and from all other transactions and other events and circumstances affecting the entity during a period, except those that result from expenses or distributions to owners.

Traditionally, the financial statements have consisted of:

1. an income statement,

2. a balance sheet,

3. a statement of retained earnings, and

4. a statement of cash flows.[13]

Proposed *CICA Handbook* Section 1530 adds one more statement: the **statement of comprehensive income**. The term comprehensive income represents a relatively new income concept that is more inclusive than the traditional notion of net income. It includes net income and all other changes in equity exclusive of owners' investments and distributions. For example, the following would be included as **other comprehensive income** (the final element) in this new statement:

- unrealized holding gains and losses on certain securities

- certain gains and losses related to foreign exchange instruments

- gains and losses relating to certain hedges

- adjustments resulting from certain related party transactions with non-owners

- other

Comprehensive income may also be presented as part of the income statement. More detail will be presented in Chapter 4.

THIRD LEVEL: FOUNDATIONAL PRINCIPLES AND CONVENTIONS

The framework's third level consists of **foundational principles and conventions** that implement the basic objectives of level one. These concepts help explain which, when, and how financial elements and events should be **recognized, measured,** and **presented** by the accounting system.

For discussion purposes, the concepts are identified as basic **assumptions, principles,** and **constraints**. Not everyone uses this classification system, so it is best to focus your attention more on understanding the concepts than on how they are classified and organ-

---

[13] *CICA Handbook*, Section 1400.10.

ized. These concepts serve as guidelines in developing rational responses to controversial financial reporting issues. They have evolved over time and are fundamental to the specific accounting principles issued by the AcSB.

Basic Assumptions

Four basic **assumptions** underlie the financial accounting structure: (1) **economic entity**, (2) **going concern**, (3) **monetary unit**, and (4) **periodicity**.

⑥ Objective
Describe the basic assumptions of accounting.

Economic Entity Assumption

The economic entity assumption (or entity concept) means that economic activity can be **identified** with a particular **unit of accountability** (e.g., a company). In other words, a company's business activity can be kept separate and distinct from its owners and any other business unit. If there were no meaningful way to separate all the economic events that occur, no basis for accounting would exist.

The **entity concept** does not apply solely to segregating activities among given **business enterprises**. An individual, a department or division, or an entire industry could be considered a separate entity if we chose to define the unit in such a manner. Thus, the entity concept **does not necessarily always refer to a legal entity**. For tax and legal purposes, the **legal entity** is the relevant unit for a company. GAAP, however, requires that a company **consolidate** the financial statements of its subsidiaries with those of the parent. A parent and its subsidiaries are separate **legal entities**, but merging their activities for accounting and reporting purposes provides more meaningful information.[14] Thus, the consolidated financial statements are prepared from the perspective of the **economic entity**. This allows the company to group the assets, liabilities, and other financial statement elements that are under the parent's **control** together in one set of statements. Control has historically been viewed as a function of number of common shares held.[15]

Illustration 2-2 depicts the notion of economic entity for consolidated financial statements.

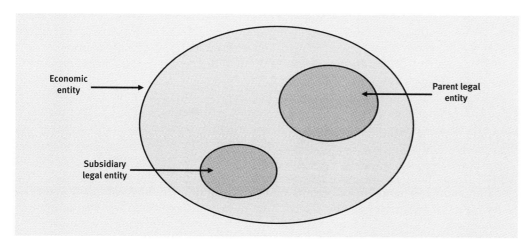

Illustration 2-2

Economic Entity as Defined for Consolidated Financial Statements

---

[14] The concept of the entity is changing. For example, it is now harder to define the outer edges of companies. There are public companies with multiple public subsidiaries, each with joint ventures, licensing arrangements, and other affiliations and strategic alliances. Increasingly, loose affiliations of enterprises in joint ventures or customer-supplier relationships are formed and dissolved in a matter of months or weeks. These virtual companies raise accounting issues about how to account for the entity. See Steven H. Wallman, "The Future of Accounting and Disclosure in an Evolving World: The Need for Dramatic Change," *Accounting Horizons*, September 1995.

[15] That is, if the parent owns more than 50% of the (voting) common shares, it can exercise voting control.

What do the Numbers Mean?

It is important to first **define the entity** for financial reporting purposes. Many companies use vehicles known as Special Purpose Entities ("SPE") or Variable Interest Entities ("VIE"). These are legal entities set up for a specific purpose, e.g., to hold leases, pension funds, or perhaps certain investments. Are SPEs part of the economic entity for consolidated financial reporting purposes? This was the centre of much of the controversy for Enron. Enron had numerous SPEs that it did not include in its definition of economic entity and therefore excluded from the consolidated financial statements. As it turned out, Enron should have included them since the liabilities and losses of these SPEs ended up being liabilities and losses of Enron in the end. Enron's accounting had the impact of understating liabilities as well as overstating income. The AcSB has issued new standards dealing with inclusion of VIE as part of the economic entity.

Going Concern Assumption

Most accounting methods are based on the going concern assumption. This assumes that the business enterprise will **continue to operate for the foreseeable future**, i.e., it will not be forced to cease operations. Experience indicates that, in spite of numerous business failures, companies have a fairly high continuance rate. Although accountants do not believe that business firms will last indefinitely, they do expect them to last long enough to fulfill their objectives and commitments.

The implications of this assumption are profound. The **historical cost principle** would have limited usefulness if **liquidation** were assumed. Under a liquidation approach, for example, asset values are better stated at **net realizable value** (sales price less costs of disposal) than at **acquisition cost**. Amortization and amortization policies are justifiable and appropriate only if we assume some permanence to the enterprise so that we can justify allocating the costs of the amortized assets to future periods to match with future revenues. If a liquidation approach were adopted, the **current-noncurrent classification** of assets and liabilities would lose much of its significance. Labelling anything a **fixed or long-term** asset would be difficult to justify. Indeed, listing liabilities in priority of liquidation would be more reasonable.

The going concern assumption applies in most business situations. Only where **liquidation appears imminent** is the assumption inapplicable. In these cases, a total **revaluation** of assets and liabilities can provide information that closely approximates the entity's **net realizable value**. Accounting problems related to an enterprise in liquidation are presented in advanced accounting courses. In order to illustrate this concept, consider the situation of Air Canada.

On April 1, 2003, Air Canada filed for bankruptcy protection under the Companies' Creditors Arrangement Act (CCAA) due to cash flow difficulties. The CCAA provides a safe harbour for companies in distress and allows them to reorganize their financial affairs in an organized manner while at the same time holding off creditors. Air Canada's protection was granted for the period ending June 30. This was subsequently extended to September 30, 2003. In the meantime, the company issued its first quarter results.

Should the statements have been prepared on a **liquidation basis** or **going concern basis**? Air Canada prepared the statements on a going concern basis using certain assumptions:

1. that management was in the process of developing a plan to restructure operations under the CCAA,

2. that it had been able to obtain "debtor in possession" financing from General Electric Canada Finance Inc., and

3. that its expectation was that the company would continue to operate as a going concern.

The financial statements fully disclosed these facts.

What do the Numbers Mean?

Monetary Unit Assumption

The monetary unit assumption means that money is the common denominator of economic activity and provides an appropriate **basis for accounting measurement** and analysis. This assumption implies that the monetary unit is the most effective means of expressing to interested parties changes in capital and exchanges of goods and services. The monetary unit is relevant, simple, universally available, understandable, and useful. Applying this assumption depends on the even more basic assumption that **quantitative data** are useful in communicating economic information and in making rational economic decisions.

In Canada and the United States, accountants have chosen generally to ignore the phenomenon of **price-level change** (inflation and deflation) by assuming that the unit of measure, the dollar, remains reasonably **stable**. This assumption about the monetary unit has been used to justify adding 1970 dollars to 2003 dollars without any adjustment. Only if circumstances change dramatically (such as if Canada or the United States were to experience high inflation similar to that in many South American countries) would the AcSB and FASB consider "inflation accounting."

Periodicity Assumption

The most accurate way to measure enterprise activity results is at the time of the enterprise's eventual liquidation. At that point there is complete certainty as to all cash flows of the company. Business, government, investors, and various other user groups, however, cannot wait that long for such information. Users need to be apprised of performance and economic status on a **timely basis** so that they can evaluate and compare firms. Therefore, information must be reported periodically. The periodicity (or time period) assumption implies that an enterprise's economic activities can be divided into **artificial time periods**. These time periods vary, but the most common are monthly, quarterly, and yearly.

The shorter the time period, the more difficult it becomes to **determine the proper net income** for the period. A month's results are usually less reliable than a quarter's results, and a quarter's results are likely less reliable than a year's results. This is because in applying accrual accounting, the shorter the time period, the more estimates there are that need to be made in terms of accruing costs and revenues. Investors desire and demand that information be quickly processed and disseminated; yet the more quickly the information is released, the more it is subject to error.

This problem of defining the time period is becoming more serious because product cycles are shorter and products become obsolete more quickly. Many believe that, given technology advances, more on-line, **real-time financial information** needs to be provided to ensure that relevant information is available. The issue of continuous financial reporting was introduced in Chapter 1.

Basic Principles of Accounting

Four basic principles of accounting are used to record transactions: (1) **historical cost**, (2) **revenue recognition**, (3) **matching**, and (4) **full disclosure**.

Historical Cost Principle—A Valuation Principle in Transition

GAAP requires that financial statements be prepared using the historical cost basis of measurement whereby transactions are initially measured at the amount of cash or cash equivalents paid or received or the fair value ascribed to them when they took place. This

International Insight

Due to their experiences with persistent inflation, several South American countries produce "constant currency" financial reports. Typically, a general price-level index is used to adjust for the effects of inflation.

IAS Note

IAS 29 sets out certain requirements for entities reporting in a hyperinflationary economy.

7 Objective

Explain the application of the basic principles of accounting.

is often referred to as the **historical cost principle**.[16] The historical cost principle has three foundational assumptions:

1. it represents a value at a **point in time**,

2. it results from a **reciprocal exchange** (i.e., a two-way exchange), and

3. the exchange includes **an outside party**.

Initial recognition. For non-financial assets, the cost includes any **laid-down costs**; that is, any cost incurred to get the asset in place (whether it be for sale or to generate income through use). Inventory, for instance, might include the **cost of material, labour, and a reasonable allocation of overhead**.[17] Similarly, for self-constructed assets, cost would include any cost incurred to get the asset **ready for its intended use**, including transportation and installation costs.[18]

Sometimes it is not possible to determine **cost**. Transactions that have some or all of the following characteristics present challenges:

- **Non-monetary or barter transactions** where **no cash or monetary consideration** is exchanged. Here the value of the assets exchanged may be more difficult to determine.

- **Non-reciprocal transactions** such as donations (where there is **no exchange**).

- **Related party transactions** where the parties to the transaction are not acting at arm's length (i.e., **no outside party**). In these cases, the exchange price may not reflect the true value of the assets exchanged.

In cases such as these, an attempt is made to estimate the **fair value**.

The historical cost principle also applies to financial instruments including financial assets and financial liabilities. Bonds, notes, and accounts payable and receivable are issued by a business enterprise in exchange for assets, or perhaps services, for which an **agreed upon exchange price** or **economic value** has usually been determined. Parties to the transaction have agreed upon the respective value of what they are giving up and what they are getting. This price, established by the exchange transaction, is the "cost" of the financial instrument and provides the figure at which it should be recognized in the financial statements.

Subsequent remeasurement. Cost has an important advantage over other valuation methods: it is **reliable**. Because it generally arises from an **arm's length transaction** or exchange, it represents a bargained, fairly arrived at value at a specific point in time. Upon initial recognitions, it usually represents fair value. Over time, however, it often becomes irrelevant in terms of **predictive value**. While subsequent remeasurements based on alternative measurement values such as fair value provide information that is more relevant, they often involve **measurement uncertainty**. Furthermore, because there is often no external exchange (i.e., with an outside party), the values may be **subjective**.

Having stated this, the trend has been toward an increasingly **mixed valuation model**. What used to be primarily a **historical cost based model**, modified by the application of conservatism (i.e., where the value of the asset declined below cost), is moving more toward a **market valuation model**. The current **mixed valuation model** is shown in Illustration 2-3.

---

[16] *CICA Handbook*, Section 1000.53.

[17] *CICA Handbook*, Section 3030.06.

[18] *CICA Handbook*, Section 3061.05.

Illustration 2-3

*Valuation of Selected
Balance Sheet Elements:
A Mixed Valuation Model*

ASSET	BASIS OF VALUATION	MANAGEMENT INTENT
Accounts receivable	Net realizable value	To collect
Financial assets and liabilities held for trading, e.g., marketable securities and derivatives	Fair value*	To sell in near term for profit (part of trading portfolio)
Financial assets available for sale, e.g., securities	Fair value* (where available— otherwise at cost)	To sell but not necessarily actively trade
Inventories	Lower of cost and market (if cost not recoverable)	To sell and replace
Capital assets	Lower of cost and fair value (if cost not recoverable)	Hold to produce revenues
Financial assets held to maturity, e.g., bonds receivable	Lower of amortized cost and NRV	Hold for the longer term and collect the face value

* proposed *Handbook* Section 3855

Illustration 2-3 identifies basic elements that are found on many balance sheets along with the basis for valuation. As noted in the illustration, the existing **mixed attribute system** permits the use of the following measurements:

1. Historical cost

2. Fair value consisting of any of the following:

    (a) market value (via lower of cost and market)

    (b) discounted cash flows

    (c) net present value/net realizable value

    (d) option pricing models and

    (e) other.

3. Lower of cost and market/fair value (conservatism)

The primary emphasis in the model is on **relevance** and therefore many financial statement elements consider market or fair value in some way. Note that the **basis for valuation is tied to management intent** with respect to the asset. Management intent gives more insight into which value might be more relevant. As a general principle, **where current values are available** and they provide more relevant information (in terms of what management intends to do with the asset or liability), they should be used as long as **measurement uncertainty levels are acceptable**.

IAS Note

IAS 39 dictates that most financial instruments be carried at fair value.

Revenue Recognition Principle

A crucial question for many enterprises is when revenue should be recognized. Revenue is generally recognized when:

- performance is achieved (**earned**) and

- **measurability is reasonably certain** and

- **collectibility is reasonably assured** (realized/realizable).[19]

---

[19] *CICA Handbook*, Section 1000.47.

This is referred to as the **revenue recognition principle**. As with the historical cost principle, the basic presumptions are that the transaction:

- results from a **reciprocal exchange** (i.e., a two-way exchange) and
- the exchange includes **an outside party**.[20]

Revenues are **realized** when products (goods or services), merchandise, or other assets are **exchanged** for cash or claims to cash. Revenues are **realizable** when assets received or held are readily convertible into cash or claims to cash. Assets are readily convertible when they are saleable or interchangeable in an active market at readily determinable prices without significant additional cost.

Performance.   Revenues are considered earned when the entity has substantially accomplished what it must do to be entitled to the benefits represented by the revenues. In other words, revenue is recognized when the **earnings process is substantially complete**. When the earnings process is a **discrete earnings process**, i.e., with one main or **critical event**, the revenue recognition point is objective. Normally revenue would be recognized when the **risks and rewards of ownership** pass to the buyer at shipping point. When the earnings process lasts over a longer period and has more than one significant event, i.e., a **continuous earnings process**, revenue recognition becomes more difficult. An example of a continuous earnings process is a long-term construction contract. In these cases, revenue is recognized as earned, over the life of the contract.

Measurability and collectibility.   Where there is **measurement or collection uncertainty**, revenue recognition should be deferred until these uncertainties have been resolved or minimized to an acceptable level. For collectibility issues, either the **instalment** or **cost recovery** methods may be used to accomplish this. These methods recognize profits as cash is received often after performance by the company.

Matching Principle

Expenses are recognized on the income statement not when wages are paid, or when the work is performed, or when a product is produced, but when the work (service) or the product actually **makes its contribution to revenue**. Thus, expense recognition is tied to revenue recognition. This practice is referred to as the **matching principle** because it dictates that efforts (expenses) be matched with accomplishment (revenues) whenever reasonable and practicable. It also illustrates the **cause and effect relationship** between the money spent to earn revenues and the revenues themselves.

For those costs for which it is difficult to establish a direct association with revenue, some other approach must be developed. Often, a **rational and systematic** allocation policy is used that will approximate the matching principle. This type of expense recognition pattern involves assumptions about the benefits that are being received as well as the cost associated with those benefits. The cost of a long-lived asset, for example, must be allocated over all accounting periods during which the asset is used because the asset contributes to revenue generation throughout its useful life.

Some costs are charged to the current period as expenses (or losses) simply because there is no basis for capitalizing or deferring the cost. The transaction occurred in the period and benefits the period. Examples of these types of costs are officers' salaries and other administrative expenses.

Costs are generally classified into two groups: **product costs** and **period costs**. Product costs such as material, labour, and overhead attach to the product and are carried

---

[20] Where there is a related party, additional care needs to be taken to ensure that a *bona fide* transaction exists from the entity's perspective and that the basis for measurement is appropriate.

into future periods if the revenue from the product is recognized in subsequent periods. Period costs such as officers' salaries and other administrative expenses are charged off immediately, even though benefits associated with these costs occur in the future, because no direct relationship between cost and revenue can be established.

Summarizing, we might say that costs are analysed to determine whether a relationship exists with revenue. Where this association holds, the costs are expensed and matched against the revenue in the period when the revenue is recognized. If no connection appears between costs and revenues, an allocation of cost on some systematic and rational basis might be appropriate. Where this method does not seem desirable, the cost may be expensed immediately.

Livent Inc., mentioned earlier, followed the policy of deferring preproduction costs associated with the creation of each separate show until the show was opened. At that time, the show would start to produce revenues and then the costs were amortized and matched with those revenues. Such costs included advertising, publicity and promotions, set construction, props, costumes, and salaries paid to the cast, crew, musicians, and creative constituents during rehearsal. In short, anything to do with the production was deferred.

On the one hand, one might argue that this was a bit aggressive. One could also argue that this treatment was acceptable given the direct and incremental nature of these costs in terms of the future production revenues. The trouble began when the company started to reclassify some of these costs to fixed assets and also to reallocate these costs to different and unrelated shows that had higher revenue streams. The company even had spreadsheets to keep track of actual results as compared with those that were publicly reported.[21]

The matching principle's conceptual validity has been a subject of debate. A major concern is that matching permits certain costs to be **deferred and treated as assets** on the balance sheet when in fact these costs **may not have future benefits**. If abused, this principle permits the balance sheet to become a dumping ground for unmatched costs. In addition, there appears to be no objective **definition of systematic and rational**. For example, assume a company purchases an asset for $100,000 that will last five years. Various amortization methods (all considered systematic and rational) might be used to allocate this cost over the five-year period. However, it is difficult to develop objective criteria to be used in determining what portion of the asset cost should be written off each period.[22]

What do the Numbers Mean?

Full Disclosure Principle

Anything that is decision relevant should be included in the financial statements. This is referred to as the **full disclosure principle**. The principle recognizes that the nature and amount of information included in financial reports reflects a series of judgemental trade-offs. These trade-offs strive for:

- **sufficient detail** to disclose matters that make a difference to users, yet

- **sufficient condensation** to make the information understandable, keeping in mind **costs** of preparing and using it.

More information is not always better. Too much information may result in a situation where the user is unable to digest or process the information. This is referred to as **information overload**. Information about financial position, income, cash flows, and investments can be found in one of three places:

---

[21] OSC Notice of Hearing and Statement of Allegations July 3, 2001.

[22] Some would even suggest that procedure is nearly impossible, given that the revenue flow from any given asset is interrelated with the remaining asset structure of the enterprise. For example, see Arthur L. Thomas, "The Allocation Problem in Financial Accounting Theory," *Studies in Accounting Research No. 3,* (Evanston, Ill.: American Accounting Association, 1969), and "The Allocation Problem: Part Two," *Studies in Accounting Research No. 9,* (Sarasota, Fla.: American Accounting Association, 1974).

1. within the **main body of financial statements**,

2. in the **notes to the financial statements**, or

3. as supplementary information including the **Management Discussion and Analysis** (MD&A).

The financial statements are a **formalized, structured means of communicating financial information**. Disclosure is not a substitute for proper accounting.[23] Certain numbers, such as earnings per share, send signals to the capital marketplace. Thus, for example, cash basis accounting for cost of goods sold is misleading, even if accrual basis amounts were disclosed in the notes to the financial statements. As mentioned in Chapter 1, and earlier in this chapter with regards to Nortel, the market watches and listens for signals about earnings in particular and does not always react well to earnings surprises—especially negative ones.

The notes to financial statements generally **amplify or explain** the items presented in the main body of the statements. If the information in the main body of the statements gives an incomplete picture of the enterprise's performance and position, additional information that is needed to complete the picture should be included in the notes.

Information in the notes does not have to be quantifiable, nor does it need to qualify as an element. Notes can be partially or totally narrative. Examples of notes are:

- **descriptions** of the accounting policies and methods used in measuring the elements reported in the statements

- **explanations** of uncertainties and contingencies

- **statistics and details** too voluminous to include in the statements.

The notes are not only helpful but essential to understanding the enterprise's performance and position.

Supplementary information may include details or amounts that present a different perspective from that adopted in the financial statements. It may be quantifiable information that is high in relevance but low in reliability, or information that is helpful but not essential. One example of supplementary information is the data and schedules provided by oil and gas companies: typically they provide information on proven reserves as well as the related discounted cash flows.

Supplementary information also includes management's explanation of the financial information and a discussion of its significance as is found in the **MD&A**. The CICA MD&A *Guidance on Preparation and Disclosure* lays out six general disclosure principles as follows:

"MD&A's should:

- enable readers to **view the company through the eyes of management**;

- **complement** as well as **supplement** financial statements;

- be **reliable, complete, fair and balanced**, providing material information—that is, information important to an investor, acting reasonably, in making a decision to invest or continue to invest in the company;

- have a **forward-looking** orientation;

- focus on **management's strategy for generating value** for investors over time;

---

[23] According to *CICA Handbook*, Section 1000.42, recognition means including an item within one or more individual statements and does not mean disclosure in the notes to the financial statements. Some might argue, however, that if markets are assumed to be efficient, then as long as the information is disclosed, the market will absorb and use the information in pricing the shares.

- be **written in plain language**, with candour and without exaggeration, and embody the qualities of understandability, relevance, comparability and consistency over reporting periods."

Thus, the MD&A is a step toward a more broad-based business reporting model that also incorporates forward-looking information. The Guideline also includes a framework that identifies five key elements that should be included in the MD&A:

1. the company's **vision, core businesses and strategy**,

2. **key performance drivers**,

3. **capabilities** (capital and other resources) to achieve desired results,

4. **results**—historical and prospective analysis, and

5. the **risks** that may shape and/or affect the achievement of results.

Hopefully, these additional disclosures will give users of the financial information a greater insight into the company's business.[24]

The content, arrangement, and display of financial statements, along with other facets of full disclosure, are discussed in Chapters 4, 5, 24, and throughout the text.

Constraints

In providing information with the qualitative characteristics that make it useful, three overriding **constraints** must be considered:

8 Objective
Describe the impact that constraints have on reporting accounting information.

1. **uncertainty**,

2. the **cost-benefit** relationship, and

3. **materiality**.

Another less dominant yet important constraint is **industry practice**.

Uncertainty

Uncertainty is considered a constraint because excessive uncertainty may preclude recognition of a financial statement element. As a general rule, **elements** are **recognized** in the financial statements if they arise from events that are **likely or probable** and **measurable** (i.e., amounts may be reasonably estimated).[25] Management must assess the likelihood of outcomes (e.g., will a company lose a lawsuit or not) based on history and corroborating or supporting evidence. Often, companies rely on specialists such as lawyers and engineers to assist in this assessment.

Measurability is a big issue for many financial statement elements. When there is a **variance** between the recognized amount and another reasonably possible amount, this is referred to as **measurement uncertainty**.[26] Accountants are continually working to develop and incorporate **measurement tools** such as the Black Scholes option pricing model, net present value model, and discounted cash flow models as well as others. When observable values are not available (e.g., market prices, cost), these methods are used to

---

[24] Although MD&A disclosures are mandated for public companies, the CICA guidance, in its executive summary, notes that the MD&A can be used by other organizations to communicate more effectively.

[25] *CICA Handbook*, Section 3290.12. and Section 1000.44.

[26] *CICA Handbook*, Section 1508.03.

cope with measurement uncertainty.[27] A tradeoff exists with uncertainty. Too much measurement uncertainty undermines the reliability of the financial statements. However, if the element is not recognized at all in the financial statement, then all relevant information is not reflected. A compromise is to measure and recognize the elements in the body of the financial statements and to disclose the existence and nature of significant measurement uncertainty in the notes to the financial statements.

Cost-Benefit Relationship

Too often, users assume that information is a cost-free commodity. But preparers and providers of accounting information know that it is not. Therefore, the **cost-benefit relationship** must be considered: the costs of providing the information must be weighed against the benefits that can be derived from using the information. Standard-setting bodies and governmental agencies now use cost-benefit analysis before making their informational requirements final. In order to justify requiring a particular measurement or disclosure, the benefits perceived to be derived from it must exceed the costs perceived to be associated with it.

The difficulty in cost-benefit analysis is that the costs and especially the benefits are not always evident or measurable. The costs are of several kinds, including the costs of:

- collecting and processing
- disseminating
- auditing
- potential litigation
- disclosure to competitors and
- analysis and interpretation.

Benefits accrue to preparers (in terms of greater management control and access to capital) and to users (in terms of allocation of resources, tax assessment, and rate regulation). Benefits, however, are generally more difficult to quantify than costs. The CICA has taken some steps to reduce the cost of providing information by developing a Differential Reporting model. This model enables smaller, private companies to follow a simplified version of GAAP.[28]

Materiality

The constraint of **materiality** relates to an item's impact on a firm's overall financial operations. An item is material if its inclusion or omission would influence or change the judgement of a reasonable person.[29] It is immaterial and, therefore, irrelevant if it would have no impact on a decision-maker. In short, it must make a difference or it need not be disclosed. The point involved here is one of **relative size** and **importance**. If the amount involved is significant when compared with the other revenues and expenses, assets and

---

[27] FASB Statement of Financial Accounting Concepts 7 addresses the use of cash flow and present value techniques in measurement. In Canada, these concepts are also being incorporated in the *Handbook*. See for instance Section 3025 on Impaired loans, Section 3063 on Impairment of long-lived assets, and other sections such as leases and employee future benefits.

[28] *CICA Handbook*, Section 1300.

[29] FASB Statement of Financial Accounting Concepts No. 2 (par. .132) sets forth the essence of materiality: The omission or misstatement of an item in a financial report is material if, in light of surrounding circumstances, the item's magnitude is such that it is probable that the judgement of a reasonable person relying upon the report would have been changed or influenced by the item's inclusion or correction. This same concept of materiality has been adopted by the CICA. See *CICA Handbook*, Section 1000.17.

liabilities, or net income of the entity, sound and acceptable standards should be followed. If the amount is so small that it is quite unimportant when compared with other items, applying a particular standard may be considered of less importance.

It is difficult to provide firm guidelines in judging when a given item is or is not material because materiality varies both with relative amount and with relative importance.

For example, the two sets of numbers presented below illustrate relative size.

	Company A	Company B
Sales	$10,000,000	$100,000
Costs and expenses	9,000,000	90,000
Income from operations	1,000,000	10,000
Unusual gain	20,000	5,000

Illustration 2-4

Materiality Comparison

During the period in question, the revenues and expenses and, therefore, the net incomes of Company A and Company B have been proportional. Each has had an unusual gain.

In looking at the abbreviated income figures for Company A, it does not appear significant whether the amount of the unusual gain is set out separately or merged with the regular operating income. It is only 2% of the operating income and, if merged, would not seriously distort the income figure. Company B has had an unusual gain of only $5,000, but it is relatively much more significant than the larger gain realized by A. For Company B, an item of $5,000 amounts to 50% of its income. Obviously, the inclusion of such an item in ordinary operating income would affect the amount of that income materially. Thus we see the importance of an item's relative size in determining its materiality.

Companies and their auditors for the most part have adopted the general rule of thumb that anything above **5% of income from continuing operations** (after tax) is considered material.[30] This is a fairly simplistic and one-dimensional view of materiality, which needs further examination. The impact of the items on other factors, for instance key financial statement ratios and management compensation—in short, **any sensitive number on the financial statements**—should also be considered. Both **quantitative** and **qualitative** factors must be considered in determining whether an item is material.[31] Qualitative factors might include illegal acts, failure to comply with regulations, or inadequate or inappropriate description of an accounting policy. Materiality is a factor in a great many internal accounting decisions, too. The amount of classification required in a subsidiary expense ledger, the degree of accuracy required in prorating expenses among the departments of a business, and the extent to which adjustments should be made for accrued and deferred items are examples of judgements that should finally be determined on a basis of reasonableness and practicability, which is the materiality constraint sensibly applied. Only by exercising good judgement and professional expertise can reasonable and appropriate answers be found.

Industry Practices

Another practical consideration is industry practice. The peculiar nature of some industries and business concerns sometimes requires unique accounting. Care should be taken to ensure that these practices are consistent with the primary sources of GAAP and the conceptual framework.[32]

---

[30] CICA Assurance and Related Services Guideline 31.

[31] *CICA Handbook*, Section 5130.07.

[32] *CICA Handbook*, Section 1100.31.

Illustration 2-5

Conceptual Framework for
Financial Reporting

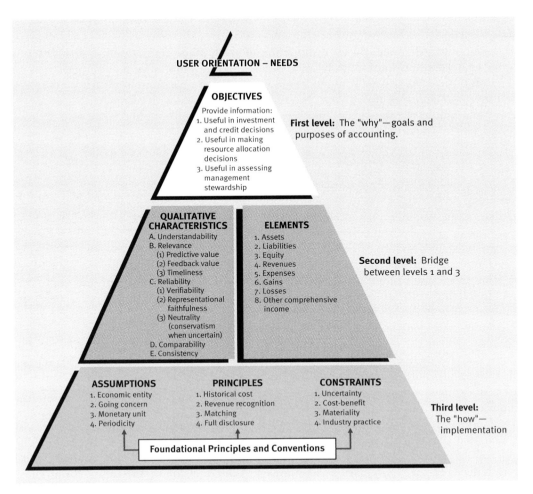

Illustration 2-5 presents the conceptual framework discussed in this chapter. It is similar to Illustration 2-1, except that it provides additional information for each level. We cannot overemphasize the usefulness of this conceptual framework in helping to understand many of the problem areas that are examined in subsequent chapters.

FINANCIAL REPORTING ISSUES

Objective 9

Explain the factors that contribute to choice in financial reporting decisions.

Making financial reporting decisions is a complex process. The next section examines the factors that make this process challenging.

Making Accounting Choices

Many factors contribute to choice in financial reporting, including:

1. GAAP in Canada is **principles-based** and therefore requires the use of professional judgement,

2. **measurement uncertainty**, and

3. **complexity** of business transactions.

The role of each of these will be examined in turn.

Principles-Based Approach

As mentioned earlier in the chapter, the main objective of financial reporting is to **provide reliable decision-relevant financial information** to users so that they can make well-informed capital allocation decisions. Capital invested in good investments will fuel the economy and spur job growth and wealth creation. To achieve this objective, judicious choices between alternative accounting concepts, methods, and means of disclosure must be made. Accounting principles and rules must be **selected and interpreted and professional judgement must be applied**.

Because accounting is **influenced by its environment** (in many cases in a negative way) and by decisions made by individuals who often act in **self-interest** or in the interests of the company (at the expense of other stakeholders), it is unrealistic to believe that the financial reporting system will always work properly. Instead of wealth creation in the capital markets and the economy, financial reporting decisions sometimes lead to wealth and value destruction.

The conceptual framework developed in this chapter is the anchor that should ground all financial reporting decisions. As noted in *CICA Handbook* Section 1100, where a primary source of GAAP does not exist,

> "... an entity should adopt accounting policies that are:
>
> (a) consistent with the primary sources of GAAP; and
>
> (b) developed through the exercise of professional judgement and the application of the concepts described in ...Section 1000"[33]

Canadian GAAP is **principles-based**—that is, most of the *Handbook* is based on a few foundational principles and concepts like those embodied in the conceptual framework noted here as well as in *Handbook* Section 1000. The benefit of this approach is that all decisions should theoretically be **consistent** if they stem from the same foundational reasoning. Another benefit is that principles-based GAAP is **flexible**. The most appropriate accounting for any new situation or novel business transaction may be reasoned through by going back to these principles (sometimes referred to as *first principles*). Principles-based GAAP is sometimes criticized for being too flexible. Some feel that it allows too much choice and therefore results in **lack of comparability**.

Care should therefore be taken to ensure that the flexible nature is not abused. The key foundational concept of **neutrality** is paramount.

Measurement Uncertainty

Because of the use of **accrual accounting**, many estimates must be used when preparing financial statements. Fundamental principles and assumptions such as the **periodicity assumption**, the **going concern assumption**, the **matching principle**, the **revenue realization principle**, and others also contribute to measurement uncertainty. Most numbers on a balance sheet and income statement are in fact quite "soft" and inexact. Measurement uncertainty was discussed earlier under Constraints. The key for accountants is to **determine an acceptable level of uncertainty**, use **measurement tools** that help deal with the uncertainty, and **disclose sufficient information** to signal the uncertainty.

Unusual and Complex Transactions

The business environment is ever-changing and becoming increasingly complex. It is difficult for the AcSB to keep abreast of all of these changes. Therefore, accountants must often sort through the complexities and determine the most appropriate treatment.

---

[33] *CICA Handbook*, Section 1100.04.

Issue Identification

Objective 10

Identify the four types of financial reporting issues and what makes certain issues more important than others.

When making financial reporting choices, some issues are more difficult to analyse and resolve than others. This is because there is more than one possible resolution as to how the item should be accounted for. All issues fall into one of four categories:

(a) **Recognition**—Should the element be recorded or not in the general ledger (and hence in the income statement or balance sheet)? E.g., revenue recognition, accrual of a liability, recognition of an asset.

(b) **Measurement**—If recognized, how much should the element be recorded at, i.e., what is the value? For example, how should an accrual for environmental damages be measured? How should a particular asset be valued?

(c) **Presentation**—Where on the key financial statements should the item be shown? E.g., as debt or equity, as extraordinary item or discontinued operations.

(d) **Disclosure**—How much detail should be given in the financial reports?

All financial reporting decisions are not the same—some are more important or material to user decision making. How do we determine the relative importance of an issue? Accountants, while ensuring the completeness, authorization, and accuracy of **all** transactions in the accounting system, must ensure that **important or material issues** receive special attention.

As previously noted, accounting decisions are not made in a vacuum. Many stakeholders depend on the information to make key decisions. As a result, some numbers in the financial statements have a **higher profile and visibility** than others since they become the **focus for decision-making**.

Contractual and regulatory focal points.   As an example, many creditors structure lending agreements such that they include requirements to adhere to certain liquidity and solvency ratios such as current and debt-to-equity ratios. The company must calculate these ratios periodically and report to the lender as to whether they adhere to the loan agreement's requirements. These requirements are often referred to as **debt covenants**. If a company does not meet the requirement, the implication is that the loan may become a demand loan and the lender may require immediate repayment. Thus, any ratios mentioned in key business agreements become important ratios and any transactions that affect these ratios become important focal points.

Similarly, ratios and key numbers are used in **management remuneration arrangements**, e.g., bonuses that depend on earnings. Sometimes regulatory restrictions exist that emphasize certain key numbers or ratios. Accountants must be aware of all of these pressure points and factor this into decision-making.

Key capital market focal points.   Capital market participants focus on **earnings** and earnings per share. As discussed in Chapter 1, negative earnings surprises are not well received by the marketplace and affect a company's share price and ability to raise capital. Therefore decisions that impact earnings are also important.

Any transactions or balances that affect key numbers or ratios by a material amount become important and significant. This is not to say that accountants should bias the accounting; rather, that they should **be aware of the impact** of their decisions on stakeholders.

Financial Engineering

Objective 11

Explain the practice of financial engineering.

Over the past decade, a practice known as **financial engineering** has emerged. Financial engineering is a process whereby a business arrangement or transaction is structured legally such that it meets the company's financial reporting objective (e.g., to maximize earnings, minimize a debt-to-equity ratio, or other). This is often done by creating complex legal arrangements and financial instruments. These arrangements and instruments are created such that the resulting accounting meets the desired objective within GAAP. For example, a company raising debt financing might want the instrument structured such that it meets the GAAP definition of equity versus debt. In this way, the debt-to-equity ratio is not affected.

Many financial institutions developed and marketed these products to their clients. These arrangements are often referred to as structured financings. Since Enron, this practice has been curtailed. Is financial engineering and the practice of structured financings acceptable under GAAP? Financial engineering has moved from being an accepted (saleable) practice and commodity to a potentially fraudulent activity.

Illustration 2-6 looks at the various shades of grey in accounting for transactions.

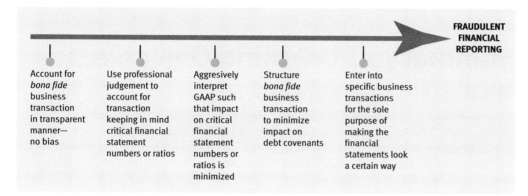

Illustration 2-6

Choice in Accounting Decision-Making

Fraudulent Financial Reporting

Keep in mind that accountants who are responsible for preparing a company's financial records seek to capture business and economic events and transactions as they occur and communicate them to interested parties. They should not use the financial statements to portray something that is not there. Similarly, good financial reporting should be a result of **well reasoned and supported analysis** that is grounded in a conceptual framework. It should not be influenced by external pressures. Pressures in the capital marketplace abound, however, and their potentially negative impact on financial reporting must be acknowledged. Pressures may arise from various sources as follows.

12 Objective

Identify factors that contribute to fraudulent financial reporting.

Economic or Business Environment

Sometimes a company experiences sudden declines in revenues or market share. The underlying reason may be unique to the company and stem from some poor strategic and business decisions or it may result from an industry or economy downturn. This may put pressures on a company to "prop up" its revenues. There may be pressure to recognize revenues before they should be or defer recognition of expenses.

Some companies use an industry or economic downturn as an opportunity to clean up their books and generally take large writedowns of assets such as inventory or goodwill. The markets expect a loss and therefore the company's share price is not unduly negatively affected. This "purging" of the balance sheet has the positive impact of making future earnings look better.

Other Pressures

Budgets put tremendous pressure on company management. Since bonuses and even jobs depend upon meeting budgets, sometimes this negative influence leaks inappropriately into accounting decisions.

Sometimes substantial pressures mount because of debt covenants or analysts' expectations. These can be significant and cause management to make biased decisions and misrepresent the company's financial position and operations.

These pressures, if not monitored and controlled properly, are a major problem. In order to minimize fraudulent financial reporting, various controls and a solid governance structure may be put in place by a company including:

(a) vigilant, knowledgeable top management,

(b) an independent audit committee,

(c) an internal audit function and

(d) other internal controls at lower levels.

Digital Tool

Glossary

www.wiley.com/canada/kieso

KEY TERMS

assets, 37
assumptions, 39
basic elements, 37
comparability, 36
comprehensive income, 38
conceptual framework, 30
conservatism, 35
consistency, 36
constraints, 47
continuous earnings
   process, 44
cost-benefit relationship,
   48
critical event (earnings),
   44
debt covenants, 52
decision usefulness, 33
discrete earnings process,
   44
earned (revenue), 43
economic entity
   assumption, 39
economic substance over
   legal form, 34
equity, 38
expenses, 38
feedback value, 33
financial engineering, 52
first principles, 51
full disclosure principle, 45

Summary of Learning Objectives

1 Describe the usefulness of a conceptual framework.

A conceptual framework is needed to (1) build on and relate to an established body of concepts and objectives, (2) provide a framework for solving new and emerging practical problems, (3) increase financial statement users' understanding of and confidence in financial reporting, and (4) enhance comparability among companies' financial statements.

2 Describe the main components of the conceptual framework for financial reporting.

The first level deals with the objective of financial reporting. The second level includes the qualitative characteristics of useful information and elements of financial statements. The third level includes foundational principles and conventions.

3 Understand the objective of financial reporting.

The objective of financial reporting is to provide information that is useful to those making investment and credit decisions.

4 Identify the qualitative characteristics of accounting information.

The overriding criterion by which accounting choices can be judged is decision usefulness; that is, providing information that is most useful for decision-making. Understandability, relevance, reliability, comparability, and consistency are the qualities that make accounting information useful for decision-making.

5 Define the basic elements of financial statements.

The basic elements of financial statements are: (1) assets, (2) liabilities, (3) equity, (4) revenues, (5) expenses, (6) gains, and (7) losses. An additional element is other comprehensive income.

6 Describe the basic assumptions of accounting.

Four basic assumptions underlying the financial accounting structure are: (1) Economic entity: the assumption that the activity of business enterprise can be kept separate and distinct from its owners and any other business unit. (2) Going concern: the assumption that the business enterprise will have a long life. (3) Monetary unit: the assumption that money is the common denominator by which economic activity is conducted, and that the monetary unit provides an appropriate basis for measurement and analysis. (4) Periodicity: the assumption that an enterprise's economic activities can be divided into artificial time periods to facilitate timely reporting.

7 Explain the application of the basic principles of accounting.

(1) Historical cost principle: existing GAAP requires that many assets and liabilities be accounted for and reported on the basis of acquisition price. Many assets are subsequently revalued. (2) Revenue recognition: revenue is generally recognized when (a) earned and measurable and (b) collectible (realizable). (3) Matching principle: expenses are recognized when the work (service) or the product actually contributes to revenue. (4) Full disclosure principle: accountants follow the general practice of providing information that is important enough to influence an informed user's judgement and decisions.

8 Describe the impact that constraints have on reporting accounting information.

The constraints and their impact are: (1) Uncertainty: excessive uncertainty makes recognition difficult or impossible. (2) Cost-benefit relationship: the costs of providing the information must be weighed against the benefits that can be derived from using the information. (3) Materiality: sound and acceptable standards should be followed if the amount involved is significant when compared with the other revenues and expenses, assets and liabilities, or net income of the entity. (4) Industry practices: sometimes the unique nature of a specific industry requires unique accounting. Ensure that the resulting statements are consistent with primary sources of GAAP and the conceptual framework.

9 Explain the factors that contribute to choice in financial reporting decisions.

Choice stems from many things including (1) principles-based approach to GAAP, (2) measurement uncertainty, and (3) increasingly complex business transactions. The conceptual framework is the foundation upon which GAAP is built. If a primary source of GAAP does not exist, then professional judgement must be used, making sure that the accounting policies chosen are consistent with the primary sources of GAAP and the conceptual framework. A principles-based approach allows flexibility but as a result may lead to inconsistencies. Accrual-based accounting requires that transactions be recognized when incurred, which often involves estimations. This leads to measurement uncertainty. The AcSB is unable to keep pace with the increasingly complex nature of business and the business environment and thus accountants must sort out how they will account for complex transactions.

10 Identify the four types of financial reporting issues and what makes certain issues more important than others.

The four types of issues are (1) recognition, (2) measurement, (3) presentation, and (4) disclosure. Any transactions or balances that affect key numbers or ratios by a material amount become important and significant.

11 Explain the practice of financial engineering.

Financial engineering is a process whereby a business arrangement or transaction is structured legally such that it meets the company's financial reporting objective.

12 Identify factors that contribute to fraudulent financial reporting.

Fraudulent financial reporting often results from pressures placed upon individuals or the company. These pressures may arise from various sources including worsening company, industry, or economic conditions, unrealistic internal budgets and financial statement focal points arising from contractual, regulatory, or capital market expectations. Weak internal controls and governance also contribute to fraudulent financial reporting.

Brief Exercises

BE2-1   Discuss whether the changes described in each of the cases below require recognition in the audit report as to consistency (assume that the amounts are material).

(a) After three years of calculating amortization under an accelerated method for income tax purposes and under the straight-line method for reporting purposes, the company adopted an accelerated method for reporting purposes.

(b) The company disposed of one of the two subsidiaries that had been included in its consolidated statements for prior years.

(c) The estimated remaining useful life of plant property was reduced because of obsolescence.

(d) The company is using an inventory valuation method that is different from the one used by other companies in its industry.

BE2-2   Identify which qualitative characteristic of accounting information is best described in each item below. (Do not use relevance and reliability.)

(a) The annual reports of Garbo Corp. are audited by public accountants.

(b) Klamoth Corp. and Kutenai, Inc. both use the straight-line depreciation method.

(c) Abbado Corp. has used straight-line amortization since it began operations.

(d) Augusta Corp. issues its quarterly reports immediately after each quarter ends.

BE2-3   For each item below, indicate to which category of elements of financial statements it belongs.

(a) Retained earnings

(b) Sales

(c) Goodwill

(d) Inventory

(e) Amortization

(f) Loss on sale of equipment investment

(g) Interest payable

(h) Dividends shares

(i) Gain on sale of equipment and investment

(j) Issuance of common shares

BE2-4   Identify which basic assumption of accounting is best described in each item below.

(a) The economic activities of Kapoor Corp. are divided into 12-month periods for the purpose of issuing annual reports.

(b) Brewer, Inc. does not adjust amounts in its financial statements for the effects of inflation.

(c) Ramsey Ltd. reports current and noncurrent classifications in its balance sheet.

(d) The economic activities of Bateau Corporation and its subsidiaries are merged for accounting and reporting purposes.

BE2-5   Identify which basic principle of accounting is best described in each item below.

(a) Ontario Corporation reports revenue in its income statement when it is earned instead of when the cash is collected.

(b) Nunavut Enterprise recognizes amortization expense for a machine over the five-year period during which that machine helps the company earn revenue.

(c) Lesfleurs, Inc. reports information about pending lawsuits in the notes to its financial statements.

(d) Springdale Farms reports land on its balance sheet at the amount paid to acquire it, even though the estimated fair market value is greater.

BE2-6   Which constraints on accounting information are illustrated by the items below?

(a) Zip's Farms, Inc. reports agricultural crops on its balance sheet at market value.

(b) Crimson Corporation does not accrue a contingent lawsuit gain of $650,000.

(c) Wildcat Ltd. does not disclose any information in the notes to the financial statements unless the value of the information to financial statement users exceeds the expense of gathering it.

(d) Xu Corporation expenses the cost of wastebaskets in the year they are acquired.

BE2-7 Presented below are four concepts discussed in this chapter.

(a) Periodicity assumption

(b) Historical cost principle

(c) Conservatism

(d) Full disclosure principle

Match these concepts to the following accounting practices. Each letter can be used only once.

1. _____ Preparing financial statements on a quarterly basis.

2. _____ Using the lower of cost and market method for inventory valuation.

3. _____ Recording equipment at its purchase price.

4. _____ Using notes and supplementary schedules in the financial statements.

BE2-8 Presented below are three different transactions related to materiality. Explain whether you would classify these transactions as material.

(a) Marcus Corp. has reported a positive trend in earnings over the last three years. In the current year, it reduces its bad debt allowance to ensure another positive earnings year. The impact of this adjustment is equal to 3% of net income.

(b) Sosa Ltd. has an extraordinary gain of $3.1 million on the sale of plant assets and a $3.3 million loss on the sale of investments. It decides to net the gain and loss because the net effect is considered immaterial. Sosa Ltd.'s income for the current year was $10 million.

(c) Mohawk Inc. expenses all capital equipment under $25,000 on the basis that it is immaterial. The company has followed this practice for a number of years.

BE2-9 If the going concern assumption is not made in accounting, what difference does it make in the amounts shown in the financial statements for the following items?

(a) Land

(b) Unamortized bond premium

(c) Amortization expense on equipment

(d) Merchandise inventory

(e) Prepaid insurance

BE2-10 What concept(s) from the conceptual framework does Accra Limited use in each of the following situations?

(a) Accra uses the lower of cost and market basis to value inventories.

(b) Accra was involved in litigation with Kinshasa Ltd. over a product malfunction. This litigation is disclosed in the financial statements.

(c) Accra allocates the cost of its depreciable (amortizable) assets over the life it expects to receive revenue from these assets.

(d) Accra records the purchase of a new PC at its cash equivalent price.

BE2-11 Explain how you would decide whether to record each of the following expenditures as an asset or an expense. Assume all items are material.

(a) Legal fees paid in connection with the purchase of land are $1,500.

(b) Bratt, Inc. paves the driveway leading to the office building at a cost of $21,000.

(c) A meat market purchases a meat-grinding machine at a cost of $345.

(d) On June 30, Alan and Chung, medical doctors, pay six months' office rent to cover the month of June and the next five months.

(e) Taylor's Hardware Company pays $9,000 in wages to labourers for construction on a building to be used in the business.

(f) Kwan's Florists pays wages of $2,100 for November to an employee who drives its delivery truck.

Exercises

E2-1 (Qualitative Characteristics) The conceptual framework identifies the qualitative characteristics that make accounting information useful. Presented below are a number of questions related to these qualitative characteristics and underlying constraints.

1. What is the quality of information that enables users to confirm or correct prior expectations?

2. Identify the pervasive constraints.

3. The SEC chairman at one time noted if it becomes accepted or expected that accounting principles are determined or modified in order to secure purposes other than economic measurement, we assume a grave risk that confidence in the credibility of our financial information system will be undermined. Which qualitative characteristic of accounting information should ensure that such a situation will not occur? (Do not use reliability.)

4. Owens Corp. switches from weighted average cost to FIFO over a two-year period. Which qualitative characteristic of accounting information is not followed?

5. Assume that the profession permits the financial services industry to defer losses on investments it sells, because immediate recognition of the loss may have adverse economic consequences on the industry. Which qualitative characteristic of accounting information is not followed? (Do not use relevance or reliability.)

6. What are the qualities that make accounting information useful for decision-making?

7. Chapman, Inc. does not issue its first-quarter report until after the second quarter's results are reported. Which qualitative characteristic of accounting is not followed? (Do not use relevance.)

8. Predictive value is an ingredient of which qualitative characteristics of useful information?

9. Victoria, Inc. is the only company in its industry to amortize its plant assets on a straight-line basis. Which qualitative characteristic of accounting information may not be followed? (Do not use industry practices.)

10. Joliet Corp. has attempted to determine the replacement cost of its inventory. Three different appraisers arrive at substantially different amounts for this value. The president, nevertheless, decides to report the middle value for external reporting purposes. Which qualitative characteristic of information is lacking in this data? (Do not use reliability or representational faithfulness.)

E2-2 (Qualitative Characteristics) The qualitative characteristics that make accounting information useful for decision-making purposes are:

Relevance	Timeliness	Representational faithfulness
Reliability	Verifiability	Comparability
Predictive value	Neutrality	Consistency
Feedback value	Understandability	Conservatism

Instructions

Identify the appropriate qualitative characteristic(s) to be used given the information provided below.

1. Qualitative characteristic being employed when companies in the same industry are using the same accounting principles.

2. Quality of information that confirms users' earlier expectations.

3. Imperative for providing comparisons of a firm from period to period.

4. Ignores the economic consequences of a standard or rule.

5. Requires a high degree of consensus among individuals on a given measurement.

6. Predictive value is an ingredient of this primary quality of information.

7. Neutrality is an ingredient of this primary quality of accounting information.

8. Two primary qualities that make accounting information useful for decision-making purposes.

9. Issuance of interim reports is an example of what primary ingredient of relevance?

E2-3 (Elements of Financial Statements) Seven interrelated elements that are most directly related to measuring an enterprise's performance and financial status are provided below.

Assets	Expenses	Liabilities
Gains	Equity	Revenues
Losses		

Instructions

Identify the element or elements associated with the 10 items below.

1. Arises from peripheral or incidental transactions.

2. Obliges a transfer of resources arising from past transaction.

3. Increases ownership interest.

4. Declares and pays cash dividends to owners.

5. Characterizes items by service potential or future economic benefit.

6. Decreases assets during period for the payment of taxes.

7. Arises from income-generating activities that constitute the entity's ongoing major or central operations.

8. Consists of residual interest in the enterprise's assets after deducting its liabilities.

9. Increases assets during a period through sale of product.

10. Decreases assets during the period by purchasing the company's own shares.

E2-4 (Assumptions, Principles, and Constraints) Presented below are the assumptions, characteristics, principles, and constraints used in this chapter.

(a) Economic entity assumption	(e) Historical cost principle	(i) Materiality
(b) Going concern assumption	(f) Matching principle	(j) Industry practices
(c) Monetary unit assumption	(g) Full disclosure principle	(k) Revenue recognition
(d) Periodicity assumption	(h) Conservatism	

Instructions

Identify by letter the accounting assumption, characteristic, principle, or constraint that describes each situation below. Do not use a letter more than once.

1. Allocates expenses to revenues in the proper period.

2. Indicates that market value changes subsequent to purchase are not recorded in the accounts. (Do not use revenue recognition principle.)

3. Ensures that all relevant financial information is reported.

4. Is the rationale why plant assets are not reported at liquidation value. (Do not use historical cost principle.)

5. Anticipates all losses, but reports no gains.

6. Indicates that personal and business record keeping should be separately maintained.

7. Separates financial information into time periods for reporting purposes.

8. Permits the use of market value valuation in certain specific situations.

9. Requires that information significant enough to affect the decision of reasonably informed users should be disclosed. (Do not use full disclosure principle.)

10. Assumes that the dollar is the measuring stick used to report on financial performance.

E2-5 (Assumptions, Principles, and Constraints) Presented below are a number of operational guidelines and practices that have developed over time.

1. Price-level changes are not recognized in the accounting records.

2. Financial information is presented so that reasonably prudent investors will not be misled.

3. Property, plant, and equipment are capitalized and amortized over periods benefited.

4. Repair tools are expensed when purchased.

5. Market value for purposes of valuation of all marketable securities is used by brokerage firms.

6. Each enterprise is kept as a unit distinct from its owner or owners.

7. All significant post-balance sheet events are reported.

8. Revenue is recorded at point of sale.

9. All important aspects of bond indentures are presented in financial statements.

10. Rationale for accrual accounting is stated.

11. The use of consolidated statements is justified.

12. Reporting must be done at defined time intervals.

13. An allowance for doubtful accounts is established.

14. Goodwill is recorded only at time of purchase.

15. Sales commission costs are charged to expense.

Instructions
Select the assumption, principle, or constraint that most appropriately justifies these procedures and practices.

E2-6   (Assumptions, Principles, and Constraints)   A number of operational guidelines used by accountants are described below.

1. The treasurer of Gretzky Corp. wishes to prepare financial statements only during downturns in its wine production, which occur periodically when the rhubarb crop fails. He states that it is at such times that the statements could be most easily prepared. In no event would more than 30 months pass without statements being prepared.

2. The Regina Power & Light Inc. has purchased a large amount of property, plant, and equipment over a number of years. It has decided that because the general price level has changed materially over the years, it will issue only price-level adjusted financial statements.

3. Smith Manufacturing Ltd. decided to manufacture its own widgets because it would be cheaper than buying them from an outside supplier. In an attempt to make its statements more comparable with those of its competitors, Smith charged its inventory account for what it felt the widgets would have cost if they had been purchased from an outside supplier. (Do not use the revenue recognition principle.)

4. Flanagan's Discount Centres buys its merchandise by the truck and train-carload. Flanagan does not defer any transportation costs in computing the cost of its ending inventory. Such costs, although varying from period to period, are always material in amount.

5. Grab & Run, Inc., a fast-food company, sells franchises for $100,000, accepting a $5,000 down payment and a 50-year note for the remainder. Grab & Run promises for three years to assist in site selection, building, and management training. Grab & Run records the $100,000 franchise fee as revenue in the period in which the contract is signed.

6. Conway Corp. faces possible expropriation (i.e., takeover) of foreign facilities and possible losses on sums owed by various customers on the verge of bankruptcy. The company president has decided that these possibilities should not be noted on the financial statements because Conway still hopes that these events will not take place.

7. Mike Singletary, manager of College Bookstore, Inc., bought a computer for his own use. He paid for the computer by writing a cheque on the bookstore chequing account and charged the Office Equipment account.

8. Enis, Inc. recently completed a new 60-storey office building that houses its home offices and many other tenants. All the office equipment for the building that had a per item or per unit cost of $1,000 or less was expensed as immaterial, even though the office equipment has an average life of 10 years. The total cost of such office equipment was approximately $26 million. (Do not use the matching principle.)

9. Brokers and other dealers in securities generally value investments at market or fair value for financial reporting purposes. The brokerage firm of James and Williams, Inc. continues to value its trading and investment accounts at cost or market, whichever is lower.

10. A large lawsuit has been filed against Big Cat Corp. by Perry Inc. Big Cat has recorded a loss and related estimated liability equal to the maximum possible amount it feels it might lose. Big Cat is confident, however, that either it will win the suit or it will owe a much smaller amount.

Instructions
For each of the foregoing, list the assumption, principle, or constraint that has been violated. List only one term for each case.

E2-7 (Full Disclosure Principle) Presented below are a number of facts related to Kelly, Inc. Assume that no mention of these facts was made in the financial statements and the related notes.

(a) The company decided that, for the sake of conciseness, only net income should be reported on the income statement. Details as to revenues, cost of goods sold, and expenses were omitted.

(b) Equipment purchases of $170,000 were partly financed during the year through the issuance of a $110,000 note payable. The company offset the equipment against the notes payable and reported plant assets at $60,000.

(c) During the year, an assistant controller for the company embezzled $15,000. Kelly's net income for the year was $2.3 million. Neither the assistant controller nor the money have been found.

(d) Kelly has reported its ending inventory at $2.1 million in the financial statements. No other information related to inventories is presented in the financial statements and related notes.

(e) The company changed its method of amortizing equipment from the double-declining balance to the straight-line method. No mention of this change was made in the financial statements.

Instructions

Assume that you are the auditor of Kelly, Inc. and that you have been asked to explain the appropriate accounting and related disclosure necessary for each of these items.

E2-8 (Accounting Principles—Comprehensive) Presented below is information related to Brooks, Inc.

(a) Amortization expense on the building for the year was $60,000. Because the building was increasing in value during the year, the controller decided to charge the amortization expense to retained earnings instead of to net income. The following entry is recorded:

Retained Earnings	60,000	
Accumulated Amortization—Buildings		60,000

(b) Materials were purchased on January 1, 2005 for $120,000 and this amount was entered in the Materials account. On December 31, 2005, the materials would have cost $141,000, so the following entry is made:

Inventory	21,000	
Gain on Inventories		21,000

(c) During the year, the company sold certain equipment for $285,000, recognizing a gain of $69,000. Because the controller believed that new equipment would be needed in the near future, the controller decided to defer the gain and amortize it over the life of any new equipment purchased.

(d) An order for $61,500 has been received from a customer for products on hand. This order was shipped on January 9, 2006. The company made the following entry in 2005.

Accounts Receivable	61,500	
Sales		61,500

Instructions

Comment on the appropriateness of the accounting procedures followed by Brooks, Inc.

Problems

P2-1 Accounting information provides useful information about business transactions and events. Those who provide and use financial reports must often select and evaluate accounting alternatives. The conceptual framework developed in this chapter examines the characteristics of accounting information that make it useful for decision-making. It also points out that various limitations inherent in the measurement and reporting process may necessitate trade-offs or sacrifices among the characteristics of useful information.

Instructions

(a) For each of the following pairs of information characteristics, give an example of a situation in which one of the characteristics may be sacrificed in return for a gain in the other:

1. Relevance and reliability.
2. Relevance and consistency.
3. Comparability and consistency.
4. Relevance and understandability.

(b) What criterion should be used to evaluate trade-offs between information characteristics?

P2-2   You are engaged to review the accounting records of Roenick Corporation prior to the closing of the revenue and expense accounts as of December 31, the end of the current fiscal year. The following information comes to your attention.

1. During the current year, Roenick Corporation changed its policy in regard to expensing purchases of small tools. In the past, these purchases had always been expensed because they amounted to less than 2% of net income, but the president has decided that capitalization and subsequent amortization should now be followed. It is expected that purchases of small tools will not fluctuate greatly from year to year.

2. Roenick Corporation constructed a warehouse at a cost of $1 million. The company had been amortizing the asset on a straight-line basis over 10 years. In the current year, the controller doubled amortization expense because the warehouse replacement cost had increased significantly.

3. When the balance sheet was prepared, detailed information as to the amount of cash on deposit in each of several banks was omitted. Only the total amount of cash under a caption "Cash in banks" was presented.

4. On July 15 of the current year, Roenick Corporation purchased an undeveloped tract of land at a cost of $320,000. The company spent $80,000 in subdividing the land and getting it ready for sale. A property appraisal at the end of the year indicated that the land was now worth $500,000. Although none of the lots was sold, the company recognized revenue of $180,000, less related expenses of $80,000, for a net income on the project of $100,000.

5. For a number of years the company used the FIFO method for inventory valuation purposes. During the current year, the president noted that all the other companies in the industry had switched to the LIFO method. The company decided not to switch to LIFO because net income would decrease $830,000.

Instructions
State whether or not you agree with the decisions made by Roenick Corporation. Support your answers with reference, whenever possible, to the generally accepted principles, assumptions, and constraints applicable in the circumstances.

P2-3   After presenting your report examining the financial statements to the board of directors of Bones Publishing Corp., one of the new directors expresses surprise that the income statement assumes that an equal proportion of the revenue is earned with the publication of every issue of the company's magazine. She feels that the critical event in the process of earning revenue in the magazine business is the cash sale of the subscription. She says that she does not understand why most of the revenue cannot be recognized in the period of the sale.

Instructions
Discuss the propriety of timing the recognition of revenue in Bones Publishing Corp.'s account with:

1. The cash sale of the magazine subscription.

2. The publication of the magazine every month.

3. Both events, by recognizing a portion of the revenue with cash sale of the magazine subscription and a portion of the revenue with the publication of the magazine every month.

P2-4   On June 5, 2005, McCoy Corporation signed a contract with Sandov Associates under which Sandov agreed (1) to construct an office building on land owned by McCoy, (2) to accept responsibility for procuring financing for the project and finding tenants, and (3) to manage the property for 35 years.

The annual net income from the project, after debt service, was to be divided equally between McCoy Corporation and Sandov Associates. Sandov was to accept its share of future net income as full payment for its services in construction, obtaining finances and tenants, and project management.

By May 31, 2006, the project was nearly completed and tenants had signed leases to occupy 90% of the available space at annual rents aggregating $4 million. It is estimated that, after operating expenses and debt service, the annual net income will amount to $1.5 million. The management of Sandov Associates believed that (a) the economic benefit derived from the contract with McCoy should be reflected on its financial statements for the fiscal year ended May 31, 2006, and directed that revenue be accrued in an amount equal to the commercial value of the services Sandor had rendered during the year, (b) this amount be carried in contracts receivable, and (c) all related expenditures be charged against the revenue.

Instructions

(a) Explain the main difference between the economic concept of business income as reflected by Sandov's management and the measurement of income under generally accepted accounting principles.

(b) Discuss the factors to be considered in determining when revenue should be recognized for the purpose of accounting measurement of periodic income.

(c) Is the belief of Sandov's management in accordance with generally accepted accounting principles for the measurement of revenue and expense for the year ended May 31, 2006? Support your opinion by discussing the application to this case of the factors to be considered for asset measurement and revenue and expense recognition.

(AICPA adapted)

P2-5 Carl Schneider sells and erects shell houses; that is, frame structures that are completely finished on the outside but are unfinished on the inside except for flooring, partition studding, and ceiling joists. Shell houses are sold chiefly to customers who are handy with tools and who have time to do the interior wiring, plumbing, wall completion and finishing, and other work necessary to make the shell houses liveable dwellings.

Schneider buys shell houses from a manufacturer in unassembled packages consisting of all lumber, roofing, doors, windows, and similar materials necessary to complete a shell house. Upon commencing operations in a new area, Schneider buys or leases land as a site for his local warehouse, field office, and display houses. Sample display houses are erected at a total cost of $20,000 to $29,000, including the cost of the unassembled packages. The chief cost of the display houses is the unassembled packages, inasmuch as erection is a short, low-cost operation. Old sample models are torn down or altered into new models every three to seven years. Sample display houses have little salvage value because dismantling and moving costs amount to nearly as much as the cost of an unassembled package.

Instructions

(a) A choice must be made between (1) expensing the costs of sample display houses in the periods in which the expenditure is made and (2) spreading the costs over more than one period. Discuss the advantages of each method.

(b) Would it be preferable to amortize the cost of display houses on the basis of (1) the passage of time or (2) the number of shell houses sold? Explain.

(AICPA adapted)

P2-6 Recently, your Uncle Waldo, who knows that you always have your eye out for a profitable investment, has discussed the possibility of you purchasing some corporate bonds. He suggests that you may wish to get in on the ground floor of this deal. The bonds being issued by the Cricket Corp. are 10-year debentures, which promise a 40% rate of return. Cricket manufactures novelty and party items.

You have told Waldo that unless you can take a look at Cricket's financial statements, you would not feel comfortable about such an investment. Thinking that this is the chance of a lifetime, Uncle Waldo has procured a copy of Cricket's most recent, unaudited financial statements, which are a year old. These statements were prepared by Mrs. John Cricket. You peruse these statements, and they are quite impressive.

The balance sheet showed a debt-to-equity ratio of .10 and, for the year shown, the company reported net income of $2,424,240.

The financial statements are not shown in comparison with amounts from other years. In addition, no significant note disclosures about inventory valuation, amortization methods, loan agreements, etc. are available.

Instructions

Write a letter to Uncle Waldo explaining why it would be unwise to base an investment decision on the financial statements that he has provided to you. Incorporate the concepts developed in this chapter.

P2-7 Hinckley Nuclear Power Plant will be "mothballed" at the end of its useful life (approximately 20 years) at great expense. The matching principle requires that expenses be matched to revenue. Accountants Jana Kingston and Pete Henning argue whether it is better to allocate the expense of mothballing over the next 20 years or ignore it until mothballing occurs.

Instructions

Discuss the issues considering stakeholders.

Writing Assignments

WA2-1 Roger Chang has some questions regarding the theoretical framework in which standards are set. He knows that the AcSB has attempted to develop a conceptual framework for accounting theory formulation. Yet Roger's supervisors have indicated that these theoretical frameworks have little value in the practical sense—in the real world. Roger did notice that accounting standards seem to be established after the fact rather than before. He thought this indicated a lack of theory structure but never really questioned the process at school because he was too busy doing the homework.

Roger feels that some of his anxiety about accounting theory and accounting semantics could be alleviated by identifying the basic concepts and definitions accepted by the profession and considering them in light of his current work. By doing this, he hopes to develop an appropriate connection between theory and practice.

Instructions

Help Roger recognize the purpose of and benefit of a conceptual framework.

WA2-2   Gordon and Medford are discussing various aspects of the *CICA Handbook*, Section 1000—Financial Statement Concepts. Gordon indicates that this pronouncement provides little, if any, guidance to the practising professional in resolving accounting controversies. He believes that the statement provides such broad guidelines that it would be impossible to apply the objectives to present-day reporting problems. Medford concedes this point but indicates that objectives are still needed to provide a starting point in helping to improve financial reporting.

Instructions

Discuss.

WA2-3   An accountant must be familiar with the concepts involved in determining earnings of a business entity. The amount of earnings reported for a business entity depends on the proper recognition, in general, of revenue and expense for a given time period. In some situations, costs are recognized as expenses at the time of product sale; in other situations, guidelines have been developed for recognizing costs as expenses or losses by other criteria.

Instructions

(a) Explain the rationale for recognizing costs as expenses at the time of product sale.

(b) What is the rationale underlying the appropriateness of treating costs as expenses of a period instead of assigning the costs to an asset? Explain.

(c) In what general circumstances would it be appropriate to treat a cost as an asset instead of as an expense? Explain.

(d) Some expenses are assigned to specific accounting periods on the basis of systematic and rational allocation of asset cost. Explain the underlying rationale for recognizing expenses on the basis of systematic and rational allocation of asset cost.

(e) Identify the conditions in which it would be appropriate to treat a cost as a loss.

(AICPA adapted)

WA2-4   Financial statements incorporate a significant amount of soft information.

Instructions

Define what is meant by "soft" versus "hard" information. Discuss the factors that contribute to soft numbers in financial reporting.

WA2-5   Many Canadian companies include in the notes to their financial statements a note that reconciles Canadian GAAP net income to U.S. GAAP net income.

Instructions

Discuss in context of the conceptual framework.

Cases

Digital Tool

www.wiley.com/
canada/kieso

Refer to the Case Primer on the Digital Tool to help you answer these cases.

CA2-1   Bre-X Minerals (Bre-X), a small mining company, announced in the early 1990s that it had discovered a fairly significant gold deposit in Indonesia. The company shares skyrocketed from pennies a share to over $280 per share. Subsequently, it was discovered that the company had been "salting the samples"[33] and that there was little, if any, gold there. This information was not disclosed to the market until long after it was discovered that there was no gold. Certain parties who had access to this information benefited; however, many investors lost a significant amount of money. Lawsuits relating to the misrepresentations are currently ongoing.

Instructions

Identify and analyse the financial reporting issues using the conceptual framework.

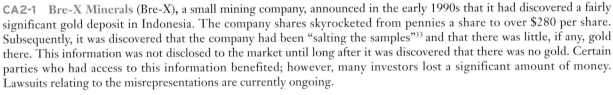

CA2-2   Bennett Environmental Inc. (Bennett) operates in North America. Its basic business is high temperature treatment services for the remediation of contaminated soils and other PCB-contaminated construction debris, according to its 2002 annual report. In 2002, its annual revenues were $48,103,845 (more than double the prior year). In June 2003, the company successfully bid on a $200 million three-year contract to treat contaminated soils from a large site in New Jersey.

[33] The term "salting" refers to the practice of someone tampering with the samples (and adding in some, or more, gold).

The cleanup site was previously operated by Federal Creosote, which made treated railroad ties until the mid-1950s. In 1997, homes in the surrounding area discovered that the creosote, which has now been determined to be carcinogenic, was leaking into their basements. In the short run, the waste will be shipped to Quebec, where it will be incinerated. The company has almost completed work on its New Brunswick plant where the rest of the waste will ultimately be incinerated.[34]

Instructions

Assume that the work has now begun and that it is early 2004. The company's year end is December 31, 2004. Discuss the financial reporting issues.

CA2-3 Presented below is a statement that appeared about Weyerhaeuser Company in a financial magazine.

> "The land and timber holdings are now carried on the company's books at a mere $422 million (U.S.). The value of the timber alone is variously estimated at $3 billion to $7 billion and is rising all the time. The understatement of the company is pretty severe, conceded Charles W. Bingham, a senior vice-president. Adds Robert L. Schuyler, another senior vice-president: We have a whole stream of profit nobody sees and there is no way to show it on our books.

Instructions

(a) What does Schuyler mean when he says that the company has a whole stream of profit nobody sees and there is no way to show it on its books?

(b) If the understatement of the company's assets is severe, why does accounting not report this information?

Research and Financial Analysis

RA2-1   Teck Cominco

Obtain the 2002 financial statements of Teck Cominco and answer the following questions.

Instructions

(a) Using the notes to the consolidated financial statements, determine the company's revenue recognition policies. Comment on whether the company uses an aggressive or conservative method for reporting revenue.

(b) Give two examples of where historical cost information is reported on the financial statements and related notes. Give two examples of the use of fair value information reported in either the financial statements or related notes.

(c) How can we determine that the accounting principles used by the company are prepared on a basis consistent with those of last year?

(d) Compare net income under Canadian versus U.S. GAAP. What are the key differences?

RA2-2   Abitibi-Consolidated Inc. versus Domtar Inc.

Instructions

Go to the Digital Tool and obtain the Annual Reports found there to answer the following questions related to Abitibi-Consolidated Inc. and Domtar Inc. for the year ended December 31, 2002.

(a) What are the primary lines of business of these two companies as shown in their notes to the financial statements? What are the key business risks?

(b) Which company has the dominant position in paper product sales? Explain how you used information in the financial statements to conclude this.

Digital Tool

Annual Reports

www.wiley.com/canada/kieso

---

[34] Based on the June 3, 2003 article from the *Globe and Mail*, "Bennett wins N.J. tainted soil contract."

(c) Review the key accounting policies for revenues, inventories, fixed assets, and environmental costs. How comparable are these two sets of statements?

(d) Domtar also reports in U.S. dollars. Why do you think it does this?

(e) Which company is more profitable and why? Support your answer.

RA2-3   Retrieval of Information on Public Company

There are several commonly available indexes and reference products that enable individuals to locate articles previously included in numerous business publications and periodicals. Articles can generally be searched by company or by subject matter. Several common sources are *Canadian Business and Current Affairs* (*CBCA Fulltext Business*), *Investex Plus*, *The Wall Street Journal Index*, *Business Abstracts* (formerly the *Business Periodical Index*), and *ABI/Inform*.

Instructions
Use one of these resources to find an article about a company in which you are interested. Read the article and answer the following questions. (Note: Your library may have hard copy or CD-ROM versions of these sources or they may be available through your library electronic database.)

(a) What is the article about?

(b) What company-specific information is included in the article?

(c) Identify any accounting-related issues discussed in the article.

RA2-4   Concepts and Quantitative Guidelines–Materiality

In 2002, the AcSB issued a new guideline entitled "Applying materiality and audit risk concepts in conducting an audit." Materiality is used to determine whether a transaction or event has decision relevance for financial reporting purposes. Materiality can be determined either quantitatively or qualitatively.

Instructions
Recap and discuss the quantitative and qualitative thresholds articulated in the guideline.

RA2-5   Research Study on Mining Company Disclosures

A recent PricewaterhouseCoopers (PwC) study disclosures in the mining industry entitled "Digging Deeper" shows that most mining companies are not disclosing enough forward-looking information about their companies.
An excerpt from the study follows:

"The traditional, predominantly financial, indicators used to measure corporate performance are becoming increasingly recognised as having their limitations. They do not tell a company's full story and are not adequate to deliver true insights into what creates value in the long term. Our survey of mining companies, investors and analysts demonstrates the case for better reporting of what creates value in the long term.

More than 70% of mining company executives surveyed believe that their companies are undervalued. Furthermore, they recognise that the market's continued focus on short-term earnings is a problem. In an industry characterised by long lead times and extended project lifespans, it is worrying to find that approximately half of all three participant groups feel that a focus on short-term earnings discourages mining companies in general from investing in long-term value creation. Interestingly, however, company executives strongly feel that the focus on short-term earnings does not inhibit their own company from investing for the long term."

Instructions

1. Download and read the report from the PwC website at www.pwc.com/mining.

2. Explain how mining companies earn income. What is the earnings process?

3. Why might the shares be undervalued?

4. Discuss the financial reporting principles that are at issue here.

5. Conclude as to how this scenario might contribute to problems in the mining industry.

Cable Connections

In 1984, certified general accountant Louise Nesterenko was vice-president, finance, for a Calgary computer company that had received a shipment of new personal computers. The computers arrived without any cables, and to order new ones from Ontario would take three weeks. The enterprising woman saw a hole in the western marketplace—and a year later, she launched Alberta Computer Cable, Inc (ACC).

The company has since grown from a single staff member and first-year revenues of less than $60,000 to 64 full-time employees and $4 million in revenue in 2003.

ACC manufactures and distributes cables and other computer connectivity products—from a single cable to orders in the thousands, often within 24 hours. This efficiency is thanks to one thing: "The accounting system was crucial to our success," Nesterenko says.

Effective cash management is important because, from the start, Nesterenko did not seek any outside funding. She relies on a good payable system. "We notify all our vendors that payments will always be made, regardless, the third Monday of the month," she says.

The accounts receivable system is similarly regimented, with statements faxed regularly to clients. "Our bad debts are so insignificant, they don't register on a scale," Nesterenko says. In 2002, there were only $2,300 in bad debts; there was none in the previous four years. In addition, Nesterenko ensures that no account represents more than 10% of the company's business.

The sophistication of the record keeping has increased with the company's growth. At the beginning, ACC used a custom software package that was updated at the end of each day. Now, it runs "Made-to-Manage" software, which updates all components— general ledger, the bank, accounts payable and receivable—instantaneously. In addition, the company has introduced digital photography technology to receiving, reducing the risk of error when managing shipments. ∎

The Accounting Information System

Learning Objectives

After studying this chapter, you should be able to:

1. Understand basic accounting terminology.
2. Explain double-entry rules.
3. Identify steps in the accounting cycle.
4. Record transactions in journals, post to ledger accounts, and prepare a trial balance.
5. Explain the reasons for preparing adjusting entries.
6. Prepare closing entries.
7. Explain how inventory accounts are adjusted at year end.
8. Prepare a 10-column work sheet.

After studying the appendix, you should be able to:

9. Identify adjusting entries that may be reversed.

Preview of Chapter 3

As illustrated in the case of ACC noted above, a reliable information system is a necessity for all companies. The purpose of this chapter is to explain and illustrate the features of an accounting information system. Even though most companies have sophisticated computerized and automated accounting systems, it is nonetheless important to understand the mechanics of bookkeeping. How do transactions get captured into the system and how and when are the financial statements produced? The content and organization of this chapter are as follows:

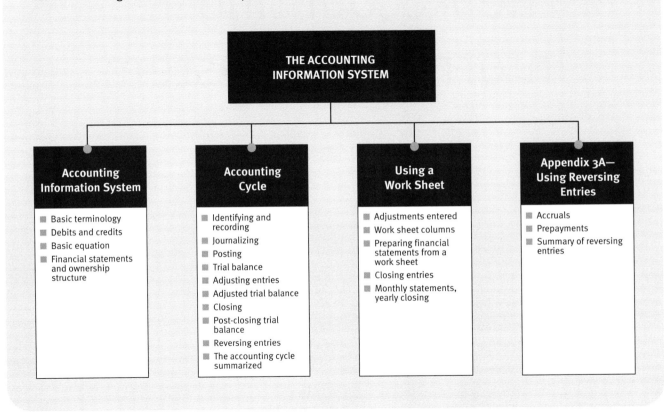

ACCOUNTING INFORMATION SYSTEM

The system of collecting and processing transaction data and disseminating financial information to interested parties is known as the **accounting information system**.

Accounting information systems vary widely from one business to another. Factors that shape these systems are the nature of the business and the transactions in which it engages, the firm's size, the volume of data to be handled, and the information demands that management and others place on the system.

Basic Terminology

Financial accounting rests on a set of concepts (discussed in Chapters 1 and 2) for identifying, recording, classifying, and interpreting transactions and other events relating to enterprises. It is important to understand the **basic terminology** employed in **collecting** accounting data.

BASIC TERMINOLOGY

Event. A happening of consequence. An **event** generally is the source or cause of changes in assets, liabilities, and equity. Events may be external or internal.

Transaction. An **external event** involving a transfer or exchange between two or more entities or parties.

Account. A systematic arrangement that accumulates transactions and other events. A separate **account** is kept for each asset, liability, revenue, expense, and for capital (owners' equity).

Permanent and temporary accounts. **Permanent** (real) **accounts** are asset, liability, and equity accounts; they appear on the balance sheet. **Temporary** (nominal) **accounts** are revenue, expense, and dividend accounts; except for dividends, they appear on the income statement. Temporary accounts are periodically closed; permanent accounts are left open.

Ledger.[1] The book (or electronic database) containing the accounts. Each account usually has a separate page. A **general ledger** is a collection of all the asset, liability, owners' equity, revenue, and expense accounts. A **subsidiary ledger** contains the details related to a given general ledger account.

Journal. The book of original entry where transactions and selected other events are initially recorded. Various amounts are transferred to the ledger from the book of original entry, the **journal**.

Posting. The process of transferring the essential facts and figures from the book of original entry to the ledger accounts.

Trial balance. A list of all open accounts in the ledger and their balances. A **trial balance** taken immediately after all adjustments have been posted is called an **adjusted trial balance**. A trial balance taken immediately after closing entries have been posted is designated as a **post-closing** or **after-closing trial balance**. A trial balance may be prepared at any time.

Adjusting entries. Entries made at the end of an accounting period to bring all accounts up to date on an accrual accounting basis so that correct financial statements can be prepared.

Financial statements. Statements that reflect the accounting data's collection, tabulation, and final summarization. Four **financial statements** are involved: (1) the **balance sheet**, which shows the enterprise's financial condition at the end of a period, (2) the **income statement**, which measures the results of operations during the period, (3) the **statement of cash flows**, which reports the cash provided and

Objective

Understand basic accounting terminology.

---

1 Most companies use accounting software systems instead of manual systems. The software allows the data to be entered into a database and then subsequently, various reports can be generated such as journals, trial balances, ledgers, and financial statements.

used by operating, investing, and financing activities during the period, and (4) the statement of retained earnings, which reconciles the balance of the retained earnings account from the beginning to the end of the period. Comprehensive Income may be shown as a separate statement—the statement of comprehensive income—or as part of the income statement.

Closing entries. The formal process by which all temporary accounts are reduced to zero and the net income or net loss is determined and transferred to an owners' equity account, also known as "closing the ledger," "closing the books," or merely "closing."

Debits and Credits

Objective 2
Explain double-entry rules.

The terms debit and credit refer to left and right sides of a general ledger account, respectively. They are commonly abbreviated as Dr. for debit and Cr. for credit. These terms do not mean increase or decrease. The terms debit and credit are used repeatedly in the recording process to describe where entries are made. For example, the act of entering an amount on the left side of an account is called debiting the account, and making an entry on the right side is crediting the account. When the totals of the two sides are compared, an account will have a debit balance if the total of the debit amounts exceeds the credits. Conversely, an account will have a credit balance if the credit amounts exceed the debits. The procedure of having debits on the left and credits on the right is an accounting custom. We could function just as well if debits and credits were reversed. However, the custom of having debits on the left side of an account and credits on the right side (like the custom of driving on the right-hand side of the road) has been adopted in Canada. This rule applies to all accounts.

The equality of debits and credits provides the basis for the double-entry system of recording transactions (sometimes referred to as double-entry bookkeeping). Under the universally used double-entry accounting system, the dual (two-sided) effect of each transaction is recorded in appropriate accounts. This system provides a logical method for recording transactions. It also offers a means of proving the accuracy of the recorded amounts. If every transaction is recorded with equal debits and credits, then the sum of all the debits to the accounts must equal the sum of all the credits.

Illustration 3-1

Double-entry (Debit and Credit) Accounting System

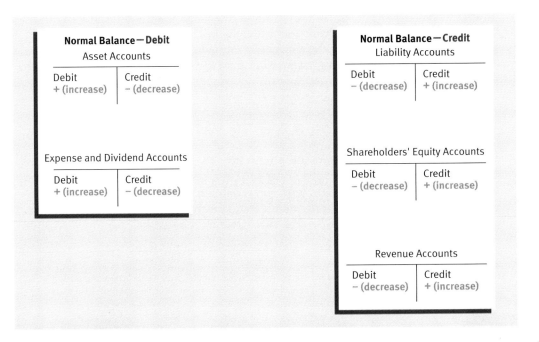

All **asset** and **expense** accounts are increased on the left (or debit side) and decreased on the right (or credit side). Conversely, all **liability** and **revenue** accounts are increased on the right (or credit side) and decreased on the left (or debit side). Shareholders' equity accounts, such as Common Shares and Retained Earnings, are increased on the credit side, whereas Dividends is increased on the debit side. The basic guidelines for an accounting system are presented in Illustration 3-1.

Basic Equation

In a double-entry system, for every debit there must be a credit and vice versa. This leads us to the basic accounting equation (Illustration 3-2).

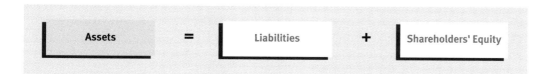

Illustration 3-2

The Basic Accounting Equation

Illustration 3-3 expands this equation to show the accounts that compose shareholders' equity. In addition, the debit/credit rules and effects on each type of account are illustrated. Study this diagram carefully. It will help you understand the fundamentals of the double-entry system. Like the basic equation, the expanded basic equation must balance (total debits equal total credits).

Illustration 3-3

Expanded Basic Equation and Debit/Credit Rules and Effects

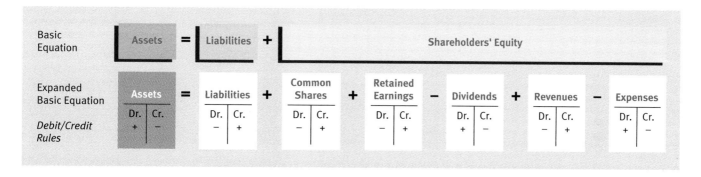

Every time a transaction occurs, the equation elements change, but the basic equality remains. To illustrate, here are eight different transactions for Perez Inc.

1 Owners invest $40,000 in exchange for common shares:

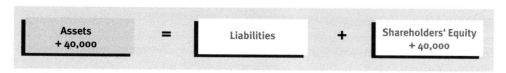

2 Disburse $600 cash for secretarial wages:

3 Purchase office equipment priced at $5,200, giving a 10% promissory note in exchange:

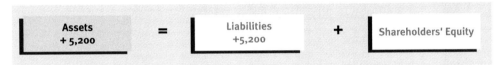

4 Receive $4,000 cash for services rendered:

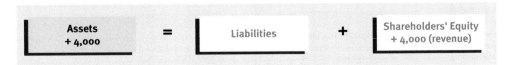

5 Pay off a short-term liability of $7,000:

6 Declare a cash dividend of $5,000:

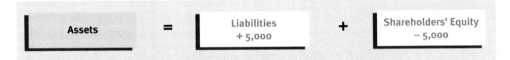

7 Convert a long-term liability of $80,000 into common shares:

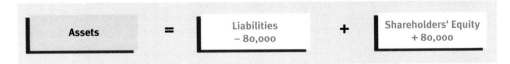

8 Pay cash of $16,000 for a delivery van:

Financial Statements and Ownership Structure

Common shares and retained earnings are reported in the shareholders' equity section of the balance sheet. Dividends are reported on the statement of retained earnings. Revenues and expenses are reported on the income statement. Dividends, revenues, and expenses are eventually transferred to retained earnings at the end of the period. As a result, a change in any one of these three items affects shareholders' equity. The relationships related to shareholders' equity are shown in Illustration 3-4.

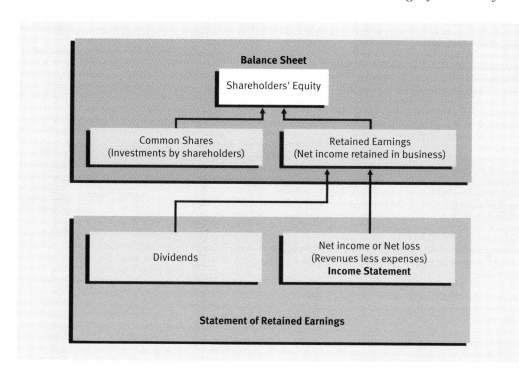

Illustration 3-4

Financial Statements and Ownership Structure

The type of ownership structure employed by a business enterprise dictates the types of accounts that are part of or affect the equity section. In a **corporation**,[2] **Common Shares, Contributed Surplus, Dividends**, and **Retained Earnings** are accounts commonly used. In a **proprietorship** or **partnership**, a **Capital** account is used to indicate the owner's or owners' investment in the company. A **Drawing** or withdrawal account may be used to indicate withdrawals by the owner(s). These two accounts are grouped or netted under **Owners' Equity**.

Illustration 3-5 summarizes and relates the transactions affecting shareholders' equity to the temporary and permanent classifications and to the types of business ownership.

Illustration 3-5

Effects of Transactions on Owners' Equity Accounts

		Ownership Structure			
		Proprietorships and Partnerships		Corporations	
Transactions Affecting Owners' Equity	Impact on Owners' Equity	Temporary Accounts	Permanent Accounts	Temporary Accounts	Permanent Accounts
Investment by owner(s)	Increase		Capital		Common Shares and related accounts
Revenues earned	Increase	Revenue	Capital	Revenue	Retained Earnings
Expenses incurred	Decrease	Expense		Expense	
Withdrawal by owner(s)	Decrease	Drawing		Dividends	

_____

2 Corporations are incorporated under a government act such as the Canada Business Corporations Act. The main reason for incorporation is to limit the liability for the owners if the corporation gets sued or goes bankrupt. When companies are incorporated, shares are issued to owners and the company becomes a separate legal entity (separate and distinct from its owners).

THE ACCOUNTING CYCLE

Objective 3
Identify steps in the accounting cycle.

Illustration 3-6 charts the steps in the accounting cycle. These are the accounting procedures normally used by enterprises to record transactions and prepare financial statements.

Illustration 3-6
The Accounting Cycle

Digital Tool
Accounting Cycle Tutorial

www.wiley.com/canada/kieso

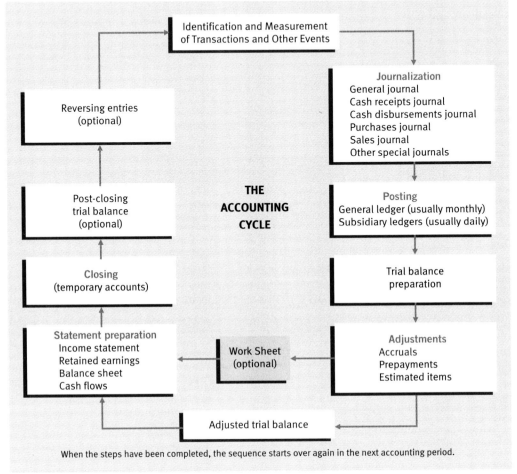

Identifying and Recording Transactions and Other Events

The first step in the accounting cycle consists of **analysing transactions** and selected other **events**. The problem is determining **what to record**. No simple rules exist that state whether an event should be recorded. Most agree that changes in personnel, changes in managerial policies, and the value of human resources, though important, should not be recorded in the accounts. On the other hand, when the company makes a cash sale or purchase—no matter how small—it should be recorded. The treatment relates to the accounting concepts presented in Chapter 2. An item should be **recognized** in the financial statements if it is an **element**, is **measurable**, and for assets and liabilities, is **probable**.

The phrase "transactions and other events and circumstances that affect a business enterprise" is used to describe the sources or causes of changes in an entity's assets, liabilities, and equity.[3] Events are of two types.

- **External events** involve interaction between an entity and its environment, such as a **transaction** with another entity, a change in the price of a good or service that an entity buys or sells, a flood or earthquake, or an improvement in technology by a competitor.

- **Internal events** occur within an entity, such as using buildings and machinery in its operations or transferring or consuming raw materials in production processes.

Many events have **both** external and internal elements. For example, acquiring the services of employees or others involves exchange transactions, which are external events; using those services (labour), often simultaneously with their acquisition, is part of production, which is internal. Events may be initiated and controlled by an entity, such as the purchase of merchandise or the use of a machine, or they may be beyond its control, such as an interest rate change, a theft or vandalism, or the imposition of taxes.

Transactions, as particular kinds of **external events**, may be an exchange in which each entity both receives and sacrifices value, such as purchases and sales of goods or services. Alternatively, transactions may be transfers in one direction (non-reciprocal) in which an entity incurs a liability or transfers an asset to another entity without directly receiving (or giving) value in exchange. Examples include distributions to owners, payment of taxes, gifts, charitable contributions, casualty losses, and thefts.

In short, as many events as possible that affect the enterprise's financial position are recorded. Some events are omitted because of tradition and others because measuring them is too complex. The accounting profession in recent years has shown signs of breaking with age-old traditions and is more receptive than ever to accepting the challenge of measuring and reporting events and phenomena previously viewed as too complex and immeasurable.[4] These areas will be studied in further depth in the rest of the textbook.

Journalizing

Differing effects on the basic business elements (assets, liabilities, and equities) are categorized and collected in accounts. The general ledger is a collection of all the asset, liability, shareholders' equity, revenue, and expense accounts. A T account (as shown in Illustration 3-8) is a convenient method of illustrating the effect of transactions on particular asset, liability, equity, revenue, and expense items.

In practice, transactions and selected other events are not recorded originally in the ledger because a transaction affects two or more accounts, each of which is on a different page in the ledger.[5] To circumvent this deficiency and to have a complete record of each transaction or other event in one place, a journal (the book of original entry) is employed. The simplest journal form is a chronological listing of transactions and other events expressed in terms of debits and credits to particular accounts. This is called a general journal. It is illustrated below for the following transactions.

4 Objective
Record transactions in journals, post to ledger accounts, and prepare a trial balance.

---

3 Elements of Financial Statements of Business Enterprises, Statement of Financial Accounting Concepts No. 6, (Stamford, Conn.: FASB, 1985), pp. 259 - 60.

4 Examples of these include accounting for defined future benefit pension plans and stock-based employee compensation. These will be covered in Chapters 20 and 17 respectively.

5 The transition to electronic bookkeeping systems and databases has dramatically changed the way bookkeeping is carried out. Much of the terminology and visual layout of the reports have been retained, however.

Nov. 11   Buys a new delivery truck on account from Auto Sales Inc., $22,400.

Nov. 13   Receives an invoice from the *Evening Graphic* for advertising, $280.

Nov. 14   Returns merchandise to Canuck Supply for credit, $175.

Nov. 16   Receives a $95 debit memo from Confederation Ltd., indicating that freight on a purchase from Confederation Ltd. was prepaid but is our obligation.

Each general journal entry consists of four parts:

1. the accounts and amounts to be debited (Dr.),

2. the accounts and amounts to be credited (Cr.),

3. a date, and

4. an explanation.

Digital Tool

Expanded
Discussion of
Special Journals

www.wiley.com/canada/kieso

Debits are entered first, followed by the credits, which are slightly indented. The explanation begins below the name of the last account to be credited and may take one or more lines. The Reference column is completed when the accounts are posted.

In some cases, businesses use **special journals** in addition to the general journal. Special journals summarize transactions possessing a common characteristic (e.g., cash receipts, sales, purchases, cash payments), thereby reducing the time necessary to accomplish the various bookkeeping tasks.

Illustration 3-7

General Journal with Sample Entries

GENERAL JOURNAL   PAGE 12

Date 2004	Account Title and Explanation	Ref.	Debit	Credit
Nov. 11	Delivery Equipment	8	$22,400	
	Accounts Payable	34		$22,400
	(Purchased delivery truck on account)			
Nov. 13	Advertising Expenses	65	280	
	Accounts Payable	34		280
	(Received invoice for advertising)			
Nov. 14	Accounts Payable	34	175	
	Purchase Returns	53		175
	(Returned merchandise for credit)			
Nov. 16	Transportation-In	55	95	
	Accounts Payable	34		95
	(Received debit memo for freight on merchandise purchased)			

Posting

The items entered in a general journal must be transferred to the general ledger. This procedure, **posting**, is part of the summarizing and classifying process.

For example, the November 11 entry in the general journal in Illustration 3-7 showed a debit to Delivery Equipment of $22,400 and a credit to Accounts Payable of $22,400. The amount in the debit column is posted from the journal to the debit side of the ledger account (Delivery Equipment). The amount in the credit column is posted from the journal to the credit side of the ledger account (Accounts Payable).

The numbers in the Ref. column of the general journal refer to the ledger accounts to which the respective items are posted. For example, the 34 placed in the column to the right of Accounts Payable indicates that this $22,400 item was posted to Account No. 34 in the ledger.

The general journal posting is completed when all the posting reference numbers have been recorded opposite the account titles in the journal. Thus the number in the posting reference column serves two purposes: (1) to indicate the ledger account number of the account involved, and (2) to indicate that the posting has been completed for the particular item. Each business enterprise selects its own numbering system for its ledger accounts. One practice is to begin numbering with asset accounts and to follow with liabilities, shareholders' equity, revenue, and expense accounts, in that order.

The various ledger accounts in Illustration 3-8 are shown after the posting process is completed. The source of the data transferred to the ledger account is indicated by the reference GJ 12 (General Journal, page 12).

Trial Balance

A trial balance is a list of accounts and their balances at a given time. Customarily, a trial balance is prepared at the end of an accounting period. The accounts are listed in the order in which they appear in the ledger, with debit balances listed in the left column and credit balances in the right column. The totals of the two columns must agree.

Delivery Equipment   No. 8

Nov.   11 GJ 12 $22,400

Accounts Payable   No. 34

Nov.   14 GJ 12 $175 | Nov. 11 GJ 12 $22,400
                           | 13 GJ 12   280
                           | 16 GJ 12   95

Purchase Returns   No. 53

Nov. 14 GJ 12 $175

Transportation-In   No. 55

Nov.   16 GJ 12 $95

Advertising Expense   No. 65

Nov.   13 GJ 12 $280

Illustration 3-8

Ledger Accounts, in T Account Format

The primary purpose of a trial balance is to prove the mathematical equality of debits and credits after posting. Under the double-entry system, this equality will occur when the sum of the debit account balances equals the sum of the credit account balances. A trial balance also uncovers errors in journalizing and posting. In addition, it is useful when preparing financial statements. The procedures for preparing a trial balance consist of:

1. Listing the account titles and their balances.

2. Totalling the debit and credit columns.

3. Proving the equality of the two columns.

The trial balance prepared from the ledger of Pioneer Advertising Agency Inc. is presented below.

Illustration 3-9

Trial Balance (Unadjusted)

PIONEER ADVERTISING AGENCY INC.
Trial Balance
October 31, 2004

	Debit	Credit
Cash	$ 80,000	
Accounts Receivable	72,000	
Advertising Supplies	25,000	
Prepaid Insurance	6,000	
Office Equipment	50,000	
Notes Payable		$ 50,000
Accounts Payable		25,000
Unearned Service Revenue		12,000
Common Shares		100,000
Dividends	5,000	
Service Revenue		100,000
Salaries Expense	40,000	
Rent Expense	9,000	
	$287,000	$287,000

Note that the total debits, $287,000, equal the total credits, $287,000. Account numbers to the left of the account titles in the trial balance are also often shown.

A trial balance does not prove that all transactions have been recorded or that the ledger is correct. Numerous errors may exist even though the trial balance columns agree. For example, the trial balance may balance even when:

1. a transaction is not journalized,

2. a correct journal entry is not posted,

3. a journal entry is posted twice,

4. incorrect accounts are used in journalizing or posting, or

5. offsetting errors are made in recording a transaction amount.

In other words, as long as equal debits and credits are posted, even to the wrong account or in the wrong amount, the total debits will equal the total credits.

Adjusting Entries

In order for revenues to be recorded in the period in which they are earned, and for expenses to be recognized in the period in which they are incurred, adjusting entries are made at the end of the accounting period. In short, **adjustments are needed to ensure that the revenue recognition and matching principles are followed.**

The use of adjusting entries makes it possible to report on the balance sheet the appropriate assets, liabilities, and owners' equity at the statement date and to report on the income statement the proper net income (or loss) for the period. However, the trial balance—the first pulling together of the transaction data—may not contain up-to-date and complete data. This is true for the following reasons.

1. Some events are **not journalized daily** because it is not expedient. Examples are the consumption of supplies and the earning of wages by employees.

2. Some costs are not journalized during the accounting period because these costs **expire with the passage of time** rather than as a result of recurring daily transactions. Examples of such costs are building and equipment deterioration and rent and insurance.

3. Some items may be **unrecorded**. An example is a utility service bill that will not be received until the next accounting period.

Adjusting entries are required every time financial statements are prepared. An essential starting point is an analysis of each trial balance account to determine whether it is complete and up to date for financial statement purposes. The analysis requires a thorough understanding of the company's operations and the interrelationship of accounts. Preparing adjusting entries is often an involved process that requires the services of a skilled professional. In accumulating the adjustment data, the company may need to take inventory counts of supplies and repair parts. Also it may be desirable to prepare supporting schedules of insurance policies, rental agreements, and other contractual commitments. Adjustments are often prepared after the balance sheet date. However, the entries are dated as of the balance sheet date.

Types of Adjusting Entries

Adjusting entries can be classified as either **prepayments** or **accruals**. Each of these classes has two subcategories as shown below.

PREPAYMENTS	ACCRUALS
1. **Prepaid Expenses.** Expenses paid in cash and recorded as assets before they are used or consumed.	3. **Accrued Revenues.** Revenues earned but not yet received in cash or recorded.
2. **Unearned Revenues.** Revenues received in cash and recorded as liabilities before they are earned.	4. **Accrued Expenses.** Expenses incurred but not yet paid in cash or recorded.

Specific examples and explanations of each type of adjustment are given in subsequent sections. Each example is based on the October 31 trial balance of Pioneer Advertising Agency Inc. (Illustration 3-9). We assume that Pioneer Advertising uses an accounting period of one month. Thus, monthly adjusting entries will be made. The entries will be dated October 31.

Adjusting Entries for Prepayments

As indicated earlier, prepayments are either **prepaid expenses** or **unearned revenues**. Adjusting entries for prepayments are required at the statement date to record the portion of the prepayment that represents the expense incurred or the revenue earned in the current accounting period. Assuming an adjustment is needed for both types of prepayments, the asset and liability are overstated and the related expense and revenue are understated. For example, in the trial balance, the balance in the asset Supplies shows only supplies purchased. This balance is overstated; the related expense account, Supplies Expense, is understated because the cost of supplies used has not been recognized. Thus the adjusting entry for prepayments will decrease a balance sheet account and increase an income statement account. The effects of adjusting entries for prepayments are depicted in Illustration 3-10.

Illustration 3-10

Adjusting Entries for Prepayments

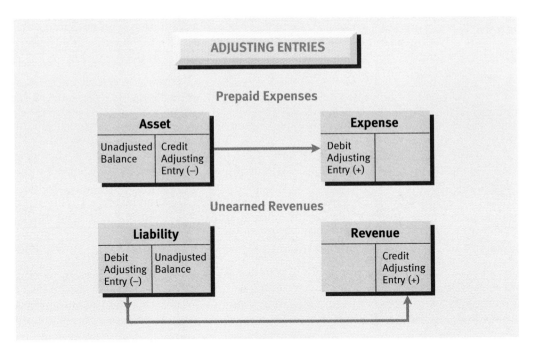

Prepaid Expenses.   As previously stated, expenses paid in cash and recorded as assets before they are used or consumed are identified as prepaid expenses. When a cost is incurred, an asset account is debited to show the service or benefit that will be received in the future. Prepayments often occur with regard to insurance, supplies, advertising, and rent.

Prepaid expenses expire either with the passage of time (e.g., rent and insurance) or through use and consumption (e.g., supplies). The expiration of these costs does not require daily recurring entries, which would be unnecessary and impractical. Accordingly, it is customary to postpone the recognition of such cost expirations until financial statements are prepared. At each statement date, adjusting entries are made to record the expenses that apply to the current accounting period and to show the unexpired costs in the asset accounts.

Prior to adjustment, assets are overstated and expenses are understated. **Thus, the prepaid expense adjusting entry results in a debit to an expense account and a credit to an asset account.**

Supplies.   Several different types of supplies are used in a business enterprise. For example, a CA firm will have office supplies such as stationery, envelopes, and accounting paper. In contrast, an advertising firm will have advertising supplies such as graph paper, video film, and poster paper. Supplies are generally debited to an asset account when they are acquired. During the course of operations, supplies are depleted or entirely consumed. However, recognition of supplies used is deferred until the adjustment process when a physical inventory (count) of supplies is taken. The difference between the balance in the Supplies (asset) account and the cost of supplies on hand represents the supplies used (expense) for the period.

Pioneer Advertising Agency purchased advertising supplies costing $25,000 on October 5. The debit was made to the asset Advertising Supplies, and this account shows a balance of $25,000 in the October 31 trial balance. An inventory count at the close of business on October 31 reveals that $10,000 of supplies is still on hand. Thus, the cost of supplies used is $15,000 ($25,000 − $10,000), and the following adjusting entry is made.

Oct. 31

Advertising Supplies Expense	15,000	
Advertising Supplies		15,000
(To record supplies used)		

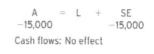

A	=	L	+	SE
−15,000				−15,000

Cash flows: No effect

Illustration 3-11

Supplies Accounts after Adjustment

After the adjusting entry is posted, the two supplies accounts in T account form show the following.

	Advertising Supplies				Advertising Supplies Expense	
10/5	$25,000	10/31 Adj. $15,000		10/31 Adj.	$15,000	
10/31 Bal.	$10,000					

The asset account Advertising Supplies now shows a balance of $10,000, which is equal to the cost of supplies on hand at the statement date. In addition, Advertising Supplies Expense shows a balance of $15,000, which equals the cost of supplies used in October. **If the adjusting entry is not made, October expenses will be understated and net income overstated by $15,000. Moreover, both assets and shareholders' equity will be overstated by $15,000 on the October 31 balance sheet.**

Insurance. Most companies have fire and theft insurance on merchandise and equipment, personal liability insurance for accidents suffered by customers, and automobile insurance on company cars and trucks. The cost of insurance protection is determined by the payment of insurance premiums. The term and coverage are specified in the insurance policy. The minimum term is usually one year, but three- to five-year terms are available and offer lower annual premiums. Insurance premiums normally are charged to the asset account Prepaid Insurance when paid. At the financial statement date, it is necessary to debit Insurance Expense and credit Prepaid Insurance for the cost that has expired during the period.

On October 4, Pioneer Advertising Agency Inc. paid $6,000 for a one-year fire insurance policy. The effective date of coverage was October 1. The premium was charged to Prepaid Insurance when it was paid, and this account shows a balance of $6,000 in the October 31 trial balance. An analysis of the policy reveals that $500 ($6,000/12) of insurance expires each month. Thus, the following adjusting entry is made.

Oct. 31

Insurance Expense	500	
Prepaid Insurance		500
(To record insurance expired)		

After the adjusting entry is posted, the accounts show the following.

	Prepaid Insurance				Insurance Expense	
10/4	$6,000	10/31 Adj. $500		10/31 Adj.	$500	
10/31 Bal.	$5,500					

A	=	L	+	SE
−500				−500

Cash flows: No effect

Illustration 3-12

Insurance Accounts after Adjustment

The asset Prepaid Insurance shows a balance of $5,500, which represents the unexpired cost applicable to the remaining 11 months of coverage. At the same time, the balance in Insurance Expense is equal to the insurance cost that has expired in October. **If** this adjustment is not made, October expenses will be understated by $500 and net income overstated by $500. Moreover, both assets and owners' equity also will be overstated by $500 on the October 31 balance sheet.

Amortization

Oct.1

Office equipment purchased; record asset ($50,000)

Office Equipment			
Oct $400	Nov $400	Dec $400	Jan $400
Feb $400	March $400	April $400	May $400
June $400	July $400	Aug $400	Sept $400
Amortization = $4,800/year			

Oct. 31 Amortization recognized; record amortization expense

Amortization/Depreciation.   A business enterprise typically owns a variety of productive facilities such as buildings, equipment, and motor vehicles. These assets provide a service for a number of years. The term of service is commonly referred to as the asset's useful life. **Because an asset such as a building is expected to provide service for many years, it is recorded as an asset, rather than an expense, in the year it is acquired.** Such assets are recorded at cost, as required by the cost principle.

According to the matching principle, a portion of the cost of a long-lived asset should be reported as an expense during each period of the asset's useful life. Amortization is the process of **allocating the cost of an asset** to expense over its useful life in a rational and systematic manner.

From an accounting standpoint, the acquisition of productive facilities is viewed essentially as a long-term prepayment for services. The need for making periodic adjusting entries for amortization is, therefore, the same as described before for other prepaid expenses; that is, to recognize the cost that has expired (expense) during the period and to report the unexpired cost (asset) at the end of the period.

In determining a productive facility's useful life, the primary causes of amortization are:

- actual use,

- deterioration due to the elements, and

- obsolescence.

At the time an asset is acquired, the effects of these factors cannot be known with certainty, so they must be estimated. Thus, you should recognize that amortization is an estimate rather than a factual measurement of the cost that has expired. A common procedure in calculating amortization expense is to divide the asset's cost by its useful life. For example, if cost is $10,000 and useful life is expected to be 10 years, annual amortization is $1,000.

For Pioneer Advertising, amortization on the office equipment is estimated at $4,800 a year (cost $50,000 less salvage value $2,000 divided by useful life of 10 years), or $400 per month. Accordingly, amortization for October is recognized by the following adjusting entry.

A = L + SE
-400   -400

Cash flows: No effect

	Oct. 31		
Amortization Expense		400	
Accumulated Amortization—Office Equipment			400
(To record monthly amortization)			

After the adjusting entry is posted, the accounts show that the balance in the accumulated amortization account will increase $400 each month.

Illustration 3-13

Accounts after Adjustment for Amortization

Office Equipment

10/1	$50,000	

Accumulated Amortization–Office Equipment

	10/31 Adj.	$400

Amortization Expense

10/31 Adj.	$400	

Therefore, after journalizing and posting the adjusting entry at November 30, the balance will be $800.

Accumulated Amortization—Office Equipment is a contra asset account. A contra asset account is an account that is offset against an asset account on the balance sheet. This means that the accumulated amortization account is offset against Office Equipment on the balance sheet and that its normal balance is a credit. This account is used instead of crediting Office Equipment in order to permit disclosure of both the original cost of the equipment and the total cost that has expired to date. In the balance sheet, Accumulated Amortization—Office Equipment is deducted from the related asset account as follows.

Office equipment	$50,000	
Less: Accumulated amortization—office equipment	400	$49,600

Illustration 3-14

Balance Sheet Presentation of Accumulated Amortization

The difference between any depreciable asset's cost and its related accumulated amortization is referred to as its book value. In Illustration 3-14, the equipment's book or carrying value at the balance sheet date is $49,600. It is important to realize that the asset's **book value and market value are generally two different values**.

Note also that amortization expense identifies that portion of the asset's cost that has expired in October. As in the case of other prepaid adjustments, **omitting this adjusting entry would cause total assets, total shareholders' equity, and net income to be overstated and amortization expense to be understated.**

If additional equipment is involved, such as delivery or store equipment, or if the company has buildings, amortization expense is recorded on each of these items. Related accumulated amortization accounts also are established. These accumulated amortization accounts would be described in the ledger as follows: Accumulated Amortization—Delivery Equipment; Accumulated Amortization—Store Equipment; and Accumulated Amortization—Buildings.

Unearned Revenues.   As stated earlier, revenues received in cash and recorded as liabilities before they are earned are called unearned revenues. Such items as rent, magazine subscriptions, and customer deposits for further service may result in unearned revenues. Airlines such as Air Canada and United Airlines treat receipts from the sale of tickets as unearned revenue until the flight service is provided. Similarly, tuition fees received by a university prior to the start of a semester is considered unearned revenue. Unearned revenues are the opposite of prepaid expenses. Indeed, unearned revenue on the books of one company is likely to be a prepayment on the books of the company that has made the advance payment. For example, if identical accounting periods are assumed, a landlord will have unearned rent revenue when a tenant has prepaid rent.

When the payment is received for services to be provided in a future accounting period, an unearned revenue account (a liability) should be credited to recognize the obligation that exists. Unearned revenues are subsequently earned through rendering service to a customer. During the accounting period, it may not be practical to make daily recurring entries as the revenue is earned. In such cases, the recognition of earned revenue is delayed until the adjustment process. Then an adjusting entry is made to record the revenue that has been earned and to show the liability that remains. In the typical case, liabilities are overstated and revenues are understated prior to adjustment. Thus, the adjusting entry for unearned revenues results in a debit (decrease) to a liability account and a credit (increase) to a revenue account.

Pioneer Advertising Agency received $12,000 on October 2 from R. Knox for advertising services expected to be completed by December 31. The payment was credited to Unearned Service Revenue, and this account shows a balance of $12,000 in the October 31 trial balance. When analysis reveals that $4,000 of these services have been earned in October, the following adjusting entry is made.

A = L + SE
   −4,000   +4,000

Cash flows: No effect

Oct. 31		
Unearned Service Revenue	4,000	
Service Revenue		4,000
(To record revenue for services provided)		

After the adjusting entry is posted, the accounts show the following.

Illustration 3-15

Service Revenue Accounts after Prepayments Adjustment

Unearned Service Revenue				Service Revenue		
10/31 Adj. $4,000	10/2	$12,000			10/31 Bal. $100,000	
	10/31	Bal. $8,000			31 Adj. 4,000	
					10/31 Bal. $104,000	

Underlying Concept

The revenue recognition principle requires revenue to be recognized when earned.

The Unearned Service Revenue now shows a balance of $8,000, which represents the remaining advertising services expected to be performed in the future. At the same time, Service Revenue shows total revenue earned in October of $104,000. If this adjustment is not made, revenues and net income will be understated by $4,000 in the income statement. Moreover, liabilities will be overstated and shareholders' equity will be understated by $4,000 on the October 31 balance sheet.

Alternative Method for Adjusting Prepayments

So far, the assumption has been that an asset (e.g., prepaid rent) or liability account (e.g., unearned revenue) is recorded when the company initially pays or receives the cash. An alternative treatment is to record the initial entry through the related income statement account and adjust later. For example, if Pioneer Advertising Agency Inc. paid $6000 for a one-year fire insurance policy on October 1, they might initially have recorded the whole amount as Insurance expense. Thus at October 31, the adjusting entry would be as follows.

A = L + SE
+5,500   +5,500

Cash flows: No effect

Oct. 31		
Prepaid Insurance	5,500	
Insurance Expense		5,500
(To record unexpired insurance)		

The same could be done for other prepayments such as supplies and revenues.

Adjusting Entries for Accruals

The second category of adjusting entries is **accruals**. Adjusting entries for accruals are required to record revenues earned and expenses incurred in the current accounting period that have not been recognized through daily entries. If an accrual adjustment is needed, the revenue account (and the related asset account) and/or the expense account (and the related liability account) is understated. Thus, the adjusting entry for accruals will increase both a balance sheet and an income statement account. Adjusting entries for accruals are depicted in Illustration 3-16.

Accrued Revenues

Oct. 31

My fee is $2,000

Service is provided; revenue and receivable are recorded

Nov.

Cash is received; receivable is reduced

Accrued Revenues.   As explained earlier, revenues **earned but not yet received** in cash or recorded at the statement date are accrued revenues. Accrued revenues may **accumulate (accrue) with the passing of time**, as in the case of interest revenue and rent revenue. Or they may result from services that have been performed but neither billed nor collected, as in the case of commissions and fees. The former are unrecorded because earning interest and rent does not involve daily transactions; the latter may be unrecorded because only a portion of the total service has been provided.

An adjusting entry is required to show the receivable that exists at the balance sheet date and to record the revenue that has been earned during the period. Prior to adjustment, both

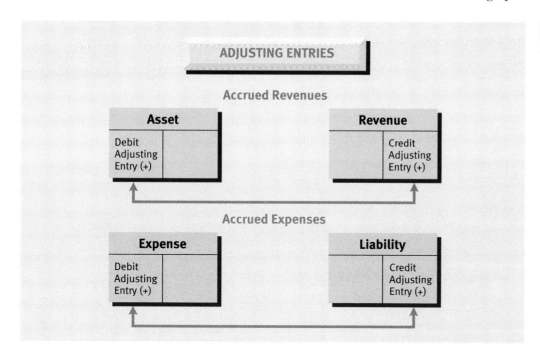

Illustration 3-16

Adjusting Entries for Accruals

assets and revenues are understated. Accordingly, an adjusting entry for accrued revenues results in a debit (increase) to an asset account and a credit (increase) to a revenue account.

In October, Pioneer Advertising Agency earned $2,000 for advertising services that were not billed to clients before October 31. Because these services have not been billed, they have not otherwise been recorded. Thus, the following adjusting entry is made.

Oct. 31		
Accounts Receivable	2,000	
Service Revenue		2,000
(To record revenue for services provided)		

A = L + SE
+2,000   +2,000
Cash flows: No effect

After the adjusting entry is posted, the accounts show the following.

Accounts Receivable			Service Revenue		
10/31	$72,000		10/31	$100,000	
31 Adj.	2,000		31	4,000	
10/31 Bal.	$74,000		31 Adj.	2,000	
			10/31 Bal. $106,000		

Illustration 3-17

Receivable and Revenue Accounts after Accrual Adjustment

The asset Accounts Receivable shows that $74,000 is owed by clients at the balance sheet date. The balance of $106,000 in Service Revenue represents the total revenue earned during the month ($100,000 + $4,000 + $2,000). If the adjusting entry is not made, assets and shareholders' equity on the balance sheet, and revenues and net income on the income statement, will all be understated.

Accrued Expenses. As indicated earlier, expenses incurred but not yet paid or recorded at the statement date are called **accrued expenses**. Interest, rent, taxes, and salaries can be accrued expenses. Accrued expenses result from the same causes as accrued revenues. In fact, an accrued expense on the books of one company is accrued revenue to another company. For example, the $2,000 accrual of service revenue by Pioneer is an accrued expense to the client that received the service.

Underlying Concept

Accrual accounting requires that expenses be accrued when incurred.

Adjustments for accrued expenses are necessary to record the obligations that exist at the balance sheet date and to recognize the expenses that apply to the current accounting period. Prior to adjustment, both liabilities and expenses are understated. Therefore, the adjusting entry for accrued expenses results in a debit (increase) to an expense account and a credit (increase) to a liability account.

Accrued Interest.   Pioneer Advertising Agency signed a three-month note payable for $50,000 on October 1. The note requires interest at an annual rate of 12%. The interest accumulation amount is determined by three factors:

- the note's face value,

- the interest rate, which is always expressed as an annual rate, and

- the length of time the note is outstanding. In this instance, the total interest due on the $50,000 note at its due date three months hence is $1,500 ($50,000 × 12% × 3/12), or $500 for one month. The formula for calculating interest and its application to Pioneer Advertising Agency for the month of October are shown in Illustration 3-18.

Illustration 3-18

Formula for Calculating Interest

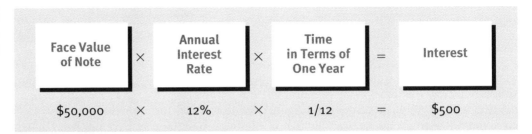

Note that the time period is expressed as a fraction of a year. The accrued expense adjusting entry at October 31 is as follows.

A = L + SE
      +500   −500
Cash flows: No effect

Oct. 31		
Interest Expense	500	
Interest Payable		500
(To record interest on notes payable)		

After this adjusting entry is posted, the accounts show the following.

Illustration 3-19

Interest Accounts after Adjustment

Interest Expense			Interest Payable		
10/31	$500			10/31	$500

Interest Expense shows the interest charges applicable to the month of October. The amount of interest owed at the statement date is shown in Interest Payable. It will not be paid until the note comes due at the end of three months. The Interest Payable account is used instead of crediting Notes Payable to disclose the two types of obligations (interest and principal) in the accounts and statements. **If this adjusting entry is not made, liabilities and interest expense will be understated, and net income and shareholders' equity will be overstated.**

Accrued Salaries.   Some types of expenses, such as employee salaries and commissions, are paid for after the services have been performed. At Pioneer Advertising, salaries were last paid on October 26; the next payment of salaries will not occur until November 9. As shown in the calendar below, three working days remain in October (October 29–31).

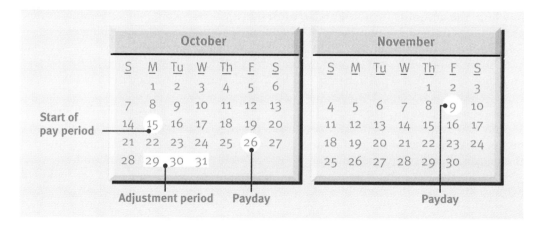

At October 31, the salaries for these days represent an accrued expense and a related liability to Pioneer Advertising. The employees receive total salaries of $10,000 for a five-day workweek, or $2,000 per day. Thus, accrued salaries at October 31 are $6,000 ($2,000 × 3), and the adjusting entry is:

Oct. 31		
Salaries Expense	6,000	
Salaries Payable		6,000
(To record accrued salaries)		

A = L + SE
    +6,000   −6,000
Cash flows: No effect

After this adjusting entry is posted, the accounts show the following.

Salaries Expense					Salaries Payable			
10/26		$40,000				10/31	Adj	$6,000
31	Adj.	6,000						
10/31	Bal.	$46,000						

Illustration 3-20

Salary Accounts after Adjustment

After this adjustment, the balance in Salaries Expense of $46,000 (23 days × $2,000) is the actual salary expense for October. The balance in Salaries Payable of $6,000 is the amount of liability for salaries owed as of October 31. **If the $6,000 adjustment for salaries is not recorded, Pioneer's expenses will be understated $6,000, and its liabilities will be understated $6,000.**

At Pioneer Advertising, salaries are payable every two weeks. Consequently, the next payday is November 9, when total salaries of $20,000 will again be paid. The payment consists of $6,000 of salaries payable at October 31 plus $14,000 of salaries expense for November (7 working days as shown in the November calendar × $2,000).

Therefore, the following entry is made on November 9.

Nov. 9		
Salaries Payable	6,000	
Salaries Expense	14,000	
Cash		20,000
(To record November 9 payroll)		

A = L + SE
−20,000   −6,000   −14,000
Cash flows: ↓ 20,000 outflow

This entry eliminates the liability for Salaries Payable that was recorded in the October 31 adjusting entry and records the proper amount of Salaries Expense for the period November 1 to November 9.

Bad Debts.   **Proper matching of revenues and expenses dictates recording bad debts as an expense of the period in which revenue is earned instead of the period**

Underlying Concept

Bad debt expense must be recognized when a loss is likely and measurable according to conservatism.

Bad Debts

Oct. 31
Uncollectible accounts;
record bad debt expense

A   =   L   +   SE
−1,600   −1,600

Cash flows: No effect

in which the accounts or notes are written off. Properly valuing the receivable balance also requires recognizing uncollectible, worthless receivables. Proper matching and valuation require an adjusting entry.

At the end of each period, an estimate is made of the amount of current period revenue on account that will later prove to be uncollectible. The estimate is based on the amount of bad debts experienced in past years, general economic conditions, how long the receivables are past due, and other factors that indicate the element of uncollectibility. Usually it is expressed as a percentage of the revenue on account for the period. Or it may be calculated by adjusting the Allowance for Doubtful Accounts to a certain percentage of the trade accounts receivable and trade notes receivable at the end of the period.

To illustrate, assume that experience indicates a reasonable estimate for bad debt expense for the month is $1,600. The adjusting entry for bad debts is:

Oct. 31		
Bad Debt Expense	1,600	
Allowance for Doubtful Accounts		1,600
(To record monthly bad debt expense)		

After the adjusting entry is posted, the accounts show the following.

Illustration 3-21

Accounts after Adjustment for Bad Debt Expense

Accounts Receivable

10/1		$72,000
31	Adj.	2,000
10/31	Bal.	$74,000

Allowance for Doubtful Accounts			**Bad Debt Expense**		
	10/31	Adj. $1,600	10/31	Adj.	$1,600

Adjusted Trial Balance

After all adjusting entries have been journalized and posted, another trial balance is prepared from the ledger accounts. This trial balance is called an **adjusted trial balance**. It shows the balance of all accounts, including those that have been adjusted, at the end of the accounting period. The purpose of an adjusted trial balance is to show the effects of all financial events that have occurred during the accounting period.

Illustration 3-22

Trial Balance (Adjusted)

PIONEER ADVERTISING AGENCY, INC.
Adjusted Trial Balance
October 31, 2004

	Debit	Credit
Cash	$80,000	
Accounts Receivable	74,000	
Allowance for Doubtful Accounts		$1,600
Advertising Supplies	10,000	
Prepaid Insurance	5,500	
Office Equipment	50,000	
Accumulated Amortization—		
Office Equipment		400
Notes Payable		50,000
Accounts Payable		25,000
Interest Payable		500
Unearned Service Revenue		8,000
Salaries Payable		6,000
Common Shares		100,000

Dividends	5,000	
Service Revenue		106,000
Salaries Expense	46,000	
Advertising Supplies Expense	15,000	
Rent Expense	9,000	
Insurance Expense	500	
Interest Expense	500	
Amortization Expense	400	
Bad Debt Expense	1,600	
	$297,500	$297,500

Closing

Basic Process

The procedure generally followed to reduce the balance of temporary accounts to zero in order to prepare the accounts for the next period's transactions is known as the **closing process**. In the closing process, all of the revenue and expense account balances (income statement items) are transferred to a clearing or suspense account called **Income Summary**, which is used only at the end of each accounting period (yearly). Revenues and expenses are matched in the Income Summary account, and the net result of this matching, which represents the net income or net loss for the period, is then transferred to an owners' equity account (retained earnings for a corporation and capital accounts or owners' equity normally for proprietorships and partnerships). All closing entries are posted to the appropriate general ledger accounts.

6 **Objective**
Prepare closing entries.

For example, assume that revenue accounts of Collegiate Apparel Shop Inc. have the following balances, after adjustments, at the end of the year.

Sales Revenue	$280,000
Rental Revenue	27,000
Interest Revenue	5,000

These revenue accounts would be closed and the balances transferred by the following closing journal entry.

Sales Revenue	280,000	
Rental Revenue	27,000	
Interest Revenue	5,000	
Income Summary		312,000
(To close revenue accounts to Income Summary)		

A = L + SE
    −312,000
    +312,000
Cash flows: No effect

Assume that the expense accounts, including Cost of Goods Sold, have the following balances, after adjustments, at the end of the year.

Cost of Goods Sold	$206,000
Selling Expenses	25,000
General and Admin. Expenses	40,600
Interest Expense	4,400
Income Tax Expense	13,000

These expense accounts would be closed and the balances transferred through the following closing journal entry.

A = L + SE		
−289,000		
+289,000		

Cash flows: No effect

Income Summary	289,000	
Cost of Goods Sold		206,000
Selling Expenses		25,000
General and Admin. Expenses		40,600
Interest Expense		4,400
Income Tax Expense		13,000
(To close expense accounts to Income Summary)		

The Income Summary account now has a credit balance of $23,000, which is net income. **The net income is transferred to retained earnings by closing the Income Summary account to Retained Earnings** as follows.

A = L + SE		
−23,000		
+23,000		

Cash flows: No effect

Income Summary	23,000	
Retained Earnings		23,000
(To close Income Summary to Retained Earnings)		

Assuming that dividends of $7,000 were declared and distributed during the year, the Dividends account is closed directly to Retained Earnings as follows.

A = L + SE		
−7,000		
+7,000		

Cash flows: No effect

Retained Earnings	7,000	
Dividends		7,000
(To close Dividends to Retained Earnings)		

After the closing process is completed, each income statement account is balanced out to zero and is ready for use in the next accounting period. Illustration 3-23 shows the closing process in T account form.

Illustration 3-23

The Closing Process

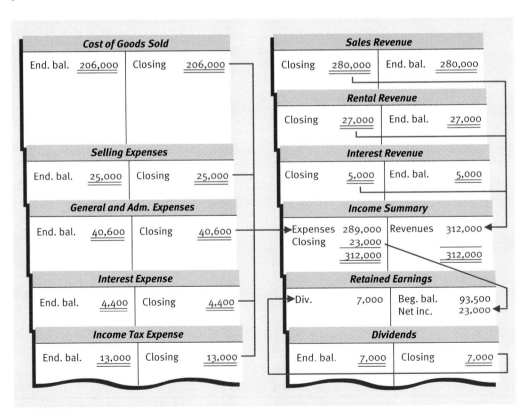

Objective 7

Explain how inventory accounts are adjusted at year end.

Inventory and Cost of Goods Sold

The closing procedures illustrated above assumed the use of the perpetual inventory system. With a **perpetual inventory system**, purchases and sales are recorded directly in the inventory account as they occur. Therefore, the balance in the Inventory account should represent the ending inventory amount, and no adjusting entries are needed.

To ensure this accuracy, a **physical count** of the items in the inventory is generally made annually. No Purchases account is used because the purchases are debited directly to the Inventory account. However, a Cost of Goods Sold account is used to accumulate the issuances from inventory. That is, when inventory items are sold, the cost of the sold goods is credited to Inventory and debited to Cost of Goods Sold.

With a periodic inventory system, a Purchases account is used, and the Inventory account is unchanged during the period. The Inventory account represents the beginning inventory amount throughout the period. At the end of the accounting period, the Inventory account must be adjusted by **closing out the beginning inventory amount** and **recording the ending inventory amount**. The ending inventory is determined by physically counting the items on hand and valuing them at cost or at the lower of cost or market. Under the periodic inventory system, cost of goods sold is, therefore, determined by adding the beginning inventory together with net purchases and deducting the ending inventory.

To illustrate how cost of goods sold is calculated with a periodic inventory system, assume that Collegiate Apparel Shop has a beginning inventory of $30,000; Purchases $200,000; Transportation-In $6,000; Purchase Returns and Allowances $1,000; Purchase Discounts $3,000; and the ending inventory is $26,000. The calculation of cost of goods sold is as follows.

Underlying Concept

Use of a periodic inventory system reflects the application of the cost benefit concept since the costs to maintain this system are lower than a perpetual inventory system. The use of computers has greatly reduced this cost.

Beginning inventory		$30,000
Purchases	$200,000	
Less: Purchase returns and allowances	$1,000	
Less: Purchase discounts	3,000	4,000
Net purchases	196,000	
Plus: Transportation-in	6,000	
Cost of goods purchased		202,000
Cost of goods available for sale		232,000
Less: Ending inventory		26,000
Cost of goods sold		$206,000

Illustration 3-24

Calculation of Cost of Goods Sold

Cost of goods sold will be the same whether the perpetual or periodic method is used.

Post-Closing Trial Balance

We already mentioned that a trial balance is taken after the period's regular transactions have been entered and that a second trial balance (the adjusted trial balance) is taken after the adjusting entries have been posted. A third trial balance may be taken after posting the closing entries. The trial balance after closing, often called the post-closing trial balance, shows that equal debits and credits have been posted to the Income Summary account. The post-closing trial balance consists only of asset, liability, and owners' equity (the permanent) accounts.

Reversing Entries

After the financial statements have been prepared and the books have been closed, it is often helpful to reverse some of the adjusting entries before recording the next period's regular transactions. Such entries are called reversing entries. A reversing entry is made at the beginning of the next accounting period and is the exact opposite of the related adjusting entry made in the previous period. The recording of reversing entries is an optional step in the accounting cycle that may be performed at the beginning of the next accounting period. Appendix 3A discusses reversing entries in more detail.

The Accounting Cycle Summarized

The steps in the accounting cycle follow a logical sequence of the accounting procedures used during a fiscal period.

1. Enter the period's transactions in appropriate journals.

2. Post from the journals to the ledger (or ledgers).

3. Take an unadjusted trial balance (trial balance).

4. Prepare adjusting journal entries and post to the ledger(s).

5. Take a trial balance after adjusting (adjusted trial balance).

6. Prepare the financial statements from the second trial balance.

7. Prepare closing journal entries and post to the ledger(s).

8. Take a trial balance after closing (post-closing trial balance).

9. Prepare reversing entries (optional) and post to the ledger(s).

This list of procedures constitutes a complete accounting cycle that is normally performed in every fiscal period.

USING A WORK SHEET

Objective 8
Prepare a 10-column work sheet.

To facilitate the end-of-period (monthly, quarterly, or annually) accounting and reporting process, a work sheet is often used. A **work sheet** is a columnar sheet of paper (or computer spreadsheet) used to adjust the account balances and prepare the financial statements. Using a work sheet helps accountants prepare financial statements on a more timely basis. It is not necessary to delay preparing the financial statements until the adjusting and closing entries are journalized and posted. The **10-column work sheet** illustrated in this chapter (Illustration 3-25) provides columns for the first trial balance, adjustments, adjusted trial balance, income statement, and balance sheet.

The work sheet does not replace the financial statements. Instead, it is an informal device for accumulating and sorting information needed for the financial statements. Completing the work sheet provides considerable assurance that all of the details related to the end-of-period accounting and statement preparation have been properly brought together.

Adjustments Entered on the Work Sheet

Items (a) through (f) below serve as the basis for the adjusting entries made in the work sheet shown in Illustration 3-25.

(a) Furniture and equipment is amortized at the rate of 10% per year based on original cost of $67,000.

(b) Estimated bad debts, one-quarter of 1% of sales ($400,000).

(c) Insurance expired during the year, $360.

(d) Interest accrued on notes receivable as of December 31, $800.

(e) The Rent Expense account contains $500 rent paid in advance, which is applicable to next year.

(f) Property taxes accrued December 31, $2,000.

The adjusting entries shown on the December 31, 2004 work sheet are as follows.

(a)	Amortization Expense-Furniture and Equipment	6,700	
	Accumulated Amortization-Furniture and Equipment		6,700
(b)	Bad Debt Expenses	1,000	
	Allowance for Doubtful Accounts		1,000
(c)	Insurance Expense	360	
	Prepaid Insurance		360
(d)	Interest Receivable	800	
	Interest Revenue		800
(e)	Prepaid Rent Expense	500	
	Rent Expense		500
(f)	Property Tax Expense	2,000	
	Property Tax Payable		2,000

These adjusting entries are transferred to the work sheet's Adjustments columns and each may be designated by letter. The accounts set up resulting from the adjusting entries that are not already in the trial balance are listed below the totals of the trial balance, as illustrated on the work sheet. The Adjustments columns are then totalled and balanced.

Work Sheet Columns

Trial Balance Columns

Data for the trial balance are obtained from the ledger balances of Uptown Cabinet Corp. at December 31. The amount for Merchandise Inventory, $40,000, is the year-end inventory amount, which results from applying a perpetual inventory system.

Adjustments Columns

After all adjustment data are entered on the work sheet, the equality of the adjustment columns is established. The balances in all accounts are then extended to the adjusted trial balance columns.

Adjusted Trial Balance

The adjusted trial balance shows the balance of all accounts after adjustment at the end of the accounting period. For example, the $2,000 shown opposite the Allowance for Doubtful Accounts in the Trial Balance Cr. column is added to the $1,000 in the Adjustments Cr. column. The $3,000 total is then extended to the Adjusted Trial Balance Cr. column. Similarly, the $900 debit opposite Prepaid Insurance is reduced by the $360 credit in the Adjustments column. The result, $540, is shown in the Adjusted Trial Balance Dr. column.

Income Statement and Balance Sheet Columns

All the debit items in the Adjusted Trial Balance columns are extended into the Income Statement or Balance Sheet columns to the right. All the credit items are similarly extended. The next step is to total the Income Statement columns; the figure necessary to balance the debit and credit columns is the pretax income or loss for the period. The income before income taxes of $15,640 is shown in the Income Statement Dr. column because revenues exceeded expenses by that amount.

Income Taxes and Net Income

The federal and provincial income tax expense and related tax liability are calculated next. The company applies an effective rate of 22% to arrive at $3,440. Because the Adjustments columns have been balanced, this adjustment is entered in the Income Statement Dr. column as Income Tax Expense and in the Balance Sheet Cr. column as Income Tax Payable.

A = L + SE
  +3,440 −3,440

Cash flows: No effect

The following adjusting journal entry is recorded on December 31, 2004, and posted to the general ledger as well as entered on the work sheet.

(g)	Income Tax Expense	3,440	
	Income Tax Payable		3,440

Illustration 3-25

Use of Work Sheet

Next, the Income Statement columns are balanced with the income taxes included. The $12,200 difference between the debit and credit columns in this illustration represents net

UPTOWN CABINET CORP.
Ten-Column Work Sheet
For the Year Ended December 31, 2004

Accounts	Trial Balance Dr.	Trial Balance Cr.	Adjustments Dr.	Adjustments Cr.	Adjusted Trial Balance Dr.	Adjusted Trial Balance Cr.	Income Statement Dr.	Income Statement Cr.	Balance Sheet Dr.	Balance Sheet Cr.
Cash	1,200				1,200				1,200	
Notes receivable	16,000				16,000				16,000	
Accounts receivable	41,000				41,000				41,000	
Allowance for doubtful accounts		2,000		(b) 1,000		3,000				3,000
Merchandise inventory	40,000				40,000				40,000	
Prepaid insurance	900			(c) 360	540				540	
Furniture and equipment	67,000				67,000				67,000	
Accumulated amortization— furniture and equipment		12,000		(a) 6,700		18,700				18,700
Notes payable		20,000				20,000				20,000
Accounts payable		13,500				13,500				13,500
Bonds payable		30,000				30,000				30,000
Common shares		50,000				50,000				50,000
Retained earnings, Jan. 1, 2004		14,200				14,200				14,200
Sales		400,000				400,000		400,000		
Cost of goods sold	316,000				316,000		316,000			
Sales salaries expense	20,000				20,000		20,000			
Advertising expense	2,200				2,200		2,200			
Travelling expense	8,000				8,000		8,000			
Salaries, office and general	19,000				19,000		19,000			
Telephone and Internet expense	600				600		600			
Rent expense	4,800			(e) 500	4,300		4,300			
Property tax expense	3,300		(f) 2,000		5,300		5,300			
Interest expense	1,700				1,700		1,700			
Totals	541,700	541,700								
Amortization expense— furniture and equipment			(a) 6,700		6,700		6,700			
Bad debt expense			(b) 1,000		1,000		1,000			
Insurance expense			(c) 360		360		360			
Interest receivable			(d) 800		800				800	
Interest revenue				(d) 800		800		800		
Prepaid rent expense			(e) 500		500				500	
Property tax payable				(f) 2,000		2,000				2,000
Totals			11,360	11,360	552,200	552,200	385,160	400,800		
Income before income taxes							15,640			
Totals							400,800	400,800		
Income before income taxes								15,640		
Income tax expense			(g) 3,440				3,440			
Income tax payable				(g) 3,440						3,440
Net income							12,200			12,200
Totals							15,640	15,640	167,040	167,040

income. The net income of $12,200 is entered in the Income Statement Dr. column to achieve equality and in the Balance Sheet Cr. column as the increase in retained earnings.

Preparing Financial Statements from a Work Sheet

The work sheet provides the information needed to prepare financial statements without referring to the ledger or other records. In addition, the data have been sorted into appropriate columns, which eases the statement preparation.

The financial statements prepared from the 10-column work sheet illustrated are: **Income Statement for the Year Ended December 31, 2004 (Illustration 3-26), Statement of Retained Earnings for the Year Ended December 31, 2004 (Illustration 3-27), and Balance Sheet as of December 31, 2004 (Illustration 3-28), as shown below.**

UPTOWN CABINET CORP.
Income Statement
For the Year Ended December 31, 2004

Net sales			$400,000
Cost of goods sold			316,000
Gross profit on sales			84,000
Selling expenses			
Sales salaries expense		$20,000	
Advertising expense		2,200	
Travelling expense		8,000	
Total selling expenses		30,200	
Administrative expenses			
Salaries, office, and general	$19,000		
Telephone and Internet expense	600		
Rent expense	4,300		
Property tax expense	5,300		
Amortization expense—furniture and equipment	6,700		
Bad debt expense	1,000		
Insurance expense	360		
Total administrative expenses		37,260	
Total selling and administrative expenses			67,460
Income from operations			16,540
Other revenues and gains			
Interest revenue			800
			17,340
Other expenses and losses			
Interest expense			1,700
Income before income taxes			15,640
Income taxes			3,440
Net income			$12,200
Earnings per share			**$1.22**

Illustration 3-26

An Income Statement

UPTOWN CABINET CORP.
Statement of Retained Earnings
For the Year Ended December 31, 2004

Retained earnings, Jan. 1, 2004	$14,200
Add net income for 2004	12,200
Retained earnings, Dec. 31, 2004	**$26,400**

Illustration 3-27

A Statement of Retained Earnings

Income Statement

The income statement presented is that of a trading or merchandising concern; if a manufacturing concern were illustrated, three inventory accounts would be involved: raw materials, work in process, and finished goods.

Illustration 3-28

A Balance Sheet

UPTOWN CABINET CORP.
Balance Sheet
As of December 31, 2004

Assets

Current assets			
Cash			$ 1,200
Notes receivable	$16,000		
Accounts receivable	41,000		
Interest receivable	800	$57,800	
Less: Allowance for doubtful accounts		3,000	54,800
Merchandise inventory			40,000
Prepaid insurance			540
Prepaid rent			500
Total current assets			97,040
Property, plant, and equipment			
Furniture and equipment		67,000	
Less: Accumulated amortization		18,700	
Total property, plant, and equipment			48,300
Total assets			$145,340

Liabilities and Shareholders' Equity

Current liabilities			
Notes payable			$ 20,000
Accounts payable			13,500
Property tax payable			2,000
Income tax payable			3,440
Total current liabilities			38,940
Long-term liabilities			
Bonds payable, due June 30, 2009			30,000
Total liabilities			68,940
Shareholders' equity			
Common shares, issued and outstanding,			
10,000 shares		$50,000	
Retained earnings		26,400	
Total shareholders' equity			76,400
Total liabilities and shareholders' equity			$145,340

Statement of Retained Earnings

The net income earned by a corporation may be retained in the business or distributed to shareholders by paying dividends. In Illustration 3-27, the net income earned during the year was added to the balance of retained earnings on January 1, thereby increasing the balance of retained earnings to $26,400 on December 31. No dividends were declared during the year.

Balance Sheet

The balance sheet prepared from the 10-column work sheet contains new items resulting from year-end adjusting entries. Interest receivable, unexpired insurance, and prepaid rent expense are included as current assets. These assets are considered current because they will be converted into cash or consumed in the ordinary routine of the business within a relatively short period of time. The amount of Allowance for Doubtful Accounts is deducted from the total of accounts, notes, and interest receivable because it is estimated that only $54,800 of $57,800 will be collected in cash.

In the property, plant, and equipment section, the accumulated amortization is deducted from the cost of the furniture and equipment; the difference represents the book or carrying value of the furniture and equipment.

Property tax payable is shown as a current liability because it is an obligation that is payable within a year. Other short-term accrued liabilities would also be shown as current liabilities.

The bonds payable, due in 2009, are long-term liabilities and are shown in a separate section. (Interest on the bonds was paid on December 31.)

Because Uptown Cabinet Corp. is a corporation, the balance sheet's capital section, called the shareholders' equity section in Illustration 3-28, is somewhat different from the capital section for a proprietorship. Total shareholders' equity consists of the common shares, which is the original investment by shareholders, and the earnings retained in the business.

Closing Entries

The entries for the closing process are as follows.

GENERAL JOURNAL
December 31, 2004

Interest Revenue	800	
Sales	400,000	
Cost of Goods Sold		316,000
Sales Salaries Expense		20,000
Advertising Expense		2,200
Travelling Expense		8,000
Salaries, Office, and General		19,000
Telephone and Internet Expense		600
Rent Expense		4,300
Property Tax Expense		5,300
Amortization Expense—Furniture and Equipment		6,700
Bad Debt Expense		1,000
Insurance Expense		360
Interest Expense		1,700
Income Tax Expense		3,440
Income Summary		12,200
(To close revenues and expenses to Income Summary)		
Income Summary	12,200	
Retained Earnings		12,200
(To close Income Summary to Retained Earnings)		

Monthly Statements, Yearly Closing

The use of a work sheet at the end of each month or quarter permits the preparation of interim financial statements even though the books are closed only at the end of each year. For example, assume that a business closes its books on December 31 but that monthly financial statements are desired. At the end of January, a work sheet similar to the one illustrated in this chapter can be prepared to supply the information needed for statements for January. At the end of February, a work sheet can be used again. Note that because the accounts were not closed at the end of January, the income statement taken from the work sheet on February 28 will present the net income for two months. To obtain an income statement for only the month of February, subtract the items in the January income statement from the corresponding items in the income statement for the two months of January and February.

A statement of retained earnings for February only also may be obtained by subtracting the January items. The balance sheet prepared from the February work sheet, however, shows assets, liabilities, and shareholders' equity as of February 28, the specific date for which a balance sheet is desired.

The March work sheet would show the revenues and expenses for three months, and the subtraction of the revenues and expenses for the first two months could be made to supply the amounts needed for an income statement for the month of March only, and so on throughout the year.

Summary of Learning Objectives

1 Understand basic accounting terminology.

It is important to understand the following terms: (1) event, (2) transaction, (3) account, (4) permanent and temporary accounts, (5) ledger, (6) journal, (7) posting, (8) trial balance, (9) adjusting entries, (10) financial statements, (11) closing entries.

2 Explain double-entry rules.

The left side of any account is the debit side; the right side is the credit side. All asset and expense accounts are increased on the left or debit side and decreased on the right or credit side. Conversely, all liability and revenue accounts are increased on the right or credit side and decreased on the left or debit side. Shareholders' equity accounts, Common Shares, and Retained Earnings are increased on the credit side, whereas Dividends is increased on the debit side.

3 Identify steps in the accounting cycle.

The basic steps in the accounting cycle are (1) identification and measurement of transactions and other events; (2) journalization; (3) posting; (4) unadjusted trial balance; (5) adjustments; (6) adjusted trial balance; (7) statement preparation; and (8) closing.

4 Record transactions in journals, post to ledger accounts, and prepare a trial balance.

The simplest journal form is a chronological listing of transactions and events expressed in terms of debits and credits to particular accounts. The items entered in a general journal must be transferred (posted) to the general ledger. An unadjusted trial balance should be prepared at the end of a given period after the entries have been recorded in the journal and posted to the ledger.

5 Explain the reasons for preparing adjusting entries.

Adjustments are necessary to achieve a proper matching of revenues and expenses so as to determine net income for the current period and to achieve an accurate statement of end-of-the-period balances in assets, liabilities, and owners' equity accounts.

6 Prepare closing entries.

In the closing process, all of the revenue and expense account balances (income statement items) are transferred to a clearing account called Income Summary, which is used only at the end of the fiscal year. Revenues and expenses are matched in the Income Summary account. The net result of this matching, which represents the net income or net loss for the period, is then transferred to a shareholders' equity account (retained earnings for a corporation and capital accounts for proprietorships and partnerships).

7 Explain how inventory accounts are adjusted at year end.

Under a perpetual inventory system, the balance in the Inventory account should represent the ending inventory amount. When the inventory records are maintained in a periodic inventory system, a Purchases account is used; the Inventory account is unchanged during the period. The Inventory account represents the beginning inventory amount throughout the period. At the end of the accounting period, the inventory account must be adjusted by closing out the beginning inventory amount and recording the ending inventory amount.

8 Prepare a 10-column work sheet.

The 10-column work sheet provides columns for the first trial balance, adjustments, adjusted trial balance, income statement, and balance sheet. The work sheet does not replace the financial statements. Instead, it is the accountant's informal device for accumulating and sorting information needed for the financial statements.

Digital Tool

Glossary

www.wiley.com/canada/kieso

KEY TERMS

account, 71
accounting cycle, 76
accounting information
   system, 70
accrued expenses, 87
accrued revenues, 86
adjusted trial balance, 71
adjusting entry, 80
amortization, 84
balance sheet, 71
book value, 85
closing entries, 72
closing process, 91
contra asset account, 85
credit, 72
debit, 72
double-entry accounting, 72
event, 71
financial statements, 71
general journal, 77
general ledger, 77
income statement, 71
journal, 71
periodic inventory
   system, 93
permanent accounts, 71
perpetual inventory
   system, 92
post-closing trial
   balance, 93
posting, 78
prepaid expenses, 82
reversing entries, 93
special journals, 78
statement of cash flows, 71
statement of com-
   prehensive income, 72
statement of retained
   earnings, 72
subsidiary ledger, 71
T account, 77
temporary accounts, 71
transaction, 71
trial balance, 79
unearned revenues, 85
useful life, 84
work sheet, 94

Using Reversing Entries

Objective 9
Identify adjusting entries that may be reversed.

The purpose of reversing entries is to simplify recording transactions in the next accounting period. The use of reversing entries does not change the amounts reported in the previous period's financial statements.

ILLUSTRATION OF REVERSING ENTRIES— ACCRUALS

Reversing entries are most often used to reverse two types of adjusting entries: accrued revenues and accrued expenses. To illustrate the optional use of reversing entries for accrued expenses, we will use the following transaction and adjustment data.

1. October 24 (initial salary entry): $4,000 of salaries incurred between October 1 and October 24 are paid.

2. October 31 (adjusting entry): Salaries incurred between October 25 and October 31 are $1,200. These will be paid in the November 8 payroll.

3. November 8 (subsequent salary entry): Salaries paid are $2,500. Of this amount, $1,200 applied to accrued wages payable at October 31 and $1,300 was incurred between November 1 and November 8.

Illustration 3A-1

Comparison of Entries for Accruals, with and without Reversing Entries

The comparative entries are shown in Illustration 3A-1.

Reversing Entries Not Used				Reversing Entries Used			
Initial Salary Entry							
Oct. 24	Salaries Expense	4,000		Oct. 24	Salaries Expense	4,000	
	Cash		4,000		Cash		4,000
Adjusting Entry							
Oct. 31	Salaries Expense	1,200		Oct. 31	Salaries Expense	1,200	
	Salaries Payable		1,200		Salaries Payable		1,200
Closing Entry							
Oct. 31	Income Summary	5,200		Oct. 31	Income Summary	5,200	
	Salaries Expense		5,200		Salaries Expense		5,200
Reversing Entry							
Nov. 1	No entry is made.			Nov. 1	Salaries Payable	1,200	
					Salaries Expense		1,200
Subsequent Salary Entry							
Nov. 8	Salaries Payable	1,200		Nov. 8	Salaries Expense	2,500	
	Salaries Expense	1,300			Cash		2,500
	Cash		2,500				

The comparative entries show that the first three entries are the same whether or not reversing entries are used. The last two entries, however, are different. The November 1 reversing entry eliminates the $1,200 balance in Salaries Payable that was created by the October 31 adjusting entry. The reversing entry also creates a $1,200 credit balance in the Salaries Expense account. As you know, it is unusual for an expense account to have a credit balance; however, the balance is correct in this instance. It is correct because the entire amount of the first salary payment in the new accounting period will be debited to Salaries Expense. This debit will eliminate the credit balance, and the resulting debit balance in the expense account will equal the salaries expense incurred in the new accounting period ($1,300 in this example).

When reversing entries are made, all cash payments of expenses can be debited to the expense account. This means that on November 8 (and every payday), Salaries Expense can be debited for the amount paid without regard to the existence of any accrued salaries payable. Being able to make the same entry each time simplifies the recording process in an accounting system.

ILLUSTRATION OF REVERSING ENTRIES—PREPAYMENTS

Up to this point, we have assumed that all prepayments are recorded as prepaid expense or unearned revenue. In some cases, prepayments are recorded directly in expense or revenue accounts. When this occurs, prepayments may also be reversed. To illustrate the use of reversing entries for prepaid expenses, we will use the following transaction and adjustment data.

December 10 (initial entry): $20,000 of office supplies are purchased with cash.

December 31 (adjusting entry): $5,000 of office supplies on hand.

The comparative entries are shown in Illustration 3A-2.

Illustration 3A-2

Comparison of Entries for Prepayments, with and without Reversing Entries

Reversing Entries Not Used				**Reversing Entries Used**			
Initial Purchase of Supplies Entry							
Dec. 10	Office Supplies	20,000		Dec. 10	Office Supplies Expense	20,000	
	Cash		20,000		Cash		20,000
Adjusting Entry							
Dec. 31	Office Supplies Expense	15,000		Dec. 31	Office Supplies	5,000	
	Office Supplies		15,000		Office Supplies Expense		5,000
Closing Entry							
Dec. 31	Income Summary	15,000		Dec. 31	Income Summary	15,000	
	Office Supplies Expense		15,000		Office Supplies Expense		15,000
Reversing Entry							
Jan. 1	No entry			Jan. 1	Office Supplies Expense	5,000	
					Office Supplies		5,000

After the adjusting entry on December 31 (regardless of whether reversing entries are used), the asset account Office Supplies shows a balance of $5,000 and Office Supplies Expense a balance of $15,000. If Office Supplies Expense initially was debited when the supplies were purchased, a reversing entry is made to return to the expense account the cost of unconsumed supplies. The company then continues to debit Office Supplies Expense for additional purchases of office supplies during the next period.

With respect to prepaid items, why are all such items not entered originally into real accounts (assets and liabilities), thus making reversing entries unnecessary? Sometimes this practice is followed. It is particularly advantageous for items that need to be apportioned over several periods (e.g., supplies and parts inventories). However, items that do not follow this regular pattern and that may or may not involve two or more periods are ordinarily entered initially in revenue or expense accounts. The revenue and expense accounts may not require adjusting and are systematically closed to Income Summary. Using the temporary accounts adds consistency to the accounting system and makes the recording more efficient, particularly when a large number of such transactions occur during the year. For example, the bookkeeper knows that when an invoice is received for other than a capital asset acquisition, the amount is expensed. The bookkeeper need not worry at the time the invoice is received whether or not the item will result in a prepaid expense at the end of the period, because adjustments will be made at that time.

SUMMARY OF REVERSING ENTRIES

A summary of guidelines for reversing entries is as follows.

1. All accrued items should be reversed.

2. All prepaid items for which the original cash transaction was debited or credited to an expense or revenue account should be reversed.

3. Adjusting entries for amortization and bad debts are not reversed.

Although reversing entries reduce potential errors and are therefore often used, they do not have to be used. Many accountants avoid them entirely. Reversing entries add an additional step to the bookkeeping process. Also there may be instances where it does not make sense to use them. Assume a company with a December 31 year end has accrued six months worth of interest on a bond (June 30 interest payment date) at year end. If the company releases financial information monthly, it would not make sense to reverse the entry in January since this would show a credit balance when the monthly reports are prepared.

Summary of Learning Objectives for Appendix 3A

9 Identify adjusting entries that may be reversed.

Reversing entries are most often used to reverse two types of adjusting entries: accrued revenues and accrued expenses. Prepayments may also be reversed if the initial entry to record the transaction is made to an expense or revenue account.

Note: All asterisked assignment material relates to the appendix to the chapter.

Brief Exercises

BE3-1 Transactions for Angel Limited for the month of May are presented below. Prepare journal entries for each of these transactions. (You may omit explanations.)

May   1   Invests $3,000 cash in exchange for common shares in a small welding corporation.
      3   Buys equipment on account for $1,100.
    13   Pays $400 to landlord for May rent.
    21   Bills Noble Corp. $500 for welding work done.

BE3-2 Fancy Repair Shop Inc. had the following transactions during the first month of business. Journalize the transactions.

August   2   Invested $12,000 cash and $2,500 of equipment in the business.
        7   Purchased supplies on account for $400. (Debit asset account.)
      12   Performed services for clients, for which $1,300 was collected in cash and $670 was billed to the clients.
      15   Paid August rent, $600.
      19   Counted supplies and determined that only $270 of the supplies purchased on August 7 are still on hand.

BE3-3 On July 1, 2006, Blondy Ltd. pays $18,000 to Hindi Insurance Ltd. for a three-year insurance contract. Both companies have fiscal years ending December 31. For Blondy, journalize the entry on July 1 and the adjusting entry on December 31 treating the expenditure as an asset *and* expense on July 1.

BE3-4 Using the data in BE3-3, journalize the entry on July 1 and the adjusting entry on December 31 for Hindi Insurance Ltd. Hindi uses the accounts Unearned Insurance Revenue and Insurance Revenue. Prepare two sets of journal entries—one where the initial cash receipt is treated as Unearned Insurance Revenue and one where it is treated as Insurance Revenue.

BE3-5 On August 1, Bell Limited paid $8,400 in advance for two years of insurance coverage. Prepare Bell's August 1 journal entry and the annual adjusting entry on December 31. Prepare two sets of journal entries treating the initial expenditure as an asset *and* an expense on August 1.

BE3-6 Modigliani Corporation owns a warehouse. On November 1, it rented storage space to a lessee (tenant) for three months for a total cash payment of $2,700 received in advance. Prepare Modigliani's November 1 journal entry and the December 31 annual adjusting entry. Prepare an alternate set of journal entries assuming that the initial cash receipt on November 1 is treated as revenue.

BE3-7 Janeway Corp's weekly payroll, paid on Fridays, totals $6,000. Employees work a five-day week. Prepare Janeway's adjusting entry on Wednesday, December 31 and the journal entry to record the $6,000 cash payment on Friday, January 2.

BE3-8 Included in Mascot Corp's December 31 trial balance is a note receivable of $10,000. The note is a four-month, 12% note dated October 1. Prepare Mascot's December 31 adjusting entry to record $300 of accrued interest, and the February 1 journal entry to record receipt of $10,400 from the borrower.

BE3-9 Prepare the following adjusting entries at December 31 for DeGroot Ltd.

1. Interest on notes payable of $400 is accrued.

2. Fees earned but unbilled total $1,400.

3. Salaries earned by employees of $700 have not been recorded.

4. Bad debt expense for year is $900.

Use the following account titles: Service Revenue, Accounts Receivable, Interest Expense, Interest Payable, Salaries Expense, Salaries Payable, Allowance for Doubtful Accounts, and Bad Debt Expense.

BE3-10 At the end of its first year of operations, the trial balance of Rafael Limited shows Equipment $30,000 and zero balances in Accumulated Amortization—Equipment and Amortization Expense. Amortization for the year is estimated to be $3,000. Prepare the adjusting entry for amortization at December 31, and indicate the balance sheet presentation for the equipment at December 31.

BE3-11   Willis Corporation has beginning inventory $81,000; Purchases $540,000; Freight-in $16,200; Purchase Returns $5,800; Purchase Discounts $5,000; and ending inventory $70,200. Calculate cost of goods sold.

BE3-12   Karen Inc. has year-end account balances of Sales $828,900; Interest Revenue $13,500; Cost of Goods Sold $556,200; Operating Expenses $189,000; Income Tax Expense $35,100; and Dividends $18,900. Prepare the year-end closing entries.

BE3-13   If the $3,900 cost of a new microcomputer and printer purchased for office use were recorded as a debit to Purchases, what would be the effect of the error on the balance sheet and income statement in the period in which the error was made?

BE3-14   What differences are there between the trial balance before closing and the trial balance after closing with respect to the following accounts?

(a) Accounts Payable

(b) Expense accounts

(c) Revenue accounts

(d) Retained Earnings account

(e) Cash

BE3-15   Manny Molitar, maintenance supervisor for Blue Jay Insurance Co., has purchased a riding lawnmower and accessories to be used in maintaining the grounds around corporate headquarters. He has sent the following information to the accounting department.

Cost of mower and		Date purchased	7/1/05
accessories	$3,000	Monthly salary of	
Estimated useful life	5 yrs	groundskeeper	$1,100
		Estimated annual	
		fuel cost	$150

Calculate the amount of amortization expense (related to the mower and accessories) that should be reported on Blue Jay's December 31, 2005 income statement. Assume straight-line amortization.

*BE3-16   Pelican Inc. made a December 31 adjusting entry to debit Salaries Expense and credit Salaries Payable for $3,600. On January 2, Pelican paid the weekly payroll of $6,000. Prepare Pelican's (a) January 1 reversing entry, (b) January 2 entry (assuming the reversing entry was prepared), and (c) January 2 entry (assuming the reversing entry was not prepared).

Exercises

E3-1   (Transaction Analysis—Service Company)   Charlie Ainsworth is a licenced CA. During the first month of operations of his business (a sole proprietorship), the following events and transactions occurred.

April	2	Invested $12,000 cash and equipment valued at $14,000 in the business.
	2	Hired a secretary-receptionist at a salary of $390 per week payable monthly.
	3	Purchased supplies on account $800 (debit an asset account).
	7	Paid office rent of $600 for the month.
	11	Completed a tax assignment and billed client $1,100 for services rendered. (Use service revenue account.)
	12	Received $3,200 advance on a management consulting engagement.
	17	Received cash of $2,300 for services completed for Botticelli Limited.
	21	Paid insurance expense $110.
	30	Paid secretary-receptionist $1,360 for the month.
	30	A count of supplies indicated that $220 of supplies had been used.
	30	Purchased a new computer for $6,100 with personal funds. (The computer will be used exclusively for business purposes.)

Instructions

Journalize the transactions in the general journal (omit explanations).

E3-2   (Corrected Trial Balance)   The trial balance of Wanda Landowska Company, a sole proprietorship, does not balance. Your review of the ledger reveals the following: (a) each account had a normal balance, (b) the debit footings in Prepaid Insurance, Accounts Payable, and Property Tax Expense were each understated $100, (c) transposition errors wcrc made in Accounts Receivable and Service Revenue; the correct balances are $2,750 and $6,690, respectively, (d) a debit posting to Advertising Expense of $300 was omitted, and (e) a $1,500 cash drawing by the owner was debited to Wanda Landowska, Capital, and credited to Cash.

WANDA LANDOWSKA COMPANY
Trial Balance
April 30, 2005

	Debit	Credit
Cash	$ 4,800	
Accounts Receivable	2,570	
Prepaid Insurance	700	
Equipment		$ 8,000
Accounts Payable		4,500
Property Tax Payable	560	
Wanda Landowska, Capital		11,200
Service Revenue	6,960	
Salaries Expense	4,200	
Advertising Expense	1,100	
Property Tax Expense		800
	$20,890	$24,500

Instructions
Prepare a correct trial balance.

E3-3   (Corrected Trial Balance)   The trial balance of Blues Corner Corporation does not balance.

BLUES CORNER CORPORATION
Trial Balance
April 30

	Debit	Credit
Cash	$ 5,912	
Accounts Receivable	5,240	
Supplies on Hand	2,967	
Furniture and Equipment	6,100	
Accounts Payable		$ 7,044
Common Shares		8,000
Retained Earnings		2,000
Service Revenue		5,200
Office Expense	4,320	
	$24,539	$22,244

An examination of the ledger shows these errors.

1. Cash received from a customer on account was recorded (both debit and credit) as $1,380 instead of $1,830.

2. The purchase on account of a computer costing $3,200 was recorded as a debit to Office Expense and a credit to Accounts Payable.

3. Services were performed on account for a client, $2,250, for which Accounts Receivable was debited $2,250 and Service Revenue was credited $225.

4. A payment of $95 for telephone charges was entered as a debit to Office Expenses and a debit to Cash.

5. The Service Revenue account was totalled at $5,200 instead of $5,280.

Instructions
From this information, prepare a corrected trial balance.

E3-4   (Corrected Trial Balance)   The trial balance of Chris Cross Inc. shown below does not balance.

CHRIS CROSS INC.
Trial Balance
June 30, 2006

	Debit	Credit
Cash		$ 2,870
Accounts Receivable	$ 3,231	
Supplies	800	
Equipment	3,800	
Accounts Payable		2,666
Unearned Service Revenue	1,200	
Common Shares		6,000
Retained Earnings		3,000
Service Revenue		2,380
Wages Expense	3,400	
Office Expense	940	
	$13,371	$16,916

Each of the listed accounts has a normal balance per the general ledger. An examination of the ledger and journal reveals the following errors.

1. Cash received from a customer on account was debited for $570 and Accounts Receivable was credited for the same amount. The actual collection was for $750.

2. The purchase of a computer printer on account for $500 was recorded as a debit to Supplies for $500 and a credit to Accounts Payable for $500.

3. Services were performed on account for a client for $890. Accounts Receivable was debited for $890 and Service Revenue was credited for $89.

4. A payment of $65 for telephone charges was recorded as a debit to Office Expense for $65 and a debit to Cash for $65.

5. When the Unearned Service Revenue account was reviewed, it was found that $325 of the balance was earned prior to June 30.

6. A debit posting to Wages Expense of $670 was omitted.

7. A payment on account for $206 was credited to Cash for $206 and credited to Accounts Payable for $260.

8. A dividend of $575 was debited to Wages Expense for $575 and credited to Cash for $575.

Instructions
Prepare a correct trial balance. (Note: It may be necessary to add one or more accounts to the trial balance.)

E3-5   (Adjusting Entries)   The ledger of Deng Rental Agency Ltd. on March 31 of the current year includes the following selected accounts before adjusting entries have been prepared.

	Debit	Credit
Prepaid Insurance	$3,600	
Supplies	2,800	
Equipment	25,000	
Accumulated Amortization—Equipment		$8,400
Notes Payable		20,000
Unearned Rent Revenue		9,300
Rent Revenue		60,000
Interest Expense	–0–	
Wage Expense	14,000	

An analysis of the accounts shows the following.

1. The equipment amortization is $350 per month.

2. One-half of the unearned rent was earned during the quarter.

3. Interest of $550 is accrued on the notes payable.

4. Supplies on hand total $950.

5. Insurance expires at the rate of $300 per month.

Instructions

Prepare the adjusting entries at March 31, assuming that adjusting entries are made quarterly. Additional accounts are: Amortization Expense, Insurance Expense, Interest Payable, and Supplies Expense.

E3-6 **(Adjusting Entries)** Karen Pain, D.D.S., opened a dental practice on January 1, 2005. During the first month of operations, the following transactions occurred.

1. Performed services for patients who had dental plan insurance. At January 31, $1,750 of such services was earned but not yet billed to the insurance companies.

2. Utility expenses incurred but not paid prior to January 31 totalled $1,520.

3. Purchased dental equipment on January 1 for $80,000, paying $20,000 in cash and signing a $60,000, three-year note payable. The equipment amortization is $400 per month. Interest is $500 per month.

4. Purchased a one-year malpractice insurance policy on January 1 for $13,000.

5. Purchased $2,600 of dental supplies. On January 31, determined that $500 of supplies were on hand.

Instructions

(a) Prepare the adjusting entries on January 31. Account titles are: Accumulated Amortization—Dental Equipment, Amortization Expense, Service Revenue, Accounts Receivable, Insurance Expense, Interest Expense, Interest Payable, Prepaid Insurance, Supplies, Supplies Expense, Utilities Expense, and Utilities Payable.

(b) Prepare the adjusting entries on January 31 assuming the company initially records prepayments through the related income statement accounts (alternate method).

E3-7 **(Analyse Adjusted Data)** A partial adjusted trial balance of Pansy Limited at January 31, 2004, shows the following.

PANSY LIMITED
Adjusted Trial Balance
January 31, 2004

	Debit	Credit
Supplies	$ 700	
Prepaid Insurance	2,400	
Salaries Payable		$800
Unearned Revenue		750
Supplies Expense	950	
Insurance Expense	400	
Salaries Expense	1,800	
Service Revenue		2,000

Instructions

Answer the following questions, assuming the year begins January 1.

(a) If the amount in Supplies Expense is the January 31 adjusting entry, and $850 of supplies was purchased in January, what was the balance in Supplies on January 1?

(b) If the amount in Insurance Expense is the January 31 adjusting entry, and the original insurance premium was for one year, what was the total premium and when was the policy purchased?

(c) If $2,500 of salaries was paid in January, what was the balance in Salaries Payable at December 31, 2003?

(d) If $1,600 was received in January for services performed in January, what was the balance in Unearned Revenue at December 31, 2003?

E3-8 **(Adjusting Entries)** Benson Balladucci is the new owner of Ace Computer Services Inc. At the end of August 2005, his first month of ownership, Mr. Balladucci is trying to prepare monthly financial statements. Below is some information related to unrecorded expenses that the business incurred during August.

1. At August 31, Mr. Balladucci owed his employees $5,000 in wages that would be paid on September 1.

2. At the end of the month, he had not yet received the month's utility bill. Based on previous experience, he estimated the bill would be approximately $700.

3. On August 1, Mr. Balladucci borrowed $50,000 from a local bank on a 10-year mortgage. The annual interest rate is 5%.

4. A telephone bill in the amount of $117 covering August charges is unpaid at August 31.

Instructions

Prepare the adjusting journal entries as of August 31, 2005, suggested by the information above.

E3-9   (Adjusting Entries)   Selected accounts of Urdu Limited are shown below.

Supplies					Accounts Receivable		
Beg. Bal.	800	10/31	470		10/17	2,400	
					10/31	1,650	

Salaries Expense					Salaries Payable		
10/15	800					10/31	600
10/31	600						

Unearned Service Revenue					Supplies Expense		
10/31	400	10/20	650		10/31	470	

Service Revenue		
	10/17	2,400
	10/31	1,650
	10/31	400

Instructions

From an analysis of the T accounts, reconstruct (a) the October transaction entries, and (b) the adjusting journal entries that were made on October 31, 2005.

E3-10   (Adjusting Entries)   The trial balance for Greco Resort Limited on August 31 is as follows.

GRECO RESORT LIMITED
Trial Balance
August 31, 2005

	Debit	Credit
Cash	$ 10,600	
Prepaid Insurance	4,500	
Supplies	2,600	
Land	20,000	
Cottages	129,000	
Furniture	16,000	
Accounts Payable		$ 4,500
Unearned Rent Revenue		4,600
Loan Payable		70,000
Common Shares		81,000
Retained Earnings		9,000
Dividends	5,000	
Rent Revenue		76,200
Salaries Expense	44,800	
Utilities Expense	9,200	
Repair Expense	3,600	
	$245,300	$245,300

Other data:

1. The balance in prepaid insurance is a one-year premium paid on June 1, 2005.

2. An inventory count on August 31 shows $450 of supplies on hand.

3. Annual amortization rates are cottages (4%) and furniture (10%). Residual value is estimated to be 10% of cost.

4. Unearned Rent Revenue of $3,800 was earned prior to August 31.

5. Salaries of $375 were unpaid at August 31.

6. Rentals of $800 were due from tenants at August 31.

7. The loan interest rate is 8% per year.

Instructions

(a) Journalize the adjusting entries on August 31 for the three-month period June 1 to August 31.

(b) Prepare an adjusted trial balance on August 31.

E3-11 **(Closing Entries)** The adjusted trial balance of Lopez Limited shows the following data pertaining to sales at the end of its fiscal year October 31, 2005: Sales $900,000, Freight-out $12,000, Sales Returns and Allowances $24,000, and Sales Discounts $25,000.

Interactive
Homework

Instructions

(a) Prepare the sales revenues section of the income statement.

(b) Prepare separate closing entries for (1) sales, and (2) the contra accounts to sales.

E3-12 **(Closing Entries)** Presented is information related to Gonzales Corporation for the month of January 2004.

Cost of goods sold	$208,000	Salary expense	$ 61,000
Freight-out	7,000	Sales discounts	8,000
Insurance expense	12,000	Sales returns and allowances	13,000
Rent expense	20,000	Sales	350,000

Instructions
Prepare the necessary closing entries.

E3-13 **(Work Sheet)** Presented below are selected accounts for Algonquin Inc. as reported in the work sheet at the end of May 2006.

Accounts	Adjusted Trial Balance		Income Statement		Balance Sheet	
	Dr.	Cr.	Dr.	Cr.	Dr.	Cr.
Cash	9,000					
Merchandise Inventory	80,000					
Sales		450,000				
Sales Returns and Allowances	10,000					
Sales Discounts	5,000					
Cost of Goods Sold	250,000					

Instructions
Complete the work sheet by extending amounts reported in the adjusted trial balance to the appropriate columns in the work sheet. Do not total individual columns.

E3-14 **(Missing Amounts)** Presented below is financial information for two different companies.

	Alatorre Ltd.	Eduardo Inc.
Sales	$90,000	(d)
Sales returns	(a)	$ 5,000
Net sales	81,000	95,000
Cost of goods sold	56,000	(e)
Gross profit	(b)	38,000
Operating expenses	15,000	23,000
Net income	(c)	15,000

Instructions
Calculate the missing amounts.

E3-15 **(Find Missing Amounts—Periodic Inventory)** Financial information is presented below for four different companies.

	Pamela's Cosmetics Inc.	Dean's Grocery Inc.	Anderson Wholesalers Ltd.	Baywatch Supply Ltd.
Sales	$78,000	(c)	$144,000	$100,000
Sales returns	(a)	$5,000	12,000	9,000
Net sales	74,000	94,000	132,000	(g)
Beginning inventory	16,000	(d)	44,000	24,000
Purchases	88,000	100,000	(e)	85,000
Purchase returns	6,000	10,000	8,000	(h)
Ending inventory	(b)	48,000	30,000	28,000
Cost of goods sold	64,000	72,000	(f)	72,000
Gross profit	10,000	22,000	18,000	(i)

Instructions

Determine the missing amounts (a - i). Show all calculations.

E3-16 **(Cost of Goods Sold Section—Periodic Inventory)** The trial balance of Maori Limited at the end of its fiscal year, August 31, 2006, includes the following accounts: Merchandise Inventory $17,500, Purchases $149,400, Sales $200,000, Freight-in $4,000, Sales Returns and Allowances $4,000, Freight-out $1,000, and Purchase Returns and Allowances $2,000. The ending merchandise inventory is $25,000.

Interactive
Homework

Instructions

Prepare a cost of goods sold section for the year ending August 31.

E3-17 **(Closing Entries)** Presented below are selected account balances for Winslow Inc. as of December 31, 2006.

Merchandise Inventory 12/31/06	$ 60,000	Cost of Goods Sold	$225,700
Common Shares	75,000	Selling Expenses	16,000
Retained Earnings	45,000	Administrative Expenses	38,000
Dividends	18,000	Income Tax Expense	30,000
Sales Returns and Allowances	12,000		
Sales Discounts	15,000		
Sales	410,000		

Instructions

Prepare closing entries for Winslow Inc. on December 31, 2006.

E3-18 **(Work Sheet Preparation)** The trial balance of Potter Roofing Inc. at March 31, 2006 is as follows.

Interactive
Homework

POTTER ROOFING INC.
Trial Balance
March 31, 2006

	Debit	Credit
Cash	$2,300	
Accounts Receivable	2,600	
Roofing Supplies	1,100	
Equipment	6,000	
Accumulated Amortization—Equipment		$ 1,200
Accounts Payable		1,100
Unearned Service Revenue		300
Common Shares		6,400
Retained Earnings		600
Service Revenue		3,000
Salaries Expense	500	
Miscellaneous Expense	100	
	$12,600	$12,600

Other data:

1. A physical count reveals only $520 of roofing supplies on hand.

2. Equipment is amortized at a rate of $120 per month.

3. Unearned service revenue amounted to $100 on March 31.

4. Accrued salaries are $850.

Instructions

Enter the trial balance on a work sheet and complete the work sheet, assuming that the adjustments relate only to the month of March. (Ignore income taxes.)

E3-19 **(Work Sheet and Balance Sheet Presentation)** The adjusted trial balance of Widijat Company's work sheet for the month ended April 30, 2005 contains the following:

WIDIJAT COMPANY
Work Sheet (partial)
For the Month Ended April 30, 2005

Account Titles	Adjusted Trial Balance Dr.	Cr.	Income Statement Dr.	Cr.	Balance Sheet Dr.	Cr.
Cash	$18,472					
Accounts Receivable	6,920					
Prepaid Rent	3,280					
Equipment	18,050					
Accumulated Amortization		$ 4,895				
Notes Payable		6,700				
Accounts Payable		4,472				
Widijat, Capital		34,960				
Widijat , Drawing	6,650					
Service Revenue		11,590				
Salaries Expense	6,840					
Rent Expense	2,260					
Amortization Expense	145					
Interest Expense	83					
Interest Payable		83				

Instructions

Complete the work sheet and prepare a balance sheet as illustrated in this chapter.

E3-20 **(Partial Work Sheet Preparation)** Jurassic Inc. prepares monthly financial statements from a work sheet. Selected portions of the January work sheet showed the following data.

JURASSIC INC.
Work Sheet (partial)
For Month Ended January 31, 2006

Account Title	Trial Balance Dr.	Cr.	Adjustments Dr.	Cr.	Adjusted Trial Balance Dr.	Cr.
Supplies	3,256			(a) 1,500	1,756	
Accumulated Amortization		6,682		(b) 257		6,939
Interest Payable		100		(c) 50		150
Supplies Expense			(a) 1,500		1,500	
Amortization Expense			(b) 257		257	
Interest Expense			(c) 50		50	

During February, no events occurred that affected these accounts, but at the end of February, the following information was available.

(a) Supplies on hand	$715
(b) Monthly amortization	$257
(c) Accrued interest	$50

Instructions

Reproduce the data that would appear in the February work sheet and indicate the amounts that would be shown in the February income statement.

E3-21 **(Transactions of a Corporation, Including Investment and Dividend)**   Scratch Miniature Golf and Driving Range Inc. was opened on March 1 by Scott Verplank. The following selected events and transactions occurred during March.

Mar.   1 Invested $50,000 cash in the business in exchange for common shares.
      3 Purchased Lee Janzen's Golf Land for $38,000 cash. The price consists of land, $10,000; building, $22,000; and equipment, $6,000. (Make one compound entry.)
      5 Advertised the opening of the driving range and miniature golf course, paying advertising expenses of $1,600.
      6 Paid cash $1,480 for a one-year insurance policy.
     10 Purchased golf equipment for $2,500 from Sluman Ltd. payable in 30 days.
     18 Received golf fees of $1,200 in cash.
     25 Declared and paid a $500 cash dividend.
     30 Paid wages of $900.
     30 Paid Sluman Ltd. in full.
     31 Received $750 of fees in cash.

Scott Verplank uses the following accounts: Cash; Prepaid Insurance; Land; Buildings; Equipment; Accounts Payable; Common Shares; Dividends; Service Revenue; Advertising Expense; and Wages Expense.

Instructions

Journalize the March transactions.

*E3-22 **(Adjusting and Reversing Entries)**   On December 31, adjusting information for Lyman Corporation is as follows.

1. Estimated amortization on equipment $1,100.

2. Property taxes amounting to $525 have accrued but are unrecorded and unpaid.

3. Employee wages earned but unpaid and unrecorded $1,200.

4. Unearned Service Revenue balance includes $1,500 that has been earned.

5. Interest of $250 on a $25,000 note receivable has accrued.

Instructions

(a) Prepare adjusting journal entries.

(b) Prepare reversing journal entries.

*E3-23 **(Closing and Reversing Entries)**   On December 31, the adjusted trial balance of Cree Inc. shows the following selected data.

Accounts Receivable	$4,300	Service Revenue	$96,000
Interest Expense	7,800	Interest Payable	2,400

Analysis shows that adjusting entries were made for (a) $4,300 of services performed but not billed, and (b) $2,400 of accrued but unpaid interest.

Instructions

(a) Prepare the closing entries for the temporary accounts at December 31.

(b) Prepare the reversing entries on January 1.

(c) Enter the adjusted trial balance data in the four accounts. Post the entries in (a) and (b) and rule and balance the accounts. (Use T accounts.)

(d) Prepare the entries to record (1) the collection of the accrued commissions on January 10, and (2) the payment of all interest due ($3,000) on January 15.

(e) Post the entries in (d) to the temporary accounts.

*E3-24 **(Adjusting and Reversing Entries)** When the accounts of Barenboim Inc. are examined, the adjusting data listed below are uncovered on December 31, the end of an annual fiscal period.

1. The prepaid insurance account shows a debit of $5,280, representing the cost of a two-year fire insurance policy dated August 1 of the current year.

2. On November 1, Rental Revenue was credited for $1,800, representing revenue from a subrental for a three-month period beginning on that date.

3. Purchase of advertising materials for $800 during the year was recorded in the Advertising Expense account. On December 31, advertising materials of $290 are on hand.

4. Interest of $770 has accrued on notes payable.

Instructions

Prepare in general journal form: (a) the adjusting entry for each item; (b) the reversing entry for each item where appropriate.

Problems

P3-1 Listed below are the transactions of Isao Aoki, D.D.S., for the month of September.

Sept. 1 Isao Aoki begins practice as a dentist and invests $20,000 cash.
2 Purchases furniture and dental equipment on account from Green Jacket Limited for $17,280.
4 Pays rent for office space, $680 for the month.
4 Employs a receptionist, Michael Bradley.
5 Purchases dental supplies for cash, $942.
8 Receives cash of $1,690 from patients for services performed.
10 Pays miscellaneous office expenses, $430.
14 Bills patients $5,120 for services performed.
18 Pays Green Jacket Limited on account, $3,600.
19 Withdraws $3,000 cash from the business for personal use.
20 Receives $980 from patients on account.
25 Bills patients $2,110 for services performed.
30 Pays the following expenses in cash: office salaries, $1,400; miscellaneous office expenses, $85.
30 Dental supplies used during September, $330.

Instructions

(a) Enter the transactions shown above in appropriate general ledger accounts. Use the following ledger accounts: Cash; Accounts Receivable; Supplies on Hand; Furniture and Equipment; Accumulated Amortization; Accounts Payable; Isao Aoki, Capital; Service Revenue; Rent Expense; Miscellaneous Office Expense; Office Salaries Expense; Supplies Expense; Amortization Expense; and Income Summary. Allow 10 lines for the Cash and Income Summary accounts, and five lines for each of the other accounts needed. Record amortization using a 5-year life on the furniture and equipment, the straight-line method, and no residual value. Do not use a drawing account.

(b) Prepare an adjusted trial balance.

(c) Prepare an income statement, a balance sheet, and a statement of owners' equity.

(d) Close the ledger. Post directly to the general ledger account without writing out the journal entry.

(e) Prepare a post-closing trial balance.

P3-2 Yancy Advertising Agency Limited was founded by Tang Min in January of 2000. Presented below are both the adjusted and unadjusted trial balances as of December 31, 2004.

YANCY ADVERTISING AGENCY LIMITED
Trial Balance
December 31, 2004

	Unadjusted Dr.	Unadjusted Cr.	Adjusted Dr.	Adjusted Cr.
Cash	$11,000		$11,000	
Accounts Receivable	20,000		21,500	
Art Supplies	8,400		5,000	
Prepaid Insurance	3,350		2,500	
Printing Equipment	60,000		60,000	
Accumulated Amortization		$28,000		$35,000
Accounts Payable		5,000		5,000
Interest Payable		–0–		150
Notes Payable		5,000		5,000
Unearned Advertising Revenue		7,000		5,600
Salaries Payable		–0–		1,300
Common Shares		10,000		10,000
Retained Earnings		3,500		3,500
Advertising Revenue		58,600		61,500
Salaries Expense	10,000		11,300	
Insurance Expense			850	
Interest Expense	350		500	
Amortization Expense			7,000	
Art Supplies Expense			3,400	
Rent Expense	4,000		4,000	
	$117,100	$117,100	$127,050	$127,050

Instructions

(a) Journalize the annual adjusting entries that were made.

(b) Prepare an income statement and a statement of retained earnings for the year ending December 31, 2004 and a balance sheet at December 31.

(c) Answer the following questions.

1. If the note has been outstanding three months, what is the annual interest rate on that note?

2. If the company paid $13,500 in salaries in 2004, what was the balance in Salaries Payable on December 31, 2003?

P3-3 A review of the ledger of Okanagen Inc. at December 31, 2006 produces the following data pertaining to the preparation of annual adjusting entries.

1. Salaries Payable $0. There are eight salaried employees. Salaries are paid every Friday for the current week. Five employees receive a salary of $700 each per week, and three employees earn $500 each per week. December 31 is a Tuesday. Employees do not work weekends. All employees worked the last two days of December.

2. Unearned Rent Revenue $369,000. The company began subleasing office space in its new building on November 1. Each tenant is required to make a $5,000 security deposit that is not refundable until occupancy is terminated. At December 31, the company had the following rental contracts that are paid in full for the entire term of the lease.

Date	Term (in months)	Monthly Rent	Number of Leases
Nov. 1	6	$4,000	5
Dec. 1	6	$8,500	4

3. Prepaid Advertising $13,200. This balance consists of payments on two advertising contracts. The contracts provide for monthly advertising in two trade magazines. The terms of the contracts are as follows.

Contract	Date	Amount	Number of Magazine Issues
A650	May 1	$6,000	12
B974	Oct. 1	7,200	24

The first advertisement runs in the month in which the contract is signed.

4. Notes Payable $80,000. This balance consists of a note for one year at an annual interest rate of 12%, dated June 1.

Instructions

Prepare the adjusting entries at December 31, 2006. (Show all calculations).

P3-4 The completed financial statement columns of the work sheet for Zhou Limited are shown below.

ZHOU LIMITED
Work Sheet
For the Year Ended December 31, 2005

Account No.	Account Titles	Income Statement Dr.	Income Statement Cr.	Balance Sheet Dr.	Balance Sheet Cr.
101	Cash			8,200	
112	Accounts Receivable			7,500	
130	Prepaid Insurance			1,800	
157	Equipment			28,000	
167	Accumulated Amortization				8,600
201	Accounts Payable				12,000
212	Salaries Payable				3,000
301	Common Shares				20,000
306	Retained Earnings				6,800
400	Service Revenue		42,000		
622	Repair Expense	3,200			
711	Amortization Expense	2,800			
722	Insurance Expense	1,200			
726	Salaries Expense	36,000			
732	Utilities Expense	3,700			
	Totals	46,900	42,000	45,500	50,400
	Net Loss		4,900	4,900	
		46,900	46,900	50,400	50,400

Instructions

(a) Prepare an income statement, retained earnings statement, and a classified balance sheet. Zhou's shareholders made an additional investment in the business of $4,000 during 2005.

(b) Prepare the closing entries.

(c) Post the closing entries and rule and balance the accounts. Use T accounts. Income Summary is No. 350.

(d) Prepare a post-closing trial balance.

P3-5 Noah's Ark has a fiscal year ending on September 30. Selected data from the September 30 work sheet are presented below.

NOAH'S ARK
Work Sheet
For the Year Ended September 30, 2005

	Trial Balance Dr.	Trial Balance Cr.	Adjusted Trial Balance Dr.	Adjusted Trial Balance Cr.
Cash	37,400		37,400	
Supplies	18,600		1,200	
Prepaid Insurance	31,900		3,900	
Land	80,000		80,000	
Equipment	120,000		120,000	
Accumulated Amortization		36,200		43,000
Accounts Payable		14,600		14,600
Unearned Admissions Revenue		2,700		1,700
Mortgage Payable		50,000		50,000

	Trial Balance		Adjusted Trial Balance	
	Dr.	Cr.	Dr.	Cr.
N.Y. Berge, Capital		109,700		109,700
N.Y. Berge, Drawing	14,000		14,000	
Admissions Revenue		278,500		279,500
Salaries Expense	109,000		109,000	
Repair Expense	30,500		30,500	
Advertising Expense	9,400		9,400	
Utilities Expense	16,900		16,900	
Property Taxes Expense	18,000		21,000	
Interest Expense	6,000		12,000	
Totals	491,700	491,700		
Insurance Expense			28,000	
Supplies Expense			17,400	
Interest Payable				6,000
Amortization Expense			6,800	
Property Taxes Payable				3,000
Totals			507,500	507,500

Instructions

(a) Prepare a complete work sheet.

(b) Prepare a classified balance sheet. (Note: $10,000 of the mortgage payable is due for payment in the next fiscal year.)

(c) Journalize the adjusting entries using the work sheet as a basis.

(d) Journalize the closing entries using the work sheet as a basis.

(e) Prepare a post-closing trial balance.

P3-6   The trial balance of Bhopal Fashion Centre Inc. contained the following accounts at November 30, the end of the company's fiscal year.

BHOPAL FASHION CENTRE INC.
Trial Balance
November 30, 2005

	Debit	Credit
Cash	$ 16,700	
Accounts Receivable	43,700	
Merchandise Inventory	45,000	
Store Supplies	5,500	
Store Equipment	85,000	
Accumulated Amortization—Store Equipment		$ 18,000
Delivery Equipment	48,000	
Accumulated Amortization—Delivery Equipment		6,000
Notes Payable		41,000
Accounts Payable		58,500
Common Shares		100,000
Retained Earnings		8,000
Sales		747,200
Sales Returns and Allowances	4,200	
Cost of Goods Sold	497,400	
Salaries Expense	140,000	
Advertising Expense	26,400	
Utilities Expense	14,000	
Repair Expense	12,100	
Delivery Expense	16,700	
Rent Expense	24,000	
	$978,700	$978,700

Adjustment data:

1. Store supplies on hand totalled $3,500.

2. Amortization is $9,000 on the store equipment and $7,000 on the delivery equipment.

3. Interest of $11,000 is accrued on notes payable at November 30.

Other data:

1. Salaries expense is 70% selling and 30% administrative.

2. Rent expense and utilities expense are 80% selling and 20% administrative.

3. $30,000 of notes payable are due for payment next year.

4. Repair expense is 100% administrative.

Instructions

(a) Enter the trial balance on a work sheet and complete the work sheet.

(b) Prepare a multiple-step income statement and retained earnings statement for the year and a classified balance sheet as of November 30, 2005.

(c) Journalize the adjusting entries.

(d) Journalize the closing entries.

(e) Prepare a post-closing trial balance.

P3-7 The Hardisty Department Store Incorporated is located near the Village shopping mall. At the end of the company's fiscal year on December 31, 2006, the following accounts appeared in two of its trial balances.

	Unadjusted	Adjusted
Accounts Payable	$79,300	$79,300
Accounts Receivable	50,300	50,300
Accumulated Amortization—Building	42,100	52,500
Accumulated Amortization—Equipment	29,600	42,900
Building	190,000	190,000
Cash	23,000	23,000
Common Shares	160,000	160,000
Retained Earnings	16,600	16,600
Cost of Goods Sold	412,700	412,700
Amortization Expense—Building		10,400
Amortization Expense—Equipment		13,300
Dividends	28,000	28,000
Equipment	110,000	110,000
Insurance Expense		7,200
Interest Expense	3,000	11,000
Interest Payable		8,000
Interest Revenue	4,000	4,000
Merchandise Inventory	75,000	75,000
Mortgage Payable	80,000	80,000
Office Salaries Expense	32,000	32,000
Prepaid Insurance	9,600	2,400
Property Taxes Expense		4,800
Property Taxes Payable		4,800
Sales Salaries Expense	76,000	76,000
Sales	628,000	628,000
Sales Commissions Expense	11,000	14,500
Sales Commissions Payable		3,500
Sales Returns and Allowances	8,000	8,000
Utilities Expense	11,000	11,000

Analysis reveals the following additional data.

1. Insurance expense and utilities expense are 60% selling and 40% administrative.

2. $20,000 of the mortgage payable is due for payment next year.

3. Amortization on the building and property tax expense are administrative expenses; amortization on the equipment is a selling expense.

Instructions

(a) Prepare a multiple-step income statement, a retained earnings statement, and a classified balance sheet.

(b) Journalize the adjusting entries that were made.

(c) Journalize the closing entries that are necessary.

P3-8 The accounts listed below appeared in the December 31 trial balance of the Alexander Theatre.

	Debit	Credit
Equipment	$192,000	
Accumulated Amortization—Equipment		$60,000
Notes Payable		90,000
Admissions Revenue		380,000
Advertising Expense	13,680	
Salaries Expense	57,600	
Interest Expense	1,400	

Instructions

(a) From the account balances listed above and the information given below, prepare the annual adjusting entries necessary on December 31.

1. The equipment has an estimated life of 16 years and a residual value of $40,000 at the end of that time. (Use straight-line method.)

2. The note payable is a 90-day note given to the bank October 20 and bearing interest at 10%.

3. In December, 2,000 coupon admission books were sold at $25 each; they could be used for admission any time after January 1.

4. Advertising expense paid in advance and included in Advertising Expense, $1,100.

5. Salaries accrued but unpaid, $4,700.

(b) What amounts should be shown for each of the following on the income statement for the year?

1. Interest expense

2. Admissions revenue

3. Advertising expense

4. Salaries expense

P3-9 Presented below are the trial balance and the other information related to Muhammad Moamar, a consulting engineer.

MUHAMMAD MOAMAR, CONSULTING ENGINEER
Trial Balance
December 31, 2006

	Debit	Credit
Cash	$31,500	
Accounts Receivable	49,600	
Allowance for Doubtful Accounts		$750
Engineering Supplies Inventory	1,960	
Unexpired Insurance	1,100	
Furniture and Equipment	25,000	
Accumulated Amortization—Furniture and Equipment		6,250
Notes Payable		7,200
Muhammad Moamar, Capital		35,010
Service Revenue		100,000
Rent Expense	9,750	
Office Salaries Expense	28,500	
Heat, Light, and Water Expense	1,080	
Miscellaneous Office Expense	720	
	$149,210	$149,210

1. Fees received in advance from clients, $6,900.

2. Services performed for clients that were not recorded by December 31, $4,900.

3. Bad debt expense for the year is $1,430.

4. Insurance expired during the year, $480.

5. Furniture and equipment is being amortized at 12½% per year.

6. Muhammad gave the bank a 90-day, 10% note for $7,200 on December 1, 2006.

7. Rent of the building is $750 per month. The rent for 2006 has been paid, as has that for January 2007.

8. Office salaries earned but unpaid December 31, 2006, $2,510.

Instructions

(a) From the trial balance and other information given, prepare annual adjusting entries as of December 31, 2006.

(b) Prepare an income statement for 2006, a balance sheet, and a statement of owners' equity. Muhammad Moamar withdrew $17,000 cash for personal use during the year.

P3-10 Andrew Advertising Corporation was founded by Jan Andrew in January 2001. Presented below are both the adjusted and unadjusted trial balances as of December 31, 2005.

ANDREW ADVERTISING CORPORATION
Trial Balance
December 31, 2005

	Unadjusted		Adjusted	
	Dr.	Cr.	Dr.	Cr.
Cash	$7,000		$ 7,000	
Accounts Receivable	19,000		22,000	
Art Supplies	8,500		5,500	
Prepaid Insurance	3,250		2,500	
Printing Equipment	60,000		60,000	
Accumulated Amortization		$ 27,000		$33,750
Accounts Payable		5,000		5,000
Interest Payable				150
Note Payable		5,000		5,000
Unearned Service Revenue		7,000		5,600
Salaries Payable				1,500
Common Shares		10,000		10,000
Retained Earnings		4,500		4,500
Service Revenue		58,600		63,000
Salaries Expense	10,000		11,500	
Insurance Expense			750	
Interest Expense	350		500	
Amortization Expense			6,750	
Art Supplies Expense	5,000		8,000	
Rent Expense	4,000		4,000	
	$117,100	$117,100	$128,500	$128,500

Instructions

(a) Journalize the annual adjusting entries that were made.

(b) Prepare an income statement and a statement of retained earnings for the year ending December 31, 2005 and a balance sheet at December 31.

(c) Answer the following questions.

   1. If the useful life of equipment is eight years, what is the expected residual value?

   2. If the note has been outstanding three months, what is the annual interest rate on that note?

   3. If the company paid $12,500 in salaries in 2005, what was the balance in Salaries Payable on December 31, 2004?

P3-11   Presented below is information related to Joachim Anderson, Realtor, at the close of the fiscal year ending December 31.

1. Joachim had paid the local newspaper $335 for an advertisement to be run in January of the next year, charging it to Advertising Expense.

2. On November 1, Joachim borrowed $9,000 from Yorkville Bank issuing a 90-day, 10% note.

3. Salaries and wages due and unpaid December 31: sales, $1,420; office clerks, $1,060.

4. Interest accrued to date on Grant Muldaur's note, which Joachim holds, $500.

5. Estimated loss on bad debts, $1,210 for the period.

6. Stamps and stationery on hand, $110, charged to Stationery and Postage Expense account when purchased.

7. Joachim has not yet paid the December rent on the building his business occupies, $1,000.

8. Insurance paid November 1 for one year, $930, charged to Prepaid Insurance when paid.

9. Property taxes accrued, $1,670.

10. On December 1, Joachim gave Laura Palmer a 60-day, 12% note for $6,000 on account.

11. On October 31, Joachim received $2,580 from Douglas Raines in payment of six months' rent for office space occupied by him in the building and credited Unearned Rent Revenue.

12. On September 1, he paid six months' rent in advance on a warehouse, $6,600, and debited the asset account Prepaid Rent Expense.

13. The bill from Light & Power Limited for December has been received but not yet entered or paid, $510.

14. Estimated amortization on furniture and equipment, $1,400.

Instructions

Prepare annual adjusting entries as of December 31.

P3-12   Following is the trial balance of the Millcraft Golf Club, Inc. as of December 31. The books are closed annually on December 31.

MILLCRAFT GOLF CLUB, INC.
Trial Balance
December 31

	Debit	Credit
Cash	$115,000	
Accounts Receivable	13,000	
Allowance for Doubtful Accounts		$ 1,100
Land	350,000	
Buildings	120,000	
Accumulated Amortization—Buildings		38,400
Equipment	150,000	
Accumulated Amortization—Equipment		70,000
Unexpired Insurance	9,000	
Common Shares		500,000
Retained Earnings		82,000
Dues Revenue		200,000
Greens Fee Revenue		8,100
Rental Revenue		15,400
Utilities Expense	54,000	
Salaries Expense	80,000	
Maintenance Expense	24,000	
	$915,000	$915,000

Instructions

(a) Enter the balances in ledger accounts. Allow five lines for each account.

(b) From the trial balance and the information given, prepare annual adjusting entries and post to the ledger accounts.

1. The buildings have an estimated life of 25 years with no salvage value (straight-line method).
2. The equipment is amortized at 10% per year.
3. Insurance expired during the year, $3,500.
4. The rental revenue represents the amount received for 11 months for dining facilities. The December rent has not yet been received.
5. It is estimated that 15% of the accounts receivable will be uncollectible.
6. Salaries earned but not paid by December 31, $3,600.
7. Dues paid in advance by members, $8,900.

(c) Prepare an adjusted trial balance.

(d) Prepare closing entries and post.

P3-13   Presented below is the December 31 trial balance of Drew Boutique Inc.

DREW BOUTIQUE INC.
Trial Balance
December 31

	Debit	Credit
Cash	$18,500	
Accounts Receivable	42,000	
Allowance for Doubtful Accounts		$700
Inventory, December 31	80,000	
Furniture and Equipment	84,000	
Accumulated Amortization—Furniture and Equipment		35,000
Prepaid Insurance	5,100	
Notes Payable		28,000
Common Shares		80,600
Retained Earnings		10,000
Sales		600,000
Cost of Goods Sold	398,000	
Sales Salaries Expense	50,000	
Advertising Expense	6,700	
Administrative Salaries Expense	65,000	
Office Expense	5,000	
	$754,300	$754,300

Instructions

(a) Construct T accounts and enter the balances shown.

(b) Prepare adjusting journal entries for the following and post to the T accounts. Open additional T accounts as necessary. (The books are closed yearly on December 31.)

1. Bad debts are estimated to be $1,400.
2. Furniture and equipment is amortized based on a six-year life (no residual).
3. Insurance expired during the year, $2,550.
4. Interest accrued on notes payable, $3,360.
5. Sales salaries earned but not paid, $2,400.
6. Advertising paid in advance, $700.
7. Office supplies on hand, $1,500, charged to Office Expense when purchased.

(c) Prepare closing entries and post to the accounts.

P3-14 The following list of accounts and their balances represents the unadjusted trial balance of Clancy Inc. at December 31, 2005.

	Dr.	Cr.
Cash	$ 32,740	
Accounts Receivable	98,000	
Allowance for Doubtful Accounts		$ 3,500
Merchandise Inventory	62,000	
Prepaid Insurance	2,620	
Investment in Casper Inc. Bonds (9%)	40,000	
Land	30,000	
Building	124,000	
Accumulated Amortization—Building		12,400
Equipment	33,600	
Accumulated Amortization—Equipment		5,600
Goodwill	26,600	
Accounts Payable		101,050
Bonds Payable (20-year; 7%)		180,000
Common Shares		121,000
Retained Earnings		21,360
Sales		190,000
Rental Income		10,800
Advertising Expense	22,500	
Supplies Expense	10,800	
Purchases	98,000	
Purchase Discounts		900
Office Salary Expense	17,500	
Sales Salary Expense	36,000	
Interest Expense	12,250	
	$646,610	$646,610

Additional information:

1. Actual advertising costs amounted to $1,500 per month. The company has already paid for advertisements in *Montezuma Magazine* for the first quarter of 2006.

2. The building was purchased and occupied January 1, 2003, with an estimated life of 20 years. (The company uses straight-line amortization.)

3. Prepaid insurance contains the premium costs of two policies: Policy A, cost of $960, one-year term taken out on Sept. 1, 2004; Policy B, cost of $1,980, three-year term taken out on April 1, 2005.

4. A portion of Clancy's building has been converted into a snack bar that has been rented to the Ono Food Corp. since July 1, 2004 at a rate of $7,200 per year payable each July 1.

5. One of the company's customers declared bankruptcy December 30, 2005, and it has been definitely established that the $2,700 due from him will never be collected. This fact has not been recorded. In addition, Clancy estimates that 4% of the Accounts Receivable balance on December 31, 2005 will become uncollectible.

6. Six hundred dollars given as an advance to a salesperson on December 31, 2005 was charged to Sales Salary Expense. Sales salaries are paid on the 1st and 16th of each month for the following half month.

7. On November 1, 2003, Clancy issued 180, $1,000 bonds at par value. Interest payments are made semiannually on April 30 and October 31.

8. The equipment was purchased January 1, 2003, with an estimated life of 12 years. (The company uses straight-line amortization.)

9. On August 1, 2005, Clancy purchased 40, $1,000, 9% bonds maturing on August 31, 2010 at par value. Interest payment dates are July 31 and January 31.

10. The inventory on hand at December 31, 2005 was $74,000 per a physical inventory count. Record the adjustment for inventory in the same entry that records the Cost of Goods Sold for the year.

Instructions

(a) Prepare adjusting and correcting entries for December 31, 2005 using the information given.

(b) Indicate which of the adjusting entries could be reversed.

P3-15 The following list of accounts and their balances represents the unadjusted trial balance of Lentil Ltd. at December 31, 2005.

	Dr.	Cr.
Cash	$ 3,350	
Accounts Receivable	49,000	
Allowance for Doubtful Accounts		$ 750
Inventory	58,000	
Prepaid Insurance	2,940	
Prepaid Rent	13,200	
Investment in Legume Inc. Bonds	18,000	
Land	10,000	
Plant and Equipment	104,000	
Accumulated Amortization		18,000
Accounts Payable		9,310
Bonds Payable		50,000
Common Shares		100,000
Retained Earnings		80,660
Sales		208,310
Rent Revenue		10,200
Purchases	170,000	
Purchase Discounts		2,400
Transportation-out	9,000	
Transportation-in	3,500	
Salaries and Wages Expense	31,000	
Interest Expense	6,750	
Miscellaneous Expense	890	
	$479,630	$479,630

Additional information:

1. On November 1, 2005, Lentil received $10,200 rent from its lessee for a 12-month lease beginning on that date. This was credited to Rent Revenue.

2. Lentil estimates that 4% of the Accounts Receivable balances on December 31, 2005 will be uncollectible. On December 28, 2005, the bookkeeper incorrectly credited Sales for a receipt on account in the amount of $1,000. This error had not yet been corrected on December 31.

3. By a physical count, inventory on hand at December 31, 2005 was $65,000. Record the adjusting entry for inventory by using a Cost of Goods Sold account.

4. Prepaid insurance contains the premium costs of two policies: Policy A, cost of $1,320, two-year term, taken out on September 1, 2005; Policy B, cost of $1,620, three-year term, taken out on April 1, 2005.

5. The regular rate of amortization is 10% of cost per year. Acquisitions and retirements during a year are amortized at half this rate. There were no retirements during the year. On December 31, 2004, the balance of Plant and Equipment was $90,000.

6. On April 1, 2005, Lentil issued 50, $1,000, 11% bonds maturing on April 1, 2013 at par value. Interest payment dates are April 1 and October 1.

7. On August 1, 2005, Lentil purchased 18, $1,000, 12% Legume Inc. bonds, maturing on July 31, 2007 at par value. Interest payment dates are July 31 and January 31.

8. On May 30, 2005, Lentil rented a warehouse for $1,100 per month, payment $13,200 in advance, debiting Prepaid Rent.

Instructions

(a) Prepare the year-end adjusting and correcting entries in general journal form using the information given.

(b) Indicate the adjusting entries that could be reversed.

Research and Financial Analysis

RA 3-1 Intrawest Corporation

The financial statements of Intrawest Corporation are presented in Appendix 5B. Refer to these financial statements and the accompanying notes to answer the following questions.

Instructions

(a) What were the company's total assets at year end for both years presented?

(b) How much cash (and cash equivalents) did the company have at year end?

(c) What were the company's total revenues for the current and preceding year? What are the three main sources of revenues and how profitable are they?

(d) Using the financial statements and related notes, identify items that may result in adjusting entries for prepayments and accruals.

(e) What were the amounts of the company's amortization expense for the past two years?

RA 3-2 Kellogg Company

Kellogg Company has its world headquarters in Battle Creek, Michigan. The company manufactures and sells ready-to-eat breakfast cereals and convenience foods including toaster pastries and cereal bars.

Selected data from Kellogg Company's 2001 annual report follow (dollar amounts and share data in millions).

	2001	2000	1999
Net sales	$8,853.3	$6,954.7	$6,984.2
Operating profit	1,167.9	989.8	828.8
Net cash flow provided by operations less capital expenditures	855.5	650.0	529.0
Net earnings	473.6	587.7	338.3

In its 2001 annual report, Kellogg Company discussed its strategy for "creating more value in the future." One of the principles designed to drive growth relates to the use of accounting measures:

"Set the Right Targets and Measures—Set targets that are both challenging and realistic and which do not risk long-term health for short-term gains."

Specifically, Kellogg has established performance incentives based on net sales, operating profit, and cash flow.

Instructions

(a) Calculate the percentage change in sales, operating profit, net cash flow, and net earnings from year to year for the years presented.

(b) Evaluate the company's performance based on the above. Which trend seems most favourable? Which trend seems least favourable? What are the implications of these trends for the company in terms of its mandate to "create value"?

RA 3-3 Financial Statement Dates

Companies normally issue their annual financial statements within weeks of year end.

Instructions

(a) Identify the top five companies (by revenue) in the following industries:

1. Banks

2. Insurance

3. Real Estate

4. Biotech and pharmaceutical

(Hint: Look on the Digital Tool for a link to the Top 1000 Canadian Companies from the *Report on Business*.)

(b) For each company, identify the year-end date as well as the date that the financial statements were produced (look at the auditor's report). You will have to go to the company websites or SEDAR (www.sedar.com) to find the statements.

(c) Why do you think that the banks have a different year end than the others?

(d) How many days does it take for the companies to produce the statements after year end? Look at the average time period by each industry. In terms of timing, within each industry group, how close are the issue dates among companies? Comment on your findings.

RA 3-4 ERP

Enterprise Resource Planning (ERP) software systems incorporate not only bookkeeping systems but also systems to monitor and manage human resource functions, quality control functions, and many other aspects of business. The software runs off a centralized database, servicing all company departments and functions.

Instructions
Research and write a one- to two-page summary detailing what ERPs are and why they have gained so much attention. Why do companies find them so useful? What are the pros and cons to these systems? (Hint: Search "Enterprise Resource Planning" on the Internet.)

Two Views

Vancouver-based Pivotal Corporation provides businesses with customer relationship management (CRM) software systems that help manage and automate customer service functions like marketing, selling, and servicing.

When reporting its financial performance, Pivotal provides users with two sets of figures, one calculated according to generally accepted accounting principles (GAAP) and one showing non-GAAP or pro-forma earnings or losses. For example, for the nine months ending March 31, 2003, the software company reported a non-GAAP net loss of $15.9 million or $0.64 per share; net loss under GAAP was $25 million or $1 per share.

Why the different numbers? "GAAP statements can be fairly complicated for a lot of users of financial statements," says Divesh Sisodraker, Pivotal's chief financial officer. "What we try to do in our performance statements is to remove some of that complexity so that the financial statement users can look at an income statement that reflects what's going on in the quarter. If they are sophisticated enough, they can always go back to the GAAP statements."

Non-GAAP statements provide a view of the company's operating performance by including or excluding amounts required under GAAP. In Pivotal's case, the figures are the result of adding back some amortization of goodwill and acquired intangibles, while also leaving out some non-recurring events like restructuring charges. Individual companies arrive at non-GAAP financial information in different ways, which means it is difficult to compare from one company to another.

GAAP statements allow users to measure a company's performance relative to its peers and their expectations.

Sisodraker expects users of Pivotal's financial information to compare the GAAP and non-GAAP figures. "That's what keeps companies honest," he quips. "They're both useful in the right context."

CHAPTER 4

Reporting Financial Performance

Learning Objectives

After studying this chapter, you should be able to:

1. Identify the uses and limitations of an income statement.
2. Prepare a single-step income statement.
3. Prepare a multiple-step income statement.
4. Explain how irregular items are reported.
5. Measure and report results of discontinued operations.
6. Explain intraperiod tax allocation.
7. Explain where earnings per share information is reported.
8. Prepare a retained earnings statement.
9. Explain how comprehensive income is reported.

After studying Appendix 4A, you should be able to:

10. Differentiate the cash basis of accounting from the accrual basis of accounting.

Preview of Chapter 4

The way items are reported within the income statement can affect its usefulness. The purpose of this chapter is to examine the many different types of revenues, expenses, gains, and losses that are represented in the income statement and related information. The content and organization of this chapter are as follows:

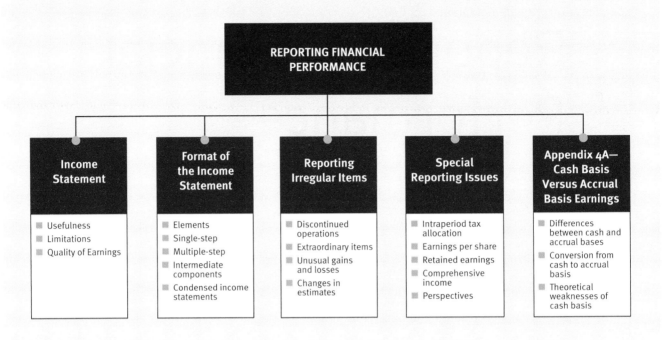

All business is based on a **business model** that involves getting cash, investing it in resources, and then using these resources to generate profits. The business model may be broken up into three distinct types of activities.

1. **Financing:** obtaining cash funding, often by borrowing, issuing shares, or (in established companies), retaining profits. Financing activities also involve repayment of debt/repurchase of shares.

2. **Investing:** using the funding to buy assets and invest in people. Investing activities also include divestitures.

3. **Operating:** utilizing the assets and people to earn profits.

In performing these three types of activities, companies take on differing levels of **risk** and are exposed to different **opportunities**. Companies must **manage** these risks in order to maximize performance and returns. Better companies develop strategies that will allow them to react to the best opportunities in order to maximize shareholder value. **Value creation** is central in any business model.

Since the objective of financial reporting is to communicate what the company is doing to interested stakeholders, the financial statements should capture these **fundamental business activities** and communicate them appropriately. In general, the information is captured and communicated as follows.

- The **balance sheet** strives to capture the **financing and investing activities**.
- The **income statement** strives to capture the **operating and performance related activities**.
- The **cash flow statement** looks at the **interrelationship** between the activities.

Illustration 4-1 depicts this overview perspective of the business model.

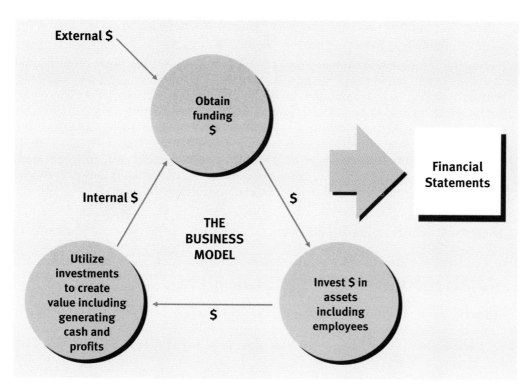

External $

Obtain funding $

Internal $

THE BUSINESS MODEL

$

Utilize investments to create value including generating cash and profits

$

Invest $ in assets including employees

$

Financial Statements

Illustration 4-1
An Overview Perspective of the Business Model

Underlying Concept

The concept of transparency mandates that the financial statements reflect the economic reality of running a business.

INCOME STATEMENT

The **income statement**, often called the statement of earnings or statement of income,[1] is the report that measures the success of enterprise operations for a given time period. The business and investment community uses this report to determine profitability, investment value, and credit worthiness. It provides investors and creditors with information that helps them allocate resources and assess management stewardship.

1 Objective
Identify the uses and limitations of an income statement.

Usefulness of the Income Statement

The income statement helps financial statement users allocate their own resources and assess management stewardship of the company's resources in a number of ways.[2] For example, investors and creditors can use the information in the income statement to:

Abitibi   Domtar

Revenues − Expenses $ Profits < Revenues − Expenses $ Profits

Which company did better last year?

[1] *Financial Reporting in Canada, 2002* (Toronto, CICA), p.98, indicates that for the 200 companies surveyed, 80 used earnings, 53 used income, and 53 used operations. The use of the latter is increasing while income and earnings are declining in terms of usage.

[2] In support of the usefulness of income information, accounting researchers have documented that the market prices of companies change when income is reported to the market. See W.H. Beaver, "The Information Content of Annual Earnings Announcements, Empirical Research in Accounting: Selected Studies," *Journal of Accounting Research* (Supplement 1968), pp. 67–92.

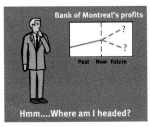

Bank of Montreal's profits

Past　Now　Future

Hmm....Where am I headed?

Income for Year Ended 12/31/04	Recurring?
Revenues	
− Operating expenses	
Operating income	Yes
± Unusual or extraordinary items	No
$ Net Income	?

Recurring items are more certain in the future.

1. **Evaluate the enterprise's past performance and profitability.** By examining revenues, expenses, gains, and losses, users can see how the company (and management) performed and compare its performance with its competitors. (Balance sheet information is also useful in assessing profitability, e.g., by calculating return on assets. See Appendix 5A.)

2. **Provide a basis for predicting future performance.** Information about past performance can be used to determine important trends that, if continued, provide information about future performance. However, success in the past does not necessarily mean the company will have success in the future.

3. **Help assess the risk or uncertainty of achieving future cash flows.** Information on the various components of income-revenues, expenses, gains, and losses highlights the relationships among them and can be used to assess the risk of not achieving a particular level of cash flows in the future. For example, segregating a company's recurring **operating** income (results from continuing operations) from nonrecurring income sources (discontinued operations, extraordinary items) is useful because **operations are usually the primary means by which revenues and cash are generated.** Thus, results from continuing operations usually have greater significance for predicting future performance than do results from nonrecurring activities.

In summary, the income statement provides feedback and predictive value, assisting stakeholders in understanding the business.

Limitations of the Income Statement

Net income is not a point estimate. Rather it is a range of possible values. This is because net income reflects a number of assumptions. By definition, accrual accounting mandates that estimates of things such as expenses and asset values be recorded. Because we report net income as a point estimate, income statement users must be made aware of certain limitations associated with information contained in the income statement. The income statement includes a mix of **hard** (easily measured with reasonable level of certainty, e.g., cash sales) and **soft** numbers (more difficult to measure, e.g., provision for bad debt). Specifically, the income statement has the following shortcomings.

Exp Exp
Rev Rev Rev
Profits
Unrealized Earnings
Brand value

You left something out!

1. **Items that cannot be measured reliably are not reported in the income statement.** Current practice prohibits recognizing certain items from the determination of income even though these items arguably affect an entity's performance from one point in time to another. For example, contingent gains may not be recorded in income, as there is uncertainty regarding whether the gains will ever be realized.

Income Using:

Straight-line amortization

Accelerated amortization

Hmm... Is the income the same?

2. **Income numbers are affected by the accounting methods employed.** For example, one company may choose to depreciate or amortize its plant assets on an accelerated basis; another chooses straight-line amortization. Assuming all other factors are equal, the first company's income will be lower, even though the companies are essentially the same. In effect, we are comparing apples with oranges.

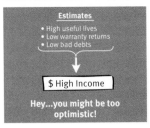

Estimates

• High useful lives
• Low warranty returns
• Low bad debts

$ High Income

Hey...you might be too optimistic!

3. **Income measurement involves the use of estimates.** For example, one company may estimate in good faith that an asset's useful life is 20 years while another company uses a 15-year estimate for the same type of asset. Similarly, some companies may make overly optimistic estimates of future warranty returns and bad debt write-offs, which result in lower expense and higher income. As mentioned above, where significant measurement uncertainty exists, the resulting numbers captured in the financial statements are referred to as "soft numbers."

Quality of Earnings

Users need **good information** about a company's earnings to make decisions; however, not all income statements provide this. This issue was addressed in part above (limitations of the income statement) and will be examined further here. When analysing earnings information, there are two aspects that must be considered:

1. **Content**

   (a) the **integrity of the information,** including whether it reflects the underlying business fundamentals and

   (b) **sustainability of the earnings**

2. **Presentation** (i.e., a clear, concise manner that fosters ease of use and is understandable)

The **nature of the content** and the **way it is presented** are referred to as the quality of earnings.

From an accountant's perspective, the emphasis is on ensuring that the information **is unbiased, reflects reality and is transparent and understandable**. From a capital market perspective, these factors are important but in addition, the focus is on whether the **earnings are sustainable**. Given the company's business model, can it continue to generate or sustain these earnings in the future? Note that accountants acknowledge this additional perspective by segregating earnings on the income statement between those that are expected to continue and those that are not. Even though the underlying business might be accurately reflected and understandable in the financial statements, the quality of the earnings might be judged to be low because the earnings are not sustainable.[3]

As inferred, earnings numbers may be judged to be of a **higher** quality or conversely, a **lower** quality. Higher quality earnings are more reliable, with a lower margin of potential misstatement, and are more representative of the underlying business and economic reality.

Companies with higher quality earnings are attributed higher values by the markets, all other things being equal. Earnings that cannot be replicated and/or are subject to significant bias are discounted by the markets.

Illustration 4-2 articulates some attributes of high quality earnings.

High quality earnings have the following characteristics:

1. Nature of content:

   - **Unbiased** (numbers not subject to manipulation) and **objectively determined** (consider need to estimate, accounting choice, application of professional judgement).

   - **Reflect economic reality**—all transactions and events appropriately captured.

   - **Reflect primarily earnings generated from ongoing core business activities** (as opposed to one-time gains or losses).

   - **Closely correlated with cash flows from operations.** Earnings that convert to cash more quickly provide a better measure of real earnings as little or no uncertainty exists as to realizability.

   - **Based on sound business strategy and business model.** (Consider riskiness of business, business strategy, industry, economic and political environments. Identify the effect of these on earnings stability, volatility and sustainability).

2. Presentation:

   - **Transparent**—no attempt to disguise or mislead; reflects the underlying business fundamentals

   - **Understandable**

Illustration 4-2

Some Attributes of High Quality Earnings

---

[3] In assessing whether earnings are sustainable, a strategic analysis of the company's positioning within the industry as well as an assessment of the business model's viability must be performed. This is beyond the scope of this course.

Is quality of earnings controllable by management? Looking at Illustration 4-2, there are some factors that are under management control, such as the integrity of the information, i.e., what information is captured and **recognized**, how it is **measured**, and how it is **presented and disclosed**. Management may also have some control over how quickly cash is generated from operations and how closely this correlates with reported earnings, e.g., through choice of sales and payment terms. Factors such as the economic and political environment are beyond the control of management for the most part, although management may certainly devise strategies to identify and minimize risks that lead to volatile earnings.

Earnings management may be defined as the process of **targeting certain earnings levels** (whether current or future) or desired earnings trends and **working backwards to determine what has to be done to ensure that these targets are met** (including selection of accounting and other company policies, use of estimates, and even execution of transactions). In many cases, earnings management is used to increase income in the current year at the expense of income in future years. For example, companies may prematurely recognize sales before they are complete in order to boost earnings. Some companies may enter into transactions with the sole objective of making the statements look better, incurring unnecessary transaction costs.

Earnings management can also be used to decrease current earnings in order to increase future income. Reserves may be established by using aggressive assumptions to estimate items such as sales returns, loan losses, and warranty returns. These reserves can then be reduced in the future to increase income. Earnings management activities have a negative effect on the quality of earnings. As long as there is full disclosure, an efficient market should see through these attempts to mask the underlying economic reality. Unfortunately, companies do not always disclose all important information and markets do not always operate efficiently.

Although many users do not believe that management intentionally misrepresents accounting results, there is concern that much of the information that companies disseminate is too promotional and that troubled companies take great pains to present their results in the best light. Preparers of financial statements must strive to present information that is of the highest quality. Users of this information must assess the quality of earnings prior to making decisions.

FORMAT OF THE INCOME STATEMENT

Elements of the Income Statement

International Insight

In some nations, financial reporting is prepared on the same basis as tax returns. In such cases, companies have incentives to minimize reported income.

Net income results from revenue, expense, gain, and loss transactions. These transactions are summarized in the income statement. This view of the income statement is **transactions-based** because it focuses on the income-related activities that have occurred during the period.[4] Income can be further classified by customer, product line, or function or by operating and non-operating, continuing and discontinued, and regular and irregular categories.[5] Income statement presentation and classification will be discussed later in the chapter.

---

[4] The most common alternative to the transaction approach, is the capital maintenance approach to income measurement. Under this approach, income for the period is determined based on the **change in equity**, after adjusting for capital contributions (e.g., investments by owners) or distributions (e.g., dividends). In other words, net income is a residual calculation. If the company is better off at the end of the year (excluding shareholder transactions), the excess is income—no matter what the source is. Canada is currently moving toward a combination of the two approaches with the new standards on **comprehensive income**. This will be discussed later in the chapter.

[5] The term "irregular" encompasses transactions and other events that are derived from developments outside the normal business operations.

More formal definitions of income-related items, referred to as the major **elements** of the income statement, are as follows.

ELEMENTS OF FINANCIAL STATEMENTS[6]

Revenues. **Increases in economic resources** either by way of:

1. inflows, or

2. enhancements of an entity's assets, or

3. settlements of liabilities resulting from its ordinary activities.

Expenses. **Decreases in economic resources**, by:

1. outflows, or

2. reductions of assets, or

3. incurrence of liabilities, resulting from an entity's ordinary revenue-generating activities.

Gains. **Increases in equity (net assets)** from **peripheral** or **incidental transactions** of an entity from all other transactions and other events and circumstances affecting the entity during a period except those that result from revenues or investment by owners.

Losses. **Decreases in equity (net assets)** from **peripheral** or **incidental transactions** of an entity and from all other transactions and other events and circumstances affecting the entity during a period except those that result from expenses or distributions to owners.

These are the same **elements** identified in Chapter 2 and the conceptual framework. **Revenues** take many forms, such as sales, fees, interest, dividends, and rents. **Expenses** also take many forms, such as cost of goods sold, amortization, interest, rent, salaries and wages, and taxes. **Gains** and **losses** also are of many types, resulting from the sale of investments, sale of plant assets, settlement of liabilities, write-offs of assets due to obsolescence or casualty, and theft.

The **distinction** between revenues and gains (and expenses and losses) depends to a great extent on how the enterprise's **ordinary** or **typical business activities** are defined. It is therefore critical to understand an enterprise's typical business activities. For example, when McDonald's sells a hamburger, the selling price is recorded as **revenue**. However, when McDonald's sells a french-fryer, any excess of the selling price over the book value would be recorded as a **gain**. This difference in treatment results because the hamburger sale is part of McDonald's regular operations while the french-fryer sale is not. Similarly, when a manufacturer of french-fryers sells a fryer, the sale proceeds would be recorded as **revenue**.

Underlying Concept

The business model should be transparent.

The importance of properly presenting these elements should not be underestimated. For many decision-makers, the **parts of a financial statement may be more useful than the whole**. A company must be able to generate cash flows from its **normal ongoing core business activities** (revenues minus expenses). Having income statement elements shown in some detail and in a format that shows prior years' data allows

---

[6] *CICA Handbook*, Section 1000.37–.40.

decision-makers to better assess whether a company does indeed **generate cash flows** from its normal ongoing core business activities and **whether it is getting better or worse at it.**

In arriving at income or loss before discontinued operations and extraordinary items, companies are required to present the following items in the income statement:[7]

- revenues
- income from investments
- finance income
- income from leases
- government assistance
- amortization
- goodwill impairment
- research and development costs
- exchange gains or losses
- interest expense
- unusual items
- income taxes

Illustration 4-3 shows the Income Statement of **Molson Inc.** for the year ended March 31, 2003. The amount of detail on this statement is comparable to the detail on the income statements of many public companies.

Illustration 4-3

Molson Inc.'s Statement of Earnings

Digital Tool

Annual Reports

www.wiley.com/canada/kieso

Molson Inc.

Consolidated Statements of Earnings

Years ended March 31, 2003 and 2002
(Dollars in millions, except share and per share amounts)

	2003	2002
Sales and other revenues	$ 3,529.2	$ 2,830.8
Brewing excise and sales taxes	1,014.0	728.5
Net sales revenue	2,515.2	2,102.3
Costs and expenses		
Cost of sales, selling and administrative costs	1,934.7	1,675.9
Gain on sale of 20% of operations in Brazil (note 3)	(64.2)	–
Provision for rationalization (note 5)	63.5	50.0
	1,934.0	1,725.9
Earnings before interest, income taxes and amortization	581.2	376.4
Amortization of capital assets	64.9	54.6
Earnings before interest and income taxes	516.3	321.8
Net interest expense (note 6)	95.4	65.5
Earnings before income taxes	420.9	256.3
Income tax expense (note 7)	115.0	80.7
Earnings before minority interest	305.9	175.6
Minority interest	6.5	–
Earnings from continuing operations	312.4	175.6
Earnings from discontinued operations (note 8)	–	2.0
Net earnings	$ 312.4	$ 177.6
Net earnings per share from continuing operations (note 9)		
Basic	$ 2.45	$ 1.46
Diluted	$ 2.41	$ 1.43
Net earnings per share (note 9)		
Basic	$ 2.45	$ 1.48
Diluted	$ 2.41	$ 1.45

---

[7] *CICA Handbook*, Section 1520.

Note that Molson presents the **cost of sales** number separately on the income statement. Many companies do not show this number as it is not a required disclosure. For example see Illustration 4-4, which shows the income statement of The Hudson's Bay Company.

Years ended January 31 (thousands of dollars except per share amounts)	Notes	**2003**	2002
Sales and revenue			
The Bay		**2,648,339**	2,667,262
Zellers		**4,656,274**	4,693,027
Other		**79,200**	85,524
		$7,383,813	7,445,813
Earnings before interest expense and income taxes			
The Bay		**104,931**	65,740
Zellers		**120,401**	134,035
Other		**(26,022)**	(14,260)
		199,310	185,515
Interest expense	17	**(45,428)**	(53,648)
Earnings before income taxes		**153,882**	131,867
Income taxes	3	**(42,421)**	(59,117)
Net earnings		**111,461**	72,750
Earnings per share—basic	18	**$ 1.40**	$0.85
Earnings per share—diluted	18	**$ 1.34**	$0.84

(See accompanying notes to the Consolidated Financial Statements)

Illustration 4-4

The Hudson's Bay Company's Statements of Earnings

Single-Step Income Statements

In reporting revenues, gains, expenses, and losses, a format known as the single-step income statement is often used. In the single-step statement, just two groupings exist: **revenues** and **expenses**. Expenses and losses are deducted from revenues and gains to arrive at net income or loss. The expression "single-step" is derived from the single subtraction necessary to arrive at net income. Frequently, income tax is reported separately as the last item before net income to indicate its relationship to income before income tax.

For example, Illustration 4-5 shows the single-step income statement of DeGrootes Corporation.

2 Objective

Prepare a single-step income statement.

DEGROOTES CORPORATION Income Statement For the Year Ended December 31, 2005	
Revenues	
Net sales	$2,972,413
Dividend revenue	98,500
Rental revenue	72,910
Total revenues	3,143,823
Expenses	
Cost of goods sold	1,982,541
Selling expenses	453,028
Administrative expenses	350,771
Interest expense	126,060
Income tax expense	66,934
Total expenses	2,979,334
Net income	$ 164,489
Earnings per common share	$1.74

Illustration 4-5

Single-Step Income Statement

The single-step form of income statement is widely used in financial reporting in smaller, private companies. The **multiple-step** form described below is used almost exclusively among public companies.[8]

The primary advantage of the single-step format lies in the **simplicity of presentation** and the **absence of any implication that one type of revenue or expense item has priority over another**. Potential classification problems are thus eliminated.

Multiple-Step Income Statements

Objective 3
Prepare a multiple-step income statement.

Some contend that **presenting other important revenue and expense data separately** makes the income statement more informative and more useful. These further classifications include:

1. A separation of the company's operating and non-operating activities. For example, enterprises often present an income from operations figure and then sections entitled **other revenues and gains** and **other expenses and losses**. These other categories include interest revenue and expense, gains or losses from sales of miscellaneous items, and dividends received.

2. A classification of expenses **by functions**, such as merchandising or manufacturing (cost of goods sold), selling, and administration. This permits immediate **comparison** with costs of previous years and with the cost of other departments during the same year.

A **multiple-step income statement** is used to recognize these additional relationships. This statement recognizes a separation between **operating** transactions and **non-operating** transactions and **matches** costs and expenses with related revenues. It highlights certain intermediate components of income that are used to calculate ratios used to assess the enterprise's performance (i.e., gross profit/margin).

To illustrate, DeGrootes Corporation's multiple-step income statement is presented in Illustration 4-6. Note, for example, that in arriving at net income, at least three main subtotals are presented: net sales revenue, gross profit, and income from operations. The disclosure of net sales revenue is useful because regular revenues are reported as a separate item. Irregular or incidental revenues are disclosed elsewhere in the income statement. As a result, trends in revenue from continuing operations (typical business activities) should be easier to identify, understand, and analyse. Similarly, the reporting of gross profit provides a useful number for evaluating performance and assessing future earnings. A study of the trend in gross profits may show **how successfully a company uses its resources** (prices paid for inventory, costs accumulated, wastage); it may also be a basis for **understanding how profit margins have changed** as a result of competitive pressure (prices the company is able to charge for its products and services). Gross profit percentage is a very important ratio in the retail business.

Underlying Concept

This disclosure helps users recognize that incidental or irregular activities are **unlikely to continue at the same level (predictive value)**.

Finally, disclosing income from operations **highlights the difference between regular and irregular or incidental activities**. Disclosure of operating earnings may assist in comparing different companies and assessing operating efficiencies. Note that if this company had **discontinued operations or extraordinary items**, these would be added to the bottom of the statement and shown separately. These items are by definition **atypical and/or nonrecurring** and therefore have **little predictive value**. They do, however, give **feedback value** as to prior decisions made by management. Net income that consists primarily of net income from continuing operations would be viewed as **higher quality**.

---

[8] *Financial Reporting in Canada, 2002* (Toronto, CICA). Of the 200 companies surveyed, 98% employed the multiple-step form, p. 98.

Illustration 4-6

*Multiple-Step
Income Statement*

DEGROOTES CORPORATION
Income Statement
For the Year Ended December 31, 2005

Sales Revenue			
Sales			$3,053,081
Less: Sales discounts		$24,241	
Less: Sales returns and allowances		56,427	80,668
Net sales revenue			2,972,413
Cost of Goods Sold			
Merchandise inventory, Jan. 1, 2005		461,219	
Purchases	$1,989,693		
Less: Purchase discounts	19,270		
Net purchases	1,970,423		
Freight and transportation-in	40,612	2,011,035	
Total merchandise available for sale		2,472,254	
Less: Merchandise inventory, Dec. 31, 2005		489,713	
Cost of goods sold			1,982,541
Gross profit on sales			989,872
Operating Expenses			
Selling expenses			
Sales salaries and commissions	202,644		
Sales office salaries	59,200		
Travel and entertainment	48,940		
Advertising expense	38,315		
Freight and transportation-out	41,209		
Shipping supplies and expense	24,712		
Postage and stationery	16,788		
Amortization of sales equipment	9,005		
Telephone and Internet expense	12,215	453,028	
Administrative expenses			
Officers' salaries	186,000		
Office salaries	61,200		
Legal and professional services	23,721		
Utilities expense	23,275		
Insurance expense	17,029		
Amortization of building	18,059		
Amortization of office equipment	16,000		
Stationery, supplies, and postage	2,875		
Miscellaneous office expenses	2,612	350,771	803,799
Income from operations			186,073
Other Revenues and Gains			
Dividend revenue		98,500	
Rental revenue		72,910	171,410
			357,483
Other Expenses and Losses			
Interest on bonds and notes			126,060
Income before income tax			231,423
Income tax			66,934
Net income for the year			$164,489
Earnings per common share			$1.74

Intermediate Components of the Income Statement

When a multiple-step income statement is used, some or all of the following sections or subsections may be prepared.

INCOME STATEMENT SECTIONS

1. *Continuing Operations*

   (a) **Operating** Section. A report of the **revenues and expenses** of the company's principal operations.

      i. **Sales or Revenue** Section. A subsection presenting sales, discounts, allowances, returns, and other related information. Its purpose is to arrive at the net amount of sales revenue.

      ii. **Cost of Goods Sold** Section. A subsection that shows the cost of goods that were sold to produce the sales.

      iii. **Selling Expenses.** A subsection that lists expenses resulting from the company's efforts to make sales.

      iv. **Administrative or General Expenses.** A subsection reporting expenses of general administration.

   (b) **Non-operating** Section. A report of revenues and expenses resulting from the company's secondary or auxiliary activities. In addition, special gains and losses that are infrequent or unusual, but not both, are normally reported in this section. Generally these items break down into two main subsections:

      i. **Other Revenues and Gains.** A list of the revenues earned or gains incurred, generally net of related expenses, from nonoperating transactions.

      ii. **Other Expenses and Losses.** A list of the expenses or losses incurred, generally net of any related incomes, from nonoperating transactions.

   (c) **Income Tax.** A short section reporting income taxes levied on income from continuing operations.

2. *Discontinued Operations.* Material gains or losses resulting from the disposition of a part of the business (net of taxes).

3. *Extraordinary Items.* Atypical and infrequent material gains and losses beyond the control of management (net of taxes).

Although the **content** of the operating section is generally the same, the **presentation** or organization of the material need not be as described above.

Usually, financial statements that are provided to external users have **less detail** than internal management reports. The latter tend to have more expense categories, usually grouped along lines of responsibility. This detail allows top management to judge staff performance.

Whether a single-step or multiple-step income statement is used, **irregular transactions** such as discontinued operations and extraordinary items are **required to be reported separately** following income from continuing operations.

Underlying Concept

This contributes to understandability as it reduces "information overload."

Condensed Income Statements

In some cases it is impossible to present all the desired expense detail in a single income statement of convenient size. This problem is solved by including only the totals of expense groups in the statement of income and preparing **supplementary schedules** of expenses to support the totals. With this format, the income statement itself may be reduced to a few lines on a single sheet. For this reason, readers who wish to study all the reported data on operations must give their attention to the supporting schedules.

The income statement shown in Illustration 4-7 for DeGrootes Corporation is a condensed version of the more detailed multiple-step statement presented earlier and is more representative of the type found in practice.

DEGROOTES CORPORATION
Income Statement
For the Year Ended December 31, 2005

Sales		$2,972,413
Cost of goods sold		1,982,541
Gross profit		989,872
Selling expenses (see Note D)	$453,028	
Administrative expenses	350,771	803,799
Income from operations		186,073
Other revenues and gains		171,410
Other expenses and losses		126,060
Income before income tax		231,423
Income tax		66,934
Net income for the year		$ 164,489
Earnings per share		$1.74

Illustration 4-7
Condensed Income Statement

An example of a supporting schedule, cross-referenced as Note D and detailing the selling expenses, is shown in Illustration 4-8.

Note D: Selling expenses	
Sales salaries and commissions	$202,644
Sales office salaries	59,200
Travel and entertainment	48,940
Advertising expense	38,315
Freight and transportation-out	41,209
Shipping supplies and expense	24,712
Postage and stationery	16,788
Amortization of sales equipment	9,005
Telephone and Internet expense	12,215
Total selling expenses	$453,028

Illustration 4-8
Sample Supporting Schedule

Deciding **how much detail** to include in the income statement is always a problem. On the one hand, a simple, summarized statement allows a reader to readily discover important factors. On the other hand, disclosure of results of all activities provides users with detailed relevant information. Certain basic elements are always included, but they may be presented in various formats.

Underlying Concept

This is an example of a tradeoff between understandability versus full disclosure.

REPORTING IRREGULAR ITEMS

Either the **single-step** or the **multiple-step** income statement may be used for financial reporting purposes: flexibility in presenting the income components is thereby permitted.

Objective

Explain how irregular items are reported.

In two important areas, however, specific guidelines have been developed. These two areas relate to what is included in income and how certain unusual or irregular items are reported.

What should be included in net income has been a controversy for many years. For example, should irregular gains and losses, corrections of revenues and prior year's expenses, and non-operating changes in equity be treated differently than ongoing revenues and expenses from operating activities? One option is to book these items directly to retained earnings or a separate equity section, i.e., not book them through the income statement.

Currently income measurement follows a modified **all-inclusive approach**. This approach indicates that most items, even irregular ones, are recorded in income.[9] Some exceptions are:

1. **errors** in prior years' income measurement

2. **changes in accounting policies applied retroactively**

Because these items relate to earnings already reported in a prior period, they are not included in current income. Rather, they are recorded as adjustments to retained earnings.[10]

Illustration 4-9 identifies the most common types and number of irregular items reported in a survey of 200 large companies.[11] As indicated, unusual items, which many times contain write-offs and other one-time items, were reported by more than 60% of the surveyed firms. About 17% of the surveyed firms reported discontinued operations. Thus, developing a framework for reporting irregular items is important to ensure that financial statement users have relevant, high quality income information.[12]

Illustration 4-9

Number of Irregular Items Reported in 2001 by 200 Public Companies

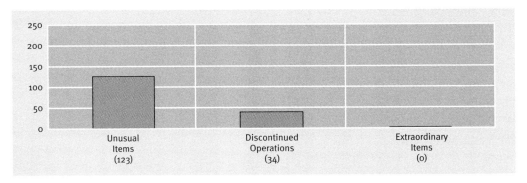

Some users advocate a **current operating performance approach** to income reporting. They argue that the most useful income measures reflect only regular and recurring revenue and expense elements or normalized, sustainable earnings. Irregular items do not reflect an enterprise's future earning power since by definition, they are irregular and atypical or nonrecurring. Operating income supporters believe that including one-time items such as write-offs and restructuring charges reduces the income measure's essentially **predictive value**.

In contrast, others warn that a focus on operating income potentially misses important information about a firm's performance. Any gain or loss experienced by the firm, whether directly or indirectly related to operations, contributes to its long-run profitability. As one

---

[9] *CICA Handbook*, Section 1000.27. The modified all-inclusive approach is substantially consistent with a **capital maintenance approach** to measuring income in that net income is equal to a change in net assets excluding capital transactions. *CICA Handbook* Section 1000.55 notes that financial statements are prepared with capital maintenance measured in financial terms.

[10] *CICA Handbook*, Section 1506.31.

[11] *Financial Reporting in Canada, 2002* (Toronto, CICA), pp. 102, 461 and 477.

[12] The AcSB, the IASB, and FASB are currently working on projects dealing with reporting financial performance. The objective is to improve the quality of information presented in the income and cash flow statements. The work to date supports the all-inclusive or comprehensive income approach.

analyst notes, "write-offs matter.... They speak to the volatility of (past) earnings."[13] Therefore, they have **feedback value**. As a result, some non-operating items can be used to assess the riskiness of future earnings—**predictive value**. Furthermore, determining which items are (regular) **operating** items and which are **irregular** requires judgement and this could lead to differences in the treatment of irregular items and to possible manipulation of income measures.

Discontinued Operations

As indicated in Illustration 4-9, one of the most common types of irregular items relates to discontinued operations. Discontinued operations include **components of an enterprise** that have been **disposed of** (by sale, abandonment, or spin-off) **or** are classified as **held for sale**, where:

- the **operations and cash flows** have been, or will be, **eliminated**, and

- the enterprise will **not have any continuing involvement.**[14]

Companies might discontinue operations as part of a downsizing strategy to improve operating results or to focus on core operations or perhaps to generate cash flows. For example, in the last decade, Molson Inc. spun off its ownership in its retail operations (consisting of the Home Depot and Beaver Lumber) as well as its sports and entertainment business (consisting of the Montreal Canadiens Hockey Club and the Molson Centre). Currently it is a brewing operation only, brewing and selling the Molson, Coors, Kaiser, and Bavaria brands.

Separate Component

In order to qualify for separate presentation on the income statement, the business being disposed of must be a **component of an entity** (business component) where the **operations, cash flows, and financial elements are clearly distinguishable** from the rest of the enterprise. A component may be one of the following:

- a **reportable** or **operating segment** as defined in *CICA Handbook* Section 1701— Segmented Reporting,

- a **reporting unit** as defined in *CICA Handbook* Section 3062 in testing for goodwill impairment,

- a **subsidiary**, or

- an **asset group** as defined in *CICA Handbook* Section 3063 for impairment of long-lived assets.[15]

Basically, a component consists of a **unit of operation**, which may be as small as a hotel or an apartment building that is being rented out, or as large as a major subsidiary. When does the **disposal of an asset** constitute a **disposal of a component** for discontinued operations purposes? **The key elements are that the asset or group of assets generates its own net cash flows and is operationally distinct.**

Illustration 4-10 below provides a conceptual view of what constitutes a component for discontinued operations purposes.

---

[13] D. McDermott, "Latest Profit Data Stir Old Debate Between Net and Operating Income," *The Wall Street Journal*, May 3, 1999.

[14] *CICA Handbook*, Section 3475.27.

[15] *CICA Handbook*, Section 3475.28.

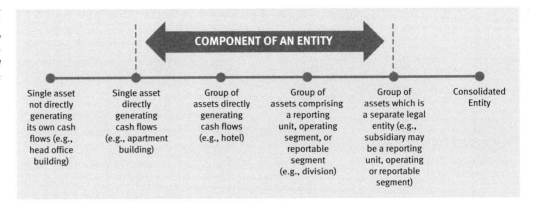

Assets Held for Sale

A component is **held for sale** when all of the following criteria are met:

- an **authorized plan** to sell exists,
- the asset is **available for immediate sale** in its current state,
- an **active program** to find a buyer exists,
- sale is **probable** within one year,
- the asset is **reasonably priced** and actively marketed, and
- **changes** to the plan are **unlikely**.[16]

In summary, an asset may be deemed held for sale where there is a formal plan to dispose of the component.

Measurement and Presentation

Where an asset is held for sale, the asset would be **remeasured** to the lower of its carrying value and fair value less cost to sell.[17] Note that if the value of an asset that has been written down subsequently increases, **the gain may be recognized up to the original loss**. Once classified as held for sale, **no further depreciation is recognized**.

Assets and related liabilities would be **presented** separately (as held for sale) in the balance sheet, retaining their original classification, i.e., as an asset (and/or liability), current or noncurrent.[18] The results of operations would be shown separately on the income statement, net of tax for both current and prior periods.[19] An example will illustrate these concepts below.

On November 1, 2004 top management of Multiplex Products, Inc., a highly diversified company, approves a detailed plan to discontinue its electronics division at December 31, 2005. The plan, among other things, identifies steps to find a buyer and includes a timeline for disposition, along with a calculation of expected gain or loss on disposition. The business is available for sale immediately.

As top management has approved the disposal and has articulated in reasonable detail which assets are to be disposed of and how, a **formal plan** exists. The division is a separate business (being a division) that is therefore operationally distinct, with separate cash flows. Since it is a division, it will also have separate financial information and is thus a business

---

[16] *CICA Handbook*, Section 3475.08

[17] *CICA Handbook*, Section 3475.13

[18] *CICA Handbook*, Section 3475.33

[19] *CICA Handbook*, Section 3475.30

component. Separate financial information is critical so that the gain or loss from discontinued operations may be properly **measured**.

Assume that during the year, the electronics division for Multiplex Products Inc. lost $300,000 (net of tax of $190,000) and that the assets were sold the following year at a loss of $500,000 (net of tax of $320,000). The assets and liabilities relating to the division would have been segregated on the balance sheet as follows:

- current assets—as "current assets held for sale/related to discontinued operations,"

- noncurrent assets—as "noncurrent assets held for sale/related to discontinued operations,"

- current liabilities—as "current liabilities related to assets held for sale/discontinued," and/or

- long-term liabilities—as "long-term liabilities related to assets held for sale/discontinued."

Assume that the company had estimated the asset impairment as at year end was $500,000 net of tax. The information would be shown on the current year's annual income statement as follows.

Digital Tool

Student Toolkit—
Additional
Disclosures
www.wiley.com/canada/kieso

Income from continuing operations		$20,000,000
Discontinued operations[a]		
Loss from operation of discontinued electronics division (net of tax of $190,000)	$300,000	
Loss from disposal of electronics division (net of tax of $320,000)	500,000	800,000
Net income		$19,200,000
Income per share from continuing operations		$2.00
Discontinued operation per share		0.08
Net income per share		$1.92

[a] Note that the detail could also be shown in the notes to the financial statements along with the other required disclosures such as the details of any plan to dispose and the facts and circumstances of the discontinuance.[20]

Illustration 4-11

Income Statement Presentation of Discontinued Operations

5 Objective

Measure and report results of discontinued operations.

The company would cease recording depreciation on the division's assets and in the following year, would show any operating losses or profits, and/or revised gain/loss on disposal as discontinued operations. Estimated future losses would not be included in the loss from operations since they would be implicitly reflected in the fair value estimate of the assets held for sale or sold. Note that the phrase "Income from continuing operations" is used only when gains or losses on discontinued operations or extraordinary items occur.

Extraordinary Items

Extraordinary items are material, non-recurring items that differ significantly from the entity's typical business activities.[21] They are presented separately on the income statement in order to provide sufficient detail for predictive purposes. The criteria for extraordinary items are as follows. All three criteria must be met:

1. **infrequent**

2. **atypical** of normal business activities of the company

3. do not depend primarily on **decisions or determinations by management** or owners[22]

International Insight

Classification of items as extraordinary differs across nations. Even in countries in which the criteria for identifying extraordinary items are similar, they are not interpreted identically; thus, what is extraordinary in North America is not necessarily extraordinary elsewhere.

---

[20] *CICA Handbook*, Section 3475.36 and .37.

[21] It is often difficult to determine what is extraordinary, because assessing the materiality of individual items requires judgement. However, in making materiality judgements, extraordinary items should be considered individually, and not in the aggregate. (*CICA Handbook*, Section 3480.09).

[22] *CICA Handbook*, Section 3480.02.

**What
do the
Numbers
Mean?**

Professional judgement must be applied in considering whether these three criteria are met and because of the third criterion, very few extraordinary items are reported. How infrequent is infrequent? Consideration should be given to how often an event has occurred in the past and may recur in the future. For instance, in 2001, a fibre optics cable supplying 315,000 high-speed Internet customers of **Rogers Cable Inc.** (Rogers) was damaged. This was the second time that it had been damaged in a month. Twice in one month would appear to meet the criteria of frequency for the current year; however, a review of the existence of past damage would confirm whether this was a frequent occurrence for the company over time.

The second criterion to determine whether or not an event is atypical also involves the use of professional judgement. As a starting point, **typical business activities** should be identified. What is the company's business and what are typical activities and business risks? Consider the Rogers example above. Rogers is a subsidiary of Rogers Communications Inc. and is in the business of supplying high-speed cable access to homes and industry for cable television and Internet services. Fixed assets, which include land and distribution cable, account for 51% of the company's total assets, which is pretty significant. Is damage to high-speed fibre optics cables considered a typical business risk? The cables are normally buried and therefore less likely to be damaged by animals and vandals; however, in this case, they were exposed, being repaired. One factor to consider is if the company insures itself against such losses. If so, this may be an acknowledgement that the company feels that this risk is typical and significant enough to cover with insurance.

If a company was completely insured against every possible risk, no loss would occur; however, sometimes companies are not able to obtain insurance for complete coverage and hence if a loss occurs, part of it would be borne by the company itself. Also, costs to completely insure against all risks would be prohibitively high. Thus, a company must make decisions about what to insure itself against.

**What
do the
Numbers
Mean?**

No recent event better illustrates the difficulties of determining whether a transaction meets the definition of extraordinary than the financial impacts of the terrorist attacks on the World Trade Center on September 11, 2001. To many, this event, which resulted in the tragic loss of lives, jobs, and in some cases, entire businesses, clearly meets the criteria for unusual and infrequent. For example, airlines, insurance companies, and other businesses recorded major losses due to property damage, business disruption, and suspension of airline travel and of securities trading. But, to the surprise of many, extraordinary item reporting was not permitted for losses arising from the terrorist attacks.

The reason? After much deliberation, the Emerging Issues Task Force (EITF) of the FASB decided that measuring the possible loss was too difficult. Take the airline industry as an example. What portion of the airlines' losses after September 11 was related to the terrorist attack, and what portion was due to the ongoing recession? There also was concern that some companies would use the attacks as a reason for reporting as extraordinary some losses that had little direct relationship to the attacks. For example, shortly after the attacks, energy company **AES** and shoe retailer **Footstar**, who both were experiencing profit pressure before the attacks, put some of the blame for their poor performance on the attacks.[23]

The third criterion looks at **management involvement**. The event must not hinge on or be precipitated by a management or owner decision. This third criterion ensures that items classified as extraordinary items are beyond management control. Thus, decisions to sell assets at losses, downsize, restructure, and other similar expenses are not considered extraordinary.

For further clarification, the CICA specifies that the following gains and losses are **not** extraordinary items:

1. losses and provisions for losses with respect to bad debt and inventories

2. gains and losses from fluctuations in foreign exchange rates

3. adjustments with respect to contract prices

---

[23] J. Creswell, "Bad News Bearers Shift the Blame," *Fortune* (October 15, 2001), p. 44.

4. gains and losses from writedowns or sale of property, plant and equipment, or other investments

5. income tax reductions on utilization of prior period losses or reversal of previously recorded tax benefits

6. changes in income tax rates or laws[24]

The items listed above are not considered extraordinary because they are **usual in nature** and may be **expected to recur** as a consequence of customary and continuing business activities.

In determining whether an item is extraordinary, the environment in which the entity operates is of primary importance. The environment includes such factors as industry characteristics, geographic location, and the nature and extent of governmental regulations. Thus, extraordinary item treatment is accorded the loss from hail damages to a tobacco grower's crops only if severe damage from hailstorms in its locality is rare. On the other hand, frost damage to a citrus grower's crop in Florida does not qualify as extraordinary because frost damage is normally experienced every three or four years. In this environment, the criterion of infrequency is not met.

Extraordinary items are to be shown **net of taxes** in a separate section in the income statement, usually just before net income.

Unusual Gains and Losses

Because of the restrictive criteria for extraordinary items, financial statement users must carefully examine the financial statements for items that meet only some of the criteria for presentation as an extraordinary item (but not all). As indicated earlier, items such as writedowns of inventories and gains and losses from fluctuation of foreign exchange are not considered extraordinary items. Thus, these items are sometimes shown with the normal, recurring revenues, costs, and expenses. If they are not material in amount, they are combined with other items in the income statement. If they are material, they are disclosed separately, but are shown above "income (loss) before extraordinary items."

Consolidated Statements of Earnings and Retained Earnings
Years ended December 31

Illustration 4-12

Income Statement Presentation of Unusual Charges

($ in millions, except per share data)	2002	2001
Revenues	$ 2,187	$ 2,379
Cost of operations	(1,805)	(1,751)
Depreciation and amortization	(199)	(226)
Operating Profit	183	402
Other Expenses		
General, administration and marketing	(53)	(58)
Interest on long-term debt	(67)	(77)
Exploration	(34)	(59)
Research and development	(19)	(15)
Other income and expense (net)	7	62
	17	255

---

[24] *CICA Handbook*, Section 3480.04.

Illustration 4-12

*Income Statement Presentation
of Unusual Charges
(continued)*

Asset valuation writedowns (Note 12)	–	(169)
Income and resource taxes (Note 13)		
On earnings from operations	(5)	(103)
On asset valuation writedowns (Note 12)	–	47
Minority interests	1	(50)
Equity earnings (loss)	17	(1)
Net Earnings (Loss)	$ 30	$ (21)
Basic and Diluted Earnings (Loss) Per Share	$ 0.15	$ (0.17)

For example, Teck Cominco Limited, a diversified mining and refining company, presented an unusual charge for asset valuation writedowns shown in Illustration 4-12 in its income statement.

As indicated in Illustration 4-9, unusual items have been common in recent years. There has been a tendency to report unusual items in a separate section just above income from operations before income taxes and extraordinary items, especially when there are multiple unusual items. For example, when General Electric Company experienced multiple unusual items in one year, it reported them in a separate unusual items section of the income statement below Income before unusual items and income taxes. [25]

Changes in Estimates

Another type of change involves change in estimates. Estimates are inherent in the accounting process. Estimates are made, for example, of useful lives and salvage values of depreciable assets, of uncollectible receivables, of inventory obsolescence, and of the number of periods expected to benefit from a particular expenditure. Not infrequently, as time passes, as circumstances change, or as additional information is obtained, even estimates originally made in good faith must be changed. Such changes in estimates are accounted for in the period of change if they affect only that period, or in the period of change and future periods if the change affects both.

To illustrate a change in estimate that affects only the period of change, assume that DuPage Materials Corp. has consistently estimated its bad debt expense at 1% of credit sales. In 2004, however, DuPage's controller determines that the estimate of bad debts for the current year's credit sales must be revised upward to 2%, or double the prior year's percentage. Using 2% results in a bad debt charge of $240,000, or double the amount using the 1% estimate for prior years. The expense is recorded at December 31, 2004, as follows.

A   = L +   SE
−$240,000   −$240,000
Cash flows: No effect

Bad Debt Expense	240,000	
Allowance for Doubtful Accounts		240,000

The entire change in estimate is included in 2004 income because it reflects decisions made and information available in the current year and no future periods are affected by the change. Changes in estimate are not handled retroactively; that is, carried back to adjust prior years.

---

[25] Some companies report items such as restructuring charges every year as unusual items. Research on the market reaction to income containing one-time items indicates that the market discounts the earnings of companies that report a series of non-recurring items. Such evidence supports the contention that these elements reduce the quality of earnings. See J. Elliot and D. Hanna, "Repeat Accounting Write-offs and the Information Content of Earnings," *Journal of Accounting Research* (Supplement, 1996).

All accounting changes (including correction of errors) will be examined further in Chapter 22.

SPECIAL REPORTING ISSUES

Intraperiod Tax Allocation

As previously noted, certain irregular items are shown on the income statement net of tax, thus providing more informative disclosure to statement users. This procedure is called **intraperiod tax allocation**; that is, allocation of tax balances within a period. Intraperiod tax allocation relates the income tax expense or benefit of the fiscal period to the underlying income statement items and events that give rise to the tax. Intraperiod tax allocation is used for the following items: (1) income from continuing operations, (2) discontinued operations, and (3) extraordinary items.

The income tax expense attributable to income from continuing operations is calculated by finding the income tax expense related to revenue and to expense transactions used in determining this income. In this tax calculation, no effect is given to the tax consequences of the items excluded from the determination of income from continuing operations. A separate tax effect is then associated with each irregular item.

In applying the concept of intraperiod tax allocation, assume that Schindler Corp. has income before income tax and extraordinary item of $250,000 and an extraordinary gain from the expropriation of land by the government of $100,000. If the income tax rate is assumed to be 40%, the following information is presented on the income statement.

6 Objective
Explain intraperiod tax allocation.

Income before income tax and extraordinary item	$250,000
Income tax	100,000
Income before extraordinary item	150,000
Extraordinary gain net of applicable taxes of (40,000)	60,000
Net income	$210,000

Illustration 4-13

Intraperiod Tax Allocation, Extraordinary Gain

The income tax of $100,000 ($250,000 × 40%) attributable to income before income tax and extraordinary item is determined from revenue and expense transactions related to this income. In this income tax calculation, the tax consequences of items excluded from the determination of income before income tax and extraordinary item are not considered. The "extraordinary gain" then shows a separate tax effect of $40,000.

Earnings per Share

The results of a company's operations are customarily summed up in one important figure: net income. As if this condensation were not enough of a simplification, the financial world has widely accepted an even more distilled and compact figure as its most significant business indicator: **earnings per share**.

The calculation of earnings per share is usually straightforward. Net income minus preferred dividends (income available to common shareholders) is divided by the weighted average of common shares outstanding to arrive at earnings per share. To illustrate, assume that Lancer Inc. reports net income of $350,000 and declares and pays preferred dividends of $50,000 for the year. The weighted average number of common shares outstanding during the year is 100,000 shares. Earnings per share is $3.00, as calculated in Illustration 4-14.

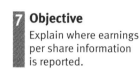

7 Objective
Explain where earnings per share information is reported.

IAS Note

IAS 33 requires presentation of earnings per share information for net income only.

Illustration 4-14

*Equation Illustrating
Calculation of Earnings
per Share*

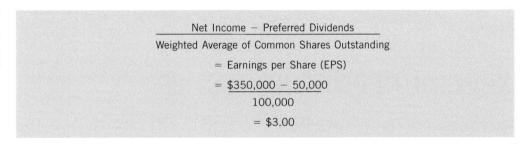

$$\frac{\text{Net Income } - \text{ Preferred Dividends}}{\text{Weighted Average of Common Shares Outstanding}}$$

$$= \text{ Earnings per Share (EPS)}$$

$$= \frac{\$350,000 - 50,000}{100,000}$$

$$= \$3.00$$

Note that the EPS figure measures the number of dollars earned by each common share but not the dollar amount paid to shareholders in the form of dividends.

"Net income per share" or "earnings per share" is a ratio commonly used in prospectuses, proxy material, and annual reports to shareholders. It is also highlighted in the financial press, by statistical services like **Standard & Poor's**, and by Bay Street securities analysts. Because of its importance, earnings per share is required to be disclosed on the face of the income statement. A company that reports a discontinued operation or an extraordinary item must report per share amounts for these line items either on the face of the income statement or in the notes to the financial statements.[26] Illustrations 4-11 and 4-12 show how earnings per share may be presented.

Many corporations have simple capital structures that include only common shares. For these companies, a presentation such as earnings per common share is appropriate on the income statement. In many instances, however, companies' earnings per share are subject to dilution (reduction) in the future because existing contingencies permit the issuance of additional common shares. Presentation for these corporations would include both basic EPS and fully diluted EPS.[27]

In summary, the simplicity and availability of figures for per share earnings lead inevitably to their widespread use. Because of the undue importance that the public—even the well-informed public—attaches to earnings per share, this information must be made as meaningful as possible.

Retained Earnings Statement

Objective 8

Prepare a retained earnings statement.

Net income increases retained earnings and a net loss decreases retained earnings. Both cash and share dividends decrease retained earnings. Retroactively applied changes in accounting principles and corrections of errors may either increase or decrease retained earnings. Information related to retained earnings may be shown in different ways. For example, many companies prepare a separate retained earnings statement,[28] as shown in Illustration 4-15.

The reconciliation of the beginning to the ending balance in retained earnings provides information about why net assets increased or decreased during the year. The association of dividend distributions with net income for the period indicates what management is doing with earnings: it may be plowing back into the business part or all of the earnings, distributing all current income, or distributing current income plus the accumulated earnings of prior years. Note that the retained earnings statement may be combined with the income statement by adding it on to the bottom of the income statement.

---

[26] *CICA Handbook*, Section 3500.60 and .61.

[27] Earnings per share will be covered in significant detail in Chapter 18.

[28] *Financial Reporting in Canada, 2002* (Toronto, CICA), p. 57, notes that in 2001, 148 out of 200 public companies showed the statement of Retained Earnings as a separate statement.

Illustration 4-15

Retained Earnings Statement

WOODS INC.
Retained Earnings Statement
For the Year Ended December 31, 2005

Balance, January 1, as reported		$1,050,000
Correction for understatement of net income in prior period		
(inventory error) (net of taxes of $35,000)		50,000
Balance, January 1, as adjusted		1,100,000
Add: Net income		360,000
		1,460,000
Less: Cash dividends	$100,000	
Less: Stock dividends	200,000	300,000
Balance, December 31		$1,160,000

Changes in Accounting Principle

Changes in accounting occur frequently in practice, because important events or conditions may be in dispute or uncertain at the statement date. One type of accounting change results when an accounting principle is adopted that is different from the one previously used. **Changes in accounting principle** would include a change in the method of inventory pricing from FIFO to average cost.

Changes in accounting principle are generally recognized through **retroactive adjustment**, which involves determining the effect of the policy change on the income of prior periods affected. The financial statements for all prior periods that are presented for comparative purposes should be restated except when the effect is not reasonably determinable. If all comparative years are not disclosed, a cumulative amount would be calculated and adjusted through opening retained earnings.

To illustrate, Gaubert Inc. decided in March 2004 to change from the FIFO method of valuing inventory to the weighted average method. If prices are rising, cost of sales would be higher and ending inventory lower for the preceding period.

The information presented in the 2004 financial statements is shown in Illustration 4-16.

Underlying Concept

Retroactive application ensures consistency.

Retained earnings, January 1, 2004 as previously reported	$120,000
Cumulative effect on prior years of retroactive application	
of new inventory costing method (net of $9,000 tax)	14,000
Adjusted balance of retained earnings, January 1, 2004	$106,000

The journal entry would be:

Taxes Receivable	9,000	
Retained Earnings	14,000	
Inventory		14,000

A = L + E
−14,000 −14,000
Cash flows: No effect

The above assumes no comparatives are shown. A note describing the change and its impact would be required.

Comprehensive Income

Comprehensive income includes all changes in equity during a period except for those resulting from investments by owners and distributions to owners. Comprehensive income, therefore, includes all revenues and gains, expenses and losses reported in net income, and in addition it includes gains and losses that bypass net income but affect shareholders' equity. These items that bypass the income statement are referred to as **other comprehensive income**.

An example of one of the items that is included in other comprehensive income is unrealized gains and losses on available-for-sale securities.[29] Why are they excluded from net income? Because disclosing them separately (1) highlights the impact on net income due to fluctuations in fair value, yet (2) informs the financial statement user of the gain or loss that would be incurred if the securities were sold at fair value.

The AcSB decided that the components of other comprehensive income must be displayed in a financial statement with the same prominence as other key financial statements.[30] This could be done by expanding the Income Statement or adding another statement. Regardless of the format used, net income must be added to other comprehensive income to arrive at comprehensive income. Earnings per share information related to comprehensive income is not required.[31]

Combined Income and Comprehensive Income Statement

To illustrate these presentation formats, assume that V. Gill Inc. reports the following information for 2004: sales revenue $800,000, cost of goods sold $600,000, operating expenses $90,000, and an unrealized holding gain on available-for-sale securities of $30,000, net of tax.

The combined income statement format is shown in Illustration 4-17 below. The relationship of the traditional income statement to the comprehensive income statement is apparent because net income is the starting point in the comprehensive income statement.

Illustration 4-17
Combined Income and Comprehensive Income Statement

V. GILL INC.	
Statements of Income and Comprehensive Income	
For the Year Ended December 31, 2004	
Sales revenue	$800,000
Cost of goods sold	600,000
Gross profit	200,000
Operating expenses	90,000
Net income	$110,000
Other comprehensive income	
Unrealized holding gain, net of tax	30,000
Comprehensive income	$140,000

The combined statement has the advantage of not requiring the creation of a new financial statement. However, burying net income in a subtotal on the statement is a disadvantage.

---

[29] Available-for-sale securities are further discussed in Chapter 10. Other examples of comprehensive items are certain translation gains and losses on foreign currency and unrealized gains and losses on certain hedging transactions.

[30] Proposed *CICA Handbook*, Section 1530.

[31] A company is required to display the components of other comprehensive income and related tax effects.

Statement of Shareholders' Equity

The statement of shareholders' equity reports the changes in each shareholder's equity account and in total shareholders' equity during the year, including comprehensive income. The statement of shareholders' equity is often **prepared in columnar form** with columns for each account and for total shareholders' equity.

To illustrate its presentation, assume the same information related to V. Gill Inc. and that the company had the following shareholders' equity account balances at the beginning of 2004: Common Shares $300,000; Retained Earnings $50,000; and Accumulated Other Comprehensive Income $60,000. No changes in the Common Shares account occurred during the year. A statement of shareholders' equity for V. Gill Inc. is shown in Illustration 4-18.

V. GILL INC.
Statement of Shareholders' Equity
For the Year Ended December 31, 2004

	Total	Compre-hensive Income	Retained Earnings	Accum. Other Comp. Income	Common Shares
Beginning balance	$410,000		$50,000	$60,000	$300,000
Net income	110,000	$110,000	110,000		
Other comprehensive income					
Unrealized holding gain, net of tax	30,000	30,000		30,000	
Comprehensive income		$140,000			
Ending balance	$550,000		$160,000	$90,000	$300,000

Illustration 4-18

Presentation of Comprehensive Income Items in Shareholders' Equity Statement

Because many companies already provide a statement of shareholders' equity, adding additional columns to display information related to comprehensive income is not costly.

Balance Sheet Presentation

Regardless of the display format used, the **accumulated other comprehensive income** of $90,000 is reported in the shareholders' equity section of the balance sheet of V. Gill Inc. as shown in Illustration 4-19.

V. GILL INC.
Balance Sheet
As of December 31, 2004
(Shareholders' Equity Section)

Shareholders' equity	
Common shares	$300,000
Retained earnings	160,000
Accumulated other comprehensive income	90,000
Total shareholders' equity	$550,000

Illustration 4-19

Presentation of Accumulated Other Comprehensive Income in the Balance Sheet

By providing information on the components of comprehensive income as well as total accumulated other comprehensive income, the company communicates information about all changes in net assets.[32] With this information, users will be better able to under-

---

[32] Note that prior period adjustments and the cumulative effect of changes in accounting principle are not considered other comprehensive income items.

stand the quality of the company's earnings. This information should help users predict the amounts, timing, and uncertainty of future cash flows.

Perspectives

Financial analysts assess quality of earnings and factor it into their decisions. They are often looking to see what additional information the income statements provide in terms of valuing the company's shares. When valuing the shares, analysts look at how good the numbers are at the financial statement date and then they determine whether the company can continue to produce similar or better earnings into the future.

Some attributes of high quality earnings were articulated in Illustration 4-2. To assess the quality of earnings, look for and analyse the following:

- **accounting policies**—aggressive accounting policies, soft numbers

- **notes to financial statements**—unrecognized liabilities and asset overstatement and in general measurement uncertainty

- **financial statements** as a whole—complexity of presentation or language (which may obscure the company performance or financial position)

- **income statement**—percentage of net income derived from ongoing operations, to see whether the company can produce profits primarily from its core business

- **cash flow statement**—cash from operating activities versus net income, to get a sense of whether net income is cash backed or not

- **balance sheet**—to see how the company is financed and what the revenue-generating assets are

- **other**—environmental factors such as the industry and economy. How is the company doing compared with its competitors? How is it positioning itself to take advantage of opportunities and manage risk? Where is the industry going? Are current earnings likely to be replicated in the future?

Companies often attempt to assist users in assessing results of operations and their financial position by providing modified GAAP information such as **pro-forma earnings**. As mentioned in the vignette, pro-forma earnings start with GAAP net income and add back or deduct non-recurring or non-operating items to arrive at an adjusted net income number. Pro-forma earnings are not bad per se. If the calculation of the pro-forma earnings is **clearly disclosed and explained** as well as being reconciled to net income, it hopefully adds value to the decision-making process. The danger with these numbers is that there are no standards to ensure that the calculation is **consistently** prepared and **comparable** between companies.

Summary of Learning Objectives

1 Identify the uses and limitations of an income statement.

The income statement provides investors and creditors with information that helps them predict the amounts, timing, and uncertainty of future cash flows. Also, the income statement helps users determine the risk (level of uncertainty) of not achieving particular cash flows. The limitations of an income statement are: (1) the statement does not include many items that contribute to general growth and well-being of an enterprise; (2) income numbers are often affected by the accounting methods used; and (3) income measures are subject to estimates.

2 Prepare a single-step income statement.

In a single-step income statement, just two groupings exist: revenues and expenses. Expenses are deducted from revenues to arrive at net income or loss—a single subtraction. Frequently, income tax is reported separately as the last item before net income to indicate its relationship to income before income tax.

3 Prepare a multiple-step income statement.

A multiple-step income statement shows two further classifications: (1) a separation of operating results from those obtained through the subordinate or non-operating activities of the company; and (2) a classification of expenses by functions, such as merchandising or manufacturing, selling, and administration.

4 Explain how irregular items are reported.

Irregular gains or losses or nonrecurring items are generally closed to Income Summary and are included in the income statement. These are treated in the income statement as follows: (1) Discontinued operation of a business component is classified as a separate item, after continuing operations. (2) The unusual, material, nonrecurring items that are significantly different from the customary business activities are shown in a separate section for extraordinary items, below discontinued operations. (3) Other items of a material amount that are of an unusual or nonrecurring nature and are not considered extraordinary are separately disclosed and are included as part of continuing operations.

5 Measure and report results of discontinued operations.

The gain or loss on disposal of a business component involves the sum of: (1) income or loss from operations to the financial statement date, and (2) the gain or loss on the disposal of the business component. These items are reported net of tax among the irregular items in the income statement.

6 Explain intraperiod tax allocation.

The tax expense for the year should be related, where possible, to specific items on the income statement, to provide a more informative disclosure to statement users. This procedure is called intraperiod tax allocation; that is, allocation within a period. Its main purpose is to relate the income tax expense for the fiscal period to the following items that affect the amount of the tax provisions: (1) income from continuing operations, (2) discontinued operations, and (3) extraordinary items.

7 Explain where earnings per share information is reported.

Because of the inherent dangers of focusing attention solely on earnings per share, the profession concluded that earnings per share must be disclosed on the face of the income statement. A company that reports a discontinued operation or an extraordinary item must report per share amounts for these line items either on the face of the income statement or in the notes to the financial statements.

8 Prepare a retained earnings statement.

The retained earnings statement should disclose net income (loss), dividends, prior period adjustments, and transfers to and from retained earnings (appropriations).

9 Explain how comprehensive income is reported.

Comprehensive Income may be presented at the bottom of the Income Statement or in another statement of equal prominence. The Statement of Shareholders' Equity must include the changes in the accumulated other Comprehensive Income items.

Digital Tool

Glossary

www.wiley.com/canada/kieso

KEY TERMS

all-inclusive approach, 142
business component, 143
capital maintenance
 approach, 134
changes in accounting
 principle, 151
changes in estimates, 148
comprehensive income, 152
current operating performance approach, 142
discontinued
 operations, 143
earnings management, 134
earnings per share, 149
extraordinary items, 145
formal plan, 144
income statement, 131
intraperiod tax
 allocation, 149
multiple-step income
 statement, 138
pro-forma earnings, 154
quality of earnings, 133
single-step income
 statement, 137
typical business
 activities, 146

Cash Basis Versus Accrual Basis Earnings

Differences between Cash and Accrual Bases

Objective 10
Differentiate the cash basis of accounting from the accrual basis of accounting.

Most companies use the **accrual basis** of accounting: they recognize revenue when it is earned and recognize expenses in the period incurred, without regard to the time of receipt or payment of cash. Some small enterprises and the average individual taxpayer, however, use a strict or modified cash basis approach. Under the **strict cash basis** of accounting, revenue is recorded only when the cash is received and expenses are recorded only when the cash is paid. The determination of income on the cash basis rests upon the collection of revenue and the payment of expenses, and the revenue recognition and the matching principles are ignored. Consequently, cash basis financial statements do not conform with generally accepted accounting principles.

To illustrate and contrast accrual basis accounting and cash basis accounting, assume that Quality Contractor signs an agreement to construct a garage for $22,000. In January, Quality Contractor begins construction, incurs costs of $18,000 on credit, and by the end of January delivers a finished garage to the buyer. In February, Quality Contractor collects $22,000 cash from the customer. In March, Quality pays the $18,000 due the creditors. The net incomes for each month under cash basis accounting and accrual basis accounting are as follows.

Illustration 4A-1
Income Statement—Cash Basis

QUALITY CONTRACTOR
Income Statement Cash Basis
For the Month of

	January	February	March	Total
Cash receipts	$-0-	$22,000	$-0-	$22,000
Cash payments	-0-	-0-	18,000	18,000
Net income (loss)	$-0-	$22,000	$(18,000)	$ 4,000

Illustration 4A-2
Income Statement—
Accrual Basis

QUALITY CONTRACTOR
Income Statement Accrual Basis
For the Month of

	January	February	March	Total
Revenues	$22,000	$-0-	$-0-	$22,000
Expenses	18,000	-0-	-0-	18,000
Net income (loss)	$ 4,000	$-0-	$-0-	$ 4,000

For the three months combined, total net income is the same under both cash basis accounting and accrual basis accounting; the difference is in the timing of net income. The balance sheet is also affected by the basis of accounting. For instance, if cash basis accounting were used, Quality Contractor's balance sheets at each month end would appear as follows.

Illustration 4A-3

Balance Sheets—Cash Basis

QUALITY CONTRACTOR
Balance Sheets Cash Basis
As of

	January 31	February 28	March 31
Assets			
Cash	$–0–	$22,000	$4,000
Total assets	$–0–	$22,000	$4,000
Liabilities and Owners' Equity			
Owners' equity	$–0–	$22,000	$4,000
Total liabilities and owners' equity	$–0–	$22,000	$4,000

If accrual basis accounting were used, Quality Contractor's balance sheets at each month-end would appear as follows.

Illustration 4A-4

Balance Sheets—Accrual Basis

QUALITY CONTRACTOR
Balance Sheets Accrual Basis
As of

	January 31	February 28	March 31
Assets			
Cash	$ –0–	$22,000	$ 4,000
Accounts receivable	22,000	–0–	–0–
Total assets	$22,000	$22,000	$4,000
Liabilities and Owners' Equity			
Accounts payable	$18,000	$18,000	$ 0
Owners equity	4,000	4,000	4,000
Total liabilities and owners' equity	$22,000	$22,000	$4,000

An analysis of the preceding income statements and balance sheets shows the ways in which cash basis accounting is inconsistent with basic accounting theory.

1. The cash basis understates revenues and assets from the construction and delivery of the garage in January. It ignores the $22,000 accounts receivable, representing a near-term future cash inflow.

2. The cash basis understates expenses incurred with the construction of the garage and the liability outstanding at the end of January. It ignores the $18,000 accounts payable, representing a near-term future cash outflow.

3. The cash basis understates owners' equity in January by not recognizing the revenues and the asset until February, and it overstates owners' equity in February by not recognizing the expenses and the liability until March.

In short, cash basis accounting violates the theory underlying the elements of financial statements.

The **modified cash basis**, a mixture of cash basis and accrual basis, is the method often followed by professional services firms (doctors, lawyers, accountants, consultants) and by retail, real estate, and agricultural operations. It is the pure cash basis of accounting with modifications that have substantial support, such as capitalizing and amortizing plant assets or recording inventory.[33]

Conversion from Cash Basis to Accrual Basis

Not infrequently, a cash basis or a modified cash basis set of financial statements is converted to the accrual basis for presentation to investors and creditors. To illustrate this conversion, assume that Dr. Diane Windsor keeps her accounting records on a cash basis. In the year 2005, Dr. Windsor received \$300,000 from her dental patients and paid \$170,000 for operating expenses, resulting in an excess of cash receipts over disbursements of \$130,000 (\$300,000 − \$170,000). At January 1 and December 31, 2005, she has accounts receivable, unearned service revenue, accrued liabilities, and prepaid expenses as follows.

Illustration 4A-5

Excerpt from General Ledger

	January 1, 2005	December 31, 2005
Accounts receivable	\$12,000	\$9,000
Unearned service revenue	–0–	4,000
Accrued liabilities	2,000	5,500
Prepaid expenses	1,800	2,700

Service Revenue Calculation

To convert the amount of cash received from patients to service revenue on an accrual basis, changes in accounts receivable and unearned service revenue during the year must be considered. Accounts receivable at the beginning of the year represents revenues earned last year that are collected this year. Ending accounts receivable indicates revenues earned this year that are not yet collected. Therefore, beginning accounts receivable is subtracted and ending accounts receivable is added to arrive at revenue on an accrual basis, as shown in Illustration 4A-6.

Illustration 4A-6

Conversion of Cash Receipts to Revenue—Accounts Receivable

Cash receipts from customers	(− Beginning accounts receivable) (+ Ending accounts receivable)	=	Revenue on an accrual basis

Using similar analysis, beginning unearned service revenue represents cash received last year for revenues earned this year. Ending unearned service revenue results from collections this year that will be recognized as revenue next year. Therefore, beginning unearned service revenue is added and ending unearned service revenue is subtracted to arrive at revenue on an accrual basis, as shown in Illustration 4A-7.

---

[33] A cash or modified cash basis might be used in the following situations:
1. A company that is primarily interested in cash flows (for example, a group of physicians that distributes cash-basis earnings for salaries and bonuses)
2. A company that has a limited number of financial statement users (small, closely held company with little or no debt)
3. A company that has operations that are relatively straightforward (small amounts of inventory, long-term assets, or long-term debt

Cash receipts from customers	(+ Beginning unearned service revenue) (− Ending unearned service revenue)	=	Revenue on an accrual basis

Illustration 4A-7

Conversion of Cash Receipts to Revenue—Unearned Service Revenue

Cash collected from customers, therefore, is converted to service revenue on an accrual basis as follows.

Cash receipts from customers		$300,000
Beginning accounts receivable	$(12,000)	
Ending accounts receivable	9,000	
Beginning unearned service revenue	–0–	
Ending unearned service revenue	(4,000)	(7,000)
Service revenue (accrual)		$293,000

Illustration 4A-8

Conversion of Cash Receipts to Service Revenue

Operating Expense Calculation

To convert cash paid for operating expenses during the year to operating expenses on an accrual basis, you must consider changes in prepaid expenses and accrued liabilities during the year. Beginning prepaid expenses should be recognized as expenses this year. (The cash payment occurred last year.) Therefore, the beginning prepaid expenses balance is added to cash paid for operating expenses to arrive at operating expense on an accrual basis.

Conversely, ending prepaid expenses result from cash payments made this year for expenses to be reported next year. (The expense recognition is deferred to a future period.) As a result, ending prepaid expenses are deducted from cash paid for expenses, as shown in Illustration 4A-9.

Cash paid for operating expenses	(+ Beginning prepaid expenses) (− Ending prepaid expenses)	Expenses on an accrual basis

Illustration 4A-9

Conversion of Cash Payments to Expenses— Prepaid Expenses

Using similar analysis, beginning accrued liabilities result from expenses recognized last year that require cash payments this year. Ending accrued liabilities relate to expenses recognized this year that have not been paid. Beginning accrued liabilities, therefore, are deducted and ending accrued liabilities added to cash paid for expenses to arrive at expense on an accrual basis, as shown in Illustration 4A-10.

Cash paid for operating expenses	(+ Beginning accrued liabilities) (− Ending accrued liabilities)	Expenses on an accrual basis

Illustration 4A-10

Conversion of Cash Payments to Expenses— Accrued Liabilities

Cash paid for operating expenses, therefore, is converted to operating expenses on an accrual basis for Dr. Diane Windsor as follows.

Cash paid for operating expenses		$170,000
Beginning prepaid expense	$1,800	
Ending prepaid expense	(2,700)	
Beginning accrued liabilities	(2,000)	
Ending accrued liabilities	5,500	2,600
Operating expenses (accrual)		$172,600

Illustration 4A-11

Conversion of Cash Paid to Operating Expenses

This entire conversion can be shown in work sheet form as follows.

Illustration 4A-12

Conversion of Statement of Cash Receipts and Disbursements to Income Statement

DIANE WINDSOR, D.D.S.
Conversion of Income Statement Data from Cash Basis to Accrual Basis
For the Year 2005

	Cash Basis	Add	Deduct	Accrual Basis
Collections from customers	$300,000			
− Accounts receivable, Jan. 1			$12,000	
+ Accounts receivable, Dec. 31		$9,000		
+ Unearned service revenue, Jan. 1		—	—	
− Unearned service revenue, Dec. 31			4,000	
Service revenue				$293,000
Disbursement for expenses				
+ Prepaid expenses, Jan. 1		1,800		
− Prepaid expenses, Dec. 31			2,700	
− Accrued liabilities, Jan. 1			2,000	
+ Accrued liabilities, Dec. 31	170,000	5,500		
Operating expenses				172,600
Excess of cash collections over Disbursements—cash basis	$130,000			
Net income—accrual basis				$120,400

Using this approach, collections and disbursements on a cash basis are adjusted to revenue and expense on an accrual basis to arrive at accrual net income. In any conversion from the cash basis to the accrual basis, depreciation or amortization expense is an expense in arriving at net income on an accrual basis.

Theoretical Weaknesses of the Cash Basis

Underlying Concept

Accrual based net income is a good predictor of future cash flows

The cash basis does report exactly when cash is received and when cash is disbursed. To many people that information represents something solid, something concrete. Isn't cash what it is all about? Does it make sense to invent something, design it, produce it, market and sell it, if you aren't going to get cash for it in the end? If so, then what is the merit of accrual accounting?

Today's economy is based more on credit than cash. And the accrual basis, not the cash basis, recognizes all aspects of the credit phenomenon. Investors, creditors, and other decision-makers seek timely information about an enterprise's future cash flows. Accrual basis accounting provides this information by reporting the cash inflows and outflows associated with earnings activities as soon as these cash flows can be estimated with an acceptable degree of certainty. Receivables and payables are forecasters of future cash inflows and outflows. In other words, accrual basis accounting aids in predicting future cash flows by reporting transactions and other events with cash consequences at the time the transactions and events occur, rather than when the cash is received and paid.

Summary of Learning Objective for Appendix 4A

Digital Tool
Glossary

10 Differentiate the cash basis of accounting from the accrual basis of accounting.

Accrual basis accounting provides information about cash inflows and outflows associated with earnings activities as soon as these cash flows can be estimated with an acceptable degree of certainty. That is, accrual basis accounting aids in predicting future cash flows by reporting transactions and events with cash consequences at the time the transactions and events occur, rather than when the cash is received and paid.

www.wiley.com/canada/kieso

KEY TERMS

accrual basis, 156
modified cash basis, 158
strict cash basis, 156

Note: All asterisked assignment material relates to the appendix to the chapter.

Brief Exercises

BE4-1 Allen Corp. had sales revenue of $740,000 in 2005. Other items recorded during the year were:

Cost of goods sold	$320,000
Wage expense	120,000
Income tax expense	115,000
Increase in value of company reputation	35,000
Other operating expenses	10,000
Unrealized gain on value of patents	20,000

Prepare a single-step income statement for Allen for 2005. Allen has 100,000 common shares outstanding.

BE4-2 Alley Corporation had net sales of $2,780,000 and investment revenue of $103,000 in 2005. Its 2005 expenses were: cost of goods sold, $2,190,000; selling expenses, $272,000; administrative expenses, $211,000; interest expense, $76,000; and income tax expense, $40,000. Prepare a single-step income statement for Alley Corporation, which has 10,000 common shares outstanding.

BE4-3 Use the information provided in BE4-2 for Alley Corporation to prepare a multiple-step income statement.

BE4-4 Green Corporation had income from continuing operations of $12.6 million in 2005. During 2005, it disposed of its restaurant division at an after-tax loss of $89,000. Prior to disposal, the division operated at a loss of $315,000 (net of tax) in 2005. Green had 10 million common shares outstanding during 2005. Prepare a partial income statement for Green beginning with income from continuing operations.

BE4-5 Boyz Corporation had income before income taxes for 2005 of $7.3 million. In addition, it suffered an unusual and infrequent pretax loss of $1,770,000 from a volcano eruption. Of this, $500,000 was insured. The corporation's tax rate is 30%. Prepare a partial income statement for Boyz beginning with income before income taxes. The corporation had 5 million common shares outstanding during 2005.

BE4-6 Kingston Limited has recorded bad debts expense in the past at a rate of 1.5% of net sales. In 2004, Kingston decides to increase its estimate to 2%. If the new rate had been used in prior years, cumulative bad debt expense would have been $380,000 instead of $285,000. In 2004, bad debt expense will be $120,000 instead of $90,000. If Kingston's tax rate is 40%, how should this be reflected in the financial statements? Show calculations.

BE4-7 In 2006, Puckett Corporation reported net income of $1.2 million. It declared and paid preferred share dividends of $250,000. During 2006, Puckett had a weighted average of 190,000 common shares outstanding. Calculate Puckett's 2006 earnings per share.

BE4-8 Turgeon Corporation had retained earnings of $529,000 at January 1, 2005. Net income in 2005 was $1,496,000 and cash dividends of $650,000 were declared and paid. Prepare a 2005 retained earnings statement for Turgeon Corporation.

BE4-9 Use the information provided in BE4-9 to prepare a retained earnings statement for Turgeon Corporation, assuming that in 2005 Turgeon discovered that it had overstated 2003 amortization by $25,000 (net of tax).

BE4-10   Garok Inc. decided on Sept. 1, 2005 to dispose of its Cardassian Division. The Cardassian Division operated at a loss of $190,000 during the first eight months of 2005 and a loss of $114,000 during the last four months of the year. Garok estimates the division will be sold at a gain of $85,000 in 2006. Garok's tax rate is 40%. Prepare the discontinued operations section of Garok's 2005 income statement.

BE4-11   On January 1, 2004 Creature Corp. had cash and common shares of $60,000. At that date, the company had no other asset, liability, or equity balances. On January 2, 2004, it purchased for cash $20,000 of equity securities that it classified as available-for-sale investments. It received cash dividends of $3,000 during the year on these securities. In addition, it has an unrealized holding gain on these securities of $5,000 net of tax. Determine the following amounts for 2004: (a) net income; (b) comprehensive income; (c) other comprehensive income; and (d) accumulated other comprehensive income (end of 2004).

*BE4-12   Smith Corp. had cash receipts from customers in 2005 of $152,000. Cash payments for operating expenses were $97,000. Smith has determined that at January 1, accounts receivable was $13,000 and prepaid expenses were $17,500. At December 31, accounts receivable was $18,600, and prepaid expenses were $23,200. Calculate (a) service revenue and (b) operating expenses.

Exercises

Interactive
Homework

E4-1   (Calculation of Net Income)   Presented below are changes in all the account balances of Reiner Furniture Ltd. during the current year, except for retained earnings.

	Increase (Decrease)		Increase (Decrease)
Cash	$ 79,000	Accounts payable	$(51,000)
Accounts receivable (net)	45,000	Bonds payable	82,000
Inventory	127,000	Common shares	125,000
Investments	(47,000)	Contributed surplus	13,000

Instructions
Calculate the net income for the current year, assuming that there were no entries in the Retained Earnings account except for net income and a dividend declaration of $19,000, which was paid in the current year.

Interactive
Homework

E4-2   (Calculation of Net Income)   Presented below is selected information pertaining to the Videohound Video Company during 2005.

Cash balance, January 1	$ 23,000
Accounts receivable, January 1	19,000
Collections from customers during year	200,000
Capital account balance, January 1	38,000
Total assets, January 1	75,000
Cash investment added, July 1	5,000
Total assets, December 31	101,000
Cash balance, December 31	20,000
Accounts receivable, December 31	36,000
Merchandise taken for personal use	11,000
Total liabilities, December 31	41,000

Instructions
Calculate the net income for 2005.

Interactive
Homework

E4-3   (Income Statement Items)   Presented below are certain account balances of Paczki Products Corp.

Rental revenue	$ 6,500	Sales discounts	7,800
Interest expense	12,700	Selling expenses	99,400
Beginning retained earnings	114,400	Sales	390,000
Ending retained earnings	134,000	Income tax	31,000
Dividends earned	71,000	Cost of goods sold	184,400
Sales returns	12,400	Administrative expenses	82,500

Instructions
From the foregoing, calculate the following: (a) total net revenue; (b) net income; (c) dividends declared during the current year.

E4-4 (Single-Step Income Statement) The financial records of Jones Inc. were destroyed by fire at the end of 2005. Fortunately the controller had kept certain statistical data related to the income statement as presented below.

1. The beginning merchandise inventory was $84,000 and decreased 20% during the current year.

2. Sales discounts amounted to $15,000.

3. 15,000 common shares were outstanding for the entire year.

4. Interest expense was $20,000.

5. The income tax rate was 40%.

6. Cost of goods sold amounted to $420,000.

7. Administrative expenses were 20% of cost of goods sold but only 8% of gross sales.

8. Four-fifths of the operating expenses related to sales activities.

Instructions

From the foregoing information, prepare an income statement for the year 2005 in single-step form.

E4-5 (Multiple-Step and Single-Step) Two accountants for the firm of Elwes and Wright are arguing about the merits of presenting an income statement in a multiple-step versus a single-step format. The discussion involves the following 2005 information related to Singh Corp. ($000 omitted).

ADMINISTRATIVE EXPENSE	
Officers' salaries	$3,900
Amortization of office furniture and equipment	3,560
Cost of goods sold	58,570
Rental revenue	15,230
SELLING EXPENSE	
Transportation-out	2,290
Sales commissions	7,280
Amortization of sales equipment	6,480
Sales	106,500
Income tax	9,070
Interest expense on bonds payable	1,860

Instructions

(a) Prepare an income statement for the year 2005 using the multiple-step form. Common shares outstanding for 2005 total 30,550 ($000 omitted).

(b) Prepare an income statement for the year 2005 using the single-step form.

(c) Which one do you prefer? Discuss.

E4-6 (Multiple-Step and Extraordinary Items) The following balances were taken from the books of Voisine Corp. on December 31, 2005.

Interest revenue	$86,000	Accumulated amortization—	
		equipment	$40,000
Cash	51,000	Accumulated amortization—	
		building	28,000
Sales	1,380,000	Notes receivable	155,000
Accounts receivable	150,000	Selling expenses	194,000
Prepaid insurance	20,000	Accounts payable	170,000
Sales returns and allowances	150,000	Bonds payable	100,000
Allowance for doubtful accounts	7,000	Administrative and general	
		expenses	97,000
Sales discounts	45,000	Accrued liabilities	32,000
Land	100,000	Interest expense	60,000
Equipment	200,000	Notes payable	100,000
Building	140,000	Loss from earthquake damage	
Cost of goods sold	621,000	(extraordinary item)	150,000
Common shares	500,000	Retained earnings	21,000

Assume the total effective tax rate on all items is 44%.

Instructions

Prepare a multiple-step income statement; 200,000 common shares were outstanding during the year.

E4-7   (Multiple-Step and Single-Step)   The accountant of Whitney Shoe Corp. has compiled the following information from the company's records as a basis for an income statement for the year ended December 31, 2005.

Rental revenue	$129,000
Interest on notes payable	18,000
Market appreciation on land above cost	51,000
Wages and salaries—sales	124,800
Materials and supplies used	17,600
Income tax	37,400
Wages and salaries—administrative	135,900
Other administrative expense	51,700
Cost of goods sold	496,000
Net sales	980,000
Amortization on plant assets	
(70% selling, 30% administrative)	65,000
Dividends declared	16,000

There were 40,000 common shares outstanding during the year.

Instructions

(a) Prepare a multiple-step income statement.

(b) Prepare a single-step income statement.

(c) Which format do you prefer? Discuss.

E4-8   (Multiple-Step and Single-Step—Periodic Inventory Method)   Presented below is income statement information related to Ying-Wai Corporation for the year 2005.

Administrative expenses:		Transportation-in	$14,000
Officers' salaries	$39,000	Purchase discounts	10,000
Amortization expense—building	28,500	Inventory (beginning)	120,000
Office supplies expense	9,500	Sales returns and allowances	15,000
Inventory (ending)	137,000	Selling expenses:	
Flood damage		Sales salaries	71,000
(pretax extraordinary item)	50,000	Amortization expense—store equipment	18,000
Purchases	600,000	Store supplies expense	9,000
Sales	930,000		

In addition, the corporation has other revenue from dividends received of $20,000 and other expense of interest on notes payable of $9,000. There are 20,000 common shares outstanding for the year. The total effective tax rate on all income is 34%.

Instructions

(a) Prepare a multiple-step income statement for 2005.

(b) Prepare a single-step income statement for 2005.

(c) Discuss the relative merits of the two income statements.

E4-9   (Multiple-Step Statement with Retained Earnings)   Presented below is information related to Gottlieb Corp. for the year 2005.

Net sales	$1,300,000	Write-off of inventory due to	
		obsolescence	$ 80,000
Cost of goods sold	780,000	Amortization expense omitted	
Selling expenses	65,000	by accident in 2004	55,000
Administrative expenses	48,000	Casualty loss (extraordinary	
		item) before taxes	50,000
Dividend revenue	20,000	Dividends declared	45,000
Interest revenue	7,000	Retained earnings at	
		December 31, 2004	980,000

Effective tax rate of 44% on all items.

Instructions

(a) Prepare a multiple-step income statement for 2005. Assume that 40,000 common shares are outstanding.

(b) Prepare a separate retained earnings statement for 2005.

E4-10 (Earnings per Share) The shareholders' equity section of Tkachuk Corporation appears below as of December 31, 2006.

8% cumulative preferred shares, authorized	
100,000 shares, outstanding 80,000 shares	$4,500,000
Common shares, authorized and issued	
10 million shares	10,000,000
Contributed surplus	10,500,000
	25,000,000
Retained earnings	177,000,000
	$202,000,000

Net income of $43 million for 2006 reflects a total effective tax rate of 44%. Included in the net income figure is a loss of $15 million (before tax) as a result of a major casualty.

Instructions

Calculate earnings per share data as they should appear on the financial statements of Tkachuk Corporation.

E4-11 (Condensed Income Statement Periodic Inventory Method) Presented below are selected ledger accounts of Sooyoun Corporation at December 31, 2004.

Cash	$185,000	Travel and entertainment	$ 69,000
Merchandise inventory	535,000	Accounting and legal services	33,000
Sales	4,275,000	Insurance expense	24,000
Advances from customers	117,000	Advertising	54,000
Purchases	2,786,000	Transportation-out	93,000
Sales discounts	34,000	Amortization of office	48,000
Purchase discounts	27,000	Amortization of sales equipment	36,000
Sales salaries	284,000	Telephone-sales	17,000
Office salaries	346,000	Utilities—office	32,000
Purchase returns	15,000	Miscellaneous office expenses	8,000
Sales returns	79,000	Rental revenue	240,000
Transportation-in	72,000	Extraordinary loss (before tax)	70,000
Accounts receivable	142,500	Interest expense	176,000
Sales commissions	83,000	Common shares	900,000

Sooyoun's effective tax rate on all items is 34%. A physical inventory indicates that the ending inventory is $686,000. The number or common shares outstanding is 90,000.

Instructions

Prepare a condensed 2004 income statement for Sooyoun Corporation.

E4-12 (Retained Earnings Statement) Zambrano Corporation began operations on January 1, 2002. During its first three years of operations, Zambrano reported net income and declared dividends as follows.

	Net income	Dividends declared
2002	$10,000	$-0-
2003	135,000	$30,000
2004	160,000	$50,000

The following information relates to 2005:

Income before income tax,	$340,000
Prior period adjustment: understatement of 2003 amortization expense (before taxes)	$45,000
Cumulative increase in prior year's income from change in inventory methods (before taxes),	$35,000
Dividends declared (of this amount, $25,000 will be paid on January 15, 2006),	$100,000
Effective tax rate is	39%

Instructions
Prepare a 2005 retained earnings statement for Zambrano Corporation.

E4-13   (Earnings per Share)   At December 31, 2004, Naoya Corporation had the following shares outstanding:

10% cumulative preferred shares,	$10,750,000
107,500 shares outstanding	
Common shares, 4,000,000 shares outstanding	20,000,000

During 2005, Naoya's only share transaction was the issuance of 400,000 common shares on April 1. During 2005, the following also occurred:

Income from continuing operations before taxes	$23,650,000
Discontinued operations (loss before taxes)	$3,225,000
Preferred dividends declared	$1,075,000
Common dividends declared	$2,200,000
Effective tax rate	35%

Instructions
Calculate earnings per share data as they should appear in the 2005 income statement of Naoya Corporation.

E4-14   (Discontinued Operations)   Assume that Alzado Inc. decides to sell CBTV, its television subsidiary, on September 30, 2004. This sale qualifies for discontinued operations treatment. Assume a formal plan exists to dispose of the subsidiary. Pertinent data regarding the operations of the TV subsidiary are as follows:

Loss from operations from beginning of year to September 30, $1,000,000 (net of tax).
Loss from operations from September 30 to end of 2004, $700,000 (net of tax).
Estimated loss on sale of net assets on disposal date June 1, 2005, $150,000 (net of tax).
The year end is December.

Instructions

(a) What is the net income/loss from discontinued operations reported in 2004? In 2005?

(b) Prepare the discontinued operations section of the income statement for the year ended 2004.

(c) If the amount reported in 2005 as gain or loss from disposal of a segment by Alzado Inc. proves to be materially incorrect, when and how is the correction reported, if at all?

E4-15   (Discontinued Operations)   On October 5, 2005, Marzook Inc.'s board of directors decided to dispose of the Song and Elwood Division. A formal plan was approved. Marzook is a real estate firm with approximately 25% of its income from management of apartment complexes. The Song and Elwood Division contracts to clean apartments after tenants move out in the Marzook complexes and several others. The board decided to dispose of the division because of unfavourable operating results.

Net income for Marzook was $91,000 after tax (assume a 30% rate) for the fiscal year ended December 31, 2005. The Song and Elwood Division accounted for only $4,200 (after tax) of this amount. The average number of common shares outstanding was 20,000 for the year.

Because of the unfavourable results and the extreme competition, the board believes selling the business intact is impossible. Its final decision is to complete all current contracts, the last of which expires on May 3, 2006, and then auction off the cleaning equipment on May 10, 2006. This, the only asset of the division, has a carrying value of $25,000 at October 5, 2005. The board believes the sale proceeds will approximate $5,000 after the auction expenses. Currently the estimated fair value of the equipment is $10,000.

Instructions

(a) Prepare the income statement and the appropriate footnotes that relate to the Song and Elwood Division for 2005. The income statement should begin with income from continuing operations before income taxes. Earnings per share calculations are not required.

(b) Explain how the assets would be valued and presented on the balance sheet.

E4-16   (Comprehensive Income)   Rosy Randall Corporation reported the following for 2004: net sales $1,200,000; cost of sales $750,000; selling and administrative expenses $320,000; and unrealized holding gains on available-for-sale securities $18,000.

Instructions
Prepare a statement of comprehensive income. Ignore taxes and EPS.

E4-17 (Comprehensive Income) DougieDoug Limited reports the following for 2004: sales revenues $700,000; cost of sales $500,000; operating expenses $80,000; and an unrealized holding loss on available-for-sale securities for 2004 of $60,000. It declared and paid a cash dividend of $10,000 in 2004. The company has January 1, 2004 balances in common shares of $350,000; accumulated other comprehensive income $80,000; and retained earnings of $90,000. It issued no shares during 2004.

Instructions
Prepare a statement of shareholders' equity.

*E4-18 (Cash and Accrual Basis) Roger Corp. maintains its financial records on the cash basis of accounting. Interested in securing a long-term loan from its regular bank, the company requests you, as an independent CA, to convert its cash basis income statement data to the accrual basis. You are provided with the following summarized data covering 2004, 2005, and 2006.

Interactive
Homework

	2004	2005	2006
Cash receipts from sales:			
On 2004 sales	$295,000	$160,000	$ 30,000
On 2005 sales	–0–	355,000	90,000
On 2006 sales	–0–		408,000
Cash payments for expenses:			
On 2004 expenses	185,000	67,000	25,000
On 2005 expenses	40,000[a]	160,000	55,000
On 2006 expenses	–0–	45,000[b]	218,000

[a]Prepayments of 2005 expense
[b]Prepayments of 2006 expense

Instructions
Using the data above, prepare abbreviated income statements for the years 2004 and 2005 on:

(a) cash basis

(b) accrual basis

Problems

P4-1 Presented below is information related to Zalev Corp. for 2005.

Retained earnings balance, January 1, 2005	$1,980,000
Sales for the year	35,000,000
Cost of goods sold	27,000,000
Interest revenue	170,000
Selling and administrative expenses	4,700,000
Write-off of goodwill (not tax deductible)	520,000
Income taxes for 2005	768,000
Assessment for additional 2003 income taxes (normal recurring)	500,000
Gain on the sale of investments (normal recurring)	110,000
Loss due to flood damage—extraordinary item (net of tax)	390,000
Loss on the disposition of the wholesale division (net of tax)	440,000
Operating loss for the wholesale division (net of tax)	90,000
Dividends declared on common shares	250,000
Dividends declared on preferred shares	70,000

Instructions
Prepare a multi-step income statement and a retained earnings statement. Zalev decided to discontinue its entire wholesale operations and to retain its manufacturing operations. On September 15, Zalev sold the wholesale operations to Roger Corp. During 2005, there were 800,000 common shares outstanding all year.

P4-2   Presented below is the trial balance of Blige Corporation at December 31, 2006.

BLIGE CORPORATION
Trial Balance
Year Ended December 31, 2006

	Debits	Credits
Purchase discounts		$10,000
Cash	$205,100	
Accounts receivable	105,000	
Rent revenue		18,000
Retained earnings		260,000
Salaries payable		18,000
Sales		1,000,000
Notes receivable	110,000	
Accounts payable		49,000
Accumulated amortization— equipment		28,000
Sales discounts	14,500	
Sales returns	17,500	
Notes payable		70,000
Selling expenses	232,000	
Administrative expenses	99,000	
Common shares		300,000
Income tax expense	38,500	
Cash dividends	45,000	
Allowance for doubtful accounts		5,000
Supplies	14,000	
Freight-in	20,000	
Land	70,000	
Equipment	140,000	
Bonds payable		100,000
Gain on sale of land		30,000
Accumulated amortization—building		19,600
Merchandise inventory	89,000	
Building	98,000	
Purchases	610,000	
Totals	$1,907,600	$1,907,600

A physical count of inventory on December 31 resulted in an inventory amount of $124,000.

Instructions
Prepare a single-step income statement and a retained earnings statement. Assume that the only changes in the retained earnings during the current year were from net income and dividends. Thirty thousand common shares were outstanding the entire year.

P4-3   Charyk Inc. reported income from continuing operations before taxes during 2005 of $1,790,000. Additional transactions occurring in 2005 but not considered in the $1,790,000 are as follows.

1. The corporation experienced an insured flood loss (extraordinary) in the amount of $80,000 during the year.

2. At the beginning of 2003, the corporation purchased a machine for $54,000 (salvage value of $9,000) that had a useful life of six years. The bookkeeper used straight-line amortization for 2003, 2004, and 2005 but failed to deduct the salvage value in calculating the amortization base.

3. Sale of securities held as a part of its portfolio resulted in a loss of $107,000 (pretax).

4. When its president died, the corporation realized $100,000 from an insurance policy. The cash surrender value of this policy had been carried on the books as an investment in the amount of $46,000 (the gain is nontaxable).

5. The corporation disposed of its recreational division at a loss of $115,000 before taxes. Assume that this transaction meets the criteria for discontinued operations.

6. The corporation decided to change its method of inventory pricing from average cost to the FIFO method. The effect of this change on prior years is to increase 2003 income by $60,000 and decrease 2004 income by $20,000 before taxes. The FIFO method has been used for 2005.

Instructions

Prepare an income statement for the year 2005 starting with income from continuing operations before taxes. Calculate earnings per share as it should be shown on the face of the income statement. Common shares outstanding for the year are 80,000 shares. (Assume a tax rate of 40% on all items, unless nontaxable as noted.)

P4-4 The following account balances were included in the trial balance of Reid Corporation at June 30, 2005.

Sales	$1,678,500	Amortization of office furniture	
Sales discounts	31,150	and equipment	$7,250
Cost of goods sold	896,770	Real estate and other local taxes	7,320
Sales salaries	56,260	Bad debt expense—selling	4,850
Sales commissions	97,600	Building expense—prorated to	
Travel expense—salespersons	28,930	administration	9,130
Freight-out	21,400	Miscellaneous office expenses	6,000
Entertainment expense	14,820	Sales returns	62,300
Telephone and Internet—sales	9,030	Dividends received	38,000
Amortization of sales equipment	4,980	Bond interest expense	18,000
Building expense prorated to sales	6,200	Income taxes	133,000
Miscellaneous selling expenses	4,715	Amortization understatement due to	
Office supplies used	3,450	error—2003 (net of tax)	17,700
Telephone and Internet—Administration	2,820	Dividends declared on preferred shares	9,000
		Dividends declared on common shares	32,000

The Retained Earnings account had a balance of $287,000 at June 30, 2005, before closing. There are 180,000 common shares outstanding.

Instructions

(a) Using the multiple-step form, prepare an income statement and an unappropriated retained earnings statement for the year ended June 30, 2005.

(b) Using the single-step form, prepare an income statement for the year ended June 30, 2005.

P4-5 Presented below is a combined single-step income and retained earnings statement for Pereira Corp. for 2006.

	($000 omitted)	
Net sales		$640,000
Cost and expenses:		
Cost of goods sold		500,000
Selling, general, and administrative expenses		66,000
Other, net		17,000
		583,000
Income before income tax		57,000
Income tax		19,400
Net income		37,600
Retained earnings at beginning of period,		
as previously reported	141,000	
Adjustment required for correction of error	(7,000)	
Retained earnings at beginning of period, as restated		134,000
Dividends on common shares		(12,200)
Retained earnings at end of period		$159,400

Additional facts are as follows:

1. "Selling, general, and administrative expenses" for 2006 included a usual but infrequently occurring charge of $10.5 million.

2. Other, net for 2006 included an extraordinary item (charge) of $9 million. If the extraordinary item (charge) had not occurred, income taxes for 2006 would have been $22.4 million instead of $19.4 million.

3. "Adjustment required for correction of an error" was a result of a change in estimate (useful life of certain assets reduced to eight years and a catch-up adjustment made).

4. Pereira Company disclosed earnings per common share for net income in the notes to the financial statements.

Instructions

Determine from these additional facts whether the presentation of the facts in the Pereira income and retained earnings statement is appropriate. If the presentation is not appropriate, describe the appropriate presentation and discuss its theoretical rationale. (Do not prepare a revised statement.)

P4-6   Below is the retained earnings account for the year 2005 for LeClair Corp.

Retained earnings, January 1, 2005		$257,600
Add:		
Gain on sale of investments (net of tax)	$41,200	
Net income	84,500	
Refund on litigation with government (net of tax)	21,600	
Recognition of income earned in 2005, but omitted from income statement in that year (net of tax)	25,400	172,700
		430,300
Deduct:		
Loss on discontinued operations (net of tax)	25,000	
Write-off of goodwill (net of tax)	60,000	
Cumulative effect on income in changing from straight-line amortization to accelerated amortization in 2005	18,200	
Cash dividends declared	32,000	135,200
Retained earnings, December 31, 2005		$295,100

Instructions

(a) Prepare a corrected retained earnings statement. LeClair Corp. normally sells investments of the type mentioned above.

(b) State where the items that do not appear in the corrected retained earnings statement should be shown.

P4-7   The Tamayo Corporation commenced business on January 1, 2002. Recently the corporation has had several unusual accounting problems related to the presentation of its income statement for financial reporting purposes.

You are the CA for Tamayo and have been asked to examine the following data.

TAMAYO CORPORATION
Income Statement
For the Year Ended December 31, 2005

Sales	$9,500,000
Cost of goods sold	5,900,000
Gross profit	3,600,000
Selling and administrative expense	1,300,000
Income before income tax	2,300,000
Income tax (30%)	690,000
Net income	$1,610,000

In addition, this information was provided:

1. The controller mentioned that the corporation has had difficulty in collecting on several of its receivables. For this reason, the bad debt write-off was increased from 1% to 2% of sales. The controller estimates that if this rate had been used in past periods, an additional $83,000 worth of expense would have been charged. The bad debt expense for the current period was calculated using the new rate and is part of selling and administrative expense.

2. Common shares outstanding at the end of 2005 totalled 400,000. No additional shares were purchased or sold during 2005.

3. The following items were not included in the income statement.

   (a) Inventory in the amount of $72,000 was obsolete.

   (b) The major casualty loss suffered by the corporation was partially uninsured and cost $127,000, net of tax (extraordinary item).

4. Retained earnings as of January 1, 2005 was $2.8 million. Cash dividends of $700,000 were paid in 2005.

5. In January 2005, Tamayo changed its method of accounting for plant assets from the straight-line method to the accelerated method (double-declining balance). The controller has prepared a schedule indicating what amortization expense would have been in previous periods if the double-declining method had been used. (The effective tax rate for past years was 30%.) Assume that this change results in more reliable and relevant presentation.

	Amortization Expense under Straight-Line	Amortization Expense under Double-Declining	Difference
2002	$275,000	$150,000	$175,000
2003	75,000	112,500	37,500
2004	75,000	84,375	9,375
	$225,000	$346,875	$121,875

Instructions

(a) Prepare the income statement for Tamayo Corporation in accordance with professional pronouncements. Do not prepare notes to the financial statements.

(b) Prepare a combined statement of net income and retained earnings.

P4-8 Rap Corp. has 100,000 common shares outstanding. In 2005, the company reports income from continuing operations before taxes of $2,210,000. Additional transactions not considered in the $2,210,000 are as follows.

1. In 2005, Rap Corp. sold equipment for $140,000. The machine had originally cost $80,000 and had accumulated amortization of $36,000. The gain or loss is considered ordinary.

2. The company discontinued operations of one of its subsidiaries during the current year at a loss of $290,000 before taxes. Assume that this transaction meets the criteria for discontinued operations. The loss on operations of the discontinued subsidiary was $90,000 before taxes; the loss from disposal of the subsidiary was $200,000 before taxes.

3. The sum of $500,000, applicable to a breached 2001 contract, was received as a result of a lawsuit. Prior to the award, legal counsel was uncertain about the outcome of the suit and had not established a receivable.

4. In 2005, the company reviewed its accounts receivable and determined that $46,000 of accounts receivable that had been carried for years appeared unlikely to be collected. No allowance for doubtful accounts was previously set up.

5. An internal audit discovered that amortization of intangible assets was understated by $35,000 (net of tax) in a prior period. The amount was charged against retained earnings.

Instructions

Analyse the above information and prepare an income statement for the year 2005, starting with income from continuing operations before income taxes. Calculate earnings per share as it should be shown on the face of the income statement. (Assume a total effective tax rate of 38% on all items, unless otherwise indicated.)

P4-9 Campbell Corporation management formally decided to discontinue operation of its Rocketeer Division on November 1, 2004. Campbell is a successful corporation with earnings in excess of $150 million before taxes for each of the past five years. The Rocketeer Division is being discontinued because it has not contributed to this profitable performance.

The principal assets of this division are the land, plant, and equipment used to manufacture engine components. The land, plant, and equipment had a net book value of $96 million on November 1, 2004.

Campbell's management has entered into negotiations for a cash sale of the facility for $87 million. The expected sale date and final disposal of the segment is July 1, 2005. Campbell Corporation has a fiscal year ending May 31. The results of operations for the Rocketeer Division for the 2004–2005 fiscal year and the estimated results for June 2005 are presented below. The before-tax losses after October 31, 2004 are calculated without amortization on the plant and equipment because the net book value as of November 1, 2004 is being used as a basis for negotiating for the sale.

Period	Before-tax Income (Loss)
June 1, 2004 to October 31, 2004	$(6,100,000)
November 1, 2004 to May 31, 2005	$(3,900,000)
June 1–30, 2005 (estimated)	$(750,000)

The Rocketeer Division will be accounted for as a discontinued operation on Campbell's 2004–2005 fiscal year financial statements. Campbell is subject to a 40% tax rate on operating income and all gains and losses.

Instructions

(a) Explain how the Rocketeer Division's assets would be reported on Campbell Corporation's balance sheet as of May 31, 2005.

(b) Explain how the discontinued operations and pending sale of the Rocketeer Division would be reported on Campbell Corporation's income statement for the year ended May 31, 2005.

(CMA adapted)

*P4-10   On January 1, 2005, Jill Monroe and Jenni Meno formed a computer sales and service enterprise in Montreal by investing $90,000 cash. The new company, Razorback Sales and Service, has the following transactions during January.

1. Pays $6,000 in advance for 3 months' rent of office, showroom, and repair space.

2. Purchases 40 personal computers at a cost of $1,500 each, 6 graphics computers at a cost of $3,000 each, and 25 printers at a cost of $450 each, paying cash upon delivery.

3. Sales, repair, and office employees earn $12,600 in salaries during January, of which $3,000 was still payable at the end of January.

4. Sells 30 personal computers at $2,550 each, 4 graphics computers for $4,500 each, and 15 printers for $750 each; $75,000 is received in cash in January and $30,750 is sold on a deferred payment plan.

5. Other operating expenses of $8,400 are incurred and paid for during January; $2,000 of incurred expenses are payable at January 31.

Instructions

(a) Using the transaction data above, prepare (1) a cash basis income statement and (2) an accrual basis income statement for the month of January.

(b) Using the transaction data above, prepare (1) a cash basis balance sheet and (2) an accrual basis balance sheet as of January 31, 2005.

(c) Identify the items in the cash basis financial statements that make cash basis accounting inconsistent with the theory underlying the elements of financial statements.

*P4-11   Dr. John Gleason, M.D., maintains the accounting records of Bones Clinic on a cash basis. During 2005, Dr. Gleason collected $146,000 in revenues and paid $55,470 in expenses.

At January 1, 2005, and December 31, 2005, he had accounts receivable, unearned service revenue, accrued expenses, and prepaid expenses as follows (all long-lived assets are rented).

	January 1	December 31
Accounts receivable	$9,250	$16,100
Unearned service revenue	2,840	1,620
Accrued expenses	3,435	2,200
Prepaid expenses	2,000	1,775

Instructions

Last week Dr. Gleason asked you, his CA, to help him determine his income on the accrual basis. Write a letter to him explaining what you did to calculate net income on the accrual basis. Be sure to state net income on the accrual basis and to include a schedule of your calculations.

P4-12   Amos Corporation was incorporated and began business on January 1, 2004. It has been successful and now requires a bank loan for additional working capital to finance expansion. The bank has requested an audited income statement for the year 2004. The accountant for Amos Corporation provides you with the following income statement, which Amos plans to submit to the bank.

AMOS CORPORATION
Income Statement

Sales		$850,000
Dividends		32,300
Gain on recovery of insurance proceeds from		
earthquake loss (extraordinary)		38,500
		920,800
Less:		
Selling expenses	$100,100	
Cost of goods sold	510,000	
Advertising expense	13,700	
Loss on obsolescence of inventories	34,000	
Loss on discontinued operations	48,600	
Administrative expense	73,400	779,800
Income before income tax		140,000
Income tax		56,000
Net income		$84,000

Instructions

Indicate the deficiencies in the income statement presented above. Assume that the corporation desires a single-step income statement.

P4-13 The following represents a recent income statement for Baring Corp.

Sales	$21,924,000,000
Costs and expenses	20,773,000,000
Income from operations	1,151,000,000
Other income	122,000,000
Interest and debt expense	(130,000,000)
Earnings before income taxes	1,143,000,000
Income taxes	(287,000,000)
Net income	$ 856,000,000

It includes only five separate numbers (which are in billions of dollars), two subtotals, and the net earnings figure.

Instructions

(a) Indicate the deficiencies in the income statement.

(b) What recommendations would you make to the company to improve the usefulness of its income statement?

P4-14 Stan Foxworthy, vice-president of finance for Hand Corp., has recently been asked to discuss with the company's division controllers the proper accounting for extraordinary items. Foxworthy prepared the factual situations presented below as a basis for discussion.

1. An earthquake destroys one of the oil refineries owned by a large multinational oil company. Earthquakes are rare in this geographical location.

2. A publicly held company has incurred a substantial loss in the unsuccessful registration of a bond issue.

3. A large portion of a cigarette manufacturer's tobacco crops are destroyed by a hailstorm. Severe damage from hailstorms is rare in this locality.

4. A large diversified company sells a block of shares from its portfolio of securities acquired for investment purposes.

5. A company sells a block of common shares of a publicly traded company. The block of shares, which represents less than 10% of the publicly held company, is the only security investment the company has ever owned.

6. A company that operates a chain of warehouses sells the excess land surrounding one of its warehouses. When the company buys property to establish a new warehouse, it usually buys more land than it expects to use for the warehouse with the expectation that the land will appreciate in value. Twice during the past five years the company sold excess land.

7. A textile manufacturer with only one plant moves to another location and sustains relocation costs of $725,000.

8. A company experiences a material loss in the repurchase of a large bond issue that has been outstanding for three years. The company regularly repurchases bonds of this nature.

9. A railroad experiences an unusual flood loss to part of its track system. Flood losses normally occur every three or four years.

10. A machine tool company sells the only land it owns. The land was acquired 10 years ago for future expansion, but shortly thereafter the company abandoned all plans for expansion but decided to hold the land for appreciation.

Instructions

Determine whether the foregoing items should be classified as extraordinary items. Present a rationale for your position.

P4-15 Grace Inc. has recently reported steadily increasing income. The company reported income of $20,000 in 2002, $25,000 in 2003, and $30,000 in 2004. A number of market analysts have recommended that investors buy the shares because they expect the steady growth in income to continue. Grace is approaching the end of its fiscal year in 2005, and it again appears to be a good year. However, it has not yet recorded warranty expense.

Based on prior experience, this year's warranty expense should be around $5,000, but some top management has approached the controller to suggest a larger, more conservative warranty expense should be recorded this year. Income before warranty expense is $43,000. Specifically, by recording an $8,000 warranty accrual this year, Grace could report an income increase for this year and still be in a position to cover its warranty costs in future years.

Instructions

(a) What is earnings management?

(b) What is the effect of the proposed accounting in 2005? In 2006?

(c) What is the appropriate accounting in this situation?

P4-16 Andy Neville, controller for Tatooed Heart Inc., has recently prepared an income statement for 2005. Mr. Neville admits that he has not examined any recent professional pronouncements, but believes that the following statement presents fairly the financial progress of this company during the current period.

TATOOED HEART INC.
Income Statement
For the Year Ended December 31, 2005

Sales			$377,852
Less: Sales returns and allowances			16,320
Net sales			361,532
Cost of goods sold:			
Inventory, January 1, 2005		$50,235	
Purchases	$192,143		
Less: Purchase discounts	3,142	189,001	
Cost of goods available for sale		239,236	
Inventory, December 31, 2005		41,124	
Cost of goods sold			198,112
Gross profit			163,420
Selling expenses		41,850	
Administrative expenses		32,142	73,992
Income before income tax			89,428
Other revenues and gains			
Dividends received			40,000
			129,428
Income tax			43,900
Net income			$ 85,528

TATOOED HEART INC.
Retained Earnings Statement
For the Year Ended December 31, 2005

Retained earnings, January 1, 2005			$216,000
Add:			
Net income for 2005	$85,528		
Gain from casualty (net of tax)	10,000		
Gain on sale of plant assets	21,400	$116,928	
Deduct:			
Loss on expropriation (net of tax)	13,000		
Correction of mathematical error (net of tax)	17,186	(60,186)	56,742
Retained earnings, December 31, 2005			$272,742

Instructions

(a) Determine whether these statements are prepared under the current operating or all-inclusive concept of income. Cite specific details.

(b) Which method do you favour and why?

(c) Which method must be used, and how should the information be presented? Common shares outstanding for the year are 50,000 shares.

For questionable items, use the classification that ordinarily would be appropriate.

P4-17 The following financial statement was prepared by employees of Klein Corporation.

KLEIN CORPORATION
Income Statement
Year Ended December 31, 2004

Revenues	
Gross sales, including sales taxes	$1,044,300
Less: Returns, allowances, and cash discounts	56,200
Net sales	988,100
Dividends, interest, and purchase discounts	30,250
Recoveries of accounts written off in prior years	13,850
Total revenues	1,032,200
Costs and expenses	
Cost of goods sold	465,900
Salaries and related payroll expenses	60,500
Rent	19,100
Freight-in and freight-out	3,400
Bad debt expense	24,000
Addition to reserve for possible inventory losses	3,800
Total costs and expenses	576,700
Income before extraordinary items	455,500
Extraordinary items	
Loss on discontinued styles (Note 1)	37,000
Loss on sale of marketable securities (Note 2)	39,050
Loss on sale of warehouse (Note 3)	86,350
Tax assessments for 2001 and 2000 (Note 4)	34,500
Total extraordinary items	196,900
Net income	258,600
Net income per common share	$2.30

Note 1: New styles and rapidly changing consumer preferences resulted in a $37,000 loss on the disposal of discontinued styles and related accessories.

Note 2: The corporation sold an investment in marketable securities at a loss of $39,050. The corporation normally sells securities of this nature.

Note 3: The corporation sold one of its warehouses at an $86,350 loss (net of taxes).

Note 4: The corporation was charged $34,500 for additional income taxes resulting from a settlement in 1999. Of this amount, $17,000 was applicable to 2003, and the balance was applicable to 2002. Litigation of this nature is recurring for this company.

Instructions
Identify and discuss the weaknesses in classification and disclosure in the single-step income statement above. You should explain why these treatments are weaknesses and what the proper presentation of the items would be in accordance with recent professional pronouncements.

P4-18 Anikan Limited has approved a formal plan to sell its head office tower to an outside party. A detailed plan has been approved by the board of directors. The building is on the books at $50 million (net book value). Estimated selling price is $49 million. The company will continue to use the building until the new head office is complete. Construction has not yet started on the new building.

Instructions
Discuss the financial reporting issues.

Writing Assignments

WA4-1 Information concerning a corporation's operations is presented in an income statement or in a combined income and retained earnings statement. Income statements are prepared on a current operating performance basis or an all-inclusive basis. Proponents of the two types of income statements do not agree upon the proper treatment of material nonrecurring charges and credits.

Instructions

(a) Define current operating performance and all-inclusive as used above.

(b) Explain the differences in content and organization of a current operating performance income statement and an all-inclusive income statement. Include a discussion of the proper treatment of material nonrecurring charges and credits.

(c) Give the principal arguments for the use of each of the three statements: all-inclusive income statement, current operating performance income statement, and a combined income and retained earnings statement.

(AICPA adapted)

*WA4-2   Ernest Banks is the manager and accountant for a small company privately owned by three individuals. Banks always has given the owners cash-based financial statements. The owners are not accountants and do not understand how financial statements are prepared. Recently, the business has experienced strong growth, and inventory, accounts receivable, and capital assets have become more significant company assets. Banks understands generally accepted accounting principles and knows that net income would be lower if he prepared accrual-based financial statements. He is afraid that if he gave the owners financial statements prepared on an accrual basis, they would think he is not managing the business well; they might even decide to fire him.

Instructions
Discuss the issues.

Cases

Digital Tool
www.wiley.com/
canada/kieso

Refer to the Case Primer on the Digital Tool to help you answer these cases.

CA4-1   Allen Corp. is an entertainment firm that derives approximately 30% of its income from the Casino Royale Division, which manages gambling facilities. As auditor for Allen Corp., you have recently overheard the following discussion between the controller and financial vice-president.

VICE-PRESIDENT: If we sell the Casino Royale Division, it seems ridiculous to segregate the results of the sale in the income statement. Separate categories tend to be absurd and confusing to the shareholders. I believe that we should simply report the gain on the sale as other income or expense without detail.

CONTROLLER: Professional pronouncements would require that we disclose this information separately in the income statement. If a sale of this type relates to a separate component and there exists a formal plan to dispose of it, it must be reported as a discontinued operation.

VICE-PRESIDENT: What about the walkout we had last month when our employees were upset about their commission income? Would this situation not also be an extraordinary item?

CONTROLLER: I am not sure whether this item would be reported as extraordinary or not.

VICE-PRESIDENT: Oh well, it doesn't make any difference because the net effect of all these items is immaterial, so no disclosure is necessary.

Instructions
Discuss.

CA4-2   Anderson Corp. is a major manufacturer of foodstuffs whose products are sold in grocery and convenience stores throughout Canada. The company's name is well known and respected because its products have been marketed nationally for over 50 years.

In April 2005, the company was forced to recall one of its major products. A total of 35 persons in Oshkosh were treated for severe intestinal pain, and eventually three people died from complications. All of the people had consumed Anderson's product.

The product causing the problem was traced to one specific lot. Anderson keeps samples from all lots of foodstuffs. After thorough testing, Anderson and the legal authorities confirmed that the product had been tampered with after it had left the company's plant and was no longer under the company's control.

All of the product was recalled from the market—the only time an Anderson product has been recalled nationally and the only incident of tampering. Persons who still had the product in their homes, even though it was not from the affected lot, were encouraged to return the product for credit or refund. A media campaign was designed and implemented by the company to explain what had happened and what the company was doing to minimize any chance of recurrence. Anderson decided to continue the product with the same trade name and same wholesale price. However, the packaging was redesigned completely to be tamper resistant and safety sealed. This required the purchase and installation of new equipment.

The corporate accounting staff recommended that the costs associated with the tampered product be treated as an extraordinary charge on the 2005 financial statements. Corporate accounting was asked to identify the various costs that could be associated with the tampered product and related recall. These costs ($000 omitted) are as follows.

1. Credits and refunds to stores and consumers	$30,000
2. Insurance to cover lost sales and idle plant costs for possible future recalls	5,000
3. Transportation costs and off-site warehousing of returned product	2,000
4. Future security measures for other Anderson products	4,000
5. Testing of returned product and inventory	900
6. Destruction of returned product and inventory	2,400
7. Public relations program to reestablish brand credibility	4,200
8. Communication program to inform customers, answer inquiries, prepare press releases, etc.	1,600
9. Higher cost arising from new packaging	800
10. Investigation of possible involvement of employees, former employees, competitors, etc.	500
11. Packaging redesign and testing	2,000
12. Purchase and installation of new packaging equipment	6,000
13. Legal costs for defence against liability suits	750
14. Lost sales revenue due to recall	32,000

Anderson's estimated earnings before income taxes and before consideration of any of the above items for the year ending December 31, 2005 are $225 million.

Instructions
Adopt the role of the company controller and discuss the issues.

CA4-3   As a receiver for the Ontario Securities Commission, you are in the process of receiving the financial statements of public companies. The following items have come to your attention.

1. A merchandising company incorrectly overstated its ending inventory two years ago by a material amount. Inventory for all other periods is correctly calculated.

2. An automobile dealer sells for $137,000 an extremely rare 1930 S type Invicta, which it purchased for $21,000 10 years ago. The Invicta is the only such display item the dealer owns.

3. A drilling company during the current year extended the estimated useful life of certain drilling equipment from 9 to 15 years. As a result, amortization for the current year was materially lowered.

4. A retail outlet changed its calculation for bad debt expense from 1% to 1/2 of 1% of sales because of changes in its customer clientele.

5. A mining company sells a foreign subsidiary engaged in uranium mining, although it continues to engage in uranium mining in other countries.

6. A steel company changes from straight-line amortization to accelerated amortization in accounting for its plant assets.

7. A construction company, at great expense, prepared a major proposal for a government loan. The loan is not approved.

8. A water pump manufacturer has had large losses resulting from a strike by its employees early in the year.

9. Amortization for a prior period was incorrectly understated by $950,000. The error was discovered in the current year.

10. A large sheep rancher suffered a major loss because the province required that all sheep in the province be killed to halt the spread of a rare disease. Such a situation has not occurred in the province for 20 years.

11. A food distributor that sells wholesale to supermarket chains and to fast-food restaurants (two major classes of customers) decides to discontinue the division that sells to one of the two classes of customers.

Instructions
Discuss the issues.

CA4-4   You are working on the audit team for October Division, a multi-divisional, calendar year-end client with annual sales of $90 million. The company primarily sells electronic transistors to small customers and has one division (the October Division) that deals in acoustic transmitters for Navy submarines. The October Division has approximately $18 million in sales.

It's an evening in February 2004, and the audit work is complete. You're working in the client's office on the report, when you overhear a conversation among the financial vice-president, the treasurer, and the controller. They're discussing the sale of the October Division, expected to take place in June of this year, and the related reporting problems.

The vice-president thinks no segregation of the sale is necessary in the income statement because separate categories tend to be abused and confuse the shareholders. The treasurer disagrees. He feels that if an item is unusual or infrequent, it should be classified as an extraordinary item, including the sale of the October Division. The controller says an item should be both infrequent and unusual to be extraordinary. He feels the sale of the October Division should be shown separately, but not as an extraordinary item. Another alternative is to show pro-forma income that excludes the October Division.

The sale is not new to you because you read about it in the minutes of the December 16, 2003 board of directors' meeting. The minutes indicated plans to sell the transmitter plant and equipment by June 30, 2004 to its major competitor, who seems interested. The board estimates that net income and sales will remain constant until the sale, on which the company expects a $700,000 profit.

You also hear the controller disagree with the vice-president that the results of the strike last year and the sale of the old transistor ovens, formerly used in manufacturing, would also be extraordinary items. In addition, the treasurer thinks the government regulation issued last month, which made much of their inventory of raw material useless, would be extraordinary. The regulations set beta emission standards at levels lower than those in the raw materials supply, and there's no alternative use for the materials.

Finally, the controller claims the discussion is academic. Since the net effect of all three items is immaterial, no disclosure is required.

Instructions
Discuss the issues.

Research and Financial Analysis

RA4-1   Intrawest Corporation

The financial statements of Intrawest and accompanying notes, as presented in the company's annual report, are in Appendix 5B.

Instructions
Refer to this information and answer the following questions.

(a) What type of income statement format does the company use?

(b) What business is the company in? (Hint: look at the Management Discussion and Analysis—MD&A.) How is this reflected in the balance sheet and income statement?

(c) What are the company's two primary revenue sources? Calculate the percentage composition of total revenues. Have revenues for the two main sources of revenues declined or increased over the last year? Calculate the percentage change and provide an explanation for the change (see MD&A). Calculate the operating profit on the two main revenue streams.

(d) Is this a seasonal business? How has management dealt with this?

(e) Are the two main revenue streams sustainable? Comment on management's strategy to deal with this.

RA4-2   Royal Bank of Canada

Obtain the 2002 annual report for the Royal Bank of Canada from the Digital Tool. Note that financial reporting for Canadian banks is also constrained by the Bank Act and monitored by the Office of the Superintendent of Financial Institutions.

Instructions

(a) Revenues and expenses are defined as arising from ordinary activities of the business. What are the ordinary activities (core business activities) of the bank? What normal expenses must they incur in order to generate core revenues?

(b) Is this reflected in the income statement? (Hint: look at the classification between revenues and other income/gains and expenses and other costs/losses.)

(c) Calculate the percentage of the various revenues/income streams to total revenues/income. Discuss the trends from year to year; i.e., are these revenue/income streams increasing as a percentage of the total revenue/income or decreasing? What are the primary sources of the revenues/income?

RA4-3   Trizec Canada Inc. and Mainstreet Equity Corp.

Instructions

Go to the Digital Tool, and use the annual reports of Trizec Canada Inc. and Mainstreet Equity Corp. to answer the following questions related to the years ended December 31, 2002 and September 30, 2002 respectively.

(a) What type of income format(s) do these two companies use? Identify any differences in income statement format between these two companies.

(b) Look at the Management Discussion and Analysis and the annual report in general. What business are both companies in?

(c) What are the main sources of revenues for both companies? Are these increasing or decreasing?

(d) Is this nature of the business reflected in the balance sheet? (Hint: what is the main asset and what percentage of total assets is this asset?)

(e) Identify the irregular items reported by these two companies in their income statements over the two-year period. Do these irregular items appear to be significant? Comment on both presentations.

RA4-4   Canadian Securities Administration

The Canadian Securities Administrators (CSA), an umbrella group of Canadian provincial securities commissions, accumulates all documents required to be filed by public companies under securities law. This electronic database may be accessed from the following website: www.sedar.com. Company financial statements may also be accessed through the company websites.

Instructions

Visit the CSA website (www.sedar.com) and find the company documents for Bank of Montreal and Royal Bank of Canada. Answer the following questions.

(a) What types of company documents may be found here that provide useful information for investors who are making investment decisions?

(b) Locate the Annual Information Form. Explain the nature of the information that it contains. As a financial statement analyst, is this information useful to you? Why?

(c) Who are the auditors of both banks?

(d) Which stock exchange(s) do the banks trade on?

(e) Go to the company websites directly (www.bmo.com and www.royalbank.com). Look under Investor relations. What type of information is on these websites and how does it differ from what is on the www.sedar.com website? Should these websites contain the same information as the CSA website?

RA4-5   Reporting Financial Performance

The accounting standard-setting bodies for Canada, the United States, the United Kingdom, and International are currently studying the issue of reporting financial performance. The United Kingdom and the IASB have articulated one overriding principle and five additional principles that should underlie any new accounting standard on reporting financial performance.

The principles are listed below.

PRIMARY PRINCIPLE:	The objective of the format of the statement of comprehensive income is to categorize, order, and display information so as to maximize predictive value with respect to forecasts of comprehensive income and its components.
PRINCIPLE 1.	A statement of comprehensive income should be able to distinguish the return on total capital employed from the return on equity
PRINCIPLE 2.	Components of gains and losses should be reported gross unless they give little information with respect to future income.
PRINCIPLE 3.	Income and expenses resulting from the re-measurement of an asset or liability should be reported separately. ("Re-measurements" are revisions of estimates embedded in the carrying amounts of assets and liabilities.)
PRINCIPLE 4.	A statement of comprehensive income should identify income and expenses where the change in economic value does not arise in the period in which it is reported.
PRINCIPLE 5.	Within the prescribed format and without the use of proscribed sub-totals, the statement of comprehensive income should allow reporting in the form of: (1) information on the entity as a whole, analysed by nature or function; (2) those activities disaggregated by business segments (geographic or product-based); and (3) additional distinctions according to managerial discretion.
PRINCIPLE A.	The format of the statement of comprehensive income should not be driven by concepts of realization or recycling.
PRINCIPLE B.	It is not practical or meaningful to make a distinction between "operating" and "non-operating" on the basis that the former are "core" or "central" and the latter are not.
PRINCIPLE C.	A distinction between trading gains and holding gains encounters the same practical difficulties as the distinction between operating and non-operating activities. In addition, it introduces a time dimension as a second subjective basis of differentiation. The trading/holding distinction does not, therefore, suggest a clear-cut conceptual basis for statement of comprehensive income components.

Instructions

Go to the FASB website and download and read the material relating to reporting financial performance.

(a) What are the main problems in reporting financial performance that the Invitation to Comment paper identifies?

(b) What is the status of the project to date?

(c) Visit the CICA website and comment on the AcSB role in this project.

(d) Review the principles articulated above. Comment on whether you believe that these principles will result in a more informative income statement.

RA4-6   Quality of Earnings Research

Quality of earnings analysis is a very important tool in assessing the value of a company and its shares. The chapter presents a framework for evaluating quality of earnings.

Instructions

Do an Internet search on the topic and write a critical essay discussing the usefulness of the quality of earnings assessment.

RA4-7   Avon Rubber PLC

Presented below is the income statement for a British company, Avon Rubber PLC.

AVON RUBBER PLC
Consolidated Profit and Loss Account
for the Year Ended 3 October 1998

	Total £ 000
Turnover	
Continuing activities	251,531
Acquisitions	15,554
Total turnover	267,085
Cost of sales	(216,174)
Gross profit	50,911
Net operating expenses	(28,586)
Share of operating profits of joint ventures and associated companies	26
Operating profit	
Continuing activities	19,361
Acquisitions	2,990
Total operating profit	22,351
Profit on sale of property	993
Loss on sale of fixed asset investment	(275)
Profit on ordinary activities before interest	23,069
Interest payable	(3,014)
Interest receivable	3,850
Profit on ordinary activities before taxation	23,905
Taxation	(7,003)
Profit on ordinary activities after taxation	16,902
Minority interests	254
Profit for the year	17,156
Basic earnings per ordinary share	62.4p

Instructions

(a) Review the Avon Rubber income statements and identify at least three differences between this British income statement and an income statement of a Canadian company as presented in this chapter.

(b) Identify irregular items reported by Avon Rubber. Is the reporting of these items in Avon's income statement similar to reporting of these items in the Canadian company's income statement? Explain.

RA4-8   Alliance Atlantis Communications Inc.

An excerpt from the annual report of Alliance Atlantis Communications Inc. is shown below. The excerpt shows a calculation of Earnings Before Interest, Tax, Depreciation, and Amortization (EBITDA)—a non-GAAP earnings measure.

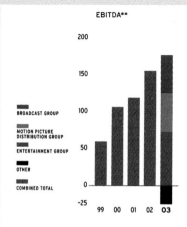

The Company reported EBITDA (excluding Developing Channels*** operating losses) of $165.2 million – up 7% compared to the prior fiscal year. EBITDA (including Developing Channels operating losses) was $151.9 million in fiscal 2003 – up 10% compared to the prior fiscal year. Consolidated EBITDA margin (excluding Developing Channels operating losses) was 19% in fiscal 2003 compared to 17% in the prior fiscal year. Operating Group EBITDA margin for fiscal 2003 as compared to fiscal 2002 is as follows: Broadcast Group – Operating Channels 39%/41%; Motion Picture Distribution Group 14%/16%; and Entertainment Group 23%/15%.

** EBITDA IS DEFINED AS EARNINGS BEFORE INTEREST, INCOME TAXES, AMORTIZATION, MINORITY INTEREST, EQUITY INTEREST IN AFFILIATES, INVESTMENT GAINS AND LOSSES, FOREIGN EXCHANGE GAINS AND LOSSES AND UNUSUAL ITEMS. EBITDA IS USED BY THE COMPANY TO MEASURE ITS OPERATING PERFORMANCE. EBITDA AND RELATED MEASURES MAY OR MAY NOT BE CONSISTENT WITH THE CALCULATION OF SIMILAR MEASURES FOR OTHER COMPANIES, AND SHOULD NOT BE VIEWED AS ALTERNATIVES TO NET EARNINGS OR OTHER MEASURES OF PERFORMANCE CALCULATED IN ACCORDANCE WITH CANADIAN GENERALLY ACCEPTED ACCOUNTING PRINCIPLES.

*** DEVELOPING CHANNELS COMPRISE SEVEN DIGITAL CHANNELS LAUNCHED IN FISCAL 2002: SHOWCASE ACTION, SHOWCASE DIVA, IFC - THE INDEPENDENT FILM CHANNEL CANADA, DISCOVERY HEALTH CHANNEL, BBC CANADA, BBC KIDS, AND NATIONAL GEOGRAPHIC CHANNEL.

Instructions

Discuss the pros and cons of management reporting additional earnings numbers outside of the traditional audited financial statements. In the case of this company, in your opinion, do you think that this presentation provides good, useful information?

Olympic Gold

The 2010 Winter Olympics set to take place in Vancouver and Whistler, British Columbia, can only improve Intrawest Corporation's already rosy financial position. The company owns the Whistler Blackcomb ski resort, where many Olympic events will be held.

"The first impact [of the Olympics] is the increase in profile, leading to an increase in visits to the resort, which obviously has a profit and cash flow impact on us," says David Blaiklock, Intrawest's vice-president and corporate controller. "If that happens, we'll have more cash and less debt because whenever we increase our business volume it generates a cash flow, which will either result in cash or paying down debt."

"The company will also benefit from significant infrastructure improvements, for example to the highway from Vancouver to Whistler," he adds.

The expected increase in visitors, revenues, and profits will of course show up on the balance sheet. Blaiklock says what's important is not so much the numbers themselves, but the relationship between the numbers: the relationship between the different assets and liabilities and between the liabilities and cash flow. Since Intrawest has two main lines of businesses—resort operations and real estate— its balance sheet reflects a hybrid capital structure combining the lower leverage of an operating company with the higher leverage of a real estate developer.

Of the 10 Canadian and U.S. resorts the company owns, Whistler Blackcomb is by far its greatest asset, with or without the Olympics. "It's the most popular ski resort in North America by a sizable margin, based on skier visits," Blaiklock says. With 2.2 million skier visits per year, Whistler Blackcomb's contribution significantly outweighs Intrawest's next largest ski resort, Mammoth, California, with 1.2 million skier visits per year.■

CHAPTER 5

Financial Position and Cash Flows

Learning Objectives

After studying this chapter, you should be able to:

1. Identify the uses and limitations of a balance sheet.
2. Identify the major classifications of a balance sheet.
3. Prepare a classified balance sheet.
4. Identify balance sheet information requiring supplemental disclosure.
5. Identify major disclosure techniques for the balance sheet.
6. Indicate the purpose of the statement of cash flows.
7. Identify the content of the statement of cash flows.
8. Understand the usefulness of the statement of cash flows.

After studying Appendix 5A, you should be able to:

9. Identify the major types of financial ratios and what they measure.

The **balance sheet** and **statement of cash flows** complement the income statement, offering information about the company's financial position and how the firm generates and uses cash. The purpose of this chapter is to examine the many different types of assets, liabilities, and shareholders' equity items that affect the balance sheet and the statement of cash flows. The content and organization of this chapter are as follows:

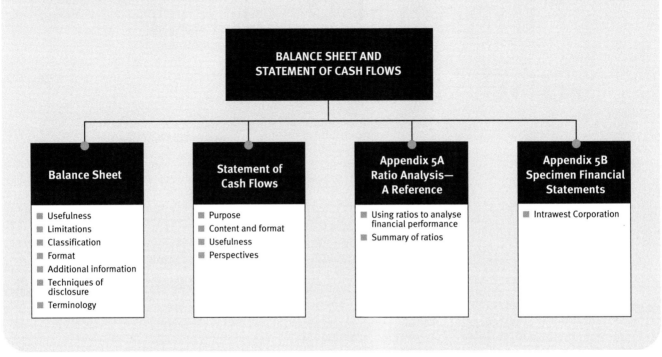

SECTION 1—BALANCE SHEET

The balance sheet, sometimes referred to as the statement of financial position, reports a business enterprise's assets, liabilities, and shareholders' equity at a specific date. This financial statement provides information about the nature and amounts of investments in enterprise resources, obligations to creditors, and the owners' equity in net resources.[1] It therefore helps in predicting the amounts, timing, and uncertainty of future cash flows.

Usefulness of the Balance Sheet

Objective **1**
Identify the uses and limitations of a balance sheet.

By providing information about assets, liabilities, and shareholders' equity, the balance sheet provides a basis for calculating rates of return on invested assets and evaluating the

[1] *Financial Reporting in Canada, 2002*, (Toronto, CICA) indicates that approximately 90% of the companies surveyed used the term "balance sheet". The term "statement of financial position" is used infrequently, although it is conceptually appealing (p. 56).

enterprise's capital structure. Information in the balance sheet is also used to assess business risk[2] and future cash flows. In this regard, **the balance sheet is useful for analysing a company's liquidity, solvency, and financial flexibility**, as described below, and helps analyse profitability (even though this is not the main focus of the statement).

Liquidity looks at the **amount of time that is expected to elapse until an asset is realized** or otherwise converted into cash or until a liability has to be paid. Does the company have sufficient cash and cash coming in to cover its short-term liabilities? Certain ratios help assess overall liquidity, including **current ratio**, **quick or acid test ratio**, and **current cash debt coverage ratio**. Liquidity of certain assets such as receivables and inventory is assessed through **turnover ratios**.[3] These ratios look at how fast the receivables or inventories are being collected or sold. Creditors are interested in **short-term** liquidity ratios, because they indicate whether the enterprise will have the resources to pay its current and maturing obligations. Similarly, shareholders assess liquidity to evaluate the possibility of future cash dividends or the buyback of shares. In general, the greater the liquidity, the lower the risk of enterprise or business failure.[4]

Solvency refers to an **enterprise's ability to pay its debts and related interest**. For example, when a company carries a high level of long-term debt relative to assets, it is at higher risk for insolvency than a similar company with a low level of long-term debt. Companies with higher debt are relatively more risky because more of their assets will be required to meet these fixed obligations (such as interest and principal payments). Certain ratios assist in assessing solvency. These are often called "coverage" ratios, referring to a company's ability to cover its interest and long-term debt payments.

Liquidity and solvency affect an entity's **financial flexibility**, which measures the **"ability of an enterprise to take effective actions to alter the amounts and timing of cash flows so it can respond to unexpected needs and opportunities."**[5] For example, a company may become so loaded with debt—so financially inflexible—that its cash sources to finance expansion or to pay off maturing debt are limited or nonexistent. An enterprise with a high degree of financial flexibility is better able to survive bad times, to recover from unexpected setbacks, and to take advantage of profitable and unexpected investment opportunities. Generally, the greater the financial flexibility, the lower the risk of enterprise or business failure.

As mentioned in Chapter 2, **Air Canada** filed for bankruptcy protection in April 2003. Factors such as outbreaks of severe acute respiratory syndrome, the Iraq war, and terrorism threats had severely curbed airline travel, thus reducing cash inflows for airlines. At that time, Air Canada's total debt exceeded total assets by $2,558 million, leaving it very little flexibility to react to changes in its environment. It was therefore very vulnerable to the decreasing demand for its services. Its current liabilities exceeded its current assets by $1,386 million, resulting in an inability to cover its day-to-day operating costs. By the end of the second quarter, the company had taken steps, while under bankruptcy protection, to ease the cash flow problems and increase flexibility. These included:

1. arranging for interim financing (called debtor in possession (DIP) financing) with General Electric Capital Canada Inc. (GE),

2. restructuring union contracts, and

3. renegotiating aircraft leases for 106 planes (with GE).

How quickly will my assets convert to cash?

Obligation Ocean

We are drowning in a sea of debt!

Opportunity Shop

Investments

Can we afford the high payoff investment?

What do the Numbers Mean?

---

[2] Risk is an expression of the unpredictability of the enterprise's future events, transactions, circumstances, and results.

[3] The formulas for these ratios and other ratios are summarized in Appendix 5A.

[4] Liquidity measures are important inputs to bankruptcy prediction models, such as those developed by Altman and others. See G. White, A. Sondhi, and D. Fried, *The Analysis of Financial Statements* (New York: John Wiley & Sons, 2003), Chapter 18.

[5] "Reporting Income, Cash Flows, and Financial Position of Business Enterprises," *Proposed Statement of Financial Accounting Concepts* (Stamford, Conn.: FASB, 1981), par. .25.

This DIP financing provided the company with an additional $700 million line of credit while the other two significant renegotiations helped reduce immediate cash needs for salaries and lease/rent payments. Note that the line of credit, while providing short-term relief, increases total debt when drawn. The company announced that it hoped to emerge from bankruptcy protection by the end of 2003. In order to be successful on a going forward basis, the company needs to continue to reduce debt and increase cash flows from operating activities, thus giving itself greater flexibility.

Limitations of the Balance Sheet

Because the income statement and the balance sheet are interrelated, it is not surprising that the balance sheet has many of the same limitations as the income statement. Here are some of the major limitations of the balance sheet.

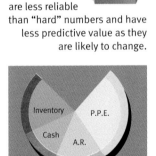

If we sell that land, we could get more than we paid.

Underlying Concept

"Soft" numbers are less reliable than "hard" numbers and have less predictive value as they are likely to change.

Hey....we left out the value of the employees!

Underlying Concept

Disclosing too much detail often obscures important information, resulting in information overload.

1. Many assets and liabilities are stated at historical cost. As a result, the information reported in the balance sheet has higher reliability but is subject to the criticism that a more relevant current fair value is not reported. Use of historical cost and other valuation methods was discussed in Chapter 2. As noted therein, we are moving towards greater use of fair value, i.e., for derivatives and investments.

2. Judgements and estimates are used in determining many of the items reported in the balance sheet. This represents the other side of the same issue identified in Chapter 4 when discussing income statement limitations. As discussed there, the financial statements consist of many "soft" numbers, meaning that they are subject to a significant amount of uncertainty.

3. The balance sheet necessarily **omits many items** that are of financial value to the business but cannot be recorded objectively.[6] These may be either assets or liabilities. Again, this represents the other side of the identical issue discussed in Chapter 4. Given that capitalization of liabilities results in worsening liquidity and solvency ratios, a company bias may exist to exclude them. Knowing this, analysts habitually look for and capitalize[7] many liabilities that may be "off balance sheet" prior to calculating key liquidity and solvency ratios. When valuing a company, mergers and acquisition specialists consider off balance sheet assets such as goodwill. Information disclosed in the notes to the financial statements and knowledge of the business and industry is critical in identifying and measuring off balance sheet items that often represent either additional risk to the company or unrecognized assets.

Classification in the Balance Sheet

Balance sheet accounts are **classified** (like the income statement) so that **similar items are grouped together** to arrive at significant subtotals. Furthermore, the material is arranged so that important relationships are shown.

As with the income statement, the balance sheet's parts and subsections can be more informative than the whole. Therefore, the reporting of summary accounts alone (total assets, net assets, total liabilities, etc.) is discouraged. Individual items should be separately reported and classified in sufficient detail to permit users to assess the amounts,

---

[6] Several of these omitted items (such as internally generated goodwill and certain commitments) are discussed in later chapters.

[7] While the term "capitalize" is often used in the context of recording costs as assets, it is sometimes used in the context noted above. The latter context deals with recognizing the liabilities on the balance sheet.

timing, and uncertainty of future cash flows, as well as the evaluation of liquidity and financial flexibility, profitability, and risk.

2 Objective
Identify the major classifications of a balance sheet.

Classification in financial statements helps analysts by **grouping items with similar characteristics** and **separating items with different characteristics**. In this regard, the balance sheet has additional information content. The following groupings help provide additional insight.

1. Assets that differ in their type or expected **function** in the central operations or other enterprise activities should be reported as separate items. For example, merchandise inventories should be reported separately from property, plant, and equipment. Inventory will be sold and property, plant and equipment used. In this way, investors can see how fast inventory is turning over or being sold.

2. Assets and liabilities with **different implications for the enterprise's financial flexibility** should be reported as separate items. For example, long-term liabilities should be reported separately from current liabilities and debt separately from equity.

3. Assets and liabilities with different **general liquidity characteristics** should be reported as separate items. For example, cash should be reported separately from accounts receivable.

4. Certain assets, liabilities, and equity instruments have **attributes that allow greater ease of measurement or valuation**. Reporting these separately takes advantage of this. Financial instruments and monetary assets and liabilities are two such groupings. Each will be discussed separately below.

    Monetary versus nonmonetary: Assets that are **convertible to known amounts of cash** are said to be monetary assets and are generally easier to measure. Examples are accounts and notes receivables. Likewise, liabilities that are to be settled in terms of fixed or determinable amounts of cash are also considered to be monetary. Accounts and notes payable and long-term debt are examples. Other assets such as inventory, property, plant and equipment, certain investments, and intangibles are nonmonetary assets in that their value is not fixed in terms of a monetary unit such as dollars.

Underlying Concept

With non monetary assets, historical cost is often a more reliable measure.

    Financial instruments versus other: Financial instruments are contracts between two or more parties. The key is that they are generally marketable or tradable and thus easy to measure.[8] They include:

- **cash,**

- **investments in other companies, and**

- **contractual rights to receive or obligations to deliver cash or another financial instrument.**[9]

    Contractual rights to **receive** cash or other financial instruments are assets, whereas contractual obligations to **pay** are liabilities. Cash, investments, accounts receivable, and all payables or debt are examples of financial instruments. Shares are also financial instruments. New accounting standards on financial instruments mandate fair value accounting for many types of financial instruments including derivatives and investments.[10] More extensive discussion of financial instrument accounting and reporting is provided in Chapters 7, 10, 14, 15, 16, and 18. Derivatives, a more complex type of financial instrument, will be covered in Chapter 17. In general, most monetary assets and liabilities are financial instruments.

---

[8] Markets often exist or can be created for these instruments because of their nature and measurability. Liabilities are included because they represent the other side of an asset contract, e.g., accounts payable to one company represents accounts receivable to another. Accounts receivables contracts or pools are often bought and sold.

[9] See *CICA Handbook*, Section 3860.05 for more complete definitions.

[10] *CICA Handbook*, Section 3855 effective October 1, 2005.

The three general classes of items included in the balance sheet are assets, liabilities, and equity. The elements related to the balance sheet are defined below.

ELEMENTS OF THE BALANCE SHEET

1. *Assets.* Probable **future economic benefits** obtained or **controlled by** a particular entity as a result of **past transactions** or events.

2. *Liabilities.* Probable future sacrifices of economic benefits arising from present **duty or responsibility** to others, as a result of **past transactions** or events, where there **is little or no discretion to avoid** the obligation.

3. *Equity/Net Assets.* **Residual interest** in an entity's assets that remains after deducting its liabilities. In a business enterprise, the equity is the ownership interest.

These are the same definitions as identified in Chapter 2 and the conceptual framework. Illustration 5-1 indicates the general format of balance sheet presentation.

Illustration 5-1

Balance Sheet Classifications

Assets	Liabilities and Owners' Equity
Current assets	Current liabilities
Long-term investments	Long-term debt
Property, plant, and equipment	Owners' equity
Intangible assets	Capital shares
Other assets	Contributed surplus
	Retained earnings
	Accumulated Other Comprehensive Income

The balance sheet may be classified in some other manner, but there is very little departure from these major subdivisions in practice except in certain industries. If a proprietorship or partnership is involved, the classifications within the owners' equity section are presented a little differently, as will be shown later in the chapter.

These classifications allow ease of calculation of important ratios such as the current ratio for assessing liquidity and debt-to-equity ratios for assessing solvency. By showing the breakdown of total assets, users can easily calculate which assets are more significant than others and how these relationships change over time.[11] This gives insight into management's strategy and stewardship. Illustration 5-2 shows a partial classified balance sheet for **Petro-Canada Corporation** (Petro-Canada).

Note that the current ratio changed significantly from 2001 to 2002. The calculations for the current ratio are as follows.

2001 = \$2,009 million/\$1,397 million = 1.4 to 1
2002 = \$2,434 million/\$2,520 million = .96 to 1

The deteriorating current ratio signals a worsening liquidity position. Understanding the company's changing business and business environment is key in interpreting this.

Digital Tool

Analyst Toolkit—
Financial
Statement Analysis
Primer
www.wiley.com/canada/kieso

[11] That is, by performing a **vertical analysis** and calculating the percentage represented by specific assets divided by total assets. This number may then be compared with the same percentage from prior years. This latter comparison is generally referred to as a **horizontal or trend analysis**. Horizontal and vertical analyses are discussed further in the Digital Tool under Financial Statement Analysis.

Illustration 5-2

Partial Classified Balance Sheet—Excerpt from Petro-Canada

(stated in millions of Canadian dollars)

As at December 31.	2002	2001
ASSETS		
CURRENT ASSETS		
Cash and short-term investments *(Note 12)*	$ 234	$ 781
Accounts receivable	1 596	758
Inventories *(Note 13)*	585	455
Prepaid expenses	19	15
	2 434	2 009
PROPERTY, PLANT AND EQUIPMENT, NET *(Note 14)*	10 084	7 460
GOODWILL *(Note 3)*	709	–
DEFERRED CHARGES AND OTHER ASSETS *(Note 15)*	212	165
	$ 13 439	$ 9 634
LIABILITIES AND SHAREHOLDERS' EQUITY		
CURRENT LIABILITIES		
Accounts payable and accrued liabilities	$ 1 901	$ 1 158
Income taxes payable	263	234
Current portion of long-term debt *(Note 16)*	356	5
	2 520	1 397

According to the management discussion and analysis, the change in ratio is due to increases in both accounts receivable and payable, reflecting significantly higher prices for both oil and natural gas. The changes also reflect the acquisition of another company on May 2, 2002 for $2,234 million.

Current Assets

Current assets are **cash and other assets ordinarily realizable within one year from the date of the balance sheet or within the normal operating cycle where that is longer than a year.**[12] The operating cycle is the average time between the acquisition of materials and supplies and the realization of cash. Cash is realized through sales of the product for which the materials and supplies were acquired. The cycle operates from cash through inventory, production, and receivables back to cash. When there are several operating cycles within one year, the one-year period is used. If the operating cycle is more than one year, the longer period is used. Illustration 5-3 depicts the operating cycle for manufacturing companies.

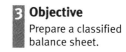

Objective
Prepare a classified balance sheet.

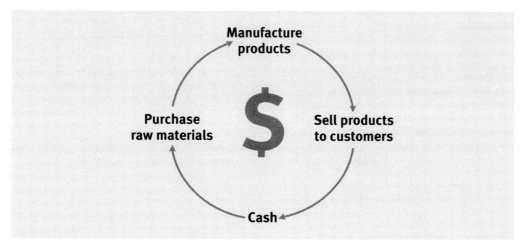

Illustration 5-3

The Business Operating Cycle for Manufacturing Companies

---

[12] *CICA Handbook*, Section 1510.01.

Current assets are generally segregated and presented in the balance sheet in order of liquidity for most industries.[13] The five major items found in the current assets section are cash, short-term (or temporary) investments, receivables, inventories, and prepayments. Cash is included at its stated value; short-term trading investments are valued at fair value;[14] accounts receivable are stated at the estimated amount collectible; inventories generally are included at cost or the lower of cost and market; and prepaid items are valued at cost.

Cash   Cash is often grouped with other cash-like liquid assets and reported as cash and cash equivalents.[15] Cash and cash equivalents are defined as **cash, demand deposits, and short-term highly liquid investments that are readily convertible into known amounts of cash and are subject to insignificant risk of changes in value.**[16] Illustration 5-4 details the cash and cash equivalents for the RBC Financial Group. Note that the bank groups cash and deposits under the heading Cash Resources. Deposits are considered cash-like as they are monetary.

Illustration 5-4

Balance Sheet Presentation of Cash and Cash Equivalents— Excerpt from the Financial Statements of RBC Financial Group

Underlying Concept

Grouping these like items together reduces the amount of redundant information on the balance sheet and therefore results in information that is easier to understand.

Consolidated financial statements

Consolidated balance sheet

As at October 31 ($ millions)	**2002**	2001
Assets		
Cash resources		
Cash and due from banks	**$ 2,534**	$ 1,792
Interest-bearing deposits with banks	**18,789**	15,743
	21,323	17,535

Any restrictions on the general availability of cash or any commitments on its probable disposition must be disclosed. If cash is restricted for purposes other than current obligations, it is excluded from current assets.

How much cash should a company hold? In general, a company needs sufficient liquid assets including cash to be able to settle current liabilities in a timely manner; however, it must also ensure that its assets do not sit idle. Cash itself is generally noninterest-bearing and so does not otherwise contribute to net income. Too much cash may make a company subject to a takeover bid.

Temporary Investments   Investments in debt and equity securities are grouped into three separate portfolios for valuation and presentation purposes. These portfolios are categorized as follows.[17]

---

[13] The real estate industry is an example of one that does not follow this approach. This is because the industry feels that a more meaningful presentation results in the most important assets being presented first. In most real estate development companies, the most important and largest asset is Revenue-producing properties. This asset includes hotels, shopping centres, leased buildings, etc. that generate revenue or profits for the company. Brookfield Properties Corporation records this asset first on the balance sheet. On the liabilities side, the corresponding debt related to the properties is recorded. For Brookfield, this asset represents 68% of total assets. Real estate companies are bound by GAAP and also by specialized industry GAAP (Real Estate GAAP as published by the Canadian Institute of Public and Private Real Estate Companies, CIPREC). Bombardier Inc. does not classify its balance sheet for different reasons. It operates in four distinct segments that have differing operating cycles and thus it feels that classification would not add value.

[14] Historically, these financial instruments have been valued primarily at historical cost in most industries. Recently released *CICA Handbook* Section 3855 on financial instruments requires investments classified as held for trading or available for sale to be valued at market or fair value.

[15] According to a survey of 200 companies, 112 reported cash and cash equivalents (up from 36 in 1998) with 28 reporting cash grouped with short-term deposits or investments (CICA, *Financial Reporting in Canada, 2002*, p. 218).

[16] *CICA Handbook*, Section 1540.06.

[17] Proposed *CICA Handbook*, Section 3855. Since this section becomes effective in 2005 there are currently very few Canadian examples of this balance sheet presentation prior to that time. More detail will be presented in Chapter 10.

Held-to-maturity securities: Debt securities that the company has positive intent and ability to hold to maturity.

Trading securities: Debt and equity securities that have the following characteristics:

1. they are bought and held primarily for sale in the near term,

2. they represent part of a portfolio that is managed for profit-taking, or

3. they are derivative instruments (forwards, options, futures, and others).[18]

Available-for-sale securities: Debt and equity securities not classified as held-to-maturity or trading securities.

Trading securities should be recorded as current assets. Available-for-sale and held-to-maturity should be classified as current or noncurrent depending on the nature of the investment and management intent. All of these securities should be measured at fair value except for the held-to-maturity securities, which are measured at amortized cost.

Companies that have excess cash often have significant amounts of temporary investments. The business models of banks, insurance companies, and pension funds are such that they result in significant amounts of temporary and long-term investments. For instance, insurance companies collect premiums upfront and invest the money so that they have funds available to pay out subsequent claims that might arise under the insurance policies. Pension plans likewise collect money upfront (pension contributions from individuals) and invest them for payout when the contributors retire. Money is a bank's inventory. The bank must decide how much of it should be invested and in which investment.

Receivables   Accounts receivable should be segregated so as to show **ordinary trade accounts**, amounts owing by **related parties**, and other **unusual items** of a substantial amount.[19] Any anticipated loss due to uncollectibles, the amount and nature of any non-trade receivables, and any receivables designated or pledged as collateral should be clearly identified. Accounts receivables are valued at net realizable value. QLT Inc. (QLT) reported its receivables in note 2 to the financial statements as follows.

NOTE 2. ACCOUNTS RECEIVABLE

(In thousands of U.S. dollars)	2002	2001
Visudyne®	$ 28,636	$ 23,044
Contract research and development	1,128	1,338
Diomed, Inc. (Note 4)	-	1,215
Trade and other	422	389
	$ 30,186	$ 25,986

Accounts receivable –Visudyne is due from Novartis Ophthalmics and consists of the Company's 50% share of pre-tax profit on sales of Visudyne, amounts due from sale of bulk Visudyne to Novartis Ophthalmics and reimbursement of specified manufacturing, royalty and other costs. The Company does not require an allowance for doubtful accounts.

Illustration 5-5

Balance Sheet Presentation of Securities—Excerpt from QLT Financial Statements

QLT is a biotechnology company specializing in the discovery, development, and commercialization of drugs, including light-activated drugs such as Visudyne. Visudyne is marketed through Novartis Ophthalmics (Novartis), the company's co-development partner. The companies share the earnings from distribution of the drug. By virtue of the relationship between QLT and Novartis, the latter is considered a related party[20] and the accounts

What do the Numbers Mean?

---

[18] Derivatives will be discussed further in Chapter 17.

[19] *CICA Handbook*, Section 3020.01.

[20] Identification and measurement of related parties and related party transactions will be covered in Chapter 24.

receivables are therefore disclosed separately. Note also that because the company markets and distributes its main product through Novartis, almost all of its receivables come from one source, creating a credit risk concentration. This is important information and is thus highlighted in the note disclosure. The category "Contract research and development" represents work done for other companies. Ordinary trade and other receivables represents a very small part of QLT's total receivables.

Underlying Concept

The lower of cost and market valuation is an example of the use of conservatism in accounting.

Inventories   **Inventories represent items held for sale in the normal course of operations.** Inventories are valued at the lower of cost and market, with cost being determined using a **cost flow assumption** such as first-in, first-out (FIFO), last-in, first-out (LIFO), weighted average cost, or other. It is important to disclose these details as this information assists users in understanding the amount of judgement involved in measuring this asset. For a manufacturing concern, the stage of the inventories' completion is also indicated (raw materials, work in progress, and finished goods). Illustration 5-6 shows the breakdown of QLT's inventory.

Illustration 5-6

Balance Sheet Presentation of Inventories—Excerpt from QLT Financial Statements

NOTE 3. INVENTORIES

(In thousands of U.S. dollars)	2002	2001
Raw materials and supplies	$ 1,706	$ 497
Work-in-process	22,057	25,882
Finished goods	13,794	14,685
Provision for non-completion of product inventory	(1,664)	(2,447)
	$ 35,892	$ 38,617

Inventories include finished goods with a cost of $12.0 million (2001 - $7.3 million) that have been shipped to and are held by Novartis Ophthalmics. These finished goods will be recognized as costs of manufacturing in the period of the related product sale by Novartis Ophthalmics to third parties and are included in deferred revenue at cost.

The Company records a provision for non-completion of product inventory to provide for potential failure of inventory batches in production to pass quality inspection. Consistent with this policy, during the second quarter of 2002, the Company reduced its provision for non-completion of product inventory by $1.3 million, as a result of the release of validation batches of verteporfin for injection previously on hold for second source supplier qualification.

What do the Numbers Mean?

QLT also discloses the following in the Significant Accounting Policy note:

"Raw materials and supplies inventories are carried at the lower of actual cost and replacement cost. Finished goods and work-in-process inventories are carried at the lower of weighted average cost and net realizable value…"

The **nature of the inventory is important in assessing value.** QLT's inventory consists primarily of manufactured pharmaceuticals, which must be made according to exacting standards and specifications. Because of this, QLT acknowledges the risk that the manufactured batches might not pass quality inspection. Retailers would consider theft and out-of-date stock in assessing inventory value. High technology companies would consider obsolescence.

Which types of companies are likely to have significant inventory? Companies that sell and manufacture goods will normally carry inventory (as compared with companies that offer services only). How much inventory is enough or, conversely, how much inventory is too much? Companies must have at least sufficient inventory to meet customer demands. On the other hand, inventory ties up significant amounts of cash flows, incurs storage costs, and subjects the company to risk of theft, obsolescence, etc. Many companies operate on a just-in-time philosophy, meaning that they streamline their production and supply channels such that they are able to order the raw materials and produce the product in a very short time. Car manufacturers often follow this philosophy, thus freeing up working capital and reducing need for storing inventory.

Prepaid Expenses **Prepaid expenses** included in current assets are **expenditures already made for benefits (usually services) to be received within one year or the operating cycle**, whichever is longer. These items are current assets because if they had not already been paid, they would require the use of cash during the next year or the operating cycle. A common example is the payment in advance for an insurance policy. It is classified as a prepaid expense at the time of the expenditure because the payment precedes receipt of the coverage benefit. Prepaid expenses are reported at the amount of the unexpired or unconsumed cost. Other common prepaid expenses include rent, advertising, taxes, and office or operating supplies.

Companies often include insurance and other prepayments for two or three years in current assets even though part of the advance payment applies to periods beyond one year or the current operating cycle. This is a matter of convention even though it is inconsistent with the definition of current assets.

Long-term Investments

Long-term investments, often referred to simply as investments, normally consist of one of four types:

1. Investments in **securities**, such as bonds, common shares, or long-term notes.

2. Investments in **tangible fixed assets not currently used** in operations, such as land held for speculation.

3. Investments set aside in **special funds** such as a sinking fund, pension fund, or plant expansion fund. The cash surrender value of life insurance may be included in this category.

4. Investments in **nonconsolidated subsidiaries** or affiliated companies.

Long-term investments are generally held for many years. These assets are not acquired with the intention of disposing of them in the near future. They are usually presented on the balance sheet just below Current Assets in a separate section called Investments. Many securities that are properly shown among long-term investments are, in fact, readily marketable. They are not included as current assets unless the intent is to convert them to cash in the short-term within a year or in the operating cycle, whichever is longer.

As mentioned earlier under Temporary Investments, securities classified as available-for-sale are valued at fair value in the balance sheet. Securities classified as held-to-maturity are valued at amortized cost. Other long-term equity investments (i.e., non-consolidated subsidiaries or affiliated companies) are accounted for using the equity method (see Chapter 10). A decline in value that is other than temporary may exist, for example, when the market value of common shares has been less than carrying value for a number of years. This will be dealt with in greater detail in Chapter 10.

The following excerpt from the financial statements of **Fairmont Hotels & Resorts Inc.** (Fairmont) reports various types of investments in partnership units, shares, investment trusts, and land separately after current assets.

	119.4	121.3
Investments in partnerships and corporations (note 5)	68.9	58.8
Investment in Legacy Hotels Real Estate Investment Trust (note 6)	96.4	56.4
Investments in land held for sale	88.8	92.1
Property and equipment (note 7)	1,441.1	1,261.9
Goodwill (note 8)	123.0	106.0
Intangible assets (note 8)	201.7	149.8
Other assets and deferred charges (note 9)	83.7	75.1
	$ 2,223.0	$ 1,921.4

Illustration 5-7

Balance Sheet Presentation of Long-term Investments— Excerpt from Fairmont Financial Statements

Fairmont's presentation shows the investment in the real estate investment trusts (REIT) separately from other investments in partnerships and corporations since REITs distribute the majority of their income to shareholders each year. This is quite different from a partnership or corporation, which will base distribution of earnings on many factors.

Property, Plant, and Equipment

Property, plant, and equipment are tangible capital assets i.e., properties of a durable nature which are **used in ongoing business operations to generate income**. These assets consist of physical or tangible property such as land, buildings, machinery, furniture, tools, and wasting resources (timberland, minerals). These assets are carried at cost or amortized cost. With the exception of land, most assets are either depreciable (such as buildings) or depletable (such as timberlands or oil reserves).

As shown in Illustration 5-8, **ClubLink Corporation** (ClubLink) has significant capital assets. In fact, in 2002, capital assets represented 95% of total assets. This is not surprising given that the company is one of Canada's largest golf club developers and operators. The bulk of these assets are in land (golf courses) and buildings. Illustration 5-8 shows the detailed breakdown of these assets as presented in note 4 to the financial statements.

Illustration 5-8

Balance Sheet Presentation of Property, Plant, and Equipment—Excerpt from ClubLink's Financial Statements

4. Capital Assets

(thousands of dollars)	Cost	Accumulated Amortization	2002 Net	2001 Net
OPERATING CAPITAL ASSETS				
Golf course lands	$ 210,784	$ –	$ 210,784	$ 209,535
Leased lands	11,354	550	10,804	10,975
Buildings	106,822	11,870	94,952	93,869
Roads, cartpaths and irrigation	45,796	7,283	38,513	36,484
Maintenance equipment	20,657	8,602	12,055	12,825
Clubhouse equipment	19,791	7,259	12,532	11,081
Golf carts	10,235	2,845	7,390	6,325
Office and computer equipment	12,373	8,458	3,915	5,450
	$ 437,812	$ 46,867	390,945	386,544
DEVELOPMENT ASSETS				
Properties under construction			32,998	13,646
Properties under development			28,102	26,535
Properties held for future development			13,201	16,340
			74,301	56,521
			$ 465,246	$ 443,065

What do the Numbers Mean?

Note that ClubLink further segregates its assets between **operating** and **development** assets. This helps users understand which assets are producing revenues already and which ones will be coming on stream to produce additional future revenues, representing growth potential. The basis of valuing the property, plant, and equipment, any liens against the properties, and accumulated amortization should be disclosed, usually in notes to the statements.

Aside from companies in the golf club business, those in real estate, manufacturing, resource-based companies, and pharmaceutical companies also have large amounts of capital assets on their balance sheets. These types of companies are often referred to as being **capital intensive** since they require large amounts of capital to invest in the long-term revenue-generating assets.

Intangible Assets

Intangible assets **are capital assets that lack physical substance** and usually have a higher degree of uncertainty concerning their future benefits. They include patents, copyrights, franchises, goodwill, trademarks, trade names, and secret processes. These intangibles are initially recorded at cost and are divided into two groups for accounting purposes:

- those with finite lives and

- those with infinite lives.

The former are amortized to expense over their useful lives. The latter are not amortized. Both are tested for impairment.

Intangibles can represent significant economic resources, yet financial analysts often ignore them. This is because **valuation and measurement is difficult**. Many intangible assets, especially those that are **internally generated** such as goodwill, are never recognized at all on the balance sheet.

A significant portion of Biovail Corporation's (Biovail) total assets is composed of Goodwill and Intangibles (49%) as shown in Illustration 5-9.

As at December 31	2002	2001
ASSETS		
Current		
Cash and cash equivalents	$ 56,080	$ 434,891
Accounts receivable	190,980	96,556
Inventories	53,047	38,506
Deposits and prepaid expenses	21,524	6,643
	321,631	576,596
Long-term investments	79,324	2,355
Property, plant and equipment, net	136,784	85,581
Goodwill, net	102,212	96,477
Intangible assets, net	1,080,503	556,360
Other assets, net	113,350	14,114
	$ 1,833,804	$ 1,331,483

Illustration 5-9

Balance Sheet Presentation of Goodwill and Intangible Assets—Excerpt from Biovail's Financial Statements

What do the Numbers Mean?

A further look at the detail behind that number shows that Biovail's intangibles include brand names, product rights, and royalty interests for several pharmaceutical products. It makes sense that the company would have a large amount of money invested in intangibles since Biovail is in the business of developing products in the controlled release drug delivery sector. The drugs are patented by the company and become main revenue generators. Having stated this, the true value of **internally generated** patents is generally not reflected in the balance sheet and it is most often the **purchased** rights to drugs that show up as intangible assets since the value is measured through the acquisition. For instance, in 2000, Biovail acquired the rights to Cardizem, a drug for the treatment of hypertension and angina. This drug accounts for 73% of the balance in Intangibles Assets.

Other Assets

The items included in the section Other Assets vary widely in practice. Some of the items commonly included are deferred charges, noncurrent receivables, intangible assets, assets in special funds, future income taxes assets, property held for sale, and advances to subsidiaries. Care should be taken to disclose these assets in sufficient detail such that users can get a better idea of their nature.

Future Income Tax Assets represent the taxes that may be avoided or saved due to deductions that a company may take when preparing **future** tax returns. For instance, when a company buys an asset, it is allowed to deduct the cost of the asset from future taxable income. This represents a benefit, which is tax effected and recognized on the balance sheet. Future Income Taxes will be discussed in greater detail in Chapter 19.

Current Liabilities

Current liabilities are the **obligations that are due within one year from the date of the balance sheet or within the operating cycle, where this is longer.**[21] This concept includes:

1. Payables resulting from the acquisition of goods and services: trade accounts payable, wages payable, taxes payable.

2. Collections received in advance for the delivery of goods or performance of services such as unearned rent revenue or unearned subscriptions revenue.

3. Other liabilities whose liquidation will take place within the operating cycle, such as the portion of long-term bonds to be paid in the current period, or short-term obligations arising from purchase of equipment.

4. Short-term financing payable on demand (such as a line of credit or overdraft).

At times, a liability payable within the year may not be included in the current liabilities section. This may occur either when the debt will be refinanced through another long-term issue,[22] or when the debt is retired out of noncurrent assets. This approach is supportable because liquidation does not result from the use of current assets or the creation of other current liabilities.

Current liabilities are not reported in any consistent order. The items most commonly listed first are accounts payable, accrued liabilities or short-term debt; those most commonly listed last are income taxes payable, current maturities of long-term debt, or other current liabilities. Any secured liability—for example, notes payable where shares are held as collateral—is fully described in the notes so that the assets providing the security can be identified.

The excess of total current assets over total current liabilities is referred to as working capital (sometimes called net working capital). Working capital represents the net amount of a company's relatively liquid resources. That is, it is the liquid buffer available to meet the operating cycle's financial demands. Working capital as an amount is seldom disclosed on the balance sheet, but it is calculated by bankers and other creditors as an indicator of a company's short-run liquidity. To determine the actual liquidity and availability of working capital to meet current obligations, however, one must analyse the current asset's composition and analyse nearness to cash.

Long-term Debt/Liabilities

Underlying Concept

Information about covenants and restrictions gives insight into the financial flexibility and therefore is disclosed under the full disclosure principle.

Long-term liabilities are **obligations that are not reasonably expected to be liquidated within the normal operating cycle but instead are payable at some date beyond that time.** Bonds payable, notes payable, some future income tax liabilities, lease obligations, and pension obligations are the most common examples. Generally, a great deal of supplementary disclosure is needed for this section, because most long-term debt is subject to various covenants and restrictions to protect lenders.[23] Long-term liabilities that

---

[21] *CICA Handbook*, Section 1510.03.

[22] A more detailed discussion of debt expected to be refinanced and its classification in the balance sheet is noted in Chapter 14.

[23] The pertinent rights and privileges of the various securities (both debt and equity) outstanding are usually explained in the notes to the financial statements. Examples of information that should be disclosed are dividend and liquidation preferences, participation rights, call prices and dates, conversion or exercise prices or rates and pertinent dates, sinking fund requirements, unusual voting rights, and significant terms of contracts to issue additional shares, (*CICA Handbook*, Sections 3210 and 3240).

mature within the current operating cycle are classified as current liabilities if their liquidation requires the use of current assets.

Generally, long-term liabilities are of three types:

1. Obligations arising from **specific financing situations**, such as the issuance of bonds, long-term lease obligations, and long-term notes payable.

2. Obligations arising from the **ordinary enterprise operations**, such as pension obligations, future income tax liabilities, and deferred or unearned revenues.

3. Obligations that are **dependent upon the occurrence or nonoccurrence of one or more future events to confirm the amount payable,** or the payee, or the date payable, such as service or product warranties and other contingencies.

It is desirable to report any premium or discount separately as an addition to or subtraction from the bonds payable. The terms of all long-term liability agreements (including maturity date or dates, interest rates, nature of obligation, and any security pledged to support the debt) are frequently described in notes to the financial statements. Future Income Tax Liabilities represent future amounts that the company owes to the government for income taxes. Deferred or unearned revenues are often treated as liabilities since a service or product is owed to the customer. They may be classified as long-term or current.

An example of the financial statement and accompanying note presentation is shown in Illustration 5-10 in the excerpt from Sobeys Inc. (Sobeys).

Liabilities			
Current			
Bankers' acceptances (*Note 6*)	$	–	$ 25.0
Accounts payable and accrued liabilities		922.9	845.1
Income taxes payable		18.8	–
Long-term debt due within one year		48.7	48.8
Current liabilities of discontinued operations (*Note 2*)		–	224.7
		990.4	1,143.6
Long-term debt (*Note 7*)		474.9	608.2
Employee future benefit obligation (*Note 17*)		70.4	59.3
Non-current future tax liabilities (*Note 11*)		43.4	–
Deferred revenue		12.8	14.1
Non-current liabilities of discontinued operations (*Note 2*)		–	2.6
		1,591.9	1,827.8

Illustration 5-10

Balance Sheet Presentation of Long-term Debt—Excerpt from Sobeys' Balance Sheet

Note that the company's long-term liabilities are composed primarily of long-term debt. The deferred revenues consist of revenues related to long-term supplier purchase agreements and rental revenue arising from the sale of subsidiaries. These are being recognized over the terms of the related agreements (which are greater than one year).

Owners' Equity

The owners' equity (shareholders' equity) section is one of the most difficult sections to prepare and understand. This is due to the complexity of capital shares agreements and the various restrictions on residual equity imposed by corporation laws, liability agreements, and boards of directors. The section is usually divided into four parts:

1. **Capital Shares:** represents the exchange value of shares issued

2. **Contributed Surplus:** includes premiums on shares issued and other

3. **Retained Earnings:** includes undistributed earnings, sometimes referred to as earned surplus

4. **Accumulated Other Comprehensive Income:** includes unrealized gains and non-impairment losses on available-for-sale securities, certain debit/credits from related party transactions, non-shareholders/non-government donations and other.

The major disclosure requirements for capital shares (or stock) are the authorized, issued, and outstanding amounts. Contributed surplus is usually presented as one amount. Retained earnings, also presented as one amount is positive if the company has undistributed accumulated profits. Otherwise, it will be a negative number and labelled "Deficit." Any capital shares reacquired by the company (treasury stock) are shown as a reduction of shareholders' equity.[24]

A corporation's ownership or shareholders' equity accounts are considerably different from those in a partnership or proprietorship. Partners' permanent capital accounts and the balance in their temporary accounts (drawing accounts) are shown separately. Proprietorships ordinarily use a single capital account that handles all of the owners' equity transactions.

Presented below is an example of the shareholders' equity section from **Alliance Atlantis Communications Inc.** (Alliance Atlantis).

<table>
<tr><td>Illustration 5-11</td><td colspan="3">SHAREHOLDERS' EQUITY</td></tr>
</table>

Balance Sheet Presentation of Shareholders' Equity— Excerpt from Alliance Atlantis' Balance Sheet

SHAREHOLDERS' EQUITY		
Share capital and other (note 13)	**714.2**	713.4
Deficit	**(183.3)**	(164.5)
Cumulative translation adjustments (note 14)	**(11.8)**	(16.8)
	519.1	532.1
	1,695.1	1,700.5

COMMITMENTS AND CONTINGENCIES (NOTE 23)
THE ACCOMPANYING NOTES FORM AN INTEGRAL PART OF THESE FINANCIAL STATEMENTS.

Note that the Retained Earnings account has turned into a deficit in 2002. Upon review of the notes to the financial statements, this is due to a change in accounting policy applied retroactively. Alliance Atlantis has chosen to show the details regarding number of shares issued and authorized as well as other details in the notes to the financial statements. This leaves the balance sheet itself uncluttered. Illustration 5-13 demonstrates how this information might be presented on the face of the balance sheet. The Cumulative Translation Adjustment account would be renamed Accumulated Other Comprehensive Income under the new accounting standard.

Balance Sheet Format

One method of presenting a classified balance sheet lists assets by sections on the left side and liabilities and shareholders' equity by sections on the right side. The main disadvantage of this format is the need for two facing pages. To avoid the use of facing pages, another format, shown in Illustration 5-12, lists liabilities and shareholders' equity directly below assets on the same page.

Most public Canadian companies use this format.[25]

---

[24] In Canada, under the CBCA, shares reacquired must be cancelled. However, some provincial jurisdictions and other countries (e.g., the United States) still allow treasury shares to exist.

[25] In a survey of 200 Canadian companies, the CICA found that 194 out of the 200 used this format (CICA, *Financial Reporting in Canada, 2002*, p. 56).

Illustration 5-12

Classified Balance Sheet

Digital Tool

Annual Reports

www.wiley.com/canada/kieso

SCIENTIFIC PRODUCTS, INC.
Balance Sheet
December 31, 2004

Assets

Current assets			
Cash		$ 42,485	
Temporary investments—trading		28,250	
Accounts receivable	$165,824		
Less: Allowance for doubtful accounts	1,850	163,974	
Notes receivable		23,000	
Inventories—at average cost		489,713	
Supplies on hand		9,780	
Prepaid expenses		16,252	
Total current assets			$ 773,454
Long-term investments—available for sale			
Investments in Warren Co.			87,500
Property, plant, and equipment			
Land—at cost		125,000	
Buildings—at cost	975,800		
Less: Accumulated amortization	341,200	634,600	
Total property, plant, and equipment			759,600
Intangible assets			
Goodwill			100,000
Total assets			$1,720,554

Liabilities and Shareholders' Equity

Current liabilities			
Accounts payable		$247,532	
Accrued interest		500	
Income taxes payable		62,520	
Accrued salaries, wages, and other liabilities		9,500	
Deposits received from customers		420	
Total current liabilities			$ 320,472
Long-term debt			
Twenty-year 12% debentures, due January 1, 2011			500,000
Total liabilities			820,472
Shareholders' equity			
Paid in on capital shares			
Preferred, 7%, cumulative			
Authorized, issued, and outstanding, 30,000 shares	$300,000		
Common—			
Authorized, 500,000 shares; issued and outstanding, 400,000 shares	400,000		
Contributed surplus	37,500	737,500	
Retained earnings		102,333	
Accumulated other comprehensive income		60,249	
Total shareholders' equity			900,082
Total liabilities and shareholders' equity			$1,720,554

Additional Information Reported

The balance sheet is not complete simply because the assets, liabilities, and owners' equity accounts have been listed. Great importance is given to supplemental information. It may be information not presented elsewhere in the statement, or it may be an elaboration or

4 Objective

Identify balance sheet information requiring supplemental disclosure.

IAS Note

IAS 30 requires specific disclosures for financial institutions such as banks. The *CICA Handbook* does not specifically deal with accounting for banks.

IAS Note

IAS 1 specifically requires disclosure of material uncertainties that cast doubt on the company's ability to continue as a going concern. The *CICA Handbook*, on the other hand, while not explicitly requiring disclosure, would expect that the disclosure be made under the full disclosure principle.

qualification of items in the balance sheet. There are normally five types of information that are supplemental to account titles and amounts presented in the balance sheet.

SUPPLEMENTAL BALANCE SHEET INFORMATION

1. *Contingencies:* material events that have an uncertain outcome.

2. *Accounting Policies:* explanations of the valuation methods used or the basic assumptions made concerning inventory valuations, amortization methods, investments in subsidiaries, etc.

3. *Contractual Situations:* explanations of certain restrictions or covenants attached to specific assets or, more likely, to liabilities.

4. *Additional Detail:* expanded details regarding specific balance sheet line items.

5. *Subsequent Events:* events that happen subsequent to the balance sheet data.

Contingencies

A contingency is defined as an **existing situation involving uncertainty as to possible gain (gain contingency) or loss (loss contingency) that will ultimately be resolved when one or more future events occur or fail to occur.**[26] In short, contingencies are material events that have an uncertain future. Examples of gain contingencies are tax operating loss carry-forwards or company litigation against another party. Typical loss contingencies relate to litigation against the company, environmental issues, possible tax assessments, or government investigation. The accounting and reporting requirements involving contingencies are examined fully in Chapter 14, and, therefore, additional discussion is not provided here.

Accounting Policies

CICA Handbook Section 1505 recommends disclosure for all significant accounting principles and methods that involve selection from among alternatives or those that are peculiar to a given industry. For instance, inventories can be calculated under several cost flow assumptions (such as LIFO, FIFO, and other); plant and equipment can be amortized under several accepted methods of cost allocation (such as double declining-balance, straight-line, and other); and investments can be carried at different valuations (such as cost, fair value, or using the equity method). More informed users of financial statements know of these possibilities and examine the statements closely to determine the methods used and the impact on net income and key ratios.

Companies are also required to disclose information about the use of estimates in preparing financial statements.[27] Disclosure of significant accounting principles and methods and of risks and uncertainties is particularly useful if given in a separate summary preceding the notes to the financial statements or as the initial note.

Contractual Situations

Objective 5

Identify major disclosure techniques for the balance sheet.

In addition to contingencies and different valuation methods, contractual situations of significance should be disclosed in the notes to the financial statements. It is mandatory, for

[26] *CICA Handbook*, Section 3290.02.

[27] *CICA Handbook*, Section 1508 and various other sections.

example, that the essential provisions of guarantees, lease contracts, pension obligations, and stock option plans be clearly stated in the notes. The analyst who examines a set of financial statements wants to know not only the liability amounts but also how the different contractual provisions affect the company at present and in the future.

Commitments related to obligations to maintain working capital, to limit the payment of dividends, to restrict asset use, and to require the maintenance of certain financial ratios must all be disclosed if material. Considerable judgement is necessary to determine whether omitting such information is misleading. The axiom in this situation is, "When in doubt, disclose." It is better to disclose a little too much information than not enough.

The accountant's judgement should reflect ethical considerations, because the manner of disclosing the accounting principles, methods, and other items that have important effects on the enterprise may subtly represent the interests of a particular stakeholder (at the expense of others). A reader, for example, may benefit by the highlighting of information in comprehensive notes, whereas the company—not wishing to emphasize certain information—may choose to provide limited (rather than comprehensive) note information.

Underlying Concept

The basis for including additional information is the full disclosure principle; that is, the information is of sufficient importance to influence the decisions of an informed user.

Additional Detail

For many balance sheet items, further detail is disclosed for clarification. This has already been discussed under the various headings of the balance sheet assets, liabilities, and equity.

Subsequent Events

A period of several weeks or months may elapse after the end of the year before the financial statements are issued. This time is used to take and price inventory, reconcile subsidiary ledgers with controlling accounts, prepare necessary adjusting entries, ensure all transactions for the period have been entered, and obtain an audit of the financial statements.

Underlying Concept

There is a tradeoff here. Timely information is more relevant but may not be as reliable.

During this period, important transactions and events may occur that materially affect the company's financial position or operating situation. These events are known as **subsequent events**. Notes to the financial statements should explain any significant financial events that take place after the formal balance sheet date, but before the issuance of the financial statements.

According to Section 3820 of the *CICA Handbook*, subsequent events fall into one of two types or categories:

1. Those that provide further evidence of **conditions that existed** at the balance sheet date (must adjust financial statements for these).

2. Those that indicate **conditions that arose subsequent** to the financial statement date (disclose in notes if the condition causes a significant change to assets, liabilities, and/or it will have a significant impact on future operations).

These will be dealt with in further detail in Chapter 24.

Techniques of Disclosure

The additional information reported should be disclosed as completely and as intelligently as possible. The following methods of disclosing pertinent information are available: parenthetical explanations, notes, cross reference and contra items, and supporting schedules.

Parenthetical Explanations

Additional information is often provided by parenthetical explanations following the item. For example, shareholders' equity may be shown as follows in Illustration 5-13:

Illustration 5-13

Parenthetical Explanations—Excerpt from Imax Corporation Financial Statements

Shareholders' equity (deficit)		
Capital stock (note 15) Common shares.		
Authorized—unlimited number		
Issued and outstanding—32,973,366 (2001—31,899,114)	64,107	61,866

This device permits disclosure of additional pertinent balance sheet information that adds clarity and completeness. It has an advantage over a note because it brings the additional information into the body of the statement where it is less likely to be overlooked. Of course, lengthy parenthetical explanations that might distract the reader from the balance sheet information must be used with care.

Notes

Notes are used if additional explanations cannot be shown conveniently as parenthetical explanations. For example, inventory-costing methods are reported in **The Quaker Oats Company**'s accompanying notes as follows.

Illustration 5-14

Notes Disclosure

THE QUAKER OATS COMPANY	
Inventories (Note 1)	
Finished goods	$326,000,000
Grain and raw materials	114,100,000
Packaging materials and supplies	39,000,000
Total inventories	479,100,000

Note 1: Inventories. Inventories are valued at the lower of cost or market, using various cost methods, and include the cost of raw materials, labour, and overhead.
The percentage of year-end inventories valued using each of the methods is as follows:

Average quarterly cost	21%
Last-in, first-out (LIFO)	65%
First-in, first-out (FIFO)	14%

If the LIFO method of valuing certain inventories was not used, total inventories would have been $60.1 million higher than reported.

The notes must present all essential facts as completely and succinctly as possible. Loose wording may mislead rather than aid readers. Notes should add to the total information made available in the financial statements, not raise unanswered questions or contradict other portions of the statements.

Cross Reference and Contra Items

A direct relationship between an asset and a liability may be cross referenced on the balance sheet. For example, on December 31, 2004, among the current assets this might be shown:

Cash on deposit with sinking fund trustee for redemption of bonds payable—see Current liabilities	$800,000

Included among the current liabilities is the amount of bonds payable to be redeemed within one year:

> Bonds payable to be redeemed in 2004 see—Current assets　　$2,300,000

This cross reference points out that $2.3 million of bonds payable are to be redeemed currently, for which only $800,000 in cash has been set aside. Therefore, the additional cash needed must come from unrestricted cash, from sales of investments, from profits, or from some other source. The same information can be shown parenthetically, if this technique is preferred.

Another common procedure is to establish contra or adjunct accounts. A contra account on a balance sheet is an item that reduces an asset, liability, or owners' equity account. Examples include Accumulated Amortization and Discount on Bonds Payable. Contra accounts provide some flexibility in presenting the financial information. With the use of the Accumulated Amortization account, for example, a reader of the statement can see the asset's original cost as well as the amortization to date.

An adjunct account, on the other hand, increases an asset, liability, or owners' equity account. An example is Premium on Bonds Payable, which, when added to the Bonds Payable account, describes the enterprise's total bond liability.

Supporting Schedules

Often a separate schedule is needed to present more detailed information about certain assets or liabilities, because the balance sheet provides just a single summary item.

> Property, plant, and equipment
> Land, buildings, equipment, and other fixed assets net
> 　(see Schedule 3)　　$643,300

Illustration 5-15

Disclosure through Use of Supporting Schedules

A separate schedule then might be presented as follows.

SCHEDULE 3
Land, Buildings, Equipment, and Other Fixed Assets

	Total	Land	Buildings	Equipment	Other Fixed Assets
Balance January 1, 2004	$740,000	$46,000	$358,000	$260,000	$76,000
Additions in 2004	161,200		120,000	38,000	3,200
	901,200	46,000	478,000	298,000	79,200
Assets retired or sold in 2004	31,700			27,000	4,700
Balance December 31, 2004	869,500	46,000	478,000	271,000	74,500
Amortization taken to January 1, 2004	196,000		102,000	78,000	16,000
Amortization taken in 2004	56,000		28,000	24,000	4,000
	252,000		130,000	102,000	20,000
Amortization on assets retired in 2004	25,800			22,000	3,800
Amortization accumulated December 31, 2004	226,200		130,000	80,000	16,200
Book value of assets	$643,300	$46,000	$348,000	$191,000	$58,300

Terminology

The account titles in the general ledger do not necessarily represent the best terminology for balance sheet purposes. Account titles are often brief and include technical terms that are understood only by accountants. But balance sheets are examined by many people who are not acquainted with the technical vocabulary of accounting. Thus, balance sheets should contain descriptions that will be generally understood and not subject to misinterpretation.

Objective 6
Indicate the purpose of the statement of cash flows.

SECTION 2—STATEMENT OF CASH FLOWS

The balance sheet, the income statement, and the statement of shareholders' equity each present, to a limited extent and in a fragmented manner, information about an enterprise's cash flows during a period. For instance, comparative balance sheets might show what new assets have been acquired or disposed of and what liabilities have been incurred or liquidated. The income statement provides information about resources, but not exactly cash, provided by operations. The statement of retained earnings shows the amount of dividends declared. None of these statements presents a detailed summary of all the cash inflows and outflows, or the sources and uses of cash during the period. To fill this need, the statement of cash flows (also called the cash flow statement) is required.[28]

Purpose of the Statement of Cash Flows

The primary purpose of a statement of cash flows is to allow users to **assess the enterprise's capacity to generate cash and cash equivalents and its needs for cash resources.**[29]

Reporting the sources, uses, and net increase or decrease in cash helps investors, creditors, and others know what is happening to a company's most liquid resource. Because most individuals maintain their chequebook and prepare their tax return on a cash basis, they can relate to the statement of cash flows and comprehend the causes and effects of cash inflows and outflows and the net increase or decrease in cash. The statement of cash flows provides answers to the following simple but important questions.

1. Where did the cash come from during the period?

2. What was the cash used for during the period?

3. What was the change in the cash balance during the period?

Content and Format of the Statement of Cash Flows

Cash receipts and cash payments during a period are classified in the statement of cash flows into three different activities: **operating, investing,** and **financing** activities. These are the main types of activities that companies enter into. These classifications are defined as follows.

Objective 7
Identify the content of the statement of cash flows.

1. **Operating activities** represent the enterprise's principal revenue-producing activities and all other activities not related to investing or financing.

2. **Investing activities** represent the acquisitions and disposal of long-term assets and other investments not included in cash equivalents.

---

[28] According to the *CICA Handbook*, Section 1540.03, the cash flow statement should be presented as an integral part of the financial statements.

[29] *CICA Handbook*, Section 1540.01.

3. **Financing activities** represent activities that result in changes in the size and composition of the enterprise's equity capital and borrowings.[30]

With cash flows classified into those three categories, the statement of cash flows has assumed the following basic format.

Statement of Cash Flows	
Cash flows from operating activities	$XXX
Cash flows from investing activities	XXX
Cash flows from financing activities	XXX
Net increase (decrease) in cash	XXX
Cash at beginning of year	XXX
Cash at end of year	$XXX

Illustration 5-16

*Basic Format of
Cash Flow Statement*

Digital Tool
Annual Reports

www.wiley.com/canada/kieso

The statement's value is that it helps users evaluate liquidity, solvency, and financial flexibility as previously defined. Chapter 23 deals with the preparation and content of the statement of cash flows in detail. Comprehensive coverage of this topic has been deferred to that later chapter so that several elements and complex topics that make up the content of a typical statement of cash flows may be covered in intervening chapters. The presentation in this chapter is introductory, a reminder of the statement of cash flows' existence and usefulness.

The inflows and outflows of cash classified by activity are shown in Illustration 5-17.

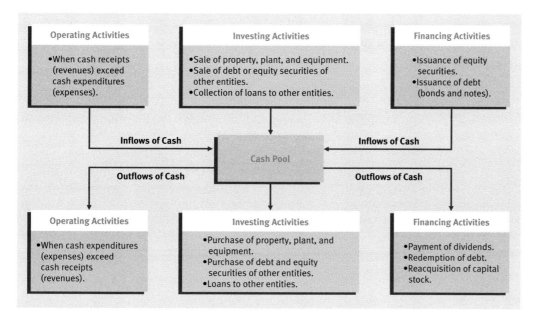

Illustration 5-17

Cash Inflows and Outflows

Usefulness of the Statement of Cash Flows

Although net income provides a long-term measure of a company's success or failure, cash is a company's lifeblood. Without cash, a company will not survive. For small and newly developing companies, cash flow is the single most important element of survival. Even medium and large companies indicate a major concern in controlling cash flow.

Creditors examine the cash flow statement carefully because they are concerned about being paid. A good starting point in their examination is to find **net cash provided by**

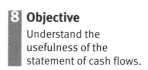

8 Objective
Understand the usefulness of the statement of cash flows.

---

[30] *CICA Handbook*, Section 1540.06.

operating activities. A high amount of net cash provided by operating activities indicates that a company was able to generate sufficient cash internally from operations in the most recent period to pay its bills without further borrowing. Conversely, a low or negative amount of net cash provided by operating activities indicates that a company did not generate enough cash internally from its operations and, therefore, had to borrow or issue equity securities to acquire additional cash. Just because a company was able to generate cash flows from operating activities in the most recent period, however, does not mean that they will be able to replicate this in future periods.

Consequently, creditors look for answers to the following questions in the company's cash flow statements.

1. How successful is the company in generating net cash provided by operating activities?

2. What are the trends in net cash flow provided by operating activities over time?

3. What are the major reasons for the positive or negative net cash provided by operating activities?

4. Are the cash flows sustainable or renewable, i.e., can they be replicated over time?

It is important to recognize that companies can fail even though they are profitable. The difference between net income and net cash provided by operating activities can be substantial. One of the main reasons for the difference between a positive net income and a negative net cash provided by operating activities is substantial increases in receivables and/or inventory. To illustrate, Hinchcliff Inc., in its first year of operations, reported a net income of $80,000. Its net cash provided by operating activities, however, was a negative $95,000, as shown in Illustration 5-18.

Illustration 5-18

Negative Net Cash Provided by Operating Activities

HINCHCLIFF INC.		
Net Cash Flow from Operating Activities		
Net income		$ 80,000
Adjustments to reconcile net income to net cash provided by operating activities:		
Increase in receivables	$(75,000)	
Increase in inventories	(100,000)	(175,000)
Net cash provided by operating activities		$(95,000)

Note that the negative net cash provided by operating activities occurred for Hinchcliff even though it reported a positive net income. The company could easily experience a "cash crunch" because it has tied up its cash in receivables and inventory. If problems in collecting receivables occur or inventory is slow-moving or becomes obsolete, the company's creditors may have difficulty collecting on their loans.

Companies that are expanding often experience this type of "cash crunch" as they must buy increasing inventory amounts to meet increasing sales demands. This means that the cash outflow to purchase the inventory occurs before the cash inflow from the customer for sale of that product. This is often referred to as a "lead-lag" factor. The cash outflow leads (occurs first) and the cash inflow from sales lags (occurs later). The lead-lag factor requires the company to use up any excess cash that it has on hand or to borrow more funds. Refer back to Illustration 5-4—the business operating cycle.

As mentioned earlier in the chapter, financial flexibility may be assessed by using information from the financial statements. The cash flow statement is especially suited for providing this type of information.

Financial Liquidity

One ratio that is used to assess liquidity is the current cash debt coverage ratio. It indicates whether the company can pay off its current liabilities in a given year from its operations. The formula for this ratio is:

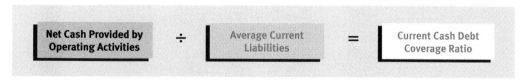

Illustration 5-19

Formula for Current Cash Debt Coverage Ratio

The higher this ratio, the less likely a company will have liquidity problems. For example, a ratio of at least 1:1 is good because it indicates that the company can meet all of its current obligations from internally generated cash flow. To benchmark, this ratio may be compared with similar companies in the industry (or with prior years for the company itself).

Financial Flexibility

A more long-run measure that provides information on financial flexibility is the cash debt coverage ratio. This ratio indicates a company's ability to repay its liabilities from net cash provided by operating activities, without having to liquidate the assets employed in its operations. The formula for this ratio is:

Illustration 5-20

Formula for Cash Debt Coverage Ratio

The higher this ratio, the less likely the company will experience difficulty in meeting its obligations as they come due. As a result, it signals whether the company can pay its debts and survive if external sources of funds become limited or too expensive.

Perspectives

Cash Flow Patterns

Below is a cash flow statement for Telemarketing Inc. The cash flow statement can yield some interesting results when users look at the various patterns between cash inflows and outflows for the following subtotals on the statement: operating, investing, and financing cash flows. For instance, Telemarketing Inc. has cash inflows ("+") from operating activities of $10,000, cash outflows ("−") from investing activities of $15,000, and cash inflows ("+") from financing activities of $31,000, yielding a "+" "−" "+" pattern.

Interpreting this, the company is getting its cash from operations (which is a very good sign) and also from issuance of common shares. It is investing this cash to expand the business. The fact that the company is able to raise funds in the capital markets by issuing shares, indicates that the capital markets have faith in the company's ability to prosper. The fact that the bulk of the money being used to finance the assets is generated from operations means that the company does not have to increase its solvency risk by issuing debt or further dilute its shareholders' equity by issuing more shares. Telemarketing Inc. appears to be a successful company in an expansionary mode.

Illustration 5-21

Statement of Cash Flows

TELEMARKETING INC.
Statement of Cash Flows
For the Year Ended December 31, 2004

Cash flows from operating activities		
Net income		$39,000
Adjustments to reconcile net income to		
net cash provided by operating activities:		
Increase in accounts receivable	$(41,000)	
Increase in accounts payable	12,000	(29,000)
Net cash provided by operating activities		10,000
Cash flows from investing activities		
Purchase of land	(15,000)	
Net cash used by investing activities		(15,000)
Cash flows from financing activities		
Issuance of common shares	50,000	
Payment of cash dividends	(14,000)	
Net cash provided by financing activities		36,000
Net increase in cash		31,000
Cash at beginning of year		–0–
Cash at end of year		$31,000

Companies that generate cash from investing activities may be selling off long-term assets. This pattern generally goes along with a company that is in a downsizing or restructuring mode. If the assets being disposed of are excess or redundant assets, then it makes sense to free up the capital that is tied up. Similarly, if the assets being disposed of relate to operations that are not profitable, disposal reflects a good management decision. However, if the company is in a position where it **must** sell off core income producing assets (e.g., to generate cash), then it may be sacrificing future profitability and revenue-producing potential. Thus, cash flow patterns have significant information content.

Free Cash Flow

A more sophisticated way to examine a company's financial flexibility is to develop a free cash flow analysis. This analysis starts with net cash provided by operating activities and ends with free cash flow, which is calculated as net cash provided by operating activities less capital expenditures and dividends.[31] Free cash flow is the amount of discretionary cash flow a company has for purchasing additional investments, retiring its debt, purchasing treasury stock, or simply adding to its liquidity. This measure indicates a company's level of financial flexibility. Questions that a free cash flow analysis answers are.

1. Is the company able to pay its dividends without resorting to external financing?

2. If business operations decline, will the company be able to maintain its needed capital investment?

3. What is the free cash flow that can be used for additional investment, retirement of debt, purchase of treasury stock, or addition to liquidity?

Presented below is a free cash flow analysis for Nestor Corporation.

---

[31] In determining free cash flows, some companies do not subtract dividends because they believe these expenditures are discretionary.

Illustration 5-22

Free Cash Flow Calculation

NESTOR CORPORATION Free Cash Flow Analysis	
Net cash provided by operating activities	$411,750
Less: Capital expenditures	(252,500)
Dividends	(19,800)
Free cash flow	$139,450

This analysis shows that Nestor has a positive, and substantial, net cash provided by operating activities of $411,750. Nestor reports on its statement of cash flows that it purchased equipment of $182,500 and land of $70,000 for total capital spending of $252,500. This amount is subtracted from net cash provided by operating activities because without continued efforts to maintain and expand facilities, it is unlikely that Nestor can continue to maintain its competitive position. Capital spending is deducted first on the free cash flow statement to indicate it is the least discretionary expenditure a company generally makes. Dividends are then deducted to arrive at free cash flow.

Nestor has more than sufficient cash flow to meet its dividend payment and therefore has satisfactory financial flexibility. Nestor used its free cash flow to redeem bonds and add to its liquidity. If it finds additional investments that are profitable, it can increase its spending without putting its dividend or basic capital spending in jeopardy. Companies that have strong financial flexibility can take advantage of profitable investments even in tough times. In addition, strong financial flexibility frees companies from worry about survival in poor economic times. In fact, those with strong financial flexibility often fare better in poor economic times because they can take advantage of opportunities that other companies cannot.

Caution

As more and more complex financial instruments are created, this results in presentation issues for financial statements preparers. Many instruments have attributes of both debt and equity. This is significant for analysts since a misclassification will affect key ratios. Note disclosure of the details of the instruments assists analysts and other users in assessing a company's liquidity and solvency. This issue will be expanded upon in subsequent chapters dealing with liabilities and equities.

Summary of Learning Objectives

1 Identify the uses and limitations of a balance sheet.

The balance sheet provides information about the nature and amounts of investments in enterprise resources, obligations to creditors, and the owners' equity in net resources. The balance sheet contributes to financial reporting by providing a basis for (1) calculating rates of return, (2) evaluating the enterprise's capital structure, and (3) assessing the enterprise's liquidity, solvency, and financial flexibility. The limitations of a balance sheet are: (1) The balance sheet often does not reflect current value because accountants have adopted a historical cost basis in valuing and reporting assets and liabilities. (2) Judgements and estimates must be used in preparing a balance sheet. The collectibility of receivables, the saleability of inventory, and the useful life of long-term tangible and intangible assets are difficult to determine. (3) The balance sheet omits many items that are of financial value to the business but cannot be recorded objectively, such as human resources, customer base, and reputation.

Digital Tool

Glossary

KEY TERMS

adjunct account, 203
available-for-sale
    securities, 191
balance sheet, 184
cash and cash
    equivalents, 190
cash debt coverage
    ratio, 207
contingency, 200
contra account, 203
current assets, 189
current cash debt
    coverage ratio, 207
current liabilities, 196
financial flexibility, 185
financial instruments, 187
financing activities, 205
future income tax
    assets, 195
future income tax
    liabilities, 197
free cash flow, 208
held-to-maturity
    securities, 191
intangible assets, 195
investing activities, 204
liquidity, 185
long-term investments, 193
long-term liabilities, 196
monetary assets, 187
nonmonetary assets, 187
operating activities, 204
other assets, 195
owners' (shareholders')
    equity, 197
prepaid expenses, 193
property, plant, and
    equipment/capital
    assets, 194
solvency, 185
statement of cash
    flows, 204
statement of financial
    position, 184
subsequent events, 201
trading securities, 191
working capital, 196

2 Identify the major classifications of a balance sheet.

The balance sheet's general elements are assets, liabilities, and equity. The major classifications within the balance sheet on the asset side are current assets; long-term investments; property, plant, and equipment; intangible assets; and other assets. The major classifications of liabilities are current and long-term liabilities. In a corporation, owners' equity is generally classified as shares, contributed surplus, retained earnings, and accumulated other comprehensive income.

3 Prepare a classified balance sheet.

The most common format lists liabilities and shareholders' equity directly below assets on the same page.

4 Identify balance sheet information requiring supplemental disclosure.

Five types of information normally are supplemental to account titles and amounts presented in the balance sheet. (1) Contingencies: Material events that have an uncertain outcome. (2) Accounting policies: Explanations of the valuation methods used or the basic assumptions made concerning inventory valuation, amortization methods, investments in subsidiaries, etc. (3) Contractual situations: Explanations of certain restrictions or covenants attached to specific assets or, more likely, to liabilities. (4) Detailed information: Clarifies in more detail the composition of balance sheet items. (5) Subsequent events: Events that happen after the balance sheet date.

5 Identify major disclosure techniques for the balance sheet.

There are four methods of disclosing pertinent information in the balance sheet: (1) Parenthetical explanations: Additional information or description is often provided by parenthetical explanations following the item. (2) Notes: Notes are used if additional explanations or descriptions cannot be shown conveniently as parenthetical explanations. (3) Cross reference and contra items: A direct relationship between an asset and a liability is cross referenced on the balance sheet. (4) Supporting schedules: Often a separate schedule is needed to present more detailed information about certain assets or liabilities, because the balance sheet provides just a single summary item.

6 Indicate the purpose of the statement of cash flows.

The primary purpose of a statement of cash flows is to provide relevant information about an enterprise's cash receipts and cash payments during a period. Reporting the sources, uses, and net increase or decrease in cash enables investors, creditors, and others to know what is happening to a company's most liquid resource.

7 Identify the content of the statement of cash flows.

Cash receipts and cash payments during a period are classified in the statement of cash flows into three different activities: (1) Operating activities: Involve the cash effects of transactions that enter into the determination of net income. (2) Investing activities: Include making and collecting loans and acquiring and disposing of investments (both debt and equity) and property, plant, and equipment. (3) Financing activities: Involve liability and owners' equity items and include (a) obtaining capital from owners and providing them with a return on their investment and (b) borrowing money from creditors and repaying the amounts borrowed.

8 Understand the usefulness of the statement of cash flows.

Creditors examine the cash flow statement carefully because they are concerned about being paid. The amount and trend of net cash flow provided by operating activities in relation to the company's liabilities is helpful in making this assessment. In addition, measures such as a free cash flow analysis provide creditors and shareholders with a better picture of the company's financial flexibility.

Appendix 5A

Ratio Analysis– A Reference

Using Ratios to Analyse Financial Performance

Companies expose themselves to many risks in carrying on business. Strategically, the goal is to identify these risks and then manage them in order to take advantage of opportunities and maximize shareholder value. How do users know whether a company is managing its risks in a manner that will maximize shareholder value? Illustration 5A-1 depicts the business model as originally introduced in Chapter 4. Risks have been added to the model along with the key management personnel responsible for managing the risks.[32]

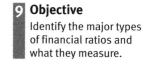

9 Objective
Identify the major types of financial ratios and what they measure.

Illustration 5A-1

The Business Model and Various Related Risks that a Company Must Manage

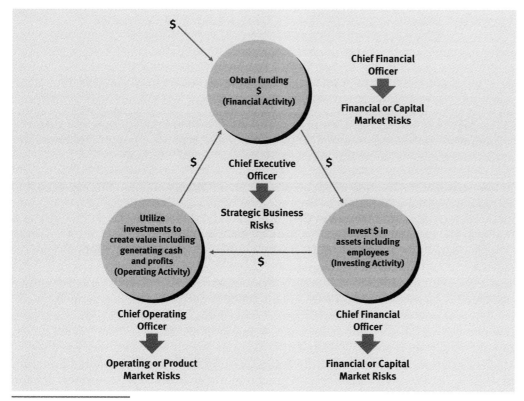

---

[32] This is a brief overview only, meant to link risk with the business model and use of financial statements in communicating information about risk management. A thorough review of risk models and risk management is beyond the scope of this text.

Financial or capital market risks are related to financing and investing activities. For example, a company, in borrowing funds, might increase its solvency and liquidity risk. **Operating or product market risks** are related to operating activities. For instance, there is a risk that a company, in manufacturing a drug, might not be able to produce quality products on time or successfully target the appropriate market for sale.

Information about risks is useful and much of this information is included in the annual report both within the financial statements and in other parts. The financial statements give information about financing, investing, and operating activities and therefore provide indirect feedback as to how related risks are managed and how this in turn affects performance. A solvent company that constantly generates cash from operations has a solid business model where risks and opportunities are appropriately managed to create value. Companies usually disclose explicit information about risks and risk management policies in the MD&A section of the annual report.

Ratio analysis helps in assessing operating and financial risks by **expressing the relationship between selected financial statement data**. Qualitative information from financial statements is gathered by **examining relationships** between items on the statements and **identifying trends** in these relationships. Relationships are often expressed in terms of either a percentage, a rate, or a simple proportion.

To illustrate, recently IBM Corporation had current assets of $42,641 million U.S. and current liabilities of $35,119 million U.S. The relationship is determined by dividing current assets by current liabilities. The alternative means of expression are:

Percentage: Current assets are 121% of current liabilities.

Rate: Current assets are 1.21 times as great as current liabilities.

Proportion: The relationship of current assets to liabilities is 1.21:1.

For analysis of financial statements, ratios are generally classified into four types, as follows.

MAJOR TYPES OF RATIOS

Liquidity Ratios. Measure of the enterprise's short-run ability to pay its maturing obligations.

Activity Ratios. Measure of how effectively the enterprise is using the assets employed. Activity ratios also measure how liquid certain assets like inventory and receivables are—how fast the asset value is realized by the company.

Profitability Ratios. Measure financial performance and shareholder value creation for a given time period.

Coverage or Solvency Ratios. Measure of the degree of protection for long-term creditors and investors or a company's ability to meet its long-term obligations.

Digital Tool

Analyst Toolkit—
Financial
Statement
Analysis Primer
www.wiley.com/canada/kieso

In Chapter 4, profitability ratios were discussed briefly and in this chapter, liquidity, activity, and coverage ratios were touched on. Throughout the remainder of the textbook, ratios are provided to help you understand and interpret the information presented in context of each subject area. The Digital Tool looks at the area of financial statement analysis, of which ratio analysis is one part. Illustration 5A-2 presents some common, basic ratios that will be used throughout the text. In practice, there are many other ratios that are also used that provide useful information.

The key to a refined, information-rich analysis rests with **understanding the business, business risks, and industry** prior to calculating and interpreting any ratios. Specialized industries focus on different ratios depending on the critical success factors in their business. As discussed throughout the chapter, different companies and businesses would be expected to have different types of assets and capital structures. Furthermore, they would be expected to have differing types of costs and revenue streams and business models.

Success in the retail industry, for instance, is reflected in the ability to set prices and target customers so that maximum market penetration is effected. Also critical is the ability to minimize inventory shrinkage (there is a high risk of theft) and keep inventory moving so that it does not become obsolete or out of fashion. A company's ability to achieve this or not is reflected in the gross profit margin (ratio). This is calculated by taking gross profit divided by revenues. Companies must achieve a sufficiently high gross profit to cover off other costs. A stable gross profit margin is a positive sign that management is dealing with all of the above issues.

Once ratios are calculated, they must then be examined and the information interpreted. Examining ratios in isolation provides very little insight. Instead, the **ratios must be compared with or benchmarked against similar ratios, perhaps for the same company from prior periods or alternatively for similar companies in the same industry**.

When benchmarking against industry comparatives, it may be necessary to create these comparatives if they are not available. Select several companies that have a similar business model and are in the same industry. Companies that are the same size are better comparators.

Note that average amounts may be approximated by taking opening and closing balances and dividing by 2.

Summary of Learning Objective for Appendix 5A

9 Identify the major types of financial ratios and what they measure.

Ratios express the mathematical relationship between one quantity and another, in terms of either a percentage, a rate, or a proportion. Liquidity ratios measure the short-run ability to pay maturing obligations. Activity ratios measure the effectiveness of asset usage. Profitability ratios measure an enterprise's success or failure. Coverage ratios measure the degree of protection for long-term creditors and investors.

Digital Tool

Glossary

www.wiley.com/canada/kieso

KEY TERMS

activity ratios, 212
coverage ratios, 212
liquidity ratios, 212
profitability ratios, 212
ratio analysis, 212
solvency ratios, 212

Illustration 5A-2

A Summary of Financial Ratios

RATIO	FORMULA	PURPOSE OR USE
I. Liquidity		
1. Current ratio	$\dfrac{\text{Current assets}}{\text{Current liabilities}}$	Measures short-term debt-paying ability
2. Quick or acid-test ratio	$\dfrac{\text{Cash, marketable securities, and receivables (net)}}{\text{Current liabilities}}$	Measures immediate short-term liquidity
3. Current cash debt coverage ratio	$\dfrac{\text{Net cash provided by operating activities}}{\text{Average current liabilities}}$	Measures a company's ability to pay off its current liabilities in a given year from its operations
II. Activity		
4. Receivable turnover	$\dfrac{\text{Net sales}}{\text{Average trade receivables (net)}}$	Measures liquidity of receivables
5. Inventory turnover	$\dfrac{\text{Cost of goods sold}}{\text{Average inventory}}$	Measures liquidity of inventory
6. Asset turnover	$\dfrac{\text{Net sales}}{\text{Average total assets}}$	Measures how efficiently assets are used to generate sales
III. Profitability		
7. Profit margin on sales	$\dfrac{\text{Net income}}{\text{Net sales}}$	Measures net income generated by each dollar of sales
8. Rate of return on assets	$\dfrac{\text{Net income}}{\text{Average total assets}}$	Measures overall profitability of assets
9. Rate of return on common share equity	$\dfrac{\text{Net income minus preferred dividends}}{\text{Average common shareholders' equity}}$	Measures profitability of owners' investment
10. Earnings per share	$\dfrac{\text{Net income minus preferred dividends}}{\text{Weighted shares outstanding}}$	Measures net income earned on each common share
11. Price earnings ratio	$\dfrac{\text{Market price of shares}}{\text{Earnings per share}}$	Measures the ratio of the market price per share to earnings per share
12. Payout ratio	$\dfrac{\text{Cash dividends}}{\text{Net income}}$	Measures percentage of earnings distributed in the form of cash dividends
IV. Coverage		
13. Debt to total assets	$\dfrac{\text{Total debt}}{\text{Total assets or equities}}$	Measures the percentage of total assets provided by creditors
14. Times interest earned	$\dfrac{\text{Income before interest charges and taxes}}{\text{Interest charges}}$	Measures ability to meet interest payments as they come due
15. Cash debt coverage ratio	$\dfrac{\text{Net cash provided by operating activities}}{\text{Average total liabilities}}$	Measures a company's ability to repay its total liabilities in a given year from its operations
16. Book value per share	$\dfrac{\text{Common Shareholders' equity}}{\text{Outstanding shares}}$	Measures the amount each share would receive if the company were liquidated at the amounts reported on the balance sheet

Appendix 5B

Specimen Financial Statements

The following pages contain the financial statements, accompanying notes, and other information from the 2003 Annual Report of Intrawest Corporation (Intrawest), a significant resort operator in Canada. The company has 9 mountain resorts, 1 warm-weather resort, 25 golf courses under management, a vacation ownership business, and 6 world-class village resorts. One of the company's significant properties is Whistler Blackcomb, which generates significant cash flows.

The Business

Intrawest has three distinct businesses:

1. Mountain resort

2. Warm-weather resort, including golf courses

3. Real estate, including rental and development and sale

One of the key drivers of the mountain resort business is skier visits. Although the number of visits was up for Intrawest in the past year, mountain resort financial performance was affected by warmer weather in the east, a slower economy, and a decrease in international travellers due to the September 11 attack. This was partially offset by an increase in skiers who drove to the resorts.

Within the real estate division, the company develops resort properties such as condominiums, townhouses, and houses and operates a resort club. The company not only sells the units it develops but also rents them out, which contributes to more skiers. The sales represent one-time revenues whereas the rentals represent sustainable income. The resort club generates less than 10% of the company's real estate revenues and therefore is not reported separately. The real estate division performed well in the year.

We do not expect that you will comprehend the company's financial statements and the accompanying notes in their entirety at your first reading. But we expect that by the time you complete the material in this text, your level of understanding and interpretive ability will have grown.

At this point we recommend that you take 20 to 30 minutes to scan the statements and notes to familiarize yourself with the contents and accounting elements. Throughout the following chapters, when you are asked to refer to specific parts of Intrawest's financials, do so. Then, when you have completed reading this book, we challenge you to reread Intrawest's financials to see how much greater and more sophisticated is your understanding of them.

Management's Discussion and Analysis

(All dollar amounts are in United States currency, unless otherwise indicated)

The following discussion and analysis should be read in conjunction with our audited consolidated financial statements for the year ended June 30, 2003 and accompanying notes included in this annual report. The discussion of our business may include forward-looking statements about our future operations, financial results and objectives. These statements are necessarily based on estimates and assumptions that are subject to risks and uncertainties. Our actual results could differ materially from those expressed or implied by such forward-looking information due to a variety of factors including, but not limited to, our ability to implement our business strategies, seasonality, weather conditions, competition, general economic conditions, currency fluctuations, world events and other risks detailed in our filings with Canadian securities regulatory authorities and the U.S. Securities and Exchange Commission.

COMPANY OVERVIEW

Intrawest is the world's leading operator and developer of village-centered resorts. We have a network of 10 mountain resorts, geographically diversified across North America's major ski regions. Our resorts include Whistler Blackcomb (77% interest) and Panorama in British Columbia, Blue Mountain (50% interest) in Ontario, Tremblant in Quebec, Stratton in Vermont, Snowshoe in West Virginia, Copper and Winter Park in Colorado, Mammoth (59.5% interest) in California and Mountain Creek in New Jersey. We assumed control of Winter Park in December 2002 under a long-term capital lease arrangement. Our resorts hosted 8.2 million skier visits in fiscal 2003, 10.7% of the North American market and the most in the mountain resort industry.

We own and operate one warm-weather resort, Sandestin, in Florida. Our resort assets include 18 golf courses and we also manage an additional 11 golf courses for other owners. We have interests in several other leisure-related businesses, including Alpine Helicopters (45% interest) and the Breeze/Max retail store chain.

We are the largest mountain resort real estate developer in North America. We develop real estate at our resorts and at six third-party owned resorts (five in the United States and one in France). We develop real estate for the purpose of sale and to June 30, 2003 we have closed 10,490 residential units at 15 different resorts.

OPERATING SUMMARY

Our operating results in 2003 were below the expectations we set at the outset of the year. The travel and leisure industry continued to feel the impact of the challenges we faced in 2002, i.e., the slow economy and the aftermath of September 11, and it also had to deal with several unforeseen events, including the war in Iraq and the SARS outbreak.

Income from continuing operations was $34.8 million in 2003 compared with $58.6 million in 2002. The decline was caused primarily by reduced profits from our real estate business and a $12.3 million write-down of technology assets. Until the beginning of March our ski and resort operations were performing well, however concerns over the war in Iraq and the SARS outbreak had a dramatic impact on destination visits to our resorts at a time that has historically been the busiest part of our season. Consequently, in the third and fourth quarters, our ski and resort operations lost the ground they had gained earlier in the season.

In Colorado, real estate sales continued to be slow. In Whistler, we had planned to close the second phase of high-end, high-margin single-family lots at Kadenwood but the market for this product type has temporarily stalled. Notwithstanding these situations, demand for real estate has generally been very strong at our resorts, as evidenced by our record backlog of pre-sales. We will realize the benefit of these pre-sales when they close in 2004 and 2005. Our real estate profits were also impacted by delays in the completion of construction of two projects that pushed closings into fiscal 2004.

The write-down of technology assets resulted from our decision to standardize various business systems across our resorts and reflects the write-off of our investment in redundant systems. We expect to realize both efficiencies and cost savings as a consequence of this decision.

Total Company EBITDA was $209.2 million in 2003, down from $211.2 million in 2002. A reconciliation between earnings reported in our statements of operations and Total Company EBITDA is included in "Additional Information" at the end of this discussion and analysis.

REVIEW OF SKI AND RESORT OPERATIONS

Our ski and resort operations are segregated into two reportable segments: mountain resort operations and warm-weather resort operations. The mountain resort operations comprise all the operating activities at our 10 mountain resorts as well as the operations of Resort Reservations (RezRez), Alpine Helicopters and Breeze/Max Retail. The warm-weather resort operations comprise all the operating activities at Sandestin as well as operations at our five stand-alone golf courses.

The key drivers of the mountain resort operations business are skier visits, revenue per visit and margins. Our strategy to increase skier visits has two main elements: improving the quality of the resort experience by upgrading and expanding the on-mountain facilities and building villages at the base to provide accommodation for destination guests. By expanding the amenities on the mountain and in the village, we are able to broaden the customer mix, extend the length of stay and capture a higher percentage of guest spending, all of which increases revenue per visit. Building the accommodation also allows visits to be spread more evenly during the week and during the season, which improves margins since a significant proportion of operating expenses at a resort are fixed. The key drivers of the warm-weather resort operations business are similar; i.e., golf rounds, revenue per round and margins.

The following table highlights the results of our ski and resort operations.

	2003	2002	CHANGE (%)
Skier visits [1]	7,302,000	6,283,000	16.2
Revenue (Millions)	$ 571.5	$ 485.1	17.8
EBITDA (Millions)	$ 116.7	$ 107.3	8.8
Margin (%)	20.4	22.1	

[1] All resorts are at 100% except Mammoth at 59.5% and Blue Mountain at 50%.

Revenue from ski and resort operations was $571.5 million in 2003 compared with $485.1 million in 2002. Revenue from mountain resorts increased from $424.8 million to $506.5 million while revenue from warm-weather resorts increased from $60.3 million to $65.0 million.

MOUNTAIN RESORTS

On December 23, 2002, we closed on a transaction with the City and County of Denver to operate Winter Park on a long-term lease arrangement. Since the lease gives us control over the resort, for financial reporting purposes Winter Park is treated in the same manner as any of our directly owned resorts. This was an important transaction for us, not only because it adds a quality resort in the largest ski market in North America to our portfolio, but also because of the synergies that it will create with Copper and our other Colorado operations. Winter Park, combined with Copper, gives us an operation with over two million skier visits, similar in scale to Whistler Blackcomb, our most profitable resort. By sharing administrative services, collaborating on marketing initiatives, harmonizing operations and developing new product and service offerings, we expect to realize higher margins than either resort could achieve individually.

The results of Winter Park were consolidated from the closing date and accounted for $33.1 million of the increase in mountain resort revenue and 793,000 of the increase in skier visits. In February 2002 we sold our smallest resort, Mont Ste. Marie, which generated $1.6 million of revenue from 62,000 skier visits in fiscal 2002.

On a same-resort basis (i.e., excluding Winter Park and Mont Ste. Marie) mountain resort revenue increased by 11.8% or $50.1 million due to various factors:

(MILLIONS)	
Increase in skier visits	$ 15.9
Increase in revenue per skier visit	15.2
Increase in non-skier visit revenue	10.8
Impact of exchange rate on reported revenue	8.2
	$ 50.1

Same-resort skier visits increased by 4.6% from 6,221,000 in 2002 to 6,509,000 in 2003, despite the difficult conditions in the travel and leisure sector. Skier visits were higher at every resort except for Whistler Blackcomb, Panorama and Tremblant. Skier visits at our eastern resorts, which experienced excellent early-season conditions, were 18.7% ahead of last year through the first week of March but then declined by 7.5% to the end of the season. The changes were somewhat less significant at our western resorts, being 2.3% ahead through the first week of March and 3.9% below for the balance of the season. The decline in visits after the first week of March came entirely from the destination market as evidenced by the fact that during this period season pass visits increased 24.4%. We estimate that the increase in skier visits increased mountain resort revenue by $15.9 million in 2003.

Same-resort revenue per skier visit increased 4.2% from $55.07 in 2002 (after adjusting for the impact of the improvement in the Canadian dollar exchange rate) to $57.40 in 2003. Revenue per skier visit is a function of ticket prices and ticket yields, and revenue from non-ticket sources such as retail and rental stores, lodging, ski school, and food and beverage services. Ticket yields reflect the mix of ticket types (e.g., adult, child, season pass and group), the proportion of day versus destination visitors (destination visitors tend to be less price-sensitive), and the amount of discounting of full-price tickets in regional markets. Revenue per visit from non-ticket sources is also influenced by the mix of day versus destination visitors, the affluence of the visitor base, and the quantity and type of amenities and services offered at the resort.

Revenue per visit from ticket sales increased 1.4% from $27.60 to $27.99. There was a relative shift in the mix of visits from "paid" visits to season pass visits as we sold 16.6% more season passes and frequency cards in 2003 than 2002 and this tended to lower ticket yields. Over the past several seasons we have deliberately sought to increase season pass and frequency card sales in order to increase pre-committed revenue. Revenue per visit from non-ticket sources increased 7.1% from $27.46 to $29.41. This increase is less than we had expected due to softness in the retail business (which was an industry trend) and lower revenues from ski school and rental due to reduced destination visits after February. Approximately half of the increase in non-ticket revenue per visit came from lodging and property management due to a 12.9% increase in the number of occupied room nights, most notably at Blue Mountain, Stratton and Snowshoe. We estimate that the increase in revenue per visit increased mountain resort revenue by $15.2 million in 2003.

For the purposes of this analysis, non-skier visit revenue comprises revenue from golf and other summer activities and revenue from businesses such as RezRez, Alpine Helicopters and Breeze/Max. Revenue from golf and other summer activities increased 8.1% across the mountain resorts from $39.5 million in 2002 to $42.7 million in 2003. Summer lodging and property management revenue increased 20.1%, led by strong room night growth at Tremblant, Blue Mountain and Snowshoe. Our central reservations business, RezRez, expanded its operations into several new warm-weather destinations, leading to a 40.9% growth in revenue to $13.5 million in 2003. We had expected much higher revenues from RezRez, however increased competition in the on-line travel sector and reduced travel by U.S. customers (which account for over 80% of RezRez's business) significantly reduced bookings. Revenue at Alpine and Breeze/Max increased by 4.0% and 1.1%, respectively. Overall, non-skier visit revenue increased by $10.8 million in 2003.

The reported amount of mountain resort revenue was increased by $8.2 million in 2003 because of the increase in the value of the Canadian dollar against the U.S. dollar. In 2003 revenue from the Canadian resorts was translated for financial statement reporting purposes at an average rate of Cdn.$1.51 to U.S.$1.00 compared with an average rate of Cdn.$1.57 to U.S.$1.00 in 2002.

WARM-WEATHER RESORTS

Revenue from warm-weather resorts increased 7.9% from $60.3 million in 2002 to $65.0 million in 2003. Revenue at Sandestin increased by $6.4 million due mainly to a 12.6% increase in occupied room nights. The opening of the new village at Baytowne Wharf in July 2002 increased the accommodation base at Sandestin and added many new amenities to the resort, driving higher lodging, retail, and food and beverage revenue. The sale of the Sabino Springs golf course in Tuscon in June 2002 reduced warm-weather resort revenue by $3.2 million, however this was partially offset by $1.1 million more revenue from Big Island Country Club in Hawaii, which we acquired in January 2002.

REVENUE BREAKDOWN

The breakdown of ski and resorts operations revenue by business was as follows:

(MILLIONS)	2003 REVENUE	2002 REVENUE	INCREASE (DECREASE)	CHANGE (%)
Mountain operations	$ 228.6	$ 193.3	$ 35.3	18.3
Retail and rental shops	95.9	85.0	10.9	12.8
Food and beverage	74.9	63.0	11.9	18.9
Lodging and property management	81.7	61.0	20.7	33.9
Ski school	37.1	30.4	6.7	22.1
Golf	28.0	29.4	(1.4)	(4.9)
Other	25.3	23.0	2.3	10.3
	$ 571.5	$ 485.1	86.4	17.8

Assuming control of Winter Park in December 2002 increased revenue from mountain operations, retail and rental shops, food and beverage, and ski school by $20.7 million, $3.4 million, $4.8 million and $3.5 million, respectively.

The proportion of revenue from mountain operations has fallen from 49.3% of total ski and resort operations revenue in 1997 to 40.0% in 2003. This trend is likely to continue as we build out the villages at our resorts, expanding the inventory of lodging units and changing the customer mix in favor of destination visitors who spend more on retail and rental, ski school, and food and beverage.

SKI AND RESORT OPERATIONS EXPENSES AND EBITDA

Ski and resort operations expenses increased from $377.8 million in 2002 to $454.9 million in 2003. Mountain resort expenses increased by $71.4 million to $397.3 million while warm-weather resort expenses increased by $5.7 million to $57.6 million.

The net impact of assuming control of Winter Park and selling Mont Ste. Marie increased mountain resort expenses by $19.5 million, leaving same-resort expense growth of $51.9 million. The strengthening of the value of the Canadian dollar increased the reported amount of mountain resort expenses by $6.7 million. The strong start in the East in 2003 compared with a very late start in 2002 impacted our expense growth. In 2002 we had a "vertical" ramp-up at Blue Mountain, Stratton, Snowshoe and Mountain Creek with essentially no pre-Christmas season, resulting in abnormally low costs. By comparison, in 2003 these eastern resorts commenced operations much earlier, ramping up more gradually, resulting in higher costs supported by higher revenues. In addition, the impact of the war in Iraq and SARS occurred in our core-operating month of March and happened suddenly, reducing visits significantly. Since we were uncertain how long the decline in visits would last and how great it would be, we had limited ability to ramp down costs. Overall, increased business volumes at these four eastern resorts during the full 2003 season resulted in a 19.3% increase in operating expenses (equivalent to $13.1 million) and a 22.6% increase in revenues.

The expansion of RezRez into new locations added $10.5 million to ski and resort operations expenses. We had set up an organization and infrastructure at RezRez to deal with a significant expected increase in business volumes. With the majority of bookings typically occurring in the period from October to February, the revenue shortfall was evident too late to institute meaningful cost savings before year-end. We have now heavily downsized and reorganized RezRez to focus on the ski and golf destinations where we have inherent advantages and away from warm-weather destinations. We expect these expense reductions, combined with revenue opportunities from the significant interest we are receiving from other travel providers in the RezRez on-line booking engine, to return this business to profitability.

The increase in warm-weather resort expenses of $5.7 million was almost entirely due to Sandestin and the opening of the new village in July 2002. The revenue growth at Sandestin more than offset the growth in expenses.

EBITDA from ski and resort operations increased from $107.3 million in 2002 to $116.7 million in 2003. EBITDA from the mountain resorts increased from $98.9 million to $109.2 million while EBITDA from the warm-weather resorts declined from $8.4 million to $7.5 million.

On a same-resort basis, mountain resorts EBITDA was $96.8 million in 2003 compared with $98.6 million in 2002. EBITDA from the resorts increased by 8.3%, however this was offset by reduced EBITDA from the non-skier visit businesses, i.e., Alpine, RezRez and the Breeze/Max retail chain.

The decrease in warm-weather resort EBITDA was due mainly to reduced profits from our Arizona golf operations due to the sale of the Sabino Springs golf course last year.

REVIEW OF REAL ESTATE OPERATIONS

We have two real estate divisions – the resort development group and the resort club group. The resort development group develops and sells three main products: condo-hotel units (typically, small village-based units that owners occupy sporadically and put into a rental pool at other times), townhome units (typically, larger units outside the main village core that owners retain for their own use) and single-family lots (serviced land on which owners or other developers build homes). In order to broaden market appeal, condo-hotel and townhome units are sold on the basis of both whole ownership and fractional ownership. Currently most of the fractional product has been quarter-share but a high-end tenth-share project is under construction at Whistler and other fractions are under consideration. The resort club group's business is a flexible form of timeshare where owners purchase points that entitle them to use accommodation at different resorts. The resort club group currently generates less than 10% of our total real estate revenue and hence is not reported as a separate business segment in the financial statements.

Our business strategy for real estate has two major elements: the maximization of profits from the sale of real estate and the provision of accommodation for destination visitors, which represents an earnings annuity for the ski and resort operations. Visitors renting the accommodation generate lodging revenue as well as revenue from purchasing lift tickets or golf fees, food and beverage, and retail.

We recognize real estate sales revenue at the time of "closing," which is when title to a completed unit is conveyed to the purchaser and the purchaser becomes entitled to occupancy. Since our standard practice is to pre-sell our real estate, any proceeds received prior to closing are recorded as deferred revenue in our balance sheet.

The following table highlights the results of the real estate business.

	2003	2002	CHANGE (%)
Units closed	1,239	1,290	(4.0)
Revenue (Millions)	$ 512.7	$ 487.8	5.1
Operating profit (Millions)	$ 75.0	$ 85.1	(11.9)
Margin (%)	14.6	17.4	

Revenue from the sale of real estate increased 5.1% from $487.8 million in 2002 to $512.7 million in 2003. Revenue generated by the resort development group increased from $449.8 million to $472.8 million while revenue generated by the resort club group increased from $38.0 million to $39.9 million.

RESORT DEVELOPMENT GROUP REVENUE

We closed a total of 528 units at the Canadian resorts in 2003 compared with 589 units last year. The average price per unit increased from Cdn.$423,000 in 2002 to Cdn.$436,000 in 2003. We also closed the sale of the majority of our commercial properties at Tremblant in 2003, recognizing revenue of $21.5 million. Currently we have approximately 500,000 square feet of remaining commercial properties at nine different resorts. Our plan is to sell all of these properties in the normal course.

We closed 611 units at the U.S. resorts in 2003 compared with 701 units in 2002. The number of units that close in a particular period is dependent on both transacting sales and the timing of construction completion. We had expected to close more units in 2003, however construction delays, due mainly to difficult site conditions, the complicated building design and construction management issues (see below), were experienced on two projects at Lake Las Vegas and Squaw Valley. The average price per unit was $457,000 at the U.S. resorts in 2003 (after adjusting the number of units for the impact of joint ventures at Keystone and Three Peaks), up from $442,000 in 2002. In 2003 we also closed our first 100 units at Les Arcs in France for proceeds of $31.1 million.

The mix of product types (i.e., condo-hotel, townhome and single-family lot) closed was not materially different in 2003 than in 2002.

During 2003 we reorganized the resort development group from a resort-based structure to a regional structure. We have six regional offices providing development and construction services to 17 different resorts. This structure allows us to share resources between resorts and gives us the critical mass in each region to be able to engage specialized development and construction experts that might be uneconomical for an individual resort. The new structure also strengthens our control systems so that, for example, the construction management issues that affected the completion of two projects in 2003 are less likely to impact our business in the future.

RESORT CLUB GROUP REVENUE

The resort club group generated $39.9 million in sales revenue in 2003, up from $38.0 million in 2002. We had expected stronger revenue growth, however sales were impacted by the slow economy and the uncertainty created by recent world events. This product type is more of a consumer purchase than our resort development group product and confidence is an important factor in the purchase consideration. Furthermore, resort club product does not have the same sense of scarcity as other types of real estate so purchasers are under less pressure to buy.

REAL ESTATE OPERATING PROFIT

Operating profit from real estate sales decreased from $85.1 million in 2002 to $75.0 million in 2003. The profit margin was 14.6% in 2003 compared with 17.4% in 2002. The reduction in margin was due to a number of factors, including:

- The write-off of $3.3 million of costs at Copper in connection with various projects that are on hold pending a strengthening of the Colorado market.
- A write-down of $3.0 million in connection with two projects at Mountain Creek. Sales of these projects had slowed because of an environmental lawsuit (that has now been settled), resulting in increased holding costs. In addition we have projected more conservative sales prices for unsold inventory.
- Lower margins in 2003 for the resort club group. Marketing and sales costs increased to 57% of revenue in 2003 from 48% in 2002 as a result of the difficult market conditions.

    Excluding the impact of the factors listed above, the profit margin in 2003 would have been 16.7%.

REAL ESTATE PRE-SALES

At August 31, 2003, we had pre-sold real estate revenue of $460 million that we expect to close in fiscal 2004. This compares with pre-sold revenue this time last year of $370 million for delivery in fiscal 2003. In addition, we have $65 million of pre-sales for delivery in fiscal 2005. This does not include projects that will be undertaken by Leisura (see Liquidity and Capital Resources), which has $260 million of pre-sales for delivery in fiscal 2004 and 2005. Our strategy of pre-selling projects before the start of construction reduces market risk and increases the predictability of real estate earnings.

CAPITALIZATION OF COSTS TO REAL ESTATE

Generally accepted accounting practice for real estate requires that all costs in connection with the development of real estate be capitalized to properties under development and then expensed in the period when the properties are closed and the revenue is recognized. Such costs include land and building costs as well as overhead costs of personnel directly involved in the development, construction and sale of real estate, and interest on debt used to fund real estate costs. The capitalized interest comprises interest on specific real estate debt (i.e., construction financing) and interest on the portion of general corporate debt used to fund real estate development expenditures.

The book value of properties increased from $867.8 million at June 30, 2002 to $1,067.3 million at June 30, 2003. The strengthening of the value of the Canadian dollar from a year-end rate of Cdn$1.52:US$1.00 in 2002 to Cdn$1.35:US$1.00 in 2003 increased the reported book value of properties by $26.3 million. Other factors responsible for the increase include:

- A net increase of $73.3 million in the book value of commercial space resulting from the completion of new properties at Whistler, Mammoth, Sandestin, Squaw Valley, Lake Las Vegas and Blue Mountain and the sale of commercial properties at Tremblant.
- An increase of $26.1 million in the book value of resort club properties mainly due to the new resort club locations under construction at Blue Mountain and Zihuatanejo, Mexico.

    The book value of properties to be sold to Leisura was $73.8 million at June 30, 2003. We expect to transfer the majority of these properties in the first two quarters of fiscal 2004.

    With the completion and closing of projects currently under construction and with the development of most new projects to take place in Leisura, the book value of our properties is expected to decline significantly in 2004.

RENTAL PROPERTIES

Effective July 1, 2002, we changed our plans for commercial properties. Instead of holding them as long-term revenue-producing investments, existing commercial properties would be sold and commercial properties developed in the future would be developed for the purpose of sale. In 2003 we sold the majority of our commercial properties at Tremblant and we plan to sell our remaining portfolio of commercial properties. Rental revenue and rental expenses relating to these properties were capitalized during 2003. In 2002 rental property revenue of $8.0 million and rental property expenses of $5.0 million were included in the statement of operations.

REVIEW OF CORPORATE OPERATIONS

INTEREST AND OTHER INCOME

Interest and other income was $2.4 million in 2003, up from $1.1 million in 2002 due mainly to dividend income from Compagnie des Alpes (CDA) and higher interest income net of losses on asset disposals.

In July 2002 we sold 55% of our investment in CDA and at the same time ceased to exercise significant influence over CDA's affairs. In 2003 we therefore accounted for CDA on a cost basis, whereas in 2002 we used the equity basis and recorded income from equity accounted investment of $3.9 million. Subsequent to June 30, 2003, we sold the balance of our investment in CDA. Both the sale in July 2002 and the sale subsequent to June 30, 2003 were for proceeds approximately equal to the book value of our investment.

INTEREST COSTS

Interest expense increased from $43.1 million in 2002 to $47.1 million in 2003. We incurred total interest costs (including financing fees and amortization of deferred financing costs) of $102.9 million in 2003 compared with $83.4 million in 2002. The increase was due mainly to interest on the $137-million 10.5% senior unsecured notes issued in October 2002, partially offset by interest on the Cdn. $125-million 6.75% unsecured debentures repaid in December 2002. In addition we had higher construction loan interest due to increased construction activity and the Winter Park capital lease added $2.2 million of interest. In total, $55.5 million of this interest was capitalized to properties under development, $14.9 million of which was subsequently expensed in 2003 when the properties were closed.

DEPRECIATION AND AMORTIZATION

Depreciation and amortization expense increased from $65.4 million in 2002 to $67.5 million in 2003. The increase was due mainly to assuming control of Winter Park.

GENERAL AND ADMINISTRATIVE COSTS

All general and administrative (G&A) costs incurred by our resorts in connection with the ski and resort operations business are included in ski and resort operations expenses. Similarly, G&A costs incurred in the development of real estate are initially capitalized to properties, and then expensed to real estate costs in the period when the properties are closed. Corporate G&A costs, which mainly comprise executive employee costs, public company costs, audit and legal fees, corporate information technology costs and head office occupancy costs are disclosed as a separate line in the statement of operations. The breakdown of G&A costs for 2003 and 2002 was as follows:

(MILLIONS)		2003	PROPORTION (%)		2002	PROPORTION (%)
Corporate G&A costs	$	14.9	12.6	$	12.2	11.1
G&A expenses of ski and resort operations business		65.1	55.2		55.9	50.8
Previously capitalized G&A costs expensed in real estate cost of sales		16.5	14.0		15.4	14.0
Total G&A costs expensed during the year		96.5	81.8		83.5	75.9
Net G&A costs of real estate business capitalized to properties		21.5	18.2		26.6	24.1
Total G&A costs incurred during the year	$	118.0	100.0	$	110.1	100.0

Corporate G&A costs increased from $12.2 million in 2002 to $14.9 million in 2003 due mainly to higher compensation and pension costs, and increased insurance, legal and audit expenses. Including the G&A costs of our operations and real estate divisions, we expensed 81.8% of general and administrative expenses in 2003 compared with 75.9% in 2002.

WRITE-DOWN OF TECHNOLOGY ASSETS

When we acquired our network of resorts we inherited many different information technology (IT) systems. This impeded our ability to share information and build synergies across resorts. Where we introduced new IT systems, we used a standardized approach, however we recognized that we needed to move to greater standardization of legacy IT systems. During the fourth quarter of 2003 we therefore wrote off $9.1 million of IT systems that we plan to replace. Furthermore, in 2003 we reorganized and downsized RezRez, our central reservations business. RezRez had expanded into several warm-weather destinations but the expansion was not successful. We therefore decided to abandon these locations to focus on our core ski destinations. In light of this, we reviewed the value of RezRez assets and took a write-down of $3.2 million for various of its IT assets in the fourth quarter.

INCOME TAXES

We provided for income taxes of $6.2 million in 2003 compared with $9.5 million in 2002. This equates to an effective tax rate of 12.0% in both years. Note 13 to the consolidated financial statements provides a reconciliation between income tax at the statutory rate (38.0% and 41.2%, respectively, in 2003 and 2002) and the actual income tax charge.

NON-CONTROLLING INTEREST

We have a 23% limited partner in the two partnerships that own Whistler Blackcomb. The results of the two partnerships are fully consolidated with the outside partner's share of earnings shown as non-controlling interest. Non-controlling interest decreased from $11.7 million in 2002 to $11.3 million in 2003, reflecting reduced ski and resort operations earnings due to the slow start to the season and the impact of the war in Iraq and SARS on business, primarily in March.

DISCONTINUED OPERATIONS

Our consolidated financial statements disclose the results of our non-resort real estate business as discontinued operations. The discontinued operations incurred a loss of $0.6 million in 2003 compared with a loss of $0.1 million in 2002. Losses (or net income) from discontinued operations accrue to the holders of the non-resort preferred ("NRP") shares and any cash flows generated by the discontinued operations are paid to the NRP shareholders to redeem their shares. In December 2002 the discontinued operations were wound up and all the remaining NRP shares were redeemed.

LIQUIDITY AND CAPITAL RESOURCES

Generating free cash flow continues to be a high priority for us. Free cash flow does not have a standardized meaning prescribed by generally accepted accounting principles ("GAAP"). We calculate it as follows:

(MILLIONS)	2003	2002
Cash provided by (used in) continuing operating activities [1]	$ (26.6)	$ 5.7
Investment in ski and resort operations assets ("capex")	(64.5)	(91.5)
Free cash flow	$ (91.1)	$ (85.8)

[1] A reconciliation between net earnings as determined by Canadian GAAP and cash provided by (used in) continuing operating activities is shown in the Consolidated Statements of Cash Flows.

In 2003 our results showed negative free cash flow of $91.1 million compared with negative free cash flow of $85.8 million in 2002. We had expected positive free cash flow in 2003, however the slowdown in the travel and leisure sector, made worse by concerns over the war in Iraq and SARS, reduced operating cash flow from our ski and resort operations businesses. Cash flow from our real estate business was impacted by delayed completions of some projects and slow sales in Colorado, although generally demand for our products has been robust. On the positive side we reduced resort capex to about $65 million, significantly below prior years, and we sold some non-core assets.

Over the past few years, as we started to build out our villages and install infrastructure, our real estate business has been a significant user of cash. In both 2003 and 2002 we were free cash flow positive before making investments to grow our real estate business. During 2003 we implemented a strategy – the Leisura partnerships – that will allow us to both reduce the capital required for real estate and to grow the business.

We are also focused on increasing cash flow from our ski and resort operations businesses. We have a number of initiatives at our resorts to increase revenue (e.g., customer relationship management (CRM) and E-commerce programs, more packaging of services and maximizing sales channels) and to reduce costs (e.g., shared-services model in Colorado and elsewhere, downsizing of RezRez and eliminating discretionary expenses). Given the strong competitive position of our resorts, we do not need to invest as much in capex as we did in 2002 and prior years. We expect future resort capex requirements to remain close to 2003 levels (at approximately the same amount as depreciation and amortization expense). We also plan to grow our fee-based businesses (e.g., golf course and lodging management) and we can do this by investing minimal capital.

We expect to generate free cash flow in fiscal 2004 and to use it to repay debt.

LEISURA PARTNERSHIPS

In 2003 we entered into two partnerships (one in Canada and one in the U.S., collectively referred to as "Leisura") that will have a significant impact on our capital structure and our capital requirements for real estate. Leisura is intended to carry out the ownership and financing of the bulk of our real estate production. By selling the bulk of our production-phase real estate to separate and independent entities we achieve several objectives, including:

■ Significantly reducing the capital requirements needed to support the real estate business.
■ Significantly reducing debt levels.
■ Limiting our exposure to the risks of the production-phase real estate business.
■ Implementing separate and appropriate capital structures for our resort business and our real estate business.

We will continue to undertake some development activity on our own account outside of the Leisura structure. This includes smaller townhome projects and single-family lots, which are not as capital intensive as condo-hotel and larger townhome projects, as well as resort club and fractional projects. In addition, we will carry out all development activity at certain resorts (e.g., Snowmass because it is a joint venture development or Les Arcs because construction is primarily purchaser-financed).

Intrawest is a minority partner in Leisura and we will account for our investment in Leisura on an equity basis. We will continue to identify land parcels for development and complete the master planning, project design and pre-sales process for all future real estate projects. Once a project has reached set pre-sale targets and construction is about to commence, Leisura will acquire the land parcels for the project from us at fair market value. By December 31, 2003, Leisura is expected to acquire land parcels for about 10 projects at seven resorts (none had been transferred at June 30, 2003). In future years, we expect to carry out the bulk of the real estate production at our resorts in a similar fashion. There is no guarantee, however, that Leisura will acquire more land parcels from us in future years. For the projects that are sold to Leisura, we will provide development management services on a fee basis.

The Leisura partnerships have sufficient capital to be strong credit-worthy entities that can comfortably finance and carry out their business on a freestanding basis. Construction financing will be secured by the projects with recourse only to Leisura.

The formation of Leisura will result in a significant reduction in our net debt in 2004. We will recover the bulk of our investment in projects currently under construction as they are completed over the next 12 months and our capital expenditures to support this part of our real estate business in future will be limited to our investment in Leisura. The difference between the large amount of capital recovered from current projects as they complete (approximately 80% of the units in these projects are pre-sold) and the much smaller investment in Leisura will generate significant cash flow that will be used to reduce debt.

CASH FLOWS IN 2003 COMPARED WITH 2002

The major sources and uses of cash in 2003 and 2002 are summarized in the table below. This table should be read in conjunction with the Consolidated Statements of Cash Flows, which are more detailed as prescribed by GAAP.

(MILLIONS)	2003	2002	CHANGE
Funds from continuing operations	$ 122.8	$ 128.6	$ (5.8)
Acquisitions, resort capex and other investments	(39.4)	(107.1)	67.7
Net cash flow from other net assets	14.6	44.3	(29.7)
Funds available before net investment in real estate	98.0	65.8	32.2
Net investment in real estate developed for sale	(163.8)	(163.2)	(0.6)
Net cash flow from operating and investing activities	(65.8)	(97.4)	31.6
Net financing inflows	115.9	87.7	28.2
Increase (decrease) in cash	$ 50.1	$ (9.7)	$ 59.8

Funds from continuing operations generated $122.8 million of cash flow in 2003, down from $128.6 million in 2002 as reduced real estate profits and increased interest and G&A expenses were partially offset by higher EBITDA from ski and resort operations.

Acquisitions, resort capex and other investments used $39.4 million of cash in 2003, down from $107.1 million in 2002. Acquisitions and resort capex used $6.0 million and $26.9 million, respectively, less cash in 2003 than 2002 while proceeds from asset disposals, net of other investments, generated $34.8 million more cash in 2003 than 2002.

Assuming control of Winter Park used $2.8 million cash in 2003 as the majority of the purchase price was financed through a capital lease. In 2002 we had acquired Big Island Country Club in Hawaii for a cash payment of $8.9 million. We do not plan to invest significant capital in acquisitions in the near term. We will continue to seek opportunities to expand our businesses but do so in ways (e.g., engaging in management contracts or entering joint ventures) that limit our capital requirements.

We spent $64.5 million on resort capex in 2003, down from $91.5 million in 2002. Each year we spend $25 million to $30 million on maintenance capex at our resorts. Maintenance capex is considered non-discretionary (since it is required to maintain the existing level of service) and comprises such things as snow grooming machine or golf cart replacement, snowmaking equipment upgrades and building refurbishments. Expansion capex (e.g., new lifts or new restaurants) is considered discretionary and the annual amount spent varies year by year. We expect maintenance and expansion capex to be approximately the same in 2004 as in 2003.

Proceeds from non-core asset sales (mainly 55% of our investment in Compagnie des Alpes and employee housing units at Whistler Blackcomb) net of new investments generated $28.0 million of cash in 2003. Subsequent to year-end we sold the balance of our investment in Compagnie des Alpes for $12.5 million. In 2002 we sold Mont Ste. Marie and Sabino Springs golf course but these sales were offset by new investments, resulting in a net investment in other assets of $6.7 million. We have identified other non-core assets for disposal and we will continue our program of selling these assets in the future.

Other net assets provided cash of $14.6 million in 2003 compared with $44.3 million in 2002. This represents the cash flow from changes in receivables, other assets, payables and deferred revenue.

Our businesses provided cash flow of $98.0 million in 2003 compared with $65.8 million in 2002, before net new investments in real estate. We invested $163.8 million in real estate in 2003, approximately the same as in 2002. We had expected our net investment to be lower in 2003, however the construction delays at Squaw Valley and Lake Las Vegas and slower transfers of properties to Leisura delayed cost recoveries until fiscal 2004. We expect to recover a portion of our investment in real estate in fiscal 2004 as units currently under construction are completed and closed and new real estate production moves to Leisura.

In total, our operating and investing activities used $65.8 million of cash in 2003, down from $97.4 million in 2002. We also paid $12.0 million and $11.3 million, respectively, in 2003 and 2002 for dividends to our shareholders and distributions to the limited partner in Whistler Blackcomb and we expect these payments to be approximately the same in 2004. Amounts paid to redeem and repurchase NRP shares were $6.7 million in 2003 and $0.4 million in 2002. We have now redeemed all the NRP shares. Net borrowings of $129.9 million and $46.3 million in 2003 and 2002, respectively, as well as proceeds of share issuances of $4.8 million and $53.0 million in 2003 and 2002, respectively, funded these cash flows.

DEBT AND LIQUIDITY POSITION

At June 30, 2003, we had net debt (i.e., bank and other indebtedness net of cash) of $1,134.1 million compared with $979.2 million at June 30, 2002. Part of the increase in net debt was due to the strengthening of the Canadian dollar, particularly in the fourth quarter. The change in the exchange rate from Cdn$1.52:US$1.00 at last year end to Cdn$1.35:US$1.00 at this year end increased the reported amount of Canadian dollar-denominated debt by $39.9 million at June 30, 2003.

As discussed above, we expect to generate significant free cash flow in fiscal 2004 and to reduce net debt. We are confident that we can achieve this objective because of the Leisura transaction and the current high level of pre-sales of real estate that is being completed within Intrawest. Not only does the Leisura transaction significantly reduce our capital requirements for real estate but it also reduces the risk that delays in construction completion will result in higher debt balances because these debt balances are obligations of Leisura, not Intrawest.

Over half of our bank and other indebtedness ($658.4 million) at June 30, 2003 is not due for repayment until after 2008. With respect to the balance of our bank and other indebtedness, $287.2 million is due to be repaid in fiscal 2004 of which $229.1 million, or approximately 80%, relates to construction financing that is covered more than 100% by real estate pre-sales. As these projects close, we will repay the construction loans as well as other debt. Our senior credit facility, which had a balance of $240.2 million at year-end, is due in fiscal 2005 and we expect to renew this facility on maturity.

We have a number of revolving credit facilities to meet our short-term capital needs. These include a $365-million facility at the corporate level, of which $240 million was drawn at June 30, 2003. In addition, several of our resorts have lines of credit in the range of $5 million to $10 million each to fund seasonal cash requirements. Since Leisura will be undertaking most of the future real estate development, we have not renewed the three revolving credit facilities that we had last year for real estate construction. Instead we will finance any projects that we develop through one-off project-specific loans. We believe that these credit facilities, combined with cash on hand and internally generated cash flow, are adequate to finance all of our normal operating needs.

BUSINESS RISKS

We are exposed to various risks and uncertainties in the normal course of our business that can cause volatility in our earnings. Our ski and resort operations and real estate businesses are managed to deal with risks that are common to most companies; i.e., the risks of severe economic downturn, competition and currency fluctuations, and the more industry-specific risks of unfavorable weather conditions, seasonality of operations and development issues.

ECONOMIC DOWNTURN

A severe economic downturn could reduce spending on resort vacations and weaken sales of recreational real estate.

Our results in both 2003 and 2002 (years that saw a significant slowdown in the economy) provide evidence of our ability to deal with an economic downturn. Ski and resort operations EBITDA for 2003 and 2002 were only 3.7% and 0.9%, respectively, below our record EBITDA in 2001, on a same-resort basis. There are two main reasons for this:

- The strong competitive position of each of our resorts due to the villages at their base and the quality of their on-mountain facilities. This has also created a loyal customer base that is strongly committed to our resorts.
- The profile of our customer base, who have incomes well above the national average and are therefore less likely to have their vacation plans impacted by a recession.

Real estate developers face two major risks from an economic downturn: land risk and completed inventory risk. Land risk arises when land is purchased with debt and economic conditions deteriorate resulting in higher holding costs and reduced profitability, or worse, loan defaults and foreclosure. We have reduced our land risk by generally acquiring land at low cost with the purchase of a resort or by securing land through options and joint ventures. Completed inventory risk arises when completed units cannot be sold and construction financing cannot be repaid. Often this risk arises because many developers are supplying units to the market and since we control most of the supply at our resorts, this risk is reduced. We have also mitigated this risk by pre-selling a significant portion of units prior to commencement of, and during, construction.

COMPETITION

The mountain resort industry has significant barriers to entry (e.g., very high start-up costs, significant environmental hurdles) that prevent new resorts from being created. Competition therefore is essentially confined to existing resorts. Our resorts compete for destination visitors with other mountain resorts in Canada, the United States, Europe and Japan, and with other leisure industry companies, such as cruise lines. They also compete for day skiers with other ski areas within each resort's local market area. Skier visits in North America have been relatively static over the past 10 years, which has increased competition between resort owners.

Our strategy has been to acquire resorts that have natural competitive advantages (e.g., in terms of location, vertical drop and quality of terrain) and to enhance those advantages by upgrading the facilities on the mountain and building resort villages at the base. Our principal strength compared with industry competitors is our ability to combine expertise in resort operations and real estate development, particularly in building master-planned resort villages. Increasingly the village has become the dominant attraction in generating visits to a resort.

We own substantially all of the supply of developable land at the base of our resorts and hence competition in real estate is somewhat restricted. Expertise in all aspects of the development process, including resort master-planning, project design, construction, sales and marketing, and property management also gives us a distinct competitive advantage.

CURRENCY FLUCTUATIONS

Over the past several years our Canadian resort operations have benefited from the lower Canadian dollar relative to other currencies, and particularly against the U.S. dollar. This has made vacationing in Canada more affordable for foreign visitors and it has encouraged Canadians to vacation at home. A significant shift in the value of the Canadian dollar, particularly against its U.S. counterpart, could impact earnings at Canadian resorts.

We finance our U.S. assets with U.S. dollar debt and our Canadian assets with Canadian dollar debt. Generally we service debt with revenue denominated in the same currency. In addition, cash flow generated by Canadian operations is generally retained in Canada and invested in expanding our Canadian assets. Similarly cash flow generated at our U.S. resorts is generally reinvested in the United States. Cross-border cash transactions and currency exchanges are kept to a minimum.

Since we report earnings in U.S. dollars but our income is derived from both Canadian and U.S. sources, we are exposed to foreign currency exchange risk in our reported earnings. Revenues and expenses of our Canadian operations will be impacted by changes in exchange rates when they are reported in U.S. dollars. We estimate that a 10% increase in the average value for the fiscal year of the Canadian dollar relative to the U.S. dollar would result in a 5% increase in our reported net income, while a 10% decline in the average value of the Canadian dollar would result in a 4% decrease in our reported net income. The impact of Canadian/U.S. dollar exchange rate changes on the balance sheet are reflected in the foreign currency translation amount included in shareholders' equity and does not affect reported earnings.

UNFAVORABLE WEATHER CONDITIONS

Our ability to attract visitors to our resorts is influenced by weather conditions and the amount of snowfall during the ski season.

We manage our exposure to unfavorable weather in three ways: by being geographically diversified, by seeking to spread visits to our resorts as evenly as possible through the season and by investing in snowmaking. Geographically diversified companies like ours can reduce the risk associated with a particular region's weather patterns. Every ski season since 1995, favorable and unfavorable weather conditions at different times across North America have offset one another, allowing us to come within 3% of our budgeted winter season ski and resort operations revenue on a same-resort basis. The more a resort can attract visitors evenly through the season the less vulnerable it is to unfavorable weather at a particular time. We seek to spread visits to our resorts by marketing to destination visitors who book in advance, stay several days and are less likely than day visitors to change their vacation plans, and by attempting to increase visits mid-week and at non-peak times. Investing in snowmaking also mitigates the impact of poor natural snow conditions. Snowmaking is particularly important in the East due to the number of competing resorts and less reliable snowfall. We have an average of 92% snowmaking coverage across our five eastern resorts.

SEASONALITY OF OPERATIONS

Ski and resort operations are highly seasonal. In fiscal 2003, 67% of our ski and resort operations revenue was generated during the period from December to March. Furthermore during this period a significant portion of ski and resort operations revenue is generated on certain holidays, particularly Christmas/New Year, Presidents' Day and school spring breaks, and on weekends. Conversely, Sandestin's peak operating season occurs during the summer months, partially offsetting the seasonality of the mountain resorts. Our real estate operations tend to be somewhat seasonal as well, with construction primarily taking place during the summer and the majority of sales closing in the December to June period. This seasonality of operations impacts reported quarterly earnings. The operating results for any particular quarter are not necessarily indicative of the operating results for a subsequent quarter or for the full fiscal year.

We have taken steps to balance our revenue and earnings throughout the year by investing in four-season amenities (e.g., golf) and growing summer and shoulder-season businesses. As a result of these initiatives, the proportion of ski and resort operations revenue earned outside the historically strong third fiscal quarter has increased to 45.2% in 2003 from 32.7% in 1997.

DEVELOPMENT ISSUES

As a real estate developer we face the following industry-specific risks:

- Zoning approvals or project permits could be withheld.
- Construction and other development costs could exceed budget.
- Project completion could be delayed.
- Purchasers could fail to close.

Our experience in resort master planning equips us to deal with municipal approval agencies. In addition, our approach of consulting with all community stakeholders during the planning process helps to ensure that we run into less resistance at public hearings.

We are not in the construction business – we engage general contractors to construct our real estate projects. Having fixed-price contracts with completion penalties reduces our exposure to cost overruns and construction delays. As our experience showed this year, some construction delays are inevitable in the real estate business, particularly given the location and variable weather conditions at our mountain resorts, however we do not anticipate that they would have a material impact on our earnings in any particular year.

Our pre-sales contracts require purchasers to put down 20% deposits, i.e., generally in the range of $50,000 to $150,000, which they forfeit if they do not close. Historically very few purchasers have failed to close.

Leisura rather than Intrawest is at risk for cost overruns, completion delays and purchaser contract defaults on any project that it purchases. We continue to be at risk for zoning and permit approvals since these approvals must be in hand before projects are sold to Leisura.

There is a risk that Leisura will not purchase land parcels from Intrawest in future years. The Leisura partners have, however, expressed a strong interest in extending their involvement in future years and we expect them to do so. In the event that the current partners decide not to participate in future projects we believe we will be able to identify alternative investors.

WORLD EVENTS

World events such as the terrorist attacks on September 11, 2001, the war in Iraq and the SARS outbreak disrupt domestic and international travel and reduce visits, or change the mix of visits, to our resorts. Often these types of events happen suddenly and cannot be prepared for. As we have shown over the past two years, we have been less impacted by these events than many other leisure and hospitality companies due to the high degree of commitment of our customers (e.g., as season pass holders or property owners), the significant proportion of our visitors who drive to our resorts (approximately 85% of all resort visits) and our ability to communicate with our database of customers and market products to them.

CRITICAL ACCOUNTING POLICIES

This discussion and analysis is based upon our consolidated financial statements, which have been prepared in accordance with GAAP in Canada. The preparation of these financial statements requires us to make estimates and judgments that affect the reported amounts of assets, liabilities, revenues and expenses and disclosure of contingencies. These estimates and judgments are based on factors that are inherently uncertain. On an ongoing basis, we evaluate our estimates based on historical experience and on various other assumptions that we believe are reasonable under the circumstances. Actual amounts could differ from those based on such estimates and assumptions.

We believe the following critical accounting policies call for management to make significant judgments and estimates.

USEFUL LIVES FOR DEPRECIABLE ASSETS　Ski and resort operations assets and administrative furniture, computer equipment, software and leasehold improvements are depreciated using both the declining balance and straight-line basis (depending on the asset category) over the estimated useful life of the asset. Assets may become obsolete or require replacement before the end of their estimated useful life in which case any remaining undepreciated costs must be written off.

FUTURE NET CASH FLOWS FROM PROPERTIES **Properties under development and held for sale, which totaled $1,067.3 million at June, 30, 2003, are recorded at the lower of cost and net realizable value. In determining net realizable value it is necessary, on a non-discounted basis, to estimate the future cash flows from each individual project for the period from the start of land servicing to the sell-out of the last unit. This involves making assumptions about project demand and sales prices, construction and other development costs, and project financing. Changes in our assumptions could affect future cash flows from properties leading to reduced real estate profits or potentially property write-downs.**

RECOVERABILITY OF AMOUNTS RECEIVABLE **At June 30, 2003, amounts receivable totaled $203.6 million. We regularly review the recoverability of amounts receivable and record allowances for any amounts that we deem to be uncollectible. Disputes with our customers or changes in their financial condition could alter our expectation of recoverability and additional allowances may be required.**

VALUE OF FUTURE INCOME TAX ASSETS AND LIABILITIES **In determining our income tax provision, we are required to interpret tax legislation in a variety of jurisdictions and to make assumptions about the expected timing of the reversal of future tax assets and liabilities. In the event that our interpretations differed from those of the taxing authorities or that the timing of reversals is not as anticipated, the tax provision could increase or decrease in future periods.**

At June 30, 2003, we had accumulated $117.2 million of non-capital loss carryforwards which expire at various times through 2023. We have determined that it is more likely than not that the benefit of these losses will be realized in the future and we have recorded future tax assets of $35.8 million related to them. If it is determined in the future that it is more likely than not that all or a part of these future tax assets will not be realized, we will make a charge to earnings at that time.

OUTLOOK

As we move into fiscal 2004 we are focused on two primary financial objectives – to improve profitability and returns on capital from our existing businesses and to generate free cash flow.

Our goal is to increase profits in the ski and resort operations business by both growing revenue and containing costs. As we build more accommodation in our villages we will open up revenue-generating opportunities in lodging management and indirectly in our other businesses. We intend to utilize our capability in CRM and direct marketing to increase occupancy levels. Given the shortened booking window, these programs have the advantage that they can be introduced quickly and, since they are targeted to existing customers and good prospects, their rate of success is enhanced. They are also more cost-effective than other marketing programs.

We expect to reduce costs at our resorts by capitalizing on our network to take advantage of economies of scale. Standardized processes and technology will allow us to consolidate operations. The consolidation of our Colorado businesses in fiscal 2004 is the first step. Since new capex for ski and resort operations is expected to remain at about the same level as annual depreciation, these revenue growth and cost containment initiatives are expected to lead to a higher return on capital.

Our new organizational structure for the real estate development group is expected to improve our efficiency and our control, leading to stronger real estate margins in the future. This structure also facilitates growth since resources for multiple resorts are pooled.

As we assembled and improved our network of resorts we were significantly cash flow negative. We are now moving to a less capital-intensive business model with lower capital expenditures for our resorts and reduced infrastructure spending for real estate. We are also focused on growing our fee-based businesses (e.g., lodging, golf course and reservations management), which require minimal capital investment. We expect the Leisura transaction to produce free cash flow from our real estate business in fiscal 2004. This will occur as we recover the book value of current projects, and expenditures for the most capital-intensive projects in the future are restricted to our investment in Leisura. As we generate free cash flow we expect to pay down debt and improve our credit ratios.

ADDITIONAL INFORMATION

The term EBITDA does not have a standardized meaning prescribed by GAAP and may not be comparable to similarly titled measures presented by other publicly traded companies. A reconciliation between net earnings as determined in accordance with Canadian GAAP and Total Company EBITDA is presented in the table below.

	YEAR ENDED JUNE 30	
(MILLIONS)	2003	2002
Income before tax	$ 52.3	$ 79.8
Depreciation and amortization	67.5	65.4
Interest expense	47.1	43.1
Interest in real estate costs	32.4	27.9
Write-down of technology assets	12.3	—
Interest and other income	(2.4)	(5.0)
Total Company EBITDA	$ 209.2	$ 211.2

QUARTERLY FINANCIAL SUMMARY

(in millions of dollars, except per share amounts)

	2003 QUARTERS				2002 QUARTERS			
	1ST	2 ND	3RD	4TH	1ST	2ND	3RD	4TH
Total revenue	$ 112.7	$ 208.0	$ 402.6	$ 363.3	$ 93.7	$ 231.4	$ 342.1	$ 318.8
Income (loss) from continuing operations	(11.1)	3.4	56.8	(14.3)	(9.8)	6.0	56.2	6.2
Results of discontinued operations	0.0	(0.6)	0.0	0.0	0.2	(0.1)	0.0	(0.1)
Net income (loss)	(11.1)	2.8	56.8	(14.3)	(9.6)	5.9	56.2	6.0
PER COMMON SHARE:								
Income (loss) from continuing operations								
Basic	(0.23)	0.07	1.20	(0.30)	(0.22)	0.14	1.28	0.14
Diluted	(0.23)	0.07	1.19	(0.30)	(0.22)	0.14	1.25	0.13
Net income (loss)								
Basic	(0.23)	0.07	1.20	(0.30)	(0.22)	0.14	1.28	0.14
Diluted	(0.23)	0.07	1.19	(0.30)	(0.22)	0.14	1.25	0.13

Management's Responsibility

The consolidated financial statements of Intrawest Corporation have been prepared by management and approved by the Board of Directors of the Company. Management is responsible for the preparation and presentation of the information contained in the consolidated financial statements. The Company maintains appropriate systems of internal control, policies and procedures that provide management with reasonable assurance that assets are safeguarded and that financial records are reliable and form a proper basis for preparation of financial statements.

The Company's independent auditors, KPMG LLP, have been appointed by the shareholders to express their professional opinion on the fairness of the consolidated financial statements. Their report is included below.

The Board of Directors ensures that management fulfills its responsibilities for financial reporting and internal control through an Audit Committee which is composed entirely of outside directors. This committee reviews the consolidated financial statements and reports to the Board of Directors. The auditors have full and direct access to the Audit Committee.

Joe S. Houssian
Chairman, President and Chief Executive Officer
SEPTEMBER 2, 2003

Daniel O. Jarvis
Executive Vice President and Chief Financial Officer

Auditors' Report to the Shareholders

We have audited the consolidated balance sheets of Intrawest Corporation as at June 30, 2003 and 2002 and the consolidated statements of operations, retained earnings, and cash flows for the years then ended. These financial statements are the responsibility of the Company's management. Our responsibility is to express an opinion on these financial statements based on our audits.

We conducted our audits in accordance with Canadian generally accepted auditing standards. Those standards require that we plan and perform an audit to obtain reasonable assurance whether the financial statements are free of material misstatement. An audit includes examining, on a test basis, evidence supporting the amounts and disclosures in the financial statements. An audit also includes assessing the accounting principles used and significant estimates made by management, as well as evaluating the overall financial statement presentation.

In our opinion, these consolidated financial statements present fairly, in all material respects, the financial position of the Company as at June 30, 2003 and 2002 and the results of its operations and its cash flows for the years then ended in accordance with Canadian generally accepted accounting principles.

KPMG LLP
Chartered Accountants
Vancouver, Canada
SEPTEMBER 2, 2003

Consolidated Statements of Operations

For the years ended June 30, 2003 and 2002
(In thousands of United States dollars, except per share amounts)

	2003	2002
REVENUE:		
Ski and resort operations	$ 571,527	$ 485,142
Real estate sales	512,695	487,775
Rental properties	—	8,038
Interest and other income	2,417	1,115
Income from equity accounted investment	—	3,901
	1,086,639	985,971
EXPENSES:		
Ski and resort operations	454,861	377,801
Real estate costs	437,690	402,700
Rental properties	—	4,963
Interest (note 16)	47,142	43,072
Depreciation and amortization	67,516	65,434
Corporate general and administrative	14,889	12,175
Write-down of technology assets (note 8(b))	12,270	—
	1,034,368	906,145
Income before undernoted	52,271	79,826
Provision for income taxes (note 13)	6,243	9,549
Income before non-controlling interest and discontinued operations	46,028	70,277
Non-controlling interest	11,274	11,675
Income from continuing operations	34,754	58,602
Results of discontinued operations (note 4)	(578)	(122)
Net income	$ 34,176	$ 58,480
INCOME FROM CONTINUING OPERATIONS PER COMMON SHARE:		
Basic	$ 0.73	$ 1.33
Diluted	0.73	1.31
NET INCOME PER COMMON SHARE:		
Basic	0.73	1.33
Diluted	0.73	1.31

See accompanying notes to consolidated financial statements.

Consolidated Balance Sheets

June 30, 2003 and 2002
(In thousands of United States dollars)

	2003	2002
ASSETS		
CURRENT ASSETS:		
Cash and cash equivalents	$ 126,832	$ 76,689
Amounts receivable (note 7)	126,725	109,948
Other assets (note 8(a))	123,610	88,062
Resort properties (note 6)	662,197	399,572
Future income taxes (note 13)	10,619	7,536
	1,049,983	681,807
Ski and resort operations (note 5)	918,727	841,841
Properties (note 6):		
Resort	405,100	461,893
Discontinued operations	—	6,325
	405,100	468,218
Amounts receivable (note 7)	76,842	64,734
Other assets (note 8(b))	65,070	94,332
Goodwill	—	15,985
	$2,515,722	$2,166,917
LIABILITIES AND SHAREHOLDERS' EQUITY		
CURRENT LIABILITIES:		
Amounts payable	$ 218,444	$ 195,254
Deferred revenue (note 10)	134,878	99,484
Bank and other indebtedness (note 9):		
Resort	287,176	279,297
Discontinued operations	—	2,750
	640,498	576,785
Bank and other indebtedness (note 9):		
Resort	973,743	773,790
Discontinued operations	—	82
	973,743	773,872
Due to joint venture partners (note 14)	5,388	3,963
Deferred revenue (note 10)	43,609	23,069
Future income taxes (note 13)	94,986	75,843
Non-controlling interest in subsidiaries	46,359	36,116
	1,804,583	1,489,648
Shareholders' equity:		
Capital stock (note 12)	460,742	466,899
Retained earnings	264,640	241,665
Foreign currency translation adjustment	(14,243)	(31,295)
	711,139	677,269
	$2,515,722	$2,166,917

Contingencies and commitments (note 15)
Subsequent event (note 8(b))

Approved on behalf of the Board:

Joe S. Houssian
Director

Paul M. Manheim
Director

See accompanying notes to consolidated financial statements.

Consolidated Statements of Retained Earnings

For the years ended June 30, 2003 and 2002
(In thousands of United States dollars)

	2003	2002
Retained earnings, beginning of year:		
As previously reported	$ 241,665	$ 187,922
Adjustment to reflect change in accounting for goodwill and intangibles, net of tax (note 2(t)(i))	(6,150)	—
As restated	235,515	187,922
Net income	34,176	58,480
Dividends	(5,051)	(4,737)
Retained earnings, end of year	$ 264,640	$ 241,665

See accompanying notes to consolidated financial statements.

Consolidated Statements of Cash Flows

For the years ended June 30, 2003 and 2002
(In thousands of United States dollars)

	2003	2002
CASH PROVIDED BY (USED IN):		
OPERATIONS:		
Income from continuing operations	$ 34,754	$ 58,602
Items not affecting cash:		
Depreciation and amortization	67,516	65,434
Future income taxes	(3,914)	(2,873)
Income from equity accounted investment	—	(3,901)
(Gain) loss on asset disposals, net of write-offs	858	(323)
Write-down of technology assets	12,270	—
Non-controlling interest	11,274	11,675
Funds from continuing operations	122,758	128,614
Recovery of costs through real estate sales	437,690	402,700
Acquisition and development of properties held for sale	(601,524)	(565,863)
Increase in amounts receivable, net	(12,109)	(8,936)
Changes in non-cash operating working capital (note 21)	26,590	49,191
Cash provided by (used in) continuing operating activities	(26,595)	5,706
Cash provided by discontinued operations	140	3,898
	(26,455)	9,604
FINANCING:		
Proceeds from bank and other borrowings	599,112	351,259
Repayments on bank and other borrowings	(469,235)	(304,933)
Issue of common shares for cash, net of issuance costs	4,782	53,037
Redemption and repurchase of non-resort preferred shares (note 12(a))	(6,697)	(358)
Dividends paid	(5,051)	(4,737)
Distributions to non-controlling interests	(6,923)	(6,534)
	115,988	87,734
INVESTMENTS:		
Expenditures on:		
Revenue-producing properties	—	(2,353)
Ski and resort operations assets	(64,546)	(91,490)
Other assets	(11,778)	(8,463)
Business acquisitions (note 3)	(2,849)	(8,876)
Proceeds from asset disposals	39,783	4,103
	(39,390)	(107,079)
Increase (decrease) in cash and cash equivalents	50,143	(9,741)
Cash and cash equivalents, beginning of year	76,689	86,430
Cash and cash equivalents, end of year	$ 126,832	$ 76,689

Supplementary information (note 21)
See accompanying notes to consolidated financial statements.

Notes to Consolidated Financial Statements

For the years ended June 30, 2003 and 2002
(Tabular amounts in thousands of United States dollars, unless otherwise indicated)

1 OPERATIONS:

Intrawest Corporation was formed by an amalgamation on November 23, 1979 under the Company Act (British Columbia) and was continued under the Canada Business Corporations Act on January 14, 2002. Through its subsidiaries, the Company is engaged in the development and operation of mountain and golf resorts principally throughout North America.

2 SIGNIFICANT ACCOUNTING POLICIES:

(a) BASIS OF PRESENTATION:

The consolidated financial statements are prepared in accordance with generally accepted accounting principles in Canada as prescribed by The Canadian Institute of Chartered Accountants ("CICA"). Information regarding United States generally accepted accounting principles as it affects the Company's consolidated financial statements is presented in note 22.

(b) PRINCIPLES OF CONSOLIDATION:

The consolidated financial statements include:

(i)   the accounts of the Company and its subsidiaries; and

(ii)   the accounts of all incorporated and unincorporated joint ventures, including non-controlled partnerships, to the extent of the Company's interest in their respective assets, liabilities, revenues and expenses.

The Company's principal subsidiaries and joint ventures are as follows:

SUBSIDIARIES	PERCENTAGE INTEREST HELD BY THE COMPANY (%)
Blackcomb Skiing Enterprises Limited Partnership	77
Whistler Mountain Resort Limited Partnership	77
Intrawest/Lodestar Limited Partnership	100
IW Resorts Limited Partnership	100
Mont Tremblant Resorts and Company, Limited Partnership	100
Copper Mountain, Inc.	100
Intrawest California Holdings, Inc.	100
Intrawest Golf Holdings, Inc.	100
Intrawest Resort Ownership Corporation	100
Intrawest Retail Group, Inc.	100
Intrawest Sandestin Company, L.L.C.	100
Intrawest/Winter Park Holdings Corporation (note 3)	100
Mountain Creek Resort, Inc.	100
Mt. Tremblant Reservations Inc.	100
Playground Real Estate Inc.	100
Resort Reservations Network Inc.	100
Snowshoe Mountain, Inc.	100
Intrawest Golf Management (Canada) Ltd.	100
The Stratton Corporation	100

2 SIGNIFICANT ACCOUNTING POLICIES: (CONTINUED)

JOINT VENTURES AND NON-CONTROLLED PARTNERSHIPS (note 14)	PERCENTAGE INTEREST HELD BY THE COMPANY (%)
Alpine Helicopters Ltd.	45
Blue Mountain Resorts Limited	50
Blue River Land Company L.L.C.	50
Chateau M.T. Inc.	50
Intrawest/Brush Creek Development Company L.L.C.	50
Intrawest/Lodestar Golf Limited Partnership	73.7
Keystone/Intrawest L.L.C.	50
Mammoth Mountain Ski Area	59.5
Resort Ventures Limited Partnership	50

All significant intercompany balances and transactions have been eliminated.

(c) ACCOUNTING FOR INVESTMENTS:

The Company accounts for investments in which it is able to exercise significant influence in accordance with the equity method. Under the equity method, the original cost of the shares is adjusted for the Company's share of post-acquisition earnings or losses, less dividends.

(d) USE OF ESTIMATES:

The preparation of financial statements in conformity with generally accepted accounting principles requires management to make estimates and assumptions that affect the reported amounts of assets and liabilities and disclosure of contingent assets and liabilities at the date of the financial statements and the reported amounts of revenues and expenses during the reporting period. Actual results could differ from those estimates.

The significant areas requiring management estimates include the estimates of future net cash flows from properties, useful lives for depreciation, the recoverability of amounts receivable, and the value of future income tax assets and liabilities.

(e) CASH EQUIVALENTS:

The Company considers all highly liquid investments with terms to maturity of three months or less when acquired to be cash equivalents.

(f) PROPERTIES:

(i) Properties under development and held for sale:

Properties under development and held for sale are recorded at the lower of cost and net realizable value. Cost includes all expenditures incurred in connection with the acquisition, development and construction of these properties. These expenditures consist of all direct costs, interest on specific debt, interest on that portion of total costs financed by the Company's pooled debt, and an allocation of indirect overhead. Incidental operations related specifically to properties under development are treated as an increase in or a reduction of costs.

Effective July 1, 2002, the Company determined that it would no longer retain the commercial properties that it developed as long-term revenue-producing properties. Instead existing commercial properties would be sold and commercial properties developed in the future would be developed for the purpose of sale. Consequently from July 1, 2002, commercial properties are classified as properties under development and held for sale and net rental income before depreciation is capitalized to the cost of the property. Properties held for sale are not depreciated.

Costs associated with the development of sales locations of the vacation ownership business, including operating and general and administrative costs incurred until a location is fully operational, are capitalized. The results of incidental operations related specifically to a location are treated as an increase in or a reduction of costs during the start-up period. These net costs are amortized on a straight-line basis over seven years.

The Company defers costs directly relating to the acquisition of new properties and resorts which, in management's judgment, have a high probability of closing. If the acquisition is abandoned, any deferred costs are expensed immediately.

The Company provides for write-downs where the carrying value of a particular property exceeds its net realizable value.

(ii) Classification:

Properties that are currently under development for sale and properties available for sale are classified as current assets. Related bank and other indebtedness is classified as a current liability.

(g) SKI AND RESORT OPERATIONS:

The ski and resort operations assets are stated at cost less accumulated depreciation. Costs of ski lifts, area improvements and buildings are capitalized. Certain buildings, area improvements and equipment are located on leased or licensed land. Depreciation is provided over the estimated useful lives of each asset category using the declining balance method at annual rates as follows:

	(%)
Buildings	3.3 to 5.0
Ski lifts	5.0 to 8.0
Golf courses	2.0 to 3.3
Area improvements	2.0 to 3.3
Automotive, helicopters and other equipment	10.0 to 50.0
Leased vehicles	20.0 to 25.0

Inventories are recorded at the lower of cost and net realizable value, and consist primarily of retail goods, food and beverage products, and mountain operating supplies.

(h) ADMINISTRATIVE FURNITURE, COMPUTER EQUIPMENT, SOFTWARE AND LEASEHOLD IMPROVEMENTS:

Administrative furniture, computer equipment and software are stated at cost less accumulated depreciation. Included in software costs are any direct costs incurred developing internal use software. Depreciation of administrative furniture is provided using the declining balance method at annual rates of between 20% and 30%. Depreciation of computer equipment and software is provided using the straight-line method at annual rates of between 10% and 33 ⅓%.

Leasehold improvements are stated at cost less accumulated amortization. Amortization is provided using the straight-line method over the lease term.

(i) DEFERRED FINANCING COSTS:

Deferred financing costs consist of legal and other fees directly related to the debt financing of the Company's ski and resort operations. These costs are amortized to interest expense over the term of the related financing.

(j) GOODWILL AND INTANGIBLE ASSETS:

Goodwill represents the excess of purchase price over the fair value of identifiable assets acquired in a purchase business combination. Intangible assets with indefinite useful lives represent costs that have been allocated to brand names and trademarks. Effective July 1, 2002, the Company no longer amortizes goodwill and intangible assets with indefinite useful lives, but they are subject to impairment tests on at least an annual basis (see note 2(t)(i)) and additionally, whenever events and changes in circumstances suggest that the carrying amount may not be recoverable.

Intangible assets with finite useful lives are costs that have been allocated to contracts and customer lists and are amortized on a straight-line basis over their estimated useful lives.

(k) DEFERRED REVENUE:

Deferred revenue mainly comprises real estate deposits, season pass revenue, club initiation deposits, government grants and the exchange gains arising on the translation of long-term monetary items that are denominated in foreign currencies (note 2(o)). Deferred revenue which relates to the sale of season passes is recognized throughout the season based on the number of skier visits. Deferred revenue which relates to club initiation deposits is recognized on a straight-line basis over the estimated membership terms. Deferred revenue which relates to government grants for ski and resort operations assets is recognized on the same basis as the related assets are amortized. Deferred revenue which relates to government grants for properties under development is recognized as the properties are sold.

Notes to Consolidated Financial Statements

2 SIGNIFICANT ACCOUNTING POLICIES: (CONTINUED)

(l) GOVERNMENT ASSISTANCE:

The Company periodically applies for financial assistance under available government incentive programs. Non-repayable government assistance relating to capital expenditures is reflected as a reduction of the cost of such assets.

(m) REVENUE RECOGNITION:

(i)   Ski and resort operations revenue is recognized as the service is provided. Commission revenues derived from airline ticket, hotel, car and cruise reservations are recognized when the customer first utilizes the service. Commission revenue is recorded at the net of the amount charged to the customer and the amount paid to the supplier.

(ii)   Revenue from the sale of properties is recorded when title to the completed unit is conveyed to the purchaser, the purchaser becomes entitled to occupancy and the purchaser has made a payment that is appropriate in the circumstances.

(iii) Points revenue associated with membership in the vacation ownership business of Club Intrawest (which revenue is included in real estate sales) is recognized when the purchaser has paid the amount due on closing, all contract documentation has been executed and all other significant conditions of sale are met.

(n) FUTURE INCOME TAXES:

The Company follows the asset and liability method of accounting for income taxes. Under such method, future tax assets and liabilities are recognized for future tax consequences attributable to differences between the financial statement carrying amounts of existing assets and liabilities and their respective tax bases.

Future tax assets and liabilities are measured using enacted or substantively enacted tax rates expected to apply to taxable income in the years in which those temporary differences are expected to be recovered or settled. The effect on future tax assets and liabilities of a change in tax rates is recognized in income in the period that includes the substantive enactment date. To the extent that it is not considered to be more likely than not that a future income tax asset will be realized, a valuation allowance is provided.

(o) FOREIGN CURRENCY TRANSLATION:

These consolidated financial statements are presented in U.S. dollars. The majority of the Company's operations are located in the United States and are conducted in U.S. dollars. The Company's Canadian operations use the Canadian dollar as their functional currency. The Canadian entities' financial statements have been translated into U.S. dollars using the exchange rate in effect at the balance sheet date for asset and liability amounts and at the average rate for the period for amounts included in the determination of income.

Cumulative unrealized gains or losses arising from the translation of the assets and liabilities of these operations into U.S. dollars are recorded as foreign currency translation adjustment, a separate component of shareholders' equity.

Effective July 1, 2002, exchange gains or losses arising on the translation of long-term monetary items that are denominated in foreign currencies to the applicable currency of measurement are included in the determination of net income (note 2(t)(ii)). Previously these gains and losses were deferred and amortized on a straight-line basis over the remaining terms of the related monetary item except for gains or losses related to foreign currency denominated long-term obligations designated as hedges of investments in self-sustaining foreign operations.

The actual exchange rates used for translation purposes were as follows:

CANADIAN DOLLAR TO U.S. DOLLAR EXCHANGE RATES	2003	2002
At June 30	1.3475	1.5162
Average during year	1.5112	1.5687

(p) PER SHARE CALCULATIONS:

Income per common share has been calculated using the weighted average number of common shares outstanding during the year. The dilutive effect of stock options is determined using the treasury stock method.

(q) STOCK OPTIONS AND STOCK-BASED COMPENSATION:

The Company has a stock option plan as described in note 12(c). Section 3870 of the CICA Accounting Handbook ("CICA 3870") requires a fair value-based method of accounting that is required for certain, but not all, stock-based transactions. CICA 3870 must be applied to all stock-based payments to non-employees, and to employee awards that are direct awards of shares, that call for settlement in cash or other assets, or are share appreciation rights that call for settlement by the issuance of equity instruments. As permitted by CICA 3870, the Company continues to account for employee stock option grants using the intrinsic value-based method under which no expense is recorded on grant and provides, on a pro forma basis, information as if a fair value methodology had been applied (note 12(h)). Accordingly, no compensation expense has been recognized for the periods presented. Any consideration paid on the exercise of options or purchase of shares is credited to capital stock.

(r) EMPLOYEE FUTURE BENEFITS:

The Company accrues its obligations under employee benefit plans and the related costs as the underlying services are provided.

(s) COMPARATIVE FIGURES:

Certain comparative figures for 2002 have been reclassified to conform with the financial statement presentation adopted in the current year.

(t) CHANGE IN ACCOUNTING POLICIES:

(i)   On July 1, 2002, the Company adopted the new recommendations of section 3062, "Goodwill and Other Intangible Assets," of the CICA Handbook, without restatement of prior periods. Under the new recommendations, goodwill and intangible assets with indefinite lives are no longer amortized but are subject to impairment tests on at least an annual basis by comparing the related reporting unit's carrying value to its fair value. Any write-down resulting from impairment tests made under the new section at adoption effective July 1, 2002 must be recognized as a charge to retained earnings at that date. Any impairment of goodwill or other intangible assets identified subsequent to July 1, 2002 will be expensed as determined. Other intangible assets with finite lives will continue to be amortized over their useful lives and are also tested for impairment by comparing carrying values to net recoverable amounts.

At June 30, 2002, the net carrying value of goodwill was $15,985,000. Upon adoption of these recommendations, it was determined that $179,000 needed to be reclassified from goodwill to ski and resort operations assets, and $3,813,000 needed to be reclassified from goodwill to depreciable intangible assets under CICA recommendations on business combinations. The Company completed its impairment testing on the balance of goodwill and intangible assets with indefinite lives as at July 1, 2002. As a result of this testing, an impairment loss of $6,150,000 (being net of taxes of $5,843,000) was required and has been recognized as an adjustment to opening retained earnings.

A reconciliation of previously reported net income and income per share (basic and diluted) to the amounts adjusted for the exclusion of goodwill amortization is as follows:

	2003	2002
Income as reported	$ 34,176	$ 58,480
Goodwill amortization	—	743
Adjusted income	$ 34,176	$ 59,223
Income per share (basic):		
Income as reported	$ 0.73	$ 1.33
Goodwill amortization	—	0.01
Adjusted income per share	$ 0.73	$ 1.34
Income per share (diluted):		
Income as reported	$ 0.73	$ 1.31
Goodwill amortization	—	0.02
Adjusted income per share	$ 0.73	$ 1.33

(ii)   On July 1, 2002, the Company retroactively adopted the new recommendations of section 1650, "Foreign Currency Translation," of the CICA Handbook which eliminated the requirement to defer and amortize unrealized translation gains and losses on long-term foreign currency denominated monetary items with a fixed or determinable life. Instead the exchange gains and losses on these items are included in the determination of income immediately. The adoption did not impact the financial position and results of operations of prior periods, or the results for the year ended June 30, 2003.

Notes to Consolidated Financial Statements

3 ACQUISITIONS:

On December 23, 2002, the Company assumed control of the assets and operations of Winter Park Resort, a major ski and resort operation in Colorado. For accounting purposes the assumption of control has been treated as a purchase of the resort. The fair value of the purchase price of the assets acquired was $47,204,000 of which $38,236,000 was assigned to ski and resort operations assets, $7,817,000 was assigned to real estate development properties and $1,151,000 was assigned to amounts receivable. The purchase was financed primarily through the issuance of a capital lease, the assumption of certain liabilities and the payment of $2,849,000 cash.

During the year ended June 30, 2002, the Company acquired the assets and business of Big Island Country Club Limited Partnership, which operates a golf course on the island of Hawaii, for cash consideration of $8,876,000.

4 DISCONTINUED OPERATIONS:

For reporting purposes, the results of operations and cash flow from operating activities of the non-resort real estate business have been disclosed separately from those of continuing operations for the periods presented.

The results of discontinued operations are as follows:

	2003	2002
Revenue	$ 441	$ 1,128
Loss before current income taxes	$ (578)	$ (104)
Provision for current income taxes	—	18
Loss from discontinued operations	$ (578)	$ (122)

5 SKI AND RESORT OPERATIONS:

	2003		
	COST	ACCUMULATED DEPRECIATION	NET BOOK VALUE
SKI OPERATIONS:			
Land	$ 58,679	$ —	$ 58,679
Buildings	300,351	59,124	241,227
Ski lifts and area improvements	443,889	140,260	303,629
Automotive, helicopters and other equipment	134,654	81,001	53,653
Leased vehicles	4,903	2,814	2,089
	942,476	283,199	659,277
RESORT OPERATIONS:			
Land	23,187	—	23,187
Buildings	68,178	7,486	60,692
Golf courses	124,919	21,173	103,746
Area improvements	95,256	23,431	71,825
	311,540	52,090	259,450
	$1,254,016	$ 335,289	$ 918,727

	2002		
	COST	ACCUMULATED DEPRECIATION	NET BOOK VALUE
SKI OPERATIONS:			
Land	$ 52,490	$ —	$ 52,490
Buildings	248,731	47,556	201,175
Ski lifts and area improvements	411,352	118,993	292,359
Automotive, helicopters and other equipment	120,681	70,499	50,182
Leased vehicles	4,614	2,311	2,303
	837,868	239,359	598,509
RESORT OPERATIONS:			
Land	21,925	—	21,925
Buildings	58,219	8,937	49,282
Golf courses	120,145	16,444	103,701
Area improvements	87,446	19,022	68,424
	287,735	44,403	243,332
	$1,125,603	$ 283,762	$ 841,841

The ski and resort operations have been pledged as security for certain of the Company's bank and other indebtedness (note 9).

6 PROPERTIES:

Summary of properties:

	2003	2002
Properties under development and held for sale	$1,067,297	$ 797,603
Revenue-producing properties	—	70,187
	$1,067,297	$ 867,790

Properties are classified for balance sheet purposes as follows:

	2003	2002
CURRENT ASSETS:		
Resort	$ 662,197	$ 399,572
LONG-TERM ASSETS:		
Resort	405,100	461,893
Discontinued operations	—	6,325
	$1,067,297	$ 867,790

Cumulative costs capitalized to the carrying value of properties under development and held for sale are as follows:

	2003	2002
Land and land development costs	$ 205,709	$ 187,269
Building development costs	704,396	478,175
Interest	103,154	80,082
Administrative	54,038	52,077
	$1,067,297	$ 797,603

During the year ended June 30, 2003, the Company capitalized interest of $55,525,000 (2002 – $38,850,000) (note 16).

Properties have been pledged as security for certain of the Company's bank and other indebtedness (note 9).

Breakdown of revenue-producing properties:

		2002	
	COST	ACCUMULATED DEPRECIATION	NET BOOK VALUE
REVENUE-PRODUCING PROPERTIES:			
Land	$ 8,217	$ —	$ 8,217
Buildings	68,298	11,340	56,958
Leasehold improvements and equipment	6,472	1,460	5,012
	$ 82,987	$ 12,800	$ 70,187

7 AMOUNTS RECEIVABLE:

	2003	2002
Receivables from sales of real estate	$ 54,576	$ 59,679
Ski and resort operations trade receivables	34,427	23,053
Loans, mortgages and notes receivable (note 20)	89,189	73,408
Funded senior employee share purchase plans (note 12(f))	4,445	4,475
Other accounts receivable	20,930	14,067
	203,567	174,682
Current portion	126,725	109,948
	$ 76,842	$ 64,734

Amounts receivable from sales of real estate primarily comprise sales proceeds held in trust which are generally paid out to the Company or to construction lenders within 60 days.

Total payments due on amounts receivable are approximately as follows:

YEAR ENDING JUNE 30,	
2004	$ 126,725
2005	19,129
2006	4,037
2007	3,310
2008	1,996
Subsequent to 2008	48,370
	$ 203,567

The loans, mortgages and notes receivable bear interest at both fixed and floating rates which averaged 10.71% per annum as at June 30, 2003 (2002 – 10.91%). Certain of these amounts have been pledged as security for the Company's bank and other indebtedness (note 9).

Notes to Consolidated Financial Statements

8 OTHER ASSETS:

(a) CURRENT:

	2003	2002
Ski and resort operations inventories	$ 34,640	$ 30,054
Restricted cash deposits	57,087	34,502
Prepaid expenses and other	31,883	23,506
	$ 123,610	$ 88,062

(b) LONG-TERM:

	2003	2002
Investment in Compagnie des Alpes	$ 12,257	$ 36,142
Deferred financing and other costs	20,053	16,481
Administrative furniture, computer equipment, software and leasehold improvements, net of accumulated depreciation of $19,644,000 (2002 – $15,769,000)	23,856	33,614
Other	8,904	8,095
	$ 65,070	$ 94,332

In July 2002 the Company sold 55% of its investment in Compagnie des Alpes ("CDA") for proceeds which approximated its carrying value. As a result, the Company changed from the equity to the cost method of accounting for its investment at the beginning of the current fiscal year. During July 2003 the Company sold its remaining interest in CDA for proceeds which approximated its carrying value.

During the year ended June 30, 2003, the Company decided to standardize certain information technology systems across its resorts in order to improve efficiencies and eliminate costs. In addition, the Company reorganized its central reservations business and assessed the value of the assets of that business. As a result, the Company wrote down the value of information technology assets by $12,270,000.

9 BANK AND OTHER INDEBTEDNESS:

The Company has obtained financing for its ski and resort operations and properties from various financial institutions by pledging individual assets as security for such financing. Security for general corporate debt is provided by general security which includes a floating charge on the Company's assets and undertakings, fixed charges on real estate properties, and assignment of mortgages and notes receivable. The following table summarizes the primary security provided by the Company, where appropriate, and indicates the applicable type of financing, maturity dates and the weighted average interest rate at June 30, 2003:

	MATURITY DATES	WEIGHTED AVERAGE INTEREST RATE(%)	2003	2002
SKI AND RESORT OPERATIONS:				
Mortgages and bank loans	Demand – 2017	3.68	$ 62,432	$ 124,578
Obligations under capital leases	2004 – 2052	9.09	45,070	3,869
			107,502	128,447
PROPERTIES:				
Interim financing on properties under development and held for sale	2004 – 2017	5.71	264,032	141,337
Resort club notes receivable credit facilities	2006	5.21	28,121	27,436
Mortgages on revenue-producing properties	2004 – 2011	nil	—	12,485
			292,153	181,258
General corporate debt	2004 – 2005	5.63	240,243	184,000
Unsecured debentures	2004 – 2010	10.20	621,021	562,214
		7.91	1,260,919	1,055,919
Current portion			287,176	282,047
			$ 973,743	$ 773,872

Principal repayments and the components related to either floating or fixed interest rate indebtedness are as follows:

| YEAR ENDING JUNE 30, | INTEREST RATES | | TOTAL |
	FLOATING	FIXED	REPAYMENTS
2004	$ 252,630	$ 34,546	$ 287,176
2005	267,620	10,680	278,300
2006	19,257	12,836	32,093
2007	80	2,942	3,022
2008	1,278	653	1,931
Subsequent to 2008	5,231	653,166	658,397
	$ 546,096	$ 714,823	$1,260,919

The Company has entered into a swap agreement to fix the interest rate on a portion of its floating rate debt. The Company had $14,126,000 (2002 – $16,000,000) of bank loans swapped against debt with a fixed interest rate ranging from 4.70% to 5.58% (2002 – 4.70% to 5.58%) per annum.

Bank and other indebtedness includes indebtedness in the amount of $306,458,000 (2002 – $263,691,000) which is repayable in Canadian dollars of $412,952,000 (2002 – $399,808,000).

The Company is subject to certain covenants in respect of some of the bank and other indebtedness which require the Company to maintain certain financial ratios. The Company is in compliance with these covenants at June 30, 2003.

10 DEFERRED REVENUE:

	2003	2002
Deposits on real estate sales	$ 109,075	$ 76,239
Government assistance (note 11)	10,992	7,901
Club initiation deposits	24,845	13,431
Season pass revenue	14,989	13,883
Other deferred amounts	18,586	11,099
	178,487	122,553
Current portion	134,878	99,484
	$ 43,609	$ 23,069

11 GOVERNMENT ASSISTANCE:

The federal government of Canada and the Province of Quebec have granted financial assistance to the Company in the form of interest-free loans and forgivable grants for the construction of specified four-season tourist facilities at Mont Tremblant. Loans totaling $10,464,000 (Cdn.$14,100,000) (2002 – $9,300,000; Cdn.$14,100,000) have been advanced and are repayable over 17 years starting in 2000. The grants, which will total $43,052,000 (Cdn.$58,013,000) (2002 – $38,318,000; Cdn.$58,013,000) when they are fully advanced, amounted to $31,400,000 (Cdn.$42,312,000) at June 30, 2003 (2002 – $24,518,000; Cdn.$37,174,000). During the year ended June 30, 2003, grants received of $3,812,000 (Cdn.$5,138,000) (2002 – $3,513,000; Cdn.$5,326,000) were credited as follows: $1,138,000 (2002 – $1,010,000) to ski and resort operations assets, $573,000 (2002 – $1,461,000) to properties and $2,101,000 (2002 – $1,042,000) to deferred government assistance.

Notes to Consolidated Financial Statements

12 CAPITAL STOCK:

(a) SHARE CAPITAL REORGANIZATION:

Effective March 14, 1997, the Company completed a reorganization of its share capital designed to separate the remaining non-resort real estate assets from the rest of the Company's business. Under the reorganization, each existing common share was exchanged for one new common share and one non-resort preferred ("NRP") share. The new common shares have the same attributes as the old common shares.

On December 18, 2002, the Company redeemed all of the remaining NRP shares at a price of Cdn.$2.02 per share for a total of $6,697,000. As a result, the carrying value of the NRP shares was reduced to zero and contributed surplus was increased by $2,661,000 representing the difference between the redemption price and the assigned value of the NRP shares less the foreign currency translation adjustment related to the NRP shares.

(b) CAPITAL STOCK:

The Company's capital stock comprises the following:

	2003	2002
Common shares	$ 458,081	$ 453,299
NRP shares	—	13,600
Contributed surplus (note 12(a))	2,661	—
	$ 460,742	$ 466,899

(i) Common shares:

Authorized: an unlimited number without par value

Issued:

	2003		2002	
	NUMBER OF COMMON SHARES	AMOUNT	NUMBER OF COMMON SHARES	AMOUNT
Balance, beginning of year	47,255,062	$ 453,299	44,026,394	$ 400,262
Issued for cash under stock option plan	305,000	2,685	270,850	1,893
Amortization of benefit plan, net (g)	—	2,097	—	—
Purchased for benefit plan (g)	—	—	(292,182)	(4,807)
Issued for cash, net of issuance costs	—	—	3,250,000	55,951
Balance, end of year	47,560,062	$ 458,081	47,255,062	$ 453,299

(ii) NRP shares:

Authorized: 50,000,000 without par value

Issued:

	2003		2002	
	NUMBER OF NRP SHARES	AMOUNT	NUMBER OF NRP SHARES	AMOUNT
Balance, beginning of year	5,163,436	$ 13,600	5,513,936	$ 13,958
Redemption	(5,163,436)	(6,697)	—	—
Transferred to contributed surplus	—	(2,661)	—	—
Foreign currency adjustment	—	(4,242)	—	—
Purchased for cancellation	—	—	(350,500)	(358)
Balance, end of year	—	$ —	5,163,436	$ 13,600

(iii) Preferred shares:

Authorized: an unlimited number without par value

Issued: nil

(c) STOCK OPTIONS:

The Company has a stock option plan which provides for grants to officers and employees of the Company and its subsidiaries of options to purchase common shares of the Company. Options granted under the stock option plan are exercisable in Canadian dollars and may not be exercised except in accordance with such limitations as the Human Resources Committee of the Board of Directors of the Company may determine.

The following table summarizes the status of options outstanding under the Plan:

	2003		2002	
	SHARE OPTIONS OUTSTANDING	WEIGHTED AVERAGE PRICE	SHARE OPTIONS OUTSTANDING	WEIGHTED AVERAGE PRICE
Outstanding, beginning of year	3,697,900	$ 16.04	3,322,500	$ 15.24
Granted	445,000	15.89	711,800	16.17
Exercised	(305,000)	9.41	(270,850)	6.99
Forfeited	(34,000)	18.03	(65,550)	17.87
Outstanding, end of year	3,803,900	$ 18.68	3,697,900	$ 16.04
Exercisable, end of year	1,867,310	$ 18.20	1,753,950	$ 14.70

The following table provides details of options outstanding at June 30, 2003:

RANGE OF EXERCISE PRICES	NUMBER OUTSTANDING JUNE 30, 2003	WEIGHTED AVERAGE LIFE REMAINING (YEARS)	WEIGHTED AVERAGE PRICE	NUMBER EXERCISABLE JUNE 30, 2003	WEIGHTED AVERAGE PRICE
$ 8.56 – $ 10.74	134,100	1.8	$ 10.17	134,100	$ 10.17
$ 11.67 – $ 17.07	233,500	4.4	14.74	205,500	15.02
$ 17.66 – $ 21.56	3,436,300	6.8	19.28	1,527,710	19.19
	3,803,900	6.4	$ 18.68	1,867,310	$ 18.20

(d) EMPLOYEE SHARE PURCHASE PLAN:

The employee share purchase plan permits certain full-time employees of the Company and its subsidiaries and limited partnerships to purchase common shares through payroll deductions. The Company contributes $1 for every $3 contributed by an employee. To June 30, 2003, a total of 65,809 (2002 – 65,809) common shares have been issued from treasury under this plan. A further 100,000 common shares have been authorized and reserved for issuance under this plan.

(e) DEFERRED SHARE UNIT PLAN:

The company has a key executive Deferred Share Unit Plan (the "DSU Plan") that allows each executive officer to elect to receive all or any portion of his annual incentive award as deferred share units. A DSU is equal in value to one common share of the Company. The units are determined by dividing the dollar amount elected by the average closing price of the common shares on the Toronto Stock Exchange for the five trading days preceding the date that the annual incentive award becomes payable. The units also accrue dividend equivalents payable in additional units in an amount equal to dividends paid on Intrawest common shares. DSUs mature upon the termination of employment, whereupon an executive is entitled to receive the fair market value of the equivalent number of common shares, net of withholdings, in cash.

The Company records the cost of the DSU plan as compensation expense. As at June 30, 2003, 74,381 units were outstanding at a value of $981,000 (2002 – 49,351 units at a value of $827,000).

(f) FUNDED SENIOR EMPLOYEE SHARE PURCHASE PLANS:

The Company has two funded senior employee share purchase plans which provide for loans to be made to designated eligible employees to be used for the purchase of common shares. At June 30, 2003, loans to employees under the funded senior employee share purchase plans amounted to $4,445,000 with respect to 247,239 common shares (2002 – $4,475,000 with respect to 374,387 common shares and 26,939 NRP shares). The loans, which are included in amounts receivable, are non-interest bearing, secured by a promissory note and a pledge of the shares ($3,259,000 market value at June 30, 2003) and mature by 2012. A further 96,400 common shares have been authorized and reserved for issuance under one of the plans.

(g) KEY EXECUTIVE EMPLOYEE BENEFIT PLAN:

The Company has a key executive employee benefit plan which permits the Company to grant awards of common shares purchased in the open market to executive officers. To June 30, 2003, a total of 292,182 (2002 – 292,192) common shares were purchased under this plan. The common shares vest to the employees in part over time and the balance on the attainment of certain future earnings levels. The value of the shares amortized to income during the year ended June 30, 2003 was $2,097,000. None of the shares were vested as at June 30, 2003.

Notes to Consolidated Financial Statements

12 CAPITAL STOCK: (CONTINUED)

(h) STOCK COMPENSATION:

Had compensation expense for stock options granted subsequent to June 30, 2001 been determined by a fair value method using the Black-Scholes option pricing model at the date of the grant, the following weighted average assumptions would have been used for options granted in the current period:

	2003	2002
Dividend yield (%)	0.9	0.6
Risk-free interest rate (%)	3.11	4.38
Expected option life (years)	7	7
Expected volatility (%)	36	55

Using the above assumptions, the Company's net income for the year ended June 30, 2003 would have been reduced to the pro forma amount indicated below:

	2003	2002
Net income, as reported	$ 34,176	$ 58,480
Estimated fair value of option grants	(1,909)	(649)
Net income, pro forma	$ 32,267	$ 57,831
PRO FORMA INCOME PER COMMON SHARE FROM CONTINUING OPERATIONS:		
Basic	$ 0.69	$ 1.31
Diluted	0.69	1.29

The estimated fair value of option grants excludes the effect of those granted before July 1, 2001. The fair value of options granted during the year ended June 30, 2003 was $6.35 per option (2002 – $9.15) on the grant date on a weighted average basis.

(i) PER SHARE INFORMATION:

The reconciliation of the net income and weighted average number of common shares used to calculate basic and diluted income per common share is as follows:

	2003		2002	
	NET INCOME	SHARES (000)	NET INCOME	SHARES (000)
BASIC INCOME PER COMMON SHARE:				
Income from continuing operations	$ 34,754	47,364	$ 58,602	44,206
Dilutive effect of stock options	—	226	—	489
Diluted income per common share	$ 34,754	47,590	$ 58,602	44,695

Options aggregating 3,675,300 (2002 – 2,399,800) have not been included in the computation of diluted income per common share as they were anti-dilutive.

13 INCOME TAXES:

(a) The provision for income taxes from continuing operations is as follows:

	2003	2002
Current	$ 10,157	$ 12,422
Future	(3,914)	(2,873)
	$ 6,243	$ 9,549

The reconciliation of income taxes calculated at the statutory rate to the actual income tax provision is as follows:

	2003	2002
Statutory rate (%)	38.0	41.2
Income tax charge at statutory rate	$ 19,683	$ 32,888
Non-deductible expenses and amortization	326	53
Large corporations tax	2,574	1,159
Taxes related to non-controlling interest share of earnings	(4,284)	(4,804)
Reduction for enacted changes in tax laws and rates	—	(2,434)
Taxes related to equity accounted investment	—	(1,605)
Foreign taxes less than statutory rate	(13,182)	(15,589)
Other	1,126	(101)
	6,243	9,567
Current income taxes related to discontinued operations	—	18
Provision for income taxes	$ 6,243	$ 9,549

(b) **The tax effects of temporary differences that give rise to significant portions of the future tax assets and future tax liabilities are presented below:**

	2003	2002
FUTURE TAX ASSETS:		
Non-capital loss carryforwards	$ 35,823	$ 27,068
Differences in working capital deductions for tax and accounting purposes	5,465	4,004
Other	3,861	727
Total gross future tax assets	45,149	31,799
Valuation allowance	(17,559)	(16,206)
Net future tax assets	27,590	15,593
FUTURE TAX LIABILITIES:		
Differences in net book value and undepreciated capital cost of ski and resort assets and properties	81,824	80,021
Differences in book value and tax basis of bank and other indebtedness	28,844	3,879
Other	1,289	—
Total gross future tax liabilities	111,957	83,900
Net future tax liabilities	$ 84,367	$ 68,307

Net future tax liabilities are classified for balance sheet purposes as follows:

	2003	2002
CURRENT ASSETS:		
Future income taxes	$ 10,619	$ 7,536
LONG-TERM LIABILITIES:		
Future income taxes	94,986	75,843
	$ 84,367	$ 68,307

(c) **At June 30, 2003, the Company has non-capital loss carryforwards for income tax purposes of approximately $117,200,000 (2002 – $101,960,000) that are available to offset future taxable income through 2023.**

14 JOINT VENTURES:

The following amounts represent the Company's proportionate interest in joint ventures and non-controlled partnerships (note 2(b)):

	2003	2002
Properties, current	$ 53,993	$ 42,178
Other current assets	20,888	21,717
	74,881	63,895
Current liabilities	(59,629)	(49,487)
Working capital	15,252	14,408
Ski and resort operations	161,609	155,964
Properties, non-current	79,032	58,713
Bank and other indebtedness, non-current	(32,213)	(40,376)
Other, net	(14,856)	(14,924)
	$ 208,824	$ 173,785

	2003	2002
Revenue	$ 128,286	$ 131,122
Expenses	122,272	119,960
Income from continuing operations before income taxes	6,014	11,162
Results of discontinued operations	419	385
	$ 6,433	$ 11,547

	2003	2002
CASH PROVIDED BY (USED IN):		
Operations	$ (5,309)	$ 29,206
Financing	30,544	(15,267)
Investments	(25,003)	(20,425)
Increase (decrease) in cash and cash equivalents	$ 232	$ (6,486)

Due to joint venture partners is the amount payable to the Company's joint venture partners on various properties for costs they have incurred on the Company's behalf. Payments to the joint venture partners are governed by the terms of the respective joint venture agreement.

Notes to Consolidated Financial Statements

15 CONTINGENCIES AND COMMITMENTS:

(a) The Company holds licenses and land leases with respect to certain of its ski operations. These leases expire at various times between 2032 and 2051 and provide for annual payments generally in the range of 2% of defined gross revenues.

(b) The Company has estimated costs to complete ski and resort operations assets and properties currently under construction and held for sale amounting to $379,019,000 at June 30, 2003 (2002 – $397,642,000). These costs are substantially covered by existing financing commitments.

(c) In addition to the leases described in (a) above, the Company has entered into other operating lease commitments, payable as follows:

YEAR ENDING JUNE 30,	
2004	$ 10,478
2005	9,919
2006	8,987
2007	7,605
2008	7,024
Subsequent to 2008	65,785
	$ 109,798

(d) The Company is contingently liable for the obligations of certain joint ventures and partnerships. The assets of these joint ventures and partnerships, which in all cases exceed the obligations, are available to satisfy such obligations.

(e) The Company and its subsidiaries are involved in several lawsuits arising from the ordinary course of business. Although the outcome of such matters cannot be predicted with certainty, management does not consider the Company's exposure to lawsuits to be material to these consolidated financial statements.

(f) Canada Customs and Revenue Agency ("CCRA") has proposed certain adjustments to reduce the amount of capital cost allowance and non-capital losses claimed by the Company. No notice of reassessment has been issued. The Company has made submissions with respect to these proposals and intends to contest any adjustments, if made. The Company believes that it is unlikely that CCRA would be successful with the proposed challenge. Whether CCRA will ultimately proceed with such proposals, and the outcome of the issues under review if the proposals proceed, cannot be determined at this time. If all of the issues raised by CCRA in the proposals were reassessed as proposed, the Company would be required to pay total cash taxes of approximately $7,500,000 plus interest of approximately $5,000,000. For accounting purposes, the effect of any reassessment would be charged to income in the year the outcome of the proposals is determined.

16 INTEREST EXPENSE:

	2003	2002
Total interest incurred	$ 102,926	$ 83,439
Less:		
Interest capitalized to ski and resort operations assets	192	1,353
Interest capitalized to properties, net of capitalized interest included in real estate cost of sales of $14,872,000 (2002 – $13,314,000)	40,653	25,536
	$ 62,081	$ 56,550

Interest was charged to income as follows:

	2003	2002
Real estate costs	$ 14,872	$ 13,314
Interest expense	47,142	43,072
Discontinued operations	67	164
	$ 62,081	$ 56,550

Real estate cost of sales also include $17,581,000 (2002 – $14,525,000) of interest incurred in prior years.

Interest incurred and interest expense include commitment and other financing fees and amortization of deferred financing costs.

17 FINANCIAL INSTRUMENTS:

(a) FAIR VALUE:

The Company has various financial instruments including cash and cash equivalents, amounts receivable, certain amounts payable and accrued liabilities. Due to their short-term maturity or, in the case of amounts receivable, their market comparable interest rates, the instruments' book value approximates their fair value. Debt and interest swap agreements are also financial instruments. The fair value of the Company's long-term debt including interest swap agreements, calculated using current rates offered to the Company for debt at the same remaining maturities, is not materially different from amounts included in the consolidated balance sheets.

(b) INTEREST RATE RISK:

As described in note 9, $546,096,000 of the Company's debt instruments bear interest at floating rates. Fluctuations in these rates will impact the cost of financing incurred in the future.

(c) CREDIT RISK:

The Company's products and services are purchased by a wide range of customers in different regions of North America and elsewhere. Due to the nature of its operations, the Company has no concentrations of credit risk.

18 PENSION PLANS:

The Company has two non-contributory defined benefit pension plans, one registered and the other non-registered, covering certain of its senior executives. The number of senior executives included in the plan increased from five to 15 in 2002. The Company partially funded the accrued benefit obligation until December 2001. The estimated market value of the plans' assets (i.e., the funded amount) was $3,252,000 at June 30, 2003 (2002 – $2,857,000). A substantial portion of the unfunded benefit obligation, the estimated present value of which was $15,479,000 at June 30, 2003 (2002 – $10,783,000), has been secured by a letter of credit. This obligation is being expensed over a period of 13 years.

In addition to the plans mentioned above, one of the Company's subsidiaries has two defined benefit pension plans covering certain employees. The estimated market value of the plans' assets was $5,989,000 and the estimated present value of the unfunded benefit obligation was $2,229,000 at June 30, 2003. The obligation is being expensed over a period of 10 years.

For the year ended June 30, 2003, the Company charged to operations pension costs of $1,992,000 (2002 – $1,070,000).

19 SEGMENTED INFORMATION:

The Company has four reportable segments: mountain resort operations, warm-weather resort operations, real estate operations, and corporate and all other. The mountain resort segment includes all of the Company's mountain resorts and associated activities. The warm-weather segment includes Sandestin and all of the Company's stand-alone golf courses. The real estate segment includes all of the Company's real estate activities.

The Company evaluates performance based on profit or loss from operations before interest, depreciation and amortization, and income taxes. Intersegment sales and transfers are accounted for as if the sales or transfers were to third parties.

The Company's reportable segments are strategic business units that offer distinct products and services, and that have their own identifiable marketing strategies. Each of the reportable segments has senior executives responsible for the performance of the segment.

The following table presents the Company's results from continuing operations by reportable segment:

	2003	2002
SEGMENT REVENUE:		
Mountain resort	$ 506,483	$ 424,835
Warm-weather resort	65,044	60,307
Real estate	512,695	495,813
Corporate and all other	2,417	5,016
	$1,086,639	$ 985,971

Notes to Consolidated Financial Statements

19 SEGMENTED INFORMATION: (CONTINUED)

	2003	2002
SEGMENT OPERATING PROFIT:		
Mountain resort	$ 109,197	$ 98,935
Warm-weather resort	7,469	8,406
Real estate	75,005	88,150
Corporate and all other	2,417	5,016
	194,088	200,507
Less:		
Interest	47,142	43,072
Depreciation and amortization	67,516	65,434
Corporate general and administrative	14,889	12,175
Write-down of technology assets	12,270	—
	141,817	120,681
Income before income taxes, non-controlling interest and discontinued operations	$ 52,271	$ 79,826

	2003	2002
SEGMENT ASSETS:		
Mountain resort	$ 978,719	$ 912,642
Warm-weather resort	145,361	151,924
Real estate	1,311,079	1,032,296
Corporate and all other	80,563	60,720
Discontinued operations	—	9,335
	$2,515,722	$ 2,166,917

	2003	2002
CAPITAL EXPENDITURES:		
Mountain resort	$ 59,674	$ 81,658
Warm-weather resort	4,872	9,832
Corporate and all other	5,025	10,237
	$ 69,571	$ 101,727

GEOGRAPHIC INFORMATION:

	2003	2002
REVENUE:		
Canada	$ 474,865	$ 424,764
United States	611,774	561,207
	$1,086,639	$ 985,971

	2003	2002
SEGMENT OPERATING PROFIT:		
Canada	$ 102,871	$ 121,707
United States	91,217	78,800
	$ 194,088	$ 200,507

	2003	2002
IDENTIFIABLE ASSETS:		
Canada	$ 886,978	$ 753,885
United States	1,628,744	1,403,697
Discontinued operations	—	9,335
	$2,515,722	$ 2,166,917

20 RELATED PARTY TRANSACTIONS:

During the year ended June 30, 2002, $3,991,000 was repaid to the Company by a partnership, one of whose partners was a corporation controlled by an officer and a director of the Company.

21 CASH FLOW INFORMATION:

The changes in non-cash operating working capital balance consist of the following:

	2003	2002
CASH PROVIDED BY (USED IN):		
Amounts receivable	$ (17,208)	$ (29,720)
Other assets	(17,557)	20,819
Amounts payable	14,866	48,676
Due to joint venture partners	1,425	(4,788)
Deferred revenue	45,064	14,204
	$ 26,590	$ 49,191
SUPPLEMENTAL INFORMATION:		
Interest paid related to interest charged to income	$ 62,091	$ 56,550
Income, franchise and withholding taxes paid	11,067	11,596
NON-CASH INVESTING ACTIVITIES:		
Notes received on asset disposals	2,226	6,902
Bank and other indebtedness incurred on acquisition	35,172	—

22 DIFFERENCES BETWEEN CANADIAN AND UNITED STATES GENERALLY ACCEPTED ACCOUNTING PRINCIPLES:

The consolidated financial statements have been prepared in accordance with generally accepted accounting principles ("GAAP") in Canada. The principles adopted in these financial statements conform in all material respects to those generally accepted in the United States and the rules and regulations promulgated by the Securities and Exchange Commission ("SEC") except as summarized below:

	2003	2002
Income from continuing operations in accordance with Canadian GAAP	$ 34,754	$ 58,602
EFFECTS OF DIFFERENCES IN ACCOUNTING FOR:		
Depreciation and amortization pursuant to SFAS 109 (d)	(690)	(1,870)
Real estate revenue recognition (i)	(8,931)	4,089
Start-up costs (j)	3,101	(4,772)
Tax effect of differences	2,478	562
Foreign exchange pursuant to SFAS 52 (g)	—	(14)
Results of discontinued operations	(578)	(122)
Income before cumulative effect of change in accounting principle	30,134	56,475
Adjustment to reflect change in accounting for goodwill, net of tax (k)	(6,150)	—
Net income in accordance with United States GAAP	23,984	56,475
Opening retained earnings in accordance with United States GAAP (b)	275,101	223,363
Common share dividends	(5,051)	(4,737)
Closing retained earnings in accordance with United States GAAP	$ 294,034	$ 275,101
INCOME BEFORE CUMULATIVE EFFECT OF CHANGE IN ACCOUNTING PRINCIPLE PER COMMON SHARE (IN DOLLARS):		
Basic	$ 0.65	$ 1.28
Diluted	0.65	1.27
INCOME PER COMMON SHARE (IN DOLLARS):		
Basic	0.52	1.28
Diluted	0.52	1.27
WEIGHTED AVERAGE NUMBER OF SHARES OUTSTANDING (IN THOUSANDS):		
Basic	47,364	44,206
Diluted	47,590	44,695

Notes to Consolidated Financial Statements

22 DIFFERENCES BETWEEN CANADIAN AND UNITED STATES GENERALLY ACCEPTED ACCOUNTING PRINCIPLES: (CONTINUED)

	2003	2002
COMPREHENSIVE INCOME:		
Net income in accordance with United States GAAP	$ 23,984	$ 56,475
Other comprehensive income (h)	17,808	2,299
	$ 41,792	$ 58,774

	2003	2002
Total assets in accordance with Canadian GAAP	$2,515,722	$2,166,917
EFFECTS OF DIFFERENCES IN ACCOUNTING FOR:		
Shareholder loans (c)	(4,445)	(4,475)
Ski and resort assets (d)	1,948	2,525
Goodwill (d)	37,471	34,696
Properties (d)	640	650
Sale-leaseback (i)	14,080	—
Start-up costs (j)	(2,551)	(5,682)
Future income taxes on differences	4,222	1,744
Total assets in accordance with United States GAAP	$2,567,087	$2,196,375

	2003	2002
Total liabilities in accordance with Canadian GAAP	$1,804,583	$1,489,648
EFFECTS OF DIFFERENCES IN ACCOUNTING FOR:		
Revenue recognition (i)	24,096	—
Total liabilities in accordance with United States GAAP	$1,828,679	$1,489,648

	2003	2002
Capital stock in accordance with Canadian GAAP	$ 460,742	$ 466,899
EFFECTS OF DIFFERENCES IN ACCOUNTING FOR:		
Extinguishment of options and warrants (a)	1,563	1,563
Shareholder loans (c)	(4,445)	(4,475)
Capital stock in accordance with United States GAAP	457,860	463,987
Closing retained earnings in accordance with United States GAAP	294,034	275,101
Accumulated other comprehensive income (h)	(13,486)	(32,361)
Shareholders' equity in accordance with United States GAAP	$ 738,408	$ 706,727

(a) EXTINGUISHMENT OF OPTIONS AND WARRANTS:

Payments made to extinguish options and warrants can be treated as capital items under Canadian GAAP. These payments would be treated as income items under United States GAAP. As a result, payments made to extinguish options in prior years impact the current year's capital stock and retained earnings. No payments were made during the years ended June 30, 2003 and 2002.

(b) RETAINED EARNINGS:

Opening retained earnings in accordance with United States GAAP for the year ended June 30, 2002 includes the effects of:

(i)   adopting SFAS 109 as described in (d). The net increase in retained earnings was $40,685,000; and

(ii)   treating payments made to extinguish options and warrants as income items as described in (a). The net decrease in retained earnings was $1,563,000.

(c) SHAREHOLDER LOANS:

The Company accounts for loans provided to senior employees for the purchase of shares as amounts receivable. Under United States GAAP, these loans, totaling $4,445,000 and $4,475,000 as at June 30, 2003 and 2002, respectively, would be deducted from share capital.

(d) INCOME TAXES:

As described in note 2(n), the Company follows the asset and liability method of accounting for income taxes. Prior to July 1, 1999, the Company had adopted the Statement of Financial Accounting Standards No. 109, "Accounting for Income Taxes" ("SFAS 109"), for the financial statement amounts presented under United States GAAP. SFAS 109 requires that future tax liabilities or assets be recognized for the difference between assigned values and tax bases of assets and liabilities acquired pursuant to a business combination except for non tax-deductible goodwill and unallocated negative goodwill, effective from the Company's year ended September 30, 1994. The effect of adopting SFAS 109 increases the carrying values of certain balance sheet amounts at June 30, 2003 and 2002 as follows:

	2003	2002
Ski and resort operations assets	$ 1,948	$ 2,525
Goodwill	37,471	34,696
Properties	640	650

(e) JOINT VENTURES:

In accordance with Canadian GAAP, joint ventures are required to be proportionately consolidated regardless of the legal form of the entity. Under United States GAAP, incorporated joint ventures are required to be accounted for by the equity method. However, in accordance with practices prescribed by the SEC, the Company has elected for the purpose of this reconciliation to account for incorporated joint ventures by the proportionate consolidation method (note 14).

(f) STOCK COMPENSATION:

As described in note 2(q), the Company accounts for stock options by the intrinsic value-based method. In addition, in note 12(h) the Company provides pro forma disclosure as if a fair value-based method had been applied for grants made subsequent to June 30, 2001. For United States GAAP purposes, the pro forma disclosures would consider the fair value of all grants made subsequent to December 15, 1995.

Had compensation expense been determined in accordance with the timing of application provisions of United States GAAP using the Black-Scholes option pricing model at the date of the grant, the following weighted average assumptions would be used for option grants in:

	2003	2002
Dividend yield (%)	0.9	0.6
Risk-free interest rate (%)	3.11	4.38
Expected option life (years)	7	7
Expected volatility (%)	36	55

Using the above assumptions, the Company's net income under United States GAAP would have been reduced to the pro forma amounts indicated below:

	2003	2002
NET INCOME IN ACCORDANCE WITH UNITED STATES GAAP:		
As reported	$ 23,984	$ 56,475
Estimated fair value of option grants	(5,228)	(5,215)
Pro forma	$ 18,756	$ 51,260
PRO FORMA INCOME PER COMMON SHARE:		
Basic	$ 0.41	$ 1.16
Diluted	0.41	1.15

Notes to Consolidated Financial Statements

22 DIFFERENCES BETWEEN CANADIAN AND UNITED STATES GENERALLY ACCEPTED ACCOUNTING PRINCIPLES: (CONTINUED)

(g) FOREIGN EXCHANGE ON BANK AND OTHER INDEBTEDNESS:

Prior to July 1, 2002 under Canadian GAAP, the Company deferred and amortized foreign exchange gains and losses on bank and other indebtedness denominated in foreign currencies over the remaining term of the debt. Under United States GAAP, foreign exchange gains and losses are included in income in the period in which the exchange rate fluctuates.

(h) OTHER COMPREHENSIVE INCOME:

Statement of Financial Accounting Standards No. 130, "Reporting Comprehensive Income" ("SFAS 130"), requires that a company classify items of other comprehensive income by their nature in a financial statement and display the accumulated balance of other comprehensive income separately from retained earnings and capital stock in the equity section of the balance sheet.

The foreign currency translation adjustment in the amount of $14,243,000 (2002 – $31,295,000) presented in shareholders' equity under Canadian GAAP would be considered accumulated other comprehensive income under United States GAAP. The change in the balance of $17,808,000 would be other comprehensive income for the year (2002 – income of $2,299,000).

(i) REAL ESTATE REVENUE RECOGNITION:

The Company recognizes profit arising on the sale of a property, a portion of which is leased back by the Company, to the extent the gain exceeds the present value of the minimum lease payments. The deferred gain is recognized over the lease term. Under United States GAAP, the Company's continued involvement in the property precludes a sale-leaseback transaction from sale-leaseback accounting. As a result, the profit on the transaction is not recognized but rather the sales proceeds are treated as a liability and the property continues to be shown as an asset of the Company until the conditions for sales recognition are met.

In accordance with Canadian GAAP, the Company recognizes revenue from the sale of serviced lots after receiving a deposit and conveying title to the purchaser. Statement of Financial Accounting Standards No. 66, "Accounting for Sales of Real Estate" ("SFAS 66"), provides that a sale of real estate should not be recognized unless the deposit received from the purchaser is at least a major part of the difference between usual loan limits and the sales value of the property. Accordingly, no revenue and cost of sales would have been recognized under United States GAAP on certain lot sales for the year ended June 30, 2001 where the deposit received was less than 10% of the sales price. During the year ended June 30, 2002, the remainder of the loans receivable was collected.

(j) START-UP COSTS:

As described in note 2(f), the Company capitalizes for Canadian GAAP purposes certain costs incurred in the start-up period of specific operations. For United States GAAP purposes, such costs would be expensed as incurred.

(k) GOODWILL AND OTHER INTANGIBLE ASSETS:

As described in note 2(t)(i), the Company restated opening retained earnings for impairment losses calculated by comparing the carrying values to fair values of goodwill and intangible assets with indefinite lives. For United States GAAP, the Company adopted effective July 1, 2002 the provisions of SFAS 142, "Goodwill and Other Intangible Assets," which are similar to Canadian GAAP except that under this standard the impairment losses are recognized as a cumulative effect of a change in accounting principle and are treated as a charge to net income in the year of adoption.

(l) DERIVATIVES AND HEDGING ACTIVITIES:

For United States GAAP purposes, the Company adopted the provisions of SFAS 133, "Accounting for Derivative Instruments and Hedging Activities," as amended, effective July 1, 2000. Under this standard, derivative instruments are initially recorded at cost with changes in fair value recognized in income except when the derivative is identified, documented and highly effective as a hedge, in which case the changes in fair value are excluded from income to be recognized at the time of the underlying transaction. The only derivative instrument outstanding at June 30, 2003 and 2002 is the interest rate swap described in note 9. As the fair value of this swap is not materially different than its cost at both dates, no reconciliation adjustment is required.

(m) RECENTLY ANNOUNCED ACCOUNTING PRONOUNCEMENTS:

In the U.S., SFAS 143, "Accounting for Asset Retirement Obligations" ("SFAS 143"), addresses financial accounting and reporting for obligations associated with the retirement of long-lived assets and the associated asset retirement costs. SFAS 143 requires the Company to record the fair value of an asset retirement obligation as a liability in the period in which it incurs a legal obligation associated with the retirement of tangible long-lived assets that result from the acquisition, construction, development and/or normal use of the assets. The fair value of the liability is added to the carrying amount of the associated asset and this additional carrying amount is depreciated over the life of the asset. Subsequent to the initial measurement of the asset retirement obligation, the obligation will be adjusted at the end of each period to reflect the passage of time and changes in the estimated future cash flows underlying the obligation. If the obligation is settled for other than the carrying amount of the liability, the Company will recognize a gain or loss on settlement. The Company was required to adopt the provisions of SFAS 143 effective July 1, 2002. Certain of the land lease arrangements related to the Company's ski and resort operations require remediation steps be taken on termination of the lease arrangement. The Company plans to operate its resorts indefinitely and thus is unable to make a reasonable estimate of the fair values of the associated asset retirement obligations.

In the U.S., SFAS 144, "Accounting for the Impairment or Disposal of Long-Lived Assets" ("SFAS 144"), provides guidance for recognizing and measuring impairment losses on long-lived assets held for use and long-lived assets to be disposed of by sale. SFAS 144 also provides guidance on how to present discontinued operations in the income statement and includes a component of an entity (rather than a segment of a business). The provisions of SFAS 144 are required to be applied prospectively after the adoption date to newly initiated disposal activities. The Company was required to adopt SFAS 144 effective July 1, 2002. The adoption of SFAS 144 did not materially impact the Company's consolidated financial position or results of operations.

The FASB has issued SFAS 146, "Accounting for Costs Associated with Exit or Disposal Activities" ("SFAS 146"), which is effective for exit or disposal activities that are initiated after December 31, 2002. SFAS 146 requires that a liability be recognized for exit or disposal costs only when the liability is incurred, as defined in the FASB's conceptual frame-work, rather than when a company commits to an exit plan, and that the liability be initially measured at fair value. The Company expects the adoption of this standard will affect the timing of recognizing liabilities, and the amount recognized, in respect of future exit activities, if any.

The FASB has issued Interpretation No. 45, "Guarantor's Accounting and Disclosure Requirements for Guarantees, Including Indirect Guarantees of Indebtedness of Others" ("FIN 45"). FIN 45 requires additional disclosures as well as the recognition of a liability by a guarantor at the inception of certain guarantees entered into or modified after December 31, 2002. The initial measurement of this liability is the fair value of the guarantee at inception. The requirements of FIN 45 have been considered in the preparation of this reconciliation.

The FASB has issued Interpretation No. 46, "Consolidation of Variable Interest Entities" ("FIN 46"). Its consolidation provisions are applicable for all entities created after January 31, 2003, and for existing variable interest entities as of July 1, 2003. With respect to entities that do not qualify to be assessed for consolidation based on voting interests, FIN 46 generally requires consolidation by the entity that has a variable interest(s) that will absorb a majority of the variable interest entity's expected losses if they occur, receive a majority of the entity's expected residual returns if they occur, or both. The Company is currently evaluating the impact of adopting the requirements of FIN 46.

Directors and Management

DIRECTORS

R. THOMAS M. ALLAN [1]
Consultant

JOE S. HOUSSIAN
Chairman, President and Chief Executive Officer,
Intrawest Corporation

DANIEL O. JARVIS
Executive Vice President and
Chief Financial Officer, Intrawest Corporation

DAVID A. KING [1, 2]
President, David King Corporation

GORDON H. MACDOUGALL [2, 3]
Partner, CC&L Financial Services Group

PAUL M. MANHEIM [1, 3]
President, HAL Real Estate Investments, Inc.

PAUL A. NOVELLY [2]
Chairman and Chief Executive Officer,
Apex Oil Company, Inc.

GARY L. RAYMOND
Chief Executive Officer, Resort
Development Group, Intrawest Corporation

BERNARD A. ROY [3]
Senior Partner, Ogilvy Renault

KHALED C. SIFRI [1]
Managing Partner, Hadef Al-Dhahiri & Associates

HUGH R. SMYTHE
President, Resort Operations Group,
Intrawest Corporation

NICHOLAS C.H. VILLIERS [2]
Consultant

[1] Audit Committee
[2] Corporate Governance and Nominating Committee
[3] Human Resources Committee

CORPORATE MANAGEMENT

JOE. S. HOUSSIAN
Chairman, President and Chief Executive Officer

DANIEL O. JARVIS
Executive Vice President
and Chief Financial Officer

  DAVID C. BLAIKLOCK
  Vice President and Corporate Controller

  JOHN E. CURRIE
  Senior Vice President, Financing and Taxation

JIM GREEHEY
Vice President, Corporate Insurance

MICHAEL M. HANNAN
Senior Vice President, Strategic
and Corporate Development

ROSS J. MEACHER
Corporate Secretary and Chief Privacy Officer

ANDREW C. MORDEN
Vice President,
Financial Planning and Systems

STEPHEN J. SAMMUT
Vice President, Project and Corporate Finance

STAN C. SPRENGER
President, Resort Reservations Network

ANDREW VOYSEY
Senior Vice President, Acquisitions

EWAN R. WILDING
Vice President, Internal Audit Services

RESORT OPERATIONS GROUP

HUGH R. SMYTHE
President, Resort Operations Group

  PAT ALDOUS
  Director, Canadian Mountain Holidays

  DAVID BARRY
  Senior Vice President, Intrawest Colorado

    GARY DEFRANGE
    Vice President/General Manager,
    Winter Park

    STEVE PACCAGNAN
    Vice President/General Manager, Copper

  DAVID B. BROWNLIE
  Senior Vice President, Finance,
  Whistler Blackcomb

    GORDON AHRENS
    Vice President and General Manager,
    Panorama Mountain Village

  DAVID A. CREASY
  Senior Vice President, Finance

  DOUG FORSETH
  Senior Vice President, Operations,
  Whistler Blackcomb

RUSTY GREGORY
Chief Executive Officer, Mammoth Mountain

DAVE HARTVIGSEN
Senior Vice President, Lodging

  R. SCOTT BUNCE
  Vice President, Sales – Lodging

  PETER A. COWLEY
  Vice President, Lodging
  Product Development

  MIKE STANGE
  Vice President and General Manager,
  Sandestin

EDWARD B. PITONIAK
Senior Vice President, Resort Enterprises

  LINDA DENIS
  Vice President,
  Customer Relationship Marketing

  MARK R. HULME
  Vice President, Retail/Rental Operations

  GRAHAM R. KWAN
  Vice President, Business Development

ANN M. MACLEAN
Vice President,
People and Organizational Development

TONY B. OSBORNE
Staff Vice President, Project Management

CATE THERO
Vice President, Marketing

STEPHEN K. RICE
Senior Vice President, Eastern Region

  MICHEL AUBIN
  President, Tremblant

  CHARLES BLIER
  Vice President and General Manager,
  Mountain Creek

  GORDON CANNING
  President, Blue Mountain

  SKY FOULKES
  Vice President and General Manager,
  Stratton

  BRUCE D. PITTET
  Vice President and General Manager,
  Snowshoe

RESORT DEVELOPMENT GROUP

GARY L. RAYMOND
Chief Executive Officer,
Resort Development Group

  LORNE D. BASSEL
  Executive Vice President,
  Northeast and Europe Regions

    ROBERT JÉRÔME
    Regional Vice President, Europe Region

    WILLIAM R. GREEN
    Regional Vice President, Northeast Region

      ROBIN CONNERS
      Vice President, Commercial,
      Northeast Region

      RICHARD LABONTÉ
      Vice President, Construction,
      Northeast Region

      CRAIG WATTERS
      Vice President, Development,
      Northeast Region

    MAX REIM
    Vice President, Commercial Development

  MICHAEL F. COYLE
  Executive Vice President

    GREG L. ASHLEY
    President, Playground

    DANAE JOHNSON
    Vice President, People Development

JIM ONKEN
President, Storied Places

DAVID S. GREENFIELD
Executive Vice President,
Northwest and Southwest Regions

  DONAL O'CALLAGHAN
  Vice President, Design

  DOUGLAS W. OGILVY
  Regional Vice President, Southwest Region

    FRED GOERS
    Vice President, Construction,
    Southwest Region

    TOM JACOBSON
    Vice President, Development,
    Southwest Region

  PAUL WOODWARD
  Vice President, Northwest Region

    ROBERT FRITZ
    Vice President, Construction,
    Northwest Region

    ERIC GERLACH
    Vice President, Development,
    Northwest Region

DAVID KLEINKOPF
Executive Vice President,
Southeast and Colorado Regions

  DON CARR
  Regional Vice President, Southeast Region

    JIM BOIVIN
    Vice President, Construction,
    Southeast Region

    TOM WALLINGTON
    Vice President, Development,
    Southeast Region

  MIKE O'CONNOR
  Vice President, Development,
  Colorado Region

  JOE WHITEHOUSE
  Vice President, Development,
  Colorado Region

  CONNIE WYNNE
  Vice President, Resort Planning,
  Southeast and Colorado Regions

  JEFF STIPEC
  President, Intrawest Golf

  DREW STOTESBURY
  Chief Financial Officer

    RASHA HODALY
    Vice President, Financial Reporting
    and Accounting

RESORT CLUB GROUP

JAMES J. GIBBONS
President, Resort Club Group

  RENÉ L. CARDINAL
  Senior Vice President,
  Finance and Administration

  R. JUDE CARRILLO
  Executive Vice President,
  Sales and Marketing

BARBARA J. JACKSON
Vice President,
Guest Experience and Communications

MICHAEL KAINE
Vice President, Technology

MURRAY PRATT
Vice President, Global Tour Generation

DOUG REGELOUS
Senior Vice President, Development

JEFF TISDALL
Vice President, Membership
Programs Marketing

RON. T. ZIMMER
Executive Vice President and
Chief Financial Officer

Note: All asterisked assignment material relates to the appendix to the chapter.

Brief Exercises

BE5-1 Broncho Corporation has the following accounts included in its 12/31/04 trial balance: Accounts Receivable $210,000; Inventories $190,000; Allowance for Doubtful Accounts $8,000; Patents $92,000; Prepaid Insurance $9,500; Accounts Payable $77,000; and Cash $7,000. Prepare the balance sheet's current assets section listing the accounts in proper sequence. Identify which items are monetary.

BE5-2 Included in Daily Limited's 12/31/04 trial balance are the following accounts: Prepaid Rent $1,200; Long-term Investments in Common Shares $51,000; Unearned Fees $7,000; Land Held for Investment $139,000; and Long-term Receivables $42,000. Prepare the balance sheet's long-term investments section. Identify which items are financial instruments.

BE5-3 Azalea Corp's 12/31/04 trial balance includes the following accounts: Inventories $20,000; Buildings $307,000; Accumulated Amortization—Equipment $119,000; Equipment $190,000; Land Held for Investment $146,000; Accumulated Amortization— Buildings $45,000; Land $261,000; and Capital Leases $170,000. Prepare the balance sheet's property, plant, and equipment section.

BE5-4 Mai Corporation has the following accounts included in its 12/31/04 trial balance: Temporary Investments $121,000; Goodwill $250,000; Prepaid Insurance $112,000; Patents $20,000; and Franchises $110,000. Prepare the balance sheet's intangible assets section.

BE5-5 Included in Euclid Limited's 12/31/04 trial balance are the following accounts: Accounts Payable $240,000; Obligations under Long-term Capital Leases $175,000; Discount on Bonds Payable $124,000; Advances from Customers $141,000; Bonds Payable $600,000; Wages Payable $127,000; Interest Payable $112,000; and Income Taxes Payable $9,000. Prepare the balance sheet's current liabilities section. Identify which items are monetary.

BE5-6 Use the information presented in BE5-5 for Euclid Limited to prepare the balance sheet's long-term liabilities section.

BE5-7 Tong Corp's 12/31/04 trial balance includes the following accounts: Investment in Common Shares $170,000; Retained Earnings $309,000; Trademarks $87,000; Preferred Shares $234,000; Common Shares $67,000; Future Income Taxes $188,000; and Contributed Surplus $4,000. Prepare the balance sheet's shareholders' equity section.

Exercises

E5-1 (Balance Sheet Classifications) Presented below are a number of balance sheet accounts of SooYoun Inc.

1. Investment in Preferred Shares
2. Common Shares Distributable
3. Cash Dividends Payable
4. Accumulated Amortization
5. Warehouse in Process of Construction
6. Petty Cash
7. Accrued Interest on Notes Payable
8. Deficit
9. Temporary Investments
10. Income Taxes Payable
11. Unearned Subscription Revenue
12. Work-in-Process
13. Accrued Vacation Pay

Instructions

For each account above, indicate the proper balance sheet classification. In the case of borderline items, indicate the additional information that would be required to determine the proper classification. (Refer to Illustration 5-1 as a guideline.) Identify which items are monetary and which are financial instruments.

E5-2 (Classification of Balance Sheet Accounts) Presented below are the captions of Farooq Limited's balance sheet.

(a) Current Assets	**(g)** Noncurrent Liabilities
(b) Investments	**(h)** Common Shares
(c) Property, Plant, and Equipment	**(i)** Preferred Shares
(d) Intangible Assets	**(j)** Contributed Surplus
(e) Other Assets	**(k)** Retained Earnings
(f) Current Liabilities	**(l)** Accumulated Other Comprehensive Income

Instructions

Indicate by letter where each of the following items would be classified.

1. Preferred shares	**12.** Notes payable (due next year)
2. Goodwill	**13.** Office supplies
3. Wages payable	**14.** Common shares
4. Trade accounts payable	**15.** Land
5. Buildings	**16.** Bond sinking fund
6. Temporary investments	**17.** Merchandise inventory
7. Current portion of long-term debt	**18.** Prepaid insurance
8. Premium on bonds payable	**19.** Bonds payable
9. Allowance for doubtful accounts	**20.** Taxes payable
10. Accounts receivable	**21.** Unrealized gain on derivatives
11. Cash surrender value of life insurance	**22.** Donation of artwork from unrelated customer

E5-3 (**Classification of Balance Sheet Accounts**)   Assume that Macy Inc. uses the following headings on its balance sheet.

(a) Current Assets	**(g)** Long-term Liabilities
(b) Investments	**(h)** Common Shares
(c) Property, Plant, and Equipment	**(i)** Contributed Surplus
(d) Intangible Assets	**(j)** Retained Earnings
(e) Other Assets	**(k)** Accumulated Other Comprehensive Income
(f) Current Liabilities	

Instructions

Indicate by letter how each of the following usually should be classified. If an item should appear in a note to the financial statements, use the letter N to indicate this. If an item need not be reported at all on the balance sheet, use the letter X. Note also whether an item is monetary and/or represents a financial instrument.

1. Unexpired insurance

2. Shares owned in affiliated companies

3. Unearned subscriptions

4. Advances to suppliers

5. Unearned rent

6. Copyrights

7. Petty cash fund

8. Sales tax payable

9. Accrued interest on notes receivable

10. Twenty-year issue of bonds payable that will mature within the next year (no sinking funds exists, and refunding is not planned)

11. Machinery retired from use and held for sale

12. Fully amortized machine still in use

13. Organization costs

14. Accrued interest on bonds payable

15. Salaries that company budget shows will be paid to employees within the next year

16. Accumulated amortization

17. Unrealized gains on available for sale securities

E5-4 **(Preparation of a Classified Balance Sheet)**   Assume that Dion Inc. has the following accounts at the end of the current year.

1. Common Shares	11. Accumulated Amortization Buildings
2. Raw Materials	12. Cash Restricted for Plant Expansion
3. Preferred Shares Investments Long-term	13. Land Held for Future Plant Site
4. Unearned Rent	14. Allowance for Doubtful Accounts
5. Work-in-Process	15. Retained Earnings
6. Copyrights	16. Unearned Subscriptions
7. Buildings	17. Receivables from Officers (due in one year)
8. Notes Receivable (short-term)	18. Finished Goods
9. Cash	19. Accounts Receivable
10. Accrued Salaries Payable	20. Bonds Payable (due in 4 years)

Instructions

Prepare a classified balance sheet in good form (no monetary amounts are necessary).

E5-5 **(Preparation of a Corrected Balance Sheet)**   Sibongilie Corp. has decided to expand its operations. The bookkeeper recently completed the balance sheet presented below in order to obtain additional funds for expansion.

Interactive
Homework

SIBONGILIE CORP.
Balance Sheet
For the Year Ended 2005

Current assets	
Cash (net of bank overdraft of $30,000)	540,000
Accounts receivable (net)	140,000
Inventories at lower of average cost or market	322,000
Trading securities at cost (fair value $120,000)	140,000
Property, plant, and equipment	
Building (net)	1,570,000
Office equipment (net)	460,000
Land held for future use	2,375,000
Intangible assets	
Goodwill	180,000
Cash surrender value of life insurance	90,000
Prepaid expense	12,000
Current liabilities	
Accounts payable	505,000
Notes payable (due next year)	125,000
Pension obligation	82,000
Rent payable	49,000
Premium on bonds payable	53,000
Long-term liabilities	
Bonds payable	500,000
Shareholders' equity	
Common shares, authorized	
400,000 shares, issued 290,000	290,000
Contributed Surplus	160,000
Retained earnings	?

Instructions
Prepare a revised balance sheet given the available information. Assume that the accumulated amortization balance for the buildings is $560,000 and for the office equipment, $105,000. The allowance for doubtful accounts has a balance of $17,000. The pension obligation is considered a long-term liability.

E5-6   (Corrections of a Balance Sheet)   The bookkeeper for Nguyen Corp has prepared the following balance sheet as of July 31, 2005.

NGUYEN CORP.
Balance Sheet
As of July 31, 2005

Cash	$ 69,000	Notes and accounts payable	$ 44,000
Accounts receivable (net)	40,500	Long-term liabilities	75,000
Inventories	60,000	Shareholders' equity	155,500
Equipment (net)	84,000		$274,500
Patents	21,000		
	$274,500		

The following additional information is provided.

1. Cash includes $1,200 in a petty cash fund and $15,000 in a bond sinking fund.

2. The net accounts receivable balance is composed of the following three items: (a) accounts receivable debit balances $52,000; (b) accounts receivable credit balances $8,000; (c) allowance for doubtful accounts $3,500.

3. Merchandise inventory costing $5,300 was shipped out on consignment on July 31, 2005. The ending inventory balance does not include the consigned goods. Receivables in the amount of $5,300 were recognized on these consigned goods.

4. Equipment had a cost of $112,000 and an accumulated amortization balance of $28,000.

5. Taxes payable of $6,000 were accrued on July 31. Nguyen Corp, however, had set up a cash fund to meet this obligation. This cash fund was not included in the cash balance, but was offset against the taxes payable amount.

Instructions
Prepare a corrected classified balance sheet as of July 31, 2005 from the available information, adjusting the account balances using the additional information.

E5-7   (Current Assets Section of the Balance Sheet)   Presented below are selected accounts of Kawabata Limited at December 31, 2005.

Finished goods	$ 152,000	Cost of goods sold	2,100,000
Revenue received in advance	90,000	Notes receivable	40,000
Bank overdraft	8,000	Accounts receivable	161,000
Equipment	453,000	Raw materials	207,000
Work-in-process	134,000	Supplies expense	60,000
Cash	97,000	Allowance for doubtful accounts	12,000
Temporary investments—trading	51,000	Licences	18,000
Customer advances	36,000	Contributed surplus	88,000
Cash restricted for plant expansion	150,000	Common shares	22,000

The following additional information is available.

1. Inventories are valued at lower of cost and market using FIFO.

2. Equipment is recorded at cost. Accumulated amortization, calculated on a straight-line basis, is $50,600.

3. The short-term investments have a fair value of $129,000.

4. The notes receivable are due April 30, 2009, with interest receivable every April 30. The notes bear interest at 12%. (Hint: Accrue interest due on December 31, 2005.)

5. The allowance for doubtful accounts applies to the accounts receivable. Accounts receivable of $50,000 are pledged as collateral on a bank loan.

6. Licences are recorded net of accumulated amortization of $14,000.

Instructions
Prepare the current assets section of Kawabata Limited's December 31, 2005 balance sheet, with appropriate disclosures.

E5-8   (Current vs. Long-term Liabilities)   Chopin Corporation is preparing its December 31, 2004 balance sheet. The following items may be reported as either a current or long-term liability.

1. On December 15, 2004, Chopin declared a cash dividend of $2.50 per share to shareholders of record on December 31. The dividend is payable on January 15, 2005. Chopin has issued 1 million common shares.

2. Also on December 31, Chopin declared a 10% stock dividend to shareholders of record on January 15, 2005. The dividend will be distributed on January 31, 2005. Chopin's common shares have a market value of $38 per share.

3. At December 31, bonds payable of $100 million are outstanding. The bonds pay 12% interest every September 30 and mature in instalments of $25 million every September 30, beginning September 30, 2005.

4. At December 31, 2003, customer advances were $12 million. During 2004, Chopin collected $30 million of customer advances, and advances of $25 million were earned.

5. At December 31, 2004, retained earnings appropriated for future inventory losses is $15 million.

Instructions
For each item above, indicate the dollar amounts to be reported as a current liability and as a long-term liability, if any.

E5-9   (Current Assets and Current Liabilities)   The current assets and liabilities sections of the balance sheet of Scarlatti Corp. appear as follows:

SCARLATTI CORP.
Balance Sheet (partial)
December 31, 2004

Cash		$ 990,000	Accounts payable	$1,061,000
Accounts receivable	$1,189,000		Notes payable	867,000
Allowance for doubtful accounts	197,000	992,000		$1,928,000
Inventories		971,000		
Prepaid expenses		19,000		
		$2,972,000		

The following errors in the corporation's accounting have been discovered.

1. January 2005 cash disbursements entered as of December 2004 included payments of accounts payable in the amount of $739,000, on which a cash discount of 2% was taken.

2. The inventory included $127,000 of merchandise that had been received at December 31 but for which no purchase invoices had been received or entered. Of this amount, $12,000 had been received on consignment; the remainder was purchased f.o.b. destination, terms 2/10, n/30.

3. Sales for the first four days in January 2005 in the amount of $430,000 were entered in the sales book as of December 31, 2004. Of these, $121,500 were sales on account and the remainder were cash sales.

4. Cash, not including cash sales, collected in January 2005 and entered as of December 31, 2004 totalled $135,324. Of this amount, $123,324 was received on account after cash discounts of 2% had been deducted; the remainder represented the proceeds of a bank loan.

Instructions

(a) Restate the balance sheet's current assets and liabilities sections. (Assume that both accounts receivable and accounts payable are recorded gross.)

(b) State the net effect of your adjustments on Scarlatti Corp's retained earnings balance.

E5-10   (Statement of Cash Flows—Classifications)   The major classifications of activities reported in the statement of cash flows are operating, investing, and financing.

Instructions
Classify each of the transactions listed below as.

1. Operating activity

2. Investing activity

3. Financing activity

4. Not reported as a cash flow

The transactions are as follows:

(a) Issuance of common shares

(g) Issuance of bonds for plant assets

(b) Purchase of land and building

(h) Payment of cash dividends

(c) Redemption of bonds

(i) Exchange of furniture for office equipment

(d) Sale of equipment

(j) Loss on sale of equipment

(e) Amortization of machinery

(k) Increase in accounts receivable during the year

(f) Amortization of patent

(l) Decrease in accounts payable during the year

E5-11 (Preparation of a Balance Sheet) Presented below is the trial balance of Kwanzu Corporation at December 31, 2004.

Interactive Homework

	Debits	Credits
Cash	$ 197,000	
Sales		$ 8,100,000
Temporary Investment—trading (at market, $245,000)	153,000	
Cost of Goods Sold	4,800,000	
Long-term Investments in Bonds—Held to maturity	299,000	
Long-term Investments in Shares—Available for sale	277,000	
(market $345,000)		
Short-term Notes Payable		90,000
Accounts Payable		455,000
Selling Expenses	2,000,000	
Investment Gains		63,000
Land	260,000	
Buildings	1,040,000	
Dividends Payable		136,000
Accrued Liabilities		96,000
Accounts Receivable	435,000	
Accumulated Amortization—Buildings		152,000
Allowance for Doubtful Accounts		25,000
Administrative Expenses	900,000	
Interest Expense	211,000	
Inventories	597,000	
Extraordinary Gain		80,000
Correction of Prior Year's Error	140,000	
Long-term Notes Payable		900,000
Equipment	600,000	
Bonds Payable		1,000,000
Accumulated Amortization—Equipment		60,000
Franchise	160,000	
Common Shares		809,000
Patent	195,000	
Retained Earnings		218,000
Accumulated Other Comprehensive Income		80,000
Totals	$12,264,000	$12,264,000

Instructions

Prepare a balance sheet at December 31, 2004. Ignore income taxes.

E5-12 (Preparation of a Balance Sheet) Worldly Corporation's balance sheet at the end of 2003 included the following items.

Interactive Homework

Current assets	$1,235,000	Current liabilities	$1,150,000
Land	30,000	Bonds payable	1,100,000
Building	1,120,000	Common shares	180,000
Equipment	190,000	Retained earnings	44,000
Accum. Amort—build.	(130,000)	Total	$2,474,000
Accum. amort.—equip.	(11,000)		
Patents	40,000		
Total	$2,474,000		

The following information is available for 2004.

1. Net income was $355,000.

2. Equipment (cost $20,000 and accumulated amortization, $8,000) was sold for $10,000.

3. Amortization expense was $4,000 on the building and $9,000 on equipment.

4. Patent amortization expense was $2,500.

5. Current assets other than cash increased by $229,000. Current liabilities increased by $213,000.

6. An addition to the building was completed at a cost of $27,000.

7. A long-term investment in shares (no quoted market value) was purchased for $16,000.

8. Bonds payable of $50,000 were issued.

9. Cash dividends of $130,000 were declared and paid.

Instructions
Prepare a balance sheet at December 31, 2004.

*E5-13 (Analysis) The comparative balance sheets of Marubeni Corporation at the beginning and end of the year 2005 appear below.

MARUBENI CORPORATION
Balance Sheets

Assets	Dec. 31, 2005	Jan. 1, 2005
Cash	$ 20,000	$ 13,000
Accounts receivable	106,000	88,000
Equipment	39,000	22,000
Less: Accumulated		
Amortization	(17,000)	(11,000)
Total	$148,000	$112,000
Liabilities and Shareholders' Equity		
Accounts payable	$ 20,000	$ 15,000
Common shares	100,000	80,000
Retained earnings	28,000	17,000
Total	$148,000	$112,000

Net income of $44,000 was reported and dividends of $33,000 were paid in 2005. New equipment was purchased and none was sold.

Instructions

(a) Calculate the current ratio and debt to total assets ratio as of January 1, 2005 and December 31, 2005.

(b) In light of the analysis above, comment on the company's liquidity and financial flexibility.

*E5-14 (Analysis) A comparative balance sheet for Nicholson Industries Inc. is presented below.

NICHOLSON INDUSTRIES INC.
Balance Sheets

	December 31	
Assets	2004	2003
Cash	$ 13,000	$ 22,000
Accounts receivable	112,000	66,000
Inventories	220,000	189,000
Land	71,000	110,000
Equipment	260,000	200,000
Accumulated amortization—equipment	(69,000)	(42,000)
Total	$607,000	$545,000

Liabilities and Shareholders' Equity

Accounts payable	$ 44,000	$ 47,000
Bonds payable	150,000	200,000
Common shares	214,000	164,000
Retained earnings	99,000	34,000
Accumulated other comprehensive income	100,000	100,000
Total	$607,000	$545,000

Additional information:

1. Net income for 2004 was $125,000.

2. Cash dividends of $60,000 were declared and paid.

3. Bonds payable amounting to $50,000 were retired through issuance of common shares.

4. Land was sold at book value.

Instructions

(a) Calculate the current and acid-test ratios for 2003 and 2004.

(b) Calculate Nicholson's current cash debt coverage ratio for 2004.

(c) Based on the analyses in (a) and (b), comment on Nicholson's liquidity and financial flexibility.

Problems

P5-1 Presented below is a list of accounts in alphabetical order.

Accounts Receivable	Inventory—Ending
Accrued Wages	Land
Accumulated Amortization—Buildings	Land for Future Plant Site
Accumulated Amortization—Equipment	Loss from Flood
Accumulated Other Comprehensive Income	Notes Payable—Current
Advances to Employees	Patent (net of amortization)
Advertising Expense	Pension Obligations
Allowance for Doubtful Accounts	Petty Cash
Available for Sale Securities—Noncurrent	Preferred Shares
Bonds Payable	Premium on Bonds Payable
Buildings	Prepaid Rent
Cash in Bank	Purchase Returns and Allowances
Cash on Hand	Purchases
Cash Surrender Value of Life Insurance	Retained Earnings
Commission Expense	Sales
Common Shares	Sales Discounts
Copyright (net of amortization)	Sales Salaries Expense
Dividends Payable	Taxes Payable
Equipment	Temporary Investments—Held for Trading
Gain on Sale of Equipment	Transportation-in
Interest Receivable	Unearned Subscriptions
Inventory—Beginning	Unrealized Gain/Loss on Available for Sale Securities

Instructions

Prepare a classified balance sheet in good form. (No monetary amounts are to be shown.)

Interactive
Homework

P5-2 Presented below are a number of balance sheet items for Li Inc. for the current year, 2005.

Goodwill	$ 125,000	Accumulated amortization	
		equipment	$ 292,000
Payroll taxes payable	177,591	Inventories	239,800
Bonds payable	300,000	Rent payable short-term	45,000
Discount on bonds payable	15,000	Taxes payable	98,362
Cash	360,000	Long-term rental obligations	480,000

Land	480,000	Common shares (20,000 shares issued)	200,000
Notes receivable	545,700	Preferred shares (15,000 shares issued)	150,000
Notes payable to banks	265,000	Prepaid expenses	87,920
Accounts payable	590,000	Equipment	1,470,000
Retained earnings	?	Temporary investments—trading	121,000
Income taxes receivable	97,630	Accumulated amortization—building	170,200
Unsecured notes payable (long-term)	1,600,000	Building	1,640,000

Instructions

Prepare a classified balance sheet in good form. 400,000 common shares were authorized, and 20,000 preferred shares were authorized. Assume that notes receivable and notes payable are short-term, unless stated otherwise. Cost and fair value of temporary investments are the same.

P5-3   The trial balance of Klix Inc. and other related information for the year 2005 is presented below.

KLIX INC.
Trial Balance
December 31, 2005

	Debits	Credits
Cash	$ 91,000	
Accounts Receivable	363,500	
Allowance for Doubtful Accounts		$ 58,700
Prepaid Insurance	5,900	
Inventory	308,500	
Long-term Investments—available for sale	339,000	
Land	85,000	
Construction Work in Progress	124,000	
Patents	36,000	
Equipment	400,000	
Accumulated Amortization—Equipment		340,000
Unamortized Discount on Bonds Payable	20,000	
Accounts Payable		148,000
Accrued Expenses		49,200
Notes Payable		94,000
Bonds Payable		400,000
Common Shares		500,000
Accumulated Other Comprehensive Income		45,000
Retained Earnings		138,000
	$1,772,900	$1,772,900

Additional information:

1. The inventory has a replacement market value of $353,000. The LIFO method of inventory value is used.

2. The fair value of the Investments is $559,000.

3. The amount of the Construction Work in Progress account represents the costs expended to date on a building in the process of construction. (The company rents factory space at the present time.) The land on which the building is being constructed cost $85,000, as shown in the trial balance.

4. The patents were purchased by the company at a cost of $40,000 and are being amortized on a straight-line basis.

5. Of the unamortized discount on bonds payable, $2,000 will be amortized in 2006.

6. The notes payable represent bank loans that are secured by long-term investments carried at $120,000. These bank loans are due in 2006.

7. The bonds payable bear interest at 11% payable every December 31, and are due January 1, 2013.

8. Six hundred thousand shares of common shares were authorized, of which 500,000 shares issued are outstanding.

Instructions

Prepare a balance sheet as of December 31, 2005, so that all important information is fully disclosed.

P5-4   Presented below is the balance sheet of Cruise Corporation as of December 31, 2005.

CRUISE CORPORATION
Balance Sheet
December 31, 2005

Assets	
Goodwill (Note 2)	$ 120,000
Buildings (Note 1)	1,640,000
Inventories	312,100
Trading securities	100,000
Land	650,000
Accounts receivable	170,000
Long-term investments—available for sale	87,000
Cash on hand	175,900
Assets allocated to trustee for plant expansion	
Cash in bank	70,000
Treasury notes, at cost and fair value	138,000
	$3,463,000

Equities	
Notes payable (Note 3)	$ 600,000
Common shares, issued, 1,000,000 shares (authorized unlimited)	1,150,000
Retained earnings	456,000
Accumulated other comprehensive income	202,000
Appreciation capital (Note 1)	570,000
Income taxes payable	75,000
Reserve for amortization of building	410,000
	$3,463,000

Note 1: Buildings are stated at cost, except for one building that was recorded at appraised value. The excess of appraisal value over cost was $570,000. Amortization has been recorded based on cost.

Note 2: Goodwill in the amount of $120,000 was recognized because the company believed that book value was not an accurate representation of the company's fair market value. The gain of $120,000 was credited to Retained Earnings.

Note 3: Notes payable are long-term except for the current instalment due of $100,000.

Note 4: Trading securities have a market value of $75,000 and Available for sale securities have a market value of $200,000.

Instructions
Prepare a corrected classified balance sheet in good form. The notes above are for information only.

P5-5   Presented below is the balance sheet of Krause Corporation for the current year, 2005.

KRAUSE CORPORATION
Balance Sheet
December 31, 2005

Current assets	$ 125,000	Current liabilities	$ 330,000
Investments	940,000	Long-term liabilities	990,000
Property, plant, and equipment	1,720,000	Shareholders' equity	1,770,000
Intangible assets	305,000		
	$3,090,000		$3,090,000

The following information is presented.

1. The current assets section includes: cash $10,000, accounts receivable $115,000 less $10,000 for allowance for doubtful accounts, inventories $15,000, and unearned revenue $5,000. The cash balance is composed of $14,000, less a bank overdraft of $4,000. Inventories are stated on the lower of FIFO cost or market.

2. The investments section includes the cash surrender value of a life insurance contract $40,000; temporary investments in common shares of another company—trading $280,000 (fair value $280,000) and long-term available for sale securities $140,000 (fair value $240,000); bond sinking fund $250,000; and organization costs $130,000.

3. Property, plant, and equipment includes buildings $1,040,000 less accumulated amortization $360,000; equipment $450,000 less accumulated amortization $180,000; land $500,000; and land held for future use $270,000.

4. Intangible assets include a franchise $165,000, goodwill $100,000, and discount on bonds payable $40,000.

5. Current liabilities include accounts payable $90,000, notes payable short-term $80,000 and long-term $120,000, and taxes payable $40,000.

6. Long-term liabilities are composed solely of 10% bonds payable due 2010.

7. Shareholders' equity has 70,000 preferred shares (authorized 200,000 shares), which were issued for $450,000, and 100,000 common shares (authorized 400,000 shares), which were issued at an average price of $10. In addition, the corporation has retained earnings of $120,000 and Accumulated Other Comprehensive Income of $200,000.

Instructions

Prepare a balance sheet in good form, adjusting the amounts in each balance sheet classification as affected by the information given above.

P5-6 Cooke Inc. had the following balance sheet at the end of operations for 2003.

COOKE INC.
Balance Sheet
December 31, 2003

Cash	$ 20,000	Accounts payable	$ 30,000
Accounts receivable	21,200	Long-term notes payable	41,000
Investments—Trading	32,000	Common shares	100,000
Plant assets (net)	81,000	Retained earnings	23,200
Land	40,000		
	$194,200		$194,200

During 2004, the following occurred.

1. Cooke Inc. sold part of its investment portfolio for $17,000. This transaction resulted in a gain of $3,400 for the firm. The company often sells and buys securities of this nature.

2. A tract of land was purchased for $18,000 cash.

3. Long-term notes payable in the amount of $16,000 were retired before maturity by paying $16,000 cash.

4. An additional $24,000 in common shares was issued.

5. Dividends totalling $8,200 were declared and paid to shareholders.

6. Net income for 2004 was $32,000 after allowing for amortization of $12,000.

7. Land was purchased through the issuance of $30,000 in bonds.

8. At December 31, 2004, Cash was $39,000, Accounts Receivable was $41,600, and Accounts Payable remained at $30,000.

Instructions

Prepare the balance sheet as it would appear at December 31, 2004.

P5-7 Anne Spier has prepared baked goods for resale since 1991. She started a baking business in her home and has been operating in a rented building with a storefront since 1996. Spier incorporated the business as MAS Inc. on January 1, 2004, with an initial shares issue of 1,000 shares of common shares for $2,500. Anne Spier is the principal shareholder of MAS Inc.

Sales have increased 30% annually since operations began at the present location, and additional equipment is needed to accommodate expected continued growth. Spier wishes to purchase some additional baking equipment and to finance the equipment through a long-term note from a commercial bank. Kelowna Bank & Trust has asked Spier to submit an income statement for MAS Inc. for the first five months of 2004 and a balance sheet as of May 31, 2004.

Spier assembled the following information from the corporation's cash basis records for use in preparing the financial statements requested by the bank.

1. The bank statement showed the following 2004 deposits through May 31.

Sale of common shares	$ 2,500
Cash sales	22,770
Rebates from purchases	130
Collections on credit sales	5,320
Bank loan proceeds	2,880
	$33,600

2. The following amounts were disbursed through May 31, 2004.

Baking materials	$14,400
Rent	1,800
Salaries and wages	5,500
Maintenance	110
Utilities	4,000
Insurance premium	1,920
Equipment	3,000
Principal and interest payment on bank loan	312
Advertising	424
	$31,466

3. Unpaid invoices at May 31, 2004, were as follows.

Baking materials	$256
Utilities	270
	$526

4. Customer records showed uncollected sales of $4,226 at May 31, 2004.

5. Baking materials costing $1,840 were on hand at May 31, 2004. There were no materials in process or finished goods on hand at that date. No materials were on hand or in process and no finished goods were on hand at January 1, 2004.

6. The note evidencing the three-year bank loan is dated January 1, 2004, and states a simple interest rate of 10%. The loan requires quarterly payments on April 1, July 1, October 1, and January 1 consisting of equal principal payments plus accrued interest since the last payment.

7. Anne Spier receives a salary of $750 on the last day of each month. The other employees had been paid through May 25, 2004, and were due an additional $240 on May 31, 2004.

8. New display cases and equipment costing $3,000 were purchased on January 2, 2004, and have an estimated useful life of five years. These are the only fixed assets currently used in the business. Straight-line amortization is to be used for book purposes.

9. Rent was paid for six months in advance on January 2, 2004.

10. A one-year insurance policy was purchased on January 2, 2004.

11. MAS Inc. is subject to an income tax rate of 20%.

12. Payments and collections pertaining to the unincorporated business through December 31, 2003 were not included in the corporation's records, and no cash was transferred from the unincorporated business to the corporation.

Instructions

Using the accrual basis of accounting, prepare for MAS Inc.:

(a) An income statement for the five months ended May 31, 2004.

(b) A balance sheet as of May 31, 2004.

(CMA adapted)

P5-8 Mansbridge Inc. had the following balance sheet at the end of operations for 2003.

MANSBRIDGE INC.
Balance Sheet
December 31, 2003

Cash	$ 20,000	Accounts payable	$ 30,000
Accounts receivable	21,200	Bonds payable	41,000
Investments—trading—at fair value	32,000	Common shares	100,000
Plant assets (net)	81,000	Retained earnings	23,200
Land	40,000		
	$194,200		$194,200

During 2004, the following occurred.

1. Mansbridge liquidated its investment portfolio at a loss of $3,000.

2. A tract of land was purchased for $38,000.

3. An additional $26,000 in common shares was issued.

4. Dividends totalling $10,000 were declared and paid to shareholders.

5. Net income for 2004 was $35,000, including $12,000 in amortization expense.

6. Land was purchased through the issuance of $30,000 in additional bonds.

7. At December 31, 2004, Cash was $66,200, Accounts Receivable was $42,000, and Accounts Payable was $40,000.

8. The fair value of the investments is equal to its cost.

Instructions

(a) Prepare the balance sheet as it would appear at December 31, 2004.

(b) Calculate the current and acid-test ratios for 2003 and 2004.

(c) Calculate Mansbridge's current cash debt coverage ratio for 2004.

P5-9 In an examination of Acevedo Corporation as of December 31, 2004, you have learned that the following situations exist. No entries have been made in the accounting records for these items.

1. The corporation erected its present factory building in 1989. Amortization was calculated by the straight-line method, using an estimated life of 35 years. Early in 2004, the board of directors conducted a careful survey and estimated that the factory building had a remaining useful life of 25 years as of January 1, 2004.

2. An additional assessment of 2003 income taxes was levied and paid in 2004.

3. When calculating the accrual for officers' salaries at December 31, 2004, it was discovered that the accrual for officers' salaries for December 31, 2003 had been overstated.

4. On December 15, 2004, Acevedo Corporation declared a common shares dividend of $1 per share on its common shares outstanding, payable February 1, 2005, to the common shareholders of record December 31, 2004.

5. Acevedo Corporation, which is on a calendar-year basis, changed its inventory method as of January 1, 2004. The inventory for December 31, 2003 was costed by the average method, and the inventory for December 31, 2004 was costed by the FIFO method.

Instructions

Describe fully how each item above should be reported in the financial statements of Acevedo Corporation for the year 2004.

P5-10   Presented below is the balance sheet of Bellemy Corporation (000s omitted).

BELLEMY CORPORATION
Balance Sheet
December 31, 2005

Assets

Current assets

Cash	$26,000	
Marketable securities—trading	18,000	
Accounts receivable	25,000	
Merchandise inventory	20,000	
Supplies inventory	4,000	
Investment in subsidiary company	20,000	$113,000

Investments

Marketable securities		25,000

Property, plant, and equipment

Buildings and land	91,000	
Less: Reserve for amortization	31,000	60,000

Other assets

Cash surrender value of life insurance		19,000
		$217,000

Liabilities and Equity

Current liabilities

Accounts payable	$22,000	
Reserve for income taxes	15,000	
Customer accounts with credit balances	1	$37,001

Deferred credits

Unamortized premium on bonds payable		2,000

Long-term liabilities

Bonds payable		60,000
Total liabilities		99,001

Shareholders' Equity

Common shares issued	85,000	
Earned surplus	24,999	
Cash dividends declared	8,000	117,999
		$217,000

Instructions

Evaluate the balance sheet presented. State briefly the proper treatment of any item criticized.

Writing Assignments

WA5-1   The partner in charge of the Spencer Corporation audit comes by your desk and leaves a letter he has started to the CEO and a copy of the cash flow statement for the year ended December 31, 2004. Because he must leave on an emergency, he asks you to finish the letter by explaining: (1) the disparity between net income and cash flow; (2) the importance of operating cash flow; (3) the sustainable source(s) of cash flow; and (4) possible suggestions to improve the cash position.

SPENCER CORPORATION
Statement of Cash Flows
For the Year Ended December 31, 2004

Cash flows from operating activities

Net income		$100,000
Adjustments to reconcile net income to net cash provided by operating activities:		
Amortization expense	$ 11,000	
Loss on sale of fixed assets	5,000	
Increase in accounts receivable (net)	(40,000)	
Increase in inventory	(35,000)	
Decrease in accounts payable	(41,000)	(100,000)
Net cash provided by operating activities		–0–
Cash flows from investing activities		
Sale of plant assets	25,000	
Purchase of equipment	(100,000)	
Purchase of land	(200,000)	
Net cash used by investing activities		(275,000)
Cash flows from financing activities		
Payment of dividends	(10,000)	
Redemption of bonds	(100,000)	
Net cash used by financing activities		(110,000)
Net decrease in cash		(385,000)
Cash balance, January 1, 2004		400,000
Cash balance, December 31, 2004		$ 15,000

Date
James Spencer III, CEO
James Spencer Corporation
125 Bay Street
Toronto, ON

Dear Mr. Spencer:

I have good news and bad news about the financial statements for the year ended December 31, 2004. The good news is that net income of $100,000 is close to what we predicted in the strategic plan last year, indicating strong performance this year. The bad news is that the cash balance is seriously low. Enclosed is the Statement of Cash Flows, which best illustrates how both of these situations occurred simultaneously . . .

Instructions
Complete the letter to the CEO, including the four components requested by the partner.

WA5-2   Andrea Pafko, corporate comptroller for Nicholson Industries, is trying to decide how to present "Property, plant, and equipment" in the balance sheet. She realizes that the statement of cash flows will show that the company made a significant investment in purchasing new equipment this year, but overall she knows the company's plant assets are rather old. She feels that she can disclose one figure titled "Property, plant, and equipment, net of amortization," and the result will be a low figure. However, it will not disclose the assets' age. If she chooses to show the cost less accumulated amortization, the assets' age will be apparent. She proposes the following.

Property, plant, and equipment, net of amortization	$10,000,000
rather than	
Property, plant and equipment	$50,000,000
Less: Accumulated amortization	(40,000,000)
Net book value	$10,000,000

Instructions
Discuss the financial reporting issues including any ethical issues.

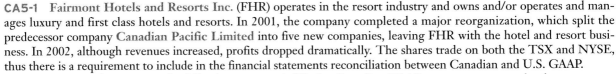

Cases

Refer to the Case Primer on the Digital Tool to help you answer these cases.

CA5-1   Fairmont Hotels and Resorts Inc. (FHR) operates in the resort industry and owns and/or operates and manages luxury and first class hotels and resorts. In 2001, the company completed a major reorganization, which split the predecessor company **Canadian Pacific Limited** into five new companies, leaving FHR with the hotel and resort business. In 2002, although revenues increased, profits dropped dramatically. The shares trade on both the TSX and NYSE, thus there is a requirement to include in the financial statements reconciliation between Canadian and U.S. GAAP.

In the reconciliation note, the following was noted: "Under Canadian GAAP, computer systems development costs for internal use software are capitalized when the project is expected to be of continuing benefit to FHR and otherwise expensed. U.S. GAAP standards require that certain costs of computer software developed for internal use be capitalized and amortized."

In addition, the following was noted under the Changes in accounting policy note: "In 2002, revenues and expenses from managed and franchised properties were included in the consolidated statements of income in response to a recent CICA Emerging Issues abstract. The 2001 and 2000 revenues and expenses have been reclassified to conform with the presentation adopted for 2002. They were previously recorded in a net basis."

Instructions

Discuss the alternative treatments and recommend which treatment reflects reality. Hint: Use the conceptual framework identified in Chapter 2.

CA5-2   In the late 1990's, **CIBC** helped **Enron** structure 34 "loans" that appeared as cash proceeds from sales of assets in the financial statements. Enron subsequently went bankrupt in 2001 and in its wake, left many unhappy investors and creditors who had lost billions of dollars. In December 2003, CIBC settled four regulatory investigations with the SEC, U.S. Federal Reserve, the U.S. Justice Department and the Canadian Office of the Superintendent of Financial Institutions. The settlement, which amounted to $80 million U.S., is one of the largest regulatory penalties levied on a Canadian bank. The regulatory authorities felt that CIBC had aided Enron in boosting its earnings and hiding debt. CIBC set aside a $109 million reserve in early 2003 in anticipation of this settlement. No additional reserves will be set aside.

As part of the settlement, CIBC agreed to get rid of its structured financing line of business (where all of these "loans" were created). Bank management noted that the decision to get rid of the structured financing business would reduce annual earnings by 10 cents a share. The bank had previously reported annual earnings of $5.21 per share. In addition, the bank must accept the appointment of an outside monitor who will, amongst other things, review the bank's compliance with the settlement. Strategically, the bank had already reduced its emphasis on corporate lending (having suffered heavy losses in 2002) in favour of increased focus on earnings from branch banking operations.

CIBC is still owed $213 million from Enron. There are many additional Enron related lawsuits pending against the bank which has stated that the lawsuits are without merit. The bank has insurance against many of these claims and plans to vigorously defend itself.

Instructions

Adopt the role of the company's auditors and discuss any financial reporting issues.

(Information drawn from the following articles published on December 23, 2003:
New York Times "Canadian bank to pay fine and drop unit in Enron case", *National Post*
"CIBC to pay US80M over Enron", and *Toronto Star* "Enron cost CIBC $80M".)

CA5-3   Brookfield Properties Corporation (BPC) announced earnings from continuing operations of $236 U.S. million and a return on equity of 20.2% for the year ended December 31, 2002. The company owns, develops and manages North American office properties and its shares trade on both the New York and Toronto stock exchanges. According to the 2002 annual report, the company prides itself upon a strong financial position and providing a foundation for growth.

The balance sheet of the company is presented below:

Consolidated Balance Sheet

December 31 (US Millions)	note	2002	2001	2000
Assets				
Commercial properties	2	**$5,661**	$5,802	$6,368
Development properties	3	**944**	575	537
Receivables and other	4	**769**	847	1,017
Cash and cash equivalents	1	**76**	195	201
Assets of Brookfield Homes Corporation	5	**879**	872	762
		$8,329	$8,291	$8,885
Liabilities				
Commercial property debt	7	**$4,038**	$4,376	$4,542
Commercial development property debt	7	**550**	230	160
Accounts payable and other liabilities	8	**429**	460	1,031
Liabilities of Brookfield Homes Corporation	5	**556**	583	549
Shareholders' interests				
Interests of others in properties	9, 14	**84**	113	159
Preferred shares—subsidiaries and corporate	10	**579**	585	607
Convertible debentures	11	**—**	—	50
Common shares	12	**2,093**	1,944	1,787
		$8,329	$8,291	$8,885

See accompanying notes to the consolidated financial statements

Instructions

Adopt the role of a financial analyst and critically evaluate the balance sheet presentation. Discuss alternative presentations and conclude on the presentation that provides the best transparency in terms of the company's business and message that it wishes to communicate.

Research and Financial Analysis

RA5-1   Intrawest Corporation

The 2002 financial statements of Intrawest Corporation appear in Appendix 5B.

Instructions

(a) What alternative formats could the company have adopted for its balance sheet? Which format did it adopt?

(b) Identify the various techniques of disclosure the company might have used to disclose additional pertinent financial information. Which techniques does it use in its financials?

(c) What were the company's cash flows from its operating, investing, and financing activities for 2002? What were its trends in net cash provided by operating activities over the period 2001–2002? Why is cash generated from operating activities significantly different from net earnings in 2002? (Identify the main reconciling items.) Explain why an increase in accounts receivables is deducted from earnings in order to arrive at net cash provided by operating activities.

(d) Calculate the company's (1) current cash debt coverage ratio, (2) cash debt coverage ratio, and (3) free cash flow for 2000. What do these ratios indicate about the company's financial condition?

RA5-2   Magna International Inc.

The financial statements for Magna International Inc. may be found on the Digital Tool.

Instructions

(a) Calculate the ratios identified in Appendix 5A for both years presented in the financial statements.

(b) Comment on the company's liquidity, solvency, and profitability.

(c) Review the cash flow patterns on the cash flow statements and comment on where the company is getting its cash from and where it is spending it.

(d) Perform a "vertical analysis" of the assets. (Calculate each asset as a percentage of total assets.) How has this changed from year to year?

RA5-3   Maple Leaf Foods Inc.

The financial statements for Maple Leaf Foods Inc. may be found on the Digital Tool.

Instructions

(a) Calculate the liquidity and solvency ratios identified in Appendix 5A for both years presented in the financial statements.

(b) Comment on the company's financial flexibility.

(c) Review the cash flow patterns on the cash flow statements and comment on where the company is getting its cash from and where it is spending it. (Hint: Identify the cash flow pattern and explain what information the pattern provides.)

(d) Perform a "horizontal analysis" for working capital. How has this changed from year to year and what are the implications for the company's financial health?

RA5-4   Goldcorp Inc.

Obtain the 2001 Annual Report for Goldcorp. Inc. (see the company's website). Read the material leading up to the financial statements and answer the following questions.

(a) Explain how the company's business changed from 2000 to 2001. What significant events occurred?

(b) What was the impact on key ratios of the event(s) identified in part (a)?

RA5-5   Abitibi-Consolidated Inc. versus Domtar Inc.

The financial statements for Abitibi Consolidated Inc. and Domtar Inc. may be found on the Digital Tool.

Instructions

(a) Is Domtar a good benchmark for comparison purposes? Explain.

(b) Identify three other companies that might be used for comparison purposes.

(c) Calculate industry averages for these five companies for the current and debt-to-total assets ratios.

(d) Based on this very brief analysis, which company is in better shape in terms of liquidity and solvency? How do these companies compare with the other three companies?

(e) Review the statement of cash flows. Describe the cash flow patterns for each company. Comment on these cash flow patterns, noting changes over the past two to three years.

RA5-6   Industry analysis

The following is an excerpt from the *Globe and Mail* Top 1000 Canadian Company.

Gold Producers

COMPANY AND YEAR END	REVENUE $000	REVENUE % CH'GE	PROFIT $000	PROFIT % CH'GE	RETURN ON CAPITAL 1-YR %	RETURN ON CAPITAL 5-YR %	GOLD RECOVERED OZ. (000)	CASH COST $ PER OZ.	PROVEN AND PROBABLE RESERVES TONS (000)	PROVEN AND PROBABLE RESERVES CONTAINED OZ. (000)
Barrick Gold(De02)[1]	(US)2,108,000	52	(US)229,000	-15	4.49	1.91	5,695	(US)177	1,229,152	86,927
Placer Dome(De02)[1]	(US)1,289,000	0	(US)119,000	163	7.02	0.18	2,823	(US)180	462,292	52,891
Kinross Gold(De02)[1]	(US)274,600	-2	(US)-30,900	15	-4.30	-18.58	889	(US)201	510,451	13,166
Echo Bay Mines(De02)[1]	(US)206,970	-13	(US)-7,690	-35	-5.11	-4.20	539	(US)237	114,930	3,400
Cambior Inc.(De02)[1]	(US)204,203	-33	(US)-8,052	37	-2.37	-17.06	569	(US)223	72,668	4,216
Goldcorp Inc.(De02)[1]	(US)189,215	9	(US)65,643	24	41.29	17.93	608	(US)93	16,298	5,537
Meridian Gold(De02)[1]	(US)135,441	14	(US)41,516	7	16.38	5.27	436	(US)87	14,661	4,281
Agnico-Eagle Mines(De02)[1]	(US)111,044	10	(US)4,023	176	2.48	-0.30	260	(US)182	41,692	4,022
Northgate Exploration(De02)[1]	(US)110,992	14	(US)-14,243	-46	-5.48	-0.37	282	(US)204	120,549	2,503
Iamgold Corp.(De02)[1]	(US)90,709	7	(US)5,535	-49	5.40	9.46	290	(US)178	236,335	3,600

1. Company reports in U.S. dollars.

Reprinted with permission from The Globe and Mail.

Instructions

(a) Review the data provided for the top 10 gold producers. What is the average production cost per ounce of gold for the 10 companies?

(b) Identify the two companies that have significantly lower costs per ounce. What is the relationship between gold cost and profit? (Look at all 10 companies.)

(c) Research the gold industry and explain why gold production costs differ for each company. (Hint: read the annual reports of several gold-producing companies.)

(d) How are gold selling prices determined? Comment on their stability.

(e) Identify the financial risks associated with gold production. How do companies manage these risks and what is the impact of risk management on profitability?

RA5-7   Tomkins PLC

Presented below is the balance sheet for Tomkins PLC, a British company. It is a large global engineering company providing jobs for over 40,000 employees. The company makes and distributes automotive products, industrial power systems and engineered and construction products. Shares of the company trade on the NYSE and LSE.

Instructions

(a) Identify at least three differences in balance sheet reporting between British and Canadian firms, as shown in Tomkins's balance sheet.

(b) Review Tomkins's balance sheet and identify how the format of this financial statement provides useful information, as illustrated in the chapter.

TOMKINS PLC
Consolidated Balance Sheet
At 31 December 2002

	£ million
Capital employed	
Fixed assets	
Intangible assets	168.4
Tangible assets	787.6
Investments	8.4
	964.4
Current assets	
Stock	400.4
Debtors	624.5
Cash	341.5
	1,366.4
Current liabilities	
Creditors: amounts falling due within one year	(490.2)
Net current assets	876.2
Total assets less current liabilities	1,840.6
Creditors: amounts falling due after more than one year	(243.3)
Provisions for liabilities and charges	(519.8)
Net assets	1,077.5
Capital and reserves	
Called up share capital	
Ordinary shares	38.7
Convertible cumulative preference shares	337.2
Redeemable convertible cumulative preference shares	386.3
	762.2
Share premium account	92.2
Capital redemption reserve	66.6
Profit and loss account	118.5
Shareholders' funds	1,039.5
Equity minority interest	38.0
	1,077.5

Boomerang Sales

Boomerang Kids, an Ottawa children's clothing store, sells a lot of merchandise on consignment. Parents bring in clothes their children have outgrown, as well as unneeded baby equipment and maternity wear, for the store to sell. The challenge in running this kind of business is recognizing when and how much of a sale is actually revenue.

Ken Peach designed Boomerang Kids' accounting software program. The system tracks the history of each consigned item in the store's inventory: when it was brought in, who brought it in, when it was sold, for how much, how much is owed the original owner, and when it was paid out.

"Each item has to remain attached to the original owner, who really still owns it even though it's in the store," Peach says. At the time of the sale, the store assumes ownership, keeping 50% of the sale on clothing and 40% on equipment, and returning the rest to the original owner.

The percentage of the sale retained by the store is its revenue on the sale. "The other part of the sale becomes a liability until such time as they pay it out," Peach points out. The store now owes the consignor for a portion of the sale.

Since the inventory is essentially not owned by the store, there is no loss in the event it doesn't sell. The tracking system will note when it is returned to the original owner, or forwarded on to charity.

The consigned items are not part of the store's assets, Peach says. Although you can assign a value to what's in the store's inventory, it's not included in the store's equity. The biggest asset in most consignment stores is goodwill, says Peach.■

CHAPTER 6

Revenue Recognition

Learning Objectives

After studying this chapter, you should be able to:

1. Apply the revenue recognition principle.
2. Describe accounting issues involved with revenue recognition for sale of goods.
3. Explain accounting for consignment sales.
4. Describe accounting issues involved with revenue recognition for services and long-term contracts.
5. Apply the percentage-of-completion method for long-term contracts.
6. Apply the completed-contract method for long-term contracts.
7. Account for losses on long-term contracts.
8. Discuss how to deal with measurement uncertainty.
9. Discuss how to deal with collection uncertainty.
10. Explain and apply the instalment sales method of accounting.
11. Explain and apply the cost recovery method of accounting.

After studying Appendix 6A, you should be able to:

12. Explain revenue recognition for franchises.

Preview of Chapter 6

When should revenue be recognized? This is a complex question. The answer lies with analysing the earnings process. The purpose of this chapter is to provide you with general principles used in recognizing revenues for most business transactions. The content and organization of the chapter are as follows:

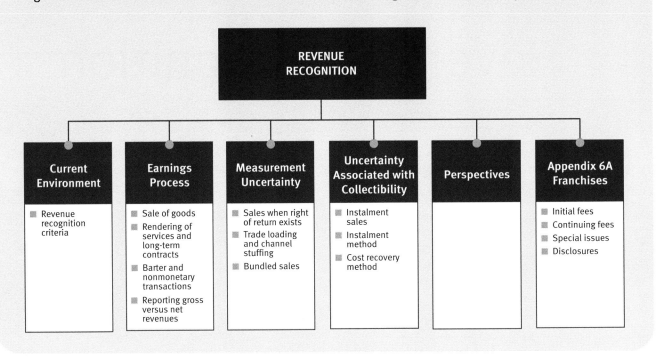

REVENUE RECOGNITION

Current Environment	Earnings Process	Measurement Uncertainty	Uncertainty Associated with Collectibility	Perspectives	Appendix 6A Franchises
▪ Revenue recognition criteria	▪ Sale of goods ▪ Rendering of services and long-term contracts ▪ Barter and nonmonetary transactions ▪ Reporting gross versus net revenues	▪ Sales when right of return exists ▪ Trade loading and channel stuffing ▪ Bundled sales	▪ Instalment sales ▪ Instalment method ▪ Cost recovery method		▪ Initial fees ▪ Continuing fees ▪ Special issues ▪ Disclosures

THE CURRENT ENVIRONMENT

Digital Tool

Student Toolkit— Additional Disclosures

www.wiley.com/canada/kieso

The issue of when to recognize revenue has continually received considerable attention. A series of highly publicized cases of companies recognizing revenue prematurely has caused the OSC and SEC to increase their enforcement actions in this area.[1]

---

[1] The OSC completed a review of revenue recognition practices in 2001 and again in 2002 as it felt that some users were placing undue emphasis on revenue growth as a key indicator of value and performance. The review targeted 75 public companies in both years. The 2001 survey findings indicated that there was need for improving the nature and extent of disclosure and the OSC identified cases that were later investigated to determine whether financial reporting practices related to revenue recognition reflected appropriate application of relevant GAAP. The 2002 survey showed improvement with only one company having to restate the financial statements and 29 making additional enhanced disclosures.

Revenue Recognition Criteria

Revenues are realized when goods and services are exchanged for cash or claims to cash (receivables). Revenue recognition[2] is governed by general principles and therefore there is a wide array of practical applications. Different companies interpret these principles in different ways.[3] Revenues are recognized according to the revenue recognition principle. Under this principle, revenue is recognized when **performance** is substantially complete and when **collection is reasonably assured.**[4]

Performance occurs when the entity can **measure** the revenue and when it has substantially accomplished what it must do to be entitled to the benefits represented by the revenues; that is, when the **earnings process is complete or substantially complete.**[5] Both these components are important. If a company cannot measure the transaction, then either there is too much uncertainty surrounding the transaction or the company has not completed all that it has to do to earn the revenues. Although the *CICA Handbook* does not make specific mention of **cost** measurability, this is also very important.

In short, revenues are recognized when the following criteria are met:

1. **Earnings process** is substantially complete,
2. **Measurability** is reasonably assured,
3. **Collectibility** is reasonably assured.

Note that there must be persuasive evidence that an agreement exists.[6] Side agreements that modify the main sales agreement may indicate that in hindsight, the arrangement was not final and that revenue should not have been recognized. Each of these will be examined in more detail below.

EARNINGS PROCESS

What does the company do to create valuable products or services that customers will pay for? How does it add value? Earnings process is a term that refers to the actions that a company undertakes to add value. It is an important part of the business model as it focuses on the operating activities.[7] The earnings process is unique to each company and each industry. Different industries add value in different ways, e.g. companies that sell goods have vastly differing earnings processes than those that sell services. Companies that are in the biotechnology business have models that are different from

1 Objective
Apply the revenue recognition principle.

Underlying Concept
The related costs must be measurable and recognized at the same time as revenues under the matching principle in order to facilitate appropriate measurement of net income.

Underlying Concept
Revenues are increases in economic resources, either by an entity's inflows or other enhancements of assets of an entity or settlement of its liabilities resulting from its ordinary activities.

IAS Note
IAS 18 also requires measurability of both revenues and related costs.

2 Objective
Describe accounting issues involved with revenue recognition for sale of goods.

---

[2] Recognition is "the process of including an item in the financial statements of an entity" (*CICA Handbook*, Section 1000). Recognition is not the same as realization, although the two are sometimes used interchangeably in accounting literature and practice. Realization is "the process of converting non-cash resources and rights into money and is most precisely used in accounting and financial reporting to refer to sales of assets for cash" or claims to cash (SFAC No. 3, par. 83).

[3] Because of this and partially due to the increased profile of the revenue recognition issues with the securities commissions, companies generally disclose the revenue recognition method in their notes to the financial statements. The number of companies disclosing their policies has increased 62% for the period 1998 to 2001 (*Financial Reporting in Canada*, 2002, CICA, 2002, p. 65).

[4] *CICA Handbook*, Section 3400.06.

[5] *CICA Handbook*, Section 3400.07.

[6] It should be noted that the SEC believes that revenue is realized or realizable and earned when all of the following criteria are met: (1) Persuasive evidence of an arrangement exists; (2) delivery has occurred or services have been rendered; (3) the seller's price to the buyer is fixed or determinable; and (4) collectibility is reasonably assured. See Revenue Recognition in Financial Statements, SEC Staff Accounting Bulletin (SAB) No. 101, December 3, 1999. The SEC has provided more specific guidance because general criteria are often difficult to interpret. EIC 141 acknowledges SAB101 as being consistent with Handbook 3400, noting that it should be referred to as interpretive guidance.

[7] A view of the business model was introduced in Chapters 4 and 5.

say real estate companies. For this reason, it is important to begin with an understanding of the earnings process.

Sale of Goods

A manufacturing company such as Magnotta Winery Corporation makes wine (among other products). Its business involves the following steps, as shown in Illustration 6-1.

Illustration 6-1

Magnotta Winery's Earnings Process

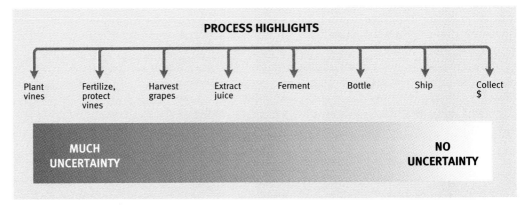

Magnotta must perform all of these acts in order to earn the revenues from sales of its wine. At the early points in the earnings process, there is significant uncertainty as to how much product will be produced and at what quality. What if the vines get diseased? What if temperatures are too low or there is excess rainfall? What if there is no market for the product? Moving along the earnings process timeline (from left to right), the conditions underlying the uncertainty resolve themselves. At the far right-hand side of the earnings process, all uncertainty related to ability to deliver the product, measurability of both costs and revenues, and collectibility is eliminated once the product is shipped and paid for.

Often, there is one main act or critical event in the earnings process that signals **substantial completion** or **performance**. At this point, although all uncertainty is not eliminated, it is at an acceptable level for the revenues to be recognized under accrual accounting. In businesses involving sale of goods, this is normally at the point of delivery. This is generally when the risks and rewards of ownership pass. Where the earnings process has a critical event, it is often referred to as a discrete earnings process.

Risks and Rewards of Ownership

The concept of risks and rewards (benefits) of ownership is a core concept in financial reporting. It helps establish ownership[8] and when ownership passes from one party to another.

Illustration 6-2 depicts some risks and rewards associated with the sale of wine at Magnotta.

Illustration 6-2

Risk and Rewards of Ownership—Case of Wine

Risks	Rewards
—wine will not age well and thus will decline in value	—wine will age well and appreciate in value
—wine will be stolen/vandalized	—wine can be consumed by owner or buyer
	—wine inventory may be used as collateral for bank loan
—wine will be stored improperly	—wine may be sold for cash

---

[8] That is, in order to recognize an asset on the balance sheet, a company must prove that it has the risks and rewards of ownership. If it no longer has the risks and rewards, they have been passed on to another party and a disposition has occurred.

In determining who has the risks and rewards of ownership and hence whether a sale has occurred at the point of delivery, it is important to look at who has possession of the goods and who has legal title. The risks and rewards usually stem from these two factors, i.e., Magnotta is not entitled to sell or pledge the inventory as collateral unless it has legal title to it. Likewise legal title and possession expose the company to risk of loss.

When determining whether legal title to the product has passed to the buyer, consider the terms of sale, e.g., f.o.b. shipping point means that the legal title belongs to the buyer when the goods leave the shipping docks. If the terms are f.o.b. destination, then the legal title does not pass until the goods reach the customer's location. Care should be taken where the customer has taken legal title but the product is being held by the vendor (bill and hold). Professional judgement would be used to determine if the risks and rewards of ownership have passed. Where a product is held by the vendor on a layaway plan, the risks and rewards are felt not to have passed until the point of delivery. Legal title remains with the vendor who also has possession.

Sales with Buyback

If a company sells inventory in one period and agrees to buy it back in the next accounting period, has the company sold the product? In essence, this is a 100% return.

When a repurchase agreement exists at a set price and this price covers all costs of the inventory plus related holding costs, the inventory and related liability remain on the seller's books since the seller retains the price risk.[9]

Underlying Concept

Legal title has transferred in this situation, but the economic substance of the transaction is that the **seller retains risks of ownership**.

Disposition of Assets other than Inventory

The risks and rewards concept deals not only with sale of inventory, as in the case of Magnotta's wine inventory, but also with items disposed of that are not sold as part of the normal earnings process, e.g., income-producing or capital assets. In these cases, a gain[10] would be generated (as opposed to revenues). Care should be taken to establish that in substance, a disposition has actually occurred. In certain cases, a company may sell a fixed asset and receive a note receivable that is secured by the asset itself. If very little other consideration is received, has the asset really been sold? Have the risks and rewards really passed?

If the purchaser does not pay, legal title to the asset may revert back to the vendor **at little or no loss to the purchaser**. This indicates that the risks and rewards may still rest with the vendor. In general, the purchaser must demonstrate substantial commitment to pay. This is normally evidenced when the purchaser makes a commitment with a fair value of not less than 15% of the consideration's fair value. An example of this is when the purchaser pays nonrefundable cash equal to at least 15% of the total consideration.[11]

Underlying Concept

Legally, a transaction may be structured as a sale. However, analysis of the economic substance might show otherwise.

Consignment Sales

Under some distribution arrangements, the point of delivery does not provide evidence of full performance because the vendor **retains legal title** to the goods. This specialized method of marketing for certain types of products makes use of a device known as a

---

[9] *CICA Handbook*, EIC Abstract 141. Accounting Guideline "Transfer of Receivables" allows recognition of a sale of accounts receivables when control over the assets is surrendered. Surrendering of control occurs when the assets are isolated from the transferor, the transferee can pledge or exchange the assets, and the transferor will not repurchase the assets. *CICA Handbook*, EIC Abstract #121 deals with accounting for wash sales of financial assets other than receivables, i.e., the transfer of financial assets with the intent to reacquire. The EIC requires the application of the Guideline test to other financial assets. These GAAP sources could also be looked to for sales of non-financial assets.

[10] Gains (as contrasted with revenues) commonly result from transactions and other events that do not involve an earnings process. For gain recognition, being earned is generally less significant than being realized or realizable.

[11] *CICA Handbook*, EIC Abstract #79.

Objective 3
Explain accounting for consignment sales.

consignment. Under this arrangement, the **consignor** (e.g., manufacturer) ships merchandise to the **consignee** (e.g., dealer), who acts as an agent for the consignor in selling the merchandise. Both consignor and consignee are interested in selling: the former to make a profit or develop a market, the latter to make a commission on the sales.

The consignee accepts the merchandise and agrees to exercise due diligence in caring for and selling it. Cash received from customers is remitted to the consignor by the consignee, after deducting a sales commission and any chargeable expenses. Revenue is recognized only after the consignor receives notification of sale. The merchandise is carried throughout the consignment as the consignor's inventory, separately classified as Merchandise on Consignment. It is not recorded as an asset on the consignee's books.

Upon sale of the merchandise, the consignee has a liability for the net amount due the consignor. The consignor periodically receives from the consignee a report that shows the merchandise received, merchandise sold, expenses chargeable to the consignment, and the cash remitted.

To illustrate consignment accounting entries, assume that Nitkin Manufacturing Corp. ships merchandise costing $36,000 on consignment to Best Value Stores. Nitkin pays $3,750 of freight costs and Best Value pays $2,250 for local advertising costs that are reimbursable from Nitkin. By the end of the period, two-thirds of the consigned merchandise has been sold for $40,000 cash. Best Value notifies Nitkin of the sales, retains a 10% commission, and remits the cash due Nitkin. The following journal entries would be made by the consignor (Nitkin) and the consignee (Best Value).

Illustration 6-3

Entries for Consignment Sales

Nitkin Mfg. Corp. (Consignor)			Best Value Stores (Consignee)		
Shipment of consigned merchandise					
Inventory on Consignment	36,000		No entry (record memo of merchandise received)		
Finished Goods Inventory		36,000			
Payment of freight costs by consignor					
Inventory on Consignment	3,750		No entry.		
Cash		3,750			
Shipment of consigned merchandise					
Payment of advertising by consignee					
No entry until notified.			Receivable from Consignor	2,250	
			Cash		2,250
Sales of consigned merchandise					
No entry until notified.			Cash	40,000	
			Payable to Consignor		40,000
Notification of sales and expenses and remittance of amount due					
Cash	33,750		Payable to Consignor	40,000	
Advertising Expense	2,250		Receivable from		
Commission Expense	4,000		Consignor		2,250
			Commission Revenue		4,000
Revenue from Consignment Sales		40,000	Cash		33,750
Adjustment of inventory on consignment for cost of sales					
Cost of Goods Sold	26,500		No entry.		
Inventory on Consignment		26,500			
[2/3 ($36,000 + $3,750) = $26,500]					

Why would companies use consignment to sell their goods? The company selling the goods will often use this type of distribution mechanism to induce consignees to take their goods and sell them. Under the consignment arrangement, the manufacturer (consignor) retains the risk that the merchandise might not sell and relieves the dealer (consignee) of the need to commit part of its working capital to inventory. Presumably, if the products sell very well to third parties, the consignor could push for the consignee to actually purchase the goods outright. A variety of different systems and account titles are used to record consignments, but they all share the common goal of postponing the recognition of revenue until it is known that a sale to a third party has occurred.

Continuing Managerial Involvement

In some cases, the vendor **retains some involvement in the product sold**, such as the responsibility to fix the product if it breaks or to provide ongoing product support to the customer.

For instance, in order to induce a sale, the company might promise that the purchaser will receive a certain amount on resale of the asset (guaranteed minimum resale value). In this case the seller still retains risk of value loss and consideration should be given to whether a sale should be recognized.[12] Alternatively, the vendor may promise, in the case of a sold building, certain cash flows from the building (e.g., rent). Has a real sale occurred? As a general rule, in order to recognize revenues, the seller should retain no continuing managerial involvement in or effective control of the goods transferred to a degree normally associated with ownership.[13] The determination of whether continuing managerial involvement precludes revenue recognition is a matter of professional judgement.

Completion of Production

Revenue may be recognized at the completion of production even though no customer has yet been identified. Examples of such situations involve precious metals or agricultural products with assured prices and ready markets. Revenue is recognized when these metals are mined or crops harvested because the sales price is reasonably assured, the units are interchangeable, and no significant costs are involved in distributing the product. Thinking back to Illustration 6-1, the argument is that earlier recognition is acceptable under accrual accounting as there is little or no uncertainty with respect to measurement (price) or finding a customer. Performance is substantially complete even though the risks and rewards of ownership still rest with the company.

Rendering of Services and Long-Term Contracts

Unlike earnings processes relating solely to sales of goods, where the benchmark or critical event for revenue recognition is normally delivery, the focus in providing services is on **performance of the service**. Often the earnings process has **numerous significant events** as opposed to one critical event or discrete act. The earnings process is said to be an ongoing or continuous earnings process as opposed to a discrete earnings process.

Consider a public accounting firm where an auditor accepts an engagement to provide assurance to a company's shareholders regarding the company's financial position and operations. The earnings process is noted in Illustration 6-4.

---

[12] *CICA Handbook*, EIC Abstract #84 suggests that no sale should be recognized.

[13] *CICA Handbook*, Section 3400.07.

Illustration 6-4

Earnings Process of Public Accounting Firm in Providing Assurance to Client on Financial Statements

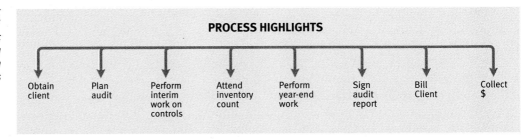

PROCESS HIGHLIGHTS

Obtain client | Plan audit | Perform interim work on controls | Attend inventory count | Perform year-end work | Sign audit report | Bill Client | Collect $

Businesses that provide services are different from businesses that sell goods since the customer is usually identified before the services are performed. (In the case of sale of goods, as noted in Illustration 6-1, the goods are produced and then a customer found). Often a contract establishing the terms of the relationship or engagement is signed upfront. This contract establishes the nature of the services to be provided and the value of the services, among other things. In the case of the auditor, an engagement letter would be signed upfront and serves as the contract.

Consider the performance "test." When does performance occur in the earnings process noted in Illustration 6-4? Should the company wait until the audit report is signed (engagement completed) before recognizing the revenue? There is no easy answer. This may be seen as a **continuous earnings process** with many significant events, e.g., the planning and the interim work. As such, it might make sense to recognize revenues bit by bit as each significant event is performed (as long as it is collectible). Judgement is required.

The issue becomes even more complicated if the process is a **long-term process** (as many service contracts are) as the services are performed over longer periods of time, often spanning one or more fiscal year ends. With these types of contracts, there may also be a "service" component and a "goods" component, e.g., a construction company building a road for the government.

Long-term contracts such as construction-type contracts, development of military and commercial aircraft, weapons delivery systems, and space exploration hardware frequently provide that the seller (builder) may bill the purchaser at intervals, as various points in the project are reached (referred to as billings). When the project consists of separable units such as a group of buildings or kilometres of roadway, passage of title and billing may take place at stated stages of completion, such as the completion of each building unit or every 10 km of road. Such contract provisions provide for delivery in instalments, and the accounting records may reflect this by recording sales when instalments are "delivered."

Two distinctly different methods of accounting for long-term construction contracts are currently recognized.[14]

1. **Percentage-of-Completion Method.** Revenues and gross profit are recognized each period based upon the construction progress; that is, the percentage of completion. Construction costs plus gross profit earned to date are accumulated in an inventory account (Construction in Process), and progress billings are accumulated in a contra inventory account (Billings on Construction in Process).

2. **Completed-Contract Method.** Revenues and gross profit are recognized only when the contract is completed. Construction costs are accumulated in an inventory account (Construction in Process), and progress billings are accumulated in a contra inventory account (Billings on Construction in Process).

---

[14] *CICA Handbook*, Section 3400.08.

The method that **best relates the revenues to be recognized to the work performed** should be used.[15] In other words, if performance requires numerous ongoing acts (**continuous earnings process**) the percentage-of-completion method should be used as long as the company is able to **measure** the transaction. Alternatively, the completed contract method should be used where performance consists of a single act (**discrete earnings process**) or when there is a **continuous earnings process but the revenues are not measurable**.

The rationale for using percentage-of-completion accounting is that under most of these contracts, the buyer and seller have obtained **enforceable rights**. The buyer has the legal right to require specific performance on the contract; the seller has the right to require progress payments that provide evidence of the buyer's ownership interest. As a result, a continuous sale occurs as the work progresses, and revenue should be recognized accordingly.

The presumption is that percentage of completion is the better method and that the completed-contract method should be used only when the percentage-of-completion method is inappropriate.[16]

Percentage-of-Completion Method

The percentage-of-completion method recognizes revenues, costs, and gross profit as progress is made toward completion on a long-term contract. To defer recognition of these items until completion of the entire contract is to misrepresent the efforts (costs) and accomplishments (revenues) of the interim accounting periods. In order to apply the percentage-of-completion method, one must have some basis or standard for measuring the progress toward completion at particular interim dates.

Objective

Describe accounting issues involved with revenue recognition for services and long-term contracts.

Measuring progress toward completion requires significant judgement. Costs, labour hours worked, tonnes produced, etc. are often used. The various measures are identified and classified as either input or output measures.[17] Input measures (costs incurred, labour hours worked) measure efforts devoted to a contract. Output measures (tonnes produced, storeys of a building completed, kilometres of a highway completed) measure results. Neither is universally applicable to all long-term projects; their use requires careful tailoring to the circumstances and the exercise of judgement.

Use of either input or output measures has certain disadvantages. The input measure is based on an established relationship between a unit of input and productivity. If inefficiencies cause the productivity relationship to change, inaccurate measurements result. Another potential problem, called front-end loading, produces higher estimates of completion by virtue of incurring significant costs upfront. Some early-stage construction costs should be disregarded if they do not relate to contract performance; for example, costs of uninstalled materials or costs of subcontracts not yet performed.

Underlying Concept

Both input and output measures have measurement uncertainty.

Output measures can result in inaccurate measures if the units used are not comparable in time, effort, or cost to complete. For example, using storeys completed can be deceiving; completing the first storey of an eight-storey building may require more than one-eighth the total cost because of the substructure and foundation construction.

One of the more popular input measures used to determine the progress toward completion is cost, sometimes referred to as the cost-to-cost basis. Under the cost-to-cost basis, the percentage of completion is measured by comparing costs incurred to date with the most recent estimate of the total costs to complete the contract, as shown in the following formula.

---

[15] *CICA Handbook*, Section 3400.08.

[16] *Accounting Trends and Techniques - 2001* reports that, of the 95 of its 600 sample companies that referred to long-term construction contracts, 90 used the percentage-of-completion method and 5 used the completed-contract method.

[17] *CICA Handbook*, EIC Abstract #78.

$$\frac{\text{Costs incurred to date}}{\text{Most recent estimate of total costs}} = \text{percent complete}$$

The percentage that costs incurred bear to total estimated costs is applied to the total revenue or the estimated total gross profit on the contract in arriving at the revenue or the gross profit amounts to be recognized to date.

| Percent complete | × | Estimated total revenue (for gross profit) | = | Revenue (or gross profit) to be recognized to date |

To find the amounts of revenue and gross profit recognized each period, we would need to subtract total revenue or gross profit recognized in prior periods, as shown in the following formula.

| Revenue (or gross profit) to be recognized to date | − | Revenue (or gross profit) recognized in prior periods | = | Current period revenue (or gross profit) |

Illustration of Percentage-of-Completion Method, Cost-to-Cost Basis

To illustrate the percentage-of-completion method, assume that Hardhat Construction Ltd. has a contract starting July 2004 to construct a $4.5 million bridge that is expected to be completed in October 2006, at an estimated cost of $4 million. The following data pertain to the construction period (note that by the end of 2005 the estimated total cost has increased from $4 million to $4,050,000).

	2004	2005	2006
Costs to date	$1,000,000	$2,916,000	$4,050,000
Estimated costs to complete	3,000,000	1,134,000	—
Progress billings during the year	900,000	2,400,000	1,200,000
Cash collected during the year	750,000	1,750,000	2,000,000

The percent complete would be calculated as follows.

	2004	2005	2006
Costs incurred to date			
Contract price	$4,500,000	$4,500,000	$4,500,000
Less estimated cost:			
Costs to date	1,000,000	2,916,000	4,050,000
Estimated costs to complete	3,000,000	1,134,000	
Estimated total costs	4,000,000	4,050,000	4,050,000
Estimated total gross profit	$ 500,000	$ 450,000	$ 450,000
Percent complete:	25%	72%	100%
	($1,000,000)	($2,916,000)	($4,050,000)
	($4,000,000)	($4,050,000)	($4,050,000)

Based on the data above, the following entries would be prepared to record (1) the costs of construction, (2) progress billings, and (3) collections. These entries appear as summaries of the many transactions that would be entered individually as they occur during the year.

	2004		2005		2006	
To record cost of construction:						
Construction in Process	1,000,000		1,916,000		1,134,000	
Materials, Cash,						
Payables, etc.		1,000,000		1,916,000		1,134,000
To record progress billings:						
Accounts Receivable	900,000		2,400,000		1,200,000	
Billings on Construction						
in Process		900,000		2,400,000		1,200,000
To record collections:						
Cash	750,000		1,750,000		2,000,000	
Accounts Receivable		750,000		1,750,000		2,000,000

Illustration 6-9

Journal Entries—Percentage-of-Completion Method, Cost-to-Cost Basis

In this illustration, the costs incurred to date as a proportion of the estimated total costs to be incurred on the project are a measure of the extent of progress toward completion.

The estimated revenue and gross profit to be recognized for each year are calculated as follows.

	2004	2005	2006
Revenue recognized in:			
2004 $4,500,000 × 25%	$1,125,000		
2005 $4,500,000 × 72%		$3,240,000	
Less: Revenue recognized in 2004		1,125,000	
Revenue in 2005		$2,115,000	
2006 $4,500,000 × 100%			$4,500,000
Less: Revenue recognized in 2004 and 2005			3,240,000
Revenue in 2006			$1,260,000
Gross profit recognized in:			
2004 $500,000 × 25%	$ 125,000		
2005 $450,000 × 72%		$ 324,000	
Less: Gross profit recognized in 2004		125,000	
Gross profit in 2005		$ 199,000	
2006 $450,000 × 100%			$ 450,000
Less: Gross profit recognized in 2004 and 2005			$ 324,000
Gross profit in 2006			$ 126,000

Illustration 6-10

Percentage of Completion, Revenue and Gross Profit, by Year

The entries to recognize revenue and gross profit each year and to record completion and final approval of the contract are shown below.

	2004		2005		2006	
To recognize revenue and gross profit:						
Construction in Process						
(gross profit)	125,000		199,000		126,000	
Construction Expenses	1,000,000		1,916,000		1,134,000	
Revenue from Long-Term						
Contract		1,125,000		2,115,000		1,260,000
To record completion of the contract:						
Billings on Construction						
in Process					4,500,000	
Construction in Process						4,500,000

Illustration 6-11

Journal Entries to Recognize Revenue and Gross Profit and to Record Contract Completion—Percentage-of-Completion Method, Cost-to-Cost Basis

Note that gross profit as calculated above is debited to Construction in Process, while Revenue from Long-Term Contract is credited for the amounts as calculated above. The difference between the amounts recognized each year for revenue and gross profit is debited to a nominal account, Construction Expenses (similar to cost of goods sold in a manufacturing enterprise), which is reported in the income statement. That amount is the actual cost of construction incurred in that period. For example, in the Hardhat cost-to-cost illustration, the actual costs of $1 million in 2004 are used to calculate both the gross profit of $125,000 and the percent complete (25%).

Costs must continue to be accumulated in the Construction in Process account to maintain a record of total costs incurred (plus recognized profit) to date. Although theoretically the percentage-of-completion method reflects a **series of sales,** the related inventory cost cannot be removed until the construction is completed and transferred to the new owner. The Construction in Process account would include the following summarized entries over the term of the construction project.

Illustration 6-12

Content of Construction in Process Account—Percentage-of-Completion Method

Construction in Process				
2004 construction costs	$1,000,000	12/31/06	to close	
2004 recognized gross profit	125,000		completed	
2005 construction costs	1,916,000		project	$4,500,000
2005 recognized gross profit	199,000			
2006 construction costs	1,134,000			
2006 recognized gross profit	126,000			
Total	$4,500,000	Total		$4,500,000

The Hardhat illustration contains a change in estimate in the second year, 2005, when the estimated total costs increased from $4 million to $4,050,000. By adjusting the percent completed to the new estimate of total costs and then deducting the amount of revenues and gross profit recognized in prior periods from revenues and gross profit calculated for progress to date, the change in estimate is accounted for in a cumulative catch-up manner. That is, the change in estimate is accounted for in the period of change so that the balance sheet at the end of that period and the accounting in subsequent periods are the same as if the revised estimate had been the original estimate.

Financial Statement Presentation—Percentage of Completion

Generally when a receivable from a sale is recorded, the Inventory account is reduced. In this case, however, both the receivable and the inventory continue to be carried. Subtracting the balance in the Billings account from Construction in Process avoids double-counting the inventory. During the life of the contract, the difference between the Construction in Process and the Billings on Construction in Process accounts is reported in the balance sheet as a current or non-current asset if a debit (liability if a credit), depending on the life of the contract.

When the costs incurred plus the gross profit recognized to date (the balance in Construction in Process) exceed the billings, this excess is reported as a current asset entitled "Cost and Recognized Profit in Excess of Billings." The unbilled portion of revenue recognized to date can be calculated at any time by subtracting the billings to date from the revenue recognized to date, as illustrated below for 2004 for Hardhat.

Illustration 6-13

Calculation of Unbilled Contract

Amount at 12/31/04

Contract revenue recognized to date: $4,500,000 \times \dfrac{\$1,000,000}{\$4,000,000} = \$1,125,000$

Billings to date	900,000
Unbilled revenue	$ 225,000

When the billings exceed costs incurred and gross profit to date, this excess is reported as a liability entitled Billings in Excess of Costs and Recognized Profit. Separate disclosures of the dollar volume of billings and costs are preferable to a summary presentation of the net difference.

Using data from the previous illustration, Hardhat would report the status and results of its long-term construction activities under the percentage-of-completion method as follows.

Illustration 6-14
Financial Statement Presentation—Percentage-of-Completion Method

HARDHAT CONSTRUCTION LTD.

Income Statement	2004	2005	2006
Revenue from long-term contracts	$1,125,000	$2,115,000	$1,260,000
Costs of construction	1,000,000	1,916,000	1,134,000
Gross profit	$ 125,000	$ 199,000	$ 126,000

Balance Sheet (12/31)		2004	2005
Current assets			
Accounts receivable		$ 150,000	$ 800,000
Inventories			
Construction in process	$1,125,000		
Less: Billings	900,000		
Costs and recognized profit in excess of billings		$ 225,000	
Current liabilities			
Billings ($3,300,000) in excess of costs and recognized profit ($3,240,000)			$ 60,000

Note 1. Summary of significant accounting policies.
LONG-TERM CONSTRUCTION CONTRACTS. The company recognizes revenues and reports profits from long-term construction contracts, its principal business, under the percentage-of-completion method of accounting. These contracts generally extend for periods in excess of one year. The amounts of revenues and profits recognized each year are based on the ratio of costs incurred to the total estimated costs. Costs included in construction in process include direct materials, direct labour, and project-related overhead. Corporate general and administrative expenses are charged to the periods as incurred and are not allocated to construction contracts.

Completed-Contract Method

Under the completed-contract method, revenue and gross profit are recognized when the contract is completed. Costs of long-term contracts in process and current billings are accumulated, but there are no interim charges or credits to income statement accounts for revenues, costs, and gross profit.

6 Objective
Apply the completed-contract method for long-term contracts.

The principal advantage of the completed-contract method is that reported revenue is based on final results rather than on estimates of unperformed work. Its major disadvantage is that it does not reflect current performance when the period of a contract extends into more than one accounting period. Although operations may be fairly uniform during the contract period, revenue is not reported until the year of completion, creating a distortion of earnings.[18]

The annual entries to record costs of construction, progress billings, and collections from customers would be identical to those illustrated under the percentage-of-completion method with the significant exclusion of the recognition of revenue and gross profit.

---

[18] *CICA Handbook* EIC Abstract #65 states that law firms must use the percentage-of-completion method, as the completed-contract method is inappropriate. The abstract further notes that other professional service firms might look to the abstract for guidance in similar revenue recognition situations.

For Hardhat's bridge project illustrated on the preceding pages, the following entries are made in 2006 under the completed-contract method to recognize revenue and costs and to close out the inventory and billing accounts.

A =   L   +   OE
    −$450,000   +$450,000
Cash flows: No effect

Billings on Construction in Process	4,500,000	
Revenue from Long-Term Contracts		4,500,000
Costs of Construction	4,050,000	
Construction in Process		4,050,000

Comparing the two methods in relation to the same bridge project, Hardhat would have recognized gross profit as follows.

Illustration 6-15

Comparison of Gross Profit Recognized under Different Methods

	Percentage-of-Completion	Completed-Contract
2004	$125,000	$ 0
2005	199,000	0
2006	126,000	$450,000

Hardhat would report its long-term construction activities as follows.

Illustration 6-16

Financial Statement Presentation—Completed-Contract Method

HARDHAT CONSTRUCTION LTD.

Income Statement	2004	2005	2006
Revenue from long-term contracts	—	—	$4,500,000
Costs of construction	—	—	4,050,000
Gross profit	—	—	$ 450,000

Balance Sheet (12/31)		2004	2005
Current assets			
Accounts receivable		$150,000	$800,000
Construction in process	$1,000,000		
Less: Billings	900,000		
Unbilled contract costs		$100,000	
Liabilities			
Billings ($3,300,000) in excess of contract			
costs ($2,916,000)			$384,000

Note 1. Summary of significant accounting policies.

LONG-TERM CONSTRUCTION CONTRACTS. The company recognizes revenues and reports profits from long-term construction contracts, its principal business, under the completed-contract method. These contracts generally extend for periods in excess of one year. Contract costs and billings are accumulated during the periods of construction, but no revenues or profits are recognized until contract completion. Costs included in construction in process include direct material, direct labour, and project-related overhead. Corporate general and administrative expenses are charged to the periods as incurred.

Long-Term Contract Losses

Two types of losses can become evident under long-term contracts.

Objective 7
Account for losses on long-term contracts.

1. **Loss in Current Period on a Profitable Contract.** This condition arises when, during construction, there is a significant increase in the estimated total contract costs but the increase does not eliminate all profit on the contract. Under the percentage-of-

completion method only, the estimated cost increase requires a current period adjustment of excess gross profit recognized on the project in prior periods. This adjustment is recorded as a loss in the current period because it is a change in accounting estimate (discussed in Chapter 22).

2. **Loss on an Unprofitable Contract.** Cost estimates at the end of the current period may indicate that a loss will result on completion of the entire contract. Under both the percentage-of-completion and the completed-contract methods, the entire expected contract loss must be recognized in the current period.

The treatment described for unprofitable contracts is consistent with the accounting custom of anticipating foreseeable losses to avoid overstatement of current and future income (conservatism).

Loss in Current Period

To illustrate a loss in the current period on a contract expected to be profitable upon completion, assume that on December 31, 2005, Hardhat estimates the costs to complete the bridge contract at $1,468,962 instead of $1,134,000. Assuming all other data are the same as before, Hardhat would calculate the percent complete and recognize the loss as shown in Illustration 6-17. Compare these calculations with those for 2005 in Illustration 6-8. The percent complete has dropped from 72% to 66½ % due to the increase in estimated future costs to complete the contract.

The 2005 loss of $48,500 is a cumulative adjustment of the excessive gross profit recognized on the contract in 2004. Instead of restating the prior period, the prior period misstatement is absorbed entirely in the current period. In this illustration, the adjustment was large enough to result in recognition of a loss.

Cost to date (12/31/05)	$2,916,000
Estimated costs to complete (revised)	1,468,962
Estimated total costs	$4,384,962
Percent complete ($2,916,000 / $4,384,962)	66½%
Revenue recognized in 2005	
($4,500,000 × 66½%) − $1,125,000	$1,867,500
Costs incurred in 2005	1,916,000
Loss recognized in 2005	$ 48,500

Illustration 6-17

Calculation of Recognizable Loss, 2005—Loss in Current Period

Hardhat would record the loss in 2005 as follows.

Construction Expenses	1,916,000	
Construction in Process (loss)		48,500
Revenue from Long-Term Contract		1,867,500

A   = L +   SE
−$48,500   −$48,500
Cash flows: No effect

The loss of $48,500 will be reported on the 2005 income statement as the difference between the reported revenues of $1,867,500 and the costs of $1,916,000.[19] Under the completed-contract method, no loss is recognized in 2002 because the contract is still expected to result in a profit to be recognized in the year of completion.

---

[19] In 2006, Hardhat will recognize the remaining 33½% of the revenue ($1,507,500) with costs of $1,468,962 as expected, and report a gross profit of $38,538. The total gross profit over the three years of the contract would be $115,038 [$125,000 (2001) − $48,500 (2002) + $38,538 (2003)], which is the difference between the total contract revenue of $4,500,000 and the total contract costs of $4,384,962.

Loss on an Unprofitable Contract

To illustrate the accounting for an overall loss on a long-term contract, assume that at December 31, 2005, Hardhat estimates the costs to complete the bridge contract at $1,640,250 instead of $1,134,000. Revised estimates relative to the bridge contract appear as follows.

	2004 Original Estimates	2005 Revised Estimates
Contract price	$4,500,000	$4,500,000
Estimated total cost	4,000,000	4,556,250*
Estimated gross profit	$ 500,000	
Estimated loss		$ (56,250)

*($2,916,000 + $1,640,250)

Under the percentage-of-completion method, $125,000 of gross profit was recognized in 2004 (see Illustration 6-10). This $125,000 must be offset in 2005 because it is no longer expected to be realized. In addition, the total estimated loss of $56,250 must be recognized in 2005 since losses must be recognized as soon as estimable. Therefore, a total loss of $181,250 ($125,000 + $56,250) must be recognized in 2005.

The revenue recognized in 2005 is calculated as follows.

Illustration 6-18

Calculation of Revenue Recognizable, 2005— Unprofitable Contract

Revenue recognized in 2005		
Contract price		$4,500,000
Percent complete		× 64%*
Revenue recognizable to date		2,880,000
Less: Revenue recognized prior to 2005		1,125,000
Revenue recognized in 2005		$1,755,000
Cost to date (12/31/05)	$2,916,000	
Estimated cost to complete	1,640,250	
Estimated total costs	$4,556,250	

*Percent complete: $2,916,000 / $4,556,250 = 64%

To calculate the construction costs to be expensed in 2005, we add the total loss to be recognized in 2005 ($125,000 + $56,250) to the revenue to be recognized in 2005. This calculation is shown below.

Illustration 6-19

Calculation of Construction Expense, 2005— Unprofitable Contract

Revenue recognized in 2005 (calculated above)		$1,755,000
Total loss recognized in 2005:		
Reversal of 2004 gross profit	$125,000	
Total estimated loss on the contract	56,250	181,250
Construction cost expensed in 2005		$1,936,250

Hardhat would record the long-term contract revenues, expenses, and loss in 2005 as follows.

A = L + SE
−$181,250   −$181,250
Cash flows: No effect

Construction Expenses	1,936,250	
Construction in Process (Loss)		181,250
Revenue from Long-Term Contracts		1,755,000

At the end of 2005, Construction in Process has a balance of $2,859,750 as shown below.[20]

Construction in Process			
2004 Construction costs	$1,000,000		
2004 Recognized gross profit	125,000		
2005 Construction costs	1,916,000	2005 Recognized loss	$181,250
Balance	2,859,750		

Illustration 6-20

Content of Construction in Process Account at End of 2005—Unprofitable Contract

Under the completed-contract method, the contract loss of $56,250 is also recognized in the year in which it first became evident through the following entry in 2005.

Loss from Long-Term Contracts	56,250	
Construction in Process (Loss)		56,250

A = L + SE
−$56,250   −$56,250
Cash flows: No effect

Just as the Billings account balance cannot exceed the contract price, neither can the balance in Construction in Process exceed the contract price. In circumstances where the Construction in Process balance exceeds the billings, the recognized loss may be deducted on the balance sheet from such accumulated costs. That is, under both the percentage-of-completion and the completed-contract methods, the provision for the loss (the credit) may be combined with Construction in Process, thereby reducing the inventory balance. In those circumstances (as in the 2005 illustration above) where the billings exceed the accumulated costs, the amount of the estimated loss must be reported separately on the balance sheet as a current liability. That is, under both the percentage-of-completion and the completed-contract methods, the amount of the loss of $56,250, as estimated in 2005, would be taken from the Construction in Process account and reported separately as a current liability entitled Estimated Liability from Long-Term Contracts.

Disclosures

In addition to making the financial statement disclosures required of all businesses, construction contractors usually make some unique disclosures. Generally these additional disclosures are made in the notes to the financial statements. For example, a construction contractor should disclose the method of recognizing revenue, the basis used to classify assets and liabilities as current (the nature and length of the operating cycle), the basis for recording inventory, the effects of any revision of estimates, the amount of backlog on uncompleted contracts, and the details about receivables (billed and unbilled, maturity, interest rates, and significant individual or group concentrations of credit risk).

Barter and Nonmonetary Transactions

Barter transactions are transactions where little or no monetary assets are received as consideration when goods or services are sold. For instance, a computer manufacturing company might sell a computer but instead of receiving cash as consideration, the company might receive another type of asset, e.g., office furniture. Is this still a sale? How

---

[20] If the costs in 2006 are $1,640,250 as projected, at the end of 2006 the Construction in Process account will have a balance of $1,640,250 + $2,859,750, or $4,500,000, equal to the contract price. When the revenue remaining to be recognized in 2006 of $1,620,000 [$4,500,000 (total contract price) − $1,125,000 (2004) − $1,755,000 (2005)] is matched with the construction expense to be recognized in 2006 of $1,620,000 [total costs of $4,556,250 less the total costs recognized in prior years of $2,936,250 (2004, $1,000,000; 2005, $1,936,250)], a zero profit results. Thus the total loss has been recognized in 2005, the year in which it first became evident.

should it be measured? As a **general rule** the transaction is treated as a sale and should be recorded at **fair value of the asset or services given up** unless the value of the asset or services received are more clearly determinable.[21]

As long as the **earnings process is substantially complete** (culmination of the earnings process),[22] then it is viewed as a sale and a purchase. Factors in considering whether the earnings process is substantially complete or culminated are the same factors as noted in the first part of the chapter: have the risks and rewards of ownership passed and/or has the company earned the revenue (performance). Just because the company takes back a different (non cash) form of consideration, this does not preclude treating the transaction as a sale as long as it is a bona fide business transaction. The problem arises when the transaction is entered into solely for making revenues look better. This topic will be dealt with in further detail in Chapter 11.

Reporting Gross versus Net Revenues

Although net income does not change if a company chooses to report revenues as the **gross amount billed to the customer** (and cost of goods sold) versus the **net amount retained**, the revenues number changes. Since revenue is the focus of many financial statement users, this is an important issue.

What do the Numbers Mean?

Consider Priceline.com, the U.S. company that allows "naming your own price" for airline tickets and hotel rooms. In its third-quarter 1999 quarterly SEC filings, Priceline reported that it earned $152 million in revenues. But that includes the full amount customers paid for tickets, hotel rooms, and rental cars. Traditional travel agencies call that amount "gross bookings," not revenues. And much like regular travel agencies, Priceline keeps only a small portion of gross bookings—namely, the spread between the customers' accepted bids and the price it paid for the merchandise. The rest, which Priceline calls "product costs," are paid to the airlines and hotels that supply the tickets and rooms. In a recent quarter, those costs came to $134 million, leaving Priceline just $18 million of what it calls "gross profit" and what most other companies would call revenues. And that's before all of Priceline's other costs—like advertising and salaries—which netted out to a loss of $102 million. The difference isn't academic: Priceline stock traded at about 23 times its reported revenues but at a mind-boggling 214 times its "gross profits."

Source: Jeremy Kahn, "Presto Chango! Sales Are Huge," *Fortune* (March 20, 2000), p. 44.

In analyzing this issue (which is essentially a **presentation** issue), the following factors should be considered:

(a) whether the company acts as a **principal** in the transaction or an **agent or broker** (who is buying and selling an item for commission),

(b) whether the company takes **title to the goods** being sold, or

(c) whether the company has the **risks and rewards of ownership** of the goods being sold.[23]

For example, a real estate agent acts as a **broker** or **agent**, finding a house for a customer and then taking a **commission** on the sale. He does not take **title** to the house nor does he have the **risks and rewards** associated with ownership of the house. Revenues associated with a sale of the house would be recorded net as commissions. On the other hand, a company such as Mattamy Homes Limited, which builds houses and then sells

---

[21] *CICA Handbook*, Section 3830.05

[22] *CICA Handbook*, Section 3830.08. Under proposed standards, the transaction must have commercial substance.

[23] *CICA Handbook*, EIC Abstract 123.

them to customers, acts as a **principal**. It has the risk and rewards of ownership of the house prior to sale (including legal title). When Mattamy sells a house, it would record its market value as revenue and the cost to build it as cost of goods sold.

MEASUREMENT UNCERTAINTY

Measurement uncertainty stems from inability to measure the consideration itself, e.g., in some barter transactions, or inability to measure returns.

8 Objective
Discuss how to deal with measurement uncertainty.

Sales when Right of Return Exists

Whether cash or credit sales are involved, a special problem arises with claims for returns and allowances. In Chapter 7, the accounting treatment for normal returns and allowances is presented. However, certain companies experience such a high rate of returns—the ratio of returned merchandise to sales—that they find it necessary to postpone reporting sales until the return privilege has substantially expired. Consideration should be given to length of return period and historical rates of returns. External factors such as obsolescence, business of economic cycles, financial health of customers and introduction of competitor's products that may render products obsolete also affect rates of return.

What do the Numbers Mean?

For example, in the publishing industry, the rate of return approaches 25% for hardcover books and 65% for some magazines. The high rate of return is a function of two factors: (1) the publishers want to induce sales and therefore overship and (2) the power rests with the retailers in the industry. Chapters Inc., formed through the merger between Smithbooks and Coles in 1995, engaged in very aggressive return activities after the merger. In 2001, Indigo Books & Music, Inc. became Canada's largest book retailer as a result of an amalgamation between Indigo and Chapters Inc.

Since this deal created an even greater concentration in the retail book industry in Canada, the deal was reviewed by the federal Competition Tribunal. The Tribunal concluded, among other things, that the deal could go through as long as 24 Chapters stores were sold to an unrelated party and the new company adhered to a business code of conduct. The code of conduct stipulated that returns would be limited and payments to publishers would have to be made within a reasonable time frame.

Returns in many industries are frequently effected either through a right of contract or as a matter of practice involving guaranteed sales agreements or consignments.

Three alternative revenue recognition methods are available when the seller is exposed to continued risks of ownership through return of the product. These are: (1) not recording a sale until all return privileges have expired; (2) recording the sale, but reducing sales by an estimate of future returns; and (3) recording the sale and accounting for the returns as they occur. Method #2 is only an option where returns are measurable but is preferable under accrual accounting.

The following situations may preclude revenue recognition where there is a right to return even though title to the goods has passed.

1. where the price is not fixed or determinable.

2. where the buyer's obligation to pay is excused until the buyer resells/consumes or uses the product

3. where the buyer's obligation would change in the event of theft or damage/destruction of the product.

4. where the returns are not estimable

These situations create measurement uncertainty, and there is a question as to who has the risks and rewards of ownership.

In some cases, the company may offer price protection to the customer, i.e., if the purchase price goes down before the customer has resold the product, the vendor will provide a cash refund. This is to stop the customer from returning the product and repurchasing at the lower price. In these cases, the company must estimate and recognize the potential loss due to cash refunds.[24] If not measurable, revenue might not be recognizable.

Trade Loading and Channel Stuffing

The domestic cigarette industry at one time engaged in a distribution practice known as trade loading. Producers would induce their wholesale customers, known as the trade, to buy more product than they could resell. As a result, the wholesalers would return significant amounts of product in the following period. In the computer software industry, this same practice is referred to as channel stuffing. Software producers would offer deep discounts to their distributors who would then overbuy and not be able to subsequently resell.

Trade loading and channel stuffing overstate sales in one period and distort operating results. If used without an appropriate allowance for sales returns, channel stuffing is a classic example of booking tomorrow's revenue today. The problem lies in the motivating factors that lie beneath these transactions. It is not a problem to engage in aggressive selling practices as long as they are sustainable and result in revenues that are realizable. The danger lies in entering into these and similar types of transactions for the sole purpose of booking more revenues.

Bundled Sales

Where the sale involves multiple deliverables, such as a product and service or several products, the revenue should be allocated between the deliverables. Revenue recognition criteria should be considered separately for each deliverable or unit. For instance, a cellular telephone company might sell a phone plus a monthly service (to provide airtime). As long as each deliverable has value to the customer on a standalone basis and has an objectively determinable value (e.g., fair value), this is relatively straightforward. The revenue for the phone would be recognized upon delivery and the revenue for the airtime as the service is provided or the airtime is used up. If it is not possible to measure each part, then revenue recognition criteria must be applied to the whole bundled sale as though it were one product or service.[25]

UNCERTAINTY ASSOCIATED WITH COLLECTIBILITY

Objective 9
Discuss how to deal with collection uncertainty.

At the point of sale, where there is reasonable assurance as to ultimate collection, revenues are recognized.[26] Note that as long as an estimate can be made of uncollectible amounts at point of sale (e.g. perhaps based on historical data) the sale is booked and the potential uncollectible amount accrued. Alternatively, when collectibility cannot be established, revenues may not be recognized. In cases such as this, the presumption is that if collectibility is not established at the time of sale, then in substance, no real sale has been made.

Certain types of sales transactions, such as those that require or allow payment over longer periods, pose greater collectibility risk. Instalment sales are an example of this type of sale. If collectibility is established but the uncollectible amounts are not estimable, one of two methods is generally employed to defer income recognition until the cash is received:

---

[24] *CICA Handbook*, EIC Abstract 141.

[25] *CICA Handbook*, EIC Abstract 142.

[26] *CICA Handbook*, Section 3400.16.

1. **instalment sales method** or

2. **cost recovery method**.

In some situations cash is received prior to delivery or transfer of the property and is recorded as a deposit because the sale transaction is incomplete.

Instalment Sales

The expression "instalment sales" is generally used to describe any type of sale for which payment is required in periodic instalments over an extended period of time. It is used in retailing, where all types of farm and home equipment and furnishings are sold on an instalment basis. It is also sometimes used in the heavy equipment industry in which machine installations are paid for over a long period.

Because of the greater risk of **collectibility**, various devices are used to protect the seller. In merchandising, the two most common are (1) the use of a **conditional sales contract** that provides that title to the item sold does not pass to the purchaser until all payments have been made, and (2) use of **notes secured by a chattel** (personal property) mortgage on the article sold. Either of these permits the seller to repossess the goods sold if the purchaser defaults on one or more payments. The repossessed merchandise is then resold at whatever price it will bring to compensate the seller for the uncollected instalments and the expense of repossession.

Instalment Method

The instalment sales method is one way of dealing with sales agreements that allow extended payment terms. It emphasizes collection rather than sale, recognizing income in the collection periods rather than the sale period. This method is justified on the basis that when there is no reasonable approach for estimating the degree of collectibility, income should not be recognized until cash is collected.

Under the instalment sales method of accounting, income recognition is deferred until the period of cash collection. Both revenues and costs of sales are recognized in the period of sale but the related gross profit is deferred to those periods in which cash is collected. Thus, instead of the sale being deferred to the future periods of anticipated collection and then related costs and expenses being deferred, only the proportional gross profit is deferred.

Other expenses, such as selling and administrative expense, are not deferred. Thus, the theory that cost and expenses should be matched against sales is applied in instalment sales transactions through the gross profit figure, but no further. Companies using the instalment sales method of accounting generally record operating expenses without regard to the fact that some portion of the year's gross profit is to be deferred. This practice is often justified on the basis that (1) these expenses do not follow sales as closely as does the cost of goods sold, and (2) accurate apportionment among periods would be so difficult that it could not be justified by the benefits gained.

Procedures for Deferring Income

For the sales in any one year:

1. During the year, record both sales and cost of sales in the regular way, using the special accounts described later, and calculate the rate of gross profit on instalment sales transactions.

10 Objective
Explain and apply the instalment sales method of accounting.

Underlying Concept

Realization is a critical part of revenue recognition. Thus, if a high degree of uncertainty exists about collectibility, revenue recognition must be deferred.

IAS Note

IAS 18 provides more extensive application guidance, e.g., revenue is measured at the PV of future cash flows when settlement of cash is deferred.

2. At year end, apply the rate of gross profit to the cash collections of the current year's instalment sales to arrive at the realized gross profit.

3. The gross profit not realized should be deferred to future years.

For sales made in prior years:

The gross profit rate of each year's sales must be applied against cash collections of accounts receivable resulting from that year's sales to arrive at the realized gross profit. From the preceding discussion of the general practice followed in taking up income from instalment sales, it is apparent that special accounts must be used. These accounts provide certain special information required to determine the realized and unrealized gross profit in each year of operations. The requirements for special accounts are as follows.

1. Instalment sales transactions must be kept separate in the accounts from all other sales.

2. Gross profit on sales sold on instalment must be determinable.

3. The amount of cash collected on instalment sales accounts receivable must be known, and the total collected on the current year's and on each preceding year's sales must be determinable.

4. Provision must be made for carrying forward each year's deferred gross profit.

In each year, ordinary operating expenses are charged to expense accounts and are closed to the Income Summary account as under customary accounting procedure. Thus, the only peculiarity in calculating net income under the instalment sales method as generally applied is the deferral of gross profit until realized by accounts receivable collection.

To illustrate the instalment sales method in accounting for the sales of merchandise, assume the following data.

	2004	2005	2006
Instalment sales	$200,000	$250,000	$240,000
Cost of instalment sales	150,000	190,000	168,000
Gross profit	$ 50,000	$ 60,000	$ 72,000
Rate of gross profit on sales	25% (a)	24% (b)	30% (c)
Cash receipts			
2004 sales	$ 60,000	$100,000	$ 40,000
2005 sales		100,000	125,000
2006 sales			80,000

(a) $50,000/200,000   (b) $60,000/250,000   (c) $72,000/240,000

To simplify the illustration, interest charges have been excluded. Summary entries in general journal form for year 2004 are shown below.

2004

Instalment Accounts Receivable, 2004	200,000	
Instalment Sales		200,000
(To record sales made on instalment in 2004)		
Cash	60,000	
Instalment Accounts Receivable, 2004		60,000
(To record cash collected on instalment receivables)		
Cost of Instalment Sales	150,000	
Inventory (or Purchases)		150,000
(To record cost of goods sold on instalment in 2004 on either a perpetual or a periodic inventory basis)		

Deferred (unrealized) Gross Profit current year (income statement)	35,000	
Deferred Gross Profit (balance sheet)		35,000
(to defer gross profit recognition for unrealized gross profits [25% ($200,000 − 60,000)])		

Summary entries in journal form for year 2 (2005) are shown below.

2005

Instalment Accounts Receivable, 2005	250,000	
Instalment Sales		250,000
(To record sales made on instalment in 2005)		
Cash	200,000	
Instalment Accounts Receivable, 2004		100,000
Instalment Accounts Receivable, 2005		100,000
(To record cash collected on instalment receivables)		
Cost of Instalment Sales	190,000	
Inventory (or Purchases)		190,000
(To record cost of goods sold on instalment in 2005)		
Deferred Gross Profit, (balance sheet)	25,000	
Realized Gross Profit—prior year sales (income statement)		25,000
(to record 2004 realized gross profits [25% × $100,000])		
Deferred (unrealized) Gross Profit— current year (income statement)	36,000	
Deferred Gross Profit (balance sheet)		36,000
(to defer gross profit recognition for unrealized gross profits [24% ($250,000 − 100,000)])		

The two income statement accounts, Realized Gross Profit Prior Year Sales and Deferred (Unrealized) Gross Profit Current Year, would generally be netted against each other. The entries in 2006 would be similar to those of 2005, and the gross profit realized on prior year's sales would be $40,000, as shown by the following calculations.

From 2004	$40,000 × 25% =	$10,000
From 2005	$125,000 × 24% =	$30,000
		$40,000

Deferred gross profit on 2006 sales would be calculated as follows.

30% ($240,000 − 80,000) = $48,000

Additional Problems of Instalment Sales Accounting

In addition to calculating realized and deferred gross profit currently, other problems are involved in accounting for instalment sales transactions. These problems are related to:

1. interest on instalment contracts,
2. uncollectible accounts, and
3. defaults and repossessions.

Interest on Instalment Contracts

Because the collection of instalment receivables is spread over a long period, it is customary to charge the buyer interest on the unpaid balance. A schedule of equal payments consisting of interest and principal is set up.

Each successive payment is attributable to a smaller amount of interest and a correspondingly larger amount attributable to principal, as shown in Illustration 6-21. This illustration assumes that an asset costing $2,400 is sold for $3,000 with interest of 8% included in the three instalments of $1,164.10.

Illustration 6-21

Instalment Payment Schedule

Date	Cash (Debit)	Interest Earned (Credit)	Instalment Receivables (Credit)	Instalment Unpaid Balance	Realized Gross Profit (20%)
1/2/04	—	—		$3,000.00	—
1/2/05	$1,164.10(a)	$240.00(b)	$924.10(c)	2,075.90(d)	$184.82(e)
1/2/06	1,164.10	166.07	998.03	1,077.87	199.61
1/2/07	1,164.10	86.23	1,077.87	–0–	215.57
					$600.00

(a) Periodic payment = Original unpaid balance / PV of an annuity of $1.00 for three periods at 8%; $1,164.10 = $3,000 / 2.57710.
(b) $3,000.00 × .08 = $240.
(c) $1,164.10 − $240.00 = $924.10.
(d) $3,000.00 − $924.10 = $2,075.90.
(e) $924.10 × .20 = $184.82.

Interest should be accounted for separately from the gross profit recognized on the instalment sales collections during the period. It is recognized as interest revenue at the time of the cash receipt.

Uncollectible Accounts

The problem of bad debts or uncollectible accounts receivable is somewhat different for concerns selling on an instalment basis because of a repossession feature commonly incorporated in the sales agreement. This feature gives the selling company an opportunity to recoup any uncollectible accounts through repossession and resale of repossessed merchandise. If the company's experience indicates that repossessions do not, as a rule, compensate for uncollectible balances, it may be advisable to provide for such losses through charges to a special bad debt expense account just as is done for other credit sales.

Defaults and Repossessions

Depending on the sales contract terms and credit department policy, the seller can repossess merchandise sold under an instalment arrangement if the purchaser fails to meet payment requirements. Repossessed merchandise may be reconditioned before being offered for sale. It may be resold for cash or instalment payments.

The accounting for repossessions recognizes that the related instalment receivable account is not collectible and that it should be written off. Along with the account receivable, the applicable deferred gross profit must be removed from the ledger using the following entry.

Repossessed Merchandise (an inventory account)	xx	
Deferred Gross Profit (balance sheet)	xx	
Instalment Accounts Receivable		xx

The entry above assumes that the repossessed merchandise is to be recorded on the books at exactly the amount of the uncollected account less the deferred gross profit applicable. This assumption may or may not be proper. The condition of the merchandise repossessed, the cost of reconditioning, and the market for second-hand merchandise of that particular type must all be considered. The objective should be to put any asset acquired on the books at its fair value or, when fair value is not ascertainable, at the best possible approximation of fair value. If the fair value of the merchandise repossessed is less than the uncollected balance less the deferred gross profit, a "loss on repossession" should be recorded at the repossession date.

To illustrate the required entry, assume that a refrigerator was sold to Marilyn Hunt for $500 on September 1, 2004. Terms require a down payment of $200 and $20 on the first of every month for 15 months, starting October 1, 2004. It is further assumed that the refrigerator cost $300 and that it is sold to provide a 40% rate of gross profit on selling price. At the year end, December 31, 2004, a total of $60 should have been collected in addition to the original down payment.

If Hunt makes her January and February payments in 2005 and then defaults, the account balances applicable to Hunt at time of default would be:

Instalment Account Receivable	
($500 − $200 − $20 − $20 − $20 − $20 − $20) =	200 (dr.)
Deferred Gross Profit (Balance Sheet)	
[40% ($500 − $200 − $20 − $20 − $20)] =	96 (cr.)

The deferred gross profit applicable to the Hunt account still has the December 31, 2004 balance ($96) because no entry has yet been made to take up gross profit realized by 2005 cash collections ($40 × 4% = $16). If the repossessed article's estimated fair value is set at $70, the following entry would be required to record the repossession. Assume that the $16 realized gross profit will be recognized at year end with the regular entry to recognize realized gross profit.

Deferred Gross Profit	80	
Repossessed Merchandise	70	
Loss on Repossession	50	
Instalment Account Receivable (Hunt)		200

A = L + SE
−130   −80   −50
Cash flows: No effect

The loss amount is determined by (1) subtracting the deferred gross profit from the amount of the account receivable, to determine the unrecovered cost (or book value) of the merchandise repossessed, and (2) subtracting the estimated fair value of the merchandise repossessed from the unrecovered cost to get the amount of the loss on repossession.

Financial Statement Presentation of Instalment Sales Transactions

If instalment sales transactions represent a significant part of total sales, full disclosure of instalment sales, the cost of instalment sales, and any expenses allocable to instalment sales is desirable. If, however, instalment sales transactions constitute an insignificant part of total sales, it may be satisfactory to include only the realized gross profit in the income statement as a special item following the gross profit on sales, as shown below.

HEALTH MACHINE CORP.	
Statement of Income	
For the Year Ended December 31, 2005	
Sales	$620,000
Cost of goods sold	490,000
Gross profit on sales	130,000
Gross profit realized on instalment sales	51,000
Total gross profit on sales	$181,000

Illustration 6-22

Disclosure of Instalment Sales Transactions— Insignificant Amount

Underlying Concept

This level of detail might result in "information overload" for some users.

If more complete disclosure of instalment sales transactions is desired, a presentation similar to the following may be used.

Illustration 6-23

Disclosure of Instalment Sales Transactions— Significant Amount

HEALTH MACHINE CORP.
Statement of Income
For the Year Ended December 31, 2005

	Instalment Sales	Other Sales	Total
Sales	$248,000	$620,000	$868,000
Cost of goods sold	182,000	490,000	672,000
Gross profit on sales	66,000	130,000	196,000
Less: Deferred gross profit on instalment sales of this year	47,000		47,000
Realized gross profit on this year's sales	19,000	130,000	149,000
Add: Gross profit realized on instalment sales of prior years	32,000		32,000
Gross profit realized this year	$ 51,000	$130,000	$181,000

The apparent awkwardness of this presentation method is difficult to avoid if full disclosure of instalment sales transactions is to be provided in the income statement. One solution, of course, is to prepare a separate schedule showing instalment sales transactions with only the final figure carried into the income statement.

In the balance sheet it is generally considered desirable to classify instalment accounts receivable by year of collectibility. There is some question as to whether instalment accounts that are not collectible for two or more years should be included in current assets. If instalment sales are part of normal operations, they may be considered current assets because they are collectible within the business operating cycle. Little confusion should result from this practice if maturity dates are fully disclosed, as illustrated in the following example.

Illustration 6-24

Disclosure of Instalment Accounts Receivable, by Year

Current assets		
Notes and accounts receivable		
Trade Customers	$78,800	
Less: Allowance for doubtful accounts	3,700	
	75,100	
Instalment accounts collectible in 2005	22,600	
Instalment accounts collectible in 2006	47,200	$144,900

On the other hand, receivables from an instalment contract, or contracts, resulting from a transaction not related to normal operations should be reported in the Other Assets section if due beyond one year.

Repossessed merchandise is a part of inventory and should be included as such in the Current Asset section of the balance sheet. Any gain or loss on repossessions should be included in the income statement in the Other Revenues and Gains or Other Expenses and Losses section.

Deferred gross profit on instalment sales may be treated either as unearned revenue (current liability) or a contra asset account (as a valuation of instalment accounts receivable).

Cost Recovery Method

Under the cost recovery method, no profit is recognized until cash payments by the buyer exceed the seller's cost of the merchandise sold. After all costs have been recovered, any additional cash collections are included in income. This method is therefore the most conservative method of recognizing income under accrual accounting.[27] The income statement for the period of sale reports sales revenue, the cost of goods sold, and the gross profit— both the amount (if any) that is recognized during the period and the amount that is deferred. The deferred gross profit is either presented as unearned revenue or offset against the related receivable (reduced by collections) on the balance sheet. Subsequent income statements report the gross profit as a separate revenue item when it is recognized as earned.

To illustrate the cost recovery method, assume that early in 2004, Fesmire Manufacturing sells inventory with a cost of $25,000 to Higley Limited for $36,000 with payments receivable of $18,000 in 2004, $12,000 in 2005, and $6,000 in 2006. If the cost recovery method applies to this sale transaction and the cash is collected on schedule, then cash collections, revenue, cost, and gross profit are recognized as follows.

Objective 11
Explain and apply the cost recovery method of accounting.

	2004	2005	2006
Cash collected	$18,000	$12,000	$6,000
Revenue	$36,000	–0–	–0–
Cost of goods sold	25,000	–0–	–0–
Deferred gross profit	$11,000	$11,000	$6,000
Recognized gross profit	–0–	5,000*	6,000
Deferred gross profit balance (end of period)	$11,000	$ 6,000	$-0–

Illustration 6-25

Calculation of Gross Profit— Cost Recovery Method

*$25,000 − $18,000 = $7,000 of unrecovered cost at the end of 2004; $12,000 − $7,000 = $5,000, the excess of cash received in 2005 over unrecovered cost.

Under the cost recovery method, total revenue and cost of goods sold are reported in the period of sale similar to the instalment sales method. However, unlike the instalment sales method, which recognizes income as cash is collected, the cost recovery method recognizes profit only when cash collections exceed the total cost of the goods sold.

The journal entry to record the deferred gross profit on this transaction (after the sale and the cost of sale were recorded in the normal manner) at the end of 2004 is as follows.

2004		
Deferred (unrealized) Gross Profit (income statement)	11,000	
Deferred Gross Profit (balance sheet)		11,000
(To record deferred gross profit on sales accounted for under the cost recovery method)		

A = L + SE
　+11,000 + −11,000
Cash flows: No effect

In 2005 and 2006, the deferred gross profit becomes realized gross profit as the cumulative cash collections exceed the total costs by recording the following entries.

2005		
Deferred Gross Profit (balance sheet)	5,000	
Realized Gross Profit (income statement)		5,000
(To recognize gross profit to the extent that cash collections in 2005 exceed costs)		

A = L + SE
　−5,000 + +5,000
Cash flows: No effect

[27] "Omnibus Opinion – 1966", *Opinions of the Accounting Principles Board No. 10* (New York: AICPA, 1969), footnote 8, page 149; "Accounting for Franchise Fee Revenue," *Statement of Financial Accounting Standards No. 45* (Stamford, Conn.: FASB, 1981), par. 6; "Accounting for Sales of Real Estate," *Statement of Financial Accounting Standards No. 66*, pars. 62 and 63. In Canada, CICA Accounting Guideline #2 (franchise fee revenue) mentions that either the instalment method or cost recovery method may be used where there is no reasonable basis for estimating collectibility.

	2006	
Deferred Gross Profit (balance sheet)	6,000	
Realized Gross Profit (income statement)		6,000
(To recognize gross profit to the extent that		
cash collections in 2006 exceed costs)		

A = L + SE
   −6,000 + +6,000
Cash flows: No effect

PERSPECTIVES

Although the revenues number shows up in several key ratios, the most important revenue analysis is normally a trend analysis (revenues year to year). Due to the sensitivity and high profile of the revenues number on the income statement, there is considerable pressure to bias the reporting. This is possible under either a principles-based accounting standards system (because there is less specific guidance) or under a rules-based accounting standards system (under a loophole mentality). Revenues are a key number that management is judged on in terms of job performance and represent a signal in the marketplace for sustainable growth potential. Firms in certain industries, such as Internet companies, are often valued based on revenues since many of these firms do not generate profits in their early years.

As mentioned in the opening statements of the chapter, this is one of the main areas of misrepresentation. Note that it is often difficult to spot these misrepresentations in financial statements since the note disclosures are often very general. Care should be taken to understand the underlying business and business model of the company and to ensure that any changes in the business model are reflected appropriately in the statements. Care should also be taken to ensure that large and unusual transactions are entered into for bona fide business reasons (e.g., to add value to the shareholders) and not for window dressing.

Summary of Learning Objectives

1 Apply the revenue recognition principle.

The revenue recognition principle provides that revenue is recognized (1) when performance is substantially complete (including measurability) and (2) collection is reasonably assured. Revenue is earned when the entity has substantially accomplished what it must do to be entitled to the benefits represented by the revenues; that is, when the earnings process is complete or virtually complete. Revenues and costs must also be measurable.

2 Describe accounting issues involved with revenue recognition for sale of goods.

The two conditions for recognizing revenue are usually met by the time product or merchandise is delivered (risks and rewards of ownership passed). Judgement must be applied in determining when the risks and rewards pass. The earnings process must be considered to determine if revenue and income is recognized prior to or after delivery.

3 Explain accounting for consignment sales.

The risks and rewards remain with the seller in this case and therefore a real sale does not occur until the goods are sold to a third party. Special accounts separate inventory on consignment.

4 Describe accounting issues involved with revenue recognition for services and long-term contracts.

The earnings process is more likely a continuous one, involving many significant events. Often, the customer is identified upfront. Therefore, revenue is recognized throughout the earnings process.

5 Apply the percentage-of-completion method for long-term contracts.

To apply the percentage-of-completion method to long-term contracts, one must have some basis for measuring the progress toward completion at particular interim dates. One of the most popular input measures used to determine the progress toward completion is the cost-to-cost basis. Using this basis, the percentage of completion is measured by comparing costs incurred to date with the most recent estimate of the total costs to complete the contract. The percentage that costs incurred bear to total estimated costs is applied to the total revenue or the estimated total gross profit on the contract in arriving at the revenue or the gross profit amounts to be recognized to date.

6 Apply the completed-contract method for long-term contracts.

Under this method, revenue and gross profit are recognized only when the contract is completed. Costs of long-term contracts in process and current billings are accumulated, but there are no interim charges or credits to income statement accounts for revenues, costs, and gross profit. The annual entries to record costs of construction, progress billings, and collections from customers would be identical to those for the percentage-of-completion method with the significant exclusion of the recognition of revenue and gross profit.

7 Account for losses on long-term contracts.

Two types of losses can become evident under long-term contracts: (1) Loss in current period on a profitable contract: Under the percentage-of-completion method only, the estimated cost increase requires a current period adjustment of excess gross profit recognized on the project in prior periods. This adjustment is recorded as a loss in the current period because it is a change in accounting estimate. (2) Loss on an unprofitable contract: Under both the percentage-of-completion and the completed-contract methods, the entire expected contract loss must be recognized in the current period.

8 Discuss how to deal with measurement uncertainty.

Transactions that involve rights of return may require remeasurement. Existence of the practice of trade loading and channel stuffing may also require remeasuring of the transaction.

9 Discuss how to deal with collection uncertainty.

Normally, if estimable, a provision for uncollectible amounts is accrued. In certain types of sales arrangements, payment is extended over the longer term. In these cases, the instalments or cost recovery methods may be used. These methods allow revenue recognition upfront but gross profits are deferred.

10 Explain and apply the instalment sales method of accounting.

The instalment sales method recognizes income in the periods of collection rather than in the period of sale. The instalment method of accounting is justified on the basis that when there is no reasonable approach for estimating the degree of collectibility, revenue should not be recognized until cash is collected.

11. Explain and apply the cost recovery method of accounting.

Under the cost recovery method, no profit is recognized until cash payments by the buyer exceed the seller's cost of the merchandise sold. After all costs have been recovered, any additional cash collections are included in income. The income statement for the period of sale reports sales revenue, the cost of goods sold, and the gross profit—both the amount that is recognized during the period and the amount that is deferred. The deferred gross profit is treated as deferred or unearned revenues on the balance sheet or offset against the related receivable on the balance sheet. Subsequent income statements report the gross profit as a separate income item when it is recognized as earned.

Digital Tool

Glossary

www.wiley.com/canada/kieso

KEY TERMS

barter transactions, 293

billings, 284

collectibility, 296

completed-contract
   method, 284

consignment, 282

continuous earnings
   process, 283

continuous sale, 285

cost recovery method, 302

cost-to-cost basis, 285

critical event, 280

discrete earnings
   process, 280

earnings process, 279

f.o.b. shipping point, 281

f.o.b. destination, 281

input measures, 285

instalment sales
   method, 297

legal title, 281

measurement
   uncertainty, 295

output measures, 285

percentage-of-completion
   method, 284

performance, 279

point of delivery, 280

possession, 281

realized, 279

revenue recognition
   principle, 279

risks and rewards of
   ownership, 280

Appendix 6A

Franchises

Objective 12

Explain revenue recognition for franchises.

As indicated throughout this chapter, revenue is recognized on the basis of two criteria: **performance and collectibility.** These criteria are appropriate for most business activities. This appendix looks at how they apply to industries characterized by franchises.

There are many different types of franchise arrangements. Below are several of the more well known franchises:

> Soft ice cream/frozen yogurt stores (Baskin Robbins, TCBY, Dairy Queen)
> Food drive-ins (McDonald's, Tim Hortons, Burger King)
> Restaurants (Swiss Chalet, Pizza Hut, Denny's)
> Motels (Holiday Inn, Ramada, Best Western)
> Auto rentals (Avis, Hertz, National)
> Others (H & R Block, Mr. Lube, Mac's Convenience Stores)

Franchise companies derive their revenue from one or both of two sources: (1) from the sale of initial franchises and related assets or services (initial franchise fee), and

(2) from continuing franchise fees based on franchise operations. The franchiser (the party that grants business rights under the franchise) normally provides the franchisee (the party that operates the franchised business) with the following services.

1. Assistance in site selection

    (a) analysing location

    (b) negotiating lease

2. Evaluation of potential income

3. Supervision of construction activity

    (a) obtaining financing

    (b) designing building

    (c) supervising contractor while building

4. Assistance in the acquisition of signs, fixtures, and equipment

5. Bookkeeping and advisory services

    (a) setting up franchisee's records

    (b) advising on income, real estate, and other taxes

    (c) advising on local regulations of the franchisee's business

6. Employee and management training

7. Quality control

8. Advertising and promotion

During the 1960s and early 1970s it was standard accounting practice for franchisers to recognize the entire franchise fee at the date of sale whether the fee was received then or was collectible over a long period of time. Frequently, franchisers recorded the entire amount as revenue in the year of sale even though many of the services were yet to be performed and uncertainty existed regarding the collection of the entire fee.[28]

However, a franchise agreement may provide for refunds to the franchisee if certain conditions are not met, and franchise fee profit can be reduced sharply by future costs of obligations and services to be rendered by the franchiser.[29]

Initial Franchise Fees

The initial franchise fee is consideration for establishing the franchise relationship and providing some initial services. Initial franchise fees are to be recorded as revenue only when and as the franchiser has established **substantial performance**,[30] i.e., it has substantially completed the services it is obligated to perform and collection of the fee is reasonably assured. Substantial performance occurs when the franchiser has no remaining obligation to refund any cash received or excuse any nonpayment of a note and has substantially performed all significant initial services required under the contract. Commencement of operations by the franchisee is normally presumed to be the earliest point at which substantial performance has occurred, unless it can be demonstrated that substantial performance has occurred before that time.

Illustration of Entries for Initial Franchise Fee

To illustrate, assume that Dino's Pizza Inc. charges an initial franchise fee of $50,000 for the right to operate as a franchisee of Dino's Pizza. Of this amount, $10,000 is payable when the agreement is signed and the balance is payable in five annual payments of $8,000 each. In return for the initial franchise fee, the franchiser will help locate the site, negotiate the site lease or purchase, supervise the construction activity, and provide the bookkeeping services. The franchisee's credit rating indicates that money can be borrowed at 8%. The present value of an ordinary annuity of five annual receipts of $8,000 each, discounted at 8%, is $31,941.68. The discount of $8,058.32 represents the interest revenue to be accrued by the franchiser over the payment period.

1. If there is reasonable expectation that the down payment may be refunded and if substantial future services remain to be performed by Dinos's Pizza Inc., the entry should be:

Cash	10,000	
Notes Receivable	40,000	
Discount on Notes Receivable		8,058
Unearned Franchise Fees		41,942

A = L + SE
+41,942 +41,942

Cash flows: ↑ 10,000 inflow

---

[28] In 1987 and 1988 the SEC ordered a half-dozen fast-growing startup franchisers, including Jiffy Lube International, Moto Photo, Inc., Swensen's, Inc., and LePeep Restaurants, Inc., to defer their initial franchise fee recognition until earned. See "Claiming Tomorrow's Profits Today," *Forbes*, October 17, 1988, p. 78.

[29] To curb the abuses in revenue recognition that existed and to standardize the accounting and reporting practices in the franchise industry, the CICA issued an Accounting Guideline and the FASB issued Statement No. 45.

[30] *CICA Handbook*, Accounting Guideline #2

2. If the probability of refunding the initial franchise fee is extremely low, if the amount of future services to be provided to the franchisee is minimal, collectibility of the note is reasonably assured, and if substantial performance has occurred, the entry should be:

A = L + SE
+41,942   +41,942

Cash flows: ↑ 10,000 inflow

Cash	10,000	
Notes Receivable	40,000	
Discount on Notes Receivable		8,058
Revenue from Franchise Fees		41,942

3. If the initial down payment is not refundable and represents a fair measure of the services already provided, with a significant amount of services still to be performed by the franchiser in future periods, and if collectibility of the note is reasonably assured, the entry should be:

A = L + SE
+41,942   +31,942   +10,000

Cash flows: ↑ 10,000 inflow

Cash	10,000	
Notes Receivable	40,000	
Discount on Notes Receivable		8,058
Revenue from Franchise Fees		10,000
Unearned Franchise Fees		31,942

4. If the initial down payment is not refundable and no future services are required by the franchiser, but collection of the note is so uncertain that recognition of the note as an asset is unwarranted, the entry should be:

A = L + SE
+10,000   +10,000

Cash flows: ↑ 10,000 inflow

Cash	10,000	
Revenue from Franchise Fees		10,000

5. Under the same conditions as those listed under 4 except that the down payment is refundable or substantial services are yet to be performed, the entry should be:

A = L + SE
+10,000   +10,000

Cash flows: ↑ 10,000 inflow

Cash	10,000	
Unearned Franchise Fees		10,000

In cases 4 and 5—where collection of the note is extremely uncertain—cash collections may be recognized using the instalment method or the cost recovery method.

Continuing Franchise Fees

Continuing franchise fees are received in return for the continuing rights granted by the franchise agreement and for providing such services as management training, advertising and promotion, legal assistance, and other support. Continuing fees should be reported as revenue when they are earned and receivable from the franchisee, unless a portion of them has been designated for a particular purpose, such as providing a specified amount for building maintenance or local advertising. In that case, the portion deferred shall be an amount sufficient to cover the estimated cost in excess of continuing franchise fees and provide a reasonable profit on the continuing services.

Special Issues

Bargain Purchases

In addition to paying continuing franchise fees, franchisees frequently purchase some or all of their equipment and supplies from the franchiser. The franchiser would account for these sales as it would for any other product sales. Sometimes, however, the franchise agreement grants the franchisee the right to make bargain purchases of equipment or supplies after the initial franchise fee is paid. If the bargain price is lower than the normal selling price of the same product, or if it does not provide the franchiser a reasonable profit, then a portion of the initial franchise fee should be deferred. The deferred portion would be accounted for as an adjustment of the selling price when the franchisee subsequently purchases the equipment or supplies.

Options to Purchase

A franchise agreement may give the franchiser an option to purchase the franchisee's business. As a matter of management policy, the franchiser may reserve the right to purchase a profitable franchised outlet, or to purchase one that is in financial difficulty. If it is probable at the time the option is given that the franchiser will ultimately purchase the outlet, then the initial franchise fee should not be recognized as revenue but should be recorded as a liability. When the option is exercised, the liability would reduce the franchiser's investment in the outlet.

Franchiser's Cost

Franchise accounting also involves proper accounting for the franchiser's cost. The objective is to match related costs and revenues by reporting them as components of income in the same accounting period. Franchisers should ordinarily defer direct costs (usually incremental costs) relating to specific franchise sales for which revenue has not yet been recognized. Costs should not be deferred, however, without reference to anticipated revenue and its realizability. Indirect costs of a regular and recurring nature such as selling and administrative expenses that are incurred irrespective of the level of franchise sales should be expensed as incurred.

Disclosures of Franchisers

Disclosure of all significant commitments and obligations resulting from franchise agreements, including a description of services that have not yet been substantially performed, is required. Any resolution of uncertainties regarding the collectibility of franchise fees should be disclosed. Initial franchise fees should be segregated from other franchise fee revenue if they are significant. Where possible, revenues and costs related to franchiser-owned outlets should be distinguished from those related to franchised outlets.

Digital Tool

Glossary

www.wiley.com/canada/kieso

Summary of Learning Objective for Appendix 6A

12 Explain revenue recognition for franchises.

In a franchise arrangement, the initial franchise fee is recorded as revenue only when and as the franchiser makes substantial performance of the services it is obligated to perform and collection of the fee is reasonably assured. Continuing franchise fees are recognized as revenue when they are earned and receivable from the franchisee.

KEY TERMS

continuing franchise
    fees, 306
initial franchise fee, 306
substantial
    performance, 307

Note: All asterisked assignment material relates to the appendix to the chapter.

Brief Exercises

BE6-1   Manchrian Music sold CDs to retailers and recorded sales revenue of $500,000. During 2005, retailers returned CDs to Manchrian and were granted credit of $38,000. Experience indicates that the normal return rate is 10%. Prepare the company's journal entries to record (a) the $38,000 of returns and (b) estimated returns at December 31, 2005.

BE6-2   Wan Inc. began work on a $9.2 million contract in 2004 to construct an office building. During 2004, Wan Inc. incurred costs of $1.3 million, billed its customers for $2.1 million, and collected $960,000. At December 31, 2004, the estimated future costs to complete the project total $5 million. Prepare Wan's 2004 journal entries using the percentage-of-completion method.

BE6-3   Use the information from BE6-2, but assume Wan uses the completed-contract method. Prepare the company's 2004 journal entries.

BE6-4   Boomer Inc. began work on a $5 million contract in 2005 to construct an office building. Boomer uses the percentage-of-completion method. At December 31, 2005, the balances in certain accounts were construction in process, $450,000; accounts receivable, $340,000; and billings on construction in process, $1 million. Indicate how these accounts would be reported in the company's December 31, 2005 balance sheet.

BE6-5   Candeloro Inc. began work on a $5 million contract in 2005 to construct an office building. Candeloro uses the completed-contract method. At December 31, 2005, the balances in certain accounts were construction in process, $915,000; accounts receivable, $560,000; and billings on construction in process, $1 million. Indicate how these accounts would be reported in Candeloro's December 31, 2005 balance sheet.

BE6-6   Tower Construction Corp. began work on a $1,420,000 construction contract in 2004. During 2004, the company incurred costs of $588,000, billed its customer for $615,000, and collected $275,000. At December 31, 2004, the estimated future costs to complete the project total $532,000. Prepare Tower's journal entry to record profit or loss using (a) the percentage-of-completion method and (b) the completed contract method, if any, for the year ended December 31, 2004.

BE6-7   Paradise Corporation began selling goods on an instalment basis on January 1, 2005. During 2005, Paradise had instalment sales of $450,000; cash collections of $254,000; and cost of instalment sales of $255,000. Prepare the company's entries to record instalment sales, cash collected, cost of instalment sales, deferral of gross profit, and gross profit recognized, using the instalment sales method.

BE6-8   Shinsui Limited sells goods on the instalment basis and uses the instalment sales method. Due to a customer default, Shinsui repossessed merchandise that was originally sold for $1,800, resulting in a gross profit rate of 40%. At the time of repossession, the uncollected balance is $960, and the fair value of the repossessed merchandise is $1,575. Prepare Shinsui's entry to record the repossession.

BE6-9   At December 31, 2006, Starskin Corporation had the following account balances.

Instalment Accounts Receivable, 2005	$165,000
Instalment Accounts Receivable, 2006	160,000
Deferred Gross Profit, 2005	63,400
Deferred Gross Profit, 2006	70,700

Most of Starskin's sales are made on a two-year instalment basis. Indicate how these accounts would be reported in the company's December 31, 2006 balance sheet. The 2006 accounts are collectible in 2008, and the 2005 accounts are collectible in 2007.

BE6-10   Brew Corporation sold equipment to Mug Limited for $120,000. The equipment is on Brew's books at a net amount of $86,000. Brew collected $60,000 in 2005, $40,000 in 2006, and $20,000 in 2007. If Brew uses the cost recovery method, what amount of gross profit will be recognized in each year?

*BE6-11   Raclette Inc. charges an initial franchise fee of $100,000 for the right to operate as a franchisee of Raclette. Of this amount, $20,000 is collected immediately. The remainder is collected in four equal annual instalments of $20,000 each. These instalments have a present value of $63,397. There is reasonable expectation that the down payment may be refunded and substantial future services be performed by Raclette Inc. Prepare the journal entry required by Raclette to record the franchise fee.

BE6-12   TGI Corporation shipped $200,000 of merchandise on consignment to Thomas Company. TGI paid freight costs of $2,000. Thomas Company paid $500 for local advertising, which is reimbursable from TGI. By year end, 60% of the merchandise had been sold for $222,300. Thomas notified TGI, retained a 10% commission, and remitted the cash due to TGI. Prepare TGI's entry when the cash is received.

Exercises

E6-1   **(Revenue Recognition on Book Sales with High Returns)**   Pebbles Publishing Inc. publishes college textbooks that are sold to bookstores on the following terms. Each title has a fixed wholesale price, terms f.o.b. shipping point, and payment is due 60 days after shipment. The retailer may return a maximum of 30% of an order at the retailer's expense. Sales are made only to retailers that have good credit ratings. Experience indicates that the normal return rate is 12% and the average collection period is 72 days.

Instructions

(a) Identify alternative revenue recognition points that Pebbles could employ concerning textbook sales.

(b) Briefly discuss the reasoning for your answers in (a) above.

(c) In late July, Pebbles shipped books and sent an invoice for $8 million. Prepare the journal entry to record this event given (a) and (b).

(d) In October, $2.4 million of the invoiced July sales were returned according to the return policy, and the remaining $5.6 million was paid. Prepare the entry recording the return and payment.

E6-2   **(Sales with Discounts)**   On June 3, Rancourt Corp. sold to Kerry Randall merchandise having a sale price of $15,000 with terms of 2/10, n/60, f.o.b. shipping point. An invoice totalling $520, terms n/30, was received by Randall on June 8 from the Olympic Transport Service for the freight cost. Upon receipt of the goods, June 5, Randall notified Rancourt that merchandise costing $4,000 contained flaws that rendered it worthless. The same day, Rancourt issued a credit memo covering the worthless merchandise and asked that it be returned at the company's expense. The freight on the returned merchandise was $124, paid by Rancourt on June 7. On June 12, the company received a cheque for the balance due from Randall.

Instructions

(a) Prepare journal entries on Rancourt's books to record all the events noted above under each of the following bases.

   1.   Sales and receivables are entered at gross selling price.

   2.   Sales and receivables are entered net of cash discounts.

(b) Prepare the journal entry under basis 2, assuming that Randall did not remit payment until August 5.

E6-3   **(Revenue Recognition on Marina Sales with Discounts)**   Wavy Marina has 500 available slips that rent for $1,000 per season. Payments must be made in full at the start of the boating season, April 1. Slips for the next season may be reserved if paid for by December 31. Under a new policy, if payment is made by December 31, a 5% discount is allowed. The boating season ends October 31, and the marina has a December 31 year end. To provide cash flow for major dock repairs, the marina operator is also offering a 25% discount to slip renters who pay for the second season following the current December 31.

For the fiscal year ended December 31, 2005, all 500 slips were rented at full price. Two hundred slips were reserved and paid for in advance of the 2006 boating season, and 160 slips were reserved and paid for in advance of the 2007 boating season.

Instructions

Prepare the appropriate journal entries for fiscal 2005.

E6-4   **(Recognition of Profit on Long-Term Contracts)**   During 2004, Pierette started a construction job with a contract price of $2.5 million. The job was completed in 2006. The following information is available.

Interactive
Homework

	2004	2005	2006
Costs incurred to date	$900,000	$1,535,000	$1,785,000
Estimated costs to complete	900,000	305,000	–0–
Billings to date	1,000,000	1,900,000	2,500,000
Collections to date	770,000	1,810,000	2,500,000

Instructions

(a) Calculate the amount of gross profit to be recognized each year assuming the percentage-of-completion method is used.

(b) Prepare all necessary journal entries for 2005.

(c) Calculate the amount of gross profit to be recognized each year assuming the completed-contract method is used.

E6-5   (Analysis of Percentage-of-Completion Method Financial Statements)   In 2005, Gage Construction Corp. began construction work under a three-year contract. The contract price was $10 million. Gage uses the percentage-of-completion method for financial accounting purposes. The income to be recognized each year is based on the proportion of cost incurred to total estimated costs for completing the contract. The financial statement presentations relating to this contract at December 31, 2005 follow.

Balance Sheet		
Accounts receivable construction contract billings		$821,500
Construction in progress	$1,665,000	
Less contract billings	1,061,500	
Cost of uncompleted contract in excess of billings		603,500

Income Statement	
Income (before tax) on the contract recognized in 2005	$713,600

Instructions

(a) How much cash was collected in 2005 on this contract?

(b) What was the initial estimated total income before tax on this contract?

(AICPA adapted)

Interactive Homework

E6-6   (Gross Profit on Uncompleted Contract)   On April 1, 2004, Buming Limited entered into a cost-plus-fixed-fee contract to construct an electric generator for Tian Corporation. At the contract date, Buming estimated that it would take two years to complete the project at a cost of $4 million. The fixed fee stipulated in the contract is $1,050,000. Buming appropriately accounts for this contract under the percentage-of-completion method. During 2004, Buming incurred costs of $1.7 million related to the project. The estimated cost at December 31, 2004 to complete the contract is $3 million. Tian was billed $600,000 under the contract.

Instructions

Prepare a schedule to calculate the amount of gross profit to be recognized by Buming under the contract for the year ended December 31, 2004. Show supporting calculations in good form.

(AICPA adapted)

E6-7   (Recognition of Profit, Percentage-of-Completion Method)   In 2005, Rendezvous Construction Inc. agreed to construct an apartment building at a price of $12 million. The information relating to the costs and billings for this contract is as follows.

	2005	2006	2007
Costs incurred in the period	$2,280,000	$3,000,000	$1,785,000
Estimated costs yet to be incurred	4,720,000	1,920,000	–0–
Customer billings in the period	3,000,000	4,000,000	5,000,000
Collection of billings to date	2,000,000	4,000,000	6,000,000

Instructions

(a) Assuming that the percentage-of-completion method is used: (1) calculate the amount of gross profit to be recognized in 2005 and 2006, and (2) prepare journal entries for 2006.

(b) For 2006, show how the details related to this construction contract would be disclosed on the balance sheet and on the income statement.

E6-8   (Recognition of Revenue on Long-Term Contract and Entries)   Van DeHoot Construction Corp. uses the percentage-of-completion method of accounting. In 2005, Van DeHoot began work under contract #E2-D2, which provided for a contract price of $5.2 million. Other details follow.

	2005	2006
Costs incurred during the year	$1,480,000	$1,785,000
Estimated costs to complete, as of December 31	1,120,000	–0–
Billings during the year	2,420,000	2,780,000
Collections during the year	2,350,000	2,850,000

Instructions

(a) What portion of the total contract price would be recognized as revenue in 2005? In 2006?

(b) Assuming the same facts as those above except that the company uses the completed-contract method of accounting, what portion of the total contract price would be recognized as revenue in 2006?

(c) Prepare a complete set of journal entries for 2005 (using percentage-of-completion method).

E6-9   (Recognition of Profit and Balance Sheet Amounts for Long-Term Contracts)   Adam Construction Corp. began operations January 1, 2004. During the year, Adam entered into a contract with Dave Corp. to construct a manufacturing facility. At that time, Adam estimated that it would take five years to complete the facility at a total cost of $6.5 million. The total contract price to construct the facility is $10.3 million. During the year, Adam incurred $3,185,800 in construction costs related to the construction project. The estimated cost to complete the contract is $4,204,200. Dave was billed and paid 30% of the contract price.

Interactive Homework

Instructions

Prepare schedules to calculate the amount of gross profit to be recognized for the year ended December 31, 2004, and the amount to be shown as cost of uncompleted contract in excess of related billings or billings on uncompleted contract in excess of related costs at December 31, 2004, under each of the following methods:

(a) completed-contract method and

(b) percentage-of-completion method.

Show supporting calculations in good form.

(AICPA adapted)

E6-10   (Long-Term Contract Reporting)   Angela Construction Ltd. began operations in 2004. Construction activity for the first year is shown below. All contracts are with different customers, and any work remaining at December 31, 2004 is expected to be completed in 2005.

Project	Total Contract Price	Billings through 12/31/04	Cash Collections through 12/31/04	Contract Costs Incurred through 12/31/04	Estimated Additional Costs to Complete
1	$2,360,000	$1,360,000	$1,040,000	$1,450,000	$1,040,000
2	2,670,000	1,220,000	1,210,000	1,126,000	504,000
3	500,000	500,000	440,000	330,000	–0–
	$5,530,000	$3,080,000	$2,690,000	$2,906,000	$1,544,000

Instructions

Prepare a partial income statement and balance sheet to indicate how the above information would be reported for financial statement purposes. Angela uses the completed-contract method.

E6-11   (Instalment Sales Method Calculations, Entries)   Harder Corporation appropriately uses the instalment sales method of accounting to recognize income in its financial statements. The following information is available for 2005 and 2006.

Interactive Homework

	2005	2006
Instalment sales	$1,900,000	$1,000,000
Cost of instalment sales	1,230,000	680,000
Cash collections on 2005 sales	670,000	350,000
Cash collections on 2006 sales	–0–	475,000

Instructions

(a) Calculate the amount of realized gross profit recognized in each year.

(b) Prepare all journal entries required in 2005 and 2006.

E6-12   (Analysis of Instalment Sales Accounts)   Humpback Ltd. appropriately uses the instalment sales method of accounting. On December 31, 2007, the books show balances as follows.

Instalment Receivables		Deferred Gross Profit (Balance Sheet Account)		Gross Profit on Sales	
2005	$101,000	2005	$ 71,000	2005	35%
2006	400,000	2006	260,000	2006	34%
2007	800,000	2007	995,000	2007	32%

Instructions

(a) Prepare the adjusting entry or entries required on December 31, 2007 to recognize 2007 realized gross profit. (Instalment receivables have already been credited for cash receipts during 2007.)

(b) Calculate the amount of cash collected in 2007 on accounts receivable each year.

E6-13   (Gross Profit Calculations and Repossessed Merchandise)   Minutto Corporation, which began business on January 1, 2004, appropriately uses the instalment sales method of accounting. The following data were obtained for the years 2004 and 2005.

	2004	2005
Instalment sales	$2,050,000	$ 840,000
Cost of instalment sales	1,525,000	604,800
General & administrative expenses	170,000	84,000
Cash collections on sales of 2004	1,010,000	840,000
Cash collections on sales of 2005	–0–	400,000

Instructions

(a) Calculate the balance in the deferred gross profit balance sheet accounts on December 31, 2004 and on December 31, 2005.

(b) A 2004 sale resulted in default in 2005. At the date of default, the balance on the instalment receivable was $112,000, and the repossessed merchandise had a fair value of $80,000. Prepare the entry to record the repossession.(AICPA adapted)

E6-14   (Interest Revenue from Instalment Sale)   Badali Corporation sells farm machinery on the instalment plan. On July 1, 2004, Badali entered into an instalment sale contract with Kogan Inc. for a 10-year period. Equal annual payments under the instalment sale are $200,000 and are due on July 1. The first payment was made on July 1, 2004.

1. The amount that would be realized on an outright sale of similar farm machinery is $1,350,000.

2. The cost of the farm machinery sold to Kogan Inc. is $900,000.

3. The finance charges relating to the instalment period are $650,000 based on a stated interest rate of 10%, which is appropriate.

4. Circumstances are such that the collection of the instalments due under the contract is reasonably assured.

Instructions

What income or loss before income taxes should Badali record for the year ended December 31, 2004 as a result of the transaction above? (AICPA adapted)

E6-15   (Instalment Method and Cost Recovery)   Cheung Corp., a capital goods manufacturing business that started on January 4, 2005 and operates on a calendar-year basis, uses the instalment method of profit recognition in accounting for all its sales. The following data were taken from the 2005 and 2006 records.

	2005	2006
Instalment sales	$1,480,000	$1,620,000
Gross profit as a percent of sale	25%	28%
Cash collections on sales of 2005	$840,000	$240,000
Cash collections on sales of 2006	–0–	$1,080,000

The amounts given for cash collections exclude amounts collected for interest charges.

Instructions

(a) Calculate the amount of realized gross profit to be recognized on the 2006 income statement, prepared using the instalment method.

(b) State where the balance of Deferred Gross Profit would be reported on the financial statements for 2006.

(c) Calculate the amount of realized gross profit to be recognized on the income statement, prepared using the cost recovery method.

(CIA adapted)

E6-16   (Instalment Sales Method and Cost Recovery Method)   On January 1, 2005, Tihal Limited sold property for $200,000. The note will be collected as follows: $100,000 in 2005, $60,000 in 2006, and $40,000 in 2007. The property had cost Tihal $150,000 when it was purchased in 2003.

Interactive
Homework

Instructions

(a) Calculate the amount of gross profit realized each year assuming Tihal uses the cost recovery method.

(b) Calculate the amount of gross profit realized each year assuming Tihal uses the instalment sales method.

E6-17   (Cost Recovery Method)   On January 1, 2005, Jacob Limited sold real estate that cost $110,000 to Kimberly Limited for $120,000. Kimberly agreed to pay for the purchase over three years by making three end-of-year equal payments of $52,557 that included 15% interest. Shortly after the sale, Jacob learns distressing news about Kimberly's financial circumstances and because collection is so uncertain decides to account for the sale using the cost recovery method.

Instructions

Applying the cost recovery method, prepare a schedule showing the amounts of cash collected, the increase (decrease) in deferred interest revenue, the balance of the receivable, the balance of the unrecovered cost, the gross profit realized, and the interest revenue realized for each of the three years, assuming the payments are made as agreed.

E6-18   (Instalment Sales—Default and Repossession)   Jitsui Imports Inc. was involved in two default and repossession cases during the year.

   1. A refrigerator was sold to Conrad White for $1,800, including a 35% gross margin. White made a down payment of 20%, 4 of the remaining 16 equal payments, and then defaulted on further payments. The refrigerator was repossessed, at which time the fair value was determined to be $800.

   2. An oven that cost $1,200 was sold to Delilah Brown for $1,600 on the instalment basis. Brown made a down payment of $240 and paid $80 a month for six months, after which she defaulted. The oven was repossessed and the estimated value at time of repossession was determined to be $750.

Instructions

Prepare journal entries to record each of these repossessions. (Ignore interest charges.)

E6-19   (Instalment Sales—Default and Repossession)   Ku Inc. uses the instalment sales method in accounting for its instalment sales. On January 1, 2005, Ku had an instalment account receivable from Kristopher King with a balance of $1,800. During 2005, $400 was collected from King. When no further collection could be made, the merchandise sold to King was repossessed. The merchandise had a fair market value of $650 after the company spent $60 for reconditioning the merchandise. The merchandise was originally sold with a gross profit rate of 40%.

Instructions

Prepare the entries on the books of Ku to record all transactions related to King during 2005. (Ignore interest charges.)

E6-20   (Cost Recovery Method)   On January 1, 2005, Richardson Inc. sells 200 acres of farmland for $600,000, taking in exchange a 10% interest-bearing note. Richardson purchased the farmland in 1987 at a cost of $100,000. The note will be paid in three instalments of $241,269 each on December 31, 2005, 2006, and 2007. Collectibility of the note is uncertain; Richardson therefore uses the cost recovery method.

Instructions

Prepare for Richardson a three-year instalment payment schedule (under the cost recovery method) that shows cash collections, deferred interest revenue, instalment receivable balances, unrecovered cost, realized gross profit, and realized interest revenue by year.

*E6-21   (Franchise Entries)   Sage Inc. charges an initial franchise fee of $170,000. Upon signing the agreement, a payment of $50,000 is due; thereafter, three annual payments of $40,000 are required. The franchisee's credit rating is such that it would have to pay interest at 10% to borrow money.

Instructions

Prepare the entries to record the initial franchise fee on the franchiser's books under the following assumptions.

   (a) The down payment is not refundable, no future services are required by the franchiser, and collection of the note is reasonably assured.

   (b) The franchiser has substantial services to perform, the down payment is refundable, and the collection of the note is very uncertain.

   (c) The down payment is not refundable, collection of the note is reasonably certain, the franchiser has yet to perform a substantial amount of services, and the down payment represents a fair measure of the services already performed.

*E6-22   (Franchise Fee, Initial Down Payment)   On January 1, 2005, Susan Sali signed an agreement to operate as a franchisee of Short-Track Inc. for an initial franchise fee of $150,000. The amount of $30,000 was paid when the agreement was signed, and the balance is payable in six annual payments of $20,000 each, beginning January 1, 2006. The agreement provides that the down payment is not refundable and that no future services are required of the franchiser. Sali's credit rating indicates that she can borrow money at 11% for a loan of this type.

Instructions

(a) How much should Short-Track record as revenue from franchise fees on January 1, 2005? At what amount should Sali record the franchise acquisition cost on January 1, 2005?

(b) What entry would be made by Short-Track on January 1, 2005 if the down payment is refundable and substantial future services remain to be performed by Short-Track?

(c) How much revenue from franchise fees would be recorded by Short-Track on January 1, 2005, if:

1. The initial down payment is not refundable, it represents a fair measure of the services already provided, a significant amount of services is still to be performed by Short-Track in future periods, and collectibility of the note is reasonably assured?

2. The initial down payment is not refundable and no future services are required by the franchiser, but collection of the note is so uncertain that recognition of the note as an asset is unwarranted?

3. The initial down payment has not been earned and collection of the note is so uncertain that recognition of the note as an asset is unwarranted?

E6-23   (Consignment Calculations)   On May 3, 2004, Branzei Limited consigned 70 freezers, costing $500 each, to Martino Inc. The cost of shipping the freezers amounted to $840 and was paid by Branzei. On December 30, 2004, an account sales report was received from the consignee, reporting that 40 freezers had been sold for $700 each. Remittance was made by the consignee for the amount due, after deducting a commission of 6%, advertising of $200, and total installation costs of $320 on the freezers sold.

Instructions

(a) Calculate the inventory value of the units unsold in the hands of the consignee.

(b) Calculate the profit for the consignor for the units sold.

(c) Calculate the amount of cash that will be remitted by the consignee.

Problems

P6-1   Dunbar Construction Ltd. has entered into a contract beginning January 1, 2005 to build a parking complex. It has been estimated that the complex will cost $6 million and will take three years to construct.

The complex will be billed to the purchasing company at $9 million. The following data pertain to the construction period.

	2005	2006	2007
Costs to date	$2,070,000	$4,020,000	$6,600,000
Estimated costs to complete	4,000,000	2,180,000	–0–
Progress billings to date	2,000,000	6,300,000	9,000,000
Cash collected to date	1,040,000	5,000,000	9,000,000

Instructions

(a) Using the percentage-of-completion method, calculate the estimated gross profit that would be recognized during each year of the construction period.

(b) Using the completed-contract method, calculate the estimated gross profit that would be recognized during each year of the construction period.

P6-2   On March 1, 2004, Stevens Inc. entered into a contract to build an apartment building. It is estimated that the building will cost $82 million and will take three years to complete. The contract price was $123 million. The following information pertains to the construction period.

	2004	2005	2006
Costs to date	$36,600,000	$66,560,000	$92,100,000
Estimated costs to complete	50,400,000	36,390,000	–0–
Progress billings to date	31,050,000	80,100,000	123,000,000
Cash collected to date	29,950,000	77,950,000	123,000,000

Instructions

(a) Calculate the amount of gross profit to be recognized each year assuming the percentage-of-completion method is used.

(b) Prepare all necessary journal entries for 2006.

(c) Prepare a partial balance sheet for December 31, 2005, showing the balances in the receivables and inventory accounts.

P6-3   On February 1, 2005, Romance Inc. obtained a contract to build an athletic stadium. The stadium was to be built at a total cost of $15.4 million and was scheduled for completion by September 1, 2007. One clause of the contract stated that Romance was to deduct $105,000 from the $15.4 million billing price for each week that completion was delayed. Completion was delayed six weeks, which resulted in a $630,000 penalty. Below are the data pertaining to the construction period.

	2005	2006	2007
Costs to date	$3,782,000	$8,850,000	$10,500,000
Estimated costs to complete	7,618,000	1,450,000	–0–
Progress billings to date	5,200,000	10,100,000	14,770,000
Cash collected to date	4,000,000	9,800,000	14,770,000

Instructions

(a) Using the percentage-of-completion method, calculate the estimated gross profit recognized in the years 2005 to 2007.

(b) Prepare a partial balance sheet for December 31, 2006, showing the balances in the receivable and inventory accounts.

P6-4   Zheng Inc. was established in 1972 by Tian Zheng and initially built high quality customized homes under contract with specific buyers. In the 1980s, Zheng's two sons joined the firm and expanded the company's activities into the high-rise apartment and industrial plant markets. Upon the retirement of the company's long-time financial manager, Zheng's sons hired Lance Ling as controller. Ling, a former university friend of Zheng's sons, has been working for a public accounting firm for the last six years.

Upon reviewing the company's accounting practices, Ling observed that the company followed the completed-contract method of revenue recognition, a carryover from the years when individual home building was the majority of the company's operations. Several years ago, the predominant portion of the company's activities shifted to the high-rise and industrial building areas. From land acquisition to the completion of construction, most building contracts cover several years. Under the circumstances, Ling believes that the company should follow the percentage-of-completion method of accounting. From a typical building contract, Ling developed the following data.

Zheng Inc.

Contract price: $10,000,000

	2004	2005	2006
Estimated costs	$2,010,000	$4,015,000	$1,675,000
Progress billings	2,000,000	2,500,000	5,500,000
Cash collections	1,800,000	2,300,000	5,900,000

Instructions

(a) Explain the difference between completed-contract revenue recognition and percentage-of-completion revenue recognition.

(b) Using the data provided for the Zheng Inc. and assuming the percentage-of-completion method of revenue recognition is used, calculate the company's revenue and gross profit for 2004, 2005, and 2006, under each of the following circumstances.

   1.   Assume that all costs are incurred, all billings to customers are made, and all collections from customers are received within 30 days of billing, as planned.

2. Further assume that, as a result of unforeseen local ordinances and the fact that the building site was in a wetlands area, the company experienced cost overruns of $1.2 million in 2004 to bring the site into compliance with the ordinances and to overcome wetlands barriers to construction.

3. Further assume that, in addition to the cost overruns of $1.2 million for this contract incurred under Instruction (b)2., inflationary factors over and above those anticipated when developing the original contract cost have caused an additional cost overrun of $1,240,000 in 2005. It is not anticipated that any cost overruns will occur in 2006.

(CMA adapted)

P6-5 On March 1, 2005, Whellan Limited contracted to construct a factory building for Vottero Manufacturing Inc. for a total contract price of $9.4 million. The building was completed by October 31, 2007. The annual contract costs incurred, estimated costs to complete the contract, and accumulated billings to Vottero for 2005, 2006, and 2007 are given below.

	2005	2006	2007
Contract costs incurred during the year	$3,600,000	$3,900,000	$1,250,000
Estimated costs to complete the contract at 12/31	4,200,000	1,200,000	–0–
Billings to Vottero during the year	3,200,000	3,500,000	2,700,000

Instructions

(a) Using the percentage-of-completion method, prepare schedules to calculate the profit or loss to be recognized as a result of this contract for the years ended December 31, 2005, 2006, and 2007. (Ignore income taxes.)

(b) Using the completed-contract method, prepare schedules to calculate the profit or loss to be recognized as a result of this contract for the years ended December 2005, 2006, and 2007. (Ignore income taxes.)

P6-6 On July 1, 2005, Wang Construction Company Inc. contracted to build an office building for Zhou Corp. for a total contract price of $1,850,000. On July 1, Wang estimated that it would take between two and three years to complete the building. On December 31, 2007, the building was deemed substantially completed. Following are accumulated contract costs incurred, estimated costs to complete the contract, and accumulated billings to Zhou for 2005, 2006, and 2007.

	12/31/05	12/31/06	12/31/07
Contract costs incurred to date	$ 450,000	$1,200,000	$1,900,000
Estimated costs to complete the contract	1,350,000	800,000	–0–
Billings to Zhou	1,300,000	2,100,000	2,950,000

Instructions

(a) Using the percentage-of-completion method, prepare schedules to calculate the profit or loss to be recognized as a result of this contract for the years ended December 31, 2005, 2006, and 2007. (Ignore income taxes.)

(b) Using the completed-contract method, prepare schedules to calculate the profit or loss to be recognized as a result of this contract for the years ended December 2005, 2006, and 2007. (Ignore income taxes.)

P6-7 Presented below is summarized information for Deng Corp., which sells merchandise on the instalment basis.

	2004	2005	2006
Sales (on instalment plan)	$350,000	$360,000	$280,000
Cost of sales	250,000	263,800	182,000
Gross	100,000	$ 96,200	$ 98,000
Collections from customers on:			
2004 instalment sales	$175,000	$100,000	$75,000
2005 instalment sales		200,000	120,000
2006 instalment sales			110,000

Instructions

(a) Calculate the realized gross profit for each of the years 2004, 2005, and 2006.

(b) Prepare in journal form all entries required in 2006, applying the instalment sales method of accounting. (Ignore interest charges.)

P6-8 Spearing Inc. sells merchandise on open account as well as on instalment terms.

	2005	2006	2007
Sales on account	$770,000	$426,000	$625,000
Instalment sales	640,000	275,000	480,000
Collections on instalment sales			
Made in 2005	220,000	90,000	80,000
Made in 2006		110,000	140,000
Made in 2007			125,000
Cost of sales			
Sold on account	540,000	277,000	441,000
Sold on instalment	428,800	167,750	224,200
Selling expenses	154,000	87,000	102,000
Administrative expenses	100,000	51,000	52,000

Instructions

From the data above, which cover the three years since Spearing Inc. commenced operations, determine the net income for each year, applying the instalment sales method of accounting. (Ignore interest charges.)

P6-9 Shao Limited sells appliances for cash and also on the instalment plan. Entries to record cost of sales are made monthly.

SHAO LIMITED
Trial Balance
December 31, 2005

	Dr.	Cr.
Cash	$153,000	
Instalment Accounts Receivable, 2004	48,000	
Instalment Accounts Receivable, 2005	91,000	
Inventory New Merchandise	123,200	
Inventory Repossessed Merchandise	24,000	
Accounts Payable		$98,500
Deferred Gross Profit, 2004		45,600
Capital Shares		170,000
Retained Earnings		93,900
Sales		343,000
Instalment Sales		200,000
Cost of Sales	255,000	
Cost of Instalment Sales	128,000	
Gain or Loss on Repossessions	800	
Selling and Administrative Expenses	128,000	
	$951,000	$951,000

The accounting department has prepared the following analysis of cash receipts for the year.

Cash sales (including repossessed merchandise)	$424,000
Instalment accounts receivable, 2004	104,000
Instalment accounts receivable, 2005	109,000
Other	36,000
Total	$673,000

Repossessions recorded during the year are summarized as follows.

	2004
Uncollected balance	$8,000
Loss on repossession	800
Repossessed merchandise	4,800

Instructions

From the trial balance and accompanying information:

(a) Calculate the rate of gross profit for 2004 and 2005.

(b) Prepare journal entries as of December 31, 2005 to record any deferred and/or realized profits under the instalment sales method of accounting.

(c) Prepare a statement of income for the year ended December 31, 2005, after booking the journal noted in (b).

P6-10 The following summarized information relates to the instalment sales activity of Greenwood Inc. for the year 2004.

Instalment sales during 2004	$500,000
Costs of goods sold on instalment basis	330,000
Collections from customers	200,000
Unpaid balances on merchandise repossessed	24,000
Estimated value of merchandise repossessed	9,200

Instructions

(a) Prepare journal entries at the end of 2004 to record on the books of Greenwood the summarized data above.

(b) Prepare the entry to record the gross profit realized during 2004.

P6-11 Racine Inc. sells merchandise for cash and also on the instalment plan. Entries to record cost of goods sold are made at the end of each year.

Repossessions of merchandise (sold in 2004) were made in 2005 and were recorded correctly as follows.

Deferred Gross Profit, 2004	7,200	
Repossessed Merchandise	8,000	
Loss on Repossessions	2,800	
Instalment Accounts Receivable, 2004		18,000

Part of this repossessed merchandise was sold for cash during 2005, and the sale was recorded by a debit to Cash and a credit to Sales.

The inventory of repossessed merchandise on hand December 31, 2005 is $4,000; of new merchandise, $127,400. There was no repossessed merchandise on hand January 1, 2005.

Collections on accounts receivable during 2005 were:

Instalment Accounts Receivable, 2004	$80,000
Instalment Accounts Receivable, 2005	50,000

The cost of the merchandise sold under the instalment plan during 2005 was $117,000.

The rate of gross profit on 2004 and on 2005 instalment sales can be calculated from the information given above.

RACINE INC.
Trial Balance
December 31, 2005

	Dr.	Cr.
Cash	$ 98,400	
Instalment Accounts Receivable, 2004	80,000	
Instalment Accounts Receivable, 2005	130,000	
Inventory, Jan. 1, 2005	120,000	
Repossessed Merchandise	8,000	
Accounts Payable		$ 47,200
Deferred Gross Profit, 2004		64,000
Common Shares		200,000
Retained Earnings		40,000
Sales		400,000
Instalment Sales		180,000
Purchases	380,000	
Loss on Repossessions		2,800
Operating Expenses	112,000	
	$931,200	$931,200

Instructions

(a) From the trial balance and other information given above, prepare adjusting and closing entries as of December 31, 2005.

(b) Prepare an income statement for the year ended December 31, 2005.

P6-12 Selected transactions of Liping Limited are presented below.

1. A television set costing $560 is sold to Wycliffe on November 1, 2004 for $800. Wycliffe makes a down payment of $200 and agrees to pay $30 on the first of each month for 20 months thereafter.

2. Wycliffe pays the $30 instalment due December 1, 2004.

3. On December 31, 2004, the appropriate entries are made to record profit realized on the instalment sales.

4. The first seven 2005 instalments of $30 each are paid by Wycliffe. (Make one entry.)

5. In August 2005, the set is repossessed after Wycliffe fails to pay the August 1 instalment and indicates that he will be unable to continue the payments. The estimated fair value of the repossessed set is $100.

Instructions

Prepare journal entries to record on the books of Liping Limited the transactions above. Closing entries should not be made.

P6-13 Truong Inc., on January 2, 2004, entered into a contract with a manufacturing company to purchase room-size air conditioners and to sell the units on an instalment plan with collections over approximately 30 months with no carrying charge.

For income tax purposes Truong elected to report income from its sales of air conditioners according to the instalment sales method.

Purchases and sales of new units were as follows.

	Units Purchased			Units Sold	
Year	Quantity	Price Each		Quantity	Price Each
2004	1,400	$130		1,100	$200
2005	1,200	112		1,500	170
2006	900	136		800	182

Collections on instalment sales were as follows.

	Collections Received		
	2004	2005	2006
2004 sales	$42,000	$88,000	$ 80,000
2005 sales		51,000	100,000
2006 sales			34,600

In 2006, 50 units from the 2005 sales were repossessed and sold for $80 each on the instalment plan. At the time of repossession, $1,440 had been collected from the original purchasers and the units had a fair value of $3,000.

General and administrative expenses for 2006 were $60,000. No charge has been made against current income for the applicable insurance expense from a three-year policy expiring June 30, 2007, costing $7,200, and for an advance payment of $12,000 on a new contract to purchase air conditioners beginning January 2, 2007.

Instructions

Assuming that the weighted-average method is used for determining the inventory cost, including repossessed merchandise, prepare schedules calculating for 2004, 2005, and 2006:

(a) 1. The cost of goods sold on instalments.

    2. The average unit cost of goods sold on instalments for each year.

(b) The gross profit percentages for 2004, 2005, and 2006.

(c) The gain or loss on repossessions in 2006.

(d) The net income from instalment sales for 2006 (ignore income taxes).

(AICPA adapted)

P6-14 Mahaher Inc. entered into a firm fixed-price contract with Nobes Clinic on July 1, 2002, to construct a four-storey office building. At that time, Mahaher estimated that it would take between two and three years to complete the project. The total contract price to construct the building is $5.5 million. Mahaher appropriately accounts for this contract under the completed-contract method in its financial statements and for income tax reporting. The building was deemed substantially completed on December 31, 2004.

Estimated percentage of completion, accumulated contract costs incurred, estimated costs to complete the contract, and accumulated billings to the clinic under the contract were as follows.

	December 31, 2002	December 31, 2003	December 31, 2004
Percentage of completion	30%	71.1%	100%
Contract costs incurred to date	$1,140,000	$4,055,000	$5,800,000
Estimated costs to complete the contract	$2,660,000	$1,645,000	–0–
Billings to Nobes Clinic	$1,500,000	$2,500,000	$5,500,000

Instructions

(a) Prepare schedules to calculate the amount to be shown as cost of uncompleted contract in excess of related billings or billings on uncompleted contract in excess of related costs at December 31, 2002, 2003, and 2004. Ignore income taxes. Show supporting calculations in good form.

(b) Prepare schedules to calculate the profit or loss to be recognized as a result of this contract for the years ended December 31, 2002, 2003, and 2004. Ignore income taxes. Show supporting calculations in good form.

(AICPA adapted)

P6-15   You have been engaged by Shen Corp. to advise it concerning the proper accounting for a series of long-term contracts. Shen commenced doing business on January 1, 2004. Construction activities for the first year of operations are shown below. All contract costs are with different customers, and any work remaining at December 31, 2004 is expected to be completed in 2005.

Project	Total Contract Price	Billings Through 12/31/04	Cash Collections Through 12/31/04	Contract Costs Incurred Through 12/31/04	Estimated Additional Costs to Complete
A	$ 300,000	$200,000	$180,000	$248,000	$ 67,000
B	350,000	110,000	105,000	67,800	271,200
C	280,000	280,000	255,000	186,000	–0–
D	200,000	35,000	25,000	123,000	87,000
E	240,000	205,000	200,000	185,000	15,000
	$1,370,000	$830,000	$765,000	$809,800	$440,200

Instructions

(a) Prepare a schedule to calculate gross profit (loss) to be reported, unbilled contract costs and recognized profit, and billings in excess of costs and recognized profit using the percentage-of-completion method.

(b) Prepare a partial income statement and balance sheet to indicate how the information would be reported for financial statement purposes.

(c) Repeat the requirements for part (a) assuming Shen uses the completed-contract method.

(d) Using the responses above for illustrative purposes, prepare a brief report comparing the conceptual merits (both positive and negative) of the two revenue recognition approaches.

Writing Assignments

WA-1   Revenue is usually recognized at the point of delivery. Under special circumstances, however, bases other than the point of delivery are used for the timing of revenue recognition.

Instructions

(a) Why is the point of delivery usually used as the basis for the timing of revenue recognition?

(b) Disregarding the special circumstances when bases other than the point of delivery are used, discuss the merits of each of the following objections to using the point of delivery of revenue recognition.

1.   It is too conservative because revenue is earned throughout the entire process of production.

2.   It is not conservative enough because accounts receivable do not represent disposable funds, sales returns and allowances may be made, and collection and bad debt expenses may be incurred in a later period.

(c) Revenue may also be recognized (1) during production and (2) when cash is received. For each of these two bases of timing revenue recognition, give an example of the circumstances in which it is properly used and discuss the accounting merits of its use in lieu of the sales basis.

(AICPA adapted)

WA-2 The earning of revenue by a business enterprise is recognized for accounting purposes when the transaction is recorded. In some situations, revenue is recognized approximately as it is earned in the economic sense. In other situations, however, accountants have developed guidelines for recognizing revenue by other criteria, such as at the point of delivery.

Instructions
(Ignore income taxes)

(a) Explain and justify why revenue is often recognized as it is earned.

(b) Explain in what situations it would be appropriate to recognize revenue as the productive activity takes place.

(c) At what times, other than those included in (a) and (b) above, may it be appropriate to recognize revenue? Explain.

Cases

Refer to the Case Primer on the Digital Tool to help you answer these cases.

Digital Tool
www.wiley.com/
canada/kieso

CA6-1 Alexi Industries has three operating divisions: Figaro Mining, Manuel Paperbacks, and Oslo Protection Devices. Each division maintains its own accounting system and method of revenue recognition. During the year, Alexi was running short of cash due to major expansion in Figaro Mining. Problems in the mining industry were also contributing to cash flow difficulties. Due to the buoyancy in the equity markets (markets had reached a 10-year high), prices of commodities such as gold, silver, and platinum were down. As a result, the company had approached the bank for a line of credit. Prior to making any adjustments, the company's draft financial statements are showing a break-even net income. The following information is available regarding each of the three operating divisions.

Figaro Mining
Figaro Mining specializes in the extraction of precious metals such as silver, gold, and platinum. During the fiscal year ended November 30, 2004, Figaro entered into contracts worth $2,250,000 and shipped metals worth $2 million. A quarter of the shipments were made from inventories on hand at the beginning of the fiscal year while the remainder were made from metals that were mined during the year. Mining production totals for the year, valued at market prices, were: silver at $750,000, gold at $1.3 million, and platinum at $490,000. Figaro uses the completion-of-production method to recognize revenue.

Manuel Paperbacks
Manuel Paperbacks sells large quantities of novels to a few book distributors that in turn sell to several national chains of bookstores. Manuel allows distributors to return up to 30% of sales, and distributors give the same terms to bookstores. While returns from individual titles fluctuate greatly, the returns from distributors have averaged 20% in each of the past five years. A total of $8 million of paperback novel sales were made to distributors during the fiscal year. On November 30, 2004, $3.2 million of fiscal 2004 sales were still subject to return privileges over the next six months. The remaining $4.8 million of fiscal 2004 sales had actual returns of 21%. Sales from fiscal 2004 totalling $2.5 million were collected in fiscal 2004, with less than 18% of sales returned. Manuel records revenue at the point of sale.

Oslo Protection Devices
Oslo Protection Devices works through manufacturers' agents in various cities. Orders and down payments for alarm systems are forwarded from agents, and Oslo ships the goods f.o.b. shipping point. Customers are billed for the balance due plus actual shipping costs. The firm received orders for $6 million of goods during the fiscal year ended November 30, 2004. Down payments of $600,000 were received, and $5 million of goods were billed and shipped. Actual freight costs of $100,000 were also billed. Commissions of 10% on product price were paid to manufacturers' agents after the goods were shipped to customers. Such goods are warranted for 90 days after shipment, and warranty returns have been about 1% of sales. Revenue is recognized at the point of sale by Oslo.

Instructions
Assume the role of the assistant controller and prepare a report to the controller discussing any financial reporting issues. The controller needs this information prior to his upcoming meeting with the bank. He does not want any unpleasant surprises in the meeting.

CA6-2   Points International Ltd. ("Points") was formed on January 6, 1999 and currently trades on the TSX Venture Exchange. Sales in 2002 were $2.4 million, with the Toronto-based company experiencing revenue growth of 240% over the prior year. Points is an on-line exchange that allows customers to combine, exchange, and purchase points or miles from various loyalty programs such as Aeroplan, American Airlines, ebay, and Priority Club. In its annual report, the company commented on the growth potential in the industry, noting that according to *The Economist*, global frequent flyer points are now worth approximately $500 billion (U.S.) (with about 8.5 trillion unredeemed miles) and that frequent flyer points are arguably the second largest currency, after the U.S. dollar.

The company partners with several major airlines such as Air Canada and American Airlines and as such, its business is susceptible to fluctuations in the airline industry. Points has dealt with this by facilitating the exchange of airline points for retail points and the consolidation of points from various different programs.

The following excerpts from the company's Annual Information Form (filed with the securities commission) and Annual Report detail the earnings process and related revenue recognition policy.

According to the company's Annual Information Form:

"Revenue from the online exchange:

Commission fee revenue: Points retains a commission on all exchanges, based on a value of the loyalty currency tendered for exchange by the loyalty program member. Through the exchange model, the participating loyalty program sets a value on the currency tendered for "sale". Based on this valuation, a percentage is remitted to Points, and the remaining balance is used to purchase a currency of another participating loyalty program. The Corporation filed a U.S. Patent Application covering this exchange process.

Consumer exchange fees: The payment by a customer of an annual fee allows unlimited *pointsxchange* transactions. Alternately, customers can pay a service fee for a single exchange."

According to note 2 of the 2002 Annual Financial Statements:

"Revenue recognition

Revenues from transaction processing are recognized as the services are provided under the terms of related contracts. Membership fees received in advance for services to be provided over a future period are recorded as deferred revenue and recognized as revenue evenly over the term of service. Related direct costs are also recognized over the term of the membership.

Revenues from the sales of loyalty program points are recorded net of costs, in accordance with Abstract 123 of the Emerging Issues Committee ("EIC") of the Canadian Institute of Chartered Accountants ("C.I.C.A."), "Reporting Revenue Gross as a Principal Versus Net as an Agent", when the collection of the sales proceeds is reasonably assured and other material conditions of the exchange are met. Gross proceeds received on the resale of loyalty program points, net of the commissions earned, are included in deposits in the attached consolidated balance sheet until remitted.

Nonrefundable partner sign-up fees with no fixed term, and for which the company is under no further obligations, are recognized as revenue when received.

Custom web site design revenues are recorded on the percentage-of-completion basis."

Although the company's revenues increased substantially in 2002, the company suffered a loss of over three times revenues. This loss was $3.3 million less than the loss from 2001.

Instructions
Assume the role of a financial analyst and critically analyse the revenue recognition policies. You are trying to establish whether you should issue a buy or sell order on these shares.

CA6-3   *Cutting Edge* is a monthly magazine that has been on the market for 18 months. It has a circulation of 1.4 million copies. Negotiations are underway to obtain a bank loan in order to update its facilities. It is producing close to capacity and expects to grow at an average of 20% per year over the next three years.

After reviewing the financial statements of *Cutting Edge*, Gary Hall, the bank loan officer, had indicated that a loan could be offered to *Cutting Edge* only if it could increase its current ratio and decrease its debt-to-equity ratio to a specified level.

Alexander Popov, the marketing manager of *Cutting Edge*, has devised a plan to meet these requirements. Popov indicates that an advertising campaign can be initiated to immediately increase circulation. The potential customers would be contacted after the purchase of another magazine's mailing list. The campaign would include:

1. An offer to subscribe to *Cutting Edge* at three quarters the normal price.

2. A special offer to all new subscribers to receive the most current world atlas whenever requested at a guaranteed price of $2.00.

3. An unconditional guarantee that any subscriber will receive a full refund if dissatisfied with the magazine.

Although the offer of a full refund is risky, Popov claims that few people will ask for a refund after receiving half of their subscription issues. Popov notes that other magazine companies have tried this sales promotion technique and experienced great success. Their average cancellation rate was 25%. On average, each company increased its initial circulation threefold and in the long run had increased circulation to twice that before the promotion. In addition, 60% of the new subscribers are expected to take advantage of the atlas premium. Popov feels confident that the increased subscriptions from the advertising campaign will increase the current ratio and decrease the debt-to-equity ratio.

You are *Cutting Edge*'s controller and must give your opinion of the proposed plan.

Instructions
Discuss the issues.

CA6-4 Pankratov Lakes is a new recreational real estate development that consists of 500 lakefront and lakeview lots. As a special incentive to the first 100 buyers of lakeview lots, the developer is offering three years of free financing on 10-year, 12% notes, no down payment, and one week at a nearby established resort (a $1,200 value). The normal price per lot is $12,000. The cost per lakeview lot to the developer is an estimated average of $2,000. The development costs continue to be incurred; the actual average cost per lot is not known at this time. The resort promotion cost is $700 per lot.

Instructions
Discuss the issues.

CA6-5 Nimble Health and Racquet Club (NHRC), which operates eight clubs in the metropolitan area of a large city, offers one-year memberships. The members may use any of the eight facilities but must reserve racquetball court time and pay a separate fee before using the court. As an incentive to new customers, NHRC advertised that any customers not satisfied for any reason could receive a refund of the remaining portion of unused membership fees. Membership fees are due at the beginning of the individual membership period; however, customers are given the option of financing the membership fee over the membership period at a 15% interest rate.

Some customers have expressed a desire to take only the regularly scheduled aerobic classes without paying for a full membership. During the current fiscal year, NHRC began selling coupon books for aerobic classes only to accommodate these customers. Each book is dated and contains 50 coupons that may be redeemed for any regularly scheduled aerobic class over a one-year period. After the one-year period, unused coupons are no longer valid.

During 2000, NHRC expanded into the health equipment market by purchasing a local company that manufactures rowing machines and cross-country ski machines. These machines are used in NHRC's facilities and are sold through the clubs and mail order catalogues. Customers must make a 20% downpayment when placing an equipment order; delivery is 60-90 days after order placement. The machines are sold with a two-year unconditional guarantee. Based on experience, NHRC expects the costs to repair machines under guarantee to be 4% of sales.

NHRC is in the process of preparing financial statements as of May 31, 2005, the end of its fiscal year. James Hogan, corporate controller, expressed concern over the company's performance for the year and decided to review the preliminary financial statements prepared by Barbara Hardy, NHRC's assistant controller. After reviewing the statements, Hogan proposed that the following changes be reflected in the May 31, 2005 published financial statements.

1. Membership revenue should be recognized when the membership fee is collected.

2. Revenue from the coupon books should be recognized when the books are sold.

3. Down payments on equipment purchases and expenses associated with the guarantee on the rowing and cross-country machines should be recognized when paid.

Hardy indicated to Hogan that the proposed changes are not in accordance with generally accepted accounting principles, but Hogan insisted that the changes be made. Hardy believes that Hogan wants to manipulate income to forestall any potential financial problems and increase his year-end bonus. At this point, Hardy is unsure what action to take.

Instructions
Discuss the financial reporting issues.

(CMA adapted)

CA6-6   The following is an excerpt from the financial statements of the Saskatchewan Wheat Pool. Among other things, the Wheat Pool buys grain from farmers and sells it to the Canadian Wheat Board.

"Notes to the Consolidated Financial Statements July 31, 2002, in thousands

Revenue Recognition

Generally, sales are recognized upon shipment of products and other operating revenues are recognized when services are performed. A large portion of the company's Grain Handling and Marketing segment revenue is derived from Canadian Wheat Board ("Board") grains. The company assumes the risk of physical loss, while promoting the value of grain deliveries through blending and cleaning. Consequently, the value of Board grains handled is recorded as a sale, and the sale is recognized when it is delivered to the Board, typically at a port terminal. Other grain handling revenues are recognized when functions are performed in accordance with the company's contract with the Board. In the case of non-Board grains, sales are recognized when grain is shipped from the company's country or port terminals, or on transfer of ownership.

Changes in Accounting Policies—prior year 2001

The company changed its revenue recognition method for receipts of grain at its country elevators. Previously, the company's policy was to recognize a portion of the grain handling revenue as earned when grain was received and recognize the balance when grain was shipped. The new revenue recognition method recognized all of these revenues when the grain is shipped or title transfers to the customer. The effect of the change resulted in a $2.1 million after-tax increase to fiscal 2001 earnings. The cumulative effect of this change on prior year financial statements was to decrease retained earnings by $6.0 million."

The Wheat Pool had experienced two years of drought in its primary operating area and there were concerns about its ability to meet upcoming principal payments on debt. At the end of 2002, the company was experiencing cash outflows from operating activities and its 2002 loss of $92 million was more than double its loss from the prior year.

Instructions

$150 million worth of debt is coming due in 2004. Adopt the role of the creditors and discuss the financial reporting issues.

Integrated Case

Treetop Pharmaceuticals (TP) is in the business of research, development, and production of over the counter pharmaceuticals. During the year, it acquired 100% of the net assets of Treeroot Drugs Limited (TDL) for $200 million. The fair value of the identifiable assets at the time of purchase was $150 million (which included $120 million for patents). The company plans to sell the patents to a third party at the end of seven years even though at that time, the remaining legal life of the patent will be five years. TP already has a commitment from a specific third party that has agreed to pay $50 million for the patents (in seven years).

In January, in an unrelated deal, the company acquired a trademark that has a remaining legal life of three years. The trademark is renewable every 10 years at little cost. TP is unsure as to whether it will renew the trademark or not.

Given these two acquisitions, TP has been a bit short of cash and has entered into the following arrangement with Drug Development Corporation (DDC). DDC paid $30 million to TP upfront when the contract was signed. Under the contract terms, the money is to be used to develop drugs as well as new channels to distribute them. TP has already spent a considerable portion of this money. TP has agreed that it will pay DDC 2% of the revenues from the subsequent sale of the drugs (which are close to the point of commercial production).

Given the cash shortage, the company has also entered into negotiations with the bank to increase its line of credit. The bank has expressed concern about the company's liquidity. TP's top management has graciously agreed to take stock options in lieu of any bonuses or raises for the next two years in order to ease cash flow constraints.

It is now year-end and TP is looking at issuing its financial statements. Of concern is the fact that one of TDL's major competitors has just come out with several new drugs that will compete directly with the drugs that TDL sells. Management is concerned that this may severely erode the market for TDL's products. As a matter of fact, TP has had preliminary meetings to discuss selling TDL and has contacted a consultant to help find a buyer.

Jack Kimble, the controller, is preparing for a planning meeting with TP's auditors. The auditors are currently analysing the draft financial statements to identify critical and high risk areas. The draft financial statements are showing the company barely breaking even. The chief financial officer has commented that the company's share price is likely to "take a tumble" given that the company has always been profitable in prior years and since the company's competitors seem to be doing well. Kimble is debating how to deal with the latest news from TP's lawyers. Apparently, the company is being sued in a class action lawsuit (i.e., by a significant number of people) for illness allegedly caused by one of TP's main pharmaceutical products. The claim is equal to revenues from last year. At this point, the lawyers have a concern that the case may be successful against TP but are having trouble trying to estimate the potential loss to the company.

Instructions:
Adopt the role of the controller and prepare an analysis of all the financial reporting issues facing TP.

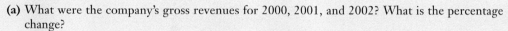

Research and Financial Analysis

RA 6-1   Barrick Gold Corporation

Barrick Gold Corporation has its head office located in Toronto. Its shares trade on the NYSE and TSX as well as others.

Instructions
Refer to the financial statements and accompanying notes in the Digital Tool and answer the following questions.

(a) What were the company's gross revenues for 2000, 2001, and 2002? What is the percentage change?

(b) Given your findings in (a), comment on the net income/loss of the company over the three-year period.

(c) Review the notes to the financial statements to determine the company's revenue recognition policy. Discuss, relating to the nature of the business and the industry. Comment on the switch in accounting policy.

(d) The company uses the U.S. dollar to present its Canadian financial statements on the basis that most of the activities take place in the United States or in U.S. dollars. Substantiate this by giving evidence from the financial statements.

(e) Even though this is a Canadian company, its primary financial statements are prepared according to U.S. GAAP. Why do you suppose it chooses to have its main financial statements according to U.S. GAAP and to downplay the Canadian GAAP financial statements? (Hint: Read the notes to the financial statements for both the U.S. GAAP and Canadian GAAP statements.)

RA6-2   Sears Canada Inc. and Hudson's Bay Company

Sears Canada Inc. and the Hudson's Bay Company are two major retailers in North America. They both have significant presence in Canada. Hbc's business strategy (through Zellers) is high volume, low cost. Sears' emphasis is on higher price, higher end products.

Instructions
Using the annual reports on the Digital Tool, answer the following.

(a) Calculate the "Earnings before interest and taxes" to "sales" percentage for each company for the most recent two years. Comment on the trend.

(b) Identify any significant or unusual items that are affecting your calculations. Recalculate the percentage.

(c) Which strategy appears to be more successful? Consider the economic environment.

(d) Compare the income statements for each company for the most current year. Comment on their comparability.

RA6-3   IASB

As capital markets become more global, accounting standards in the countries where the major capital markets exist are converging.

Instructions
Go to the International Accounting Standards Board website (www.iasb.org) and research the current project on revenue recognition. Compare and contrast the proposed standard with the Canadian standards (*CICA Handbook* 3400).

RA6-4   Qwest Communications International

There have been a significant number of cases, particularly in the United States where companies have overstated their revenues in the past several years. The Securities and Exchange Commission (SEC) has been vigilant in tracking these cases down. Qwest Communications International is one such case where the revenues were misstated in numerous instances.

Instructions

There are various sources available that deal with the misstatements. Research the issue by visiting the company website (www.qwest.com) and the SEC website (www.sec.gov).

List and quantify the main types of misstatements related to revenues. Discuss the way the company had treated the revenues originally and after restatement. How is it possible that the auditors gave the company a clean audit opinion originally?

Sales Factor

For its first 17 or so years, Montreal-based Hollywood Jeans insured receipt of payment by using factors, finance companies that provide insurance on any receivables. But the 22-year-old denim design manufacturer found the cost of factoring was beginning to outweigh its benefits.

With the changing retail landscape and the consolidation of many factoring companies, the criteria for covering a company's receivables became more stringent. "We found the total annual cost [of factoring] exceeded our true losses," says Allen Gauthier, vice-president, sales. "After a thorough analysis of our receivables' performances, we discovered that, with a strong credit team, good prior investigation, and a continuous investigation process, the total cost of maintaining a support staff in the department would be less than the factoring costs."

Hollywood Jeans still uses Export Development Canada (EDC) to factor United States-based accounts, but its in-house credit staff handles all other accounts. Like its previous arrangements with other factors, the EDC factoring is for insurance purposes only, not for capital purposes.

Although factoring is not cost-effective for Hollywood Jeans, Gauthier says the arrangement is essential for new companies, unless they have access to a significant amount of capital. "In the apparel industry, it's dangerous from an account perspective. You've bought the material, you've done the sewing, and sent the shipment. Everything's been paid for, but you're waiting for your money, sometimes up to 90 days."

Even though factors may have deemed the apparel industry high-risk, Gauthier says, if collecting receivables becomes high-risk in other businesses, it is probably the result of poor preparation. He describes some companies as putting blinders on to possible credit risk when they hold a super sale.

"Our company philosophy is, 'It's only a sale when the money is in our bank.'"■

Cash, Temporary Investments, and Receivables

Preview of Chapter 7

The purpose of this chapter is to discuss the most liquid of financial assets—cash, temporary investments, and receivables. The accounting standards associated with financial instruments are in the midst of change, so the coverage of temporary investments in this chapter reflects the standards in proposed *Handbook* Section 3855, effective in 2005. Chapter 10 describes recent progress in moving toward fair value accounting for financial instruments and the appendix to Chapter 10 describes the accounting standards in place as the text went to print. The content and organization of the chapter are as follows:

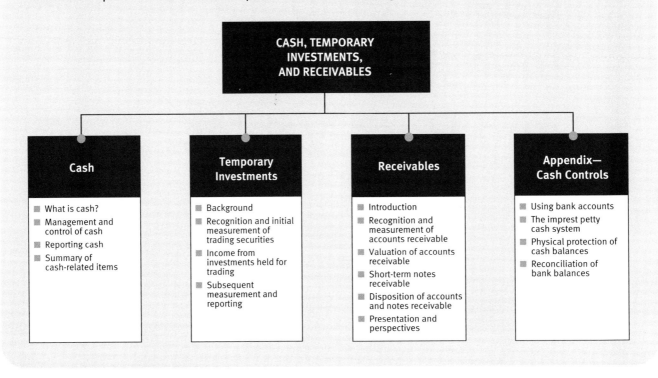

Objective 1
Define financial assets.

As you begin your detailed study of balance sheet accounts and the recognition and measurement concepts applied to each category of asset, liability, and shareholders' equity, the first assets encountered are the most liquid and they are financial assets. A **financial asset** is defined by *CICA Handbook* Section 3860 as "any asset that is:

(i) cash;

(ii) a contractual right to receive cash or another financial asset from another party;

(iii) a contractual right to exchange financial instruments with another party under conditions that are potentially favourable; or

(iv) an equity instrument of another entity."

Financial assets are covered in various chapters throughout this text. Chapter 7 deals with cash, cash equivalents, temporary investments in debt and equity securities, accounts, and short-term notes receivable. Chapter 10 covers longer term investments in loans and receivables, and in debt and equity instruments of other companies. The financial assets in these two chapters meet parts (i), (ii), and (iv) of the definition. The more complex instruments referred to in part (iii) are dealt with in Chapter 17.

The fact that accounting is anything but static is evidenced by the profession's movement from the longstanding transactions-based historical cost model toward one that relies more and more on fair values. Evidence of this is the recent proposal to change to a fair value measurement basis for most financial assets that are not expected to be held to maturity. Watch for references throughout the text to other requirements for the measurement and disclosure of fair values.

SECTION 1—CASH

What is Cash?

Cash, the most liquid of assets, is the standard medium of exchange and the basis for measuring and accounting for all other items. It meets the definition of a financial asset, and is generally classified as a current asset. To be reported as a current asset, it must be readily available to pay current obligations, and it must be free from any contractual restriction that limits its use in satisfying debts.

Cash consists of coin, currency, and available funds on deposit at the bank. Negotiable instruments such as money orders, certified cheques, cashier's cheques, personal cheques, and bank drafts are also viewed as cash. Savings accounts are usually classified as cash, although the bank may have a legal right to demand notice before withdrawal. But because prior notice is rarely demanded by banks, savings accounts are considered cash.

Money market funds, certificates of deposit (CDs), and similar types of deposits and "short-term paper"[1] that provide investors with an opportunity to earn interest are more appropriately classified as **cash equivalents** or **temporary investments** than as cash. The reason is that these securities usually contain restrictions or penalties on their conversion to cash. Money market funds that provide chequing account privileges, however, are usually classified as cash.

Certain items present classification problems: for example, postdated cheques from customers and IOUs are treated as receivables. Travel advances are properly treated as receivables if the advances are to be collected from the employees or deducted from their salaries. Otherwise, classifying the travel advance as a prepaid expense is more appropriate. Postage stamps on hand are classified as part of office supplies inventory or as a prepaid expense. Petty cash funds and change funds are included in current assets as cash because these funds are used to meet current operating expenses and to liquidate current liabilities.

2 Objective
Identify items considered cash and cash equivalents.

Management and Control of Cash

Cash is the asset most susceptible to improper diversion and use. Management must overcome two problems of accounting for cash transactions by (1) establishing proper controls to ensure that no unauthorized transactions are entered into by officers, employees, or others; and (2) providing information necessary to properly manage cash on hand and cash transactions. Yet even with sophisticated control devices, errors can and do happen. *The Wall Street Journal* once ran a story entitled "A $7.8 Million Error Has a Happy Ending for

---

[1] A variety of short-term paper is available for investment. For example, CDs represent formal evidence of indebtedness, issued by a bank. They must usually be held until maturity, although some CDs in excess of $100,000 are negotiable. Guaranteed investment certificates (GICs) are similar time deposits issued by trust companies. The short-term certificates mature in 30 to 360 days and generally pay interest at the short-term rate in effect at the date of issuance. In money market funds, a variation of the mutual fund, the yield is determined by the mix of Treasury bills and commercial paper making up the fund's portfolio. Treasury bills are Canadian government obligations with 3-, 6-, and 12-month maturities; they are sold only in integral multiples of $1,000 (face value) denominations at weekly government auctions. Commercial paper is short-term unsecured debt notes issued by corporations with good credit ratings, usually in minimum denominations of $50,000.

a Horrified Bank," which described how Manufacturers Hanover Trust Co. mailed about $7.8 million too much in cash dividends to its shareholders. As implied in the headline, most of the monies were subsequently returned.

To safeguard cash and ensure the accuracy of the accounting records for cash, effective internal control over cash is imperative. There are new challenges to maintaining control over liquid assets as more and more transactions are conducted with the swipe of a debit or credit card. For example, a recent survey conducted by the Bank for International Settlements reported that Canadians use debit cards more than any other country in the world, with 71.7 transactions per person in 2001, compared with 43.7 in the United States! The same survey also indicated that Canadians were the top automated bank machine (ABM) users with 47.8 such transactions per inhabitant in 2001 compared with 47.7 in the U.S. and 37.7 in Sweden.[2] In addition, electronic commerce conducted over the Internet continues to grow. Each of these trends contributes to the shift from cold cash to digital cash and poses new challenges for the control of cash. The appendix to this chapter discusses some basic control procedures used to ensure that cash is reported correctly.

Reporting Cash

Objective 3
Indicate how cash and related items are reported.

Although reporting cash is relatively straightforward, there are a number of issues that merit special attention. These issues relate to the reporting of:

1. restricted cash

2. cash in foreign currencies

3. bank overdrafts

4. cash equivalents

Restricted Cash

International Insight

Among other potential restrictions, companies need to determine whether any of the cash in accounts outside Canada is restricted by regulations against exportation of currency.

Petty cash and special payroll and dividend bank accounts are examples of cash set aside for a particular purpose. In most situations, these fund balances are not material and therefore are not segregated from cash when reported in the financial statements. When material in amount, restricted cash is segregated from regular cash for reporting purposes. The restricted cash is separately disclosed and reported in Current Assets or classified separately in the Long-term Assets section, depending on the date of availability or disbursement. In general, classification in the current section is not appropriate if there are restrictions that prevent it from being used for current purposes.[3] Cash classified in the long-term section is often set aside for investment or financing purposes such as for plant expansion, long-term debt retirement, or as collateral. Illustration 7-1 indicates how Hudson's Bay Company reports restricted cash.

Some lending institutions require customers to whom they lend money to maintain minimum cash balances in chequing or savings accounts. These minimum balances, called compensating balances, are defined as that portion of any demand deposit (or any time deposit or certificate of deposit) maintained by a corporation that constitutes support for its existing borrowing arrangements with a lending institution.[4] By requiring a compensating balance, the bank achieves an effective interest rate on a loan that is higher than the stated rate because it can use the restricted amount that must remain on deposit.

---

[2] As reported by the Canadian Bankers Association, Media Room Fast Facts, Electronic Banking (April 2003) found at www.cba.ca.

[3] *CICA Handbook*, Section 3000.01.

[4] *Accounting Series Release No. 148*, "Amendments to Regulations S-X and Related Interpretations and Guidelines Regarding the Disclosure of Compensating Balances and Short-Term Borrowing Arrangements," Securities and Exchange Commission (November 13, 1973).

Illustration 7-1

Disclosure of Restricted Cash—Hudson's Bay Company

Consolidated Balance Sheets
thousands of dollars

January 31	**2003**	2002
Current assets		
Cash in stores	**$7,308**	$7,392

Notes to Consolidated Financial Statements
Years ended January 31, 2003 and January 31, 2002

1. **Accounting principles and policies**
    These consolidated financial statements have been prepared by Management in accordance with accounting principles generally accepted in Canada. The significant accounting policies are as follows:

e) **Cash and Cash Equivalents**
    Cash and cash equivalents consist of short-term deposits with maturities of less than three months and exclude restricted funds. Cash in stores is considered restricted, as it is required as a cash float for store operations.

To ensure that investors are not mislead about the amount of cash available to meet recurring obligations, such legally restricted balances are required to be reported separately within current assets or noncurrent assets as appropriate. Compensating balances are more commonly required by U.S. than by major Canadian banks.

Digital Tool

Student Toolkit—Additional Disclosures

www.wiley.com/canada/kieso

Cash in Foreign Currencies

Many companies maintain bank accounts in other countries, especially if they have recurring transactions in that country's currency. The foreign currency is translated into Canadian dollars at the exchange rate on the balance sheet date and, in situations where there is no restriction on the transfer of those funds to the Canadian company, it is included as Cash in current assets. If there are restrictions on the flow of capital out of a country, the cash is reported as restricted. The classification of the cash as current or non-current is based on the circumstances and, in extreme cases, the restrictions may be so severe that the foreign balances may not qualify for recognition as assets.

Bank Overdrafts

Bank overdrafts occur when cheques are written for more than the amount in the cash account. They should be reported in the Current Liabilities section and are often added to the amount reported as accounts payable. If material, these items should be separately disclosed either on the face of the balance sheet or in the related notes.

Bank overdrafts in general should not be offset against the Cash account. A major exception is when available cash is present in another account in the same bank on which the overdraft occurred. Offsetting in this case is appropriate.

Cash Equivalents

Cash is often reported with a category of asset that is known as cash equivalents. Cash equivalents tend to be held for meeting upcoming cash requirements and are defined as "short-term, highly liquid investments that are readily convertible to known amounts of cash and which are subject to an insignificant risk of changes in value."[5] Generally only investments with original maturities of three months or less qualify under this definition,

---

[5] *CICA Handbook*, Section 1540.06(b).

and equity investments are excluded. Examples of cash equivalents are Treasury bills, commercial paper, and money market funds.

In some circumstances, bank overdrafts may be deducted in determining the amount of cash and cash equivalents. If overdrafts are part of the firm's cash management activities, are repayable on demand, and the bank balance fluctuates often between a positive and negative balance, the overdraft may be considered a component of cash and cash equivalents.[6]

Because some companies report investments that qualify as cash equivalents in other categories of current assets such as short-term or temporary investments, it is important for them to disclose their reporting policy in a note to the financial statements. Illustration 7-2 provides an example of such disclosure by **QLT Inc.**

Illustration 7-2

Reporting of Cash and Cash Equivalents—QLT Inc.

Consolidated Balance Sheets
In thousands of U.S. dollars

As at December 31	**2002**	2001
ASSETS		
Current assets		
Cash and cash equivalents	**$128,138**	$ 70,362
Short-term investment securities	**79,797**	93,111

Notes to the Consolidated Financial Statements

1. **Significant Accounting Policies (excerpt)**
    Cash, Cash Equivalents and Short-term Investment Securities
    Cash equivalents include highly liquid investments with insignificant interest rate risk and original maturities of ninety days or less at the date of purchase. Investments with maturities between ninety days and one year at the date of purchase are considered to be short-term investment securities. Short-term investment securities consist primarily of investment-grade commercial paper (R-1 DBRS rating), bankers' acceptances and certificates of deposit.

Because investments classified as cash equivalents are very short-term, they have tended to be measured at cost, or at cost plus accrued interest to the balance sheet date. This measurement is generally representative of the instruments' fair value. Proposed *CICA Handbook* Section 3855, "Financial Instruments—Recognition and Measurement," requires these trading securities to be measured at fair value, with all changes in value reported in income. The accounting procedures are explained below in the section on temporary investments.

Summary of Cash-Related Items

Cash and cash equivalents include the medium of exchange and most negotiable instruments. If the item cannot be converted to coin or currency on short notice, it is separately classified as an investment, as a receivable, or as a prepaid expense. Cash that is not available for payment of currently maturing liabilities is segregated and classified in the long-term assets section. Illustration 7-3 summarizes the classification of cash-related items.

Illustration 7-3

Classification of Cash-Related Items

Classification of Cash, Cash Equivalents, and Noncash Items

Item	Classification	Comment
Cash	Cash	If unrestricted, report as cash. If restricted, identify and classify as current and noncurrent assets.

---

[6] *CICA Handbook*, Section 1540.10.

Item	Classification	Comment
Petty cash and change funds	Cash	Report as cash.
Short-term paper	Cash equivalents	Investments with maturity of less than 3 months, often combined with cash.
Short-term paper	Temporary investments	Investments with maturity of 3 to 12 months.
Postdated cheques and IOUs	Receivables	Assumed to be collectible.
Travel advances	Receivables, or as prepaid expenses	Assumed to be collectable from employees or deducted from their salaries, or spent on travel in the future.
Postage on hand (as stamps or in postage meters)	Prepaid expenses	May also be classified as office supplies inventory.
Bank overdrafts	Current liability	If right of offset exists, reduce cash.
Compensating balances	Cash separately classified as a deposit maintained as compensating balance	Classify as current or noncurrent in the balance sheet. Disclose separately in notes details of the arrangement.

SECTION 2—TEMPORARY INVESTMENTS

Background

Often, companies will invest excess cash in temporary investments with the intention of maximizing returns on their assets. These investments are usually highly marketable, providing the company with the flexibility to liquidate the investments when the cash is needed. Examples of such investments include short-term paper (certificates of deposit, treasury bills, and commercial paper), debt securities (government and corporate bonds), and equity instruments (preferred and common shares, options, and warrants). While similar to cash equivalents, these investments may be longer term and include equity as well as debt and money market instruments.

Until 2004, Canadian accounting standards for temporary investments reported as current assets were required to be recognized initially at cost, and subsequently adjusted at each balance sheet date to the lower of cost and market. Unrealized losses in value and loss recoveries were reported in income.

In 2005 it is expected that the Accounting Standards Board will have new standards covering the accounting for financial instruments.[7] The new standards as drafted are consistent with the FASB standards applied in the United States, and are generally based on current international standards. The new *CICA Handbook* requirements are extensive and are explained more fully in Chapters 10 and 17.

The coverage in this chapter is limited to the accounting for and reporting of basic financial asset investments that are held for trading and that are reported as current assets. Available-for-sale and held-to-maturity investments, usually reported outside of current

International Insight

Like Canada, the IAS provide for classification as trading, available-for-sale, or held-to-maturity for all types of financial assets. U.S. GAAP applies these classifications only to securities.

---

[7] The new *Handbook* sections, expected to be effective in 2005, are Section 3855, Financial Instruments—Recognition and Measurement; Section 3865, Hedges; and Section 1530, Comprehensive Income.

assets, are discussed in Chapter 10, along with more detail on how to differentiate among these classifications.[8]

Recognition and Initial Measurement of Trading Securities

Objective 4

Explain how temporary investments and related income are measured and reported.

In general, a financial asset held for trading (or held-for-trading investment) is one that is acquired for the purpose of selling in the near term, or is part of a portfolio of managed short-term investments with a history of short-term profit-taking, and that is not a loan or receivable. "Trading" in this context means frequent buying and selling, and trading securities are usually used to generate profits from short-term differences in price. "Near term" is defined as not exceeding one year from the date of the financial statements.[9] Section 3855 specifically states that "designation of a financial instrument as held for trading is not precluded simply because the entity does not intend to sell" it in the short term.[10] **In order to qualify as a current asset, however, the investment has to be readily marketable, with the intention to sell it within one year from the balance sheet date, or operating cycle, if longer.**

When acquired, financial assets are recorded at the fair value of the consideration given. Fair value is defined in *Handbook* Section 3855 as "the amount of the consideration that would be agreed upon in an arm's length transaction between knowledgeable, willing parties who are under no compulsion to act." Debt security prices are usually quoted as a percentage of par or face value. For example, a $25,000 face value bond priced at 99 sells at 99% of $25,000, or $24,750. If priced at 103.5, it will sell for 103.5% of $25,000, or $25,875. Shares traded on the stock exchange are usually quoted at the market price per share in dollars and cents.

In some cases, fair value or initial cost may not be obvious. For example, while financial assets acquired in exchange for noncash consideration (property or services) should be recognized at the fair value of the consideration given, there may not be clearly determinable values available for the property or services given up or quoted prices in an active market for the asset acquired. In this case, valuation techniques incorporating information about market conditions that affect the investment's fair value are used to estimate the instrument's fair value and cost. The input required would include the time value of money, credit risk, indexes of prices of traded equities, market risk premiums, and other market-related information.

In addition, investments in shares may be acquired on margin. This means that the investor pays only part of the purchase price to acquire the shares. The remainder is financed by the broker. Since the shares legally belong to the investor, the full amount of the share price should be recorded with a corresponding liability to the broker.

Accounting for costs incidental to the acquisition transaction such as fees, commissions, or transfer taxes, is not addressed in the new *Handbook* sections.[11] The obvious choices are to expense these amounts immediately, or to add them to the cost of the assets acquired. In the past, when they are an integral part of the purchase transaction, incidental direct costs such as brokerage commissions, legal fees, and taxes have tended to be included in the cost of the

---

[8] Available-for-sale investments are defined in terms of what they are not: they are financial assets that are not loans or receivables, and are not held for trading or held-to-maturity. Held-to-maturity investments are those with fixed or determinable payments and a fixed maturity date, and which a company intends to and is financially capable of holding until then. (*Handbook* Section 3855.)

[9] *CICA Handbook*, Section 1508.02

[10] In fact, Section 3855 permits any financial instrument to be designated, on acquisition, as a "trading" security. This is to allow fair values to be reported on the balance sheet and the related holding gains and losses in income, and to facilitate hedge accounting.

[11] Companies also have a choice of when to recognize the acquisition of the financial asset—either on the trade date or on the settlement date, usually a short time thereafter, and the policy chosen must be disclosed.

asset.[12] Wherever a choice of policy exists, as in this situation, the accounting policy used is disclosed in the notes to the financial statements.

Income from Investments Held for Trading

Income from trading investments **in debt securities** is generally in the form of interest. Interest income is received in one of two ways, depending on whether the security is interest bearing or noninterest-bearing. **If it is interest-bearing**, the company holding the security on the interest payment date receives all the interest since the last interest payment date. Because debt securities are bought and sold throughout the year, the practice has developed for the purchaser of such an instrument to pay the seller an amount equal to the interest since the last interest payment date—over and above the agreed exchange price for the security.

Assume Investor Inc. acquires a held-for-trading investment in $20,000 face value Sorfit Ltd. 10% bonds on June 15. The bonds pay interest semi-annually on January 15 and July 15 each year. Investor pays $21,300 for the bonds, and sells the bonds on August 31 for $21,350 when Investor requires the cash for operations. Illustration 7-4 explains how interest revenue is calculated and recorded.

June 15	Cost of bonds	$21,300	
	Interest purchased since last interest payment date:		
	$20,000 × 10% × 5/12	833	
	Cash payment	$22,133	
	Trading Securities	21,300	
	Interest Revenue	833	
	Cash		22,133
	(To record purchase of Sorfit Ltd. bonds and accrued interest)		
July 15	Cash	1,000	
	Interest Revenue		1,000
	$20,000 × 10% × 6/12		
	(To record receipt of semi-annual interest on Sorfit Ltd. bonds)		
Aug 31	Selling price of bonds	$21,350	
	Interest sold since last interest payment date		
	$20,000 × 10% × 1½/12	250	
	Cash received	$21,600	
	Selling price of bonds	$21,350	
	Carrying value of bonds	21,300	
	Gain on sale of bonds	$ 50	
	Cash	21,600	
	Trading Securities		21,300
	Interest Revenue		250
	Gain on Sale of Bonds		50
	(To record sale of bonds and interest accrued since the last interest payment date)		

Illustration 7-4

Interest Income on an Interest-Bearing Debt Instrument

---

[12] Brokerage commissions are usually incurred when buying and selling most securities. Commissions vary with the share value and the number of shares/units purchased and are often between 1% and 3% of the trade value for smaller trades. For larger trades, the commissions are often substantially lower in terms of percentage. Discount brokerages offer significant discounts even on smaller trades. Transactions involving mutual funds may have no commission attached to them (no load funds) but a commission may be charged upon redemption (back end commission).

Note that the interest revenue reported by Investor over the two and one-half months the company held the bonds is $1,000 − $833 + $250 = $417. This is exactly equal to 10% × $20,000 × 2½/12, the amount Investor should have earned based on the period the investment was held. **Also note that any discount or premium that may exist on debt instruments held for trading is not amortized.**

For a noninterest-bearing debt investment, the difference between the security's purchase price and maturity value represents the interest earned. Treasury bills, for example, are usually traded in this manner. Assume Investor Inc. pays $19,231 on March 15 for a $20,000 six-month Treasury bill that matures on September 15. The investment was purchased to yield an 8% return and is designated as a held-for-trading investment. Illustration 7-5 indicates how to account for the interest revenue from this investment.

<table>
<tr><td>**Illustration 7-5**

Interest Income on a NonInterest-Bearing Debt Instrument</td><td>March 15</td><td>Trading Securities
   Cash
(To record purchase of a six-month,
$20,000 Treasury bill)</td><td align="right">19,231</td><td align="right">
19,231</td></tr>
<tr><td></td><td>Sept. 15</td><td>Cash
   Trading Securities
   Interest Revenue
(To record the proceeds on maturity
of a $20,000 Treasury bill)</td><td align="right">20,000</td><td align="right">
19,231
769</td></tr>
</table>

Note that the interest revenue reported is equal to an 8% yield on the amount paid for the investment: $19,231 × 8% × 6/12 = $769.

If Investor needed cash prior to September 15 and sold the investment before maturity, the difference between its cost and the proceeds on disposal would be recognized as interest revenue.[13]

Investments in equity securities that are held for trading may pay dividends. If so, these are recorded as dividend (or investment) revenue as they are received. Because entitlement to the dividend goes to the holder of the shares on the date of record, generally a few weeks before the paying company mails the dividend cheques, a dividend receivable and the related revenue may be recognized before the cash is received. When the equity security is sold, its cost is removed from the Trading Securities account, and a gain or loss on disposal is recognized.

Subsequent Measurement and Reporting

Trading securities are remeasured and reported at fair value at each balance sheet date, with unrealized holding gains and losses reported as part of net income. (A holding gain or loss is the net change in a security's fair value from one period to another, exclusive of dividend or interest revenue recognized but not received.) Instead of directly increasing or decreasing the securities' account to fair value, a valuation allowance account is used. The valuation allowance is a contra account, a credit, to the Trading Securities account **if the fair value is less than cost**, and an adjunct account, a debit, **if the fair value is greater than cost**. The Allowance account is adjusted at each balance sheet date and is always reported with the Trading Securities account, which is maintained at the cost of the securities.

---

[13] In theory, the difference between the proceeds and the investment's cost is made up of interest revenue at the 8% rate, and a gain or loss on disposal. Interest at a rate of 8% should be recognized and added to the investment's carrying value. The difference between the proceeds on disposal and the adjusted carrying value is the gain or loss. Because the difference in amounts are usually immaterial, interest revenue alone is generally credited.

To illustrate, assume that on December 31, 2005, Western Publishing Corporation determined its trading securities portfolio to be as shown in Illustration 7-6. (Assume that 2005 is the first year that Western Publishing held trading securities.) At the date of acquisition, these trading securities were recorded at cost in the account entitled Trading Securities. This is the first valuation of this recently purchased portfolio.

TRADING SECURITY PORTFOLIO
December 31, 2005

Investments	Cost	Fair Value	Unrealized Gain (Loss)
Burlington 10% bonds	$ 43,860	$ 51,500	$ 7,640
Genesta Corp. 8% bonds	184,230	175,200	(9,030)
Warner 11% bonds	86,360	91,500	5,140
Total of portfolio	$314,450	$318,200	
Balance needed in Allowance account—debit			3,750
Allowance account balance before adjustment			0
Adjustment needed to Allowance account—debit			$ 3,750

Illustration 7-6

Calculation of Fair Value Adjustment—Trading Security Portfolio, December 31, 2005

The total cost of Western's trading portfolio is $314,450. The gross unrealized gains are $12,780 ($7,640 + $5,140) and the gross unrealized losses are $9,030, resulting in a net unrealized gain of $3,750. The fair value of trading securities at the reporting date is $3,750 greater than their cost.

At December 31, an adjusting entry is made to the valuation allowance to record the increase in value and to an income statement account to record the unrealized holding gain.

December 31, 2005

Allowance to Adjust Trading Securities to Fair Value	3,750	
Unrealized Holding Gain or Loss		3,750

A = L + SE
+3,750   +3,750
Cash flows: No effect

Because the Allowance account balance of $3,750 is a debit, it is added to the cost of the Trading Securities account of $314,450 to arrive at a reported value for the trading securities on the balance sheet of $318,200, their fair value. The Unrealized Holding Gain or Loss account (in this case, a gain) is included in net income on the income statement.

Now, further assume that the next reporting date is December 31, 2006. The Trading Securities portfolio account at this date is provided in Illustration 7-7. Remember that this account is made up of the cost of the trading securities, and that no adjustments have been made to the Allowance account since the previous reporting date.

TRADING SECURITY PORTFOLIO
December 31, 2006

Investments	Cost	Fair Value	Unrealized Gain (Loss)
Ace Corp. 6% bonds	$37,150	$37,700	$ 550
Next Ltd. shares	49,990	48,135	(1,855)
Total of portfolio	$87,140	$85,835	
Balance needed in Allowance account—credit			(1,305)
Allowance account balance before adjustment—debit			3,750
Adjustment needed to Allowance account—credit			$(5,055)

Illustration 7-7

Calculation of Fair Value Adjustment—Trading Security Portfolio, December 31, 2006

At December 31, 2006, the balance in the Trading Securities portfolio account is their cost of $87,140. Because the portfolio's fair value at this date is only $85,835, an Allowance account with a credit balance of $1,305 is needed for the balance sheet. Therefore, a credit adjustment of $5,055 is needed to bring the Allowance account to its proper balance. The adjusting entry follows.

A = L + SE
−5,055   −5,055
Cash flows: No effect

December 31, 2006

Unrealized Holding Gain or Loss	5,055	
Allowance to Adjust Trading Securities		
To Fair Value		5,055

The Unrealized Holding Gain or Loss account (in this case, a loss) is included in net income on the 2006 income statement. The trading securities are reported on the 2005 and 2006 balance sheets as follows.

	2006	2005
Current assets:		
Trading securities, at fair value	$85,835	$318,200

Underlying Concept

Investments in securities that are held for trading and, therefore, are generally marketable, are reported at fair value, not only because the information is relevant, but also because it is reliable.

Particularly when securities are actively traded, the AcSB believes that financial reporting is improved when the economic events affecting the company (changes in fair value) and related unrealized gains and losses are reported in the same period. Including changes in fair value in income provides more relevant information to current shareholders whose composition may be different next period.

In addition, companies must disclose how fair values have been determined, whether the trade date or settlement date is used in accounting for purchases and sales, and how transaction costs are accounted for. Holdings of securities of affiliated companies must also be reported separately.

Changes in Classification

What happens when management changes its intentions about securities the company holds? Proposed *Handbook* Section 3855 is very clear on this matter: "An entity should not reclassify a financial instrument into or out of the trading category while it is held." The decision relative to the trading classification, made when the instrument is acquired, should not be reversed.

SECTION 3—RECEIVABLES

Introduction

Objective 5
Define receivables and identify the different types of receivables.

Receivables are claims held against customers and others for money, goods, or services. When receivables represent contractual rights to receive cash or other financial assets from another party, they are termed financial assets. For financial statement purposes, receivables are classified as either current (short-term) or noncurrent (long-term). Current receivables are expected to be collected within a year or during the current operating cycle, whichever is longer. All other receivables are classified as noncurrent. Receivables are further classified in the balance sheet as either trade or nontrade receivables.

Trade receivables are amounts owed by customers for goods sold and services rendered as part of normal business operations. Trade receivables, usually the most significant an enterprise possesses, may be subclassified into accounts receivable and notes receivable. Accounts receivable are the purchaser's oral promises to pay for goods and services sold and represent "open accounts" resulting from short-term extensions of credit. They are normally collectible within 30 to 60 days, but credit terms may be longer—or shorter—depending on the industry. Notes receivable are written promises to pay a certain sum of money on a specified future date. They may arise from sales, financing, or other transactions. Notes may be short-term or long-term.

Nontrade receivables arise from a variety of transactions and can be written promises either to pay or to deliver. Some examples of nontrade receivables are:

1. advances to officers and employees

2. advances to subsidiaries

3. deposits to cover potential damages or losses

4. deposits as a guarantee of performance or payment

5. dividends and interest receivable

6. claims against:

    (a) insurance companies for casualties sustained

    (b) defendants under suit

    (c) governmental bodies for tax refunds

    (d) common carriers for damaged or lost goods

    (e) creditors for returned, damaged, or lost goods

    (f) customers for returnable items (crates, containers, etc.)

Because of the peculiar nature of nontrade receivables, they are generally classified and reported as separate items in the balance sheet or in a note cross-referenced to the balance sheet. Illustration 7-8 shows the separate reporting of trade and nontrade receivables in the financial statements of Alcan Inc. as does the more complex Illustration 7-19 later in the chapter for Intrawest Corporation.

Consolidated Balance Sheet (in millions of US$)			
December 31	**2002**	2001 (Restated – note 3)	2000 (Restated – note 3)
ASSETS			
Current assets			
Cash and time deposits	**110**	119	261
Trade receivables (net of allowances of $59 in 2002, $52 in 2001 and $55 in 2000) (notes 2 and 11)	**1,300**	1,216	1,721
Other receivables	**553**	532	559

Illustration 7-8

Receivables Reporting—Alcan Inc.

The basic issues in accounting for accounts and notes receivable are the same: **recognition, measurement, valuation, and disposition.** We will discuss these basic issues of accounts and notes receivable in the following sequence:

1. recognition and measurement of accounts receivable

2. valuation of accounts receivable

3. recognition, measurement, and valuation of short-term notes receivable

4. disposition of receivables

Recognition and Measurement of Accounts Receivable

Objective 6
Explain accounting issues related to recognition and measurement of accounts receivable.

In most receivables transactions, the amount to be recognized is the exchange price between the two parties. **The exchange price is the amount due from the debtor** (a customer or a borrower) and is generally evidenced by a business document, often an invoice. Two factors that may complicate the measurement of the exchange price are (1) the availability of discounts (trade and cash discounts) and (2) the length of time between the sale and the payment due date (the interest element).

Trade Discounts

Customers are often quoted prices on the basis of list or catalogue prices that may be subject to a trade or quantity discount. Such trade discounts are used to avoid frequent changes in catalogues, to quote different prices for different quantities purchased, or to hide the true invoice price from competitors.

Trade discounts are commonly quoted in percentages. For example, if your textbook has a list price of $90.00 and the publisher sells it to college bookstores for list less a 30% trade discount, the receivable recorded by the publisher is $63.00 per textbook. The normal practice is simply to deduct the trade discount from the list price and bill the customer net.

Cash Discounts (Sales Discounts)

Cash discounts (sales discounts) are offered to induce prompt payment. They are communicated in terms that read, for example, 2/10, n/30 (2% if paid within 10 days, gross amount due in 30 days), or 2/10, E.O.M. (2% if paid within 10 days of the end of the month).

Companies buying goods or services that fail to take sales discounts are usually not using their money advantageously. An enterprise that receives a 1% reduction in the sales price for payment within 10 days, total payment due within 30 days, is effectively earning 18.25% (0.01 divided by 20/365), or at least avoiding that rate of interest cost. For this reason, companies usually take the discount unless their cash is severely limited.

The easiest and most commonly used method of recording sales and related sales discount transactions is to enter the receivable and sale at the gross amount. Under this method, sales discounts are recognized in the accounts only when payment is received within the discount period. Sales discounts would then be shown in the income statement as a deduction from sales to arrive at net sales.

Some accountants contend that sales discounts not taken reflect penalties added to an established price to encourage prompt payment. That is, the seller offers sales on account at a slightly higher price than if selling for cash, and the increase is offset by the cash discount offered. Thus, customers who pay within the discount period purchase at the cash price; those who pay after the discount period expires are penalized because they must pay more than the cash price. If this reasoning is used, sales and receivables should be recorded net, and any discounts not taken should be recognized as Sales Discounts Forfeited, similar to an interest or financing revenue. The following entries illustrate the difference between the gross and net methods.

Gross Method			Net Method		
Sales of $10,000, terms 2/10, n/30:					
Accounts Receivable	10,000		Accounts Receivable	9,800	
Sales		10,000	Sales		9,800
Payment on $4,000 received within discount period:					
Cash	3,920		Cash	3,920	
Sales Discounts	80		Accounts Receivable		3,920
Accounts Receivable		4,000			
Payment on $6,000 received after discount period:					
Cash	6,000		Accounts Receivable	120	
Accounts Receivable		6,000	Sales Discounts		
			Forfeited		120
			Cash	6,000	
			Accounts Receivable		6,000

If the gross method is used, sales discounts are reported as a deduction from sales in the income statement. Proper matching would dictate that a reasonable estimate of material amounts of expected discounts to be taken also should be charged against sales. An Allowance for Sales Discounts, a contra account to Accounts Receivable, would be credited. If the net method is used, Sales Discounts Forfeited are considered an 'other revenue' item.[14]

Theoretically, recognizing Sales Discounts Forfeited is preferred because the receivable is stated closer to its realizable value and the net sales figure measures the revenue earned from the sale. As a practical matter, however, the net method is seldom used because it requires additional analysis and bookkeeping. For one thing, the net method requires adjusting entries to record sales discounts forfeited on accounts receivable that have passed the discount period.

Nonrecognition of Interest Element

Ideally, receivables should be measured in terms of their present value; that is, the amount of cash that would be required at the date of sale to satisfy the outstanding claim. This is equivalent to the discounted value of the cash to be received in the future. When expected cash receipts require a waiting period, the receivable face amount is not a good measure of the debt today.

To illustrate, assume that a company makes a sale on account for $1,000. The applicable annual rate of interest is 12%, and payment is made at the end of four months. The receivable's present value is not $1,000 but $961.54 ($1,000 × .96154, Table A-2; $n = 1, i = 4\%$). In other words, $1,000 to be received in four months is equivalent to $961.54 received today.

Theoretically, any revenue after the period of sale is interest revenue. **In practice, accountants have generally chosen to ignore this for accounts receivable because the discount amount is not usually material in relation to the net income for the period.** Generally, receivables that arise from transactions with customers in the normal course of business, and that are due in customary trade terms not exceeding approximately one year, are excluded from present value considerations.[15]

> **Underlying Concept**
>
> Materiality means it must make a difference to a decision-maker. Standard setters believe that present value concepts can be ignored for short-term receivables and payables.

---

[14] To the extent that discounts not taken reflect a short-term financing situation, some argue that an interest revenue account could be used to record these amounts.

[15] *CICA Handbook*, Section 3020, Accounts and Notes Receivable, is silent on the issue of interest. However, in the U.S., *APB Opinion No. 21*, Interest on Receivables and Payables, provides that all receivables are subject to present value measurement techniques and interest imputation, if necessary, except for the following specifically excluded types: (a) normal accounts receivable due within one year (b) security deposits, retainages, advances, or progress payments (c) transactions between parent and subsidiary (d) receivables due at some determinable future date.

Valuation of Accounts Receivable

Objective 7

Explain accounting issues related to valuation of accounts receivable.

Having recorded receivables at their face value (the amount due), the issue of financial statement presentation is dealt with next. Reporting of receivables involves (1) classification and (2) valuation on the balance sheet.

Classification involves determining the length of time each receivable will be outstanding. For companies that present classified balance sheets, receivables intended to be collected within a year or the operating cycle, if longer, are classified as current; all other receivables are classified as long-term.

The valuation of receivables is more complex. Short-term receivables are valued and reported at **net realizable value**—the net amount expected to be received in cash, which is not necessarily the amount legally receivable. Determining net realizable value requires estimating both uncollectible receivables and any returns or allowances to be granted.

Uncollectible Accounts Receivable

As one accountant so aptly noted, the credit manager's idea of heaven probably would be a place where everyone (eventually) paid his or her debts.[16] The recent experience of **Sears Canada Inc.**, as shown in Illustration 7-10, indicates the importance of credit sales for many companies.

Illustration 7-10

Sears Canada Customer Method of Payment

	2002	2001
Sears Card	60.6%	60.5%
Third Party Credit Cards	16.5%	15.6%
Debit Cards	8.6%	8.5%
Cash	14.3%	15.4%
Total	100.0%	100.0%

from: Sears Canada Inc. Annual Report, 2002

Sales on any basis other than for cash raise the possibility of failure to collect the account. An uncollectible account receivable is a loss of revenue that requires, through proper entry in the accounts, a decrease in the asset accounts receivable and a related decrease in income and shareholders' equity. The loss in revenue and related decrease in income are recognized by recording bad debt expense.

The chief problem in recording uncollectible accounts receivable **is establishing the time at which to record the loss**. Two general procedures are used.

METHODS FOR RECORDING UNCOLLECTIBLE ACCOUNTS

1. **Direct Write-Off Method.** No entry is made until a specific account has definitely been established as uncollectible. Then the loss is recorded by crediting Accounts Receivable and debiting Bad Debt Expense.

2. **Allowance Method.** An estimate is made of the expected uncollectible amounts from all sales made on account or from the total of outstanding receivables. This estimate is entered as an expense and an indirect reduction in accounts receivable (via an increase in the allowance account) in the period in which the sale is recorded.

---

[16] William J. Vatter, *Managerial Accounting* (Englewood Cliffs, N.J.: Prentice-Hall, 1950), p. 60.

Direct Write-off Method

The **direct write-off method** records bad debt expense in the year it is determined that a specific receivable cannot be collected. When an account is determined to be uncollectible, the specific account receivable is written off with the debit recognized as bad debt expense:

Bad Debt Expense	$$	
Accounts Receivable		$$

A = L + SE
−$$ −$$
Cash flows: No effect

If amounts are subsequently collected on an account previously written off, a notation is made in the customer's record, and the cash collected and a revenue account entitled Uncollectible Amounts Recovered are recognized:

Cash	$$	
Uncollectible Amounts Recovered		$$

A = L + SE
+$$ +$$
Cash flows: ↑ inflow

No allowance account is used.

Supporters of the **direct write-off method** contend that facts, not estimates, are recorded. It assumes that a good account receivable resulted from each sale, and that later events proved certain accounts to be uncollectible and worthless. From a practical standpoint this method is simple and convenient to apply, although receivables do not generally become worthless at an identifiable moment of time. The direct write-off method is theoretically deficient because it usually does not match the period's costs with revenues, nor does it result in receivables being stated at estimated realizable value on the balance sheet. **As a result, the direct write-off method is not considered appropriate, except when the amount uncollectible is immaterial.**

Allowance Method

The **allowance method** recognizes expense on an estimated basis in the accounting period in which the sales on account are made. Advocates of the allowance method believe that bad debt expense should be recorded in the same period as the sale to obtain a proper matching of expenses and revenues and to achieve a proper carrying value for accounts receivable. They support the position that although estimates are involved, the percentage of sales that will not be collected can be predicted from past experience, present market conditions, and an analysis of the outstanding balances. Many companies set their credit policies to provide for a certain percentage of uncollectible accounts. In fact, many feel that failure to reach that percentage means that sales are being lost by credit policies that are too restrictive.

Within the allowance method, there are two approaches to estimating bad debt expense. As a receivable is a prospective cash inflow, the probability of its collection must be considered in valuing this inflow. These estimates normally are made either on (1) the basis of percentage of sales or (2) the basis of outstanding receivables.

Percentage-of-Sales (Income Statement) Approach. If there is a fairly stable relationship between previous years' credit sales and bad debts, then that relationship can be turned into a percentage and used to determine this year's bad debt expense.

The **percentage-of-sales approach** matches costs with revenues because it relates the charge (the expense) to the period in which the sale is recorded. To illustrate, assume that Dockrill Corp. estimates from past experience that about 2% of net credit sales become uncollectible. If Dockrill Corp. has net credit sales of $400,000 in 2004, the entry to record bad debt expense in 2004 using the percentage-of-sales method is as follows:

International Insight

In the People's Republic of China, the rates for providing for bad debts are established by state regulation.

Underlying Concept

The percentage-of-sales method is a good illustration of the use of the matching principle, which relates expenses to revenues earned.

A	=	L	+	SE
−8,000				−8,000

Cash flows: No effect

Bad Debt Expense	8,000	
Allowance for Doubtful Accounts		8,000

The Allowance for Doubtful Accounts is a valuation account (i.e., a contra asset) and is subtracted from trade receivables on the balance sheet.[17] The amount of bad debt expense and the related credit to the allowance account are unaffected by any balance currently existing in the allowance account. Because the bad debt expense estimate is related to a nominal account (Sales), and any balance in the allowance is ignored, this method is frequently referred to as the **income statement approach**. An excellent matching of cost and revenues is therefore achieved.

Percentage-of-Receivables (Balance Sheet) Approach.   Using past experience, a company can estimate the percentage of its outstanding receivables that will become uncollectible, without identifying specific accounts. This procedure provides a reasonably accurate estimate of the receivables' realizable value, but does a poorer job of matching cost and revenues. Rather, its objective is to report receivables in the balance sheet at net realizable values; hence it is referred to as the **percentage-of-receivables** (or **balance sheet) approach**.

The percentage used in this approach may be a composite rate that reflects an overall estimate of the uncollectible receivables. Another approach that is more sensitive to the actual status of the accounts receivable sets up an **aging schedule**. This approach determines the age of each account receivable and applies a different percentage to each of the various age categories, based on past experience. An aging schedule is commonly used in practice. It indicates which accounts require special attention by highlighting how long various accounts receivable have been outstanding. The schedule of Wilson & Co. in Illustration 7-11 is an example.

Illustration 7-11

Accounts Receivable Aging Schedule

WILSON & CO.
Aging Schedule

Name of Customer	Balance Dec. 31	Under 60 days	61-90 days	91-120 days	Over 120 days
Western Stainless Steel Corp.	$ 98,000	$ 80,000	$18,000		
Brockville Steel Company	320,000	320,000			
Freeport Sheet & Tube Co.	55,000				$55,000
Manitoba Iron Works Ltd.	74,000	60,000		$14,000	
	$547,000	$460,000	$18,000	$14,000	$55,000

Summary

Age	Amount	Percentage Estimated to be Uncollectible	Required Balance in Allowance
Under 60 days old	$460,000	4%	$18,400
61-90 days old	18,000	15%	2,700
91-120 days old	14,000	20%	2,800
Over 120 days	55,000	25%	13,750
Year-end balance of Allowance for Doubtful Accounts should =			$37,650

[17] In Canada, many companies do not actually make reference to or disclose the amount of the Allowance for Doubtful Accounts. The assumption is that an adequate allowance has been made for potentially uncollectible accounts in the absence of a statement to the contrary.

Assuming that no balance existed in the Allowance account before this adjustment, the bad debt expense to be reported for this year would be $37,650.

To change the illustration slightly, **assume that the Allowance account had a credit balance of $800 before adjustment**. In this case, the amount to be added to the Allowance account to bring it to the desired balance of $37,650 is $36,850 ($37,650 – $800), and the following entry is made.

Bad Debt Expense	36,850	
Allowance for Doubtful Accounts		36,850

A   = L +   SE
−36,850   −36,850
Cash flows: No effect

The balance in the Allowance account is therefore reported at $37,650. **If the Allowance balance before adjustment had a debit balance of $200**, then the amount to be recorded for bad debt expense would be $37,850 ($37,650 desired balance + $200 debit balance). In the percentage-of-receivables method, the balance in the Allowance account before the adjusting entry is made **cannot be ignored**, because it is used to calculate the amount of the adjustment needed.

An aging schedule is usually not prepared for the sole purpose of determining the amount of bad debt expense. Rather, it is prepared as an internal control measure to determine the composition of receivables and to identify delinquent accounts. The estimated loss percentage developed for each category is based on previous loss experience and the advice of credit department personnel. Regardless of whether a composite rate or an aging schedule is used, the percentage of receivables method's primary objective for financial statement purposes is to report receivables in the balance sheet at net realizable value. However, while it does result in bad debt expense being recognized, it does not do as good a job as the percentage-of-sales method does of matching bad debt expense to the period in which the sale takes place.

The allowance for doubtful accounts as a percentage of receivables will vary considerably, depending upon the industry and the economic climate. Imperial Oil Limited, for example, reports an allowance for doubtful accounts of less than 1% of its accounts receivable at December 31, 2002, while Alcan Inc.'s allowance is over 4.3% of its receivables.

In summary, the percentage-of-receivables method results in a more accurate valuation of receivables on the balance sheet. From a matching viewpoint, the percentage-of-sales approach provides the better results. Illustration 7-12 relates these methods to the basic theory.

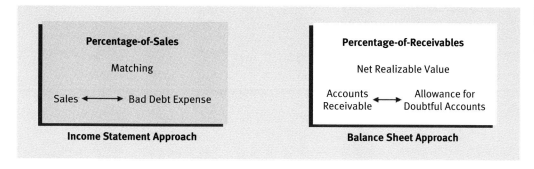

Illustration 7-12

Comparison of Methods for Estimating Uncollectibles

Regardless of the method chosen, "accounts and notes receivable, net of the allowance should be the best possible estimate of the amount for which reasonable assurance of collection exists, in the light of current conditions and assuming the continuation of the business as a 'going concern.'"[18]

---

[18] *CICA Handbook*, Section 3020.12.

Accounts Receivable Written Off.   Under the Allowance method, when a specific account is determined to be uncollectible, its balance is removed from the Accounts Receivable and the Allowance is reduced. For example, assuming the account of Brown Ltd. of $550 is considered uncollectible, the write-off entry is as follows:

A = L + SE
0   0   0
Cash flows: No effect

Allowance for Doubtful Accounts	550	
Accounts Receivable		550
(To write off the account of Brown Ltd.)		

Note that there is no effect on the income statement from writing off an account. This is because bad debt expense was estimated, recognized, and matched with revenue in the period of the sale. There is also no effect on the net amount of the receivables because the Accounts Receivable and its contra account are **both** reduced by equal amounts.

If a collection is made on a receivable that was previously written off, the procedure is first to reestablish the receivable by reversing the write-off entry, and then recognize the cash inflow as a regular receipt on account. To illustrate, assume that Brown Ltd. subsequently remits $300, but indicates that this is all that will be paid. The entries to record this transaction are as follows.

A = L + SE
0   0   0
Cash flows: No effect

Accounts Receivable	300	
Allowance for Doubtful Accounts		300
(To reinstate the account written off now determined to be collectible.)		

A = L + SE
0   0   0
Cash flows: ↑ 300 inflow

Cash	300	
Accounts Receivable		300
(To record the receipt of cash on account from Brown Ltd.)		

Sales Returns and Allowances.   To properly measure sales revenues and receivables, it is sometimes necessary to establish additional allowance accounts. Probable sales returns and price concessions are estimated and deducted as contra accounts against sales on the income statement and accounts receivable on the balance sheet. Net sales and the net realizable amount of accounts receivable are therefore properly reported on the financial statements.

This procedure is carried out so that the sales returns or price allowances (called sales returns and allowances) are reported in the same period as the sales to which they relate. However, if this adjustment is not made, the amount of mismatched returns and allowances is usually not material if such items are handled consistently from year to year. Yet if a company completes a few special orders involving large amounts near the end of the accounting period, sales returns and allowances should be anticipated and recognized in the period of the sale to avoid distorting the current period's income statement. There are some companies that by their nature have significant returns and customarily establish an allowance for sales returns.

As an example, assume that Astro Corporation estimates that approximately 5% of its $1 million trade receivables outstanding will be returned or some adjustment made to the sale price. Omission of a $50,000 charge could have a material effect on net income for the period. The entry to reflect anticipated sales returns and allowances is:

A = L + SE
−50,000   −50,000
Cash flows: No effect

Sales Returns and Allowances	50,000	
Allowance for Sales Returns and Allowances		50,000

The account Sales Returns and Allowances is reported as an offset to sales revenue in the income statement. Returns and price allowances are accumulated separately instead of debited directly to the Sales account simply to provide better information for management and the statement reader. The Allowance is an asset valuation account (contra asset) and is deducted from total Accounts Receivable.

In most cases, reporting all returns and allowances made during the period in the income statement, whether or not they resulted from the current period's sales, is an acceptable accounting procedure justified by practicality and immateriality.[19]

Recognition, Measurement, and Valuation of Short-Term Notes Receivable

A note receivable is similar to an account receivable, except that the former is supported by a formal **promissory note**, a written promise to pay a certain sum of money at a specific future date. Such a note is a negotiable instrument that is signed by a **maker** in favour of a designated **payee** who may legally and readily sell or otherwise transfer the note to others. **Notes always contain an interest element** because of the time value of money, but they may be classified as interest-bearing or noninterest-bearing. **Interest-bearing notes** have a stated rate of interest that is payable over and above the face value of the note; **zero-interest-bearing notes** (or **noninterest-bearing notes**) also include interest, but it is equal to the difference between the amount borrowed (the proceeds) and the face amount paid back. The rate may not be stated explicitly.

Notes receivable are frequently accepted from customers who need to extend the payment period of an outstanding receivable. Notes are also sometimes required of high-risk or new customers. In addition, notes are often used in loans to employees and subsidiaries and in the sales of property, plant, and equipment. In some industries (e.g., the pleasure and sport boat industry) all credit sales are supported by notes. The majority of notes, however, originate from lending transactions. The basic issues in accounting for notes receivable are the same as those for accounts receivable: recognition, measurement, valuation, and disposition. This chapter addresses only short-term notes. Long-term notes and loans receivable are covered in Chapter 10.

To illustrate the accounting for notes receivable, assume that on March 14, 2005, Prime Corporation agreed to allow its customer, Gouneau Ltd., to substitute a six-month note for the account receivable of $1,000 it was unable to pay when it came due for payment. It was agreed that **the note would bear interest** at a rate of 6%. Prime's entries to record the substitution and payment of the note are as follows.

March 14, 2005		
Note Receivable	1,000	
Account Receivable		1,000
September 14, 2005		
Cash	1,030	
Note Receivable		1,000
Interest Revenue		30*

*$1,000 × .06 × 6/12

8 Objective
Explain accounting issues related to recognition, measurement, and valuation of short-term notes receivable.

A = L + SE
0   0   0
Cash flows: No effect

A = L + SE
+30   +30
Cash flows: ↑ 1,030 inflow

---

[19] An interesting sidelight to the entire problem of returns and allowances is determining when a sale is a sale. In certain circumstances, the seller is exposed to such a high risk of ownership through possible return of the property that the sale is not recognized. Such situations have developed, particularly in sales to related parties. This subject is discussed in more detail in Chapter 6.

Alternatively, a note could be taken back in exchange for lending money to an employee or subsidiary company, for example, in a **noninterest-bearing note** situation. In this case, the interest is the difference between the amount of cash provided and the face or maturity value of the note receivable. Assume that the president of Ajar Ltd. borrowed money from the company on February 23, 2005 with $5,000 repayable in nine month's time. An interest rate of 8% is appropriate for this type of loan. Instead of borrowing $5,000 and repaying this amount with 8% interest added on the maturity date, only $4,717 is given to the president on February 23. The $283 difference between the $4,717 borrowed and the $5,000 repaid represents 8% interest for the nine-month period the note is outstanding. Ajar's entries would be as follows.[20]

A = L + OE
0   0   0

Cash flows: ↓ 4,717 outflow

A   = L | OE
+283   +283

Cash flows: ↑ 5,000 inflow

	February 23, 2005	
Note Receivable	4,717	
Cash		4,717

	November 23, 2005	
Cash	5,000	
Note Receivable		4,717
Interest Revenue		283*

*4,717 × .08 × 9/12

In both cases, if financial statements were prepared while the note receivable was still outstanding, interest must be accrued to the balance sheet date.

Like accounts receivable, short-term notes receivable are recorded and reported at their net realizable value; that is, at their face amount less all necessary allowances. The primary notes receivable allowance account is Allowance for Doubtful Accounts. The calculations and estimations involved in valuing short-term notes receivable and in recording bad debt expense and the related allowance **are exactly the same as for trade accounts receivable**. Either a percentage of sales revenue or an analysis of the receivables can be used to estimate the amount of uncollectibles.

Disposition of Accounts and Notes Receivable

Objective 9

Explain accounting issues related to disposition of accounts and notes receivable.

In the normal course of events, accounts and notes receivable are collected when due and removed from the books. However, as credit sales and receivables have grown in size and significance, this "normal course of events" has evolved. **In order to accelerate the receipt of cash from receivables, the owner may transfer accounts or notes receivable to another company for cash.**

---

[20] Alternatively, the entries could recognize the Note Receivable initially at maturity value along with the Discount, a contra account to the Note Receivable:

February 23	Note Receivable	5,000	
	Cash		4,717
	Discount on Note Receivable		283
November 23	Cash	5,000	
	Note Receivable		5,000
	Discount on Note Receivable	283	
	Interest Revenue		283

The balance sheet effects and cash flows are identical, regardless of the entries made. If financial statements were prepared while this note is still outstanding, the discount is reduced and Interest Revenue earned to the balance sheet date is recognized.

There are various reasons for this early transfer. First, for competitive reasons, providing sales financing for customers is virtually mandatory in many industries. In the sale of durable goods, such as automobiles, trucks, industrial and farm equipment, computers, and appliances, a large majority of sales are on an instalment contract basis. Many major companies in these industries have created wholly owned subsidiaries specializing in receivables financing. For example, General Motors of Canada Ltd. has General Motors Acceptance Corp. of Canada (GMAC).

Second, the **holder** may sell receivables because money is tight and access to normal credit is not available or is prohibitively expensive. A firm may have to sell its receivables, instead of borrowing, to avoid violating existing lending agreements. In addition, billing and collecting of receivables is often time-consuming and costly. Credit card companies such as MasterCard, VISA, and others take over the collection process and provide merchants with immediate cash, in return for a fee to cover their collection and bad debt costs. On the other hand, some **purchasers** of receivables buy them to obtain the legal protection of ownership rights afforded a purchaser of assets versus the lesser rights afforded a secured creditor. In addition, banks and other lending institutions may be forced to purchase receivables because of legal lending limits; that is, they cannot make any additional loans but they can buy receivables and charge a fee for this service.

Receivables can be used to generate immediate cash for a company in one of two ways:

1. secured borrowings

2. sales of receivables

Secured Borrowings

Receivables, as is the case with many other assets, are often used as collateral in borrowing transactions. A creditor may require that the debtor designate (assign) or pledge receivables as security for the loan, but the receivables remain under the control of the borrowing company. The note or loan payable, a liability, is reported on the balance sheet and, if it is not paid when due, the creditor has the right to convert the collateral to cash; that is, to collect the receivables.

Accounting Guideline 12[21] recommends that a company should account for the transferred assets in a secured borrowing after the transaction **in the same way it did prior to the borrowing**, and account for the liability according to accounting policies for similar liabilities. The debtor recognizes interest expense on the borrowed amount, and may have to pay an additional finance charge, which is expensed.

In addition to recording the collection of receivables, all discounts, returns and allowances, and bad debts must be recognized. Each month the proceeds from collecting accounts receivable are used to retire the loan obligation.

Sales of Receivables

Sales of receivables have increased substantially in recent years. One common type is a sale to a factor. **Factors** are finance companies or banks that buy receivables from businesses for a fee and then collect the remittances directly from the customers. Factoring receivables is traditionally associated with the textile, apparel, footwear, furniture, and home furnishing industries. An illustration of a factoring arrangement is shown below.

---

[21] *CICA Handbook*, "Transfers of Receivables," March 2001.

Illustration 7-13

Basic Procedures in Factoring

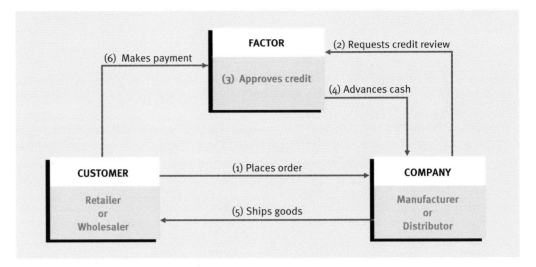

Increasingly common is the **transfer of receivables** through a process known as **securitization**. Securitization is defined as the transformation of financial assets such as loans and receivables into securities, often called **asset-backed securities**. The process takes a pool of assets such as credit card receivables, mortgage receivables, or car loan receivables and sells shares in these pools of interest and principal payments (in effect, creating securities backed by these pools of assets). Virtually every asset with a payment stream and a long-term payment history is a candidate for securitization.

For example, instead of Sears Canada Inc. owning all of its credit card receivables throughout the collection period, Sears sells customer charge account receivable balances to one or more independent trusts. The trusts exist to hold the receivables as an investment, and are financed by the issue of debt and equity securities in large part to independent third parties. Therefore, ownership of the receivables is transformed into securities of a **special purpose entity (SPE)**, the trust.

The arrangements that are made in a securitization transaction differ from company to company. Sears, for example, "receives proceeds equal to fair value for the assets sold and retains rights to future cash flows arising after the investors in the securitization trust have received the return for which they have contracted."[22] Sears continues to service the receivables; that is, it manages the accounts, including the collection activity.

What do the Numbers Mean?

What is the motivation for this type of transaction? In short, it is a financing transaction, providing an attractive means of raising funds by Sears instead of issuing a corporate bond or note. The credit risk associated with a bond or note issued by Sears is higher than the credit risk associated with the special purpose entity set up to hold the receivables. Sears reports a credit rating of AAA and R-1 (High) **for its trust securitized debt issues and commercial paper**, respectively, the highest ratings assigned to these debt classifications. Compare these with BBB and BBB (High) ratings for **Sears' senior unsecured debt**. The higher credit rating is due to the fact that the receivables transferred to the SPE are often credit enhanced[23] and the cash flows to the SPE are much more predictable than the cash flows to the operating company because of the absence of operating risks. With lower risk comes a lower financing cost. The net result is that the transferor company accesses lower cost financing that it can use to pay out debt with a higher cost of capital.

The differences between factoring and securitization are that **factoring** usually involves sale to only one company, fees are high, the receivables quality is low, and the

---

[22] Sears Canada Inc. 2002 Annual Report, p. 56.

[23] Credit enhancement can take the form of guaranteeing payment through recourse or third party guarantee provisions, the use of cash reserve accounts, or overcollateralization—providing security with a greater fair value than the amount at risk.

seller afterward does not service the receivables. In a **securitization**, many investors are involved, margins are tight, the receivables are of higher quality, and the seller usually continues to service the receivables. Where transferors have some form of continuing involvement with the transferred assets, and measurement of the underlying transaction amounts is subject to some uncertainty, numerous disclosures are required for such transactions.

Underlying Principles

Before identifying the criteria that must exist to justify sale treatment, it is important to understand two basic concepts that underlie the decisions of the Accounting Standards Board. The first principle, and one that is applied in many analogous situations, is that an entity should recognize on its balance sheet only assets it can control. Once control is given up, the asset should no longer be recognized—it should be derecognized. The second concept, and one that has only recently been applied to assets such as accounts receivable, is that receivables can be disaggregated into a variety of financial components. This approach permits the assignment of values to such components as the recourse provision, servicing rights, agreements to reacquire, and rights to returns in excess of specified limits, for example. Previous standards treated receivables as an inseparable unit that could be only "entirely sold or entirely retained."[24]

Criteria for Treatment as a Sale

Prior to the Accounting Standards Board pronouncements in *Accounting Guideline 12*, companies tended to account for many transactions as sales of receivables, even when they had substantial continuing interest in and control over the receivables transferred. Their financial statements indicated a reduction in receivables, no additional debt, and often a gain on sale. The purpose of *Accounting Guideline 12* is to identify when a transfer of receivables qualifies for **sale treatment**, and when it is merely a **secured borrowing**. In addition, it covers how to account for **the sale of receivables**, particularly where the transferor has a continuing interest in the transferred assets.

International Insight

The IASB has a similar approach to the sale of receivables, although it provides more flexibility in implementation.

The ASB concluded that a sale occurs when the seller surrenders control of all or a portion of the receivables to the buyer and receives in exchange consideration other than a beneficial interest in the transferred asset. **The following three conditions must be met before a sale can be recorded:**

1. The transferred assets have been isolated from the transferor—put beyond the reach of the transferor and its creditors, even in bankruptcy or receivership.

2. Each transferee has the right to pledge or exchange the assets (or beneficial interests) it received, and no condition both constrains the transferee from taking advantage of this right and provides more than a trivial benefit to the transferor.

3. The transferor does not maintain effective control over the transferred assets through either an agreement to repurchase or redeem them before their maturity or through an ability to unilaterally cause the holder to return specific assets.[25]

If all three conditions **are not met**, the transferor should record the transfer as a secured borrowing. **Only when all three conditions are satisfied** is control over the assets assumed to be given up, and the transaction accounted for as a sale. If sale accounting is appropriate, it is necessary to identify the specific assets obtained and liabilities incurred in the transaction. The general rules of accounting for transfers of receivables are summarized in Illustration 7-20.

---

[24] *Accounting Guideline 12*, par. 6.

[25] *Accounting Guideline 12*, par. 9.

Illustration 7-14

Accounting for Transfers of Receivables

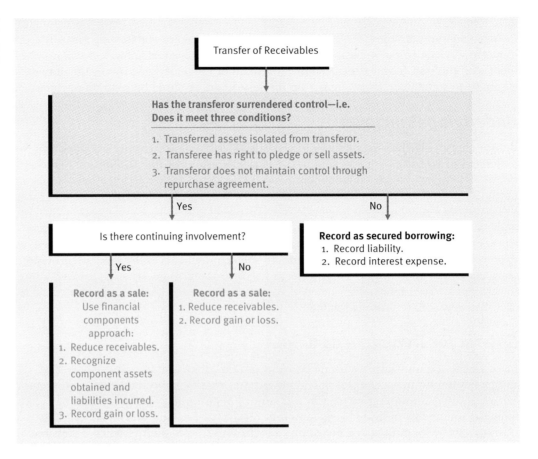

Applying the accounting and disclosure guidance for the transfer of receivables is complicated by specialized contracts among companies that differ in their terms and conditions, the securitization of receivables, and special purpose entities. The illustrations that follow are somewhat simplified to provide a basic understanding of the accounting for such transactions. A discussion of the complex issues and requirements is beyond the purview of an intermediate accounting text.

Sale With No Continuing Involvement by Transferor

The most straightforward situation is one where the receivables are sold outright to another unrelated party such as a factor, and they are sold without recourse.

When receivables are sold **without recourse**, the purchaser assumes the risk of collectibility and absorbs any credit losses.[26] The transfer of accounts receivable in a nonrecourse transaction is an outright sale of the receivables both in form (transfer of title) and substance (transfer of control). In nonrecourse transactions, as in any sale of assets, Cash is debited for the proceeds. Accounts Receivable is credited for the receivables' face value. The difference, reduced by any provision for probable adjustments (discounts, returns, allowances, etc.), is recognized as a Gain or Loss on the Sale of Receivables. Where appropriate, the seller uses a Due from Factor account (reported as a receivable) to account for the proceeds retained by a factor to cover probable sales discounts, sales returns, and sales allowances.

To illustrate, Crest Textiles Ltd. factors $500,000 of accounts receivable with Commercial Factors, Inc., on a **without recourse** basis. The receivable records are trans-

Digital Tool

Expanded
Discussion

www.wiley.com/canada/kieso

---

[26] *Accounting Guideline 12* defines recourse as the right of a transferee of receivables to receive payment from the transferor of those receivables for (i) failure of debtors to pay when due, (ii) the effects of prepayments, or (iii) adjustments resulting from defects in the eligibility of the transferred receivables.

ferred to Commercial Factors, Inc., which will receive the collections. Commercial Factors assesses a finance charge of 3% of the amount of accounts receivable and withholds initially an amount equal to 5% of the accounts receivable. The journal entries for both Crest Textiles and Commercial Factors for the receivables transferred without recourse are as follows:

Illustration 7-15

Entries for Sale of Receivables Without Recourse

Crest Textiles Ltd.			Commercial Factors, Inc.		
Cash	460,000		Accounts (Notes)		
Due from Factor	25,000*		Receivable	500,000	
Loss on Sale of Receivables	15,000**		Due to Crest Textiles		25,000
Accounts (Notes)			Financing Revenue		15,000
Receivable		500,000	Cash		460,000
*(5% × $500,000)					
**(3% × $500,000)					

To recognize the sale of all the financial components of the receivables, Crest Textiles records a loss of $15,000. The factor's net income will be the difference between the financing revenue of $15,000 and the amount of any uncollectible receivables.

Sale With Continuing Involvement by Transferor

Recourse Component Retained. If receivables are sold **with recourse**, the seller or transferor guarantees payment to the purchaser in the event the debtor fails to pay. To record this type of transaction, a **financial components approach** is used, because the seller has a continuing involvement with the receivable. Each party to the sale recognizes the assets and liabilities that it controls after the sale and no longer recognizes the assets and liabilities that were sold or extinguished.

To illustrate, assume the same information as in Illustration 7-15 for Crest Textiles and Commercial Factors except that the receivables are sold on a **with recourse** basis. It is determined that the recourse obligation has a fair value of $6,000. This is Crest Textile's estimate of the fair value of the cost of its contract to make good on any receivables where the debtor fails to pay. To determine the loss on the sale of receivables by Crest Textiles, the net proceeds from the sale are calculated and compared with the carrying value of the assets sold. Net proceeds are cash or other assets received in a sale less any liabilities incurred.

Illustration 7-16

Calculation of Net Proceeds and Loss on Sale

Calculation of net proceeds:		
Cash received	$460,000	
Due from factor	25,000	$485,000
Less: Recourse obligation		6,000
Net proceeds		$479,000
Calculation of loss on sale:		
Carrying (book) value		$500,000
Net proceeds		479,000
Loss on sale of receivables		$ 21,000

The journal entries for both Crest Textiles and Commercial Factors for the receivables sold with a recourse component retained are as follows:

Crest Textiles Ltd.				Commercial Factors, Inc.		
Cash	460,000			Accounts Receivable	500,000	
Due from Factor	25,000			Due to Crest Textiles		25,000
Loss on Sale of Receivables	21,000			Financing Revenue		15,000
Accounts (Notes)				Cash		460,000
Receivable		500,000				
Recourse Liability		6,000				

In this case, Crest Textiles recognizes a loss of $21,000. In addition, a liability of $6,000 is recorded to indicate the probable payment to Commercial Factors for uncollectible receivables. If all the receivables are collected, Crest Textiles would eliminate its recourse liability and increase income. Commercial Factors' net income is the financing revenue of $15,000 because it will have no bad debts related to these receivables.

Servicing and Other Components. Often, the transferor in a securitization will retain the responsibility for servicing the receivables. This usually includes collecting principal and interest, monitoring slow paying accounts, and remitting cash to those who hold beneficial interests in the receivables, but may include other specified services. If the transferor receives no reimbursement for these activities or receives less than the estimated cost of carrying them out, a **servicing liability component** will be recorded. This decreases the net proceeds on disposal. Alternatively, a **servicing asset component** is recognized if the benefits of servicing (servicing fees under contract, late charges, etc.) are greater than the estimated cost of the obligation. Accounting for this latter case is beyond the purview of this text.

Other financial components identified and recognized in a securitization might include:

Interest-only strip receivable — The contractual right to receive some or all of the interest due on an interest-bearing receivable.

Call option — The right of the transferor to repurchase similar loans or receivables from the transferee.

Disclosure

Accounting Guideline 12 requires considerable disclosure related to securitized receivables accounted for as sales. These are designed to inform the reader about fair value measurements used, key assumptions and some sensitivity analysis, characteristics of the securitizations, information about cash flows between the special purpose entity and the transferor, and detail about balances of and risk associated with servicing assets and liabilities.

Illustration 7-18 provides an example of the main securitization disclosures made by Sears Canada Inc. for its year ended December 28, 2002.

Presentation and Perspectives

Presentation of Receivables

The general disclosure and presentation standards related to typical transactions and balances in the accounts and notes receivables section are:

1. segregate the different types of receivables that an enterprise possesses, if material, so that ordinary trade accounts, amounts owing by related parties, and other significant amounts are separately reported;

2. report the amounts and maturity dates of instalment accounts with a maturity extending beyond one year;

Illustration 7-18

Sears Canada Inc. Disclosures

Sears Canada Inc. (excerpts)
In millions

As at December 28, 2002 and December 29, 2001	2002	2001
Assets		
Current assets		
Accounts receivable (note 2)	**$1,384.2**	$ 871.9

Notes to Consolidated Financial Statements

1. **Summary of Accounting Policies**

   Transfer of Receivables

   Effective July 1, 2001, the Company adopted, on a prospective basis, the new Accounting Guideline—12 Transfers of Receivables, issued by The Canadian Institute of Chartered Accountants. Under the new policy, the Company recognizes gains or losses on transfers of receivables that qualify as sales and recognizes certain financial components that are created as a result of such sales, which consist primarily of the retained interest in the form of a cash reserve account and the retained rights to future excess yield from the transferred receivables (interest-only strip). A gain or loss on sale of the receivables depends in part on the previous carrying amount of the receivables involved in the transfer. Retained interests are initially recorded at fair value, which is estimated based upon the present value of the expected future cash flows and discount rates. Any subsequent decline in the value of the retained interest, other than a temporary decline, will be recorded as a reduction to income.

2. **Accounts Receivable**

in millions	2002	2001
Charge account receivables—current	**$1,882.4**	$1,885.9
Charge account receivables—deferred	**870.6**	755.7
Managed accounts	**2,753.0**	2,641.6
Less: co-ownership interest held by third parties (note 3)	**(1,423.5)**	(1,804.2)
Co-ownership retained by the Company	**1,329.5**	837.4
Interest-only strip receivable (note 3)	**20.6**	36.1
Miscellaneous receivables	**34.1**	(1.6)
	$1,384.2	$ 871.9

3. **Transfer of Receivables**

   The Company sells an undivided co-ownership interest in a pool of current and deferred charge account receivables on a fully serviced basis in securitization transactions and receives no fee for ongoing servicing responsibilities. The Company receives proceeds equal to fair value for the assets sold and retains rights to future cash flows arising after the investors in the securitization trust have received the return for which they contracted. The co-owners have no recourse to the Company's retained interest in the receivables sold other than in respect of amounts in the cash reserve account (Note 5) and the interest only strip receivable. The co-owners have no recourse to the Company's other assets.

   During the year ended December 28, 2002, the Company recognized a pre-tax reduction in revenue of $21.1 million on the securitization of charge account receivables (2001—pre-tax gain of $54.0 million). As at December 28, 2002, the interest-only strip was recorded at $20.6 million (2001—$36.1 million). The following table shows the key economic assumptions used in measuring the interest-only strip and securitization gains. The table also displays the sensitivity of the current fair value of residual cash flows to immediate 10% and 20% adverse changes in yield, payment rate, net charge-off rate and discount rate assumptions.

in millions	Assumptions	10%	20%
Yield (annual rate)	24.03%	$3.4	$6.7
Principal payment rate (monthly)	25.00%	2.7	4.4
Net charge-off rate (annual rate)	4.48%	1.7	2.3
Discount rate (annual rate)	12.00%	1.1	1.1

   The table below summarizes certain cash flows related to the transfer of receivables which have been accounted for under the provisions of Accounting Guideline-12:

in millions	2002	2001
Proceeds from new transfers	$128.0	$1,002.0
Proceeds from collections	756.2	259.4
Other cash flows relating to retained interests	(10.4)	30.6

International Insight

Holding receivables that will be paid in a foreign currency represents risk that the exchange rate may move against the company, causing a decrease in the amount collected in terms of Canadian dollars. Companies engaged in cross-border transactions often "hedge" these receivables by buying contracts to exchange currencies at specified amounts at future dates.

3. report in current assets amounts receivable within one year from the balance sheet date, or an operating cycle, if longer;

4. deduct any allowances necessary to report short-term trade receivables at an appropriate balance sheet valuation; and

5. disclose the nature and carrying value of receivables designated or pledged as collateral for liabilities.[27]

As receivables are financial assets, the general disclosure requirements for financial instruments also apply: (1) disclose information about their terms and conditions; (2) provide information about exposure to interest rate risk and credit risk, including any significant concentrations of credit risk arising from receivables; and (3) disclose their fair value, if practicable.[28] Special disclosures related to transfers of receivables have previously been alluded to.

Excerpts from the June 30, 2002 balance sheet of Intrawest Corporation and the notes cross-referenced to the balance sheet illustrate many of the disclosures required for receivables.

Illustration 7-19

Disclosure of Receivables—Intrawest Corporation

Digital Tool

Student Toolkit—Additional Disclosures

www.wiley.com/canada/kieso

Intrawest Corporation (excerpts)
In thousands of United States dollars

June 30, 2003 and 2002	**2003**	2002
Assets		
Current assets		
Amounts receivable (note 7)	**$126,725**	$109,948
Outside current assets		
Amounts receivable (note 7)	**$ 76,842**	$ 64,734

Notes
7. **Amounts Receivable**

	2003	2002
Receivable from sale of real estate	**$ 54,576**	$ 59,679
Ski and resort operations trade receivables	**34,427**	23,053
Loans, mortgages and notes receivable (note 20)	**89,189**	73,408
Funded senior employee share purchase plans (note 12(f))	**4,445**	4,475
Other accounts receivable	**20,930**	14,067
	203,567	174,682
Current portion	**126,725**	109,948
	$ 76,842	$ 64,734

Amounts receivable from sales of real estate primarily comprise sales proceeds held in trust which are generally paid out to the Company or to construction lenders within 60 days.

Total payments due on amounts receivable are approximately as follows:

Year ending June 30	
2004	$126,725
2005	19,129
2006	4,037
2007	3,310
2008	1,996
Subsequent to 2008	48,370
	$203,567

The loans, mortgages and notes receivable bear interest at both fixed and floating rates which averaged 10.71% per annum as at June 30, 2003 (2002—11.91%). Certain of these amounts have been pledged as security for the Company's bank and other indebtedness (note 9).

---

[27] *CICA Handbook*, Sections 1500.12, 1510.01, and 3020.01, .02, and .12.

[28] Concentrations of credit risk exist when receivables have common characteristics that may affect their collection. These common characteristics might be companies in the same industry or same region of the country. For example, financial statement users want to know if a substantial amount of receivables are with companies in the Middle East, or start-up companies in the high-tech sector.

20. Related Party Transactions:
   During the year ended June 30, 202, $3,991,000 was repaid to the Company by a partnership, one of whose partners was a corporation controlled by an officer and a director of the Company

Illustration 7-19

*Disclosure of Receivables—
Intrawest Corporation
(continued)*

Perspectives

Analysts often calculate financial ratios to evaluate the liquidity of a company's accounts receivable. The ratio used to assess the receivables' liquidity is the **receivables turnover ratio**. This ratio measures the number of times, on average, receivables are collected during the period. The ratio is calculated by dividing net sales by average receivables (net) outstanding during the year. Theoretically, the numerator should include only credit sales. This information is frequently not available, however, and if the relative amounts of credit and cash sales remain fairly constant, the trend indicated by the ratio will still be valid. Unless seasonal factors are significant, average receivables outstanding can be calculated from the beginning and ending balances of net trade receivables.

To illustrate, Canadian Utilities Limited reported 2002 revenue of $2,975.9 million and accounts receivable balances at December 31, 2001 and 2002 of $445.4 million and $459.4 million, respectively. Its accounts receivable turnover ratio is calculated as follows:

Illustration 7-20

*Calculation of Accounts
Receivable Turnover*

$$\text{Accounts Receivable Turnover} = \frac{\text{Net Sales/Revenue}}{\text{Average trade receivables (net)}}$$

$$= \frac{\$2,975.9}{(\$445.4 + \$459.4)/2}$$

$$= 6.58 \text{ times, or every 55 days}$$
$$(365 \text{ days} \div 6.58) \,[29]$$

This information provides some indication of the receivables' quality. It also gives an idea of how successful the firm is in collecting its outstanding receivables, particularly when compared with the credit terms offered by the company. Management, internally, would also prepare an aging schedule to determine how long receivables have been outstanding. It is possible that a satisfactory receivables turnover may have resulted because certain receivables were collected quickly though others have been outstanding for a relatively long period. An aging schedule would reveal such patterns.

Because the expense associated with uncollectible accounts is subject to a large degree of judgement, there has been some concern that companies can use this judgement to manage earnings. By overestimating the amount of uncollectible loans in a good earnings year, a bank, for example, can "save for a rainy day." In future, less profitable periods, the overly conservative allowance for its loan loss account can be reduced to increase earnings.[30]

Further analysis should be carried out on the changes in the basic related accounts. Ordinarily, sales, accounts receivable, and the allowance for doubtful accounts should all

Underlying Concept

Providing information that will help users assess an enterprise's current liquidity and prospective cash flows is a primary objective of accounting.

---

[29] Often the receivables turnover is converted to "days to collect accounts receivable" or "days sales outstanding"—an average collection period. In this case, 6.58 is divided into 365 days to obtain 55 days. Several figures other than 365 could be used here; a common alternative is 360 days because it is divisible by 30 (days) and 12 (months). Use 365 days in any homework calculations.

[30] Recall from the earnings management discussion in Chapter 4 that increasing or decreasing income through management manipulation can reduce the quality of financial reports.

move in the same direction. Higher sales should generate more receivables and an increased allowance. If sales have increased as well as receivables, but the allowance has not increased proportionately, the reader should be alert to the possibility of earnings management. If the allowance grows faster than receivables, particularly in the absence of increased sales, this could indicate a deterioration in credit quality. Alternatively, perhaps the company has built up its allowance account so that there is a cushion for poorer performing years ahead. The answers are not always obvious, but this type of analysis can identify concerns.

With the increased use of the disposition of receivables through securitization transactions, especially where a company retains servicing (such as collection) responsibilities, the financial ratios have to be calculated and interpreted carefully. Consider the following.

- While the company has sold its receivables and received cash earlier than if the receivables were collected in the ordinary course of business, the cash flows are actually from financing transactions, not operating activities.

- Comparing growth in sales to growth in receivables on the balance sheet is not appropriate when calculating receivables turnover and days sales uncollected. Adjustments are needed to the receivable balances for the sold but uncollected accounts. Companies are required to provide this information through note disclosures.

- The securitization is "off-balance sheet" in that the receivables sold are removed from the current assets and the amount "borrowed" is not reported in current liabilities. Therefore, liquidity ratios such as the current and quick ratios are also affected. Even though the same dollar amount is missing from the assets and liabilities, the ratios could be significantly affected.

Securitization transactions can be complex, making it necessary to exercise considerable caution when interpreting basic financial statement ratios. Companies are increasingly being required by regulators to provide full discussion in the MD&A of critical issues such as liquidity, especially where dependent on the use of off-balance sheet financing arrangements such as securitization of receivables.

Digital Tool

Glossary

www.wiley.com/canada/kieso

KEY TERMS

accounts receivable, 343
adjunct account, 340
aging schedule, 348
allowance method, 347
asset-backed
    securities, 354
available-for-sale
    investments, 338
balance sheet
    approach, 348
bank overdrafts, 335
cash, 333
cash discounts, 344

Summary of Learning Objectives

1 Define financial assets.

Financial assets are a major type of asset, and are clearly defined as cash, a contractual right to receive cash or another financial asset, an equity holding in another company, or a contractual right to exchange financial instruments under potentially favourable conditions.

2 Identify items considered cash and cash equivalents.

To be reported as cash, an asset must be readily available to pay current obligations and free from contractual restrictions that limit its use in satisfying debts. Cash consists of coin, currency, and available funds on deposit at the bank. Negotiable instruments such as money orders, certified cheques, cashier's cheques, personal cheques, and bank drafts are also viewed as cash. Savings accounts are usually classified as cash. Cash equivalents include highly liquid short-term (mature less than three months from the date of purchase) investments exchangeable for known amounts of cash, with an insignificant chance of a change in value. Examples include Treasury bills, commercial paper, and money market funds. In certain circumstances, temporary bank overdrafts may be deducted in determining the balance of cash and cash equivalents.

3 Indicate how cash and related items are reported.

Cash is reported as a current asset in the balance sheet, with foreign currency balances reported in the Canadian dollar equivalent at the balance sheet date. The reporting of other related items are: (1) Restricted cash: legally restricted deposits held as compensating balances against short-term borrowing should be stated separately among the cash and cash equivalent items in Current Assets. Restricted deposits held against long-term borrowing arrangements should be separately classified as noncurrent assets in either the Investments or Other Assets sections. (2) Bank overdrafts: They should be reported in the current liabilities section and are usually added to the amount reported as accounts payable. If material, these items should be separately disclosed either on the face of the balance sheet or in the related notes. (3) Cash equivalents: This item is often reported together with cash as cash and cash equivalents.

4 Explain how temporary investments and related income are measured and reported.

Temporary investments that are held for trading are recognized originally at their fair value (cost), and are subsequently adjusted to, and reported at, their fair value at each balance sheet date. This is accounted for by using a valuation allowance account. All unrealized holding gains and losses are taken directly into income. Interest income is earned on investments in debt securities, and there is no amortization of any purchase discount or premium from face value. Dividend income may be earned on equity investments.

5 Define receivables and identify the different types of receivables.

Receivables are claims held against customers and others for money, goods, or services. Most receivables are financial assets. The receivables are classified into three types: (1) current or noncurrent; (2) trade or nontrade; (3) accounts receivable or notes receivable.

6 Explain accounting issues related to recognition and measurement of accounts receivable.

Two issues that may complicate the measurement of accounts receivable are: (1) The availability of discounts (trade and cash discounts) and (2) the length of time between the sale and the payment due dates (the interest element). Ideally, receivables should be measured in terms of their present value; that is, the discounted value of the cash to be received in the future. Receivables arising from normal business transactions that are due in customary trade terms are excluded from present value considerations.

7 Explain accounting issues related to valuation of accounts receivable.

Short-term receivables are valued and reported at net realizable value—the net amount expected to be received in cash, which is not necessarily the amount legally receivable. Determining net realizable value requires estimating both uncollectible receivables and any returns or allowances.

8 Explain accounting issues related to recognition, measurement, and valuation of short-term notes receivable.

The accounting issues related to short-term notes receivable are identical to those of accounts receivable. However, because notes always contain an interest element, interest revenue must be properly recognized. Notes receivable either bear interest on the face amount (interest bearing) or have an interest element that is the difference between the amount lent (or the purchase price) and the maturity value (non-interest bearing).

9 Explain accounting issues related to disposition of accounts and notes receivable.

To accelerate the receipt of cash from receivables, the owner may transfer the receivables to another company for cash. The transfer of receivables to a third party for cash may be accomplished in one of two ways: (1) Secured borrowing: A creditor often requires that the debtor designate or pledge receivables as security for the loan. (2) Sales (factoring or securitization) of receivables: Factors are finance companies or banks that buy receivables from businesses and then collect the remittances directly from the customers. Securitization involves the transfer of receivables to a special purpose entity financed principally by highly rated debt instruments. In many cases, transferors have some continuing involvement with the receivables sold. A financial components approach is used to record this type of transaction whereby the receivables are broken up into a variety of their asset and liability components and the components actually sold or related liabilities taken on are accounted for separately.

10 Explain how receivables are reported and analysed.

Disclosure of receivables requires that valuation accounts be appropriately offset against receivables, receivables be appropriately classified as current or noncurrent, pledged or designated receivables be identified, and concentrations of risks arising from receivables be identified. Receivables are analysed relative to turnover, their age (number of days outstanding), and the relative changes in the related sales, receivables, and allowance accounts.

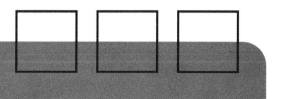

Appendix 7A

Cash Controls

As indicated in Chapter 7, cash creates many management and control problems. The purpose of this appendix is to discuss some of the basic control issues related to cash.

11 Objective
Explain common techniques employed to control cash.

Using Bank Accounts

A company can vary the number and location of banks and the types of bank accounts to obtain desired control objectives. For large companies operating in multiple locations, the location of bank accounts can be important. Establishing collection accounts in strategic locations can accelerate the flow of cash into the company by shortening the time between a customer's payment mailing and the company's use of the cash. Multiple collection centres generally are used to reduce the size of a company's **collection float**, which is the difference between the amount on deposit according to the company's records and the amount of collected cash according to the bank record.

The **general chequing account** is the principal bank account in most companies and frequently the only bank account in small businesses. Cash is deposited in and disbursed from this account as all transactions are cycled through it. Deposits from and disbursements to all other bank accounts are made through the general chequing account.

Imprest bank accounts are used to make a specific amount of cash available for a limited purpose. The account acts as a clearing account for a large volume of cheques or for a specific type of cheque. The specific and intended amount to be cleared through the imprest account is deposited by transferring that amount from the general chequing account or other source. Imprest bank accounts are often used for disbursing payroll cheques, dividends, commissions, bonuses, confidential expenses (e.g., officers' salaries), and travel expenses.

Lockbox accounts are often used by large, multilocation companies to make collections in cities within areas of heaviest customer billing. The company rents a local post office box and authorizes a local bank to pick up the remittances mailed to that box number. The bank empties the box at least once a day and immediately credits the company's account for collections. The greatest advantage of a lockbox is that it accelerates the availability of collected cash. Generally, in a lockbox arrangement the bank microfilms the cheques for record purposes and provides the company with a deposit slip, a list of collections, and any customer correspondence. If the control over cash is improved and if the income generated from accelerating the receipt of funds exceeds the cost of the lockbox system, then it is considered a worthwhile undertaking.

International Insight

Multinational corporations often have cash accounts in more than one currency. For financial statement purposes, these currencies are typically translated into Canadian dollars using the exchange rate in effect at the balance sheet date.

The Imprest Petty Cash System

Almost every company finds it necessary to pay small amounts for a great many things such as employee's lunches, taxi fares, minor office supplies, and other miscellaneous expenses. It is usually impractical to require that such disbursements be made by cheque, yet some control over them is important. A simple method of obtaining reasonable control, while adhering to the rule of disbursement by cheque, is the **imprest system for petty cash** disbursements.

This is how the system works:

1. Someone is designated petty cash custodian and given a small amount of currency from which to make small payments. The transfer of funds to petty cash is recorded as:

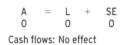

Petty Cash	300	
Cash		300

2. As disbursements are made, the petty cash custodian obtains signed receipts from each individual to whom cash is paid. If possible, evidence of the disbursement should be attached to the petty cash receipt. Petty cash transactions are not recorded until the fund is reimbursed, and then such entries are recorded by someone other than the petty cash custodian.

3. When the petty cash supply runs low, the custodian presents to the general cashier a request for reimbursement supported by the petty cash receipts and other disbursement evidence. The custodian receives a company cheque to replenish the fund. At this point, transactions are recorded based on petty cash receipts:

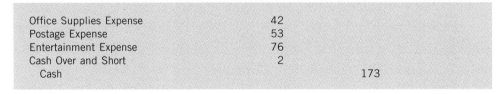

Office Supplies Expense	42	
Postage Expense	53	
Entertainment Expense	76	
Cash Over and Short	2	
Cash		173

4. If it is decided that the amount of cash in the petty cash fund is excessive, an adjustment may be made as follows, lowering the fund balance from $300 to $250:

Cash	50	
Petty Cash		50

Entries are made to the Petty Cash account only to increase or decrease the size of the fund.

A **Cash Over and Short** account is used when the petty cash fund fails to prove out. When this occurs, it is usually due to an error, such as a failure to provide correct change, overpayment of expense, lost receipt, etc. If cash proves out short (i.e., the sum of the receipts and cash in the fund is less than the imprest amount), the shortage is debited to the Cash Over and Short account. If it proves out over, the overage is credited to Cash Over and Short. This account is left open until the end of the year, when it is closed and generally shown on the income statement as an "other expense or revenue."

There are usually expense items in the fund except immediately after reimbursement; therefore, if accurate financial statements are desired, the funds must be reimbursed at the end of each accounting period and also when nearly depleted.

Under the imprest system, the petty cash custodian is responsible at all times for the amount of the fund on hand either in the form of cash or signed receipts. These receipts provide the evidence required by the disbursing officer to issue a reimbursement cheque. Two additional procedures are followed to obtain more complete control over the petty cash fund:

1. Surprise counts of the fund are made from time to time by a superior of the petty cash custodian to determine that the fund is being accounted for satisfactorily.

2. Petty cash receipts are cancelled or mutilated after they have been submitted for reimbursement, so that they cannot be used to secure a second reimbursement.

Physical Protection of Cash Balances

Not only must cash receipts and cash disbursements be safeguarded through internal control measures, but also the cash on hand and in banks must be protected. Because receipts become cash on hand and disbursements are made from cash in banks, adequate control of receipts and disbursements is a part of protecting cash balances. Certain other procedures, however, should be given some consideration.

Physical protection of cash is so elementary a necessity that it requires little discussion. Every effort should be made to minimize the cash on hand in the office. A petty cash fund, the current day's receipts, and perhaps funds for making change should be all that is on hand at any one time. Insofar as possible, these funds should be kept in a vault, safe, or locked cash drawer. Each day's receipts should be transmitted **intact** to the bank as soon as practicable. Intact means that the total receipts are accounted for together with no use of the funds for other purposes. A trail is left, therefore, from the receipts activity into the bank. Accurately stating the amount of available cash both in internal management reports and in external financial statements is also extremely important.

Every company has a record of cash received, disbursed, and the balance. Because of the many cash transactions, however, errors or omissions may be made in keeping this record. Therefore, it is necessary periodically to prove the balance shown in the general ledger. Cash actually present in the office—petty cash, change funds, and undeposited receipts—can be counted for comparison with the company records. Cash on deposit is not available for count and is proved by preparing a bank reconciliation—a reconciliation of the company's record and the bank's record of the company's cash.

Reconciliation of Bank Balances

At the end of each calendar month, the bank supplies each customer with a bank statement (a copy of the bank's account with the customer) together with the customer's cheques that have been paid by the bank during the month.[31] (Increasingly, less and less hard copy will be returned as banks provide companies with electronic access to this information.) If no errors were made by the bank or the customer, if all deposits made and all cheques drawn by the customer reached the bank within the same month, and if no unusual transactions occurred that affected either the company's or the bank's record of cash, the balance of cash reported by the bank to the customer would be the same as that shown in the customer's own records. This condition seldom occurs for one or more of the following reasons.

---

[31] As mentioned in Chapter 7, use of paper cheques continues to be a popular means of payment. However, ready availability of desktop publishing software and hardware has created new opportunities for cheque fraud in the form of duplicate, altered, and forged cheques. At the same time, new fraud-fighting technologies, such as ultraviolet imaging and high-capacity barcodes, are being developed. These technologies convert paper documents into document files that are processed electronically, thereby reducing the risk of fraud.

RECONCILING ITEMS

1. **Deposits in Transit.** End-of-month deposits of cash recorded on the depositor's books in one month are received and recorded by the bank in the following month.

2. **Outstanding Cheques.** Cheques written by the depositor are recorded when written but may not be recorded by (or "clear") the bank until the next month.

3. **Bank Charges.** Charges recorded by the bank against the depositor's balance for such items as bank services, printing cheques, **not-sufficient-funds (NSF) cheques**, and safe-deposit box rentals. The depositor may not be aware of these charges until the bank statement is received.

4. **Bank Credits.** Collections or deposits by the bank for the depositor's benefit may or may not be known to the depositor until receipt of the bank statement. These are reconciling items to the extent they have not yet been recorded on the company's records. Examples are note collection for the depositor, interest earned on interest-bearing chequing accounts, and direct deposits by customers and others.

5. **Bank or Depositor Errors.** Errors on either the part of the bank or the depositor cause the bank balance to disagree with the depositor's book balance.

Hence, differences between the depositor's record of cash and the bank's record are usual and expected. Therefore, the two must be reconciled to determine the nature of the differences between the two amounts.

A **bank reconciliation** is a schedule explaining any differences between the bank's and the company's records of cash. If the difference results only from transactions not yet recorded by the bank, the company's record of cash is considered correct. But, if some part of the difference arises from other items, the bank's records or the company's records must be adjusted.

Two forms of bank reconciliation may be prepared. One form reconciles from the bank statement balance to the book balance or vice versa. The other form reconciles both the bank balance and the book balance to a correct cash balance. This latter form is more widely used. A sample of that form and its common reconciling items are shown in Illustration 7A-1.

Illustration 7A-1	**Balance per bank statement (end of period)**		$$$
Bank Reconciliation Form and Content	Add: Deposits in transit	$$	
	Undeposited receipts (cash on hand)	$$	
	Bank errors that understate the bank statement balance	$$	$$
			$$$
	Deduct: Outstanding cheques	$$	
	Bank errors that overstate the bank statement balance	$$	$$
	Correct cash balance		$$$
	Balance per company's books (end of period)		$$$
	Add: Bank credits and collections not yet recorded in the books	$$	
	Book errors that understate the book balance	$$	$$
			$$$
	Deduct: Bank charges not yet recorded in the books	$$	
	Book errors that overstate the book balance	$$	$$
	Correct cash balance		$$$

This form of reconciliation consists of two sections: (1) "Balance per bank statement" and (2) "Balance per company's books." Both sections end with the same correct cash balance. The correct cash balance is the amount to which the books must be adjusted and is the amount reported on the balance sheet. **Adjusting journal entries are prepared for**

all the addition and deduction items appearing in the "Balance per company's books" section. Any errors attributable to the bank should be called to the bank's attention immediately.

To illustrate, Nugget Mining Company's books show a cash balance at the Ottawa National Bank on November 30, 2005, of $20,502. The bank statement covering the month of November shows an ending balance of $22,190. An examination of Nugget's accounting records and November bank statement identified the following reconciling items:

1. A deposit of $3,680 was mailed to the bank on November 30 but does not appear on the bank statement.

2. Cheques written in November but not charged to (deducted from) the November bank statement are:

Cheque #7327	$ 150
#7348	4,820
#7349	31

3. Nugget has not yet recorded the $600 of interest collected by the bank on November 20 on Sequoia Co. bonds held by the bank for Nugget.

4. Bank service charges of $18 are not yet recorded on Nugget's books.

5. One of Nugget's customer's cheques for $220 was returned with the bank statement and marked "NSF." The bank treated this bad cheque as a disbursement.

6. Nugget discovered that cheque #7322, written in November for $131 in payment of an account payable, had been incorrectly recorded in its books as $311.

7. A cheque written on Nugent Oil Co.'s account in the amount of $175 that had been incorrectly charged to Nugget Mining accompanied the bank statement.

The reconciliation of bank and book balances to the correct cash balance of $21,044 would appear as follows:

Illustration 7A-2

Sample Bank Reconciliation

NUGGET MINING COMPANY
Bank Reconciliation
Ottawa National Bank, November 30, 2005

Balance per bank statement, November 30/05			$22,190
Add: Deposit in transit	(1)	$3,680	
Bank error—incorrect cheque charged to account by bank	(7)	175	3,855
			26,045
Deduct: Outstanding cheques	(2)		5,001
Correct cash balance, November 30/05			$21,044
Balance per books, November 30/05			$20,502
Add: Interest collected by the bank	(3)	$ 600	
Error in recording cheque #7322	(6)	180	780
			21,282
Deduct: Bank service charges	(4)	18	
NSF cheque returned	(5)	220	238
Correct cash balance, November 30/05			$21,044

The journal entries required to adjust and correct Nugget Mining's books in early December 2005 are taken from the items in the "Balance per books" section and are as follows:

A   =   L   +   SE
+762   +180   +582

Cash flows: ↑ 542 inflow

Digital Tool

Expanded
Discussion

www.wiley.com/canada/kieso

Cash	600	
Interest Revenue		600
(To record interest on Sequoia Co. bonds, collected by bank)		
Cash	180	
Accounts Payable		180
(To correct error in recording amount of cheque #7322)		
Office Expense—Bank Charges	18	
Cash		18
(To record bank service charges for November)		
Accounts Receivable	220	
Cash		220
(To record customer's cheque returned NSF)		

Alternatively, one entry could be made with a net $542 debit to cash, the difference between the balance before adjustment of $20,502 and the correct balance of $21,044. When the entries are posted, Nugget's cash account will have a balance of $21,044. Nugget should return the Nugent Oil Co. cheque to Ottawa National Bank, informing the bank of the error.

Digital Tool

Glossary

www.wiley.com/canada/kieso

KEY TERMS

bank reconciliation, 368

imprest system for petty cash, 366

not-sufficient-funds (NSF) cheques, 368

Summary of Learning Objectives for Appendix 7A

11. Explain common techniques used to control cash.

The common techniques employed to control cash are: (1) Using bank accounts: a company can vary the number and location of banks and the types of accounts to obtain desired control objectives. (2) The imprest petty cash system: It may be impractical to require small amounts of various expenses be paid by cheque, yet some control over them is important. (3) Physical protection of cash balances: Adequate control of receipts and disbursements is part of protection of cash balances. Every effort should be made to minimize the cash on hand in the office. (4) Reconciliation of bank balances: Cash on deposit is not available for count and is proved by preparing a bank reconciliation.

Note: All asterisked assignment material relates to the appendix to the chapter.

Brief Exercises

BE7-1   Stowe Enterprises owns the following assets at December 31, 2005:

Cash in bank-savings account	63,000	Chequing account balance	15,000
Cash on hand	9,300	Postdated cheque from Yu Co.	450
Cash refund due, overpayment of income taxes	31,400	Certificates of deposit (180-day)	90,000

What amount should be reported as cash?

BE7-2   On October 1, Robinson Ltd. purchased bonds with a face value of $20,000 as a trading investment. The bonds were priced at $20,500 and the accrued interest purchased was $1,500. At December 31, Robinson received annual interest of $2,000, and the bonds' fair value was $20,900. Prepare Robinson's journal entries for the (a) purchase of the investment and accrued interest, (b) the interest received, and (c) the fair value adjustment.

BE7-3 Peaman Corporation purchased 300 shares of Galactica Inc. common shares as a trading investment for $9,900 on September 8. In December, Galactica declared and paid a cash dividend of $1.25 per share. At year end, December 31, Galactica shares were selling for $34.50 per share. Prepare Peaman Corporation's journal entries to record (a) the purchase of the investment, (b) the dividends received, and (c) the fair value adjustment.

BE7-4 Civic Company made sales of $40,000 with terms 1/10, n/30. Within the discount period it received payment from customers owing $30,000; after the discount period it received payment from customers owing $10,000. Assuming Civic uses the gross method of recording sales, prepare journal entries for the transactions described above.

BE7-5 Use the information presented for Civic Company in BE7-4. If Civic uses the net method of recording sales, prepare journal entries for the transactions described.

BE7-6 Yoshi Corp. uses the gross method to record sales made on credit. On June 1, the company made sales of $40,000 with terms 3/15, n/45. On June 12, Yoshi received full payment for the June 1 sale. Prepare the required journal entries for Yoshi Corp.

BE7-7 Use the information from BE7-6, assuming Yoshi Corp. uses the net method to account for cash discounts. Prepare the required journal entries for Yoshi Corp.

BE7-8 Battle Tank Limited had net sales in 2005 of $1.2 million. At December 31, 2005, before adjusting entries, the balances in selected accounts were: Accounts Receivable, $250,000 debit, and Allowance for Doubtful Accounts, $2,100 credit. If Battle Tank estimates that 2% of its net sales will prove to be uncollectible, prepare the December 31, 2005, journal entry to record bad debt expense.

BE7-9 Use the information presented for Battle Tank Limited in BE7-8.

(a) Instead of estimating the uncollectibles at 2% of net sales, assume it is expected that 10% of accounts receivable will prove to be uncollectible. Prepare the entry to record bad debt expense.

(b) Instead of estimating uncollectibles at 2% of net sales, assume Battle Tank prepares an aging schedule that estimates total uncollectible accounts at $24,600. Prepare the entry to record bad debt expense.

BE7-10 Addams Family Importers sold goods to Acme Decorators for $20,000 on November 1, 2005, accepting Acme's $20,000, six-month, 12% note. Prepare Addams' November 1 entry, December 31 annual adjusting entry, and May 1 entry for the collection of the note and interest.

BE7-11 Aero Acrobats lent $19,417 to Afterburner Limited, accepting Afterburner's three-month, $20,000, zero-interest-bearing note. The implied interest is 12%. Prepare Aero's journal entries for the initial transaction and the collection of $20,000 at maturity assuming (i) the Note Receivable account was debited for $19,417, and (ii) the Note Receivable account was debited for $20,000.

BE7-12 On October 1, 2005, Akira, Inc. assigns $1 million of its accounts receivable to Alberta Provincial Bank as collateral for a $700,000 loan evidenced by a note. The bank assesses a finance charge of 2% of the receivables assigned and interest on the loan of 13%. Prepare the October 1 journal entries for both Akira and Alberta.

BE7-13 Landstalker Enterprises sold $400,000 of accounts receivable to Leander Factors, Inc. on a without recourse basis. The transaction meets the criteria for a sale, and no asset or liability components of the receivables are retained by Landstalker. Leander Factors assesses a finance charge of 4% of the amount of accounts receivable and retains an amount equal to 5% of accounts receivable. Prepare journal entries for both Landstalker and Leander.

BE7-14 Use the information presented for Landstalker Enterprises in BE7-13. Assume the receivables are sold with recourse. Prepare the journal entry for Landstalker to record the sale, assuming the recourse obligation has a fair value of $6,000.

BE7-15 Keyser Woodcrafters sells $200,000 of receivables with a fair value of $210,000 to Keyser Trust in a securitization transaction that meets the criteria for a sale. Keyser Woodcrafters receives full fair value for the receivables and agrees to continue to service the receivables, estimating that the fair value of this service liability component is $18,000. Prepare the journal entry for Keyser Woodcrafters to record the sale.

BE7-16 The financial statements of Andrés Wines Ltd. report net sales for its year ended March 31, 2002 of $139,008 thousand. Accounts receivable are $11,603 thousand at March 31, 2001 and $11,497 thousand at March 31, 2002. Calculate the company's accounts receivable turnover ratio and the average collection period for accounts receivable in days.

BE7-17 Refer to Illustration 7-20 in Chapter 7 and the information provided about Canadian Utilities Limited. Given that the company's accounts receivable balance at December 31, 2000 was $629.2 million and 2001 sales were $3,513.6 million, calculate the company's accounts receivable turnover ratio for 2001. Did it improve in 2002?

*BE7-18 Genesis Ltd. designated Alexa Kidd as petty cash custodian and established a petty cash fund of $200. The fund is reimbursed when the cash in the fund is at $21. Petty cash receipts indicate funds were disbursed for office supplies, $94, and miscellaneous expense, $87. Prepare journal entries for the establishment of the fund and the reimbursement.

*BE7-19 Use the information in BE7-18. Assume that Genesis decides (a) to increase the size of the petty cash fund to $300 immediately after the reimbursement or (b) to reduce the size of the petty cash to $125 immediately after the reimbursement. Prepare the entries necessary to record the (a) and (b) transactions.

*BE7-20 Jaguar Corporation is preparing a bank reconciliation and has identified the following potential reconciling items. For each item, indicate if it is (1) added to the balance per bank statement, (2) deducted from the balance per bank statement, (3) added to the balance per books, or (4) deducted from the balance per books.

(a) Deposit in transit	$5,500	**(d)** Outstanding cheques	$7,422
(b) Interest credited to Jaguar's account	$31	**(e)** NSF cheque returned	$377
(c) Bank service charges	$25		

*BE7-21 Use the information presented for Jaguar Corporation in BE7-20. Prepare any entries necessary to make Jaguar's accounting records correct and complete.

Exercises

E7-1 (Determining Cash Balance) The controller for Eastwood Co. is attempting to determine the amount of cash to be reported on its December 31, 2005, balance sheet. The following information is provided:

1. Commercial savings account of $600,000 and a commercial chequing account balance of $900,000 are held at First National Bank, and a bank overdraft of $35,000 in a chequing account at the Royal Scotia Bank.

2. Eastwood has agreed to maintain a cash balance of $100,000 at all times in its chequing account at First National Bank to ensure future credit availability.

3. Investment in the Commercial Bank of Montreal money market mutual fund, $5 million.

4. Travel advances of $18,000 for executive travel for the first quarter of next year (employees to complete expense reports after travel completed).

5. A separate cash fund in the amount of $1.5 million is restricted for the retirement of long-term debt.

6. Petty cash fund of $1,000.

7. An IOU from Marianne Koch, a company officer, in the amount of $1,900, to be withheld from her salary in January 2006.

8. Twenty cash floats for retail operation cash registers: 8 at $75 and 12 at $100.

9. The company has two certificates of deposit, each totalling $500,000. These certificates of deposit each had a maturity of 120 days when acquired. One was purchased October 15 and the other on December 27.

10. Eastwood has received a cheque dated January 12, 2006 in the amount of $25,000 from a customer owing funds at December 31, and another dated January 8, 2006 in the amount of $11,500 from another customer as an advance on an order placed December 29 to be delivered February 1, 2006.

11. Eastwood holds $2.1 million of commercial paper of Sergio Leone Co., which is due in 60 days.

12. Currency and coin on hand amounted to $7,700.

13. Eastwood acquired 1,000 shares of Sortel for $3.90 in late November to be held for trading. These are still on hand at year end and have a market value of $4.10 on December 31, 2005.

Instructions

(a) Calculate the amount of cash to be reported on Eastwood Co.'s balance sheet at December 31, 2005.

(b) Indicate the proper reporting for items that are not reported as cash on the December 31, 2005 balance sheet.

E7-2 **(Determine Cash Balance)** Presented below are a number of independent situations. For each situation, determine the amount that should be reported as cash. If the item(s) is not reported as cash, explain the rationale.

1. Chequing account balance $925,000; certificate of deposit $1.4 million; cash advance to subsidiary of $980,000; utility deposit paid to gas company $180.

2. Chequing account balance $600,000; an overdraft in special chequing account at same bank as normal chequing account of $17,000; cash held in a bond sinking fund $200,000; petty cash fund $300; coins and currency on hand $1,350.

3. Chequing account balance $590,000; postdated cheque from customer $11,000; cash restricted due to maintaining compensating balance requirement of $100,000; certified cheque from customer $9,800; postage stamps on hand $620.

4. Chequing account balance at bank $37,000; money market balance at mutual fund (has chequing privileges) $48,000; NSF cheque received from customer $800.

5. Chequing account balance $700,000; cash restricted for future plant expansion $500,000; short-term (60 day) Treasury bills $180,000; cash advance received from customer $900 (not included in chequing account balance); cash advance of $7,000 to company executive, payable on demand; refundable deposit of $26,000 paid to federal government to guarantee performance on construction contract.

E7-3 **(Trading Securities Entries)** On December 31, 2004, Tiger Corp. provided you with the following information regarding its trading securities.

December 31, 2004

Investments (Trading)	Cost	Fair Value	Unrealized Gain (Loss)
Clemson Corp. shares	$20,000	$19,000	$(1,000)
Colorin Corp. shares	10,000	9,000	(1,000)
Buffald Ltd. shares	20,000	20,600	600
Total of portfolio	$50,000	$48,600	(1,400)
Previous balance, fair value allowance account			–0–
Adjustment needed to allowance account—Cr.			$(1,400)

During 2005, Colorin Corp. shares were sold for $9,400. The fair value of the securities on December 31, 2005 was: Clemson Corp. shares—$19,100; Buffald Ltd. shares—$20,500.

Instructions

(a) Prepare the adjusting journal entry needed on December 31, 2004.

(b) Prepare the journal entry to record the sale of the Colorin Corp. shares during 2005.

(c) Prepare the adjusting journal entry needed on December 31, 2005.

E7-4 **(Investment in Debt Security Held for Trading)** Alberta Corp. purchased a $100,000 face value bond of Myers Corp. on July 31, 2004 for $105,490 plus accrued interest. The bond pays interest annually each November 1 at a rate of 9%. On November 1, 2004, Alberta Corp. received the annual interest. On December 31, 2004, Alberta's year end, a newspaper indicated a market value for these bonds of 103.2. Alberta sold the bonds on January 15, 2005 for $102,600 plus accrued interest.

Interactive Homework

Instructions

(a) Prepare the journal entries to record the purchase of the bond, the receipt of interest, any adjustments required at year end, and the subsequent sale of the bonds.

(b) Calculate the number of months the bonds were held by Alberta in 2004 and the amount of interest they should have reported as earned in 2004. How much interest revenue is reported by Alberta on its 2004 income statement?

(c) If these bonds were acquired to earn a return on excess funds, did the company meet its objective? If so, how much return did they earn while the bonds were held? If not, why not?

E7-5 **(Held-for-Trading Securities Entries)** Lazier Corporation has the following securities in its trading portfolio of securities on December 31, 2004.

Investments (Trading)	Cost	Fair Value
1,500 shares of David Jones Inc., common	$ 73,500	$ 69,000
5,000 shares of Hearn Corp., common	180,000	175,000
400 shares of Alessandro Inc., preferred	60,000	61,600
	$313,500	$305,600

All of the securities were purchased in 2004.

In 2005, Lazier completed the following securities transactions.

| March | 1 | Sold the 1,500 shares of David Jones Inc., common, at $45 per share less fees of $500. |
| April | 1 | Bought 700 shares of Oberto Ltd., common, at $75 per share plus fees of $1,300. Lazier's policy is to include any fees and commissions paid on the purchase of securities as part of their cost. |

Lazier Corporation's portfolio of trading securities appeared as follows on December 31, 2005.

Investments (Trading)	Cost	Fair Value
5,000 shares of Hearn Corp., common	$180,000	$175,000
700 shares of Oberto Ltd., common	53,800	50,400
400 shares of Alessandro Inc., preferred	60,000	58,000
	$293,800	$283,400

Instructions

Prepare the general journal entries for Lazier Corporation for:

(a) The 2004 adjusting entry.

(b) The sale of the David Jones Inc. shares.

(c) The purchase of the Oberto Ltd. shares.

(d) The 2005 adjusting entry for the trading portfolio.

E7-6   (Financial Statement Presentation of Receivables)   Gleason Inc. shows a balance of $221,140 in the Accounts Receivable account on December 31, 2005. The balance consists of the following:

Instalment accounts due in 2006	$ 23,000
Instalment accounts due after 2006	34,000
Overpayments to creditors	2,640
Due from regular customers, of which $40,000 represents accounts pledged as security for a bank loan	79,000
Advances to employees	1,500
Advance to subsidiary company (made in 2000)	81,000
	$221,140

Instructions

Illustrate how the information above should be shown on the balance sheet of Gleason Inc. on December 31, 2005.

E7-7   (Determine Ending Accounts Receivable)   Your accounts receivable clerk, Mitra Adams, to whom you pay a salary of $1,500 per month, has just purchased a new Cadillac. You decided to test the accuracy of the accounts receivable balance of $82,000 as shown in the ledger.

Interactive Homework

The following information is available for your first year in business:

1. Collections from customers $198,000

2. Merchandise purchased $320,000

3. Ending merchandise inventory $90,000

4. Goods are marked to sell at 40% above cost

Instructions

Estimate the ending balance of accounts receivable from customers that should appear in the ledger and any apparent shortages. Assume that all sales are made on account.

E7-8   (Recording Sales Transactions)   Presented below is information from Perez Computers Ltd.

July	1	Sold $20,000 of computers to Robertson Corp. with terms 3/15, n/60.
July	5	Robertson Corp. returned for full credit one computer with an invoice price of $2,200.
July	10	Perez received payment from Robertson for the full amount owed from the July transactions.
July	17	Sold $200,000 in computers and peripherals to the Clarkson Store with terms of 2/10, n/30.
July	26	The Clarkson Store paid Perez for half of its July purchases.
August	30	The Clarkson Store paid Perez for the remaining half of its July purchases.

Instructions

(a) Prepare the entries for Perez Computers Ltd. assuming the gross method is used to record sales and cash discounts.

(b) Prepare the entries for Perez Computers Ltd. assuming the net method is used to record sales and cash discounts.

E7-9 (Record Sales Gross and Net) On June 3, Arnold Limited sold to Chester Arthur merchandise having a sale price of $3,000 with terms of 2/10, n/60, f.o.b. shipping point. An invoice totalling $90, terms n/30, was received by Chester on June 8 from the John Booth Transport Service for the freight cost. On receipt of the goods, June 5, Chester notified Arnold that merchandise costing $500 contained flaws that rendered it worthless; the same day Arnold Limited issued a credit memo covering the worthless merchandise and asked that it be returned at company expense. The freight on the returned merchandise was $25, paid by Arnold on June 7. On June 12, the company received a cheque for the balance due from Chester Arthur.

Instructions

(a) Prepare journal entries on Arnold Limited's books to record all the events noted above under each of the following bases:

1. Sales and receivables are entered at gross selling price.

2. Sales and receivables are entered at net of cash discounts.

(b) Prepare the journal entry under basis 2, assuming that Chester Arthur did not remit payment until July 29.

E7-10 (Recording Bad Debts) At the end of 2004, Juan Corporation has accounts receivable of $800,000 and an allowance for doubtful accounts of $40,000. On January 16, 2005, Juan determined that its receivable from Maximillian Ltd. of $6,000 will not be collected, and management has authorized its write-off.

Instructions

(a) Prepare the journal entry for Juan Corporation to write off the Maximillian receivable.

(b) What is the net realizable value of Juan's accounts receivable before the write-off of the Maximillian receivable? What is the book value of Juan's accounts receivable before the write-off?

(c) What is the net realizable value of Juan's accounts receivable after the write-off of the Maximillian receivable? What is the book value of Juan's accounts receivable after the write-off?

E7-11 (Calculating Bad Debts and Preparing Journal Entries) The trial balance before adjustment of Kline Ltd. shows the following balances.

Interactive Homework

	Debit	Credit
Accounts receivable	$50,000	
Allowance for doubtful accounts	1,750	
Sales (75% on credit)		$680,000

Instructions

Give the entry for estimated bad debts assuming that the allowance is to provide for doubtful accounts on the basis of (a) 4% of gross accounts receivable, and (b) 1% of net credit sales.

E7-12 (Calculating Bad Debts) At January 1, 2005, the credit balance in the Allowance for Doubtful Accounts of Amos Corp. was $400,000. For 2005, the provision for doubtful accounts is based on a percentage of net sales. Net sales for 2005 were $70 million. Based on the latest available facts, the 2005 provision for doubtful accounts is estimated to be 0.8% of net sales. During 2005, uncollectible receivables amounting to $500,000 were written off against the allowance for doubtful accounts.

Instructions

Prepare a schedule calculating the balance in Amos' Allowance for Doubtful Accounts at December 31, 2005.

E7-13 (Bad Debt Reporting) The chief accountant for Dickinson Corporation provides you with the following list of accounts receivable written off in the current year.

Date	Customer	Amount
March 31	Eli Masters Ltd.	$7,700
June 30	S. Crane Associates	6,800
September 30	Annie Lowell's Dress Shop	12,000
December 31	Richard Frost	6,830

Dickinson Corporation follows the policy of debiting Bad Debt Expense as accounts are written off. The chief accountant maintains that this procedure is appropriate for financial statement purposes.

All of Dickinson Corporation's sales are on a 30-day credit basis. Sales for the current year total $2.2 million, and research has determined that bad debt losses approximate 2% of sales.

Instructions

(a) Do you agree or disagree with the Dickinson Corporation policy concerning recognition of bad debt expense? Why or why not?

(b) By what amount would net income differ if bad debt expense was calculated using the allowance method and percentage-of-sales approach?

E7-14   (Calculating Bad Debts and Preparing Journal Entries)   The trial balance before adjustment of Chloe Inc. shows the following balances:

	Dr.	Cr.
Accounts Receivable	$92,000	
Allowance for Doubtful Accounts	1,950	
Sales (all on credit)		$684,000
Sales Returns and Allowances	30,000	

Instructions

Give the entry for bad debt expense for the current year assuming:

(a) the allowance should be 4% of gross accounts receivable

(b) historical records indicate 1% of net sales will not be collected.

E7-15   (Bad Debts—Aging)   Gerard Manley, Inc. includes the following account among its trade receivables.

Hopkins Co.

1/1	Balance forward	700	1/28	Cash (#1710)	1,100
1/20	Invoice #1710	1,100	4/2	Cash (#2116)	1,350
3/14	Invoice #2116	1,350	4/10	Cash (1/1 Balance)	155
4/12	Invoice #2412	1,710	4/30	Cash (#2412)	1,000
9/5	Invoice #3614	490	9/20	Cash (#3614 and	
10/17	Invoice #4912	860		part of #2412)	790
11/18	Invoice #5681	2,000	10/31	Cash (#4912)	860
12/20	Invoice #6347	800	12/1	Cash (#5681)	1,250
			12/29	Cash (#6347)	800

Instructions

Age the Hopkins Co. account and specify any items that may require particular attention at year end.

E7-16   (Interest-bearing and Noninterest-bearing Notes)   Saleh Corp. was experiencing cash flow problems and was unable to pay its $32,000 account payable to Amirkal Corp. when it fell due on September 30, 2004. Saleh agreed to substitute a one-year note for the open account. The following two options were presented to Saleh by Amirkal Corp.:

Option 1   A one-year note for $32,000 due September 30, 2005. Interest at a rate of 8% would be payable at maturity.

Option 2   A one-year noninterest-bearing note for $34,560. The implied rate of interest is 8%.

Assume that Amirkal Corp. has a December 31 year end.

Instructions

(a) Prepare the entries required on Amirkal Corp.'s books on September 30, 2004, December 31, 2004, and September 30, 2005 assuming Option 1 is chosen by Saleh Corp.

(b) Prepare the entries required on Amirkal Corp.'s books on September 30, 2004, December 31, 2004, and September 30, 2005 assuming Option 2 is chosen by Saleh Corp.

(c) Compare the amount of interest revenue earned by Amirkal Corp. in 2004 and 2005 under both options. Comment briefly.

E7-17   (Journalizing Various Receivable Transactions)   Presented below is information related to Janut Corp.

July	1	Janut Corp. sold to Harding Ltd. merchandise having a sales price of $9,000 with terms 1/10, net/60. Janut records its sales and receivables net.
	3	Harding Ltd. returned defective merchandise having a sales price of $700.
	5	Accounts receivable of $15,000 (gross) are factored with Jackson Credit Corp. without recourse at a financing charge of 9%. Cash is received for the proceeds; collections are handled by the finance company. (These accounts were subject to a 2% discount and were all past the discount period.)
	9	Specific accounts receivable of $15,000 (gross) are pledged to Landon Credit Corp. as security for a loan of $11,000 at a finance charge of 2% of the loan amount plus 9% interest on the outstanding balance. Janut will continue to make the collections. All the accounts receivable are past the discount period.
Dec.	29	Harding Ltd. notifies Janut that it is bankrupt and will pay only 10% of its account. Give the entry to write off the uncollectible balance using the allowance method. (Note: First record the increase in the receivable on July 11 when the discount period passed.)

Instructions

Prepare all necessary entries in general journal form for Janut Corp.

E7-18   (Assigning Accounts Receivable)   On April 1, 2005, Rasheed Corporation assigns $400,000 of its accounts receivable to the First Provincial Bank as collateral for a $200,000 loan due July 1, 2005. The assignment agreement calls for Rasheed to continue to collect the receivables. First Provincial Bank assesses a finance charge of 2% of the accounts receivable, and interest on the loan is 10%, a realistic rate for a note of this type.

Instructions

(a) Prepare the April 1, 2005 journal entry for Rasheed Corporation.

(b) Prepare the journal entry for Rasheed's collection of $350,000 of the accounts receivable during the April 1 to June 30, 2005 period.

(c) On July 1, 2005, Rasheed paid First Provincial all that was due on the loan.

E7-19   (Transfer of Receivables with Recourse)   Quartet Ltd. factors receivables with a carrying amount of $200,000 to Joffrey Company for $160,000 on a with-recourse basis.

Instructions

The recourse provision has a fair value of $1,000. Assuming this transaction should be recorded as a sale, prepare the appropriate journal entry to record the transaction on the books of Quartet Ltd.

Interactive Homework

E7-20   (Transfer of Receivables with Recourse)   Houseman Corporation factors $175,000 of accounts receivable with Battle Financing, Inc. on a with-recourse basis. Battle Financing will collect the receivables. The receivable records are transferred to Battle Financing on August 15, 2005. Battle Financing assesses a finance charge of 2% of the amount of accounts receivable and also reserves an amount equal to 4% of accounts receivable to cover probable adjustments.

Instructions

(a) What conditions must be met for a transfer of receivables to be accounted for as a sale?

(b) Assume the conditions from part (a) are met. Prepare the journal entry on August 15, 2005, for Houseman to record the sale of receivables, assuming the recourse obligation has a fair value of $2,000.

(c) What effect will the factoring of receivables have on calculating the accounts receivable turnover for Houseman? Comment briefly.

E7-21   (Transfer of Receivables with Servicing Retained)   Lute Retail Ltd. transfers $300,000 of its accounts receivable to an independent trust in a securitization transaction on July 11, 2005, receiving 96% of the receivables balance as proceeds. Lute will continue to manage the customer accounts, including their collection. Lute estimates this obligation has a liability value of $12,500. In addition, the agreement includes a recourse provision with an estimated value of $9,900. The transaction is to be recorded as a sale.

Instructions

(a) Prepare the journal entry on July 11, 2005, for Lute Retail Ltd. to record the securitization of the receivables.

(b) What effect will the securitization of receivables have on the account receivable turnover calculated for Lute Retail Ltd.? Comment briefly.

E7-22   (Analysis of Receivables)   Presented below is information for Jones Company.

1. Beginning of the year Accounts Receivable balance was $15,000.

2. Net sales for the year were $185,000. (Credit sales were $100,000 of the total sales.) Jones does not offer cash discounts.

3. Collections on accounts receivable during the year were $70,000.

Instructions

(a) Prepare (summary) journal entries to record the items noted above.

(b) Calculate Jones's accounts receivable turnover ratio for the year. How old is the average receivable?

(c) Use the turnover ratio calculated in (b) to analyse Jones's liquidity. The turnover ratio last year was 4.85.

E7-23   (Receivables Turnover)   The Becker Milk Company Limited, a real estate management company since November 1996, reports the following information in their financial statements for their years ended April 30, 2003, 2002 and 2001:

Accounts receivable, net of allowance for	
doubtful accounts (note 4)—April 30, 2003	$ 575,118
April 30, 2002	68,559
April 30, 2001	286,372
Revenue (note 4), year ended April 30, 2003	3,691,698
April 30, 2002	4,482,241
April 30, 2001	4,092,828

Note 4: Accounts Receivable and Revenue
As at April 30, 2003, the Company's largest single tenant accounted for approximately nil% (2002 – 67%, 2001 – 82%) of accounts receivable and 84% (2002 – 85%, 2001 – 82%) of revenue. Included in revenue in fiscal 2002 is $540,000 from the tenant to terminate a lease at one location.

Instructions

(a) Calculate the receivables turnover and days sales outstanding (or average age of receivables) for the two most recent years provided.

(b) Comment on your results.

*E7-24   (Petty Cash)   Keene, Inc. decided to establish a petty cash fund to help ensure internal control over its small cash expenditures. The following information is available for the month of April.

1. On April 3, a petty cash fund is established in the amount of $200.

2. A summary of the petty cash expenditures made by the petty cash custodian as of April 13 is as follows:

Delivery charges paid on merchandise purchased	$60.00
Supplies purchased and used	25.00
Postage expense	33.00
IOU from employees	17.00
Miscellaneous expense	36.00

The petty cash fund was replenished on April 13. The balance in the fund was $27.

3. The petty cash fund balance was increased by $100 to $300 on April 20.

Instructions
Prepare the journal entries to record transactions related to petty cash for the month of April.

Interactive
Homework

*E7-25   (Petty Cash)   The petty cash fund of Luigi's Auto Repair Service, a sole proprietorship, contains the following:

1. Coins and currency		$15.20
2. An IOU from Bob Cunningham, an employee, for cash advance		43.00
3. Cheque payable to Luigi's Auto Repair from Pat Webber, an employee, marked NSF		34.00
4. Vouchers for the following:		
Stamps	$ 21.00	
Two NHL play-off tickets for Al Luigi	170.00	
Printer cartridge	14.35	205.35
		$297.55

The general ledger account Petty Cash has a balance of $300.00.

Instructions

Prepare the journal entry to record the reimbursement of the petty cash fund.

*E7-26 (Bank Reconciliation and Adjusting Entries) Ling Corp. deposits all receipts intact and makes all payments by cheque. The following information is available from the cash records.

April 30 Bank Reconciliation

Balance per bank	$7,000
Add: Deposits in transit	1,540
Deduct: Outstanding cheques	(2,000)
Balance per books	$6,540

Month of May Results

	Per Bank	Per Books
Balance May 31	$8,640	$9,250
May deposits	5,000	5,810
May cheques	4,000	3,100
May note collected (not included in May deposits)	1,000	—
May bank service charge	25	—
May NSF cheque from a customer, returned by the bank (recorded by bank as a charge)	335	—

Instructions

(a) Prepare a bank reconciliation going from balance per bank and balance per books to correct cash balance.

(b) Prepare the general journal entry or entries to correct the Cash account at May 31.

*E7-27 (Bank Reconciliation and Adjusting Entries) Bruno Corp. has just received the August 31, 2005 bank statement, which is summarized below:

National Bank of Ottawa	Disbursements	Receipts	Balance
Balance, August 1			$ 9,369
Deposits during August		$32,200	41,569
Note collected for depositor, including $40 interest		1,040	42,609
Cheques cleared during August	$34,500		8,109
Bank service charges	20		8,089
Balance, August 31			8,089

The general ledger Cash account contained the following entries for the month of August:

Cash			
Balance, August 1	10,050	Disbursements in August	34,903
Receipts during August	35,000		

Deposits in transit at August 31 are $3,800, and cheques outstanding at August 31 total $1,050. Cash on hand at August 31 is $310. The bookkeeper improperly entered one cheque in the books at $146.50 that was written for $164.50 for supplies (expense); it cleared the bank during the month of August.

Instructions

(a) Prepare a bank reconciliation dated August 31, 2005, proceeding to a correct balance.

(b) Prepare any entries necessary to make the books correct and complete.

(c) What amount of cash should be reported in the August 31 balance sheet?

Problems

P7-1 Mainet Equipment Corp. closes its books regularly on December 31, but at the end of 2005 it held its cash book open so that a more favourable balance sheet could be prepared for credit purposes. Cash receipts and disbursements for the first 10 days of January were recorded as December transactions.

The following information is given.

1. January cash receipts recorded in the December cash book totalled $39,640, of which $22,000 represents cash sales and $17,640 represents collections on account for which cash discounts of $360 were given.

2. January cash disbursements recorded in the December cheque register liquidated accounts payable of $26,450 on which discounts of $250 were taken.

3. The ledger has not been closed for 2005.

4. The amount shown as inventory was determined by physical count on December 31, 2005.

Instructions

(a) Prepare any entries you consider necessary to correct Mainet's accounts at December 31.

(b) To what extent was Mainet Equipment Co. able to show a more favourable balance sheet at December 31 by holding its cash book open? (Use ratio analysis.) Assume that the balance sheet that was prepared by the company showed the following amounts:

	Dr.	Cr.
Cash	$39,000	
Receivables	42,000	
Inventories	67,000	
Accounts payable		$45,000
Other current liabilities		14,200

P7-2 Gypsy Clothing Corp. has the following portfolio of trading securities at September 30, 2004, its last reporting date.

Trading Securities	Cost	Fair Value
Alpha Inc., 5,000 common shares	$225,000	$200,000
Epsilon Ltd., 3,500 preferred shares	133,000	140,000
Sigma Supply Inc., 1,000 common shares	180,000	179,000

On October 10, 2004, the Alpha shares were sold at a price of $54 per share. On November 2, 2004, 3,000 common shares of Gamma Corp. were purchased at $59.50 per share. Gypsy pays a 1% commission on both purchases and sales of all securities and follows a policy of including the commission in the calculation of proceeds and investment cost. The December 31, 2004 fair values of the shares held were: Epsilon $96,000, Gamma $132,000, and Sigma $193,000.

Instructions

(a) Prepare the journal entries to record the sale, purchase, and adjusting entries related to the trading securities in the last quarter of 2004.

(b) Indicate how the investments would be reported on the December 31, 2004 balance sheet.

P7-3 The following information relates to the 2005 debt and equity investment transactions of Yellowjackets Ltd., all of which have been designated as held for trading.

1. On February 1, the company purchased 12% bonds of Williams Corp. having a par value of $500,000 at 106.5 plus accrued interest. Interest is payable April 1 and October 1.

2. On April 1, semiannual interest is received on the Williams bond.

3. On July 1, 9% bonds of Saint, Inc. were purchased. These bonds, with a par value of $200,000, were purchased at 101 plus accrued interest. Interest dates are June 1 and December 1.

4. On August 12, 3,000 shares of the Royal Bank of Canada were acquired at a cost of $59 per share. A 1% commission was paid. (Include in the investment cost.)

5. On September 1, Williams Corp. bonds with a par value of $100,000 were sold at 104 plus accrued interest.

6. On September 28, a dividend of $0.50 per share is received on the Royal Bank shares.

7. On October 1, semiannual interest is received on the remaining Williams Corp. bonds.

8. On December 1, semiannual interest is received on the Saint, Inc. bonds.

9. On December 28, a dividend of $0.52 per share is received on the Royal Bank shares.

10. On December 31, the following fair values are determined: Williams bonds 103.75; Saint bonds 99; Royal Bank shares $62.50.

Instructions

(a) Prepare all journal entries you consider necessary, including year-end adjusting entries at December 31. Assume there were no trading securities on hand at the end of 2004.

(b) Identify the effect on the 2005 Income Statement of Yellowjackets Ltd. of the 2005 transactions.

(c) Assume instead that there were trading securities on hand at December 31, 2004 made up of shares with a cost of $400,000 and a fair value of $390,000. These non-dividend-paying shares were sold in early 2005 and their original cost was recovered exactly. How would your answer to part (b) differ as a result of this information?

P7-4 Presented below are a series of unrelated situations.

1. Atlantic Inc.'s unadjusted trial balance at December 31, 2005 included the following accounts:

	Debit	Credit
Allowance for doubtful accounts	$ 4,000	
Sales		$1,600,000
Sales returns and allowances	67,000	
Sales discounts	2,300	

Atlantic estimates its bad debt expense to be 1.5% of net sales. Determine its bad debt expense for 2005.

2. An analysis and aging of Central Corp. accounts receivable at December 31, 2005 disclosed the following:

Amounts estimated to be uncollectible	$ 180,000
Accounts receivable	1,790,000
Allowance for doubtful accounts (per books)	125,000

What is the net realizable value of Central's receivables at December 31, 2005?

3. Western Co. provides for doubtful accounts based on 3% of credit sales. The following data are available for 2005.

Credit sales during 2005	$2,100,000
Allowance for doubtful accounts 1/1/05	17,000
Collection of accounts written off in prior years	
(customer credit was reestablished)	8,000
Customer accounts written off as uncollectible	
during 2005	26,000

What is the balance in the Allowance for Doubtful Accounts at December 31, 2005?

4. At the end of its first year of operations, December 31, 2005, Pacific Inc. reported the following information:

Accounts receivable, net of allowance for	
doubtful accounts	$950,000
Customer accounts written off as uncollectible	
during 2005	24,000
Bad debt expense for 2005	84,000

What should be the balance in accounts receivable at December 31, 2005, before subtracting the allowance for doubtful accounts?

5. The following accounts were taken from Northern Inc.'s unadjusted trial balance at December 31, 2005.

	Debit	Credit
Sales (all on credit)		$750,000
Sales discounts	$ 11,400	
Allowance for doubtful accounts	14,000	
Accounts receivable	410,000	

If doubtful accounts are 3% of accounts receivable, determine the bad debt expense to be reported for 2005.

Instructions

Answer the questions relating to each of the five independent situations as requested.

P7-5 Paderewski Corporation operates in an industry that has a high rate of bad debts. Before any year-end adjustments, the balance in Paderewski's Accounts Receivable account was $595,000 and the Allowance for Doubtful Accounts had a credit balance of $35,000. The year-end balance reported in the balance sheet for the Allowance for Doubtful Accounts will be based on the aging schedule shown below.

Days Account Outstanding	Amount	Probability of Collection
Less than 16 days	$340,000	0.97
Between 16 and 30 days	100,000	0.92
Between 31 and 45 days	80,000	0.80
Between 46 and 60 days	40,000	0.75
Between 61 and 75 days	20,000	0.40
Over 75 days	15,000	0.00

Instructions

(a) What is the appropriate balance for the Allowance for Doubtful Accounts at year end?

(b) Show how accounts receivable would be presented on the balance sheet.

(c) What is the dollar effect of the year-end bad debt adjustment on the before-tax income?

P7-6   From inception of operations to December 31, 2005, Madden Corporation provided for uncollectible accounts receivable under the allowance method: provisions were made monthly at 2% of credit sales; bad debts written off were charged to the allowance account; recoveries of bad debts previously written off were credited to the allowance account; and no year-end adjustments to the allowance account were made. Madden's usual credit terms are net 30 days.

The balance in the Allowance for Doubtful Accounts was $154,000 at January 1, 2005. During 2005, credit sales totalled $9 million, interim provisions for doubtful accounts were made at 2% of credit sales, $95,000 of bad debts were written off, and recoveries of accounts previously written off amounted to $15,000. Madden upgraded its computer facility in November, 2005 and an aging of accounts receivable was prepared for the first time as of December 31, 2005. A summary of the aging is as follows:

Classification by Month of Sale	Balance in Each Category	Estimated % Uncollectible
November–December 2005	$1,080,000	2%
July–October	650,000	10%
January–June	420,000	35%
Prior to 1/1/05	150,000	75%
	$2,300,000	

Based on the review of collectibility of the account balances in the "prior to 1/1/05" aging category, additional receivables totalling $60,000 were written off as of December 31, 2005. The 75% uncollectible estimate applies to the remaining $90,000 in the category. Effective with the year ended December 31, 2005, Madden adopted a new accounting method for estimating the allowance for doubtful accounts at the amount indicated by the year-end aging analysis of accounts receivable.

Instructions

(a) Prepare a schedule analysing the changes in the Allowance for Doubtful Accounts for the year ended December 31, 2005. Show supporting calculations in good form. (Hint: In calculating the 12/31/05 allowance, subtract the $60,000 write-off.)

(b) Prepare the journal entry for the year-end adjustment to the Allowance for Doubtful Accounts balance as of December 31, 2005.

(AICPA adapted)

P7-7   Presented below is information related to Shea Inc.'s Accounts Receivable during the current year 2005.

1. An aging schedule of the accounts receivable as of December 31, 2005, is as follows:

Age	Net Debit Balance	% to Be Applied after Correction Is Made
Under 60 days	$172,342	1%
61–90 days	136,490	3%
91–120 days	39,924*	7%
Over 120 days	23,644	$4,200 definitely uncollectible; estimated remainder uncollectible is 20%
	$372,400	

*The $2,740 write-off of receivables is related to the 91–120 day category.

2. The Accounts Receivable control account has a debit balance of $372,400 on December 31, 2005.

3. Two entries were made in the Bad Debt Expense account during the year: (1) a debit on December 31 for the amount credited to Allowance for Doubtful Accounts, and (2) a credit for $2,740 on November 3, 2005, and a debit to Allowance for Doubtful Accounts because of a bankruptcy.

4. The Allowance for Doubtful Accounts is as follows for 2005:

Allowance for Doubtful Accounts				
Nov. 3	Uncollectible accounts written off	2,740	Jan. 1 Beginning balance	8,750
			Dec. 31 5% of $372,400	18,620

5. A credit balance exists in the Accounts Receivable (61–90 days) of $4,840, which represents an advance on a sales contract.

Instructions

Assuming that the books have not been closed for 2005, make the necessary correcting entries.

P7-8 The balance sheet of Reynolds Corp. at December 31, 2004 includes the following:

Notes receivable	$26,000	
Accounts receivable	182,100	
Less: Allowance for doubtful accounts	(17,300)	$190,800

Transactions in 2005 include the following:

1. Accounts receivable of $138,000 were collected, including accounts (gross) of $40,000, on which 2% sales discounts were allowed.

2. An additional $6,300 was received in payment of an account that was written off the books as worthless in 2002.

3. Customer accounts of $17,500 were written off during the year.

4. At year end, the Allowance for Doubtful Accounts was estimated to need a balance of $20,000. This estimate is based on an analysis of aged accounts receivable.

Instructions

Prepare all journal entries necessary to reflect the information above.

(AICPA adapted)

P7-9 On October 1, 2005, Farm Equipment Corp. sold a harvesting machine to Stead Industries. In lieu of a cash payment, Stead Industries gave Farm Equipment a two-year, $100,000, 12% note, a realistic rate for a note of this type. The note required interest to be paid annually on October 1. Farm Equipment's financial statements are prepared on a calendar-year basis.

Instructions

Assuming Stead Industries fulfills all the terms of the note, prepare the necessary journal entries for Farm Equipment for the entire term of the note.

P7-10 Logo Limited manufactures sweatshirts for sale to athletic-wear retailers. The following summary information was available for Logo for the year ended December 31, 2004:

Cash	$20,000
Trade accounts receivable (net)	40,000
Inventories	85,000
Accounts payable	65,000
Other current liabilities	15,000

Part 1

During 2005, Logo had the following transactions:

1. Total sales were $465,000.

2. $215,000 of total sales were made on a credit basis.

3. On June 30, an account receivable of $50,000 to a major customer was settled with Logo accepting a one-year $50,000 note, bearing 11% interest, payable at maturity.

4. Logo collected $160,000 on trade accounts receivable during the year.

5. At December 31, 2005, Cash had a balance of $15,000, Inventories had a balance of $80,000, Accounts Payable were $70,000, and other current liabilities were $16,000.

Instructions

(a) Prepare (summary) journal entries to record the items noted above.

(b) Calculate the current ratio and the receivables turnover ratio for Logo at December 31, 2005. Use these measures to assess Logo's liquidity. The receivables turnover ratio last year was 4.85.

Part 2

Now assume that at year end 2005, Logo enters into the following transactions related to the company's receivables:

1. Logo sells the note receivable to Prairie Bank for $50,000 cash plus accrued interest. Given the creditworthiness of Logo's customer, the bank accepts the note without recourse and assesses a finance charge of 1.5%. Prairie Bank will collect the note directly from the customer.

2. Logo factors some accounts receivable at the end of the year. Accounts totalling $40,000 are transferred to First Factors, Inc. with recourse. First Factors retains 6% of the balances and assesses a finance charge of 4% on the transfer. First Factors will collect the receivables from Logo's customers. The fair value of the recourse obligation is $4,000.

Instructions

(c) Prepare the journal entry to record the transfer of the note receivable to Prairie Bank.

(d) Prepare the journal entry to record the sale of receivables to First Factors.

(e) Calculate the current ratio and the receivables turnover ratio for Logo at December 31, 2005. Use these measures to assess Logo's liquidity. The receivables turnover ratio last year was 4.85.

(f) Discuss how the ratio analysis in (e) would be affected if Logo had transferred the receivables in secured borrowing transactions.

P7-11   Ibran Corp. requires additional cash for its business. Management has decided to use accounts receivable to raise the additional cash and has asked you to determine the income statement effects of the following contemplated transactions.

1. On July 1, 2005, Ibran assigned $400,000 of accounts receivable to Provincial Finance Corporation as security for a loan. Ibran received an advance from Provincial of 85% of the assigned accounts receivable less a commission of 3% on the advance. Prior to December 31, 2005, Ibran collected $220,000 on the assigned accounts receivable, and remitted $232,720 to Provincial, $12,720 of which represented interest on the advance from Provincial.

2. On December 1, 2005, Ibran sold $300,000 of accounts receivable to Wunsch Corp. for $250,000. The receivables were sold outright on a without recourse basis and Ibran has no continuing interest in the receivables.

3. On December 31, 2005, an advance of $120,000 was received from First Bank by pledging $160,000 of Ibran's accounts receivable. Ibran's first payment to First Bank is due on January 30, 2006.

Instructions

Prepare a schedule showing the income statement effects for the year ended December 31, 2005 as a result of the above facts.

*P7-12   Joseph Howe is reviewing the cash accounting for Connolly Corporation, a local mailing service. Howe's review will focus on the petty cash account and the bank reconciliation for the month ended May 31, 2005. He has collected the following information from Connolly's bookkeeper for this task.

Petty Cash

1. The petty cash fund was established on May 10, 2005 in the amount of $300.00.

2. Expenditures from the fund by the custodian as of May 31, 2005 were evidenced by approved receipts for the following:

Postage expense	$33.00
Mailing labels and other supplies	40.00
Coffee supplies (milk, sugar, cups)	35.00
IOU from employees	30.00
Shipping charges	57.45
Newspaper advertising	22.80
Miscellaneous expense	15.35

On May 31, 2005, the petty cash fund was replenished and increased to $400.00; currency and coin in the fund at that time totalled $64.99.

Bank Reconciliation

SCOTIA IMPERIAL BANK
Bank Statement

	Disbursements	Receipts	Balance
Balance, May 1, 2005			$8,769
Deposits		$28,000	
Note payment direct from customer (interest of $30)		930	
Cheques cleared during May	$31,150		
Bank service charges	37		
Balance, May 31, 2005			$6,512

Connolly's Cash Account

Balance, May 1, 2005	$ 9,150
Deposits during May 2005	31,000
Cheques written during May 2005	(31,835)

Deposits in transit are determined to be $3,000, and cheques outstanding at May 31 total $550. Cash on hand (besides petty cash) at May 31, 2005 is $246.

Instructions

(a) Prepare the journal entries to record the transactions related to the petty cash fund for May.

(b) Prepare a bank reconciliation dated May 31, 2005, proceeding to a correct balance, and prepare the journal entries necessary to make the books correct and complete.

(c) What amount of cash should be reported in the May 31, 2005 balance sheet?

*P7-13 The cash account of Villa Corp. shows a ledger balance of $3,969.85 on June 30, 2005. The bank statement as of that date indicates a balance of $4,150. Upon comparing the statement with the cash records, the following facts were determined:

1. There were bank service charges for June of $25.00.

2. A bank memo stated that Bao Dai's note for $900 and interest of $36 had been collected on June 29, and the bank had made a charge of $5.50 on the collection. (No entry had been made on Villa's books when Bao Dai's note was sent to the bank for collection.)

3. Receipts for June 30 of $2,890 were not deposited until July 2.

4. Cheques outstanding on June 30 totalled $2,136.05.

5. The bank had charged the Villa Corp.'s account for a customer's uncollectible cheque amounting to $453.20 on June 29.

6. A customer's cheque for $90 had been entered as $60 in the cash receipts journal by Villa on June 15.

7. Cheque no. 742 in the amount of $491 had been entered in the cashbook as $419, and cheque no. 747 in the amount of $58.20 had been entered as $582. Both cheques had been issued to pay for purchases of equipment.

8. In May 2005, the bank had charged a cheque of the Wella Corp. for $27.50 against the Villa Corp. account. The June bank statement indicated that the bank had reversed this and corrected its error.

Instructions

(a) Prepare a bank reconciliation dated June 30, 2005, proceeding to a correct cash balance.

(b) Prepare any entries necessary to make the books correct and complete.

*P7-14 Presented below is information related to Bonzai Books Ltd. Balance per books at October 31, $41,847.85; November receipts, $173,528.91; November disbursements, $166,193.54.

Balance per bank statement November 30, $56,270.20. The following cheques were outstanding at November 30:

1224	$1,635.29
1230	2,468.30
1232	3,625.15
1233	482.17

Included with the November bank statement and not recorded by the company were a bank debit memo for $31.40 covering bank charges for the month, a debit memo for $572.13 for a customer's cheque returned and marked NSF, and a credit memo for $1,400 representing bond interest collected by the bank in the name of Bonzai Books Ltd. Cash on hand at November 30 recorded and awaiting deposit amounted to $1,920.40.

Instructions

(a) Prepare a bank reconciliation (to the correct balance) at November 30 for Bonzai Books Ltd. from the information above.

(b) Prepare any journal entries required to adjust the cash account at November 30.

*P7-15   Presented below is information related to Quartz Industries Ltd.

QUARTZ INDUSTRIES LTD.
Bank Reconciliation
May 31, 2005

Balance per bank statement		$30,928.46
Less: Outstanding cheques		
No. 6124	$2,125.00	
No. 6138	932.65	
No. 6139	960.57	
No. 6140	1,420.00	5,438.22
		25,490.24
Add deposit in transit		4,710.56
Balance per books (correct balance)		$30,200.80

CHEQUE REGISTER-JUNE

Date	Payee	No.	Invoice Amount	Discount	Cash
June 1	Ren Mfg.	6141	$237.50		$237.50
1	Stimpy Mfg.	6142	915.00	$9.15	905.85
8	Rugrats Co., Inc.	6143	122.90	2.45	120.45
9	Ren Mfg.	6144	306.40		306.40
10	Petty Cash	6145	89.93		89.93
17	Muppet Babies Photo	6146	706.00	14.12	691.88
22	Hey Dude Publishing	6147	447.50		447.50
23	Payroll Account	6148	4,130.00		4,130.00
25	Dragnet Tools, Inc.	6149	390.75	3.91	386.84
28	Dare Insurance Agency	6150	1,050.00		1,050.00
28	Get Smart Construction	6151	2,250.00		2,250.00
29	M M T, Inc.	6152	750.00		750.00
30	Lassie Co.	6153	400.00	8.00	392.00
			$11,795.98	$37.63	$11,758.35

PROVINCIAL BANK
Bank Statement
General Chequing Account of Quartz Industries – June, 2005

Debits			Date	Credits	Balance
					$30,928.46
$2,125.00	$237.50	$905.85	June 1	$4,710.56	32,370.67
932.65	120.45		12	1,507.06	32,824.63
1,420.00	447.50	306.40	23	1,458.55	32,109.28
4,130.00		*11.05	26		27,968.23
89.93	2,250.00	1,050.00	28	4,157.48	28,735.78

*Bank charges

Cash received June 29 and 30 and deposited in the mail for the general chequing account June 30 amounted to $4,607.96. Because the cash account balance at June 30 is not given, it must be calculated from other information in the problem.

Instructions

From the information above, prepare a bank reconciliation (to the correct balance) as of June 30, 2005 for Quartz Industries.

P7-16 The Cormier Corporation sells office equipment and supplies to many organizations in the city and surrounding area on contract terms of 2/10, n/30. In the past, over 75% of the credit customers have taken advantage of the discount by paying within 10 days of the invoice date. The number of customers taking the full 30 days to pay has increased within the last year. Current indications are that less than 60% of the customers are now taking the discount. Bad debts as a percentage of gross credit sales have risen from the 1.5% provided in past years to about 4% in the current year.

The controller has responded to a request for more information on the deterioration in collections of accounts receivable with the report reproduced below.

THE CORMIER CORPORATION
Finance Committee Report—Accounts Receivable Collections
May 31, 2005

The fact that some credit accounts will prove uncollectible is normal. Annual bad debt write-offs have been 1.5% of gross credit sales over the past five years. During the last fiscal year, this percentage increased to slightly less than 4%. The current Accounts Receivable balance is $1.6 million. The condition of this balance in terms of age and probability of collection is as follows:

Proportion of Total	Age Categories	Probability of Collection
68%	not yet due	99%
15%	less than 30 days past due	96.5%
8%	30 to 60 days past due	95%
5%	61 to 120 days past due	91%
2.5%	121 to 180 days past due	70%
1.5%	more than 180 days past due	20%

The Allowance for Doubtful Accounts had a credit balance of $43,300 on June 1, 2004. The Cormier Corporation has provided for a monthly bad debt expense accrual during the current fiscal year based on the assumption that 4% of gross credit sales will be uncollectible. Total gross credit sales for the 2004–05 fiscal year amounted to $4 million. Write-offs of bad accounts during the year totalled $145,000.

Instructions

(a) Prepare an accounts receivable aging schedule for the Cormier Corporation using the age categories identified in the controller's report to the Finance Committee showing (1) the amount of accounts receivable outstanding for each age category and in total, and (2) the estimated amount that is uncollectible for each category and in total.

(b) Calculate the amount of the year-end adjustment necessary to bring the Allowance for Doubtful Accounts to the balance indicated by the age analysis. Then prepare the necessary journal entry to adjust the accounting records.

(c) In a recessionary environment with tight credit and high interest rates:

　1.　Identify steps the Cormier Corporation might consider to improve the accounts receivable situation.

　2.　Evaluate each step identified in terms of the risks and costs involved.

(CMA adapted)

Writing Assignments

WA7-1 The trial balance of Imotex Ltd. contains the following accounts.

(a) Accounts receivable, trade

(b) Accounts receivable, related company

(c) Accounts receivable, to be exchanged for shares in another company

(d) Note receivable, receivable in grams of a precious metal

(e) Cash

(f) Investment in Royal Bank common shares (long-term investment)

(g) Interest rate swap: contract to receive fixed rate (at 8%) and to pay variable rate (current rates are 6%) on debenture debt.

(h) U.S. dollar cash holdings in a U.S. subsidiary's bank account

Instructions

For (a) to (h), indicate whether each is or is not a financial asset. Provide an explanation for your choice.

WA7-2   Sib Mukandi conducts a wholesale merchandising business that sells approximately 5,000 items per month with a total monthly average sales value of $250,000. The company's annual bad debt ratio has been approximately 1.5% of sales. In recent discussions with her bookkeeper, Ms. Mukandi has become confused by all the alternatives apparently available in handling the Allowance for Doubtful Accounts. The following information has been shown.

1. An allowance can be set up (a) on the basis of a percentage of sales or (b) on the basis of a valuation of all past due or otherwise questionable accounts receivable—those considered uncollectible being charged to such allowance at the close of the accounting period, or specific items charged off directly against (1) Gross Sales, or to (2) Bad Debt Expense in the year in which they are determined to be uncollectible.

2. Collection agency fees, legal fees, and so on incurred in connection with the attempted recovery of bad debts can be charged to (a) Bad Debt Expense, (b) Allowance for Doubtful Accounts, (c) Legal Expense, or (d) General Expense.

3. Debts previously written off in whole or in part but currently recovered can be credited to (a) Other Revenue, (b) Bad Debt Expense, or (c) Allowance for Doubtful Accounts.

Instructions

Which of the foregoing methods would you recommend to Ms. Mukandi in regard to (1) allowances and charge-offs, (2) collection expenses, and (3) recoveries? State briefly and clearly the reasons supporting your recommendations.

WA7-3   Soon after beginning the year-end audit work on March 10 at Arkin Corp., the auditor has the following conversation with the controller.

Controller:	The year ended March 31st should be our most profitable in history and, as a consequence, the Board of Directors has just awarded the officers generous bonuses.
Auditor:	I thought profits were down this year in the industry, according to your latest interim report.
Controller:	Well, they were down, but 10 days ago we closed a deal that will give us a substantial increase for the year.
Auditor:	Oh, what was it?
Controller:	Well, you remember a few years ago our former president bought shares of Hi-Tek Enterprises Ltd. because he had those grandiose ideas about becoming a conglomerate. For six years we have not been able to sell the shares, which cost us $3 million and has not paid a nickel in dividends. Thursday we sold the shares to Campbell Inc. for $4 million. So, we will have a gain of $700,000 ($1 million pretax) which will increase our net income for the year to $4 million, compared with last year's $3.8 million. As far as I know, we'll be the only company in the industry to register an increase in net income this year. That should help the market value of our shares!
Auditor:	Do you expect to receive the $4 million in cash by March 31st, your fiscal year end?
Controller:	No. Although Campbell Inc. is an excellent company, they are a little tight for cash because of their rapid growth. Consequently, they are going to give us a $4 million noninterest-bearing note due $400,000 per year for the next 10 years. The first payment is due on March 31 of next year.
Auditor:	Why is the note noninterest-bearing?
Controller:	Because that's what everybody agreed to. Since we don't have any interest-bearing debt, the funds invested in the note do not cost us anything and besides, we were not getting any dividends on the Hi-Tek Enterprises shares.

Instructions

Do you agree with the way the controller has accounted for the transaction? If not, how should the transaction be accounted for?

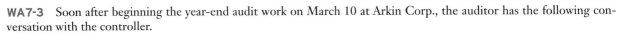

WA7-4   Rudolph Corp. is a subsidiary of Huntley Corp. The controller believes that the yearly charge for doubtful accounts for Rudolph should be 2% of net credit sales. The president, nervous that the parent company might expect the subsidiary to sustain its 10% growth rate, suggests that the controller increase the charge for doubtful accounts to 3% yearly. The supervisor thinks that the lower net income, which reflects a 6% growth rate, will be a more sustainable rate for Rudolph.

Instructions

(a) Should the controller be concerned with Rudolph Corp.'s growth rate in estimating the allowance? Explain your answer.

(b) Does the president's request pose an ethical dilemma for the controller? Give your reasons.

Cases

Refer to the Case Primer on the Digital Tool to help you answer these cases.

CA7-1   Hanley Limited (HL) manufactures camera equipment. The company is looking to list its shares on the TSX Venture Exchange. As such it must meet the following initial listing requirements (amongst others):

1. net tangible assets must be at least $500,000

2. pre-tax earnings must be $50,000 and

3. the company must have adequate working capital.

Hanley has experienced significant growth in terms of sales and is having difficulty estimating its bad debt expense. During the year, the sales team has been extending credit on a more aggressive basis in order to increase commissions revenues. Under the percentage of receivables approach using past percentages, the estimate is $50,000. Hanley has performed an aging and estimates the bad debts as $57,000. Finally, using a percentage of sales, the expense is estimated at $67,000. Prior to booking the allowance, net tangible assets are approximately $550,000. The controller decides to accrue $50,000 which results in pre-tax earnings of $60,000.

Instructions
Adopt the role of the TSX Venture exchange staff making the decision as to whether the company meets the financial aspects of the initial listing requirements for listing on the TSX Venture Exchange.

CA 7-2   Telus Corporation (Telus) is one of Canada's largest telecommunications companies providing both products and services. Its shares are traded on the Toronto and New York Stock Exchanges. 21% of the voting and non-voting shares are owned by Verizon and 73% are widely held. In its 2002 Management Discussion and Analysis, Telus noted that its business plans could be negatively affected if existing financing was insufficient. Its plan is to finance future capital requirements with internally generated funds as well as utilizing its bank line of credit. Because of disruptions in the capital market and reduced lending to the telecommunications sector, as well as downgradings and negative outlooks on Telus debt, additional borrowing is not really an option.

According to the 2002 Annual Report:

> "On July 26, 2002, Telus entered into an agreement with an arms-length securitization trust under which it is able to sell an interest in certain of its trade receivables up to a maximum of $650 million. As at December 31, 2002, Telus had received aggregate cash proceeds of $475 million. Under the program, Telus is required to maintain at least a BBB (low) credit rating by Dominion Bond Rating Service. In the event this rating is not maintained, the Company may be required to wind down the program. A change in credit rating could impact Telus' cost of and access to capital…"

Under the terms of the agreement, Telus will still service the receivables. In structuring the transaction, the following assumptions were made:

Expected credit loss	2.4%
Discount rate	4.2%
Servicing costs	1.0%

Instructions
Adopt the role of the controller of Telus and discuss the financial reporting issues.

Integrated case

IC7-1   Franklyn's Furniture (FF) is a mid sized owner operated business started twenty-five years ago by Fred Franklyn. The retail furniture business is a cyclical business with business dropping off in times of economic downturn as is the case currently. In order to induce sales, the store offers its own credit cards to good customers. Franklyn has run into a bit of a cash crunch and is planning to go to the bank to obtain an increase in his line of credit in order to replenish and expand the stock. At present the line of credit is capped at 70% of the credit card receivables and inventory. The receivables and inventory have been pledged as security for the loan.

Franklyn has identified two possible sources of the cash shortage—a build-up in old inventory and outstanding credit card receivables. He has come up with two strategies to deal with the problem:

Excess inventory—a new sales promotion has been advertised in the newspaper for the past two months. Under the terms of the promotion, customers need not pay anything up front and will be able to take the furniture home and begin payments the following year. Response to the advertisement has been very good and a significant amount of inventory has been moved to date, leaving room for new inventory once the bank financing comes through.

Credit card receivables – for the existing receivables, Franklyn has found a company Factors Inc. (FI) that will buy the receivables for 93% of their face value. They are currently negotiating the terms of the deal. So far, FF has agreed to transfer legal title to the receivables to FI. FF will maintain and collect the receivables. The one term that is still under consideration is whether FI will have any recourse to FF should the amounts be uncollectible.

Instructions
Assume the role of Franklyn's bookkeeper and advise him as to the financial reporting implications of the strategies.

Research and Financial Analysis

RA7-1 Maple Leaf Foods Inc.

Selected excerpts from the financial statements of Maple Leaf Foods Inc. for the year ended December 31, 2002 are reproduced below. In addition, the company reported accounts receivable of $246,966 thousand at December 31, 2000; fiscal year 2000 sales of $3,943,289 thousand; and securitized receivables of $102 million at December 31, 2000.

Consolidated Balance Sheet
In thousands of Canadian dollars

As at December 31	2002	2001
ASSETS		
Current assets		
Cash	$156,866	$ 52,611
Accounts receivable (note 3)	243,121	248,064
Inventories (note 4)	266,889	231,918
Prepaid expenses and other assets	14,806	14,725
Total current assets (note 1)	$681,682	$547,318

Consolidated Statement of Earnings
In thousands of Canadian dollars, except per share amounts

Years ended December 31	2002	2001
Sales	$5,075,879	$4,775,358

Notes to the consolidated financial statements

3. **Accounts receivable**
   Under revolving securitization programs, the Company has sold, with limited recourse, certain of its trade accounts receivable to financial institutions. The Company retains servicing responsibilities and assumes limited recourse obligation for delinquent receivables. At year end, trade accounts receivable amounting to $194.6 million (2001—$163.4 million) had been sold under these programs.

Instructions

(a) Calculate the accounts receivable turnover for 2001 and 2002 and the average age of the accounts receivable at December 31, 2001 and 2002 without taking the securitized receivables into account. Comment on your results.

(b) Calculate the percentage growth in sales and accounts receivable in 2001 and 2002 without taking the securitized receivables into account. Comment on your results.

(c) Suggest how, if at all, the securitized receivables should be taken into account in the calculations in (a) and (b) above. Recalculate your ratios and percentages. Did the securitizations have an effect on your assessment of the company? Explain.

RA7-2 Canadian Tire Corporation, Limited

Canadian Tire Corporation, Limited is one of Canada's best-known retailers. The company operates over 450 "hard-goods" retail stores through Associate Dealers, over 300 corporate and franchise stores under its subsidiary, Mark's Work Wearhouse, has over 200 independently operated gasoline sites, and increasingly offers financial services through its branded credit cards.

Instructions
Access the financial statements of Canadian Tire Corporation, Limited for its year ended December 28, 2002, either on the Digital Tool or on the SEDAR website (www.sedar.com). Refer to these financial statements, including the accompanying notes, to answer the following questions.

(a) How does Canadian Tire define cash and cash equivalents on its balance sheet?

(b) What criteria does the company use to determine what short-term investments to include in this category?

(c) Review the full financial statements provided and identify all the locations where the company has provided information about its receivables.

(d) Accounting standards require companies to disclose information about their exposure to credit risk. What is credit risk? What does Canadian Tire report? What is your assessment of its exposure to credit risk?

(e) Canadian Tire uses its accounts receivable to generate cash prior to when they fall due. Briefly describe what form of "transfer" activities the company is engaged in. Are the receivables used as security for loans, are they sold outright with no continuing interest, or do they have a continuing relationship with the accounts? What financial components do they retain, if any?

RA7-3 Sears Canada Inc. versus Hudson's Bay Company

Instructions
Hudson's Bay Company has been ranked as the largest Canadian retailer (by total revenue) by *The Globe and Mail*'s *Report on Business Magazine* (July 2003). Sears Canada Inc. was ranked #4.

Access both companies' financial statements covering the 2002 year, either on the Digital Tool or on SEDAR (www.sedar.com). Use this information to answer the following questions.

(a) Compare how the two companies report cash and cash equivalents on the statement of financial position. What is included in the cash and cash equivalents of each? Is there any restricted cash reported by either company? If so, have both companies reported it in a similar manner?

(b) What types of receivables do Sears and Hudson's Bay have? Are they common to both companies?

(c) What amount of "trade" accounts receivable (net) do Sears and Hudson's Bay have? Can you tell which company reports the greater allowance for doubtful accounts (amount and percentage of gross receivable) at the end of the most recent year?

(d) Does either company dispose of receivables prior to the due date to generate cash? Comment.

(e) Calculate, compare, and comment on the Accounts Receivable Turnover ratio for both companies for the most recent year. How does securitization of receivables affect this ratio? Be specific.

RA7-4 Research Issue

Financial Reporting in Canada, published annually by the Canadian Institute of Chartered Accountants, is a survey of 200 Canadian company annual reports to shareholders. The survey covers companies from all of the TSX 300 industry groups with the exception of financial institutions.

Instructions
Examine the sections dealing with cash, temporary investments, and accounts and notes receivable. Write a short report summarizing Canadian practice and trends in reporting these financial assets.

Last In, First Out

At Petro-Canada, one of Canada's largest integrated oil and gas companies, inventory is valued based on cost—the cost of crude oil, plus refining and distribution costs. "Inventories are stated at the lower of cost and net realizable value," says controller Chris Smith.

The Calgary-based company, which has an inventory of around 15 million barrels of crude oil and refined petroleum products at any given time, uses the LIFO (last in, first out) method to determine inventory costs. "Under LIFO, it is the most recent cost of commodity purchases that is reflected in the cost of sales," Smith says. "As a result, LIFO provides us with a better matching of costs and revenues."

Petro-Canada and its Canadian competitors have used this valuation method since the early '90s. Prior to the 1991 war in the Persian Gulf, the standard method was FIFO, where the first goods manufactured are the first ones to come out of inventory and be included in sales. "Under FIFO, in times of rising prices, the carrying value of the closing inventory would be increasing and earnings would be higher," Smith explains. Similarly, if crude oil prices fell, so would the value of the inventory and the company's earnings.

With oil prices rising prior to the Gulf war and subsequently falling, Canadian companies found that selling a high-cost inventory into a lower-priced market resulted in significant losses. Petro-Canada changed from FIFO to LIFO in 1992 and thus reduced its inventory carrying value by $130 million.

Both methods have advantages and disadvantages, Smith explains. "LIFO provides a better matching in the earnings statement, but can provide an out-of-date valuation in the balance sheet. FIFO gives a more current valuation in the balance sheet, but a less current matching in the earnings statement."

CHAPTER 8

Inventory: Recognition and Measurement

Learning Objectives

After studying this chapter, you should be able to:

1. Identify major classifications of inventory.

2. Distinguish between perpetual and periodic inventory systems.

3. Identify the effects of inventory errors on the financial statements.

4. Identify the items that should be included as inventory cost.

5. Explain the difference between variable costing and absorption costing in assigning manufacturing costs to inventory.

6. Distinguish between the physical flow of inventory and the cost flow assigned to inventory.

7. Identify possible objectives for inventory valuation decisions.

8. Describe and compare the cost flow assumptions used in accounting for inventories.

9. Evaluate LIFO as a basis for understanding the differences among the cost flow methods.

10. Explain the importance of judgement in selecting an inventory cost flow method.

Preview of Chapter 8

Inventories are often a significant portion of a company's total assets. As indicated in the opening story, accounting and reporting for this asset can materially affect both the income statement and the balance sheet. Many decisions must be made in determining the final amounts reported for inventory on the balance sheet and for cost of goods sold on the income statement: the quantity of inventory on hand, which costs are to be included in inventory cost, what cost flow assumption is to be used, and whether cost is the appropriate value for the balance sheet.

Some related topics are covered in other chapters of the text: issues associated with accounting for long-term construction contract inventories were examined in Chapter 6; and balance sheet valuation and methods of estimating inventory are discussed in Chapter 9. **The purpose of this chapter is to introduce the basic issues related to the recognition and initial measurement of inventory costs and to discuss the choices available within GAAP for assigning costs to inventory and to cost of goods sold.** The content and organization of the chapter are as follows:

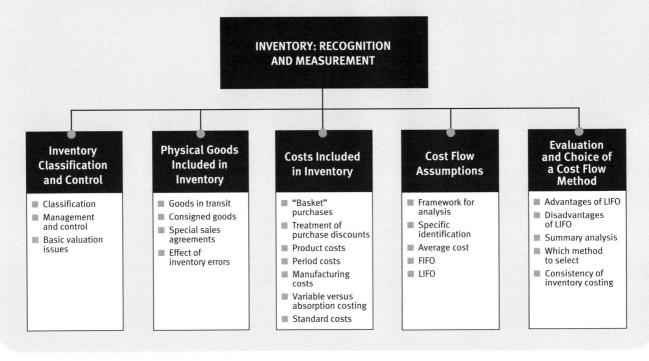

INVENTORY CLASSIFICATION AND CONTROL

Classification

Objective 1
Identify major classifications of inventory

Inventories are asset items held for sale in the ordinary course of business or goods that will be used or consumed in the production of goods to be sold. Identification, measurement, and disclosure of inventories require careful attention because the investment in inventories is frequently the largest current asset of merchandising (retail) and manufacturing businesses. Costco Wholesale Corporation, with about 400 warehouse stores from the Pacific Rim to the United Kingdom, reports merchandise inventories in excess of $3 billion (U.S.), making up 67.5% of its current assets and 30% of total assets![1]

A **merchandising concern**, such as Hudson's Bay Company, ordinarily purchases its merchandise in a form ready for sale. It reports the cost assigned to unsold units left on hand as merchandise inventory. Only one inventory account, Merchandise Inventories, appears in the financial statements.

Manufacturing concerns, on the other hand, produce goods to be sold to merchandising firms. Many of the largest Canadian businesses—Bombardier, General Motors of Canada, and Magna International Inc., for example—are manufacturers. Although the products they produce may be quite different, manufacturers normally have three inventory accounts: Raw Materials, Work in Process, and Finished Goods. The cost assigned to goods and materials on hand but not yet placed into production is reported as raw materials inventory. Raw materials include the wood to make a baseball bat or the steel to make a car. These materials ultimately can be traced directly to the end product. At any point in a continuous production process, some units are not completely processed. The cost of the raw material on which production has been started but not completed, plus the direct labour cost applied specifically to this material and an applicable share of manufacturing overhead costs, constitutes the work-in-process inventory. The costs identified with the completed but unsold units on hand are reported as finished goods inventory.

The current assets sections presented in Illustration 8-1 contrast the financial statement presentation of inventories of a merchandising company and those of a manufacturing company. The remainder of the balance sheet is essentially similar for the two types of companies.

Illustration 8-1

Comparison of Inventory Presentation for Merchandising and Manufacturing Companies

MERCHANDISING COMPANY
Hudson's Bay Company
Balance Sheet, January 31, 2003

(thousands of dollars)	Notes	2003	2002
Current assets			
Cash in stores		7,308	7,392
Short-term deposits		51,418	331,350
Credit card receivables	2	559,151	487,281
Other accounts receivable		117,412	73,494
Merchandise inventories		1,551,104	1,489,049
Prepaid expenses and other current assets		122,860	169,092
		2,409,253	2,557,658

MANUFACTURING COMPANY
Domtar Inc.
Balance Sheet, December 31, 2002

(In millions of Canadian dollars)	2002	2001
Assets		
Current assets		
Cash and cash equivalents	38	36
Receivables (Note 9)	304	300
Inventories (Note 10)	736	779
Prepaid expenses	22	24
Future income taxes (Note 7)	76	29
	1,176	1,168
Note 10		
Inventories		
Work in process and finished goods	406	430
Raw materials	150	166
Operating and maintenance supplies	180	183
	736	779

---

[1] Based on the company's financial statements for the 52 weeks ended September 1, 2002.

A manufacturing company also might include a manufacturing or factory supplies inventory account, such as that reported by Domtar above. In it would be items such as machine oils, nails, cleaning materials, and the like that are used in production but are not the primary materials being processed. The flow of costs through a merchandising company is different from that of a manufacturing company, as shown in Illustration 8-2.

Management and Control

Management is vitally interested in inventory planning and control. An accurate accounting system with up-to-date records is essential. If unsaleable items have accumulated in the inventory, a potential loss exists. Sales and customers may be lost if products ordered by customers are not available in the desired style, quality, and quantity. Inefficient purchasing procedures, faulty manufacturing techniques, or inadequate sales efforts may saddle management with excessive and unusable inventories. Businesses must monitor inventory levels carefully to limit the financial and other costs associated with carrying these assets. In recent years, with the introduction and use of "just-in-time" (JIT) inventory order systems and better supplier relationships, inventory levels have become leaner for many enterprises.

What do the Numbers Mean?

Technology has played an important role in the development of inventory systems. Radio-frequency data communications warehouse systems, for example, have helped companies such as Eli Lilly Canada Inc. and BC Hot House Foods increase the accuracy of inventory information and the efficiency and productivity of their inventory management activities. Toyota uses bar codes, electronic data interchange, and radio frequency communication terminals to control the shipment of parts throughout North America, much of it through its Ontario parts centre. This has resulted in delivery times and safety stock that are one-third of previous levels.

From a perspective of accounting for inventory, management is well aware that the level of year-end inventory can significantly affect the amount of net income as well as cur-

Illustration 8-2

Flow of Costs Through Manufacturing and Merchandising Companies

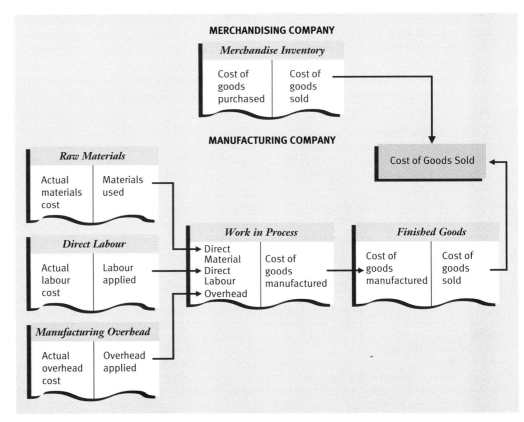

rent assets, total assets, and retained earnings (through the amount of net income reported). As indicated in Chapter 2, **these amounts or totals including them are used to calculate ratios that, in turn, are used to evaluate management's performance (e.g., payment of bonuses) and adherence to debt restrictions (e.g., to not exceed a specified debt-to-total-asset ratio or dividend payout ratio).**

For these and other reasons, management is very interested in having an inventory accounting system that provides accurate, up-to-date information on quantities. As discussed later, the choice of a cost method to value inventories is also of concern.

Perpetual System

As indicated in Chapter 3, inventory records may be maintained on a perpetual or periodic basis. Under a perpetual inventory system, **a continuous or perpetual record of inventory changes is maintained in the Inventory account**. That is, the dollar cost of all purchases and the cost of the items sold (or issued out of inventory) are recorded directly in the Inventory account as they occur. The accounting features of a perpetual inventory system are:

2 Objective
Distinguish between perpetual and periodic inventory systems.

1. Purchases of merchandise for resale or raw materials for production are debited to Inventory rather than to Purchases.

2. Freight-in, purchase returns and allowances, and purchase discounts are recorded in Inventory rather than in separate accounts.

3. Cost of goods sold is recognized for each sale by debiting the account, Cost of Goods Sold, and crediting Inventory.

4. Inventory is a control account that is supported by a subsidiary ledger of individual inventory records. The subsidiary records show the quantity and cost of each type of inventory on hand.

The perpetual inventory system provides a continuous record of the balances in both the Inventory account and the Cost of Goods Sold account.

Under a computerized record-keeping system, additions to and issuances from inventory can be recorded nearly instantaneously. The popularity and affordability of computerized accounting software have made the perpetual system cost-effective for many kinds of businesses. Recording sales with optical scanners at the cash register now is commonly incorporated into perpetual inventory systems at most retail stores of any size.

Periodic System

Under a periodic inventory system, the quantity of inventory on hand is determined, as its name implies, only periodically. All inventory acquisitions during the accounting period are recorded by debits to a Purchases account. The total in the Purchases account at the end of the accounting period is added to the cost of the inventory on hand at the beginning of the period to determine the total cost of the goods available for sale during the period. The cost of ending inventory is subtracted from the cost of goods available for sale to calculate the cost of goods sold.

Note that under a periodic inventory system, the cost of goods sold is a residual amount that depends upon separately calculating the cost of the ending inventory. This can be based on a physically counted ending inventory with its cost determined according to methods explained in this chapter, or on an estimate of the cost of the ending inventory as explained in Chapter 9.

If based on a physical inventory count, the inventory count is taken once a year at the end of the year.[2] However, most companies need more current information about their

---

[2] In recent years, many companies have developed methods of determining inventories, including statistical sampling, that are sufficiently reliable to make an annual physical count of each inventory item unnecessary.

inventory levels to protect against stockouts or overpurchasing and to help prepare monthly or quarterly financial data. As a consequence, many companies use a modified perpetual inventory system in which **increases and decreases in quantities—not dollar amounts** are kept in a detailed inventory record. **It is merely a memorandum device outside the double-entry system that helps determine the level of inventory at any point in time.**

Whether a company maintains a perpetual inventory in quantities and dollars, quantities only, or has no perpetual inventory record at all, it probably takes a physical inventory once a year. No matter what type of inventory records are used or how well-controlled the procedures for recording purchases and requisitions are, the danger of loss and error is always present. Waste, breakage, theft, improper entry, failure to prepare or record requisitions, and any number of similar possibilities may cause the inventory records to differ from the actual inventory on hand. This requires periodic verification of the inventory records by actual count, weight, or measurement. **These counts are compared with the detailed inventory records. The records are corrected to agree with the quantities actually on hand.**

Insofar as possible, the physical inventory should be taken near the end of a company's fiscal year so that correct inventory quantities are available for use in preparing annual accounting reports and statements. Because this is not always possible, however, physical inventories taken within two or three months of the year end are satisfactory, **if the detailed inventory records are maintained with a fair degree of accuracy.**

To illustrate the difference between a perpetual and a periodic system, assume that Fesmire Limited had the following balances and transactions during the current year:

Beginning inventory	100 units at $ 6	=	$600
Purchases	900 units at $ 6	=	$5,400
Sales	600 units at $12	=	$7,200
Ending inventory	400 units at $ 6	=	$2,400

The entries to record these transactions during the current year are shown in Illustration 8-3.

Illustration 8-3

Comparative Entries— Perpetual vs. Periodic

Perpetual Inventory System			Periodic Inventory System		
1. Beginning Inventory, 100 units at $6:					
The inventory account shows the inventory on hand at $600.			The inventory account shows the inventory on hand at $600.		
2. Purchase 900 units at $6:					
Inventory	5,400		Purchases	5,400	
Accounts Payable		5,400	Accounts Payable		5,400
3. Return 50 defective units:					
Accounts Payable	300		Accounts Payable	300	
Inventory		300	Purchase returns and allowances		300
4. Sale of 600 units at $12:					
Accounts Receivable	7,200		Accounts Receivable	7,200	
Sales		7,200	Sales		7,200
Cost of Goods Sold	3,600				
(600 at $6)					
Inventory		3,600	(No entry)		
5. End-of-period entries for inventory accounts, 350 units at $6:					
No entry necessary.			Purchase returns	300	
The account, Inventory, shows the ending			and allowances		
balance of $2,100			Inventory (ending,	2,100	
($600 + $5,400 − $300 − $3,600).			by count)		
			Cost of Goods Sold	3,600	
			Purchases		5,400
			Inventory (beginning)		600

When a perpetual inventory system is used and a difference exists between the perpetual inventory balance and the physical inventory count, a separate entry is needed to adjust the perpetual inventory account. To illustrate, assume that at the end of the reporting period, the perpetual inventory account reported an inventory balance of $4,000, but a physical count indicated $3,800 was actually on hand. The adjusting entry is as follows.

Inventory Over and Short	200	
Inventory		200

A = L + SE
−200   −200

Cash flows: No effect

Perpetual inventory overages and shortages may be recorded as an adjustment of (i.e., closed to) Cost of Goods Sold. This would be appropriate if its cause related to incorrect record keeping. Alternatively, the Inventory Over and Short account may be reported in the Other Revenues and Gains or Other Expenses and Losses section, depending on its balance. If so, an overage or shortage would not be a component of Cost of Goods Sold, and the gross profit percentage would not be distorted because of such things as shrinkage, breakage, and theft. **Note that in a periodic inventory system, the account Inventory Over and Short does not arise, because there are no accounting records available against which to compare the physical count.** Thus, inventory overages and shortages are buried in cost of goods sold.

Basic Valuation Issues

Because the goods sold or used during an accounting period seldom correspond exactly with the goods bought or produced during that period, the physical inventory either increases or decreases. In addition, the cost of the same number of items could be higher or lower at the end of the period than at the beginning. The cost of all the goods available for sale or use must be allocated between the goods that were sold or used and those that are still on hand. The cost of goods available for sale or use is the total of (1) the cost of the goods on hand at the beginning of the period and (2) the cost of the goods acquired or produced during the period. The cost of goods sold is the difference between those available for sale during the period and those on hand at the end of the period, as shown in Illustration 8-4.

Beginning inventory, Jan. 1	$100,000
Cost of goods acquired or produced during the year	800,000
Total cost of goods available for sale	900,000
Ending inventory, Dec. 31	200,000
Cost of goods sold during the year	$700,000

Illustration 8-4

Calculation of Cost of Goods Sold

Determining the cost of ending inventory requires a number of steps. It can be a complex process that requires answers to each of the following questions.

1. **Which physical goods should be included as part of inventory?** Who owns inventory still in transit at the balance sheet date, or inventory on consignment? What about inventory under special sales agreements?

2. **What costs should be included as part of inventory cost?** Consider purchase discounts, product vs. period costs, manufacturing costs, variable costing vs. absorption costing, standard costs.

3. **What cost flow assumption should be adopted?** Consider specific identification, average cost, FIFO, or LIFO.

We will explore these three basic issues in the next three sections of the chapter.

PHYSICAL GOODS INCLUDED IN INVENTORY

Technically, purchases should be recorded when legal title to the goods passes to the buyer, as this is usually when the risks and rewards of ownership are transferred.

General practice, however, is to record acquisitions when the goods are received, because it is difficult for the buyer to determine the exact time of legal passage of title for every purchase. In addition, no material error is likely to result from such a practice if it is consistently applied. Illustration 8-5 indicates the general guidelines used in evaluating whether the seller or the buyer reports an item as inventory.

Illustration 8-5

Guidelines for Determining Ownership

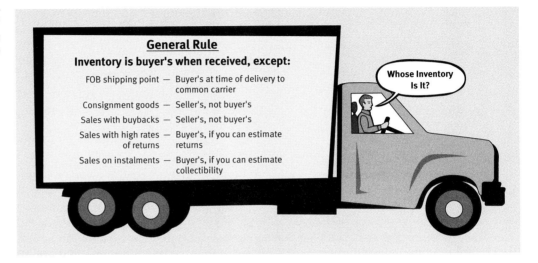

Goods in Transit

Sometimes purchased merchandise is in transit—not yet received—at the end of a fiscal period. **The accounting for these goods depends on who owns them**. This can be determined by applying the "transfer of risks and rewards" test. If the goods are shipped **f.o.b. shipping point**, the risks and rewards of ownership, usually associated with legal title, pass to the buyer when the seller delivers the goods to the common carrier (transporter) who acts as an agent for the buyer. (The abbreviation "f.o.b." stands for free on board.) If the goods are shipped **f.o.b. destination**, ownership and its associated risks and rewards do not pass until the goods reach the destination. "Shipping point" and "destination" are often designated by a particular location, for example, f.o.b. Medicine Hat.[3]

Goods in transit at the end of a fiscal period that were sent f.o.b. shipping point should be recorded by the buyer as purchases of the period and should be included in ending inventory. **To disregard such purchases would result in understating inventories and accounts payable in the balance sheet, and understating purchases and ending inventories when calculating cost of goods sold for the income statement.**

---

[3] Terms other than f.o.b. shipping point or f.o.b. destination (e.g., CIF for cost, insurance, freight) are often used to identify when legal title passes. The f.o.b. terms are used in this text to reflect that an agreement as to when title passes must be reached between the buyer and seller in the purchase-sale contract. In a particular situation, the terms of the sale contract would be examined to determine when the risks and rewards of ownership pass from the seller to the buyer.

The accountant normally prepares a purchase cut-off schedule for the end of a period to ensure that goods received from suppliers around the end of the year are recorded in the appropriate period. Cut-off procedures can be extensive and include controls such as:

- curtailing and controlling the receipt and shipment of goods around the time of the count,

- marking freight and shipping documents as "before" and "after" the inventory count, and

- ensuring that receiving reports covering goods received prior to the count are linked to invoices that also are recorded in the same period.

Because goods bought f.o.b. shipping point may have been in transit at the period's end, the cut-off schedule is not completed until a few days after the period's end, providing sufficient time for goods shipped at year end to be received. In cases where there is some question as to whether title has passed, the accountant exercises judgement by taking into consideration industry practices, the sales agreement's intent, the policies of the parties involved, and any other available information.

Consigned Goods

In Chapter 6, the nature of consignment shipments and accounting for consignment sales was discussed. In terms of accounting for inventory, **it is important to recognize that goods out on consignment remain the consignor's property and must be included in the consignor's inventory** at purchase price or production cost plus the cost of handling and shipping involved in the transfer to the consignee. When the consignee sells the consigned goods, the revenue less a selling commission and expenses incurred in accomplishing the sale is remitted to the consignor.

Occasionally, the inventory out on consignment is shown as a separate item or reported in notes, but unless the amount is large, there is little need for this. No entry is made by the consignee to adjust the Inventory account for goods received because they are the consignor's property. The consignee should be extremely careful not to include any goods consigned as a part of inventory.

Special Sales Agreements

While the transfer of legal title is a general guideline used to determine whether the risks and rewards of ownership have passed from a seller to a buyer, **transfer of legal title and the underlying economic substance of the situation (passage of risks and rewards) may not match.** For example, it is possible that legal title has passed to the purchaser but the seller of the goods retains the risks of ownership. Conversely, transfer of legal title may not occur, but the economic substance of the transaction is that the seller no longer retains the risks and rewards of ownership. Three special sale situations, discussed in Chapter 6 from a revenue recognition perspective, are considered below in terms of inventory implications. These are:

1. sales with buyback agreement

2. sales with high rates of return

3. sales on instalment

Sales with Buyback Agreement

Sometimes an enterprise finances its inventory without reporting either the liability or the inventory on its balance sheet. Such an approach—often referred to as a product financing arrangement—usually involves a "sale" with either an implicit or explicit "buyback" agreement. These are sometimes referred to as "parking transactions" because the seller simply parks the inventory on another enterprise's balance sheet for a short period of time.

To illustrate, Hill Enterprises transfers ("sells") inventory to Chase Ltd. and simultaneously agrees to repurchase this merchandise at a specified price over a specified period of time. Chase then uses the inventory as collateral and borrows against it. Chase uses the loan proceeds to pay Hill. Hill repurchases the inventory in the future, and Chase uses the proceeds from repayment to meet its loan obligation.

The essence of this transaction is that Hill Enterprises is financing its inventory—and retaining risk of ownership—even though technical legal title to the merchandise was transferred to Chase Ltd. The advantage to Hill in structuring a transaction in this manner is the removal of the current liability from its balance sheet, and the ability to manipulate income. The advantages to Chase are that the goods purchased may solve a LIFO liquidation problem (discussed later), or that Chase may be interested in a reciprocal agreement at a later date.

The Canadian accounting standards for revenue recognition tend to curtail this practice, at least in terms of enabling a "selling company" to remove the inventory and liability from its balance sheet. This is because the *CICA Handbook* requires the seller to transfer the risks and rewards of ownership before a sale can be recognized.[4] By implication, a "buying company" should not recognize the goods received as its inventory. Canadian practitioners, however, continue to exercise judgement regarding substance over form in such situations.

Sales with High Rates of Return

Formal or informal agreements often exist in industries such as publishing, music, and toys and sporting goods that permit inventory to be returned for a full or partial refund.

To illustrate, Quality Publishing Limited sells textbooks to Campus Bookstores Inc. with an agreement that any books not sold may be returned for full credit. In the past, approximately 25% of the textbooks sold to Campus Bookstores were returned. Should Quality Publishing report its deliveries to Campus Bookstores as sales transactions, or should it treat the delivered books as inventory until being notified of how many were sold? **An acceptable accounting treatment is that if a reasonable prediction of the returns can be established, then the goods should be considered sold. Conversely, if returns are unpredictable, removal of these goods from inventory is inappropriate.** Essentially, the choice of treatment depends on whether there is reasonable assurance of the measurement of the ultimate consideration to be derived from the sale given that goods may be returned.[5] If not, only the items actually sold by the purchaser are accounted for as revenue, with all remaining items being part of the seller's inventory.

Sales on Instalment

Because the risk of loss from uncollectibles is higher in instalment sale situations than in other sale transactions, the seller often withholds legal title to the merchandise until all payments have been made. Should the inventory be considered sold, even though legal title has not passed? **The goods should be excluded from the seller's inventory and the sale recorded if the cost of the outstanding risk, i.e., the bad debts, can be reasonably estimated and matched with the related revenue.** This issue is raised here to illustrate that in some cases, goods should be removed from inventory, even though legal title may not have passed.

---

[4] *CICA Handbook*, Section 3400.07.

[5] *CICA Handbook*, Section 3400.07.

Effect of Inventory Errors

Items incorrectly included or excluded in determining ending inventory will result in both income statement and balance sheet errors in the financial statements. Therefore, decisions made using financial statement amounts affected by the errors (e.g., bonus paid to management based on net income) would be in error and comparability would be impaired. Let's look at two cases and the effects on the financial statements.

3 Objective
Identify the effects of inventory errors on the financial statements.

Ending Inventory Misstated

What would happen if the beginning inventory and purchases are recorded correctly, but some items are not included in ending inventory in error (e.g., were on the premises but were missed in the physical count or were out on consignment)? In this situation, the effects on the financial statements at the end of the period would be as follows.

Balance Sheet		Income Statement	
Inventory	Understated	Cost of goods sold	Overstated
Retained earnings	Understated		
Working capital	Understated	Net income	Understated
(current assets less current liabilities)			
Current ratio	Understated		
(Current assets divided by current liabilities)			

Illustration 8-6

Financial Statement Effects of Misstated Ending Inventory

Working capital and the current ratio are understated because a portion of the ending inventory is omitted; net income is understated because cost of goods sold is overstated.

To illustrate the effect on net income over a two-year period, assume that the ending inventory of Weiseman Ltd. is understated by $10,000 and that all other items are correctly stated. The effect of this error is an understatement of net income in the current year and an overstatement of net income in the following year relative to the correct net income amounts. The error affects the following year because the beginning inventory of that year is understated, thereby causing net income to be overstated. Both net income figures are misstated, but the total for the two years is correct as the two errors will be counterbalanced (offset), as shown in Illustration 8-7.

Underlying Concept
When inventory is misstated, its presentation lacks representational faithfulness.

Illustration 8-7

Effect of Ending Inventory Error on Two Periods

	Incorrect Recording		Correct Recording	
WEISEMAN LTD. (All figures assumed)	2004	2005	2004	2005
Revenues	$100,000	$100,000	$100,000	$100,000
Cost of goods sold				
Beginning inventory	25,000	20,000	25,000	30,000
Purchased or produced	45,000	60,000	45,000	60,000
Goods available for sale	70,000	80,000	70,000	90,000
Less: Ending inventory*	20,000	40,000	30,000	40,000
Cost of goods sold	50,000	40,000	40,000	50,000
Gross profit	50,000	60,000	60,000	50,000
Administrative and selling expenses	40,000	40,000	40,000	40,000
Net income	$ 10,000	$ 20,000	$ 20,000	$ 10,000

Total income for two years = $30,000   Total income for two years = $30,000

*Ending inventory understated by $10,000 in 2004.

If the error were discovered in 2004 just before the books were closed, the correcting entry in 2004 is:

A = L + SE
+10,000   +10,000
Cash flows: No effect

| Inventory | 10,000 | |
| Cost of Goods Sold | | 10,000 |

If the error was not discovered until 2005, after the books were closed for 2004, the correcting entry in 2005 is:

A = L + SE
+10,000   +10,000
Cash flows: No effect

| Inventory | 10,000 | |
| Retained Earnings | | 10,000 |

If discovered after the books for 2005 were closed, no entry is required as the error is self-correcting over the two-year period. The inventory on the balance sheet at the end of 2005 is correct, as is the total amount of retained earnings. **However, whenever comparative financial statements are prepared that include 2004 or 2005, the inventory and net income would be adjusted and reported at the correct figures.**

If ending inventory is **overstated**, the reverse effect occurs. Inventory, working capital, current ratio, and net income are overstated and cost of goods sold is understated.

The error's effect on net income will be counterbalanced in the next year, but both years' net income figures are incorrect, thus destroying the usefulness of any analysis of trends in earnings and ratios.

Purchases and Inventory Misstated

Suppose that certain goods that the company owns are not recorded as a purchase and are not counted in ending inventory. The effect on the financial statements, assuming this is a purchase on account, is as follows.

Illustration 8-8

Financial Statement Effects of Misstated Purchases and Inventory

Balance Sheet		Income Statement	
Inventory	Understated	Purchases	Understated
Retained earnings	No effect	Inventory (ending)	Understated
Accounts payable	Understated	Cost of goods sold	No effect
Working capital	No effect	Net income	No effect
Current ratio	Overstated		

Omitting goods from purchases and inventory results in understating inventory and accounts payable on the balance sheet and understating purchases and ending inventory on the income statement. **Net income for the period is not affected by omitting such goods because purchases and ending inventory are both understated by the same amount—the error thereby offsetting itself in cost of goods sold.**[6] Total working capital is unchanged, but the current ratio is overstated (assuming it was greater than 1 to 1) because of the omission of equal amounts from inventory and accounts payable.

---

[6] To correct the error in the year of the error before the books are closed and assuming inventories are adjusted prior to the closing entries, the following entries are needed.

Periodic Method				**Perpetual Method**			
Purchases	$x			Inventory	$x		
Accounts Payable		$x		Accounts Payable		$x	
Inventory	$x						
Cost of Goods Sold		$x					

To determine an error's effect on any particular financial statement amount or ratio, it is helpful to construct a comparison chart based on assumed (if not real) numbers.

The chart would include columns based on amounts that include the error(s) and on amounts that would result if there were no error(s). To illustrate the effect on the current ratio, assume that a company understated accounts payable and ending inventory by $40,000. The understated and correct data are shown below.

Purchases and Ending Inventory Understated		Purchases and Ending Inventory Correct	
Current assets	$120,000	Current assets	$160,000
Current liabilities	$ 40,000	Current liabilities	$ 80,000
Current ratio	3 to 1	Current ratio	2 to 1

Illustration 8-9

Effects of Purchases and Ending Inventory Errors

The correct current ratio is 2 to 1 rather than 3 to 1. Thus, understating accounts payable and ending inventory can lead to a "window dressing" of the current ratio—making it appear better than it is.

If both purchases (on account) and ending inventory are overstated, then the effects on the balance sheet are exactly the reverse. Inventory and accounts payable are overstated and the current ratio is understated; working capital is not affected. Cost of goods sold and net income are not affected because the errors offset one another. While these examples illustrate the nature of some errors that may occur and their consequences, many other types of error are possible: not recording a purchase but counting the acquired inventory; not recording a sale in the current period although the items have been delivered; omitting the adjusting entry to update the Allowance for Future Returns in situations where sales are subject to a high rate of return, etc. The approach illustrated to determine the effect of errors helps in analysing such situations.

The importance of accurately calculating purchases and inventory to ensure reliable amounts are presented in the financial statements cannot be overemphasized. One has only to read the financial press to learn how misstating inventory can generate high income numbers. For example, the practice of some Canadian farm equipment manufacturers of treating deliveries to dealers as company sales (with concurrent reductions in inventory) can result in significantly inflating reported income when sales to the ultimate consumer do not keep pace with the deliveries to dealers.

As indicated in Chapter 5, the correction of an error of a prior period is accounted for retroactively as an adjustment to retained earnings. Full disclosure requires a description of the error, and a statement of the effect on the current and prior period financial statements.

COSTS INCLUDED IN INVENTORY

Having decided what physical goods are included in ending inventory, the next issue in determining the inventory amount for the balance sheet is deciding what costs should be included in "cost."

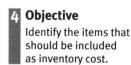

4 Objective

Identify the items that should be included as inventory cost.

One of the most important issues in dealing with inventories concerns the amount at which the inventory should be carried in the accounts. As indicated in Chapter 2, **the acquisition of inventories, like other non-financial assets, is generally accounted for on a basis of cost.** (Other bases are discussed in Chapter 9.) How is cost determined, and what should be included in cost?

"Basket" Purchases

A special problem arises when a group of varying units is purchased at a single lump sum price, a so-called basket purchase. Assume that Woodland Developers purchases land for $1 million that can be subdivided into 400 lots. These lots are of different sizes and shapes but can be roughly sorted into three groups graded A, B, and C. The purchase cost of $1 million must be apportioned among the lots so that the cost of those sold (cost of goods sold) and those remaining on hand (ending inventory) can be calculated.

It is inappropriate to use the average lot cost of $2,500 (the total cost of $1 million divided by the 400 lots) because the lots vary in size, shape, and attractiveness. When such a situation is encountered—and it is not at all unusual—the most reasonable practice is to allocate the total cost among the various units **based on their relative sales value**. For the example given, the cost allocation works as follows.

Illustration 8-10

Allocation of Costs, Using Relative Sales Values

Lots	Number of Lots	Sales Price Per Lot	Total Sales Value	Relative Sales Value	Total Cost	Cost Allocated to Lots	Cost Per Lot
A	100	$10,000	$1,000,000	100/250	$1,000,000	$ 400,000	$4,000
B	100	6,000	600,000	60/250	1,000,000	240,000	2,400
C	200	4,500	900,000	90/250	1,000,000	360,000	1,800
			$2,500,000			$1,000,000	

The cost per lot determined above is then used in calculating the cost of ending inventory as well as the cost of lots sold. **Brookfield Properties Corporation**, which owns, develops, and manages properties—including the World Financial Center in New York and BCE Place in Toronto—includes the following accounting policy note relating to its residential development properties in its financial statements:

> "Costs are allocated to the saleable acreage of each project or subdivision in proportion to the anticipated revenue."

The relative sales value method is commonly used whenever there is a joint product cost that needs to be allocated. Other examples include the petroleum industry, which uses it to value (at cost) the many products and by-products obtained from a barrel of crude oil, and the food processing industry, where different cuts of meat of varying value are "split off" from one animal carcass.

Treatment of Purchase Discounts

When suppliers offer cash discounts to purchasers, there are two methods available to account for the purchases: the gross method and the net method. Under the gross method, **both the purchases and payables are recorded at the gross amount of the invoice and any** purchase discounts **subsequently taken are credited to a Purchase Discount account.** This account should be reported as a contra account to Purchases, as a reduction in the cost of purchases.

The alternative approach, called the net method, **is to record the purchases and accounts payable initially at an amount net of the cash discounts.** If the account payable is paid within the discount period, the cash payment is exactly equal to the amount credited to the payable account. **If paid after the discount period lapses, the discount foregone is recorded in a Purchase Discounts Lost account, for which**

someone is held responsible. This treatment is considered more theoretically appropriate because it (1) provides a correct reporting of the asset cost and related liability, and (2) presents the opportunity to measure the inefficiency of financial management if the discount is not taken. To illustrate the difference between the gross and net methods, assume the following transactions.

Gross Method			Net Method		
Purchase cost of $10,000, terms 2/10, net 30:					
Purchases	10,000		Purchases	9,800	
Accounts Payable		10,000	Accounts Payable		9,800
Invoices of $4,000 are paid within discount period:					
Accounts Payable	4,000		Accounts Payable	3,920	
Purchase Discounts		80	Cash		3,920
Cash		3,920			
Invoices of $6,000 are paid after discount period:					
Accounts Payable	6,000		Accounts Payable	5,880	
Cash		6,000	Purchase Discounts Lost	120	
			Cash		6,000

Illustration 8-11

Entries Under Gross and Net Methods

Under the gross method, purchase discounts are deducted from purchases in determining cost of goods sold. If the net method is used, purchase discounts lost are considered a financial expense and are reported in the income statement's Other Expenses section. Many believe that the difficulty involved in using the somewhat more complicated net method is not worth the resulting benefits. Also, some contend that management is reluctant to report the amount of purchase discounts lost in the financial statements. These reasons may account for the widespread use of the less logical but simpler gross method.

Underlying Concept

Not using the net method because of resultant difficulties is an example of the application of the cost-benefit constraint.

Product Costs

Product costs are those costs that "attach" to the inventory and are recorded in the inventory account. These costs are directly connected with bringing goods to the buyer's place of business and converting such goods to a saleable condition. Such charges would include freight charges on goods purchased, other direct costs of acquisition, and labour and other production costs incurred in processing the goods up to the time of sale.

Nonrecoverable taxes (e.g., some provincial sales taxes) paid on goods purchased for resale or manufacturing purposes are a cost of inventory. Since value-added taxes (e.g., the federal Goods and Services Tax) are recoverable by a manufacturer, wholesaler, or retailer, they should not normally be treated as a cost of inventory. Chapter 14 discusses this type of tax.

It would be theoretically correct to allocate to inventories a share of any buying costs or expenses of a purchasing department, storage costs, and other costs incurred in storing or handling the goods before they are sold. **Because of the practical difficulties involved in allocating such costs and expenses, however, these items are not ordinarily included in inventory cost.**

Underlying Concept

Product costs are a direct application of the historical cost principle.

IAS Note

IAS 41 on agricultural activity recommends that agricultural production at the point of harvest be measured at fair value less estimated costs to sell.

Period Costs

Selling expenses and, under ordinary circumstances, **general and administrative expenses** are not considered directly related to the acquisition or production of goods and, therefore, are not considered a part of inventories. Such costs are period costs.

Conceptually, these expenses are as much a cost of the product as the initial purchase price and related freight charges attached to the product. Why then are these costs not considered inventoriable items? Selling expenses are generally considered more directly related to the cost of goods sold than to the unsold inventory. In most cases, though, these costs, especially administrative expenses, are so unrelated or indirectly related to the immediate production process that any allocation is purely arbitrary.

Interest costs associated with getting inventories ready for sale usually are expensed as incurred. A major argument for this approach is that interest costs are really a cost of financing. Additionally, it may be argued that the informational benefit of capitalizing interest costs to inventory does not justify the cost of doing it. Others have argued, however, that interest costs incurred to finance activities associated with bringing inventories to a condition and place ready for sale are as much a cost of the asset as materials, labour, and overhead and, therefore, should be capitalized.[7] While the FASB has ruled that interest costs related to assets constructed for internal use or assets produced as discrete projects (such as ships or real estate projects) for sale or lease should be capitalized, the *CICA Handbook* requires only that **if interest is capitalized, this policy and the amount capitalized in the current period be disclosed.**[8]

Brookfield Properties Corporation, referred to above, provides the following accounting policy note to its financial statements related to its inventory of properties under development.

Underlying Concept

In capitalizing interest, the constraints of materiality and cost/benefit are both applied.

Illustration 8-12

Development Property Inventory Costs

NOTE 1: SIGNIFICANT ACCOUNTING POLICIES

(d) Capitalized costs

Costs are capitalized on commercial and residential properties which are under development, home building properties and other properties held for sale, including all expenditures incurred in connection with the acquisition, development, construction and initial predetermined leasing period. These expenditures consist of all direct costs, interest on debt that is related to these assets and certain administrative expenses. Ancillary income relating specifically to such properties during the development period is treated as a reduction of costs.

NOTE 3: DEVELOPMENT PROPERTIES (Excerpt)

Development properties include commercial developments, primarily for office development and residential land under and held for development.

(Millions)	2002	2001	2000
Commercial developments	$ 720	$344	$193
Residential development land	224	231	344
Total	$ 944	$575	$537

Commercial developments include commercial land, and rights and options which represent developable land and construction costs. Residential development land includes fully entitled lots and land in processing. The company capitalizes interest and administrative and development costs to both commercial and residential development properties. During 2002, the company capitalized construction and related costs of $189 million (2001 – $61 million, 2000 – $16 million) and $28 million (2001 – $17 million, 2000 – nil) of interest to its commercial development sites. During 2002, after interest recoveries of $20 million (2001 – $35 million, 2000 – recovered net $4 million) of interest and capitalized a net nil (2001 – nil, 2000 – 1 million) of administrative and development costs. In connection with residential land development operations, these costs are expensed as land is sold.

Manufacturing Costs

As previously indicated, a business that manufactures goods uses three inventory accounts: Raw Materials, Work in Process, and Finished Goods. Work in process and finished goods include direct materials, direct labour, and manufacturing overhead costs. Manufacturing

---

[7] The reporting rules related to interest capitalization have their greatest impact in accounting for property, plant, and equipment and, therefore, are discussed in detail in Chapter 11. This brief overview provides the basic issues when inventories are involved.

[8] *CICA Handbook*, Section 3850.03.

overhead costs include indirect material, indirect labour, and such items as amortization, taxes, insurance, heat, and electricity incurred in the manufacturing process. The raw materials and work-in-process inventories are incorporated into a **statement of cost of goods manufactured**, as shown in Illustration 8-13.

Illustration 8-13

Statement of Cost of Goods Manufactured

STATEMENT OF COST OF GOODS MANUFACTURED
For the Year Ended December 31, 2005

Raw materials consumed			
Raw materials inventory, Jan. 1, 2005			$ 14,000
Add net purchases:			
Purchases		$126,000	
Less: Purchase returns and allowances	$1,800		
Purchase discounts	1,200	3,000	123,000
Raw material available for use			137,000
Less **raw materials inventory, Dec. 31, 2005**			17,000
Cost of raw materials consumed			120,000
Direct labour			200,000
Manufacturing overhead			
Supervisors' salaries		$ 63,000	
Indirect labour		20,000	
Factory supplies used		18,000	
Heat, light, power, and water		13,000	
Amortization of building and equipment		27,000	
Tools expense		2,000	
Patent amortization		1,000	
Miscellaneous factory expenses		6,000	150,000
Total manufacturing costs for the period			470,000
Work-in-process inventory, Jan. 1, 2005			33,000
Total manufacturing costs			503,000
Less **work-in-process inventory, Dec. 31, 2005**			28,000
Cost of goods manufactured during the year			**$475,000**

Cost of goods manufactured statements are prepared primarily for internal use; such details are rarely disclosed in published financial statements. The cost of goods sold reported in a manufacturing firm's income statement is determined in a manner similar to that for a merchandising concern except that **the cost of goods manufactured during the year is substituted for the cost of goods purchased**. For example, if the inventory of finished goods for the company in Illustration 8-13 was $16,000 at the beginning of the year and $10,000 at the end of the year, the calculation of cost of goods sold for the income statement would be as shown in Illustration 8-14.

Illustration 8-14

Cost of Goods Sold Calculation: Manufacturing Company

Cost of goods sold	
Finished goods inventory, Jan. 1, 2005	$ 16,000
Cost of goods manufactured during 2005	475,000
Cost of goods available for sale	491,000
Finished goods inventory, Dec. 31, 2005	10,000
Cost of goods sold	**$481,000**

One issue of importance for costing a manufacturing company's inventory is whether or not fixed manufacturing overhead costs will be included in inventory (absorption costing) or charged to expenses of the period (variable costing). This issue is discussed next.

Variable Costing Versus Absorption Costing

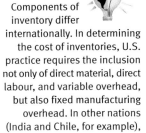

Fixed manufacturing overhead costs present a special problem in costing inventories because two points of view exist about the costs that should attach to the product as it flows through the manufacturing process. These two concepts are variable costing, frequently called direct costing, and absorption costing, also called full costing. In a variable costing system, all costs must be classified as variable or fixed. Variable costs are those that fluctuate in direct proportion to changes in output, and fixed costs are those that remain constant in spite of changes in output. Under variable costing, **only costs that vary directly with the production volume are charged to products** as manufacturing takes place. Direct material, direct labour, and variable manufacturing overhead are charged to work-in-process and finished goods inventories and subsequently become part of cost of goods sold. **Fixed overhead costs** such as property taxes, insurance, amortization on plant building, and supervisors' salaries **are considered period costs**. These costs are considered necessary to operate at a given level of capacity and are not viewed as costs of the products being manufactured. **All fixed costs are charged as expenses to the current period.**

Under an absorption costing system, **all manufacturing costs**, variable and fixed, direct and indirect, that are incurred in the factory or production process **attach to the product**. Both fixed and variable overhead are charged to output and are allocated to the cost of inventory, and eventually, cost of goods sold.

Proponents of the variable costing system believe that it provides information on accounting reports that is more useful to management in formulating pricing policies and in controlling costs. Also, because fixed costs are included in inventory under the absorption approach, it may be argued that such a system results in distorting net income from period to period when production volume fluctuates. If such is the case, variable costing may be a more appropriate basis for reporting income. Absorption costing, however, is the dominant basis for external financial reporting. Its supporters believe it more reasonably represents a firm's investment in inventories.

The Canadian accounting standard for assigning costs to work-in-process and finished goods inventories requires only that the "**applicable share of overhead expense properly chargeable to production**" be captured in inventory cost.[9] This leaves the decision of treating fixed overhead costs to one's judgement. The *CICA Handbook* also allows for a portion of overhead to be excluded from inventory cost if, by being included, it would distort the income reported due to fluctuating production volume. These statements suggest that while variable costing is acceptable, it is more the exception than the rule for external reporting.

Standard Costs

A manufacturing company that uses a standard cost system predetermines the unit costs for material, labour, and manufacturing overhead. Usually the standard costs are determined based on the costs that should be incurred per unit of finished goods when the plant is operating at normal capacity. Deviations from actual costs are recorded in variance accounts that are examined by management so that appropriate action can be taken to achieve greater control over costs.

For financial statement purposes, reporting inventories at standard costs is acceptable if there is no significant difference between the aggregate actual and standard costs. If there is a significant difference, the inventory amounts should be adjusted to estimated actual cost.[10] Otherwise the net income, assets, and retained earnings would be misstated.

---

[9] *CICA Handbook*, Section 3030.06.

[10] *CICA Handbook*, Section 3030.04.

An interesting related inventory costing issue is Bombardier Inc.'s change in its method of accounting for the costs related to its inventory of regional and business aircraft, during its year ended January 31, 2003. Aerospace companies generally use "program costing" when a new aircraft is developed. Under this method, the company estimates the number of aircraft to be produced and the total costs associated with all production of that model expected over the life of that model, which could be 15 to 20 years. From this, the aircraft's average unit production cost is determined, and this is the inventory cost of each unit of that model in inventory—in effect, its standard cost.

However, **there is a considerable learning curve in the production of each model**. The earlier units produced take considerably more time and cost than the production toward the end of the program. The difference between the actual costs incurred and the average unit production cost are included in the inventory account as well, called "excess over-average production costs." In theory, when the future actual costs are lower than the average, this account is reduced, falling to zero as the program is completed. In reality, the total program costs are subject to considerable revision as cost estimates are updated and better information is generated about the market for the aircraft and the number to be produced and sold.

Previously, Bombardier deferred any increase in estimated costs (i.e., included them in inventory), spreading the higher cost revisions over the remaining units to be produced. In 2003, the company changed its method of accounting to charge the effect of the revisions directly to income as a cumulative catch-up adjustment. While both methods are acceptable under GAAP, there can be a significant difference in reported income. This change, along with a change in method of writing off associated non-recurring costs, retroactively applied, resulted in a $753.9 million after-tax reduction in Bombardier's opening retained earnings!

A detailed examination of standard costing is available in most managerial and cost accounting texts, but is beyond the scope of this book.

What do the Numbers Mean?

COST FLOW ASSUMPTIONS

Two issues have now been addressed in determining inventory cost—the physical items to include, and which costs should be included for these units and which excluded. The next issue needing resolution is deciding, when purchases are made at different cost amounts during the year, whether to assign the earlier costs, the most recent costs, an average, or some other basis to the items left in ending inventory.

6 Objective

Distinguish between the physical flow of inventory and the cost flow assigned to inventory.

A Framework for Analysis

During any given fiscal period, it is likely that merchandise will be purchased at several different prices. **If inventories are to be priced at cost and numerous purchases have been made at different unit costs, which of the various cost prices should be assigned to Inventory on the balance sheet and which costs should be charged to Cost of Goods Sold on the income statement?** Conceptually, to match actual costs with the physical flow of goods, a specific identification of the items sold and unsold seems appropriate, but this is often not only expensive but impossible to achieve. Consequently, the accountant must consistently apply one of several other cost methods that are based on differing but systematic inventory cost flow assumptions. Indeed, the actual physical flow of goods and the cost flow assumption applied are often quite different. **There is no requirement that the cost flow assumption adopted be consistent with the physical movement of goods.**

Issues regarding the various cost flow methods will be illustrated and discussed using the data in Illustration 8-15, which summarizes inventory-related activities of Call-Mart

Inc. for the month of March. For illustrative purposes, the beginning inventory's cost per unit is assumed to be the same for all methods. **It is important to note that the company experienced increasing unit costs for its purchases throughout the month.**

The problem is which cost or costs should be assigned to the 6,000 units of ending inventory and which to the 4,000 units sold. The solution depends on what one wishes to accomplish. There are, as previously indicated, several acceptable alternative cost flow methods that may be chosen. These methods are based on different assumptions and accomplish different objectives. A suggested approach to selecting a method is as follows.

1. Identify possible objectives to be accomplished.

2. Know the different acceptable methods, their assumptions, and how they work.

3. Evaluate the advantages and disadvantages of the different methods for achieving the objectives.

4. Choose the method appropriate to the situation and the objective(s) to be accomplished.

Objectives of Inventory Valuation

Objective 7
Identify possible objectives for inventory valuation decisions.

The following general objectives are often associated with choosing an inventory cost-flow method:

1. to match expenses (cost of goods sold) realistically against revenue,

2. to report inventory on the balance sheet at a realistic amount, and

3. to minimize income taxes, maximizing cash flow.

While the first two are legitimate objectives of financial reporting, the third should not be relevant to financial accounting; however, it sometimes enters into financial accounting decisions for the very real reason that it affects cash flows and therefore share value.

The financial statement objectives of inventory valuation are inherently logical and useful when assessing the various cost flow methods' merits and limitations within the framework of generally accepted accounting principles. They do, however, beg the question, "What is realistic?" The answer depends on the purpose of preparing financial statements. More will be said about this later in the chapter under the heading "Which Method to Select?"

To illustrate the application of the various cost flow assumptions, assume that Call-Mart Inc. had the following transactions for the month of March.

Illustration 8-15

Data Used to Illustrate Inventory Calculation: Cost Flow Assumptions

CALL-MART INC.			
Date	Purchases	Sold or Issued	Balance
March 1	(beginning inventory)		
	500 @ $3.80		500 units
March 2	1,500 @ $4.00		2,000 units
March 15	6,000 @ $4.40		8,000 units
March 19		4,000 units	4,000 units
March 30	2,000 @ $4.75		6,000 units

From this information, we can calculate the ending inventory of 6,000 units and the cost of goods available for sale (beginning inventory + purchases) of $43,800 [(500 @ $3.80) + (1,500 @ $4.00) + (6,000 @ $4.40) + (2,000 @ $4.75)]. **The question is, which price or prices should represent the cost of the 6,000 units of ending inventory?** The answer depends on which cost flow assumption is chosen.

Specific Identification

8 Objective
Describe and compare the cost flow assumptions used in accounting for inventories.

Specific identification calls for identifying each item sold and each item in inventory. The costs of the specific items sold are included in the cost of goods sold, and the costs of the specific items on hand are included in the ending inventory. This method may be used only in instances where it is practical to segregate specific items as coming from separate purchases. It can be successfully applied in situations where a relatively small number of costly, easily distinguishable (e.g., by physical characteristics, serial numbers, or special markings) items are handled. In the retail trade this includes some types of jewellery, fur coats, automobiles, and some furniture. In manufacturing it includes special orders and many products manufactured under a job cost system.

To illustrate the specific identification method, assume that Call-Mart Inc.'s 6,000 units of inventory is composed of 100 units from the opening inventory, 900 from the March 2 purchase, 3,000 from the March 15 purchase, and 2,000 from the March 30 purchase. The ending inventory and cost of goods sold would be calculated as shown in Illustration 8-16.

Units from	No. of Units	Unit Cost	Total Cost
Beginning inventory	100	$3.80	$ 380
March 2 purchase	900	4.00	3,600
March 15 purchase	3,000	4.40	13,200
March 30 purchase	2,000	4.75	9,500
Ending inventory	**6,000**		**$26,680**
Cost of goods available for sale (beginning inventory + purchases)		$43,800	
Deduct: Ending inventory		26,680	
Cost of goods sold		**$17,120**	

Illustration 8-16
Specific Identification Method

Conceptually, this method appears ideal because actual costs are matched against actual revenue, and ending inventory is reported at actual cost. In other words, under specific identification, the cost flow matches the goods' physical flow. On closer observation, however, this method has certain deficiencies.

One argument against specific identification is that it makes it possible to manipulate net income. For example, assume that a wholesaler purchases otherwise identical plywood early in the year at three different prices. When the plywood is sold, the wholesaler can select either the lowest or the highest price to charge to expense simply by selecting the plywood from a specific lot for delivery to the customer. A business manager, therefore, can manipulate net income simply by delivering to the customer the higher- or lower-priced item, depending on whether lower or higher reported income is desired for the period.

Another problem relates to the arbitrary allocation of costs that sometimes occurs with specific inventory items. In certain circumstances, **it is difficult to relate adequately, for example, shipping charges, storage costs, and discounts directly to a given inventory item.** The alternative, then, is to allocate these costs somewhat arbitrarily, which leads to a breakdown in the precision of the specific identification method.[11]

IAS Note

For inventory items that are not interchangeable, IAS6 requires the specific costs to be assigned to individual items. For interchangeable goods, the benchmark methods are FIFO or weighted average cost. For now, LIFO is an allowed alternative.

---

[11] A good illustration of the cost allocation problem arises in the motion picture industry. Often actors and actresses receive a percentage of net income for a given movie or television program. Some actors who had these arrangements have alleged that their programs have been extremely profitable to the motion picture studios but they have received little in the way of profit-sharing. Actors contend that the studios allocate additional costs to successful projects to ensure that there will be no profits to share. Such contentions illustrate the type of problems that can emerge when contracts are based on accounting numbers that incorporate arbitrary allocations. One way to help overcome such problems is to establish specific measurement rules regarding how the accounting numbers are to be determined, rather than just stating the numbers to be used. This should be done before the contract is signed so that all parties clearly understand what they are getting into.

Average Cost

As the name implies, the **average cost method** prices inventory items based on the average cost of the goods available for sale during the period. To illustrate, assuming that Call-Mart Inc. used the periodic inventory method (or a perpetual system in units only), the ending inventory and cost of goods sold would be calculated as follows using a **weighted-average method**.

Illustration 8-17

*Weighted-Average Method—
Periodic Inventory*

	Date	No. Units	Unit Cost	Total Cost
Inventory	Mar. 1	500	$3.80	$ 1,900
Purchases	Mar. 2	1,500	4.00	6,000
Purchases	Mar. 15	6,000	4.40	26,400
Purchases	Mar. 30	2,000	4.75	9,500
Total goods available		10,000		$43,800

Weighted average cost per unit $\dfrac{\$43,800}{10,000} = \$4.38$

Ending inventory in units	6,000	
Cost of ending inventory	**6,000** × **$4.38 = $26,280**	
Cost of goods available for sale	$43,800	
Deduct ending inventory	26,280	
Cost of goods sold	**$17,520**	(= 4,000 × $4.38)

Note that the beginning inventory is included both in the total units available and in the total cost of goods available in calculating the average cost per unit.

Another average cost method is the **moving-average method**, which is **used with perpetual inventory records kept in both units and dollars**. Application of the average cost method for full perpetual records is shown in Illustration 8-18.

Illustration 8-18

*Moving-Average Method—
Perpetual Inventory*

Date	Purchased	Sold or Issued	Balance	
Mar. 1	Beginning inventory		(500 @ $3.80)	$ 1,900
Mar. 2	(1,500 @ $4.00) $6,000		(2,000 @ $3.95)	7,900
Mar. 15	(6,000 @ $4.40) 26,400		(8,000 @ $4.2875)	34,300
Mar. 19		(4,000 @ $4.2875) $17,150	(4,000 @ $4.2875)	17,150
Mar. 30	(2,000 @ $4.75) 9,500		(6,000 @ $4.4417)	26,650

Calculation of moving-average cost per unit:
After March 2 purchase
= Cost of units available / Units available
= [$1,900 + (1,500 × $4.00)] / (500 + 1,500)
= ($1,900 + $6,000) / 2,000
= $7,900 / 2,000
= $3.95

After March 15 purchase
= [$7,900 + (6,000 × $4.40)] / (2,000 + 6,000)
= $34,300 / 8,000
= $4.2875

After March 30 purchase
= [17,150 + (2,000 × $4.75)] / (4,000 + 2,000)
= $26,650 / 6,000
= $4.4417

In this method, a new average unit cost is calculated each time a purchase is made. On March 15, after 6,000 units are purchased for $26,400, 8,000 units costing $34,300 ($7,900 plus $26,400) are on hand. The average unit cost is $34,300 divided by 8,000, or $4.2875. This unit cost is used in costing withdrawals until another purchase is made, when a new average unit cost is calculated. Accordingly, the cost of the 4,000 units withdrawn on March 19 is shown at $4.2875, a total cost of goods sold of $17,150. On March 30, following the purchase of 2,000 units for $9,500, a new unit cost of $4.4417 is determined for an ending inventory of $26,650.

The use of the average cost method is usually justified with practical rather than conceptual reasons. These methods are simple to apply, objective, and not as subject to income manipulation as some other inventory costing methods. In addition, proponents of the average cost method argue that it is often impossible to measure a specific physical flow of inventory and therefore it is better to cost items on an average price basis. This argument is particularly persuasive when the inventory involved is relatively homogeneous in nature.

In terms of achieving financial statement objectives, an average cost method results in an average of costs being used to determine the cost of goods sold in the income statement and ending inventory in the balance sheet. Compared with the FIFO method (discussed below), an average cost method results in more recent costs being reflected in the cost of goods sold, but older costs in ending inventory. Relative to the LIFO method (discussed below), an average cost method reflects more recent costs in ending inventory, but older costs in cost of goods sold. Therefore, the average cost method may be viewed as a compromise between the FIFO and LIFO methods. Some would argue that, as a compromise, an average cost method has the advantages of neither and the disadvantages of both of these other methods. For income taxes, an average cost method can be used in Canada and it may provide some income tax advantages during periods of rising prices.

First-In, First-Out (FIFO)

The **FIFO method** assigns costs assuming that goods are used in the order in which they are purchased. In other words, it assumes that **the first goods purchased are the first used** (in a manufacturing concern) **or sold** (in a merchandising concern). The inventory remaining must, therefore, represent the most recent purchases.

To illustrate, assume that Call-Mart Inc. uses the periodic inventory system (or a perpetual system in units only), where the inventory cost is calculated only at the end of the month. **The ending inventory's cost is calculated by taking the cost of the most recent purchase and working back until all units in the ending inventory are accounted for.** The ending inventory and cost of goods sold are determined as shown in Illustration 8-19.

Date	No. Units	Unit Cost	Total Cost
March 30	2,000	$4.75	$ 9,500
March 15	4,000	4.40	17,600
Ending inventory	6,000		$27,100
	Cost of goods available for sale	$43,800	
	Deduct: Ending inventory	27,100	
	Cost of goods sold	$16,700	

Illustration 8-19

FIFO Method—Periodic Inventory

If a perpetual inventory system in quantities and dollars is used, a cost figure is attached to each withdrawal from inventory when the units are sold. In the example, the cost of the 4,000 units removed on March 19 would be made up first from the items in the beginning inventory, then the purchases on March 2, and finally from the March 15 purchases. The inventory record on a FIFO basis perpetual system for Call-Mart Inc. is shown in Illustration 8-20, which indicates an ending inventory of $27,100 and a cost of goods sold of $16,700.

Illustration 8-20

*FIFO Method—
Perpetual Inventory*

Date	Purchased	Sold or Issued	Balance	
Mar. 1	Beginning inventory		500 @ $3.80	$ 1,900
Mar. 2	(1,500 @ $4.00) $ 6,000		500 @ 3.80 ⎫ 1,500 @ 4.00 ⎬	7,900
Mar. 15	(6,000 @ $4.40) 26,400		500 @ 3.80 ⎫ 1,500 @ 4.00 ⎬ 6,000 @ 4.40 ⎭	34,300
Mar. 19		500 @ $3.80 ⎫ 1,500 @ 4.00 ⎬ 2,000 @ 4.40 ⎭ **$16,700**	4,000 @ 4.40	17,600
Mar. 30	(2,000 @ $4.75) 9,500		4,000 @ 4.40 ⎫ 2,000 @ 4.75 ⎬	27,100

Notice that in these two FIFO examples, the cost of goods sold and ending inventory are the same. **In all cases where FIFO is used, the inventory and cost of goods sold would be the same at the end of the month whether a perpetual or periodic system is used.** This is true because the same costs will always be first in and, therefore, first out—whether cost of goods sold is calculated as goods are sold throughout the accounting period (the perpetual system) or as a residual at the end of the accounting period (the periodic system).

One objective of FIFO is to approximate the physical flow of goods. When the physical flow of goods is actually first-in, first-out, the FIFO method very nearly represents specific identification. At the same time, it does not permit manipulation of income because the enterprise is not free to choose a certain cost to be charged to expense.

Another advantage of the FIFO method is that the ending inventory is close to its current cost. Because the costs of the first goods in are transferred to cost of goods sold, the ending inventory amount will be composed of the most recent purchases. This approach generally approximates replacement cost for inventory on the balance sheet when the inventory turnover is rapid and/or price changes have not occurred since the most recent purchases.

As indicated by the controller of Petro-Canada in this chapter's opening vignette, the FIFO method's basic disadvantage is that current costs are not matched against current revenues on the income statement. The oldest costs are charged against current revenue, which can lead to distortions in gross profit and net income when prices are changing rapidly.

Last-In, First-Out (LIFO)

**International
Insight**

Until recently,
LIFO was typically
used only in the United States.
It is found primarily in
countries where it is allowed
for tax purposes, such as in
Belgium, Germany, Japan,
South Korea, and Taiwan.

The LIFO method assigns costs on the assumption that the cost of the most recent purchase is the first cost to be charged to cost of goods sold. The cost assigned to the inventory remaining would therefore come from the earliest acquisitions (i.e., "first-in, still-here").

If a periodic inventory system (or a perpetual system in units only) is used, it is assumed that **the total quantity sold or issued during the period would have come from the most recent purchases, even though such purchases may have taken place**

after the actual date of sale. Conversely, the ending inventory costs would consist first of costs from the beginning inventory and then from purchases early in the period. Using the example for Call-Mart Inc., the assumption is made that the 4,000 units withdrawn and sold consisted of the 2,000 units purchased on March 30 and 2,000 of the 6,000 units purchased on March 15. Therefore, the cost of the ending inventory of 6,000 units is assumed to come from the cost of any beginning inventory (500 units) and then the earliest purchases in the period (1,500 units on March 2 and 4,000 units on March 15). The inventory and related cost of goods sold are calculated as shown in Illustration 8-21.

Date of Invoice	No. Units	Unit Cost	Total Cost
Beginning inventory	500	$3.80	$ 1,900
Mar. 2 purchase	1,500	4.00	6,000
Mar. 15 purchase	4,000	4.40	17,600
Ending inventory	**6,000**		**$25,500**

Cost of goods available for sale	$43,800	
Deduct: Ending inventory	25,500	
Cost of goods sold	**$18,300**	

Illustration 8-21

*LIFO Method—
Periodic Inventory*

If a perpetual inventory system is kept in quantities and dollars, applying the last-in, first-out method will result in different ending inventory and cost of goods sold amounts, as shown in Illustration 8-22.

Date	Purchased	Sold or Issued	Balance	
Mar. 1	Beginning inventory		500 @ $3.80	$ 1,900
Mar. 2	(1,500 @ $4.00) $ 6,000		500 @ 3.80 1,500 @ 4.00	7,900
Mar. 15	(6,000 @ $4.40) 26,400		500 @ 3.80 1,500 @ 4.00 6,000 @ 4.40	34,300
Mar. 19		(4,000 @ $4.40) **$17,600**	500 @ 3.80 1,500 @ 4.00 2,000 @ 4.40	16,700
Mar. 30	(2,000 @ $4.75) 9,500		500 @ 3.80 1,500 @ 4.00 2,000 @ 4.40 2,000 @ 4.75	26,200

Illustration 8-22

*LIFO Method—
Perpetual Inventory*

The month-end **periodic** inventory calculation presented in Illustration 8-21 (inventory $25,500 and cost of goods sold $18,300) shows a different amount from the **perpetual** inventory calculation (inventory $26,200 and cost of goods sold $17,600). This is because the periodic system matches the total withdrawals for the month with the total purchases for the month, whereas the perpetual system matches each withdrawal with the immediately preceding purchases. In effect, the periodic calculation assumed that the goods that were not purchased until March 30 were included in the sale or issue of March 19. While this is not physically possible, remember that it is not necessary to match physical item flows with cost flows when measuring cost of goods sold. The perspective to be taken is that of understanding which costs are matched against the revenues.

EVALUATION AND CHOICE OF A COST FLOW METHOD

Use of the LIFO method is controversial. Some do not believe it is appropriate for conceptual reasons, while others believe it is conceptually superior to other approaches given that financial statements are prepared on a historical cost basis. Arguments for and against the use of LIFO necessarily reflect a perception regarding many fundamental issues about financial accounting: What is relevant? Which is more important, the income statement or the balance sheet? Should income tax requirements dictate methods to be selected for preparing financial statements?

While reaching a conclusion about LIFO's acceptability is a matter of judgement, its major advantages and disadvantages should be considered. Careful reflection on this listing will indicate that, for most points, the advantages of LIFO become the disadvantages of other cost flow methods (FIFO and average cost) and vice versa.

Major Advantages of LIFO

Matching

Objective 9
Evaluate LIFO as a basis for understanding the differences among the cost flow methods.

The matching principle requires that we match costs to the same period as related revenues are recognized. **The principle, however, does not say which costs should be matched when alternatives are available.** Therefore, for inventory valuation, the various methods available leave open the choice of matching recent costs (LIFO), average costs (average methods), or older costs (FIFO) against revenues.

In LIFO, the more recent costs are matched against current revenues to provide what may be viewed as a more realistic measure of current earnings in periods of changing prices. For example, in the early 1990s, many Canadian oil companies changed to the LIFO method. The explanation given in **Petro-Canada**'s financial report, reiterated at the beginning of this chapter, was: "The change was made to more closely match current costs with current revenues in determination of the results of the Company's operations."

During periods of rising prices, many challenge the quality of non-LIFO historical cost-based earnings, noting that by failing to match current costs against current revenues, **transitory "paper" or "inventory profits"** are created. **Inventory profits** occur because old low inventory costs that are matched against sales are less than the recent, higher costs to replace the inventory. The cost of goods sold therefore is perceived to be understated and profit is overstated. By using LIFO (rather than FIFO or average cost), more recent costs are matched against revenues and inventory profits are thereby reduced.

Future Earnings Hedge

With LIFO, in a period of rising prices, a company's future reported earnings will not be affected substantially by future price declines due to writedowns under the lower of cost and market rule (examined in Chapter 9). LIFO eliminates or substantially minimizes writedowns to market as a result of price decreases. The reason: since the most recent (higher cost) inventory is assumed to be sold first, the ending inventory value ordinarily will be lower than net realizable value. In contrast, inventory costed under FIFO is more vulnerable to price declines, which can reduce net income substantially. When prices are declining, however, this aspect of LIFO becomes a disadvantage.

Major Disadvantages of LIFO

Reduced Earnings

Many corporate managers view the lower profits reported under the LIFO method, relative to other methods, as a distinct disadvantage. They fear that the effect on net income from using LIFO may be misunderstood and that, as a result of the lower profits, the company's share price will fall. In fact, though, there is some evidence to refute this contention. Studies have indicated that users of financial data exhibit a sophistication that enables them to recognize the impact on reported income from using LIFO compared with other methods and, as a consequence, reflect this when assessing a company's share price.

This disadvantage of reduced earnings assumes that prices are increasing; when prices are declining, the opposite effect may occur. For example, oil prices to refineries were declining when many Canadian oil companies switched to LIFO in the early 1990s.

Inventory Distortion

Under LIFO, the inventory valuation on the balance sheet is normally outdated because the oldest costs remain in inventory. This results in several problems, especially in evaluating the amounts, ratios, and related trends that include the ending inventory. The extent of the problem depends on the degree and direction of the changes in price and the rate of inventory turnover.

Physical Flow

LIFO does not approximate the items' physical flow except in a few situations. Imagine a coal pile: the last coal bought is the first coal out, since the coal remover will not take coal from inside the pile. However, matching more recent costs against revenues may be viewed as a higher priority objective than reflecting the physical flow of goods when choosing an inventory valuation method.

Inventory Liquidation

Use of LIFO raises the problem of LIFO liquidation. If the base or layers of old costs in beginning inventory are eliminated (e.g., when units sold during a period exceed the units purchased for a period), strange results can occur. The matching advantage of LIFO would be lost because old, irrelevant costs would be matched against current revenues, resulting in a severe distortion in reported income at least for the given period. For example, Allied Corporation reported net earnings of $0.09 per share in a year in which its inventory reductions resulted in liquidations of LIFO inventory quantities. The inventory reduction's effect was to increase income by $13 million or $0.17 per share!

Poor Buying Habits

Because of the liquidation problem, LIFO may cause poor buying habits. A company may simply purchase more goods and match the cost of these goods against revenue to ensure that old costs are not charged to expense. Furthermore, the possibility always exists with LIFO that a company will attempt to manage (manipulate) its earnings at year end simply by altering its purchasing pattern.

Not Acceptable for Tax Purposes

Because of definitions in the Income Tax Act as to how inventory amounts may be determined, **LIFO inventory valuation is not accepted by Canada Customs and Revenue**

Agency for purposes of determining taxable income except in a few special circumstances. If Canadian companies want to use LIFO, they are required to maintain information on one of the acceptable methods as well, for use on their tax return.

Current Cost Income Not Measured

LIFO falls short of measuring current cost (replacement cost) income, though not as far short as FIFO. When measuring current cost income, the cost of goods sold should consist not of the most recently incurred costs but rather of the cost that will be incurred to replace the goods that have been sold. Using replacement cost is referred to as the next-in, first-out method, which is not currently acceptable for purposes of inventory valuation.

Summary Analysis of FIFO, Weighted-Average, and LIFO Methods

For review and comparison purposes, a summary of the three major cost flow methods' differing effects on the financial statements is shown in Illustration 8-23. The numbers were derived from the illustrations of each method for Call-Mart Inc. for the month of March, using the periodic system or a perpetual system maintained in units only. The sales revenue reflects that the 4,000 units were sold for $10 each. The difference in gross profit and, therefore, net income (other expenses would be the same) is due to the differing cost flow assumptions associated with each method. Since the example assumed a period of rising prices, the gross profit (and, therefore, net income) is highest under FIFO and lowest under LIFO.

Illustration 8-23

Comparison of FIFO, Weighted-Average, and LIFO Methods

	Method		
	FIFO	Weighted-Average	LIFO
Partial Income Statement:			
Sales Revenue	$40,000	$40,000	$40,000
Cost of Goods Sold:			
Beginning inventory	$ 1,900	$ 1,900	$ 1,900
Purchases	41,900	41,900	41,900
Goods Available	$43,800	$43,800	$43,800
Deduct:			
Ending inventory	27,100	26,280	25,500
Cost of Goods Sold	16,700	17,520	18,300
Gross Profit	$23,300	$22,480	$21,700
Balance Sheet:			
Inventory	$27,100	$26,280	$25,500
Objectives:			
1. Matching	Old costs against current revenue	Average cost against current revenue	"Current" costs against current revenue*
2. Balance sheet valuation	"Current" costs*	Average cost	Old costs
3. Income tax minimization	Results in higher taxable income in periods of rising prices.	Best in Canada in periods of rising prices as results in highest cost of goods sold next to LIFO.*	Not allowed in Canada in most situations. If it were, it would be best in periods of rising prices.

*Results in a realistic accomplishment of objective relative to other methods. The * regarding matching for LIFO assumes no liquidation of beginning inventory.

At the bottom of the comparative results is a listing of the three objectives previously identified as being most commonly associated with choosing an inventory method. As developed in the prior discussion, the strongest argument favouring LIFO for financial statement reporting purposes is that it matches more current costs against current revenue. FIFO results in the most current cost for inventory on the balance sheet.

In terms of minimizing income tax or deferring tax payments, the method resulting in the lowest taxable income for the period is preferred. While LIFO results in the lowest income in periods of rising prices (assuming there is little or no beginning inventory liquidation), it is not permitted for calculating taxable income in Canada for most businesses. Consequently, the average-cost method, which is permitted under income tax legislation, more effectively accomplishes this objective in a period of rising prices.

The fact that LIFO is generally not allowed for determining taxable income in Canada is in direct contrast to the situation in the United States, where it is accepted for tax purposes. While non-LIFO disclosures may be made as supplemental information, the Internal Revenue Service in the United States requires that if LIFO is used for income tax purposes, it must also be used for financial reporting purposes (this is known as the LIFO conformity rule). Though one may argue the merits of LIFO for financial reporting purposes on a more conceptual level, the IRS ruling is likely primarily responsible for the much higher use of the LIFO method in financial statements in the United States compared with Canada.[12] In fact, due to falling raw material costs and other savings from using EDI (electronic data interface) and just-in-time technologies, many companies using LIFO no longer are experiencing substantial tax benefits, and are moving to FIFO and average cost methods.

Which Method to Select?

The *CICA Handbook* indicates that specific identification, FIFO, average cost, and LIFO are generally acceptable and commonly used methods for determining inventory cost for financial reporting purposes.[13] The *CICA Handbook* also recommends that the method selected should result in the fairest matching of costs against revenues, whether or not the method is consistent with the physical flow of goods.[14]

What method will provide the fairest matching? The answer can be derived only by exercising professional judgement, given knowledge of the particular circumstances and the consequences desired in terms of the financial statements' objectives. As indicated in Chapter 1, a primary objective of financial reporting is to communicate information that is useful to investors, creditors, and others in making their resource allocation decisions and/or assessing management stewardship. Therefore, the inventory valuation method that accomplishes this objective would certainly be the fairest (most relevant) one to choose. Making the appropriate choice, however, depends on awareness of a number of things, such as who the users are, the decisions they are making, and what information fits their decision models. If one method was fairest for all situations, then the accounting profession would certainly not have acceptable alternative methods. Consequently, professional judgement is the basis for determining the method to use.

10 **Objective**
Explain the importance of judgement in selecting an inventory cost flow method.

 IAS Note

 As part of the project to improve its standards, the IAS is eliminating the use of LIFO as an allowed alternative.

---

[12] *Financial Reporting in Canada—2002* reported that of the 142 inventory cost method disclosures, 39% used FIFO, 35% used average cost, 2% used LIFO, 3% used other methods, and 22% used more than one method. For comparison, a similar U.S. study, *Accounting Trends and Techniques—2001*, reported that of 887 inventory method disclosures, 44% used FIFO, 20% used average cost, 32% used LIFO, and 4% used other methods. Data from the United States indicate that a significant shift from FIFO to LIFO took place in the 1970s and early 1980s. The rate of inflation and tax advantages were, no doubt, at least partially responsible for the shift. Although inflation was also significant in Canada, no shift to LIFO was evident.

[13] *CICA Handbook*, Section 3030.07. Noteworthy about this section is that it does not explicitly identify these methods as the only ones that are acceptable.

[14] *CICA Handbook*, Section 3030.09.

An important point is that a company can use one method (e.g., FIFO) for financial statement reporting and another method (average cost) for tax purposes. This is legal and reasonable as financial reporting objectives are different from those of income tax determination. Having "two sets of books" may, however, be inefficient—a judgement requiring the accountant to be fully cognizant of the circumstances. If methods used for preparing financial statements differ from those used for determining taxable income, a difference results between the inventory's book value and tax value. The tax effect on the amount of the temporary difference is accounted for as an interperiod allocation, a topic that is examined in Chapter 19.

Consistency of Inventory Costing

Underlying Concept

Consistent application of the same method enhances the comparability of the financial statements.

All the inventory costing methods described in this chapter are used to some extent. Indeed, a company may use different methods for different types of inventory.

It can be seen that freedom to shift from one inventory costing method to another at will would permit a wide range of possible net income figures for a given company for any given period. This would affect the comparability of the financial statements. The variety of methods has been devised to assist appropriate financial reporting rather than to permit manipulation. Hence, it is necessary that the costing method most suitable to a company be selected and, once selected, be applied consistently thereafter. If conditions indicate that another accounting policy would result in a reliable and more relevant presentation in the financial statements, a change may be made. Such a change should be accounted for retroactively, clearly explained, and its effect disclosed in the financial statements.[15]

Summary of Learning Objectives

1 Identify major classifications of inventory.

Only one inventory account, Merchandise Inventory, appears in the financial statements of a merchandising concern. A manufacturer normally has three inventory accounts: Raw Materials, Work in Process, and Finished Goods. Factory or manufacturing supplies inventory may also exist.

2 Distinguish between perpetual and periodic inventory systems.

Under a perpetual inventory system, a continuous record of changes in inventory is maintained in the Inventory account. That is, all purchases and transfers of goods out (issues) are recorded directly in the Inventory account as they occur. No such record is kept under a periodic inventory system. Under the periodic system, year-end inventory must be determined by a physical count upon which the amount of ending inventory and cost of goods sold is based. Even under the perpetual system, an annual count is needed to test the records' accuracy.

3 Identify the effects of inventory errors on the financial statements.

If the ending inventory is misstated, (1) the inventory, retained earnings, working capital, and current ratio in the balance sheet will be incorrect, and (2) the cost of goods sold and net income in the income statement will be incorrect. If purchases and inventory are misstated, (1) the inventory, accounts payable, and current ratio will be incorrect, and (2) purchases and ending inventory in the income statement will be incorrect.

---

[15] *CICA Handbook*, Section 1506 *Exposure Draft*.

4 Identify the items that should be included as inventory cost.

Product costs are directly connected with the bringing of goods to the buyer's place of business and converting such goods to a saleable condition. Such charges would include freight charges on goods purchased, other direct costs of acquisition, and labour and other production costs incurred in processing the goods up to the time of sale. Manufacturing overhead costs that include indirect material, indirect labour, and such items as amortization, taxes, insurance, heat, and electricity incurred in the manufacturing process are also usually allocated to inventory, although some companies include only the costs of direct or variable overhead.

5 Explain the difference between variable costing and absorption costing in assigning manufacturing costs to inventory.

Under variable (direct) costing, direct material, direct labour, and variable manufacturing overhead are charged to inventories and fixed manufacturing overhead is treated as a period cost. In absorption (full) costing, direct material, direct labour, and all manufacturing costs (variable and fixed) are treated as product costs and are included in the cost of inventory.

6 Distinguish between the physical flow of inventory and the cost flow assigned to inventory.

If the unit cost is different for various purchases, the question is which costs will be assigned to ending inventory and, as a consequence, to cost of goods sold. In accounting there is no requirement that the costs charged to goods sold be consistent with the goods' physical movement. Consequently, various cost flow methods for assigning costs to cost of goods sold and ending inventory are generally acceptable. The primary methods are specific identification, average cost, FIFO, and LIFO.

7 Identify possible objectives for inventory valuation decisions.

The general objectives are (1) to match expenses realistically against revenues; (2) to report inventory on the balance sheet at a realistic amount; and (3) to minimize income taxes. Inevitably, trade-offs exist between the cost flow methods and the objectives such that no one method will likely satisfy all objectives.

8 Describe and compare the cost flow assumptions used in accounting for inventories.

(1) Average cost prices items in the ending inventory based on the average cost of all similar goods available during the period. (2) First-in, first-out (FIFO) assumes that goods are used in the order in which they are purchased. The inventory remaining must therefore represent the most recent purchases. (3) Last-in, first-out (LIFO) matches the cost of the last goods purchased against revenue.

9 Evaluate LIFO as a basis for understanding the differences among the cost flow methods.

In a period of rising prices, LIFO may be viewed as providing a more realistic matching in the income statement (recent costs against revenues) and offering a greater future earnings hedge. Disadvantages include a reduction in net income and old costs for inventory on the balance sheet. In addition, it does not generally reflect physical flow, matching is destroyed when beginning inventory is liquidated, it provides an opportunity to manage (manipulate) earnings, and it is not acceptable for income tax purposes in Canada. To an extent, the advantages and disadvantages of LIFO are the disadvantages and advantages of FIFO. Average cost methods fall between these two extremes.

Digital Tool
Glossary

www.wiley.com/canada/kieso

KEY TERMS

absorption costing
  system, 410
average cost method, 414
basket purchase, 406
consigned goods, 401
cost flow assumptions, 411
cost of goods available for
  sale or use, 399
cost of goods sold, 399
current ratio, 404
cut-off schedule, 401
finished goods
  inventory, 395
first-in, first-out (FIFO)
  method, 415
fixed costs, 410
f.o.b. destination, 400
f.o.b. shipping point, 400
gross method, 406
inventories, 394
last-in, first-out (LIFO)
  method, 416
LIFO liquidation, 416
merchandise inventory, 395
modified perpetual
  inventory system, 398
moving-average
  method, 414
net method, 406
period costs, 407
periodic inventory
  system, 397
perpetual inventory
  system, 397
product costs, 407
product financing
  arrangement, 401
purchase discounts, 406
raw materials
  inventory, 395
relative sales value
  method, 406
specific identification, 413
standard cost system, 410
statement of cost of goods
  manufactured, 409

10 Explain the importance of judgement in selecting an inventory cost flow method.

The only guidance provided in the *CICA Handbook* is that the method chosen should result in the fairest matching of costs against revenues regardless of whether or not the method corresponds to the physical flow of goods. Consequently, exercise of judgement is required when choosing a cost flow method.

Brief Exercises

BE8-1 Included in the December 31 trial balance of Joel Corp. are the following assets.

Cash	$ 190,000	Work in process	$200,000
Equipment (net)	1,100,000	Receivables (net)	400,000
Prepaid insurance	41,000	Patents	110,000
Raw materials	335,000	Finished goods	150,000

Prepare the current assets section of the December 31 balance sheet.

BE8-2 Alanis Ltd. uses a perpetual inventory system. Its beginning inventory consists of 50 units that cost $30 each. During June, the company purchased 150 units at $30 each, returned 6 units for credit, and sold 125 units at $50 each. Journalize the June transactions.

BE8-3 Data for Alanis Ltd. are presented in BE8-2. Journalize the June transactions assuming Alanis uses a periodic inventory system.

BE8-4 Data for Alanis Ltd. are presented in BE8-2 and 3. Assume Alanis uses a periodic system and prepares financial statements at the end of each month. An inventory count determines that there are 69 units of inventory remaining at June 30. Prepare the necessary adjusting entry at June 30.

BE8-5 Ahmed Corp. purchases inventory costing $5,000 on July 11 on terms 2/10, n/30, and pays the invoice in full on July 15. Prepare the required entries to record the two transactions assuming Ahmed uses (i) the gross method of recording purchases, and (ii) the net method of recording purchases. Assume the periodic method is used.

BE8-6 Data for Ahmed Corp. are presented in BE8-5. Journalize the two transactions under (i) the gross method and (ii) the net method assuming the invoice was paid on July 31 instead of July 15.

BE8-7 PC Plus buys 1,000 computer game CDs from a distributor that is discontinuing those games. The purchase price for the lot is $6,000. PC Plus will group the CDs into three price categories for resale, as indicated below.

Group	No. of CDs	Price per CD
1	100	$ 5.00
2	800	10.00
3	100	15.00

Determine the cost per CD for each group, using the relative sales value method.

BE8-8 Paige Ltd. reports the following per unit costs related to the current year's production: Direct Material, $4.00, Direct Labour, $7.50, Variable Overhead, $3.75, Fixed Overhead, $6.50. There are 800 units left in ending inventory. (i) Calculate the cost of ending inventory assuming Paige applies the direct costing method. (ii) Calculate the cost of ending inventory assuming Paige applies the absorption costing method.

BE8-9 Mayberry Ltd. took a physical inventory on December 31 and determined that goods costing $200,000 were on hand. Not included in the physical count were $15,000 of goods purchased from Taylor Corporation, f.o.b. shipping point; and $22,000 of goods sold to Mount Pilot Ltd. for $30,000, f.o.b. destination. Both the Taylor purchase and the Mount Pilot sale were in transit at year end. What amount should Mayberry report as its December 31 inventory?

BE8-10 Bryars Enterprises Ltd. reported cost of goods sold for 2005 of $1.4 million and retained earnings of $5.2 million at December 31, 2005. Bryars later discovered that its ending inventories at December 31, 2004 and 2005 were overstated by $110,000 and $45,000, respectively. Determine the corrected amounts for 2005 cost of goods sold and December 31, 2005 retained earnings.

BE8-11 Jose Zorilla Corp. uses a periodic inventory system. For April, when the company sold 600 units, the following information is available.

	Units	Unit Cost	Total Cost
April 1 inventory	250	$10	$ 2,500
April 15 purchase	400	12	4,800
April 23 purchase	350	13	4,550
	1,000		$11,850

Calculate the April 30 inventory and the April cost of goods sold using the average cost method.

BE8-12 Data for Jose Zorilla Corp. are presented in BE8-11. Calculate the April 30 inventory and the April cost of goods sold using the FIFO method.

BE8-13 Data for Jose Zorilla Corp. are presented in BE8-11. Calculate the April 30 inventory and the April cost of goods sold using the LIFO method.

BE8-14 HTM Corp. uses a perpetual inventory system. The following information is available for April.

	Units	Unit Cost	Total Cost
April 1 inventory	250	$10	$ 2,500
April 15 purchase	400	12	4,800
April 23 purchase	350	13	4,550
	1,000		$11,850

500 units of this product were sold on April 19. Calculate the April 30 inventory and the April cost of goods sold using the average (moving average) cost method.

BE8-15 Data for HTM Corp. are presented in BE8-14. Calculate the April 30 inventory and the April cost of goods sold using the FIFO method.

BE8-16 Data for HTM Corp. are presented in BE8-14. Calculate the April 30 inventory and the April cost of goods sold using the LIFO method.

Exercises

E8-1 **(Inventoriable Costs)** Presented below is a list of items that may or may not be reported as inventory in a company's December 31 balance sheet.

1. Goods out on consignment at another company's store ✓

2. Goods sold on an instalment basis ✓

3. Goods purchased f.o.b. shipping point that are in transit at December 31 ✓

4. Goods purchased f.o.b. destination that are in transit at December 31 ✗

5. Goods sold to another company, for which our company has signed an agreement to repurchase at a set price that covers all costs related to the inventory

6. Goods sold where large returns are predictable ✓

7. Goods sold f.o.b. shipping point that are in transit at December 31 ✓

8. Freight charges on goods purchased ✓

9. Factory labour costs incurred on goods still unsold ✓

10. Interest costs incurred for inventories that are routinely manufactured ✓

11. Costs incurred to advertise goods held for resale

12. Materials on hand not yet placed into production by a manufacturing firm

13. Office supplies

14. Raw materials on which a manufacturing firm has started production, but which are not completely processed

15. Factory supplies

16. Goods held on consignment from another company

17. Costs identified with units completed by a manufacturing firm, but not yet sold

18. Goods sold f.o.b. destination that are in transit at December 31

19. Temporary investments in shares and bonds that will be resold in the near future

20. Costs of uncleared land to be developed by a property development company

Instructions

Indicate which of these items would typically be reported as inventory in the financial statements. If an item should not be reported as inventory, indicate how it should be reported in the financial statements.

E8-2   (Determining Merchandise Amounts—Periodic)   Two or more items are omitted in each of the following tabulations of income statement data. Fill in the amounts that are missing.

	2004	2005	2006
Sales	$290,000	$_____	$410,000
Sales returns	11,000	13,000	_____
Net sales	_____	347,000	_____
Beginning inventory	20,000	32,000	_____
Ending inventory	_____	_____	_____
Purchases	_____	260,000	298,000
Purchase returns and allowances	5,000	8,000	10,000
Transportation-in	8,000	9,000	12,000
Cost of goods sold	233,000	_____	293,000
Gross profit on sales	46,000	91,000	97,000

E8-3   (Inventoriable Costs)   In your audit of the Oliva Corp., you find that a physical inventory on December 31, 2005 indicated merchandise with a cost of $441,000 was on hand at that date. You also discover the following items were all excluded from the $441,000.

1. Merchandise of $61,000 that is held by Oliva on consignment. The consignor is Max Company Limited.

2. Merchandise costing $38,000 that was shipped by Oliva f.o.b. destination to a customer on December 31, 2005. The customer was expected to receive the merchandise on January 6, 2006.

3. Merchandise costing $46,000 that was shipped by Oliva f.o.b. shipping point to a customer on December 29, 2005. The customer was scheduled to receive the merchandise on January 2, 2006.

4. Merchandise costing $83,000 shipped by a vendor f.o.b. destination on December 30, 2005, and received by Oliva on January 4, 2006.

5. Merchandise costing $51,000 shipped by a vendor f.o.b. shipping point on December 31, 2005 and received by Oliva on January 5, 2006.

Instructions

Based on the above information, calculate the amount that should appear on Oliva's balance sheet at December 31, 2005 for inventory.

E8-4   (Inventoriable Costs)   In an annual audit of Majestic Company Limited at December 31, 2005, you find the following transactions near the closing date.

1. A special machine, fabricated to order for a customer, was finished and specifically segregated in the back part of the shipping room on December 31, 2005. The customer was billed on that date and the machine excluded from inventory although it was shipped on January 4, 2006.

2. Merchandise costing $2,800 was received on January 3, 2006, and the related purchase invoice recorded January 5. The invoice showed the shipment was made on December 29, 2005, f.o.b. destination.

3. A packing case containing a product costing $3,400 was standing in the shipping room when the physical inventory was taken. It was not included in the inventory because it was marked "Hold for shipping instructions." Your investigation revealed that the customer's order was dated December 18, 2005, but that the case was shipped and the customer billed on January 10, 2006. The product was a stock item of your client.

4. Merchandise received on January 6, 2006 costing $680 was entered in the purchase journal on January 7, 2006. The invoice showed shipment was made f.o.b. supplier's warehouse on December 31, 2005. Because it was not on hand at December 31, it was not included in inventory.

5. Merchandise costing $720 was received on December 28, 2005, and the invoice was not recorded. You located it in the hands of the purchasing agent; it was marked "on consignment."

Instructions

Assuming that each amount is material, state whether the merchandise should be included in the client's inventory and give your reason for your decision on each item.

E8-5 (Inventoriable Costs—Perpetual) The Davis Machine Corporation maintains a general ledger account for each class of inventory, debiting such accounts for increases during the period and crediting them for decreases. The transactions below relate to the Raw Materials inventory account, which is debited for materials purchased and credited for materials requisitioned for use.

1. An invoice for $8,100, terms f.o.b. destination, was received and entered January 2, 2006. The receiving report shows that the materials were received December 28, 2005.

2. Materials costing $28,000, shipped f.o.b. destination, were not entered by December 31, 2005 because they were in a railroad car on the company's siding on that date and had not been unloaded.

3. Materials costing $7,300 were returned to the creditor on December 29, 2005 and were shipped f.o.b. shipping point. The return was entered on that date, even though the materials are not expected to reach the creditor's place of business until January 6, 2006.

4. An invoice for $7,500, terms f.o.b. shipping point, was received and entered December 30, 2005. The receiving report shows that the materials were received January 4, 2006, and the bill of lading shows that they were shipped January 2, 2006.

5. Materials costing $19,800 were received December 30, 2005, but no entry was made for them because they were ordered with a specified delivery of no earlier than January 10, 2006.

Instructions

Prepare correcting journal entries required at December 31, 2005, assuming that the books have not been closed. Also indicate which entries must be reversed after closing so the next period's accounts will be correct.

E8-6 (Inventoriable Costs—Error Adjustments) Craig Corporation asks you to review its December 31, 2005 inventory values and prepare the necessary adjustments to the books. The following information is given to you.

1. Craig uses the periodic method of recording inventory. A physical count reveals $234,890 of inventory on hand at December 31, 2005, although the books have not yet been adjusted to reflect the ending inventory.

2. Not included in the physical count of inventory is $13,420 of merchandise purchased on December 15 from Browser. This merchandise was shipped f.o.b. shipping point on December 29 and arrived in January. The invoice arrived and was recorded on December 31.

3. Included in inventory is merchandise sold to Champy on December 30, f.o.b. destination. This merchandise was shipped after it was counted. The invoice was prepared and recorded as a sale on account for $12,800 on December 31. The merchandise cost $7,350, and Champy received it on January 3.

4. Included in inventory was merchandise received from Dudley on December 31 with an invoice price of $15,630. The merchandise was shipped f.o.b. destination. The invoice, which has not yet arrived, has not been recorded.

5. Not included in inventory is $8,540 of merchandise purchased from Glowser Industries. This merchandise was received on December 31 after the inventory had been counted. The invoice was received and recorded on December 30.

6. Included in inventory was $10,438 of inventory held by Craig on consignment from Jackel Industries.

7. Included in inventory is merchandise sold to Kemp f.o.b. shipping point. This merchandise was shipped after it was counted on December 31. The invoice was prepared and recorded as a sale for $18,900 on December 31. The cost of this merchandise was $10,520, and Kemp received the merchandise on January 5.

8. Excluded from inventory was a carton labelled "Please accept for credit." This carton contains merchandise costing $1,500, which had been sold to a customer for $2,600. No entry had been made to the books to reflect the return, but none of the returned merchandise seemed damaged.

Instructions

(a) Determine the proper inventory balance for Craig Corporation at December 31, 2005.

(b) Prepare any adjusting entries to bring inventory to its proper amount at December 31, 2005. Assume the books have not been closed.

E8-7   (Financial Statement Presentation of Manufacturing Amounts—Periodic)   Haida Ltd. is a manufacturing firm. Presented below is selected information from its 2005 accounting records.

Interactive
Homework

Raw materials inventory, 1/1/05	$ 30,800	Transportation-out	$8,000
Raw materials inventory, 12/31/05	37,400	Selling expenses	300,000
Work-in-process inventory, 1/1/05	72,600	Administrative expenses	180,000
Work-in-process inventory, 12/31/05	61,600	Purchase discounts	10,640
Finished goods inventory, 1/1/05	35,200	Purchase returns and allowances	6,460
Finished goods inventory, 12/31/05	22,000	Interest expense	15,000
Purchases	278,600	Direct labour	440,000
Transportation-in	6,600	Manufacturing overhead	330,000

Instructions

(a) Calculate the cost of raw materials used.

(b) Calculate the cost of goods manufactured.

(c) Calculate cost of goods sold.

(d) Indicate how inventories would be reported in the December 31, 2005 balance sheet.

E8-8   (Purchases Recorded Net/Gross)   Presented below are transactions related to Jennings Limited.

May   10   Purchased goods billed at $15,000 subject to cash discount terms of 2/10, n/60.
      11   Purchased goods billed at $13,200 subject to terms of 1/15, n/30.
      19   Paid invoice of May 10.
      24   Purchased goods billed at $11,500 subject to cash discount terms of 2/10, n/30

Instructions

(a) Prepare general journal entries for the transactions above, assuming that purchases are to be recorded at net amounts after cash discounts and that discounts lost are to be treated as financial expense. Assume a periodic inventory system.

(b) Assuming no purchase or payment transactions other than those given above, prepare the adjusting entry required on May 31 if financial statements are to be prepared as of that date.

(c) Prepare general journal entries for the transactions above, assuming that purchases are to be recorded using the gross method. Assume a periodic inventory system.

(d) Indicate whether there are entries required at May 31 in addition to those in (c) if financial statements are to be prepared. Explain.

E8-9   (Purchases Recorded, Gross Method and Net Method)   Cruise Industries Ltd. purchased $10,800 of merchandise on February 1, 2005, subject to a trade discount of 10% and with credit terms of 3/15, n/60. It returned $2,500 of goods (gross price before trade or cash discount) on February 4. The invoice was paid on February 13.

Instructions

(a) Assuming that Cruise uses the perpetual method for recording merchandise transactions, record the purchase, return, and payment using the gross method.

(b) Assuming that Cruise uses the periodic method for recording merchandise transactions:

   1.   record the purchase, return, and payment using the gross method.

   2.   at what amount would the purchase on February 1 be recorded if the net method were used?

E8-10   (Relative Sales Value Method)   Lu Realty Corporation purchased a tract of unimproved land for $55,000. This land was improved and subdivided into building lots at an additional cost of $34,460. These building lots were all the same size but owing to differences in location were offered for sale at different prices as follows.

Group	No. of Lots	Price per Lot
1	9	$3,000
2	15	4,000
3	17	2,400

Operating expenses for the year allocated to this project totalled $18,200. Lots unsold at year end were as follows.

Group 1	5 lots
Group 2	7 lots
Group 3	2 lots

Instructions

Determine the year-end inventory and net income of Lu Realty Corporation.

E8-11   (Relative Sales Value Method)   During 2005, Trainor Furniture Limited purchased a carload of wicker chairs. The manufacturer sold the chairs to Trainor for a lump sum of $59,850, because it was discontinuing manufacturing operations and wished to dispose of its entire stock. Three types of chairs are included in the carload. The three types and the estimated selling price for each are listed below.

Type	No. of Chairs	Estimated Selling Price Each
Lounge chairs	400	$90
Armchairs	300	80
Straight chairs	700	50

During 2005, Trainor sells 200 lounge chairs, 100 armchairs, and 120 straight chairs, all at the same prices as estimated.

Instructions

What is the amount of gross profit earned during 2005? What is the amount of inventory of unsold lounge chairs on December 31, 2005?

E8-12   (Periodic versus Perpetual Entries)   The Fong Corporation sells one product. Presented below is information for January for the Fong Corporation.

Interactive
Homework

Jan.	1	Inventory	100 units at $5 each
	4	Sale	80 units at $8 each
	11	Purchase	150 units at $6 each
	13	Sale	120 units at $8.75 each
	20	Purchase	160 units at $7 each
	27	Sale	100 units at $9 each

Fong uses the FIFO cost flow assumption. All purchases and sales are on account.

Instructions

(a) Assume Fong uses a periodic system. Prepare all necessary journal entries, including the end-of-month adjusting entry to record cost of goods sold. A physical count indicates that the ending inventory for January is 110 units.

(b) Calculate gross profit using the periodic system.

(c) Assume Fong uses the periodic system, and a count on January 31 reports only 102 units in ending inventory. How would your entries in (a) change, if at all? Explain briefly.

(d) Assume Fong uses a perpetual system. Prepare all January journal entries.

(e) Calculate gross profit using the perpetual system.

(f) Assume Fong uses the perpetual system, and a count on January 31 reports only 102 units in ending inventory. How would your entries in (d) change, if at all? Explain briefly.

E8-13   (Inventory Errors—Periodic)   Martine Limited makes the following errors during the current year. Each is an independent case.

1. Ending inventory is overstated by $120, but purchases are recorded correctly.

2. Both ending inventory and purchases on account are understated. (Assume this purchase of $550 was recorded in the following year.)

3. Ending inventory is correct, but a purchase on account was not recorded. (Assume this purchase of $710 was recorded in the following year.)

Instructions

Indicate the effect of each error on working capital, current ratio (assume that the current ratio is greater than 1), retained earnings, and net income for the current year and the subsequent year.

E8-14   (Inventory Errors) Walker Limited has a calendar-year accounting period. The following errors have been discovered in 2005.

1. The December 31, 2003 merchandise inventory had been understated by $21,000.

2. Merchandise purchased on account during 2004 was recorded on the books for the first time in February 2005, when the original invoice for the correct amount of $5,430 arrived. The merchandise had arrived December 28, 2004, and was included in the December 31, 2004 merchandise inventory. The invoice arrived late because of a mixup by the wholesaler.

3. Accrued interest of $1,300 at December 31, 2004 on notes receivable had not been recorded until the cash for the interest was received in March 2005.

Instructions

(a) Calculate the effect each error had on the 2004 net income.

(b) Calculate the effect, if any, each error had on the related December 31, 2004 balance sheet items.

E8-15   (Inventory Errors) At December 31, 2005, McGill Corporation reported current assets of $370,000 and current liabilities of $200,000. McGill uses a periodic inventory system. The following items may have been recorded incorrectly.

1. Goods purchased costing $22,000 were shipped f.o.b. shipping point by a supplier on December 28. McGill received and recorded the invoice on December 29, but the goods were not included in McGill's physical count of inventory because they were not received until January 4.

2. Goods purchased costing $15,000 were shipped f.o.b. destination by a supplier on December 26. McGill received and recorded the invoice on December 31, but the goods were not included in McGill's physical count of inventory because they were not received until January 2.

3. Goods held on consignment from Kishi Company were included in McGill's physical count of inventory at $13,000.

4. Freight-in of $3,000 was debited to advertising expense on December 28.

Instructions

(a) Calculate the current ratio based on McGill's balance sheet.

(b) Recalculate the current ratio after corrections are made.

(c) By what amount will income (before taxes) be adjusted up or down as a result of the corrections?

E8-16   (Inventory Errors) The net income per books of Patrice Limited was determined without knowledge of the errors indicated. The 2000 year was Patrice's first year in business. No dividends have been declared or paid.

Year	Net Income per Books	Error in Ending Inventory	
2000	$50,000	Overstated	$ 3,000
2001	52,000	Overstated	9,000
2002	54,000	Understated	11,000
2003	56,000	No error	
2004	58,000	Understated	2,000
2005	60,000	Overstated	8,000

Instructions

(a) Prepare a work sheet to show the adjusted net income figure for each of the six years after taking into account the inventory errors.

(b) Prepare a schedule indicating the original retained earnings balance reported at the end of each year as well as the corrected amount.

Interactive Homework

E8-17   (FIFO and LIFO—Periodic and Perpetual) Inventory information for Part 311 of Monique Limited discloses the following information for the month of June.

June 1	Balance	300 units @ $10	June 10	Sold	200 units @ $24
11	Purchased	800 units @ $12	15	Sold	500 units @ $25
20	Purchased	500 units @ $13	27	Sold	300 units @ $27

Instructions

(a) Assuming that the periodic inventory method is used, calculate the cost of goods sold and ending inventory under (1) LIFO and (2) FIFO.

(b) Assuming that the perpetual inventory record is kept in dollars and costs are calculated at the time of each withdrawal, what is the LIFO cost of the ending inventory?

(c) Assuming that the perpetual inventory record is kept in dollars and costs are calculated at the time of each withdrawal, what is the gross profit if the inventory is reported at a FIFO cost?

(d) Why is it stated that LIFO usually produces a lower gross profit than FIFO?

E8-18 (FIFO, LIFO, and Average Cost Determination) The J.A. Corporation record of transactions for the month of April is as follows.

Purchases				Sales		
April 1 (balance on hand)	600	@ $6.00		April 3	500	@ 10.00
4	1,500	@ 6.08		9	1,400	@ 10.00
8	800	@ 6.40		11	600	@ 11.00
13	1,200	@ 6.50		23	1,200	@ 11.00
21	700	@ 6.60		27	900	@ 12.00
29	500	@ 6.79			4,600	
	5,300					

Instructions

(a) Assuming that perpetual inventory records are kept in units only, calculate the inventory cost at April 30 using (1) LIFO and (2) average cost.

(b) Assuming that perpetual inventory records are kept in dollars, determine the inventory cost using (1) FIFO and (2) LIFO.

(c) Calculate cost of goods sold assuming periodic inventory procedures and inventory priced at FIFO cost.

(d) In an inflationary period, which inventory method—FIFO, LIFO, or average cost—will show the highest net income? Explain briefly.

E8-19 (Calculate FIFO, LIFO, Average Cost—Periodic) Presented below is information related to the inventory of mini radios for Cleartone Company Limited for the month of July.

Date	Transaction	Units In	Unit Cost	Total	Units Sold	Unit Price	Total
July 1	Balance	100	$4.10	$ 410			
6	Purchase	800	4.20	3,360			
7	Sale				300	$7.00	$ 2,100
10	Sale				300	7.30	2,190
12	Purchase	400	4.50	1,800			
15	Sale				200	7.40	1,480
18	Purchase	300	4.60	1,380			
22	Sale				400	7.40	2,960
25	Purchase	500	4.58	2,290			
30	Sale				200	7.50	1,500
	Totals	2,100		$9,240	1,400		$10,230

Instructions

(a) Assuming that the periodic inventory method is used, calculate the inventory cost at July 31 under each of the following cost flow assumptions:

1. FIFO
2. LIFO
3. Weighted-average (Round the weighted-average unit cost to the nearest one-tenth of one cent.)

(b) Answer the following questions:

1. Which of the methods used above will yield the lowest figure for gross profit for the income statement? Explain why.
2. Which of the methods used above will yield the highest figure for the current ratio? Explain why.

E8-20   (Calculate FIFO, LIFO, Average Cost—Perpetual)   Presented above in E8-19 is information related to the inventory of mini radios for Cleartone Company Limited for the month of July.

Instructions

Assuming that the perpetual inventory method (units and dollars) is used, calculate the inventory cost at July 31 under each of the following cost flow assumptions:

(a) FIFO

(b) LIFO

(c) Moving (weighted) average (Round all unit costs to the nearest one-tenth of one cent.)

(d) Explain where and why the inventory costs calculated in this exercise might differ from those in E8-19.

E8-21   (FIFO and LIFO Periodic and Perpetual)   The following is a record of Ellison Corp.'s transactions for ceramic plates for the month of May 2005.

May 1 Balance 400 units @ $20	May 10 Sale 300 units @ $38	
12 Purchase 600 units @ $25	20 Sale 540 units @ $38	
28 Purchase 400 units @ $30		

Instructions

(a) Assuming that perpetual inventories are not maintained and that a physical count at the end of the month shows 560 units on hand, what is the cost of the ending inventory using (1) FIFO and (2) LIFO?

(b) Based on your answers to (a), prepare partial income statements for May 2005 for Ellison up to the Gross Profit line. Provide a full Cost of Goods Sold section.

(c) Assuming that perpetual records are maintained and they tie into the general ledger, calculate the ending inventory using (1) FIFO and (2) LIFO.

E8-22   (Alternative Inventory Methods)   Amos Corporation began operations on December 1, 2005. The only inventory transaction in 2005 was the purchase of inventory on December 10, 2005, at a cost of $20 per unit. None of this inventory was sold in 2005. Relevant information is as follows.

Ending inventory units		
December 31, 2005		100
December 31, 2006, by purchase date		
December 2, 2006	100	
July 20, 2006	50	150

During 2006, the following purchases and sales were made.

Purchases		Sales	
March 15	300 units at $24	April 10	200
July 20	300 units at $25	August 20	300
September 4	200 units at $28	November 18	150
December 2	100 units at $30	December 12	200

The company uses the periodic inventory method.

Instructions

Determine ending inventory under (1) specific identification, (2) FIFO, (3) LIFO periodic, and (4) average cost.

Problems

P8-1   You are the vice-president of finance of Javid Corporation, a retail company that prepared two different schedules of gross margin for the first quarter ended March 31, 2006. These schedules appear below.

	Sales ($5 per unit)	Cost of Goods Sold	Gross Margin
Schedule 1	$150,000	$124,900	$25,100
Schedule 2	150,000	129,400	20,600

The calculation of cost of goods sold in each schedule is based on the following data.

	Units	Cost per Unit	Total Cost
Beginning inventory, January 1	10,000	$4.00	$40,000
Purchase, January 10	8,000	4.20	33,600
Purchase, January 30	6,000	4.25	25,500
Purchase, February 11	9,000	4.30	38,700
Purchase, March 17	11,000	4.40	48,400

Jane Preya, the corporation president, cannot understand how two different gross margins can be calculated from the same data set. As the vice-president of finance you have explained to Ms. Preya that the two schedules are based on different assumptions concerning the flow of inventory costs, i.e., first-in, first-out; and last-in, first-out. Schedules 1 and 2 were not necessarily prepared in this sequence of cost flow assumptions.

Instructions
Prepare two separate schedules calculating cost of goods sold and supporting schedules showing the composition of the ending inventory under both cost flow assumptions.

P8-2 Digby Limited stocks a variety of sports equipment for sale to institutions. The following stock record card for footballs was taken from the records at the December 31, 2005 year end.

Interactive Homework

Date	Voucher	Terms	Units Received	Unit Invoice Cost	Gross Invoice Amount
1/1	balance	Net 30	90	$20.00	$1,800.00
1/15	10624	Net 30	50	20.00	1,000.00
3/15	11437	1/5, net 30	65	16.00	1,040.00
6/20	21332	1/10, net 30	90	15.00	1,350.00
9/12	27644	1/10, net 30	84	12.00	1,008.00
11/24	31269	1/10, net 30	76	11.00	836.00
	Totals		455		$7,034.00

A physical inventory on December 31, 2005 reveals that 100 footballs were in stock. The bookkeeper informs you that all the discounts were taken. Assume that Digby Limited uses a periodic inventory system, and the invoice price less discount for recording purchases. During 2005, the average sales price per football was $21.50.

Instructions
(a) Calculate the December 31, 2005 inventory using the FIFO method.

(b) Calculate the 2005 cost of goods sold using the LIFO method.

(c) Calculate the December 31, 2005 inventory using the weighted-average cost method (round unit cost to nearest cent).

(d) Prepare income statements for the year ended December 31, 2005 as far as the gross profit line under each of the FIFO, LIFO, and weighted average methods, and calculate the gross profit rate for each. Comment.

(e) If the selling prices for the footballs sold follow the same pattern as their wholesale prices from the supplier, might this have an effect on the inventory cost reported on the December 31, 2005 balance sheet? (Hint: review your answers to parts (a) to (c).)

(f) What method would you recommend to minimize income taxes in 2005, using the inventory information for footballs as a guide?

P8-3 The following independent situations relate to inventory accounting.

1. Jag Co. purchased goods with a list price of $150,000, subject to trade discounts of 20% and 10%, with no cash discounts allowable. How much should Jag Co. record as the cost of these goods?

2. Francis Company's inventory of $1.1 million at December 31, 2005 was based on a physical count of goods priced at cost and before any year-end adjustments relating to the following items.

(a) Goods shipped f.o.b. shipping point on December 24, 2005 from a vendor at an invoice cost of $69,000 to Francis Company were received on January 4, 2006.

(b) The physical count included $29,000 of goods billed to Sakic Corp. f.o.b. shipping point on December 31, 2005. The carrier picked up these goods on January 3, 2006.

What amount should Francis report as inventory on its balance sheet?

3. Messier Corp. had 1,500 units of part 54169 on hand May 1, 2005, costing $21 each. Purchases of part 54169 during May were as follows.

	Units	Unit Cost
May 9	2,000	$22.00
17	3,500	23.00
26	1,000	24.00

A physical count on May 31, 2005 shows 2,100 units of part 54169 on hand. Using the FIFO method, what is the cost of part 54169 inventory at May 31, 2005? Using the LIFO method, what is the inventory cost? Using the average cost method, what is the inventory cost?

4. Lindros Ltd., a retail store chain, had the following information in its general ledger for the year 2005.

Merchandise purchased for resale	$909,400
Interest on notes payable to vendors	8,700
Purchase returns	16,500
Freight-in	22,000
Freight-out	17,100
Cash discounts on purchases	6,800

What is Lindros' inventoriable cost for 2005?

Instructions

Answer each of the questions above about inventories and explain your answers.

P8-4 Kirk Limited, a manufacturer of small tools, provided the following information from its accounting records for the year ended December 31, 2005.

Inventory at December 31, 2005 (based on physical count of goods in Kirk's plant, at cost, on December 31, 2005)	$1,520,000
Accounts payable at December 31, 2005	1,200,000
Net sales (sales less sales returns)	8,150,000

Additional information is as follows.

1. Included in the physical count were tools billed to a customer f.o.b. shipping point on December 31, 2005. These tools had a cost of $31,000 and were billed at $40,000. The shipment was on Kirk's loading dock waiting to be picked up by the common carrier.

2. Goods were in transit from a vendor to Kirk on December 31, 2005. The invoice cost was $71,000, and the goods were shipped f.o.b. shipping point on December 29, 2005.

3. Work-in-process inventory costing $30,000 was sent to an outside processor for plating on December 30, 2005.

4. Tools returned by customers and held pending inspection in the returned goods area on December 31, 2005 were not included in the physical count. On January 8, 2006, tools costing $32,000 were inspected and returned to inventory. Credit memos totalling $47,000 were issued to the customers on the same date.

5. Tools shipped to a customer f.o.b. destination on December 26, 2005 were in transit at December 31, 2005 and had a cost of $21,000. Upon notification of receipt by the customer on January 2, 2006, Kirk issued a sales invoice for $42,000.

6. Goods, with an invoice cost of $27,000, received from a vendor at 5:00 p.m. on December 31, 2005 were recorded on a receiving report dated January 2, 2006. The goods were not included in the physical count, but the invoice was included in accounts payable at December 31, 2005.

7. Goods received from a vendor on December 26, 2005 were included in the physical count. However, the related $56,000 vendor invoice was not included in accounts payable at December 31, 2005, because the accounts payable copy of the receiving report was lost.

8. On January 3, 2006, a monthly freight bill in the amount of $6,000 was received. The bill specifically related to merchandise purchased in December 2005, one-half of which was still in the inventory at December 31, 2005. The freight charges were not included in either the inventory or in accounts payable at December 31, 2005.

Instructions

Using the format shown below, prepare a schedule of adjustments as of December 31, 2005 to the initial amounts per Kirk's accounting records. Show separately the effect, if any, of each of the eight transactions on the December 31, 2005 amounts. If the transactions would have no effect on the initial amount shown, enter NONE.

	Inventory	Accounts Payable	Net Sales
Initial amounts	$1,520,000	$1,200,000	$8,150,000
Adjustments increase (decrease)			
1			
2			
3			
4			
5			
6			
7			
8			
Total adjustments			
Adjusted amounts	$	$	$

(AICPA adapted)

P8-5 Some of the transactions of Dubois Corp. during August are listed below. Dubois uses the periodic inventory method.

August 10	Purchased merchandise on account, $9,000, terms 2/10, n/30.
13	Returned part of the purchase of August 10, $1,200, and received credit on account.
15	Purchased merchandise on account, $12,000, terms 1/10, n/60.
25	Purchased merchandise on account, $15,000, terms 2/10, n/30.
28	Paid invoice of August 15 in full.

Instructions

(a) Assuming that purchases are recorded at gross amounts and that discounts are to be recorded when taken:

1. Prepare general journal entries to record the transactions.

2. Describe how the various items would be shown in the financial statements.

(b) Assuming that purchases are recorded at net amounts and that discounts lost are treated as financial expenses:

1. Prepare general journal entries to enter the transactions.

2. Prepare the adjusting entry necessary on August 31 if financial statements are to be prepared at that time.

3. Describe how the various items would be shown in the financial statements.

(c) Which method results in a higher reported gross profit ratio? Explain.

(d) Which of the two methods do you prefer and why?

P8-6 Some of the information found on a detailed inventory card for Leif Letter Ltd. for January is as follows.

Date	Received No. of Units	Unit Cost	Issued, No. of Units	Balance, No. of Units
January 1 (opening balance)	150	$2.90		150
2	1,050	3.00		1,200
7			700	500
10	600	3.20		1,100
13			500	600
18	1,000	3.30	300	1,300
20			1,100	200
23	1,300	3.40		1,500
26			800	700
28	1,500	3.60		2,200
31			1,300	900

Instructions

(a) From these data, calculate the ending inventory on each of the following bases. Assume that perpetual inventory records are kept in units only. Carry unit costs to the nearest cent and ending inventory to the nearest dollar.

1. First-in, first-out (FIFO)

2. Last-in, first-out (LIFO)

3. Average cost

(b) Assuming an average selling price per unit during January of $6.75, prepare partial income statements to the gross profit on sales line, based on your results in part (a). Calculate the gross profit percentage under each method of costing inventory. Comment on your results.

(c) If the perpetual inventory record is kept in dollars, and costs are calculated at the time of each withdrawal, would the amounts shown as ending inventory in 1, 2, and 3 above be the same? Explain. Recalculate under this revised assumption, carrying average unit costs to four decimal places.

P8-7 B.C. Corporation is a multi-product firm. Presented below is information concerning one of its products, the Hawkeye.

Date	Transaction	Quantity	Price/Cost
1/1	Beginning inventory	1,000	$12
2/4	Purchase	2,000	18
2/20	Sale	2,500	30
4/2	Purchase	3,000	23
11/4	Sale	2,000	33

Instructions

Calculate cost of goods sold, assuming B.C. uses:

(a) Periodic system, FIFO cost flow

(b) Perpetual system, FIFO cost flow

(c) Periodic system, LIFO cost flow

(d) Perpetual system, LIFO cost flow

(e) Periodic system, weighted-average cost flow

(f) Perpetual system, moving-average cost flow

P8-8 The management of Ontario Ltd. has asked its accounting department to describe the effect on the company's financial position and its income statements of accounting for inventories on the weighted average cost rather than the FIFO basis during 2005 and 2006. The accounting department is to assume that the change to average cost would have been effective on January 1, 2005, and that the initial average cost of inventory would have been the inventory value on December 31, 2004. Presented below are the company's financial statements and other data for the years 2005 and 2006 when the FIFO method was employed.

	Financial Position as of		
	12/31/04	12/31/05	12/31/06
Cash	$ 90,000	$130,000	$141,600
Accounts receivable	80,000	100,000	120,000
Inventory	120,000	140,000	180,000
Other assets	160,000	170,000	200,000
Total assets	$450,000	$540,000	$641,600
Accounts payable	$ 40,000	$ 60,000	$ 80,000
Other liabilities	70,000	80,000	110,000
Common shares	200,000	200,000	200,000
Retained earnings	140,000	200,000	251,600
Total equities	$450,000	$540,000	$641,600

	Income for Years Ended	
	12/31/05	12/31/06
Sales	$900,000	$1,350,000
Less: Cost of goods sold	505,000	770,000
Other expenses	205,000	304,000
	710,000	1,074,000
Net income before income taxes	190,000	276,000
Income taxes (40%)	76,000	110,400
Net income	$114,000	$ 165,600

Other data:

1. Inventory on hand at 12/31/04 consisted of 40,000 units valued at $3.00 each.
2. Sales (all units sold at the same price in a given year):

    2005—150,000 units @ $6.00 each   2006—180,000 units @ $7.50 each

3. Purchases (all units purchased at the same price in a given year):

    2005—150,000 units @ $3.50 each   2006—180,000 units @ $4.50 each

4. Income taxes at the effective rate of 40% are paid on December 31 each year.

Instructions

Name the account(s) presented in the financial statements that would have different amounts for 2006 if the weighted average cost method rather than FIFO had been used, and state the new amount for each account that is named. Show calculations. Both FIFO and weighted average cost are accepted for income tax purposes.

P8-9 Yama Ltd. sells two products: figure skates and speed skates. Effective January 1, 2006, Yama was acquired by a large U.S. chain. At December 31, 2005, Yama used the first-in, first-out (FIFO) inventory method. Effective January 1, 2006, Yama changed to the last-in, first-out (LIFO) inventory method in order to be consistent with the policy used by its parent company. The cumulative effect of this change is not determinable and, as a result, the ending inventory of 2005 for which the FIFO method was used is also the beginning inventory for 2006 for the LIFO method.

    The following information was available from Yama's inventory records for the two most recent years.

	Figure Skates		Speed Skates	
	Units	Unit Cost	Units	Unit Cost
2005 purchases				
January 7	7,000	$40.00	22,000	$20.00
April 16	12,000	45.00		
November 8	17,000	54.00	18,500	34.00
December 13	9,000	62.00		
2006 purchases				
February 11	3,000	66.00	23,000	36.00
May 20	8,000	75.00		
October 15	20,000	81.00		
December 23			15,500	42.00
Units on hand				
December 31, 2005	15,100		15,000	
December 31, 2006	18,000		13,200	

Instructions

Calculate the effect on income before income taxes for the year ended December 31, 2006 resulting from the change from the FIFO to the LIFO inventory method.

(AICPA adapted)

P8-10 Zeda Limited is a wholesale distributor of automotive replacement parts. Initial amounts taken from Zeda's accounting records are as follows.

Inventory at December 31, 2005 (based on physical count of goods in Zeda's warehouse, Dec. 31/05)			$1,520,000

Accounts payable at December 31, 2005:

Vendor	Terms	Amount
Sonny Company Ltd.	2/10, n30	$ 260,000
Avalon Corporation	Net 30	190,000
Bottler Company	Net 30	405,000
Mindle Enterprises	Net 30	20,000
Boot Products	Net 30	—
Cameo Company	Net 30	—
		$ 875,000

Sales in 2005	$9,650,000

Additional information is as follows.

1. Parts received on consignment from Avalon Corporation by Zeda, the consignee, amounting to $150,000 were included in the physical count of goods in Zeda's warehouse on December 31, 2005 and in accounts payable at December 31, 2005.

2. In early January 2006, it was discovered that an invoice from Bottler covering purchases of $17,000 in early December 2005 had been entered twice in the accounting records.

3. Parts costing $20,000 were purchased from Boot and paid for in December 2005. These parts were sold in the last week of 2005 and recorded as sales of $38,000. The parts were included in the physical count of goods in the warehouse on December 31, 2005 because the parts were on the loading dock waiting to be picked up by customers who had been informed the parts were ready and had stated they would pick them up as soon as possible.

4. On January 7, 2006, a credit memo for $4,200 was received from Voltz Company, a regular supplier to Zeda for products purchased earlier in 2005. Because Zeda's purchases had exceeded an established minimum in 2005, Voltz issued Zeda the credit memo that allows Zeda to deduct $4,200 from its 2006 purchases from the company. Approximately 10% of the purchases from Voltz remain in Zeda's year-end inventory.

5. Parts in transit to customers on December 31, 2005, shipped f.o.b. shipping point on December 28, 2005, amounted to $43,000. The customers received the parts on January 6, 2006. Invoices for $65,000, including sales taxes of $8,500, were sent to the customers for the parts and were recorded by Zeda on January 2, 2006.

6. Early in January 2006, it was discovered that an invoice had not been sent to one of Zeda's regular customers for a rush order shipped just before the Christmas break. An invoice in the amount of $14,000, including sales taxes of $1,800, was sent immediately.

7. Retailers were holding $233,000 of goods at cost ($310,000 at retail) on consignment from Zeda, the consignor, at their retail stores on December 31, 2005.

8. Goods were in transit from Cameo to Zeda on December 31, 2005. The goods cost $36,000 and were shipped f.o.b. shipping point on December 29.

9. A quarterly freight bill for $4,700 relating specifically to merchandise purchased in December 2005, all of which was still in inventory at December 31, 2005, was received on January 3, 2006. The freight bill was not included in the inventory or accounts payable at December 31, 2005.

10. All of the purchases from Sonny occurred during the last seven days of the year. These items have been recorded in accounts payable and accounted for in the physical inventory at cost before discount. Zeda's policy is to pay invoices in time to take advantage of all cash discounts, adjust inventory accordingly, and record accounts payable, net of cash discounts.

Instructions

Set up a schedule with the amount of Inventory, Accounts Payable, and Sales as reported in the general ledger of Zeda at December 31, 2005 across the top of the page. Analyse each of the 10 situations above. Show the effect, if any, of each situation described, on each of the three general ledger accounts. If the item has no effect on the amount shown, state "N/A" or "no effect." Complete the schedule by determining the correct balance of each of the three accounts.

P8-11   The summary financial statements of DeliMart Ltd. on December 31, 2005 are presented below.

DELIMART LTD.
Balance Sheet, December 31, 2005

Assets

Cash	$ 2,000
Accounts and notes receivable	36,000
Inventory	60,000
Property, plant, and equipment (net)	100,000
	$198,000

Liabilities and Shareholders' Equity

Accounts and notes payable	$ 50,000
Long-term debt	50,000
Common shares	50,000
Retained earnings	48,000
	$198,000

The following errors were made by the inexperienced accountant on December 31, 2004 and were not corrected: the inventory was overstated by $15,000, prepaid expense of $2,400 was omitted (was fully expensed in 2004), accrued revenue of $2,500 was omitted (recognized when cash was received in 2005), and a supplier's invoice for $1,700 relating to 2004 purchases was not recorded until 2005. On December 31, 2005, the inventory was understated by $18,000, prepaid expense of $800 was omitted, accrued December 2005 salaries of $1,100 were not recognized, and unearned income of $2,300 was recorded in 2005 revenue. In addition, it was determined that $20,000 of the accounts payable were long-term, and that a $500 dividend was reported as dividend expense and deducted in calculating net income.

The net income reported on the books for 2005 was $55,000.

Instructions

(a) Calculate the working capital, current ratio, and the debt-to-equity ratio for DeliMart Ltd. based on the original balance sheet information provided above.

(b) Calculate the corrected net income for 2005.

(c) Prepare a corrected balance sheet at December 31, 2005.

(d) Re-calculate the ratios identified in part (a). Comment.

P8-12 Count Controllers Corporation (CCC) was incorporated early in January 2005 to manufacture electronic control devices to monitor traffic, of automobiles or people, past specific locations. CCC built a small manufacturing plant and office building in a new industrial park and was in operation by mid-March. General ledger accounts at December 31, 2005 indicated the following.

Sales salaries and expenses	$ 75,000
Supervisory salaries, production	65,000
Executive salaries	100,000
Raw material purchases	123,500
Miscellaneous plant supplies	12,400
Amortization, plant building	26,000
Amortization, office building	8,000
Amortization, plant equipment	10,000
Property taxes on real property (1/5 office building, 4/5 plant building)	6,600
Sales	427,000
Direct labour	62,000
Maintenance labour	27,500
Raw material inventory, December 31, 2005	14,600
Utilities expense (1/10 related to the office)	22,000
General administration expenses	38,800

At December 31, 2005 there was no work in process, but 20% of the units manufactured remained in ending finished goods inventory.

Instructions

(a) Prepare an income statement as far as "income from operations" for CCC for the year ended December 31, 2005, assuming the decision is made to adopt variable costing.

(b) Prepare an income statement as far as "income from operations" for CCC, assuming absorption costing is preferred.

(c) Make a recommendation to the company president on which method CCC should choose, supported with your rationale.

P8-13 John Potter established Dilemma Co. as a sole proprietorship on January 5, 2005. The accounts on December 31, 2005, the company's year end, had balances as follows. The balances are in thousands.

Current assets, excluding inventory		$ 10
Other assets		107
Current liabilities		30
Long-term bank loan		50
Owner's investment (excluding income)		40
Purchases during year		
January 2:	5,000 @ $11	
June 30:	8,000 @ $12	
December 10:	6,000 @ $16	247
Sales		284
Other expenses		40

A count of ending inventory on December 31, 2005 showed there were 4,000 units on hand.

Potter is now preparing financial statements for the year. He is aware that inventory may be costed using the FIFO, LIFO, or weighted-average method. He is unsure of which one to use and requests your assistance. In discussions with Potter, you learn the following.

1. Suppliers to Dilemma provide goods at regular prices as long as the current ratio is at least 2 to 1. If this ratio is lower, the suppliers increase the price charged by 10% in order to compensate for what they consider to be a substantial credit risk.

2. The long-term bank loan terms include the bank's ability to call the loans for immediate repayment if the debt-to-total-asset ratio exceeds 45%.

3. Potter thinks that, for the company to be a success, the rate of return on total assets should be at least 30%.

4. Potter has an agreement with the company's only employee that, for each full percentage point above a 25% rate of return on total assets, she will be given an additional one day off with pay in the following year.

Instructions

(a) Prepare an income statement and a year-end balance sheet assuming the company applies:

   1. the FIFO method

   2. the weighted-average method

   3. the LIFO method

(b) Identify the advantages of each method in (a).

(c) Identify the disadvantages of each method in (a).

(d) What is your recommendation? Explain briefly.

P8-14   Grass Corp. is considering changing its inventory valuation method from FIFO to weighted average because of the potential tax savings. However, management wishes to consider all of the effects on the company, including its reported performance, before making the final decision.

The inventory account, currently valued on the FIFO basis, consists of 1 million units at $7 per unit on January 1, 2005. There are 1 million common shares outstanding as of January 1, 2005 and the cash balance is $400,000.

The company has made the following forecasts for the period 2005–2007.

	2005	2006	2007
Unit sales (in millions of units)	1.1	1.0	1.3
Sales price per unit	$10	$10	$12
Unit purchases (in millions of units)	1.0	1.1	1.2
Purchase price per unit	$7	$8	$9
Annual amortization (in thousands of dollars)	$300	$300	$300
Cash dividends per share	.15/sh	.15/sh	.15/sh
Cash payments for additions to and replacement of plant and equipment (in thousands of dollars)	$350	$350	$350
Income tax rate	40%	40%	40%
Operating expense (exclusive of amortization) as a percent of sales	15%	15%	15%
Common shares outstanding (in millions)	1	1	1

Instructions

(a) Prepare a schedule that illustrates and compares the following data for Grass Corp. under the FIFO and the weighted average inventory method for 2005–2007. Assume the company would begin the weighted average method at the beginning of 2005.

   1. Year-end inventory balances   3. Earnings per share

   2. Annual net income   4. Cash balance

   Assume all sales are collected in the year of sale and all purchases, operating expenses, and taxes are paid during the year incurred.

(b) Using the data above, your answer to (a), and any additional issues you believe need to be considered, prepare a report that recommends whether or not Grass Corp. should change from the FIFO inventory method. Support your conclusions with appropriate arguments.

(CMA adapted)

Writing Assignments

WA8-1 You are asked to travel to Moncton to observe and verify the inventory of a client's Moncton branch. You arrive on Thursday, December 30, and find that the inventory procedures have just been started. You spot a railway car on the sidetrack at the unloading door and ask the warehouse superintendent Donnie Coggins how he plans to inventory the car contents. He responds: "We are not going to include the contents in the inventory."

Later in the day, you ask the bookkeeper for the invoice on the carload and the related freight bill. The invoice lists the various items, prices, and extensions of the goods in the car. You note that the carload was shipped December 24 from Montreal, f.o.b. Montreal, and that the total invoice price of the car's goods was $35,300. The freight bill called for a payment of $1,500. Terms were net 30 days. The bookkeeper affirms the fact that this invoice is to be held for recording in January.

Instructions

(a) Does your client have a liability that should be recorded at December 31? Discuss.

(b) Prepare a journal entry(ies), if required, to reflect any accounting adjustment required. Assume a perpetual inventory system is used by your client.

(c) For what possible reason(s) might your client wish to postpone recording the transaction?

WA8-2 Jack McDowell, the controller for McDowell Lumber Corporation, has recently hired you as assistant controller. He wishes to determine your expertise in the area of inventory accounting and therefore asks you to answer the following unrelated questions.

(a) A company is involved in the wholesaling and retailing of automobile tires for foreign cars. Most of the inventory is imported, and it is valued on the company's records at the actual inventory cost plus freight-in. At year end, the warehousing costs are prorated over cost of goods sold and ending inventory. Are warehousing costs considered a product cost or a period cost?

(b) A certain portion of a company's inventory is composed of obsolete items. Should obsolete items that are not currently consumed in the production of goods or services to be available for sale be classified as part of inventory?

(c) A company purchases airplanes for sale to others. However, until they are sold, the company charters and services the planes. What is the proper way to report these airplanes in the company's financial statements?

(d) A company wants to buy coal deposits but does not want the financing for the purchase to be reported on its financial statements. The company therefore establishes a trust to acquire the coal deposits. The company agrees to buy the coal over a certain period of time at specified prices. The trust is able to finance the coal purchase and pay off the loan as it is paid by the company for the minerals. How should this transaction be reported?

WA8-3 Akihito Ltd. is a manufacturing business with relatively heavy fixed costs and large inventories of finished goods. These inventories constitute a very material item on the balance sheet. The company has a departmental cost accounting system that assigns all manufacturing costs to the product each period.

Edward Gierek, company controller, has informed you that management is seriously considering adopting variable (direct) costing as a method of accounting for plant operations and inventory valuation. Management wants your opinion of the effect, if any, that such a change would have on: (1) the year-end financial position, and (2) the net income for the year.

Instructions
Draft a reply to the request and the reasons for your conclusions.

WA8-4 Jeanne Honore, president of Assiniboine Corp., a Manitoba company, had previously read articles about U.S. companies adopting the LIFO method for valuing inventories. The reasons given were that LIFO better neutralizes the effect of inflation in financial statements, eliminated inventory profits, and reduced income taxes.

Assiniboine currently uses the first-in, first-out (FIFO) method of inventory valuation in its periodic inventory system. The company's inventory investment has been declining due to technological improvements and a high inventory turnover rate, although inventories still represent a significant proportion of the assets.

Instructions
Write a report to Ms. Honore on how economic and industry conditions could influence a company's choice of inventory costing method. Limit your discussion to LIFO and FIFO. Make sure you explain such statements as "LIFO better neutralizes the effect of inflation" and what "inventory profits" are.

WA8-5   Local Drilling Inc. is a Canadian drilling site company. All the company's drilling material is purchased by the head office and stored at a local warehouse before being shipped to the drilling sites. The price of drilling material has been steadily decreasing over the past few years. The drilling material is sent to various sites upon request of the site manager, where it is stored and then used in drilling. Managers are charged the inventory cost when it is sent based on the cost assigned to the item in the head office records. At any given time, it is estimated that about one-half of the company's drilling material inventory will be at the local warehouse. A site manager's performance is partially evaluated on the net income reported for the site.

Instructions

Given the options of choosing the FIFO, moving-average, or LIFO inventory costing methods and use of a perpetual inventory system:

(a) Which costing method would you, as a site manager, want to be used? Why?

(b) As a site manager, what might you do regarding the requesting of inventory if FIFO were used? Why, and what might the implications be for the company as a whole?

(c) As the decision-maker at head office, which method would you recommend if you wanted the results to be fair for all site managers? Why?

(d) Which method would you recommend for determining the company's taxable income? Why?

(e) Which method would you recommend for financial statement purposes? Why?

WA8-6   Gamble Corporation uses the LIFO method for inventory costing. In an effort to lower net income, company president Oscar Gamble tells the plant accountant to take the unusual step of recommending to the purchasing department a large purchase of inventory at year end. The price of the item to be purchased has nearly doubled during the year, and the item represents a major portion of inventory value.

Instructions

Answer the following questions.

(a) Explain the consequences on the financial statements of the year-end purchase.

(b) Identify the major stakeholders. If the plant accountant recommends the purchase, what are the consequences?

(c) If Gamble Corporation were using the FIFO method of inventory costing, would Oscar Gamble give the same order? Why or why not?

Cases

Refer to the Case Primer on the Digital Tool to help you answer these cases.

Digital Tool

www.wiley.com/
canada/kieso

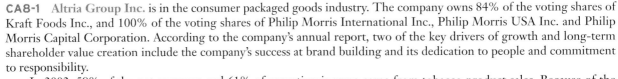

CA8-1   Altria Group Inc. is in the consumer packaged goods industry. The company owns 84% of the voting shares of Kraft Foods Inc., and 100% of the voting shares of Philip Morris International Inc., Philip Morris USA Inc. and Philip Morris Capital Corporation. According to the company's annual report, two of the key drivers of growth and long-term shareholder value creation include the company's success at brand building and its dedication to people and commitment to responsibility.

In 2002, 59% of the net revenues and 61% of operating income came from tobacco product sales. Because of the health risks related to the use of tobacco products, the industry is increasingly regulated and the company is the subject of substantial tobacco-related litigation.

During 1997 and 1998, the company entered into agreements in the United States in settlement of asserted and unasserted health care recovery costs and other claims. The agreements, known as the State Settlement Agreements (SSA), provide restrictions on the company relating primarily to advertising. They also provide for payments by the domestic tobacco industry into a fund in the following amounts.

2003	$10.9 billion
2004–2007	$8.4 billion each year
Thereafter	$9.4 billion each year.

The fund will be used to settle claims and aid tobacco growers. Each company's share of these payments is based on its market share and Philip Morris records its portion of the settlement costs as cost of goods sold upon shipment. These amounts may increase based on several factors including inflation and industry volume. In 1999, 2000 and 2001, the company accrued costs in excess of $5 billion each year.

Another significant lawsuit, the "Engle Class Action", is still in process. In July 2000, the jury returned a verdict assessing punitive damages against various defendants, of which the company's share was $74 billion. The company is contesting this and the lawsuit continues. As a result of preliminary judicial stipulations, the company has placed $500 million into a separate interest bearing escrow account. This money will be kept by the court and distributed to the plaintiffs regardless of the outcome of the trial. The company also placed $1.2 billion into another escrow account which will be returned to the company should they win the case.

Instructions

Assume the role of a financial analyst and discuss the related financial reporting issues noting alternative accounting treatments for each issue and recommending how each issue should be treated in the financial statements.

CA8-2   Philex Gold Inc. was created in 1996 and is 81% owned by Philex Mining Corporation. Its shares trade on the TSX Venture Exchange and its objective is to become a substantial low cost mineral producer in the Philippines. Philex Mining has provided substantial financial support to the company over the past five years as the company is primarily in the exploration stages. In 2002, the company decommissioned its Bulawan gold mine, which had been in production since 1996. At this point, rehabilitation and reforestation activity is the only activity in the mine.

Over the five year period, the company carried its gold bullion inventory at net realizable value and recognized revenues on gold sales (net of refining and selling costs) at net realizable value, when the minerals were produced. Gold is a commodity which trades actively and whose prices fluctuate subject to supply and demand. Below is a chart which shows the price of gold over the past 5 years.

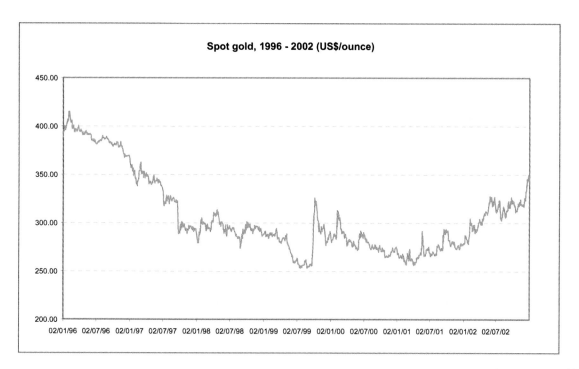

Source: www.gold.org

Instructions

Assume the role of the company's parent company and assess the financial reporting policies relating to inventory valuation and revenue recognition. Identify any other potential financial reporting issues.

Research and Financial Analysis

RA8-1   Imperial Oil Limited

Imperial Oil Limited, according to its 2002 Annual Report, is "one of the largest producers of crude oil in Canada and a major producer of natural gas. The company is the largest refiner and marketer of petroleum products—sold primarily under the Esso brand name—and a major producer of petrochemicals." Imperial has been involved in the Canadian oil industry for more than 120 years.

Imperial Oil reported net earnings of $1,210 million for the year ended December 31, 2002, and excerpts from the company's 2002 financial statements are reproduced below.

Consolidated balance sheet

millions of dollars At December 31	2002	2001
Assets		
Current assets		
Cash	766	872
Marketable securities	–	–
Accounts receivable (note 12)	1,348	992
Inventories of crude oil and products (note 12)	433	478
Materials, supplies and prepaid expenses	110	116
Future income tax assets (note 5)	323	227
Total current assets	2,980	2,685
Investments and other long-term assets	134	139
Property, plant and equipment (note 1)	8,526	7,709
Goodwill (notes 1 and 2)	204	204
Other intangible assets (note 1)	24	24
Total assets (note 1)	**11,868**	10,761

Summary of significant accounting policies

Inventories

Inventories are recorded at the lower of cost or net realizable value. The cost of crude oil and products is determined primarily using the last-in, first-out (LIFO) method. LIFO was selected over the alternative first-in, first out and average cost methods because it provides a better matching of current costs with the revenues generated in the period.

Costs include purchase costs and other applicable operating expenses. Selling and general administrative expenses are excluded.

12.   Miscellaneous financial information

In 2002, net earnings included an after-tax loss of $2 million (2001 – $18 million gain; 2000 – $25 million gain) attributable to the effect of changes in LIFO inventories. The replacement cost of inventories was estimated to exceed their LIFO carrying values at December 31, 2002, by $941 million (2001 – $506 million).

Research and development costs in 2002 were $64 million (2001 – $71 million; 2000 – $55 million) before investment tax credits earned on these expenditures of $10 million (2001 – $6 million, 2000 – $6 million). The net costs are included in expenses, due to the uncertainty of future benefits.

Accounts receivable included allowance for doubtful accounts of $13 million in 2002 (2001 – $12 million).

Instructions

(a) Identify what cost flow method Imperial Oil uses and the reasons provided for the choice. Is there anything particular about the oil and gas industry that would make this more likely than in other industries? Comment.

(b) From the information reported, estimate what the ending inventories would have been at December 31, 2002 and 2001 if the FIFO cost flow method had been applied. Is the result materially different? Comment.

(c) Assume you were analysing Imperial Oil's financial statements and comparing them with other companies in the same industry that use the FIFO cost flow method. Identify what you would have to adjust on the Imperial Oil financial statements to make them comparable to the others.

(d) Identify what common financial statement ratios would be affected if these adjustments weren't made.

RA8-2   Pacific Safety Products Inc.

Pacific Safety Products Inc., founded in 1984 in British Columbia, operates out of facilities in Kelowna, B.C., and Brampton and Arnprior, Ont. According to a company news release, it is "an established industry leader in the production, distribution and sale of high performance safety products such as: ballistic, stab and fragment protection vests; bomb and land mine retrieval suits; tactical clothing; emergency medical kits and rescue equipment; and flame resistant and industrial clothing." It is the only major manufacturer of body armour in Canada, and has seen a significant increase in sales since the events of September 11, 2001. The company engages in considerable research and development activities, and some of the products the company developed were featured in the hit movie Terminator 3: Rise of the Machines, starring Arnold Schwarzenegger!

Excerpts from the financial statements of Pacific Safety Products (PSP) follow.

CONSOLIDATED BALANCE SHEETS

As at June 30	2002	2001
ASSETS		
CURRENT ASSETS		
Cash	$ 223,351	$ 48,190
Accounts receivable	3,866,029	1,800,418
Corporation taxes recoverable	-	180,000
Inventory (Note 3)	1,877,765	2,362,447
Prepaid expenses	118,876	126,494
Future income taxes recoverable (Note 4)	288,500	-
Total Current Assets	6,374,521	4,517,549

CONSOLIDATED STATEMENTS OF OPERATIONS AND RETAINED EARNINGS (DEFICIT)

For the years ended June 30	2002	2001
SALES (Note 12)	$ 19,331,937	$ 11,441,267
COST OF SALES		
Amortization of capital assets	208,817	176,078
Material, labour, and manufacturing overhead	14,314,108	8,525,431
TOTAL COST OF SALES	14,522,925	8,701,509
GROSS MARGIN	4,809,012	2,739,758

SIGNIFICANT ACCOUNTING POLICIES

Inventory
Raw materials are stated at the lower of weighted average cost and net realizable value. Work in process and finished goods are stated at the lower of average cost, which includes direct manufacturing expenses and an allocation of overhead, and net realizable value.

Note 3
INVENTORY

	2002	2001
Raw materials	$ 1,435,985	$ 1,717,782
Work in process	64,576	170,651
Finished goods and samples	377,204	474,014
	$ 1,877,765	$ 2,362,447

Instructions

(a) Does PSP apply direct or absorption costing for its manufactured products? Explain.

(b) What cost flow assumption does the company use?

(c) PSP manufactures products designed by others to rigid client specifications. The company also develops and manufactures many of its own products, which it protects by patent. Briefly identify how these two processes differ in the type of costs incurred. Do you think all the development and manufacturing costs for its own products are product costs that should be charged to the Inventory account? Explain.

RA8-3   Intrawest Corporation

Refer to the financial statements of Intrawest Corporation (Intrawest) included as Appendix 5B.

Instructions

(a) What business is Intrawest in?

(b) Does Intrawest report any inventory on its balance sheet? Explain.

(c) "Properties under development and held for sale" is very similar to inventory. Does this meet the definition of inventory? Explain. Review the financial statements provided, including the notes to the statements. Identify what type of costs are considered product costs by Intrawest.

(d) Where does Intrawest report its holdings of properties under development and held for sale? Explain this classification.

(e) If this property *is* an inventory asset, where does the company report its associated cost of goods sold?

RA8-4   Canadian Tire Corporation, Limited

Refer to the most recent financial statements of Canadian Tire Corporation, Limited provided on the Digital Tool or available on SEDAR (www.sedar.com). Note that the company provides a 10-year financial review at the end of its Annual Report. This summary provides relevant comparative information useful for determining trends and predicting future results and position.

Instructions (all amounts in $000)

(a) Prepare three graphs covering the 1998 to 2002 period. The first graph is for net earnings from continuing operations over this five-year period, the second for working capital, and the third for the current ratio. Based on the graphs, predict the values you might expect for the following fiscal period.

(b) Assume the following errors were discovered after the latest year's financial statements were released.

1. Invoices representing the December 2001 purchases from a major supplier in the amount of $20,000 were not processed through the accounting system until late January 2002 in error, although the ending inventory at year end was correctly stated.

2. At the end of 2002, $10,000 of inventory was excluded from the physical count as it was set aside for delivery to associate dealers. The stock purchase had been appropriately recorded in December. The sales invoice to the associate dealers was issued and accounted for in early January 2003 upon delivery. (You might want to determine what the company's revenue recognition policy is for shipments of merchandise to dealers.)

(c) Assuming an effective income tax rate of 35%, calculate the correct amount of net earnings from continuing operations, working capital, and the current ratio for all years affected by these errors.

(d) Redraw the trend lines on the graphs developed in part (a).

(e) Do the revised numbers change your expectations for the following year? Comment.

RA8-5 Research

Many companies, such as **HydroMississauga** and **Matsushita Electric of Canada Ltd.**, have invested in technology to improve their inventory management systems.

Instructions
Research the topic of improvements to inventory management systems, zeroing in on two examples where companies have been able to change the way they manage this critical asset. Identify what improvements the companies have made. How do these efficiencies affect the balance sheet and income statement, if at all? Be specific.

Tracking Sales

BROCK'S

The first Brock general store opened in Port Perry, Ontario, in 1881. Now the fifth generation of Brocks, sisters Marina and Juliana, run a much larger department store and two satellite stores in Ontario's Kawartha Lakes region, selling brand name fashion and footwear. Brocks uses the retail inventory method to estimate its inventory.

Computer software keeps track of inventory by season, department, and class of item, such as sportswear or outerwear.

"We run an on-hand inventory value report at month end," Marina Brock says. "We try to get as close to a realizable value as possible, so the current season inventory is taken at full value, and then as we go back we discount it slightly to reflect that it would be harder to sell at market value." The computer allocates the percentages of merchandise from the current and previous seasons to get a clearer picture of the stock's entire value.

"Each sale is recorded and the cost of the goods is recorded at the time of sale," Brock explains. "It's taken out of the inventory at that time at the original cost. Everything is done on an individual transaction basis, then summarized at the end of the day."

The Brocks also take a physical inventory each January. They scan each item using hand-held scanners, and every return to the vendor is manually transferred out of the computer records. The computer then updates the inventory records and creates a variance, indicating the inventory's actual value vs. book value. Brock says the variance usually indicates a shrinkage of about 1% of sales, due to clerical errors and shoplifting.

Keeping close tabs on the store's inventory value helps control investment in merchandise, which is critical to business success. The computer program, Softwear POS, tracks the inventory very accurately. "We know pretty much to the dollar what we've got everywhere," Brock says.■

CHAPTER 9

Inventory Valuation and Estimation

Learning Objectives

After studying this chapter, you should be able to:

1. Recognize that the lower of cost and market (LCM) basis is a departure from the historical cost principle, and understand why this is appropriate.

2. Explain various definitions of possible market amounts that may be used when applying lower of cost and market.

3. Explain how LCM works and how it is determined.

4. Know how to account for inventory on the lower of cost and market basis.

5. Identify when inventories are carried regularly at net realizable value.

6. Explain accounting issues related to purchase commitments.

7. Estimate ending inventory by applying the gross profit method.

8. Explain the limitations of the gross profit method.

9. Estimate ending inventory by applying the retail inventory method.

10. Identify required disclosures and explain how inventory is reported and analysed.

Preview of Chapter 9

Information on inventories and changes in inventory are relevant to predicting profits.

Chapter 8 dealt with determining the total cost of inventory on hand at the end of the accounting period. Chapter 9 completes the process of determining the balance sheet value of inventory by examining when "cost" may not be appropriate. If the company cannot realize as much as "cost" when the inventory is sold, then an amount lower than cost should be reported as inventory on the balance sheet. This is the subject of the first part of the chapter.

The remainder of the chapter discusses and illustrates other valuation and estimation concepts used to develop relevant inventory information. The valuation of inventory at net realizable value instead of historic cost is discussed. In addition, the accounting for outstanding purchase commitments is explained. What happens if there is a fire and a physical count of lost inventory cannot be made? How is the amount of the destroyed inventory determined so that an insurance claim can be justified? What happens in department stores where monthly inventory figures are needed, but monthly counts are not feasible? These questions involve the development and use of estimation techniques to value the ending inventory without a physical count. The gross profit method and the retail inventory method are widely used estimation methods and are discussed in this chapter. The chapter ends with inventory disclosure requirements and a discussion of ratios and other information used to analyse inventories and related accounts to help users assess performance. The content and organization of the chapter are as follows:

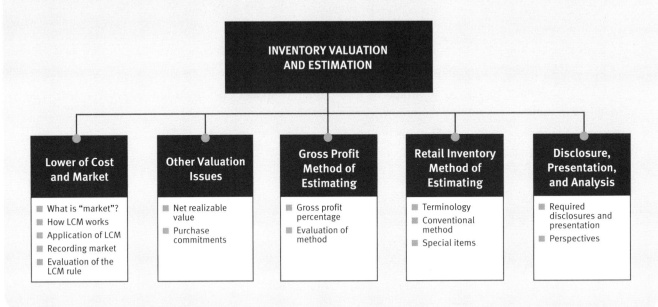

INVENTORY VALUATION AND ESTIMATION

Lower of Cost and Market	**Other Valuation Issues**	**Gross Profit Method of Estimating**	**Retail Inventory Method of Estimating**	**Disclosure, Presentation, and Analysis**
▪ What is "market"? ▪ How LCM works ▪ Application of LCM ▪ Recording market ▪ Evaluation of the LCM rule	▪ Net realizable value ▪ Purchase commitments	▪ Gross profit percentage ▪ Evaluation of method	▪ Terminology ▪ Conventional method ▪ Special items	▪ Required disclosures and presentation ▪ Perspectives

LOWER OF COST AND MARKET

As noted in Chapter 8, inventories are initially recorded at their original cost. However, a departure from the historical cost principle occurs if inventory declines in value below its original cost. Whatever the reason for a decline (e.g., obsolescence, price-level changes, damaged goods), the inventory should be written down to reflect this loss. **The general rule is that the historical cost principle is adjusted when the asset's future utility (its ability to generate net cash flows) is no longer as great as its original cost.** Inventories that experience a decline in utility are valued therefore on the basis of the lower of cost and market, instead of on the original cost.

A departure from cost is justified for two primary reasons. First, readers presume that **current assets can be converted into at least as much cash as the value reported for them on the balance sheet**; and second, **matching requires that a loss of utility be charged against revenues in the period in which the loss occurs**, not in the period in which the inventory is sold. In addition, the lower of cost and market method is a **conservative approach to inventory valuation**. That is, when doubt exists about an asset's value, it is preferable to undervalue rather than to overvalue it.

> **1 Objective**
> Recognize that the lower of cost and market (LCM) basis is a departure from the historical cost principle, and understand why this is appropriate.

> **Underlying Concept**
> The use of the lower of cost and market method is an excellent example of the conservatism constraint and the matching principle.

What is "Market"?

As we learned in Chapter 8, **cost** is the acquisition price of inventory calculated using one of the historical cost-based methods: specific identification, average cost, FIFO, or LIFO. The term market in the phrase "the lower of cost and market" (LCM) requires a specific definition as it has a number of different meanings. The *CICA Handbook*, recognizing this, states that it is desirable to use a more specific description in lieu of the term "market."[1] Other, more descriptive terms include replacement cost, net realizable value, and net realizable value less a normal profit margin.

Replacement cost generally means the amount that would be needed to acquire an equivalent item, by purchase or production, as would be incurred in the normal course of business operations (i.e., buying from usual sources or manufacturing in normal quantities). Net realizable value (NRV) is the item's estimated selling price in the ordinary course of business, less reasonably predictable future costs to complete and dispose of the item. Net realizable value (NRV) less a normal profit margin is determined by deducting a normal profit margin from the previously defined net realizable value amount. For example, a retailer may have some calculator wristwatches on hand that cost $30.00 each when purchased. If the supplier's catalogue price is now $28.00, that would be their replacement cost. If their selling price today is $50.00, and there were no additional costs to sell them, then this amount would be their net realizable value. If a normal profit margin is 35% of selling price, the net realizable value less a normal profit margin would be $32.50 (i.e., $50 − [.35 × $50]). Consequently, in this example, the inventory would be valued at $30.00 per unit (its historical cost) under the lower of cost and market rule if market were either net realizable value or net realizable value less a normal profit margin, but would be valued at $28.00 per unit if market were replacement cost.

Given different interpretations as to what market is, the question becomes: What definition of market should be used when determining the lower of cost and market? The *CICA Handbook* recognizes several possibilities, all of which are generally accepted, but is silent on which is appropriate in particular circumstances. (Some of these considerations are identified later under the heading "Evaluation of the Lower of Cost and Market

> **2 Objective**
> Explain various definitions of possible market amounts that may be used when applying lower of cost and market.

> **IAS Note**
> IAS 2 requires that inventory be valued at the lower of cost and net realizable value.

---

[1] *CICA Handbook*, Section 3030.11.

Rule.") However, **net realizable value is the most common method of determining market in Canada.**[2] Why is there such support for this method?

The use of replacement cost as "market" is based on the assumption that a decline in an item's replacement cost usually results in a decline in selling price. If selling prices fall, a company holding units of that inventory will report an eventual loss, or at least a lower profit margin. It is true that products in a very competitive market are likely to experience declines in selling price if production costs decline. However, it is not reasonable to assume that prices will fall in the same proportion as input costs, nor below inventory cost, nor that such market conditions exist for all products. Replacement cost may be appropriate in limited specific circumstances.

This leaves net realizable value and net realizable value less a normal profit margin to consider. To illustrate the effects of reducing the carrying value of inventory under these two methods, assume that a company has unfinished inventory at December 31, 2005 with a cost of $760, a completed sales value of $1,000, estimated cost of completion of $275, and a normal profit margin of 10% of sales. The determination of both "market" calculations follows.

Illustration 9-1

Calculation of Net Realizable Value

Inventory—sales value	$1,000
Less: Estimated cost of completion and disposal	275
Net realizable value	725
Less: Allowance for normal profit margin (10% of sales)	100
Net realizable value less a normal profit margin	$ 625

To understand the arguments related to the use of these terms, it is important to understand what the effects are on the financial statements of the current and subsequent periods. Illustration 9-2 first summarizes the effects of using net realizable value as the definition of market, and then the effects of using the more conservative net realizable value less a normal profit margin.

Those who support the idea that any loss to be recognized should not be greater than the estimated costs that will not be recovered would argue for the first definition of market as net realizable value. In this situation, the total expected costs are $760 + $275, or $1,035. With a selling price of $1,000, there is $35 of expected unrecoverable cost, and this is the amount recognized in 2005 in the inventory writedown. In 2006 when the inventory is sold, the result is a break-even because the unrecoverable costs were recognized in 2005 when the actual reduction in value took place.

Others support a higher inventory writedown. **They believe the inventory should be reduced sufficiently in the current period so that a normal profit will be reported when the inventory is subsequently sold.** This results when market is defined as net realizable value less a normal profit margin, and is illustrated in the bottom part of Illustration 9-2. In this example, a loss of $135 is reported in 2005 and a normal profit of $100 is recognized in 2006 when the inventory is sold.

Because the normal process of matching deducts cost from revenue when determining income, any downward adjustment of the inventory carrying amount to market **shifts income from one period to the next.** In the first example above using NRV, the loss of $35 was shifted from 2006 to 2005, leaving $0 income in 2006. In the second example

Underlying Concept

Regardless of the definition of "market" used, the intent is the same: current assets should not be reported at more than their realizable value to the company.

---

[2] *Financial Reporting in Canada, 2002* (Toronto: CICA, 2002) reports that, of the interpretations of market disclosed in 2001 financial statements of 162 of the surveyed companies, 80 used only net realizable value or estimated net realizable value, 7 used only replacement cost, 1 used only net realizable value less a normal profit margin, and 3 reported only another method. Sixty-seven companies used more than one method, and of these, 57 used replacement cost, most often in conjunction with net realizable value. Only 4 companies did not disclose how they defined market.

Illustration 9-2

Income Statement Effects of Using Net Realizable Value

	Inventory Value December 31, 2005 Balance Sheet	Profit (loss) recognized	
		in 2005	in 2006
If Market = NRV			
Cost = $760			
Market = $725			
LCM =	$725		
Effect on 2005 Income Statement:			
$760 − $725		($ 35)	
Effect on 2006 Income Statement:			
Revenue			$1,000
Expenses: Carrying value, Dec. 31/05			(725)
2006 costs to complete			
and sell			(275)
			$0
If Market = NRV less a normal profit margin			
Cost = $760			
Market = $625			
LCM =	$625		
Effect on 2005 Income Statement:			
$760 − $625		($135)	
Effect on 2006 Income Statement:			
Revenue			$1,000
Expenses: Carrying value, Dec. 31/05			(625)
2006 costs to complete			
and sell			(275)
			$ 100

using NRV less a normal profit margin, a loss of $135 was shifted into 2005 so that a normal profit of $100 could be recognized in 2006. Many consider this latter approach to be **too arbitrary in shifting profits between periods**, and too far removed from an appropriate application of the matching principle. **For this reason, net realizable value remains the most commonly used definition of "market" in Canada.**

The accounting profession in the United States has adopted a different approach for determining "market".[3] Generally, market is the item's replacement cost. When applying the lower of cost and market rule, however, "market" cannot exceed net realizable value (a ceiling or upper limit value) or be less than net realizable value less a normal profit margin (a floor or lower limit value).[4] Therefore, the value designated as "market" is the middle value of these three possibilities. Once the designated market has been determined, it is compared with the cost and the lower amount is used for inventory valuation. These guidelines are shown in Illustration 9-3.

---

[3] Generally, we do not identify U.S. financial reporting standards in this Canadian text, particularly when a specific Canadian position exists. We do so in this case because awareness of the U.S. standard may help to better understand the rationale of Canadian practice. Also, the comparison serves to illustrate that different countries can come to different conclusions when trying to account for the same phenomenon—a problem that is faced head-on by the International Accounting Standards Board when it is trying to develop international accounting standards, or by international finance professionals when they are assessing financial statements of companies from different countries.

[4] "Restatement and Revision of Accounting Research Bulletins," *Accounting Research Bulletin No. 43*, (New York: AICPA, 1953), Ch. 4, par. 8.

Illustration 9-3

*U.S. Inventory Valuation—
Lower of Cost and Market*

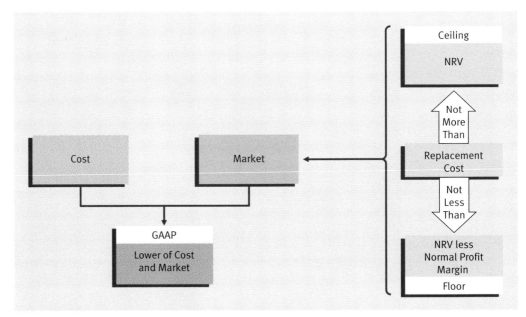

The U.S. approach is based on the premise that declines in replacement cost are reflective of or predict a decline in selling price (realizable value). The ceiling and floor limits are introduced to protect against situations where this premise is in serious error. Consequently, while the underlying objective of reflecting a decline in utility of inventory is common in both Canada and the United States, each has reached a different conclusion as to how this is best accomplished.

How Lower of Cost and Market Works

Objective 3
Explain how LCM works and how it is determined.

The **lower of cost and market (LCM)** rule requires that the inventory be valued at cost unless market is lower than cost, in which case the inventory is valued at market. To apply this rule, regardless of whether a Canadian or U.S. definition of market is used:

1. Determine the cost using an acceptable historical cost flow method.

2. Determine the market value to be used.

3. Compare the cost with the market.

4. Use the lower of the cost and market figures for inventory valuation on the financial statements.

To demonstrate, consider the following information relative to the inventory of Regner Foods Limited.

Illustration 9-4

Possible Market Values

Food	Replacement Cost	Net Realizable Value	Net Realizable Value Less a Normal Profit Margin
Spinach	$ 88,000	$120,000	$104,000
Carrots	90,000	100,000	70,000
Cut beans	45,000	40,000	27,500
Peas	36,000	72,000	48,000
Mixed vegetables	105,000	92,000	80,000

Under Canadian GAAP, company management specifies which of the three definitions of market it will adopt. If net realizable value is designated as the "market" value, as is commonly the case for Canadian companies, the net realizable values provided in the middle column of Illustration 9-4 will be the values compared with cost in establishing the lower of cost and market. Illustration 9-5 completes the inventory valuation process by choosing the lower of the two values for each inventory item. Cost is the lower amount for spinach, net realizable value is lower for cut beans, peas, and mixed vegetables, and cost and NRV are identical for carrots. The inventory value reported on Regner Foods' balance sheet is $384,000.

Illustration 9-5

Determining Final Inventory Value Using NRV

Food	Cost	Net Realizable Value	LCM
Spinach	$ 80,000	$120,000	$ 80,000
Carrots	100,000	100,000	100,000
Cut beans	50,000	40,000	40,000
Peas	90,000	72,000	72,000
Mixed vegetables	95,000	92,000	92,000
Final inventory value			$384,000

If management uses NRV less a normal profit margin as its definition of market, a lower market value in each case is compared with cost, and the final balance sheet valuation for inventory would be significantly lower.

To determine market under U.S. rules, the first step is to calculate amounts for all three possible market values, as indicated in Illustration 9-4. Given this, the next step is to determine which of these is the **designated market value**. The designated market value is always the middle value of three amounts: replacement cost, net realizable value (the ceiling), and net realizable value less a normal profit margin (the floor).

The designated market value is then compared with cost to determine the lower of cost and market. The choice of designated market value and the application of LCM in determining the final inventory value for Regner Foods is illustrated below.

Illustration 9-6

Determining Final Inventory Value—U.S. Approach

Food	Cost	Replacement Cost	Net Realizable Value (Ceiling)	Net Realizable Value Less a Normal Profit Margin (Floor)	Designated Market Value	Final Inventory Value
Spinach	$ 80,000	$ 88,000	$120,000	$104,000	$104,000	$ 80,000
Carrots	100,000	90,000	100,000	70,000	90,000	90,000
Cut beans	50,000	45,000	40,000	27,500	40,000	40,000
Peas	90,000	36,000	72,000	48,000	48,000	48,000
Mixed vegetables	95,000	105,000	92,000	80,000	92,000	92,000
						$350,000

Final Inventory Value:

Spinach	Cost ($80,000) is selected because it is lower than designated market value (net realizable value less a normal profit margin).
Carrots	Designated market value (replacement cost, $90,000) is selected because it is lower than cost.
Cut beans	Designated market value (net realizable value, $40,000) is selected because it is lower than cost.
Peas	Designated market value (net realizable value less a normal profit margin, $48,000) is selected because it is lower than cost.
Mixed vegetables	Designated market value (net realizable value, $92,000) is selected because it is lower than cost.

For spinach and peas, the "floor" value of NRV less a normal profit margin is chosen as the designated market value because it is the middle value. For carrots, replacement cost is designated as market because it is the middle value. For the cut beans and mixed vegetables, net realizable value is designated as market because it is the middle value. In Illustration 9-6, the Designated Market Value column contains the values that are compared with Cost in determining the lower of cost and market.

Under both Canadian and U.S. standards, applying the lower of cost and market rule incorporates only losses in value that occur in the normal course of business from such causes as style changes, shift in demand, or regular shop wear. Damaged or deteriorated goods are reduced directly to net realizable value. If the amount is significant, such goods may be carried in separate inventory accounts. For example, the $7.3 million writedown due to the discontinuation of the Martha Stewart product line was separately reported by **Hudson's Bay Company** relative to its **Zellers** subsidiary in the first quarter of 2003.

Methods of Applying Lower of Cost and Market

Objective 4
Know how to account for inventory on the lower of cost and market basis.

In the previous illustration for Regner Foods, we assumed that the lower of cost and market rule was applied to each type of food. However, the lower of cost and market rule may be applied on an **item-by-item basis**, a **category basis**, or a **total inventory basis**. Increases in market prices of some goods tend to offset decreases in market prices of others if a major category or total inventory approach is followed. To illustrate, assume that Regner Foods separates its food products into frozen and canned to designate major categories. **Note that market is defined as net realizable value in this illustration.**

As indicated in Illustration 9-7, if the lower of cost and market rule is applied to individual items, the LCM valuation of inventory is $384,000; if applied to major categories, it is $394,000; if applied to the total inventory, it is $415,000. The reason for the difference is that market values lower than cost are offset against market values higher than cost when the major categories or total inventory approach is adopted. For Regner Foods, the lower market values for cut beans, peas, and mixed vegetables are partially offset by the higher market value for spinach when the major categories approach is adopted, and is totally offset when the total inventory approach is used. Therefore, **the item-by-item approach is the most conservative of the three methods** because market values above cost are never taken into account.

	Cost	Market (NRV)	Lower of Cost and Market By: Individual Items	Lower of Cost and Market By: Major Categories	Lower of Cost and Market By: Total Inventory
Frozen					
Spinach	$ 80,000	$120,000	$ 80,000		
Carrots	100,000	100,000	100,000		
Cut beans	50,000	40,000	40,000		
Total frozen	230,000	260,000		$230,000	
Canned					
Peas	90,000	72,000	72,000		
Mixed vegetables	95,000	92,000	92,000		
Total canned	185,000	164,000		164,000	
Total	$415,000	$424,000	$384,000	$394,000	$415,000

The Canada Customs and Revenue Agency dictates that "in comparing 'cost' and 'fair market value' in order to determine which is the lower, the comparison should be made separately and individually in respect of each item (or each usual class of items if specific items are not readily distinguishable) in the inventory." A comparison of total cost and total market is permitted by exception where the cost of the specific items (using specific identification, FIFO or average cost) is not known and only an average cost is available.[5] The tax rules in the United States require that an individual item basis be used unless it involves practical difficulties. **Whichever method is selected, it should be applied consistently from one period to another.**

Recording "Market" Instead of Cost

Two methods are used for recording inventory at market. One method, referred to as the direct method, simply records the ending inventory at the market figure at the year end (if lower than cost), substituting the market value figure for cost when valuing the inventory. As a result, no loss is reported separately in the income statement because the loss is buried in cost of goods sold. The second method, referred to as the indirect method or allowance method, does not change the cost amount, but establishes a separate contra asset account and a loss account to record the write-off.

The following illustrations of entries under both methods are based on the following inventory data.

Inventory	At Cost	At Market
Beginning of the period	$65,000	$65,000
End of the period	82,000	70,000

The following entries assume the use of a **periodic** inventory system.

Ending Inventory Recorded at Market (Direct Method)			Ending Inventory Recorded at Cost and Reduced to Market Using An Allowance		
To transfer out beginning inventory balance:					
Cost of Goods Sold			Cost of Goods Sold		
(or Income Summary)	65,000		(or Income Summary)	65,000	
Inventory		65,000	Inventory		65,000
To record ending inventory:					
Inventory	70,000		Inventory	82,000	
Cost of Goods Sold			Cost of Goods Sold		
(or Income Summary)		70,000	(or Income Summary)		82,000
To write down inventory to market:					
No entry			Loss Due to Market		
			Decline of Inventory	12,000	
			Allowance to Reduce		
			Inventory to Market		12,000

Illustration 9-8

Accounting for the Reduction of Inventory to Market— Periodic Inventory System

If the company used a **perpetual** inventory system, the entries would be as follows.

---

[5] *CCRA Interpretation Bulletin—473R*, December 21, 1998 on "Inventory Valuation," par. .3.

(No inventory closing entries are necessary under the perpetual method; only the reduction to market is recorded.)

Direct Method			Indirect or Allowance Method		
To reduce inventory from cost to market:					
Cost of Goods Sold	12,000		Loss Due to Market		
Inventory		12,000	Decline of Inventory	12,000	
			Allowance to Reduce		
			Inventory to Market		12,000

The advantage of identifying the loss due to market decline is that it may be shown separately from cost of goods sold in the income statement, without distorting the cost of goods sold for the year. The data from the preceding illustration are used to contrast the differing amounts reported in the income statements below.

Direct Method

Sales		$200,000
Cost of goods sold		
Inventory, Jan. 1	$ 65,000	
Purchases (assumed)	125,000	
Goods available	190,000	
Inventory, Dec. 31 (at market which is lower than cost)	70,000	
Cost of goods sold		120,000
Gross profit on sales		$ 80,000

Indirect or Allowance Method

Sales		$200,000
Cost of goods sold		
Inventory, Jan. 1	$ 65,000	
Purchases (assumed)	125,000	
Goods available	190,000	
Inventory, Dec. 31 (at cost)	82,000	
Cost of goods sold		108,000
Gross profit on sales		92,000
Loss due to market decline of inventory (reported in other expenses and losses)		12,000
		$ 80,000

Underlying Concept

The income statement under the first presentation lacks representational faithfulness. The cost of goods sold does not represent what it purports to represent. However, allowing the first presentation illustrates the concept of materiality. The presentation does not affect net income and usually would not "change the judgement of a reasonable person."

The second presentation is preferable. It clearly discloses the loss resulting from the market decline of inventory prices instead of burying the loss in the cost of goods sold. This method permits both the income statement and the balance sheet to show the ending inventory of $82,000, with the Allowance to Reduce Inventory to Market reported on the balance sheet as a $12,000 deduction from the inventory cost. **It also keeps subsidiary inventory ledgers and records in correspondence with the control account without changing unit costs.**

Although using an allowance account permits balance sheet disclosure of the inventory at cost and at the lower of cost and market, it raises the problem of how to dispose of the new account balance in the following period. If the merchandise in question is still on hand, the allowance account should be retained. Otherwise, beginning inventory and cost of goods are overstated. But if the goods have been sold, then the account should be closed. A new allowance account balance is then established for any decline in inventory value that has taken place in the current year.

Some accountants leave this account on the books and merely adjust the balance at the next balance sheet date to agree with the discrepancy between cost and the lower of cost and market at that time. Thus, if prices are falling, a loss is recorded. If prices are rising, a loss recorded in prior years is recovered and a gain (which is not really a gain, but **a recovery of a previously recognized loss**) is recorded, as illustrated in the example below.

Date	Inventory at Cost	Inventory at Market	Amount Required in Allowance Account	Adjustment of Allowance Account Balance	Effect on Net Income
Dec. 31, 2003	$188,000	$176,000	$12,000 cr.	$12,000 inc.	Loss
Dec. 31, 2004	194,000	187,000	7,000 cr.	5,000 dec.	Gain
Dec. 31, 2005	173,000	174,000	0	7,000 dec.	Gain
Dec. 31, 2006	182,000	180,000	2,000 cr.	2,000 inc.	Loss

Illustration 9-11

Effect on Net Income of Adjustments to the Allowance Account

Any net "gain" can be thought of as the excess of the credit effect of closing the beginning allowance balance over the debit effect of setting up the current year-end allowance account. Recognizing a separate gain or loss has the same effect on net income as would closing the allowance balance to beginning inventory or to cost of goods sold. Recovering the loss up to the original cost is permitted, **but it may not exceed original cost.**

Evaluation of the Lower of Cost and Market Rule

The lower of cost and market rule suffers some conceptual deficiencies.

1. Decreases in the asset's value and the charge to expense are recognized in the period in which the loss in utility occurs, not in the period of sale. On the other hand, increases in the asset's value are recognized only at the point of sale. This treatment is inconsistent and can lead to distortions in income data.

2. Applying the rule results in inconsistency because a company's inventory may be valued at cost in one year and at market in the next year.

3. Lower of cost and market values the balance sheet inventory conservatively, but its effect on the income statement may or may not be conservative. Net income for the year in which the loss is taken is definitely lower; net income of the subsequent period may be higher than normal if the expected reduction in sales price does not materialize.

4. Applying the lower of cost and market rule may use a "normal" profit in determining inventory values. Since "normal" profit is an estimated figure based upon past experience and one that might not be attained in the future, it is not objective and presents an opportunity for income manipulation.

5. In general, using acceptable accounting methods arbitrarily to transfer income from one period to another reduces the quality of reported earnings.

On the other hand, many financial statement users appreciate the lower of cost and market rule because they at least know that the inventory is not overstated. In addition, recognizing all losses but anticipating no gains always results in a lower, more conservative measure of income.

Underlying Concept

The inconsistency in the presentation of inventory is an example of the trade-off between relevance and reliability. Market is more relevant than cost, and cost is more reliable than market. Apparently, relevance takes precedence in a down market, and reliability is more important in an up market.

OTHER VALUATION ISSUES

Valuation at Net Realizable Value

Objective 5
Identify when inventories are carried regularly at net realizable value.

For most companies and in most situations, inventory is recorded at cost or the lower of cost and market. Some believe that inventory should always be valued at market defined as net realizable value, since that is the net amount that will be collected in cash from the inventory in the future. Under limited circumstances, **support exists for recording inventory at net realizable value (selling price less estimated costs to complete and sell) even if that amount is above cost.** This exception to the normal recognition rule is permitted where:

1. there is a controlled market with a quoted price applicable to all quantities, and

2. no significant costs of disposal are involved.

Inventories of certain minerals (rare metals especially) are ordinarily reported at selling prices because there is often a controlled market without significant costs of disposal. A similar treatment is given agricultural products that are immediately marketable at quoted prices. **This is consistent with recognition of revenue on completion of production** as discussed in Chapter 6. The Saskatchewan Wheat Pool reports such a policy in the notes to its financial statements as reported in Illustration 9-12.

Illustration 9-12
Inventory Valued at Net Realizable Value

Saskatchewan Wheat Pool *(excerpted from its 2002 annual report)*

Inventories
Grain purchased for sale to the Canadian Wheat Board (CWB) is valued on the basis of CWB initial prices less freight and handling costs. Non-Board grains are valued on the basis of open sales contracts and futures contracts, after freight and handling costs.

IAS Note

IAS 41 on accounting for agricultural activity recommends that agricultural produce be measured at fair value at the point of harvest reduced by selling costs. However, fair value measurement stops at harvest.

Another reason for allowing this method of valuation is that sometimes the cost figures are too difficult to obtain. In a manufacturing plant, various raw materials and purchased parts are put together to create a finished product. The various items in inventory, whether completely or partially finished, can be accounted for on a basis of cost because the cost of each individual component part is known. In some cases, however, marketable by-products are produced where the costs are indistinguishable. Rather than engage in a costly exercise of arbitrary cost allocation, the by-products are measured at the market price of the by-product less any costs to bring them to market.

Purchase Commitments—A Special Problem

Objective 6
Explain accounting issues related to purchase commitments.

In many lines of business, a firm's survival and continued profitability depend on having a sufficient stock of merchandise to meet all customer demands. Consequently, it is quite common for a company to agree to buy inventory weeks, months, or even years in advance. Such arrangements may be made based on estimated or firm sales commitments by the company's customers. Generally, title to the merchandise or materials described in these **purchase commitments** has not passed to the buyer. Indeed, the goods may exist only as natural resources or, in the case of commodities, as unplanted seed, or in the case of a product, as work in process.

Usually it is neither necessary nor proper for the buyer to make any entries to reflect commitments for purchases of goods that have not been shipped by the seller. Ordinary orders, for which the prices are determined at the time of shipment and **are subject to can-**

cellation by the buyer or seller, do not represent either an asset or a liability to the buyer. Therefore, they need not be recorded in the books or reported in the financial statements.

Even with formal, **non-cancellable purchase contracts**, no asset or liability is recognized at the date of inception, **because the contract is "executory" in nature**: neither party has performed, i.e., fulfilled its part of the contract. However, if material, such contract details should be disclosed in the buyer's balance sheet in a note, such as in the following examples.

Illustration 9-13

Disclosure of Purchase Commitments—Cameco Corporation

24. Commitments and Contingencies

    c) Commitments

        At December 31, 2002, Cameco's purchase commitments, the majority of which are fixed-price uranium and conversion purchase arrangements, were as follows:

	(Millions (US))
2003	$ 118
2004	102
2005	114
2006	114
2007	117
thereafter	561
Total	**$1,126**

Note 1: Contracts for the purchase of raw materials in 2005 have been executed in the amount of $600,000. The market price of such raw materials on December 31, 2004 is $640,000.

Illustration 9-14

Disclosure of Purchase Commitment

In Illustration 9-14, the contracted price was less than the market price at the balance sheet date. **If the contracted price exceeds the market price and losses are reasonably determinable and likely to occur at the time of purchase, losses should be recognized in the period during which such declines in prices take place.**[6] For example, if purchase contracts for delivery in 2005 have been executed at a firm price of $640,000 and the material's market price on the company's year end of December 31, 2004 is $600,000, the following entry is made on December 31, 2004.

Loss on Purchase Contracts	40,000	
Accrued Liability on Purchase Contracts		40,000

$$A = L + SE$$
$$+40,000 \quad -40,000$$

Cash flows: No effect

This loss is shown on the income statement under Other Expenses and Losses. The Accrued Liability on Purchase Contracts is reported in the balance sheet's liability section. When the goods are delivered in 2005, the entry (perpetual system) is:

Inventory	600,000	
Accrued Liability on Purchase Contracts	40,000	
Accounts Payable		640,000

$$A = L + SE$$
$$+600,000 \quad +600,000$$

Cash flows: No effect

If the price has partially or fully recovered before the inventory is received, the Accrued Liability on Purchase Contracts would be reduced. A resulting gain (Recovery of Loss) is then reported in the period of the price increase for the amount of the partial or full recovery.

The purchasers in purchase commitments can protect themselves against the possibility of market price declines of goods under contract by hedging. **Hedging** is accomplished through a futures contract in which the purchaser in the purchase commitment simultaneously contracts for a future sale of the same quantity of the same or similar goods at a fixed price. When a company holds a buy position in a purchase commitment and a sell position in a futures contract in the same commodity, **it will be better off under one contract by**

Underlying Concept

Reporting the loss is conservative. However, reporting the decline in market price is debatable because no asset is recorded. This area demonstrates the need for good definitions of assets and liabilities.

---

[6] *CICA Handbook*, Section 3290.12.

approximately (maybe exactly) the same amount by which it is worse off under the other contract. That is, a loss on one will be offset by a gain on the other.[7]

Accounting for purchase commitments (and, for that matter, all commitments) is unsettled and controversial. Some argue that these contracts should be reported as assets and liabilities when the contract is signed; others believe that recognition at the delivery date is more appropriate.[8] Clearly, the treatment of such contracts in particular situations rests on judgement being exercised within the context of generally accepted accounting principles and experience.

THE GROSS PROFIT METHOD OF ESTIMATING INVENTORY

Objective 7

Estimate ending inventory by applying the gross profit method.

Recall that the basic purpose of taking a physical inventory is to verify the perpetual inventory records' accuracy or, if no perpetual records exist, to arrive at an inventory amount. Sometimes, taking a physical inventory is impractical or impossible. Then, estimation methods are used to approximate inventory on hand. One such method is called the gross profit (or gross margin) method. This method is used in situations where only an estimate of inventory is needed (e.g., preparing interim reports or testing the reasonableness of the cost derived by some other method) or where inventory has been destroyed by fire or other catastrophe. It may also be used to provide a rough check on the accuracy of a physical inventory count (e.g., compare the estimated amount with physical count amount to see if they are reasonably close; if not, a reason should be found).

The **gross profit method** is based on three assumptions:

1. the beginning inventory plus purchases equal the cost of goods available for sale that must be accounted for,

2. goods not sold must be on hand in ending inventory, and

3. when the net sales, reduced to cost, are deducted from the cost of goods available for sale, the result is the ending inventory.

To illustrate, assume that a company has a beginning inventory of $60,000 and purchases of $200,000, both at cost. Sales at selling price amount to $280,000. The gross profit on selling price is 30%. The gross margin method is applied as follows.

Illustration 9-15

Application of Gross Profit Method

Beginning inventory (at cost)		$ 60,000
Purchases (at cost)		200,000
Goods available for sale (at cost)		260,000
Sales (at selling price)	$280,000	
Less: Gross profit (30% of $280,000)	84,000	
Sales at cost = Estimated cost of goods sold		196,000
Estimated inventory (at cost)		$ 64,000

---

[7] A discussion of hedging and the use of derivatives such as futures is provided in Chapter 17.

[8] *FASB Concepts Statement No. 6*, "Elements of Financial Statements," (Stamford, Conn.: FASB, 1985) states in paragraphs 251 to 253 that a purchase commitment involves both an item that might be recorded as an asset and an item that might be recorded as a liability. That is, it involves both a right to receive assets and an obligation to pay. If both the right to receive assets and the obligation to pay were recorded at the time of the purchase commitment, the nature of the loss and the valuation account that records it when the price falls would be clearly seen. Although the discussion in *Concepts Statement No. 6* does not exclude the possibility of recording assets and liabilities for purchase commitments, it contains no conclusions or implications about whether they should be recorded.

Note that the estimated cost of goods sold could also have been calculated directly as 70% of sales, i.e., 100% less 30%. **The cost of goods sold percentage is always the complement of the gross profit percentage.**

All the information needed to estimate the inventory at cost, except for the gross profit percentage, is available in the current period's records. The gross profit percentage is determined by reviewing company policies and prior period records. In some cases, this percentage must be adjusted if prior periods are not considered representative of the current period.[9]

Calculation of Gross Profit Percentage

In most situations, the gross profit percentage is used and it is the gross profit as a percentage of selling price. The previous illustration, for example, used a 30% gross profit on sales. Gross profit on selling price is the common method for quoting the profit for several reasons: (1) Most goods are stated on a retail basis, not a cost basis. (2) A profit quoted on selling price is lower than one based on cost, and this lower rate gives a favourable impression to the consumer. (3) The gross profit based on selling price can never exceed 100%.[10]

In the previous example, the gross profit was a given. But how was that figure derived? To see how a gross profit percentage is calculated, assume that an article cost $15.00 and sells for $20.00, a gross profit of $5.00. This markup of $5.00 is ¼ or 25% of the selling price (i.e., retail) but is only ⅓ or 33⅓% of cost (see Illustration 9-16).

$$\frac{\text{Gross profit}}{\text{Selling price}} = \frac{\$\ 5.00}{\$20.00} = 25\% \text{ of selling price} \qquad \frac{\text{Gross profit}}{\text{Cost}} = \frac{\$\ 5.00}{\$15.00} = 33\tfrac{1}{3}\% \text{ of cost}$$

Illustration 9-16

Gross Profit Percentage versus Percentage of Markup on Cost

Although it is normal to calculate the gross profit on the basis of selling price, you should understand the basic relationship between this ratio and the percentage of markup on cost.

For example, assume that you were told that the **markup on cost** for a given item is 25%. What, then, is the **gross profit on selling price**? To find the answer, assume that the item's selling price is $1.00. In this case, the following formula applies.

---

[9] An alternative approach to estimating inventory using the gross profit percentage, considered by some to be less complicated than the method illustrated above, uses the standard income statement format as follows (assume the same data as in the illustration above).

Sales		$280,000		$280,000
Cost of sales				
Beginning inventory	$ 60,000		$ 60,000	
Purchases	200,000		200,000	
Goods available for sale	260,000		260,000	
Ending inventory	(3) ?		(3) 64,000 Est.	
Cost of goods sold		(2) ?		(2)196,000 Est.
Gross profit on sales (30%)		(1) ?		(1) 84,000 Est.

Calculate the unknowns as follows: first the gross profit amount, then cost of goods sold, and then the ending inventory.

(1) $280,000 × 30% = $84,000 (gross profit on sales)

(2) $280,000 − $84,000 = $196,000 (cost of goods sold)

(3) $260,000 − $196,000 = $64,000 (ending inventory)

[10] The terms "gross profit percentage," "gross margin percentage," "rate of gross profit," and "rate of gross margin" are synonymous, reflecting **the relationship of gross profit to selling price**. The terms "percentage markup" or "rate of markup" are used to describe **the relationship of gross profit to cost**. It is very important to understand the difference.

$$
\begin{aligned}
\text{Cost} + \text{Gross profit} &= \text{Selling price} \\
C + .25C &= \$1.00 \\
1.25C &= \$1.00 \\
C &= \$0.80
\end{aligned}
$$

The gross profit equals $0.20 ($1.00 − $0.80), and the rate of gross profit on selling price is therefore 20% ($0.20/$1.00).

Conversely, assume that you were told that the **gross profit on selling price** is 20%. What is the **markup on cost**? To find the answer, again assume that the selling price is $1.00. You'll find the same formula holds.

$$
\begin{aligned}
\text{Cost} + \text{Gross profit} &= \text{Selling price} \\
C + .20SP &= SP \\
C &= .80SP \\
C &= .80(\$1.00) \\
C &= \$0.80
\end{aligned}
$$

Here, as in the example above, the markup or gross profit equals $0.20 ($1.00 − $0.80), and the markup on cost is 25% ($0.20/$0.80).

Retailers use the following formulas to express these relationships.

Illustration 9-17

Formulas Relating to Gross Profit

$$
\text{1. Percent gross profit on selling price} = \frac{\text{Percent markup on cost}}{100\% + \text{Percent markup on cost}}
$$

$$
\text{2. Percent markup on cost} = \frac{\text{Percent gross profit on selling price}}{100\% - \text{Percent gross profit on selling price}}
$$

Because selling price is greater than cost, and with the gross profit amount the same for both, **gross profit on selling price will always be less than the related percentage based on cost.** Sales should never be multiplied by a cost-based markup percentage—it must be a percentage based on selling price.

What do the Numbers Mean?

Gross profits are closely followed by management and analysts. A small change in the gross profit rate can significantly affect the bottom line. In the mid-1990s, Apple Computer suffered a textbook case of shrinking gross profits. In response to pricing wars in the personal computer market, Apple was forced to quickly reduce the price of its signature Macintosh computers, cutting prices more quickly than it could reduce its costs. As a result, its gross profit rate fell 4% relative to the prior year. Although a drop of 4% may appear small, its impact on the bottom line caused Apple's share price to drop from $57 per share to $27.50 over a six-week period following release of the lower numbers.

More recently, Debenham Plc, the second largest department store in the United Kingdom, experienced a 14% share price decline in the summer of 2002. The cause? Markdowns on slow-moving inventory, which reduced its gross margin.[11]

Evaluation of Gross Profit Method

Objective 8

Explain the limitations of the gross profit method.

What are the major disadvantages of the gross profit method? One is that **it provides an estimate**; as a result, a physical inventory must be taken once a year to verify that the inventory is actually on hand. Second, the gross profit method uses **past percentages** in determining the markup. Although the past can often provide predictions about the future, a current rate is more appropriate. It is important to emphasize that whenever significant fluctuations occur, the percentage should be adjusted appropriately. Third, **care must be taken in applying a blanket gross profit rate.** Often, a store or department handles merchandise with widely varying rates of gross profit. In these situations, the gross

---

[11] Alison Smith, "Debenham's Shares Hit by Warning," *Financial Times* (July 24, 2002), p. 21.

profit method may have to be applied by subsections, lines of merchandise, or a similar basis that classifies merchandise according to their respective rates of gross profit.

The gross profit method is **not normally acceptable for financial reporting purposes** because it provides only an estimate. A physical inventory is needed as additional verification that the inventory indicated in the records is actually on hand. Nevertheless, the gross profit method is used to estimate ending inventory for **interim** (monthly and quarterly) **reporting** and for **insurance purposes** (e.g., fire losses). Note that the results of applying the gross profit method will follow closely the inventory method used (FIFO, LIFO, average cost) because it is based on historical records.

THE RETAIL INVENTORY METHOD OF ESTIMATING INVENTORY

Accounting for inventory in a retail operation presents several challenges. Retailers with certain types of inventory may use the specific identification method to value their inventories. Such an approach makes sense when individual inventory units are significant, such as automobiles, pianos, or fur coats. However, imagine attempting to use such an approach at Canadian Tire, Zellers, or Sears—high-volume retailers that have many different types of merchandise at relatively low unit costs! It would be extremely difficult to determine the cost of each sale, to enter cost codes on the tickets, to change the codes to reflect declines in value of the merchandise, to allocate costs such as transportation, and so on.

An alternative is to estimate inventory cost when necessary by taking a physical inventory at retail prices. In most retail concerns, an observable pattern between cost and selling prices exists. Retail prices can then be converted to cost simply by multiplying them by the cost-to-retail ratio. This method, called the retail inventory method, **requires that a record be kept of (1) the total cost and retail value of goods purchased, (2) the total cost and retail value of the goods available for sale, and (3) the sales for the period.**

Here is how it works: The sales for the period are deducted from the retail value of the goods available for sale to produce an estimate of the inventory at retail or selling prices. The ratio of cost to retail for all goods passing through a department or company is determined by dividing the total goods available for sale at cost by the total goods available for sale at retail. The ending inventory valued at retail is converted to ending inventory at cost by applying the cost-to-retail ratio. Use of the retail inventory method is very common. For example, Hart Stores Inc., Reitmans (Canada) Limited, and Hudson's Bay Company all report using the retail inventory method in determining their inventory cost. Excerpts from the notes to their financial statements are reproduced below.

9 Objective
Estimate ending inventory by applying the retail inventory method.

Hart Stores Inc. *(excerpted from its 2003 annual report)*

Inventory is valued at the lower of cost and net realizable value. Cost is determined using the retail method.

Reitmans (Canada) Limited *(excerpted from its 2003 annual report)*

Merchandise inventories are valued at the lower of cost, determined principally on an average basis using the retail inventory method, and net realizable value.

Hudson's Bay Company *(excerpted from its 2002 annual report)*

Merchandise inventories are carried at the lower of cost and net realizable value less normal gross profit margins. The cost of inventories is determined principally on an average basis by the use of the retail inventory method.

Illustration 9-18

Examples of Companies Using the Retail Inventory Method

The retail inventory method is illustrated below.

Illustration 9-19

Retail Inventory Method

	Cost	Retail
Beginning inventory	$14,000	$ 20,000
Purchases	63,000	90,000
Goods available for sale	$77,000	110,000
Deduct: Sales		85,000
Ending inventory, at retail		$ 25,000
Ratio of cost to retail ($77,000 ÷ $110,000)		70%
Ending inventory at cost (70% of $25,000)		$ 17,500

To avoid a potential misstatement of the inventory, periodic inventory counts are made, especially in retail operations where loss due to shoplifting and breakage is common. **When a physical count at retail is taken, the inventory cost is determined by multiplying the resulting amount at retail by the cost-to-retail ratio.** Discrepancies between the records and the physical count require an adjustment to make the records agree with the count.

The retail method is sanctioned by various retail associations and the accounting profession, and is allowed (except for methods approximating a LIFO valuation) by the CCRA (Canada Customs and Revenue Agency). **One advantage of the retail inventory method is that the inventory balance can be approximated without a physical count.** This makes the method particularly useful when preparing interim reports. Insurance adjusters use this approach to estimate losses from fire, flood, or other type of casualty.

This method also acts as a control device because any deviations from a physical count at year end have to be explained. In addition, the retail method expedites the physical inventory count at the year end. The crew taking the inventory need record only the retail price of each item. There is no need to determine each item's invoice cost, thus saving time and expense.

Retail Method Terminology

The amounts shown in the Retail column of Illustration 9-19 represent the original retail or selling prices (cost plus an original markup or mark-on), assuming no price changes.

Sales prices, however, are frequently marked up or down from the original sales price. For retailers, the term markup means an increase in the price above the original sales price. Markup cancellations are decreases in merchandise prices that had been marked up above the original retail price. Markup cancellations cannot be greater than markups. Net markups refer to markups less markup cancellations.

Markdowns are decreases in price below the original selling price. They are a common phenomenon and occur because of a decline in general price levels, special sales, soiled or damaged goods, overstocking, and competition. Markdown cancellations occur when the markdowns are later offset by increases in the prices of goods that had been marked down, such as after a one-day sale. A markdown cancellation cannot exceed the original markdown. Markdowns less markdown cancellations are known as net markdowns.

To illustrate these different concepts, assume that the Designer Clothing Store recently purchased 100 dress shirts from a supplier. The cost for these shirts was $1,500, or $15 a shirt. Designer Clothing established the selling price on these shirts at $30 each.

The manager noted that the shirts were selling quickly, so she added $5 to the price of each shirt. This markup made the price too high for customers and sales lagged. Consequently, the manager reduced the price to $32. To this point there has been a **markup of $5** and a **markup cancellation of $3** on the original selling price of a shirt. When the major marketing season ended, the manager set the price of the remaining shirts at $23. This price change constitutes a **markup cancellation of $2** and a **$7 markdown**. If the shirts are later priced at $24, a **markdown cancellation of $1** occurs.

Retail Inventory Method with Markups and Markdowns—Conventional Method

To determine the ending inventory figures using the retail inventory method, a decision must be made on the treatment of markups, markup cancellations, markdowns, and markdown cancellations **when calculating the ratio of cost to retail**.

To illustrate the different possibilities, consider the data for In-Fashion Stores Inc., shown in Illustration 9-20. In-Fashion's ending inventory at cost can be calculated under two different cost-to-retail ratios.

Ratio A: Reflects a cost percentage that includes net markups but excludes net markdowns.

Ratio B: Reflects a cost ratio that incorporates both the net markups and net markdowns.

Illustration 9-20

Retail Inventory Method with Markups and Markdowns: In-Fashion Stores Inc.

Information in Records

	Cost	Retail
Beginning inventory	$ 500	$ 1,000
Purchases (net)	20,000	35,000
Markups		3,000
Markup cancellations		1,000
Markdowns		2,500
Markdown cancellations		2,000
Sales (net)		25,000

Retail Inventory Method

	Cost		Retail
Beginning inventory	$ 500		$ 1,000
Purchases (net)	20,000		35,000
Merchandise available for sale	20,500		36,000
Add:			
Markups		$3,000	
Less: Markup cancellations		(1,000)	
Net markups			2,000
	20,500		38,000
Cost-to-retail ratio $\frac{\$20,500}{\$38,000} = 53.9\%$ .... (A)			
Deduct:			
Markdowns		2,500	
Less: Markdown cancellations		(2,000)	
Net markdowns			500
	$20,500		37,500
Cost-to-retail ratio $\frac{\$20,500}{\$37,500} = 54.7\%$ .... (B)			
Deduct: Sales (net)			25,000
Ending inventory at retail			$12,500

The calculations to determine the cost of ending inventory for In-Fashion Stores are.

Ending inventory at retail × Cost ratio = Ending inventory, at cost
Under **(A)**: $12,500 × 53.9%   = $6,737.50
Under **(B)**: $12,500 × 54.7%   = $6,837.50

Which percentage should be used to calculate the ending inventory? The answer depends on what the ending inventory amount is expected to reflect.

The conventional retail inventory method **uses the cost-to-retail ratio incorporating net markups but excluding net markdowns** as shown in the calculation of **Ratio A. It is designed to approximate the lower of average cost and market, with market being net realizable value less normal profit margin.** To understand why net markups but not net markdowns are included in the cost-to-retail ratio, we must understand how a retail outlet operates. When a company has a net markup on an item, it normally indicates that the item's market value has increased. On the other hand, if the item has a net markdown, it means that the item's utility has declined. Therefore, to approximate the lower of cost and market, net markdowns are considered a current loss and are not included in calculating the cost-to-retail ratio. **This makes the denominator a larger number and the ratio a lower percentage.** With a lower cost-to-retail ratio, the result approximates a lower of cost and market amount.

To help clarify, assume two different items were purchased for $5 each, and the original sales price was established at $10 each. One item was subsequently marked down to a selling price of $2. Assuming no sales for the period, if markdowns are included in the cost-to-retail ratio (**Ratio B** above), the ending inventory is calculated as shown in Illustration 9-21.

Illustration 9-21

Retail Inventory Method Including Markdowns— Cost Method

	Markdowns Included in Cost-to-Retail Ratio		
		Cost	Retail
Purchases		$10.00	$20.00
Deduct: Markdowns			8.00
Ending inventory, at retail			$12.00

Cost-to-retail ratio $\dfrac{\$10.00}{\$12.00} = 83.3\%$

Ending inventory at average cost ($12.00 × .833) = $10.00

This approach is the **cost method.** It results in ending inventory at the average cost of the two items on hand without considering the loss on the one item.

If markdowns are excluded from the ratio (**Ratio A** above), the result is ending inventory at the lower of average cost and market. The calculation is shown in Illustration 9-22.

Illustration 9-22

Real Inventory Method Excluding Markdowns— Conventional Method (LCM)

	Markdowns Not Included in Cost-to-Retail Ratio		
		Cost	Retail
Purchases		$10.00	$20.00

Cost-to-retail ratio $\dfrac{\$10.00}{\$20.00} = 50\%$

Deduct: Markdowns			8.00
Ending inventory, at retail			$12.00

Ending inventory at lower of average cost and market ($12 × .50) = $6.00

The $6 inventory valuation includes two inventory items, onc inventoried at $5 and the other at $1. Basically, for the item with the market decline, the sales price was reduced from $10 to $2 and the cost reduced from $5 to $1.[12] Therefore, to approximate the lower of average cost and market, the cost-to-retail ratio must be established by dividing the cost of goods available by the sum of the original retail price of these goods plus the net markups; the net markdowns are excluded from the ratio.

The basic format for the retail inventory method using the conventional approach and the In-Fashion Stores Inc. information is shown in Illustration 9-23.

Illustration 9-23

Comprehensive Conventional Retail Inventory Method Example

In-Fashion Stores Inc.

	Cost		Retail
Beginning inventory	$ 500		$ 1,000
Purchases (net)	20,000		35,000
Totals	20,500		36,000
Add: Net markups			
Markups		$3,000	
Markup cancellations		(1,000)	2,000
Totals	$20,500		38,000
Deduct: Net markdowns			
Markdowns		2,500	
Markdown cancellations		(2,000)	500
Goods available, at retail			37,500
Deduct: Sales (net)			25,000
Ending inventory, at retail			$12,500

$$\text{Cost-to-retail ratio} = \frac{\text{Cost of goods available}}{\text{Original retail price of goods available, plus net markups}}$$

$$= \frac{\$20,500}{\$38,000} = 53.9\%$$

Ending inventory at lower of average cost and market (53.9% × $12,500) $6,737.50

Many possible cost-to-retail ratios could be calculated, depending upon whether or not the beginning inventory, net markups, and net markdowns are included. The schedule below summarizes some inventory valuation methods approximated by the inclusion or exclusion of various items in the cost-to-retail ratio, given that net purchases are always included in the ratio.

Beginning Inventory	Net Markups	Net Markdowns	Inventory Valuation Method Approximated
Include	Include	Include	Average cost
Include	Include	Exclude	Lower of average cost and market (conventional method)
Exclude	Include	Include	FIFO cost
Exclude	Include	Exclude	Lower of FIFO cost and market

---

[12] The conventional method defines market as net realizable value less the normal profit margin. In other words, the sale price of the item marked down is $2, but after subtracting a normal profit of 50% of selling price, the inventoriable amount becomes $1.

Using the FIFO method, the estimated ending inventory (and its cost) will, by definition, come from the purchases of the current period. **Therefore, the opening inventory, at cost and retail, is excluded in determining the cost ratio.** The retail price of the opening inventory is added subsequently to determine the total selling price of goods available for the period.

Special Items Relating to Retail Method

The retail inventory method becomes more complicated when such items as freight-in, purchase returns and allowances, and purchase discounts are involved. **Freight costs** are treated as a part of the purchase cost. **Purchase returns and allowances** are ordinarily considered a reduction of the cost price and retail price and **purchase discounts** usually are considered a reduction of the purchases' cost. In short, the treatment for the items affecting the cost column of the retail inventory approach follows the calculation of cost of goods available for sale.

Note also that **sales returns and allowances** are considered proper adjustments to gross sales; **sales discounts to customers**, however, are not recognized when sales are recorded gross. To adjust for the Sales Discount account in such a situation would provide an ending inventory figure at retail that would be overvalued.

In addition, a number of special items require careful analysis. **Transfers-in** from another department, for example, are reported in the same way as purchases from an outside enterprise. **Normal shortages** (breakage, damage, theft, shrinkage) reduce the retail column because these goods are no longer available for sale. Such costs are reflected in the selling price because a certain amount of shortage is considered normal in a retail enterprise. As a result, this amount is not considered in calculating the cost-to-retail percentage. Rather, it is shown as a deduction similar to sales to arrive at ending inventory at retail. **Abnormal shortages** are deducted from both the cost and retail columns prior to calculating the cost-to-retail ratio and reported as a special inventory amount or as a loss. To do otherwise distorts the cost-to-retail ratio and overstates ending inventory. Finally, companies often provide their employees with special discounts to encourage loyalty, better performance, and so on. **Employee discounts** are deducted from the retail column in the same way as sales. These discounts should not be considered in the cost-to-retail percentage because they do not reflect an overall change in the selling price.

Illustration 9-24 shows some of these treatments in more detail, using the conventional retail inventory method to determine the ending inventory.

	Cost	Retail
Beginning inventory	$ 1,000	$ 1,800
Purchases	30,000	60,000
Freight-in	600	—
Purchase returns	(1,500)	(3,000)
Totals	30,100	58,800
Net markups		9,000
Abnormal shrinkage	(1,200)	(2,000)
Totals	$28,900	65,800
Deduct:		
Net markdowns		1,400
Sales	$36,000	
Sales returns	(900)	35,100
Employee discounts		800
Normal shrinkage		1,300
Ending inventory at retail		$27,200

Cost-to-retail ratio $\dfrac{\$28,900}{\$65,800} = 43.9\%$

Ending inventory, lower of average cost and market (43.9% × $27,200) = $11,940.80

Illustration 9-24

Conventional Retail Inventory Method— Special Items Included

Evaluation of Retail Inventory Method

The retail inventory method of calculating inventory is used:

1. to permit the calculation of net income without a physical count of inventory,

2. as a control measure in determining inventory shortages,

3. in controlling quantities of merchandise on hand, and

4. as a source of information for insurance and tax purposes.

One characteristic of the retail inventory method is that it **has an averaging effect for varying rates of gross profit**. When applied to an entire business where rates of gross profit vary among departments, no allowance is made for possible distortion of results because of these differences. Many companies refine the retail method under such conditions by calculating inventory separately by departments or by classes of merchandise with similar rates of gross profit. In addition, this method's reliability rests on the assumption that the distribution of inventory items is similar to the mix in the total goods available for sale.

DISCLOSURE, PRESENTATION, AND ANALYSIS

Required Disclosures and Presentation of Inventories

Inventories are one of the most significant assets of manufacturing and merchandising enterprises. The *CICA Handbook* requires disclosure of the basis of inventory valuation and a description of the method used to determine cost if it is materially different from recent cost. The standards also require that the basis of inventory valuation be consistently applied. Any change in the basis from that used in the previous period must be reported along with the change's effect on the period's results. It is also desirable that the amounts of the major categories making up the total inventory be disclosed, e.g., finished goods, work in process, and raw materials.

The following excerpts from the financial statements of Canfor Corporation and Magna International Inc. illustrate the presentation of the companies' disclosure of the basis for inventory valuation, the cost flow method, and the definition of market used for the major categories making up the total inventory. It is quite acceptable, as shown in the illustrations, for a company to use different methods for different inventory components. The use of notes is the basic means of disclosing such information. Note that Magna includes a type of inventory (tooling and engineering) that is accounted for under the completed contract method explained in Chapter 6.

10 Objective

Identify required disclosures and explain how inventory is reported and analysed.

International Insight

In Switzerland, inventory may be reported on the balance sheet at amounts substantially (one-third or more) below cost and market due to tax code provisions. Further, Swiss accounting principles do not require any specific disclosures related to inventories.

Illustration 9-25

Inventory Disclosures—Canfor Corporation

(continued)

Consolidated Balance Sheets
In millions of dollars

As at December 31	2002	2001
Assets		
Current assets		
Cash	$ 18.4	$ 8.3
Temporary investments	4.5	24.0
Accounts receivable		
Trade	148.9	176.3
Other	29.7	24.9
Future income taxes (Note 15)	25.4	13.2
Inventories (Note 2)	422.2	411.9
Prepaid expenses	20.7	20.0
Total current assets	**$669.8**	$678.6

Illustration 9-25
(continued)
*Inventory Disclosures—
Canfor Corporation*

1. **Significant Accounting Policies**
   Valuation of Inventories
   Inventories of wood products, pulp and kraft paper are valued at the lower of average cost and net realizable value. Logs and chips are valued at average cost or the greater of net realizable value and replacement cost if lower than average cost. Processing materials and supplies are valued at the lower of average cost and replacement cost.

2. **Inventories**

millions of dollars	2002	2001
Wood products, pulp and kraft paper	$253.5	$215.9
Logs and chips	101.3	127.3
Processing materials and supplies	67.4	68.7
	$422.2	$411.9

Illustration 9-26
*Inventory Disclosures—
Magna International Inc.*

Digital Tool

Student Toolkit—
Additional
Disclosures

www.wiley.com/canada/kieso

Consolidated Balance Sheets
U.S. dollars in millions

As at December 31	Note	2002	2001
Assets			
Current assets			
Cash and cash equivalents		$1,227	$890
Accounts receivable		2,140	1,752
Inventories	11	918	842
Prepaid expenses and other		84	74
		$4,369	$3,558

Significant Accounting Policies

Inventories

Inventories are valued at the lower of cost and net realizable value, with cost being determined substantially on a first-in, first-out basis. Cost includes the cost of materials plus direct labour applied to the product and the applicable share of manufacturing overhead.

11. **Inventories**
    Inventories consist of:

	2002	2001
Raw materials and supplies	$306	$243
Work-in-process	118	106
Finished goods	138	125
Tooling and engineering	356	368
	$918	$842

Tooling and engineering inventory represents costs incurred on separately priced tooling and engineering services contracts in excess of billed and unbilled amounts included in accounts receivable.

Perspectives

IAS Note

SIC (Interpretation) 1 states that the same cost formula (such as FIFO or weighted average) should be used for all inventories having the same characteristics.

Because the amount of inventory that a company carries can have significant economic consequences, it is crucial that inventories be managed effectively. Inventory management, however, is a double-edged sword. On the one hand, management wants to have a wide variety and high quantities on hand so customers have the greatest selection and always find what they want in stock. On the other hand, such an inventory policy may result in excessive carrying costs (e.g., investment, storage, insurance, taxes, obsolescence, and damage). Low inventory levels, which incur minimum carrying costs, lead to stockouts, lost sales, and disgruntled customers. Financial ratios can be used to help management chart a middle course between these two dangers and to help investors assess management's performance. Common ratios used to evaluate inventory levels are inventory turnover and a related measure, average days to sell the inventory.

The **inventory turnover ratio** measures the number of times on average the inventory was sold during the period. Its purpose is to measure the liquidity of the investment in inventory. A manager may use past turnover experience to determine how long the inventory now in stock will take to be sold. The inventory turnover is calculated by dividing the cost of goods sold by the average inventory on hand during the period. Unless seasonal factors are significant, average inventory can be calculated from the beginning and ending inventory balances.[13] For example, in its 2002 annual report, Tesma International Inc. reported a beginning inventory of $93,735 thousand, an ending inventory of $105,829 thousand, and cost of goods sold of $1,047,294 thousand for the year. The calculation of the 2002 inventory turnover of Tesma International is shown below.

$$\text{Inventory Turnover} = \frac{\text{Cost of Goods Sold}}{\text{Average Inventory}}$$

$$= \frac{\$1,047,294}{\dfrac{\$93,735 + \$105,829}{2}}$$

$$= 10.5 \text{ times}$$

Illustration 9-27

Inventory Turnover Ratio

A variant of the inventory turnover ratio is the **average days to sell inventory**, which represents the average age of the inventory on hand or the number of days it takes to sell inventory once purchased. For example, if Tesma International's inventory turns over 10.5 times per year, that means it takes, on average, 365 days divided by 10.5 or approximately 35 days to sell its average investment in inventory.

In Canada, companies are not required to disclose separately the amount of cost of goods sold. Corporate management has so far successfully fought against such disclosure on the basis that public disclosure of cost of goods sold and gross profit on sales would provide company-specific pricing information to competitors. Most public companies, therefore, combine cost of goods sold with other selling and administrative expenses and report an aggregate number.[14] This makes it difficult to calculate the inventory turnover. Some analysts attempt to measure something similar by using Sales as the numerator. This is not a very good proxy for Cost of Goods Sold because Sales includes the markup or profit as well as the cost of the items sold. However, consistent use of this less-than-perfect ratio can provide insights into trends and permit inter-company comparisons if used across the board.

Is Tesma's a good turnover ratio? If the company sells fresh fruit and vegetables, you would know that this is not a good number. However, for other products, it is not as easy to come to a firm conclusion. (Tesma provides components and systems to the automotive industry.) Each industry has its norms, so the industry average is one standard against which the company's ratio could be compared. Because the choice of inventory cost flow method may significantly affect the inventory reported on the balance sheet and the cost of goods sold, such differences would require adjustment in any inter-company comparisons. This holds true, not only for turnover ratios, but any analysis that includes inventory: amount of working capital, working capital ratio, and the gross profit percentage, for example. Internally, company management compares these numbers with what they had budgeted and set as objectives for the year.

There is no absolute standard of comparison for most ratios, but generally speaking, companies that are able to keep their inventory at lower levels with higher turnovers than those of their competitors, and still satisfy customer needs, are the most successful.

---

[13] Some seasonality is common in most companies. The fiscal year end is usually chosen at a low activity point in the year's operations, so that inventories in the annual financial statements are usually at one of the lowest levels in the year. Internally, management has access to additional information and can adjust to use the average monthly inventory level. External users, without access to monthly financial reports, are limited to using the average between the opening and closing annual inventory balances. Public companies are required to report to shareholders on a quarterly basis. In this case, the average can be based on five data points.

[14] Some companies do provide additional information in the Management Discussion & Analysis, however.

Digital Tool

Glossary

www.wiley.com/canada/kieso

KEY TERMS

allowance method, 457
average days to sell
    inventory, 473
conventional retail
    inventory method, 468
cost-to-retail ratio, 465
designated market
    value, 455
direct method, 457
gross profit method, 462
gross profit
    percentage, 463
hedging, 461
indirect method, 457
inventory turnover
    ratio, 473
lower of cost and market
    (LCM), 454
markdown
    cancellations, 466
markdowns, 466
market (for LCM), 451
markup, 466
markup on cost, 463
markup cancellations, 466
net markdowns, 466
net markups, 466
net realizable value
    (NRV), 451
net realizable value
    less a normal profit
    margin, 451
purchase
    commitments, 460
replacement cost, 451
retail inventory
    method, 465

Summary of Learning Objectives

1 Recognize that the lower of cost and market (LCM) basis is a departure from the historical cost principle, and understand why this is appropriate.

The lower of cost and market approach is a departure from historical cost. It is justified on the basis that assets in general, and current assets in particular, should not be reported at an amount greater than the cash expected to be realized from their use, sale, or conversion. It is also justified based on the matching principle. Any decline in an asset's utility (represented by a reduction in the future cash flows expected) should be recognized in the accounting period when the loss in utility occurs.

2 Explain various definitions of possible market amounts that may be used when applying lower of cost and market.

Replacement cost is the amount needed to acquire an equivalent item in the normal course of business. Net realizable value is an item's estimated selling price in the ordinary course of business less reasonably predictable future costs to complete and dispose of it. Net realizable value less a normal profit margin is determined by deducting a normal profit margin from an item's net realizable value. All three are acceptable definitions of market, although net realizable value is the one used by a large majority of Canadian companies. The U.S. rules are more prescriptive and require that the middle value be chosen. Some Canadian companies follow this latter approach.

3 Explain how LCM works and how it is determined.

Under the lower of cost and market approach, the cost (specific identification, FIFO, average cost, or LIFO) and market (replacement cost, net realizable value, or net realizable value less a normal profit margin) of inventory are separately determined. The inventory value for the balance sheet is then the lower of the two amounts. The lower of cost and market may be determined on an item-by-item basis, major category basis, or total inventory basis.

4 Know how to account for inventory on the lower of cost and market basis.

If it is determined that market is less than cost, inventory may be written down directly to market (direct method) or the difference may be accounted for in a contra inventory allowance account (indirect or allowance method).

5 Identify when inventories are carried regularly at net realizable value.

Inventories are valued at net realizable value when (1) there is a controlled market with a quoted price applicable to all quantities, and no significant costs of disposal are involved, and (2) the cost figures are too difficult or not possible to obtain.

6 Explain accounting issues related to purchase commitments.

Accounting for purchase commitments is controversial. Some argue that these contracts should be reported as assets and liabilities when the contract is signed; others believe that recognition at the delivery date is more appropriate. Generally, if purchase commitments are significant relative to the company's financial position and operations, they should be disclosed in a note to the financial statements. If a contract requires future payment of a price in excess of market value at the balance sheet date, the contingent loss should be recognized.

7 Estimate ending inventory by applying the gross profit method.

The steps in estimating ending inventory by applying the gross profit method are as follows: (1) calculate the gross profit percentage, (2) calculate gross profit by multiplying net sales by the gross profit percentage, (3) calculate cost of goods sold by subtracting gross profit from net sales, and (4) calculate ending inventory by subtracting cost of goods sold from total cost of goods available for sale.

8 Explain the limitations of the gross profit method.

Care must be taken in applying the gross profit method. The resulting estimate of ending inventory is only as good as the gross profit percentage is appropriate to the current period's mix of sales and operations.

9 Estimate ending inventory by applying the retail inventory method.

The retail inventory method is based on multiplying the retail price of ending inventory (determined by a count or from the accounting records) by a cost-to-retail percentage (derived from information in the accounting and supplementary records). To apply the retail inventory method, records must be kept of the costs and retail prices for beginning inventory, net purchases, and abnormal spoilage, as well as the retail amount of net markups, net markdowns, and net sales. Which items go into the numerator and denominator of the cost-to-retail ratio depends on the type of inventory valuation estimate desired.

10 Identify required disclosures and explain how inventory is reported and analysed.

Disclosure of the basis of inventory valuation and any change in the basis are required by the *CICA Handbook*. Also, it is desirable to disclose major categories of inventory, the method used to determine cost, and the definition of market applied under the lower of cost and market method. Common ratios used in the management and evaluation of inventory levels are inventory turnover and a related measure: average days to sell the inventory, often called the average age of inventory.

Brief Exercises

BE9-1 Presented below is information related to Lovemore Inc.'s inventory at its fiscal year end.

(per unit)	Skis	Boots	Parkas
Historical cost (FIFO basis)	$190.00	$106.00	$53.00
Selling price	217.00	145.00	73.75
Cost to distribute	19.00	8.00	2.50
Current replacement cost	203.00	105.00	51.00
Normal profit margin	40%	25%	30%
Number of units	30	40	25

Determine (a) the net realizable value per unit and (b) the net realizable value less a normal profit margin per unit of each of the items in Lovemore's inventory.

BE9-2 Refer to the information provided for Lovemore Inc. in BE9-1. Assuming Lovemore values ending inventory at LCM using a "net realizable value" definition of market based on total inventory, determine the appropriate inventory value for the year-end balance sheet.

BE9-3 Refer to the information provided for Lovemore Inc. in BE9-1 and BE9-2. Assuming Lovemore values ending inventory at LCM using a "net realizable value less normal profit margin" definition of market based on individual items, determine the appropriate inventory value for the year-end balance sheet. Is this materially different from the result obtained in BE9-2?

BE9-4 Robin Corporation has the following four items in its ending inventory.

Item	Cost	Replacement Cost	Net Realizable Value (NRV)	NRV Less Normal Profit Margin
Jokers	$2,000	$1,900	$2,100	$1,600
Penguins	5,000	5,100	4,950	4,100
Riddlers	4,400	4,550	4,625	3,700
Scarecrows	3,200	2,990	3,830	3,070

Determine the total lower of cost and market inventory value for the ending inventory using the most widely used Canadian approach applied on a total inventory basis.

BE9-5 Battle Inc. uses a perpetual inventory system. At January 1, 2005, inventory was $214,000 at both cost and market value. At December 31, 2005, the inventory was $286,000 at cost and $269,000 at market value. Prepare the necessary December 31 entry under (a) the direct method and (b) the indirect method.

BE9-6 Golden Enterprises Ltd.'s records reported an inventory cost of $45,600 and a market value of $44,000 at December 31, 2004. At December 31, 2005, the records indicated a cost of $57,200 and a market value of $54,000. If Golden Enterprises uses a perpetual inventory system, prepare the necessary December 31, 2005 entry under (a) the direct method and (b) the indirect method.

BE9-7 Refer to the information provided about Golden Enterprises in BE9-6. Assume at December 31, 2006 the records indicate inventory with a cost of $60,000 and a market value of $60,900. Prepare the necessary December 31, 2006 entry under (a) the direct method and (b) the indirect method.

BE9-8 Beaver Corp. signed a long-term noncancellable purchase commitment with a major supplier to purchase raw materials in 2006 at a cost of $1 million. At December 31, 2005, the raw materials to be purchased have a market value of $930,000. Prepare any necessary December 31 entry.

BE9-9 Use the information for Beaver Corp. from BE9-8. In 2006, Beaver paid $1 million to obtain the raw materials, which were worth $930,000. Prepare the entry to record the purchase.

BE9-10 Big Hunt Corporation's April 30 inventory was destroyed by fire. January 1 inventory was $150,000, and purchases for January through April totalled $500,000. Sales for the same period were $700,000. Big Hunt's normal gross profit percentage is 31%. Using the gross profit method, estimate Big Hunt's April 30 inventory that was destroyed by fire.

BE9-11 Refer to the information for Big Hunt Corporation in BE9-10. Assume that instead of a 31% gross profit rate, Big Hunt's markup on cost is 100%. Using the gross profit method, estimate Big Hunt's April 30 inventory that was destroyed by fire.

BE9-12 Bikini Inc. had beginning inventory of $12,000 at cost and $20,000 at retail. Net purchases were $120,000 at cost and $170,000 at retail. Net markups were $10,000; net markdowns were $7,000; and sales were $157,000. Calculate ending inventory at cost using the conventional retail method.

BE9-13 In its 2002 Annual Report, Costco Wholesale Corporation reported inventory of $3,127.2 million at the end of its 2002 fiscal year, $2,738.5 million at the end of its 2001 fiscal year, cost of goods sold of $33,983.1 million, and net sales of $37,993.1 million for fiscal year 2002. Calculate Costco's inventory turnover and the average days to sell inventory for the fiscal year 2002.

Exercises

E9-1 **(Lower of Cost and Market)** The inventory of 3T Corporation on December 31, 2005 consists of the following items.

Part No.	Quantity	Cost per Unit	Net Realizable Value per Unit
110	600	$ 90	$100
111	1,000	60	52
112	500	80	76
113	200	170	180
120	400	205	208
121[a]	1,600	16	?
122	300	240	235

[a]Part No. 121 is obsolete and has a realizable value of $0.20 each as scrap.

Instructions

(a) Determine the December 31, 2005 balance sheet value of inventory using the lower of cost and market method on an individual item basis.

(b) Determine the December 31, 2005 balance sheet value of inventory using the lower of cost and market method applied to the inventory total.

E9-2 (Lower of Cost and Market) Singing Pump Corp. uses the lower of cost and market method on an individual item basis in pricing its inventory items. The inventory at December 31, 2005 consists of products D, E, F, G, H, and I. Relevant per-unit data for these products appear below.

	Item D	Item E	Item F	Item G	Item H	Item I
Estimated selling price	$120	$110	$95	$90	$110	$90
Cost	75	80	80	80	50	36
Replacement cost	120	72	70	30	70	30
Estimated selling expense	30	30	30	25	30	30
Normal profit	20	20	20	20	20	20

Instructions

Using the lower of cost and market rule, determine the proper unit value for balance sheet reporting purposes at December 31, 2005 for each inventory item above using (1) the most commonly used Canadian definition of market and (2) the U.S. rules to determine market.

E9-3 (Lower of Cost and Market) Bollo Ltd. follows the practice of pricing its inventory at the lower of cost and market on an individual item basis.

Item No.	Quantity	Cost per Unit	Cost to Replace	Estimated Selling Price	Cost of Completion and Disposal	Normal Profit
1320	1,200	$3.20	$3.00	$4.50	$.35	$1.25
1333	900	2.70	2.30	3.50	.50	.50
1426	800	4.50	3.70	5.00	.40	1.00
1437	1,000	3.60	3.10	3.20	.25	.90
1510	700	2.25	2.00	3.25	.80	.60
1522	500	3.00	2.70	3.80	.40	.50
1573	3,000	1.80	1.60	2.50	.75	.50
1626	1,000	4.70	5.20	6.00	.50	1.00

Instructions

(a) From the information above, determine the amount of Bollo's inventory assuming use of (1) the most commonly used definition of market in Canadian practice and (2) U.S. rules to determine market.

(b) Assume that the item number identifies different categories of inventory, for example, 1300, 1400, 1500, and 1600 categories. Determine the amount of Bollo's inventory assuming (1) the most commonly used definition of market in Canadian practice and (2) U.S. rules to determine market, both applied to categories of inventory rather than individual items.

(c) Briefly explain why one method (individual basis versus categories) is more conservative than the other.

E9-4 (Lower of Cost and Market, Periodic Method—Journal Entries) As a result of its annual inventory count, Zinck Corp. determined its ending inventory at cost and at lower of cost and market at December 31, 2004 and December 31, 2005. This information is presented below.

	Cost	Lower of Cost and Market
12/31/04	$346,000	$327,000
12/31/05	410,000	395,000

Instructions

(a) Prepare the journal entries required at 12/31/04 and 12/31/05 assuming that the inventory is recorded directly at market, and a periodic inventory system is used.

(b) Prepare journal entries required at 12/31/04 and 12/31/05, assuming that the inventory is recorded at cost and an allowance account is adjusted at each year end under a periodic system.

(c) Which of the two methods above provides the higher net income in each year?

E9-5   (Lower of Cost and Market, Perpetual Method—Journal Entries)   Refer to the information in E9-4 for Zinck Corp. Assume that Zinck uses a perpetual inventory system and the allowance or indirect method of adjusting to LCM. The balances in the inventory cost accounts before the inventory count were $348,000 and $405,000 at December 31, 2004 and 2005, respectively.

Instructions

Prepare the necessary adjusting entries required at December 31, 2004 and 2005 for Zinck Corp.

E9-6   (Lower of Cost and Market Valuation Account)   Presented below is information related to Candlebox Enterprises Ltd.

	Jan. 31	Feb. 28	Mar. 31	Apr. 30
Inventory at cost	$15,000	$15,100	$17,000	$13,000
Inventory at the lower of cost and market	14,500	12,600	15,600	12,300
Purchases for the month		20,000	24,000	26,500
Sales for the month		29,000	35,000	40,000

Instructions

(a) From the information, prepare (as far as the data permit) monthly income statements in columnar form for February, March, and April. Show the inventory in the statement at cost, show the gain or loss due to market fluctuations separately, and set up a valuation account for the difference between cost and the lower of cost and market.

(b) Prepare the journal entry required to establish the valuation account at January 31 and entries to adjust it monthly thereafter.

E9-7   (Lower of Cost and Market Error Effect)   Oickle Corporation uses the lower of FIFO cost and net realizable value method, on an individual item basis, applying the direct method. The inventory at December 31, 2005 included product MX. Relevant per-unit data for product MX appear below:

Estimated selling price	$45
Cost	40
Replacement cost	35
Estimated selling expense	14
Normal profit	9

There were 1,000 units of product MX on hand at December 31, 2005. Product MX was incorrectly valued at $35 per unit for reporting purposes. All 1,000 units were sold in 2006.

Instructions

(a) Was net income for 2005 over or understated? By how much (ignore income tax aspects)?

(b) Was net income for 2006 over or understated? By how much?

(c) Indicate whether the current ratio, inventory turnover ratio, and debt-to-total asset ratio would be overstated, understated, or not affected for the years ended December 31, 2005 and December 31, 2006. Explain briefly.

E9-8   (Cost Allocation and LCM)   During 2005, Trainor Furniture Limited purchased a carload of wicker chairs. The manufacturer sold the chairs to Trainor for a lump sum of $59,850, because it was discontinuing manufacturing operations and wished to dispose of its entire stock. Three types of chairs are included in the carload. The three types and the estimated selling price for each are listed below.

Type	No. of Chairs	Estimated Selling Price Each
Lounge chairs	400	$90
Armchairs	300	80
Straight chairs	700	50

Trainor estimates that the costs to sell this inventory would amount to $2 per chair. During 2005, Trainor sells 350 lounge chairs, 210 armchairs, and 120 straight chairs, all at the same prices as estimated. At December 31, 2005, the remaining chairs were put on sale: the lounge chairs at 25% off the regular price, the armchairs at 30% off, and the straight chairs at 40% off. All were expected to be sold at these prices.

Instructions

(a) What is the total cost of the chairs remaining in inventory at the end of 2005?

(b) What is the net realizable value of the chairs remaining in inventory?

(c) What is the appropriate inventory value to be reported on the December 31, 2005 balance sheet assuming LCM is applied on an individual item basis?

E9-9 **(Purchase Commitments)**   Chunmei Corp. has been having difficulty obtaining key raw materials for its manufacturing process. The company therefore signed a long-term noncancellable purchase commitment with its largest supplier of this raw material on November 30, 2005 at an agreed price of $400,000. At December 31, 2005, the raw material had declined in price to $365,000. It was further anticipated that the price will drop another $15,000 so that, at the date of delivery, the inventory value will be $350,000.

Instructions

(a) What entry would you make on December 31, 2005 to recognize these facts? Explain.

(b) What entry would you make if the price was expected to recover $15,000 before the date of delivery, so that the inventory value will be $380,000? Explain.

E9-10 **(Purchase Commitments)**   At December 31, 2005, Indigo Ltd. has outstanding noncancellable purchase commitments for 36,000 litres, at $3.00 per litre, of raw material to be used in its manufacturing process. The company prices its raw material inventory at cost or market, whichever is lower.

Instructions

(a) Assuming that the market price as of December 31, 2005 is $3.30 per litre, how would this commitment be treated in the accounts and statements? Explain.

(b) Assuming that the market price as of December 31, 2005 is $2.70 per litre instead of $3.30, how would you treat this commitment in the accounts and statements?

(c) Provide the entry in January 2006, when the 36,000 litre shipment is received, assuming that the situation given in (b) existed at December 31, 2005, and that the market price in January 2006 is $2.70 per litre. Give an explanation of your treatment.

E9-11 **(Gross Profit Method)**   Each of the following percentages is expressed in terms of markup on cost.

1. 20%	**3.** 33 1/3%
2. 25%	**4.** 50%

Interactive
Homework

Instructions

Indicate the gross profit percentage for each of the above.

E9-12 **(Gross Profit Method)**   Terry Arthur Company Limited uses the gross profit method to estimate inventory for monthly reporting purposes. Presented below is information for the month of May.

Interactive
Homework

Inventory, May 1	$160,000
Purchases	640,000
Freight-in	30,000
Sales	1,000,000
Sales returns	70,000
Purchase discounts	12,000

Instructions

(a) Calculate the estimated inventory at May 31, assuming that the gross profit is 30% of sales.

(b) Calculate the estimated inventory at May 31, assuming that the markup on cost is 30%.

E9-13 **(Gross Profit Method)**   Tim Cheng requires an estimate of the cost of goods lost by fire on March 9. Merchandise on hand on January 1 was $38,000. Purchases since January 1 were $72,000; freight-in, $3,400; purchase returns and allowances, $2,400. Sales are made at a markup of 33 1/3% on cost and totalled $100,000 to March 9. Goods costing $10,900 were left undamaged by the fire; the remaining goods were destroyed.

Instructions

(a) Estimate the cost of goods destroyed.

(b) Estimate the cost of goods destroyed, assuming that the gross profit is 33 1/3% of sales.

E9-14   (Gross Profit Method)   Rashid Corp. lost most of its inventory in a fire in December just before the year-end physical inventory was taken. The corporation's books disclosed the following.

Beginning inventory	$340,000	Sales	$1,300,000
Purchases for the year	780,000	Sales returns	48,000
Purchase returns	60,000	Gross margin on sales	40%

Merchandise with a selling price of $42,000 remained undamaged after the fire. Damaged merchandise with an original selling price of $30,000 had a net realizable value of $10,600.

Instructions
Calculate the amount lost due to the fire, assuming that the corporation had no insurance coverage.

E9-15   (Gross Profit Method)   You are called by Brenda Madden of Vision Corp. on July 22 and asked to prepare an insurance claim resulting from a theft that took place the night before. You suggest that an inventory be taken immediately. The following data are available.

Inventory, July 1	38,000
Purchases—goods placed in stock July 1-21	80,000
Goods purchased—in transit, f.o.b. shipping	
point, received July 22	5,000
Sales—goods delivered to customers	116,000
Sales returns—goods returned to stock	4,000

Your client reports that the goods on hand on July 22 prior to receipt of the goods in transit cost $30,500, but you determine that this figure includes goods held on consignment of $4,500. Your past records show that sales are made at approximately 40% above cost.

Instructions
Calculate the claim against the insurance company.

E9-16   (Gross Profit Method)   Chernin Lumber Ltd. handles three principal lines of merchandise with these varying rates of markup on cost.

Lumber	25%
Millwork	30%
Hardware and fittings	40%

On August 18, a fire destroyed the office, lumber shed, and a considerable portion of the lumber stacked in the yard. To file a report of loss for insurance purposes, the company must know what the inventories were immediately preceding the fire. No detail or perpetual inventory records of any kind were maintained. The only pertinent information you are able to obtain is the following facts from the general ledger, which was kept in a fireproof vault and thus escaped destruction.

	Lumber	Millwork	Hardware
Inventory, Jan. 1, 2005	$ 250,000	$ 90,000	$ 45,000
Purchases to Aug. 18, 2005	1,500,000	375,000	160,000
Sales to Aug. 18, 2005	2,080,000	533,000	210,000

Instructions
Submit your estimate of the inventory amounts immediately preceding the fire.

E9-17   (Gross Profit Method)   Mahon Corporation's retail store and warehouse had been closed down for the entire weekend while the year-end inventory was counted. The controller gathered all the count books and information from the clerical staff, completed the ending inventory calculations, and prepared the following partial income statement for the general manager for Monday morning.

Sales		$2,500,000
Beginning inventory	$ 600,000	
Purchases	1,500,000	
Total goods available for sale	2,100,000	
Less ending inventory	550,000	
Cost of goods sold		1,550,000
Gross profit		$ 950,000

The general manager called the controller into her office after quickly reviewing the preliminary statements. "You've made an error in the inventory," she stated. "My pricing all year has been carefully controlled to provide a gross profit of 40%, and I know the sales are correct."

Instructions

(a) How much should the ending inventory have been?

(b) If this was due to error, suggest where the error might have occurred.

E9-18 (Retail Inventory Method) Presented below is information related to Gleneau Corporation.

	Cost	Retail
Beginning inventory	$ 58,000	$100,000
Purchases (net)	122,000	200,000
Net markups		10,345
Net markdowns		26,135
Sales		186,000

Instructions

(a) Calculate the ending inventory at retail.

(b) Calculate a cost-to-retail percentage (round to two decimals):

  1. excluding both markups and markdowns

  2. excluding markups but including markdowns

  3. excluding markdowns but including markups

  4. including both markdowns and markups

(c) Which of the methods in (b) above (1, 2, 3, or 4):

  1. provides the most conservative estimate of ending inventory?

  2. provides an approximation of lower of cost and market?

  3. is used in the conventional retail method?

(d) Calculate ending inventory at lower of cost and market (round to nearest dollar).

(e) Calculate cost of goods sold based on (d).

(f) Calculate gross margin based on (d).

E9-19 (Retail Inventory Method) Presented below is information related to Salole Limited for its year ended July 31, 2005.

	Cost	Retail
Beginning inventory	$ 200,000	$ 280,000
Purchases	1,375,000	2,140,000
Markups		95,000
Markup cancellations		15,000
Markdowns		35,000
Markdown cancellations		5,000
Sales		2,200,000

Instructions

(a) Estimate the July 31, 2005 inventory by the conventional retail inventory method.

(b) If a physical count of the inventory determined that the actual ending inventory at retail prices at July 31, 2005 was $250,000, estimate the loss due to shrinkage and theft.

E9-20 (Retail Inventory Method) The records of Elena's Boutique report the following data for the month of April.

Sales	$99,000	Purchases (at cost)	$48,000
Sales returns	2,000	Purchases (at sales price)	88,000
Additional markups	10,000	Purchase returns (at cost)	2,000
Markup cancellations	1,500	Purchase returns (at sales price)	3,000
Markdowns	9,300	Beginning inventory (at cost)	30,000
Markdown cancellations	2,800	Beginning inventory (at sales price)	46,500
Freight on purchases	2,400		

Instructions

(a) Estimate the ending inventory by the conventional retail inventory method.

(b) Identify four reasons why the estimate of inventory may differ from the actual inventory at cost.

E9-21   (Retail Inventory Method—Conventional and Average Cost)   A. Randall Smith Limited began operations on January 1, 2005, adopting the conventional retail inventory system. None of its merchandise was marked down in 2005 and, because there was no beginning inventory, the ending inventory for 2005 of $38,100 would have been the same under either the conventional retail system or the average cost system. All pertinent data regarding purchases, sales, markups, and markdowns are shown below.

Interactive
Homework

	Cost	Retail
Inventory, Jan. 1, 2006	$ 38,100	$ 60,000
Markdowns (net)		13,000
Markups (net)		22,000
Purchases (net)	130,900	178,000
Sales (net)		167,000

Instructions

Determine the cost of the 2006 ending inventory under (a) the conventional retail method and (b) the average cost retail method.

E9-22   (Retail Inventory Method—Conventional and Lower of FIFO Cost and Market) Clilverd Corp. began operations late in 2004 and adopted the conventional retail inventory method. Because there was no beginning inventory for 2004 and no markdowns during 2004, the ending inventory for 2004 was $14,000 under both the conventional retail method and the lower of FIFO cost and market retail method.

At the end of 2005, management wants to compare the results of applying the conventional method, which assumes the lower of average cost and market with a lower of FIFO cost and market method. The following data are available for calculations.

	Cost	Retail
Inventory, January 1, 2005	$14,000	$20,000
Sales		80,000
Net markups		9,000
Net markdowns		1,600
Purchases	58,800	81,000
Freight-in	7,500	
Estimated theft		2,000

Instructions

Calculate the value of the 2005 ending inventory under both (a) the conventional retail method and (b) the lower of FIFO cost and market retail method.

E9-23   (Analysis of Inventories)   The financial statements of The Forzani Group Ltd. for the 53 weeks ended February 2, 2003 and the 52 weeks ended January 27, 2002 and January 28, 2001 disclose the following information.

(in $000)	Feb. 2, 2003	Jan. 27, 2002	Jan. 28, 2001
Inventory	$268,519	$229,270	$157,923

	53/52 weeks ended	
	Feb. 2, 2003	Jan. 27, 2002
Sales	$923,795	$758,257
Gross margin	320,469	260,499
Net income	30,531	20,629

Instructions

(a) Calculate Forzani Group's (1) inventory turnover and (2) the average days to sell inventory for the two years ending in 2003 and 2002.

(b) Calculate Forzani Group's gross profit percentage and percentage markup on cost for each fiscal year.

(c) Is the growth in inventory levels over the last year consistent with its increase in sales?

E9-24 **(Ratios)** Partial information is provided about a Canadian manufacturing company.

	Year 6	Year 5	Year 4
Sales	$19,331.9	$_____	$11,870.0
Cost of goods sold	_____	8,701.5	7,881.1
Gross margin	_____	2,739.8	
Ending inventory	1,877.8	_____	$ 1,341.0
Gross profit %	24.9%	_____	_____
Inventory turnover	6.85	_____	
Days sales in inventory	_____	_____	

Instructions

(a) Complete the schedule above where indicated for Years 4, 5, and 6.

(b) Comment on the profitability and inventory management trends, suggesting possible reasons for these results.

Problems

P9-1 The Pendse Wood Corporation manufactures desks. Most of the company's desks are standard models sold at catalogue prices. At December 31, 2005, the following finished desks appear in the company's inventory.

Finished Desks—Type	A	B	C	D
2005 catalogue selling price	$460	$490	$890	$1,040
FIFO cost per inventory list 12/31/05	410	450	830	960
Estimated current cost to manufacture				
(at December 31, 2005 and early 2006)	460	440	790	1,000
Sales commissions and estimated other costs				
of disposal	45	60	90	130
2006 catalogue selling price	550	550	870	1,210
Quantity on hand	5	17	13	10

The 2005 catalogue was in effect through November 2005, and the 2006 catalogue is effective as of December 1, 2005. All catalogue prices are net of the usual discounts. Generally, the company attempts to obtain a 20% gross margin on selling price and has usually been successful in doing so.

Instructions

(a) At what total inventory value will the desks appear on the company's December 31, 2005 balance sheet, assuming that the company has adopted a lower of FIFO cost and market approach for the valuation of inventories, applied on a total inventory basis? Use net realizable value as the definition of market.

(b) Assume 78% of the shares of Pendse Wood were acquired during 2005 by Shripad Inc., a U.S. wood products company. The controller of Shripad advises that, for consolidation purposes, Pendse's inventory valuation methods should be consistent with those of the parent company. Shripad uses the U.S. rules for determining the lower of cost and market, and applies it on an individual item basis. What inventory value should Pendse's controller report to the parent company?

(c) As controller of Pendse, report to its president what the accounting and reporting implications are of using the valuation determined in (b) for reporting under Canadian GAAP.

P9-2 Secord Home Improvement Limited installs replacement siding, windows, and louvered glass doors for single family homes and condominium complexes in southern Ontario. The company is in the process of preparing its annual financial statements for the fiscal year ended May 31, 2005, and Judi MacAskill, controller for Secord, has gathered the following data concerning inventory.

At May 31, 2005, the balance in Secord's Raw Material Inventory account was $408,000, and the Allowance to Reduce Inventory to Market had a credit balance of $29,500. The controller summarized the relevant inventory cost and market data at May 31, 2005 in the schedule below.

Judi MacAskill assigned Michael O'Shea, an intern from a local college, the task of calculating the amount that should appear on Secord's May 31, 2005 financial statements for inventory under the lower of cost and market rule as applied to total inventory. Secord uses a net realizable value definition of market. O'Shea expressed concern over departing from the cost principle.

	Cost	Replacement Cost	Sales Price	Net Realizable Value	Normal Profit
Aluminum siding	$ 70,000	$ 62,500	$ 64,000	$ 56,000	$ 5,100
Cedar shake siding	86,000	79,400	94,000	84,800	7,400
Louvered glass doors	112,000	124,000	186,400	168,300	18,500
Thermal windows	140,000	122,000	154,800	140,000	15,400
Total	$408,000	$387,900	$499,200	$449,100	$46,400

Instructions

(a) Determine the proper balance in the Allowance to Reduce Inventory to LCM account at May 31, 2005 and make the necessary entry to adjust the accounts.

(b) Explain the rationale for using the lower of cost and market rule as it applies to inventories.

(c) Peter Secord, the company president, takes great care in analysing his company's financial statements, and he often compares notes with his cousin, who operates a similar company in northern New York. The use of different accounting methods makes their financial statements less comparable than they otherwise would be. For example, his cousin uses the standard U.S. approach to the valuation of inventory, and applies it on an item-by-item basis. Determine the impact on Secord Home Improvement's reported income before tax of the two approaches. (Assume a zero balance in the opening Allowance account.)

(d) What other ratios or relationships would also be affected by the different approaches? Explain.

P9-3 Capeland Boats Limited, which began operations in 2002, always values its inventories at current replacement cost. Its annual inventory figure is arrived at by taking a physical count and then pricing each item in the physical inventory at current prices determined from recent vendors' invoices or catalogues. The condensed income statements for the company's past four years are as follows.

	2002	2003	2004	2005
Sales	$850,000	$880,000	$950,000	$990,000
Cost of Goods Sold	560,000	590,000	630,000	650,000
Gross Profit	290,000	290,000	320,000	340,000
Operating expenses	190,000	180,000	200,000	210,000
Income before taxes	$100,000	$110,000	$120,000	$130,000

Instructions

(a) Comment on the procedures Capeland uses for valuing inventories.

(b) Assuming that the inventory at cost and as determined by the corporation (using replacement cost) at the end of each of the four years is as follows, restate the condensed income statements using an acceptable method of inventory valuation.

Year	At Cost	At Replacement Cost
2002	$130,000	$144,000
2003	140,000	158,000
2004	170,000	157,000
2005	150,000	159,000

(c) Compare the trend in income for the four years using the corporation's approach versus using a method acceptable under GAAP for valuing ending inventory. What observations do you make?

P9-4 Fournier Corp. follows the practice of valuing its inventory at the lower of cost and market. The following information is available from the company's inventory records as of December 31, 2005.

Item	Quantity	Unit Cost	Replacement Cost/Unit	Estimated Selling Price/Unit	Completion & Disposal Cost/Unit	Normal Profit Margin/Unit
A	1,100	$7.50	$8.40	$10.50	$1.50	$1.80
B	800	8.20	8.00	9.40	.90	1.20
C	1,000	5.60	5.40	7.20	1.10	.60
D	1,000	3.80	4.20	6.30	.80	1.50
E	1,400	6.40	6.30	6.80	.70	1.00

Instructions

(a) Indicate the inventory amount that should be used for each item under the lower of cost and market rule assuming (1) the definition of market used most commonly in Canada and (2) U.S. rules.

(b) Fournier applies the lower of cost and market rule directly to each item in the inventory but maintains its inventory account at cost to account for the items above. Give the adjusting entry, if one is necessary, to adjust the ending inventory to the lower of cost and market assuming (1) the definition of market used most commonly in Canada and (2) U.S. rules.

(c) Fournier applies the lower of cost and market rule to the inventory total. What is the dollar amount for inventory as of December 31, 2005, assuming (1) the definition of market used most commonly in Canada and (2) U.S. rules?

P9-5   Kile Inc., an audit client of your employer, provided the following information about its inventory at the end of its 2005 fiscal year, November 30, 2005.

	Product Number			
	075936	078310	079104	081111
Selling price per unit, November 30, 2005	$15.00	$23.00	$28.00	$13.00
Standard cost per unit, as included in inventory at November 30, 2005	$ 8.00	$11.25	$14.26	$ 7.40
Number in inventory	5,000	4,500	6,000	5,100

In discussion with Kile's marketing and sales personnel you were told that there would be a general 9% (rounded to the next highest five cents) increase in selling prices, effective December 1, 2005. This increase will affect all products except those having 081 as the first three digits of the product code. The 081 codes are assigned to new product introductions, and for product code 081111, the selling price will be $9.00 effective December 1, 2005.

In addition, you were told by the controller that Kile attempts to earn a 40% gross profit on all its products. From the cost department you obtained the following standard costs, which will be used for fiscal 2006.

Product number	2006 Standard
075936	$ 8.25
078310	$10.75
079104	$14.71
081111	$ 7.51

Sales commissions and estimates of other costs of disposal approximate 25% of fiscal 2006 standard costs to manufacture. Assume that standard costs provide a reasonable approximation of the product's replacement cost.

Instructions

(a) Determine the net realizable value of each item expected for fiscal 2006.

(b) Assuming the net realizable values for (a) are to be used in determining the lower of cost and market valuation for the November 30, 2005 inventory, how and at what amount would the inventory be shown on the balance sheet using an item-by-item approach? A total inventory approach?

(c) When market is lower than cost, why should inventories be reported at market? Why are inventories reported at cost when market is greater than cost?

P9-6   Yaolin Inc. manufactures and sells four products, the inventories of which are carried at the lower of cost and market. A normal profit margin of 30% is usually maintained on each product. The following information was compiled as of December 31, 2005.

Product	Number of Units in Inventory	Original Cost	Cost to Replace	Estimated Cost to Dispose	Expected Selling Price
A	650	$17.50	$14.00	$ 6.00	$ 30.00
B	340	48.00	78.00	26.00	100.00
C	375	35.00	42.00	15.00	80.00
D	190	47.50	45.00	20.50	95.00

Instructions

(a) Why are expected selling prices important in the valuation of inventory at the lower of cost and market?

(b) Prepare a schedule identifying three possible acceptable definitions of market for each product.

(c) Determine the range of acceptable inventory valuations for the December 31, 2005 balance sheet. What would be the effect on Yaolin's 2005 income statement if the highest valuation was chosen instead of the lowest valuation? Explain briefly.

(d) Comment on how a company should choose which combination of alternatives is best for its particular circumstances.

P9-7 The Bateman Company determined its ending inventory at cost and at lower of cost and market at December 31, 2004, December 31, 2005, and December 31, 2006, as shown below.

	Cost	Lower of Cost and Market
12/31/04	$650,000	$650,000
12/31/05	780,000	722,000
12/31/06	900,000	830,000

Instructions

(a) Prepare the journal entries required at 12/31/05 and 12/31/06, assuming that a periodic inventory system and the direct method of adjusting to market is used.

(b) Prepare the journal entries required at 12/31/05 and 12/31/06, assuming that a periodic inventory is recorded at cost and reduced to market through the use of an allowance account.

P9-8 Hasselholf Ltd. lost most of its inventory in a fire in December just before the year-end physical inventory was taken. Corporate records disclose the following.

Inventory (beginning)	$ 80,000	Sales	$415,000
Purchases	280,000	Sales returns	21,000
Purchase returns	28,000	Gross profit on sales	34%

Purchases includes an in-transit shipment from a supplier, shipped f.o.b. shipping point, with an invoice cost of $535. Merchandise on hand with a selling price of $30,000 remained undamaged after the fire, and damaged merchandise has a salvage value of $7,150. The company does not carry fire insurance on its inventory.

Instructions

(a) Prepare a schedule calculating the fire loss incurred by Hasselholf. (Do not use the retail inventory method.)

(b) While the gross profit percentage has averaged 34% over the past five years, it has been as high as 38% and as low as 32%. Given this information, should a range of possible loss be provided instead of a single figure? Comment.

P9-9 On April 15, 2005, fire damaged the office and warehouse of John Kimmel Corporation. The only accounting record saved was the general ledger, from which the trial balance below was prepared.

JOHN KIMMEL CORPORATION
Trial Balance
March 31, 2005

Cash	$ 20,000	
Accounts receivable	40,000	
Inventory, December 31, 2004	75,000	
Land	35,000	
Building and equipment	110,000	
Accumulated amortization		$ 41,300
Other assets	3,600	
Accounts payable		23,700
Other expense accruals		10,200
Common shares		100,000
Retained earnings		52,000
Sales		135,000
Purchases	52,000	
Other expense	26,600	
	$362,200	$362,200

The following data and information have been gathered.

1. The corporation's fiscal year ends on December 31.

2. An examination of the April bank statement and cancelled cheques revealed that cheques written during the period April 1–15 totalled $13,000: $5,700 paid on accounts payable as of March 31, $3,400 for April merchandise shipments, and $3,900 paid for other expenses. Deposits during the same period amounted to $12,950, which consisted of receipts on account from customers with the exception of a $950 refund from a vendor for merchandise returned in April.

3. Correspondence with suppliers revealed unrecorded obligations at April 15 of $10,600 for April merchandise shipments, including $2,300 for shipments in transit (f.o.b. shipping point) on that date.

4. Customers acknowledged indebtedness of $36,000 at April 15, 2005. It was also estimated that customers owed another $8,000 that will never be acknowledged or recovered. Of the acknowledged indebtedness, $600 will probably be uncollectible.

5. The companies insuring the inventory agreed that the corporation's fire-loss claim should be based on the assumption that the overall gross profit ratio for the past two years was in effect during the current year. The corporation's audited financial statements disclosed this information.

	Year Ended December 31	
	2004	2003
Net sales	$530,000	$390,000
Net purchases	280,000	235,000
Beginning inventory	50,000	75,200
Ending inventory	75,000	50,000

6. Inventory with a cost of $7,000 was salvaged and sold for $3,500. The balance of the inventory was a total loss.

Instructions

Prepare a schedule calculating the amount of inventory fire loss. The supporting schedule to calculate the gross profit should be in good form.

(AICPA adapted)

P9-10 The records for the Clothing Department of Dar's Discount Store are summarized below for the month of January.

Inventory, January 1: at retail, $25,000; at cost, $17,000
Purchases in January: at retail, $137,000; at cost, $86,500
Freight-in: $7,000
Purchase returns: at retail, $3,000; at cost, $2,300
Purchase allowances: $2,200
Transfers in from suburban branch: at retail, $13,000; at cost, $9,200
Net markups: $8,000
Net markdowns: $4,000
Inventory losses due to normal breakage, etc.: at retail, $400
Sales at retail: $85,000
Sales returns: $2,400

Instructions

(a) Estimate the inventory for this department as of January 31 at (1) retail and (2) lower of average cost and market.

(b) If a physical inventory count taken at retail prices after the close of business on January 31 indicated an inventory $450 less than estimated in (a) (1), explain what could have caused this discrepancy.

P9-11 Presented below is information related to S. Babcock Inc.

	Cost	Retail
Inventory, 12/31/04	$250,000	$ 390,000
Purchases	914,500	1,460,000
Purchase returns	60,000	80,000
Purchase discounts	18,000	—
Gross sales (after employee discounts)	—	1,460,000
Sales returns	—	97,500
Markups	—	120,000
Markup cancellations	—	40,000
Markdowns	—	45,000
Markdown cancellations	—	20,000
Freight-in	79,000	—
Employee discounts granted	—	8,000
Loss from breakage (normal)	—	2,500

Instructions

(a) Assuming that S. Babcock Inc. uses the conventional retail inventory method, calculate the cost of its ending inventory at December 31, 2005.

(b) A department store using the conventional retail inventory method estimates the ending inventory as $60,000. An accurate physical count reveals only $47,000 of inventory at lower of average cost and market. List the factors that may have caused the difference between the estimated inventory and the physical count.

P9-12   As of January 1, 2005, Akbari Inc. began to use the retail method of accounting for its merchandise inventory. To prepare the store's financial statements at June 30, 2005, you obtain these data.

	Cost	Selling Price
Inventory, January 1	$ 30,000	$ 43,000
Markdowns		10,500
Markups		9,200
Markdown cancellations		6,500
Markup cancellations		3,200
Purchases	108,800	155,000
Sales		159,000
Purchase returns and allowances	2,800	4,000
Sales returns and allowances		8,000

Instructions

(a) Prepare a schedule to calculate Akbari's June 30, 2005 inventory under the conventional retail method of accounting for inventories.

(b) Prepare as much of the income statement as possible for Akbari Inc. for the six months ended June 30, 2005 from the data provided.

(c) Determine the inventory turnover for the six-month period, and the average age of the inventory. Comment on the relationships you calculated and what additional information you need before evaluating the company's inventory management performance.

P9-13   Late in 2002, Sara Teasdale and four other investors took the chain of Sprint Department Stores Ltd. private, and the company has just completed its third year of operations under the investment group's ownership. Elinor Wylie, controller of Sprint Department Stores, is in the process of preparing the year-end financial statements. Based on the preliminary statements, Teasdale has expressed concern over inventory shortages, and she has asked Wylie to determine whether an abnormal amount of theft and breakage has occurred. The accounting records of Sprint Department Stores Ltd. contain the following amounts on November 30, 2005, the fiscal year end.

	Cost	Retail
Beginning inventory	$ 68,000	$100,000
Purchases	248,200	400,000
Net markups		50,000
Net markdowns		110,000
Sales		330,000

According to the November 30, 2005 physical inventory, the actual inventory at retail is $107,000.

Instructions

(a) Describe the circumstances under which the retail inventory method would be applied, and the advantages of using the retail inventory method.

(b) Assuming that prices have been stable, calculate the lower of cost and market value of Sprint Department Stores' ending inventory using the conventional retail method. Furnish supporting calculations.

(c) Estimate the amount of shortage, at retail, that has occurred at Sprint Department Stores during the year ended November 30, 2005.

(d) Complications in the retail method can be caused by such items as (1) freight-in expense, (2) purchase returns and allowances, (3) sales returns and allowances, and (4) employee discounts. Explain how each of these four special items is handled in the retail inventory method.

(CMA adapted)

P9-14   Brooks Specialty Corp., a division of FH Inc., manufactures three models of gear shift components for bicycles that are sold to bicycle manufacturers, retailers, and catalogue outlets. Since beginning operations in 1969, Brooks has used normal absorption costing and has assumed a first-in, first-out cost flow in its perpetual inventory system. Except for overhead, manufacturing costs are accumulated using actual costs. Overhead is applied to production using predetermined overhead rates. The balances of the inventory accounts at the end of Brooks' fiscal year, September 30, 2005, are shown below. The inventories are stated at cost before any year-end adjustments.

Finished goods	$647,000
Work in process	112,500
Raw materials	240,000
Factory supplies	69,000

The following information relates to Brooks' inventory and operations.

1. The finished goods inventory consists of the items analysed below.

	Cost	Market
Down tube shifter		
Standard model	$ 67,500	$ 67,000
Click adjustment model	94,500	87,000
Deluxe model	108,000	110,000
Total down tube shifters	270,000	264,000
Bar end shifter		
Standard model	83,000	90,050
Click adjustment model	99,000	97,550
Total bar end shifters	182,000	187,600
Head tube shifter		
Standard model	78,000	77,650
Click adjustment model	117,000	119,300
Total head tube shifters	195,000	196,950
Total finished goods	$647,000	$648,550

2. One-half of the head tube shifter finished goods inventory is held by catalogue outlets on consignment.

3. Three-quarters of the bar end shifter finished goods inventory has been pledged as collateral for a bank loan.

4. One-half of the raw materials balance represents derailleurs acquired at a contracted price 20% above the current market price. The market value of the rest of the raw materials is $127,400.

5. The total market value of the work-in-process inventory is $108,700.

6. Included in the cost of factory supplies are obsolete items with a historical cost of $4,200. The remaining factory supplies' market value is $65,900.

7. Brooks applies the lower of cost and market method to each of the three types of shifters in finished goods inventory. For each of the other three inventory accounts, Brooks applies the lower of cost and market method to the total of each inventory account.

8. Consider all amounts presented above to be material in relation to Brooks' financial statements taken as a whole.

Instructions

(a) Prepare the inventory section of Brooks' statement of financial position as of September 30, 2005, including any required note(s).

(b) Without prejudice to your answer to requirement (a), assume that the market value of Brooks' inventories is less than cost. Explain how this decline would be presented in Brooks' income statement for the fiscal year ended September 30, 2005.

(c) Assume that Brooks has a firm purchase commitment for the same type of derailleur included in the raw materials inventory as of September 30, 2005, and that the purchase commitment is at a contracted price 15% greater than the current market price. These derailleurs are to be delivered to Brooks after September 30, 2005. Discuss the impact, if any, that this purchase commitment would have on Brooks' financial statements prepared for the fiscal year ended September 30, 2005.

(CMA adapted)

Writing Assignments

WA9-1   Part of the criteria for evaluating management's performance is the inventory turnover ratio and the number of days sales in inventory. The market value of Norway Corporation's inventory has recently declined below its cost. The controller, Harry Fiord, has suggested to management that it may wish to switch from the direct method to the allowance method in applying the lower of cost and market rule because it more clearly discloses the decline in market value, and it does not distort the cost of goods sold. The financial vice-president, Krista Mallot, prefers the direct method to write down inventory because it does not call attention to the decline in market value.

Instructions

Answer the following questions.

(a) Is there an ethical issue involved here? Briefly explain.

(b) Is any stakeholder harmed if Krista Mallot's suggestion is used?

(c) What should Harry Fiord do?

WA9-2   The balance sheet valuation of inventory should represent the lower of cost and market of all inventory owned by the company. The following audit procedures are listed in the external auditor's working papers.

1. Review sales invoices subsequent to year end.

2. Review freight documents around year end.

3. Test count a sample of items during the client's physical inventory count and compare with client's count sheets.

4. Review suppliers' invoices and receiving reports both before and after year end.

5. Calculate the gross profit ratio and compare it with the previous year's ratio.

6. During the client's inventory count, select a sample of items from the client's inventory count sheets and count the quantities actually on hand.

Instructions

Suggest reasons why each of these audit procedures is required.

WA9-3   Harvey Corporation, your client, manufactures paint. The company's president, Andy Harvey, has decided to open a retail store to sell his specialty paint products as well as wallpaper and other supplies that would be purchased from other suppliers. He has asked you for information about the conventional retail method of determining the cost of inventories at the retail store.

Instructions

Prepare a report to the president explaining the retail method of valuing inventories. Your report should include these points:

(a) description and accounting features of the method

(b) the conditions that may distort the results under the method

(c) a comparison of the advantages of using the retail method with those of using cost methods of inventory pricing

(d) the accounting theory underlying the treatment of net markdowns and net markups under the method

WA9-4   A. Pox Corporation, a retailer and wholesaler of national brand-name household lighting fixtures, purchases its inventories from various suppliers.

Instructions

(a) Pox uses the lower of cost and market rule for its wholesale inventories. What are the theoretical arguments for that policy?

(b) The inventories' replacement cost is below the net realizable value less a normal profit margin, which in turn is below the original cost. Net realizable value, however, is greater than cost. What amount should be used to value the inventories? Why?

(c) Pox calculates the estimated cost of its ending inventories held for sale at retail using the conventional retail inventory method. How would Pox treat the beginning inventories and net markdowns in calculating the cost ratio used to determine its ending inventories? Why?

Cases

Refer to the Case Primer on the Digital Tool to help you answer these cases.

Digital Tool

www.wiley.com/
canada/kieso

CA9-1 Petro-Canada is one of Canada's largest oil and gas companies operating in Canada and internationally. Its shares trade on both the Toronto and New York stock exchanges. The value of the shares rose 88% over a five-year period ending in 2002. Management noted that this growth reflected the company's commitment to creating shareholder value. Natural gas, one of the company's products, is a commodity and thus, its price is subject to supply and demand which is influenced by weather, political events, and level of industry inventories.

According to the 2002 annual report, gas prices in 2001 and 2002 were very volatile. Demand decreased due to warmer than normal weather conditions and supply increased due to a build-up of gas in storage. These two factors contributed to lower prices. The spot rate for gas declined from $6.57 in 2001 to $4.24 in 2002 (AECO spot price per thousand cubic feet). The company was concerned about continued volatility into 2003 due to the disharmony between the United States and Iraq as well as a political crisis in Venezuela. The January 2003 cold weather increased demand for natural gas, thus driving prices up.

The company has commitments to purchase natural gas to reduce its exposure to the gas price volatility and to manage its fuel costs on fixed price product sales. They have locked in to buy 600 million cubic feet at $5.99 per thousand cubic feet. Inventory is valued using LIFO and has increased from $455 million to $585 million.

During the year, Deloitte & Touche LLP assumed the audit after Arthur Andersen LLP, the prior auditor, ceased to operate.

Instructions

Adopt the role of Deloitte and Touche LLP and critically evaluate the accounting issues related to the inventory.

CA9-2 Fuego Limited (FL) is a mid-sized business that produces computer paper. During the year, raw material had been increasing significantly and FL was finding it difficult to compete since it could not increase its selling prices sufficiently to generate a profit. Its customers, which were primarily "big box" stores (i.e., very large stores that dealt with office supplies), threatened to take their business elsewhere if FL did not hold the prices. By year end, the company had significant amounts of inventory and were in the process of negotiating with their two largest customers about a price increase. Luckily raw material prices had begun to decline and so future sales would not be a problem but FL needed to sell the high priced inventory on hand to at least recover their costs.

Franco Fuego, the company owner, was happy that at least some progress was being made in the discussions and hoped to move the inventory out before year end. Unfortunately, during the night, he was called by the fire department. His warehouse and the entire inventory had been burned to the ground. They wanted him to see the damages and to ask a few questions to determine the cause of the fire. Apparently, they had found traces of gasoline in the warehouse. Franco immediately called his insurance company (the inventory and building were fully covered at replacement value as long as there was no foul play).

The insurance company asked whether the company records had also been destroyed. Luckily, Franco kept a backup copy in another location and so he would hopefully be able to help the insurance people determine the value. FL used the periodic inventory method and the last count had been at the end of the prior year. Franco needs to get draft financial statements to the bank within the next few days since the bank has been monitoring his cash flow situation carefully given his almost fully drawn line of credit.

Instructions

Adopt the role of Franco and discuss the financial reporting issues related to the preparation of the current financial statements.

CA9-3 Vineland Limited signed a long-term purchase contract to buy timber from the British Columbia Forest Service at $300 per thousand board feet. Under this contract, Vineland must cut and pay $6 million for the timber during the next year. Currently the market value is $250 per thousand board feet. Ruben Walker, the controller, wants to recognize the loss in value in the year-end financial statements, but the financial vice-president, Billie Hands, argues that the loss is temporary and should be ignored. Walker notes that market value has remained near $250 for many months, and he sees no sign of significant change.

Instructions

Discuss the financial reporting issues.

Research and Financial Analysis

RA9-1   Domtar Inc.

Domtar Inc. is a well-known Canadian company that manufactures and distributes communication and specialty papers (as well as pulp), produces lumber and veneer from its forest resources, sawmill operations, and remanufacturing facilities, and has a major interest in a company that manufactures and distributes containerboard and corrugated products. Domtar reports the following information for its fiscal years ending December 31, 2002, 2001, and 2000.

DOMTAR INC.
(in millions of Canadian dollars)

	2002	2001	2000
Current assets			
Cash	$ 38	$ 36	$ 29
Receivables	304	300	404
Inventories	736	779	546
Prepaid expenses	22	24	19
Future income taxes	76	29	30
	$1,176	$1,168	$1,028
Net sales	$5,490	$4,377	$3,598
Cost of sales	$4,321	$3,514	$2,703
Inventories			
Work-in-process and finished goods	$ 406	$ 430	$ 311
Raw materials	150	166	131
Operating and maintenance supplies	180	183	104
	$ 736	$ 779	$ 546

Significant accounting policy

Inventories of operating and maintenance supplies and raw materials are valued at the lower of average cost and replacement cost. Work-in-process and finished goods are valued at the lower of average cost and net realizable value, and include the cost of raw materials, direct labour, and manufacturing overhead expenses.

Instructions

(a) Suggest reasons why Domtar uses two different definitions of market in valuing its inventory.

(b) Calculate the inventory turnover for Domtar's 2002 and 2001 fiscal years using only the raw materials, work-in-process, and finished goods inventories. Also determine the average number of days to sell the inventory.

(c) Calculate the inventory turnover for Domtar's 2002 and 2001 fiscal years using all of the inventories reported. Also determine the average number of days to sell the inventory.

(d) Briefly discuss whether your results in (b) or in (c) provide the better information.

(e) Determine Domtar's percentage gross profit on sales and its markup on cost.

(f) Suggest possible reasons why the gross profit percentage has varied over the three-year period. What would have been the effect on Domtar's income before taxes in 2002 if the company generated the same gross profit in 2002 that it did in 2000?

RA9-2   Magnotta Winery Corporation

Access the annual financial statements of **Magnotta Winery Corporation** for the year ended January 31, 2003 on the Digital Tool or on SEDAR (www.sedar.com).

Instructions

Refer to these financial statements and the accompanying notes to answer the following questions.

(a) How significant are the inventories relative to total current assets? What categories of inventory does Magnotta Winery report?

(b) How does Magnotta value its inventories? Which inventory costing method does the company use as a basis for reporting its inventories?

(c) Identify the types of costs included in each inventory category.

(d) What was Magnotta's inventory turnover ratio for the most recent year? What is the average age of the inventory? Comment briefly.

(e) Compare the gross profit ratios for the two most recent years. Comment briefly.

RA9-3 Sears Canada Inc. versus Hudson's Bay Company

Instructions

From the Digital Tool or the SEDAR website (www.sedar.com), access the annual financial statements of Sears Canada Inc. and Hudson's Bay Company. Review the financial statements and answer the following questions.

(a) What is the amount of inventory reported by Sears Canada at December 28, 2002, and by Hudson's Bay at January 31, 2003? What percent of total assets is invested in inventory by each company? How does this compare with the preceding year?

(b) What inventory costing methods are used by Sears Canada and Hudson's Bay? How does each company value its inventories?

(c) Calculate and compare the inventory turnover ratios and days to sell inventory for the two companies. If cost of goods sold is not reported, use a surrogate. What choices are there? Identify the limitations of the surrogate you chose.

(d) Comment on the results of your calculations in (c) above. Would any differences identified in (b) above help explain differences in the ratios between the two companies?

RA9-4 Research

Identify a company in your local community that develops a product through some form of manufacturing process. Consider a farming operation, a bakery, cement supplier, or other company that converts or assembles inputs to develop a different product.

Instructions

Write a report on the company's inventory. Suggestions: visit the manufacturing site, view a video of the operation, or speak to company management. Identify what types of costs are incurred in the manufacturing process. Determine which costs are included in inventory cost in the accounting records, and provide an explanation of why some may be treated as period costs. Does the company use a periodic or a perpetual system? Does the company use an LCM policy? How does this company determine "market" in order to apply LCM? How does the company determine NRV?

RA9-5 Falconbridge Limited

Falconbridge Limited, a Canadian company, is "a leading low-cost producer of nickel, copper, cobalt and platinum group metals." The financial results of companies such as this depend to a great extent on the prices of these major metal groups.

Instructions

(a) Access the 2002 Annual Report of Falconbridge Limited. Review what the report says about the company's operations.

(b) The company provides considerable detail in the Ten-Year Review and the Consolidated Results by Quarter about its level of production and sales activity. Calculate and graph the gross profit ratio for each quarter of 2001 and 2002.

(c) Can you explain differences in this profitability ratio by referring to changes in the average prices realized for the various metals the company sold? Prepare a short but informative analysis.

Food Fortunes

In the 1920s and 30s, when Frank Sobey was expanding his family's grocery business in Nova Scotia, he realized the company would need a real estate arm to maintain control of store locations. This became even more evident through the 1960s and 70s, when large competitors from central Canada could easily win bids for good locations from local developers. "Frank realized he was better off if he bought the site," says Stewart Mahoney, vice-president, treasury and investor relations, at Sobeys' holding company, Empire Company.

Now the Stellarton, Nova Scotia-based Empire Company, which was incorporated in 1983, has three distinct branches: a retail food branch with 64.5% ownership of Sobeys; a real estate branch with 100% ownership of Crombie Properties; and corporate investments, which include 100% ownership of Empire Theatres as well as $425 million of investments in "others," says Mahoney. "All the company's various assets and revenues are matched to these three divisions."

Empire is now the largest commercial property owner in Atlantic Canada, with more than 10 million square feet of retail space in 32 enclosed shopping malls plus several strip malls and big box stores.

The initial investment strategy was control, but enhancing shareholder value "through income and cash flow growth and equity participation" in other businesses has since become a motivation.

Empire's recent investments include the purchase of Oshawa Foods, creating a national food company with more than 1,300 stores, and the acquisition of 35% of Genstar Development Partnership, a land developer based in Western Canada, for $21 million, which has since generated $75 million in cash returns.

Although Empire does not have controlling interest in Genstar, it is able to use line-by-line consolidation of the investment on its financial statements. "As they grow, we grow due to our proportionate interest in the company," Mahoney says.

CHAPTER 10

Investments

Learning Objectives

After studying this chapter, you should be able to:

1. Identify the categories of debt investments and describe the accounting and reporting requirements for those that are long-term investments.

2. Apply the accounting procedures for discount and premium amortization on notes, bonds, and other long-term investments in debt securities.

3. Identify the categories of long-term equity securities and describe the accounting and reporting treatment for each category.

4. Explain the equity method of accounting.

5. Explain the basics of consolidation.

6. Explain the accounting for impairments in value of long-term investments in debt and equity securities.

7. Describe how to account for the transfer of investment securities between categories.

8. Describe the reporting and disclosure requirements for long-term investments in debt and equity securities.

After studying Appendix 10A, you should be able to:

9. Identify how the accounting standards are changing for financial asset investments from reliance on historical cost to a focus on fair values.

Preview of Chapter 10

As the opening vignette implies, companies make long-term investments in the debt and equity securities of other entities for a variety of reasons. This chapter emphasizes the nature of and accounting for primary financial asset investments:[1] long-term loans and receivables; investment in debt securities that are held-to-maturity or available-for-sale; and investments in equity securities. This latter category includes those where the investor has little or no influence over the policies of the company invested in and that are available for sale; those where the investor has significant influence, but not control over the investee company; and those where the investor or parent controls the key policies of the investee or subsidiary.

Accounting for long-term investments is in a state of flux. The chapter material explains the standards that were in exposure draft form as this text went to print and the existing standards that are unlikely to change in the near future. Appendix 10A summarizes and reviews the standards in place in 2004, including those in the process of being phased out.

The content and organization of this chapter are explained below.

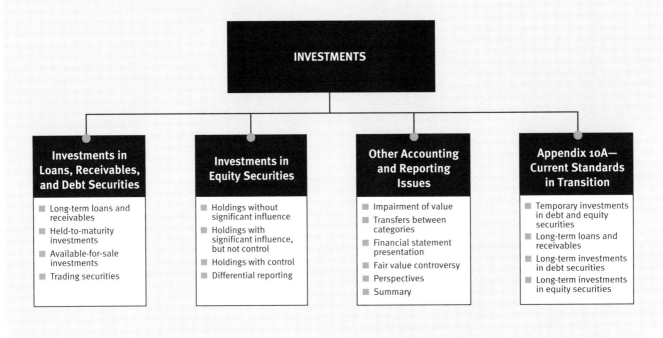

INVESTMENTS			
Investments in Loans, Receivables, and Debt Securities	**Investments in Equity Securities**	**Other Accounting and Reporting Issues**	**Appendix 10A— Current Standards in Transition**
▪ Long-term loans and receivables ▪ Held-to-maturity investments ▪ Available-for-sale investments ▪ Trading securities	▪ Holdings without significant influence ▪ Holdings with significant influence, but not control ▪ Holdings with control ▪ Differential reporting	▪ Impairment of value ▪ Transfers between categories ▪ Financial statement presentation ▪ Fair value controversy ▪ Perspectives ▪ Summary	▪ Temporary investments in debt and equity securities ▪ Long-term loans and receivables ▪ Long-term investments in debt securities ▪ Long-term investments in equity securities

---

[1] *CICA Handbook* Section 3860 defines **financial asset** as any asset that is cash, a contractual right to receive cash or other financial asset from another party, a contractual right to exchange financial instruments under conditions that are potentially favourable, or an equity instrument of another entity (para. .05). **Primary financial instruments** are receivables, payables, and equity securities that we have traditionally recognized in the financial statements. **Derivative instruments**, such as forwards, futures, and options, create rights and obligations that have the effect of transferring between parties to the instrument one or more financial risks inherent in an underlying primary instrument (para. .10). The basics of derivatives are covered in Chapter 17.

The deficiencies of the historic cost model in accounting for financial instruments have long been recognized. Because of this, accounting for investments has been on the agendas of standard-setting bodies around the world for more than a decade. While many of the inadequacies deal with more complex issues such as accounting for derivatives and hedging activities, accounting for ordinary investments in other companies' debt and equity securities are also at issue. The following recent events have taken place in Canada.

1995—*CICA Handbook* Section 3860 was released, dealing with **disclosure and presentation standards** for financial instruments. This section did not attempt to cover the more complicated and controversial recognition and measurement issues.

1997—A joint committee of the CICA and the International Accounting Standards Committee (now the IASB) released a discussion paper, *Accounting for Financial Assets and Financial Liabilities*. The paper set out a variety of options for accounting for financial instruments, concluding with **a strong preference and support for a full fair value model** for both primary and derivative securities rather than one based on historic costs.

2001—The CICA, along with standard setters in nine other international jurisdictions, issued a draft standard, an Invitation to Comment on **proposals for a comprehensive fair value model** on *Financial Instruments and Similar Items.*

2003—Without enough support to move to a full fair value model, the AcSB of the CICA issued three exposure drafts that would have the result of substantially harmonizing Canadian standards with those of the United States and the IASB.[2] This was seen by many as an interim step toward eventual full fair value accounting for financial instruments. The three exposure drafts were as follows.

Proposed Section	Proposed *Handbook* Title
1530	Comprehensive Income
3855	Financial Instruments—Recognition and Measurement
3865	Hedges

In late 2003, after considerable input from a variety of interested parties, the AcSB delayed the likely effective date for these new sections until 2005. Because the reasons for the delay relate to issues that are beyond an intermediate financial accounting level, and because harmonization with the FASB and international standards is substantially assured, **this chapter provides the basics of accounting for long-term investments under these exposure drafts.**[3]

The topic of financial instruments is a broad one. The coverage in this chapter is limited to basic investments in long-term loans and receivables, and primary debt and equity instruments. Chapter 7 included temporary investments in trading securities, Chapter 14 and 15 handle financial liabilities including guarantees, Chapter 16 reviews the issue of equity securities from the issuing company's perspective, and Chapter 17 covers the basics of stock options, rights and warrants, and other derivative instruments. The more complex aspects are left to a course in advanced financial accounting.

Those who prefer to study the Canadian standards in place as this text went to print are referred to Appendix 10A. The appendix indicates which parts of the chapter material cover standards in place in 2004 and explains the cost method used to account for portfolio investments in equity securities.

International Insight

IAS 39 provides for classification as trading, available-for-sale, or held-to-maturity for all types of financial assets. U.S. GAAP applies these classifications only to securities.

---

[2] Much of the problem was the continuing uncertainty about the ability to reliably measure fair values in many cases.

[3] The IASB approved a similar standard, IAS 39, effective 2001. Both the Canadian draft standards and the IASB standards cover recognition and measurement of financial instruments, a much broader topic than the FASB standards on investments in debt and equity securities. The relevant FASB standards are found in SFAS 115, 130, and 135.

INTRODUCTION

Before beginning the accounting for investments, we should understand the **different motivations companies have for investing** in securities issued by other companies.[4] One motivation relates to **the returns provided by investments**, i.e., through interest, dividends, or capital gains (an increase in underlying value of the investment). Note that some types of investments provide guaranteed returns (such as term deposits), while others are more risky (such as investments in shares of other companies). Managers may intend to invest for **short-term returns** or **longer-term returns** depending on their business and whether they need the excess cash for other purposes.

Another motivation for investing in equity securities deals more **with strategy** than returns. Companies may invest in common shares of other companies, allowing the holder's management to vote on key company decisions, and have some influence or control over the operations of that company. For instance, a strategic investment may give the investing company access to distribution channels or a guaranteed supply of raw materials.

Consider the situation of Empire Company in the opening vignette. What started out as a strategy of control over the property in which its stores were located, has become a primary strategy of enhancing shareholder returns and share value. Another example occurred in 2003, when Montreal-based Saputo Inc. acquired Molfino Hermanos, the third-largest dairy processor in Argentina, as part of its strategy to become a world-class cheese company. Invariably, strategic investments are made to enhance returns to shareholders.

Accounting for investments is a function of both **the type of instrument** (debt or equity) **and management's intent**, which, as noted above, may be quite different from security to security.

INVESTMENTS IN LOANS, RECEIVABLES, AND DEBT SECURITIES

Debt securities are instruments representing a creditor relationship with an enterprise. These include Government of Canada, provincial, or municipal bonds, corporate bonds, convertible debt, commercial paper, and all securitized debt instruments. Trade accounts receivable and loans receivable technically are not debt securities because they do not meet the definition of a security, but are included here as they do represent a liability of the issuing company.

According to proposed *CICA Handbook* Section 3855, financial assets classified as "debt" investments are grouped into four separate categories for accounting and reporting purposes.

Loans and receivables: These financial assets result from the delivery of cash or other assets by a lender to a borrower in return for a promise to pay an amount on a specified date(s) or on demand, usually with interest.[5]

---

[4] A **security** is a share, participation, or other interest in property or in an enterprise of the issuer or an obligation of the issuer that: (a) either is represented by an instrument issued in bearer or registered form or, if not represented by an instrument, is registered in books maintained to record transfers by or on behalf of the issuer; (b) is of a type commonly dealt in on securities exchanges or markets or, when represented by an instrument, is commonly recognized in any area in which it is issued or dealt in as a medium for investment; and (c) either is one of a class or series or by its terms is divisible into a class or series of shares, participations, interests, or obligations. From "Accounting for Certain Investments in Debt and Equity Securities," *Statement of Financial Accounting Standards No. 115* (Norwalk, Conn.: FASB, 1993), p. 48, par. 137.

[5] *Exposure Draft* Section 3855.17(h). Exclusions are loans and receivables that have been securitized, that the entity has elected to designate as held for trading, or that are quoted in an active market.

Held-to-maturity investments: These are financial assets with fixed or determinable payments and fixed maturity that an entity has the positive intent and ability to hold to maturity, excluding those classified as available for sale or that are loans and receivables.[6]

Held-for-trading investments: Financial assets that upon initial recognition are designated by the entity as held for trading. For the purposes of this chapter, these are bought and held primarily for sale in the near term to generate income on short-term price differences.[7]

Available-for-sale investments: Financial assets that are not classified as loans and receivables, held-to-maturity, or held-for-trading.[8]

Illustration 10-1 identifies these categories and provides a summary of the accounting and reporting required for each.

Category	Valuation	Unrealized Holding Gains or Losses	Other Income Statement Effects
Loans and receivables	Amortized cost	Not recognized	Interest when earned; gains and losses from sale.
Held-to-maturity	Amortized cost	Not recognized	Interest when earned; gains and losses from sale.
Held-for-trading	Fair value	Recognized in net income	Interest when earned; gains and losses from sale.
Available-for-sale	Fair value	Recognized as other comprehensive income	Interest when earned; gains and losses from sale. and as separate component of shareholders' equity

Illustration 10-1

Accounting for Investments in Loans, Receivables, and Debt Securities

Amortized cost is the amount recognized when acquired, reduced by principal payments received, and adjusted for amortization of discount or premium if appropriate, and write-downs for impairment or uncollectibility. **Fair value** is the amount that would be agreed upon in an arm's length transaction between knowledgeable, willing parties who are under no compulsion to act.[9] **Note that all investments in debt securities except loans and receivables and those held to maturity are measured at fair value.**

Long-term Loans and Receivables

A note or loan receivable is similar to an account receivable, except that the former is supported by a formal **promissory note**, a written promise to pay a certain sum of money at a specific future date. Such a note is a negotiable instrument that is signed by a **maker** in favour of a designated **payee** who may legally and readily sell or otherwise transfer the note to others. **Notes always contain an interest element** because of the time value of money, but they may be classified as interest-bearing or noninterest-bearing. **Interest-bearing notes** have a stated rate of interest that is payable over and above the face value of the note; **zero-interest-bearing notes** (or **noninterest-bearing notes**) also include interest, but it is equal to the difference between the amount borrowed (the proceeds) and the face amount paid back. The rate may not be stated explicitly. Notes receivable are considered fairly liquid, even if long-term, because they can be easily converted to cash.

Notes receivable are frequently accepted from customers who need to extend the payment period of an outstanding receivable. Notes are also sometimes required of high-risk

---

[6] *Exposure Draft* Section 3855.17(g).

[7] *Exposure Draft* Section 3855.17(f).

[8] *Exposure Draft* Section 3855.17(i).

[9] *Exposure Draft* Section 3855.17(l) and (j).

or new customers. In addition, notes are often used in loans to employees and subsidiaries and in the sales of property, plant, and equipment. In some industries (e.g., the pleasure and sport boat industry), all credit sales are supported by notes. The majority of long-term notes and loans, however, originate from lending transactions. The basic issues in accounting for these receivables are recognition, valuation, and disposition.

Long-term loans and notes receivable are recorded and reported **at the present value of the cash expected to be collected.** When the interest stated on an interest-bearing note is equal to the effective (market) rate of interest, the note sells at face value.[10] When the stated rate differs from the market rate, the cash exchanged (the note's **present value**) is different from the note's **face value**. The difference between the face value and the cash exchanged, either a discount or a premium, is then recorded and amortized over the note's life so that interest revenue reported approximates the effective or market rate. This is illustrated below.

Notes Issued at Face Value

To illustrate an interest-bearing note issued at face value, assume that Bigelow Corp. lends Scandinavian Imports $10,000 in exchange for a $10,000, three-year note bearing interest at 10% annually. The market rate of interest for a note of similar risk is also 10%. The first step always is to identify the amounts and timing of the cash flows. A time diagram depicting both interest and principal cash flows is shown below.

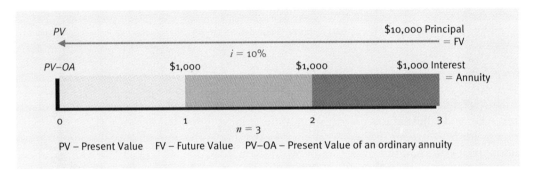

The note's present value or exchange price is calculated as follows.

Illustration 10-2

Present Value of Note—Stated and Market Rates the Same

Face value of the note		$10,000
Present value of the principal:		
$10,000 (PVF*$_{3,10\%}$) = $10,000 (0.75132) (Table A-2)	$7,513	
Present value of the interest:		
$1,000 (PVF*–OA$_{3,10\%}$) = $1,000 (2.48685) (Table A-4)	2,487	
Present value of the note		10,000
Difference		$ –0–
*Present Value Factors found in Tables A1-A5		

In this case, the note's present value and face value are the same ($10,000) **because the effective and stated interest rates are the same.** The note's receipt is recorded by Bigelow Corp. as follows.

A = L + SE
0   0   0

Cash flows: ↓ 10,000 outflow

Notes Receivable	10,000	
Cash		10,000

---

[10] The stated interest rate, also referred to as the **face rate** or the **coupon rate**, is the rate contracted as part of the note. The effective interest rate, also referred to as the market rate or the yield rate, is the rate used in the market to determine the note's value—that is, the discount rate used to determine its present value.

Bigelow Corp. recognizes the interest earned each year as follows.

Cash	1,000	
Interest Revenue		1,000

A = L + SE
+1,000   +1,000
Cash flows: ↑ 1,000 inflow

Notes Not Issued at Face Value

Zero-Interest-Bearing Notes. If a zero-interest-bearing note is received in exchange for cash, its present value is the cash paid to the issuer. Because both the note's future amount and present value are known, the interest rate can be calculated, i.e., it is implied. The **implicit interest rate** is the rate that equates the cash paid with the amounts receivable in the future. The difference between the future (face) amount and the present value (cash paid) is recorded as a discount and is amortized to interest revenue over the life of the note using the effective interest method.

To illustrate, assume Jeremiah Company receives a three-year, $10,000 zero-interest-bearing note, the present value of which is known to be $7,721.80. The implied rate of interest of 9% can be determined as follows.

PV of note = PV of future cash flows
PV of note = FV of note × $PVF_{3, ?\%}$ (Table A-2)
$7,721.80 = $10,000 × $PVF_{3, ?\%}$

$$PVF_{3, ?\%} = \frac{\$7,721.80}{\$10,000}$$

$PVF_{3, ?\%}$ = 0.77218

Table A-2: Where n = 3 and PVF = 0.77218, i = 9%

Illustration 10-3

Determination of Implicit Interest Rate

Thus, the implicit rate that equates the total cash to be received ($10,000 at maturity) to the present value of the future cash flows ($7,721.80) is 9%. Note that if any two of the three variables in the equation on the second line of Illustration 10-3 are known, the third variable can be determined. For example, if the note's maturity value (**future value**) and **present value factor** were known, the note's **present value** could be determined.

The time diagram depicting the one cash flow of Jeremiah's note is shown below.

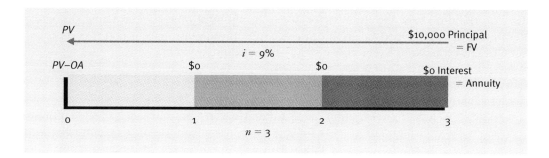

The entry to record the transaction is as follows.

Notes Receivable	10,000.00	
Discount on Notes Receivable ($10,000 − $7,721.80)		2,278.20
Cash		7,721.80

A = L + SE
0   0   0
Cash flows: ↓ 7,721.80 outflow

Objective 2

Apply the accounting procedures for discount and premium amortization on notes, bonds, and other long-term investments in debt securities.

The Discount on Notes Receivable is reported on the balance sheet as a contra-asset account to Notes Receivable. The discount is then amortized, and interest revenue is recognized annually using the **effective interest method**.[11] This method requires that the effective interest or yield rate be calculated at the time of investment. This rate is subsequently used to calculate interest revenue by applying the rate to the carrying (book) value of the investment for each interest period. The note's carrying amount is increased by the amortized discount or decreased by the amortized premium in each period. **Thus the carrying amount is always equal to the present value of the note's cash flows (principal and interest payments) discounted at the market rate at acquisition.** Jeremiah's three-year discount amortization and interest revenue schedule is shown in Illustration 10-4.

Illustration 10-4

Discount Amortization Schedule—Effective Interest Method

SCHEDULE OF NOTE DISCOUNT AMORTIZATION
Effective Interest Method
0% Note Discounted at 9%

	Cash Received	Interest Revenue	Discount Amortized	Carrying Amount of Note[a]
Date of issue				$ 7,721.80
End of year 1	$ –0–	$ 694.96[b]	$ 694.96[c]	8,416.76[d]
End of year 2	–0–	757.51	757.51	9,174.27
End of year 3	–0–	825.73[e]	825.73	10,000.00
	$ –0–	$2,278.20	$2,278.20	

[a] Note Receivable less Discount on Note Receivable
[b] $7,721.80 × 0.09 = $694.96
[c] $694.96 − 0 = $694.96
[d] $7,721.80 + $694.96 = $8,416.76 or
   $10,000 − ($2,278.20 − $694.96)
   = $8,416.76
[e] 5¢ adjustment for rounding

Interest revenue at the end of the first year using the effective interest method is recorded as follows.

A   = L +   SE
+694.96   +694.96

Cash flows: No effect

Discount on Notes Receivable	694.96	
Interest Revenue ($7,721.80 × 9%)		694.96

Underlying Concept

The use of some simpler method that yields results similar to the effective-interest method is an application of the materiality concept.

Note that the amount of the discount, $2,278.20 in this case, represents the interest revenue on the note over the three years. It can be thought of as an Unearned (Interest) Revenue account that gets taken into income over three years, except that it is reported netted against the Note Receivable instead of as a liability account.

Interest-Bearing Notes. Often the stated rate and the effective rate are different as in the zero-interest-bearing case above.

To illustrate a different situation, assume that Morgan Corp. made a loan to Marie Co. and received in exchange a three-year, $10,000 note bearing interest at 10% annually. The market rate of interest for a note of similar risk is 12%. The time diagram depicting both cash flows is shown at the top of the next page.

Note that the interest cash flows are determined by the stated rate (10%), but that **all flows are discounted at the market rate** (12%) in determining the note's present value. The present value ($9,520) of the two streams of cash is calculated in Illustration 10-5.

---

[11] Under proposed *CICA Handbook* Section 3855, the effective interest method is required.

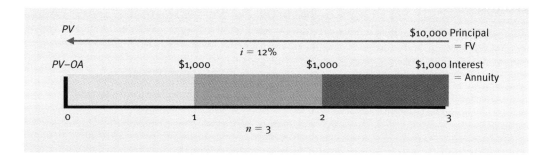

Illustration 10-5

Calculation of Present Value—Effective Rate Different from Stated Rate

Because the **effective interest rate** (12%) is greater than the stated rate (10%), the note's present value is less than the face value; that is, the note was exchanged at a **discount**. This makes intuitive sense. If you were to invest in a note that promises 10% when you could get 12% elsewhere in the market at the same level of risk, you would not be willing to pay face value for the note. The receipt of the note at a discount is recorded by Morgan as follows.

Notes Receivable	10,000	
Discount on Notes Receivable		480
Cash		9,520

A	=	L	+	SE
0		0		0

Cash flows: ↓ 9,520 outflow

The discount of $480 represents interest revenue over and above the 10% or $1,000 to be received each year. Interest revenue is recognized and the discount account is amortized annually using the effective interest method. Morgan's three-year discount amortization and interest revenue schedule is shown in Illustration 10-6.

Illustration 10-6

Discount Amortization Schedule—Effective Interest Method

SCHEDULE OF NOTE DISCOUNT AMORTIZATION
Effective Interest Method
10% Note Discounted at 12%

	Cash Received	Interest Revenue	Discount Amortized	Carrying Amount of Note[a]
Date of issue				$ 9,520
End of year 1	$1,000[b]	$1,142[c]	$142[d]	9,662[e]
End of year 2	1,000	1,159	159	9,821
End of year 3	1,000	1,179	179	10,000
	$3,000	$3,480	$480	

[a] Note Receivable less Discount on Note Receivable
[b] $10,000 × 10% = $1,000
[c] $9,520 × 12% = $1,142
[d] $1,142 − $1,000 = $142
[e] $9,520 + $142 = $9,662 or
    $10,000 − ($480 − $142) = $9,662

On the date of issue, the note has a present value of $9,520. Its unamortized discount—interest revenue to be spread over the three-year life of the note—is $480.

At the end of year one, Morgan receives $1,000 in cash. But its interest revenue is $1,142 ($9,520 × 12%). The difference between $1,000 and $1,142 is the discount to be amortized, $142. Receipt of the annual interest and amortization of the discount for the first year are recorded by Morgan as follows (amounts per amortization schedule).

A = L + SE		
+1,142 +1,142		
Cash flows: ↑ 1,000 inflow		

Cash	1,000	
Discount on Notes Receivable	142	
Interest Revenue		1,142

The note's carrying amount is now $9,662 ($9,520 + $142), or the balance in the Note Receivable of $10,000 reduced by the adjusted balance of the Discount on Note Receivable account of $338 ($480 − $142). This process is repeated until the end of year 3.

When the stated rate is greater than the effective interest rate, the note's present value exceeds its face value and the note is exchanged at a **premium**. The premium on a note receivable is recorded as a debit and amortized using the effective interest method over the life of the note as annual reductions in the amount of interest revenue recognized.

Notes Received for Property, Goods, or Services

When property, goods, or services are sold and a note is received as the consideration instead of cash or a short-term receivable, there may be an issue in determining the selling price. If an appropriate market rate of interest is known for the note, or for a note of similar risk, there is no problem. The sales proceeds are equal to the present value of the cash flows promised by the note, discounted at the market rate of interest. **Remember that if the stated rate and the market rate are the same, the note's face value and fair value are the same.** Where the two rates are not the same, the note's fair value must be determined by discounting the cash flows at the market rate.

If an appropriate market rate is not known, two approaches can be used.

1. The fair value of the property, goods, or services given up can be used as a surrogate for the fair value of the note received. In this case, because the note's fair (present) value, the cash flow amount, and the timing of the cash flows are all known, the market or yield interest rate can be determined. This is needed in order to amortize any resulting discount or premium on the note.

2. An appropriate interest rate can be imputed. **Imputation** is the process of interest-rate approximation, and the resulting interest rate is called an **imputed interest rate**. This rate is used to establish the note's present value by discounting, at that rate, all future cash receipts of interest and principal on the note. The objective for calculating the appropriate interest rate is to approximate the rate that would have been agreed upon if an independent borrower and lender had negotiated a similar transaction. The choice of a rate is affected by the prevailing rates for similar instruments of issuers with similar credit ratings. It is also affected by such factors as restrictive covenants, collateral, payment schedule, and the existing prime interest rate.

To illustrate, assume Oasis Corp. sold a corner lot in exchange for a five-year note having a maturity value of $35,247 and no stated interest rate. The land originally cost Oasis $14,000. What are the proceeds on disposal of the land; that is, what selling price should be recorded in this transaction?

Situation 1: Assume the market rate of interest of 12% is known. In this case, the proceeds on sale are equal to the present value of the note, or $20,000. This is a non-interest-bearing note, so the only cash flow is the $35,247 received in five periods' time: $35,247 × .56743 (Table A-2) = $20,000. The entry to record the sale is:

Notes Receivable	35,247	
Discount on Notes Receivable ($35,247 − $20,000)		15,247
Land		14,000
Gain on Sale of Land ($20,000 − $14,000)		6,000

A = L + SE
+6,000   +6,000
Cash flows: No effect

Situation 2: Assume the market rate of interest is unknown, but that the land has been appraised recently for $20,000. In this case, the property's fair value determines the amount of the proceeds and the note's fair value. The entry is the same as in Situation 1. To amortize the discount, however, the implicit interest rate must be determined. This is done by finding the interest rate that equates the present value of the future cash flow ($35,247) with its present value ($20,000). The present value factor is $20,000 ÷ $35,247 = .567424. Table A-2 identifies the interest rate for 5 periods and a factor of .567424 as 12%.

Situation 3: Assume neither the market rate nor the land's fair value is known. In this case, a market rate must be imputed, and then used to determine the note's present value. It will also be used to recognize interest revenue over the five years and amortize the discount. If a 12% rate is estimated for Oasis, then the entry will be the same as in Situation 1. If a different rate results, the Discount on the note and the Gain on Sale will differ.

Held-to-Maturity Investments

Only debt securities are classified as held-to-maturity because equity securities usually have no maturity date. A debt security is classified as held-to-maturity only if the reporting entity has **both (1) the positive intent** and **(2) the ability to hold the investment to maturity**. A company should not classify a debt investment as held-to-maturity if it intends to hold the financial asset for an indefinite period of time. Likewise, if the enterprise anticipates that a sale may be necessary due to changes in interest rates, foreign currency risk, liquidity needs, or other asset-liability management reasons, **the security should not be classified as held-to-maturity**.[12]

Held-to-maturity investments are accounted for **at amortized cost**, not fair value. If management intends to hold certain securities to maturity and has no plans to sell them, fair values (selling prices) are not relevant for measuring and evaluating the cash flows associated with these securities. Finally, because held-to-maturity investments are not adjusted to fair value, they do not increase the volatility of either reported earnings or reported capital as do financial assets held for trading or available-for-sale.

Accounting for held-to-maturity debt investments is almost identical to accounting for long-term notes and loans receivable. To illustrate, assume that Robinson Limited purchased $100,000 of 8% bonds of Chan Corporation on January 1, 2005, paying $92,278.[13] The bonds mature January 1, 2010, and interest is payable each July 1 and January 1. The discount of $7,722 ($100,000 − $92,278) provides an effective interest yield of 10%. Assume Robinson Limited has an August 31 year end. The entry to record the investment is.

---

[12] Proposed *CICA Handbook* Section 3855.20.

[13] As previously mentioned, the value is determined by the investment community and is equal to the present value of the stream of principal and interest payments on the bond, discounted at the market rate. This is relatively straightforward if the bond is bought/sold on its issue date or on an interest payment due date. At other times the purchase price of a bond can be estimated as follows:

PV of cash flows at immediately preceding interest payment date	= $x
Increase in PV to date of sale/purchase at yield rate: $x × annual yield rate × portion of year since interest payment date	= y
Less cash interest earned since last interest payment date: Face value × annual stated rate × portion of year since last interest date	= (z)
Purchase price of a bond bought/sold between interest payment dates	x + y − z

A = L + SE
0   0   0

Cash flows: ↓ 92,278 outflow

	January 1, 2005	
Held-to-Maturity Investment in Bonds	92,278	
Cash		92,278

A Held-to-Maturity Investment account is used to indicate the type of debt security purchased. Unlike the previous example for notes receivable, **the discount or premium on a bond investment in practice tends not to be reported separately**, although it would not be incorrect to do so. Instead, the Investment account is reported net of the discount, as indicated, or with the premium added. The effective-interest method is applied to bond investments in the same way as that described for long-term notes receivable. The investment carrying amount is increased by the amortized discount or decreased by the amortized premium in each period.

Illustration 10-7 shows the effect of the discount amortization on the interest revenue recorded **each interest period** for the investment in Chan Corporation bonds.

Illustration 10-7

Schedule of Interest Revenue and Bond Discount Amortization— Effective Interest Method

	8% Bonds Purchased to Yield 10%			
Date	Cash Received	Interest Revenue	Bond Discount Amortization	Carrying Amount of Bonds
1/1/05				$92,278
7/1/05	$ 4,000ª	$ 4,614ᵇ	$614ᶜ	92,892ᵈ
1/1/06	4,000	4,645	645	93,537
7/1/06	4,000	4,677	677	94,214
1/1/07	4,000	4,711	711	94,925
7/1/07	4,000	4,746	746	95,671
1/1/08	4,000	4,783	783	96,454
7/1/08	4,000	4,823	823	97,277
1/1/09	4,000	4,864	864	98,141
7/1/09	4,000	4,907	907	99,048
1/1/10	4,000	4,952	952	100,000
	$40,000	$47,722	$7,722	

ª $4,000 = $100,000 × .08 × 6/12
ᵇ $4,614 = $92,278 × .10 × 6/12
ᶜ $614 = $4,614 − $4,000
ᵈ $92,892 = $92,278 + $614

The journal entry to record the receipt of the first semiannual interest payment on July 1, 2005 (using the data in Illustration 10-7) is:

A   = L + SE
+4,614   +4,614

Cash flows: ↑ 4,000 inflow

	July 1, 2005	
Cash	4,000	
Held-to-Maturity Investment in Bonds	614	
Interest Revenue		4,614

At year end, Robinson recognizes the interest income that has accrued since July 1 and amortizes the discount for the two month period, using the table in Schedule 10-7.

A   = L + SE
+1,548   +1,548

Cash flows: No effect

	August 31, 2005	
Interest Receivable	1,333	
Held-to-Maturity Investment in Bonds	215	
Interest Revenue		1,548

$4,000 × 2/6 = $1,333
$4,645 × 2/6 = $1,548
$ 645 × 2/6 = $ 215

When the interest payment is received on January 1, 2006, the following entry is made, assuming reversing entries are not used by Robinson.

January 1, 2006		
Cash	4,000	
Held-to-Maturity Investment in Bonds	430	
Interest Receivable		1,333
Interest Revenue		3,097

$ 645 × 4/6 = $ 430
$4,645 × 4/6 = $3,097

A = L + SE
+3,097   +3,097
Cash flows: ↑ 4,000 inflow

Financial Statement Presentation

Robinson Limited reports the following items related to its investment in Chan bonds in its August 31, 2005 financial statements.

BALANCE SHEET	
Current assets	
Interest receivable	$ 1,333
Long-term investments	
Held-to-maturity investments in bonds,	
at amortized cost	$93,107[a]
INCOME STATEMENT	
Other revenue and gains	
Interest revenue	$ 6,162[b]

[a] $92,278 + $614 + $215 = $93,107
[b] $4,614 + $1,548 = $6,162

Illustration 10-8
Reporting of Held-to-Maturity Investments

Sale of Held-to-Maturity Investments

Assume Robinson Limited sells its investment in Chan bonds on November 1, 2009 at 99¾ plus accrued interest. The discount would have been amortized up to the company's August 31, 2009 year end in the amount of $317 (i.e., 2/6 × $952), and interest receivable of $1,333 (i.e., 2/6 × $4,000) set up at that date. The following entry is made to further amortize the discount from September 1 to November 1, 2009, with the effect of bringing the investment to its correct book value at the date of disposal. The discount amortization for this two-month period is $317 (2/6 × $952).

November 1, 2007		
Held-to-Maturity Investment in Bonds	317	
Interest Revenue		317

A = L + SE
+317   +317
Cash flows: No effect

The calculation of the realized gain on the sale is shown in Illustration 10-9.

Selling price of bonds ($100,000 × .9975)		$99,750
Less: Carrying amount of bonds on November 1, 2009:		
Amortized cost, July 1, 2009 (see amortization schedule)	$99,048	
Add: Discount amortized for the period July 1, 2009		
to November 1, 2009 ($317 to August 31 + $317		
from September 1 to November 1)	634	99,682
Gain on sale of bonds		$ 68

Illustration 10-9
Calculation of Gain on Sale of Bonds

The entry to record the sale of the bonds is:

A = L + SE
+1,401   +1,401

Cash flows: ↑ 102,416 inflow

	November 1, 2007	
Cash	102,416*	
Interest Receivable		1,333
Interest Revenue (2/6 × $4,000)		1,333
Held-to-Maturity Investment in Bonds		99,682
Gain on Sale of Bonds		68

* $99,750 for the bonds + $2,666 for four months' interest

The credit to Interest Receivable represents the two months' interest accrued at August 31, 2009, and the credit to Interest Revenue represents interest earned from September 1 to November 1, all of which the purchaser pays in cash to Robinson. The debit to Cash represents the selling price of the bonds, $99,750, plus accrued interest of $2,666. The credit to the Held-to-Maturity Investment in Bonds account represents the bond's book value on the sale date and the credit to Gain on Sale of Bonds represents the excess of the selling price over the book value of the bonds.

Available-for-Sale Investments

Underlying Concept

Recognizing unrealized gains and losses is an application of the concept of comprehensive income.

Investments in debt securities that are available-for-sale are initially recognized at cost (fair value at acquisition),[14] and any discount or premium is amortized while the investment is owned. Subsequent to acquisition, the securities are reported at fair value. The unrealized gains and losses related to changes in the fair value of available-for-sale debt securities are recorded in an unrealized holding gain or loss account. This account is included as a component of other comprehensive income and as a separate component of Shareholders' Equity until realized. Thus, **changes in fair value are not reported as part of net income until the investment is sold**. This approach results in a lower volatility of income than if the value changes were recognized in the income statement each period.

As explained in Chapter 4, the concept of comprehensive income is new to Canadian financial reporting. Unrealized gains and losses on fair valued available-for-sale financial instruments are held here in a separate component of shareholders' equity until realized.

According to proposed *CICA Handbook* Section 1530, comprehensive income is the change in equity or net assets of an entity during a period from transactions and events from non-owner sources. Net income is a major component of comprehensive income. Other comprehensive income (OCI) is made up of revenues, gains, expenses, and losses that accounting standards say are included in comprehensive income, but excluded from net income. Accumulated other comprehensive income (AOCI) is the balance of all past charges and credits to other comprehensive income to the balance sheet date. The following illustrates how these financial statement categories are related.

Illustration 10-10

Comprehensive Income

STATEMENT OF COMPREHENSIVE INCOME	
Net income	$ xx
Add/subtract **other comprehensive income** items	
(generally unrealized gains, losses)	xx
Comprehensive income	$ xx

[14] Complications may arise when the fair value of the security changes between the trade date (the date when the commitment to purchase or sell the security is made) and the settlement date (the date when delivery occurs and title is transferred). When the period between these dates is short (termed a regular-way purchase or sale), either trade-date accounting or settlement-date accounting may be used, with disclosure of the method in the notes to the financial statements. This chapter's illustrations assume the trade and settlement dates are the same.

Opening balance, **accumulated other comprehensive income**		$ xx
Other comprehensive income, current period		xx
Ending balance, **accumulated other comprehensive income**		$ xx
Shareholders' equity section on the balance sheet:		
Share capital		$ xx
Retained earnings		xx
Accumulated other comprehensive income		xx
Shareholders' Equity		$ xx

Illustration 10-10

Comprehensive Income (continued)

Illustration: Single Security

To illustrate the accounting for available-for-sale securities, assume that Graff Corporation purchases $100,000, 10%, five-year bonds on January 1, 2005, with interest payable on July 1 and January 1. The bonds sell for $108,111, which results in a bond premium of $8,111 and an effective interest rate of 8%.

The entry to record the purchase of the bonds is as follows.

January 1, 2005		
Available-for-Sale Investment in Bonds	108,111	
Cash		108,111

A = L + SE
0   0   0

Cash flows: ↓ 108,111 outflow

Illustration 10-11 indicates the effect of premium amortization on interest revenue recorded each period using the effective interest method. The entry to record interest revenue on July 1, 2005 is as follows.

July 1, 2005		
Cash	5,000	
Available-for-Sale Investment in Bonds		676
Interest Revenue		4,324

A = L + SE
+4,324   +4,324

Cash flows: ↑ 5,000 inflow

10% BONDS PURCHASED TO YIELD 8%

Date	Cash Received	Interest Revenue	Bond Premium Amortization	Carrying Amount of Bonds
1/1/05				$108,111
7/1/05	$ 5,000[a]	$ 4,324[b]	$ 676[c]	107,435[d]
1/1/06	5,000	4,297	703	106,732
7/1/06	5,000	4,269	731	106,001
1/1/07	5,000	4,240	760	105,241
7/1/07	5,000	4,210	790	104,451
1/1/08	5,000	4,178	822	103,629
7/1/08	5,000	4,145	855	102,774
1/1/09	5,000	4,111	889	101,885
7/1/09	5,000	4,075	925	100,960
1/1/10	5,000	4,040	960	100,000
	$50,000	$41,889	$8,111	

[a] $5,000 = $100,000 × .10 × 6/12
[b] $4,324 = $108,111 × .08 × 6/12
[c] $676 = $5,000 − $4,324
[d] $107,435 = $108,111 − $676 or $100,000 + ($8,111 − $676)

Illustration 10-11

Schedule of Interest Revenue and Bond Premium Amortization— Effective Interest Method

At December 31, 2005, Graff makes the following entry to recognize interest revenue.

A = L + SE
+4,297   +4,297

Cash flows: No effect

	December 31, 2005	
Interest Receivable	5,000	
Available-for-Sale Investment in Bonds		703
Interest Revenue		4,297

As a result, Graff reports interest revenue for 2005 of $8,621 ($4,324 + $4,297).

As available-for-sale investments are required to be fair valued, their fair value and carrying value are compared. Assume that at December 31, 2005 the fair value of the bonds is $105,000, and that the carrying amount of the investments at this time is $106,732, as indicated in Illustration 10-11, at January 1, 2006. Comparing the fair value with the carrying amount (amortized cost) of the bonds, Graff recognizes an unrealized holding loss of $1,732 ($106,732 − $105,000). This loss is reported as an item of other comprehensive income and is included in the accumulated other comprehensive income component of shareholders' equity. The entry is as follows.

A = L + SE
−1,732   −1,732

Cash flows: No effect

	December 31, 2005	
Unrealized Holding Gain/Loss on Available-for-Sale Investments (OCI)	1,732	
Fair Value Allowance on Available-for-Sale Investments		1,732

An allowance or valuation account is used instead of crediting the Available-for-Sale Investment in Bonds account directly. The use of the **Fair Value Allowance account** enables the company to maintain a record of its amortized cost. Because the allowance account has a credit balance in this case, it is subtracted from the balance of the Available-for-Sale Investment in Bonds account to arrive at fair value. The fair value is the amount reported on the balance sheet. At each reporting date, the bonds are reported at fair value with an adjustment to the Unrealized Holding Gain/Loss account.

Illustration: Portfolio of Securities

To illustrate the accounting for a portfolio of securities, assume that Webb Corporation has two debt securities that are classified as available-for-sale. Illustration 10-12 provides information on amortized cost, fair value, and the unrealized gain or loss.

Illustration 10-12

Calculation of Fair Value Allowance—Available-for-Sale Investments (2006)

AVAILABLE-FOR-SALE DEBT INVESTMENT PORTFOLIO December 31, 2006			
Investments	Amortized Cost	Fair Value	Unrealized Gain (Loss)
Watson Corporation 8% bonds	$ 93,537	$103,600	$10,063
Sherlock Corporation 10% bonds	200,000	180,400	(19,600)
Total of portfolio	$293,537	$284,000	(9,537)
Balance of fair value allowance account before adjustment			–0–
Adjustment needed to fair value allowance account—credit			$ (9,537)

The total fair value of Webb's available-for-sale portfolio is $284,000. The gross unrealized gains are $10,063, and the gross unrealized losses are $19,600, resulting in a net unrealized loss of $9,537. That is, the fair value of available-for-sale investments is $9,537 less than its amortized cost. An adjusting entry is made to a valuation allowance account to record the decrease in value.

December 31, 2006		
Unrealized Holding Gain/Loss on Available- for-Sale Investments (OCI)	9,537	
Fair Value Allowance on Available- for-Sale Investments		9,537

A = L + SE
−9,537   −9,537
Cash flows: No effect

The unrealized holding loss of $9,537 is reported as an item of other comprehensive income and it, therefore, is included as a reduction in the accumulated other comprehensive income component of shareholders' equity. As indicated earlier, unrealized holding gains and losses related to investments that are classified in the available-for-sale category **are not included in net income**.

Sale of Available-for-Sale Investments

If bonds carried as investments in available-for-sale securities are sold before the maturity date, entries must be made to remove the amortized cost of the bonds sold from the Available-for-Sale Investment account. To illustrate, assume that Webb Corporation sold the Watson bonds (from Illustration 10-12) on July 1, 2007 for $90,000, at which time they had an amortized cost of $94,214 (assumed). The calculation of the realized loss is as follows.

Amortized cost of investment in Watson bonds	$94,214
Less: proceeds on sale of bonds	90,000
Loss on sale of bonds	$ 4,214

Illustration 10-13

Calculation of Loss on Sale of Bonds

The entry to record the sale of the Watson bonds, ignoring any related interest is as follows.

July 1, 2007		
Cash	90,000	
Loss on Sale of Investment in Bonds	4,214	
Available-for-Sale Investment in Bonds		94,214

A = L + SE
−4,214   −4,214
Cash flows: ↑ 90,000 inflow

This realized loss is reported in the "Other expenses and losses" section of the income statement. Assuming no other purchases and sales of available-for-sale investments in 2007, Webb Corporation prepares the information shown in Illustration 10-14 at year end, December 31, 2007, **after adjusting for accrued interest and amortizing any related discount or premium**.

Illustration 10-14

Calculation of Fair Value Allowance—Available-for-Sale Investments (2007)

AVAILABLE-FOR-SALE INVESTMENT PORTFOLIO December 31, 2007			
Investments	Amortized Cost	Fair Value	Unrealized Gain (Loss)
Sherlock Corporation 10% bonds (total portfolio)	$200,600	195,600	$(5,000)
Balance of fair value allowance account before adjustment			$(9,537) Cr.
Adjustment needed to fair value allowance account—debit			$ 4,537

At December 31, 2007, an unrealized holding loss of $5,000 remains and the valuation allowance account must be adjusted to a $5,000 credit balance. Because the Fair Value Allowance account has a credit balance of $9,537 before adjustment, a $4,537 debit adjustment is needed to this account to bring it to its correct balance.

A   = L +   SE
+4,537   +4,537
Cash flows: No effect

	December 31, 2007	
Fair Value Allowance on Available-for-Sale Investments	4,537	
Unrealized Holding Gain/Loss on Available-for-Sale Investments (OCI)		4,537

Financial Statement Presentation

Webb Corporation's December 31, 2007 balance sheet and the 2007 income statement contain the following items and amounts.

Illustration 10-15

Reporting of Available-for-Sale Investments

BALANCE SHEET	
Current assets	
Interest receivable	$ **xxx**
Long-term investments	
Available-for-sale investment, at fair value	**$195,600**
Shareholders' equity	
Accumulated other comprehensive loss	**$ (5,000)**

INCOME STATEMENT	
Other revenue and gains	
Interest revenue	$ **xxx**
Other expenses and losses	
Loss on sale of investment in bonds	**$ 4,214**

Excluding the unrealized gains and losses from net income is appealing to most companies as it reduces the volatility in reported earnings. This is particularly relevant to companies with significant holdings of such investments.

Trading Securities

Held-for-trading investments or **trading securities** are those acquired with the intention of being sold in a short period of time. "Trading" in this context means active and frequent buying and selling, and trading securities are used to generate profits from short-term differences in price. The holding period for such investments is generally short-term so that they are reported in current assets. **These securities are reported at fair value, with unrealized holding gains and losses reported as part of net income.**

Proposed *Handbook* Section 3855 allows a company to designate any financial instrument as held for trading when it is acquired. Therefore, those companies who wish to simplify their hedge accounting and move a little faster to a complete fair value model for investments with changes in fair value reported in income, can do so.

Refer to Chapter 7 for an explanation of the accounting and reporting requirements for this type of investment.

INVESTMENTS IN EQUITY SECURITIES

Equity Instruments

Equity instruments are securities representing ownership interests such as common, preferred, or other capital stock or shares. They also include rights to acquire or dispose of ownership interests at an agreed-upon or determinable price, such as warrants, rights, and call or put options. Convertible debt securities and redeemable preferred shares, discussed in Chapter 17, are often not treated as equity securities.

Equity investments when acquired are **recognized initially at the fair value of the consideration given**. As fair value, by definition, does not include transaction costs such as commissions, fees, and transfer taxes, such costs that traditionally have been included as part of an asset's original cost can instead be expensed as incurred.[15] Wherever a choice of policy exists as in this situation, the accounting policy used is disclosed in the notes to the financial statements.

When equity securities are acquired **in a non-monetary transaction**, the fair value of the investment acquired may be used if it is more clearly evident than the fair value of the consideration given up. The absence of clear values for the property or services or a market price for the security acquired may require the use of appraisals or estimates to arrive at a cost.

Common Shares

Common or residual shares carry **voting rights**—the more shares held, the more votes and therefore the more say the investor has in the decisions made by the company invested in.

Accounting for investments in common shares of another corporation subsequent to acquisition depends, for the most part, on the relationship between the investor (the corporation acquiring the shares) and the investee (the company whose shares are acquired). The relationships are classified by the level of influence exercised by the investor and these, in turn are generally related to degree of share ownership. The levels of interest and corresponding reporting methods that are applied to investments are displayed in Illustration 10-16. Note that the percentages given are guidelines rather than rigid standards.

3 Objective

Identify the categories of long-term equity securities and describe the accounting and reporting treatment for each category.

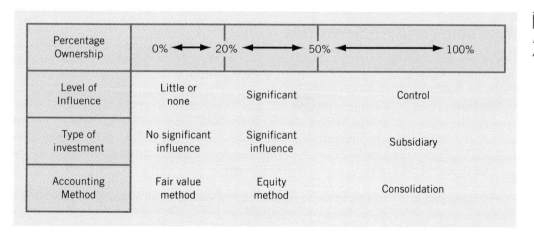

Illustration 10-16

Levels of Influence Determine Accounting Methods

---

[15] *Exposure Draft, CICA Handbook* Section 3855.53 and .56.

Accounting and reporting for equity investments therefore depends upon the level of influence, as shown in Illustration 10-17.[16]

Illustration 10-17

Accounting and Reporting for Equity Investments by Category

Category	Valuation	Unrealized Holding Gains or Losses	Other Income Statement Effects
No significant influence			
1. Available-for-sale	Fair value*	Recognized in "Other comprehensive income" and as separate component of shareholders' equity	Dividends as received or receivable; gains and losses from sale.
2. Trading	Fair value	Recognized in net income	Dividends as received or receivable; gains and losses from sale.
Significant influence	Equity	Not recognized	Investment income recognized; equal to investor's proportionate share of investee's net income reported
Control: subsidiary	Consolidation	Not recognized	Line-by-line consolidation of revenues, expenses, gains and losses

* Unless market prices not available

Holdings without Significant Influence

When an investor has an interest of less than 20%, **it is presumed that the investor has little or no influence over the investee**. This may not be the case, however. For example, a 16% interest may allow an investor to very significantly influence decisions if the remaining shares are widely held. Alternatively, ownership of 30% of a company's shares may not entitle an investor company to any influence at all if a 70% majority shareholder doesn't permit it. Therefore, the percentages serve as a guide only.

In cases **where there is no significant influence**, the investment is classified as either available-for-sale or held-for-trading. Because equity securities have no maturity date, they cannot be classified as held-to-maturity.

Available-for-Sale Securities

Equity investments classified as available-for-sale are recorded at their cost or fair value at acquisition. Subsequent to acquisition, they are reported at fair value, provided market prices are available.[17]

If market prices are not available, the investment remains at cost in periods subsequent to acquisition. This approach is the cost method. Under this method, dividends are recognized as revenue when received or receivable, and the portfolio continues to be carried and reported at acquisition cost. No gains or losses are recognized until the securities are sold, unless there is a permanent decline in value.

---

[16] Joint ventures are another type of equity investment. They may take the form of incorporated companies and therefore issue shares. Joint ventures are characterized by **joint control** (versus **unilateral control**). The accounting method used for joint ventures is the **proportionate consolidation** method (*CICA Handbook*, Section 3055.17). The key to determining whether the investment is a joint venture or not is determining whether there is joint control. This is usually evidenced through a contractual agreement that states that the venturers (investors) must **share key decision-making**.

[17] Proposed *CICA Handbook* Section 3855.59(c) requires that the securities have a "quoted market price in an active market."

Where market values are available, the **fair value method** is used. To illustrate, assume that on November 3, 2004, Manitoba Corporation purchased common shares of three companies, each investment representing less than a 20% interest. Manitoba was not able to exercise significant influence over the key operating, financing, and investing decisions of any of these companies.

	Cost (Fair value at acquisition)
Nova Industries Ltd.	$259,700
Columbia Soup Corp.	317,500
St. Boniface Pulp Ltd.	141,350
Total cost	$718,550

The purchase of the investments is recorded as follows.

November 3, 2004		
Available-for-Sale Investments	718,550	
Cash		718,550

A = L + SE
0   0   0

Cash flows: ↓ 718,550 outflow

On December 6, 2004, Manitoba Corp. receives a cash dividend of $4,200 on its investment in the common shares of Columbia Soup Corp. The cash dividend is recorded as follows.

December 6, 2004		
Cash	4,200	
Dividend Revenue		4,200

A = L + SE
+4,200   +4,200

Cash flows: ↑ 4,200 inflow

All three of the investee companies report net income for the year, but only Columbia Soup declared and paid a dividend to Manitoba Corporation. When an investor company has relatively little influence over an investee, the investor is not able to influence the conversion of its share of the investee's earnings to cash (i.e., influence them to pay out a dividend). Instead the investor must wait until the investee company declares a dividend. Although the investor can measure its share of the earnings of the investee, and has "earned" the income, its conversion to cash is not sufficiently assured **until a dividend is declared by the investee**. Only then can the investor recognize income equal in amount to the dividend received. Note the similarity of this approach to the cash basis of accounting.

At December 31, 2004, Manitoba's available-for-sale equity investment portfolio has the following cost and fair value.

Underlying Concept

Revenue should not be recognized until earned, measurable, and convertibility to cash is reasonably assured. A low level of ownership indicates that the income from an investee should be deferred until cash is received or imminently receivable (i.e., when dividend is declared).

Illustration 10-18

Calculation of Investment Fair Value Allowance— Available-for-Sale Equity Investment Portfolio (2004)

AVAILABLE-FOR-SALE EQUITY INVESTMENT PORTFOLIO
December 31, 2004

Investments	Cost	Fair Value	Unrealized Gain (Loss)
Nova Industries Ltd.	$259,700	$275,000	$ 15,300
Columbia Soup Corp.	317,500	304,000	(13,500)
St. Boniface Pulp Ltd.	141,350	104,000	(37,350)
Total of portfolio	$718,550	$683,000	(35,550)
Balance of fair value allowance account before adjustment			–0–
Adjustment needed to fair value allowance account—credit			$(35,550)

For Manitoba's available-for-sale equity investment portfolio, the gross unrealized gains are $15,300, and the gross unrealized losses are $50,850 ($13,500 + $37,350), resulting in a net unrealized loss of $35,550. The fair value of the available-for-sale portfolio is $35,550 less than its cost. As with available-for-sale **debt** securities, the net unrealized gains and losses related to changes in the fair value of available-for-sale **equity** securities are recorded in an Unrealized Holding Gain or Loss account. This is reported as a **part of other comprehensive income and as a component of shareholders' equity until realized**. In this case, Manitoba's entry is as follows.

A = L + SE
−35,550   −35,550
Cash flows: No effect

December 31, 2004		
Unrealized Holding Gain/Loss on Available-for-Sale Investments (OCI)	35,550	
Fair Value Allowance on Available-for-Sale Investments		35,550

On January 23, 2005, Manitoba sells all of its Nova Industries common shares, receiving net proceeds of $287,220. If Manitoba had purchased the Nova Industries shares at various times and at various costs in the past, the average cost is used when determining gains or losses on disposal. The realized gain on the sale is calculated as follows.

Illustration 10-19

Calculation of Gain on Sale of Shares

Net proceeds from sale	$287,220
Cost of Nova Industries shares	259,700
Gain on sale of shares	$ 27,520

The sale is recorded as follows.

A = L + SE
+27,520   +27,520
Cash flows: ↑ 287,220 inflow

January 23, 2005		
Cash	287,220	
Available-for-Sale Investments		259,700
Gain on Sale of Shares		27,520

In addition, assume that on February 10, 2005, Manitoba purchases 20,000 shares of Provincial Trucking at a market price of $12.75 per share plus brokerage commissions of $1,850. Manitoba follows a policy of capitalizing transaction costs, therefore the total cost of the new investment is $256,850.

On December 31, 2005, Manitoba's available-for-sale portfolio is as follows.

Illustration 10-20

Calculation of Investment Fair Value Allowance—Available-for-Sale Equity Investment Portfolio (2005)

AVAILABLE-FOR-SALE EQUITY INVESTMENT PORTFOLIO			
December 31, 2005			
Investments	Cost	Fair Value	Unrealized Gain (Loss)
Provincial Trucking Ltd.	$256,850	$278,350	$21,500
Columbia Soup Corp.	317,500	362,550	45,050
St. Boniface Pulp Ltd.	141,350	139,050	(2,300)
Total of portfolio	$715,700	$779,950	64,250
Balance of fair value allowance account before adjustment			(35,550)
Adjustment needed to fair value allowance account—debit			$99,800

At December 31, 2005, the fair value of Manitoba's available-for-sale equity portfolio exceeds cost by $64,250 (unrealized gain). The Fair Value Allowance account has a credit balance of $35,550 at December 31, 2005 before adjustment, as there have been no entries made to this account since the last reporting date. Therefore, a $99,800 debit adjustment is needed to bring the fair value allowance to its required balance of $64,250. The entry to record this adjustment is as follows.

December 31, 2005		
Fair Value Allowance on Available-for-Sale Investments	99,800	
Unrealized Holding Gain/Loss on Available-for-Sale Investments (OCI)		99,800

A   =   L   +   SE
+99,800   +99,800
Cash flows: No effect

Trading Securities

The accounting entries to record and account for trading equity securities (current assets) using the fair value method were previously illustrated in Chapter 7. The entries are the same as for available-for-sale equity securities illustrated above, except that the unrealized holding gain or loss is **reported as part of net income** instead of other comprehensive income. The Unrealized Holding Gain or Loss is therefore reported on the income statement. When a sale is made, the remainder of the gain or loss is recognized in income.

Holdings with Significant Influence, but not Control

While an equity interest of less than 50% of an investee corporation does not give an investor legal control, it could give the investor the ability to exercise significant influence over the strategic policies of the investee. To provide a guide for accounting for investors when 50% or less of the voting common shares are held and to develop an operational definition of "**significant influence**," the AcSB of the CICA noted in *CICA Handbook* Section 3050 that ability to exercise influence over another company's operating, investing, and financing activities may be indicated in several ways. Examples include: representation on the board of directors, participation in policy-making processes, material intercompany transactions, interchange of managerial personnel, or provision of technical information.[18]

To achieve a reasonable degree of uniformity in application of the significant influence criterion, the profession concluded that an investment (direct or indirect) of 20% or more of the voting shares of an investee should lead to a presumption that, in the absence of evidence to the contrary, an investor has the ability to exercise significant influence over an investee. With less than a 20% voting interest, the assumption is that the investor cannot exercise the required degree of influence, unless such influence is clearly demonstrated.[19]

Where significant influence—but not control—is evident, **use of the equity method is required**.

The extent of control or influence for an equity investor, given a level of investment, can vary internationally. This was illustrated when DaimlerChrysler made a 33.4% investment in Mitsubishi Motors. Under Japanese commercial law, that level of investment gives DaimlerChrysler regular seats on the board and gives it the power to veto board decisions. Whether this is a good deal for Mitsubishi will depend on whether and how DaimlerChrysler exercises its control over Mitsubishi operations. Mitsubishi is said to have sought assurances that DaimlerChrysler would not push for job cuts, but may have been willing to give DaimlerChrysler more control in exchange for the financial boost it provided and for access to the German-American carmaker's engineering and production expertise.

What
do the
Numbers
Mean?

Source: S. Miller and N. Shirouzu, "DaimlerChrysler to Acquire a Stake in Mitsubishi Motors for $1.94 Billion," *Wall Street Journal Online* (March 27, 2000).

---

[18] *CICA Handbook* Section 3050.04.

[19] *CICA Handbook* Section 3050.04.

Equity Method

Objective 4
Explain the equity method of accounting.

Under the equity method, a substantive economic relationship is acknowledged between the investor and the investee. The investment is originally recorded at the cost of the shares acquired but is subsequently adjusted each period for changes in the net assets of the investee. That is, **when the investee's net assets increase** because it earned income, **the investor increases the carrying amount of its investment** for its proportionate share of the investee's increase in net assets, and **reports its share of the investee's income as investment income. When the investee's net assets decrease** because the company pays a dividend, **the investor decreases the carrying amount of the investment** by its share of the decrease in the investee's net assets, and **recognizes the cash received**. The investment account is changed, therefore, to mirror the changes in the investee's net assets, and **investment income is recognized by the investor as it is earned by the investee.**

The equity method sounds complex at first, but it is only **the accrual basis of accounting applied to investment income.** Income is recognized by the investor as earned (i.e., as the investee earns income and its net assets increase) with a debit to an asset and a credit to investment income. When cash is received (the dividend), this is the conversion of the asset previously recognized—recorded with a debit to cash and a credit to the asset account. The asset is the Investment account, rather than an account receivable.

To illustrate the equity method and **compare it with the fair value method**, assume that Maxi Corp. purchases a 20% interest in Mini Corp. To apply the fair value method in this example, assume that Maxi does not have the ability to exercise significant influence and the securities are classified as available-for-sale. Where the equity method is applied in this example, assume that the 20% interest permits Maxi to exercise significant influence. The entries are shown in Illustration 10-21. Study the equity method first, noting the effect on the investment account and on the income statement.

Illustration 10-21

Comparison of Fair Value Method and Equity Method

ENTRIES BY MAXI CORP.

Fair Value Method		Equity Method	

On January 2, 2004, Maxi Corp. acquired 48,000 shares (20% of Mini Corp. common shares) at a cost of $10 a share.

Available-for-Sale Investment	480,000			Investment in Mini Corp.	480,000	
Cash		480,000		Cash		480,000

For the year 2004, Mini Corp. reported net income of $200,000; Maxi Corp.'s share is 20%, or $40,000.

No entry			Investment in Mini Corp.	40,000	
			Investment Revenue		40,000

At December 31, 2004, the 48,000 shares of Mini Corp. have a fair value (market price) of $12 a share, or $576,000.

Fair Value Adjustment on Available-for-Sale Investments	96,000		No entry
Unrealized Holding Gain/Loss on Available-for-Sale Investments		96,000	

On January 28, 2005, Mini Corp. announced and paid a cash dividend of $100,000; Maxi Corp. received 20%, or $20,000.

Cash	20,000			Cash	20,000	
Dividend Revenue		20,000		Investment in Mini Corp.		20,000

For the year 2005, Mini reported a net loss of $50,000; Maxi Corp.'s share is 20%, or $10,000.

No entry			Investment Loss	10,000	
			Investment in Mini Corp.		10,000

At December 31, 2005, the Mini Corp. 48,000 shares have a fair value (market price) of $11 a share, or $528,000.

Unrealized Holding Gain/Loss on Available-for-Sale Investments	48,000		No entry
Fair Value Adjustment on Available-for-Sale Investments		48,000	

Note that under the fair value method, only the dividends received from Mini Corp. are reported as revenue by Maxi Corp. **This is an application of the cash basis of accounting where the revenue is not recognized until collectibility is assured.** Mini's increased net assets resulting from profitable operations may be permanently retained in the business by the investee and the investor has no authority or influence to require a pay-out to shareholders by way of dividend.

Under the equity method, **the accrual basis is applied** in that Maxi Corp. reports investment revenue as Mini Corp. earns income. Revenue recognition is permitted earlier in this case because of the degree of influence the investor has over the decisions of the investee. If the investee company suffers a loss, as Mini Corp. did in 2005, the investor accrues its share of the loss and reduces the carrying value of its investment in the investee.

One of the benefits of this method is that the investor's income statement reports the economics of the situation: if the influence exerted results in the investee performing well, the investor's income statement reflects positive investment income. If the influence results in poor decisions and the investee incurs losses, the investor's income statement reflects its share of the loss. Other aspects of applying the equity method are discussed below.

Underlying Concept

The equity method of accounting results in income statement amounts that more faithfully represent the underlying economic reality of investor company management performance.

When the Acquisition Price Exceeds The Investor's Share of The Investee's Book Value. It is unusual for the investor to pay an amount on acquisition exactly equal to its share of the other company's book value. The excess payment (usually it is extra) could be due to a number of reasons: there may be unrecorded assets; there may be assets whose fair value exceeds the carrying amount on the investee's books or liabilities whose fair value is less than book value; there may be goodwill of value in the investee company; etc. **Any payment in excess of (or less than) the investor's share of book value is included in the cost of the investment, and subsequent to acquisition, must be dealt with.**

International Insight

International Standards permit significant-influence investments to be measured using the equity, cost, or fair value methods.

If the difference is due to long-lived assets, the extra amount must be amortized; if it relates to inventory with a fair value in excess of carrying value, it must be recognized as an increased "expense" as it is sold. There also may be assets with fair values lower than book value or liabilities with present values higher than book value. **These differences are not on the investee's records, but are included as part of the purchase cost of the investment**, so it is the investment account itself that is adjusted subsequently. The differences are accounted for according to their nature subsequent to acquisition and details of these differences are required to be disclosed in the notes to the financial statements. Accounting for these adjustments is left to an advanced financial accounting course.

Components of Net Income. Because the equity method recognizes the investor's share of the investee company's income on its income statement, it is important to also recognize the separate components of income according to their nature. The portion that is the investor's share of the investee's discontinued operations or extraordinary items is reported separately from its share of income before discontinued operations and extraordinary items. The same principle holds true for the investor's portion of the investee's other comprehensive income, changes in accounting policy reported in retained earnings, and capital charges, as these are required to be reported in the appropriate financial statement of the investor.[20]

Investee Losses Exceed Carrying Amount. If an investor's share of the investee's losses exceeds the carrying amount of the investment, should the investor recognize additional losses? Ordinarily the investor discontinues applying the equity method and no additional losses are recognized. However, if the investor's potential loss is not limited to the amount of its original investment (by guarantee of the investee's obligations or other commitment to provide further financial support), or if the investees' imminent return to profitable operations appears to be assured, it is appropriate for the investor to recognize additional losses.

[20] *CICA Handbook* Section 3050.

Principles Governing the Equity Method of Accounting. Application of the equity method is closely related to consolidation principles. *CICA Handbook* Section 3050.08 states that equity method "investment income" is the same amount that is needed to increase or decrease the investor's income to the amount that would be reported if the investor had consolidated the results of the investee with those of the investor. Therefore it is necessary to understand the requirements of *Handbook* Section 1600 on Consolidated Financial Statements in order to fully apply the equity method. This is left to an advanced course.

What do the Numbers Mean?

Bema Gold Corporation, a Canadian company based inVancouver, is engaged in the exploration, extraction, processing, and reclamation of gold. The company operates through subsidiaries and investments accounted for using the equity method. One of the significantly influenced investments reported by Bema at the end of its second quarter in 2002 was a 42% equity interest in Victoria Resource Corporation. The carrying value of Victoria on the balance sheet at that time was $644 thousand (U.S.), less than 1% of Bema's total assets. Bema reported an equity in losses of this associated company of $407 thousand (U.S.) for the six months ended June 30, 2002, representing 136% of Bema's net loss for the period! The notes to the financial statements explain that this was due mainly to Bema's share of a write-off of deferred exploration costs by Victoria Resource. This illustrates well how the performance and results of equity accounted for investments are reflected on the investor's operating statement, mirroring the results of the investor company's influence on the investee's decisions.

Holdings with Control

When one corporation acquires a voting interest of more than 50%—a **controlling interest**—in another corporation, the investor corporation is referred to as the **parent** and the investee corporation as the **subsidiary**. By virtue of holding a majority of the votes at the board of directors meetings of the investee company, the parent company's management virtually controls all the subsidiary's net assets and operations.

The investment in the common shares of the subsidiary is presented as a long-term investment on the separate financial statements of the parent, which usually applies the equity method of accounting for this investment internally. **However, when the parent company prepares its financial statements in accordance with GAAP, it must report on a line-by-line basis all the assets and liabilities over which it has control.**

Objective 5
Explain the basics of consolidation.

This means that instead of reporting the investment in the subsidiary as a one-line long-term investment, the parent replaces the investment account with 100% of each of the assets and liabilities over which it has control. Instead of reporting a single line investment income on the income statement, 100% of each of the revenues and expenses reported by the subsidiary is reported on a line-by-line basis with those of the parent company. That is, the parent presents **consolidated financial statements**. This method of reporting an investment in a controlled company is much more informative than a single line balance sheet and income statement account.[21]

The requirement to include 100% of the assets and liabilities and 100% of the revenues, expenses, gains, and losses under the parent's control when the ownership is less than 100% leads to the need to report a unique balance sheet and a unique income statement account. These accounts, termed **noncontrolling interest** or **minority interest**, represents the percentage of the net assets not owned (reported as a liability on the balance sheet,) or the percentage of net income that does not accrue to the parent company (reported as a deduction from the combined net income on the income statement.)

Underlying Concept

The consolidation of financial results of different companies follows the economic entity assumption and disregards legal entities. The key objective is to provide useful information to financial statement users.

Consolidated financial statements disregard the distinction between separate legal entities and treat the parent and subsidiary corporations as a single economic

[21] For this reason, investments in joint ventures, where the investor exercises joint control with other venturers, are accounted for by proportionate consolidation. The opening vignette explains that Empire Company uses proportionate consolidation to report its real estate investment in Genstar Development.

entity. Subsequent to acquisition, this means that all intercompany balances and unrealized intercompany gains and losses must be eliminated for reporting purposes, because an entity cannot report sales or make a profit selling to itself. The subject of when and how to prepare consolidated financial statements is discussed extensively in advanced financial accounting.

The rules for consolidation seem very straightforward: If a company owns more than 50% of another company, it generally should be consolidated. If it owns less than 50%, it is generally not consolidated. However, with complex modern business relationships, standard setters realize that this test is too artificial, and that determining who really has control is often based on factors other than share ownership.

In fact, specific guidelines have been developed that force consolidation even though share ownership is not above 50% in certain situations. For example, the well known Enron failure to consolidate three special purpose entities that were effectively controlled by Enron led to an overstatement of income of $569 million (U.S.) and overstatement of equity of $1.2 billion (U.S.). In these three cases, the GAAP answer would have led to consolidation. That is, the following factors indicate that consolidation should have occurred: the majority owner of the special purpose entity made only a modest investment, the activities of the entity were virtually to benefit Enron, and the substantive risks and rewards related to the special entity's assets or debt rested directly or indirectly with Enron. These arrangements were not unique to Enron! Many companies used non-consolidated special purpose entities to window-dress their financial statements.

Such actions prompted the CICA to issue *Accounting Guideline* AcG-15 "Consolidation of Variable Interest Entities" (VIEs) in 2003 to provide guidance on such arrangements, harmonizing with similar FASB guidance. The guideline requires a company to consolidate a **variable interest entity** **when it is the primary beneficiary of such an entity**; that is, when it will absorb a majority of a VIE's expected losses, receive a majority of its expected residual returns, or both. The guideline applies to entities established in such a way that control is achieved in ways other than through ownership of voting interests.

What do the Numbers Mean?

Differential Reporting

As referred to in Chapter 2 and 19 and again in Chapter 24, *CICA Handbook* Section 1300, "Differential Reporting," recognizes that there may be circumstances where the costs associated with providing certain financial information may be greater than the benefits accruing to users. Therefore, **companies that are not publicly accountable and whose owners unanimously agree may select alternative methods** specified by Section 1300.

Accounting for investments in equity securities subject to significant influence is one area where qualifying companies may elect to use a simpler method. The allowed alternative is to account for the investment at cost (instead of using the equity method), reporting dividends as revenue.

Qualifying entities may also elect not to consolidate subsidiary companies. The allowed alternative in this case is to account for the investments under either the equity method or at cost.

Companies that select these differential reporting options must also meet strict disclosure requirements.

OTHER ACCOUNTING AND REPORTING ISSUES

The basic issues involved in accounting for investments in debt and equity securities have been identified above. In addition, the following issues relate to both of these types of securities.

Impairment of Value

Objective 6

Explain the accounting for impairments in value of long-term investments in debt and equity securities.

Every investment should be evaluated at each reporting date to determine if it has suffered impairment—a loss in value that is other than temporary. A bankruptcy or a significant liquidity crisis being experienced by an investee are examples of situations in which a loss in value to the investor may be permanent. Alternatively, significant adverse changes in the particular markets the investee operates in may also indicate that its carrying value may not be recoverable.

For debt securities, the impairment test is to determine whether "it is probable that the investor will be unable to collect all amounts due according to the contractual terms." **For equity securities,** the guideline is less precise. Any time realizable value is lower than the carrying amount of the investment, impairment must be considered. Factors involved include the length of time and the extent to which the fair value has been less than cost; the financial condition and near-term prospects of the issuer; and the intent and ability of the investor company to retain its investment to allow for any anticipated recovery in fair value.

If the decline is judged to be 'other than temporary,' the carrying amount of the investment is written down to a new cost basis. The amount of the writedown is accounted for as if it were a realized loss and is included in net income. The standards, which differ somewhat among the various categories of instrument, are explained below.

For long-term receivables and loans, *CICA Handbook* Section 3025 is applied when accounting for the impairment of this type of asset. In general, when the collection of the full amount of interest and principal on a timely basis of an individual loan or portfolio of loans is in doubt, the carrying amount of the loan should be reduced. The writedown, either through a direct reduction in the investment or through an allowance account, is recognized in income. The writedown is measured as the difference between the carrying amount of the loan and its estimated realizable amount; that is, the present value of the expected remaining cash flows, discounted at the historical interest rate inherent in the loan.

The standards are complicated by the difficulty in estimating the remaining cash flows and by the fact that the loans often have collateral whose fair value is considered in measuring any impairment loss. The appendix to Chapter 15 discusses the accounting for troubled debt and application of *CICA Handbook* Section 3025 in more detail.

For financial assets (other than loans and receivables) carried at cost or amortized cost, or using the equity method, the impairment loss is the difference between the carrying amount of the investment and its fair value. The loss is recognized in income, and no reversal of the writedown is permitted. Amortization of any discount stops with the writedown.

For available-for-sale financial assets, the impairment standards differ because this type of investment requires valuation at fair value every reporting period. Therefore, it is likely that **much of the reduction in value has already been recognized in other comprehensive income.** Because of this, in the period there is objective evidence of an other-than-temporary decline in fair value, the cumulative net loss previously recognized in other comprehensive income is removed from OCI and is recognized in net income.

The amount transferred is the difference between the amortized acquisition cost (net of principal repayments) and its current fair value. No reversal is permitted of amounts recognized in net income until the security is sold.

To illustrate, assume that Strickler Corp. holds available-for-sale bond securities with a par value and amortized cost of $1 million. Strickler has previously reported an unrealized loss on these securities of $200,000 as part of other comprehensive income. The fair value of these securities is now $800,000 and Strickler determines it is probable that it will not be able to collect all amounts due. In this case, the unrealized loss of $200,000 will be reported as a loss on impairment of $200,000 and included in income, with the bonds stated at their new cost basis. The journal entry to record this impairment and to transfer the loss from other comprehensive income to the income statement is as follows.

Impairment Loss	200,000		A	=	L	+	SE
Unrealized Holding Gain/Loss on			0		0		0
Available-for-Sale Investments (OCI)		200,000	Cash flows: No effect				

To eliminate the previous unrealized holding losses from the Allowance account and, instead, directly reduce the carrying value of the investment to its new cost basis, the following entry is required.

Fair Value Allowance on Available-			A	=	L	+	SE
for-Sale Investments	200,000		0		0		0
Available-for-Sale Investments		200,000	Cash flows: No effect				

The new cost basis of the investment is $800,000 and amortization of any discount stops at this time. Subsequent increases and decreases in the fair value of impaired available-for-sale securities are included in other comprehensive income.

Transfers between Categories

Transfers between categories of investment are accounted for at fair value. Thus, if available-for-sale securities are transferred to held-to-maturity investments, the new held-to-maturity investment is recorded at **fair value** at the date of transfer in the new category. Similarly, if held-to-maturity investments are transferred to available-for-sale investments, the new available-for-sale investments are recorded at **fair value**. This **fair value rule** assures that a company cannot escape recognition of fair value simply by transferring securities to the held-to-maturity category. Illustration 10-22 summarizes the accounting treatment for transfers.

7 Objective
Describe how to account for the transfer of investment securities between categories.

Type of Transfer	Measurement Basis	Effect of Transfer on Other Comprehensive Income	Effect of Transfer on Net Income
To and from the trading category	n/a – reclassification into or out of trading category is not permitted	n/a	n/a
Transfer from held-to-maturity to available-for-sale	Investment is transferred at fair value at the date of transfer	Unrealized gain/loss is recognized in other comprehensive income at the date of transfer	None
Transfer from available-for-sale to held-to-maturity	Investment is transferred at fair value at the date of transfer = new cost or amortized cost	Amortize the unrealized gain/loss in OCI at date of transfer to net income over remaining life of the investment	None at date of transfer, but over life of investment

Illustration 10-22
Accounting for Transfers

Financial Statement Presentation

The objective of the disclosure requirements for investments in financial assets is to "provide information to enhance understanding of the significance of financial instruments to an entity's financial position, performance, and cash flows and assist in assessing the amounts, timing, and certainty of future cash flows associated with those instruments."[22]

8 Objective
Describe the reporting and disclosure requirements for long-term investments in debt and equity securities.

[22] Proposed consequential amendments to *CICA Handbook* Section 3860.43, *Exposure Draft* of Section 3855, March 2003.

Companies are required to present individual amounts for the three categories of investments either on the balance sheet or in the related notes, with separate disclosure of investments in affiliated companies. Trading securities should be reported at aggregate fair value as current assets (see Chapter 7). Individual long-term notes and receivables, held-to-maturity, and available-for-sale investments are classified as current or noncurrent, depending upon the circumstances.

Notes and receivables and held-to-maturity securities are classified as current or noncurrent, based on the maturity date of the individual securities. **Debt securities identified as available-for-sale** are classified as current or noncurrent, based on maturities and expectations as to sales and redemptions in the following year. **Equity securities identified as available-for-sale** are classified as current if these securities are available for use in current operations. Thus, if the invested cash used to purchase the equity securities is considered a contingency fund to be used whenever a need arises, then the securities should be classified as current. **Investments in significantly influenced companies** are classified outside the current category.

For **each class of financial asset** reported, the following are required:

1. the fair value of that class of assets or additional information related to why fair values are not presented

2. the methods and assumptions used in determining fair values

3. information about the extent and nature of the investments, including significant terms and conditions that may affect future cash flows

4. information about exposure to interest rate and credit risk and

5. total interest revenue for financial assets not designated as held-for-trading.

For **investments classified as available-for-sale**, a company should disclose the gain or loss recognized in other comprehensive income in the period and the amount removed from OCI and transferred or reclassified to net income. Reclassification adjustments are explained below.

In classifying investments, management's expressed intent should be supported by evidence, such as the history of the company's investment activities, events subsequent to the balance sheet date, and the nature and purpose of the investment.

Although Canadian companies had not applied these new standards as this text went to print, the experience in the United States is that **companies have to be extremely careful with debt securities held to maturity**. If a debt security in this category is sold prematurely, the sale may "taint" the entire held-to-maturity portfolio. That is, management's statement regarding "intent" is no longer as credible, and therefore the securities might have to be reclassified. This could lead to unfortunate consequences. An interesting by-product of this situation is that companies that wish to retire their debt securities early are finding it difficult to do so; the holder will not sell because the securities are classified as held-to-maturity.

Disclosures Required under the Equity Method

Digital Tool

Student Toolkit—
Additional
Dislosures
www.wiley.com/canada/kieso

The significance of an investment to the investor's financial position and operating results should determine the extent of disclosure. The following disclosures generally apply to investments where the equity method has been applied.

1. separate disclosure of the category on the balance sheet or in the notes to the financial statements

2. separate disclosure of the income from investments accounted for using the equity method

3. the difference, if any, between the amount in the investment account and the amount of underlying equity in the net assets of the investee, along with an explanation of the accounting treatment of the components of the difference.

Although not required, the investor is expected to disclose the reasons for **not** using the equity method in cases of 20% or more ownership interest and **for** using the equity method in cases of less than 20% ownership interest.

Reclassification Adjustments

As indicated above, changes in unrealized holding gains and losses related to available-for-sale securities are reported as part of other comprehensive income. The reporting of changes in unrealized gains or losses in other comprehensive income is straightforward **unless securities are sold during the year**. In this case, double counting results when realized gains or losses are reported as part of net income but also are shown as part of other comprehensive income in the current period or in previous periods. To ensure that gains and losses are not counted twice when a sale occurs, a reclassification adjustment is necessary. To illustrate, assume that Open Corporation has the following two available-for-sale securities in its portfolio at the end of 2004 (its first year of operations).

Investments	Cost	Fair Value	Unrealized Holding Gain (Loss)
Lehman Inc. common shares	$ 80,000	$105,000	$25,000
Woods Corp. common shares	120,000	135,000	15,000
Total of portfolio	$200,000	$240,000	40,000
Balance of fair value allowance account before adjustment			–0–
Adjustment needed to fair value allowance account—debit			$40,000

Illustration 10-23

Available-for-Sale Security Portfolio (2004)

If Open Corporation reports net income in 2004 of $350,000, a statement of comprehensive income is reported as follows.

OPEN CORPORATION
Statement of Comprehensive Income
For the Year Ended December 31, 2004

Net income	$350,000
Other comprehensive income—Holding gains arising during period	40,000
Comprehensive income	$390,000

Illustration 10-24

Statement of Comprehensive Income (2004)

During 2005, Open Corporation sells the Lehman Inc. common shares for $105,000 and realizes a gain on the sale of $25,000 ($105,000 − $80,000), which is reported in net income. By the end of 2005, the fair value of the Woods Corp. common shares has increased an additional $20,000 to $155,000. The change in the fair value allowance account is calculated as follows.

Illustration 10-25

*Available-for-Sale Security
Portfolio (2005)*

Investments	Cost	Fair Value	Unrealized Holding Gain (Loss)
Woods Corp. common shares	$120,000	$155,000	$35,000
Balance of fair value allowance account before adjustment			(40,000)
Adjustment needed to fair value allowance account—credit			$ (5,000)

Illustration 10-25 indicates that an unrealized holding loss of $5,000 should be reported in comprehensive income in 2005. The appropriate entry is made to record this. In addition, Open Corporation realized and reported a gain of $25,000 on the sale of the Lehman common shares. The total holding gain (loss) recognized in 2005 is $20,000, calculated as follows.

Illustration 10-26

*Calculation of Total
Holding Gain/Loss*

Unrealized holding gain (loss)—adjustment made to the Allowance account	($ 5,000)
Realized holding gain (loss) reported on income statement, to be reclassified	25,000
Total holding gain (loss) in period	$20,000

Open Corporation reports net income of $720,000 in 2005, which includes the $25,000 realized gain on sale of the Lehman securities. A statement of comprehensive income for 2005 is shown in Illustration 10-27, indicating how the components of holding gains (losses) are reported. Note that no further journal entries are needed—this is a disclosure and reporting issue only. The $5,000 net unrealized loss in 2005 is reported as two components in the statement of comprehensive income.

Illustration 10-27

*Statement of Comprehensive
Income (2005)*

OPEN CORPORATION
Statement of Comprehensive Income
For the Year Ended December 31, 2005

Net income (includes $25,000 realized gain on Lehman shares)		$720,000
Other comprehensive income:		
Holding gains arising during period ($155,000 – $135,000)	$20,000	
Less: Reclassification adjustment for gains included in net income	(25,000)	(5,000)
Comprehensive income		$715,000

In 2004, the unrealized gain on the Lehman Corp. common shares was included in comprehensive income. In 2005, it was sold, and the realized gain reported in net income increases comprehensive income again. To avoid double counting this gain, a reclassification adjustment is made to eliminate the realized gain from the calculation of comprehensive income. This also serves to identify **what portion of the total holding gains or losses arising during the period were actually realized gains or losses**.

A company has the option to display reclassification adjustments on the face of the financial statement in which comprehensive income is reported, or it may disclose these reclassification adjustments in the notes to the financial statements. Any associated income tax expense or benefit is reported along with the reclassification adjustment.

Comprehensive Illustration

To illustrate the reporting of investments and the related gain or loss on available-for-sale securities, assume that on January 1, 2004, Hinges Corp. had cash and shareholders' equity made up of common shares of $50,000.[23] At that date the company had no other asset, liability, or equity balance. On January 2, Hinges Corp. purchased for cash $50,000 of equity securities that are classified as available-for-sale. On June 30, Hinges Corp. sold 40% of the available-for-sale security portfolio, realizing a gain as follows.

Proceeds on sale of securities sold	$22,000
Less: cost of securities sold	20,000
Realized gain	**$ 2,000**

Illustration 10-28
Calculation of Realized Gain

Hinges Corp. did not purchase or sell any other securities during 2004. It received $3,000 in dividends during the year. At December 31, 2004, the remaining portfolio is as follows.

Fair value of portfolio	$34,000
Less: cost of portfolio	30,000
Unrealized gain	**$ 4,000**

Illustration 10-29
Calculation of Unrealized Gain

The company's income statement for 2004 is shown in Illustration 10-30.

HINGES CORP.
Income Statement
Year Ended December 31, 2004

Dividend revenue	$3,000
Realized gains on investment in securities	2,000
Net income	**$5,000**

Illustration 10-30
Income Statement

The company reports its change in the unrealized holding gain in a statement of comprehensive income as follows.

HINGES CORP.
Statement of Comprehensive Income
For the Year Ended December 31, 2004

Net income		$5,000
Other comprehensive income:		
Holding gains arising during the period	$6,000	
Less: Reclassification adjustment for gains included in net income	2,000	4,000
Comprehensive income		$9,000

Illustration 10-31
Statement of Comprehensive Income

---

[23] This example is adapted from Dennis R. Beresford, L. Todd Johnson, and Cheri L. Reither, "Is a Second Income Statement Needed?" *Journal of Accountancy* (April 1996), p.71.

If a full statement of shareholders' equity is prepared, it reports the following.

Illustration 10-32
Statement of Shareholders' Equity

HINGES CORP.
Statement of Shareholders' Equity
For the Year Ended December 31, 2004

	Common Shares	Retained Earnings	Accumulated Other Comprehensive Income	Total
Beginning balance	$50,000	$–0–	$–0–	$50,000
Add: Net income		5,000		5,000
Other comprehensive Income			4,000	4,000
Ending balance	$50,000	$5,000	$4,000	$59.000

A comparative balance sheet is shown below.

Illustration 10-33
Comparative Balance Sheet

HINGES CORP.
Comparative Balance Sheet

	1/1/04	12/31/04
Assets		
Cash	$50,000	$25,000
Available-for-sale investments		34,000
Total assets	$50,000	$59,000
Shareholders' equity		
Common shares	$50,000	$50,000
Retained earnings		5,000
Accumulated other comprehensive income		4,000
Total shareholders' equity	$50,000	$59,000

This example indicates how an unrealized gain or loss on available-for-sale investments affects all the financial statements. Note that the components that make up accumulated comprehensive income must be disclosed.

Fair Value Controversy

The move to recognize fair values for some financial instruments is seen as a step forward. Investments reported at fair values represent more faithfully the underlying economic reality of the entity's resources. In addition, the changes in fair value, even though unrealized, are quantified and captured in Shareholders' Equity. Proposed *CICA Handbook* Section 3855, however, leaves many issues unresolved. Some parties are dissatisfied with its results: some think it goes too far, others think it does not go far enough. Some think the FASB standards should have been more closely mirrored rather than those of the IASB. In this section we look at some of the major unresolved issues.

Measurement Based on Intent

Debt instruments can be classified as held-to-maturity, available-for-sale, or trading. As a result, three identical debt securities could be reported in three different ways in the financial statements. Some argue such treatment is confusing. Furthermore, the held-to-maturity category is based solely on intent, which is a subjective evaluation. What is not subjective is the market price of the debt instrument, which is observable in the market-place. In other words, the three classifications are subjective, and therefore arbitrary classifications will result.

Gains Trading

Certain debt securities can be classified as held-to-maturity and therefore reported at amortized cost. Other debt and equity securities can be classified as available-for-sale and reported at fair value with the unrealized gain or loss reported as other comprehensive income. In either case, a company can become involved in gains trading (also referred to as "cherry picking"). In **gains trading**, companies sell their winners, reporting the gains in income, and hold on to the losers.

Liabilities Not Fairly Valued

Many argue that if investment securities are going to be reported at fair value, so also should liabilities. They note that by recognizing changes in value on only one side of the balance sheet (the asset side), a high degree of volatility can occur in the income and share-holders' equity amounts. It is further argued that financial institutions are involved in asset and liability management (not just asset management) and that viewing only one side may lead managers to make uneconomic decisions as a result of the accounting. Although the proposals require derivatives and some financial liabilities to be measured at fair value, other financial liabilities continue to be measured at amortized cost. The Accounting Standards Board noted that certain debt investments were still reported at amortized cost, and that fair value measurement issues were still of concern for many companies.

Subjectivity of Fair Values

Some people question the relevance of fair value measures for investments in securities, arguing in favour of reporting based on amortized cost. They believe that amortized cost provides relevant information: it focuses on the decision to acquire the asset, the earning effects of that decision that will be realized over time, and the ultimate recoverable value of the asset. They argue that fair value ignores those concepts. Instead, fair value focuses on the effects of transactions and events that do not involve the enterprise, reflecting opportunity gains and losses whose recognition in the financial statements is, in their view, not appropriate until they are realized.

The move to fair values for measuring many financial instruments is seen as the thin end of the wedge. Technology and financial modelling have improved accounting measures, and as these continue to evolve, we will move increasingly away from the conventional historical cost model.

Perspectives

To effectively analyse a company's performance and position, it is essential to understand the accounting and reporting for the entity's investments. Some of the key aspects an analyst watches for are:

1. separation of investment results from operating results

2. relationship between investment asset and investment returns and

3. obscuring of information in the process of consolidation.

Because the income statement reports on management's performance in operating the company's assets, it is important to separate the results of active operating income from the more passive investment returns. Because gains or losses on sale of investments, or special dividends can obscure a company's operating performance, these must be separately identified and assessed.

Accounting standards require disclosures that enable a reader to relate the investment category on the balance sheet with the investment income reported on the income statement, and with the holding gains and losses in other comprehensive income. Understanding the effect of the accounting methods used for different categories of investments is a key requirement for the analyst. If an entity has significant investments in companies accounted for by the equity method, for example, some information is not available, as the one-line investment account hides the debt and risk characteristics of the investee company to which the entity is exposed.

Consolidation of subsidiary companies also presents problems. While the financial statements reflect the combined operations of the economic entity, important information is lost through the process of summarizing. This is the reason that segmented information, discussed in Chapter 24, is required to be reported in the notes. Analysts must also watch for major acquisitions during the current or previous year. The balance sheet contains all the assets of the subsidiary, but the income statement includes only the income earned by the subsidiary since it was acquired by the parent. Any analysis that looks at relationships between income and assets has to adjust for major acquisitions in the period(s) in question.

Summary

The major investments in debt and equity securities and their reporting treatment are summarized in Illustration 10-34.

Illustration 10-34

Summary of Treatment of Major Debt and Equity Investments

Category	Balance Sheet	Income Statement
Loans and receivables	Investments reported at amortized cost. Current or long-term assets.	Interest is recognized as revenue.
Trading (debt and equity securities)	Investments shown at fair value. Current assets.	Interest and dividends are recognized as revenue. Unrealized holding gains and losses are included in net income.
Available-for-sale (debt and equity securities)	Investments shown at fair value. Current or long-term assets. Unrealized holding gains and losses are a separate component of shareholders' equity.	Interest and dividends are recognized as revenue. Unrealized holding gains and losses are **not** included in net income but in other comprehensive income.
Held-to-maturity (debt securities)	Investments shown at amortized cost. Current or long-term assets.	Interest is recognized as revenue.
Equity method (equity securities)	Investments originally are carried at cost, are periodically adjusted for the investor's share of the changes in the investee's net assets from earning income and paying dividends. Classified as long-term.	Revenue is recognized to the extent of the share of the investee's earnings or losses reported subsequent to the date of investment.
Parent/subsidiary (control)—consolidation	Assets and liabilities of both are added together on a line-by-line basis.	Revenues, expenses, gains, and losses are added together on a line-by-line basis.

Summary of Learning Objectives

Digital Tool

Glossary

www.wiley.com/canada/kieso

1. **Identify the categories of debt investments and describe the accounting and reporting requirements for those that are long-term investments.**

   (1) *Long-term loans and receivables* and (2) *held-to-maturity debt securities* are carried and reported at amortized cost. (3) *Available-for-sale debt securities* are valued for reporting purposes at fair value, with unrealized holding gains or losses reported as other comprehensive income and as a separate component of shareholders' equity. (4) *Trading debt securities*, reported as current assets, are valued for reporting purposes at fair value, with unrealized holding gains or losses included in net income.

2. **Apply the accounting procedures for discount and premium amortization on notes, bonds, and other long-term investments in debt securities.**

   Discounts or premiums on long-term investments in debt securities should be amortized using the effective-interest method. The effective-interest rate or yield is applied to the beginning carrying value of the investment for each interest period in order to calculate interest revenue. The difference between interest revenue and the "cash" interest earned is the amount of discount or premium to be amortized.

3. **Identify the categories of long-term equity securities and describe the accounting and reporting treatment for each category.**

   The degree to which one corporation (investor) acquires an interest in the common shares of another corporation (investee) generally determines the accounting treatment for the investment. Where the investor controls the investee, the investor (parent company) reports its investment on a consolidated basis. Where the investor can exert significant influence over the operating, investing, and financing decisions of the investee, the equity method of accounting is used. Where the investor does not have significant influence, and this is a long-term investment, the security is classified as available-for-sale. If fair values are available, the investment is revalued at fair value with the unrealized gains and losses recognized in other comprehensive income.

4. **Explain the equity method of accounting.**

   Under the equity method, a substantive economic relationship is acknowledged between the investor and the investee. The investment is originally recorded at cost but is subsequently adjusted each period for changes in the net assets of the investee. That is, the investment's carrying amount is periodically increased (decreased) by the investor's proportionate share of the earnings (losses) of the investee, and is decreased by all dividends received by the investor from the investee.

5. **Explain the basics of consolidation.**

   Consolidation is a process of substituting the balance in the investment in subsidiary account with 100% of the assets and liabilities of the subsidiary company, offset by a noncontrolling interest account representing the portion of the net assets of the investee company not owned by the parent. The parent investor adds in all the revenues, expenses, gains, and losses of the investee on a line-by-line basis to those of the investor company again reduced by any non-controlling interest in the investee's income. Any unrealized intercompany gains and losses and intercompany balances are eliminated on consolidation.

6. **Explain the accounting for impairments in value of long-term investments in debt and equity securities.**

   Impairments of debt and equity securities are losses in value that are determined to be other than temporary, are based on a fair value test, and are charged to income.

KEY TERMS

accumulated other comprehensive income (AOCI), 508

amortized cost, 499

available-for-sale, 508

available-for-sale investments, 499

comprehensive income, 508

consolidated financial statements, 520

controlling interest, 520

cost method, 514

debt securities, 498

derivative instruments, 496

discount, 503

economic entity, 520

effective interest method, 502

effective interest rate, 500

equity instruments, 513

equity method, 518

face value, 500

fair value, 499

Fair Value Allowance account, 510

fair value method, 514

financial asset, 496

gains trading, 529

held-for-trading investments, 499

held-to-maturity, 505

held-to-maturity investments, 499

impairment, 522

implicit interest rate, 501

imputed interest rate, 504

interest-bearing notes, 499

investee, 513

investor, 513

loans and receivables, 498

market rate, 500

minority interest, 520

noncontrolling interest, 520

7. Describe how to account for the transfer of investment securities between categories.

Transfers of securities between categories of investments are accounted for at fair value, with unrealized holding gains or losses treated in accordance with the nature of the transfer.

8. Describe the reporting and disclosure requirements for long-term investments in debt and equity securities.

Individual held-to-maturity and available-for-sale securities are classified as current or noncurrent depending upon the circumstances. For available-for-sale and held-to-maturity securities, a company should describe: aggregate fair value, amortized cost basis by type (debt and equity), and information about the contractual maturity of debt securities. Where the equity method is used, disclosure should be made of the difference between the investment cost and the underlying net book value of the investee's net assets at the date of purchase as well as the treatment of the components of the difference. The following must be disclosed: terms and conditions, interest rate risk, and credit risk concentrations. A reclassification adjustment is necessary when realized gains or losses are reported as part of net income but also are shown as part of other comprehensive income in the current or in previous periods. Unrealized holding gains or losses related to available-for-sale securities should be reported in other comprehensive income and the aggregate balance as accumulated comprehensive income on the balance sheet.

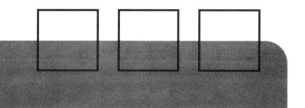

Appendix 10A

Current Standards in Transition

As explained in Chapter 10, the accounting standards for financial instruments, which include investments in debt and equity securities, are in a state of transition. This appendix provides information about the standards in place as this text went to print, and that are likely to be in force until 2005.

9 Objective
Identify how the accounting standards are changing for financial asset investments from reliance on historical cost to a focus on fair values.

Temporary Investments in Debt and Equity Securities

Illustration 10A-1 summarizes the accounting standards for temporary investments in debt and equity securities prior to the release of proposed *CICA Handbook* Sections 1530 and 3855.

CICA Handbook	Valuation	Included in Income
Section 3010	Recognized at cost at acquisition; subsequently adjusted to the lower of cost and market (LCM)	Interest revenue as earned; dividend revenue as received or receivable; unrealized holding losses and loss recoveries; realized gains and losses on disposal

Illustration 10A-1

Temporary Investments in Debt and Equity Securities— Pre-2005

Investments in both debt and equity securities are recognized at their acquisition cost. Cost includes both the purchase price and incidental direct costs such as brokerage commissions, legal fees, and taxes, if applicable. Assuming the investments are readily marketable and management intends to hold them for the short-term, the securities are subsequently valued for balance sheet purposes, at the **lower of cost and market (LCM)**.

Valuation at LCM requires recognition of declines in market values and of subsequent increases up to, but not above, the original cost. The unrealized losses (and loss recoveries) are measured by the amount necessary to bring the valuation allowance account to the proper balance sheet value and the charge (or credit) is reported on the income statement. The process is very similar to the application of LCM on a total portfolio basis to inventories.

Interest revenue is recognized as earned, and dividend revenue is recognized as dividends are received, or receivable. Realized gains or losses are recognized on disposal.

Accounting for temporary investments under the 2004 standards and the proposed 2005 standards for trading securities are very similar. The **major difference in the revised standards** for trading securities lies in their valuation at fair value rather than at LCM. That is, the new standards will permit recognition of **increases as well as decreases** in fair value after acquisition.

Long-term Loans and Receivables

Illustration 10A-2 summarizes the accounting standards for long-term loans and receivables prior to the release of proposed *CICA Handbook* Sections 1530 and 3855.

CICA Handbook	Valuation	Included in Income
Section 3025	Recognized at cost (fair value) at acquisition; subsequently adjusted and reported at amortized cost. (Impairment provisions of Section 3025 apply.)	Interest revenue as earned, including effect of premium or discount amortization; impairment losses; recognized gains and losses on disposal.

Accounting for this category of financial asset will not change under the new standards; therefore, the description of accounting for long-term loans and receivables in Chapter 10 describes practice in 2004.

Long-term Investments in Debt Securities

Illustration 10A-3 summarizes the accounting standards for long-term investments in debt securities prior to the release of proposed *CICA Handbook* Sections 1530 and 3855.

CICA Handbook	Valuation	Included in Income
No specific section	Recognized at cost (fair value) at acquisition; subsequently adjusted and reported at amortized cost. (Impairment provisions of Section 3025 apply to some debt securities.)	Interest revenue as earned, including effect of premium or discount amortization; impairment losses; recognized gains and losses on disposal

The pre-2005 requirements for this category of investment are almost identical to the requirements for long-term loans and receivables described in Illustration 10A-2. Regardless of whether the investor expects to hold the instruments until maturity or whether they are available for sale (there is no such distinction under the pre-2005 rules) **the accounting is the same as that proposed for held-to-maturity investments in Section 3855.** This method is explained in Chapter 10.

The major change with the "new" standard relates to the new category of debt securities that are designated as available-for-sale. These investments will need to be fair valued with the unrealized holding gains and losses reported in other comprehensive income.

Long-term Investments in Equity Securities

Illustration 10A-4 summarizes the accounting standards for long-term investments in equity securities prior to the release of proposed *CICA Handbook* Sections 1530 and 3855.

The investment in shares of another entity is required to be categorized according to the extent of influence exerted by the investor. The discussion in Chapter 10 of the three categories of influence—no significant influence, significant influence, and control—applies both prior to and after the proposed accounting changes. **Accounting for those classified as significantly influenced investments and parent-subsidiary relationships will not change, so the discussion in Chapter 10 is also the status quo.**

Category	Valuation and *CICA Handbook* Section	Included in Income
No significant influence (0%–20%): portfolio investment	At cost; cost method. Section 3050 applies.	Dividend revenue as received or receivable; impairment losses; gains and losses on disposal
Significant influence (20%–50%): equity method investment	At equity; equity method. Section 3050 applies.	Investment income recognized equal to investor's proportionate share of investee's reported net income; impairment losses; gains and losses on disposal
Control (>50%): subsidiary	Line-by-line consolidation of all the assets and liabilities controlled by investor. Section 1590 applies.	Line-by-line consolidation of all revenues, expenses, gains, and losses of subsidiary

Illustration 10A-4

Long-term Investments in Equity Securities—Pre-2005

Compare Illustration 10A-4 with Illustration 10-17. The one area of difference relates to those holdings with no significant influence, known in *CICA Handbook* Section 3050 as **portfolio investments**. (This category will be eliminated when Section 3855 is released.) Accounting for portfolio equity investments requires the cost method, the same as that applied to available-for-sale equity investments where a quoted market price in an active market is not available.

The following procedures apply to the **cost method**.

1. It recognizes the investment originally at its acquisition cost.

2. At subsequent balance sheet dates, the investment continues to be reported at its cost.

3. Dividend revenue is recognized as dividends are received or receivable from the investee company.

4. If there has been an other-than-temporary decline in value of the investment, the investment's carrying value is reduced directly to its lower fair value and this becomes its new cost basis. No adjustments are made for temporary declines in value.

5. When the shares are sold, the realized gain or loss on disposal is recognized in income.

With the change in standards, these long-term investments with an active market value will be fair valued at each balance sheet date, with the unrealized holding gain or loss recognized in other comprehensive income.

Summary of Learning Objective for Appendix 10A

9. Identify how the accounting standards are changing for financial asset investments from reliance on historical cost to a focus on fair values.

The proposed standards described in the Section 3855 *Exposure Draft* take one step toward fair value measurements and away from historic cost measures. If securities are held on a short-term basis for trading, they will be reported at fair value, with the unrealized gains and losses reported on the income statement. Whenever the intent is that a long-term investment is available for sale, and a market value is readily determinable, fair values are used, with the unrealized gains and losses recognized in other comprehensive income. The absence of reliable fair value measures is the primary cause for this partial step only toward the use of fair values for financial instruments.

Digital Tool

Glossary

www.wiley.com/canada/kieso

KEY TERMS

cost method, 535
lower of cost and market
  (LCM), 533
portfolio investments, 535

Note: All asterisked assignment material relates to the appendix to the chapter.

Brief Exercises

BE10-1 Lin Du Corp. lent $15,944 to Prefax Ltd., accepting Prefax's two-year, $20,000, zero-interest-bearing note. The implied interest is 12%. Prepare Lin Du's journal entries for the initial transaction, recognition of interest each year, and the collection of $20,000 at maturity.

BE10-2 Bartho Products sold used equipment with a cost of $15,000 and a carrying amount of $2,500 to Vardy Corp. in exchange for a three-year $5,000 note receivable. Although no interest was specified, the market rate for a loan of that risk would be 9%. Prepare the entries to record the sale of Bartho's equipment and receipt of the note, the recognition of interest each year, and the collection of the note at maturity.

BE10-3 Montreal Limited purchased, as a held-to-maturity investment, $50,000 of the 9%, five-year bonds of Parry Sound Corporation for $46,304, which provides an 11% return. Prepare Montreal's journal entries for (a) the investment purchase and (b) the receipt of annual interest and discount amortization. Use the effective interest method of amortization.

BE10-4 Use the information from BE10-3, but assume the bonds are purchased as an available-for-sale investment. Prepare Montreal's journal entries for (a) the purchase of the investment, (b) the receipt of the annual interest and discount amortization, and (c) the year-end fair value adjustment. The bonds have a year-end fair value of $47,200.

BE10-5 Mu Corporation purchased, as a held-to-maturity investment, $40,000 of the 8%, five-year bonds of Phang Inc. for $43,412, which provides a 6% return. The bonds pay interest semiannually. Prepare Mu's journal entries for (a) the investment purchase and (b) the receipt of semiannual interest and premium amortization. Use the effective interest method of amortization.

BE10-6 Pacioli Corporation purchased 300 shares of Galetti Inc. common shares as an available-for-sale investment for $9,900. During the year, Galetti paid a cash dividend of $3.25 per share. At year end, Galetti shares were selling for $34.50 per share. Prepare Pacioli's journal entries to record (a) the investment purchase, (b) the dividends received, and (c) the fair value adjustment.

BE10-7 Penn Corporation purchased for $300,000 a 25% interest in Teller, Inc. This investment enables Penn to exert significant influence over Teller. During the year, Teller earned net income of $180,000 and paid dividends of $60,000. Prepare Penn's journal entries related to this investment.

BE10-8 Muhammad Corporation has a portfolio of shares with a fair value of $40,000. Its cost was $35,000. If the Fair Value Allowance account (Available-for-Sale) has a debit balance of $2,000 before adjustment, prepare the journal entry at year end.

BE10-9 The following information relates to Cargall Corp. for 2005: net income $800,000; unrealized holding gain of $20,000 related to available-for-sale investments during the year; accumulated other comprehensive income of $60,000 on January 1, 2005. Determine (a) other comprehensive income for 2005, (b) comprehensive income for 2005, and (c) accumulated other comprehensive income at December 31, 2005.

Exercises

E10-1 **(Investment Classifications)** Identify whether each of the following investments is a trading, available-for-sale, or held-to-maturity security. Each case is independent of the others.

1. A bond that will mature in four years was bought one month ago when the price dropped. As soon as the value increases, which is expected next month, it will be sold.

2. 10% of the outstanding shares of Farm Corp. were purchased. The company is planning on eventually getting a total of 30% of the outstanding shares.

3. 10-year bonds were purchased this year. The bonds mature at the first of next year.

4. Bonds that will mature in five years are purchased. The company would like to hold them until they mature, but money has been tight recently and they may need to be sold.

5. A bond that matures in 10 years was purchased. The company is investing money set aside for an expansion project planned 10 years from now.

E10-2 (Notes Receivable with Zero and Unrealistic Interest Rates) On July 1, 2005, Agincourt Inc. made two sales.

1. It sold excess land having a fair market value of $700,000 in exchange for a four-year noninterest-bearing promissory note in the face amount of $1,101,460. The land's carrying value is $590,000.

2. It rendered services in exchange for an eight-year promissory note having a face value of $400,000. Interest at a rate of 3% is payable annually.

Agincourt recently had to pay 8% interest for money it borrowed from British National Bank. The customers in these two transactions have credit ratings that require them to borrow money at 12% interest.

Instructions

Record the two journal entries that should be recorded by Agincourt Inc. for the transactions of July 1, 2005.

E10-3 (Notes Receivable with Zero Interest Rate) By December 31, 2004, Golf Corp. had performed a significant amount of environmental consulting services for Rank Ltd. Rank was short of cash, and Golf agreed to accept a $200,000 noninterest-bearing note due December 31, 2006 as payment in full. Rank is somewhat of a credit risk and typically borrows funds at a rate of 15%. Golf is much more credit worthy and has various lines of credit at 6%.

Interactive
Homework

Instructions

a) Prepare the journal entry to record the transaction of December 31, 2004 for Golf Corp.

b) Assuming Golf Corp.'s fiscal year end is December 31, prepare the journal entry required at December 31, 2005.

c) Assuming Golf Corp.'s fiscal year end is December 31, prepare the journal entry required at December 31, 2006.

E10-4 (Entries for Held-to-Maturity Securities) On January 1, 2005, Dagwood Corp. purchased at par 12% bonds having a maturity value of $300,000. They are dated January 1, 2005, and mature January 1, 2010, with interest receivable December 31 of each year. The bonds are classified in the held-to-maturity category.

Instructions

(a) Prepare the journal entry at the date of the bond purchase.

(b) Prepare the journal entry to record the interest received for 2005.

(c) Prepare the journal entry to record the interest received for 2006.

E10-5 (Entries for Held-to-Maturity Securities) On January 1, 2005, Mo'd Limited purchased 12% bonds, having a maturity value of $300,000 for $322,744.44. The bonds provide the bondholders with a 10% yield. They are dated January 1, 2005, and mature January 1, 2010, with interest receivable December 31 of each year. The bonds are classified in the held-to-maturity category.

Instructions

(a) Prepare the journal entry at the date of the bond purchase.

(b) Prepare a bond amortization schedule.

(c) Prepare the journal entry to record the interest received and the amortization for 2005.

(d) Prepare the journal entry to record the interest received and the amortization for 2006.

E10-6 (Entries for Available-for-Sale Securities) Assume the same information as in E10-5 except that the securities are classified as available-for-sale. The fair values of the bonds at December 31 of each year are as follows.

2005: $320,500	2008: $310,000
2006: $309,000	2009: $300,000
2007: $308,000	

Instructions

(a) Prepare the journal entry at the date of the bond purchase.

(b) Prepare the journal entries to record the interest received and recognition of fair value for 2005.

(c) Prepare the journal entry to record the recognition of fair value for 2006.

E10-7 (Effective Interest versus Straight-Line Bond Amortization) On January 1, 2005, Phantom Corp. acquires $200,000 of Spiderman Products, Inc. 9% bonds at a price of $185,589. The interest is payable each December 31, and the bonds mature December 31, 2007. The investment will provide Phantom Corp. with a 12% yield. The bonds are classified as held-to-maturity.

Instructions

(a) Prepare a three-year schedule of interest revenue and bond discount amortization, applying the effective interest method.

(b) Prepare the journal entry for the interest receipt of December 31, 2006 and the discount amortization under the effective-interest method.

(c) If a straight-line approach were taken to amortization of the bond discount, how much discount would be amortized each year? How much interest revenue would be reported each year? Prepare the journal entry for the interest receipt of December 31, 2006 and the discount amortization under the straight-line method.

(d) Under what circumstances might it be acceptable to use the straight-line method instead of the effective interest method?

E10-8 (**Entries for Available-for-Sale and Trading Equity Investments**)   The following information is available for Barkley Corp. at December 31, 2005 regarding its investments.

Securities	Cost	Fair Value
3,000 shares of Myers Corporation common shares	$40,000	$48,000
1,000 shares of Cole Inc. preferred shares	25,000	22,000
	$65,000	$70,000

Instructions

(a) Prepare the adjusting entry (if any) at December 31, 2005, assuming the securities are classified as trading.

(b) Prepare the adjusting entry (if any) at December 31, 2005, assuming the securities are classified as available-for-sale.

(c) Discuss how the amounts reported in the financial statements are affected by the entries in (a) and (b).

Interactive
Homework

E10-9 (**Available-for-Sale Investments—Entries**)   On December 21, 2005, Niger Corp. provided you with the following information regarding its available-for-sale securities.

December 31, 2005

Investments	Cost	Fair Value	Unrealized Gain (Loss)
Clemson Corp. shares	$20,000	$19,000	$(1,000)
Colora Corp. shares	10,000	9,000	(1,000)
British Corp. shares	20,000	20,600	600
Total of portfolio	$50,000	$48,600	(1,400)
Balance of fair value allowance account before adjustment			–0–
Adjustment needed to allowance account—credit			$(1,400)

During 2006, Colora Corp. shares were sold for $9,400. The fair values of the shares on December 31, 2006 were: Clemson Corp. shares—$19,100; British Corp. shares—$20,500.

Instructions

(a) Prepare the adjusting journal entry needed on December 31, 2005.

(b) Prepare the journal entry to record the sale of the Colora Corp. shares during 2006.

(c) Prepare the adjusting journal entry needed on December 31, 2006.

(d) Early in 2007, an announcement was made that British Corp.'s major patent that was responsible for 75% of its income had lost most of its value due to a technological improvement by a competitor. As a result, British's share price fell to $0.20 per share. Niger assessed the value of the shares to be impaired. Provide the necessary adjusting entry to recognize the impairment, and advise Niger what additional effect the impairment has on its 2007 financial statements.

E10-10 (**Available-for-Sale Securities Entries and Reporting**)   Ramsco Ltd. purchases equity securities costing $73,000 and classifies them as available-for-sale. At December 31, the fair value of the portfolio is $65,000.

Instructions

Prepare the adjusting entry to report the securities properly. Indicate the statement presentation of the accounts in your entry.

E10-11 (Available-for-Sale Securities Entries and Financial Statement Presentation) At December 31, 2005, the available-for-sale equity portfolio for Steffi Inc. is as follows.

Security	Cost	Fair Value	Unrealized Gain (Loss)
A	$17,500	$15,000	($2,500)
B	12,500	14,000	1,500
C	23,000	25,500	2,500
Total	$53,000	$54,500	1,500
Balance in fair value allowance account before adjustment—debit			400
Adjustment needed to allowance account—debit			$1,100

On January 20, 2006, Steffi Inc. sold security A for $15,100. The sale proceeds are net of brokerage fees.

Instructions

(a) Prepare the adjusting entry at December 31, 2005 to report the portfolio at fair value.

(b) Show the balance sheet presentation of the investment-related accounts at December 31, 2005. (Ignore notes presentation.)

(c) Prepare the journal entry for the 2006 sale of security A.

E10-12 (Comprehensive Income Disclosure) Assume the same information as E10-11 and that Steffi Inc. reports net income in 2005 of $120,000 and in 2006 of $140,000. The adjustment to the allowance account at the end of 2006 increased it by $40,000.

Instructions

(a) Prepare a statement of comprehensive income for 2005 starting with net income.

(b) Prepare a statement of comprehensive income for 2006 starting with net income.

E10-13 (Equity Securities Entries) Arantxa Corporation made the following cash purchases of securities during 2005, the first year in which Arantxa invested in securities.

1. On January 15, purchased 10,000 shares of Sanchez Corp.'s common shares at $33.50 per share plus commission of $1,980.

2. On April 1, purchased 5,000 shares of Vicario Corp.'s common shares at $52.00 per share plus commission of $3,370.

3. On September 10, purchased 7,000 shares of WTA Corp.'s preferred shares at $26.50 per share plus commission of $4,910.

On May 20, 2005, Arantxa sold 4,000 shares of Sanchez common shares at a market price of $35 per share less brokerage commissions of $3,850. The year-end fair values per share were: Sanchez $30, Vicario $55, and WTA $28. In addition, the chief accountant of Arantxa told you that Arantxa Corporation holds these securities with the intention of selling them in order to earn profits from appreciation in prices.

Instructions

(a) Prepare the journal entries to record the above three security purchases. Arantxa follows a policy of capitalizing transaction costs on acquisition and reducing the proceeds on disposal.

(b) Prepare the journal entry for the security sale on May 20.

(c) Calculate the unrealized gains or losses and prepare the adjusting entries for Arantxa on December 31, 2005.

E10-14 (Journal Entries for Fair Value and Equity Methods) Presented below are two independent situations.

Situation 1

Conchita Cosmetics acquired 10% of the 200,000 common shares of Martinez Fashion at a total cost of $13 per share on March 18, 2005. On June 30, Martinez declared and paid a $75,000 cash dividend. On December 31, Martinez reported net income of $122,000 for the year. At December 31, the market price of Martinez Fashion was $15 per share. The securities are classified as available-for-sale.

Situation 2

Monica, Inc. obtained significant influence over Gurion Corporation by buying 30% of Gurion's 30,000 outstanding common shares at a cost of $9 per share on January 1, 2005. On June 15, Gurion declared and paid a cash dividend of $36,000. On December 31, Gurion reported a net income of $85,000 for the year.

Instructions

Prepare all necessary journal entries in 2005 for both situations.

E10-15 **(Equity Method)** Pareau Ltd. invested $1 million in Salut Corp. for 25% of its outstanding shares. At the time of the purchase, Salut Corp. had a book value of $3.2 million. Salut Corp. pays out 40% of net income in dividends each year.

Instructions

Use the information in the following T account for the investment in Salut to answer the following questions.

Investment in Salut Corp.

1,000,000	
110,000	
	44,000

(a) How much was Pareau Ltd.'s share of Salut Corp.'s net income for the year?

(b) How much was Pareau Ltd.'s share of Salut Corp.'s dividends for the year?

(c) What was Salut Corp.'s total net income for the year?

(d) What was Salut Corp.'s total dividends for the year?

E10-16 **(Available-for-Sale Securities Entries—Buy and Sell)** Lazier Corporation has the following securities in its long-term available-for-sale investment portfolio on December 31, 2005.

Investments	Cost	Fair Value
1,500 shares of DJ, Inc., Common	$ 73,500	$ 69,000
5,000 shares of RH Corp., Common	180,000	175,000
400 shares of AZ, Inc., Preferred	60,000	61,600
	$313,500	$305,600

All the securities were purchased in 2005. In 2006, Lazier completed the following securities transactions.

March 1   Sold the 1,500 shares of DJ, Inc., @ $45 less fees of $1,200.
April 1   Bought 700 shares of RG Corp., @ $75 plus fees of $1,300.

Lazier Company's portfolio of securities appeared as follows on December 31, 2006.

Investments	Cost	Fair Value
5,000 shares of RH Corp., Common	$180,000	$175,000
700 shares of RG Corp., Common	53,800	50,400
400 shares of AZ Inc., Preferred	60,000	58,000
	$293,800	$283,400

Instructions

(a) Prepare the general journal entries for Lazier for:

1. the 2005 valuation adjusting entry
2. the sale of the DJ shares
3. the purchase of the RG shares
4. the 2006 valuation adjusting entry

(b) Determine the amount of the 2006 reclassification adjustment needed in Other Comprehensive Income.

E10-17 **(Fair Value and Equity Method Compared)** Jaycie Inc. acquired 20% of the outstanding common shares of Kulikowski Inc. on December 31, 2004. The purchase price was $1.2 million for 50,000 shares. Kulikowski declared and paid an $0.85 per share cash dividend on June 30 and on December 31, 2005. Kulikowski reported net income of $730,000 for 2005. The fair value of Kulikowski's shares was $27 per share at December 31, 2005.

Instructions

(a) Prepare the journal entries for Jaycie for 2005, assuming that Jaycie cannot exercise significant influence over Kulikowski. The securities should be classified as available-for-sale.

(b) Prepare the journal entries for Jaycie for 2005, assuming that Jaycie can exercise significant influence over Kulikowski.

(c) At what amount is the investment in securities reported on the balance sheet under each of these methods at December 31, 2005? What amount of income is reported and included in net income by Jaycie in 2005 under each of these methods?

E10-18 **(Long-term Equity Investments and Impairment)** On January 1, 2005, Warner Corporation purchased 30% of the common shares of Martz Limited for $180,000. During the year, Martz earned net income of $10,000 and paid out a small $8,000 dividend. The investment in Martz had a fair value of $185,000 at December 31, 2005. During 2006, Martz incurred a loss of $80,000 and paid no dividends. At December 31, 2006, the fair value of the investment was $140,000.

Instructions

(a) Prepare all relevant journal entries to record the information about Warner's investment in Martz for 2005 and 2006, assuming this is its only investment and Warner cannot exercise significant influence over Martz's policies. The decline in fair value in 2006 is considered a permanent decline. Identify any amounts that affect Other Comprehensive Income in 2005 and 2006. Briefly explain.

(b) Prepare all relevant journal entries to record the information about Warner's investment in Martz for 2005 and 2006, assuming this is its only investment and Warner exercises significant influence over Martz's policies. The decline in fair value in 2006 is considered a permanent decline. Identify any amounts that affect Other Comprehensive Income in 2005 and 2006. Briefly explain.

E10-19 **(Impairment of Debt Securities)** Moceanu Corporation owns corporate bonds classified as available-for-sale at December 31, 2005. These bonds have a par value of $800,000, an amortized cost of $800,000, and a fair value of $720,000. The unrealized loss of $80,000 previously recognized as other comprehensive income and as a separate component of shareholders' equity is now determined to be other than temporary. That is, the company believes that the value of the bonds is impaired.

Instructions

(a) Prepare the journal entry(ies) to recognize the impairment.

(b) What is the new cost basis of the municipal bonds? Given that the maturity value of the bonds is $800,000, should Moceanu Corporation accrete (i.e., increase) the difference between the carrying amount and the maturity value over the life of the bonds?

(c) At December 31, 2006, the fair value of the corporate bonds is $760,000. Prepare the entry (if any) to record this information.

E10-20 **(Determine Proper Income Reporting)** Presented below are two independent situations that you are to solve.

1. Bacall Inc. received dividends from its common share investments during the year ended December 31, 2005 as follows.

   (a) A cash dividend of $12,000 is received from Sleep Corporation. (Bacall owns a 2% interest in Sleep.)

   (b) A cash dividend of $60,000 is received from Largo Corporation. (Bacall owns a 30% interest in Largo.) A majority of Bacall's directors are also directors of Largo Corporation.

   (c) A cash dividend of $72,000 is received from Orient Inc., a subsidiary of Bacall.

   Determine how much dividend revenue Bacall should report in its 2005 consolidated income statement.

2. On January 3, 2005, Bach Corp. purchased as a long-term available-for-sale investment 5,000 common shares of Starr Ltd. for $79 per share, which represents a 2% interest. On December 31, 2005, the shares' market price was $83 per share. On March 3, 2006, Bach sold all 5,000 shares of Starr for $102 per share. Determine the amount of gain or loss on disposal that should be included in net income in 2006. The investment in Starr Ltd. was Bach's only investment.

Problems

P10-1 On December 31, 2005 Zhang Ltd. rendered services to Beggy Corp. at an agreed price of $91,844.10, accepting $36,000 down and agreeing to accept the balance in four equal instalments of $18,000 receivable each December 31. An interest rate of 11% is imputed.

Instructions

Prepare the entries recorded by Zhang Ltd. for the sale and for the receipts and interest on the following dates.

(a) December 31, 2005   (c) December 31, 2007   (e) December 31, 2009

(b) December 31, 2006   (d) December 31, 2008

P10-2 Desrosiers Ltd. had the following long-term receivable account balances at December 31, 2004.

Note receivable from sale of division	$1,800,000
Note receivable from officer	400,000

Transactions during 2005 and other information relating to Desrosiers' long-term receivables were as follows.

1. The $1.8 million note receivable is dated May 1, 2004, bears interest at 9%, and represents the balance of the consideration received from the sale of Desrosiers' electronics division to New York Company. Principal payments of $600,000 plus appropriate interest are due on May 1, 2005, 2006, and 2007. The first principal and interest payment was made on May 1, 2005. Collection of the note instalments is reasonably assured.

2. The $400,000 note receivable is dated December 31, 2004, bears interest at 8%, and is due on December 31, 2007. The note is due from Mark Cumby, president of Desrosiers Ltd. and is secured by 10,000 Desrosiers' common shares. Interest is payable annually on December 31, and all interest payments were paid on their due dates through December 31, 2005. The quoted market price of Desrosiers' common shares was $45 per share on December 31, 2005.

3. On April 1, 2005, Desrosiers sold a patent to Pinot Company in exchange for a $200,000 noninterest-bearing note due on April 1, 2007. There was no established exchange price for the patent, and the note had no ready market. The prevailing rate of interest for a note of this type at April 1, 2005 was 12%. The present value of $1 for two periods at 12% is 0.79719 (use this factor). The patent had a carrying value of $40,000 at January 1, 2005, and the amortization for the year ended December 31, 2005 would have been $8,000. The collection of the note receivable from Pinot is reasonably assured.

4. On July 1, 2005, Desrosiers sold a parcel of land to Harris Inc. for $200,000 under an instalment sale contract. Harris made a $60,000 cash down payment on July 1, 2005 and signed a four-year 11% note for the $140,000 balance. The equal annual payments of principal and interest on the note will be $45,125 payable on July 1, 2006 through July 1, 2009. The land could have been sold at an established cash price of $200,000. The cost of the land to Desrosiers was $150,000. Circumstances are such that the collection of the instalments on the note is reasonably assured.

Instructions

(a) For each note:

  1. Describe the relevant cash flows in terms of amount and timing.

  2. Determine the amount of interest revenue that should be reported in 2005.

  3. Determine the portion of the note and any interest that should be reported in current assets at December 31, 2005.

  4. Determine the portion of the note that should be reported as a long-term investment at December 31, 2005.

(b) Prepare the long-term receivables section of Desrosiers' balance sheet at December 31, 2005.

(c) Prepare a schedule showing the current portion of the long-term receivables and accrued interest receivable that would appear in Desrosiers' balance sheet at December 31, 2005.

(d) Determine the total interest revenue from the long-term receivables that would appear on Desrosiers' income statement for the year ended December 31, 2005.

P10-3 Presented below is an amortization schedule related to Baker Corp.'s five-year, $100,000 bond with a 7% interest rate and a 5% yield, purchased on December 31, 2004, for $108,660.

Date	Cash Received	Interest Revenue	Bond Premium Amortization	Carrying Amount of Bonds
12/31/04				$108,660
12/31/05	$7,000	$5,433	$1,567	107,093
12/31/06	7,000	5,354	1,646	105,447
12/31/07	7,000	5,272	1,728	103,719
12/31/08	7,000	5,186	1,814	101,905
12/31/09	7,000	5,095	1,905	100,000

The following schedule presents a comparison of the amortized cost and fair value of the bonds at year end.

	12/31/05	12/31/06	12/31/07	12/31/08	12/31/09
Amortized cost	$107,093	$105,447	$103,719	$101,905	$100,000
Fair value	$106,500	$107,500	$105,650	$103,000	$100,000

Instructions

(a) Prepare the journal entry to record the purchase of these bonds on December 31, 2004, assuming the bonds are classified as held-to-maturity securities.

(b) Prepare the journal entry(ies) related to the held-to-maturity bonds for 2005.

(c) Prepare the journal entry(ies) related to the held-to-maturity bonds for 2007.

(d) Prepare the journal entry(ies), if required, to transfer the held-to-maturity bond investment to the available-for-sale category on December 31, 2007, and any entry(ies) required on December 31, 2008 and 2009.

(e) Prepare the journal entry(ies) to record the purchase of these bonds, assuming they are classified as available-for-sale.

(f) Prepare the journal entry(ies) related to the available-for-sale bonds for 2005.

(g) Prepare the journal entry(ies) related to the available-for-sale bonds for 2007.

(h) Prepare the journal entry(ies), if required, to transfer the available-for-sale bond investment to the held-to-maturity category on December 31, 2007, and any entry(ies) required on December 31, 2008 and 2009.

P10-4 On January 1, 2006, Jovi Inc. purchased $200,000, 8% bonds of Mercury Ltd. for $184,557. The bonds were purchased to yield 10% interest. Interest is payable semiannually on July 1 and January 1. The bonds mature on January 1, 2011. Jovi uses the effective interest method to amortize discount or premium. On January 1, 2008, Jovi sold the bonds for $185,363 (after receiving interest) to meet its liquidity needs.

Interactive
Homework

Instructions

(a) Prepare the journal entry to record the purchase of bonds on January 1. Assume that the bonds are classified as available-for-sale.

(b) Prepare the amortization schedule for the bonds.

(c) Prepare the journal entries to record the semiannual interest on July 1, 2006 and December 31, 2006.

(d) If the fair value of Mercury bonds is $186,363 on December 31, 2007, prepare the necessary adjusting entry. (Assume the securities' fair value allowance balance on January 1, 2007 is a debit of $3,375.)

(e) Prepare the journal entry to record the sale of the bonds on January 1, 2008.

P10-5 Octavio Corp. carries an account in its general ledger called Investments, which contained the following debits for investment purchases, and no credits.

Feb. 1, 2005	Chiang Corp. common shares, no par value, 200 shares	$ 37,400
April 1	Government of Canada bonds, 11%, due April 1, 2015, interest payable April 1 and October 1, 100 bonds of $1,000 par each	100,000
July 1	Monet Corp. 12% bonds, par $50,000, dated March 1, 2005 purchased at 104 plus accrued interest, interest payable annually on March 1, due March 1, 2025	54,000

Instructions

(a) Prepare entries necessary to classify the amounts into proper accounts, assuming that all the securities are classified as available-for-sale.

(b) Prepare the entry to record the accrued interest and the amortization of premium on December 31, 2005. Use a straight-line method to amortize the premium instead of the effective interest method.

(c) The fair values of the securities on December 31, 2005 were:

Chiang Corp. common shares	$ 33,800
Government of Canada bonds	124,700
Monet Corp. bonds	58,600

What entry or entries, if any, would you recommend be made?

(d) The Government of Canada bonds were sold on July 1, 2006 for $119,200 plus accrued interest. Give the proper entry to record this transaction.

P10-6   Presented below is information taken from a bond investment amortization schedule with related fair values provided. These bonds are classified as available-for-sale.

	12/31/05	12/31/06	12/31/07
Amortized cost	$491,150	$519,442	$550,000
Fair value	$499,000	$506,000	$550,000

Instructions

(a) Indicate whether the bonds were purchased at a discount or at a premium.

(b) Prepare the adjusting entry to record the bonds at fair value at December 31, 2005. The Securities Fair Value Allowance account has a debit balance of $1,000 prior to adjustment.

(c) Prepare the adjusting entry to record the bonds at fair value at December 31, 2006.

Interactive
Homework

P10-7   Incognito Corp. has the following securities in its investment portfolio on December 31, 2005 (all securities were purchased in 2005): (1) 3,000 shares of Bush Corp. common shares, which cost $58,500, (2) 10,000 shares of Sanborn Ltd. common shares, which cost $580,000, and (3) 6,000 shares of Abba Corp. preferred shares, which cost $255,000. The Securities Fair Value Allowance account shows a credit of $10,100 at the end of 2005.

In 2006, Incognito completed the following securities transactions.

1. On January 15, sold 3,000 shares of Bush's common shares at $23 per share less fees of $2,150.

2. On April 17, purchased 1,000 shares of Tractors' common shares at $31.50 per share plus fees of $1,980.

On December 31, 2006, the market values per share of these securities were: Bush $20, Sanborn $62, Abba $40, and Tractors $29. In addition, the accounting supervisor of Incognito told you that even though all these securities have readily determinable fair values, Incognito will not actively trade these securities because top management intends to hold them for more than one year.

Instructions

(a) Prepare the entry for the sale of the investment on January 15, 2006.

(b) Prepare the journal entry to record the investment's purchase on April 17, 2006.

(c) Calculate the unrealized gains or losses and prepare the adjusting entry for Incognito on December 31, 2006.

(d) How should the unrealized gains or losses be reported on Incognito's balance sheet?

P10-8   Gypsy Corporation has the following portfolio of investments at September 30, 2005, its last reporting date.

Available-for-Sale Investments	Cost	Fair Value
Fogelberg, Inc. common (5,000 shares)	$225,000	$200,000
Petra, Inc. preferred (3,500 shares)	133,000	140,000
Weisberg Corp. common (1,000 shares)	180,000	179,000

On October 10, 2005, the Fogelberg shares were sold at a price of $54 per share. In addition, 3,000 shares of Los Tigres common shares were acquired at $59.50 per share on November 2, 2005. The December 31, 2005 fair values were: Petra $96,000, Los Tigres $132,000, and the Weisberg common $193,000. All the investments are classified as available-for-sale.

Instructions

(a) Prepare the journal entries to record the sale, purchase, and adjusting entries related to the available-for-sale securities in the last quarter of 2005.

(b) What amount of unrealized holding gains or losses must be reclassified out of Other Comprehensive Income in the last quarter?

(c) How would the entries in part (a) change if the securities were classified as trading investments?

P10-9   The information on the next page relates to the debt securities investments of Yellowjackets Corporation.

1. On February 1, the company purchased 12% bonds of Vanessa Corp. having a face value of $500,000 at 100 plus accrued interest. Interest is payable April 1 and October 1.

2. On April 1, semiannual interest is received.

3. On July 1, 9% bonds of Chieftains, Inc. were purchased. These bonds with a par value of $200,000 were purchased at 100 plus accrued interest. Interest dates are June 1 and December 1.

4. On September 1, bonds with a par value of $100,000, purchased on February 1, are sold at 99 plus accrued interest.

5. On October 1, semiannual interest is received.

6. On December 1, semiannual interest is received.

7. On December 31, the fair value of the bonds purchased February 1 and July 1 are 95 and 93, respectively.

Instructions

(a) Prepare any journal entries you consider necessary, including year-end entries (December 31), assuming these are available-for-sale securities.

(b) If Yellowjackets classified these as held-to-maturity securities, explain how the journal entries would differ from those in part (a).

P10-10   Pacers Corp. is a medium-sized corporation specializing in quarrying stone for building construction. The company has long dominated the market, at one time achieving a 70% market penetration. During prosperous years, the company's profits, coupled with a conservative dividend policy, resulted in funds available for outside investment. Over the years, Pacers has had a policy of investing idle cash in equity securities. In particular, Pacers has made periodic investments in the company's principal supplier, Pierce Industries Limited. Although the firm currently owns 12% of the outstanding common shares of Pierce, Pacers does not have significant influence over the operations of this investee company.

Cheryl Miller has recently joined Pacers as assistant controller, and her first assignment is to prepare the 2005 year-end adjusting entries for the accounts that are valued by the fair value rule for financial reporting purposes. Miller has gathered the following information about Pacers' pertinent accounts.

1. Pacers has trading securities related to Davis Motors and Smits Electric. During this fiscal year, Pacers purchased 100,000 shares of Davis Motors for $1.4 million; these shares currently have a market value of $1.6 million. Pacers' investment in Smits Electric has not been profitable; the company acquired 50,000 shares of Smits in April 2005 at $20 per share, a purchase that currently has a value of $620,000.

2. Prior to 2005, Pacers invested $22.5 million in Pierce Industries and has not changed its holdings this year. This investment in Pierce Industries was valued at $21.5 million on December 31, 2004. Pacers' 12% ownership of Pierce Industries has a current market value of $22,275,000.

Instructions

(a) Prepare the appropriate adjusting entries for Pacers as of December 31, 2005 to reflect the application of the fair value rule for both classes of securities described above.

(b) For both classes of securities presented above, describe how the results of the valuation adjustments made in (a) would be reflected in the body of and/or notes to Pacers' 2005 financial statements.

P10-11   Woolford Corporation has the following portfolio of available-for-sale securities at December 31, 2005.

| | | Percent | Per Share | |
Security	Quantity	Interest	Cost	Market
Favre, Inc.	2,000 shares	8%	$11	$16
Walsh Corp.	5,000 shares	14%	23	17
Dilfer Ltd.	4,000 shares	2%	31	24

Instructions

(a) What should be reported on Woolford's December 31, 2005 balance sheet relative to these long-term available-for-sale securities?

Early in 2006, Woolford sold all the Favre, Inc. shares for $17 per share, less a 1% commission on the sale. On December 31, 2006, Woolford's portfolio of available-for-sale securities consisted of the following common shares.

| | | Percent | Per Share | |
Security	Quantity	Interest	Cost	Market
Walsh Corp.	5,000 shares	14%	$23	$30
Dilfer Ltd.	4,000 shares	2%	31	23
Dilfer Ltd.	2,000 shares	1%	25	23

(b) What should be reported on the face of Woolford's December 31, 2006 balance sheet relative to available-for-sale securities investments? What should be reported to reflect the transactions above in Woolford's 2006 income statement?

(c) What amount of unrealized holding gains or losses must be reclassified as a result of the sale of the Favre, Inc. shares?

(d) Assuming that comparative financial statements for 2005 and 2006 are presented, draft the footnote necessary for full disclosure of Woolford's transactions and position in equity securities.

P10-12   Big Brother Holdings, Inc. had the following available-for-sale investment portfolio at January 1, 2004.

Earl Corp.	1,000 shares @ $15 each	$15,000
Josie Corp.	900 shares @ $20 each	18,000
David Corp.	500 shares @ $ 9 each	4,500
Available-for-sale securities at cost		37,500
Fair value allowance: Available-for-sale securities		(7,500)
Available-for-sale securities at fair value		$30,000

During 2004, the following transactions took place.

1. On March 1, Josie Corp. paid a $2 per share dividend.

2. On April 30, Big Brother Holdings, Inc. sold 300 shares of David Corp. for $10 per share.

3. On May 15, Big Brother Holdings, Inc. purchased 50 more Earl Corp. shares at $16 per share.

4. At December 31, 2004, the shares had the following market prices per share: Earl $17, Josie $19, and David $8.

During 2005, the following transactions took place.

5. On February 1, Big Brother Holdings, Inc. sold the remaining David shares for $7 per share.

6. On March 1, Josie Corp. paid a $2 per share dividend.

7. On December 21, Earl Corp. declared a cash dividend of $3 per share to be paid in the next month.

8. At December 31, 2005, the shares had the following market prices per share: Earl $19 and Josie $21.

Instructions

(a) Prepare journal entries for each of the above transactions.

(b) Prepare a partial balance sheet showing how the investments are reported at December 31, 2004 and 2005.

(c) Identify the amounts, if any, that have to be reclassified out of other comprehensive income in 2004 and 2005.

P10-13   Alvarez Corp. invested its excess cash in available-for-sale securities during 2004. As of December 31, 2004, the portfolio of available-for-sale securities consisted of the following common shares.

Security	Quantity	Cost	Fair Value
Jones, Inc.	1,000 shares	$ 15,000	$ 21,000
Eola Corp.	2,000 shares	50,000	42,000
Yevette Aircraft Ltd.	2,000 shares	72,000	60,000
Totals		$137,000	$123,000

Instructions

(a) What should be reported on Alvarez's December 31, 2004 balance sheet relative to these securities? What should be reported on Alvarez's 2004 income statement?

On December 31, 2005, Alvarez's portfolio of available-for-sale securities consisted of the following common shares.

Security	Quantity	Cost	Fair Value
Jones, Inc.	1,000 shares	$ 15,000	$20,000
Jones, Inc.	2,000 shares	38,000	40,000
King Corp.	1,000 shares	16,000	12,000
Yevette Aircraft Ltd.	2,000 shares	72,000	22,000
Totals		$141,000	$94,000

During 2005, Alvarez Corp. sold 2,000 shares of Eola Corp. for $38,200 and purchased 2,000 more shares of Jones, Inc. and 1,000 shares of King Corp.

(b) What should be reported on Alvarez's December 31, 2005 balance sheet? What should be reported on Alvarez's 2005 income statement?

On December 31, 2006, Alvarez's portfolio of available-for-sale securities consisted of the following common shares.

Security	Quantity	Cost	Fair Value
Yevette Aircraft Ltd.	2,000 shares	$72,000	$82,000
King Corp.	2,500 shares	8,000	6,000
Totals		$80,000	$88,000

During the year 2006, Alvarez Corp. sold 3,000 shares of Jones, Inc. for $39,900 and 500 shares of King Corp. at a loss of $2,700.

(c) What should be reported on the face of Alvarez's December 31, 2006 balance sheet? What should be reported on Alvarez's 2006 income statement?

(d) What would be reported in a statement of comprehensive income at (1) December 31, 2004, and (2) December 31, 2005?

In the first quarter of 2006, the market value of King Corp. continued to fall as major customers were lost, and its share price stabilized at $1.00 per share. Alvarez assessed this investment as impaired.

(e) Prepare any entries required to recognize the impairment and explain the effect of this impairment on the 2006 balance sheet, income statement, and accumulated other comprehensive income.

P10-14 Fuentes Incorporated is a publicly traded manufacturing company in the technology industry. The company grew rapidly during its first 10 years and made three public offerings during this period. During its rapid growth period, Fuentes acquired common shares in Yukasato Inc. and Dimna Importers. In 1994, Fuentes acquired 25% of Yukasato's common shares for $588,000 and properly accounts for this investment using the equity method. For its fiscal year ended November 30, 2005, Yukasato Inc. reported net income of $250,000 and paid dividends of $100,000. In 1996, Fuentes acquired 10% of Dimna Importers common shares for $204,000 and properly accounts for this investment as an available-for-sale financial asset. Fuentes has a policy of investing idle cash in equity securities. The following data pertain to the securities in Fuentes trading investment portfolio.

TRADING INVESTMENTS
at November 30, 2004

Security	Cost	Fair Value
Craxi Electric	$326,000	$314,000
Renoir Inc.	184,000	81,000
Seferis Inc.	95,000	98,500
	$605,000	$593,500

AVAILABLE-FOR-SALE INVESTMENTS
at November 30, 2004

Dimna Importers	$204,000	$198,000

TRADING INVESTMENTS
at November 30, 2005

Security	Cost	Fair Value
Craxi Electric	$326,000	$323,000
Renoir Inc.	184,000	180,000
Mer Limited	105,000	108,000
	$615,000	$611,000

AVAILABLE-FOR-SALE INVESTMENTS
at November 30, 2004

Dimna Importers	$204,000	$205,000

On November 14, 2005, Tasha Yan was hired by Fuentes as assistant controller. Her first assignment was to prepare the entries to record the November activity and the November 30, 2005 year-end adjusting entries for the investments in the current trading securities and the long-term available-for-sale investment in common shares. Using Fuentes' ledger of investment transactions and the data given above, Yan proposed the following entries and submitted them to Miles O'Brien, controller, for review.

Entry 1 (November 8, 2005)

Cash	99,500	
Trading Investments		98,500
Investment Income		1,000
To record the sale of Seferis Inc. shares for $99,500.		

Entry 2 (November 26, 2005)

Trading Investments	105,000	
Cash		105,000
To record the purchase of Mer common shares for $102,200 plus brokerage fees of $2,800.		

Entry 3 (November 30, 2005)

Investment Income	3,000	
Investment Allowance		3,000
To recognize a loss equal to the excess of cost over market value of equity securities.		

Entry 4 (November 30, 2005)

Cash		38,500	
Investment Income			38,500
To record dividends received from securities.			
Yukasato Inc.	$25,000		
Dimna Importers	9,000		
Craxi Electric	4,500		

Entry 5 (November 30, 2005)

Investment in Yukasato Inc.	62,500	
Investment Income		62,500
To record share of Yukasato Inc. income under the equity method, $250,000 × 0.25		

Instructions

(a) Distinguish between the characteristics of trading and available-for-sale investments.

(b) The journal entries proposed by Tasha Yan will establish the value of Fuentes' equity investments to be reported on the company's external financial statements. Review each journal entry proposed by Yan and indicate whether or not it is in accordance with the applicable accounting standards. If an entry is incorrect, prepare the correct entry or entries that should have been made.

(c) Because Fuentes owns more than 20% of Yukasato Inc., Miles O'Brien has adopted the equity method to account for the investment in Yukasato Inc. Under what circumstances would it be inappropriate to use the equity method to account for a 25% interest in the common shares of Yukasato Inc.?

Writing Assignments

WA10-1   Fran Song looked at the Consolidated Financial Statements of Vixen Manufacturing Limited and shook her head. "I was asked to look at the accounting for Vixen's investments," she said, "but I can't find any investments listed on the balance sheet!" Fran has just begun her work term with Potts and Palmer, a CGA firm in public practice, and she has approached you for help.

Instructions

(a) Explain to Fran what type of investments Vixen likely holds and how they have been accounted for.

(b) Explain the rationale for the reporting standards for this type of investment.

(c) Identify what other evidence there might be on the financial statements that would indicate this type of investment.

WA10-2   Addison Manufacturing holds a large portfolio of debt and equity securities as an investment. The fair value of the portfolio is greater than its original cost, even though some securities have decreased in value. Ted Abernathy, the financial vice-president, and Donna Nottebart, the controller, are near year end in the process of classifying for the first time this securities portfolio in accordance with proposed *CICA Handbook* Section 3855. Abernathy wants to classify those investments that have increased in value during the period as trading securities in order to increase net income this year. He wants to classify all the securities that have decreased in value as available-for-sale (the equity securities) and as held-to-maturity (the debt securities).

Nottebart disagrees. She wants to classify those investments that have decreased in value as trading securities and those that have increased in value as available-for-sale (equity) and held-to-maturity (debt). She contends that the company is having a good earnings year and that recognizing the losses will help to smooth the income this year. As a result, the company will have built-in gains for future periods when the company may not be as profitable.

Instructions

Answer the following questions.

(a) Will classifying the portfolio as each proposes actually have the effect on earnings that each says it will?

(b) Is there anything unethical in what each of them proposes? Who are the stakeholders affected by their proposals?

(c) Assume that Abernathy and Nottebart properly classify the entire portfolio into trading, available-for-sale, and held-to-maturity categories. But then each proposes to sell just before year end the securities with gains or with losses, as the case may be, to accomplish their effect on earnings. Is this unethical?

WA10-3   You have just started work for Andrelli Corp. as part of the controller's group involved in current financial reporting problems. Jackie Franklin, controller for Andrelli, is interested in your accounting background because the company has experienced a series of financial reporting surprises over the last few years. Recently, the controller has learned from the company's auditors that a new *CICA Handbook* standard will apply to its financial asset investments. She assumes that you are familiar with these changes in accounting standards as well as other standards relating to investments and asks how the following situations should be reported in the financial statements under the new standard.

Situation 1

Trading securities in the current assets section have a fair value of $4,200 lower than cost.

Situation 2

A trading security whose fair value is currently less than cost is transferred to the available-for-sale category.

Situation 3

An available-for-sale security whose fair value is currently less than cost is classified as noncurrent but is to be reclassified as current.

Situation 4

A company's portfolio of available-for-sale securities consists of the common shares of one company. At the end of the prior year, the fair value of the security was 50% of original cost, and this reduction in market value was reported as an other than temporary impairment. However, at the end of the current year, the fair value of the security had appreciated to twice the original cost.

Situation 5

The company has purchased 20% of the common shares of a supplier and has been able to get three of its nominees elected to the supplier's 10-person board of directors. The supplier reported record earnings of $100,000 this year, but unfortunately wasn't able to pay out a dividend.

Instructions

What is the effect upon carrying value and earnings for each of the situations above? Assume that these situations are unrelated.

WA10-4   On July 1, 2005, Munns Corp. purchased for cash 25% of the outstanding shares of Huber Corporation. Both Munns and Huber have a December 31 year end. Huber Corporation, whose common shares are actively traded on the Toronto Stock Exchange, paid a cash dividend on November 15, 2005 to Munns Corp. and its other shareholders. It also reported a net income for 2005 of $920,000.

Instructions

Prepare a one-page memorandum of instructions on how Munns Corp. should report the above facts on its December 31, 2005 balance sheet and its 2005 income statement, as well as what additional disclosure might be required in the notes to the financial statements. In your memo, identify and describe the method of valuation you recommend. If additional information is needed, identify what other information would be useful. Provide rationale where you can. Address your memo to the chief accountant at Munns Corp.

WA10-5   The Accounting Standards Board of the CICA issued proposed *CICA Handbook* Section 3855 to specify the recognition and measurement standards for financial instruments. These standards cover the accounting methods and procedures with respect to certain debt and equity securities. An important part of the statement concerns the distinction between held-to-maturity, available-for-sale, and trading securities.

Instructions

(a) Why does a company maintain an investment portfolio of held-to-maturity, available-for-sale, and trading securities?

(b) What factors should be considered in determining whether investments in securities should be classified as held-to-maturity, available-for-sale, and trading? How do these factors affect the accounting treatment for unrealized losses?

Cases

Digital Tool

www.wiley.com/
canada/kieso

Refer to the Case Primer on the Digital Tool to help you answer these cases.

CA10-1   Investment Company Limited (ICL) is a private company owned by ten doctors. The objective of the company is to manage the doctors' investment portfolios. It actually began as an investment club ten years ago. At that time, each doctor invested equal amounts of cash and the group met every other week to determine where the money should be invested. Eventually, they decided to incorporate the company and each doctor now owns one tenth of the voting shares of the company. The company employs two managers who look after the business on a full time basis and make the investment decision with input from the owners. After tax earnings per year now average $1.5 million. During the year, the following transactions took place and information is available:

Investment A (IA): Purchased common shares of IA for $1,000,000. IA allows researchers to use expensive lab equipment (which is owned by the company) on a pay-per-use basis. These shares represent 15% of the total outstanding common shares of the company. As such, ICL is allowed to appoint 1 member of the Board of Directors. There are a total of 3 members on the Board. One of the ICL owners has also been hired as a consultant to the company to advise on equipment acquisitions. These shares have not been designated as trading and the company is unsure as to how long they will keep them. At least two of the owners of the company are interested in holding on to the investments for the longer term as they use the services of IA.

Investment in B (IB): Purchased preferred shares of IB representing 25% of the total outstanding shares. The shares will likely be resold within two months although no decision has yet been made.

Investment in C (IC): Purchased 25% interest in voting common shares of IC for $1 million two years ago. The current carrying value is $950,000 since the company has been in the drug development stage. IC develops drug delivery technology. In the past week, a major drug that the company has spent substantial amounts (approximately $10 million) in terms of research and development was declined by the Food and Drug Administration for sale in North America. Most of the $10 million had previously been capitalized in the financial statements of IC. This is a significant blow to IC as it had been projecting that 50% of its future revenues would stem from this drug. IC does not produce financial statement until two months after the ICL year end.

Although the investments to date have been primarily in private companies, the doctors are thinking of revising the investment strategy and investing in more public companies. They feel that the stock market is poised for recovery. Therefore, they are planning to borrow some funds for investment. The accountant is currently reviewing the above transactions in preparation for a meeting with the bank.

Instructions

Adopt the role of the company's accountant and analyze the financial reporting issues.

CA10-2   CanWest Global Communications Corp. (CWG) owns and operates 16 broadcast television stations and several specialty cable channels, 17 newspapers (including the *National Post*) and many other non-daily publications. It has a 57.6% economic interest in Network Ten (Australia), a 45% interest in TV3 (Republic of Ireland) and 29.9% interest in UTV (Northern Ireland).

According to note 3 to the financial statements, the company owns approximately 15% of the shares and all of the convertible and subordinated debentures of Network TEN. The convertible debentures are convertible into shares which would represent 50% of the total issued shares of the company at the time of conversion. In total, including the debentures, the investment in Network TEN yields a distribution equivalent to 57.5% of all distributions paid by Network TEN. CWG has a contractual right to representation on the Board of Directors and has appointed 3 of the 13 members on the Board.

The investment in TV3 is the subject of a joint venture agreement with another company. Under the terms of the agreement, control of the company is shared between the two parties.

Although the company has made an attempt to influence the decisions made by UTV management, they have been unsuccessful and presently do not have any representation on the Board of Directors.

Investments represent approximately $167 million (approximately 3% of total assets). Even though revenues were up 17%, net income was only $13 million for the year ended August 31, 2002, down from $47 million the prior year.

Instructions

Adopt the role of a financial analyst and critically analyze the financial reporting issues.

Research and Financial Analysis

RA10-1 Cara Operations Limited

Refer to the financial statements of Cara Operations Limited for its year ended March 30, 2003. These can be found on www.sedar.com or on the Digital Tool. These financial statements were prepared under the accounting standards in effect in 2003 and therefore do not incorporate the changes in proposed *CICA Handbook* Section 3855.

Instructions

(a) Review Cara's balance sheet. Identify all long-term financial asset investments reported. You may need to read the notes to the financial statements to get the necessary details.

(b) Does Cara have any investments in subsidiary companies? Does it own 100% of all its subsidiaries? Can you tell this by looking at the balance sheet? At the income statement?

(c) Briefly summarize Cara's investments in debt and equity securities during its year ended March 30, 2003.

(d) What accounting policies does the company apply to its long-term investments in debt and equity securities? Are these consistent with the CICA standards proposed for 2005? How might you expect the company's stated policies to change?

RA10-2 MOSAID Technologies Incorporated

Refer to the financial statements of MOSAID Technologies Incorporated for its year ended April 25, 2003. These can be found on www.sedar.com or on the Digital Tool. These financial statements were prepared under the accounting standards in effect in 2003 and therefore do not incorporate the changes in proposed *CICA Handbook* Section 3855.

Instructions

(a) Identify MOSAID Technologies' investments in debt and equity securities. Refer to the notes to the financial statements if necessary.

(b) Identify the accounting policies used in accounting for and reporting these investments.

(c) Identify the decisions MOSAID Technologies will have to make when proposed *CICA Handbook* Section 3855 is approved.

(d) The company recognized an impairment in value of one of its investments during its 2003 fiscal year. Explain the reason for the impairment and what the effect was on 2003's reported earnings.

(e) The company sold a long-term investment during its 2003 fiscal year. Reconstruct to the extent possible the entry that would have been made on disposal of the investment.

RA10-3 Canadian Imperial Bank of Commerce

Refer to the 2002 financial statements and accompanying notes of Canadian Imperial Bank of Commerce included in the Digital Tool or accessed through www.sedar.com.

Instructions

(a) What percentage of total assets is held in securities (2002 versus 2001)? Note that CIBC holds a significant loan portfolio also. What is the business reason for holding loans versus securities? Comment on how the investments are classified and presented in the balance sheet.

(b) What percentage of total interest income comes from securities (2002 versus 2001)? Are there any other lines on the income statement relating to securities? What percentage of net income relates to securities (2002 versus 2001)? Calculate a rough return on the investments in securities. Comment, looking at the nature of the securities invested in.

(c) Read the notes to the financial statements relating to securities and note the valuation method. Is this consistent with GAAP prior to new Section 3855, or with the proposed standards?

(d) Discuss briefly your findings in (c).

RA10-4 Research Issue—Variable Interest Entities (VIEs)

In June 2003, the CICA released new *Accounting Guideline AcG-15*—Consolidation of Variable Interest Entities. This topic has been high on the agendas of the accounting standard-setting communities around the world—particularly since the fall of Enron in 2001.

Instructions

Research and write a one to two page report on variable interest entities. What is a VIE? What is the accounting issue that needs resolution? What is the effect of applying the guideline? That is, how will financial statements differ from what was previously reported? Identify at least one company whose financial statements will be affected and quantify the effect on the statements.

RA10-5 The Coca-Cola Company and PepsiCo, Inc.

Instructions

Gain access to the 2002 financial statements of The Coca-Cola Company and PepsiCo, Inc. on the Digital Tool.

(a) Based on the information contained in these financial statements, determine each of the following for each company.

   1. Cash used in (for) investing activities during 2002 (from the Statement of Cash Flows).

   2. Cash used for acquisitions and investments in unconsolidated affiliates (or principally bottling companies) during 2002.

   3. Total investment in unconsolidated affiliates (or investments and other assets) at December 31, 2002.

   4. What conclusions concerning the management of investments can be drawn from these data?

(b) Briefly identify from Coca-Cola's December 31, 2002 balance sheet the investments it reported as being accounted for under the equity method. What is the amount of investments that Coca-Cola reported in its 2002 balance sheet as "cost method investments," and what is the nature of these investments?

(c) In its note number 9 on Financial Instruments, what total amounts did Coca-Cola report at December 31, 2002 as: (1) trading securities, (2) available-for-sale securities, and (3) held-to-maturity securities? What types of investments were included in each category?

Expansion Incentive

On-Line Support Inc. has a huge call centre facility in Dartmouth, Nova Scotia, which until recently had been underutilized. Although the building could house up to 140 workstations, the help desk and technical support services provider had installed only 40 or 50. In 2003, On-Line Support expanded this facility to almost full capacity with approximately $250,000 in office and computer equipment purchases, says Director of Finance Lane Pineau.

These capital asset purchases were helped indirectly through a payroll rebate the company received from the province's development agency, Nova Scotia Business Inc. The rebate will offset wage costs and is contingent on On-Line Support employing at least 250 people in the Halifax area within five years. The Prince Edward Island-based company also runs a site in Kentville, Nova Scotia.

"Whatever funds that we receive basically go back to expansion, and go back to the community," Pineau says.

With the payroll rebate, the company receives a certain percentage of its annual wage costs after indicating the number of staff and the hours they work. Although the contributions help with cash flow, for accounting purposes, they are treated as a reduction of the wage expense rather than capital costs. The rebate will be accounted for as an adjustment at year end and will be disclosed in the notes to the financial statements.

The contribution allows the company to acquire additional facilities by freeing up resources. "In this industry, our clients, which are typically Internet service providers or telephone service providers, require us to grow very rapidly," Pineau says.

CHAPTER 11

Acquisition of Property, Plant, and Equipment

Learning Objectives

After studying this chapter, you should be able to:

1. Describe the major characteristics of property, plant, and equipment.
2. Identify the costs included in the initial valuation of land, buildings, and equipment.
3. Describe the accounting issues associated with self-constructed assets.
4. Identify the costs included in the initial valuation of natural resources.
5. Describe the accounting issues associated with interest capitalization.
6. Understand other accounting issues related to the initial measurement of plant assets.
7. Describe the accounting treatment for costs subsequent to acquisition.

After studying Appendix 11A, you should be able to:

8. Calculate the amount of capitalizable interest on projects involving expenditures over a period of time and borrowings from different sources at varying rates.

Preview of Chapter 11

The purpose of this chapter is to discuss (1) the proper accounting for costs related to the initial acquisition of property, plant, and equipment, including natural resources, and (2) the treatment of capital asset costs subsequent to acquisition. The amortization (allocation of long-term plant asset costs to accounting periods), impairment, and disposition of property, plant, and equipment are presented in Chapter 12 as are the disclosure requirements and analysis issues related to capital assets.

The content and organization of this chapter are as follows:

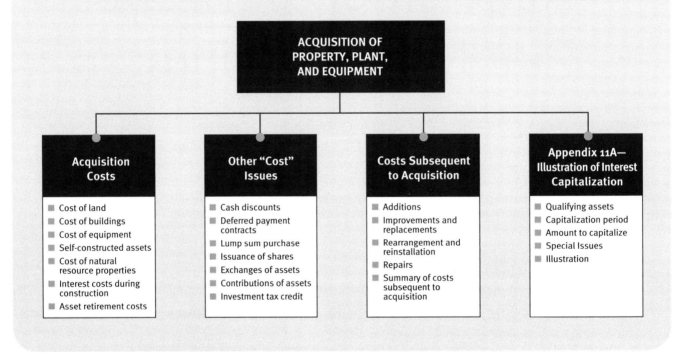

ACQUISITION OF PROPERTY, PLANT, AND EQUIPMENT

Acquisition Costs	Other "Cost" Issues	Costs Subsequent to Acquisition	Appendix 11A— Illustration of Interest Capitalization
▪ Cost of land ▪ Cost of buildings ▪ Cost of equipment ▪ Self-constructed assets ▪ Cost of natural resource properties ▪ Interest costs during construction ▪ Asset retirement costs	▪ Cash discounts ▪ Deferred payment contracts ▪ Lump sum purchase ▪ Issuance of shares ▪ Exchanges of assets ▪ Contributions of assets ▪ Investment tax credit	▪ Additions ▪ Improvements and replacements ▪ Rearrangement and reinstallation ▪ Repairs ▪ Summary of costs subsequent to acquisition	▪ Qualifying assets ▪ Capitalization period ▪ Amount to capitalize ▪ Special Issues ▪ Illustration

Objective 1

Describe the major characteristics of property, plant, and equipment.

Almost every business enterprise of any size or activity uses assets of a durable nature. Such long-term assets include both those that have physical substance—property, plant, and equipment—and those without physical substance—intangible assets. The accounting for intangible assets is the subject of Chapter 13. Property, plant, and equipment, also commonly referred to as tangible capital assets, plant assets, or fixed assets, include land, building structures (offices, factories, warehouses), equipment (machinery, furniture, tools), and natural resource properties. These terms are used interchangeably by organizations and throughout this textbook. In the past, the term "depreciation" was used to denote the amortization of property, plant, and equipment, "depletion" was used for the amortization of natural resource properties, and "amortization" was used for intangibles. While these terms are still in common usage, **amortization** is generally used throughout this text to refer to the allocation of the cost of all long-lived assets to accounting periods.

The major characteristics of property, plant, and equipment are:

1. **They are acquired and held for use in operations and are not intended for sale in the ordinary course of business.** Only assets used in normal business operations should be classified as property, plant, and equipment.[1]

2. **They are long-term in nature and usually subject to amortization.** Property, plant, and equipment yield services over a number of years. The investment in these assets is assigned to the periods benefiting from their use through periodic amortization charges. The exception is land, which is not amortized unless a material decline in value occurs; for example, due to a loss of agricultural land fertility because of poor crop rotation, drought, or soil erosion.

3. **They possess physical substance.** Property, plant, and equipment are characterized by physical existence or substance and thus are differentiated from intangible assets, such as patents or goodwill.

ACQUISITION COSTS

Historical cost is the usual basis for valuing property, plant, and equipment. **Historical cost is measured by the cash or cash equivalent price of obtaining the asset and bringing it to the location and condition necessary for its intended use.** The purchase price, freight costs, most provincial sales taxes, and a productive asset's installation costs are considered part of the asset's cost. These costs are allocated to future periods through the amortization process. Any related costs incurred after the asset's acquisition, such as additions, improvements, or replacements, are added to the asset's cost **if they provide future service potential**. Otherwise they are expensed immediately.

Cost should be the basis used at the acquisition date because the cash or cash equivalent price best measures the asset's value at that time. However, there is some disagreement about what to do with changes in value after acquisition. Should the asset value be adjusted to recognize changes in its replacement cost or its fair market value? Writing up fixed asset values is not considered appropriate in ordinary circumstances. Although minor exceptions are noted (during financial reorganizations, for example), current standards indicate that departures from historical cost for non-financial assets are rare.

The main reasons for this position are (1) at the acquisition date, cost reflects fair value; (2) historical cost involves actual, not hypothetical, transactions, and as a result is more objective; and (3) gains should not be anticipated and recognized before they are realized; that is, before the asset is sold.

Several other valuation methods have been considered, such as (1) constant dollar accounting (adjustments for general price-level changes), (2) current cost accounting (adjustments for specific price-level changes), (3) net realizable value, or (4) a combination of constant dollar accounting and current cost or net realizable value.

International Insight

In many nations, such as Great Britain and Brazil, companies are allowed to revalue their fixed assets at amounts above historical cost. These revaluations may be at appraisal values or at amounts linked to a specified index. Other nations, such as Japan and Germany, do not allow such revaluations.

Underlying Concept

Historical costs are verifiable and therefore considered more reliable.

Cost of Land

All expenditures made to acquire land and to ready it for use should be considered part of the land cost. Land costs typically include (1) the purchase price; (2) closing costs, such as title to the land, legal fees, and recording fees; (3) costs incurred to condition the land for its intended use, such as grading, filling, draining, and clearing; (4) assumption of any

2 Objective

Identify the costs included in the initial valuation of land, buildings, and equipment.

---

[1] Use in normal business operations includes the production or supply of goods and services, administrative purposes, for rental to others, or for the development and maintenance of other property, plant, and equipment (*CICA Handbook* Section 3061.04 (a)).

liens, such as taxes in arrears or mortgages or encumbrances on the property; and (5) any additional land improvements that have an indefinite life.

When land has been purchased to construct a building, all costs incurred up to the excavation for the new building are considered land costs. **Removal of old buildings, clearing, grading, and filling are considered land costs because these costs are necessary to get the land in condition for its intended purpose.** Any proceeds obtained in the process of getting the land ready for its intended use, such as salvage receipts on the demolition of an old building or the sale of timber that has been cleared, are treated as reductions in the land cost.

In some cases, the land purchaser has to take on responsibility for certain obligations on the land such as back taxes or liens. In such situations, the cost of the land is the cash paid for it, plus the encumbrances. In other words, if the land purchase price is $50,000 cash, but accrued property taxes of $5,000 and liens of $10,000 are assumed by the purchaser, the land cost is $65,000.

Special assessments for local improvements, such as pavements, street lights, sewers, and drainage systems, are usually charged to the Land account because they are relatively permanent in nature and are maintained and replaced by the local government body. In addition, permanent improvements made by the owner, such as landscaping, are properly chargeable to the Land account. Improvements with limited lives, such as private driveways, walks, fences, and parking lots, are recorded separately as Land Improvements so they can be amortized over their estimated lives.

Generally, land is considered part of property, plant, and equipment. If the major purpose of acquiring and holding land is speculative, however, it is more appropriately classified as an investment. If the land is held by a real estate concern for resale, by land developers or subdividers, it should be classified as inventory.

In cases where land is held as an investment, what accounting treatment should be given taxes, insurance, and other direct costs incurred while holding the land? Many believe these costs should be capitalized as part of the land's cost until it is sold and a gain is recognized. This approach is reasonable as long as the total amount capitalized does not exceed the property's fair value, and seems justified except in cases where the asset is currently producing revenue, such as with rental property.

Cost of Buildings

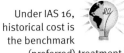

IAS Note

Under IAS 16, historical cost is the benchmark (preferred) treatment for property, plant, and equipment. However, it is also allowable to use revalued amounts. If revaluation is used, companies are required to revalue the class of assets regularly.

The cost of buildings should include all expenditures related directly to their acquisition or construction. These costs include (1) materials, labour, and overhead costs incurred during construction and (2) professional fees and building permits. Generally, companies contract to have their buildings constructed. All costs incurred, from excavation to completion, are considered part of the building costs.

One accounting issue relates to the cost of an old building that is on the site of a newly proposed building. Is the cost to remove the old building a cost of the land, or of the new building? The answer is that if land is purchased with an old building on it, then the demolition cost less its salvage value is a cost of getting the land ready for its intended use and relates to the land rather than to the new building. As indicated earlier, all costs of getting an asset ready for its intended use are costs of that asset. On the other hand, if an old building owned and previously used by a company is razed (torn down) so that a new building can be built on that land, the costs of demolition net of any cost recoveries are incorporated in the cost of disposing of the old building, thus increasing any loss on disposal of the old asset.

What is the proper accounting when expenditures of a capital nature are made to property that is being leased or rented? Long-term leases ordinarily provide that any such leasehold improvements revert to the lessor at the end of the lease. If the lessee constructs new buildings on leased land or reconstucts and improves existing buildings, the lessee has the right to use such facilities during the life of the lease, but they become the property of the lessor when the lease expires. The lessee charges the facilities' cost to a separate Leasehold Improvements account which is amortized as an operating expense over the remaining life of the lease, or the useful life of the improvements, whichever is shorter.

Cost of Equipment

The term "equipment" in accounting includes delivery equipment, office equipment, machinery, furniture and fixtures, furnishings, factory equipment, and similar tangible capital assets. The cost of such assets includes the purchase price, freight, and handling charges incurred, insurance on the equipment while in transit, cost of special foundations if required, assembling and installation costs, and costs of conducting trial runs. Costs thus include all reasonable and necessary expenditures incurred in acquiring the equipment and preparing it for use. The Goods and Services Tax (GST) or Harmonized Sales Tax (HST) paid on assets acquired is treated as an Input Tax Credit used to reduce the amount of GST or HST payable—it does not increase the acquisition cost of the assets.

Self-Constructed Assets

Often, companies construct their own assets. Determining the cost of such machinery and other capital assets can be a problem. Without a purchase price or contract price, the company must allocate costs and expenses to arrive at the cost of the self-constructed asset. Materials and direct labour used in construction pose no problem; these costs can be traced directly to work and material orders related to the assets constructed.

3 Objective
Describe the accounting issues associated with self-constructed assets.

However, assigning indirect costs of manufacturing creates special problems. These indirect costs, called **overhead or burden**, include power, heat, light, insurance, property taxes on factory buildings and equipment, factory supervisory labour, amortization of fixed assets, and supplies. These costs may be handled in one of three ways.

1. **Assign no fixed overhead to the cost of the constructed asset.** The major argument for this treatment is that indirect overhead is generally fixed in nature and does not increase as a result of constructing one's own plant or equipment. This approach assumes that the company will have the same costs regardless of whether the company constructs the asset or not, so to charge a portion of the overhead costs to the equipment will normally relieve current expenses and consequently overstate the current period's income. In contrast, variable overhead costs that increase as a result of the construction are assigned to the asset cost.

2. **Assign a portion of all overhead to the construction process.** This approach, a full costing concept, is appropriate if one believes that costs attach to all products and assets manufactured or constructed. This procedure assigns overhead costs to construction as it would to normal production. Advocates say that failure to allocate overhead costs understates the initial cost of the asset and results in an inaccurate future allocation.

3. **Allocate on the basis of lost production.** A third alternative is to allocate to the construction project the cost of any curtailed production that occurs because the asset is built instead of purchased. This method is conceptually appealing, but is based on what might have occurred—an opportunity cost concept, which is difficult to measure.

CICA Handbook Section 3061 indicates that the cost of a constructed or developed asset includes direct construction and development costs and "overhead costs directly attributable to the construction or development activity." This guidance allows for some flexibility in allocating fixed overhead, but generally a pro rata portion of the fixed overhead is assigned to the asset to obtain its cost. This treatment is used extensively because many believe a better matching of costs with revenues is obtained.[2] If the allocated overhead results in recording construction costs exceeding the costs that would be charged by an outside independent producer, the excess overhead should be recorded as a period loss rather than be capitalized. This avoids capitalizing the asset at more than the expected cash flows to be generated from its use and eventual salvage—its **net recoverable amount**.

Cost of Natural Resource Properties

Objective 4
Identify the costs included in the initial valuation of natural resources.

Natural resources, sometimes called wasting assets, include oil and gas and mining properties. They are characterized by two main features: (1) complete removal (consumption) of the asset, and (2) replacement of the asset only by an act of nature. Unlike buildings and machinery, natural resources are consumed physically over the period of use and do not retain their physical characteristics. Still, the accounting problems associated with natural resources are similar to those encountered with other tangible capital assets.

Sizeable expenditures are needed to find natural resources, and for every success there are many attempts where nothing is discovered. Furthermore, long delays are encountered between the time the costs are incurred and benefits are obtained from the extracted resources. The capitalizable costs of natural resource properties are related to three types of activity:

1. acquisition of properties,

2. exploration, and

3. development.

Costs incurred by a company that are directly identified with these three activities are generally added to the asset cost. In addition, company overhead costs that are necessary and can be directly related to exploration and development activities can also be capitalized.

Acquisition Cost

Acquisition cost is the price paid to obtain the property rights to search and find an undiscovered natural resource, or the price paid for an already discovered resource. In some cases, property is leased and special royalty payments are paid to the lessor if a productive natural resource is found and is commercially profitable. Generally, the acquisition cost is placed in an account titled Undeveloped or Unproved Property and held in that account pending the results of exploration efforts.

Exploration Costs

After the enterprise has the right to use the property, **exploration costs** are incurred to identify areas that have potential and to more closely examine areas previously identified. Exploration costs include the applicable **operating costs, including depreciation, of equipment and facilities dedicated to exploration activities**. The accounting treatment for these costs varies: some firms expense all exploration costs, others capitalize those costs that are directly related to successful projects (**successful efforts approach**), and still others capitalize all these costs whether or not they are related to successful or unsuccessful projects (**full-cost approach**)[3].

---

[2] There is increasing support by some, such as the Accounting Standards Executive Committee of the AICPA, to capitalize only the direct costs of such activities. They contend that permitting fixed overhead costs to be allocated may lead to overly aggressive deferral of costs and corresponding overstatement of income. This issue is on the agenda of the Accounting Standards Board of the CICA.

[3] The CICA's *Accounting Guideline 16—Oil and Gas Accounting—Full Cost* explains the policies and procedures for applying the full cost method of accounting.

The debate between the use of the successful efforts and the full-cost approach is particularly prevalent in the oil and gas industry. Supporters of the full-cost approach believe that unsuccessful ventures are a necessary cost of those that are successful, because the cost of drilling a dry hole is a cost of the process of finding commercially profitable wells. Those who believe that only the costs of successful projects should be capitalized contend that the costs associated with unsuccessful wells do not provide future economic benefits and, therefore, do not meet the definition of an asset. Under the full cost method, unsuccessful companies end up capitalizing many costs that will enable them, in the short run, to show an income that will be similar to a successful company. In addition, it is contended that to appropriately measure cost and effort for a single property unit, the only relevant measure is the cost directly related to that unit. The remainder of the costs should be absorbed as period charges, like advertising costs.

Under both the successful efforts and full-cost approaches, exploration costs can be initially capitalized to the Undeveloped or Unproved Property account. Only when it is determined whether or not the result is successful and extraction will be commercially viable do the accounting methods differ in determining the cost of the natural resource to be reported on the balance sheet. Under **successful efforts**, the costs for unsuccessful exploration activities are charged to earnings, whereas under the **full-cost method**, they remain capitalized as part of the cost of the natural resource.[4]

Canadian practice is mixed in terms of these two approaches. Larger companies such as Imperial Oil and Petro-Canada use the successful efforts approach. Small to medium-sized companies favour the full-cost approach. Exceptions to this generality regarding size include Canadian Natural Resources Ltd. and EnCana Corporation, which are large companies that use the full-cost method; others, like Paramount Resources Ltd., although relatively small, use the successful efforts method. In the mining industry, more established companies tend to write off exploration costs as incurred, while the "juniors" generally defer these costs. The difference in net income under the two methods can be staggering.

Development Costs

Development costs are costs incurred to obtain access to reserves and to provide facilities for extracting, treating, gathering, and storing the resource.[5] Such costs include amortization and operating costs of support equipment (e.g., moveable heavy machinery) and facilities necessary for development activities. These costs include such items as drilling costs, tunnels, shafts, and wells that are needed to produce the natural resource. Because machinery and equipment can be moved from one drilling or mining site to another, **their costs are normally capitalized separately** as Equipment, and only the amortization of the equipment as it is used is included in the development cost component of the natural resource.

The preproduction costs that become components of the asset's capital cost, therefore, are based on the approach used. Accounting for natural resources is complex and specialized. Illustration 11-1 summarizes the general flow of costs assuming use of the successful

---

[4] In 1978, the Securities and Exchange Commission (SEC) in the United States argued in favour of a yet-to-be developed method, **reserve recognition accounting (RRA)**, which it believed would provide more relevant information. Under RRA, as soon as a company discovers oil, the value of the oil would be reported on the balance sheet and in the income statement—a current value approach. By 1981, the SEC renounced this method for use in primary financial statements because of the inherent uncertainty of determining and valuing recoverable quantities of proved oil and gas reserves. In 1982, the FASB issued *Statement No. 69*, which required current value **disclosures** only. The use of RRA would make a substantial difference in the balance sheets and income statements of oil companies. For example, Atlantic Richfield Co. at one time reported net producing property of $2.6 billion (U.S.). If RRA were adopted, the same properties would be valued at $11.8 billion!

[5] *CICA Handbook*, Accounting Guideline 16.

efforts method. Under the full cost approach, the costs associated with the dry holes, within certain limits, are included as part of the natural resource account on the balance sheet.

The practice of deferring exploration and development costs as fixed assets is currently on the agenda of the Accounting Standards Board as part of standards harmonization projects. In the United States the general standard is to expense all preoperating costs.

Illustration 11-1

Flow of Costs: Oil and Gas Industry—Successful Efforts Approach

	Balance Sheet		**Income Statement**
Activity	Capital Assets	Inventory	
Incur acquisition costs (AC)	AC		
Incur exploration costs (EC)	+ EC		
	= cost of unproved property		
Dry holes drilled	− (AC + EC) of dry holes ⟶		expense
	= AC + EC of proven resources		
Incur development costs (DC)	+ DC		
	= AC + EC + DC of proven resources		
Extraction activity • depletion of resource • operating costs	− depletion ⟶	depletion expense + extraction costs	
Sale of product		− cost of sales ⟶	cost of sales
	= oil & gas property less accumulated depletion	= oil & gas inventories	

Interest Costs During Construction

Objective 5

Describe the accounting issues associated with interest capitalization.

The proper accounting for interest costs has been a long-standing controversy. Three approaches have been suggested to account for the interest incurred in financing the construction or acquisition of property, plant, and equipment.

1. **Capitalize no interest charges during construction.** Under this approach, interest is considered a cost of financing. If the company had used equity financing rather than debt financing, this expense would not have been incurred. The major argument against this approach is that an implicit interest cost is associated with using cash regardless of its source; in equity financing, a real cost exists to the shareholders, even if a contractual claim does not develop.

2. **Charge construction with all costs of funds employed, whether identifiable or not.** This method maintains that one part of construction cost is the cost of financing, whether by debt, equity, or internal financing. An asset should be charged with all costs necessary to get it ready for its intended use. Interest, whether actual or imputed, is a cost of building, just as labour, materials, and overhead are costs. A major criticism of this approach is that imputing a cost of equity capital is subjective and outside the framework of a historical cost system.

IAS Note

Under international accounting standards, capitalization of interest is allowed, but it is not the preferred treatment. The benchmark treatment is to expense interest in the period incurred.

3. **Capitalize only the actual interest costs incurred during construction.** This approach relies on the historical cost concept that only actual transactions are recorded. It is argued that interest incurred is as much a cost of acquiring the asset as the cost of the materials, labour, and other resources used. As a result, a company that uses debt financing will have an asset of higher cost than an enterprise that uses equity financing. The results achieved by this approach are considered unsatisfactory by some because an asset's cost should be the same regardless of how it was financed.

In Canada, capitalization of interest is permitted, and although there is no guidance provided, many companies apply the third approach.[6] This position is likely based on two grounds.

- The third method is consistent with the primary sources of GAAP. The cost principle assumes that "cost" includes all costs incurred to acquire the asset and bring it to the condition and location necessary for its intended use. This includes the interest cost that would have been included as part of its cost if the company had purchased a completed asset from another entity.

- Where there is a choice of policy permitted, many companies apply the method recognized as GAAP in the United States. FASB recommends that the actual interest incurred during construction be capitalized.

Interest capitalization can have a substantial effect on the financial statements. When earnings of Jim Walter Corporation dropped from $1.51 to $1.17 per share, the building manufacturer, looking for ways to regain its profitability, was able to pick up an additional 11 cents per share by capitalizing the interest on coal mining projects and several plants under construction.

What do the Numbers Mean?

How can statement users determine the effect of interest capitalization on a company's bottom line? The amount of interest capitalized is required to be disclosed in the notes to the financial statements.[7] For example, Clublink Corporation, a major Canadian owner, operator, and developer of golf clubs across the country, reported $2,391,000 of interest capitalized in 2001, an amount equal to 25% of the interest expense deducted on its income statement. The 2002 numbers were lower: about 12%.

While many Canadian companies apply the FASB standard, others use different methods. Many believe that interest should be capitalized on all pre-earning assets while others argue that no interest cost should be capitalized.[8]

Asset Retirement Costs

In some industries, companies take on obligations associated with the eventual retirement of their long-lived assets. For example, a nuclear facility must be decommissioned at the end of its useful life; mine sites must be closed, dismantled, and the property restored; and landfill sites have significant closure and post-closure costs associated with the termination of their operations.

In order to capture the benefits of these long-lived assets, entities generally assume responsibility for the costs associated with their retirement. *CICA Handbook* Section 3110,

---

[6] *Financial Reporting in Canada, 27th Edition* (CICA) reports that of 200 Canadian companies surveyed, 75 reported having capitalized interest in 2001.

[7] *CICA Handbook* Section 3850.03.

[8] See John M. Boersema and Mark van Helden, "The Case Against Interest Capitalization," *CAMagazine*, December 1986, pp. 58-60, and J. Alex Milburn, *Incorporating the Time Value of Money Within Financial Accounting*, (Toronto: CICA, 1988).

"Asset Retirement Obligations," requires the recognition of a liability for an asset retirement obligation in the period it is incurred, and concurrently, the recognition of "an asset retirement cost by increasing the carrying amount of the related long-lived asset by the same amount as the liability." While a fuller discussion of liability recognition and measurement issues is left to Chapter 14, students should be aware that the cost of property, plant, and equipment will often include such a charge. This component of a long-lived asset's cost may change in future periods due to changes in the estimate of the amount and/or timing of the eventual cash flows required to remediate the asset. Both the original amount recognized in the asset's cost and subsequent revisions are allocated to expense through periodic amortization.

OTHER "COST" ISSUES

Objective 6
Understand other accounting issues related to the initial measurement of plant assets.

We have seen that assets should be recorded at their initial fair value or cost, i.e., the amount of cash or cash equivalents paid to acquire the asset. For non-monetary transactions, cost is usually the fair market value of what is given up or the fair value of the asset received, whichever is more clearly evident. **Cost and fair market value, however, are sometimes obscured by the process through which an asset is acquired.** As an example, assume that land and buildings are bought together for one price. How are separate costs for the land and buildings determined? A number of accounting issues of this nature are examined in the following sections.

Cash Discounts

When plant assets are purchased subject to cash discounts for prompt payment, how should the discount be reported? If the discount is taken, it should be considered a reduction in the asset's purchase price. What is not clear, however, is whether a reduction in the asset cost should occur even if the discount is not taken.

Two points of view exist on this matter. Under one approach, the net-of-discount amount, **regardless of whether the discount is taken or not**, is considered the asset's cost. The rationale for this approach is that an asset's cost is its cash or cash equivalent price. In addition, some argue that the terms of cash discounts are so attractive that failure to take them indicates management error or inefficiency. Proponents of the other approach argue that the discount should not always be deducted because the terms may be unfavourable or because it might not be prudent for the company to take the discount. At present, both methods are employed in practice. The former method is generally preferred.

Deferred Payment Contracts

Often, plant assets are purchased on long-term credit contracts through the use of notes, mortgages, bonds, or equipment obligations. To properly reflect cost, **assets purchased on long-term credit contracts should be accounted for at the present value of the consideration exchanged** between the contracting parties at the transaction date. For example, an asset purchased today in exchange for a $10,000 noninterest-bearing note payable four years from now should not be recorded at $10,000. The $10,000 note's present value establishes the transaction's exchange price and the asset's "cash cost." Assuming an appropriate interest rate of 12% at which to discount this single payment of $10,000 due four years from now, the asset is recognized at a cost of $6,355.20 [$10,000 × 0.63552; see Table A-2 for the present value of a single sum, PV = $10,000 $(PVF_{4,12})$].

When no interest rate is stated, or if the specified rate is unreasonable, an appropriate interest rate must be imputed. The objective is to approximate the interest rate that the buyer and seller would negotiate at arm's length in a similar borrowing transaction. Factors to consider in imputing an interest rate are the borrower's credit rating, the note's amount and maturity date, and prevailing interest rates. **If determinable, the acquired asset's cash exchange price is used as the basis for measuring the cost of the asset and the interest element.**

To illustrate, Sutter Corporation purchases a specially built robot spray painter for its production line. The company issues a $100,000, 5-year, noninterest-bearing note to Wrigley Robotics Ltd. for the new equipment when the prevailing market interest rate for obligations of this nature is 10%. Sutter is to pay off the note in five $20,000 instalments made at the end of each year. Assume the fair market value of this specially built robot is not readily determinable and must be approximated by establishing the note's fair value (present value). This calculation and the entries at the purchase and payment dates are as follows.

At date of purchase		
Equipment	75,816	
Discount on Notes Payable	24,184	
Notes Payable		100,000
Present value of note = $20,000 (PVF − OA$_{5, 10\%}$)		
= $20,000 (3.79079) (Table A-4)		
= $75,816		

A   =   L   +   SE
+75,816   +75,816
Cash flows: No effect

The difference between the asset's cash cost, $75,816, and the $100,000 cash eventually payable represents the discount or interest on the amount borrowed of $75,816.

At end of first year		
Interest Expense	7,582	
Discount on Notes Payable		7,582
Notes Payable	20,000	
Cash		20,000

A   =   L   +   SE
+7,582   −7,582
Cash flows: No effect

A   =   L   +   SE
−20,000   −20,000
Cash flows: ↓ 20,000 outflow

Interest expense under the effective interest approach is $7,582 [($100,000 − $24,184) × 10%]. The entries at the end of the second year to record interest and to pay off a portion of the note are as follows.

At end of second year		
Interest Expense	6,340	
Discount on Notes Payable		6,340
Notes Payable	20,000	
Cash		20,000

A   =   L   +   SE
+6,340   −6,340
Cash flows: No effect

A   =   L   +   SE
−20,000   −20,000
Cash flows: ↓ 20,000 outflow

Interest expense in the second year is determined by applying the 10% interest rate to the net book value of the outstanding Note Payable, that is, the Note Payable less its contra account, Discount on Notes Payable. At the end of the first year, the Note Payable account was reduced to $80,000 ($100,000 − $20,000) and the Discount account was reduced to $16,602 ($24,184 − $7,582). The note's net book value, therefore, was $63,398 throughout the second year. The second year's interest expense is thus $63,398 × 10% or $6,340.

If an interest rate is not imputed in such deferred payment contracts, the asset will be recorded at an amount greater than its fair value. In addition, interest expense reported in the income statement will be understated for all periods involved.

Lump Sum Purchase

Underlying Concept

This is the same principle applied to a basket purchase of inventory.

A special problem of determining the cost of capital assets arises when a group of such assets is purchased for a single **lump sum price**. When such a situation occurs, and it is not at all unusual, the practice is to allocate the total cost among the various assets based on their relative fair market values. The assumption is that costs will vary in direct proportion to their relative values.

To determine fair value, any of the following might be used: an appraisal for insurance purposes, the assessed valuation for property taxes, or simply an independent appraisal by an engineer or other appraiser.

To illustrate, assume that a company decides to purchase several assets of a smaller company in the same business for a total price of $80,000. The assets purchased are as follows.

	Seller's Book Value	Fair Market Value
Inventory	$30,000	$ 25,000
Land	20,000	25,000
Building	35,000	50,000
	$85,000	$100,000

The $80,000 purchase price is allocated based on the relative fair values as shown in Illustration 11-2. Note that the assets' carrying values on the seller's books are not representative of the assets' fair values. They are irrelevant.

Illustration 11-2

Allocation of Purchase Price—Relative Fair Market Value Basis

				Asset Cost
Inventory	$\frac{\$25,000}{\$100,000}$	× $80,000	=	$20,000
Land	$\frac{\$25,000}{\$100,000}$	× $80,000	=	$20,000
Building	$\frac{\$50,000}{\$100,000}$	× $80,000	=	$40,000
				$80,000

Issuance of Shares

When property is acquired by issuing securities, such as common shares, the property's cost is not measured by the par, stated, or book value of such shares. **If the shares are actively traded**, the issued shares' market value is a good indicator of the fair value of the property acquired because the shares are a good measure of the current cash equivalent price.[9]

For example, a hardware enterprise decides to purchase adjacent land to expand its carpeting and cabinet operation. In lieu of paying cash for the land, it issues to the seller

---

[9] *CICA Handbook* Section 1581 on Business Combinations and *EIC-76*, Fair Value of Shares Issued as Consideration in a Purchase Business Combination, provide guidance in using quoted market prices for shares.

5,000 no par value common shares with a fair market value of $12 per share. The purchasing company makes the following entry.

Land (5,000 × $12)	60,000	
Common Shares		60,000

A = L + SE
+$60,000   +$60,000
Cash flows: No effect

If the market value of the shares given up is not determinable, the market value of the property should be established and used as the basis for determining the asset's cost and the amount credited to the common shares.[10]

Exchanges of Assets

When nonmonetary assets such as property, plant, and equipment **are acquired for cash or other monetary assets**, the cost of the acquired asset is measured by the fair value (present value) of the cash or other monetary assets given up. Monetary assets are cash or other assets whose amounts in terms of the amount of currency to be exchanged are fixed, usually by contract. Cash and accounts and notes receivable are the most common types of monetary assets. Nonmonetary assets, on the other hand, are items whose price in terms of the monetary unit may change over time. Examples include inventory, long-lived plant assets, and equity investments in other companies.

When nonmonetary assets such as property, plant, and equipment **are disposed of and the company receives monetary assets in exchange**, a gain or loss on disposal is recognized in income. The gain can be recognized in income because it is realized, i.e., converted to cash or a claim to cash, indicating that the earnings process is complete. The earnings process is basically the cash-to-cash cycle. Net monetary assets are given up when goods and services are purchased. When they are sold and converted back to cash or a claim to cash, the earnings process is said to be substantially complete.

However, when an existing **nonmonetary asset is exchanged for a new nonmonetary asset**, the proper accounting has been controversial. The underlying issues are twofold.

1. What should be the cost of the new nonmonetary asset acquired?

2. Should a gain or loss on disposal be recognized on the nonmonetary asset given up?

Some argue that the new asset's cost should be determined by its fair value, or by the **fair value** of the asset given up, with a **gain or loss recognized** on the disposal of the old asset. Others believe that the cost of the new asset should be determined by the **book value** of the asset given up, with **no gain or loss recognized**. Still others favour an approach that would **recognize losses** in all cases, but **defer gains** in special situations.

Guidance in Canada related to nonmonetary transactions is found in *CICA Handbook* Section 3830. As this text went to print, the Accounting Standards Board had just approved an *Exposure Draft* of proposed amendments to this section in order to converge Canadian standards with those of the IASB and with proposed changes to U. S. GAAP. The discussion below is based on these amendments on the basis that they are likely to be adopted.

Nonmonetary transactions, by definition, include both **nonmonetary exchanges** and **nonmonetary non-reciprocal transfers**. A nonmonetary exchange is an exchange of nonmonetary assets (or liabilities or services) for other nonmonetary assets (or liabilities or services) with little or no monetary consideration involved.[11] Before the amendments to

International Insight

In 2004, the U. S. moved to harmonize APB Opinion No. 29 with amended IAS 16 to require that exchanges of productive assets be recorded at fair values. The CICA standard is broader, dealing with exchanges of assets, liabilities or services.

---

[10] When the shares' fair market value is used as the basis of valuation, careful consideration must be given to the effect that the issuance of additional shares will have on the existing market price. In the unusual case where the fair market value of the shares or asset cannot be determined objectively, the corporation's board of directors may set the value.

[11] *CICA Handbook* Section 3830.04(e). A non-reciprocal transfer is a transfer with no consideration given or received.

Section 3830, the definition indicated this meant, in general, that cash and other monetary assets made up less than 10% of the fair value of the total consideration given up or received. The proposals for Section 3830 amendments omit reference to a specific percentage on the basis that the transaction's economic substance is required to be determined. This economic substance test substitutes for a need to identify a limitation on the cash component of the exchange.

The **general standard** is that **nonmonetary transactions are accounted for on the same basis as monetary transactions**: the cost of the asset acquired is equal to the fair value of the asset(s) given up unless the fair value of the asset received is more clearly evident. Resulting gains and losses are recognized in income. The rationale for immediate recognition is that the earnings process related to the assets given up is completed and, therefore, it is appropriate to recognize a gain or loss. Although cash or claims to cash have not been received in a nonmonetary transaction, the earnings process is considered substantially complete if the assets differ in their specific values to the entity.

Application of the general rule that **nonmonetary exchanges be measured at fair value is required unless**:

- the transaction lacks commercial substance;

- fair values are not determinable; or

- the exchange transaction was merely to facilitate a sale to customers.

In these situations, the exchange is recorded at the carrying value of the asset(s) given up.

Transaction Lacks Commercial Substance.   Because the general standard results in the entity replacing the book or carrying value of one asset with the fair value of the asset received in exchange, and reporting the gain (or loss) in income, it is important that the underlying economic situation of the company has changed as a result of the transaction. If the company is in exactly the same position after the exchange as it was before, there is little or no justification for bypassing the cost and revenue recognition principles!

A transaction has commercial substance only if there is a change in the entity's expected future cash flows. This could be evidenced by a change in:

1. the configuration of the cash flows underlying the assets exchanged, such as in their expected risk, timing, or amount; or

2. the assets' value-in-use or entity-specific value. This relates to an asset's value within the context of a specific firm, using the entity's expectations rather than those of the market.[12]

In either case, the difference must be significant relative to the fair values of the assets exchanged.

Fair Values Are Not Determinable.   As might be expected, the exchange cannot be recorded at fair value if neither the fair value of the asset given up nor the asset received is reliably measurable.

Transaction Was Merely to Facilitate a Sale to Customers.   The third exception covers inventory exchanges—an exchange of a product or property held for sale in the ordinary course of business for a product or property to be sold in the same line of business to facilitate sales to customers other than the parties to the exchange. Consider the case where a company exchanges its inventory items with inventory of another company because of colour, size, etc. to meet the immediate needs of a customer. This is a reasonable exception to

---

[12] *Proposed Statement of Financial Accounting Standards* on "Exchanges of Productive Assets," an Amendment of APB Opinion No. 29, Appendix A11 and *Statement of Financial Accounting Concepts No. 7*, FASB, 2000.

the use of the fair value rule as the entity's economic situation hasn't changed as a result of the transaction, the earnings process is not complete, and the company's investment in inventory has not been realized. Only when the sale to the customer is made is income recognized.

An overriding principle that may have to be applied in a non-monetary exchange is that an asset cannot be recognized at an amount that exceeds its fair value at acquisition. That is, where the exchange is an exception to the fair value rule and the old asset's carrying value is greater than the fair value of the new asset, the new asset is recorded at the lower fair value amount and a loss is recognized.

Asset exchange situations are summarized in Illustration 11-3. To illustrate, we will look first at the accounting for a monetary exchange, then a nonmonetary exchange applying the general standard, and then at a nonmonetary exchange where the general standard cannot be applied.

Monetary Exchange of Assets

Often when assets are exchanged or traded in, the transaction also requires a payment or receipt of cash or other monetary asset, sometimes called boot. Where the monetary component is significant, the transaction is considered a **monetary exchange**.

For example, Information Processing, Inc. trades its used machine for a new model. The machine given up has a book value of $8,000 (original cost $12,000 less $4,000 accumulated amortization) and a fair value of $6,000. It is traded for a new model that has a list price of $16,000. In negotiations with the seller, a trade-in allowance of $9,000 is finally agreed on for the used machine. The cash payment needed and the cost of the new machine are calculated in Illustration 11-4. Because the cash paid is significant relative to the fair value of the total consideration, this is considered a monetary transaction. What proportion is significant? This is a matter of professional judgement, but as the percentage gets smaller, the requirement to evaluate whether the transaction has commercial substance increases.

Type of Exchange	Accounting Guidance	Rationale
Monetary exchange	New asset(s) at FV of asset(s) given up Recognize gains and losses immediately	Company's economic situation has changed, and earnings process is complete
Nonmonetary exchange —general rule	New asset(s) at FV of asset(s) given up Recognize gains and losses immediately	Company's economic situation has changed, and earnings process is complete
Nonmonetary exchange to facilitate sale, fair values not available, or lacking commercial substance	New asset(s) at BV of asset(s) given up No gains recognized; losses recognized immediately	Company's economic situation has not changed (or is not measurable) or earnings process is not complete

Illustration 11-3

Accounting for Asset Exchanges

Illustration 11-4

Calculation of Cost of New Machine

Fair value of assets given up:		
Fair value of cash given up:		
List price less trade-in allowance $16,000 − $9,000	=	$ 7,000
Fair value of machine given up		6,000
Cost of new machine = fair value of consideration given up		$13,000

The journal entry to record this transaction is:

A = L + SE
−2,000   −2,000
Cash flows: ↓ 7,000 outflow

Equipment (new)	13,000	
Accumulated Amortization—Equipment (old)	4,000	
Loss on Disposal of Equipment	2,000	
Equipment (old)		12,000
Cash		7,000

The loss on the disposal of the used machine can be verified as follows.

Illustration 11-5

Calculation of Loss on Disposal of Used Machine

Fair value of used machine	$6,000
Book value of used machine	8,000
Loss on disposal of used machine	$2,000

Why was the trade-in allowance not used as a basis for the new equipment? The **trade-in allowance** is not used because it included a price concession (similar to a price discount) to the purchaser. Few individuals pay list price for a new car, for example. Trade-in allowances on cars traded in are often inflated so that the customers think they are benefiting. In reality, the dealer is just prepared to sell the new car at an amount below list price. To record the car at list price would state it at an amount exceeding its cash equivalent price.

Nonmonetary Exchange—Application of Fair Value Standard

To illustrate the general standard for a nonmonetary exchange of assets, assume that Cathay Corporation exchanges a number of used trucks plus cash for vacant land that might be used for a future plant site. The trucks have a combined book value of $42,000 (cost $64,000 less $22,000 accumulated amortization). Cathay's purchasing agent, who has had previous dealings in the second-hand market, indicates that the trucks have a fair value of $49,000. In addition to the trucks, Cathay must pay $4,000 cash for the land.

This exchange is deemed to be a **nonmonetary exchange** where the general fair value standard is applied. The exchange has commercial substance because the pattern and timing of cash flows from the investment in land are very different from those of the trucks. In addition, fair values are determinable and the transaction's purpose was not to facilitate a sale to customers. Assuming the land's fair value is not known, or its fair value is not as reliable as that of the trucks, the cost of the land is calculated as follows.

Illustration 11-6

Calculation of Land's Acquisition Cost

Cost of land = fair value of consideration given up:	
Fair value of trucks exchanged	$49,000
Fair value of cash given up	4,000
Acquisition cost of the land	$53,000

The journal entry to record the exchange transaction is:

Land	53,000	
Accumulated Amortization—Trucks	22,000	
Trucks		64,000
Cash		4,000
Gain on Disposal of Trucks		7,000

A = L + SE
+7,000   +7,000
Cash flows: ↓ 4,000 outflow

The gain is the difference between the fair value of the trucks of $49,000 and their book value of $42,000. It follows that if the fair value of the trucks was $39,000 instead of $49,000, a loss on the exchange of $3,000 ($42,000 − $39,000) would be reported. In either case, the earnings process on the used trucks is considered complete and a gain or loss on disposal is recognized. Note that the accounting is identical to that used for a monetary transaction.

Nonmonetary Exchange—Exception to Fair Value Standard

The real estate industry provides a good example of why the accounting profession decided not to recognize gains on exchanges of nonmonetary assets without commercial substance. In this industry, it is common practice for companies to swap real estate holdings. Assume that Landmark Corp. and Hillfarm, Inc. each had undeveloped land on which they intended to build shopping centres. Appraisals indicated that both companies' land had increased significantly in value since they had been acquired but were similar in the configuration of their future cash flows and value-in-use. The companies decided to exchange (swap) their undeveloped land, record a gain, and report their new land parcels at current fair values. Should gains be recognized at this point? No: **the companies remain in the same economic position after the swap as before.** Therefore, the asset(s) acquired should be recorded at the book value of the asset(s) given up with no gain recognized.

In contrast, if the book value of the asset(s) given up exceeds the fair value of the asset(s) acquired, a loss is indicated. **When a loss is indicated, it is recognized immediately.** Assets cannot be recognized at amounts exceeding their fair value!

To illustrate a similar exchange, assume Davis Rent-A-Car has an automobile rental fleet consisting primarily of Ford Motor Company products. Davis' management is interested in **increasing the variety of automobiles in its rental fleet** by adding numerous General Motors models. Davis arranges with Ned's Rent-A-Car to exchange a group of Ford automobiles with a fair value of $160,000 and a book value of $135,000 (cost $150,000 less accumulated depreciation $15,000) for a number of General Motors models with a fair value of $170,000; Davis is required to pay $10,000 cash in addition to the Ford automobiles exchanged. As the cash component is a minor portion of the fair value of the total consideration, this is considered a nonmonetary exchange.

Book value of Ford automobiles given up	$135,000
Book value of cash given up	10,000
Acquisition cost of GM automobiles	$145,000

Illustration 11-7

Calculation of the Cost of GM Automobiles Acquired

The earnings process is not considered completed in this transaction because it is assumed that the exchange was undertaken only to facilitate sales to customers or it has been determined that the exchange did not have commercial substance. While the gain is not recognized, it could be considered deferred—with the cost of the General Motors automobiles determined as follows.

Illustration 11-8

Alternative Measurement of Acquisition Cost

Fair value of GM automobiles	$170,000
Less unrecognized (deferred) gain on Ford automobiles	25,000
Acquisition cost of GM automobiles	$145,000

The entry by Davis to record this transaction is as follows.

A = L + SE
0   0   0

Cash flows: ↓ 10,000 outflow

Automobiles (GM)	145,000	
Accumulated Amortization (Ford)	15,000	
Automobiles (Ford)		150,000
Cash		10,000

The "gain" that reduces the new automobiles' cost will be recognized through lower depreciation charges as the automobiles are used to generate rental income.

An enterprise that engages in nonmonetary exchanges during a period should disclose the nature, the basis of measurement, and the amount of any resulting gains or losses in its financial statements.[14]

The revisions to *Handbook* Section 3830 eliminate one more area of different accounting treatment among FASB, the IASB, and the AcSB in Canada.

Contributions of Assets

Companies sometimes receive contributions of assets as a donation, gift, or government grant. Such contributions are referred to as **nonreciprocal transfers** because they are transfers of assets in one direction only—nothing is given in exchange. Contributions are usually assets (such as cash, securities, land, buildings, or use of facilities), but they also could be the forgiveness of a debt.

When assets are acquired as a donation, a strict cost concept dictates that the asset's valuation should be zero. A departure from the cost principle seems justified, however, because the only costs incurred (legal fees and other relatively minor expenditures) do not constitute a reasonable basis of accounting for the assets acquired. To record nothing is to ignore the economic realities of an increase in wealth and resources. **Therefore, CICA Handbook Section 3830 requires the asset's fair value to be used to establish its value on the books.**

Two general approaches have been used to record the credit in this transaction. Some believe the credit should be to Donated Capital, a contributed surplus account. This is termed a **capital approach**. The increase in assets is viewed more as contributed capital than as earned revenue. To illustrate, assume a company has recently accepted the donation of a land parcel with a fair value of $150,000 from a major shareholder.

The company makes the following entry.

A = L + SE
+$150,000   +$150,000

Cash flows: No effect

Land	150,000	
Donated Capital		150,000

This entry is acceptable on the basis that business owners can make capital contributions to a company, and *Handbook* Section 3250 acknowledges that such a donation is included in contributed surplus[15]. This type of transaction, however, is very rare. It is more common for assets to be contributed by various levels of government. Because inflows of assets **from non-**

---

[14] *CICA Handbook* Section 3830.

[15] If received from a non-owner source other than government, the resulting "gain" meets the definition of "other comprehensive income."

owner sources are generally income components, government contributions that benefit an enterprise should be reported as revenue. Whether the revenue should be reported immediately or over the period that the asset is used is another consideration.

To attract new industry, a municipality may offer land, but the receiving enterprise may incur additional costs in the future (transportation, higher taxes, etc.) because the location is not the most desirable. As a consequence, some argue that the revenue should be deferred and recognized as these increased costs are incurred.

Regardless of whether assets or funds to acquire assets are received from federal, provincial, or municipal governments, Section 3800 of the *CICA Handbook* requires that recipients follow prescribed accounting methods. These methods are based on an **income approach** that requires the amount received to be deferred and recognized over the period that the related assets are used. This is accomplished by either reducing the asset cost and future amortization by the amount of government assistance received (the **cost reduction method**), or recording the amount of assistance received as a deferred credit, amortizing it to revenue over the life of the related asset (the **deferral method**).

To illustrate, assume a company receives a grant of $225,000 from the federal government to upgrade its sewage treatment facility. The entry to record the receipt of the grant if the **cost reduction method** is used is as follows.

International Insight

There is no U.S. standard on accounting for government assistance, although SFAS No. 116 takes the position that, in general, contributions received should be recognized as revenues in the period received.

Cash	225,000	
Equipment		225,000

A = L + SE
0   0   0

Cash flows: ↑ 225,000 inflow

This results in the equipment being carried on the books **at cost less the related government assistance**. Assuming a 10-year life and straight-line amortization, the annual depreciation expense for the equipment will be reduced by $22,500 and net income will be increased each year.

Alternatively, a deferred revenue account can be credited with the grant amount. This amount will then be recognized in income **on the same basis as the underlying asset is amortized.** The entries to record receipt of the grant and its amortization for the first year under the **deferral method** is as follows.

IAS Note

The Canadian standard is consistent with IAS 20, which allows either the cost reduction or deferral method to be used.

Cash	225,000	
Deferred Revenue—Government Grants		225,000
Deferred Revenue—Government Grants	22,500	
Revenue—Government Grants		22,500

A = L + SE
+225,000   +225,000

Cash flows: ↑ 225,000 inflow

A = L + SE
    −22,500   +22,500

Cash flows: No effect

The donation **of land** by a government cannot be deferred and taken into income over the period it is used **as it has an infinite life**. Three choices are available: do not recognize the land transaction; recognize the full fair value of the land, offset by an equal credit to Other Comprehensive Income; or recognize the full fair value of the land, offset by an equal credit to a revenue account. The policy chosen must be disclosed.

Government grants awarded to a company for incurring current expenditures, such as for research and development or for payroll, are recognized in income in the same period as the related expenses. If grants or donations received are contingent upon the occurrence of a future event, such as being required to construct a plant or maintain a specified number of employees on the payroll as indicated in this chapter's opening vignette, the contingency is reported in the notes to the financial statements.

Considerable disclosure is required about the amounts, terms and conditions, and accounting treatment accorded government assistance received.[16] This enables readers to evaluate the effect of such assistance on the entity's financial performance and position.

---

[16] *CICA Handbook* Section 3800.18, .22, .24, .26, .29, and .30.

Investment Tax Credit

From time to time, federal and provincial governments have attempted to stimulate the economy, particularly in areas of high unemployment, by permitting special tax advantages to enterprises that invest in qualifying capital assets. The **investment tax credit (ITC)** is one such incentive where tax legislation permits enterprises to deduct a specified percentage of the cost of eligible new capital assets directly from their income tax liability.

To illustrate, assume an enterprise purchases an asset for $100,000 that qualifies for a 10% investment tax credit. If the company has a tax liability of $30,000 before the credit, its final tax liability for the year is determined as follows.

Illustration 11-9

Determination of Tax Liability after an Investment Tax Credit

Taxes payable prior to ITC	$30,000
Less investment tax credit ($100,000 × 10%)	10,000
Final tax liability	$20,000

There has been much debate within the accounting profession about the appropriate way to account for the benefit provided by an investment tax credit. Many believe the ITC is a reduction in the cost of the asset similar to a purchase discount, and that it should be accounted for over the same period as that of the related asset; that is, by the cost reduction or deferral approach. Others believe the ITC is a selective reduction in income tax expense in the purchase year. This latter approach—called the **flowthrough approach**—takes the full benefit into income in the year of the asset acquisition by recognizing the full reduction in income tax expense. The justification for this treatment is that the tax credit is earned by the act of investment, not by the asset's use or nonuse, retention, or nonretention.

The Accounting Standards Board concluded that investment tax credits **are a form of government assistance that should be accounted for on a basis consistent with government grants as described above.**[17] That is, the benefit should be taken into income on the same basis as the underlying asset, using either the cost reduction or deferral method.

COSTS SUBSEQUENT TO ACQUISITION

Objective 7

Describe the accounting treatment for costs subsequent to acquisition.

After plant assets are installed and ready for use, additional costs are incurred that range from ordinary repair to significant additions. The major problem is allocating these costs to the proper time periods. **In general, costs incurred to achieve greater future benefits should be capitalized, whereas expenditures that simply maintain a given level of service should be expensed.** In order for costs to be capitalized, one of four conditions must be present.

1. The asset's useful life is increased.

2. The quantity of units produced from the asset is increased.

3. The quality of the units produced is enhanced.

4. The associated operating costs are reduced.

Expenditures that do not increase an asset's future benefits should be expensed. Ordinary repairs that maintain the asset's existing condition or restore it to normal operating efficiency should be expensed immediately.

---

[17] *CICA Handbook* Section 3805.

Most expenditures below an established arbitrary minimum amount are expensed rather than capitalized. Many enterprises adopt a rule that expenditures below, say, $500 or $10,000 (depending on the size of the company) should always be expensed. Although conceptually this treatment may not be correct, a cost-benefit assessment demands it.

The distinction between a capital expenditure (an asset) and a revenue expenditure (an expense) is not always clear-cut and **this accounting choice can have a significant effect on reported income**. By capitalizing costs as assets on the balance sheet, the income statement is relieved of charges that would otherwise reduce the bottom line.

Underlying Concept

Expensing long-lived staplers, pencil sharpeners, and wastebaskets is an application of the materiality constraint.

What do the Numbers Mean?

This "managing" of earnings has been behind many of the well-publicized accounting scandals of recent years. WorldCom executives accounted for billions of dollars of current operating costs as capital additions. Adelphia Communications Corp. aggressively deferred operating items as assets on the balance sheet. Closer to home, Livent has been accused of similar actions. Toronto-based Atlas Cold Storage Income Trust, the second largest cold storage firm in North America, announced in 2003 that expenditures of approximately $3.6 million were inappropriately recorded as additions to capital assets during 2002. Atlas also adjusted the 2001 financial statements for another $1.6 million of expenditures previously recognized as assets. While these examples appear to represent situations where management set out intentionally to exaggerate profits and mislead investors, decisions are made on a daily basis where the distinction between whether an expenditure should be capitalized or expensed is not always clear cut.

One issue that affects the capitalization decision is determining the **property unit** with which costs should be associated. If a fully equipped steamship is considered a property unit, then replacing the engine might be considered an expense. On the other hand, if the ship's engine is considered a property unit, then its replacement would be capitalized. Section 3061.30 of the *CICA Handbook* indicates that where an item of property, plant, and equipment is made up of significant separable component parts with useful lives that can be estimated, the costs of each component should be recognized separately, where practicable. In most cases, consistent application of a capital/expense policy is more important than attempting to provide specific guidelines for each transaction.

Generally, four major types of expenditures are incurred relative to existing assets.

MAJOR TYPES OF EXPENDITURES

Additions. Increase or extension of existing assets.

Improvements and replacements. Substitution of an improved asset for an existing one.

Rearrangement and reinstallation. Movement of assets from one location to another.

Repairs. Expenditures that maintain assets in good operating condition.

Additions

Additions should present no major accounting problems. By definition, any **addition to plant assets is capitalized** because a new asset has been created. Adding a wing to a hospital or an air conditioning system to an office, for example, increases the service potential of that facility. Such expenditures are capitalized and matched against the revenues that will result in future periods.

One problem that develops in this area is how to account for any changes related to the existing structure as a result of the addition. Is the cost that is incurred to tear down an old wall to make room for an addition a cost of the addition or an expense or loss of the period? Normally, because of practical difficulties in determining the wall's cost, its original carrying amount remains in the accounts, and the cost to tear down the wall is included in the cost of the addition.

Improvements and Replacements

Improvements (often referred to as betterments) and replacements are substitutions of one asset for another. What is the difference between an improvement and a replacement? An improvement is the substitution of a **better asset** for the one currently used (say, a concrete floor substituted for a wooden floor). A replacement, on the other hand, is the substitution of a **similar asset** (a wooden floor for a wooden floor).

Many times improvements and replacements result from a general policy to modernize or rehabilitate an older building or piece of equipment. The problem is differentiating these types of expenditure from normal repairs. Does the expenditure increase the asset's **future service potential**, or does it merely **maintain the existing service level**? Service potential is increased when an asset's physical or service capacity is increased, operating costs are reduced, useful life is extended, or the quality of the output is improved.[18] Often, the answer is not clear-cut, and good judgement must be used in order to classify these expenditures.

If it is determined that the expenditure increases the asset's future service potential and, therefore, should be capitalized, the accounting is handled in one of three ways, depending on the circumstances.

1. **Substitution approach.** Conceptually, the substitution approach is the correct procedure if the old asset's carrying amount is known. If that amount can be determined, it is a simple matter to remove the book value of the old asset and replace it with the cost of the new asset. This is consistent with the principle of recognizing separate cost components of assets on acquisition to the extent practicable—a components approach.

   To illustrate, Instinct Enterprises Ltd. decides to replace its plumbing pipes. A plumber suggests that in place of the cast iron pipes and copper tubing, a newly developed plastic tubing be used. The old pipe and tubing have a book value of $15,000 (cost of $150,000 less accumulated amortization of $135,000), and a scrap value of $1,000. The plastic tubing system has a cost of $125,000. Assuming that Instinct has to pay $124,000 for the new tubing after exchanging the old tubing, the entry is:

A   =   L   +   SE
−14,000   −14,000
Cash flows: ↓ 124,000 outflow

Plumbing System	125,000	
Accumulated Amortization	135,000	
Loss on Disposal of Plant Assets	14,000	
Plumbing System		150,000
Cash ($125,000 − $1,000)		124,000

The problem with this approach is determining the old asset's book value. Generally, the components of a given asset depreciate at different rates, but often no separate accounting is made. As an example, a truck's tires, motor, and body depreciate at different rates, but most companies use only one amortization rate for the entire truck. Separate amortization rates could be set for each component, but it would be impractical. **If the old asset's carrying amount cannot be determined**, one of two other approaches is adopted.

---

[18] *CICA Handbook* Section 3061.26.

2. **Capitalizing the new cost.** The justification for capitalizing the improvement or replacement cost is that even though the old asset's carrying amount is not removed from the accounts, sufficient amortization was taken on the item to reduce the carrying amount almost to zero. Although this assumption may not be true in every case, the differences are often not significant. Improvements are usually handled in this manner.

3. **Charging to accumulated amortization.** There are times when the production quantity or quality of the asset itself has not been improved, but its useful life has been extended. Replacements, particularly, may extend the asset's useful life, yet may not improve the quality or quantity of its output. In these circumstances, the expenditure may be debited to Accumulated Amortization rather than to the plant asset account. The theory behind this approach is that the replacement extends the asset's useful life and thereby recaptures some or all of the past amortization. The net carrying amount of the asset is the same whether the asset is debited or the accumulated amortization is debited.

Rearrangement and Reinstallation

Rearrangement and reinstallation costs, which are expenditures intended to benefit future periods, are different from additions, replacements, and improvements. An example is the rearrangement and reinstallation of a group of machines to facilitate future production. If the original installation cost and the accumulated amortization taken to date can be determined or estimated, the rearrangement and reinstallation cost is handled as a replacement. These amounts, however, are rarely known.

Conceptually, in order to match the costs with the periods expecting to benefit, the new costs should be capitalized as an asset and amortized over those future periods. This is the accounting treatment generally followed in the past and still acceptable today. Increasingly, however, accounting standard setters are requiring similar expenditures to be recognized as expenses of the current period. This treatment is more consistent with the asset and liability view of the accounting model set out in *CICA Handbook* Section 1000 that requires an asset to meet the definition of an "economic resource." Most deferred costs result from an income statement or matching emphasis.

Repairs

Ordinary repairs are expenditures made to maintain plant assets in good operating condition; they are charged to an expense account in the period in which they are incurred on the basis that **it is the primary period benefited.** Replacing minor parts, lubricating and adjusting equipment, repainting, and cleaning are examples of maintenance charges that occur regularly and are treated as ordinary operating expenses. It is often difficult to distinguish a repair from an improvement or replacement. The major consideration is the extent to which the costs incurred achieve greater future economic benefits. If a major repair is made, such as an overhaul where several periods will benefit, practice has been to account for it as an addition, improvement, or replacement. Some, however, argue that costs involved for planned major expenditures should be expensed as incurred unless they represent an additional component or the replacement of an existing component. That is, if they serve only to restore other assets to their original operating condition, an "expense as incurred" approach is justified.

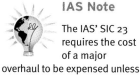

IAS Note

The IAS' SIC 23 requires the cost of a major overhaul to be expensed unless the overhauled item has been depreciated as a separate asset component.

Summary of Costs Subsequent to Acquisition

The following schedule summarizes the accounting treatment for various costs incurred subsequent to the acquisition of capitalized assets.

Illustration 11-10

Summary of Costs Subsequent to Acquisition of Property, Plant, and Equipment

Type of Expenditure	Normal Accounting Treatment
Additions	Capitalize cost of addition to asset account.

Improvements and replacements	(a) **Carrying value known:** Remove cost of and accumulated amortization on old asset, recognizing any gain or loss. Capitalize cost of improvement or replacement.
	
	(b) **Carrying value unknown:**
	  1. If the asset's useful life is extended, debit accumulated amortization for cost of improvement/replacement.
	  2. If the quantity or quality of the asset's productivity is increased, capitalize cost of improvement/replacement to asset account.

Rearrangement and reinstallation	(a) If original installation cost is **known**, account for cost of rearrangement/reinstallation as a replacement (carrying value known). (b) If original installation cost is unknown and rearrangement/reinstallation cost is **material** in amount and benefits future periods, capitalize as an asset. (c) If original installation cost is **unknown** and rearrangement/reinstallation cost is **not material or future benefit is questionable**, expense the cost when incurred.
Repairs	(a) **Ordinary:** Expense cost of repairs when incurred. (b) **Major:** As appropriate, treat as an addition, improvement, or replacement.

Inco Limited, a Canadian mining and metals company and the second largest producer of nickel in the world, reported property, plant, and equipment of $6,345 (U.S.) million on its December 31, 2002 balance sheet. Illustration 11-11 includes excerpts from Notes 1 and 9 to Inco's financial statements that provide explanatory information about the acquisition costs of these assets.

Illustration 11-11

Property, Plant, and Equipment Disclosure

Digital Tool

Student Toolkit—
Additional
Disclosures

www.wiley.com/canada/kieso

NOTES TO CONSOLIDATED FINANCIAL STATEMENTS

Note 1. Summary of significant accounting policies
Property, plant and equipment
Property, plant and equipment are stated at cost. Such cost, in the case of mines and undeveloped properties, represents related acquisition and development expenditures. Financing costs, including interest, are capitalized when they arise from indebtedness incurred to finance the development, construction or expansion of significant mineral properties and facilities. When the net carrying value of an item of property, plant and equipment, less its related provision for future removal and site restoration costs and deferred income and mining taxes, exceeds the estimated undiscounted future net cash flows together with its residual value, the excess is charged to earnings. Estimates of future cash flows are subject to risks and uncertainties.

Exploration
Exploration expenditures are expensed as incurred except in areas currently under development, where production is probable, or in areas under feasibility study, where there is production potential, in which case they are capitalized and amortized using the unit-of-production method.

Note 9. Property, plant and equipment
Property, plant and equipment consisted of the following:

December 31	2002	2001	2000
Mining and mining plants	$ 2,745	$ 2,682	$ 2,646
Processing facilities	3,281	3,169	3,176
Voisey's Bay project	3,338	5,532	5,647
Goro project	637	180	96
Other	595	604	575
Total property, plant and equipment, at cost	10,596	12,167	12,140

Accumulated depreciation	3,095	2,874	2,780
Accumulated depletion	1,156	1,076	1,008
Total accumulated depreciation and depletion	4,251	3,950	3,788
Property, plant and equipment, net	$ 6,345	$ 8,217	$ 8,352

Evaluation of the future cash flows from major development projects such as the Voisey's Bay and Goro projects entails a number of assumptions regarding project scope, the timing, receipt and terms of regulatory approvals, estimates of future metals prices, estimates of the ultimate size of the deposits, ore grades and recoverability, timing of commercial production, commercial viability of new technological processes, production volumes, operating and capital costs, and foreign currency exchange rates. Inherent in these assumptions are significant risks and uncertainties.

At December 31, 2002, the net carrying value of property, plant and equipment under construction or development not subject to depreciation or depletion was $4,109 million (2001–$5,761 million; 2000–$5,929 million). Capitalized interest costs included in capital expenditures were $27 million in 2002 (2001–$13 million; 2000–$15 million).

Summary of Learning Objectives

Digital Tool

Glossary

www.wiley.com/canada/kieso

1. **Describe the major characteristics of property, plant, and equipment.**

   The major characteristics of property, plant, and equipment are: (1) they are acquired for use in operations and not for resale; (2) they are long-term in nature and usually subject to amortization; and (3) they possess physical substance.

2. **Identify the costs included in the initial valuation of land, buildings, and equipment.**

   Cost of land: Includes all expenditures made to acquire land and to ready it for use. Land costs typically include (1) the purchase price; (2) closing costs, such as title to the land, legal fees, and registration fees; (3) costs incurred to condition the land for its intended use, such as grading, filling, draining, and clearing; (4) assumption of any liens, mortgages, or encumbrances on the property; and (5) any additional land improvements that have an indefinite life. Cost of buildings: Includes all expenditures related directly to their acquisition or construction. These costs include (1) materials, labour, and overhead costs incurred during construction and (2) professional fees and building permits. Cost of equipment: Includes the purchase price, freight, and handling charges incurred, insurance on the equipment while in transit, cost of special foundations if required, assembling and installation costs, and costs of conducting trial runs. In addition, costs associated with asset retirement obligations are required in many cases to be capitalized and included as part of the asset's cost.

3. **Describe the accounting problems associated with self-constructed assets.**

   The assignment of indirect costs of manufacturing creates special problems because these costs cannot be traced directly to work and material orders related to the fixed assets constructed. These costs might be handled in one of three ways: (1) assign no fixed overhead to the cost of the constructed asset, (2) assign a portion of all overhead to the construction process, or (3) allocate on the basis of lost production. The second method is used extensively in practice.

4. **Identify the costs included in the initial valuation of natural resources.**

   Three types of costs are involved in establishing the cost of natural resource assets such as oil and gas and mining properties: (a) acquisition costs, (b) exploration costs, and (c) development costs. In the oil and gas industry, both the full cost and successful efforts methods are acceptable in determining the costs to be capitalized.

KEY TERMS

additions, 575
betterments, 576
boot, 569
capital approach, 572
capital expenditure, 575
commercial substance, 568
cost reduction
    method, 573
deferral method, 573
development costs, 561
earnings process, 567
exploration costs, 560
fixed assets, 556
flowthrough approach, 574
full-cost approach, 560
improvements, 576
income approach, 573
investment tax credit
    (ITC), 574
leasehold
    improvements, 558
lump sum price, 566
major repair, 577
monetary assets, 567
natural resources, 560
net recoverable
    amount, 560
nonmonetary assets, 567

5. **Describe the accounting issues associated with interest capitalization.**

Companies may choose whether to expense or capitalize interest during the construction of property, plant, and equipment. However, only actual interest (with modifications) may be capitalized. The rationale for capitalization is that during construction, interest incurred is a cost necessary to acquire the asset, put it in place, and ready for use. Once construction is completed, the asset is ready for its intended use. Also, if the asset had been purchased fully constructed, the manufacturer's costs, such as interest, would make up part of the costs recovered in the selling price to the buyer. Any interest cost incurred in financing the purchase of an asset that is ready for its intended use should be expensed.

6. **Understand other accounting issues related to the initial measurement of plant assets.**

The following issues may affect the initial cost of plant assets: (1) *Cash discounts*: Whether taken or not, they are generally considered a reduction in the asset's cost; its real cost is its cash or cash equivalent price. (2) *Assets purchased on long-term credit contracts*: Account for these at the present value of the consideration exchanged between the contracting parties. (3) *Lump sum purchase*: Allocate the total cost among the various assets based on their relative fair market values. (4) *Issuance of shares*: If the shares are actively traded, the issued shares' market value is a fair indication of the acquired property's cost. If the exchanged shares' market value is not determinable, the acquired property's fair value should be determined and used as the basis for recording the asset's cost and amount credited to the common shares. (5) *Exchanges of assets*: When assets are acquired with little or no cash or other monetary assets as part of the consideration, the exchange transaction is accounted for using fair values, with gains/losses recognized in income. Exceptions to this general standard include exchanges which lack commercial substance or where the transaction was merely to facilitate a sale to customers, or when fair values are not reasonably determinable. In these cases, the acquisition cost of the new asset is equal to the carrying value of the asset(s) exchanged. No gains are recognized. (6) *Contributions*: Assets contributed by government are recorded at the asset's fair value with a related credit that is taken to income over the same period as the asset contributed is used. (7) *Investment tax credits*: An immediate tax reduction benefit should be accounted for in the same manner as a government contribution.

7. **Describe the accounting treatment for costs subsequent to acquisition.**

The accounting treatment of costs incurred subsequent to acquisition depends on whether the cost is a capital expenditure or a revenue expenditure (i.e., an expense). In general, a capital expenditure—one that results in an increase in the asset's useful life, or in the efficiency of the output obtained from that asset—is charged to the asset account. A revenue expenditure, one that does not increase the asset's future benefits, should be expensed immediately. The specific accounting treatment depends on the circumstances.

Appendix 11A

Illustration of Interest Capitalization

Chapter 11 introduced some of the issues associated with the capitalization of interest during construction. Appendix 11A continues the discussion in more detail and provides an illustration of the application guidance in FASB's *Statement of Financial Accounting Standards No. 34*, often used by Canadian companies.

Implementing this approach requires considering three issues:

1. qualifying assets

2. capitalization period

3. amount to capitalize

8 Objective
Calculate the amount of capitalizable interest on projects involving expenditures over a period of time and borrowings from different sources at varying rates.

Qualifying Assets

To qualify for interest capitalization, assets must require a time period to get them ready for their intended use. Interest costs may be capitalized starting with the first expenditure related to the asset, and continuing until the asset is substantially completed and ready for its intended use.

Assets that qualify for interest cost capitalization include assets under construction for an enterprise's own use (including buildings, plants, and large machinery) and assets intended for sale or lease that are constructed or otherwise produced as discrete projects (e.g., ships or real estate developments).

Examples of assets that do not qualify for interest capitalization are (1) assets that are in use or ready for their intended use and (2) assets that are not being used in the enterprise's earnings activities and that are not undergoing the activities necessary to get them ready for use (such as land that is not being developed and assets not being used because of obsolescence, excess capacity, or need for repair).

Capitalization Period

The **capitalization period** is the time period during which interest may be capitalized. It begins when three conditions are present.

1. Expenditures for the asset have been made.

2. Activities that are necessary to get the asset ready for its intended use are in progress.

3. Interest cost is being incurred.

Interest capitalization continues as long as these three conditions are present. The capitalization period ends when the asset is substantially complete and ready for its intended use.

Amount to Capitalize

To be capitalized, interest must be directly attributable to the project, and is limited to the lower of actual interest cost incurred during the period and avoidable interest. **Avoidable interest** is the amount of interest cost during the period that theoretically could have been avoided if expenditures for the asset had not been made. If the actual interest cost for the period is $90,000 and the avoidable interest is $80,000, only $80,000 may be capitalized. Or, if the actual interest cost is $80,000 and the avoidable interest is $90,000, a maximum of $80,000 would be capitalized. In no situation should interest cost include a cost of capital charge for shareholders' equity.

To apply the avoidable interest concept, the potential amount of interest to be capitalized during an accounting period is determined by multiplying the **weighted-average accumulated expenditures** for qualifying assets during the period by the interest rate(s).

Weighted-Average Accumulated Expenditures

In calculating the weighted-average accumulated expenditures, the construction expenditures are weighted by the amount of time (fraction of a year or accounting period) that interest cost could be incurred on the expenditure. To illustrate, assume a 17-month bridge construction project with current-year payments to the contractor of $240,000 on March 1, $480,000 on July 1, and $360,000 on November 1. The weighted-average accumulated expenditures for the year ended December 31 is calculated as follows.

Illustration 11A-1

Calculation of Weighted-Average Accumulated Expenditures

Date	Expenditures Amount	×	Capitalization Period*	=	Weighted-Average Accumulated Expenditures
March 1	$ 240,000		10/12		$200,000
July 1	480,000		6/12		240,000
November 1	360,000		2/12		60,000
	$1,080,000				$500,000

*Months between the date of expenditure and the date interest capitalization stops or end of year, whichever comes first (in this case December 31)

To calculate the weighted-average accumulated expenditures, we weight the expenditures by the amount of time that interest cost could be incurred on each one. For the March 1 expenditure, 10 months' interest cost can be associated with the expenditure, whereas for the expenditure on July 1, only 6 months' interest costs can be incurred. For the expenditure made on November 1, only 2 months of interest cost can be incurred.

Interest Rates

The principles used to select the appropriate interest rates to be applied to the weighted-average accumulated expenditures are:

1. For the portion of weighted-average accumulated expenditures that is less than or equal to any amounts borrowed specifically to finance construction of the assets, use the interest rate incurred on the specific borrowings.

2. For the portion of weighted-average accumulated expenditures that is greater than any debt incurred specifically to finance construction of the assets, use a weighted average of interest rates incurred on all other outstanding debt during the period.[18]

An illustration of the calculation of a weighted-average interest rate for debt greater than the amount incurred specifically to finance construction of the assets is shown below. It assumes that the principal amounts were outstanding for the full year.

	Principal	Interest
12%, 2-year note	$ 600,000	$ 72,000
9%, 10-year bonds	2,000,000	180,000
7.5%, 20-year bonds	5,000,000	375,000
	$7,600,000	$627,000

$$\text{Weighted-average interest rate} = \frac{\text{Total interest}}{\text{Total principal}} = \frac{\$627,000}{\$7,600,000} = 8.25\%$$

Illustration 11A-2

Calculation of Weighted-Average Interest Rate

The avoidable interest in this example, assuming there were no specific borrowings, is the weighted-average amount of accumulated expenditures multiplied by the weighted-average interest rate, or $500,000 \times 8.25\% = \$41,250$.

Special Issues Related to Interest Capitalization

Two issues related to interest capitalization merit special attention:

1. expenditures for land
2. interest revenue

Expenditures for Land

When land is purchased with the intention of developing it for a particular use, interest costs associated with those expenditures may be capitalized. If the land is purchased as a site for a structure (such as a plant site), interest costs capitalized during the construction period are part of the cost of the plant, not of the land. Conversely, if land is being developed for lot sales, any capitalized interest cost should be part of the developed land's acquisition cost. However, interest costs involved in purchasing land held for speculation should not be capitalized because the asset is ready for its intended use.

Interest Revenue

Companies frequently borrow money to finance construction of assets and temporarily invest any excess borrowed funds in interest-bearing securities until the funds are needed to pay for construction. During the early stages of construction, interest revenue earned may exceed the interest cost incurred on the borrowed funds. The question is whether it is appropriate to offset interest revenue against interest cost when determining the amount

---

[18] The interest rate to be used may be based exclusively on an average rate of all the borrowings, if desired. For our purposes, we will use the specific borrowing rate followed by the average interest rate because we believe it to be more conceptually consistent. Either method can be used; FASB *Statement 34* does not provide explicit guidance on this measurement. For a discussion of this issue and others related to interest capitalization, see Kathryn M. Means and Paul M. Kazenski, "SFAS 34: Recipe for Diversity," *Accounting Horizons*, September 1988; and Wendy A. Duffy, "A Graphical Analysis of Interest Capitalization," *Journal of Accounting Education*, Fall 1990.

of interest to be capitalized as part of the asset's construction cost. If it is assumed that short-term investment decisions are not related to the interest incurred as part of the acquisition cost of assets, then interest revenue should not be netted with capitalized interest. Some are critical of this accounting because a company may defer the interest cost but report the interest revenue in the current period.

Illustration

Assume that on November 1, 2004, Shalla Corporation contracted with Pfeifer Construction Co. Ltd. to have a building constructed for $1.4 million on land costing $100,000. The land is acquired from the contractor and its purchase price is included in the first payment. Shalla made the following payments to the construction company during 2005.

January 1	March 1	May 1	December 31	Total
$210,000	$300,000	$540,000	$450,000	$1,500,000

Construction was completed and the building was ready for occupancy on December 31, 2005. Shalla had the following debt outstanding at December 31, 2005.

Specific Construction Debt	
1. 15%, three-year note to finance construction of the building, dated December 31, 2004, with interest payable annually on December 31	$750,000
Other Debt	
2. 10%, five-year note payable, dated December 31, 2001, with interest payable annually on December 31	$550,000
3. 12%, 10-year bonds issued December 31, 2000, with interest payable annually on December 31	$600,000

The weighted-average accumulated expenditures during 2005 are calculated as follows.

Illustration 11A-3

Calculation of Weighted-Average Accumulated Expenditures

Date	Expenditures Amount	×	Current Year Capitalization Period	=	Weighted-Average Accumulated Expenditures
January 1	$ 210,000		12/12		$210,000
March 1	300,000		10/12		250,000
May 1	540,000		8/12		360,000
December 31	450,000		0		0
	$1,500,000				$820,000

Note that the expenditure made on December 31, the last day of the year, gets a zero weighting in the calculation, and thus will have no interest cost assigned to it.

The avoidable interest is calculated as follows.

Weighted-Average Accumulated Expenditures	×	Interest Rate	=	Avoidable Interest
$750,000		0.15 (construction note)		$112,500
70,000[a]		0.1104 (weighted average of other debt)[b]		7,728
$820,000				$120,228

[a] The amount by which the weighted-average accumulated expenditures exceeds the specific construction loan.

[b] Weighted-average interest rate calculation:

	Principal	Interest
10%, 5-year note	$ 550,000	$ 55,000
12%, 10-year bonds	600,000	72,000
	$1,150,000	$127,000

Weighted-average interest rate: $\dfrac{\text{Total interest}}{\text{Total principal}} = \dfrac{\$127,000}{\$1,150,000} = 11.04\%$

The actual interest cost, which represents the maximum amount of interest that may be capitalized during 2005, is calculated as shown below.

Construction note	$750,000 × 0.15	=	$112,500
5-year note	$550,000 × 0.10	=	55,000
10-year bonds	$600,000 × 0.12	=	72,000
Actual interest			$239,500

The interest cost to be capitalized is the lesser of $120,228 (avoidable interest) and $239,500 (actual interest), which is $120,228.

The journal entries to be made by Shalla Company during 2005 are as follows.

Digital Tool

Tutorial on Interest Capitalization

www.wiley.com/canada/kieso

January 1		
Land	100,000	
Building (or Construction in Process)	110,000	
Cash		210,000
March 1		
Building	300,000	
Cash		300,000
May 1		
Building	540,000	
Cash		540,000
December 31		
Building	450,000	
Cash		450,000
Building	120,228	
Interest Expense		120,228

The capitalized interest of $120,228 will be written off as part of the asset's amortization. It is thus recognized in expense over the useful life of the asset and not over the term of the debt.

At December 31, 2005, Shalla reports the total amount of interest capitalized in a note to the financial statements. Illustration 11A-6 provides an example of Clublink Corporation's note in its 2002 financial statements.

Illustration 11A-6

Disclosure of Interest Capitalized

Clublink Corporation

Notes to Consolidated Financial Statements

4. **Capital Assets (excerpt)**
    Interest of $1,271,000 (2001—$2,391,000) and direct project development and management costs in the amount of $1,241,000 (2001—$1,147,000) have been capitalized during the year to properties under construction.

Digital Tool

Glossary

Summary of Learning Objective for Appendix 11A

KEY TERMS

avoidable interest, 582
capitalization period, 581
weighted-average accumulated expenditures, 582

8. Calculate the amount of capitalizable interest on projects involving expenditures over a period of time and borrowings from different sources at varying rates.

    The amount of interest capitalized usually depends on the length of the capitalization period, the amount of avoidable interest, and the weighted-average accumulated expenditures on qualified assets during the period. The amount must be disclosed in the notes to the financial statements.

Note: All asterisked assignment material relates to the appendix to the chapter.

Brief Exercises

BE11-1   Bonanza Brothers Inc. purchased land at a price of $27,000. Closing costs were $1,400. An old building was removed at a cost of $12,200. What amount should be recorded as the land cost?

BE11-2   Central Utilities Ltd. incurred the following costs during the fiscal period in which it constructed a new maintenance building. What costs should be included in the cost of the new building?

a) Direct labour	$35,000
b) Allocation of president's salary	30,000
c) Material purchased for building	40,500
d) Interest on loan to finance construction until completed	1,500
e) Allocation of plant overhead based on labour hours worked on building	29,000
f) Architectural drawings for building	7,500

BE11-3   Khan Corporation acquires a coal mine at a cost of $400,000. Development costs incurred total $100,000, including $12,300 of depreciation on moveable equipment to construct mine shafts. The obligation to restore the property after the mine is exhausted relative to construction to date has a present value of $75,000. Prepare the journal entries to record the cost of the natural resource.

BE11-4 Junior Oil Corp. purchased the rights to explore a previously undeveloped property in northern Canada at a cost of $20,000. After incurring $80,000 on personnel and transportation costs and another $35,200 on seismic testing, it was determined that there were economic reserves that could be developed, but no further work was done in this area due to the onset of winter. Identify the effect on Junior's balance sheet and income statement of the expenditures made to date.

BE11-5 Chavez Corporation purchased a truck by issuing an $80,000, 4-year, noninterest-bearing note to Equinox Inc. The market interest rate for obligations of this nature is 12%. Prepare the journal entry to record the truck purchase.

BE11-6 Martin Corporation purchased a truck by issuing an $80,000, 12% note to Equinox Inc. Interest is payable annually and the note is payable in four years' time. Prepare the journal entry to record the truck purchase.

BE11-7 Cool Spot Inc. purchased land, building, and equipment from Pinball Wizard Corporation for a cash payment of $306,000. The assets' estimated fair values are land $60,000; building $220,000; and equipment $80,000. At what amounts should each of the three assets be recorded?

BE11-8 Wizard Corp. obtained land by issuing 2,000 of its no par value common shares. The land was recently appraised at $85,000. The common shares are actively traded at $41 per share. Prepare the journal entry to record the land acquisition.

BE11-9 Strider Corporation traded a used truck (cost $20,000, accumulated amortization $18,000) for another used truck worth $3,700. Strider also paid $300 in the transaction. Prepare the journal entry to record the exchange assuming the transaction lacks commercial substance.

BE11-10 Sloan Ltd. traded a used welding machine (cost $9,000, accumulated amortization $3,000) for office equipment with an estimated fair value of $5,000. Sloan also paid $2,000 cash in the transaction. Prepare the journal entry to record the exchange. The machinery and equipment result in differential cash flows to Sloan.

BE11-11 Bulb Ltd. traded a used truck for a new truck. The used truck cost $30,000 and has accumulated amortization of $27,000. The new truck is worth $35,000. Bulb also made a cash payment of $33,000. Prepare Bulb's entry to record the exchange.

BE11-12 Cogswell Corp. recently purchased a building to house its manufacturing operations in Moose Jaw for $400,000. The company agreed to lease the land the building stood on for $5,000 per year from the industrial park owner, and the municipality donated $100,000 to Cogswell as an incentive to locate in the area and acquire the building. Prepare entries to record the cash exchanged in each of the transactions assuming the cost reduction method is used.

BE11-13 Use the information for Cogswell Corp. in BE11-12. Prepare the entries to record the three cash transactions assuming the deferral method is used.

BE11-14 Indicate which of the following costs should be expensed when incurred.

(a) $13,000 paid to rearrange and reinstall machinery

(b) $200 paid for tune-up and oil change on delivery truck

(c) $200,000 paid for addition to building

(d) $7,000 paid to replace a wooden floor with a concrete floor

(e) $2,000 paid for a major overhaul on a truck, which extends useful life

(f) $700,000 paid for relocation of company headquarters

*BE11-15 Brent Hill Company is constructing a building. Construction began on February 1 and was completed on December 31. Expenditures were $1.5 million on March 1, $1.2 million on June 1, and $3 million on December 31. Calculate Hill's weighted-average accumulated expenditures for interest capitalization purposes.

*BE11-16 Brent Hill Company (see BE11-15) borrowed $1 million on March 1 on a 5-year, 12% note to help finance the building construction. In addition, the company had outstanding all year a 13%, 5-year, $2 million note payable and a 15%, 4-year, $3.5 million note payable. Calculate the weighted-average interest rate used for interest capitalization purposes.

*BE11-17 Use the information for Brent Hill Company from BE11-15 and BE11-16. Calculate avoidable interest for Brent Hill Company.

Exercises

E11-1 (Acquisition Costs of Realty) The following expenditures and receipts are related to land, land improvements, and buildings acquired for use in a business enterprise. The receipts are enclosed in parentheses.

(a) Money borrowed to pay building contractor (signed a note)	$(275,000)
(b) Payment for construction from note proceeds	275,000
(c) Cost of land fill and clearing	8,000
(d) Delinquent real estate taxes on property assumed by purchaser	7,000
(e) Premium on six-month insurance policy during construction	6,000
(f) Refund of one month's insurance premium because construction was completed early	(1,000)
(g) Architect's fee on building	22,000
(h) Cost of real estate purchased as a plant site (land $200,000 and building $50,000)	250,000
(i) Commission fee paid to real estate agency	9,000
(j) Installation of fences around property	4,000
(k) Cost of razing and removing building	11,000
(l) Proceeds from salvage of demolished building	(5,000)
(m) Interest paid during construction on money borrowed for construction	13,000
(n) Cost of parking lots and driveways	19,000
(o) Cost of trees and shrubbery planted (permanent in nature)	14,000
(p) Excavation costs for new building	3,000
(q) GST on excavation cost	210

Instructions

Identify each item by letter and list the items in columnar form, as shown below. All receipt amounts should be reported in parentheses. For any amounts entered in the Other Accounts column, also indicate the account title.

Item	Land	Land Improvements	Building	Other Accounts

E11-2 (Acquisition Costs of Realty) Martin Buer Corp. purchased land as a factory site for $400,000. The property tax assessment on this property was $350,000: $250,000 for the land and the remainder for the buildings. The process of tearing down two old buildings on the site and constructing the factory required six months.

The company paid $42,000 to raze the old buildings and sold salvaged lumber and brick for $6,300. Legal fees of $1,850 were paid for title investigation and drawing the purchase contract. Payment to an engineering firm was made for a land survey, $2,200, and for drawing the factory plans, $68,000. The land survey had to be made before definitive plans could be drawn. The liability insurance premium paid during construction was $900. The contractor's charge for construction was $2,740,000. The company paid the contractor in two instalments: $1.2 million at the end of three months and $1,540,000 upon completion. Interest costs of $170,000 were incurred to finance the construction.

Instructions

Determine the land and building costs as they should be recorded on the books of Martin Buer Corp. Assume that the land survey was for the building.

E11-3 (Purchase and Cost of Self-Constructed Assets) Wen Corp. both purchases and constructs various equipment it uses in its operations. The following items for two different types of equipment were recorded in random order during the calendar year 2005.

Purchase

Cash paid for equipment, including sales tax of $8,000 and GST of $7,000	$115,000
Freight and insurance cost while in transit	2,000
Cost of moving equipment into place at factory	3,100
Wage cost for technicians to test equipment	4,000
Materials cost for testing	500

Insurance premium paid during first year of operation on the equipment	1,500
Special plumbing fixtures required for new equipment	8,000
Repair cost incurred in first year of operations related to the equipment	1,300
Cash received from provincial government as incentive to purchase equipment	25,000

Construction

Material and purchased parts (gross cost $200,000; failed to take 2% cash discount)	$200,000
Imputed interest on funds used during construction (share financing)	14,000
Labour costs	190,000
Overhead costs (fixed—$20,000; variable—$30,000)	50,000
Profit on self-construction	30,000
Cost of installing equipment	4,400

Instructions

Calculate the total cost for each of these two pieces of equipment. If an item is not capitalized as an equipment cost, indicate how it should be reported.

E11-4 (Treatment of Various Costs) Siska Supply Ltd., a newly formed corporation, incurred the following expenditures related to Land, to Buildings, and to Machinery and Equipment.

Legal fees for title search		$ 520
Architect's fees		2,800
Cash paid for land and dilapidated building thereon		87,000
Removal of old building	$20,000	
Less: Salvage	5,500	14,500
Surveying before construction		370
Interest on short-term loans during construction		7,400
Excavation before construction for basement		19,000
Machinery purchased (subject to 2% cash discount, which was not taken)		55,000
Freight on machinery purchased		1,340
Storage charges on machinery, necessitated by noncompletion of building when machinery was delivered		2,180
New building constructed (building construction took six months from date of purchase of land and old building)		485,000
Assessment by city for drainage project		1,600
Hauling charges for delivery of machinery from storage to new building		620
Installation of machinery		2,000
Trees, shrubs, and other landscaping after completion of building (permanent in nature)		5,400
One-year property tax holiday (for first year of operations) to promote locating in the municipality		8,000

Instructions

Determine the amounts that should be included in the cost of Land, of Buildings, and of Machinery and Equipment. Assume Siska follows a policy of capitalizing interest on self-constructed assets. Indicate how any amounts not included in these accounts should be recorded.

E11-5 (Natural Resource—Minerals) At the beginning of 2005, Plato Corporation acquired property, including all mineral rights, for $790,000. Of this amount, $80,000 was ascribed to the land itself. Plato, an international player in the mining industry, incurred the following costs during the first six months of the year.

Interactive
Homework

Clearing the trees from the mine site	$23,400
Cash received for the timber cleared	1,250
Cost of roads into the mine site	100,000
Mine site office building, to be demolished when the mine is closed	50,000
Purchase of moveable heavy equipment for the above	88,000
Depreciation on heavy equipment used for the costs incurred above	5,800
Allocation of Plato head office costs	14,000
Salary of engineer overseeing above activities	52,000

Instructions

Calculate the costs appropriately capitalized to the mining property. Provide a brief explanation for any amounts not included.

E11-6   (Natural Resource—Oil)   Tacoma Oil Limited leases property on which oil has been discovered. The lease provides for an outright payment of $500,000 to the lessor before drilling is begun and an annual rental of $31,500. In addition, the lessee is responsible for cleaning up the waste and debris from drilling and for the costs associated with reconditioning the land for farming when the wells are abandoned. It is estimated that the clean-up and reconditioning obligation has a present value of $30,000.

Instructions

Determine the amount that should be capitalized in the Oil Property asset account as a result of the lease agreement.

Interactive
Homework

E11-7   (Acquisition Costs of Trucks)   Alexei Corporation operates a retail computer store. To improve delivery services to customers, the company purchases four new trucks on April 1, 2005. The terms of acquisition for each truck are described below.

1. Truck #1 has a list price of $15,000 and is acquired for a cash payment of $13,900.

2. Truck #2 has a list price of $16,000 and is acquired for a down payment of $2,000 cash and a noninterest-bearing note with a face amount of $14,000. The note is due April 1, 2006. Alexei would normally have to pay interest at a rate of 10% for such a borrowing, and the dealership has an incremental borrowing rate of 8%.

3. Truck #3 has a list price of $16,000. It is acquired in exchange for a computer system that Alexei carries in inventory. The computer system cost $12,000 and is normally sold by Alexei for $15,200. Alexei uses a perpetual inventory system.

4. Truck #4 has a list price of $14,000. It is acquired in exchange for 1,000 common shares of Alexei Corporation. The common shares are no par value shares with a market value of $13 per share.

Instructions

Prepare the appropriate journal entries for the foregoing transactions for Alexei Corporation. Where there is some uncertainty as to the amount, provide justification for your choice.

E11-8   (Correction of Improper Cost Entries)   Plant acquisitions for selected companies are as follows.

1. Bella Industries Inc. acquired land, buildings, and equipment from a bankrupt company, Torres Co., for a lump sum price of $700,000. At the time of purchase, Torres' assets had the following book and appraisal values.

	Book Values	Appraisal Values
Land	$200,000	$150,000
Buildings	250,000	350,000
Equipment	300,000	300,000

To be conservative, the company decided to take the lower of the two values for each asset acquired. The following entry was made.

Land	150,000	
Buildings	250,000	
Equipment	300,000	
Cash		700,000

2. Hari Enterprises purchased store equipment by making a $2,000 cash down payment and signing a one-year, $23,000, 10% note payable. The purchase was recorded as follows.

Store Equipment	27,300	
Cash		2,000
Note Payable		23,000
Interest Payable		2,300

3. Kim Company purchased office equipment for $20,000, terms 2/10, n/30. Because the company intended to take the discount, it made no entry until it paid for the acquisition. The entry was:

Office Equipment	20,000	
Cash		19,600
Purchase Discounts		400

4. Kaiser Inc. recently received, at zero cost, land from the Village of Chester as an inducement to locate its business in the village. The appraised value of the land is $27,000. The company made no entry to record the land because it had no cost basis.

5. Zimmerman Company built a warehouse for $600,000. It could have contracted out and purchased the building for $740,000. The controller made the following entry.

Warehouse	740,000	
Cash		600,000
Profit on Construction		140,000

Instructions

(a) Prepare the entry that should have been made at the date of each acquisition.

(b) Prepare the correcting entry required in each case to correct the accounts. That is, do not reverse the incorrect entry and replace it with the entry in part (a).

E11-9   (Entries for Equipment Acquisitions)   Geddes Engineering Corporation purchased conveyor equipment with a list price of $50,000. Presented below are three independent cases related to the equipment. Assume that the equipment purchases are recorded gross. (Round to nearest dollar.)

(a) Geddes paid cash for the equipment 15 days after the purchase, along with 7% GST and provincial sales tax of $3,210. The vendor's credit terms were 1/10, n/30.

(b) Geddes traded in equipment with a book value of $2,000 (initial cost $40,000), and paid $40,500 in cash one month after the purchase. The old equipment could have been sold for $8,000 at the date of trade, but was accepted for a trade-in allowance of $9,500 on the new equipment.

(c) Geddes gave the vendor a $10,000 cash down payment and a 9% note payable with blended principal and interest payments of $20,000 each, due at the end of each of the next two years.

Instructions
Prepare the general journal entries required to record the acquisition and payment in each of the independent cases above. Round to the nearest dollar.

E11-10   (Entries for Asset Acquisition, Including Self-Construction)   Below are transactions related to Frede Corporation.

(a) The City of Piedmont gives the company five hectares of land as a plant site. This land's market value is determined to be $81,000.

(b) 13,000 no-par common shares are issued in exchange for land and buildings. The property has been appraised at a fair market value of $810,000, of which $180,000 has been allocated to land and $630,000 to buildings. The Frede shares are not listed on any exchange, but a block of 100 shares was sold by a shareholder 12 months ago at $65 per share, and a block of 200 shares was sold by another shareholder 18 months ago at $58 per share.

(c) No entry has been made to remove from the accounts for Materials, Direct Labour, and Overhead the amounts properly chargeable to plant asset accounts for machinery constructed during the year. The following information is given relative to costs of the machinery constructed.

Construction materials used	$12,500 ✓
Direct materials used in calibrating the equipment	375 ✓
Factory supplies used	900
Direct labour incurred	15,000 ✓
Additional overhead (over regular) caused by construction of machinery, excluding factory supplies used	2,700 ✓
Fixed overhead rate applied to regular manufacturing operations	60% of direct labour cost
Cost of similar machinery if it had been purchased from outside suppliers	44,000

Instructions
Prepare journal entries on the books of Frede Corporation to record these transactions.

E11-11   (Entries for Acquisition of Assets)   Presented below is information related to Zoe Limited.

1. On July 6, Zoe acquired the plant assets of Desbury Company, which had discontinued operations. The property's appraised value is:

Land	$ 400,000
Building	1,200,000
Machinery and equipment	800,000
Total	$2,400,000

Zoe gave 12,500 of its no par value common shares in exchange. The shares had a market value of $168 per share on the date of the property purchase.

Interactive
Homework

2. Zoe Ltd. expended the following amounts in cash between July 6 and December 15, the date when it first occupied the building.

Repairs to building	$105,000
Construction of bases for machinery to be installed later	135,000
Driveways and parking lots	122,000
Remodelling of office space in building, including new partitions and walls	161,000
Special assessment by city on land	18,000

3. On December 20, the company paid cash for machinery, $260,000, subject to a 2% cash discount, and freight on machinery of $10,500. The machine was dropped while being placed in position, requiring repairs costing $12,000.

Instructions

Prepare entries on the books of Zoe Ltd. for these transactions.

E11-12   (Purchase of Equipment with Noninterest-Bearing Debt)   Mohawk Inc. decided to purchase equipment from Central Ontario Industries on January 2, 2005 to expand its production capacity to meet customers' demand for its product. Mohawk issues an $800,000, 5-year, noninterest-bearing note to Central Ontario for the new equipment when the prevailing market interest rate for obligations of this nature is 12%. The company will pay off the note in five $160,000 instalments due at the end of each year over the life of the note.

Instructions

(a) Prepare the journal entry(ies) at the date of purchase. (Round to nearest dollar in all calculations.)

(b) Prepare the journal entry(ies) at the end of the first year to record the payment and interest, assuming that the company uses the effective interest method.

(c) Prepare the journal entry(ies) at the end of the second year to record the payment and interest.

(d) Assuming that the equipment has a 10-year life and no residual value, prepare the journal entry necessary to record amortization in the first year. (Straight-line method is used.)

E11-13   (Purchase of Computer with Noninterest-Bearing Debt)   Sparrow Corporation purchased a computer on December 31, 2004, paying $30,000 down and agreeing to make a further $75,000 payment on December 31, 2007. An interest rate of 10% is implicit in the purchase price. Sparrow uses the effective interest method and has a December 31 year end.

Instructions

(a) Prepare the journal entry(ies) at the purchase date. (Round to two decimal places.)

(b) Prepare any journal entry(ies) required at December 31, 2005, 2006, and 2007.

E11-14   (Asset Exchange, Monetary Transaction)   Cannondale Company purchased an electric wax melter on April 30, 2006 by trading in its old gas model and paying the balance in cash. The following data relate to the purchase.

List price of new melter	$15,800
Cash paid	10,000
Cost of old melter (5-year life, $700 residual value)	11,200
Accumulated amortization old melter (straight-line)	6,300
Second-hand market value of old melter	5,200

Instructions

Prepare the journal entry(ies) necessary to record this exchange. Cannondale's fiscal year ends on December 31, and amortization has been recorded through December 31, 2005.

E11-15   (Nonmonetary Exchange)   Carlos Company Limited exchanged equipment used in its manufacturing operations plus $1,500 in cash for similar equipment used in the operations of LoBianco Company Limited. The following information pertains to the exchange.

	Carlos Co.	LoBianco Co.
Equipment (cost)	$28,000	$28,000
Accumulated amortization	19,000	10,000
Fair value of equipment	15,500	17,000
Cash paid	1,500	

Instructions

Prepare the journal entries to record the exchange on the books of both companies if the exchange is determined to (a) have commercial substance, and (b) not have commercial substance.

E11-16 (Nonmonetary Exchanges) Ashbrook Inc. has negotiated the purchase of a new piece of automatic equipment at a price of $4,000 plus trade-in, f.o.b. factory. Ashbrook Inc. paid $4,000 cash and traded in used equipment. The used equipment had originally cost $62,000; it had a book value of $42,000 and a secondhand market value of $47,800, as indicated by recent transactions involving similar equipment. Freight and installation charges for the new equipment required a cash payment of $1,100.

Instructions

(a) Prepare the general journal entry to record this transaction, assuming that the assets Ashbrook Inc. exchanged are similar in nature with little or no difference in the configuration of cash flows.

(b) Assuming the same facts as in (a) except that the asset exchange is determined to have commercial substance, prepare the general journal entry to record this transaction.

E11-17 (Government Assistance) Lightstone Equipment Ltd., looking to expand into New Brunswick and impressed by the provincial government's grant program for new industry, purchased property in downtown Saint John on June 15, 2005. The property cost $235,000 and Lightstone spent the next two months gutting the inside of the building and reconstructing the two floors to meet the company's needs. The building has a useful life of 20 years and an estimated residual value of $65,000. In late August, the company moved in to the building and began operations. Additional information follows.

(a) The property was assessed at $195,000 with $145,000 allocated to the land.

(b) Architectural drawings and engineering fees related to the construction cost $18,000.

(c) The company paid $17,000 to the contractor for gutting the inside of the building and $108,400 for construction.

(d) The provincial government contributed $75,000 toward the building costs.

Instructions

(a) What is the cost of the building on Lightstone Equipment's balance sheet at August 31, 2005, its fiscal year end?

(b) What is the effect of this capital asset on the company's income statement for the company's year ended August 31, 2006?

E11-18 (Analysis of Subsequent Expenditures) Donovan Resources Group has been in its plant facility for 15 years. Although the plant is quite functional, numerous repair costs are incurred to maintain it in sound working order. The company's plant asset book value is currently $800,000, as indicated below.

Original cost	$1,200,000
Accumulated amortization	400,000
	$ 800,000

During the current year, the following expenditures were made to the plant facility.

(a) Because of increased demands for its product, the company increased its plant capacity by building a new addition at a cost of $270,000.

(b) The entire plant was repainted at a cost of $23,000.

(c) The roof was an asbestos cement slate; for safety purposes it was removed at a cost of $4,000 and replaced with a wood shingle roof at a cost of $61,000. The original roof's cost had been $40,000 and it was being amortized over an expected life of 20 years.

(d) The electrical system was completely updated at a cost of $22,000. The cost of the old electrical system was not known. It is estimated that the building's useful life will not change as a result of this updating.

(e) A series of major repairs was made at a cost of $47,000, because parts of the wood structure were rotting. The cost of the old wood structure was not known. These extensive repairs are estimated to increase the building's useful life.

Instructions

Indicate how each of these transactions would be recorded in the accounting records.

E11-19 (Analysis of Subsequent Expenditures) The following transactions occurred during 2005. Assume that amortization of 10% per year is charged on all machinery and 5% per year on buildings, on a straight-line basis, with no estimated residual value. Amortization is charged for a full year on all fixed assets acquired during the year, and no amortization is charged on fixed assets disposed of during the year.

Jan. 30   A building that cost $132,000 in 1988 is torn down to make room for a new building. The wrecking contractor was paid $5,100 and was permitted to keep all materials salvaged.

Mar. 10   A new part costing $2,900 was purchased and added to a machine that was purchased in 2003 for $16,000. The new part replaced an original machine part, and results in a 25% increase in the efficiency of the equipment. The old part's cost was not separable from the original machine's cost.

Mar. 20   A gear breaks on a machine that cost $9,000 in 2000, and is replaced at a cost of $385. The replacement does not extend the machine's useful life.

May 18   A special base installed for a machine in 1999 when it was purchased has to be replaced at a cost of $5,500 because of defective workmanship on the original base. The cost of the machinery was $14,200 in 1999; the cost of the base was $3,500, and this amount was charged to the Machinery account in 1999.

June 23   One of the buildings is repainted at a cost of $6,900. It had not been painted since it was constructed in 2001.

Instructions
Prepare general journal entries for the transactions. (Round to nearest dollar.)

E11-20   (Analysis of Subsequent Expenditures)   Plant assets often require expenditures subsequent to acquisition. It is important that they be accounted for properly. Any errors will affect both the balance sheets and income statements for a number of years.

Instructions
For each of the following items, indicate whether the expenditure should be capitalized (C) or expensed (E) in the period incurred.

1. _____   Betterment

2. _____   Replacement of a minor broken part on a machine

3. _____   Expenditure that increases an existing asset's useful life

4. _____   Expenditure that increases the efficiency and effectiveness of a productive asset but does not increase its residual value

5. _____   Expenditure that increases the efficiency and effectiveness of a productive asset and its residual value

6. _____   Expenditure that increases the productive asset's output quality

7. _____   Improvement to a machine that increased its fair market value and its production capacity by 30% without extending the machine's useful life

8. _____   Ordinary repairs

9. _____   Improvement

10. _____   Interest on borrowing necessary to finance a major overhaul of machinery that extended its life

11. _____   Expenditure that results in a 10% per year production cost saving

12. _____   Costs of a major overhaul that brings the asset's condition back to "new," with no change in the estimated useful life.

*E11-21   (Capitalization of Interest)   On December 31, 2004, Omega Inc. borrowed $3 million at 12% payable annually to finance the construction of a new building. In 2005 the company made the following expenditures related to this building: March 1, $360,000; June 1, $600,000; July 1, $1.5 million; December 1, $1.5 million. Additional information is provided as follows.

1. Other debt outstanding:
   10-year, 13% bond, December 31, 1998, interest payable annually $4,000,000
   6-year, 10% note, dated December 31, 2002, interest payable annually $1,600,000
2. March 1, 2005 expenditure included land costs of $150,000
3. Interest revenue earned in 2005 $49,000

Instructions

(a) Determine the interest amount that could be capitalized in 2005 in relation to the building construction.

(b) Prepare the journal entry to record the capitalization of interest and the recognition of interest expense, if any, at December 31, 2005.

*E11-22 (**Capitalization of Interest**) On July 31, 2005, Amsterdam Corporation engaged Minsk Tooling Company to construct a special-purpose piece of factory machinery. Construction was begun immediately and was completed on November 1, 2005. To help finance construction, on July 31 Amsterdam issued a $300,000, 3-year, 12% note payable at Netherlands National Bank, on which interest is payable each July 31. $200,000 of the note's proceeds was paid to Minsk on July 31. The remainder of the proceeds was temporarily invested in short-term marketable securities at 10% until November 1. On November 1, Amsterdam made a final $100,000 payment to Minsk. Other than the note to Netherlands, Amsterdam's only outstanding liability at December 31, 2005 is a $30,000, 8%, 6-year note payable, dated January 1, 2002, on which interest is payable each December 31.

Instructions

(a) Calculate the interest revenue, weighted-average accumulated expenditures, avoidable interest, and total interest cost that could be capitalized during 2005. Round all calculations to the nearest dollar.

(b) Prepare the journal entries needed on the books of Amsterdam Corporation at each of the following dates, assuming the company follows a policy of capitalizing interest.

1. July 31, 2005

2. November 1, 2005

3. December 31, 2005

*E11-23 (**Capitalization of Interest**) The following three situations involve the capitalization of interest.

Situation I

On January 1, 2005, Oksana Inc. signed a fixed-price contract to have Builder Associates construct a major head office facility at a cost of $4 million. It was estimated that it would take three years to complete the project. Also on January 1, 2005, to finance the construction cost, Oksana borrowed $4 million payable in 10 annual instalments of $400,000, plus interest at the rate of 10%. During 2005, Oksana made deposit and progress payments totalling $1.5 million under the contract; the weighted-average amount of accumulated expenditures was $800,000 for the year. The excess borrowed funds were invested in short-term securities, from which Oksana realized investment income of $250,000.

Instructions

What amount should Oksana report as capitalized interest at December 31, 2005?

Situation II

During 2005, Midori Ito Corporation constructed and manufactured certain assets and incurred the following interest cost in connection with those activities.

	Interest costs Incurred
Warehouse constructed for Ito's own use	$30,000
Special-order machine for sale to unrelated customer, produced according to customer's specifications	9,000
Inventories routinely manufactured, produced on a repetitive basis	8,000

All of these assets required an extended time period for completion.

Instructions

Assuming the effect of interest capitalization is material, what is the total amount of interest costs to be capitalized?

Situation III

Fleming, Inc. has a fiscal year ending April 30. On May 1, 2005, Fleming borrowed $10 million at 11% to finance construction of its own building. Repayments of the loan are to commence the month following the building's completion. During the year ended April 30, 2006, expenditures for the partially completed structure totalled $7 million. These expenditures were incurred evenly throughout the year. Interest earned on the loan's unexpended portion amounted to $650,000 for the year.

Instructions

How much should be shown as capitalized interest on Fleming's financial statements at April 30, 2006?

(CPA adapted)

Problems

P11-1   At December 31, 2004, certain accounts included in the property, plant, and equipment section of Cilantro Corporation's balance sheet had the following balances:

Land	$230,000
Buildings	883,000
Leasehold improvements	665,000
Machinery and equipment	845,000

During 2005, the following transactions occurred.

Land site number 621 was acquired for $790,000 and a payment of $47,000 to the real estate agent. Costs of $33,500 were incurred to clear the land. During the course of clearing the land, timber and gravel were recovered and sold for $11,000.

A second tract of land (site number 622) with a building was acquired for $420,000. The closing statement indicated that the land's assessed tax value was $309,000 and the building value was $102,000. Shortly after acquisition, the building was demolished at a cost of $28,000. A new building was constructed for $340,000 plus the following costs.

Excavation fees	$38,000
Architectural design fees	11,000
Building permit fee	2,500
Imputed interest on funds used during construction (share financing)	8,500

The building was completed and occupied on September 30, 2005.

A third tract of land (site number 623) was acquired for $250,000 and was put on the market for resale.

During December 2005, costs of $89,000 were incurred to improve leased office space. The related lease will terminate on December 31, 2007 and is not expected to be renewed. (Hint: Leasehold improvements should be handled in the same manner as land improvements.)

A group of new machines was purchased under a royalty agreement that provides for payment of royalties based on units of production for the machines. The machines' invoice price was $87,000, freight costs were $3,300, installation costs were $2,400, and royalty payments for 2005 were $15,300.

Instructions

(a) Prepare a detailed analysis of the changes in each of the following balance sheet accounts for 2005: Land, Leasehold Improvements, Buildings, and Machinery and Equipment. Disregard the related accumulated amortization accounts.

(b) List the items in the situation that were not used to determine the answer to (a) above, and indicate where, or if, these items should be included in Cilantro's financial statements.

(AICPA adapted)

P11-2   Selected accounts included in the property, plant, and equipment section of Webb Corporation's balance sheet at December 31, 2004 had the following balances.

Land	$ 300,000
Land improvements	140,000
Buildings	1,100,000
Machinery and equipment	960,000

During 2005, the following transactions occurred.

1. A tract of land was acquired for $150,000 as a potential future building site.

2. A plant facility consisting of land and building was acquired from Knorman Company in exchange for 20,000 of Webb's common shares. On the acquisition date, Webb's shares had a closing market price of $37 per share on the Toronto Stock Exchange. The plant facility was carried on Knorman's books at $110,000 for land and $320,000 for the building at the exchange date. Current appraised values for the land and building, respectively, are $230,000 and $690,000.

3. Items of machinery and equipment were purchased at a total cost of $400,000. Additional costs were incurred as follows.

Freight and unloading	$13,000
Sales taxes	20,000
GST	28,000
Installation	26,000

4. Expenditures totalling $95,000 were made for new parking lots, streets, and sidewalks at the corporation's various plant locations. These expenditures had an estimated useful life of 15 years.

5. A machine costing $80,000 on January 1, 1997 was scrapped on June 30, 2005. Double declining-balance amortization has been recorded on the basis of a 10-year life.

6. A machine was sold for $20,000 on July 1, 2005. Its original cost was $44,000 on January 1, 2002 and it was amortized on the straight-line basis over an estimated useful life of seven years and a residual value of $2,000.

Instructions

(a) Prepare a detailed analysis of the changes in each of the following balance sheet accounts for 2005: Land, Land Improvements, Buildings, Machinery and Equipment. (Hint: Disregard the related accumulated amortization accounts.)

(b) List the items in the transactions above that were not used to determine the answer to (a), showing the pertinent amounts and supporting calculations in good form for each item. In addition, indicate where, or if, these items should be included in Webb's financial statements.

(AICPA adapted)

P11-3 Kiev Corp. was incorporated on January 2, 2005 but was unable to begin manufacturing activities until July 1, 2005 because new factory facilities were not completed until that date. The Land and Building account at December 31, 2005 was as follows.

January 31, 2005	Land and building	$166,000
February 28, 2005	Cost of removal of building	9,800
May 1, 2005	Partial payment of new construction	60,000
May 1, 2005	Legal fees paid	3,770
June 1, 2005	Second payment on new construction	40,000
June 1, 2005	Insurance premium	2,280
June 1, 2005	Special tax assessment	4,000
June 30, 2005	General expenses	36,300
July 1, 2005	Final payment on new construction	40,000
December 31, 2005	Asset write-up	43,800
		405,950
December 31, 2005	Amortization 2005 at 1%	4,060
Account balance		$401,890

The following additional information is to be considered.

1. To acquire land and building, the company paid $80,400 cash and 800 of its no par value 8% cumulative preferred shares. Fair market value is $107 per share.

2. Cost of removal of old buildings amounted to $9,800, and the demolition company retained all the building materials.

3. Legal fees covered the following:

Cost of organization	$ 610
Examination of title covering purchase of land	1,300
Legal work in connection with construction contract	1,860
	$3,770

4. The insurance premium covered the building for a two-year term beginning May 1, 2005.

5. The special tax assessment covered street improvements that are permanent in nature.

6. General expenses covered the following for the period from January 2, 2005 to June 30, 2005.

President's salary	$32,100
Plant superintendent covering supervision of new building	4,200
	$36,300

7. Because of a general increase in construction costs after entering into the building contract, the board of directors increased the building's value by $43,800, believing that such an increase was justified to reflect the current market at the time the building was completed. Retained Earnings was credited for this amount.

8. Estimated life of building 50 years.
   Write-off for 2005 was 1% of asset value (1% of $405,950, or $4,060).

Instructions
Prepare entries to adjust the Land and Building account to reflect correct Land, Building, and Accumulated Amortization accounts at December 31, 2005.

(AICPA adapted)

P11-4   You have been engaged to examine the financial statements of Oilco Limited for the year ending December 31, 2005. Oilco was organized in January 2005 by Messrs. Duff and Henderson, original owners of options to acquire oil leases on 5,000 hectares of land for $1.2 million. They expected that (1) the oil leases would be acquired by the corporation and (2) subsequently 180,000 common shares of the corporation would be sold to the public at $20 per share. In February 2005, they exchanged their options, $400,000 cash, and $200,000 of other assets for 75,000 common shares of the corporation. The corporation's board of directors appraised the leases at $2.1 million, basing its appraisal on the price of other parcels recently leased in the same area. The options were, therefore, recorded at $900,000 ($2.1 million minus the $1.2 million option price).

The options were exercised by the corporation in February 2005, prior to the sale of the common shares to the public in March 2005. Oilco incurred significant exploration costs over the summer, including seismic testing ($32,500), salaries and wages for work crews ($159,000), materials and supplies ($44,400), and vehicle operating costs ($11,900). In addition, Oilco recognized depreciation charges ($23,600) on the equipment used in the exploration activity. Leases on approximately 500 hectares of land were abandoned as worthless during the year. Development activities were postponed until the next spring.

Instructions

(a) 1. What reasoning might Oilco use to support valuing the leases at $2.1 million—the amount of the appraisal by the board of directors?

   2. Assuming that the board's appraisal was sincere, what steps might Oilco have taken to strengthen its position to use the $2.1 million value and to provide additional information if questions were raised about possible overvaluation of the leases?

(b) Determine the balance in the Oil and Gas Property account at December 31, 2005 assuming Oilco uses the successful efforts method of accounting.

(c) Determine the balance in the Oil and Gas Property account at December 31, 2005 assuming Oilco uses the full cost method of accounting. (Assume this is the only venture Oilco is engaged in.)

(d) Determine the balance in the Oil and Gas Property account at December 31, 2005 assuming Oilco expenses all exploration costs as incurred.

(e) What is the effect on the company's 2005 financial statements of this choice of method of accounting? Comment.

 P11-5   On June 28, 2005, HTM Corp. purchased a property comprising two hectares of land and an unused building for $225,000 plus taxes in arrears of $4,500. The company paid a real estate broker's commission of $12,000 and legal fees associated with the purchase transaction of $6,000. The closing statement indicated that the assessed values for tax purposes were $175,000 for the land and $35,000 for the building. Shortly after acquisition, the building was razed at a cost of $24,000.

HTM Corp. entered into a $1.3 million fixed-price contract with Murphy Builders, Inc. on August 1, 2005 for the construction of an office building on this site. The building was completed and occupied on April 29, 2006, along with a separate maintenance building constructed by HTM's employees. Additional costs related to the property included:

Plans, specifications, and blueprints	$21,000
Architects' fees for design and supervision	82,000
Landscaping	39,000
Extras on contract for upgrading of windows	46,000
External signage	18,000
Advertisement in newspaper and television announcing the opening of the building	10,600
Gala opening party for customers, suppliers, and friends of HTM	18,800
Costs of internal direct labour and materials for garage	60,000
Allocated plant overhead based on direct labour hours worked on garage	10,000
Allocated cost of executive time spent on project	45,000
Interest costs on debt incurred to pay contractor's progress billings up to building completion	61,000
Interest costs on short-term loan to finance garage costs	3,200

The municipality has agreed to forego 2006 calendar year property taxes as an incentive for HTM to locate and build in the town. This incentive is valued at approximately $33,000 based on tax rates in the area. The building and garage are estimated to have a 40-year life from date of completion and will be amortized using the straight-line method.

HTM has an April 30 year end, and the company accountant is analysing the New Building account set up to capture all expenditures and credits explained above that relate to the property.

Instructions

(a) Prepare a schedule that identifies the costs that would be capitalized and included in the Building account on the April 30, 2006 balance sheet assuming the accountant wants to comply with GAAP, but tends to be very conservative in nature; i.e., does not want to overstate income or assets. Briefly justify your calculations.

(b) Prepare a schedule that identifies the costs that would be capitalized and included in the Building account on the April 30, 2006 balance sheet assuming the accountant wants to comply with GAAP, but is aware that HTM needs to report increased income to support a requested increase in its bank loan next month. Briefly justify your calculations.

(c) Comment on the difference in results above. What else should be considered in determining the amount to be capitalized?

*P11-6 Jehri Landscaping began constructing a new plant on December 1, 2005. On this date the company purchased a parcel of land for $142,000 in cash. In addition, it paid $2,000 in surveying costs and $4,000 for title transfer fees. An old dwelling on the premises was demolished at a cost of $3,000, with $1,000 being received from the sale of materials.

Architectural plans were also formalized on December 1, 2005, when the architect was paid $30,000. The necessary building permits costing $3,000 were obtained from the city and paid for on December 1 as well. The excavation work began during the first week in December with payments made to the contractor as follows.

Date of Payment	Amount of Payment
March 1	$240,000
May 1	360,000
July 1	60,000

The building was completed on July 1, 2006.

To finance the plant construction, Jehri borrowed $600,000 from the bank on December 1, 2005. Jehri had no other borrowings. The $600,000 was a 10-year loan bearing interest at 8%.

Instructions

(a) Calculate the balance in each of the following accounts at December 31, 2005 and December 31, 2006. Assume Jehri follows a policy of capitalizing interest on self-constructed assets.

1. Land
2. Buildings
3. Interest Expense

(b) Identify the effects on Jehri's financial statements for the years ending December 31, 2005 and 2006 if its policy was to expense all interest costs as incurred.

*P11-7 Wordcrafters Inc. is a book distributor that had been operating in its original facility since 1979. The increase in certification programs and continuing education requirements in several professions has contributed to an annual growth rate of 15% for Wordcrafters since 1999. Wordcrafters' original facility became obsolete by early 2005 because of the increased sales volume and the fact that Wordcrafters now carries tapes and disks in addition to books.

On June 1, 2005, Wordcrafters contracted with Favre Construction to have a new building constructed for $5 million on land owned by Wordcrafters. The payments made by Wordcrafters to Favre Construction are shown in the schedule below.

Date	Amount
July 30, 2005	$1,200,000
January 30, 2006	1,500,000
May 30, 2006	1,300,000
Total payments	$4,000,000

Construction was completed and the building was ready for occupancy on May 27, 2006. Wordcrafters had no new borrowings directly associated with the new building but had the following debt outstanding at May 31, 2006, the end of its fiscal year.

14½%, 5-year note payable of $2 million, dated April 1, 2002, with interest payable annually on April 1.

12%, 10-year bond issue of $3 million sold at par on June 30, 1998, with interest payable annually on June 30.

The company follows a policy of capitalizing interest during construction of major assets.

Instructions

(a) Calculate the weighted average accumulated expenditures on Wordcrafters' new building during the capitalization period.

(b) Calculate the avoidable interest on Wordcrafters' new building.

(c) Some interest cost of Wordcrafters Inc. is capitalized for the year ended May 31, 2006.

   1.   Identify the item(s) relating to interest costs that must be disclosed in Wordcrafters' financial statements.

   2.   Calculate the amount of the item(s) that must be disclosed.

(CMA adapted)

P11-8   The production manager of Chesley Corporation wishes to acquire another machine by exchanging the machine currently in use in operations with the brand of equipment being used by others in the industry. He has received the following offers from other companies.

   1. Secord Corp. offered to give Chesley a similar machine plus $23,000 in exchange for Chesley's machine.

   2. Bateman Corp. offered a straight exchange for a similar machine.

   3. Shripad Corp. offered to exchange a similar machine, but wanted $8,000 in addition to Chesley's machine.

The production manager has also contacted Ansong Corporation, a dealer in machines. To obtain a new machine, Chesley must pay $93,000 in addition to trading in its old machine. Chesley's equipment has a cost of $160,000, a net book value of $110,000, and a fair value of $92,000.

	Secord	Bateman	Shripad	Ansong
Machine cost	$120,000	$147,000	$160,000	$130,000
Accumulated amortization	45,000	71,000	75,000	–0–
Fair value	69,000	92,000	100,000	185,000

Instructions

For each of the four independent situations, prepare the journal entries to record the exchange on the books of each company. (Round to nearest dollar.) Where necessary, state the assumptions required to justify your entries.

P11-9   During the current year, Garrison Construction trades in two relatively new small cranes (crane # 6RT and #S79) for a larger crane that Garrison expects to be more useful given the contracts the company has committed itself to over the next couple of years. The new crane is acquired from Keillor Manufacturing, which has agreed to take the smaller equipment as trade-ins and pay $17,500 cash to Garrison as well. The new crane cost Keillor $165,000 to manufacture and is classified as inventory. The following information is available.

	Garrison Const.	Keillor Mfg.
Cost of crane #6RT	$130,000	
Cost of crane #S79	120,000	
Accumulated amortization, #6RT	15,000	
Accumulated amortization, #S79	18,000	
Fair value, #6RT	120,000	
Fair value, #S79	87,500	
Fair market value of new crane		$190,000
Cash paid		17,500
Cash received	17,500	

Instructions

(a) Assume that this exchange is considered to have commercial substance. Prepare the journal entries on the books of (1) Garrison Construction and (2) Keillor Manufacturing. Keillor uses a perpetual inventory system.

(b) Assume that this exchange is considered to lack commercial substance. Prepare the journal entries on the books of (1) Garrison Construction and (2) Keillor Manufacturing. Keillor uses a perpetual inventory system.

(c) Assume you have been asked to recommend which accounting method is appropriate in this circumstance. Develop separate arguments for presentation to the controllers of both Garrison Construction and Keillor Manufacturing to justify both methods. Which arguments are more persuasive?

P11-10   Fayne Mining Corp. received a $760,000 low bid from a reputable manufacturer for the construction of special production equipment needed by Fayne in an expansion program. Because the company's own plant was not operating at capacity, Fayne decided to construct the equipment there and recorded the following production costs related to the construction.

Services of consulting engineer	$ 40,000
Work subcontracted	31,000
Materials	300,000
Plant labour normally assigned to production	114,000
Plant labour normally assigned to maintenance	160,000
Total	$645,000

Management prefers to record the equipment cost under the incremental cost method. Approximately 40% of the company's production is devoted to government supply contracts that are all based in some way on cost. The contracts require that any self-constructed equipment be allocated its full share of all costs related to the construction.

The following information is also available.

1. The production labour was for partial fabrication of the plant equipment. Skilled personnel were required and were assigned from other projects. The maintenance labour represents idle time of nonproduction plant employees who would have been retained on the payroll whether or not their services were used.

2. Payroll taxes and employee fringe benefits are approximately 35% of labour cost and are included in manufacturing overhead cost. Total manufacturing overhead for the year was $6,084,000, including the $160,000 maintenance labour used to construct the equipment.

3. Manufacturing overhead is approximately 60% variable and is applied based on production labour cost. Production labour cost for the year for the corporation's normal products totalled $8,286,000.

4. General and administrative expenses include $27,000 of allocated executive salary cost and $13,750 of postage, telephone, supplies, and miscellaneous expenses identifiable with this equipment construction.

Instructions

(a) Prepare a schedule calculating the amount that should be reported as the full cost of the constructed equipment to meet the government contract requirements. Any supporting calculations should be in good form.

(b) Prepare a schedule calculating the incremental cost of the constructed equipment.

(c) What is the greatest amount that should be capitalized as the equipment cost? Why?

(AICPA adapted)

P11-11 Adamski Corporation manufactures ballet shoes and is experiencing a period of sustained growth. In an effort to expand its production capacity to meet the increased demand for its product, the company recently made several acquisitions of plant and equipment. Tim Mullinger, newly hired in the position of Capital Asset Accountant, requested that Walter Kaster, Adamski's controller, review the following transactions.

Transaction 1
On June 1, 2005, Adamski Corporation purchased equipment from Venghaus Corporation. Adamski issued a $20,000, 4-year, noninterest-bearing note to Venghaus for the new equipment. Adamski will pay off the note in four equal instalments due at the end of each of the next four years. At the transaction date, the prevailing market interest rate for obligations of this nature was 10%. Freight costs of $425 and installation costs of $500 were incurred in completing this transaction. The new equipment qualifies for a $2,000 government grant.

Transaction 2
On December 1, 2005, Adamski purchased several assets of Haukap Shoes Inc., a small shoe manufacturer whose owner was retiring. The purchase amounted to $210,000 and included the assets listed below. Adamski engaged the services of Tennyson Appraisal Inc., an independent appraiser, to determine the assets' fair market values, which are also provided.

	Haukap Book Value	Fair Market Value
Inventory	$ 60,000	$ 50,000
Land	40,000	80,000
Building	70,000	120,000
	$170,000	$250,000

During its fiscal year ended May 31, 2006, Adamski incurred $8,000 for interest expense in connection with the financing of these assets.

Transaction 3
On March 1, 2006, Adamski traded in four units of specialized equipment plus $25,000 cash for a technologically up-to-date machine that should do the same job as the other machines, but much more efficiently and profitably. The equipment

traded in had a combined carrying value of $35,000, as Adamski had recorded $45,000 of accumulated amortization against these assets. It was agreed between Adamski's controller and the supplier company's sales manager that the new equipment had a fair value of $64,000.

Instructions

(a) Tangible capital assets such as land, buildings, and equipment receive special accounting treatment.

Describe the major characteristics of these assets that differentiate them from other types of assets.

(b) For each of the three transactions described above, determine the value at which Adamski Corporation should record the acquired assets. Support your calculations with an explanation of the underlying rationale.

(c) The books of Adamski Corporation show the following additional transactions for the fiscal year ended May 31, 2006.

   1.   acquisition of a building for speculative purposes

   2.   purchase of a two-year insurance policy covering plant equipment

   3.   purchase of the rights for the exclusive use of a process used in the manufacture of ballet shoes

For each of these transactions, indicate whether the asset should be classified as an item of property, plant, and equipment. If it is, explain why. If it is not, explain why not, and identify the proper classification.

(CMA adapted)

P11-12 Vidi Corporation made the following purchases related to its property, plant, and equipment during its fiscal year ended December 31, 2005. The company uses the straight-line method of amortization for all its capital assets.

   1. In early January, Vidi issued 140,000 common shares with a market value of $6 per share (based on a recent sale of 1,000 shares on the Toronto Stock Exchange) in exchange for property consisting of land and a warehouse. The company's property management division estimated the market value of the land to be $600,000 and the warehouse to be $300,000. The seller advertised in a commercial retail magazine a price of $860,000 for the land and warehouse, or best offer. Vidi paid a local real estate broker a finder's fee of $35,000.

   2. On March 31, the company acquired equipment on credit. Terms were $7,000 cash down payment plus payments of $5,000 at the end of each of the next two years. The implicit interest rate was 12%. The equipment's list price was $17,000. Additional costs incurred to install the equipment included $1,000 to tear down and replace a wall, and $1,500 to rearrange existing equipment to make room for the new equipment. $500 was spent repairing the equipment after it was dropped during installation.

During the year, the following events also occurred.

   3. A new motor was purchased for $50,000 for a large grinding machine (original cost of the machine, $350,000; accumulated amortization at the replacement date, $100,000). The motor will not improve the quality or quantity of production; however, it will extend the grinding machine's useful life from 8 to 10 years.

   4. On September 30, the company purchased a small building in a nearby town for $125,000 to use as a display and sales location. The municipal tax assessment indicated that the property was assessed for $95,000; $68,000 for the building and $27,000 for the land. The building had been empty for six months and required considerable maintenance work before it could be used. The following costs were incurred in 2005: previous owner's unpaid property taxes on the property for the previous year $900; current year's (2005) taxes $1,000; reshingling of roof $2,200; cost of hauling refuse out of the basement $230; cost of spray cleaning the outside walls and washing windows $750; cost of painting inside walls $3,170; and incremental fire and liability insurance of $940 for 15 months.

   5. The company completely overhauled the plumbing system in its factory for $55,000. The original plumbing costs were not known.

   6. On June 30, the company replaced a freezer with a new one that cost $20,000 cash (market value of the new freezer of $21,000 less trade-in value of old freezer). The cost of the old freezer was $15,000. At the beginning of the year, the company had amortized 60% of the asset, that is, 10% per year of use.

   7. The company painted the factory exterior at a cost of $12,000.

Instructions

(a) Prepare the journal entries required to record the acquisitions and/or costs incurred in the above transactions.

(b) In any case where there are alternative methods to account for the transactions, indicate what the alternatives are and the reason why you chose the method you did.

Writing Assignments

WA11-1 You have been working as a professional accounting trainee for about three months when the accountant for your client, Portables Inc., asks for your input about two transactions that took place in the current year. Portables, Inc., previously wholly-owned and managed by Angus Dickson, now has 12 shareholders and a sizeable bank loan. Mr. Dickson still owns a majority of the outstanding shares. The accountant is in the process of finalizing the company's financial statements for the year ended June 30, 2005. You are working on the year-end audit and will also prepare the company's tax return.

Situation 1

Management found three suitable sites, each having certain unique advantages, for a new plant facility. In order to ensure there was time to thoroughly investigate the advantages and disadvantages of each site, one-year options were purchased for an amount equal to 6% of the contract price of each site. The costs of the options cannot be applied against the contracts. Before the options expired, one of the sites was purchased at the contract price of $200,000. The option on this site had cost $12,000. The two options not exercised had cost $8,000 each.

Instructions

Present arguments in support of recording the land cost at each of the following amounts: (a) $200,000, (b) $212,000, (c) $228,000. What would you advise? (AICPA adapted)

Situation 2

Portables, Inc. operates a very successful automobile dealership and has been increasing its real estate holdings. The accountant tells you that the company has just purchased a rental property for $200,000. "The municipal assessment indicates that the land itself is worth about half that amount, but I want you to allocate no more than 10% of the purchase price to the land. We all know that land isn't deductible for tax purposes! The building was in terrible shape, so a new roof was put on, a new furnace installed, the structure was completely rewired, and the whole place was painted. These are just maintenance expenses, aren't they?"

You know that the more expenses your client can recognize, the better tax position the company will be in, the lower the cash outflows, and the higher the share value.

Instructions

Identify the relevant issues and explain how you should handle this situation.

WA11-2 Gomi Medical Labs, Inc. began operations five years ago producing stetrics, a new type of instrument it hoped to sell to doctors, dentists, and hospitals. The demand for stetrics far exceeded initial expectations, and the company was unable to produce enough stetrics to meet demand. The company was manufacturing its product on equipment that had been built at the start of its operations.

To meet demand, more efficient equipment was needed. The company decided to design and build the equipment, because the equipment currently available on the market was unsuitable for producing this product.

In 2002, a section of the plant was devoted to developing the new equipment and a special staff was hired. Within six months, a machine, developed at a cost of $714,000, increased production dramatically and reduced labour costs substantially. Elated by the new machine's success, the company built three more machines of the same type at a cost of $441,000 each.

Instructions

(a) In general, what costs should be capitalized for self-constructed equipment?

(b) Discuss the propriety of including in the capitalized cost of self-constructed assets:

   1. the increase in overhead caused by the self-construction of fixed assets

   2. a proportionate share of overhead on the same basis as that applied to goods manufactured for sale

(c) Discuss the proper accounting treatment of the $273,000 ($714,000 − $441,000) by which the cost of the first machine exceeded the cost of the subsequent machines. This additional cost should not be considered research and development costs.

WA11-3 Zucker Airline is converting from piston-type planes to jets. Delivery time for the jets is three years, during which substantial progress payments must be made. The planes' multimillion-dollar cost cannot be financed from working capital; Zucker must borrow funds for the payments.

Because of high interest rates and the large sum to be borrowed, management estimates that interest costs in the second year of the period will be equal to one-third of income before interest and taxes, and one-half of such income in the third year.

After conversion, Zucker's passenger-carrying capacity will be doubled with no increase in the number of planes, although the investment in planes will be substantially increased. The jets have a seven-year service life.

Instructions

Give your recommendation concerning the proper accounting for interest during the conversion period. Support your recommendation with reasons and suggested accounting treatment. (Disregard income tax implications.)

(AICPA adapted)

WA11-4 You have two clients that are considering trading machinery with each other. Although the machines are different, you believe that they have many features that make them similar in nature. The facts are as follows.

	Client A	Client B
Original cost	$100,000	$150,000
Accumulated amortization	40,000	80,000
Market value	90,000	120,000
Cash received (paid)	(30,000)	30,000

Instructions

(a) Write a memo to the accountant of Client A explaining how this transaction should be recorded on A's books. Ensure you explain the rationale for this treatment.

(b) You receive a voice mail message from the accountant at Client B. She doesn't remember the accounting standard for asset exchanges, but recalls that if the assets are similar, she may not be able to recognize a gain on the transaction. She asks you to respond to her idea of recognizing a portion of the gain equal to the proportion of the fair value received in cash, an alternative she thinks makes sense.

WA11-5 A machine's invoice price is $40,000. Various other costs relating to the acquisition and installation of the machine, including transportation, electrical wiring, special base, and so on, amount to $7,500. The machine has an estimated life of 10 years, with no residual value at the end of that period.

The business owner suggests that the incidental costs of $7,500 be charged to expense immediately for the following reasons.

1. If the machine should be sold, these costs cannot be recovered in the sale price.

2. The inclusion of the $7,500 in the machinery account on the books will not necessarily result in a closer approximation of this asset's market price over the years, because demand and supply levels could change.

3. Charging the $7,500 to expense immediately will reduce income taxes.

Instructions

Discuss each point raised by the business owner.

(AICPA adapted)

Cases

Refer to the Case Primer on the Digital Tool to help you answer these cases.

CA11-1 In 1997, **Legacy Hotels Real Estate Investment Trust** (LH) was created to hold hotel properties. LH currently holds twenty-two luxury and first class hotels in Canada and the United States. The entity is structured as an investment trust, thus the trust does not pay income taxes on the earnings from assets it holds directly, rather, income taxes are paid by the unit holders—those who own ownership units in the trust. The other key feature of the trust is that 85-90% of the distributable income is required to be paid to unit holders every year. The units of LH trade on the TSE under the ticker symbol LGY.UN.

Distributable income is calculated as net income before special charges, plus depreciation and amortization less capital replacement reserve and interest on the debentures. LH distributed 127% and 112% of distributable income in 2002 and 2001 respectively. Management determines the calculation of distributable income as it is not defined by GAAP. As at 2002, Property and equipment was $1.7 billion compared to $1.9 billion in total assets. Net income for the year was $55 million.

According to the notes to the financial statements, LH capitalizes major renewals and replacement and interest incurred during the renovation period of major renovations. Capitalization of interest is based on the borrowing rate of debt for the project or the average cost of borrowing. Maintenance, repairs and minor renewals and replacements are expensed.

Instructions

Assume the role of PricewaterhouseCoopers LLP, the entity's auditors and discuss any financial reporting issues.

Integrated Case

IC11-1   TransAlta Corporation (TC) is a non-regulated power generation and wholesale marketing company. The company had a BBB+ credit rating in 2002 and its goals were articulated in its annual report as follows:

- maintain investment-grade credit ratings

- improve interest coverage ratio from 1.4 to between 4 and 6 times

- other

Property, plant and equipment consists of coal-fired, gas-fired, hydro and renewable generation assets with a 2002 carrying value of $6 billion (total assets $7.4 billion). The following is an excerpt from the notes to the financial statements:

> "The corporation does not provide for the removal costs associated with its hydroelectric generating structures as the costs are not reasonable estimated because of the long service life of these assets. With either maintenance efforts or rebuilding, the water control structures are assumed to be required for the foreseeable future and therefore, no amounts have been provided for site restoration costs for these facilities. Provisions are made for removal of hydro generating equipment."

In August 2000, the company shut down one of its plants due to safety concerns. The plant was repaired and returned to service June 2001. Under the terms of an agreement related to this plant, the company had been obligated to supply electricity starting in January 2001 unless an unforeseen event precluded the company from fulfilling this liability. In the case of the said unforeseen event, both parties would have to agree that the inability to fulfill the contract was due to an acceptable event. If both parties did not agree, the company would be liable to pay a penalty equal to the cost of obtaining an alternate source of electricity.

When the decision went to arbitration in July 2001 and in May 2002, the arbitrator confirmed that the shut down exempted the company from having to deliver the electricity. The arbitrator did find however that the company could have returned the plant to service more quickly and therefore levied a penalty of $39 million on the company. The amount was recorded as an offset to revenues.

In 2001, the company sold its Fort Nelson gas-fired facility resulting in a gain of $1.3 million after tax. It was not treated as discontinued operations. On August 31, 2000, the corporation sold its Alberta D&R division resulting in an after tax gain of $262.4 million. As part of the agreement the corporation must share the benefit or burden of future regulatory decisions affecting the pre-disposition operations. This disposition was treated as a discontinued operation.

In 2002, the Canadian government ratified the Kyoto protocol which will place the responsibility for pollution minimization on the shoulders of those who pollute. The additional costs for implementation of the protocol have not been estimated nor accrued in the TC financial statements. Certain of the power purchase arrangements relating to the corporation's coal-fire plants contain provisions that may allow compliance costs to be recovered from the corporations' customers.

Instructions

Adopt the role of a financial analyst and critically evaluate the financial reporting choices open to the company relating to the 2001 and 2002 financial statements.

Research and Financial Analysis

RA11-1 Intrawest Corporation

Refer to the financial statements of Intrawest Corporation presented in Appendix 5B. Review the information provided and answer the following questions about the company.

Instructions

(a) What major business(es) is Intrawest Corporation in?

(b) For each major line of business, identify the major categories of assets you would expect that type of industry to have. List the major categories of assets that Intrawest reports for each line of business.

(c) Do all the company's "Properties" meet the definition of property, plant, and equipment? Discuss.

(d) Excluding policies on amortization, identify the policies Intrawest reports relative to the accounting for its fixed assets.

(e) If Intrawest had chosen different acceptable accounting policies, would there have been much of an effect on the income they report?

RA11-2 Sobeys Inc. and Loblaw Companies Limited

Companies in the same line of business usually have similar investments, capital structures, and an opportunity for similar rates of return. One of the key performance indicators used to assess the profitability of companies is the Return on Assets ratio. This ratio is a function of two key relationships—the profit margin and the total asset turnover—and in general terms can be written:

Return on assets = Total asset turnover (or Sales/Total assets) × Profit margin (or Income/Sales)

This says that profitability depends directly on how many sales dollars you can generate per dollar of invested assets (total asset turnover) and on how you control costs per dollar of sales (profit margin). An increase in either ratio results in an increase in return on assets employed. As property, plant, and equipment are often the largest single asset on the balance sheet, companies must have strategies in place to manage the investment in such assets.

Instructions

Access the financial statements of two companies in the food distribution business: Sobeys Inc. for the year ended May 3, 2003 and Loblaw Companies Limited for the year ended December 31, 2002. These are available either on the Digital Tool or through www.sedar.com. Review the financial statements and respond to the following questions.

(a) At each company's most recent year end, determine the percentage of property, plant, and equipment to total assets.

(b) Calculate each company's fixed asset turnover, total asset turnover, and profit margin (using net income) for the most recent year.

(c) Determine the return on assets for each company. Which company is more profitable?

(d) Which company uses its total assets more effectively in generating sales? Its fixed assets?

(e) Are there any differences in accounting policies that might explain the differences in fixed asset turnover?

(f) Which company has better control over its expenses per dollar of sales?

(g) Explain why the company with the higher return is more profitable. Does it appear that the two companies may have different strategies? Comment briefly.

RA 11-3 Homburg Invest Inc.

Usually an international comparison assignment involves comparing two similar companies reporting under different GAAP. If possible, it would be better to compare the same company's financial reports prepared on two different bases. Homburg Invest Inc., a Canadian company, does just that, and notes that the most significant differences relate to its fixed assets.

Instructions

Access the financial statements of Homburg Invest Inc. under both bases of accounting for its year ended December 31, 2002 on SEDAR at www.sedar.com. Review the statements presented and respond to the following questions.

(a) What business is Homburg Invest Inc. in? What two accounting standards does it report under? Why does the company report under two different sets of generally accepted accounting principles?

(b) Identify the single most significant GAAP difference, and what effect this has on the income statement. Be specific.

(c) What other GAAP differences are there, if any? What is the effect of these on the income statement?

(d) Which set of financial statements do you think comes closer to meeting the objectives of financial reporting? Discuss briefly.

RA 11-4 Research Issue

In groups, identify eight different companies, taking one from each of the following industry groups: Consumer products autos and parts; Consumer products biotechnology/pharmaceuticals; Film production; Financial services investment companies and funds; Industrial products steel; Merchandising specialty stores; Metals and minerals integrated mines; and Utilities telephone utilities. An excellent source is the SEDAR website at www.sedar.com. If you search the database by industry group for financial statements for the most recent 12-month period, you will be able to choose from the large number of public companies on the site.

Instructions

(a) Determine for each company the relative importance of tangible capital assets to total assets invested, and the percentage that depreciation or amortization expense is of total expenses.

(b) For each company, determine the percentage of total assets that is financed by long-term debt.

(c) What industries require the highest relative investment in tangible capital assets?

(d) Is there any relationship between the investment in tangible capital property and financing by long-term debt? Comment.

(e) How might the strategies of companies with significant investment in fixed assets or property, plant, and equipment differ from those with little investment in such assets?

Rolling Stock

VIA Rail Canada operates 480 intercity train trips each week, or almost 25,000 trips a year, using a fleet of 76 locomotives and 350 passenger cars to carry almost four million passengers annually. VIA trains run over 14,000 km of track and serve more than 450 Canadian communities. These are no small numbers, and neither are the numbers required to allocate the cost of these trains to the Crown corporation.

Corporate comptroller Anthony Rumjahn says VIA Rail follows the standard accounting theory of amortizing its tangible capital assets, such as the trains. Of the total capital assets of $1,175.2 million, VIA Rail's trains, or "rolling stock," amounted to $614.3 million in 2002. Of that amount, $313.1 million was amortized to date, leaving a net book value of $301.2 million.

VIA Rail calculates the amortization of tangible capital assets on a "straight-line basis" at rates high enough to amortize the cost of the assets, less their residual value, over their estimated lives. The corporation maintains detailed subsidiary records for each car's cost and accumulated depreciation. In the month following the date that trains are put into service, transfers to specific capital asset accounts are done and amortization is charged up to the month of disposal, Rumjahn explains. The fleet's economic useful life is calculated in consultation with the engineering group and equipment manufacturers. For current rolling stock, that figure varies from 12 to 29 years.

The trains' purchase price, refurbishment costs, and any other upgrading costs are capitalized if they were incurred to improve the trains' service value or extend their useful lives; otherwise, these costs are expensed.

"VIA Rail introduced more than 100 new state-of-the-art 'Renaissance' passenger cars to the fleet in 2003, so I expect the [future] amortization calculation to be even more impressive," Rumjahn says.

CHAPTER 12

Amortization, Impairment, and Disposition

Learning Objectives

After studying this chapter, you should be able to:

1. Explain the concept of amortization.
2. Identify and describe the factors that must be considered when determining amortization charges.
3. Determine amortization charges using the activity, straight-line, and decreasing charge methods and compare the methods.
4. Explain the accounting procedures for depletion of natural resources.
5. Explain special amortization methods.
6. Identify and understand reasons why amortization methods are selected.
7. Explain the accounting procedures for a change in the amortization rate.
8. Explain the accounting issues related to asset impairment.
9. Explain the accounting standards for long-lived assets to be disposed of.
10. Describe the accounting treatment for the disposal of property, plant, and equipment.
11. Explain how property, plant, and equipment are reported and analysed.

After studying Appendix 12A, you should be able to:

*12. Describe the income tax method of determining capital cost allowance.

Preview of Chapter 12

As indicated in the opening story, capital assets represent a considerable investment for many companies. Because of this, the alternatives involved in charging these costs to operations, the potential for impairment in their values, and the contention by some that financial statement readers don't need to be concerned with these noncash expenses, it is important to have a firm grounding in this chapter's topics. The purpose of this chapter is to examine the amortization process: the methods of writing off the cost of property, plant, equipment, and natural resources, as well as issues related to asset impairment and disposal. An appendix outlines key aspects of the capital cost allowance method required for income tax purposes. The content and organization of the chapter are as follows:

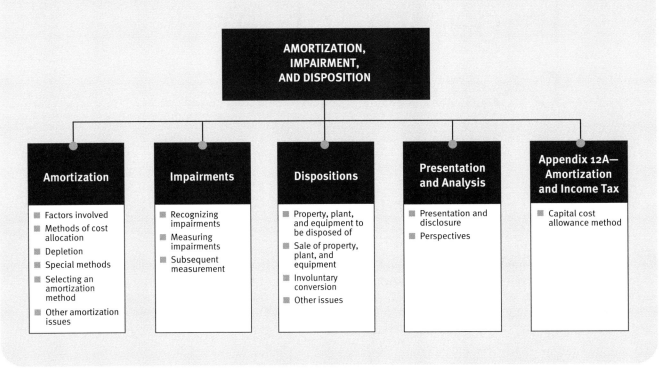

AMORTIZATION—A METHOD OF COST ALLOCATION

Objective 1
Explain the concept of amortization.

Many individuals at one time or another purchase and trade in an automobile. In discussions with the automobile dealer, depreciation is a consideration on two points. First, how much has the old car depreciated? That is, what is its trade-in value? Second, how fast will the new car depreciate? That is, what will its trade-in value be? In both cases depreciation is thought of as a loss in value.

To accountants, however, **depreciation—or amortization—is not a matter of valuation but a means of cost allocation**. Assets are not amortized based on their decline in market value, but on the basis of a systematic allocation of their cost to expense.

It is undeniably true that an asset's value will fluctuate between the time it is purchased and the time it is sold or scrapped. An allocation rather than a valuation approach is used, however, because measuring the interim value changes in an objective manner is often difficult and costly. Therefore, the asset's cost is charged to amortization expense over its estimated life, making no attempt to value the asset at fair market value between acquisition and disposition. The cost allocation approach is consistent with the historical cost model and results in a matching of costs with benefits (revenues).

The CICA defines the term "amortization" as **the charge to income that recognizes that life is finite and that the cost less salvage or residual value of a capital asset is allocated to the periods of service provided by the asset.**[1] The *CICA Handbook* also says that amortization may also be termed depreciation or depletion. In the past, the term "depreciation" was used to denote the amortization of tangible capital assets such as buildings, plant, and equipment. Depletion referred to the amortization of natural resources such as timber, oil, or mineral deposits, and amortization was reserved for intangible assets such as patents and goodwill.[2] These terms are still in common use. "Amortization" is used throughout this text to refer to the general process of allocating the cost of long-lived assets to the accounting periods benefiting from their use, although "depletion" has been retained when referring specifically to natural resource assets.

IAS Note

IAS 16 permits capital assets to be remeasured to fair value and requires that the amortization be based on the revalued amount.

Underlying Concept

Under the going concern concept, capital assets are expected to be held for use, not sale; therefore interim market value changes are not considered relevant.

Factors Involved in the Amortization Process

Three basic questions must be answered before the dollar amount of amortization expense can be determined:

1. What amount of the asset's cost is to be amortized?

2. What is the asset's useful life?

3. What pattern and method of cost apportionment is best for the asset?

The answers to these questions distill several estimates into the resulting amortization charge. A perfect measure of amortization for each period is not attainable because, except perhaps for the asset's acquisition cost, all other variables involved in the calculations are estimates.

2 **Objective**

Identify and describe the factors that must be considered when determining amortization charges.

Amount to Be Amortized

The amount of the asset's cost to be amortized—its **amortizable amount**—is a function of two factors: the asset's acquisition cost, discussed in Chapter 11, and its residual value. Residual value is defined as the estimated net realizable value of an item of property, plant, and equipment **at the end of its useful life to the entity.**[3] It is the amount to which the asset is amortized or written down during its useful life. The residual value is an estimate of the amount recoverable from disposal, based to the extent possible, on experience with similar assets operating under similar conditions.

Technically, the amortization charge should be based on the greater of (1) the cost less salvage value over the life of the asset and (2) the cost less residual value over its useful life. Salvage value is the asset's estimated net realizable value **at the end of its life** and is nor-

---

[1] *CICA Handbook*, Section 3061.29.

[2] The Accounting Standards Board of the CICA and FASB worked together to develop revised standards for business combinations and the associated issue of accounting for goodwill. In mid-2001, new accounting standards were released that specified goodwill is no longer amortized. See Chapter 13 for details.

[3] *CICA Handbook*, Section 3061.12.

mally negligible.[4] The effect is to ensure that the charges to the income statement as the asset is used are adequate. For simplicity, the discussions and illustrations that follow consider **cost less residual value** as the amortizable amount.

Illustration 12-1 shows that if an asset has a cost of $10,000 and a residual value of $1,000, only $9,000 of its cost is amortized.

Illustration 12-1

Calculation of Amount to Be Amortized

Original cost	$10,000
Less: residual value	1,000
Amortizable amount	$ 9,000

From a practical standpoint, residual value is often considered to be zero because the amount is immaterial. Some long-lived assets, however, have substantial net realizable values at the end of their useful lives to a specific enterprise. Companies with similar assets may calculate different amortizable amounts and amortization expense because of differences in estimates of these final values.

Estimation of Useful Life

A capital asset's useful life is the period over which the asset is expected to contribute economic benefits to the organization. Useful life can also be stated in terms of the number of units of product or service the asset is expected to produce or provide to the enterprise.

Useful or service life and physical life are often not the same. A piece of machinery may be physically capable of producing a given product for many years beyond its service life, but the equipment may not be used for all of those years because the cost of producing the product in later years may be too high. For example, many tractors in the Saskatchewan Western Development Museum at Saskatoon are preserved in remarkable physical condition and could be used, although their service lives were terminated many years ago. The opening vignette also indicates that the "economic useful life" of VIA Rail's fleet is determined in conjunction with engineering and manufacturing specialists. The reasons for scrapping an asset before its physical life expires are varied. New processes or techniques or improved machines may provide the same service at lower cost and with higher quality. Changes in the product may shorten an asset's service life. Environmental factors can also influence a decision to retire a given asset.

Physical factors set the outside limit for an asset's service life. Physical factors relate to such things as decay or wear and tear that result from use and the passage of time. Whenever the asset's physical nature is the primary determinant of useful life, maintenance plays a vital role. The better the maintenance, the longer the life of the asset.[5] Economic factors (e.g., technological or commercial obsolescence) also limit an asset's useful life.

Economic or functional factors can be classified into three categories: inadequacy, supersession, and obsolescence. Inadequacy results when an asset ceases to be useful to a given enterprise because the firm's demands have changed. For example, a company may require a larger building to handle increased production. Although the old building may still be sound, it may have become inadequate for the enterprise's purposes. Supersession is the replacement of one asset with a more efficient and economical asset. Examples include the replacement of a mainframe computer with a PC network, or the replacement

---

[4] *CICA Handbook*, Section 3061.13 and .28.

[5] The airline industry illustrates the type of problem involved in estimation. In the past, aircraft were assumed not to wear out, they just became obsolete. However, some jets have been in service as long as 20 years, and maintenance of these aircraft has become increasingly expensive. In addition, the public's concern about worn-out aircraft has been heightened by some recent air disasters. As a result, some airlines are finding it necessary to replace aircraft, not because of obsolescence, but because of physical deterioration.

of a Boeing 767 with a Boeing 777. Obsolescence is the catchall for situations not involving inadequacy and supersession. Because the distinctions among these categories are fuzzy, it is probably best to consider economic factors in total instead of trying to make distinctions that are not clear-cut.

To illustrate these concepts, consider a new nuclear power plant. Which do you think are the more important factors that determine its useful life: physical factors or economic factors? The limiting factors seem to be (1) ecological considerations, (2) competition from other power sources (non-nuclear), and (3) safety concerns. Physical life does not appear to be the primary factor affecting useful life. Although the plant's physical life may be far from over, the plant may become obsolete in 10 years.

The problem of estimating service life is difficult; experience and judgement are the primary means of determining service lives. In some cases, arbitrary lives are selected; in others, sophisticated statistical methods are employed to establish a useful life for accounting purposes. In many cases, the primary basis for estimating an asset's useful life is the enterprise's past experience with the same or similar assets. In an industrial economy such as Canada's, where research and innovation are so prominent, economic and technological factors have as much effect, if not more, on service lives of tangible assets as do physical factors.

Some companies try to imply that amortization is not a cost. For example, in their press releases they have often drawn more attention to earnings before interest, taxes, depreciation, and amortization (often referred to as EBITDA) or pro forma earnings other than net income under GAAP. Some companies like the EBITDA figure because it "dresses up" their earnings numbers, and they sell it on the basis that the excluded costs aren't operating costs or that amortization and depreciation are non-cash charges. Regardless, when all is said and done, companies must generate enough cash from revenues to cover all their costs, as amounts borrowed to finance long-term asset acquisitions have to be repaid. Investors need to understand the differences between these various indicators of financial performance.

Consider Aliant Inc.'s review of results for its year ended December 31, 2002. EBITDA were reported at $941.6 million, while net income under GAAP amounted to $177.6 million. Hollinger International Inc. reported 2002 EBITDA of $111.4 million (U.S.) and a GAAP net loss of $238.8 million (U.S.)! Because of concerns that investors may be confused or mislead by non-GAAP earnings measures, the Canadian Securities Administrators, the umbrella group for provincial regulators, issued specific guidance in 2002 for certain disclosures associated with non-GAAP earnings measures. These included a reconciliation of the non-GAAP measure(s) with audited GAAP results.

While EBITDA and other pro forma reporting haven't been prohibited, it appears that the reporting requirements have reduced the enthusiasm for reporting these results as prominently as was previously the case.

What do the Numbers Mean?

Methods of Cost Allocation (Amortization)

The third factor involved in the amortization decision is the pattern and method of cost allocation. The accounting profession requires that the amortization method be rational and systematic, and be used in a "manner appropriate to the nature of an item of property, plant, and equipment with a limited life and its use by the enterprise."[6]

A number of amortization methods may be used, classified as follows.

1. Activity methods (units of use or production)

2. Straight-line method

Underlying Concept

Amortization is an attempt to match an asset's cost to the periods that benefit from its use.

---

[6] *CICA Handbook*, Section 3061.28.

3. Decreasing charge (or accelerated) methods:

   (a) Declining-balance

   (b) Sum-of-the-years'-digits

4. Increasing charge methods

5. Special depreciation methods:

   (a) Group and composite methods

   (b) Hybrid or combination methods[7]

To illustrate, assume that a company recently purchased a crane for heavy construction purposes. Pertinent data concerning the crane's purchase are as follows.

Illustration 12-2

*Data Used to Illustrate
Amortization Methods*

Cost of crane	$500,000
Estimated useful life in years	5 years
Productive life in hours	30,000 hours
Estimated residual value	$ 50,000

Activity Methods

Objective 3

Determine amortization charges using the activity, straight-line, and decreasing charge methods and compare the methods.

The **activity method**, sometimes called a variable charge approach, determines amortization as **a function of use or productivity instead of the passage of time**. The asset's life is defined in terms of either the output it provides (units it produces), or the input required (the number of hours it works) to produce the output. Conceptually, a better cost association is established by using an output measure rather than the hours put in, but often the output is not homogeneous or is difficult to measure. In such cases, an input measure such as machine hours is an appropriate basis for determining the amount of the amortization charge for the accounting period.

The crane poses no particular problem because the usage (hours) is relatively easy to measure. If the crane is used 4,000 hours the first year, the amortization charge is as follows.

Illustration 12-3

*Amortization Calculation,
Activity Method—
Crane Example*

$$\frac{\text{Cost less residual value}}{\text{Total estimated hours}} = \text{Amortization expense per hour}$$

$$\frac{\$500,000 - \$50,000}{30,000 \text{ hours}} = \$15 \text{ per hour}$$

First year amortization expense: 4,000 hours × $15 = $60,000

Where reduction in utility is a result of use, activity, or productivity, the activity method will best match costs and revenues. Companies that adopt this approach will have low amortization during periods of low usage and high charges during high usage.

This method's major limitation is that it is not appropriate in situations where depreciation is a function of time instead of activity. For example, a building is subject to a great deal

---

[7] Clarence Byrd, Ida Chen, and Heather Chapman, *Financial Reporting in Canada, 2002*, (CICA, Toronto, 2002) report that, of the companies surveyed in 2001 that used only one method of amortization, 91% used straight-line, 5% used diminishing balance, 2% used units of production, and 2% used an increasing charge method. A small majority of the surveyed companies reported using only one method. Those that used a combination of methods tended to use straight-line and either a diminishing balance (i.e., a decreasing charge) or an activity method.

of steady deterioration from the elements (a function of time) regardless of its use. In addition, where an asset's useful life is subject to economic or functional factors independent of its use, the activity method loses much of its appeal. For example, if a company is expanding rapidly, a particular building may soon become obsolete for its intended purposes. The level of activity is irrelevant. Another limitation in using an activity method is that the total units of output or service hours to be received over the useful life are often difficult to determine.

Straight-Line Method

Under the straight-line method, depreciation is considered **a function of the passage of time**. This method is widely used in practice because of its simplicity. The straight-line approach is often the most conceptually appropriate, as well. When creeping obsolescence is the primary reason for a limited service life, the decline in usefulness may be constant from period to period. The amortization charge for the crane is calculated as follows.

Underlying Concept

If the benefits flow evenly over time, then justification exists for matching the asset's cost with the benefits on a straight-line basis.

Illustration 12-4

Amortization Calculation, Straight-Line Method— Crane Example

$$\frac{\text{Cost less residual value}}{\text{Estimated service life}} = \text{Amortization charge}$$

$$\frac{\$500,000 - \$50,000}{5 \text{ years}} = \$90,000$$

The major objection to the straight-line method is that it rests on two tenuous assumptions: (1) the asset's economic usefulness is the same each year, and (2) maintenance expense is about the same each period (given constant revenue flows). If such is not the case, a rational matching of expense with revenues will not result from applying this method.

Another problem stems from distortions that can develop in the rate of return analysis (income ÷ assets). Illustration 12-5 indicates how the rate of return increases, given constant revenue flows, because the asset's book value decreases. Relying on the increasing trend of the rate of return in such circumstances can be very misleading as a basis for evaluating the success of operations. The increase in the rate of return is solely the result of the accounting method used. It is not due to significant improvement in underlying economic performance. With the exception of the compound interest methods, the rate of return trend can be similarly distorted by other amortization methods.

Year	Amortization Expense	Unamortized Asset Balance (net book value)	Income (after amortization expense)	Rate of Return (income ÷ assets)
0		$500,000		
1	$90,000	410,000	$100,000	24.4%
2	90,000	320,000	100,000	31.2%
3	90,000	230,000	100,000	43.5%
4	90,000	140,000	100,000	71.4%
5	90,000	50,000	100,000	200.0%

Illustration 12-5

Amortization and Rate of Return Analysis— Crane Example

Underlying Concept

The matching concept does not justify a constant charge to income. If the asset's benefits decline as it gets older, then a decreasing charge to income would better match costs with benefits.

Decreasing Charge Methods

Decreasing charge methods, often called accelerated amortization or diminishing balance methods, provide for a higher amortization expense in the earlier years and lower charges in later periods. The main justification for this approach is that more amortization should be charged in earlier years when the asset offers the greatest benefits. Another argument is that repair and maintenance costs are often higher in later periods, and the accelerated method therefore provides a fairly constant total expense (for amortization plus repairs and maintenance) because the amortization charge is lower in the later periods. When a decreasing charge approach is used by Canadian companies, it is usually a version of what is called the declining-balance method.[8]

Declining-Balance Method.

The **declining-balance method** uses an amortization rate (expressed as a percentage and called the declining-balance rate) that remains constant throughout the asset's life, assuming no change in estimates occurs. This rate is applied to the reducing book or carrying value (cost less accumulated amortization) each year to determine amortization expense. The rate is usually calculated as a multiple of the straight-line rate.[9] For example, the double-declining-balance rate for a 10-year life asset is 20% (the straight-line rate, which is 100% ÷ 10 or 10%, multiplied by 2). For an asset with a 20-year life, the triple-declining-balance rate is 15% (the straight-line rate of 100% ÷ 20 or 5%, multiplied by 3), while the double-declining-balance rate is 10% (100% ÷ 20 or 5%, multiplied by 2).

Unlike other methods, in the declining-balance method **the residual value of the asset is not deducted** in calculating an amortizable amount. Instead, this method applies the appropriate rate to the asset's net book value or carrying amount at the beginning of each period. Since the asset's book value is reduced each period by the amortization charge, the rate is applied to a lower book value each period, resulting in a reduced amortization charge. This process continues until the asset's book value is reduced to its estimated residual value, **at which time amortization ceases**.

Application of the **double-declining-balance method** using the crane example is illustrated below.

Illustration 12-6

Amortization Calculation, Double-Declining-Balance Method—Crane Example

Year	Book Value of Asset First of Year	Rate on Declining Balance[a]	Amortization Expense	Balance of Accumulated Amortization	Net Book Value, End of Year
1	$500,000	40%	$200,000	$200,000	$300,000
2	300,000	40%	120,000	320,000	180,000
3	180,000	40%	72,000	392,000	108,000
4	108,000	40%	43,200	435,200	64,800
5	64,800	40%	14,800[b]	450,000	50,000

[a](100% ÷ 5) × 2
[b]Limited to $14,800 because book value should not be less than residual value.

---

[8] Another decreasing charge approach called the **sum-of-the-years'-digits method** exists but is used infrequently in Canada. Under this method, the amortizable amount (i.e., cost less residual value) is multiplied each year by a decreasing fraction. The **denominator** of the fraction equals the sum of the digits of an asset's useful life. For example, the sum of the digits of the life of an asset with a five-year life is 1 + 2 + 3 + 4 + 5 = 15. The **numerator** decreases year by year and the denominator stays constant. Because this is a decreasing charge approach, amortization expense is 5/15 of the amortizable amount in the first year, 4/15 of the amortizable amount in the second year, 3/15 in the third, 2/15 in the fourth, and 1/15 in the fifth year. At the end of the asset's useful life, its net book value should be equal to the estimated residual value. Similarly for an asset with a 10-year life, the sum of the years' digits 1 through 10 equals 55. Amortization in the first year is 10/55 of the amortizable amount, in the second year is 9/55, etc.

[9] The straight-line rate (%) is equal to 100% divided by the estimated useful life of the asset being amortized. A pure form of the declining-balance method (sometimes called the fixed percentage of book value method) has also been suggested as a possibility, but is not used extensively in practice. This approach finds a rate that amortizes the asset exactly to residual value at the end of its expected useful life. The formula for determining this rate is as follows:

Amortization rate = 1 − [the nth root of (the Residual value ÷ Acquisition cost)]

The life in years is n. Once the rate is calculated, it is applied to the asset's declining book value from period to period, which means that amortization expense will be successively lower.

Increasing Charge Methods

Increasing charge methods, such as **compound interest and sinking fund approaches**, provide for lower amortization charges in the early years and higher amounts in the later years of an asset's life. This method is not widely used except by companies with significant real estate holdings. Real estate tends to be financed heavily by debt, making interest expense one of the most significant expenses, especially in the early years. Over time, as the debt is paid down, interest charges become smaller and smaller. Companies with this pattern of interest expense want an amortization policy with the opposite effect on expense; that is, one with low charges in the early years and higher expense in later years. The result is a fairly stable level of total expenses over time.

The most common application of this pattern of amortization is called the sinking fund method. In general, the amount of amortization expense is the annual increase in a virtual sinking fund designed to accumulate the amortizable amount over the asset's useful life.[10] As the sinking fund increases in size, so too does the amount of the annual increase representing principal plus interest. This industry-specific method in Canada is not permitted in the United States. The CICA's Accounting Standards Board recently indicated that the elimination of this GAAP difference may be added to the scope of its Accounting Standards Improvement project now under way.

IAS Note

IAS16 identifies only three patterns of allocating depreciable amounts to expense: equal charges, reducing amounts, and amounts that vary with expected use or output.

Depletion

Chapter 11 discusses the issues associated with determining the cost, and therefore the amortizable base, of natural resource assets, which could include capitalized acquisition, exploration, development, and restoration costs. Because the resource is depleted over time as it is removed, the capitalized costs must be amortized. The amortization, or **depletion expense**, is a product cost, becoming a direct cost of the inventory of timber or petroleum products produced during the period. Illustration 11-1 summarizes this flow of costs for the oil and gas industry.

The accounting problems associated with the depletion of natural resources are similar to those encountered with the amortization of other types of property, plant, and equipment:

1. Determination of the pattern of depletion (amortization) to be used.

2. Difficulty of estimating useful life.

   In addition, the issue of liquidating dividends is associated with natural resource companies.

4 Objective

Explain the accounting procedures for depletion of natural resources.

Depletion of Resource Cost

Once the amortizable base is established, the next decision is determining how the cost of the natural resource will be allocated to accounting periods. Normally, **depletion is calculated using an activity approach such as the units of production method**. Using this method, the natural resource's total cost less any residual value is divided by the estimated recoverable reserves (number of units estimated to be in the resource deposit) to obtain a cost per unit of product. The cost per unit is multiplied by the number of units extracted to determine the period's depletion.

For example, assume a mining company acquired the right to use 1,000 ha of land in the Northwest Territories to mine for gold. The lease cost is $50,000; the related exploration costs on the property are $100,000; and development costs incurred in opening the

---

[10] This is termed a "virtual" sinking fund because no amounts are set aside in an actual sinking fund.

mine are $850,000, all of which have been capitalized. Total costs related to the mine before the first ounce of gold is extracted are, therefore, $1 million. The company estimates that the mine will provide approximately 100,000 ounces of gold. The depletion rate established is calculated in the following manner.

Illustration 12-7

Calculation of Depletion Rate

$$\frac{\text{Total cost} - \text{residual value}}{\text{Total estimated units available}} = \text{Depletion cost per unit}$$

$$\frac{\$1,000,000}{100,000} = \$10 \text{ per ounce}$$

If 25,000 ounces are extracted in the first year, the depletion for the year is $250,000 (25,000 ounces at $10). The entry to record the depletion is:

A = L + SE
0   0   0

Cash flows: No effect

Inventory (Depletion Expense)	250,000	
Accumulated Depletion		250,000

The depletion charge for the resource extracted (in addition to labour and other direct production costs) is initially charged (debited) to inventory. When sold, the inventory costs are transferred to cost of goods sold and matched with the period's revenue. This cost flow is similar to that of amortization of factory buildings in a manufacturing company. The amortization is charged initially to inventory as it is a cost of the goods manufactured. The amortization is charged to the income statement only in the period in which the related goods are sold.

The natural resource is reported as part of property, plant, and equipment. The balance sheet presents the property cost and the amount of accumulated depletion entered to date as follows.

Gold mine (at cost)	$1,000,000	
Less: Accumulated depletion	250,000	$750,000

The tangible equipment used in extracting the resource may also be amortized on a units of production basis, especially if the equipment's useful life can be directly assigned to one specific resource deposit. If the equipment is used on more than one job, other cost allocation methods such as the straight-line or an accelerated depreciation method may be more appropriate.

Estimating Recoverable Reserves

Not infrequently, the estimate of recoverable (proven) reserves has to be changed either because new information becomes available or because production processes become more sophisticated. Natural resources such as oil and gas deposits and some rare metals have provided the greatest challenges. Estimates of these reserves are in large measure knowledgeable guesses.

This problem is the same as that faced in accounting for changes in estimates of the useful lives of plant and equipment. The procedure is to revise the depletion rate on a prospective basis by dividing the remaining cost by the estimate of the new recoverable reserves. This approach has much merit because the required estimates are so tenuous.

Liquidating Dividends

A company may own a property from which it intends to extract natural resources as its only major asset. If the company does not expect to purchase additional properties, it may distribute gradually to shareholders their capital investment by paying dividends equal to the accumulated amount of net income (after depletion) plus the amount of depletion charged. The major accounting issue is to distinguish between dividends that are a return of capital and those that are not. A company issuing a liquidating dividend should reduce the appropriate Share Capital account for that portion related to the original investment instead of Retained Earnings, because the dividend is a return of part of the investor's original contribution. Shareholders must be informed that the total dividend consists of the liquidation of capital as well as a distribution of income.

To illustrate, a mining company has a retained earnings balance of $1,650,000, accumulated depletion on mineral properties of $2.1 million, and common share capital of $5.4 million. The board of directors declares a dividend of $3 per share on the 1 million shares outstanding. The entry to record the $3 million dividend is as follows:

Retained Earnings	1,650,000	
Common Shares	*1,350,000	
Cash		3,000,000

*($3,000,000 − $1,650,000)

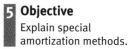

A   = L +   SE
−$3,000,000   −$3,000,000

Cash flows: ↓ 3,000,000 outflow

The $3 dividend represents a $1.65 ($1,650,000 ÷ 1,000,000) per share **return on investment** and a $1.35 ($1,350,000 ÷ 1,000,000) per share liquidating dividend, or **return of capital**.

Special Methods of Amortization

Sometimes an enterprise does not select one of the more popular amortization methods because the assets involved have unique characteristics, or the nature of the industry dictates that a special amortization method be adopted. A company may develop its own special or tailor-made amortization method. GAAP requires only that the method result in an allocation of the asset's cost over the periods benefitting in a rational and systematic manner.

Group and Composite Methods

Amortization is usually applied to a single asset. In some circumstances, however, a company may place related assets (regardless of type, use, or life) into a single multiple-asset account that is then amortized using one rate. For example, a telecommunications company might amortize telephone poles, microwave systems, or switchboards by groups.

Two methods of amortizing multiple-asset accounts can be used: the group method and the composite method. **The calculations involved are the same for both: calculate an average rate and amortize on that basis**. The different names for the methods merely reflect the degree of similarity of the assets. The group method is used when the assets are fairly homogeneous and have approximately the same useful lives. The composite method is used when the assets are dissimilar and have different lives. The group method more closely approximates a single-unit cost procedure because the variation from the average is not as great.

To illustrate, a vehicle leasing company amortizes its fleet of cars, trucks, and campers on a composite basis. The amortization rate is determined as shown in Illustration 12-8.

5 Objective
Explain special amortization methods.

Illustration 12-8

*Amortization Calculation,
Composite Basis*

Asset	Original Cost	Residual Value	Amortizable Amount	Estimated Life (yrs.)	Amortization per Year (straight-line)
Cars	$145,000	$25,000	$120,000	3	$40,000
Trucks	44,000	4,000	40,000	4	10,000
Campers	35,000	5,000	30,000	5	6,000
	$224,000	$34,000	$190,000		$56,000

$$\text{Composite amortization rate on original cost} = \frac{\$56,000}{\$224,000} = 25\%$$

$$\text{Composite life} = 3.39 \text{ years } (\$190,000 \div \$56,000)$$

The **composite amortization rate** is determined by dividing the total amortization per year for the collection of assets by their total original cost. If there are no changes in the assets, they will be amortized in the amount of $56,000 per year (the original cost of $224,000 × the composite rate of 25%) until the residual value remains. It will take the company 3.39 years (composite life as indicated in the exhibit) to amortize these assets.

The differences between the group or composite method and the single-unit amortization method are more pronounced when dealing with asset retirements. If an asset is retired before or after the average service life of the group is reached, the resulting gain or loss is buried in the Accumulated Amortization account rather than being recognized separately. This practice is justified because some assets will be retired before the average service life, while others will be retired after the average life. For this reason, **the difference between original cost and cash received is debited to Accumulated Amortization. No gain or loss on disposition is recorded**.

To illustrate, suppose that one of the campers with a cost of $5,000 is sold for $2,600 at the end of the third year. The entry is:

A = L + SE
0   0   0

Cash flows: ↑ 2,600 inflow

Accumulated Amortization	2,400	
Cash	2,600	
Cars, Trucks, and Campers		5,000

As new assets of the type identified in the group are purchased, there is no need to calculate a new amortization rate—they are amortized using the same group rate. Material changes in the relative weightings of assets in the group, however, would require that a new group rate be calculated.

A typical financial statement disclosure of the group amortization method is shown in Illustration 12-4 for Canadian National Railway Company.

The group or composite method significantly simplifies the bookkeeping process and tends to average out errors caused by over- or under-amortization. As a result, periodic income is not distorted by gains or losses on asset disposals.

On the other hand, the single-asset approach (1) simplifies the calculation mathematically; (2) identifies gains and losses on disposal; (3) isolates amortization on idle assets; and (4) represents the best estimate of the amortization of each individual asset. As a consequence, it is generally used in practice. Recently there has been increased support in the United States and internationally for a **components approach** to depreciation. Under component depreciation, any part or portion of property, plant, and equipment that can be separately identified as an asset should be depreciated over its individual expected useful life. For example, a building might be divided into various components such as roof, heating and cooling system, elevator, leasehold improvements, and so on. The useful life of each component would be separately determined.

Digital Tool

Expanded
Discussions—
Special
Amortization Methods
www.wiley.com/canada/kieso

Canadian National Railway Company

Notes to Consolidated Financial Statements

1. **Summary of Significant Accounting Policies**

    g) **Properties**

    Railroad properties are carried at cost less accumulated depreciation including asset impairment write-downs. All costs of materials associated with the installation of rail, ties, ballast and other track improvements are capitalized to the extent they meet the Company's minimum threshold for capitalization. The related labor and overhead costs are also capitalized for the installation of new, non-replacement track. All other labor and overhead costs and maintenance costs are expensed as incurred. Related interest costs are charged to expense. Included in property additions are the costs of developing computer software for internal use.

    The cost of railroad properties, less net salvage value, retired or disposed of in the normal course of business is charged to accumulated depreciation, in accordance with the group method of depreciation. The Company reviews the carrying amounts of properties whenever events or changes in circumstances indicate that such carrying amounts may not be recoverable based on future undiscounted cash flows or estimated net realizable value. Assets that are deemed impaired as a result of such review are recorded at the lower of carrying amount or net recoverable amount.

    h) **Depreciation**

    The cost of properties, net of asset impairment write-downs, is depreciated on a straight-line basis over their estimated useful lives as follows:

Asset class	Annual rate
Track and roadway	2%
Rolling stock	3%
Buildings	6%
Other	4%

    The Company follows the group method of depreciation and as such conducts comprehensive depreciation studies on a periodic basis to assess the reasonableness of the lives of properties based upon current information and historical activities. Such a study was conducted in 2001 for the Company's Canadian properties. The study did not have a significant effect on depreciation expense as the benefit of increased asset lives was offset by deficiencies in certain accumulated depreciation balances. Changes in estimated useful lives are accounted for prospectively.

Illustration 12-9

Disclosure of Group Amortization Method

Hybrid or Combination Methods

In addition to the amortization methods described above, companies may develop their own tailor-made methods. A hybrid amortization method used by some companies in the steel industry is referred to as the **production variable method**. One example is a modified units of production approach used for equipment whose depreciation is a function of physical wear and tear as well as time. The annual charge for amortization is a straight-line amount adjusted by the level of raw steel production. Therefore, in some periods the amortization expense is larger than the straight-line amount and in others it is less.

Selecting an Amortization Method

Which amortization method should be selected, and why? Conceptually, an amortization method should be selected based on which method best matches the asset's cost against the benefits or revenues received. If this is how the best method is chosen, it is first necessary to identify the pattern of benefits to be received. Possible benefit patterns are indicated in Illustration 12-10.

Pattern (1) represents an asset providing roughly the same level of benefits in each year of its life. A warehouse could be an example. For such assets, the straight-line method

6 Objective

Identify and understand reasons why amortization methods are selected.

Illustration 12-10

Possible Benefit Patterns for Assets

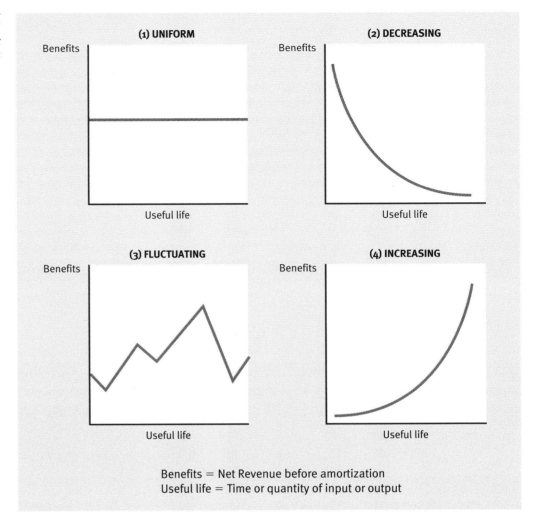

Benefits = Net Revenue before amortization
Useful life = Time or quantity of input or output

International Insight

In most non-English-speaking nations, companies are not permitted to use one amortization method for financial statements and a different method for tax returns. The financial statements must conform to the tax return.

Underlying Concept

Failure to consider the economic consequences of accounting principles is a frequent criticism of the profession. However, the neutrality concept requires that the statements be free from bias. Freedom from bias requires that the statements reflect economic reality, even if undesirable effects occur.

would be rational because it results in a constant amortization expense each period. An airplane may be an example of an asset with a decreasing benefit pattern (2). When it is new, it is constantly in service on major routes but, as it gets older, it may be repaired more often and used for more peripheral routes. Therefore, amortization expense should decline each year. The use of a truck, in terms of kilometres driven, may fluctuate considerably from period to period, yielding a benefit pattern that varies (3). An activity method would rationally match amortization expense against such a benefit pattern. An increasing benefit pattern (4) may result from ownership of a hotel. Over time, the net revenues may increase as occupancy rates increase. As such, a compound interest or sinking fund method may be most appropriate for matching.

Because it may be difficult in many cases to develop projections of future revenues, **simplicity** of method may govern. In such cases, it might be argued that the straight-line method of amortization should be used. However, others might argue that whatever is used for tax purposes should be used for book purposes because it **eliminates some record-keeping costs**. Because Canadian companies must use the capital cost allowance approach for income tax purposes (discussed in Appendix 12A), they may decide to use the same for financial reporting purposes. This is common for smaller companies. The objectives of financial reporting differ, however, from those of income tax determination, so it is not uncommon for companies to have two sets of records when accounting for amortization. While perfectly acceptable given the differences in objectives, a consequence is that financial statement amounts for property, plant, and equipment and for income before taxes will differ from the tax basis of the capital assets and taxable income. The financial accounting consequences of such differences are examined in Chapter 19.

Management sometimes appears to choose the method of amortization based on the **perceived economic consequences** of the amounts reported. Companies wishing to appear more profitable change from the declining balance method to a straight-line approach. Because share value tends to be related to reported income, management feels that such a change would favourably affect the firm's market value. In fact, research in this area has found just the opposite, with companies switching to more liberal accounting policies experiencing declines in share values. One rationale is that such changes signal that the company is in trouble and also leads to scepticism about management's attitudes and behaviour.

The real estate industry in the United States is frustrated with amortization accounting because it argues that real estate often does not decline in value. In addition, because real estate is highly debt financed, most U.S. real estate concerns report losses in early years when the sum of amortization and interest charges exceeds the revenues from the real estate project. The industry argues for some form of increasing charge method of amortization (lower amortization at the beginning and higher amortization at the end), so that higher total assets and net income are reported in the earlier years of the project. Some even use an economic consequences argument that Canadian real estate companies (which can and do use increasing charge methods) have a competitive edge over American ones. In support of this view, some American firms have pointed to the increasing number of acquisitions by Canadian real estate companies of U.S. real estate companies and properties. It will be interesting to see what stance the AcSB takes as it attempts to eliminate U.S.-Canada GAAP differences and harmonize with international standards.

Choice of an amortization method will affect both the balance sheet (i.e., the carrying value of property, plant, and equipment) and the income statement (i.e., amortization expense). Therefore, various ratios will be affected by the choice made. These ratios include the rate of return on total assets, debt-to-total assets, and the total asset turnover. Consequently, contractual commitments based on financial statement ratios (e.g., agreements related to management compensation plans and bond indentures) are potentially important aspects that are considered in selecting an amortization method.

What do the Numbers Mean?

Other Amortization Issues

Two additional issues related to amortization remain to be discussed.

1. How should amortization be calculated for partial periods?

2. How are revisions in amortization rates handled?

Amortization and Partial Periods

Plant assets are seldom purchased on the first day of a fiscal period or disposed of on the last day of a fiscal period. A practical question is: How much amortization should be charged for the partial periods involved?

Assume, for example, that an automated drill machine with a five-year life is purchased for $45,000 (no residual value) on June 10, 2004. The company's fiscal year ends December 31, and amortization is charged for 6 2/3 months during that year. The total amortization for a full year, assuming the straight-line method, is $9,000 ($45,000 ÷ 5), and the amortization for the partial year is $5,000 ($9,000 × [$6\frac{2}{3}$ ÷ 12]).

Rather than making a precise allocation of cost for a partial period, many companies establish a policy to simplify the calculations. For example, amortization may be calculated for the full period on the opening balance in the asset account and no depreciation charged on acquisitions during the year. Other variations charge a full year's amortization on assets used for a full year and charge one-half year's amortization in the years of acquisition and disposal. Alternatively, they may charge a full year's amortization in the year of acquisition and none in the year of disposal.

A company is at liberty to adopt any one of these fractional-year policies in allocating cost to the first and last years of an asset's life, provided the method is applied consistently. As indicated in the opening story, VIA Rail follows a policy of beginning amortization in the month after the train is put into service and continuing it up to the month of disposal. For purposes of the illustrations and problem material in this text, amortization is calculated on the basis of the nearest full month, unless otherwise directed. Illustration 12-11 shows amortization allocated under five different fractional-year policies using the straight-line method on the automated drill machine purchased above for $45,000 on June 10, 2004.

Illustration 12-11

Fractional-Year Amortization Policies

Machine Cost = $45,000	Amortization Allocated per Period Over 5-Year Life*					
Fractional-Year Policy	2004	2005	2006	2007	2008	2009
1. Nearest fraction of a year	$5,000[a]	$9,000	$9,000	$9,000	$9,000	$4,000[b]
2. Nearest full month	5,250[c]	9,000	9,000	9,000	9,000	3,750[d]
3. Half year in period of acquisition and disposal	4,500	9,000	9,000	9,000	9,000	4,500
4. Full year in period of acquisition, none in period of disposal	9,000	9,000	9,000	9,000	9,000	0
5. None in period of acquisition, full year in period of disposal	0	9,000	9,000	9,000	9,000	9,000

[a]6.667/12 ($9,000)   [b]5.333/12 ($9,000)   [c]7/12 ($9,000)   [d]5/12 ($9,000)
*Rounded to nearest dollar

The partial period calculation is relatively simple when the straight-line method is used. But how is partial period amortization handled when an accelerated method is used? To illustrate, assume that an asset was purchased for $10,000 on July 1, 2004, with an estimated useful life of five years. The amortization expense for 2004, 2005, and 2006 using the double-declining-balance method is shown in Illustration 12-12.

Illustration 12-12

Calculation of Partial Period Amortization, Double-Declining-Balance Method

1st full year	(40% × $10,000) = $4,000
2nd full year	(40% × 6,000) = 2,400
3rd full year	(40% × 3,600) = 1,440

Amortization July 1, 2004, to December 31, 2004:

6/12 × $4,000 = $2,000

Amortization for 2005:

6/12 × $4,000 = $2,000
6/12 × $2,400 = 1,200
$3,200

or ($10,000 − $2,000) × 40% = $3,200

Amortization for 2006:

6/12 × $2,400 = $1,200
6/12 × $1,440 = 720
$1,920

or ($10,000 − $2,000 − $3,200) × 40% = $1,920

In calculating amortization expense for partial periods in this example, the amortization charge for a full year was determined first. This amount was then prorated on a straight-line basis between the two accounting periods involved. A simpler approach when using the declining-balance method is to calculate the partial year amortization expense for the acquisition year (e.g., $2,000 for 2004 as shown in the example) and then apply the amortization rate (40%) to the book value at the beginning of each successive year. This is shown in the illustration as the "or" calculations. The charge for each year is the same regardless of the alternative arithmetic applied.

Revision of Amortization Rates

When a plant asset is purchased, amortization rates are carefully determined based on past experience with similar assets and other pertinent information. Amortization is only an estimate, however, and it may be necessary to revise the calculations during the life of the asset. *CICA Handbook* Section 3061.33 states that the amortization method and estimates of the life and useful life of property, plant, and equipment should be reviewed on a regular basis. Unexpected physical deterioration or unforeseen obsolescence may make the asset's useful life less than originally estimated. Improved maintenance procedures, revision of operating policies, or similar developments may prolong the asset's life beyond the expected period.

7 Objective
Explain the accounting procedures for a change in the amortization rate.

For example, assume that machinery that cost $90,000 was estimated to have a 20-year life with no residual value and has already been amortized for 10 years. In year 11 it is estimated that its total life is now expected to be 30 years. Amortization has been recorded at the rate of 1/20 of $90,000, or $4,500 per year, by the straight-line method. On the basis of a 30-year life, amortization should have been 1/30 of $90,000, or $3,000 per year. Amortization expense, therefore, has been overestimated, and net income understated for each of the past 10 years. The dollar differences are calculated as follows.

	Per Year	For Ten Years
Amortization charged per books (1/20 × $90,000)	$4,500	$45,000
Amortization based on a 30-year life (1/30 × $90,000)	3,000	30,000
Excess amortization charged	$1,500	$15,000

Illustration 12-13

Calculation of Accumulated Difference Due to Revision of Estimate

Canadian accounting standards **do not permit companies to go back and correct the records** when a change in an estimate is made, **nor to make a "catch up" adjustment** for the accumulated difference. Section 1506 of the *CICA Handbook* requires instead that the effects of any changes in estimates **be accounted for in the period of change and applicable future periods**. The reason is that changes in estimates are a continual and inherent part of the accounting process. As new information becomes available, it is incorporated into current and future reports.

Therefore, when a change in estimate occurs, no change is made to previously recorded amounts. Instead, a new amortization schedule is prepared for the asset using the unamortized costs remaining on the books, and the most recent estimates of residual value and remaining useful life. Charges for amortization in the current and subsequent periods are based on the revised calculations as illustrated below.

Machinery cost	$90,000
Less: Accumulated amortization to date	45,000
Carrying amount of machinery at end of tenth year	$45,000

Revised amortization = $45,000 carrying amount ÷ 20 years remaining life = $2,250

Illustration 12-14

Calculating Amortization after Revision of Estimated Life

The entry to record amortization for each of the remaining 20 years is:

A   =   L   +   SE
−2,250   −2,250
Cash flows: No effect

Amortization Expense	2,250	
Accumulated Amortization—Machinery		2,250

If the machinery now has an estimated residual value of $5,000 at the end of its revised useful life, the revised amortization rate is $2,000 ([$45,000 − $5,000] ÷ 20) each year.

If the double-declining-balance method were used, the change in estimated life would result in a new amortization rate to be applied to the book value in the current (11th) and subsequent years.[11] In this example, a revised remaining life of 20 years results in a revised 5% straight-line and a 10% double-declining rate, coincidentally the same as the rate used for the first 10 years. As this method ignores residual value in determining amortization expense, a change in residual value is ignored in the revised calculation.

AKITA Drilling Ltd., an oil and gas drilling contractor with operations in western Canada and the territories, includes the following note in its 2002 financial statements about its change in the estimate of useful life of its drilling rigs. Note that this was initiated by a change in company operating procedures.

Illustration 12-15

Change in Estimate
of Useful Life

Akita Drilling Limited
Notes to Financial Statements

1. **Summary of Significant Accounting Policies (excerpt)**

    Depreciation
    Drilling rigs are depreciated using the unit of production method based on an initial estimated life of 2,000 operating days per rig. Commencing in 2002, certain large rigs had lives re-estimated to 3,600 operating days per rig. The estimate of 3,600 operating days for specific rigs was based upon these rigs being moved relatively less often than certain smaller capacity rigs thereby encountering less wear and tear than smaller rigs and that AKITA's remaining large rigs were used when AKITA acquired them. If AKITA had adopted the effects of this change in estimate at the beginning of 2001, depreciation expense would have been reduced by $246,000 in that year.

IMPAIRMENTS

Objective 8

Explain the accounting issues related to asset impairment.

Unlike current assets such as inventories, **the lower of cost and market valuation rule does not apply to property, plant, and equipment**. Because current assets are expected to be converted into cash within the operating cycle, it is important to report them on the balance sheet at no more than the net cash you expect to receive. Property, plant, and equipment assets, however, are not held to be converted into cash, but instead are ordinarily used in operations over the long term. Therefore, the lower of cost and market is not an appropriate valuation rule for these assets.

Even when long-lived capital assets suffer partial obsolescence, accountants have been reluctant to reduce the assets' carrying amount. This reluctance occurs because, unlike inventories, it is difficult to arrive at a fair value for property, plant, and equipment that is not subjective and arbitrary. For example, Falconbridge Ltd. Nickel Mines had to decide whether all or a part of its property, plant, and equipment in a nickel-mining operation in

---

[11] To determine the unamortized book value to date when using the double-declining-balance method, the following formula can be used:

Book value = $C(1 − r)^n$ where C = cost of asset; r = amortization rate; and n = number of full years from the asset's acquisition date. For example, if the machinery in the illustration had been amortized using the double-declining-balance method instead of the straight-line method, C = $90,000; r = 2 × (100% ÷ 20) = 10%; and n = 10.

The asset's book value at the end of year 10, therefore, is $90,000(1 − .10)^{10}$ or $31,381.

the Dominican Republic should be written off. The project had been incurring losses because nickel prices were low and operating costs were high. Only if nickel prices increased by approximately 33% would the project be reasonably profitable. Whether a write-off was appropriate depended on the future price of nickel. Even if a decision were made to write down the asset, the amount to be written off was not clear.

Recognizing Impairments

Impairment is a condition that exists when the carrying amount of a long-lived asset exceeds its fair value, indicating a write-off is needed.[12] Various events and changes in circumstances might lead to an impairment. Examples include:

(a) A significant decrease in an asset's market value.

(b) A significant change in the extent or manner in which an asset is used.

(c) A significant adverse change in legal factors or in the business climate that affects an asset's value.

(d) An accumulation of costs significantly in excess of the amount originally expected to acquire or construct an asset.

(e) A projection or forecast that demonstrates continuing losses associated with an asset.

If these events or changes in circumstances indicate that the asset's carrying amount may not be recoverable, a **recoverability test** is used to determine whether an impairment has occurred. This entails estimating the future net cash flows expected **from the use of the asset and its eventual disposition**. If the sum of these (undiscounted) expected future cash flows is **less than the asset's carrying amount**, the asset is considered impaired. Conversely, if the sum of the (undiscounted) expected future net cash flows is equal to or greater than the asset's carrying amount, no impairment has occurred.

The future cash flows associated with a particular long-lived asset are, of necessity, estimated amounts and they can extend far into the future. The recoverable amounts, therefore, are **much more difficult to determine than the realizable values associated with accounts receivable and inventories**, for example. The recoverability test requires that only future net cash flows directly associated with the asset that are expected to arise as a direct result of its use or disposition should be included. Further complications arise when an asset does not generate cash flows independently of other assets, so that such individual assets must be combined with others to form an asset group. In this case, the recoverability test is applied to the asset group.[13]

The recoverability test is a screening device to determine whether an impairment has occurred. For example, if the expected future net cash flows from an asset are $400,000 and its carrying amount is $350,000, no impairment has occurred. However, if the expected future net cash flows are $300,000, an impairment has occurred. The rationale for the recoverability test is the basic presumption that a balance sheet should report long-lived assets at no more than an amount that is recoverable.

Measuring Impairments

If the recoverability test indicates that an asset is impaired, a loss is calculated. **The impairment loss is the amount by which the carrying amount of the asset exceeds its fair value**. Fair value is defined as the amount of the consideration that would be agreed upon in an arm's length transaction between knowledgeable, willing parties who

Underlying Concept

The going concern concept assumes that the firm can recover the cost of the investment in its assets. Under GAAP, the fair value of long-lived assets is not reported because a going concern does not plan to sell such assets. However, if the assumption of being able to recover the investment cost is not valid, then a reduction in value should be reported.

IAS Note

An asset's recoverable amount under IAS 36 is the greater of its net selling price and the discounted present value of its estimated future cash flows from use and disposal.

---

[12] *CICA Handbook*, Section 3063.03(c).

[13] Section 3063 of the *CICA Handbook* provides considerable application guidance for these complexities.

are under no compulsion to act.[14] Fair value is best measured by quoted market prices in active markets, but if there is no active market, other valuation methods are used. The **present value of expected future net cash flows** is considered the next best approach.

To summarize, the process of determining an impairment loss involves three steps.

1. Review events or changes in circumstances for possible impairment.

2. If the review indicates potential impairment, apply the recoverability test. If the sum of the expected future net cash flows (undiscounted) from the long-lived asset is less than the carrying amount, the asset is considered impaired.

3. Determine the fair value of the asset, based on a method that discounts the future flows to their present value. The impairment loss is the difference between the carrying amount and the fair value.

These general impairment provisions are explained in *Handbook* Section 3063 and their specific application to oil and gas assets accounted for using the full cost method are explained in Accounting Guideline AcG-16.

Illustration One

Assume a company has equipment that, due to changes in its use, is reviewed for possible impairment. The asset's carrying amount is $600,000 ($800,000 cost less $200,000 accumulated amortization). The expected future net cash flows (undiscounted) from the use of the asset and its eventual disposition are estimated to be $650,000.

The recoverability test indicates that the $650,000 of expected future net cash flows from the asset's use exceed its carrying amount of $600,000. As a result, no impairment is evident. The undiscounted future net cash flows must be less than the carrying amount for an asset to be deemed impaired and for the impairment to be measured.

Illustration Two

Assume the same facts as in Illustration One, except that the expected future net cash flows from the equipment are $580,000, instead of $650,000. The recoverability test indicates that the expected future net cash flows of $580,000 from the use and disposal of the asset are less than its carrying amount of $600,000. Therefore, the asset is considered impaired. If the asset's market value is $525,000, the impairment loss is calculated as follows.

Illustration 12-16

Calculation of Impairment Loss

Carrying amount of the equipment	$600,000
Fair value of equipment (market value)	525,000
Loss on impairment	$ 75,000

The entry to record the impairment loss is as follows.

A = L + SE
−75,000   −75,000

Cash flows: No effect

Loss on Impairment	75,000	
Accumulated Amortization		75,000

IAS Note

For assets carried at cost, impairment losses are recognized in the income statement. If carried at revalued amounts, the asset's impairment is treated as a decrease of the revaluation surplus in equity.

Assuming the asset will continue to be used in operations, the impairment loss is reported as part of income from continuing operations. It is not an extraordinary item. Costs associated with an impairment loss are the same costs that would otherwise flow through operations and be reported as part of continuing operations.

While crediting the asset account directly would accomplish the objective of reducing the asset's carrying value, crediting the Accumulated Amortization account has the benefit of preserving the asset's original cost. For intangible assets that are not amortized, a credit

[14] *CICA Handbook*, Section 3063.03(b).

to a valuation allowance contra account (e.g., Allowance for Impairment) instead of the asset's cost would accomplish the same objective. The amount of any writedown of a capital asset is required to be charged to expense, and disclosed in the period the impairment is recognized. After the writedown, it may be necessary to revise the amortization estimates and methods for the asset, but this is done only after recording the impairment loss.

A company that recognizes an impairment loss is required to describe the asset, the circumstances that led to the impairment, and the method of determining fair value. In addition, if not reported separately on the face of the income statement, the amount of the loss and where on the income statement it has been reported must be disclosed.

TransAlta Utilities Corporation, Canada's largest non-regulated power generation and wholesale marketing company, deducted an "asset impairment charge" of $110 million on its statement of earnings in determining operating income for its year ended December 31, 2002. The following information was provided in Note 4 to the company's financial statements.

Illustration 12-17

Disclosure of Impairment Loss

Transalta Utilities Corporation

4. **Property, Plant and Equipment (excerpt)**
   After a detailed unit-by-unit engineering assessment, a review of environmental issues and a review of short- and long-term market forecasts, the corporation implemented a phased decommissioning of its 537 MW coal-fired Wabamun facility in November 2002. As a result of this decision, the corporation recognized a pre-tax impairment charge of $110.0 million during the year, included in thermal generation equipment. The impairment charge was calculated as the excess of carrying value over fair value. The fair value of the facility was determined by estimating the present value of future cash flows.

Digital Tool

Student Toolkit—
Additional
Disclosures
www.wiley.com/canada/kieso

Subsequent Measurement

Once an impairment loss is recorded, the reduced carrying amount of an asset **held for use** becomes its new cost basis. As a result, the new cost basis is not changed except for amortization in future periods or for additional impairments. To illustrate, assume that at December 31, 2004, equipment with a carrying amount of $500,000 is considered impaired and is written down to its fair value of $400,000. At the end of 2005, the fair value of this asset has increased to $480,000. The asset's carrying amount should not change in 2005 except for the amortization recorded in 2005. **The impairment loss is not restored for an asset held for use.**[15]

Long-lived assets to be disposed of and that are "held for sale" are subsequently remeasured at the lower of their carrying amount and net realizable value, as explained in the next section.

IAS Note

IAS 36 permits write-ups for subsequent recoveries of impairment when there has been a change in the estimates used to determine the recoverable amount.

DISPOSITIONS

Property, Plant, and Equipment to Be Disposed of

What happens if long-lived assets are intended to be disposed of instead of continuing in use? In short, the answer depends on whether the asset is intended to be disposed of by sale or other than sale. This latter category includes situations where the asset is expected to be abandoned in the future, or exchanged for other similar productive assets, or perhaps distributed to owners through a spinoff.[16]

9 Objective

Explain the accounting standards for long-lived assets to be disposed of.

---

[15] *CICA Handbook*, Section 3063.06.

[16] *CICA Handbook*, Section 3475.05.

Long-lived Assets to Be Disposed of through Sale

If an item of property, plant, and equipment is to be disposed of by sale, it is classified as **held for sale**, and subsequently remeasured at the lower of its carrying amount and fair value less cost to sell (net realizable value). Because the criteria for classifying a long-lived asset as held for sale are very stringent, including the requirement to be disposed of in a short period of time, net realizable value is used in order to provide a better measure of the net cash flows that will be received from the asset. These criteria, identified in *CICA Handbook* Section 3475.08, were identified previously in Chapter 4 when discussing the accounting for discontinued operations.

Such assets are not amortized during the period in which they are held.[17] The rationale is that amortization is inconsistent with the notion of assets not in use, whose sale is probable, and with lower of cost and net realizable value valuation. In other words, **these assets are similar to inventory and should be reported at the lower of their carrying amount and net realizable value.** A long-lived asset classified as held for sale will continue to be written down and further losses recognized if its net realizable value continues to deteriorate. Gains (loss recoveries) are recognized for subsequent increases in net realizable value, but only to the extent of the cumulative losses previously recognized.

If the long-lived asset is part of a component of an entity that meets the criteria for reporting as a discontinued operation, the losses and subsequent recoveries are reported as part of discontinued operations on the income statement. Otherwise, they are reported in income from continuing operations. Regardless, long-lived assets classified as held for sale **are reported separately in the balance sheet as long-term assets.**

Long-lived Assets to Be Disposed of other than by Sale

An item of property, plant, and equipment to be disposed of other than through sale (expected to be abandoned, exchanged, or spun off to owners) continues to be accounted for as a "held for use" asset. Such assets continue to be amortized, tested for impairment, and reported with Property, Plant, and Equipment until disposed of.

The timing of disposal depends on the method of disposal:

- Abandonment—disposed of when it ceases to be used

- Exchange—disposed of when exchanged

- Spun off—disposed of when distributed

The accounting and disclosure requirements are complex for long-lived assets to be disposed of. While many of the issues are beyond the scope of an intermediate text, Illustration 12-18 below summarizes the key classification and measurement requirements of *CICA Handbook* Section 3063, "Impairment of Long-Lived Assets" and section 3475, "Disposal of Long-lived Assets and Discontinued Operations." Note that the classification of the asset drives the accounting. These standards are now consistent with those in the United States.

Sale of Property, Plant, and Equipment

Objective 10
Describe the accounting treatment for the disposal of property, plant, and equipment.

Unless the asset has previously been classified as "held for sale," amortization is taken up to the date of disposition, and then all accounts related to the retired asset are removed. Ideally, the specific asset's book value would equal its disposal value, but this is rarely the case. As a result, a gain or loss is usually reported. What is the reason for this? The amortization amount is an estimate of the cost to be allocated to each period, and not the result of a process of valuation. The gain or loss is really a correction of net income for the years during which the capital asset was used. If it had been possible at the time of acquisition to forecast the exact date of disposal and the amount to be realized at disposi-

---

[17] *CICA Handbook*, Section 3475.13.

	Assets held for use	Assets to be disposed of other than by sale	Assets to be disposed of by sale
		Handbook Section 3063 "Impairment of Long-Lived Assets"	
			Handbook Section 3475 "Disposal of Long-Lived Assets and Discontinued Operations"
Classify as	held for use	held for use, until disposed of	held for sale
Balance Sheet Classification	property, plant, and equipment	property, plant, and equipment	separately in long-term assets*
Impairment	Section 3063 Two-step test: • recoverability • if impaired, writedown to fair value	Section 3063 Two-step test: • recoverability • if impaired, writedown to fair value	Section 3475 Carry at lower of carrying amount and net realizable value
	No restoration of impairment loss	No restoration of impairment loss	Remeasure at balance sheet date. Recognize all losses and loss recoveries up to cumulative losses recognized
Amortization	Amortize	Amortize until disposed of (reassess useful life)	No amortization

*Unless sold prior to completion of financial statements and otherwise meets definition of current assets. If so, report in current assets.

Illustration 12-18

Summary of Long-Lived Assets

tion, then a more accurate estimate of amortization would have been recorded and no gain or loss would result.

Gains or losses on the retirement of plant assets are shown in the income statement along with other items that arise from customary business activities. However, any gain or loss from disposal of a component of a discontinued business is reported "below the line" with discontinued operations.

To illustrate the disposition of an asset classified as held for use, a machine costing $18,000 has been used for nine years and amortized at a rate of $1,200 per year. If the machine is sold in the middle of the tenth year for $7,000, the entry to record amortization to the sale date is:

Amortization Expense	600	
Accumulated Amortization—Machinery		600

A = L + SE
−600   −600
Cash flows: No effect

This separate entry may not be made because many companies enter all amortization, including this amount, in one entry at the year end. In either case the entry for the asset's sale is:

Cash	7,000	
Accumulated Amortization—Machinery	11,400	
[($1,200 × 9) + $600]		
Machinery		18,000
Gain on Disposal of Machinery		400

A = L + SE
+400   +400
Cash flows: ↑ 7,000 inflow

With the machinery's book value at the time of the sale of $6,600 ($18,000 − $11,400) and proceeds on disposal of $7,000, the gain on the sale is $400.

An asset previously recognized as held for sale is carried at its fair value less costs to sell. The net proceeds on sale, therefore, should be close to the asset's carrying value and it is likely that only minor gains or losses would be recognized when the actual disposition takes place.

Involuntary Conversion

Sometimes an asset's service is terminated through an involuntary conversion such as fire, flood, theft, or expropriation. The gains or losses are calculated no differently than those in any other type of disposition except that **they are often reported, if sufficiently material, as extraordinary items in the income statement**.

To illustrate, assume a company was forced to sell a plant located on company property that stood directly in the path of a planned major highway. For a number of years the provincial government had sought to purchase the land on which the plant stood, but the company resisted. The government ultimately exercised its right of eminent domain and its actions were upheld by the courts. In settlement, the company received $500,000, which substantially exceeded the $100,000 book value of the plant (cost of $300,000 less accumulated amortization of $200,000) and the $100,000 book value of the land. The following entry was made.

A   = L +   SE
+$300,000   +$300,000

Cash flows: ↑ 500,000 inflow

Cash	500,000	
Accumulated Amortization—Plant Assets	200,000	
Plant Assets		300,000
Land		100,000
Gain on Expropriation of Land and Plant Assets		300,000

The gain or loss that develops on this type of unusual, nonrecurring transaction that is not a result of management actions is normally shown as an extraordinary item.

Similar treatment is given to other types of involuntary conversions such as those resulting from a major nonrecurring casualty, such as an earthquake or flood, or theft, assuming that it meets other conditions for extraordinary item treatment. The difference between the amount recovered (such as an insurance recovery), if any, and the asset's carrying value is reported as a gain or loss.

Other Issues

Donations of Capital Assets

In a situation where a company donates or contributes a nonmonetary asset, the donation is recorded as an expense at the donated asset's fair value. If a difference exists between the asset's fair value and its book value, a gain or loss is recognized. To illustrate, assume that Kline Industries donates land that cost $30,000 and a small building located on the property that cost $95,000 with accumulated amortization to the contribution date of $45,000 to the City of Saskatoon for a city park. The land and building together have a fair value of $110,000. The entry to record the donation is:

A   = L +   SE
−80,000   −80,000

Cash flows: No effect

Contribution (or Donations) Expense	110,000	
Accumulated Amortization—Building	45,000	
Building		95,000
Land		30,000
Gain on Disposal of Land and Building		30,000

Miscellaneous Problems

If an asset is scrapped or abandoned without any cash recovery, a loss should be recognized equal to the asset's net carrying amount or book value. If scrap value exists, the gain or loss that results is the difference between the asset's scrap value and its book value. If an asset still can be used even though it is fully amortized, it may be kept on the books at historical cost less its related amortization.

PRESENTATION AND ANALYSIS

Presentation and Disclosure

For each major category of property, plant, and equipment, Section 3061 of the *CICA Handbook* requires disclosure of:

- the cost,

- accumulated amortization, including the amount of any writedowns, and

- the method and rate or period of amortization.

  In addition, disclosure is required of:

- the net book value of property, plant, and equipment (including natural resources) not currently being amortized because it is under construction or development or because it has been removed from service for an extended period of time, and

- the amortization expense recognized in the current period's income statement.[18]

11 Objective
Explain how property, plant, and equipment are reported and analysed.

The requirement for separate disclosure of both the cost and accumulated amortization provides financial statement readers with more information than if only the net book value is disclosed. As an example, consider two companies, each having capital assets with a carrying amount of $100,000. You determine that the first company's assets cost $1 million with accumulated amortization of $900,000 charged against them. The second company, on the other hand, has assets with a cost of $105,000, and accumulated amortization of $5,000. With the additional data, information is provided about the size of the original investment in property, plant, and equipment and their relative age. Information about amortization amounts and rates are important disclosures as this is generally the largest non-cash expense recognized by most enterprises.

IAS Note

IAS 16 requires a reconciliation of the opening and closing balances in the capital asset accounts, disclosure of their historical cost, and the change in any revaluation surplus.

General standards of financial statement presentation call for the disclosure of the **nature of and extent to which assets have been pledged as collateral** for liabilities.[19] As these long-lived assets are often used as security for debt instruments, such disclosures are common. Further, whenever a company has a **choice among alternative accounting policies**, the method chosen must be reported. Companies in the oil and gas industry, for example, must disclose whether they follow the full-cost or successful efforts method for their development costs. Additional guidance on financial reporting in this industry is provided by the CICA's *Accounting Guideline 16—Oil and Gas Accounting—Full Cost* and U.S. standards. These documents require disclosure about the manner of determining and disposing of costs related to development activities. Some of the most relevant information about natural resource companies is information about their estimated reserves, and whether they are proved or unproved in nature. This information is generally reported as supplementary disclosures outside the summary financial statements.

Digital Tool

Student Toolkit—Additional Disclosures
www.wiley.com/canada/kieso

Illustration 12-19 shows the disclosures underlying Canfor Corporation's property, plant, equipment, and timber of $1,424.2 million on the December 31, 2002 balance sheet, and amortization of $115.1 million reported on the 2002 income statement.

---

[18] *CICA Handbook*, Section 3061.38 to .40.

[19] *CICA Handbook*, Section 1400.14.

Illustration 12-19

Disclosures for Property, Plant, and Equipment

Canfor Corporation
Notes to the Consolidated Financial Statements
December 31, 2002

1. **Significant Accounting Policies**
   Property, Plant, Equipment and Timber
   Canfor capitalizes the costs of major replacements, extensions and improvements to plant and equipment, together with related interest incurred during the construction period on major projects.

   Assets are amortized over the following estimated productive lives:

Buildings	10 to 50 years
Mobile equipment	3 to 20 years
Pulp and kraft paper machinery and equipment	20 years
Sawmill machinery and equipment	5 to 12 years
Logging machinery and equipment	4 to 20 years
Logging roads and bridges	5 to 20 years
Other machinery and equipment	3 to 20 years

   Amortization of logging and manufacturing assets is calculated on a unit of production basis.

   Amortization of plant and equipment not employed in logging and manufacturing is calculated on a straight-line basis.

   Amortization of logging roads and timber is calculated on a basis related to the volume of timber harvested.

4. **Property, Plant, Equipment and Timber**

December 31, 2002 (millions of dollars)	Cost	Accumulated Amortization	Net Book Value
Land	$ 12.7	$ –	$ 12.7
Pulp and kraft paper mills	1,134.6	500.9	633.7
Wood products mills	520.0	319.2	200.8
Logging buildings and equipment	65.4	54.0	11.4
Logging roads and bridges	245.7	174.5	71.2
Other equipment and facilities	127.9	69.2	58.7
Timber	481.7	46.0	435.7
	$2,588.0	$1,163.8	$1,424.2

   Included in the above are assets under construction in the amount of $18.3 million (2001–$10.3 million), which are not being amortized.

Perspectives

Because property, plant, and equipment and their amortization are so significant on most companies' balance sheets and income statements, respectively, it is important to understand their nature, and to ensure management is generating an acceptable rate of return on the investment in these long-lived assets.

Amortization and Replacement of Assets

A common misconception about amortization is that it provides funds to replace capital assets. Amortization is similar to any other expense in that it reduces net income, but it differs in that **it does not involve a current cash outflow**.

To illustrate why amortization does not provide funds for replacing plant assets, assume that a business starts operating with plant assets of $500,000, with a useful life of five years. The company's balance sheet at the beginning of the period is:

Plant assets	$500,000	Owners' equity	$500,000

Now if we assume that the enterprise earns no revenue over the five years, the income statements are:

	Year 1	Year 2	Year 3	Year 4	Year 5
Revenue	$ –0–	$ –0–	$ –0–	$ –0–	$ –0–
Amortization	(100,000)	(100,000)	(100,000)	(100,000)	(100,000)
Loss	$(100,000)	$(100,000)	$(100,000)	$(100,000)	$(100,000)

The balance sheet at the end of the five years is:

Plant assets	–0–	Owners' equity	–0–

This extreme example illustrates that amortization in no way provides funds to replace assets. **Funds for the replacement of assets come from the revenues** (generated through use of the asset); without the revenues that generate receivables and ultimately cash, no income is earned and no cash inflow results. A separate decision must be made by management to set aside cash to accumulate asset replacement funds.

Analysis of Property, Plant, and Equipment

Investors need to be concerned about the efficiency with which management uses the long-lived assets they have invested in. Incurring capital costs provides operations with a certain capacity and often commits significant amounts of fixed costs far into the future.

What ratios might an investor use to get an indication of asset utilization? Assets may be analysed relative to activity (turnover) and profitability. How efficiently a company uses its assets to generate revenue is measured by the **asset turnover ratio**. This ratio is determined by dividing net revenue or sales by average total assets for the period. The resulting number is the dollars of revenue or sales produced by each dollar invested in assets. **For a given level of investment in assets, a company that generates more revenue is likely to be more profitable.** While this may not hold true if the profit margin on each dollar of revenue is lower than another company's, the asset turnover ratio is one of the key components of return on investment.

To illustrate, the following data are provided from Andrés Wines Ltd.'s financial statements for its year ended March 31, 2003.

ANDRÉS WINES LTD.
(in thousands)

Sales	$147,856
Total assets, March 31, 2003	132,006
Total assets, March 31, 2002	133,300
Net income	6,929

$$\text{Asset turnover} = \frac{\text{Net revenue}}{\text{Average total assets}}$$

$$= \frac{\$147,856}{\dfrac{\$132,006 + \$133,300}{2}}$$

$$= 1.11$$

Illustration 12-20

Asset Turnover Ratio

The asset turnover ratio shows that **Andrés Wines** generated $1.11 revenue for each dollar of assets in the year ended March 31, 2003.

Asset turnover ratios vary considerably among industries. For example, a power utility like **TransAlta Corporation** has a ratio of 0.23 times, and a grocery chain like **Loblaw Companies Limited** has a ratio of 2.18 times.

Use of the profit margin ratio in conjunction with the asset turnover ratio offers an interplay that leads to the rate of return earned on total assets. By using the Andrés Wines data shown above, the profit margin ratio and the rate of return on total assets are calculated as follows.

Illustration 12-21
Profit Margin

$$\text{Profit margin} = \frac{\text{Net income}}{\text{Net revenue}}$$

$$= \frac{\$6,929}{\$147,856}$$

$$= 4.7\%$$

$$\text{Rate of return on assets} = \text{Profit margin} \times \text{Asset turnover}$$

$$= 4.7\% \times 1.11$$

$$= 5.2\%$$

The profit margin indicates how much is left over from each sales dollar after all expenses are covered. In the Andrés Wines example, a profit margin of 5.2% indicates that 5.2 cents of profit remained from each dollar of revenue generated. By combining the profit margin with the asset turnover, it is possible to determine the rate of return on assets for the period. This makes intuitive sense. All else being equal, the more revenue generated per dollar invested in assets, the better off the company. The more of each sales dollar that is profit, the better off the company should be. Combined, the ratio provides a measure of the profitability of the company's investment in assets. To the extent that long-lived assets make up a significant portion of total assets, fixed asset management has a definite effect on profitability.

The rate of return on assets (ROA) can be directly calculated by dividing net income by average total assets.[20] By using Andrés Wines Ltd. data, the ratio is calculated as follows.

Illustration 12-22
Rate of Return on Assets

$$\text{Rate of return on assets} = \frac{\text{Net income}}{\text{Average total assets}}$$

$$= \frac{\$6,929}{\dfrac{\$132,006 + \$133,300}{2}}$$

$$= 5.2\%$$

The 5.2% rate of return calculated in this manner is identical to the 5.2% rate calculated by multiplying the profit margin by the asset turnover. The rate of return on assets is a good measure of profitability because it combines the effects of cost control (profit margin) and asset management (asset turnover).

Care must be taken in interpreting the numbers, however. A manager who is interested in reporting a high return on assets ratio can achieve this in the short run by not investing in new plant and equipment and by holding back on expenditures such as those for research and development and employee training—decisions that will result in lower long-term corporate value. In the short run, the result is a higher return on investment because the net income number (the numerator) will be higher and the total asset number (the denominator) lower.

---

[20] A more sophisticated calculation adds back the after-tax interest expense to net income so that the results aren't skewed by how the assets are financed. The ratio can then be used more legitimately for inter-company comparisons.

Summary of Learning Objectives

1. **Explain the concept of amortization.**

   Amortization is the accounting process of allocating the cost of long-lived assets to expense in a systematic and rational manner to those periods expected to benefit from the use of the asset. The objective is matching, not adjusting assets to their fair values. Amortization is a generic term. The allocation of the cost of intangible capital assets is termed "amortization" as well, while that of property, plant, and equipment is usually referred to as "depreciation." The allocation of capitalized costs of natural resources is termed "depletion."

2. **Identify and describe the factors that must be considered when determining amortization charges.**

   Three factors involved in determining amortization expense are: (1) the amount to be amortized (amortizable amount), (2) the estimated useful life, and (3) the pattern and method of cost allocation to be used.

3. **Determine amortization charges using the activity, straight-line, and decreasing charge methods and compare the methods.**

   The activity method assumes that the benefits provided by the asset are a function of use or productivity instead of the passage of time. The asset's life is considered in terms of either the output it provides or an input measure such as the number of hours it works. The amortization charge per unit of activity (cost less residual value divided by estimated total units of output or input) is determined and multiplied by the units of activity produced or consumed in a period to derive amortization expense for the period. The straight-line method assumes that the provision of asset benefits is a function of time. As such, cost less residual value is divided by the useful economic life to determine amortization expense per period. This method is widely used in practice because of its simplicity. The straight-line procedure is the most conceptually appropriate when the decline in usefulness is constant from period to period. The decreasing charge method provides for a higher amortization charge in the early years and lower charges in later periods. For this method, a constant rate (e.g., double the straight-line rate) is multiplied by the net book value (cost less accumulated amortization) at the start of the period to determine each period's amortization expense. The main justification for this approach is that the asset provides more benefits in the earlier periods.

4. **Explain the accounting procedures for depletion of natural resources.**

   After the depletion base has been established through accounting decisions related to the acquisition, exploration, and development costs of natural resources, these costs are allocated to the natural resources removed. Depletion is normally calculated on the units of production method. In this approach, the natural resource's total cost less residual value is divided by the number of units estimated to be in the resource deposit, to obtain a cost per unit of product. The cost per unit is multiplied by the number of units withdrawn in the period to calculate depletion expense. Depletion expense is usually added to the cost of the inventory of product removed.

5. **Explain special amortization methods.**

   Two special depreciation methods are the group and composite methods, and hybrid or combination methods. The term "group" refers to a collection of assets that are similar in nature, while "composite" refers to a collection of assets that are dissimilar in nature. The group and composite methods develop one average rate of amortization for all the assets involved and apply this rate as if they were a single asset. The hybrid or combination methods develop an amortization expense that is based on two or more approaches and that suits the specific circumstances of the assets involved.

Digital Tool

Glossary

www.wiley.com/canada/kieso

KEY TERMS

accelerated amortization, 615

activity method, 614

amortization, 611

asset turnover ratio, 635

components approach, 620

composite amortization rate, 620

composite method, 619

declining-balance method, 616

decreasing charge methods, 615

depletion, 611

depreciation, 611

double-declining-balance method, 616

fair value, 627

group method, 619

impairment, 627

inadequacy, 612

liquidating dividend, 619

obsolescence, 613

profit margin ratio, 635

rate of return on assets (ROA), 636

recoverability test, 627

residual value, 611

salvage value, 611

sinking fund method, 617

straight-line method, 615

sum-of-the-years'-digits method, 616

supersession, 612

useful life, 612

6. Identify and understand reasons why amortization methods are selected.

Various amortization methods are generally acceptable. The accountant must exercise judgement when selecting and implementing the method that is most appropriate for the circumstances. Rational matching, tax reporting, simplicity, perceived economic consequences, and impact on ratios are factors that influence such judgements.

7. Explain the accounting procedures for a change in the amortization rate.

Because all the variables in determining amortization are estimates with the exception, perhaps, of the asset's original cost, it is common for a change in those estimates to result in a change in the depreciation rate. When this occurs, there is no retroactive change and no catch-up adjustment. The change is accounted for in the current and future periods.

8. Explain the accounting issues related to asset impairment.

The Canadian standards for asset impairments have recently been made consistent with those of the FASB. The process to determine an impairment loss is as follows: (1) Review events and changes in circumstances for possible impairment. (2) If events or changes suggest impairment, determine if the sum of the undiscounted expected future net cash flows from the long-lived asset is less than the asset's carrying amount. (3) If less, determine the impairment loss by measuring the difference between the asset's carrying amount and its fair value. For assets held for use, the reduced carrying amount of the long-lived asset is considered its new cost basis and no subsequent increase in value is recognized.

9. Explain the accounting standards for long-lived assets to be disposed of.

Assets to be disposed of through sale are no longer amortized but are remeasured to their fair value less selling costs at each balance sheet date. Recoveries in value may be recognized to the extent of previous losses. Held for sale items of property, plant, and equipment are separately reported in long-term assets, unless sold before the financial statements are prepared. In this case, if they otherwise meet the definition of current assets, they are reported in this category.

Assets to be disposed of other than by sale continue to be classified as held for use, and are amortized until disposed of. The two-step impairment test is applied and no subsequent increases in value are permitted. Held for use assets are reported in property, plant, and equipment.

10. Describe the accounting treatment for the disposal of property, plant, and equipment.

If long-term assets are held and used, amortization continues up to the date of disposition, and then all accounts related to the retired asset are removed from the books. Gains and losses from the disposal of plant assets are shown on the income statement in income before discontinued operations, unless the conditions for reporting as a discontinued operation are met. Gains or losses on involuntary conversions may meet the definition of an extraordinary item. For property, plant, and equipment donated to an organization outside the reporting entity, the donation should be reported at its fair value with a gain or loss reported.

11. Explain how property, plant, and equipment are reported and analysed.

Wherever there is a choice of accounting methods, the accounting methods applied are required to be reported. Any liability secured by property, plant, equipment, and natural resources should be disclosed. Both the assets' carrying value and accumulated amortization are reported. Companies engaged in significant oil and gas producing activities must provide special additional disclosures about these activities. Analysis may be performed to evaluate the efficiency of use of a company's investment in assets through the calculation and interpretation of the asset turnover rate, the profit margin, and the rate of return on assets.

Appendix 12A

Amortization and Income Tax

The Capital Cost Allowance Method

For the most part, issues related to the calculation of income taxes are not discussed in a financial accounting course. However, because the concepts of tax amortization or tax depreciation are similar to those of amortization for financial reporting purposes and because the tax method is sometimes adopted for book purposes, an overview of this subject is presented.

The **capital cost allowance method** is used **to determine amortization in calculating taxable income and the tax value of assets by Canadian businesses regardless of the method used for financial reporting purposes**. Because companies use this method for tax purposes, some—particularly small businesses—also use it for financial reporting, judging that the benefits of keeping two sets of records, one for financial reporting and one for tax purposes, are less than the costs involved.[21] Such an action, while expedient, may not provide a rational allocation of costs in the financial reports. Therefore, many companies keep a record of capital cost allowance for tax purposes and use another method to determine amortization for their financial statements.

The mechanics of this method are similar to the declining-balance method covered in the chapter except that:

1. Instead of being labelled amortization or depreciation expense, it is called **capital cost allowance (CCA)** in tax returns.

2. The Income Tax Act (Income Tax Regulations, Schedule II) specifies the rate to be used for an asset class. This rate is called the capital cost allowance (CCA) rate. The Income Tax Act identifies several different classes of assets and the maximum CCA rate for each class. Examination of the definition of each asset class and the examples given in the Act is necessary to determine the class into which a particular asset falls. Illustration 12A-1 provides examples of various CCA classes, the maximum rate attached to the class, and the type of assets included in each.

 Objective

Describe the income tax method of determining capital cost allowance.

---

[21] The widespread availability of accounting software, capable of maintaining detailed records for property, plant, and equipment, the related amortization expense, and accumulated amortization under a variety of methods has significantly reduced the cost of record keeping and the possibility for errors.

Class	Rate	Examples of assets included in the class
1	4%	buildings, including component parts such as plumbing, elevators, sprinkler systems, etc.
4	6%	railway, tramway, or trolley bus system
6	10%	frame, log, stucco on frame, galvanized iron or corrugated metal building; greenhouse; oil or water storage tank
8	20%	manufacturing or processing machinery or equipment not included in other specified classes
10	30%	automotive equipment, general purpose electronic data processing equipment
16	40%	taxicab, coin-operated video game
33	15%	timber resource property
42	12%	fibre optic cable

Source: David M. Sherman, Ed., 2003 *Practitioner's Income Tax Act*, 24th edition, Thompson Canada Limited, 2003.

3. CCA is determined separately for each asset class and can be claimed only on year-end amounts in each class. Assuming no net additions (purchases less disposals, if any) to a class during a year, the maximum CCA allowed is the undepreciated capital cost (UCC) at year end multiplied by the CCA rate for the class. In a year when there is a net addition (regardless of when it occurs), the maximum CCA on the net addition is one-half of the allowed CCA rate multiplied by the amount of the net addition. This is usually referred to as the half-year rule. The CCA for the net addition plus the CCA on the remaining UCC is the total CCA for the asset class. If there is only one asset in a class, the maximum CCA allowed in the acquisition year is the acquisition cost multiplied by one-half of the CCA rate, even if the asset was purchased one week before year end. No CCA is allowed in the year of disposal for this single asset, even if it is sold just before year end.

4. The government, through the Income Tax Act, requires that the benefits received by a company from government grants and investment tax credits on the acquisition of a capital asset reduce the cost basis of the capital asset acquired for tax purposes. For investment tax credits, the capital cost of the asset and the undepreciated capital cost (UCC) of the class of asset are reduced **in the taxation year following the year of acquisition**.

5. CCA can be taken even if it results in an undepreciated capital cost (UCC) that is less than the estimated residual value.

6. It is not required that the maximum rate, or that any CCA, be taken in a given year, although that would be the normal case as long as a company had taxable income. If less than the maximum CCA is taken in one year, the remainder cannot be added to the amount claimed in a subsequent year. In every year, the maximum that can be claimed is limited to the UCC times the specified capital cost allowance rate.

To illustrate amortization calculations under the CCA system, assume the following facts for a company's March 28, 2004 acquisition of manufacturing equipment, the only asset in the CCA class.

Cost of equipment	$500,000	CCA class	Class 8
Estimated useful life	10 years	CCA rate for Class 8	20%
Estimated residual value	$30,000		

Illustration 12A-2 shows the calculations necessary to determine the CCA for the first three years and the UCC at the end of each of the three years.[22]

---

[22] CCA is subject to rules set by government legislation and, as such, is subject to change from time to time. Furthermore, various provincial governments can have different rules with regard to determining CCA for purposes of calculating the income on which provincial taxes are based. The examples in this chapter are based on the Federal Income Tax Act for 2003.

Class 8—20%	CCA	UCC
January 1, 2004		0
Additions during 2004		
Cost of new asset acquisition		$500,000
Disposals during 2004		0
CCA 2004: $500,000 × ½ × 20%	$50,000	(50,000)
December 31, 2004		**$450,000**
Additions less disposals, 2005		0
		$450,000
CCA, 2005: $450,000 × 20%	$90,000	(90,000)
December 31, 2005		**$360,000**
Additions less disposals, 2006		0
		$360,000
CCA, 2006: $360,000 × 20%	$72,000	(72,000)
December 31, 2006		**$288,000**

Illustration **12A-2**

CCA Schedule for Equipment

The **undepreciated capital cost (UCC)** at any point in time is known as the capital asset's **tax value**. Note that the capital asset's carrying amount (or net book value) on the balance sheet will differ from its tax value for any method of amortization for financial reporting used other than the tax method. The significance of this difference is explained in Chapter 19.

Illustration 12A-3 is a continuation of Illustration 12A-2. It incorporates the following complexities.

1. In 2007, the company bought another Class 8 asset for $700,000.

2. In 2008, the company sold the equipment purchased in 2004 for $300,000.

3. In 2009, the company sold the remaining Class 8 asset for $500,000. This resulted in no assets remaining in Class 8.

International Insight

German companies amortize their property, plant, and equipment at a much faster rate than Canadian companies because German tax laws permit accelerated amortization of up to triple the straight-line rate. Canadian tax rates, for the most part, are designed to be double the straight-line rate.

Class 8—20%	CCA	UCC
December 31, 2006		**$288,000**
Additions less disposals, 2007		
Cost of new asset		700,000
		$988,000
CCA, 2007		
$288,000 × 20% =	$57,600	
$700,000 × 1/2 × 20% =	70,000	$127,600	(127,600)
December 31, 2007		**$860,400**
Additions less disposals, 2008		
Manufacturing equipment purchased in 2004 (lesser of original cost of $500,000 and proceeds of disposal of $300,000)		(300,000)
		$560,400
CCA, 2008: $560,400 × 20% =	$112,080	(112,080)
December 31, 2008		**$448,320**
Additions less disposals, 2009		
2007 asset acquisition (lesser of original cost of $700,000 and proceeds of disposal of $500,000)		(500,000)
		($51,680)
Recaptured CCA, 2009	($51,680)	51,680
December 31, 2009		**0**

Illustration **12A-3**

CCA Schedule for Class 8

Additions to Asset Class

The purchase of another Class 8 asset in 2007 resulted in a **net addition** of $700,000 to the undepreciated capital cost at the end of 2007. Consequently, the balance of the UCC at the end of 2007 prior to determining CCA for the year is made up of this $700,000 plus the $288,000 UCC of the original equipment. The capital cost allowance for 2007 is, therefore, 20% of $288,000 ($57,600) plus one-half of 20% of the net addition of $700,000 ($70,000) for a total of $127,600.

If a government grant of $35,000 was received in 2007 to help finance the acquisition of this asset, the addition in 2007 is reported net of the government grant, i.e., at $700,000 − $35,000 = $665,000. If the 2007 acquisition was eligible instead for an investment tax credit (ITC) of $35,000, the tax legislation specifies that the ITC should reduce the asset's capital cost and the UCC of the class of assets **in the year following** the year of acquisition.[23] Assuming the Class 8 asset acquired in 2007 in Illustration 12A-3 was eligible for a $35,000 ITC, the $700,000 addition is recognized in 2007, and the UCC is reduced by the $35,000 ITC in 2008 along with the $300,000 proceeds on the original manufacturing equipment. The CCA claimed in 2008 is reduced accordingly.

Retirements from an Asset Class, Continuation of Class

While the CCA class is increased by the cost of additions, it is usually reduced **by the proceeds on the asset's disposal**, not its cost. However, if the proceeds on disposal are greater than the asset's original capital cost, the class is reduced by the cost only. There is a good reason for this. If the proceeds on disposal are greater than the original cost, there has been a capital gain on the disposal. Capital gains are taxed separately from ordinary business income in the tax system, thus the portion that is capital gain must be identified as such. This leaves only the cost to be deducted from the CCA class. It is not common for depreciable assets to be sold at amounts in excess of their cost, but when this does occur, it is important to separate out the portion that is a capital gain.

In 2008, the original manufacturing equipment is sold for $300,000. Since this is less than its $500,000 capital cost, there is no capital gain on disposal. Therefore, Class 8 is reduced by the proceeds on disposal of $300,000, and the CCA for the year is calculated on the remaining balance in the class.

Retirements from an Asset Class, Elimination of Class

When disposing of an asset eliminates an asset class, either because there are no more assets remaining in the class or because the disposal results in the elimination of the UCC balance of the class, the following may result.

1. A recapture of capital cost allowance, with or without a capital gain.

2. A terminal loss, with or without a capital gain. This occurs only when the last asset in the class is disposed of and an undepreciated capital cost balance still exists in the class after deducting the appropriate amount on the asset disposal.

The amount of proceeds, the asset's original cost, and the balance of the undepreciated capital cost for the class must be examined to determine which of these results occurs.

A **recapture** of capital cost allowance occurs when, after deducting the appropriate amount from the class on disposal of an asset, a negative amount is left as the UCC balance. The negative balance is the amount of CCA that must be recaptured and included in

---

[23] The rationale is that the ITC is not calculated until after the company's year end, when the tax return is completed and filed.

the calculation of taxable income in the year, subject to income tax at the normal rates. In effect, events have shown that too much CCA was deducted throughout the lives of the assets, and the taxing of the recaptured capital cost allowance adjusts for this. This is what occurred in 2009. When the proceeds of disposal (being less than the original cost of the asset) were deducted from the UCC, the UCC became negative. The excess of $51,680 is included in taxable income in 2009.

As indicated above, if an asset is sold for more than its cost, a *capital gain* results. This may occur whether or not the class is eliminated. For tax purposes, a capital gain is treated differently from a recapture of capital cost allowance. Essentially, the **taxable** capital gain (i.e., the amount subject to tax) is only a portion of the capital gain as defined above.[24] The taxable capital gain is included with other taxable income.

If the Class 8 asset purchased in 2007 had been sold in 2009 for $750,000, a capital gain and a recapture of capital cost allowance would have resulted. The capital gain would be $50,000, but only 50% or $25,000 would be the taxable capital gain. In this case, Class 8 would be reduced by $700,000 and the recapture would be $251,680 ($700,000 less the $448,320 UCC).

A *terminal loss* occurs when a positive balance remains in the class after the appropriate reduction is made to the CCA class from the disposal of the last asset. This remaining balance is a terminal loss that is deductible in full when calculating taxable income for the period. If the remaining equipment had been sold in 2009 for $300,000, a terminal loss of $148,320 would have resulted (the UCC of $448,320 less the $300,000 proceeds).

This example illustrating the basic calculations of capital gains, taxable capital gains, recaptured capital cost allowance, and terminal losses has necessarily been oversimplified. In essence, the tax rate on taxable capital gains is specified by tax law, which may change from time to time and have implications in terms of other considerations (e.g., refundable dividend tax on hand). Similarly, the tax rate applicable to recaptured CCA is subject to the particular circumstances of the nature of taxable income being reported, of which the recaptured amount is a component. These and other technical and definitional aspects are beyond the scope of this text. The reader is warned that specialist knowledge regarding tax laws is often required to determine income taxes payable.

International Insight

In Switzerland, amortization in the financial statements conforms to that on the tax returns. As a consequence, companies may amortize as much as 80% of the cost of assets in the first year.

Summary of Learning Objective for Appendix 12A

Digital Tool

Glossary

www.wiley.com/canada/kieso

12. Describe the income tax method of determining capital cost allowance.

Capital cost allowance is the term used for amortization when calculating taxable income in income tax returns. The CCA method mechanics are similar to those of the declining-balance method except that rates are specified for asset classes and the amount claimed is based on year-end balances. The half-year rule is applied to net additions in the year whereby only 50% of the normal rate is permitted. For an asset class, retirements are accounted for under specific rules that govern the determination of taxable income. Capital gains will occur if the proceeds on disposal exceed the asset's original cost. When an asset class is eliminated, a terminal loss or recapture of capital cost allowance can occur. When a CCA class ends in a negative balance, a recapture of CCA occurs.

KEY TERMS

capital cost allowance (CCA), 639
capital cost allowance method, 639
capital gain, 643
half-year rule, 640
net addition, 642
recapture, 642
tax value, 641
terminal loss, 643
undepreciated capital cost (UCC), 641

---

[24] The percentage of the capital gain that is taxable has varied in recent years. In 2003, the inclusion rate—the portion taxable—was 50%.

Note: All asterisked assignment material relates to the appendix to the chapter.

Brief Exercises

BE12-1   Castle Corporation purchased a truck at the beginning of 2005 for $42,000. The truck is estimated to have a residual value of $2,000 and a useful life of 250,000 km. It was driven 38,000 km in 2005 and 52,000 km in 2006. Calculate amortization expense for 2005 and 2006.

BE12-2   Cheetah Ltd. purchased machinery on January 1, 2005 for $60,000. The machinery is estimated to have a residual value of $6,000 after a useful life of eight years. (a) Calculate 2005 amortization expense using the straight-line method. (b) Calculate 2005 amortization expense using the straight-line method assuming the machinery was purchased on September 1, 2005.

BE12-3   Use the information for Cheetah Ltd. given in BE12-2. (a) Calculate 2005 amortization expense using the sum-of-the-years'-digits method. (b) Calculate 2005 amortization expense using the sum-of-the-years'-digits method assuming the machinery was purchased on April 1, 2005.

BE12-4   Use the information for Cheetah Ltd given in BE12-2. (a) Calculate 2005 amortization expense using the double-declining-balance method. (b) Calculate 2005 amortization expense using the double-declining-balance method assuming the machinery was purchased on October 1, 2005.

BE12-5   Garfield Corp. purchased a machine on July 1, 2004 for $25,000. Garfield paid $200 in title fees and a legal fee of $125 related to the machine. In addition, Garfield paid $500 shipping charges for delivery, and $475 was paid to a local contractor to build and wire a platform for the machine on the plant floor. The machine has an estimated useful life of six years with a residual value of $3,000. Determine the amortization base of Garfield's new machine. Garfield uses straight-line amortization.

BE12-6   Khan Corporation acquires a coal mine at a cost of $400,000. Capitalized development costs total $100,000. After the mine is exhausted, $75,000 will be spent to restore the property, after which it can be sold for $160,000. Khan estimates that 4,000 tonnes of coal can be extracted. If 700 tonnes are extracted the first year, prepare the journal entry to record depletion.

BE12-7   Battlesport Inc. owns the following assets.

Asset	Cost	Residual	Estimated Useful Life
A	$70,000	$17,000	10 years
B	50,000	10,000	15 years
C	82,000	14,000	12 years

Calculate the composite amortization rate and the composite life of Battlesport's assets.

BE12-8   Mystic Limited purchased a computer for $7,000 on January 1, 2004. Straight-line amortization is used, based on a five-year life and a $1,000 residual value. In 2006, the estimates are revised. Mystic now feels the computer will be used until December 31, 2007, when it can be sold for $500. Calculate the 2006 amortization.

BE12-9   Dinoland Corp. owns machinery that cost $900,000 and has accumulated amortization of $360,000. The expected future net cash flows from the use of the asset are expected to be $500,000. The equipment's fair value is $400,000. Prepare the journal entry, if any, to record the impairment loss.

BE12-10   Use the information for Dinoland Corp. given in BE12-9. By the end of the following year, the machinery's fair value has increased to $490,000. Assuming the machinery continues to be used in production, prepare the journal entry required, if any, to record the increase in its fair value.

BE12-11   Simcoe City Corporation owns machinery that cost $20,000 when purchased on January 1, 2002. Amortization has been recorded at a rate of $3,000 per year, resulting in a balance in accumulated amortization of $9,000 at December 31, 2004. The machinery is sold on September 1, 2005 for $10,500. Prepare journal entries to (a) update amortization for 2005 and (b) record the sale.

BE12-12   Use the information presented for Simcoe City Corporation in BE12-11, but assume the machinery is sold for $5,200 instead of $10,500. Prepare journal entries to (a) update amortization for 2005 and (b) record the sale.

BE12-13 In its 2002 annual report, CP Ships Limited reports beginning-of-the-year total assets of $1,923 million (U.S.), end-of-the-year total assets of $2,487 million (U.S.), total revenue of $2,687 million (U.S.), and net income of $52 million (U.S.). (a) Calculate CP Ship's asset turnover ratio. (b) Calculate CP Ship's profit margin. (c) Calculate CP Ship's rate of return on assets (1) using asset turnover and profit margin and (2) using net income.

*BE12-14 Timecap Limited purchased an asset at a cost of $40,000 on March 1, 2005. The asset has a useful life of eight years and an estimated residual value of $4,000. For tax purposes, the asset belongs in CCA Class 8, with a rate of 20%. Calculate the CCA for each year 2005 to 2008, assuming this is the only asset in Class 8.

Exercises

E12-1 (Match Amortization Method with Assets) The following assets have been acquired by various companies over the past year:

1. boardroom table and chairs for the corporate head office
2. dental equipment in a new dental clinic
3. long-haul trucks for the trucking business
4. weight and aerobic equipment in a new health club facility
5. classroom computers in a new community college

Instructions
For each long-lived asset listed above:

(a) identify the factors to consider in establishing the useful life of the asset and

(b) recommend the pattern of amortization that most closely represents the pattern of economic benefits received by the entity owning the asset, defending your position.

E12-2 (Terminology, Calculations—SL, DDB) Shih-Shan Corp. acquired a property on September 15, 2004 for $235,000, paying $2,000 in transfer tax and a $1,500 real estate fee. Based on the provincial assessment information, 75% of the property's value was related to the building and 25% to the land. It is estimated that the building, with proper maintenance, will last for 35 years, at which time it will be torn down. Shih-Shan, however, expects to use it for 10 years, at which time it would no longer suit the company's purposes. The company should be able to sell the property for $95,000 at that time, with $40,000 attributable to the land.

Instructions
Assume a December 31 year end. Identify:

(a) the building's cost

(b) the building's amortizable amount

(c) the building's useful life

(d) amortization expense for 2004, assuming the straight-line method

(e) amortization expense for 2005, assuming the double-declining-balance method and

(f) the building's carrying amount at December 31, 2005, assuming the double-declining-balance method.

E12-3 (Amortization Calculations—SL, DDB) Deluxe Company Ltd. purchases equipment on January 1, 2005 at a cost of $469,000. The asset is expected to have a service life of 12 years and a residual value of $40,000.

Interactive Homework

Instructions

(a) Calculate the amount of amortization for each of 2005, 2006, and 2007 using the straight-line amortization method.

(b) Calculate the amount of amortization for each of 2005, 2006, and 2007 using the double-declining-balance method. (In performing your calculations, round constant percentage to the nearest one-hundredth and round answers to the nearest dollar.)

E12-4 (Amortization Conceptual Understanding) Chesley Company Ltd. acquired a plant asset at the beginning of Year 1. The asset has an estimated service life of five years. An employee has prepared amortization schedules for this asset using two different methods to compare the results of using one method with the results of using the other. You are to assume that the following schedules have been correctly prepared for this asset using (1) the straight-line method and

(2) the double-declining-balance method.

Year	Straight-line	Double-declining-Balance
1	$15,000	$30,000
2	15,000	18,000
3	15,000	10,800
4	15,000	1,200
5	15,000	0
Total	$60,000	$60,000

Instructions

Answer the following questions.

(a) What is the cost of the asset being amortized?

(b) What amount, if any, was used in the amortization calculations for the residual value for this asset?

(c) Which method will produce the higher net income in Year 1?

(d) Which method will produce the higher charge to income in Year 4?

(e) Which method will produce the higher book value for the asset at the end of Year 3?

(f) Which method will produce the higher cash flow in Year 1? In Year 4?

(g) If the asset is sold at the end of Year 3, which method would yield the higher gain (or lower loss) on disposal of the asset?

E12-5   (Amortization Calculations—SL, DDB; Partial Periods)   Judds Corporation purchased a new plant asset on April 1, 2005 at a cost of $711,000. It was estimated to have a service life of 20 years and a residual value of $60,000. Judds' accounting period is the calendar year.

Interactive Homework Instructions

(a) Calculate the amortization for this asset for 2005 and 2006 using the straight-line method.

(b) Calculate the amortization for this asset for 2005 and 2006 using the double-declining-balance method.

E12-6   (Amortization Calculations—Four Methods; Partial Periods)   Parish Corporation purchased a new machine for its assembly process on August 1, 2005. The cost of this machine was $117,900. The company estimated that the machine would have a trade-in value of $12,900 at the end of its service life. Its useful life was estimated to be five years and its working hours were estimated to be 21,000 hours. Parish's year end is December 31.

Instructions

Calculate the amortization expense under the following methods:

(a) straight-line amortization for 2005,

(b) activity method for 2005, assuming that machine usage was 800 hours,

(c) double-declining-balance for 2006, and

*(d) capital cost allowance for 2005 and 2006 using a CCA rate of 25%.

E12-7   (Amortization Calculations—Five Methods)   Seceda Furnace Corp. purchased machinery for $315,000 on May 1, 2004. It is estimated that it will have a useful life of 10 years, residual value of $15,000, production of 240,000 units, and working hours of 25,000. During 2005, Seceda Corp. uses the machinery for 2,650 hours and the machinery produces 25,500 units.

Interactive Homework

Instructions

From the information given, calculate the amortization charge for 2005 under each of the following methods, assuming Seceda has a December 31 year end. (Round to three decimal places.)

(a) Straight-line

(b) Units-of-output

(c) Working hours

(d) Declining balance, using a 20% rate

(e) Sum-of-the-years'-digits

E12-8 **(Different Methods of Amortization)** Jackson Industries Ltd. presents you with the following information.

Description	Date Purchased	Cost	Residual Value	Life in Years	Amortization Method	Accumulated Amortization to 12/31/04	Amortization for 2005
Machine A	2/12/03	$142,500	$16,000	10	(a)	$39,900	(b)
Machine B	8/15/02	(c)	21,000	5	SL	29,000	(d)
Machine C	7/21/01	75,400	23,500	8	DDB	(e)	(f)

Instructions

Complete the table for the year ended December 31, 2005. The company amortizes all assets for a half year in the year of acquisition and the year of disposal.

E12-9 **(Amortization for Fractional Periods)** On March 10, 2006, Lotus Limited sold equipment that it purchased for $192,000 on August 20, 1999. It was originally estimated that the equipment would have a life of 12 years and a residual value of $16,800 at the end of that time, and amortization has been calculated on that basis. The company uses the straight-line method of amortization.

Instructions

(a) Calculate the amortization charge on this equipment for 1999, for 2006, and the total charge for the period from 2000 to 2005, inclusive, under each of the six following assumptions with respect to partial periods.

1. Amortization is calculated for the exact period of time during which the asset is owned. (Use 365 days for base.)

2. Amortization is calculated for the full year on the January 1 balance in the asset account.

3. Amortization is calculated for the full year on the December 31 balance in the asset account.

4. Amortization for one-half year is charged on plant assets acquired or disposed of during the year.

5. Amortization is calculated on additions from the beginning of the month following acquisition and on disposals to the beginning of the month following disposal.

6. Amortization is calculated for a full period on all assets in use for over one-half year, and no amortization is charged on assets in use for less than one-half year. (Use 365 days for base.)

(b) Briefly evaluate the methods above, considering them from the point of view of basic accounting theory as well as simplicity of application.

E12-10 **(Depletion Calculations—Timber)** Stanislaw Timber Inc. owns 9,000 ha of timberland purchased in 1993 at a cost of $1,400 per hectare. At the time of purchase the land without the timber was valued at $400 per hectare. In 1994, Stanislaw built fire lanes and roads, with a life of 30 years, at a cost of $84,000 and separately capitalized these costs. Every year Stanislaw sprays to prevent disease at a cost of $3,000 per year and spends $7,000 to maintain the fire lanes and roads. During 1995, Stanislaw selectively logged and sold 700,000 m³ of the estimated 3.5 million m³ of timber. In 1996, Stanislaw planted new seedlings to replace the trees cut at a cost of $100,000.

Interactive Homework

Instructions

(a) Determine the depletion charge and the cost of timber sold related to depletion for 1995.

(b) Stanislaw has not logged since 1995. If Stanislaw logged and sold 900,000 m³ of timber in 2006, when the timber cruise (appraiser) estimated a total resource of 5 million m³, determine the cost of timber sold related to depletion for 2006.

E12-11 **(Depletion Calculations—Oil)** Sunglee Drilling Limited leases property on which oil has been discovered. Wells on this property produced 18,000 barrels of oil during the current year that sold at an average $15 per barrel. Total oil resources of this property are estimated to be 250,000 barrels.

The lease provided for an outright payment of $500,000 to the lessor before drilling commenced and an annual rental of $31,500. Development costs of $625,000 were incurred before any oil was produced, and Sunglee follows a policy of capitalizing these preproduction costs. A premium of 5% of the sales price of every barrel of oil removed is to be paid annually to the lessor. In addition, the lessee is to clean up all the waste and debris from drilling and to bear the costs of reconditioning the land for farming when the wells are abandoned. It is estimated that the present value of the obligations for the existing wells is $30,000.

Instructions

From the information given, provide the journal entry made by Sunglee Drilling Limited to record depletion for the current year.

E12-12 (Depletion Calculations—Timber)   Forda Lumber Inc. owns a 7,000 ha timber tract purchased in 1998 at a cost of $1,300 per hectare. At the time of purchase the land was estimated to have a value of $300 per hectare without the timber. Forda Lumber Inc. has not logged this tract since it was purchased. In 2005, Forda had the timber cruised (appraised). The cruise (appraiser) estimated that each hectare contained 8,000 m³ of timber. In 2005, Forda built 10 km of roads at a cost of $7,840 per km. After the roads were completed, Forda logged and sold 3,500 trees containing 850,000 m³.

Instructions

(a) Determine the cost of timber sold related to depletion for 2005.

(b) If Forda amortizes the logging roads based on timber cut, determine the amortization expense for 2005.

(c) If Forda plants five seedlings at a cost of $4 per seedling for each tree cut, how should Forda treat the reforestation costs?

E12-13 (Depletion Calculations—Mining)   Belinda Mining Corp. purchased a mining property on February 1, 2005 at a cost of $1,190,000. The company estimated that a total of 60,000 tonnes of mineral was available for mining. After the natural resource has been removed, the company is required to restore the property to its previous state because of strict environmental protection laws, and it estimates the present value of this restoration obligation at $90,000 based on mining to date. Belinda believes it will be able to sell the property afterwards for $100,000. Developmental costs of $200,000 were incurred before Belinda was able to extract any of the ore. Belinda capitalizes these costs as part of the natural resource. In 2005, 30,000 tonnes were removed, and 22,000 tonnes were sold.

In 2006, a geological survey increased the estimate of the volume of total ore in the mine to 100,000 tonnes. Revised estimates also put the present value of land reclamation and restoration costs for the existing mine at $150,000. In 2006, 25,000 tonnes were mined and 27,000 tonnes sold.

Instructions
(round to two decimal places)

(a) Calculate the following information for 2005: (1) depletion cost per tonne mined in 2005; (2) total depletion cost in cost of goods sold in 2005.

(b) Assume Belinda uses the FIFO cost flow assumption. Calculate the following information for 2006: (1) depletion cost per tonne mined in 2006; (2) total depletion cost in cost of goods sold in 2006.

E12-14 (Amortization Calculation—Replacement, Trade-in)   Zidek Corporation bought a machine on June 1, 2002 for $31,000, f.o.b. the place of manufacture. Freight costs were $200, and $500 was spent to install it. The machine's useful life was estimated at 10 years, with a residual value of $2,500.

On June 1, 2003, a part costing $1,980, designed to reduce the machine's operating costs, was added to the machine. On June 1, 2006, the company bought a new machine with a larger capacity for $35,000 delivered. A trade-in value was received on the old machine equal to its fair market value of $20,000. Removing the old machine from the plant cost $75, and installing the new one cost $1,500. It was estimated that the new machine would have a useful life of 10 years, with a residual value of $4,000.

Instructions
Assuming that amortization is calculated on the straight-line basis, determine the amount of gain or loss on the disposal of the first machine on June 1, 2006, and the amount of amortization that should be provided during the company's fiscal year, which begins on June 1, 2006.

Interactive
Homework

E12-15 (Composite Amortization)   Presented below is information related to Nguyen Manufacturing Corporation.

Asset	Cost	Estimated Residual	Estimated Life (in years)
A	$25,500	$4,500	8
B	36,600	2,800	10
C	46,000	3,200	7
D	19,700	500	6
E	13,500	1,000	9

Instructions

(a) Calculate the rate of amortization per year to be applied to the plant assets under the composite method, and the composite life of the plant assets.

(b) Prepare the adjusting entry necessary at year end to record amortization for a year.

(c) Prepare the entry to record the sale of asset D for cash of $1,100. It was used for six years, and amortization was entered under the composite method.

E12-16 **(Amortization—Change in Estimate)** Machinery purchased for $60,000 by Cheng Corp. in 2001 was originally estimated to have an eight-year life with a residual value of $4,000. Amortization has been entered for five years on this basis. In 2006, it is determined that the total estimated life (including 2006) should have been 10 years with a residual value of $4,500 at the end of that time. Assume straight-line amortization.

Instructions

(a) Prepare the entry required to correct the prior years' amortization, if any.

(b) Prepare the entry to record amortization for 2006.

E12-17 **(Amortization Calculation—Addition, Change in Estimate)** In 1977, Applied Science Limited completed the construction of a building at a cost of $2 million and occupied it in January 1978. It was estimated that the building would have a useful life of 50 years and a residual value of $500,000.

Early in 1988, an addition to the building was constructed at a cost of $700,000. At that time no changes were expected in its useful life, but the residual value with the addition was estimated to increase by $100,000. The addition would not be of economic use to the company beyond the life of the original structure.

In 2006, as a result of a thorough review of its amortization policies, company management determined that the original life of the building should have been estimated at 40 years. Because the area the building is located in has witnessed the tearing down of older buildings and new ones built, it is now expected that the building and the addition are unlikely to have any residual value at the end of the 40-year period.

Instructions

(a) Using the straight-line method, calculate the annual amortization that would have been charged from 1978 through 1987.

(b) Calculate the annual amortization that would have been charged from 1988 through 2005.

(c) Prepare the entry, if necessary, to adjust the account balances because of the revision of the estimated life in 2006.

(d) Calculate the annual amortization to be charged beginning with 2006.

E12-18 **(Amortization Replacement—Change in Estimate)** Orel Limited constructed a building at a cost of $2.2 million and has occupied it since January 1985. It was estimated at that time that its life would be 40 years, with no residual value. In January 2005, a new roof was installed at a cost of $300,000, and it was estimated then that the building would have a useful life of 25 years from that date. The cost of the old roof was $160,000.

Instructions

(a) What amount of amortization was charged annually from the years 1985 through 2004? (Assume straight-line amortization.)

(b) What entry should be made in 2005 to record the roof replacement?

(c) Prepare the entry in January 2005 to record the revision in the building's estimated life, if necessary.

(d) What amount of amortization should be charged for the year 2005?

E12-19 **(Error Analysis and Amortization)** The Devereaux Company Ltd. shows the following entries in its Equipment account for 2005; all amounts are based on historical cost.

Equipment					
Jan. 1	Balance	134,750	June 30	Cost of equipment sold	
Aug. 10	Purchases	32,000		(purchased prior	
12	Freight on equipment			to 2005)	23,000
	purchased	700			
25	Installation costs	2,700			
Nov. 10	Repairs	500			

Instructions

(a) Prepare any correcting entries necessary.

(b) Assuming that amortization is to be charged for a full year on the ending balance in the asset account, calculate the proper amortization charge for 2005 under both methods listed below. Assume an estimated life of 10 years, with no residual value. The machinery included in the January 1, 2005 balance was purchased in 2003.

1. Straight-line

2. Declining-balance (assume twice the straight-line rate)

E12-20   (Impairment)   Presented below is information related to equipment owned by Gobi Limited at December 31, 2005.

Cost	$9,000,000
Accumulated amortization to date	1,000,000
Expected future net cash flows	7,000,000
Fair value	6,200,000

Assume that Gobi will continue to use this asset in the future. As of December 31, 2005, the equipment has a remaining useful life of four years. Gobi uses the straight-line method of amortization.

Instructions

(a) Prepare the journal entry (if any) to record the impairment of the asset at December 31, 2005.

(b) Prepare the journal entry (if any) to record amortization expense for 2006.

(c) The equipment's fair value at December 31, 2006 is $6.3 million. Prepare the journal entry, if necessary, to record this increase in fair value.

E12-21   (Impairment)   Assume the same information as E12-20, except that Gobi, at December 31, 2005, discontinues use of the equipment, intending to dispose of the equipment in the coming year through sale to a competitor. It is expected that the disposal cost will be $50,000.

Instructions

(a) Prepare the journal entry, if any, to record the impairment of the asset at December 31, 2005.

(b) Prepare the journal entry, if any, to record amortization expense for 2006.

(c) The asset was not sold by December 31, 2006. The equipment's fair value on this date is $6.3 million. Prepare the journal entry, if any, to record this increase in fair value. It is expected that the cost of disposal is still $50,000.

(d) Identify where, and in what amount, this asset will be reported on the December 31, 2006 balance sheet.

E12-22   (Impairment)   The management of Luis Inc. was discussing whether certain equipment should be written down as a charge to current operations because of obsolescence. The assets in question had a cost of $900,000 with amortization taken to December 31, 2005 of $400,000. On December 31, 2005, management projected the future net cash flows from this equipment to be $300,000 and its fair value to be $230,000. The company intends to use this equipment in the future.

Instructions

(a) Prepare the journal entry, if any, to record the impairment at December 31, 2005.

(b) Where should the gain or loss, if any, on the writedown be reported in the income statement?

(c) At December 31, 2006, the equipment's fair value increased to $260,000. Prepare the journal entry, if any, to record this increase in fair value.

(d) Assume instead that the future net cash flows from the equipment on December 31, 2005 were expected to be $510,000 and its fair value was $450,000 on this date. Prepare the journal entry, if any, to record the impairment at December 31, 2005.

E12-23   (Entries for Disposition of Assets)   On December 31, 2005, Travis Inc. owns a machine with a carrying amount of $940,000. The original cost and related accumulated amortization at this date are as follows.

Machine	$1,300,000
Accumulated amortization	360,000
	$ 940,000

Amortization is calculated at $60,000 per year on a straight-line basis.

Instructions

Presented below is a set of independent situations. For each independent situation, indicate the journal entry to be made to record the transaction. Make sure that amortization entries are made to update the machine's book value prior to its disposal.

(a) A fire completely destroys the machine on August 31, 2006. An insurance settlement of $430,000 was received for this casualty. Assume the settlement was received immediately.

(b) On April 1, 2006, Travis sold the machine for $1,040,000 to Yoakam Company.

(c) On July 31, 2006, the company donated this machine to the Mountain City Council. The machine's fair market value at the time of the donation was estimated to be $1.1 million.

E12-24 (Disposition of Assets) On April 1, 2005, Estefan Corp. received an award of $430,000 cash as compensation for the forced sale of the company's land and building, which stood in the path of a new highway. The land and building cost $60,000 and $280,000, respectively, when they were acquired. At April 1, 2005, the accumulated amortization relating to the building amounted to $160,000. On August 1, 2005, Estefan purchased a piece of replacement property for cash. The new land cost $90,000 and the new building cost $400,000.

Instructions
Prepare the journal entries to record the transactions on April 1 and August 1, 2005.

E12-25 (Ratio Analysis) The 2003 annual report of Alimentation Couche-Tard Inc. contains the following information:

(in thousands)	April 27, 2003	April 28, 2002
Total assets	$1,071,348	$787,167
Total liabilities	626,178	410,044
Consolidated sales	3,374,463	2,443,592
Net earnings	66,234	49,062

Instructions

(a) Calculate the following ratios for Alimentation Couche-Tard Inc. for 2003.

   1. Asset turnover ratio

   2. Rate of return on assets

   3. Profit margin on sales

(b) How can the asset turnover ratio be used to calculate the rate of return on assets?

(c) Briefly comment on the results of 1. to 3. above in part (a).

*E12-26 (CCA) During 2005, Frum Limited sold its only Class 3 asset. At the time of sale, the balance of the undepreciated capital cost for this class was $37,450. The asset originally cost $129,500. Indicate what the resulting amounts would be for any recapture of CCA, capital gain, and terminal loss, if any, assuming the asset was sold for proceeds of (a) $132,700, (b) $ 51,000, and (c) $22,000.

*E12-27 (Book vs. Tax Amortization) Chunmei Inc. purchased computer equipment on March 1, 2004 for $31,000. The computer equipment has a useful life of five years and a residual value of $1,000. Chunmei uses a double-declining-balance method of amortization for this type of capital asset. For tax purposes, the computer is assigned to Class 10 with a 30% rate.

Interactive
Homework

Instructions

(a) Prepare a schedule of amortization for financial reporting purposes for the new asset purchase covering 2004, 2005, and 2006. The company follows a policy of taking a full year's amortization in the year of purchase and none in the year of disposal.

(b) Prepare a schedule of CCA and UCC for this asset covering 2004, 2005, and 2006 assuming it is the only Class 10 asset owned by Chunmei.

(c) How much amortization is deducted over the three-year period on the financial statements? In determining taxable income? What is the carrying value of the computer equipment on the December 31, 2006 balance sheet? What is the tax value of the computer equipment at December 31, 2006?

Problems

P12-1 Onyx Corp. purchased Machine #201 on May 1, 2005. The following information relating to Machine #201 was gathered at the end of May.

Price	$73,500
Credit terms	2/10, n/30
Freight-in costs	$ 970
Preparation and installation costs	$ 3,800
Labour costs during regular production operations	$10,500

It was expected that the machine could be used for 10 years, after which the residual value would be zero. Onyx intends to use the machine for only eight years, however, after which it expects to be able to sell it for $1,200. The invoice for Machine #201 was paid May 5, 2005. Onyx has a September 30 year end.

Instructions

(a) Calculate the amortization expense for the years indicated using the following methods. (Round to the nearest dollar.)

1. Straight-line method for the fiscal years ended September 30, 2005 and 2006.

2. Double-declining-balance method for the fiscal years ended September 30, 2005 and 2006.

*(b) Calculate the capital cost allowance for the 2005 and 2006 tax returns, assuming a CCA class with a rate of 25%.

(c) The president of Onyx tells you that because the company is a new organization, she expects it will be several years before production and sales reach optimum levels. She asks you to recommend an amortization method that will allocate less of the company's amortization expense to the early years and more to later years of the assets' lives. What method would you recommend? Explain.

P12-2 On June 15, 2002, a second-hand machine was purchased for $77,000. Before being put into service, the equipment was overhauled at a cost of $5,200, and direct material costing $400 and direct labour of $800 were spent in fine-tuning the controls. The machine has an estimated residual value of $5,000 at the end of its five-year useful life. The machine is expected to operate for 100,000 hours before it will be replaced and is expected to produce 1,200,000 units in this time. Operating data for the next five fiscal years are as follows.

Year	Hours of operation	Units produced
2002	10,000	115,000
2003	25,000	310,000
2004	25,000	294,000
2005	30,000	363,000
2006	10,000	118,000

The company has an October 31 year end.

Instructions

(a) Calculate the amortization charges assigned to each fiscal year for each of the following amortization methods.

1. Straight-line method   4. Double-declining-balance method

2. Activity method: based on output   *5. CCA, Class 8, 20%

3. Activity method: based on input

(b) What is the carrying value of the machine on the October 31, 2005 balance sheet under the first four methods indicated above?

(c) Compare your answers in (b) with the asset's tax value at the same date.

(d) What happens if the actual hours of operation or units produced do not correspond to those estimated in setting the rate?

P12-3 Goran Tool Corp. records amortization annually at the end of the year. Its policy is to take a full year's amortization on all assets used throughout the year and amortization for one-half a year on all machines acquired or disposed of during the year. The amortization rate for the machinery is 10% applied on a straight-line basis, with no estimated scrap or residual value.

The balance of the Machinery account at the beginning of 2005 was $172,300; the Accumulated Amortization on Machinery account had a balance of $72,900. The following transactions affecting the machinery accounts took place during 2005.

Jan. 15   Machine No. 38, which cost $9,600 when acquired June 3, 1998, was retired and sold as scrap metal for $600.

Feb. 27   Machine No. 81 was purchased. The fair market value of this machine was $12,500. It replaced Machines No. 12 and No. 27, which were traded in on the new machine. Machine No.12 was acquired Feb. 4, 1993 at a cost of $5,500 and was still carried in the accounts although fully depreciated and not in use. Machine No. 27 was acquired June 11, 1998 at a cost of $8,200. In addition to these two used machines, $9,000 was paid in cash.

Apr. 7   Machine No. 54 was equipped with electric controls at a cost of $940. This machine, originally equipped with simple hand controls, was purchased Dec. 11, 2001 for $1,800. The new electric controls can be attached to any one of several machines in the shop.

12   Machine No. 24 was repaired at a cost of $720 after a fire caused by a short circuit in the wiring burned out the motor and damaged certain essential parts.

July 22   Machines No. 25, 26, and 41 were sold for $3,100 cash. The purchase dates and cost of these machines were:

No. 25	$4,000	May 8, 1997
No. 26	3,200	May 8, 1997
No. 41	2,800	June 1, 1999

Instructions

(a) Record each transaction in general journal form.

(b) Calculate and record amortization for the year. No machines now included in the balance of the account were acquired before January 1, 1996.

P12-4 On January 1, 2005, Dayan Corporation, a small machine-tool manufacturer, acquired new industrial equipment for $1,100,000. The new equipment had a useful life of five years and the residual value was estimated to be $50,000. Dayan estimates that the new equipment can produce 12,000 machine tools in its first year. It estimates that production will decline by 1,000 units per year over the remaining useful life of the equipment.

The following amortization methods may be used: (1) straight-line, (2) double-declining-balance; and (3) units-of-output. For tax purposes, the CCA class is Class 10—30%.

Instructions

(a) Which of the three amortization methods would maximize net income for financial statement reporting purposes for the three-year period ending December 31, 2007? Prepare a schedule showing the amount of accumulated amortization at December 31, 2007 under the method selected.

***(b)** Over the same three-year period, how much capital cost allowance would have been written off for tax purposes?

(c) Prepare one graph covering the five-year period with separate chart lines representing each of the three methods identified as well as one for the CCA method. Which pattern of amortization do you feel best reflects the benefits provided by the new equipment? Explain briefly.

P12-5 The following data relate to the Plant Assets account of Fiedler Inc. at December 31, 2004.

	A	B	C	D
Original cost	$35,000	$51,000	$80,000	$80,000
Year purchased	1999	2000	2001	2003
Useful life	10 years	15,000 hours	15 years	10 years
Residual value	$3,100	$3,000	$5,000	$5,000
Amortization method	straight-line	activity	straight-line	double-declining
Accumulated amortization				
through 2004[a]	$15,950	$35,200	$15,000	$16,000

[a] In the year an asset is purchased, Fiedler does not record any amortization expense on the asset. In the year an asset is retired or traded in, Fiedler takes a full year's amortization on the asset.

The following transactions occurred during 2005.

(a) On May 5, Asset A was sold for $13,000 cash. The company's bookkeeper recorded this retirement in the following manner.

Cash	13,000	
Asset A		13,000

(b) On December 31, it was determined that Asset B had been used 2,100 hours during 2005.

(c) On December 31, before calculating amortization expense on Asset C, the management of Fiedler decided the useful life remaining as of year end was nine years.

(d) On December 31, it was discovered that a plant asset purchased in 2004 had been expensed completely in that year. The asset cost $22,000 and had a useful life of 10 years when it was acquired and had no residual value. Management has decided to use the double-declining-balance method for this asset, which can be referred to as "Asset E."

Instructions

Prepare the necessary correcting entries for the year 2005 and any additional entries necessary to record the appropriate amortization expense on the above-mentioned assets.

P12-6 Soon after December 31, 2005, Qing Manufacturing Corp. was requested by its auditor to prepare an amortization schedule for semitrucks that showed the additions, retirements, amortization, and other data affecting the income of the company in the four-year period 2002 to 2005, inclusive. The following data were obtained.

Balance of Semitrucks account, Jan. 1, 2002:	
Truck No. 1 purchased Jan. 1, 1999, cost	$18,000
Truck No. 2 purchased July 1, 1999, cost	22,000
Truck No. 3 purchased Jan. 1, 2001, cost	30,000
Truck No. 4 purchased July 1, 2001, cost	24,000
Balance, Jan. 1, 2002	$94,000

The Semitrucks—Accumulated Amortization account had a correct balance of $30,200 on January 1, 2002 (amortization on the four trucks from the respective dates of purchase, based on a five-year life, no residual value). No charges had been made against the account before January 1, 2002.

Transactions between January 1, 2002 and December 31, 2005 and their record in the ledger were as follows.

July 1, 2002	Truck No. 3 was traded for a larger one (No. 5); the agreed purchase price (fair market value) was $34,000. Qing Manufacturing paid the automobile dealer $15,000 cash on the transaction. The entry was a debit to Semitrucks and a credit to Cash, $15,000.
Jan. 1, 2003	Truck No. 1 was sold for $3,500 cash; the entry was a debit to Cash and a credit to Semitrucks, $3,500.
July 1, 2004	A new truck (No. 6) was acquired for $36,000 cash and was charged at that amount to the Semitrucks account. (Assume truck No. 2 was not retired.)
July 1, 2004	Truck No. 4 was damaged in an accident to such an extent that it was sold for scrap for $700 cash. Qing Manufacturing received $2,500 from the insurance company. The entry made by the bookkeeper was a debit to Cash, $3,200, and credits to Miscellaneous Income, $700, and Semitrucks, $2,500.

Entries for amortization had been made at the close of each year as follows: 2002, $20,300; 2003, $21,100; 2004, $24,450; 2005, $27,800.

Instructions

(a) For each of the four years, calculate separately the increase or decrease in net income arising from the company's errors in determining or entering amortization or in recording transactions affecting trucks. Ignore income tax considerations.

(b) Prepare one compound journal entry as of December 31, 2005 for adjustment of the Semitrucks account to reflect the correct balances as revealed by your schedule, assuming that the books have not been closed for 2005.

P12-7   Linda Monkland established Monkland Ltd. as the sole shareholder in mid-2004. The accounts on June 30, 2005, the company's year end, just prior to preparing required adjusting entries, indicated the following amounts.

Current assets		$100,000
Capital assets		
Land	$40,000	
Building	90,000	
Equipment	50,000	180,000
Current liabilities		40,000
Long-term bank loan		120,000
Share capital		90,000
Net income prior to amortization		30,000

All the capital assets were acquired and put into operation in early July 2004. Estimates regarding these assets include:

Building: 25-year life, $15,000 residual value
Equipment: Five-year life, 15,000 hours of use, $5,000 residual value. The equipment was used for 1,000 hours in 2004 and 1,400 hours in 2005 up to June 30.

Linda Monkland is now considering which amortization method or methods would be appropriate. She has narrowed the choices down for the building to the straight-line or double-declining method, and for the equipment to the straight-line, double-declining-balance, or activity method. She has requested your advice and recommendation. In discussions with her, the following concerns were raised.

1. The company acquires goods from suppliers with terms of 2/10, n/30. The suppliers have indicated that these terms will continue as long as the current ratio does not fall below 2 to 1. If the ratio were less, then no purchase discounts would be given.

2. The bank will continue the loan from year to year as long as the ratio of long-term debt to total assets does not exceed 46%.

3. Linda Monkland has contracted with the company's manager to pay him a bonus equal to 50% of any net income in excess of $14,000. She prefers to minimize or pay no bonus as long as conditions of agreements with suppliers and the bank can be met.

4. In order to provide a strong signal to attract potential investors to join her in the company, Ms. Monkland believes that a rate of return on total assets of at least 5% must be achieved.

Instructions

Prepare a report for Linda Monkland that presents tables, analyses the situation, provides a recommendation on which method or methods should be used, and justifies your recommendation in light of her concerns and the requirement that the method(s) used be considered generally accepted accounting principle(s).

P12-8 Wright Mining Ltd. purchased a tract of land for $600,000. After incurring exploration costs of $95,000, the company estimated that this tract will yield 120,000 tonnes of ore with sufficient mineral content to make mining and processing profitable. It is further estimated that 6,000 tonnes of ore will be mined the first and last year and 12,000 tonnes every year in between. The land is expected to have a residual value of $30,000.

The company built necessary bunkhouses and sheds on the site at a cost of $36,000. It estimated that these structures would have a physical life of 15 years but, because they must be dismantled if they are to be moved, they have no residual value. The company does not intend to use the buildings elsewhere. Mining machinery installed at the mine was purchased second-hand at a cost of $48,000. This machinery cost the former owner $100,000 and was 50% depreciated when purchased. Wright Mining estimated that about half of this machinery will still be useful when the present mineral resources are exhausted but that dismantling and removal costs would just about offset their value at that time. The company does not intend to use the machinery elsewhere. The remaining machinery is expected to last until about one-half the present estimated mineral ore has been removed and will then be worthless. Cost is to be allocated equally between these two classes of machinery.

Wright also spent another $76,500 in opening up the mine so that the ore could be extracted and removed for shipping. The company estimates that contractual site reclamation and restoration costs when the mine is depleted (related to the existing site) has a present value of $37,000. Wright follows a policy of expensing exploration costs and capitalizing development costs.

Instructions

(a) As chief accountant for the company, you are to prepare a schedule showing estimated depletion and amortization costs for each year of the mine's expected life.

(b) Draft entries in general journal form to record amortization and depletion for the first year. Assume actual production of 7,000 tonnes. Nothing occurred during the year to cause the company engineers to change their estimates of either the mineral resources or the life of the structures and equipment.

(c) Assume 6,500 tonnes of product were processed and sold during the first year. Identify all costs discussed above that will be included on the first year income statement of Wright Mining Ltd.

P12-9 Copernicus Logging and Lumber Inc. owns 3,000 ha of timberland on the north side of a mountain in western Canada, purchased in 1988 at a cost of $550 per hectare. In 2004, Copernicus began selectively logging this timber tract. In May of 2004, a forest fire destroyed most of the timber on the Copernicus tract. In addition, the logging roads, built at a cost of $150,000, were destroyed, as was logging equipment that had a net book value of $300,000.

At the time of the fire, Copernicus had logged 20% of the estimated 500,000 m³ of timber. Prior to the fire, Copernicus estimated the land to have a value of $200 per hectare after the timber was harvested. Copernicus includes the logging roads in the depletion base.

Copernicus estimates it will take three years to salvage the burned timber at a cost of $700,000. The timber can be sold for pulp wood at an estimated price of $3 per cubic metre. The land value is unknown, but until it will grow vegetation again—which scientists say may be as long as 50 to 100 years—the value is nominal.

Instructions

(a) Determine the depletion cost per cubic metre for the timber harvested prior to the fire.

(b) Prepare the journal entry to record the depletion prior to the fire.

(c) If this tract represents approximately half of Copernicus' timber holdings, determine the amount of the estimated loss before income taxes and show how the losses of roads, machinery, and timber and the timber salvage value should be reported in the financial statements of Copernicus for the year ended December 31, 2004.

P12-10 Western Paper Products Ltd. purchased 10,000 ha of forested timberland in March 2005. The company paid $1,700 per hectare for this land, which was above the $800 per hectare most farmers were paying for cleared land. During April, May, June, and July 2005, Western cut enough timber to build roads using moveable equipment purchased on April 1, 2005. The cost of the roads was $195,000, and the cost of the equipment was $189,000; the equipment was expected to have a $9,000 residual value and would be used for the next 15 years. Western selected the straight-line method of amortization for the moveable equipment. The company began actively harvesting timber in August and by December had harvested and sold 472,500 m³ of timber of the estimated 6,750,000 m³ available for cutting.

In March 2006, Western planted new seedlings in the area harvested during the winter. Cost of planting these seedlings was $120,000. In addition, Western spent $8,000 in road maintenance and $6,000 for pest spraying during 2006. The road maintenance and spraying are annual costs. During 2006, Western harvested and sold 774,000 m³ of timber of the estimated 6,450,000 m³ available for cutting.

In March 2007, Western again planted new seedlings at a cost of $150,000, and also spent $15,000 on road maintenance and pest spraying. During 2007, the company harvested and sold 650,000 m³ of timber of the estimated 6.5 million m³ available for cutting.

Instructions

Calculate the amount of amortization and depletion expense for each of the three years. Assume that the roads are usable only for logging and therefore are included in the depletion base.

P12-11   Release Corporation uses special strapping equipment in its packaging business. The equipment was purchased in January 2004 for $8 million and had an estimated useful life of eight years with no residual value. In early April 2005, a part costing $969,000 designed to increase the efficiency of the machinery was added, although there was no change in its estimated useful life. At December 31, 2005, new technology was introduced that would accelerate the obsolescence of Release's equipment. Release's controller estimates that expected future net cash flows on the equipment will be $5.5 million and that the fair value of the equipment is $4.8 million. Release intends to continue using the equipment, but estimates that its remaining useful life is four years. Release uses straight-line amortization.

Instructions

(a) Prepare the journal entry (if any) to record the impairment at December 31, 2005.

(b) Prepare any journal entries for the equipment at December 31, 2006. The fair value of the equipment at December 31, 2006 is estimated to be $5 million.

(c) Repeat the requirements for (a) and (b), assuming that Release intends to dispose of the equipment, but continues to use it until it gets a satisfactory offer and that it has not been disposed of as of December 31, 2006.

(d) Repeat the requirements for (a) and (b), assuming that Release designates the equipment as "held for sale." Due to matters beyond Release's control, a potential sale falls through in 2006 and the equipment is still on hand at December 31, 2006.

(e) For each situation underlying (b), (c), and (d), indicate where the equipment will be reported on the December 31, 2005 and 2006 balance sheets.

P12-12   Presented below is a schedule of property dispositions for Tomasino Corp.

SCHEDULE OF PROPERTY DISPOSITIONS

	Cost	Accumulated Amortization	Cash Proceeds	Fair Market Value	Nature of Disposition
Land	$40,000	—	$31,000	$31,000	Expropriated
Building	15,000	—	3,600	—	Demolition
Warehouse	70,000	$11,000	74,000	74,000	Destruction by fire
Machine	8,000	3,200	900	7,200	Trade-in
Furniture	10,000	7,850	—	3,100	Contribution
Automobile	8,000	3,460	2,960	2,960	Sale

The following additional information is available.

Land
On February 15, land held primarily as an investment was expropriated by the city and on March 31, another parcel of unimproved land to be held as an investment was purchased at a cost of $35,000.

Building
On April 2, land and building were purchased at a total cost of $75,000, of which 20% was allocated to the building on the corporate books. The real estate was acquired with the intention of demolishing the building, and this was accomplished during November. Cash proceeds received in November represent the net proceeds from the building demolition.

Warehouse
On June 30, the warehouse was destroyed by fire. The warehouse was purchased January 2, 1991 and accumulated amortization of $11,000 had been reported. On December 27, the insurance proceeds and other funds were used to purchase a replacement warehouse at a cost of $90,000.

Machine
On December 26, the machine was exchanged for another machine having a fair market value of $6,300 and cash of $900 was received.

Furniture
On August 15, furniture was contributed to a registered charitable organization. No other contributions were made or pledged during the year.

Automobile

On November 3, the automobile was sold to Una Guillen, a shareholder.

Instructions

Indicate how these items would be reported on the income statement of Tomasino Corp.

(AICPA adapted)

P12-13   Huston Corporation, a manufacturer of steel products, began operations on October 1, 2003. Huston's accounting department has started the capital asset and amortization schedule presented below. You have been asked to assist in completing this schedule. In addition to determining that the data already on the schedule are correct, you have obtained the following information from the company's records and personnel.

1. Amortization is calculated from the first of the month of acquisition to the first of the month of disposition.

2. Land A and Building A were acquired from a predecessor corporation. Huston paid $820,000 for the land and building together. At the time of acquisition, the land had an appraised value of $90,000 and the building had an appraised value of $810,000.

3. Land B was acquired on October 2, 2003 in exchange for 2,500 newly issued common shares. At the date of acquisition, the shares had a fair value of $30 each. During October 2003, Huston paid $16,000 to demolish an existing building on this land so it could construct a new building.

4. Construction of Building B on the newly acquired land began on October 1, 2004. By September 30, 2005, Huston had paid $320,000 of the estimated total construction costs of $450,000. It is estimated that the building will be completed and occupied by July 2006.

5. Certain equipment was donated to the corporation by a local university. An independent appraisal of the equipment when donated placed the fair market value at $30,000 and the residual value at $3,000.

6. Machinery A's total cost of $164,900 includes installation expense of $600 and normal repairs and maintenance of $14,900. Residual value is estimated at $6,000. Machinery A was sold on February 1, 2005.

7. On October 1, 2004, Machinery B was acquired with a down payment of $5,740 and the remaining payments to be made in 11 annual instalments of $6,000 each, beginning October 1, 2004. The prevailing interest rate was 8%. The following data were abstracted from present-value tables (rounded).

PV of $1 at 8%		PV of an ordinary annuity of $1 at 8%	
10 years	0.463	10 years	6.710
11 years	0.429	11 years	7.139
15 years	0.315	15 years	8.559

HUSTON CORPORATION
Capital Asset and Amortization Schedule
For Fiscal Years Ended September 30, 2004 and September 30, 2005

Assets	Acquisition Date	Cost	Residual	Amortization Method	Estimated Life in Years	Amortization Expense Year Ended September 30 2004	2005
Land A	Oct. 1, 2003	$ (1)	N/A	N/A	N/A	N/A	N/A
Building A	Oct. 1, 2003	(2)	$40,000	Straight-line	(3)	$17,450	(4)
Land B	Oct. 2, 2003	(5)	N/A	N/A	N/A	N/A	N/A
Building B	Under Construction	$320,000 to date	—	Straight-line	30	—	(6)
Donated Equipment	Oct. 2, 2003	(7)	3,000	150% declining-balance	10	(8)	(9)
Machinery A	Oct. 2, 2003	(10)	6,000	Double-declining-balance	8	(11)	(12)
Machinery B	Oct. 1, 2004	(13)	—	Straight-line	20	—	(14)

N/A – Not applicable

Instructions

For each numbered item on the foregoing schedule, supply the correct amount. Round each answer to the nearest dollar.

P12-14   Situation 1   Zitar Corporation purchased electrical equipment at a cost of $12,400 on June 2, 2001. From 2001 through 2004, the equipment was amortized on a straight-line basis, under the assumption that it would have a 10-year useful life and a $2,400 residual value. After more experience and before recording 2005's amortization, Zitar revised its estimate of the machine's useful life downward from a total of 10 years to eight years, and revised the estimated residual value to $2,000.

On April 29, 2006, after recording part of a year's amortization for 2006, the company traded in the equipment on a newer model, receiving a $4,000 trade-in allowance, although its fair value was only $2,800. The new asset had a list price of $15,300 and the supplier accepted $11,300 cash for the balance. The new equipment was amortized on a straight-line basis under the assumption of a seven-year useful life and a $1,300 residual value.

Instructions

Determine the amount of amortization expense reported by Zitar for each fiscal year ending on December 31, 2001 through to December 31, 2006.

Situation 2   Boda Limited acquired a truck to deliver and install its specialized products at the customer's site. The vehicle's list price was $45,000, but customization added another $10,000 of costs. Boda took delivery of the truck on September 30, 2005 with a down payment of $5,000, signing a four-year 8% note for the remainder, payable in equal payments of $14,496 beginning September 30, 2006.

Boda expects the truck to be usable for 500 deliveries and installations, by which time the product's technology will have changed so as to make the vehicle obsolete. In late July 2008, the truck was destroyed when a concrete garage collapsed. Boda used the truck for 45 deliveries in 2005, 125 in 2006, 134 in 2007, and 79 in 2008. The company received a cheque for $12,000 from the insurance company and paid what remained on the note.

Instructions

Prepare all entries to record the events and activities related to the truck, including the amortization expense on the truck each year. Assume Boda uses an activity approach to amortize the truck, based on deliveries.

Situation 3   A group of new machines was purchased on February 17, 2005 under a royalty agreement that provides for Townsand Corp. to pay a royalty of $1 to the machinery supplier for each unit of product produced by the machines each year. The machines are expected to produce 200,000 units over their useful lives. The invoice price of the machines was $75,000, freight costs were $2,000, unloading charges were $1,500, and royalty payments for 2005 were $13,000. Townsand uses the units of production method to amortize its machinery.

Instructions

Prepare journal entries to record the purchase of the new machines, the related amortization for 2005, and the royalty payment.

*P12-15   Taber Limited reports the following information in its tax files covering the five-year period from 2002 to 2006. All assets relate to Class 10 with a 30% maximum CCA rate.

2002	Purchased assets A, B, and C for $20,000, $8,000, and $1,200 respectively.
2003	Sold asset B for $7,000; bought asset D for $4,800.
2004	Purchased asset F for $5,000; received an investment tax credit of $1,000.
2005	Sold asset A for $9,900 and asset C for $1,800.
2006	Uninsured asset D was destroyed by fire; asset E was sold to an employee for $500.

Instructions

(a) Prepare a capital cost allowance schedule for Class 10 assets covering the 2002 to 2006 period.

(b) Identify any capital gains, terminal losses, or recapture of CCA and indicate how each would be taxed.

*P12-16   Quadros Limited was attracted to the Town of LePage by its municipal industry commission. The Town donated a plant site to Quadros, and the provincial government provided $100,000 toward the cost of the new manufacturing facility. The total cost of plant construction came to $335,000 and it was ready for use in early October 2005. Quadros expects the plant to have a useful life of 15 years before it becomes obsolete and is demolished. The company uses the straight-line method of amortization for buildings and is required to include the plant in Class 6 (10% rate) for tax purposes.

Instructions

(a) Prepare the entry(ies) required in 2005 to record the payment to the contractor for the building and the receipt of the provincial government assistance. Assume the company treats the assistance as a reduction of the asset's cost. Also prepare any adjusting entries needed at the company's year end, December 31, 2005 and 2006.

(b) Prepare the entry(ies) required in 2005 to record the payment to the contractor for the building and the receipt of the provincial government assistance. Assume the company treats the assistance as a deferred credit. Also prepare any adjusting entries needed at the company's year end, December 31, 2005 and 2006.

(c) If Quadros reports 2006 income of $79,000 before amortization related to the plant and government assistance, what income before tax will the company report assuming (a) above? Assuming (b) above?

(d) What is the building's tax value at December 31, 2006?

Writing Assignments

WA12-1   Prophet Manufacturing Limited was organized January 1, 2005. During 2005, it used the straight-line method of amortizing its plant assets in its reports to management.

On November 8 you are having a conference with Prophet's officers to discuss the amortization method to be used for income tax and for reporting to shareholders. Fred Peretti, president of Prophet, has suggested the use of a new method, which he feels is more suitable than the straight-line method for the company's needs during the period of rapid expansion of production and capacity that he foresees. Following is an example in which the proposed method is applied to a capital asset with an original cost of $248,000, an estimated useful life of five years, and a residual value of approximately $8,000.

Year	Years of Life Used	Fraction Rate	Amortization Expense	Accumulated Amortization at End of Year	Book Value at End of Year
1	1	1/15	$16,000	$ 16,000	$232,000
2	2	2/15	32,000	48,000	200,000
3	3	3/15	48,000	96,000	152,000
4	4	4/15	64,000	160,000	88,000
5	5	5/15	80,000	240,000	8,000

The president favours the new method because he has heard that:

1. It will increase the funds recovered during the years near the end of the assets' useful life when maintenance and replacement disbursements are high.

2. It will result in increased write-offs in later years when the company is likely to be in a better operating position.

Instructions

(a) What is the purpose of accounting for amortization?

(b) Is the president's proposal within the scope of generally accepted accounting principles? In making your decision, discuss the circumstances, if any, under which using the method would be reasonable and those, if any, under which it would not be reasonable.

(c) Do amortization charges recover or create funds? Explain.

WA12-2   Billy Williams, HK Corporation's controller, is concerned that net income may be lower this year. He is afraid upper-level management might recommend cost reductions by laying off accounting staff, himself included.

Williams knows that amortization is a major expense for HK. The company currently uses the same method for financial reporting as it uses for tax purposes, i.e., a declining-balance method, and he's thinking of a change to the straight-line method. A change in an accounting method such as this is required to be disclosed in the financial statements along with the effect on the current year's income, and a retroactive adjustment made to opening retained earnings. Williams does not want to highlight the increasing of income in this manner. He thinks, "Why don't I increase the estimated useful lives and the residual values of the property, plant, and equipment? They are only estimates anyway. The effect will be to decrease amortization expense and since the changes are accounted for prospectively, this will not be disclosed in the income statement. I may be able to save my job and those of my staff."

Instructions

Discuss. Ensure you identify the objectives of amortization, who the stakeholders are in this situation, whether any ethical issues are involved, and what Williams should do.

WA12-3   Recently, Brunet Company Ltd. experienced a strike that affected a number of its operating plants. The company president indicated that it was not appropriate to report amortization expense during this period because the equipment did not depreciate and an improper matching of costs and revenues would result. She based her position on the following points.

1. It is inappropriate to charge the period with costs for which there are no related revenues arising from production.

2. The basic factor of amortization in this instance is wear and tear, and because equipment was idle, no wear and tear occurred.

Instructions
Comment on the appropriateness of the president's comments.

WA12-4   Carnago Corporation manufactures home electrical appliances. Company engineers have designed a new type of blender that, through the use of a few attachments, will perform more functions than any other blender currently on the market. Demand for the new blender can be projected with reasonable probability. In order to manufacture the blenders, Carnago needs a specialized machine that is not available from outside sources. It has been decided to make such a machine in Carnago's own plant.

Instructions

(a) Discuss the effect of projected demand in units for the new blenders (which may be steady, decreasing, or increasing) on the determination of an amortization method for the machine.

(b) What other matters should be considered in determining the amortization method? Ignore income tax considerations.

WA12-5   Puma Paper Company Ltd. operates a 300-tonnes-per-day kraft pulp mill and four sawmills in New Brunswick. The company is expanding its pulp mill facilities to a capacity of 1,000 tonnes per day and plans to replace three of its older, less efficient sawmills with an expanded facility. One of the mills to be replaced did not operate for most of 2005 (current year), and there are no plans to reopen it before the new sawmill facility becomes operational.

In reviewing the amortization rates and in discussing the residual values of the sawmills that were to be replaced, it was noted that if present amortization rates were not adjusted, substantial amounts of plant costs on these three mills would not be depreciated by the time the new mill comes on stream.

Instructions
What is the proper accounting for the four sawmills at the end of 2005?

WA12-6   As a cost accountant for Digby Cannery Inc., you have been approached by Merle Morash, canning room supervisor, about the 2003 costs charged to his department. In particular, he is concerned about the line item amortization. Morash is very proud of the excellent condition of his canning room equipment. He has always been vigilant about keeping all equipment serviced and well oiled. He is sure that the huge charge to amortization is a mistake; it does not at all reflect the cost of minimal wear and tear that the machines have experienced over the last year. He believes that the charge should be considerably lower.

The machines being amortized are six automatic canning machines. All were put into use on January 1, 2003. Each cost $469,000, having a residual value of $40,000 and a useful life of 12 years. Digby depreciates this and similar assets using the double-declining-balance method. Morash has also pointed out that if you used straight-line amortization, the charge to his department would not be so great.

Instructions
Write a memo to Merle Morash to clear up his misunderstanding of the term "amortization." Also, calculate the first year amortization on all machines using both methods. Explain the theoretical justification for double-declining-balance and why, in the long run, the aggregate charge to amortization will be the same under both methods.

Integrated Cases

Refer to the Case Primer on the Digital Tool to help you answer these cases.

Digital Tool
www.wiley.com/
canada/kieso

IC12-1   ClubLoop Corporation (CL) is a large owner, operator, and developer of golf clubs and resorts. The company is privately owned by several wealthy individuals. During the current year, according to the draft financial statements, revenues increased 7.2% and net operating income increased 13% to $22.5 million. Net income dropped from $2.9 million to $822,000. The decrease was largely due to two events, a change in accounting policy and costs related to settlement of a lawsuit.

One of the objectives of the company is to ensure that capital resources are readily available to meet approved capital expenditures and to take advantage of growth opportunities. According to the draft year end financial statements, the company has current assets of $12 million and current liabilities of $28 million, resulting in a working capital deficit.

Included in the current liabilities are long-term debts that are currently due. The company is working with the related financial institutions to renew or replace these facilities. CL has received unsolicited expressions of interest from several financial institutions concerning these facilities and management believes that these facilities will be replaced—hopefully before the current financial statements are issued.

The company owns most of the land on which CL's golf courses are developed. Currently, the company follows a rigorous "weed and feed" program in order to keep the grass on the golf course in top shape. The chemicals in these fertilizers, herbicides, and insecticides are felt by some in the community to be toxic to the environment. The company has met with several community groups and has undertaken to study the issue further. In a current meeting of the Board of Directors, the CEO committed to spend $1 million to mitigate any potential damage. As at year end, none of this has yet been spent. There is a concern that the community groups are going to launch a lawsuit and the company feels that this move will help CL's position should a lawsuit arise. Part of this money is for landscaping to curtail the spread and part of it is for advertising to promote the company as a good corporate citizen.

The company is currently developing new golf courses. All direct costs related to the acquisition, development, and construction of these properties, including interest and management costs, are capitalized. For one such location, which was just purchased and developed in the current year, they have run into a small problem. After having spent several million dollars on development, the planned golf course is being blocked by environmentalist groups. The costs to develop the land have been capitalized as previously mentioned, on the basis that they would be recoverable from future membership revenues. The company has decided to sell the land to a real estate developer.

CL's stock based compensation plan consists of stock options. The company does not recognize any expense for this plan when stock options are issued to employees. It has been the policy of the company to repurchase any shares issued under these stock option plans although this year, the company has indicated that this might not be the case since they are planning to revamp the stock based compensation system.

On July 1, CCRA issued notices of assessment to the company in respect of a dispute relating to recognition of revenues. Although the outcome of the assessment appeals is not determinable, the company feels that the amount owed if unsuccessful, will be $8.7 million.

Instructions

Adopt the role of the company's auditor and prepare an analysis of the financial reporting issues. Hint: If there are issues here that are new – use the conceptual framework to reason through the analysis.

IC12-2   Talisman Energy Inc. (TE) is an international company whose main business activities include exploration, development, production, and marketing of crude oil, natural gas, and natural gas liquids. Its strategy is to continue to develop its North American gas business while at the same time expanding internationally. Where it makes sense, the company owns and operates key assets and infrastructure and plans to grow through exploration and acquisition.

On October 20, 2002, the company announced that it had entered into an agreement to sell its controversial stake in Sudan. Although the company felt that the investment was a good one (the Sudan operations were profitable), they feared that shareholders were getting tired of the controversy surrounding the political conflict in Sudan. The sale is conditional upon obtaining certain governmental and consortium member consents. TE expects a gain on sale of $351 million. Revenues and costs have not been segregated in the financial statements.

During the year, the company was also forced to lower its previously announced 2003 growth targets. This caused some concern in the marketplace and resulted in investors questioning whether the company could meet its new targets on a going forward basis.

TE follows what is known as the successful efforts method of accounting for exploration and development costs. Under this method, the costs related to drilling exploratory wells are written off to "dry hole expense" when they are determined to be unsuccessful. Until that time, they are included in property, plant, and equipment as non-depleted capital. As at December 31, 2002, costs related to exploration wells included in non-depleted capital were 3% ($ 309 million) of property plant and equipment. Dry hole expense was $174 million with net income being $524 million. Note that the alternative treatment—full cost accounting—capitalizes all related costs as property, plant, and equipment, even those related to unsuccessful wells.

TE monitors its reserves and reserve estimates are made using available geological and reservoir data as well as production performance data. The reserves impact the income statement through depletion charges since oil and gas related property plant and equipment is amortized using the units of production method over proven developed reserves. $1.2 billion of the capital assets are not currently subject to depletion since they are not yet in the production phase.

Revenues are recognized using the entitlement method which means that the sales value of the production is recognized as revenue when produced.

Instructions

Adopt the role of company management and discuss the financial reporting issues.

Research and Financial Analysis

RA12-1   Canadian Tire Corporation, Limited

Canadian Tire Corporation, Limited is one of Canada's best-known retailers. Obtain a copy of Canadian Tire's financial statements for the year ended December 31, 2002, either through the Digital Tool or through SEDAR at www.sedar.com. Include the Ten Year Financial Review produced as supplementary information in the annual report, if necessary, as a basis for answering the following questions.

Instructions

(a) How significant is Canadian Tire's investment in Property, Plant, and Equipment relative to its investment in other assets? Compare this with sample companies in other industries, such as financial services, utilities, and technology. Comment.

(b) Calculate the company's total asset turnover for 2000, 2001, and 2002.

(c) Calculate the company's profit margin for the same three years.

(d) Calculate the company's return on assets for the same three years by using the ratios calculated in (b) and (c) above.

(e) Based on your calculations in (d), suggest ways in which Canadian Tire might increase the return it earns on its investment in assets.

RA12-2   McDonald's Corporation

McDonald's Corporation is the largest and best-known global food service retailer, with more than 30,000 restaurants in 121 countries. The company's system-wide sales in 2002 exceeded $41 billion (U.S.). Presented below is information related to property and equipment.

McDONALD'S CORPORATION
Significant Accounting Policies Section
Property and Equipment. Property and equipment are stated at cost, with depreciation and amortization provided using the straight-line method over the following estimated useful lives: buildings up to 40 years; leasehold improvements—the lesser of useful lives of assets or lease terms including option periods; and equipment—3 to 12 years.

Property and Equipment

(in millions of $U.S.)	Dec. 31, 2002	2001
Land	$4,169.6	$3,975.6
Buildings and improvements on owned land	8,747.2	8,127.0
Buildings and improvements on leased land	8,872.5	8,020.2
Equipment, signs, and seating	3,765.1	3,371.7
Other	664.2	611.5
	26,218.6	24,106.0
Accumulated depreciation and amortization	(7,635.2)	(6,816.5)
Net property and equipment	$18,583.4	$17,289.5

Depreciation and amortization expense was (in millions):
2002—$971.1; 2001—$945.6; 2000—$900.9.

Other information

(in millions)	2002	2001	2000
Cash provided by operations	$2,890.1	$2,688.3	$2,751.5
Capital expenditures	$2,003.8	$1,906.2	$1,945.1
Free cash flow	$ 886.3	$ 782.1	$ 806.4
Cash provided by operations as a percent of capital expenditures	144%	141%	141%
Cash provided by operations as a percent of year-end long-term debt	30%	31%	35%

Instructions

(a) What method of amortization is used by McDonald's? Does this method seem appropriate given the type of assets McDonald's has? Comment.

(b) Does depreciation and amortization expense cause cash flow from operations to increase? Explain.

(c) What is "free cash flow"? What is its significance?

(d) Comment on the level of McDonald's cash flow from operations.

RA12-3 Canadian National Railway Company & Canadian Pacific Railway Limited

Two well-known company names in the transportation industry in Canada are Canadian National Railway Company and Canadian Pacific Railway Limited. Either through SEDAR (www.sedar.com) or the Digital Tool, gain access to the financial statements of these companies for their year ended December 31, 2002.

Instructions

(a) How significant are the investments made by these companies in property, plant, and equipment? Describe in terms of percentage of total assets.

(b) Compare the types of property, plant, and equipment each company reports.

(c) Do the companies follow similar policies in what they capitalize as part of property, plant, and equipment?

(d) What methods of amortization are used by each company?

(e) Where the companies have similar types of assets, compare the useful lives and/or rates of amortization. Are they similar or would their application result in differences in reported results on a year-by-year basis? Explain briefly.

RA12-4 Loblaw Companies Limited & Sobeys Inc.

Loblaw Companies Limited and Sobeys Inc. are competitors in the Canadian food industry. Either through the Digital Tool or through SEDAR (www.sedar.com), gain access to the financial statements of Loblaw Companies Limited for its year ended December 28, 2002, and Sobeys Inc. for its year ended May 3, 2003.

Instructions

(a) What amount is reported in the balance sheets as property, plant, and equipment (net) of Loblaw Companies at December 28, 2002 and of Sobeys Inc. at May 3, 2003? What percentage of total assets is invested in this type of asset by each company?

(b) What amortization methods are used by Loblaw and Sobeys? What types of property, plant, and equipment do both companies report? Are they similar? Are their amortization policies and rates similar? How much amortization was reported by each company in each of its last two years?

(c) Calculate, compare, and comment on the following ratios for Loblaw and Sobeys for their most recent year.

1. Asset turnover

2. Profit margin on sales

3. Return on assets

(d) What amount was spent in its most recent year for capital expenditures by Loblaw? By Sobeys? Where do you find this information in the financial statements? What amount of interest, if any, was capitalized?

(e) Do Loblaw or Sobeys make any reference to impairments of long-lived assets? Comment.

RA12-5   Research Topic

Canfor Corporation, Bowater Canada Inc., Cascades Inc., Doman Industries Limited, and Tembec Industries Inc. are all large companies in the paper and forest products industry in Canada. Their latest annual financial statements can be accessed through their company websites or through SEDAR at www.sedar.com.

Instructions

(a) Because these companies are all in the same industry, it is likely that they have similar types of assets, including tangible capital assets. Because of the similarity of their operations, the expectation might be that their capitalization policies, amortization policies, and amortization rates are similar. Is this the case? Prepare a report on your findings.

(b) It is unlikely that major companies in a single industry earn the same return on the assets employed. Determine, for each of the companies identified above, the total asset turnover, the profit margin, and the return on assets calculated in two ways. Which companies perform the best measured by the return on assets? Do they do this by virtue of generating more revenue with the assets they have at work, or through good cost control? Review the companies' income statements to determine if any anomalies exist. Write a report on your findings.

RA12-6   Research Topic

A topic of significance to not-for-profit organizations that is related to long-lived assets is that of "deferred maintenance." Canadian schools and universities are particularly concerned about this issue.

Instructions

(a) Research the topic of deferred maintenance sufficiently that you understand the term. Explain the concept in 50 words or less.

(b) Interview the chief financial officer of your school, university, or other not-for-profit or government organization to discuss the issue. Can you determine from an organization's financial statements that it has a deferred maintenance problem? Should you be able to? Discuss.

The Intangible Value of Exposure

NETTWERK

With the availability of music free to download off the Internet, record companies have complained loudly about copyright infringement and the threat to their businesses. But one music industry executive isn't worried. Jennifer Beavis is the director of publishing at Nettwerk Songs Publishing, Ltd. in Toronto, a division of Vancouver-based music producer Nettwerk. She represents songwriters, exploiting their copyright through CD sales and the use of their music in film, television, and commercials.

While CD sales have decreased in recent years, film and television companies and advertising agencies have taken a greater interest in the music they include in their productions, and may look to the Internet to find new talent—thus increasing the value of the songwriters' copyright. "You earn an established income from record sales; the industry standard is seven cents per track," Beavis says. "But when it comes to use in TV, film, or commercials, you can attach any value to that song. We're really ramping up this side of the business." Of the 75 or so Nettwerk staff members in Vancouver, Toronto, New York, and Los Angeles, five work exclusively on negotiating synchronization rights, the right to use a song in a production. "Music has increasingly become important in television shows and films. Every movie that comes out, the first thing they think about is the soundtrack album," Beavis says, adding that this is another offshoot in negotiating copyright since it involves a whole other set of rights.■

CHAPTER 13

Goodwill and Other Intangible Assets

Learning Objectives

After studying this chapter, you should be able to:

1. Describe the characteristics of intangible assets.

2. Discuss the recognition and measurement issues of acquiring intangibles.

3. Explain how identifiable intangibles are valued subsequent to acquisition.

4. Identify the types of intangible assets.

5. Explain the conceptual issues related to goodwill.

6. Describe the accounting procedures for recording goodwill at acquisition.

7. Explain the accounting issues related to intangible asset impairments.

8. Differentiate between research and development expenditures, and describe and explain the rationale for the accounting for each.

9. Identify other examples of deferred charges and the accounting requirements for them.

10. Identify the disclosure requirements for intangibles, including deferred charges, and issues related to the analysis of this category of asset.

After studying the appendix to this chapter, you should be able to:

11. Explain various approaches to valuing goodwill.

As the opening story indicates, technology is one factor that plays a major role in the growth of and risk associated with intangible values for companies. The accounting for and reporting of intangible assets takes on increasing importance in this information age. The purpose of this chapter is to explain the basic conceptual and reporting issues related to intangible assets. The content and organization of the chapter are as follows.

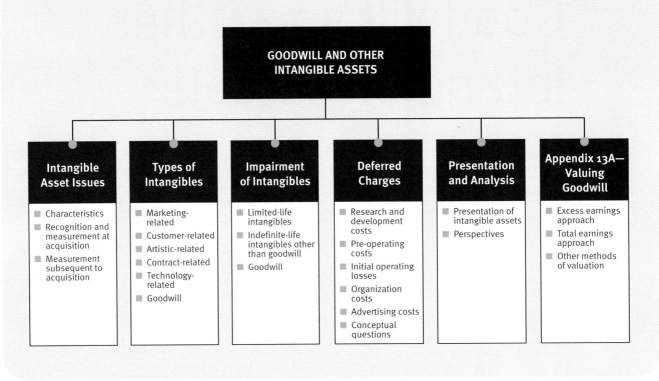

GOODWILL AND OTHER INTANGIBLE ASSETS

Intangible Asset Issues
- Characteristics
- Recognition and measurement at acquisition
- Measurement subsequent to acquisition

Types of Intangibles
- Marketing-related
- Customer-related
- Artistic-related
- Contract-related
- Technology-related
- Goodwill

Impairment of Intangibles
- Limited-life intangibles
- Indefinite-life intangibles other than goodwill
- Goodwill

Deferred Charges
- Research and development costs
- Pre-operating costs
- Initial operating losses
- Organization costs
- Advertising costs
- Conceptual questions

Presentation and Analysis
- Presentation of intangible assets
- Perspectives

Appendix 13A—Valuing Goodwill
- Excess earnings approach
- Total earnings approach
- Other methods of valuation

INTANGIBLE ASSET ISSUES

Characteristics

Objective 1
Describe the characteristics of intangible assets.

Roots Canada's most important asset is not store fixtures—it's the brand image. The major asset of Coca-Cola is not its plant facilities—it's the secret formula for making Coke. Sympatico's most important asset is not its Internet connection equipment—it's the subscriber base. We have an economy increasingly dominated by information and service providers, and their major assets are often intangible in nature. Accounting for these intangibles is difficult, and as a result many intangibles have not been captured on companies' balance sheets.

What are intangible assets? Broadly defined, **intangible assets** are assets that lack physical substance and are not financial assets.[1]

---

[1] *CICA Handbook*, Section 3062.05(c).

1. **They lack physical substance.**   Unlike tangible assets such as inventory and property, plant, and equipment, intangible assets derive their value from the rights and privileges granted to the company using them.

2. **They are not financial instruments.**   Assets such as bank deposits, accounts receivable, and long-term investments in bonds and shares lack physical substance, but they are not classified as intangible assets. These assets are **financial instruments**. They derive their value from the right (or claim) to receive cash or cash equivalents in the future.

In most cases, intangible assets provide benefits over a period of years. As a result, they are normally classified as long-term assets. Examples of intangibles under this definition include widely diverse assets such as patents, copyrights, franchises or licensing agreements, trademarks or trade names, secret formulas, customer lists, computer software, goodwill, technological know-how, superior management, deferred charges, prepayments, and some development costs. The *CICA Handbook* covers goodwill and the more traditional, specifically identifiable intangibles in Section 3062 on "Goodwill and Other Intangible Assets." Others are covered in Section 3450 on research and development costs, Accounting Guideline AcG-12 on servicing assets as a result of transfers of receivables, and Section 3070 on deferred charges, for example.

Recognition and Measurement at Acquisition

Purchased Intangibles

Consistent with the valuation of most assets, **purchased intangible assets are measured at cost—their fair value at acquisition**. Cost includes the acquisition cost and all expenditures necessary to make the intangible asset ready for its intended use; for example, the purchase price, legal fees, and other incidental expenses. Cost, as we've seen in earlier chapters, is the cash cost. If there are delayed payment terms, any portion of the payments representing interest must be recognized as financing expenses rather than part of the capitalized asset cost. If acquired for shares or in exchange for other non-monetary assets, the **cost of the intangible is the fair value of the consideration given or the fair value of the intangible received, whichever is more clearly evident**.

When several intangibles, or a combination of intangibles and tangibles, are bought in a "basket purchase," the cost is allocated on the basis of fair values. Essentially, application of the cost principle for purchased intangibles parallels that for purchased tangible assets.

When an enterprise purchases intangible assets as single assets, the accounting is straightforward. When acquired as part of a group of assets, however, such as in a business combination, the extent to which intangible assets should be given separate recognition and the extent to which they should be considered a part of goodwill must be determined. A **business combination** occurs when one entity acquires control over the net assets of another business either by acquiring the net assets directly or the equity interests representing control over the net assets. In either case, the purchase price must be allocated among all the assets and liabilities to which a value can be attributed—the company's **identifiable net assets**—with any unidentified excess recognized as goodwill.[2]

Identifiable intangibles result from contractual or other legal rights, or can be separated from the entity and sold, transferred, licensed, rented, or exchanged.[3] For example, the right to lease space at favourable rates arises from contractual arrangements and the

2 Objective
Discuss the recognition and measurement issues of acquiring intangibles.

Underlying Concept

The basic attributes of intangibles, their uncertainty as to future benefits, and their uniqueness have discouraged valuation in excess of cost.

IAS Note

IAS 38 allows intangibles that have an active market to be revalued periodically to fair value.

---

[2] If net assets are acquired directly, the purchase price must be allocated directly to the individual assets and liabilities acquired. If control over the assets is acquired through the acquisition of voting shares, the purchase price must be allocated to the identifiable assets and liabilities through the consolidation process.

[3] *CICA Handbook*, Section 1581.48.

right may or may not be transferable to others. A subscription list of a newspaper or successful magazine has value in contributing to future revenue streams and is saleable. These are examples of identifiable intangibles that are given separate recognition.

Goodwill and other intangibles, on the other hand, are not separable from the rest of the entity, and control over the future benefits does not result from contractual or legal rights. For example, the synergies of a combined sales force or a superior management team can be identified as intangibles, but the inability to separately hive off these benefits to exchange them with others or the inability to control the benefits through contractual or other legal rights means that they cannot be granted recognition as separate identifiable intangibles. They, therefore, are considered part of goodwill.

While it is **important to distinguish one identifiable intangible from another**, financial reporting objectives are not well met if each and every identifiable intangible is recognized separately. At a minimum, those with similar characteristics (such as continuity, stability, and risk) should be grouped and recognized together. Because knowledge-based and high-technology companies with large investments in "soft" intangible assets are an important component of our modern economy, the accounting treatment accorded them is a substantive issue.

Lastly, similar to other long-lived assets, subsequent direct costs incurred to enhance the service potential of the intangibles are accounted for as betterments and are capitalized.

Internally Created Intangibles

Costs incurred internally to create intangible assets are **generally expensed as incurred**. For example, even though a company incurs substantial research costs that result in eventually being granted a patent, these costs generally are expensed as incurred. The direct costs of obtaining the intangible asset, such as legal costs, are capitalized.

Various reasons are given for this approach. The primary argument relates to the uncertainty of the future benefits to be derived from the expenditures **when the expenditures are made**. Some argue that the costs incurred internally to create intangibles such as patents and brand names bear no relationship to their real value, and it is difficult to associate the costs incurred with specific intangible assets. Expensing these costs, therefore, is appropriate. When future benefits are reasonably assured, however, both the direct development costs and overhead costs directly attributable to the development activity are capitalized.[4]

Deferred Charges

Some costs incurred currently may be deemed to provide the enterprise with future benefits in excess of the costs incurred. In this situation, a case can be made to defer the costs' recognition until the future benefits are received. Over the last 25 years or so, with the shift toward an accounting model focused on asset and liability definition and away from a revenue and expense approach, it has become less acceptable to recognize deferred charges as assets.[5] As a consequence, accounting standards have been tightened to permit the capitalization of deferred costs only where specific requirements are met.

For subsequent discussion, intangibles are classified into intangible assets that are specifically identifiable, goodwill-type intangible assets, and those that represent deferred charges. The accounting treatment accorded these three types of intangible is shown in Illustration 13-1.

---

[4] *CICA Handbook*, Section 3062.07.

[5] *CICA Handbook* Section 1000.29 defines assets as economic resources controlled by an entity as a result of past transactions or events and from which future economic benefits may be obtained. Many accountants contend that because deferred charges cannot be considered economic resources, they should not be accorded asset status.

Type of Intangible	Manner Acquired	
	Purchased	Internally Created
Identifiable intangibles	Capitalize	Expense, except certain costs
Goodwill-type intangibles	Capitalize	Expense
Deferred charges	Capitalize restricted amounts	Capitalize restricted amounts

Illustration 13-1

Accounting for the Acquisition Costs of Intangibles

Measurement Subsequent to Acquisition

As indicated above, intangibles are a diverse mix of assets. Some intangibles have values based on rights that are conveyed legally by contract, statute, or similar means. Examples include a Tim Hortons franchise or licences granted by government to cable companies. Some of these rights have finite legal lives that can be easily renewed; others have lives that are not renewable, or are renewable at a significant cost. Some may be granted into perpetuity and be saleable, or they may not be exchangeable. Internally developed intangibles such as customer lists and databases have a wide range of useful lives, some of which may even be indefinite if the asset is maintained. An **indefinite life** does not mean "infinite"—that the asset will last forever—but means that there are no legal, regulatory, contractual, competitive, economic, or other factors that appear to limit its useful life to the entity.[6]

Accounting standards used to require all intangibles to be amortized over their useful lives, over a period not exceeding 40 years. While this simplified the accounting, the reality is that intangibles are diverse, and the approach to their valuation subsequent to acquisition should be based on their specific characteristics. Under current standards, if an intangible has a finite useful life, it is amortized over that useful life. If the intangible has an indefinite life and gives no indication of impairment, financial reporting is better served by retaining the asset in the accounts unless the asset is determined to be impaired or its life becomes finite.

3 Objective

Explain how identifiable intangibles are valued subsequent to acquisition.

IAS Note

IAS 38 specifies that intangibles should be amortized over a maximum period of 20 years, but is in the process of harmonizing with the Canadian and U.S. standards.

Limited-Life Intangibles

An intangible asset with a finite or limited life is amortized by systematic charges to expense over its useful life. The useful life should reflect the periods over which these assets will contribute to cash flows. Factors considered in determining useful life are:

1. The expected use of the asset by the entity.

2. The expected useful life of another asset or a group of assets to which the useful life of the intangible asset may relate (such as mineral rights to depleting assets).

3. Any legal, regulatory, or contractual provisions that may limit the useful life.

4. Any legal, regulatory, or contractual provisions that enable renewal or extension of the asset's legal or contractual life without substantial cost. This factor assumes that there is evidence to support renewal or extension and that either can be accomplished without material modifications of the existing terms and conditions.

5. The effects of obsolescence, demand, competition, and other economic factors. Examples include the stability of the industry, known technological advances, legislative action that results in an uncertain or changing regulatory environment, and expected changes in distribution channels.

6. The level of maintenance expenditure required to obtain the expected future cash flows from the asset. For example, a material level of required maintenance in relation to the carrying amount of the asset may suggest a very limited useful life.[7]

---

[6] *CICA Handbook*, Section 3062.15.

[7] *CICA Handbook*, Section 3062.15.

The amount of amortization expense for a limited-life intangible asset should reflect the pattern in which the asset is consumed or used up, if that pattern can be reliably determined. For example, assume that Second Wave, Inc. has purchased a licence to manufacture a limited quantity of a gene product, called Mega. The cost of the licence should be amortized following the pattern of production of Mega. If the pattern of production or consumption cannot be determined, the straight-line method is used. For the assignment material, assume use of the straight-line method unless stated otherwise. The amortization charges are shown **as expenses**, and the credits are made to **separate accumulated amortization accounts**.

The amount of an intangible asset to be amortized is its cost less residual value. Uncertainties about residual values for intangibles are greater than those for items of property, plant, and equipment. Because of this, an intangible asset's residual value is assumed to be zero unless there is a commitment from a third party to purchase the asset at the end of its useful life, or there is an observable market for the asset that is expected to exist at the end of its useful life to the enterprise.[8]

What happens if a limited-life intangible asset's useful life is changed? In that case, the remaining carrying amount is amortized over the revised remaining useful life. Limited-life intangibles are also **evaluated for impairment**. Similar to property, plant, and equipment, an impairment loss is recognized if the intangible's carrying amount is not recoverable and its carrying amount exceeds its fair value.

Indefinite-Life Intangibles

An intangible asset with an indefinite life **is not amortized**. For example, assume that Double Clik, Inc. acquired a trademark that is used to distinguish a leading consumer product. The trademark is renewable every 10 years at minimal cost. All evidence indicates that this trademark product will generate cash flows for an indefinite period of time. In this case, the trademark has an indefinite life because it is expected to contribute to cash flows indefinitely.

Indefinite-life intangibles should be tested for impairment at least annually. The impairment test **compares the fair value of an intangible asset with its carrying amount. This impairment test is different** from the one used for limited-life intangibles and property, plant, and equipment. For indefinite-life intangibles, **there is no recoverability test**—the intangible's carrying amount is compared directly with its fair value and written down where the fair value is lower, with no reversal if the fair value subsequently increases.

A summary of the accounting treatment for intangible assets subsequent to acquisition is shown in Illustration 13-2.

Illustration 13-2

Accounting Treatment of Intangible Assets after Acquisition

Type of intangible	Amortization	Impairment test
Limited-life intangible	Over useful life	Recoverability test and then fair value test
Indefinite-life intangible	Do not amortize	Fair value test

TYPES OF INTANGIBLES

Objective 4
Identify the types of intangible assets.

As indicated, the accounting for intangible assets depends on whether the intangible has a limited or an indefinite life. The many different types of intangibles are often classified into the following six major categories.[9]

---

[8] *CICA Handbook*, Section 3062.13.

[9] This classification framework is used in "Business Combinations," *CICA Handbook* Section 1581, Appendix A.

1. Marketing-related intangible assets

2. Customer-related intangible assets

3. Artistic-related intangible assets

4. Contract-related intangible assets

5. Technology-related intangible assets

6. Goodwill

Marketing-Related Intangible Assets

Marketing-related intangible assets are those assets primarily used in the marketing or promotion of products or services. Examples are trademarks or trade names, newspaper mastheads, Internet domain names, and non-competition agreements.

A very common form of a marketing-related intangible asset is a trademark or trade name. A trademark or trade name is one or more words, or a series of letters or numbers, or a design or shape that distinguishes or identifies a particular enterprise or product. The right to use a trademark or trade name in Canada is granted by the federal government and the registration system is administered by its Trade-marks Office. In order to obtain and maintain a protected trademark or trade name, the owner must have made prior and continuing use of it. Trade names like Kraft Dinner, Pepsi-Cola, Oldsmobile, Excedrin, Shreddies, and Sunkist create immediate product recognition in our minds, thereby enhancing their marketability. Company names themselves identify qualities and characteristics that the companies have worked hard and spent much to develop.[10]

If a trademark or trade name is purchased, its capitalizable cost is the purchase price and other direct costs of acquisition. If a trademark or trade name is developed by the enterprise itself and its future benefits to the company are reasonably assured, the costs capitalized include lawyers' fees, registration fees, design costs, consulting fees, successful legal defence costs, expenditures related to securing the trademark or trade name, direct development costs, and overhead costs directly related to its development. When a trademark or trade name's total cost is insignificant or if future benefits are uncertain, it is expensed rather than capitalized.

Trademark registrations in Canada last for 15 years, and are renewable at a reasonable cost. Although the legal life of a trademark, trade name, or company name in substance **may be unlimited**, the period over which they provide benefits to the enterprise **may be finite**. Trademarks could be determined to provide benefits to an enterprise indefinitely. A trade name such as Coca-Cola, worth billions of dollars, may reasonably be determined to have an indefinite useful life. In this case, the trade name is not amortized.

Customer-Related Intangible Assets

Customer-related intangible assets occur as a result of interactions with outside parties. Examples are customer lists, order or production backlogs, and both contractual and non-contractual customer relationships.

To illustrate, assume that We-Market Inc. acquired the customer list of a large newspaper for $6 million on January 1, 2005. The customer list is a database that includes

---

[10] To illustrate how various intangibles might arise from a given product, consider what the creators of the highly successful game, Trivial Pursuit, did to protect their creation. First, they copyrighted the 6,000 questions that are at the heart of the game. Then they shielded the Trivial Pursuit name by applying for a registered trademark. As a third mode of protection, the creators obtained a design patent on the playing board's design because it represents a unique graphic creation.

name, contact information, order history, and demographic information for a list of customers. We-Market expects to benefit from the information on the acquired list for three years, and it believes that these benefits will be spread evenly over the three years. In this case, the customer list is a limited-life intangible that should be amortized on a straight-line basis over the three-year period.

The entries to record the purchase of the customer list and its amortization at the end of each year are as follows.

A = L + SE
0   0   0

Cash flows: ↓ 6,000,000 outflow

January 1, 2005		
Customer List	6,000,000	
Cash		6,000,000
To record purchase of customer list.		

A = L + SE
−2,000,000   −2,000,000

Cash flows: No effect

December 31, 2005, 2006, 2007		
Amortization Expense—Customer List	2,000,000	
Accumulated Amortization—Customer List		2,000,000
To record amortization expense.		

In this example it is assumed that the customer list has no residual value. But what if We-Market determines that it can sell the list for $60,000 to another company at the end of three years? In that case, this residual value is subtracted from the cost in order to determine the amortizable amount. *CICA Handbook* Section 3062.13 assumes a residual value of zero, unless the asset's useful life is less than the economic life and there is reliable evidence concerning the existence and amount of residual value.

Artistic-Related Intangible Assets

Artistic-related intangible assets involve ownership rights to plays, literary works, musical works, pictures, photographs, and video and audiovisual material. These ownership rights are protected by copyrights.

A **copyright** is a federally granted right that all authors, painters, musicians, sculptors, and other artists have in their creations, whatever the mode or form of expression. A copyright is granted for the life of the creator plus 50 years, and gives the owner or heirs the exclusive right to reproduce and sell an artistic or published work. Copyrights are not renewable. Like trade names, they may be assigned or sold to other individuals. The costs of acquiring and defending a copyright may be capitalized, but the research costs involved are expensed as incurred.

Generally, the copyright's useful life is less than its legal life, and determination of its useful life is unique to the facts and circumstances in each case. Consumer habits, market trends, and prior experience all play a part, as indicated in the opening story to this chapter. The difficulty in determining the periods benefiting normally encourages companies to write these costs off over a fairly short period of time. Amortization of the copyright should be charged to the years in which the benefits are expected to be received.

Copyrights can be valuable. Really Useful Group is a company that consists of copyrights on the musicals of Andrew Lloyd Webber: *Cats*, *Phantom of the Opera*, *Jesus Christ Superstar*, and others. It has little in the way of hard assets, yet it has been valued at $300 million (U.S.). The Walt Disney Co. faced the loss of its copyright on Mickey Mouse on January 1, 2004, a loss that might affect sales of billions of dollars of Mickey-related goods and services, including theme parks. How this plays out will be determined by whether Disney can use its trademarks on Mickey (which can be renewed indefinitely) to protect itself, and how successful it, and other large entertainment companies are at lobbying the U.S. Congress for copyright extension.

Contract-Related Intangible Assets

Contract-related intangible assets represent the value of rights that arise from contractual arrangements. Examples are licensing arrangements, leaseholds, construction permits, broadcast rights, and service or supply contracts. A very common form of contract-based intangible asset is a franchise.

When you drive down the street in an automobile purchased from a Toyota dealer, fill your tank at the corner Petro-Canada station, grab a coffee at Tim Hortons, eat lunch at McDonald's, cool off with a Baskin-Robbins cone, work at a Coca-Cola bottling plant, live in a home purchased through a Royal Le Page real estate broker, or vacation at a Holiday Inn resort, you are dealing with franchises. A **franchise** is a contractual arrangement under which the franchisor grants the franchisee the right to sell certain products or services, to use certain trademarks or trade names, or to perform certain functions, usually within a designated geographical area. **Licensing agreements** work in a similar way, such as when Kraft Foods Inc. recently paid $19.5 million to acquire the rights to the Life Savers candy brand in Canada.

The franchisor, having developed a unique concept or product, protects its concept or product through a patent, copyright, trademark, or trade name. The franchisee acquires the right to exploit the franchisor's idea or product by signing a franchise agreement. Another type of franchise is the arrangement commonly entered into by a municipality (or other government body) and a business enterprise that uses public property. In such cases, a privately owned enterprise is permitted to use public property in performing its services. Examples are the use of public waterways for a ferry service, the use of public land for telephone or electric lines, the use of city streets for a bus line, or the use of the airwaves for radio or TV broadcasting. Such operating rights, obtained through agreements with governmental units or agencies, are frequently referred to as **licences** or **permits**.

Franchises and licences may be granted for a definite period of time, for an indefinite period of time, or in perpetuity. The enterprise securing the franchise or licence recognizes an intangible asset account entitled Franchise, Licence, or Brand on its books only when there are costs (such as a lump sum payment in advance or legal fees and other expenditures) that are identified with the acquisition of the operating right. The cost of a franchise or licence **with a limited life** is amortized over the lesser of its legal or useful life. A franchise **with an indefinite life**, **or a perpetual franchise**, is amortized if its useful life to the enterprise is deemed to be limited. Otherwise, it is not amortized. It continues to be carried at cost.

Annual payments made under a franchise agreement are entered as operating expenses in the period in which they are incurred. They do not represent an asset to the enterprise since they do not relate to future rights.

Another contract-related intangible asset is a **leasehold**: a contractual understanding between a lessor (property owner) and a lessee (property renter) that grants the lessee **the right to use specific property, owned by the lessor, for a specific period of time in return for stipulated, and generally periodic, cash payments**. In most cases, the periodic rent is included as an expense on the lessee's books. Special problems may develop in situations where there is a lease prepayment, or where the contract results in a **capital lease**.

If the rent for the lease period is paid in advance, or if a lump sum payment is made in advance in addition to periodic rental payments, both **lease prepayments**, it is necessary to allocate this rent to the proper periods. The lessee has purchased the exclusive right to use the property for an extended period of time. These prepayments are reported as a prepaid expense or deferred charge rather than an identifiable intangible asset.

Leasehold improvements—improvements made to leased property by the lessee—revert to the lessor at the end of the lease. These are usually recognized and accounted for as property, plant, and equipment rather than as intangible assets. The rationale for intangible asset treatment is that the improvements revert to the lessor at the end of the lease and are therefore more of a right than a tangible asset.

In cases where the lease agreement transfers substantially all of the benefits and risks incident to property ownership so that the economic effect on both parties is similar to that of an instalment purchase, the lease is capitalized as a tangible rather than an intangible asset. Such a lease is referred to as a **capital lease**. Accounting for leases is covered in more detail in Chapter 21.

Technology-Related Intangible Assets

Technology-related intangible assets relate to innovations or technological advances such as patented technology and trade secrets. To illustrate, patents are granted by the federal government. The two principal kinds of patents are product patents, which cover actual physical products, and process patents, which govern the process by which products are made. A patent gives the holder the right to exclude others from making, selling, or using a product or process for a period of 20 years from the date of application. Fortunes can be made by holding patents, as companies such as Bombardier, IMAX, Polaroid, and Xerox can attest.[11]

If a patent is purchased from an inventor or other owner, the purchase price represents its cost. Other costs incurred in connection with securing a patent, as well as legal fees and other unrecovered costs of a successful lawsuit to protect the patent, can be capitalized as part of the patent cost. Research and development costs related to developing the product, process, or idea that is subsequently patented, however, are usually expensed as incurred. A more complete discussion of accounting for research and development costs is found later in this chapter.

The cost of a patent is amortized over its legal life or its useful life (the period during which benefits from the product or process are expected to be received), **whichever is shorter**. If a patent is owned from the date it is granted, and it is expected to be useful during its entire legal life, it should be amortized over 20 years. If it appears that it will be useful for a shorter period of time, say, for five years, its cost should be amortized to expense over five years. Changing demand, new inventions superceding old ones, inadequacy, and other factors often limit the useful life of a patent to less than the legal life. For example, the useful life of patents in the pharmaceutical and drug industry is often less than the legal life because of the testing and approval period that follows their issuance. A typical drug patent has five to 11 years knocked off its 20-year legal life because one to four years must be spent on tests on animals, four to six years on human tests, and two to three years for government agencies to review the tests—all after the patent is issued but before the product goes on the pharmacist's shelves.

Legal fees and other costs associated with a successful defence of a patent are capitalized as part of the asset's cost because such a suit establishes the legal rights of the patent holder. Such costs are amortized along with acquisition cost over the remaining useful life of the patent.

Ideally, patent amortization should follow a pattern consistent with the benefits received, if that pattern can be reliably determined. This could be based on time or on units produced. To illustrate, assume that on January 1, 2005, Harcott Ltd. either pays $180,000 to acquire a patent or incurs $180,000 in legal costs to successfully defend an internally developed patent. Further, assume the patent has a remaining useful life of 12 years, and is amortized on a straight-line basis. The entries to record the $180,000 expenditure and the amortization at the end of each year are as follows.

---

[11] Consider the opposite result: Sir Alexander Fleming, who discovered penicillin, decided not to use a patent to protect his discovery. He hoped that companies would produce it more quickly to help save sufferers. Companies, however, refused to develop it because they did not have the protection of a patent and, therefore, were afraid to make the investment.

January 1, 2005		
Patents	180,000	
Cash		180,000
To record expenditure related to patent.		

December 31, 2005		
Patent Amortization Expense	15,000	
Accumulated Amortization, Patents		15,000
To record amortization of patent.		

A = L + SE
0   0   0
Cash flows: ↓ 180,000 outflow

A = L + SE
−15,000   −15,000
Cash flows: No effect

Although a patent's useful life may be limited by its legal life, small modifications or additions may lead to a new patent and an extension of the life of the old patent. In that case it is permissible to apply the unamortized costs of the old patent to the new patent if the new patent provides essentially the same benefits.[12] Alternatively, if a patent's value is reduced because demand drops for the product, for example, the asset should be tested for impairment.

Coca-Cola has managed to keep the recipe for the world's best-selling soft drink under wraps for more than 100 years. How has it done so? The company, offers almost no information about its lifeblood. The only written copy of the formula resides in a bank vault in Atlanta, Georgia. This handwritten sheet isn't available to anyone except by vote of the Coca-Cola board of directors.

Why can't science offer some clues? Coke contains 17 to 18 ingredients. That includes the usual caramel colour and corn syrup, as well as a blend of oils known as 7X—rumoured to be a mix of orange, lemon, cinnamon, and others. Distilling natural products like these is complicated, since they're made of thousands of compounds. One ingredient you won't find is cocaine. Although the original formula contained trace amounts, today's Coke doesn't. When was it removed? That is a secret, too. Some experts indicate that the power of this formula and related brand image account for almost 95% of Coke's $150 billion (U.S.) share value.

Source: Adapted from Reed Tucker, "How Has Coke's Formula Stayed a Secret?" *Fortune* (July 24, 2000), p.42.

What do the Numbers Mean?

Another common technology-based intangible relates to **computer software costs**, either for internal use or for sale as a product. Costs incurred in the development of software as a product **for external use** is discussed under research and development costs later in this chapter. The accounting for "costs of activities directly attributable to the development, betterment or acquisition of computer software **for internal use**" is covered by the capitalization criteria in *CICA Handbook* Section 3062 on "Goodwill and Other Intangible Assets."[13] This means that the cost of software purchased, and the direct costs and overhead costs directly attributable to the development of software for internal use may be recognized as intangible assets—provided future benefits are reasonably assured. The cost of any modifications to the computer software may be capitalized only when they meet the definition of a betterment.

What about the costs a company incurs in developing its own website? The Emerging Issues Committee of the CICA concluded in EIC-118 that the **costs incurred in**

---

[12] **Eli Lilly's** well known drug Prozac, used to treat depression, accounted for 43% of the company's U.S. sales in 1998. The patent on Prozac expired in 2001 and the company was unable to extend its protection with a second-use patent for the use of Prozac to treat appetite disorders. Sales of Prozac were off substantially in 2001 as generic equivalents entered the market. *The Economist* reported that by 2006 patents would expire for an estimated 11 biotech drugs with combined sales of more than $13 billion U.S. a year, spurring competition from generic drugs. (October 11–17, 2003)

[13] *CICA Handbook*, EIC-86.

developing a website were varied, and that the accounting treatment should be contingent on the type of activity. In general, costs incurred in the planning stage, costs to convert existing content to the new system, and regular operating costs should be expensed as incurred. On the other hand, costs incurred in the website application and infrastructure development stage and expenditures to develop the initial graphics that provide the overall design of the web page should be capitalized. In effect, the principles that underlie the recognition and measurement criteria in *CICA Handbook* Sections 3061 and 3062 on tangible and intangible long-lived assets are applied here as well.

Goodwill

Objective 5
Explain the conceptual issues related to goodwill.

Although companies are permitted to capitalize certain costs to develop specifically identifiable assets such as patents and copyrights, the amounts capitalized are generally not significant. Material amounts of intangible assets are recorded, however, when companies purchase intangible assets, particularly in situations involving the purchase of another business, often referred to as a business combination.

In a business combination, the cost (purchase price) of the business is assigned where possible to the identifiable tangible and intangible net assets acquired, and the remainder is recorded in an intangible asset account called goodwill. **Goodwill** is the excess of the cost of the acquired enterprise over the net of the amounts assigned to identifiable assets acquired and liabilities assumed.[14] Goodwill is often referred to as the most intangible of the intangibles. It is an unidentified excess, and it can only be calculated in relation to the business as a whole. The only way it can be sold is to sell the business.

Recognition of Goodwill

Internally Created Goodwill

Objective 6
Describe the accounting procedures for recording goodwill at acquisition.

Goodwill generated internally is not capitalized in the accounts. Measuring the components of goodwill is simply too complex and associating any costs with future benefits too difficult. The future benefits of goodwill may have no relationship to the costs incurred in its development. To add to the mystery, goodwill may even exist in the absence of specific costs to develop it. In addition, because no objective transaction with outside parties has taken place, a great deal of subjectivity—even misrepresentation—might be involved in trying to measure it.

Purchased Goodwill

Underlying Concept

Capitalizing goodwill only when it is purchased in an arm's length transaction and not capitalizing any goodwill generated internally is another example of reliability winning out over relevance.

Goodwill is recognized for accounting purposes only in a business combination, because the value of goodwill cannot be separated from the business as a whole. The problem of determining the proper cost to allocate to identifiable intangible assets in a business combination is complex because of the many different types of intangibles that might be acquired. Because goodwill is a residual amount, every dollar that is allocated to other assets, including identifiable intangible assets, is one less dollar assigned to goodwill. Thus, goodwill is often described as a residual, a "plug" amount—**the excess of cost over the fair value of the identifiable net assets acquired**.

To illustrate, Multi-Diversified, Inc. decides that it needs a parts division to supplement its existing tractor distributorship. The president of Multi-Diversified is interested in buying Tractorling, a small concern near Toronto that has an established reputation and is seeking a merger candidate. The balance sheet of Tractorling Ltd. is presented in Illustration 13-3.

---

[14] *CICA Handbook*, Section 1581.06(c).

Illustration 13-3

Tractorling Balance Sheet

TRACTORLING LTD.
Balance Sheet
December 31, 2004

Assets		Equities	
Cash	$ 25,000	Current liabilities	$ 55,000
Receivables	35,000	Share capital	100,000
Inventories	42,000	Retained earnings	100,000
Property, plant, and equipment, net	153,000		
Total assets	$255,000	Total equities	$255,000

After considerable negotiation, Tractorling Ltd. shareholders decide to accept Multi-Diversified's offer of $400,000. What is the value of the goodwill, if any?

The answer is not obvious. The fair values of Tractorling's identifiable assets are not disclosed in its cost-based balance sheet. It is likely, though, that as the negotiations progressed, Multi-Diversified conducted an investigation of Tractorling's underlying assets to determine their fair values. Such an investigation may be undertaken through a purchase audit by Multi-Diversified's auditors, or an independent appraisal from some other source. The following valuations are determined.

Illustration 13-4

Fair Values of Tractorling's Identifiable Net Assets

Fair Values, December 31, 2004

Cash	$ 25,000
Receivables	35,000
Inventories	122,000
Property, plant, and equipment, net	205,000
Patents	18,000
Liabilities	(55,000)
Fair value of identifiable net assets	$350,000

Normally, differences between current fair value and book value are more common among long-term assets, although significant differences can also develop in the current asset category. Cash obviously poses no problems as to value and receivables normally are fairly close to current valuation, although at times adjustments need to be made because of inadequate bad debt provisions. The fair values of liabilities usually are relatively close to recorded book values. However, if interest rates have changed since long-term liabilities were incurred, their current value, determined using current interest rates, may differ substantially from book value. Careful analysis must be undertaken to determine that no unrecorded liabilities exist.

The $80,000 difference between the cost and fair value of inventories ($122,000 − $42,000) could result from a number of factors. One explanation might be that Tractorling uses a LIFO cost valuation, in which ending inventory is made up of inventory at older, lower costs.

In many cases, the values of long-lived assets such as property, plant, and equipment and intangibles may have increased substantially over the years. Any difference could be due to inaccurate estimates of useful lives, a policy of continual expensing of small expenditures (say, less than $1,000), inaccurate estimates of residual values, or substantial increases in replacement costs. Alternatively, there may be assets that have not been given accounting recognition. In Tractorling's case, internally developed patents had not been recognized in the accounts, yet they have a fair value of $18,000.

Since the fair value of net assets is determined to be $350,000, why would Multi-Diversified pay $400,000? Undoubtedly, the seller points to an established reputation, good credit rating, a top management team, well-trained employees, and so on as factors that make the value of the business as a going concern greater than $350,000. At the same time, Multi-Diversified places a premium on the future earning power of these attributes as well as the enterprise's basic asset structure today. At this point in the negotiations, price can be a function of many factors; the most important is probably sheer skill at the bargaining table.[15]

The difference between the purchase price of $400,000 and the fair value of the identifiable net assets of $350,000 is labelled goodwill. Goodwill is viewed as one or a group of unidentifiable values plus the value of the identifiable intangibles that don't meet the criteria for separate recognition. The cost assigned to goodwill is the difference between the cost to the purchaser of the business as a whole and the costs assigned to the identifiable net assets acquired. This procedure for valuation, shown in Illustration 13-5, is referred to as a master valuation approach, because goodwill is assumed to cover all the values that cannot be specifically identified with any identifiable tangible or intangible asset.

Illustration 13-5

Determination of Goodwill—
Master Valuation Approach

Cash	$ 25,000
Receivables	35,000
Inventories	122,000
Property, plant, and equipment	205,000
Patents	18,000
Liabilities	(55,000)
Fair value of identifiable net assets	$350,000
Purchase price	400,000
Value assigned to goodwill	$ 50,000

The entry to record the purchase of the net assets of Tractorling is as follows.[16]

A   =   L   +   SE
+55,000   +55,000

Cash flows: ↓ 375,000 outflow

Cash	25,000	
Receivables	35,000	
Inventories	122,000	
Property, plant, and equipment	205,000	
Patents	18,000	
Goodwill	50,000	
Liabilities		55,000
Cash		400,000

Negative Goodwill—Badwill

Negative goodwill, occasionally dubbed badwill, or bargain purchase, arises when the fair value of the identifiable net assets acquired is higher than the purchase price of the acquired entity. This situation is a result of market imperfection because the seller would be better off to sell the assets individually than in total. However, situations do occur in which the pur-

IAS Note

Under IAS 22, negative goodwill due to expected future losses or expenses is deferred and recognized in income when the losses or expenses are recognized; amounts up to the fair value of the identifiable assets are recognized over the life of those assets; any excess is recognized in income immediately.

[15] Sometimes the excess paid is a function of the purchaser's stubbornness or ego, i.e., wanting the business at any price. In this situation, the price paid in excess of the business' fair value should be recognized as a loss.

[16] If Multi-Diversified purchased all of Tractorling's shares instead of the net assets directly, the entry would be:

Investment in Shares of Tractorling	400,000	
Cash		400,000

When Multi-Diversified prepares consolidated financial statements, the Investment account is removed from the balance sheet and is replaced with the underlying assets and liabilities it represents. Regardless of the transaction's legal form, the goodwill appears on the investor's balance sheet.

chase price is less than the value of the identifiable net assets and therefore a credit develops. This credit is referred to as **negative goodwill** or **excess of acquired net assets over cost**.

How should this resulting credit be handled in the accounts? Should it be taken to retained earnings directly, to the income statement in the year of purchase, or amortized to income over a reasonable future period? *CICA Handbook* Section 1581 recommends that the excess be used to reduce the amounts assigned to other acquired assets that are generally non-financial in nature. If their values are reduced to zero and some of the excess still remains, the excess amount is treated as an extraordinary gain. While many do not agree with the recognition of a gain **on the purchase of assets**, this treatment appears to be a practical approach to a situation that rarely occurs. Further discussion is left to an advanced course in financial accounting.

Valuation after Acquisition

Once goodwill has been recognized in the accounts, how should it be treated in subsequent periods? Three basic approaches have been suggested.

1. **Charge goodwill off immediately to shareholders' equity.** Goodwill differs from other types of assets and demands special treatment. Unlike other assets, it is not separable and distinct from the business as a whole and therefore is not an asset in the same sense as cash, receivables, or plant assets. In other words, goodwill cannot be sold without selling the business.

   Supporters of this approach further justify this treatment because the accounting for purchased goodwill and goodwill created internally would be consistent. Goodwill created internally is immediately expensed and does not appear as an asset; the same treatment, they argue, should be accorded purchased goodwill. Amortization of purchased goodwill leads to double counting, because net income is reduced by amortization of the purchased goodwill as well as by the internal expenditure made to maintain or enhance the value of assets. In addition, perhaps the best rationale for direct write-off is that determining the periods over which the future benefits are to be received is so difficult that immediate charging to shareholders' equity is justified.

2. **Amortize goodwill over its useful life.** Others believe that goodwill has value when acquired, but that its value eventually disappears and it is proper that the asset be charged to expense over the periods affected. Supporters of this view contend that to the extent goodwill represents wasting assets, this method provides a better matching of costs and revenues than other methods, even though the useful life may be difficult to determine.

3. **Retain goodwill indefinitely unless reduction in value occurs.** Many believe that goodwill can have an indefinite life and should be retained as an asset until a decline in value occurs. They contend that some form of goodwill should always be an asset inasmuch as internal goodwill is being expensed to maintain or enhance the purchased goodwill. In addition, without sufficient evidence that a decline in value has occurred, a write-off of goodwill is both arbitrary and capricious and leads to distortions in net income.

Prior to 2002, companies were required to amortize goodwill over a period not exceeding 40 years. Goodwill acquired in a business combination **is now considered to have an indefinite life and is no longer amortized**. The standard setters' position is that investors find the amortization charge of little use in evaluating performance. In addition, although goodwill may decrease over time, predicting the actual life of goodwill and an appropriate pattern of amortization is extremely difficult. Therefore, **income statements are not charged with any costs of goodwill unless it is determined that the goodwill has been impaired**.

International Insight

Standard setters have had difficulty determining the most appropriate method. Until recently, companies in the UK were allowed to write off goodwill immediately against equity. In 1998, UK companies were required to capitalize and amortize goodwill. Now they will likely move with the IAS to a non-amortization and test-for-impairment policy.

IAS Note

The **international standard currently** is to amortize goodwill over its useful life to a maximum of 20 years, unless a longer period can be justified. Amendments are being proposed to move to a non-amortization and test-for-impairment approach.

The Accounting Standards Board decided that **nonamortization of goodwill combined with an adequate impairment test** provides the most useful financial information to the investment community. With no amortization of goodwill, the onus is on management to ensure the carrying value of this intangible asset is tested for impairment.

This change in accounting standard has had a significant effect on the income statements of many companies, because goodwill is often a major asset on a company's balance sheet. Quebecor Inc., for example, reported an income of $91.9 million for its year ended December 31, 2002. **If the accounting standard had not changed**, the company would have had an additional $123.3 million of amortization expense (after tax and non-controlling interest) related to goodwill and reported a loss of $31.4 million. In addition, because companies were also required to review their existing goodwill and recognize any impairments as an adjustment to their opening balance of retained earnings when the new standard was first applied, Quebecor recognized a goodwill impairment loss of $2.163 billion at January 1, 2002—a charge that never saw nor will see an income statement!

IMPAIRMENT OF INTANGIBLE ASSETS

Objective 7

Explain the accounting issues related to intangible asset impairments.

In some cases, the carrying amount of a long-lived asset—whether property, plant, and equipment or an intangible—exceeds its fair value and therefore an impairment in its value has occured. This requires a writedown of its carrying amount and the recognition of an impairment loss.

Impairment of Limited-Life Intangibles

The rules that apply to **impairments of long-lived tangible assets also apply to limited-life intangibles**.[17] As indicated in Chapter 12, long-lived assets to be held and used by a company are to be reviewed for impairment whenever events or changes in circumstances indicate that **the carrying amount of the assets may not be recoverable**. In applying the recoverability test, the company estimates the future net cash flows expected to result from the use of the asset and its eventual disposition. If the sum of the **undiscounted** expected future net cash inflows is less than the carrying amount of the asset, an impairment loss must be measured and recognized. Otherwise, no impairment loss is recognized.[18] The impairment loss is the amount by which the carrying amount of the asset fails the fair value test; that is, the amount by which it exceeds the asset's fair value. As with other impairments, the loss is usually reported as part of income from continuing operations.

To illustrate, assume an enterprise has a patent on a process to extract oil from shale rock. Unfortunately, reduced oil prices have made the shale oil technology somewhat unprofitable, and the patent has provided little income to date. As a result, a recoverability test is performed, and it is found that the expected net future cash flows from this patent are $3.5 million. The patent has a carrying amount of $6 million. Because the net recoverable amount of $3.5 million is less than the carrying amount of $6 million, an impairment loss must be measured. Discounting the expected net future cash flows at the market rate of interest, the fair value of the patent is determined to be $2 million. The impairment loss calculation—the fair value test—is shown in Illustration 13-6.

---

[17] *CICA Handbook*, Section 3062.18.

[18] *CICA Handbook*, Section 3063.04 and .05.

Carrying amount of patent	$6,000,000
Fair value (based on discounted cash flows)	2,000,000
Loss on impairment	$4,000,000

Illustration 13-6

Calculation of Loss on Impairment of Patent

The journal entry to record this loss is:

Loss on Impairment	4,000,000	
Accumulated Amortization, Patents		4,000,000

A   = L +   SE
−4,000,000   −4,000,000
Cash flows: No effect

After the impairment is recognized, the patent's reduced carrying amount is its new cost basis. The patent's revised net book value is amortized over its useful life or legal life, whichever is shorter. If oil prices increase in subsequent periods and the patent's net recoverable amount recovers, **restoration of the previously recognized impairment loss is not permitted**.

Impairment of Indefinite-Life Intangibles other than Goodwill

Indefinite-life intangibles other than goodwill should be tested for impairment at least annually, or more often if changes in circumstances indicate an asset may be impaired.[19] The impairment test for an indefinite-life asset other than goodwill is a **fair value test**. This test compares the fair value of the intangible asset with the asset's carrying amount. If its fair value is less than the carrying amount, an impairment loss is recognized. Why is there a different standard for indefinite-life intangibles? This one-step test is used because it would be relatively easy for many indefinite-life assets to meet the recoverability test—the cash flows would extend many years into the future. **As a result, the recoverability test is not used.**

To illustrate, assume a company purchases a broadcast licence for $2.1 million. The licence is renewable every 10 years if the company provides appropriate service and does not violate the rules and regulations of the Canadian Radio-television and Telecommunications Commission (CRTC). The licence has been renewed with the CRTC twice, at a minimal cost. Cash flows were expected to last indefinitely, and therefore, the licence has been reported as an indefinite-life intangible asset. Assume that the CRTC decides to no longer renew broadcast licences, but to auction these licences to the highest bidder. With two years remaining in the life of the existing licence, the company performs an impairment test and determines that the fair value of the intangible asset is $750,000. As shown in Illustration 13-7, an impairment loss of $1,350,000 is indicated and recorded in the accounts.

Carrying amount of broadcast licence	$2,100,000
Fair value of broadcast licence	750,000
Loss on impairment	$1,350,000

Illustration 13-7

Calculation of Loss on Impairment of Broadcast Licence

Because there is no accumulated amortization account for the licence, the asset account itself is reduced. The licence will now be reported at $750,000, its fair value. Even if the value of the licence increases in the remaining two years, restoration of the previously recognized impairment loss is not permitted.[20]

---

[19] Entities that qualify for differential reporting under *CICA Handbook* Section 1300 may elect to test for impairment only when an event or circumstance occurs that indicates the asset's carrying value may not be recoverable (*CICA Handbook*, Section 3062.59).

[20] *CICA Handbook*, Section 3062.21.

Impairment of Goodwill

Goodwill is required to be tested for impairment on an annual basis unless specific criteria are met that indicate there is a remote possibility of an impairment in value.[21] The impairment rule for goodwill is a **two-step process specific to this unique type of asset**.

1. Compare the fair value of the reporting unit against its carrying amount including goodwill.[22] If the fair value of the reporting unit exceeds its book value, goodwill is considered not to be impaired. Nothing further is required. If the fair value is less than the book value of the unit, proceed to step 2.

2. Determine if goodwill is impaired by:

   (a) calculating its implied current fair value, and

   (b) comparing its current fair value with its carrying amount.

   Its implied current fair value is calculated by comparing the fair value of the reporting unit as a whole with the fair value of its identifiable net assets. If the goodwill's current fair value exceeds its book or carrying value, no adjustment is necessary. If less than its book value, impairment has occurred.

To illustrate, assume that Coburg Corporation has three divisions. One division, Pritt Products, was purchased four years ago for $2 million and has been identified as a reporting unit. Unfortunately, it has experienced operating losses over the last three quarters and management is reviewing the reporting unit to determine whether there has been an impairment of goodwill. The carrying amounts of Pritt Division's net assets including the associated goodwill of $900,000 are listed in Illustration 13-8.

Illustration 13-8

*Pritt Reporting Unit—
Book Value of Net Assets
Including Goodwill*

Cash	$ 200,000
Receivables	300,000
Inventory	700,000
Property, plant, and equipment (net)	800,000
Goodwill	900,000
Less: Accounts and notes payable	(500,000)
Net assets, at carrying amounts	$2,400,000

The fair value of the Pritt Division reporting unit as a whole is estimated to be $2.8 million. As a result, no impairment is recognized because the fair value of the division is greater than the carrying amount of the net assets.

However, if the fair value of Pritt Division is $1.9 million, i.e., less than the carrying amount of the net assets, **then the second step must be taken** to determine whether goodwill has been impaired. Assume that the carrying values of the identifiable net assets (i.e., excluding goodwill) are equal to their fair values. The implied fair value of the goodwill in this case is calculated in Illustration 13-9 as $400,000.

---

[21] *CICA Handbook*, Section 3062.39. Section 3062.55 indicates that an entity that qualifies for differential reporting under *CICA Handbook* Section 1300 is not required to test annually. Instead, an impairment test is required only when an event or circumstance occurs that indicates the fair value of a reporting unit may be less than its carrying amount.

[22] Section 3062.05(d) defines a reporting unit as the same level or one level below an operating segment as defined in *CICA Handbook* Section 1701 on Segment Disclosures. "A component of an operating segment is a reporting unit when the component constitutes a business for which discrete financial information is available and segment management regularly reviews the operating results of that component."

Fair value of Pritt Division	$1,900,000
Fair value of identifiable net assets of Pritt Division ($2,400,000 − $900,000)	1,500,000
Implied fair value of goodwill	$ 400,000

Illustration 13-9

Determination of Implied Current Value of Goodwill

Note that if the carrying amounts of the net identifiable assets are not the same as their fair values, the fair values must be used in this calculation. This makes intuitive sense. **There is goodwill only if** the value of a company or reporting unit is greater than the fair value of the individual net assets making up the company.

The implied value of the goodwill is then compared with the recorded goodwill to determine whether an impairment loss exists, as indicated in Illustration 13-10.

Carrying amount of goodwill	$900,000
Implied value of goodwill	400,000
Impairment loss	$500,000

Illustration 13-10

Measurement of Goodwill Impairment

The entry to record the impairment is:

Loss on Impairment of Goodwill	500,000	
Goodwill		500,000

A = L + SE
−$500,000   −$500,000
Cash flows: No effect

Illustration 13-11 summarizes the impairment tests for various intangible assets.

Type of Intangible Asset	Impairment Test
Limited life	Recoverability test, then fair value test
Indefinite life other than goodwill	Fair value test
Goodwill	Fair value test on reporting unit, then fair value test on implied goodwill

Illustration 13-11

Summary of Intangible Asset Impairment Tests

DEFERRED CHARGES

Deferred charges is a classification often used to describe a number of different items that have debit balances, including certain types of intangibles. Intangibles sometimes classified as deferred charges include deferred development costs, pre-operating and start-up costs, and organization costs.

Deferred charges also includes such items as debt discount and issue costs as well as long-term prepayments for insurance, rent, taxes, and other down payments. The deferred charge classification probably should be abolished because it cannot be clearly differentiated from other amortizable assets (which are also deferred costs), and a more informative disclosure could be made of the smaller items often found in this section of the balance sheet. Such a classification has even less relevance today because the conceptual framework in *CICA Handbook* Section 1000 establishes a definition for assets that seems to exclude many items now included in this category.

Although there are far fewer deferred charges recognized on the balance sheet than in the past, *CICA Handbook* Section 3070 still requires separate disclosure of deferred charges as well as the amount charged for amortization of this asset type.[23] The Accounting Standards Board has included Section 3070 in its short-term Accounting Standards Improvements project. Parts of this section that are of marginal use or "incorrect" may be revised, and additional disclosures required. The larger question of what charges may be appropriately deferred is being left to another future AcSB project.

Research and Development Costs

Objective 8

Differentiate between research and development expenditures, and describe and explain the rationale for the accounting for each.

Research and development (R&D) costs are not in themselves intangible assets. The accounting for R&D costs is presented here, however, for two reasons. The first is because research and development activities are often significant and they frequently result in the development of something that is eventually patented or copyrighted. Examples include a new product, process, idea, formula, composition, or literary work. Secondly, some development costs are capitalized as deferred charges, a type of intangible asset.

Many businesses spend considerable sums of money on research and development to create new products or processes, to improve present products, and to discover new knowledge that may be valuable at some future date. The following schedule shows the outlays for R&D reported by selected Canadian companies with December 2002 and early 2003 year ends.

Illustration 13-12

R&D Expenditures, as a Percentage of Revenue and Net Income

International Insight

Contrary to practice in Canada and most other nations (The Netherlands and Japan, for example), in the United States, all research and development costs are required to be expensed.

Company	R&D Expenditures	% of Revenue	% of Net Income
Alcan Inc.	$115 million (U.S.)	1	30.7
Bombardier Inc.	$284.6 million	1.2	(46.3)
MOSAID Technologies Inc.	$25,754 thousand	67.5	(129.4)
Nortel Networks Ltd.	$2,230 million (U.S.)	21.1	(62.2)
QLT Inc.	$42,502 thousand (U.S.)	38.5	342.6
Research in Motion Limited	$64,952 thousand (U.S.)	21.2	(43.7)

The difficulties in accounting for research and development expenditures are (1) identifying the costs associated with particular activities, projects, or achievements, and (2) determining the magnitude of the future benefits and length of time over which such benefits may be realized. Because of these latter uncertainties, the accounting profession, through *CICA Handbook* Section 3450, has standardized and simplified accounting practice in this area by requiring that **all research costs be charged to expense when incurred. Development costs should also be expensed when incurred except in certain narrowly defined circumstances.**[24]

Identifying R&D Activities

To differentiate research and development costs from each other and from similar costs, the CICA adopted the following definitions.

Research is planned investigation undertaken with the hope of gaining new scientific or technical knowledge and understanding. Such investigation may or may not be directed toward a specific practical aim or application.

Development is the translation of research findings or other knowledge into a plan or design for new or substantially improved materials, devices, products, processes, systems, or services prior to the commencement of commercial production or use.[25]

---

[23] *Financial Reporting in Canada, 2002*, Clarence Byrd, Ida Chen, and Heather Chapman, CICA, 2002 reported that 56.5% of the companies surveyed in 2001 made reference to a Deferred Charges category on their balance sheets.

[24] If a company acquires **in-process R&D**, in a business combination, Canadian standards permit this intangible asset to be recognized as an identifiable intangible.

[25] *CICA Handbook*, Section 3450.02.

Examples of each are provided in Illustration 13-13.[26]

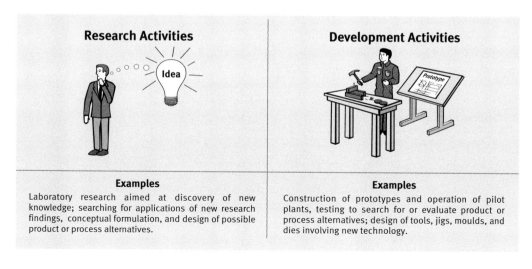

Illustration 13-13

Examples of Research and Development Activities

Research Activities

Idea

Development Activities

Prototype

Examples

Laboratory research aimed at discovery of new knowledge; searching for applications of new research findings, conceptual formulation, and design of possible product or process alternatives.

Examples

Construction of prototypes and operation of pilot plants, testing to search for or evaluate product or process alternatives; design of tools, jigs, moulds, and dies involving new technology.

It should be emphasized that R&D activities do not include routine or periodic alterations to existing products, production lines, manufacturing processes, and other ongoing operations, even though these alterations may represent improvements. Routine ongoing efforts to refine, enrich, or improve the qualities of an existing product are not considered R&D activities. They also do not include expenditures related to engineering follow-through, quality control, or trouble shooting during any part of the commercial production phase, nor routine or promotional market research activities.

A special problem arises in distinguishing R&D costs from selling and administrative activities. Research and development costs may include expenditures associated with any product or process regardless of whether they are related to production, marketing, or administrative activities. For example, the costs of software incurred by an airline in acquiring, developing, or improving its computerized reservation system or for developing general management information system would be considered development costs.

Accounting for R&D Activities

The costs associated with R&D activities are as follows:[27]

1. materials and services consumed

2. direct costs of personnel such as salaries, wages, payroll taxes, and other related costs

3. amortization of equipment and facilities used in R&D activities

4. amortization of intangibles related to R&D activities

5. a reasonable allocation of overhead

Consistent with (3) above, if an enterprise conducts R&D activities using its own research facility consisting of buildings, laboratories, and equipment that has alternative future uses (in other R&D projects or otherwise), the facility should be accounted for as a capitalized operational asset. The amortization and other costs related to such research facilities are accounted for as R&D expenses.

---

[26] *CICA Handbook*, Section 3450.04 and .05.

[27] *CICA Handbook*, Section 3450.13.

IAS Note

International
accounting
standards also
identify certain circumstances
that justify the capitalization
and deferral of appropriate
development costs.

Sometimes enterprises conduct R&D activities for other entities **under a contractual arrangement**. In this case, the contract usually specifies that all direct costs, certain specific indirect costs, plus a profit element should be reimbursed to the enterprise performing the R&D work. Because reimbursement is expected, such R&D costs should be recorded as inventory or a receivable. It is the company for whom the work has been performed that reports these costs as R&D activities.

As previously emphasized, Canadian firms must write off research costs incurred as expenses of the period. Development costs must be expensed as well, **except when all of the following criteria are met**.

1. The product or process is clearly defined and the costs attributable to it can be identified.

2. The technical feasibility of the product or process has been established.

3. Management has indicated its intention to produce and market or use the product or process.

4. The future market for the product or process is clearly defined or, if it is to be used internally rather than sold, its usefulness to the enterprise has been established.

5. Adequate resources exist or are expected to be available to complete the project.

Underlying Concept

The require-
ment that all
research and most development costs be expensed as
incurred is an example of the
conflict between relevance and
reliability, with this requirement leaning strongly in
support of reliability and
comparability. The matching of
costs with revenues is not as
important as ensuring assets
are not overstated.

Having to meet all five criteria indicates that deferral of development costs is permitted **only when the future benefits are reasonably certain**. Costs expensed in previous periods before the criteria were met should not be restated as assets, nor should amounts be deferred that are greater than the amount expected to be recovered from the sale or use of the product or process.[28] Deferred development costs are subsequently amortized to expense, preferably on a basis related to the sale or use of the underlying product or process.

Consistent with other intangibles, unamortized development costs must be reviewed at the end of each accounting period. If the criteria justifying deferral of the costs are no longer valid, the remaining costs are written off. Alternatively, if their carrying amount exceeds their net recoverable amount, the excess is written off as a charge to the income statement.

To illustrate the identification of R&D activities and the accounting treatment of related costs, assume an enterprise develops, produces, and markets laser machines for medical, industrial, and defence uses. The types of expenditures related to its laser machine activities, along with the recommended accounting treatment, are listed in Illustration 13-14.

Acceptable accounting practice requires that disclosure be made in the financial statements of the total R&D costs charged to expense in each period for which an income statement is presented. Because income tax incentives are associated with this type of activity, it is common for companies to disclose their R&D expenses net of tax recoveries, either on the face of the income statement or in the notes to the financial statements. Excerpts from the financial statements of **MOSAID Technologies Incorporated** for the year ended April 25, 2003 provided in Illustration 13-15 provide a good example of such disclosures.

Costs of development activities **unique to companies in the extractive industries** (prospecting, acquisition of mineral rights, exploration, drilling, mining, and related mineral development) are covered by *CICA Handbook* Section 3061 on Property, Plant, and Equipment. Research and development activities similar in nature to those of other industries, however, are governed by the accounting standards in Section 3450.

Many costs have characteristics similar to research and development costs. Examples include start-up costs for a new operation, initial operating losses, organization costs, and advertising costs. Explanations of these are provided next.

---

[28] *CICA Handbook*, Section 3450.21 and .23.

Illustration 13-14

Sample R&D Expenditures and their Accounting Treatment

Type of Expenditure	Accounting Treatment
1. Construction of long-range research facility (three-storey, 100,000 m² building) for use in current and future projects.	Capitalize and amortize as R&D expense.
2. Acquisition of R&D equipment for use on current project only.	Capitalize and amortize as R&D expense.
3. Purchase of materials to be used on current and future R&D projects.	Inventory and allocate to R&D projects as consumed.
4. Salaries of research staff designing new laser bone scanner.	Expense immediately as research.
5. Research costs incurred under contract for customer and billable monthly.	Expense as operating expense in period of related revenue recognition.
6. Material, labour, and overhead costs of prototype laser scanner.	Capitalize as development cost if all criteria are met, otherwise expense.
7. Costs of testing prototype and design modifications.	Capitalize as development cost if all criteria are met, otherwise expense.
8. Legal fees to obtain patent on new laser scanner.	Capitalize as patent and amortize to cost of goods manufactured as used.
9. Executive salaries.	Expense as operating expense (general and administrative).
10. Cost of marketing research related to promotion of new laser scanner.	Expense as operating expense (selling).
11. Engineering costs incurred to advance the laser scanner to full production stage.	Capitalize as development cost if all criteria are met, otherwise expense.
12. Costs of successfully defending patent on laser scanner.	Capitalize as patent and amortize to cost of goods manufactured as used.
13. Commissions to sales staff marketing new laser scanner.	Expense as operating expense (selling).

Notes to the Consolidated Financial Statements

Year ended April 25, 2003 (tabular dollar amounts in thousands, except per share amounts)

1. Accounting Policies

The financial statements have been prepared in accordance with Canadian generally accepted accounting principles and include the following significant accounting policies:

Research and development

Research costs are expensed as incurred. Development costs are deferred once technical feasibility has been established and all criteria for deferral under generally accepted accounting principles are met. Such costs are amortized commencing when the product is released, over the expected life of the product. To date, no development costs have met the criteria for deferral.

Government assistance and investment tax credits

Government assistance and investment tax credits are recorded as a reduction of the related expense or cost of the asset acquired. The benefits are recognized when the Company has complied with the terms and conditions of the approved grant program or applicable tax legislation.

9. Research and Development

Investment tax credits were applied to reduce current research and development expenses in the statements of earnings and retained earnings as summarized below:

	2003	2002
Total current research and development	$25,754	$30,549
Less: Investment tax credits	(1,767)	(2,410)
Net research and development	$23,987	$28,139

As part of a Research and Development Contribution Agreement with the Government of Canada, the government contributed $6.2 million towards research and development work. The terms of the Agreement require the Company to pay royalties to the government based upon the revenues of the resulting products, for a period extending no later than March 31, 2011. During the year ended April 25, 2003, the Company recorded repayments in the amount of $192,000 (2002—$424,000). To date, the Company has recorded repayments in the amount of $1,000,000.

Illustration 13-15

R&D Disclosures—Mosaid Technologies Incorporated

Digital Tool

Student Toolkit— Additonal Disclosures

www.wiley.com/canada/kieso

Pre-operating Costs

Objective 9
Identify other examples of deferred charges and the accounting requirements for them.

Companies that are in the development stage face numerous questions about which costs should be expensed and which should be capitalized. The general principle is that **the type of expenditure, not the enterprise's stage of development**, dictates the accounting treatment. Standards exist for property, plant, and equipment, intangible assets, and research and development activities, and these standards should be followed regardless of the maturity of the business. Revenues and expenditures in the pre-operating period, however, are a separate issue.

Pre-operating costs are costs incurred by an entity during the period prior to the commencement of commercial operations of a new facility or business. These might include costs incurred for such purposes as employee training and relocation, promotional activities, and the use of materials and supplies. A company may realize small amounts of revenue during this period as well. To what extent should such costs that are not capitalized as part of the cost of a capital asset be deferred?

The Emerging Issues Committee of the CICA, in *EIC-27*, agreed that an expenditure incurred during the pre-operating period could be deferred if the following three criteria are all met.

1. It relates directly to placing the new business into service.

2. It is incremental in nature, and would not have been incurred in the absence of the new business.

3. It is probable that the expenditure is recoverable from the future operations of the new business.[29]

The **pre-operating period** is the period prior to when the new business is ready to begin commercial operations—that is, is capable of consistently providing its intended product or service. This period will differ depending on circumstances and the industry involved, and should be predefined by management in terms of the activity level attained or the time period passed.

When the pre-operating period is over, the deferral of expenditures and any offsetting revenues ceases, and the amortization of the deferred charges begins. The amortization is based on the pattern of benefits received and the expected period of benefit. A five-year period is assumed to be the likely maximum period for amortization.[30]

To illustrate the type of costs that are permitted to be deferred as pre-operating costs, assume that Canadian-based Hilo Beverage Inc. decides to construct a new plant in Brazil. This represents Hilo's first entry into the Brazilian market. As part of its overall strategy, Hilo plans to introduce the company's major Canadian brands into Brazil, on a locally produced basis. Following are some of the pre-operating costs that might be involved with these start-up activities:

1. travel-related costs, costs related to employee salaries, and costs related to feasibility studies, accounting, tax, and government affairs

2. training of local employees related to product, maintenance, computer systems, finance, and operations

3. recruiting, organizing, and training related to establishing a distribution network

Unlike the U.S. approach, which calls for these costs to be expensed as incurred, the Canadian standard specifies that these costs qualify for deferral. They meet the three criteria imposed and are incurred during the predetermined pre-operating period.

---

[29] *CICA* EIC-27, Revenues and Expenditures during the Pre-Operating Period.

[30] *CICA* EIC-27, Issue 3.

It is not uncommon for development activities to occur at the same time as other activities, such as the acquisition or development of assets. For example, property, plant, and equipment for Hilo's new plant should be capitalized and a careful analysis of costs during the pre-operating is needed to ensure all capital asset costs are appropriately accounted for.

Initial Operating Losses

Some contend that initial operating losses incurred in a business start-up should be capitalized, since they are unavoidable and are a cost of starting a business. For example, assume that Hilo lost money in its first year of operations and wished to capitalize this loss, arguing that as the company becomes profitable, it will offset these losses in future periods. What do you think?

Deferring losses after commercial operations have begun is unsound. Losses have no future service potential and therefore cannot be considered an asset. This position is supported by CICA's *Accounting Guideline 11*—Enterprises in the Development Stage. This guideline, which clarifies the accounting and reporting practices for development stage enterprises, concludes that the accounting practices and reporting standards should be a function of the type of transaction, not an entity's maturity.

Organization Costs

Deferred costs include **organization costs**. These are costs incurred in the formation of a corporation, such as fees to underwriters (investment bankers) for handling issues of shares or bonds, legal fees, provincial or federal fees of various sorts, and promotional expenditures involving the organization of a business.

These items are usually charged to an account called Organization Costs and may be carried as an asset on the balance sheet as expenditures that will benefit the company over its life. If recognized as a deferred charge, the costs are amortized over an arbitrary period of time, since the corporation's life is indeterminable. However, the amortization period is usually short (perhaps up to five years) because the amounts tend not to be significant or because it is assumed that the early years benefit most from these expenditures.

Advertising Costs

Recently, PepsiCo hired pop star Britney Spears and soccer icon David Beckham to advertise its products. How should these advertising costs be reported? These costs could be expensed at a variety of times:

1. when the superstars complete the singing or photo-shoot assignment

2. the first time the advertising takes place

3. over the estimated useful life of the advertising

4. in an appropriate fashion to each of the three periods identified above

5. over the period revenues are expected to result

Because there is no specific Canadian standard on advertising costs, GAAP requires that methods consistent with the conceptual framework and analogous situations be used. As future benefits from advertising generally are not sufficiently defined or measurable with a degree of reliability that is required to recognize these costs as an asset, for the most part,

advertising costs are expensed as incurred or when the advertising first takes place. Whichever approach is followed, the results are essentially the same. Tangible assets used in advertising, such as billboards or blimps, are recorded as assets because they do have alternative future uses. A conservative approach is generally taken to recording advertising costs because identifying and measuring the future benefits is so difficult.[31]

Conceptual Questions

The requirement that most costs mentioned above be expensed immediately is a conservative, practical solution that ensures consistency in practice and uniformity among companies. But the practice of immediately writing off expenditures made in the expectation of benefiting future periods cannot be justified on the grounds that it is good accounting theory.

Those who support immediate expensing contend that from an income statement standpoint, long-run application of these standards usually makes little difference. They contend, for example, that the amount of R&D cost charged to expense each accounting period would be about the same whether there is immediate expensing or capitalization and subsequent amortization because of the ongoing nature of most companies' R&D activities. Critics argue that the balance sheet should report an intangible asset related to expenditures that have future benefit. To preclude capitalization of all R&D and similar expenditures removes from the balance sheet what may be a company's most valuable assets. These decisions represent some of the many trade-offs made between relevance and reliability, and cost-benefit considerations.[32]

PRESENTATION AND ANALYSIS

A recent survey indicates that the most common types of intangible assets reported other than goodwill were broadcast rights, publishing rights, trademarks, patents, licences, customer lists, non-competition agreements, franchises, and purchased R&D.[33] These, along with goodwill, have become a greater and greater proportion of companies' reported assets.

Presentation of Intangible Assets

Balance Sheet

Objective 10

Identify the disclosure requirements for intangibles, including deferred charges, and issues related to the analysis of this category of asset.

On the balance sheet, goodwill is the only intangible requiring separate, single line item disclosure. Details of the changes in the carrying amount of goodwill on the balance

---

[31] This mirrors "Reporting on Advertising Costs," *Statement of Position 93-7*, (New York: AICPA, 1993). Note that there are some exceptions to immediate expensing of advertising costs when they relate to direct-response advertising, but this subject is beyond the scope of this text.

[32] Recent research suggests that capitalizing research and development costs may be helpful to investors. For example, one study showed that a significant relationship exists between R&D outlays and subsequent benefits in the form of increased productivity, earnings, and shareholder value for R&D-intensive companies. (Baruch Lev and Theodore Sougiannis, "The Capitalization, Amortization, and Value-Relevance of R&D," *Journal of Accounting and Economics*, February 1996.) In another study, it was found that there was a significant decline in earnings usefulness for companies that were forced to switch from capitalizing to expensing R&D costs and that the decline appears to persist over time. (Martha L. Loudder and Bruce K. Behn, "Alternative Income Determination Rules and Earnings Usefulness: The Case of R&D Costs," *Contemporary Accounting Research*, Fall 1995.)

[33] *Financial Reporting in Canada, 2000*, Clarence Byrd, Ida Chen, and Heather Chapman; CICA, 2000, pp. 284-285.

sheet are also required. This includes goodwill acquired, writedowns due to impairment, and goodwill included in the disposition of any part of a reporting unit. All other intangible assets other than goodwill should be aggregated and reported as a separate line item on the balance sheet. For intangibles subject to amortization, the amount of such assets acquired during the period should be disclosed along with the cost and accumulated amortization for major intangible asset classes and in total. For intangibles not subject to amortization, similar disclosures are required, excluding the amount of accumulated amortization.[34]

Major items included in deferred charges should be reported separately, along with disclosure of the fact, where applicable, that they are reported net of amortization.[35]

Income Statement

For intangibles subject to amortization, disclosure is required of the amortization methods and rates used, as well as the amount of amortization expense charged to income for the period. Each goodwill impairment loss is required to be reported separately in the income statement before extraordinary items and discontinued operations, unless the impairment loss is associated with a discontinued operation. In addition, the enterprise must describe the facts and circumstances leading to the impairment; identify the loss amount and the adjusted carrying amount of goodwill along with the associated reporting unit (and segment, if applicable); and provide explanatory information if the loss is only an estimate.

Impairment losses associated with other intangibles do not require separate line disclosure on the face of the income statement, but a description of each impaired asset, the amount of the loss, where it is reported, and the business segment affected must be identified.[36]

In addition, amounts recognized for amortization of deferred charges should be separately disclosed along with the basis of amortization.[37]

Illustrative Presentations and Disclosures

Excerpts from the financial statements of **FirstService Corporation** for its year ended March 31, 2003 are provided in Illustration 13-16. This Canadian company provides property and business services to commercial, residential, and institutional customers in the United States and Canada. Business activities are conducted through four segments: residential property management, integrated security services, consumer services, and business services. Note that the intangibles, including goodwill, make up in excess of 52% of the company's March 31, 2003 reported assets.

It is interesting to read FirstService's Management Discussion and Analysis section of its annual report for this same year. Management identifies (i) goodwill and indefinite life intangible assets impairment testing and (ii) the determination of intangible assets acquired relative to the amount classified as goodwill in corporate acquisitions **as two of their three most critical accounting policies**. The company deems these "to be most important to the portrayal of our financial condition and results, and that require management's most difficult, subjective or complex judgments, due to the need to make estimates about the effects of matters that are inherently uncertain."

Digital Tool

Student Toolkit—
Additonal
Disclosures

www.wiley.com/canada/kieso

---

[34] *CICA Handbook*, Section 3062.48 to .51.

[35] *CICA Handbook*, Section 3070.02 to .03.

[36] *CICA Handbook*, Section 3062.49 to .54.

[37] *CICA Handbook*, Section 3070.04.

Illustration 13-16

Balance Sheet Presentation and Related Notes on Intangible Assets

FIRSTSERVICE CORPORATION
CONSOLIDATED BALANCE SHEETS
(in thousands of U.S. Dollars) – in accordance with Canadian generally accepted accounting principles

As at March 31	2003	2002
Assets		
Current assets		
Cash and cash equivalents	**$ 5,378**	$ 7,332
Accounts receivable, net of an allowance of $5,343 (2002 - $4,084)	**85,484**	88,290
Inventories (note 6)	**15,095**	10,518
Prepaids and other (note 6)	**13,617**	12,160
Deferred income taxes (note 13)	**2,808**	2,571
	122,382	120,871
Other receivables (note 7)	**$ 5,839**	4,908
Fixed assets (note 8)	**46,600**	45,367
Other assets (note 8)	**2,777**	5,411
Deferred income taxes (note 13)	**103**	972
Intangible assets (note 9)	**33,539**	29,422
Goodwill (note 10)	**164,610**	151,254
	253,468	237,334
	$ 375,850	$ 358,205

NOTES TO THE CONSOLIDATED FINANCIAL STATEMENTS
(in thousands of U.S. Dollars, except per share amounts) – in accordance with Canadian generally accepted accounting principles

2. Summary of significant accounting policies (excerpt)

Goodwill and intangible assets

Goodwill and intangible assets are accounted for in accordance with Canadian Institute of Chartered Accountants ("CICA") standard 1581, *Business Combinations* ("CICA 1581") and CICA standard 3062 *Goodwill and Other Intangible Assets* ("CICA 3062"). Goodwill represents the excess of purchase price over the fair value of identifiable assets acquired in a business combination and is not subject to amortization.

Amortizable intangible assets are recorded at cost and are amortized using the straight-line method over their estimated useful lives as follows:

Management contracts and other	over life of contract
Customer lists and relationships	2 to 15 years
Franchise rights	15 to 40 years

The Company reviews the carrying value of amortizable intangible assets for impairment whenever events and circumstances indicate that the carrying value of an asset may not be recoverable from the estimated future cash flows expected to result from its use and eventual disposition. If the sum of the expected future cash flows is less than the carrying amount of the asset, an impairment loss is recognized. Measurement of the impairment loss is based on the excess of the carrying amount of the asset over fair value calculated using discounted expected future cash flows.

Goodwill and indefinite-life franchise intangible assets are tested for impairment annually or more frequently if events or changes in circumstances indicate the asset might be impaired, in which case the carrying value of the asset is written down to fair value. Impairment of goodwill is tested at the reporting unit level by comparing the reporting unit's carrying amount, including goodwill, to the fair value of the reporting unit. The fair values of the reporting units are estimated using a discounted cash flows approach. If the carrying amount of the reporting unit exceeds its fair value, then a second step is performed to measure the amount of impairment loss, if any.

Continued on next page

Perspectives

Intellectual Capital and Knowledge Assets

During the 1990s, there was increased criticism about the inability of the conventional financial accounting model to capture many of the aspects that give a business value. In November 1997, for example, **Microsoft** had a total book value of $10.8 billion (U.S.), but

9. Intangible assets (excerpt)

Illustration 13-16

Balance Sheet Presentation and Related Notes on Intangible Assets (continued)

2003	Gross carrying amount	Accumulated amortization	Net 2003
Amortized intangible assets			
Management contracts and other	$ 2,085	$ 1,067	$ 1,018
Customer lists and relationships	6,506	1,122	5,384
Franchise rights	3,247	654	2,593
	11,838	2,843	8,995
Indefinite-life franchise intangible assets			
Trademarks and trade names	11,327	-	11,327
Franchise rights	13,217	-	13,217
	24,544	-	24,544
	$ 36,382	$ 2,843	$ 33,539

During the year ended March 31, 2003, the company acquired the following intangible assets:

	Amount	Weighted average amortization period in years
Amortized intangible assets		
Management contracts and other	$ 259	12
Customer lists and relationships	4,407	10
Franchise rights	392	12
	$ 5,058	10

The following is the estimated annual amortization expense for each of the next five years ending March 31:

2004	$ 1,278
2005	1,019
2006	810
2007	810
2008	595

10. Goodwill (excerpt)

	Residential Property Management	Integrated Security Services	Consumer Services	Business Services	Corporate	Consolidated
Balance, March 31, 2002	55,483	24,812	18,544	52,415	-	151,254
Goodwill resulting from adjustments to purchase price allocations	(238)	69	(143)	19	-	(293)
Goodwill resulting from contingent acquisition payments	1,450	1,693	-	-	-	3,143
Goodwill resulting from purchases of minority shareholders' interests	3,013	380	-	960	-	4,353
Goodwill acquired during year	2,557	-	2,208	-	-	4,765
Foreign exchange	-	34	149	1,205	-	1,388
Balance, March 31, 2003	$ 62,265	$ 26,988	$ 20,758	$ 54,599	$ -	$ 164,610

its market capitalization (i.e., the market value of its outstanding shares) was $166.5 billion (U.S.). Nortel Networks Corporation traded at a high of $125 per share in mid-2000 although its book value was closer to $5 per share. Why such significant differences?

The answer is that financial accounting is not able to capture and report many of the assets that contribute to future cash flows, and this is seen by some as the greatest challenge facing the accounting profession today. Many of the missing values belong to unrecognized, internally developed intangible assets known as knowledge assets or intellectual capital. These include the value of key personnel—not only Bill Gates, but the many creative and technologically proficient personnel in general, investment in and the potential for products from research and development, organizational adaptability, customer retention, strategic direction, flexible and innovative management, customer service capability, and effective advertising programs, to name some.

Our conventional financial accounting model, for the most part, captures the results of past transactions. This has been considered a very significant benefit in the past as it is responsible for the verifiability of the reported measures and hence the reliability of the financial statements. In most cases, the intellectual capital and knowledge assets identified above are not measurable in financial terms with sufficient reliability to give them accounting recognition. Some cannot be included as assets because of the enterprise's inability to control access to the benefits. Investments made in employee education and development, for example, walk out the door when employees leave the company to work elsewhere.

These indicators of longer term value that has been created in an organization will ultimately result in realized values through future transactions and, therefore, is relevant information for financial statement readers. Companies increasingly disclose more of this soft information in annual reports outside of the financial statements, in news releases, and in interviews with market analysts. While some believe that standard setters should work to ensure more of these intangibles are captured on the balance sheet, others believe that new performance reporting frameworks need to be developed in conjunction with, or even to displace, the existing financial reporting model. Much research is being carried out in the search for solutions to the discrepancies between what gets reported as having value on the financial statements and what the capital markets perceive as value in share prices.

Alternatively, the sceptics point to the decline in market value of technology shares in particular, from summer 2000 to summer 2001. Nortel, for example, lost 90% of its value over this period, supporting the arguments of many that the historical cost model still has much to recommend it! The "truth" of course, lies somewhere in between. While inflated market values are not sufficiently reliable to support the recognition of previously unrecognized intangible asset value, the historical cost model certainly fails to capture many of the things that lie at the heart of corporate value. As the accounting community begins to accept the recognition of fair value measures for financial instruments, perhaps sufficiently reliable measurement techniques for other asset values may not be far behind.

Analysis of Performance

When comparing the operating results of companies—either one company over time or between companies—it is important to pay close attention to how deferred charges, intangibles, and goodwill have been accounted for. In the United States, accounting standards are much stricter in expensing any costs that do not result in an objectively measurable asset, whereas in Canada, more liberal accounting policies are used.

Note also that the standards dealing with intangibles have just changed significantly. The Quebecor Inc. example earlier in the chapter illustrated the effect this change in accounting principle had on the company's results. The "big bath" Quebecor took by writing down goodwill previously reported as an asset means that these asset costs will never flow through the income statement, and future operating statements are relieved of these costs. In addition, net income for companies with significant investments in goodwill and other indefinite life intangibles are not comparable to earnings reported for years before the change in policy. Care must be exercised in calculating and interpreting any ratios that include earnings and asset numbers, especially on a comparative basis.

Summary of Learning Objectives

Digital Tool

Glossary

www.wiley.com/canada/kieso

1 Describe the characteristics of intangible assets.

Intangible assets have two main characteristics: (1) they lack physical substance and (2) they are not financial instruments. In most cases, intangible assets provide services over a period of years. As a result, they are normally classified as long-term assets.

2 Discuss the recognition and measurement issues of acquiring intangibles.

Intangibles, like other assets, are recorded at cost. When several intangibles, or a combination of intangibles and tangibles, are bought in a basket purchase, the cost is allocated on the basis of relative fair values. Costs incurred to develop an intangible internally are generally expensed immediately because of the uncertainty of the future benefits, and the inability to relate the costs with specific intangible assets. When acquired in a business combination, it is necessary that any identifiable intangibles be recognized separately from the goodwill component. Only those that can be exchanged or whose future benefits can be controlled through contractual or other legal means should be recognized separately as identifiable intangibles. Deferred charges are permitted in restricted circumstances where the future benefits associated with the costs incurred can be identified.

3 Explain how identifiable intangibles are valued subsequent to acquisition.

An intangible with a finite or limited useful life is amortized over its useful life to the entity. Except in unusual and specific circumstances, the residual value is assumed to be zero. The amount to report for amortization expense should reflect the pattern in which the asset is consumed or used up if that pattern can be reliably determined. Otherwise a straight-line approach is used. An intangible with an indefinite life is not amortized until its life is determined to be no longer indefinite. All intangibles are tested for impairment.

4 Identify the types of intangible assets.

Major types of intangibles are: (1) marketing-related intangibles that are used in the marketing or promotion of products or services; (2) customer-related intangibles that are a result of interactions with outside parties; (3) artistic-related intangibles that involve ownership rights to such items as plays and literary works; (4) contract-related intangibles that represent the value of rights that arise from contractual arrangements; (5) technology-related intangible assets that relate to innovations or technological advances; and (6) goodwill that arises in business combinations. In addition, a variety of deferred charges are intangible assets, whose costs are carried forward to be matched with revenues of future periods.

5 Explain the conceptual issues related to goodwill.

Goodwill is unique because unlike receivables, inventories, and patents that can be sold or exchanged individually in the marketplace, goodwill can be identified only with the business as a whole. Goodwill is a "going concern" valuation and is recorded only when an entire business is purchased. Goodwill generated internally is not capitalized in the accounts, because measuring the components of goodwill is simply too complex and associating any costs with future benefits too difficult. The future benefits of goodwill may bear no relationship to the costs incurred in developing that goodwill. Also, goodwill may exist even in the absence of specific costs to develop it. A variety of accounting treatments for purchased goodwill have been justified in the past.

KEY TERMS

6 Describe the accounting procedures for recording goodwill at acquisition.

To calculate goodwill, the fair value of the identifiable assets acquired and liabilities assumed is compared with the purchase price of the acquired business. The difference is goodwill: the excess of cost over fair value of the identifiable net assets acquired.

7 Explain the accounting issues related to intangible asset impairments.

Impairment occurs when the carrying amount of the intangible asset exceeds its fair value. Impairment for limited-life intangible assets is based on a recoverability test and then a fair value test, similar to that for property, plant, and equipment. Indefinite-life intangibles use only a fair value test. Goodwill impairments use a two-step process: First, test the fair value of the reporting unit, then do the fair value test on implied goodwill.

8 Differentiate between research and development expenditures and describe and explain the rationale for the accounting for each.

R&D costs are not in themselves intangible assets, but research and development activities frequently result in the development of something that is patented or copyrighted. Research is planned investigation undertaken with the hope of gaining new scientific or technical knowledge and understanding. Development is the translation of research findings or other knowledge into a plan or design for new or substantially improved products or processes prior to commercial production or use. The difficulties in accounting for R&D expenditures are (1) identifying the costs associated with particular activities, projects, or achievements and (2) determining the magnitude of the future benefits and length of time over which such benefits may be realized. Accounting practice requires that all research expenditures be expensed, and that all development costs be expensed except in prescribed circumstances. The circumstances require reasonable assurance of realization of future benefits.

9 Identify other examples of deferred charges and the accounting requirements for them.

Other deferred charges include long-term prepayments, debt discount and issue costs, pre-operating costs, organization costs, and advertising costs. In general, only costs determined to have specific future benefits may be deferred. They are then charged to income on the same basis that the future benefits are realized.

10 Identify the disclosure requirements for intangibles, including deferred charges and issues related to the analysis of this category of asset.

Similar to property, plant, and equipment, the cost and any accumulated amortization is reported on the balance sheet, with separate disclosure of the amortization expense on the income statement. For intangibles that are not amortized, companies must indicate the amount of any impairment losses recognized as well as information about the circumstances requiring the writedown. Goodwill is required to be separately reported, as are the major classes of intangible assets. Because of the difficulty in measuring intangibles, some resources such as intellectual capital do not get captured on the balance sheet, and sometimes other intangibles are reported where value very quickly disappears. For these reasons and the recent changes in accounting policy related to intangibles, care must be taken in the analysis of financial statement information related to earnings and total assets.

Appendix 13A

Valuing Goodwill

In this chapter we discussed the generally accepted method of measuring and recording goodwill **as the excess of cost over fair value of the identifiable net assets acquired in a business acquisition**. Accountants are often asked to participate in the valuation of a business as part of a planned business acquisition.

The determination of a purchase price for a business and the resulting goodwill is an inexact process. As indicated, it is usually possible to determine the fair value of specifically identifiable assets. But how does a buyer value intangible factors such as superior management, a good credit rating, and so on?

11 **Objective**
After studying Appendix 13A, you should be able to: Explain various approaches to valuing goodwill.

Excess Earnings Approach

One widely used method to calculate the amount of goodwill a business possesses is the excess earnings approach. This approach works as follows.

1. Calculate the annual average "normalized" earnings the company is expected to earn in the future.

2. Calculate the annual average earnings the company would be expected to earn if it generated the same return on investment as the average firm in the same industry. The return on investment is the percentage that income is of the net assets or shareholders' equity employed.

3. Calculate the excess earnings: the difference between what the firm is expected to earn in the future and what the industry earns. The ability to generate a higher income indicates that the business has an unidentifiable value (intangible asset) that provides this incremental earning power. It is this ability to earn a higher rate of return than the industry average that is the crux of what goodwill is.

4. Estimate the value of the goodwill by discounting the excess future earnings to their present value.

This approach is a systematic and logical way to determine goodwill, as its value is directly related to what makes a company worth more than the sum of its parts. The Tractorling Corporation example referred to in Illustration 13-4 will be extended to explain each of the four steps identified. Tractorling's identifiable net assets have a fair value of $350,000.

1. **Calculate the company's expected annual average "normalized" earnings.**
   Because the past often provides useful information about the future, past earnings is a good starting place to estimate a company's likely future earnings. Going back three to six years is usually adequate.

Assume Tractorling's net incomes for the last five years and the calculation of the company's average earnings over this period are as follows.

EARNINGS HISTORY—TRACTORLING CORPORATION	
2000	$ 60,000
2001	55,000
2002	110,000[a]
2003	70,000
2004	80,000
Total for 5 years	$375,000
Average earnings	$375,000 ÷ 5 years = $75,000

[a] Includes extraordinary gain of $25,000

Based on the average annual earnings of $75,000, a rate of return on investment of approximately 21.4% is initially indicated: $75,000 ÷ $350,000. Before we go further, however, we need to know whether $75,000 is representative of Tractorling's **future earnings**. A company's past earnings need to be analysed to determine whether any adjustments are needed in estimating expected future earnings. This process is often called normalizing earnings and the income that results is termed **normalized earnings**.

First, **the accounting policies applied should be consistent with those of the purchaser**. For example, assume that the purchasing company measures earnings using the FIFO inventory valuation method rather than LIFO, which Tractorling uses. Further assume that the use of LIFO had the effect of reducing Tractorling's net income by $2,000 each year below a FIFO-based net income. In addition, Tractorling uses accelerated amortization while the purchaser uses straight-line. As a result, the reported earnings were $3,000 lower each year than they would have been on a straight-line basis.

Secondly, because the purchaser will pay current prices for the company, **future earnings should be based on the net assets' current fair values** rather than the carrying amount on Tractorling's books. That is, differences between the carrying amounts and fair values of the assets may affect reported earnings in the future. For example, internally developed patent costs not previously recognized as an asset would be recognized on the purchase of Tractorling. This asset will need to be amortized, say, at the rate of $1,000 per period.

Finally, because we are attempting to estimate future earnings, **amounts not expected to recur should be adjusted out of our calculations**. The extraordinary gain of $25,000 is an example of such an item. An analysis can now be made of what the purchaser expects the annual future earnings of Tractorling to be.

Average past earnings of Tractorling (from Illustration 13A-1)		$75,000
Add		
Adjustment for change from LIFO to FIFO	$2,000	
Adjustment for change from accelerated to straight-line amortization	3,000	5,000
		80,000
Deduct		
Extraordinary gain ($25,000 ÷ 5)	5,000	
Patent amortization on straight-line basis	1,000	6,000
Expected future earnings of Tractorling		$74,000

Note that it was necessary to divide the extraordinary gain of $25,000 by five years to adjust it correctly. The whole $25,000 was included in the total income earned over the five-year history, but only one-fifth of it, or $5,000, is included in the average earnings.[38]

2. **Calculate the annual average earnings the company would generate if it earned the same return as the industry average.**

Determining the industry-average rate of return earned on net assets requires analysis of companies similar to the enterprise in question. An industry average may be determined by examining annual reports or data from statistical services. Assume that a rate of 15% is found to be average for companies in Tractorling's industry. **This is the level of earnings expected from a company without any goodwill.** In this case, the estimate of Tractorling's earnings considered normal for the industry is calculated in the following manner.

Fair value of Tractorling's net identifiable assets	$350,000
Industry average rate of return	15%
Tractorling's earnings if no goodwill	$ 52,500

Illustration 13A-3

Calculation of Normal Earnings for the Industry

The net assets' fair value—not their historical cost—is used to calculate the "normal" income. This is because the cost of the net identifiable assets to any company interested in purchasing Tractorling will be their fair value, not their carrying value on Tractorling's books. Therefore, their fair value is the relevant measure.

3. **Calculate the company's excess earnings.**

The next step is to calculate the extent of the company's earnings in excess of the industry norm. This is what gives the company value in excess of the fair value of its identifiable net assets. Tractorling's excess earnings are determined in Illustration 13A-4.

Expected future earnings of Tractorling	$74,000
Tractorling's earnings if no goodwill	52,500
Tractorling's excess annual earnings	$21,500

Illustration 13A-4

Calculation of Excess Earnings

4. **Estimate the value of the goodwill based on the excess earnings.**

Because the excess earnings are expected to continue for a number of years, they are discounted back to their present value to determine how much a purchaser would pay for them now. A discount rate must be chosen as well as the length of the discount period.

Discount rate. The choice of discount rate is fairly subjective.[39] The lower the discount rate, the higher the goodwill value and vice versa. To illustrate, assume that the excess

---

[38] If this isn't clear, start with the total earnings of $375,000 over the past five years and make the necessary adjustments. This would include adding 5 × $2,000 for the LIFO/FIFO adjustment; 5 × $3,000 for the amortization, then deducting 5 × $1,000 for the patent amortization and $25,000 for the extraordinary gain. The adjusted total five-year earnings of $370,000 are then divided by 5 to get the expected future annual earnings. The result is $74,000.

[39] The following illustration shows how the capitalization or discount rate might be calculated for a small business.

A Method of Selecting a Capitalization Rate

	%
Long-term Canadian government bond rate	10
Add: Average premium return on small company shares over government bonds	10
Expected total rate of return on small publicly held shares	20
Add: Premium for greater risk and illiquidity	6
Total required expected rate of return, including inflation component	26
Deduct: Consensus long-term inflation expectation	6
Capitalization rate to apply to current earnings	20

From Warren Kissin and Ronald Zulli, "Valuation of a Closely Held Business," *The Journal of Accountancy*, June 1988, p. 42.

earnings of $21,500 are expected to continue indefinitely. If the excess earnings are capitalized at a rate of 25% in perpetuity, for example, the results are as follows.

Capitalization at 25%

$$\frac{\text{Excess earnings}}{\text{Capitalization rate}} = \frac{\$21,500}{0.25} = \$86,000$$

If the excess earnings are capitalized in perpetuity at a somewhat lower rate, say 15%, a much higher goodwill figure results.[40]

Capitalization at 15%

$$\frac{\text{Excess earnings}}{\text{Capitalization rate}} = \frac{\$21,500}{0.15} = \$143,333$$

What do these numbers mean? In effect, if a company pays $86,000 over and above the fair value of Tractorling's identifiable net assets because the company generates earnings above the industry norm, and Tractorling actually does generate these excess profits into perpetuity, the $21,500 of extra earnings per year represents a 25% return on the amount invested: a $21,500 return relative to the $86,000 invested.

If the purchaser invests $143,333 for the goodwill, the extra $21,500 represents a 15% return on investment: $21,500 relative to the $143,333 invested.

Because the continuance of excess profits is uncertain, a conservative rate (higher than the normal rate) tends to be used. Factors that are considered in determining the rate are the stability of past earnings, the speculative nature of the business, and general economic conditions.

Discount period. Determining the period over which excess earnings are expected to continue is perhaps the most difficult problem associated with estimating goodwill. The perpetuity examples above assume the excess earnings will last indefinitely. Usually, however, the excess earnings are assumed to last a limited number of years. The earnings are then discounted over that period only.

Assume that the company interested in purchasing Tractorling's business believes that the excess earnings will last only 10 years and, because of general economic uncertainty, chooses 25% as an appropriate rate of return. The present value of a 10-year annuity of excess earnings of $21,500 discounted at 25% is $76,766.[41] This is the amount that a purchaser should be willing to pay above the fair value of identifiable net assets (that is, for goodwill) given the assumptions stated.

---

[40] Why do we divide by the capitalization or discount rate to arrive at the goodwill amount? Recall that the present value of an ordinary annuity is equal to:

$$P\overline{n}|i = \frac{1 - \frac{1}{(1+i)^n}}{i}$$

When a number is capitalized into perpetuity, $(1 + i)^n$ becomes so large that $1/(1 + i)^n$ essentially equals zero, which leaves $1/i$ or, as in the case above, $21,500/0.25$, or $21,500/0.15$.

[41] The present value of an annuity of $1 received in a steady stream for 10 years in the future discounted at 25% is $3.57050. The present value of an annuity of $21,500, therefore, is $21,500 × 3.57050 = $76,765.75.

Total Earnings Approach

There is another way to estimate goodwill that is similar and that should increase your understanding of the process and the resulting numbers. Under this approach, the value of the company as a whole is determined, based on the total expected earnings, not just the excess earnings. The fair value of the identifiable net assets is then deducted from the value of the company as a whole. The difference is goodwill. The calculations under both approaches are provided in Illustration 13A-7, assuming the purchaser is looking for a 15% return on amounts invested in Tractorling, and the earnings are expected to continue into perpetuity.

Assumptions:	Expected future earnings			$74,000
	Normal earnings			$52,500
	Expected excess future earnings			$21,500
	Discount rate			15%
	Discount period			perpetuity, ∞
Excess Earnings Approach:	Goodwill	=	present value of the annuity of excess future earnings	
		=	present value of annuity of $21,500 (n = ∞, i = 0.15)	
		=	$\dfrac{\$21,500}{0.15}$	= $143,333
Total Earnings Approach:	Goodwill	=	difference between the fair value of the company and the fair value of its identifiable net assets	
	Fair value of company	=	present value of the annuity of future earnings	
		=	present value of annuity of $74,000 (n = ∞, i = 0.15)	
		=	$\dfrac{\$74,000}{0.15}$	= $493,333
	Fair value of identifiable net assets	=	present value of the annuity of normal earnings	
		=	present value of annuity of $52,500 (n = ∞, i = 0.15)	
		=	$\dfrac{\$52,500}{0.15}$	= 350,000
	Goodwill	=		$143,333

Illustration 13A-7

Total Earnings Approach to the Calculation of Goodwill

Other Methods of Valuation

A number of methods of valuing goodwill exist, some "quick and dirty" and some very sophisticated. The methods illustrated here are some of the least complex approaches. Others include simply multiplying excess earnings by the number of years the excess earnings are expected to continue. Often referred to as the **number of years method**, it is used to provide a rough measure of the goodwill factor. The approach has only the advantage of simplicity; it fails to discount the future cash flows and consider the time value of money.

An even simpler method is one that relies on multiples of average yearly earnings that are paid for other companies in the same industry. If Skyward Airlines was recently acquired for five times its average yearly earnings of $50 million, or $250 million, then Worldwide Airways, a close competitor with $80 million in average yearly earnings, would be worth $400 million.

Another method (similar to discounting excess earnings) is the **discounted free cash flow method**, which involves a projection of the company's free cash flow over a long period, typically 10 or 20 years. The method first projects into the future a dozen or so important financial variables, including production, prices, noncash expenses such as amortization, taxes, and capital outlays—all adjusted for inflation. The objective is to determine the amount of operating cash flow that will be generated over and above the amount needed to maintain existing capacity. The present value of the free cash flow is then calculated. This amount represents the value of the business.

For example, if Magnaputer Ltd. is expected to generate $1 million a year of free cash flow for 20 years, and the buyer's rate-of-return objective is 15%, the buyer would be willing to pay about $6.26 million for Magnaputer. (The present value of $1 million to be received for 20 years discounted at 15% is $6,259,330.) The goodwill, then, is the difference between the $6.26 million and the fair value of the company's identifiable net assets.

In practice, prospective buyers use a variety of methods to produce a valuation curve or range of prices. But the actual price paid may be more a factor of the buyer's or seller's ego and horse-trading acumen.

Valuation of a business and its inherent goodwill is at best a highly uncertain process.[42] The estimated value of goodwill depends on a number of factors, all of which are tenuous and subject to bargaining.

Digital Tool

Glossary

www.wiley.com/canada/kieso

KEY TERMS

discounted free cash flow
   method, 704
excess earnings
   approach, 699
normalized earnings, 700
number of years
   method, 703

Summary of Learning Objective for Appendix 13A

11 Explain various approaches to valuing goodwill.

One method of valuing goodwill is the excess earnings approach. Using this approach, the total future (normalized) earnings the company is expected to generate is calculated. The next step is to calculate the average earnings that would be generated on net assets in that industry. The difference between what the firm earns and what the industry earns is referred to as the excess earnings. This excess earning power indicates that there are unidentifiable underlying asset values that result in the higher than average earnings. Finding the value of goodwill is a matter of discounting these excess future earnings to their present value. Another method involves determining the total value of the business by capitalizing total earnings, and then deducting the fair values of the identifiable net assets. The number of years method of valuing goodwill, which simply multiplies the excess earnings by the number of years of expected excess earnings, is used to provide a rough measure of goodwill. Another method of valuing goodwill is the discounted free cash flow method, which projects the future operating cash that will be generated over and above the amount needed to maintain current operating levels. The present value of the free cash flows is today's value of the firm.

---

[42] Business valuation is a specialist field. The Canadian Institute of Chartered Business Valuators (CICBV) oversees the granting of the specialist designation, Chartered Business Valuator (CBV), to professionals who meet the education, experience, and examination requirements.

Note: All asterisked assignment material relates to the appendix to the chapter.

Brief Exercises

BE13-1 Troopers Corporation purchases a patent from MacAskill Corp. on January 1, 2005, for $64,000. The patent has a remaining legal life of 16 years. Troopers feels the patent will be useful for 10 years. Prepare Troopers' journal entries to record the patent purchase and 2005 amortization.

BE13-2 Use the information provided in BE13-1. Assume that at January 1, 2007, the carrying amount of the patent on Troopers' books is $51,200. In January, Troopers spends $24,000 successfully defending a patent suit. Troopers still feels the patent will be useful until the end of 2014. Prepare the journal entries to record the $24,000 expenditure and 2007 amortization.

BE13-3 Stauder, Inc. spent $60,000 in legal fees while developing the trade name of its new product, the Mean Bean Machine. Prepare the journal entries to record the $60,000 expenditure and the first year's amortization, assuming a useful life of eight years.

BE13-4 Knickle Corporation obtained a franchise from Sonic Products Inc. for a cash payment of $100,000 on April 1. The franchise grants Knickle the right to sell certain products and services for a period of 12 years. Prepare Knickle's April 1 journal entry and December 31 adjusting entry.

BE13-5 Lager Industries Ltd. had one patent recorded on its books as of January 1, 2005. This patent had a book value of $240,000 and a remaining useful life of eight years. During 2005, Lager incurred research costs of $96,000 and brought a patent infringement suit against a competitor. On December 1, 2005, Lager received the good news that its patent was valid and that its competitor could not use the process Lager had patented. The company incurred $85,000 to defend this patent. At what amount should patent(s) be reported on the December 31, 2005 balance sheet, assuming monthly straight-line amortization of patents?

BE13-6 Wiggens Industries Ltd. acquired two copyrights during 2005. One copyright related to a textbook that was developed internally at a cost of $9,900. This textbook is estimated to have a useful life of three years from September 1, 2005, the date it was published. The second copyright, for a history research textbook, was purchased from University Press on December 1, 2005, for $19,200. This textbook has an indefinite useful life. How should these two copyrights be reported on Wiggens' balance sheet as of December 31, 2005? Assume that Wiggens will use the maximum period of amortization for intangibles, whenever possible.

BE13-7 HTM Ltd. decided that it needed to update its computer programs associated with their supplier relationships. They purchased an off-the-shelf program and modified it internally to link to HTM's other programs. The following costs may be relevant to the accounting for the new software:

Net carrying amount of old software	$ 800
Purchase price of new software	5,000
Direct cost of internal programmer's time spent on conversion	$1,720

Prepare journal entries to record the software replacement.

BE13-8 Indicate whether the following items are capitalized or expensed in the current year:

 (a) purchase cost of a patent from a competitor

 (b) product research costs

 (c) organization costs and

 (d) costs incurred internally to create goodwill.

BE13-9 Earthworm Corp. has capitalized software costs of $700,000 related to a product for external sale, and sales of this product the first year totalled $420,000. Earthworm anticipates earning $980,000 in additional future revenue from this product, which is estimated to have an economic life of four years. Calculate the amount of software amortization assuming amortization is based on the pattern by which Earthworm receives benefits from the software program.

BE13-10 On September 1, 2005, Dunvegan Corporation acquired Edinburgh Enterprises for a cash payment of $750,000. At the time of purchase, Edinburgh's balance sheet showed assets of $620,000, liabilities of $200,000, and owners' equity of $420,000. The fair value of Edinburgh's assets is estimated to be $800,000. (a) Calculate the amount of goodwill acquired by Dunvegan. (b) Prepare the December 31 entry to record amortization, if any, based on a 10-year life.

BE13-11   Nobunaga Corporation owns a patent that has a carrying amount net of accumulated amortization of $330,000. Nobunaga expects future net cash flows from this patent to total $190,000. The patent's fair value is $110,000. Prepare Nobunaga's journal entry, if necessary, to record the impairment loss.

BE13-12   Evans Corporation purchased Filo Company three years ago and at that time recorded goodwill of $400,000. The carrying amount of the goodwill today is $340,000. The Filo Division's net assets, including the goodwill, have a carrying amount of $800,000. Evans expects net future cash flows of $700,000 from the Filo Division. The division's fair value is estimated to be $525,000. Prepare Evans' journal entry, if necessary, to record impairment of the goodwill.

BE13-13   Dorsett Corporation incurred the following costs in 2005:

Cost of laboratory research aimed at discovery of new knowledge	$140,000
Cost of testing in search for product alternatives	100,000
Cost of engineering activity required to advance the design of a product to the manufacturing stage	210,000
	$450,000

Prepare the necessary 2005 journal entry for Dorsett.

BE13-14   Haysom Corporation began operations in early 2005. The corporation incurred $70,000 of costs such as fees to underwriters, legal fees, provincial incorporation fees, and promotional expenditures during its formation. Prepare journal entries to record the $70,000 expenditure and 2005 amortization. If applicable, assume a full year's amortization based on a five-year life.

*BE13-15   Nigel Corporation is interested in purchasing Lau Car Company Ltd. The total of Lau's net incomes over the last five years is $600,000. During one of those years, Lau reported an extraordinary gain of $80,000. The fair value of Lau's net identifiable assets is $560,000. A normal rate of return is 15%, and Nigel wishes to capitalize excess earnings at 20%. Calculate the estimated value of Lau's goodwill.

Exercises

E13-1   (Classification Issues—Intangibles)   Presented below is a list of items that could be included in the intangible assets section of the balance sheet.

1. investment in a subsidiary company

2. timberland

3. cost of engineering activity required to advance a product's design to the manufacturing stage

4. lease prepayment (six months' rent paid in advance)

5. cost of equipment obtained under a capital lease

6. cost of searching for applications of new research findings

7. costs incurred in forming a corporation

8. operating losses incurred in the start-up of a business

9. training costs incurred in start-up of new operation

10. purchase cost of a franchise

11. goodwill generated internally

12. cost of testing in search for product alternatives

13. goodwill acquired in the purchase of a business

14. cost of developing a patent

15. cost of purchasing a patent from an inventor

16. legal costs incurred in securing a patent

17. unrecovered costs of a successful legal suit to protect the patent

18. cost of conceptual formulation of possible product alternatives

19. cost of purchasing a copyright

20. product development costs

21. long-term receivables

22. cost of developing a trademark

23. cost of purchasing a trademark

24. cost of annual update on payroll software

25. estimated fair value of rights to advertising for number one hockey player in Canada

Instructions

(a) Indicate which items on the list above would be reported as intangible assets on the balance sheet.

(b) Indicate how, if at all, the items not reportable as intangible assets would be reported in the financial statements.

E13-2 **(Classification Issues—Intangibles)** Presented below is selected account information related to Maro Inc. as of December 31, 2005. All these accounts have debit balances.

Cable television franchises	Film contract rights
Music copyrights	Customer lists
Research costs	Prepaid expenses
Goodwill	Covenants not to compete
Cash	Brand names
Discount on notes payable	Notes receivable
Accounts receivable	Investments in affiliated companies
Property, plant, and equipment	Organization cost
Leasehold improvements	Land
Annual franchise fee paid	Excess of purchase price over fair value of identifiable net assets, X Corp.

Instructions

Identify which items should be classified as intangible assets. For those items not classified as an intangible asset, indicate where they would be reported in the financial statements.

E13-3 **(Classification Issues—Intangibles)** Hyde Inc. has the following amounts included in its general ledger at December 31, 2005.

Organization costs	$24,000
Trademarks	15,000
Discount on bonds payable	35,000
Deposits with advertising agency for ads to promote goodwill of company	10,000
Excess of cost over fair value of identifiable net assets of acquired subsidiary	75,000
Cost of equipment acquired for research and development projects; the equipment has an alternative future use	90,000
Costs of developing a secret formula for a product that is expected to be marketed for at least 20 years	80,000
Payment for a favourable lease, lease term of 10 years	25,000

Instructions

(a) Based on the information above, calculate the total amount to be reported by Hyde for intangible assets on its balance sheet at December 31, 2005.

(b) If an item is not to be included in intangible assets, explain its proper treatment for reporting purposes.

E13-4 **(Intangible Amortization)** Presented below is selected information for Torrens Corporation.

Interactive Homework

1. Torrens purchased a patent from Vania Co. for $1 million on January 1, 2003. The patent is being amortized over its remaining legal life of 10 years, expiring on January 1, 2013. During 2005, Torrens determined that the patent's economic benefits would not last longer than six years from the date of acquisition. What amount should be reported in the balance sheet for the patent, net of accumulated amortization, at December 31, 2005?

2. Torrens bought a perpetual franchise from Alexander Inc. on January 1, 2004 for $400,000. Its carrying amount on Alexander's books at January 1, 2004 was $500,000. Torrens has decided to amortize the franchise over the maximum period permitted. Assume that Torrens can substantiate clearly identifiable cash flows only for 25 years, but thinks it could have value for up to 60 years. What amount of amortization expense should be reported for the year ended December 31, 2005?

3. On January 1, 2001, Torrens incurred organization costs of $275,000. Torrens is amortizing these costs over five years. What amount, if any, should be reported as unamortized organization costs as of December 31, 2005?

Instructions

Respond to the question asked in each situation presented.

E13-5   (Correct Intangible Asset Account)   As the recently appointed auditor for Durnford Corporation, you have been asked to examine selected accounts before the six-month financial statements of June 30, 2005 are prepared. The controller for Durnford Corporation mentions that only one account (shown below) is kept for Intangible Assets.

INTANGIBLE ASSETS

		Debit	Credit	Balance
January 4	Research costs	940,000		940,000
January 5	Legal costs to obtain patent	75,000		1,015,000
January 31	Payment of seven months' rent on property leased by Durnford (Feb. to Aug.)	91,000		1,106,000
February 11	Proceeds from issue of common shares		250,000	856,000
March 31	Unamortized bond discount on bonds payable due March 31, 2025	84,000		940,000
April 30	Promotional expenses related to start-up of business	207,000		1,147,000
June 30	Operating losses for first six months	241,000		1,388,000

Instructions

Prepare the entry or entries necessary to correct this account. Assume that the patent has a useful life of 10 years.

E13-6   (Recognition and Amortization of Intangibles)   Bateman Limited, organized late in 2004, has set up a single account for all intangible assets. The following summary discloses the entries (all debits) that have been recorded since then.

1/2/05	Purchased patent (8-year life)	$ 350,000
4/1/05	Purchased goodwill (indefinite life)	360,000
7/1/05	Purchased franchise with 10-year life; expiration date 7/1/15	450,000
8/1/05	Payment for copyright (5-year life)	156,000
9/1/05	Research and development costs	215,000
		$1,531,000

Instructions

Prepare the necessary entries to clear the Intangible Assets account and to set up separate accounts for distinct types of intangibles. Make the entries as of December 31, 2005, recording any necessary amortization and reflecting all balances accurately as of that date.

E13-7   (Accounting for Trade Name)   In early January of 2005, Crystal Corporation applied for and received a trade name, incurring legal costs of $16,000. In January of 2006, Crystal incurred $7,800 of legal fees in a successful defence of its trade name.

Interactive
Homework **Instructions**

(a) Identify the variables that must be considered in determining the appropriate amortization period for this trade name.

(b) Calculate 2005 amortization, 12/31/05 book value, 2006 amortization, and 12/31/06 book value if the company amortizes the trade name over its 15-year legal life.

(c) Repeat part (b), assuming a useful life of five years.

E13-8   (Accounting for Lease Transaction)   Benet Inc. leases an old building that it intends to improve and use as a warehouse. To obtain the lease, the company paid a bonus of $72,000. Annual rental for the six-year lease period is $120,000. No option to renew the lease or right to purchase the property is given.

After the lease is obtained, improvements costing $144,000 are made. The building has an estimated remaining useful life of 17 years.

Instructions

(a) What is the annual lease or rent expense to Benet Inc.?

(b) What amount of annual amortization, if any, on a straight-line basis should Benet record?

E13-9   (Accounting for Organization Costs)   Greeley Corporation was organized in 2004 and began operations at the beginning of 2005. The company is involved in interior design consulting services. The following costs were incurred prior to the start of operations.

Legal fees in connection with organization of the company	$15,000
Improvements to leased offices prior to occupancy	25,000
Costs of meetings of incorporators to discuss organizational activities	7,000
Provincial filing fees to incorporate	1,000
	$48,000

Instructions

(a) Calculate the total amount of organization costs incurred by Greeley.

(b) Prepare a summary journal entry to record the $48,000 of expenditures in 2005.

E13-10   (Accounting for Patents, Franchises, and R&D)   Carter Corp. has provided information on intangible assets as follows.

A patent was purchased from Gerald Inc. for $2 million on January 1, 2005. Carter estimated the patent's remaining useful life to be 10 years. The patent was carried in Gerald's accounting records at a net book value of $2.3 million when Gerald sold it to Carter.

During 2006, a franchise was purchased from Reagan Ltd. for $480,000. In addition, 5% of revenue from the franchise must be paid to Reagan. Revenue from the franchise for 2006 was $2.5 million. Carter estimates the franchise's useful life to be 10 years and takes a full year's amortization in the year of purchase.

Carter incurred research and development costs in 2006 as follows.

Materials and equipment	$142,000
Personnel	189,000
Indirect costs	102,000
	$433,000

Carter estimates that these costs will be recouped by December 31, 2009. On January 1, 2006, Carter, because of recent events in the field, estimates that the remaining life of the patent purchased on January 1, 2005 is only five years from January 1, 2006.

Instructions

(a) Prepare a schedule showing the intangibles section of Carter's balance sheet at December 31, 2006. Show supporting calculations in good form.

(b) Prepare a schedule showing the income statement effect for the year ended December 31, 2006 as a result of the facts above. Show supporting calculations in good form.

(AICPA adapted)

E13-11   (Accounting for Patents)   During 2001, Weinstein Corporation spent $170,000 on research and development costs. As a result, a new product called the New Age Piano was patented at additional legal and other costs of $18,000. The patent obtained on October 1, 2001 had a legal life of 20 years and a useful life of 10 years.

Interactive
Homework

Instructions

(a) Prepare all journal entries required in 2001 and 2002 as a result of the transactions above.

(b) On June 1, 2003, Weinstein spent $9,480 to successfully prosecute a patent infringement. As a result, the estimate of useful life was extended to 12 years from June 1, 2003. Prepare all journal entries required in 2003 and 2004.

(c) In 2005, Weinstein determined that a competitor's product would make the New Age Piano obsolete and the patent worthless by December 31, 2006. Prepare all journal entries required in 2005 and 2006.

E13-12   (Accounting for Patents)   Tona Industries Ltd. has the following patents on its December 31, 2006, balance sheet.

Patent Item	Initial Cost	Date Acquired	Useful Life at Date Acquired
Patent A	$30,600	3/1/03	17 years
Patent B	$15,000	7/1/04	10 years
Patent C	$14,400	9/1/05	4 years

The following events occurred during the year ended December 31, 2007.

1. Research and development costs of $245,700 were incurred during the year.

2. Patent D was purchased on July 1 for $36,480. This patent has a useful life of 9½ years.

3. As a result of reduced demands for certain products protected by Patent B, a possible impairment of Patent B's value may have occurred at December 31, 2007. The controller for Tona estimates the future cash flows from Patent B will be as follows.

For the Year Ended	Future Cash Flows
December 31, 2008	$2,000
December 31, 2009	2,000
December 31, 2010	2,000

The proper discount rate to be used for these flows is 8%. (Assume that the cash flows occur at the end of the year.)

Instructions

(a) Calculate the total carrying amount of Tona's patents on its December 31, 2006 balance sheet.

(b) Calculate the total carrying amount of Tona's patents on its December 31, 2007 balance sheet.

E13-13   (Accounting for Goodwill)   Fred Moss, owner of Moss Interiors Inc., is negotiating for the purchase of Zweifel Galleries Ltd. The condensed balance sheet of Zweifel is given in an abbreviated form below.

ZWEIFEL GALLERIES LTD.
Balance Sheet
As of December 31, 2005

Assets		Liabilities and Shareholders' Equity		
Cash	$100,000	Accounts payable		$ 50,000
Land	70,000	Long-term notes payable		300,000
Building (net)	200,000	Total liabilities		350,000
Equipment (net)	175,000	Common shares	$200,000	
Copyright (net)	30,000	Retained earnings	25,000	225,000
Total assets	$575,000	Total liabilities and shareholders' equity		$575,000

Moss and Zweifel agree that land is undervalued by $30,000 and equipment is overvalued by $5,000. Zweifel agrees to sell the gallery to Moss for $350,000.

Instructions
Prepare the entry to record the purchase of the gallery's net assets on Moss' books.

E13-14   (Accounting for Goodwill)   On July 1, 2005, Bing Corporation purchased the net assets of Young Company by paying $250,000 cash and issuing a $100,000 note payable to Young Company. At July 1, 2005, the balance sheet of Young Company was as follows.

Cash	$ 50,000	Accounts payable	$200,000
Receivables	90,000	Young, capital	235,000
Inventory	100,000		$435,000
Land	40,000		
Buildings (net)	75,000		
Equipment (net)	70,000		
Trademarks (net)	10,000		
	$435,000		

The recorded amounts all approximate current values except for land (worth $60,000), inventory (worth $125,000), and trademarks (worthless).

Instructions

(a) Prepare the July 1, 2005 entry for Bing Corporation to record the purchase.

(b) Assume that Bing tested Goodwill for impairment on December 31, 2006 and determined that it had an implied value of $55,000. Prepare the entry, if any, on December 31, 2006.

E13-15   (Intangible Impairment)   Presented below is information related to copyrights owned by La Mare Corp. at December 31, 2005.

Cost	$8,600,000
Carrying amount	4,300,000
Expected future net cash flows	4,000,000
Fair value	3,200,000

Assume that La Mare Corp. will continue to use this copyright in the future. As of December 31, 2005, the copyright is estimated to have a remaining useful life of 10 years.

Instructions

(a) Prepare the journal entry, if any, to record the asset's impairment at December 31, 2005.

(b) Prepare the journal entry to record amortization expense for 2006 related to the copyrights.

(c) The copyright's fair value at December 31, 2006 is $3.4 million. Prepare the journal entry, if any, necessary to record the increase in fair value.

E13-16   (Accounting for Intangibles)   Argot Corporation, organized on July 1, 2004, provided you with the following information.

1. Purchased a franchise for $42,000 on July 2, 2004. The rights to the franchise expire on July 2, 2012 and cannot be renewed. The franchise is expected to be profitable over this entire period.

2. Incurred a net loss of $33,000 in 2004, including a provincial incorporation fee of $2,000 and related legal fees associated with organizing the company of $5,000.

3. Purchased a patent on January 2, 2005 for $80,000. It is estimated to have a 10-year life.

4. Costs incurred to develop a secret formula as of March 1, 2005 were $90,000. The formula has an indefinite life.

5. On March 30, 2005, Argot Corporation purchased a small manufacturing concern for $700,000. The fair value of the company's identifiable net assets acquired was $520,000.

6. On June 29, 2005, legal fees for the successful defence of the patent purchased in January were $11,400.

7. Research costs incurred in 2005 were $110,000.

Instructions

(a) Prepare the journal entries to record the transactions described in 2004 and 2005 as well as any adjusting entries required at December 31, 2004 and 2005. If necessary, assume a five-year life for any intangibles where a useful life has not been given.

(b) At December 31, 2005, an impairment test is performed on the franchise purchased in 2004. It is estimated that the net cash flows to be received from the franchise will be $25,000, and its fair value is $13,000. Calculate the amount of impairment, if any, to be recorded on December 31, 2005. Prepare any necessary journal entries.

(c) Prepare the Intangible Asset section of the balance sheet for Argot Corporation at December 31, 2005.

E13-17   (Goodwill Impairment)   Presented below is net asset information (including associated goodwill of $200 million) related to the Solar Division of Claus, Inc.

SOLAR DIVISION
Net Assets
as of December 31, 2005

(in millions)	Book Value	Fair Value
Cash	$ 50	$50
Receivables	200	150
Property, plant, and equipment (net)	2,600	2,800
Goodwill	200	
Less: Notes payable	(2,700)	(2,700)
Net assets	$ 350	

The purpose of this division (also identified as a reporting unit) is to develop a nuclear-powered aircraft. If successful, travelling delays associated with refuelling could be substantially reduced. Many other benefits would also occur. To date, management has not had much success and is deciding whether a writedown is appropriate at this time. Management estimates its future net cash flows from the project to be $400 million. Management has also received an offer to purchase the division for $345 million.

Instructions

(a) Prepare the journal entry, if any, to record the impairment at December 31, 2005.

(b) At December 31, 2006, it is estimated that the division's fair value increased to $400 million. Prepare the journal entry, if any, to record this increase in fair value.

E13-18   (Accounting for R&D Costs)   Leontyne Corp. from time to time embarks on a research program when a special project seems to offer possibilities. In 2005, the company expends $325,000 on a research project, but by the end of 2005, it is impossible to determine whether any benefit will be derived from it.

Instructions

(a) What account should be charged for the $325,000, and how should it be shown in the financial statements?

(b) The project is completed in 2006, and a successful patent is obtained. The research costs to complete the project are $110,000. The administrative and legal expenses incurred in obtaining patent number 472-1001-84 in 2006 total $16,000. The patent has an expected useful life of five years. Record these costs in journal entry form. Also, record patent amortization (full year) in 2006.

(c) In 2007, the company successfully defends the patent in extended litigation at a cost of $47,200, thereby extending the patent life to 12/31/14. What is the proper way to account for this cost? Also, record patent amortization (full year) in 2007.

(d) Additional engineering and consulting costs incurred in 2007 required to advance a product design to the manufacturing stage total $60,000. These costs enhance the product design considerably. Discuss the proper accounting treatment for this cost.

E13-19   (Accounting for R&D Costs)   Heifitz Ltd. incurred the following costs during 2005.

Quality control during commercial production, including routine product testing	$58,000
Laboratory research aimed at discovery of new knowledge	68,000
Testing for new product evaluation	23,000
Modification of the formulation of a plastics product	4,500
Engineering follow-through in an early phase of commercial production	15,000
Adaptation of an existing capability to a particular requirement or customer's need as a part of continuing commercial activity	13,000
Trouble-shooting in connection with breakdowns during commercial production	29,000
Searching for applications of new research findings	19,000

Instructions
Calculate the total amount Heifitz should classify and expense as research and development costs for 2005.

E13-20   (Accounting for R&D Costs)   Listed below are four independent situations involving research and development costs.

1. During 2005, Sisco Corp. incurred the following costs.

Research and development services performed by Miles Limited for Sisco	$350,000
Testing for evaluation of new products	300,000
Laboratory research aimed at discovery of new knowledge	425,000

For the year ended December 31, 2005, how much research and development expense should Sisco Corp. report?

2. Odo Corp. incurred the following costs during the year ended December 31, 2005.

Design, construction, and testing of preproduction prototypes and models	$290,000
Routine, ongoing efforts to refine, enrich, or otherwise improve upon the qualities of an existing product	250,000
Quality control during commercial production including routine product testing	300,000
Laboratory research aimed at discovery of new knowledge	420,000

What is the total amount to be classified and expensed as research and development for 2005?

3. Quark Ltd. incurred costs in 2005 as follows.

Equipment acquired for use in various research and development projects	$900,000
Amortization on the equipment above	210,000
Materials used in R&D	300,000
Compensation costs of personnel in R&D	400,000
Outside consulting fees for R&D work	220,000
Indirect costs appropriately allocated to R&D	260,000

What is the total amount of research and development that should be reported in Quark's 2005 income statement?

4. Julian Inc. incurred the following costs during the year ended December 31, 2005.

Laboratory research aimed at discovery of new knowledge	$200,000
Radical modification to the formulation of a chemical product	145,000
Research and development costs reimbursable under a contract to perform research and development for Bashir Inc.	350,000
Testing for evaluation of new products	225,000

What is the total amount to be classified and expensed as research and development for 2005?

Instructions

Provide the correct answer to each of the four situations.

E13-21 (Accounting for R&D Costs)   During 2004, Manitoba Enterprises Ltd. spent $5 million developing a new software product called "Dover." Of this amount, $2.2 million was spent before technological feasibility was established for the product, which is to be marketed to third parties. The package was completed by December 31, 2004. Manitoba expects a useful life of eight years for this product with total revenues of $16 million. During 2005, Manitoba realized revenues of $3.2 million from sales of the product.

Instructions

(a) Prepare journal entries required in 2004 to record the transaction described above.

(b) Prepare the entry to record amortization at December 31, 2005.

(c) At what amount should the computer software costs be reported in the December 31, 2005 balance sheet? Could the net realizable value of this asset at December 31, 2005 affect your answer? Explain briefly.

*E13-22 (Calculate Normalized Earnings)   Amanjeet Corporation's pretax accounting income of $850,000 for the year 2005 included the following items.

Amortization of identifiable intangibles	$87,000
Amortization of building	110,000
Loss from discontinued operations	44,000
Extraordinary gains	150,000
Profit-sharing payments to employees	65,000

Ewing Industries Ltd. is seeking to purchase Amanjeet Corporation. In attempting to measure Amanjeet's normalized earnings for 2005, Ewing determines that the building's fair value is triple the book value and the remaining economic life is double that used by Amanjeet. Ewing would continue the profit-sharing payments to employees; such payments are based on income before amortization.

Instructions

Calculate the normalized earnings (for purposes of calculating goodwill) of Amanjeet Corporation for the year 2005.

*E13-23   (Calculate Goodwill)   Net income figures for Ontario Ltd. are as follows:

2001—$64,000	2004—$80,000
2002—$50,000	2005—$75,000
2003—$81,000	

Future incomes are expected to continue at the average of the past five years. Identifiable net assets of this company are appraised at $400,000 on December 31, 2005. This business is to be acquired by Annapolis Corp. early in 2006. The normal rate of return on net assets for the industry is 12%.

Instructions

What amount should be paid for goodwill, and for the company as a whole, if:

(a) Goodwill is equal to average excess earnings capitalized at 25%?

(b) A 15% return is expected on the total investment in the company into perpetuity?

(c) Goodwill is equal to five years' excess earnings?

(d) Goodwill is equal to the present value of five years' excess earnings capitalized at 18%?

*E13-24   (Calculate Goodwill)   Labrador Inc. is considering acquiring Alberta Company as a going concern. Labrador makes the following calculations and conclusions.

1. The fair value of the identifiable assets of Alberta Company is $720,000.

2. Alberta Company's liabilities are $380,000.

3. A fair estimate of annual earnings for the indefinite future is $120,000 per year.

4. Considering the risk and potential of Alberta Company, Labrador feels that it must earn a 25% return on its investment.

Instructions

(a) How much should Labrador be willing to pay for Alberta Company?

(b) How much of the purchase price would be goodwill?

*E13-25   (Calculate Goodwill)   As the president of Manitoba Recording Corp., you are considering purchasing Moose Jaw CD Corp., whose balance sheet is summarized as follows.

Current assets	$ 300,000	Current liabilities	$ 300,000
Plant & equipment (net)	700,000	Long-term liabilities	500,000
Other assets	300,000	Common shares	400,000
		Retained earnings	100,000
Total	$1,300,000	Total	$1,300,000

The current assets' fair value is $250,000 higher than carrying value because of inventory undervaluation. All other assets and liabilities have a carrying value that approximates fair value. The normal rate of return on net assets for the industry is 15%. The expected annual earnings projected for Moose Jaw CD Corp. is $140,000.

Instructions

Assuming that the excess earnings are expected to continue for five years, how much would you be willing to pay for goodwill, and for the company? (Estimate goodwill by the present value method.)

Problems

P13-1   Esplanade Corp., incorporated June 28, 2004, has set up a single account for all intangible assets. The following summary discloses the debit entries that have been recorded during 2004 and 2005:

INTANGIBLE ASSETS

7/1/04	8-year franchise; expiration date 6/30/12	$ 42,000
10/1/04	Advance payment on leasehold (2-year lease)	28,000
12/31/04	Net loss for 2004 including incorporation fee, $1,000; related legal fees of organizing, $5,000; expenses of recruiting and training staff for start-up of new business, $3,700	16,000
15/2/05	Patent purchased (10-year life)	74,000

3/1/05	Direct costs of acquiring a 5-year licensing agreement	75,000
4/1/05	Goodwill purchased (indefinite life)	278,400
6/1/05	Legal fee for successful defence of patent (see above)	12,650
12/31/05	Costs of research department for the year	160,000
12/31/05	Royalties paid under licensing agreement (see above)	2,350

The new business started up on July 2, 2004. No amortization has been recorded for 2004 or 2005.

Instructions

Prepare the necessary entries to clear the Intangible Assets account and to set up separate accounts for distinct types of intangibles. Make the entries as of December 31, 2005, recording any necessary amortization and reflecting all appropriate balances as of that date. State any assumptions you need to make to support your entries.

P13-2 Ankara Laboratories holds a valuable patent (No. 758-6002-1A) on a precipitator that prevents certain types of air pollution. Ankara does not manufacture or sell the products and processes it develops; it conducts research and develops products and processes that it patents, and then assigns the patents to manufacturers on a royalty basis. Occasionally it sells a patent. The history of Ankara patent number 758-6002-1A is as follows.

Date	Activity	Cost
1995-1996	Research conducted to develop precipitator	$384,000
Jan. 1997	Design and construction of a prototype	87,600
March 1997	Testing of models	42,000
Jan. 1998	Fees paid engineers and lawyers to prepare patent application; patent granted July 1, 1998	62,050
Nov. 1999	Engineering activity necessary to advance the precipitator design to the manufacturing stage	81,500
Dec. 2000	Legal fees paid to successfully defend precipitator patent	35,700
April 2001	Research aimed at modifying the patented precipitator design	43,000
July 2005	Legal fees paid in unsuccessful patent infringement suit against a competitor	34,000

Ankara assumed a useful life of 17 years when it received the initial precipitator patent. In early 2003, it revised its useful life estimate downward to five remaining years. Amortization is calculated for a full year if the cost is incurred prior to July 1, and no amortization for the year if the cost is incurred after June 30. The company's year end is December 31.

Instructions

Calculate the carrying value of patent No. 758-6002-1A on each of the following dates:

(a) December 31, 1998

(b) December 31, 2002

(c) December 31, 2005

P13-3 Information concerning Haerhpin Corporation's intangible assets is as follows.

1. On January 1, 2005, Haerhpin signed an agreement to operate as a franchisee of Hsian Copy Service, Inc. for an initial franchise fee of $75,000. Of this amount, $15,000 was paid when the agreement was signed and the balance is payable in four annual payments of $15,000 each, beginning January 1, 2006. The agreement provides that the down payment is not refundable and no future services are required of the franchisor. The present value at January 1, 2005 of the four annual payments discounted at 14% (the implicit rate for a loan of this type) is $43,700. The agreement also provides that 5% of the franchisee's revenue must be paid to the franchisor annually. Haerhpin's revenue from the franchise for 2005 was $950,000. Haerhpin estimates the franchise's useful life to be 10 years. (Hint: Refer to Appendix 6A to determine the proper accounting treatment for the franchise fee and payments.)

2. Haerhpin incurred $65,000 of experimental costs in its laboratory to develop a patent, which was granted on January 2, 2005. Legal fees and other costs associated with patent registration totalled $13,600. Haerhpin estimates that the useful life of the patent will be eight years.

3. A trademark was purchased from Shanghai Company for $32,000 on July 1, 2002. Expenditures for successful litigation in defence of the trademark totalling $8,160 were paid on July 1, 2005. Haerhpin estimates that the trademark's useful life will be 20 years from the acquisition date.

Instructions

(a) Prepare a schedule showing the intangible section of Haerhpin's balance sheet at December 31, 2005. Show supporting calculations in good form.

(b) Prepare a schedule showing all expenses resulting from the transactions that would appear on Haerhpin's income statement for the year ended December 31, 2005. Show supporting calculations in good form.

(AICPA adapted)

P13-4 The following information relates to the intangible assets of Goldberg Products Limited.

	Renewable Licence	Goodwill	Purchased Patent Costs
Original cost at 1/1/2005	$100,000	$280,000	$48,000
Useful life at 1/1/2005 (estimated)	Indefinite	Indefinite	6 years
Implied fair value 12/31/2005	95,000	200,000	38,000
Implied fair value 12/31/2006	97,000	210,000	32,000
Implied fair value 12/31/2007	101,000	220,000	14,600
Net recoverable amount 12/31/2005	105,000	N/A	41,500
Net recoverable amount 12/31/2006	108,000	N/A	37,000
Net recoverable amount 12/31/2007	120,000	N/A	17,000

Just before Goldberg's 2004 fiscal year end at December 31, 2004, the company acquired the three intangible assets identified above in a business combination. In early 2006, the company incurred $6,000 of legal costs in successfully defending the rights to the patent. One year later, in early 2007, Goldberg discovered that a competitor had developed a product that will eventually make the company's patent obsolete. Goldberg decided that the patent had only two years of useful life remaining, with no residual value. The company uses straight-line amortization.

Instructions

(a) Prepare all journal entries required over the period January 1, 2005 to December 31, 2007.

(b) Prepare the balance sheet disclosures required at December 31, 2005, 2006, and 2007. Identify items, if any, that require separate disclosure.

(c) Identify all amounts that will be included on the company's income statements for 2005, 2006, and 2007, and which items, if any, require separate disclosure.

P13-5 During 2003, Nightingale Tool Ltd. purchased a building site for its proposed product development laboratory at a cost of $60,000. Construction of the building was started in 2003. The building was completed in late December 2004 at a cost of $280,000 and placed in service on January 2, 2005. The building's estimated useful life for amortization purposes is 20 years; the straight-line method of amortization is used and there is no estimated residual value.

Management estimates that about 50% of the development projects will result in long-term benefits (i.e., at least 10 years) to the corporation. The remaining projects either benefited the current period or were abandoned before completion. A summary of the number of projects and the direct costs incurred in conjunction with the development activities for 2005 appears below.

Upon recommendation of the research and development group, Nightingale Tool Ltd. acquired a patent for manufacturing rights at a cost of $80,000. The patent was acquired on April 1, 2004 and has an economic life of 10 years.

	Number of Projects	Salaries and Employee Benefits	Other Expenses (Excluding Building Amortization Charges)
Development of viable products (management intent and capability criteria are met)	15	$ 90,000	$50,000
Abandoned projects or projects that benefit the current period only	10	65,000	15,000
Projects in process—results indeterminate	5	40,000	12,000
Total	30	$195,000	$77,000

Instructions

If generally accepted accounting principles are followed, how should the items above relating to product development activities be reported on the company's:

(a) income statement for 2005?

(b) balance sheet as of December 31, 2005?

Be sure to give account titles and amounts, and briefly justify your presentation.

(CMA adapted)

P13-6 In late July 2004, Postera Ltd. paid $3 million to acquire all of the net assets of Muntz Corp., which became a division of Postera. Muntz reported the following balance sheet at the time of acquisition.

Current assets	$800,000	Current liabilities	$600,000
Noncurrent assets	2,700,000	Long-term liabilities	500,000
		Shareholders' equity	2,400,000
	$3,500,000		$3,500,000

It was determined at the date of the purchase that the fair value of the identifiable net assets of Muntz was $2,650,000. Over the next six months of operations, the newly purchased division experienced operating losses. In addition, it now appears that it will generate substantial losses for the foreseeable future. At December 31, 2004, the Muntz Division reports the following balance sheet information.

Current assets	$450,000
Noncurrent assets (including goodwill recognized in purchase)	2,400,000
Current liabilities	(700,000)
Long-term liabilities	(500,000)
Net assets	$1,650,000

It is determined that the fair value of the Muntz Division is $1,850,000. The recorded amount for Muntz' net assets (excluding goodwill) is the same as fair value, except for property, plant, and equipment, which has a fair value $150,000 above the carrying value.

Instructions

(a) Calculate the amount of goodwill recognized, if any, in late July 2004.

(b) Determine the impairment loss, if any, to be recognized on December 31, 2004.

(c) Assume the fair value of the Muntz Division is $1.5 million instead of $1,850,000 on December 31, 2004. Determine the impairment loss, if any, to be recognized on December 31, 2004.

(d) Prepare the journal entry to record the impairment loss, if any, and indicate where the loss would be reported in the income statement.

P13-7 Sato Corporation was incorporated on January 3, 2004. The corporation's financial statements for its first year's operations were not examined by a public accountant. You have been engaged to audit the financial statements for the year ended December 31, 2005, and your audit is substantially complete. The corporation's trial balance appears below.

SATO CORPORATION
Trial Balance
December 31, 2005

	Debit	Credit
Cash	$ 47,000	
Accounts Receivable	73,000	
Allowance for Doubtful Accounts		$ 1,460
Inventories	50,200	
Machinery	82,000	
Equipment	37,000	
Accumulated Amortization		26,200
Patents	128,200	
Leasehold Improvements	36,100	
Prepaid Expenses	13,000	
Goodwill	30,000	
Licensing Agreement No. 1	60,000	
Licensing Agreement No. 2	56,000	
Accounts Payable		73,000
Unearned Revenue		17,280
Common Shares		300,000
Retained Earnings, January 1, 2005		159,060
Sales		720,000
Cost of Goods Sold	475,000	
Selling and General Expenses	180,000	
Interest Expense	9,500	
Extraordinary Losses	20,000	
Totals	$1,297,000	$1,297,000

The following information relates to accounts that may yet require adjustment.

1. Patents for Sato's manufacturing process were acquired January 2, 2005 at a cost of $93,500. An additional $34,700 was spent in December 2005 to improve machinery covered by the patents and was charged to the Patents account. Amortization on fixed assets was properly recorded for 2005 in accordance with Sato's practice, which provides a full year's amortization for property on hand June 30 and no amortization otherwise. Sato uses the straight-line method for all amortization and amortized its patents over their legal life, which was 17 years when granted. All amortization is accumulated in one account.

2. At December 31, 2005, management determined that the net future cash flows expected from use of the patent would be $80,000, and that the resale value of the patent on this date is approximately $55,000.

3. On January 3, 2004, Sato purchased licensing agreement No. 1, which management believed had an unlimited useful life. Licences similar to this are frequently bought and sold. Sato could only clearly identify cash flows from agreement No. 1 for 18 years, after which further cash flows are possible, but somewhat uncertain. The balance in the Licensing Agreement No. 1 account includes its purchase price of $57,000 and expenses of $3,000 related to the acquisition. On January 1, 2005, Sato purchased licensing agreement No. 2, which has a life expectancy of 10 years. The balance in the Licensing Agreement No. 2 account includes its $54,000 purchase price and $6,000 in acquisition expenses, but it has been reduced by a credit of $4,000 for the advance collection of 2006 revenue from the agreement. In late December 2004, an explosion caused a permanent 70% reduction in the expected revenue-producing value of licensing agreement No. 1, and in January 2006, a flood caused additional damage that rendered the agreement worthless.

4. The balance in the Goodwill account results from legal expenses of $30,000 incurred for Sato's incorporation on January 3, 2004. Although management assumes the $30,000 cost will benefit the entire life of the organization, it decided late in 2005 that these costs should be amortized over a limited life of 30 years. No entry has been made yet.

5. The Leasehold Improvements account includes (a) the $15,000 cost of improvements with a total estimated useful life of 12 years, which Sato, as tenant, made to leased premises in January 2004, (b) movable assembly line equipment costing $15,000 that was installed in the leased premises in December 2005, and (c) real estate taxes of $6,100 paid by Sato in 2005, which under the terms of the lease should have been paid by the landlord. Sato paid its rent in full during 2005. A 10-year nonrenewable lease was signed January 3, 2004, for the leased building that Sato used in manufacturing operations. No amortization has been recorded on any amounts related to the lease or improvements.

Instructions

Prepare an eight-column work sheet to adjust accounts that require adjustment and include columns for an income statement and a balance sheet. A separate account should be used for the accumulation of each type of amortization. Formal adjusting journal entries and financial statements are not required.

(AICPA adapted)

P13-8   Presented below are six examples of purchased intangible assets reported on the balance sheet of Hamm Enterprises Limited, including information about their useful and legal lives.

Intangible #1(a): The trade name for one of the company's subsidiaries. The trade name has a remaining legal life of 16 years, but it can be renewed indefinitely at a very low cost. The subsidiary has grown quickly, has been very successful, and its name is well known to Canadian consumers. Hamm management has concluded that it can identify positive cash flows from the use of the trade name for another 25 years, and assumes they will continue beyond this as well.

Intangible #1(b): The trade name is as identified above, but assume instead that Hamm Enterprises expects to sell this subsidiary in three years time as the subsidiary operates in a non-core area.

Intangible #2: A licence granted by the federal government to Hamm to permit it to provide essential services to a key military installation overseas. The licence expires in five years, but is renewable indefinitely at little cost. Because of the profitability associated with this licence, Hamm expects to renew it indefinitely. The licence is very marketable, and will generate cash flows indefinitely.

Intangible #3: Magazine subscription list. Hamm expects to use this subscriber list to generate revenues and cash flows for at least 25 years. It has determined the cash flow potential of this intangible by analysing renewal history, the behaviour of the group, and its responses to questionnaires.

Intangible #4: Non-competition covenant. Hamm acquired this intangible asset when the company bought out a major owner-managed competitor. The seller signed an agreement contracting not to set up or work for another business that was in direct or indirect competition with Hamm. The projected cash flows resulting from this agreement are expected to continue for at least 25 years.

Intangible #5: Medical files. One of Hamm's subsidiary companies owns a number of medical clinics. A recent purchase of a retiring doctor's practice required a significant payment for the practice's medical files and clients. Hamm considers that this base will benefit the business throughout its organizational existence, providing cash flows indefinitely.

Intangible #6: Favourable lease. Hamm acquired a sub-lease on a large warehouse property that requires annual rentals that are 50% below competitive rates in the area. The lease extends for 35 years.

Instructions

For each intangible asset and situation described above:

(a) identify the appropriate method of accounting for the asset subsequent to acquisition, justify your response, and

(b) provide an example of a specific situation that would prompt you to test the intangible asset for impairment.

P13-9   MMG Inc. is a large, publicly held corporation. Listed below are six selected expenditures made by the company during the current fiscal year ended April 30, 2005. The proper accounting treatment of these transactions must be determined in order to ensure MMG's annual financial statements are prepared in accordance with generally accepted accounting principles.

1. MMG Inc. spent $3 million on a program designed to improve relations with its dealers. This project was favourably received by the dealers and MMG's management believes that significant future benefits will be received from this program. The program was conducted during the fourth quarter of the current fiscal year.

2. A pilot plant was constructed during 2004-05 at a cost of $5.5 million to test a new production process. The plant will be operated for approximately five years. At that time, the company will make a decision regarding the economic value of the process. The pilot plant is too small for commercial production, so it will be dismantled when the test is over.

3. During the year, MMG began a new manufacturing operation in Newfoundland, its first plant east of Montreal. To get the plant into operation, the following costs were incurred: (a) $100,000 to make the building fully wheelchair accessible; (b) $41,600 to outfit the new employees with MMG uniforms; (c) $12,700 for the reception to introduce the company to others in the industrial mall where the plant was located; and (d) $64,400 payroll costs covering the new employees while being trained.

4. MMG Inc. purchased Eagle Company for $6 million in cash in early August 2004. The fair value of Eagle's net identifiable assets was $5.2 million.

5. The company spent $14 million on advertising during the year: $2.5 million was spent in April 2005 to introduce a new product to be released during the first quarter of the 2006 fiscal year; $200,000 was dedicated to advertising the opening of the new plant in Newfoundland; $5 million was spent on the company product catalogue for the 2005 calendar year. The remaining expenditures were for recurring advertising and promotion coverage.

6. During the first six months of the 2004-05 fiscal year, $400,000 was expended for legal work in connection with a successful patent application. The patent became effective November 2004. The patent's legal life is 20 years and its economic life is expected to be approximately 10 years.

Instructions

For each of the six items presented, determine and justify:

(a) The amount, if any, that should be capitalized and included on MMG's statement of financial position prepared as of April 30, 2005.

(b) The amount that should be included in MMG's statement of income for the year ended April 30, 2005.

(CMA adapted)

*P13-10   Anshan Inc. has recently become interested in acquiring a South American plant to handle many of its production functions in that market. One possible candidate is La Paz Inc., a closely held corporation, whose owners have decided to sell their business if a proper settlement can be obtained. La Paz's balance sheet appears as follows.

Current assets	$150,000
Investments	50,000
Plant assets (net)	400,000
Total assets	$600,000
Current liabilities	$ 80,000
Long-term debt	100,000
Share capital	220,000
Retained earnings	200,000
Total equities	$600,000

Anshan has hired Palermo Appraisal Corporation to determine the proper price to pay for La Paz Inc. The appraisal firm finds that the investments have a fair market value of $150,000 and that inventory is understated by $80,000. All other assets and liabilities have book values that approximate their fair values. An examination of the company's income for the last four years indicates that the net income has steadily increased. In 2005, the company had a net operating income of $100,000, and this income should increase 20% each year over the next four years. Anshan believes that a normal return in this type of business is 18% on net assets. The asset investment in the South American plant is expected to stay the same for the next four years.

Instructions

(a) Palermo Appraisal Corporation has indicated that the company's fair value can be estimated in a number of ways. Prepare an estimate of the value of La Paz Inc., assuming a value based on the following.

1. Goodwill is based on the purchase of average excess earnings over the next four years.

2. Goodwill is equal to the capitalization of average excess earnings of La Paz Inc. at 24%.

3. Goodwill is equal to the present value of the average excess earnings over the next four years discounted at 15%.

4. The value of the business is based on the capitalization of future earnings of La Paz Inc. at 20%.

(b) La Paz Inc. is willing to sell the business for $1 million. How do you believe Palermo Appraisal should advise Anshan?

(c) If Anshan were to pay $770,000 to purchase the assets and assume the liabilities of La Paz Inc., how would this transaction be reflected on Anshan's books?

*P13-11   The president of Birch Corp., Joyce Pollachek, is considering purchasing Balloon Bunch Company. She thinks that the offer sounds fair but she wants to consult a professional accountant to be sure. Balloon Bunch Company is asking $78,000 in excess of the fair value of the identifiable net assets. Balloon Bunch's net income figures for the last five years are as follows.

2001—$64,000	2004—$80,000
2002—$50,000	2005—$70,000
2003—$81,000	

The company's identifiable net assets were appraised at $400,000 on December 31, 2005.

You have done some initial research on the balloon industry and discovered that the normal rate of return on identifiable net assets is 13%. After analysing variables such as stability of past earnings, the nature of the business, and general economic conditions, you have decided that the average excess earnings for the last five years should be capitalized at 25% and that the excess earnings will continue for about five more years. Further research led you to discover that the Happy Balloon Company, a competitor of similar size and profitability, was recently sold for $540,000, six times its average yearly earnings of $90,000.

Instructions

(a) Prepare a schedule that includes the calculation of Balloon Bunch Company's goodwill and purchase price under at least three methods.

(b) Write a letter to Joyce Pollachek that includes:

1. An explanation of the nature of goodwill.

2. An explanation of the different acceptable methods of determining its fair value. (Include with your explanation of the different methods the rationale of how each method arrives at a goodwill value.)

3. Advice for Joyce Pollachek on how to determine her purchase price.

Writing Assignments

WA13-1   After securing lease commitments from several major stores, Kolber Shopping Centres Ltd. was organized and it built a shopping centre in a growing suburb. The shopping centre would have opened on schedule on January 1, 2005, if it had not been struck by a severe flood in December; it opened for business on October 1, 2005. All of the additional construction costs that were incurred as a result of the flood were covered by insurance.

In July 2004, in anticipation of the scheduled January opening, a permanent staff had been hired to promote the shopping centre, obtain tenants for the uncommitted space, and manage the property.

A summary of some of the costs incurred in 2004 and the first nine months of 2005 follows.

	2004	January 1, 2005 through September 30, 2005
Interest on mortgage bonds	$720,000	$540,000
Cost of obtaining tenants	300,000	360,000
Promotional advertising	540,000	557,000

The promotional advertising campaign was designed to familiarize shoppers with the centre. Had it been known in time that the centre would not open until October 2005, the 2004 expenditure for promotional advertising would not have been made. The advertising had to be repeated in 2005.

All of the tenants who had leased space in the shopping centre at the time of the flood accepted the October occupancy date on condition that the monthly rental charges for the first nine months of 2005 be cancelled.

Instructions

Explain how each of the costs for 2004 and the first nine months of 2005 should be treated in the accounts of the shopping centre corporation. Give the reasons for each treatment.

(AICPA adapted)

WA13-2   Waveland Corporation's research and development department has an idea for a project it believes will culminate in a new product that would be very profitable for the company. Because the project will be very expensive, the department requests approval from Waveland Corporation's controller, Ron Santo.

Santo recognizes that corporate profits have been down lately and is hesitant to approve a project that will incur significant expenses that cannot be capitalized under *CICA Handbook* Section 3450 on Research and Development Costs. He knows that if Waveland Corporation hires an outside firm that does the work and obtains a patent for the process, the company can purchase the patent from the outside firm and record the expenditure as an asset. Santo knows that the company's own R&D department is first-rate, and he is confident it can do the work well.

Instructions

Advise Ron Santo on what he should do. Ensure your answer identifies who the stakeholders are in this situation and what ethical issues are involved.

WA13-3   On June 30, 2005, your client, Bearcat Limited, was granted two patents covering plastic cartons that it had been producing and marketing profitably for the past three years. One patent covers the manufacturing process and the other covers related products.

Bearcat executives tell you that these patents represent the most significant breakthrough in the industry in the past 30 years. The products have been marketed under the registered trademarks Evertight, Duratainer, and Sealrite. Licences under the patents have already been granted by your client to other manufacturers in Canada and abroad and are producing substantial royalties.

On July 1, Bearcat commenced patent infringement actions against several companies whose names you recognize as those of substantial and prominent competitors. Bearcat's management is optimistic that these suits will result in a permanent injunction against the manufacture and sale of the infringing products and collection of damages for loss of profits caused by the alleged infringement.

The financial vice-president has suggested that the patents be recorded at the discounted value of expected net royalty receipts.

Instructions

(a) What is the meaning of discounted value of expected net receipts? Explain.

(b) How would such a value be calculated for net royalty receipts?

(c) What basis of valuation for Bearcat's patents would be generally accepted in accounting? Give supporting reasons for this basis.

(d) Assuming no practical problems of implementation and ignoring generally accepted accounting principles, what is the preferred basis of valuation for patents? Explain.

(e) What would be the preferred theoretical basis of amortization? Explain.

(f) What recognition, if any, should be made of the infringement litigation in the financial statements for the year ending September 30, 2005? Discuss.

(AICPA adapted)

WA13-4 Echo Corp., a retail propane gas distributor, has increased its annual sales volume to a level three times greater than the annual sales of a dealer it purchased in 2003 in order to begin operations. The board of directors of Echo Corp. recently received an offer to negotiate the sale of Echo to a large competitor. As a result, the majority of the board wants to increase the stated value of goodwill on the balance sheet to reflect the larger sales volume developed through intensive promotion and the product's current market price. A few of the board members, however, would prefer to eliminate goodwill altogether from the balance sheet in order to prevent possible misinterpretations. Goodwill was recorded properly in 2003.

Instructions

(a) Discuss the meaning of the term "goodwill."

*(b) List the techniques used to calculate an estimated value for goodwill in negotiations to purchase a going concern.

(c) Why are the book and fair values of Echo Corp.'s goodwill different?

(d) Discuss the appropriateness of

1. Increasing the stated value of goodwill prior to the negotiations.

2. Eliminating goodwill completely from the balance sheet.

(AICPA adapted)

WA13-5 Nova Jones Ltd. is developing a revolutionary new product. A new division of the company was formed to develop, manufacture, and market this new product. As of year end (December 31, 2005), the new product had not been manufactured for resale; however, a prototype unit was built and is in operation. Throughout 2005, the new division incurred costs. These costs include design and engineering studies, prototype manufacturing costs, administrative expenses (including salaries of administrative personnel), and market research costs. In addition, approximately $900,000 in equipment (estimated useful life of 10 years) was purchased to develop and manufacture the new product. Approximately $315,000 of this equipment was built specifically for the design development of the new product; the remaining $585,000 of equipment was used to manufacture the pre-production prototype and will be used to manufacture the new product once it is in commercial production.

Instructions

(a) How are research and development defined in *CICA Handbook* Section 3450?

(b) Briefly indicate the practical and conceptual reasons for the conclusions reached by the Accounting Standards Board on accounting and reporting practices for research and development costs.

(c) In accordance with Section 3450, how should the various costs of Nova Jones described above be recorded on its financial statements for the year ended December 31, 2005? Provide support for your conclusions.

Cases

Digital Tool
www.wiley.com/
canada/kieso

Refer to the Case Primer on the Digital Tool to help you answer these cases.

CA13-1 Acquisitions Limited (AL) is a privately owned business which operates in the biotechnology business and has recently been on an acquisitions binge. It is now nearing year end and the company has been signaling to its bankers that 2003 has been a good year with substantial revenue growth. At present, the controller is preparing the adjustment for the year-end financial statements in preparation for a meeting with the bank next week. The bank is worried that the company has been overpaying for the acquired businesses and is looking for assurance that profitability and cash flows of the company will not be harmed.

The following intangible assets have been acquired in several acquisitions:

Health care industry contact lists—the company plans to use these lists for sales purposes and expects that it will be able to derive benefit from the information on the lists for two to three years.

Patents for drug delivery systems—the legal life remaining is 12 years however, due to the competitive nature of this branch of research, the protection will only last approximately 8 years. The vendor has agreed to buy back the patent for approximately 50% of the value in 5 years. AL has committed to resell.

Trademarks for certain over the counter allergy drugs – the legal life remaining on the trademark is three years but it is renewable every five years at little cost. AL is planning to add this drug to its stable of core revenue producing drugs and has already invested significant amounts in advertising. Research in the area of treating allergies has led AL scientists to believe that there will not be a better drug nor cure for allergies in the near to mid term.

AL has also started up a new online distribution business. So far, the company has relocated 40 employees, developed a new website/database and spent significant amounts training and advertising. It is now December 15 and preparations to get ready have been ongoing for 6 months. Management originally estimated that it would take 7 months to be up and running. AL is already serving its first few customers in the new business although there are still many wrinkles to iron out. It is estimated that the business will break even in about 5 more months.

Instructions

Adopt the role of the company's auditors and critically evaluate the financial reporting choices available to the company.

Integrated Case

IC13-1   The following is an excerpt from Biovail Corporation's (BC) Annual Report:

> "Biovail Corporation is a full-service pharmaceutical company that applies its proprietary drug delivery technologies in developing "oral controlled-release" products throughout North America. Biovail applies its proprietary drug delivery technologies to successful drug compounds that are free of patent protection to develop oral controlled-release pharmaceutical products. Branded oral controlled-release products improve on existing formulations, providing better therapeutic and economic benefits.
>
>   Biovail engages in the formulation, clinical testing, registration, manufacturing, sales and marketing of these oral controlled-release products throughout North America. To date, Biovail technologies have been used to develop 18 products that have been sold in more than 55 countries. Biovail's proven technologies are being applied to over 20 new products currently under development."

In 2003 and 2004 several class action lawsuits were launched against the company for misleading investors. Amongst other things, the lawsuits allege that the company's growth in revenues is primarily due to acquisitions (as opposed to core business growth).

On October 1, 2003, a large shipment of the company's Wellbutrin XL drug was involved in a fatal multi-vehicle traffic accident that killed 8 people. The truck was rear ended in the accident, suffering a reported $10-20 million in damages (no product spilled on the ground). The shipment was on its way to GlaxoSmithKline. BC stated that they had to take the drug back to the plant for inspection to be on the safe side. News reporters speculated that insurance would only cover the actual manufacturing costs (not resale value) if the entire order were destroyed.

The company stated that the loss caused them to miss their expected quarterly profit target. On October 3, the company announced that it would have to lower revenue expectations by up to 22% for the third quarter, citing the traffic accident as contributing significantly to this.

A week later, Banc of America Securities LLC issued a research report that included commentary by three forensic accountants who reviewed the financial reporting of the company and raised a list of concerns over "aggressive accounting". As a result of the report, many investors sold their shares, driving the price of stock down significantly. The company responded to the comment in the report by announcing that they were considering a lawsuit against the analyst for what they termed as irresponsible comments.

Other analysts noted that a substantial portion of Biovail's earnings in the first half of the year came from one-time items. Sixty percent of the company's assets are represented by intangible and goodwill. Net income for the nine months ended September 30, 2003 was approximately $75 (U.S.) million.

Instructions

Adopt the role of the controller of BC and discuss the financial reporting issues.

Research and Financial Analysis

RA13-1   Intrawest Corporation (A)

Refer to the financial statements and accompanying notes of Intrawest Corporation presented in Appendix 5B and answer the following questions.

Instructions

(a) Does Intrawest Corporation report any intangible assets (broadly defined) in its 2003 financial statements and accompanying notes? Identify all intangibles, their reported balance sheet amounts at June 30, 2003, and the accounting policies applied to these assets.

(b) What was Intrawest's opening balance of goodwill for the year ended June 30, 2003? Its ending balance? Reconcile these amounts, clearly explaining the reasons for each change.

(c) The notes to the financial statements indicate that the company entered into two business combinations in 2003. Did Intrawest acquire any goodwill as a result of these acquisitions? Explain why, or why not.

RA13-2   Intrawest Corporation (B)

As indicated throughout this text, the Canadian and U.S. standard-setting bodies are attempting to eliminate differences in the accounting standards between their two countries. Refer to the financial statements and accompanying notes of Intrawest Corporation presented in Appendix 5B and answer the following questions.

Instructions

(a) What accounting policies related to intangible assets (broadly defined) are applied by Intrawest that differ from the U.S. standard?

(b) What would have been the effect on net income, ending retained earnings, and total assets if Intrawest had used the same policies that were required in the United States? Explain each clearly.

RA13-3   The Descartes Systems Group Inc.

Gain access to the financial statements and accompanying notes of The Descartes Systems Group Inc. for its year ended January 31, 2003 either on the Digital Tool or through SEDAR (www.sedar.com). Descartes provides two sets of financial statements—one set prepared under Canadian GAAP and one set prepared under U.S. GAAP. Ensure you obtain the Canadian GAAP financial statements.

Instructions
Review the financial statements of Descartes for the year ended January 31, 2003 and respond to the following questions.

(a) What business is Descartes in?

(b) Identify each separate type of intangible asset (broadly defined) to which Descartes makes a reference, and specify the accounting policy applied to each.

(c) Descartes discloses information about its acquisition of Tradevision AB for $7.6 million. What was the fair value of the identifiable net assets in this business combination? What makes up the identifiable net assets? How did Descartes determine their fair values? How was the goodwill calculated?

(d) Briefly review the information provided about acquisitions for the years ended January 31, 2002 and 2001. What makes up the majority of the identifiable asset values of these acquisitions? How much goodwill was purchased as a result of the acquisitions over these two fiscal years?

(e) Prepare a reconciliation of the carrying amount of goodwill (net) over the year ended January 31, 2003, clearly explaining all changes.

RA13-4   Merck and Johnson & Johnson

Merck & Co., Inc. and Johnson & Johnson are two leading producers of health care products. Each has considerable assets, and each expends considerable funds each year toward the development of new products. The development of a new health care product is often very expensive, and risky. New products frequently must undergo considerable testing before approval for distribution to the public. For example, it took Johnson & Johnson four years and $200 million (U.S.) to develop its 1-DAY ACUVUE contact lenses. Below are some basic data compiled from the financial statements of these two companies.

(in $ millions U.S.)	Johnson & Johnson	Merck
Total assets	$15,668	$21,857
Total revenue	15,734	14,970
Net income	2,006	2,997
Research and development expense	1,278	1,230
Intangible assets	2,403	7,212

Instructions

(a) What kinds of intangible assets might a health care products company have? Does the composition of these intangibles matter to investors; that is, would it be perceived differently if all of Merck's intangibles were goodwill, than if all of its intangibles were patents?

(b) Suppose the president of Merck has come to you for advice. He has noted that by eliminating research and development expenditures, the company could have reported $1.3 billion more in net income. He is frustrated because much of the research never results in a product, or the products take years to develop. He says shareholders are eager for higher returns, so he is considering eliminating research and development expenditures for at least a couple of years. What would you advise?

(c) The notes to Merck's financial statements indicate that Merck has goodwill of $4.1 billion. Where does recorded goodwill come from? Is it necessarily a good thing to have a lot of goodwill on your books?

RA13-5 Comparative Analysis

Instructions

Go to the SEDAR website (www.sedar.com) and choose two companies from each of four different industry classifications. Choose from a variety of industries such as real estate and construction, foodstores (under merchandising), biotechnology and pharmaceuticals (under consumer products), publishing (under communications and media), etc. From the companies' most recent financial statements, identify the intangibles and deferred charges, the total assets, and the accounting policies for each type of intangible and deferred charge reported.

(a) 1. What amounts were reported for intangible assets and deferred charges by each company?

  2. What percentage of total assets does each company have invested in intangible assets and deferred charges?

  3. Does the type of intangible and deferred charge differ depending on the type of industry? Does the relative investment in this category of asset differ among industries? Comment.

(b) 1. List all the intangible assets you identified and the policies used by these companies in amortizing them, if applicable. Do the policies differ by type of intangible? By type of industry?

  2. Are the amounts of accumulated amortization reported by these companies? Have any impairments been reported in the current period? If so, what disclosure was made about the impairment?

RA13-6 CoolBrands International Inc.

CoolBrands International Inc., based in Markham, Ontario, is a market leader in the consumer products and franchising segments of the frozen dessert industry. Its brands include such well-known names as Yoplait, Betty Crocker, and Weight Watchers. In the fourth quarter of its fiscal year ended August 31, 2003, CoolBrands paid out $13.4 million (U.S.) for an acquisition that gave the company rights to other recognized ice-cream brands.

Instructions

(a) Obtain access to CoolBrands' financial statements and provide a summary of the identifiable net assets acquired in the business combination referred to above.

(b) Identify all intangibles acquired as a result of this acquisition.

(c) Summarize the intangible assets reported by CoolBrands and reconcile the change from August 31, 2002 to August 31, 2003.

(d) What effect would you expect this acquisition to have on the company, its financial statements, and market value? What has been the effect of this acquisition on the company and its share price?

Time Value of Money

Table A-1

FUTURE VALUE OF 1

(FUTURE VALUE OF A SINGLE SUM)

$$FVF_{n,\,i} = (1 + i)^n$$

(n) periods	2%	2½%	3%	4%	5%	6%	8%	9%	10%	11%	12%	15%
1	1.02000	1.02500	1.03000	1.04000	1.05000	1.06000	1.08000	1.09000	1.10000	1.11000	1.12000	1.15000
2	1.04040	1.05063	1.06090	1.08160	1.10250	1.12360	1.16640	1.18810	1.21000	1.23210	1.25440	1.32250
3	1.06121	1.07689	1.09273	1.12486	1.15763	1.19102	1.25971	1.29503	1.33100	1.36763	1.40493	1.52088
4	1.08243	1.10381	1.12551	1.16986	1.21551	1.26248	1.36049	1.41158	1.46410	1.51807	1.57352	1.74901
5	1.10408	1.13141	1.15927	1.21665	1.27628	1.33823	1.46933	1.53862	1.61051	1.68506	1.76234	2.01136
6	1.12616	1.15969	1.19405	1.26532	1.34010	1.41852	1.58687	1.67710	1.77156	1.87041	1.97382	2.31306
7	1.14869	1.18869	1.22987	1.31593	1.40710	1.50363	1.71382	1.82804	1.94872	2.07616	2.21068	2.66002
8	1.17166	1.21840	1.26677	1.36857	1.47746	1.59385	1.85093	1.99256	2.14359	2.30454	2.47596	3.05902
9	1.19509	1.24886	1.30477	1.42331	1.55133	1.68948	1.99900	2.17189	2.35795	2.55803	2.77308	3.51788
10	1.21899	1.28008	1.34392	1.48024	1.62889	1.79085	2.15892	2.36736	2.59374	2.83942	3.10585	4.04556
11	1.24337	1.31209	1.38423	1.53945	1.71034	1.89830	2.33164	2.58043	2.85312	3.15176	3.47855	4.65239
12	1.26824	1.34489	1.42576	1.60103	1.79586	2.01220	2.51817	2.81267	3.13843	3.49845	3.89598	5.35025
13	1.29361	1.37851	1.46853	1.66507	1.88565	2.13293	2.71962	3.06581	3.45227	3.88328	4.36349	6.15279
14	1.31948	1.41297	1.51259	1.73168	1.97993	2.26090	2.93719	3.34173	3.79750	4.31044	4.88711	7.07571
15	1.34587	1.44830	1.55797	1.80094	2.07893	2.39656	3.17217	3.64248	4.17725	4.78459	5.47357	8.13706
16	1.37279	1.48451	1.60471	1.87298	2.18287	2.54035	3.42594	3.97031	4.59497	5.31089	6.13039	9.35762
17	1.40024	1.52162	1.65285	1.94790	2.29202	2.69277	3.70002	4.32763	5.05447	5.89509	6.86604	10.76126
18	1.42825	1.55966	1.70243	2.02582	2.40662	2.85434	3.99602	4.71712	5.55992	6.54355	7.68997	12.37545
19	1.45681	1.59865	1.75351	2.10685	2.52695	3.02560	4.31570	5.14166	6.11591	7.26334	8.61276	14.23177
20	1.48595	1.63862	1.80611	2.19112	2.65330	3.20714	4.66096	5.60441	6.72750	8.06231	9.64629	16.36654
21	1.51567	1.67958	1.86029	2.27877	2.78596	3.39956	5.03383	6.10881	7.40025	8.94917	10.80385	18.82152
22	1.54598	1.72157	1.91610	2.36992	2.92526	3.60354	5.43654	6.65860	8.14028	9.93357	12.10031	21.64475
23	1.57690	1.76461	1.97359	2.46472	3.07152	3.81975	5.87146	7.25787	8.95430	11.02627	13.55235	24.89146
24	1.60844	1.80873	2.03279	2.56330	3.22510	4.04893	6.34118	7.91108	9.84973	12.23916	15.17863	28.62518
25	1.64061	1.85394	2.09378	2.66584	3.38635	4.29187	6.84847	8.62308	10.83471	13.58546	17.00000	32.91895
26	1.67342	1.90029	2.15659	2.77247	3.55567	4.54938	7.39635	9.39916	11.91818	15.07986	19.04007	37.85680
27	1.70689	1.94780	2.22129	2.88337	3.73346	4.82235	7.98806	10.24508	13.10999	16.73865	21.32488	43.53532
28	1.74102	1.99650	2.28793	2.99870	3.92013	5.11169	8.62711	11.16714	14.42099	18.57990	23.88387	50.06561
29	1.77584	2.04641	2.35657	3.11865	4.11614	5.41839	9.31727	12.17218	15.86309	20.62369	26.74993	57.57545
30	1.81136	2.09757	2.42726	3.24340	4.32194	5.74349	10.06266	13.26768	17.44940	22.89230	29.95992	66.21177
31	1.84759	2.15001	2.50008	3.37313	4.53804	6.08810	10.86767	14.46177	19.19434	25.41045	33.55511	76.14354
32	1.88454	2.20376	2.57508	3.50806	4.76494	6.45339	11.73708	15.76333	21.11378	28.20560	37.58173	87.56507
33	1.92223	2.25885	2.65234	3.64838	5.00319	6.84059	12.67605	17.18203	23.22515	31.30821	42.09153	100.69983
34	1.96068	2.31532	2.73191	3.79432	5.25335	7.25103	13.69013	18.72841	25.54767	34.75212	47.14252	115.80480
35	1.99989	2.37321	2.81386	3.94609	5.51602	7.68609	14.78534	20.41397	28.10244	38.57485	52.79962	133.17552
36	2.03989	2.43254	2.88928	4.10393	5.79182	8.14725	15.96817	22.25123	30.91268	42.81808	59.13557	153.15185
37	2.08069	2.49335	2.98523	4.26809	6.08141	8.63609	17.24563	24.25384	34.00395	47.52807	66.23184	176.12463
38	2.12230	2.55568	3.07478	4.43881	6.38548	9.15425	18.62528	26.43668	37.40434	52.75616	74.17966	202.54332
39	2.16474	2.61957	3.16703	4.61637	6.70475	9.70351	20.11530	28.81598	41.14479	58.55934	83.08122	232.92482
40	2.20804	2.68506	3.26204	4.80102	7.03999	10.28572	21.72452	31.40942	45.25926	65.00087	93.05097	267.86355

Table A-2

PRESENT VALUE OF 1

(PRESENT VALUE OF A SINGLE SUM)

$$PVF_{n,\,i} = \frac{1}{(1+i)^n} = (1+i)^{-n}$$

(n) periods	2%	2½%	3%	4%	5%	6%	8%	9%	10%	11%	12%	15%
1	.98039	.97561	.97087	.96156	.95238	.94340	.92593	.91743	.90909	.90090	.89286	.86957
2	.96117	.95181	.94260	.92456	.90703	.89000	.85734	.84168	.82645	.81162	.79719	.75614
3	.94232	.92860	.91514	.88900	.86384	.83962	.79383	.77218	.75132	.73119	.71178	.65752
4	.92385	.90595	.88849	.85480	.82270	.79209	.73503	.70843	.68301	.65873	.63552	.57175
5	.90583	.88385	.86261	.82193	.78353	.74726	.68058	.64993	.62092	.59345	.56743	.49718
6	.88797	.86230	.83748	.79031	.74622	.70496	.63017	.59627	.56447	.53464	.50663	.43233
7	.87056	.84127	.81309	.75992	.71068	.66506	.58349	.54703	.51316	.48166	.45235	.37594
8	.85349	.82075	.78941	.73069	.67684	.62741	.54027	.50187	.46651	.43393	.40388	.32690
9	.83676	.80073	.76642	.70259	.64461	.59190	.50025	.46043	.42410	.39092	.36061	.28426
10	.82035	.78120	.74409	.67556	.61391	.55839	.46319	.42241	.38554	.35218	.32197	.24719
11	.80426	.76214	.72242	.64958	.58468	.52679	.42888	.38753	.35049	.31728	.28748	.21494
12	.78849	.74356	.70138	.62460	.55684	.49697	.39711	.35554	.31863	.28584	.25668	.18691
13	.77303	.72542	.68095	.60057	.53032	.46884	.36770	.32618	.28966	.25751	.22917	.16253
14	.75788	.70773	.66112	.57748	.50507	.44230	.34046	.29925	.26333	.23199	.20462	.14133
15	.74301	.69047	.64186	.55526	.48102	.41727	.31524	.27454	.23939	.20900	.18270	.12289
16	.72845	.67362	.62317	.53391	.45811	.39365	.29189	.25187	.21763	.18829	.16312	.10687
17	.71416	.65720	.60502	.51337	.43630	.37136	.27027	.23107	.19785	.16963	.14564	.09293
18	.70016	.64117	.58739	.49363	.41552	.35034	.25025	.21199	.17986	.15282	.13004	.08081
19	.68643	.62553	.57029	.47464	.39573	.33051	.23171	.19449	.16351	.13768	.11611	.07027
20	.67297	.61027	.55368	.45639	.37689	.31180	.21455	.17843	.14864	.12403	.10367	.06110
21	.65978	.59539	.53755	.43883	.35894	.29416	.19866	.16370	.13513	.11174	.09256	.05313
22	.64684	.58086	.52189	.42196	.34185	.27751	.18394	.15018	.12285	.10067	.08264	.04620
23	.63416	.56670	.50669	.40573	.32557	.26180	.17032	.13778	.11168	.09069	.07379	.04017
24	.62172	.55288	.49193	.39012	.31007	.24698	.15770	.12641	.10153	.08170	.06588	.03493
25	.60953	.53939	.47761	.37512	.29530	.23300	.14602	.11597	.09230	.07361	.05882	.03038
26	.59758	.52623	.46369	.36069	.28124	.21981	.13520	.10639	.08391	.06631	.05252	.02642
27	.58586	.51340	.45019	.34682	.26785	.20737	.12519	.09761	.07628	.05974	.04689	.02297
28	.57437	.50088	.43708	.33348	.25509	.19563	.11591	.08955	.06934	.05382	.04187	.01997
29	.56311	.48866	.42435	.32065	.24295	.18456	.10733	.08216	.06304	.04849	.03738	.01737
30	.55207	.47674	.41199	.30832	.23138	.17411	.09938	.07537	.05731	.04368	.03338	.01510
31	.54125	.46511	.39999	.29646	.22036	.16425	.09202	.06915	.05210	.03935	.02980	.01313
32	.53063	.45377	.38834	.28506	.20987	.15496	.08520	.06344	.04736	.03545	.02661	.01142
33	.52023	.44270	.37703	.27409	.19987	.14619	.07889	.05820	.04306	.03194	.02376	.00993
34	.51003	.43191	.36604	.26355	.19035	.13791	.07305	.05340	.03914	.02878	.02121	.00864
35	.50003	.42137	.35538	.25342	.18129	.13011	.06763	.04899	.03558	.02592	.01894	.00751
36	.49022	.41109	.34503	.24367	.17266	.12274	.06262	.04494	.03235	.02335	.01691	.00653
37	.48061	.40107	.33498	.23430	.16444	.11579	.05799	.04123	.02941	.02104	.01510	.00568
38	.47119	.39128	.32523	.22529	.15661	.10924	.05369	.03783	.02674	.01896	.01348	.00494
39	.46195	.38174	.31575	.21662	.14915	.10306	.04971	.03470	.02430	.01708	.01204	.00429
40	.45289	.37243	.30656	.20829	.14205	.09722	.04603	.03184	.02210	.01538	.01075	.00373

Time Value of Money

Table A-3

FUTURE VALUE OF AN ORDINARY ANNUITY OF 1

$$FVF-OA_{n,\,i} = \frac{(1+i)^n - 1}{i}$$

(n) periods	2%	2½%	3%	4%	5%	6%	8%	9%	10%	11%	12%	15%
1	1.00000	1.00000	1.00000	1.00000	1.00000	1.00000	1.00000	1.00000	1.00000	1.00000	1.00000	1.00000
2	2.02000	2.02500	2.03000	2.04000	2.05000	2.06000	2.08000	2.09000	2.10000	2.11000	2.12000	2.15000
3	3.06040	3.07563	3.09090	3.12160	3.15250	3.18360	3.24640	3.27810	3.31000	3.34210	3.37440	3.47250
4	4.12161	4.15252	4.18363	4.24646	4.31013	4.37462	4.50611	4.57313	4.64100	4.70973	4.77933	4.99338
5	5.20404	5.25633	5.30914	5.41632	5.52563	5.63709	5.86660	5.98471	6.10510	6.22780	6.35285	6.74238
6	6.30812	6.38774	6.46841	6.63298	6.80191	6.97532	7.33592	7.52334	7.71561	7.91286	8.11519	8.75374
7	7.43428	7.54743	7.66246	7.89829	8.14201	8.39384	8.92280	9.20044	9.48717	9.78327	10.08901	11.06680
8	8.58297	8.73612	8.89234	9.21423	9.54911	9.89747	10.63663	11.02847	11.43589	11.85943	12.29969	13.72682
9	9.75463	9.95452	10.15911	10.58280	11.02656	11.49132	12.48756	13.02104	13.57948	14.16397	14.77566	16.78584
10	10.94972	11.20338	11.46338	12.00611	12.57789	13.18079	14.48656	15.19293	15.93743	16.72201	17.54874	20.30372
11	12.16872	12.48347	12.80780	13.48635	14.20679	14.97164	16.64549	17.56029	18.53117	19.56143	20.65458	24.34928
12	13.41209	13.79555	14.19203	15.02581	15.91713	16.86994	18.97713	20.14072	21.38428	22.71319	24.13313	29.00167
13	14.68033	15.14044	15.61779	16.62684	17.71298	18.88214	21.49530	22.95339	24.52271	26.21164	28.02911	34.35192
14	15.97394	16.51895	17.08632	18.29191	19.59863	21.01507	24.21492	26.01919	27.97498	30.09492	32.39260	40.50471
15	17.29342	17.93193	18.59891	20.02359	21.57856	23.27597	27.15211	29.36092	31.77248	34.40536	37.27972	47.58041
16	18.63929	19.38022	20.15688	21.82453	23.65749	25.67253	30.32428	33.00340	35.94973	39.18995	42.75328	55.71747
17	20.01207	20.86473	21.76159	23.69751	25.84037	28.21288	33.75023	36.97371	40.54470	44.50084	48.88367	65.07509
18	21.41231	22.38635	23.41444	25.64541	28.13238	30.90565	37.45024	41.30134	45.59917	50.39593	55.74972	75.83636
19	22.84056	23.94601	25.11687	27.67123	30.53900	33.75999	41.44626	46.01846	51.15909	56.93949	63.43968	88.21181
20	24.29737	25.54466	26.87037	29.77808	33.06595	36.78559	45.76196	51.16012	57.27500	64.20283	72.05244	102.44358
21	25.78332	27.18327	28.67649	31.96920	35.71925	39.99273	50.42292	56.76453	64.00250	72.26514	81.69874	118.81012
22	27.29898	28.86286	30.53678	34.24797	38.50521	43.39229	55.45676	62.87334	71.40275	81.21431	92.50258	137.63164
23	28.84496	30.58443	32.45288	36.61789	41.43048	46.99583	60.89330	69.53194	79.54302	91.14788	104.60289	159.27638
24	30.42186	32.34904	34.42647	39.08260	44.50200	50.81558	66.76476	76.78981	88.49733	102.17415	118.15524	184.16784
25	32.03030	34.15776	36.45926	41.64591	47.72710	54.86451	73.10594	84.70090	98.34706	114.41331	133.33387	212.79302
26	33.67091	36.01171	38.55304	44.31174	51.11345	59.15638	79.95442	93.32398	109.18177	127.99877	150.33393	245.71197
27	35.34432	37.91200	40.70963	47.08421	54.66913	63.70577	87.35077	102.72314	121.09994	143.07864	169.37401	283.56877
28	37.05121	39.85990	42.93092	49.96758	58.40258	68.52811	95.33883	112.96822	134.20994	159.81729	190.69889	327.10408
29	38.79223	41.85630	45.21885	52.96629	62.32271	73.63980	103.96594	124.13536	148.63093	178.39719	214.58275	377.16969
30	40.56808	43.90270	47.57542	56.08494	66.43885	79.05819	113.28321	136.30754	164.49402	199.02088	241.33268	434.74515
31	42.37944	46.00027	50.00268	59.32834	70.76079	84.80168	123.34587	149.57522	181.94343	221.91317	271.29261	500.95692
32	44.22703	48.15028	52.50276	62.70147	75.29883	90.88978	134.21354	164.03699	201.13777	247.32362	304.84772	577.10046
33	46.11157	50.35403	55.07784	66.20953	80.06377	97.34316	145.95062	179.80032	222.25154	275.52922	342.42945	644.66553
34	48.03380	52.61289	57.73018	69.85791	85.06696	104.18376	158.62667	196.98234	245.47670	306.83744	384.52098	765.36535
35	49.99448	54.92821	60.46208	73.65222	90.32031	111.43478	172.31680	215.71076	271.02437	341.58955	431.66350	881.17016
36	51.99437	57.30141	63.27594	77.59831	95.83632	119.12087	187.10215	236.12472	299.12681	380.16441	484.46312	1014.34568
37	54.03425	59.73395	66.17422	81.70225	101.62814	127.26812	203.07032	258.37595	330.03949	422.98249	543.59869	1167.49753
38	56.11494	62.22730	69.15945	85.97034	107.70955	135.90421	220.31595	282.62978	364.04343	470.51056	609.83053	1343.62216
39	58.23724	64.78298	72.23423	90.40915	114.09502	145.05846	238.94122	309.06646	401.44778	523.26673	684.01020	1546.16549
40	60.40198	67.40255	75.40126	95.02552	120.79977	154.76197	259.05652	337.88245	442.59256	581.82607	767.09142	1779.09031

Table A-4

PRESENT VALUE OF AN ORDINARY ANNUITY OF 1

$$PVF-OA_{n,\,i} = \frac{1 - \dfrac{1}{(1+i)^n}}{i}$$

(n) periods	2%	2½%	3%	4%	5%	6%	8%	9%	10%	11%	12%	15%
1	.98039	.97561	.97087	.96154	.95238	.94340	.92593	.91743	.90909	.90090	.89286	.86957
2	1.94156	1.92742	1.91347	1.88609	1.85941	1.83339	1.78326	1.75911	1.73554	1.71252	1.69005	1.62571
3	2.88388	2.85602	2.82861	2.77509	2.72325	2.67301	2.57710	2.53130	2.48685	2.44371	2.40183	2.28323
4	3.80773	3.76197	3.71710	3.62990	3.54595	3.46511	3.31213	3.23972	3.16986	3.10245	3.03735	2.85498
5	4.71346	4.64583	4.57971	4.45182	4.32948	4.21236	3.99271	3.88965	3.79079	3.69590	3.60478	3.35216
6	5.60143	5.50813	5.41719	5.24214	5.07569	4.91732	4.62288	4.48592	4.35526	4.23054	4.11141	3.78448
7	6.4/199	6.34939	6.23028	6.00205	5.78637	5.58238	5.20637	5.03295	4.86842	4.71220	4.56376	4.16042
8	7.32548	7.17014	7.01969	6.73274	6.46321	6.20979	5.74664	5.53482	5.33493	5.14612	4.96764	4.48732
9	8.16224	7.97087	7.78611	7.43533	7.10782	6.80169	6.24689	5.99525	5.75902	5.53705	5.32825	4.77158
10	8.98259	8.75206	8.53020	8.11090	7.72173	7.36009	6.71008	6.41766	6.14457	5.88923	5.65022	5.01877
11	9.78685	9.51421	9.25262	8.76048	8.30641	7.88687	7.13896	6.80519	6.49506	6.20652	5.93770	5.23371
12	10.57534	10.25776	9.95400	9.38507	8.86325	8.38384	7.53608	7.16073	6.81369	6.49236	6.19437	5.42062
13	11.34837	10.98319	10.63496	9.98565	9.39357	8.85268	7.90378	7.48690	7.10336	6.74987	6.42355	5.58315
14	12.10625	11.69091	11.29607	10.56312	9.89864	9.29498	8.24424	7.78615	7.36669	6.98187	6.62817	5.72448
15	12.84926	12.38138	11.93794	11.11839	10.37966	9.71225	8.55948	8.06069	7.60608	7.19087	6.81086	5.84737
16	13.57771	13.05500	12.56110	11.65230	10.83777	10.10590	8.85137	8.31256	7.82371	7.37916	6.97399	5.95424
17	14.29187	13.71220	13.16612	12.16567	11.27407	10.47726	9.12164	8.54363	8.02155	7.54879	7.11963	6.04716
18	14.99203	14.35336	13.75351	12.65930	11.68959	10.82760	9.37189	8.75563	8.20141	7.70162	7.24967	6.12797
19	15.67846	14.97889	14.32380	13.13394	12.08532	11.15812	9.60360	8.95012	8.36492	7.83929	7.36578	6.19823
20	16.35143	15.58916	14.87747	13.59033	12.46221	11.46992	9.81815	9.12855	8.51356	7.96333	7.46944	6.25933
21	17.01121	16.18455	15.41502	14.02916	12.82115	11.76408	10.01680	9.29224	8.64869	8.07507	7.56200	6.31246
22	17.65805	16.76541	15.93692	14.45112	13.16800	12.04158	10.20074	9.44243	8.77154	8.17574	7.64465	6.35866
23	18.29220	17.33211	16.44361	14.85684	13.48857	12.30338	10.37106	9.58021	8.88322	8.26643	7.71843	6.39884
24	18.91393	17.88499	16.93554	15.24696	13.79864	12.55036	10.52876	9.70661	8.98474	8.34814	7.78432	6.43377
25	19.52346	18.42438	17.41315	15.62208	14.09394	12.78336	10.67478	9.82258	9.07704	8.42174	7.84314	6.46415
26	20.12104	18.95061	17.87684	15.98277	14.37519	13.00317	10.80998	9.92897	9.16095	8.48806	7.89566	6.49056
27	20.70690	19.46401	18.32703	16.32959	14.64303	13.21053	10.93516	10.02658	9.23722	8.45780	7.94255	6.51353
28	21.28127	19.96489	18.76411	16.66306	14.89813	13.40616	11.05108	10.11613	9.30657	8.60162	7.98442	6.53351
29	21.84438	20.45355	19.18845	16.98371	15.14107	13.59072	11.15841	10.19828	9.36961	8.65011	8.02181	6.55088
30	22.39646	20.93029	19.60044	17.29203	15.37245	13.76483	11.25778	10.27365	9.42691	8.69379	8.05518	6.56598
31	22.93770	21.39541	20.00043	17.58849	15.59281	13.92909	11.34980	10.34280	9.47901	8.73315	8.08499	6.57911
32	23.46833	21.84918	20.38877	17.87355	15.80268	14.08404	11.43500	10.40624	9.52638	8.76860	8.11159	6.59053
33	23.98856	22.29188	20.76579	18.14765	16.00255	14.23023	11.51389	10.46444	9.56943	8.80054	8.13535	6.60046
34	24.49859	22.72379	21.13184	18.41120	16.19290	14.36814	11.58693	10.51784	9.60858	8.82932	8.15656	6.60910
35	24.99862	23.14516	21.48722	18.66461	16.37419	14.49825	11.65457	10.56682	9.64416	8.85524	8.17550	6.61661
36	25.48884	23.55625	21.83225	18.90828	16.54685	14.62099	11.71719	10.61176	9.67651	8.87859	8.19241	6.62314
37	25.96945	23.95732	22.16724	19.14258	16.71129	14.73678	11.77518	10.65299	9.70592	8.89963	8.20751	6.62882
38	26.44064	24.34860	22.49246	19.36786	16.86789	14.84602	11.82887	10.69082	9.73265	8.91859	8.22099	6.63375
39	26.90259	24.73034	22.80822	19.58448	17.01704	14.94907	11.87858	10.72552	9.75697	8.93567	8.23303	6.63805
40	27.35548	25.10278	23.11477	19.79277	17.15909	15.04630	11.92461	10.75736	9.77905	8.95105	8.24378	6.64178

Time Value of Money

Table A-5

PRESENT VALUE OF AN ANNUITY DUE OF 1

$$PVF - AD_{n,\,i} = 1 + \frac{1 - \dfrac{1}{(1+i)^{n-1}}}{i}$$

(n) periods	2%	2½%	3%	4%	5%	6%	8%	9%	10%	11%	12%	15%
1	1.00000	1.00000	1.00000	1.00000	1.00000	1.00000	1.00000	1.00000	1.00000	1.00000	1.00000	1.00000
2	1.98039	1.97561	1.97087	1.96154	1.95238	1.94340	1.92593	1.91743	1.90909	1.90090	1.89286	1.86957
3	2.94156	2.92742	2.91347	2.88609	2.85941	2.83339	2.78326	2.75911	2.73554	2.71252	2.69005	2.62571
4	3.88388	3.85602	3.82861	3.77509	3.72325	3.67301	3.57710	3.53130	3.48685	3.44371	3.40183	3.28323
5	4.80773	4.76197	4.71710	4.62990	4.54595	4.46511	4.31213	4.23972	4.16986	4.10245	4.03735	3.85498
6	5.71346	5.64583	5.57971	5.45182	5.32948	5.21236	4.99271	4.88965	4.79079	4.69590	4.60478	4.35216
7	6.60143	6.50813	6.41719	6.24214	6.07569	5.91732	5.62288	5.48592	5.35526	5.23054	5.11141	4.78448
8	7.47199	7.34939	7.23028	7.00205	6.78637	6.58238	6.20637	6.03295	5.86842	5.71220	5.56376	5.16042
9	8.32548	8.17014	8.01969	7.73274	7.46321	7.20979	6.74664	6.53482	6.33493	6.14612	5.96764	5.48732
10	9.16224	8.97087	8.78611	8.43533	8.10782	7.80169	7.24689	6.99525	6.75902	6.53705	6.32825	5.77158
11	9.98259	9.75206	9.53020	9.11090	8.72173	8.36009	7.71008	7.41766	7.14457	6.88923	6.65022	6.01877
12	10.78685	10.51421	10.25262	9.76048	9.30641	8.88687	8.13896	7.80519	7.49506	7.20652	6.93770	6.23371
13	11.57534	11.25776	10.95400	10.38507	9.86325	9.38384	8.53608	8.16073	7.81369	7.49236	7.19437	6.42062
14	12.34837	11.98319	11.63496	10.98565	10.39357	9.85268	8.90378	8.48690	8.10336	7.74987	7.42355	6.58315
15	13.10625	12.69091	12.29607	11.56312	10.89864	10.29498	9.24424	8.78615	9.36669	7.98187	7.62817	6.72448
16	13.84926	13.38138	12.93794	12.11839	11.37966	10.71225	9.55948	9.06069	8.60608	8.19087	7.81086	6.84737
17	14.57771	14.05500	13.56110	12.65230	11.83777	11.10590	9.85137	9.31256	8.82371	8.37916	7.97399	6.95424
18	15.29187	14.71220	14.16612	13.16567	12.27407	11.47726	10.12164	9.54363	9.02155	8.54879	8.11963	7.04716
19	15.99203	15.35336	14.75351	13.65930	12.68959	11.82760	10.37189	9.75563	9.20141	8.70162	8.24967	7.12797
20	16.67846	15.97889	15.32380	14.13394	13.08532	12.15812	10.60360	9.95012	9.36492	8.83929	8.36578	7.19823
21	17.35143	16.58916	15.87747	14.59033	13.46221	12.46992	10.81815	10.12855	9.51356	8.96333	8.46944	7.25933
22	18.01121	17.18455	16.41502	15.02916	13.82115	12.76408	11.01680	10.29224	9.64869	9.07507	8.56200	7.31246
23	18.65805	17.76541	16.93692	15.45112	14.16300	13.04158	11.20074	10.44243	9.77154	9.17574	8.64465	7.35866
24	19.29220	18.33211	17.44361	15.85684	14.48857	13.30338	11.37106	10.58021	9.88322	9.26643	8.71843	7.39884
25	19.91393	18.88499	17.93554	16.24696	14.79864	13.55036	11.52876	10.70661	9.98474	9.34814	8.78432	7.43377
26	20.52346	19.42438	18.41315	16.62208	15.09394	13.78336	11.67478	10.82258	10.07704	9.42174	8.84314	7.46415
27	21.12104	19.95061	18.87684	16.98277	15.37519	14.00317	11.80998	10.92897	10.16095	9.48806	8.89566	7.49056
28	21.70690	20.46401	19.32703	17.32959	15.64303	14.21053	11.93518	11.02658	10.23722	9.54780	8.94255	7.51353
29	22.28127	20.96489	19.76411	17.66306	15.89813	14.40616	12.05108	11.11613	10.30657	9.60162	8.98442	7.53351
30	22.84438	21.45355	20.18845	17.98371	16.14107	14.59072	12.15841	11.19828	10.36961	9.65011	9.02181	7.55088
31	23.39646	21.93029	20.60044	18.29203	16.37245	14.76483	12.25778	11.27365	10.42691	9.69379	9.05518	7.56598
32	23.93770	22.39541	21.00043	18.58849	16.59281	14.92909	12.34980	11.34280	10.47901	9.73315	9.08499	7.57911
33	24.46833	22.84918	21.38877	18.87355	16.80268	15.08404	12.43500	11.40624	10.52638	9.76860	9.11159	7.59053
34	24.98856	23.29188	21.76579	19.14765	17.00255	15.23023	12.51389	11.46444	10.56943	9.80054	9.13535	7.60046
35	25.49859	23.72379	22.13184	19.41120	17.19290	15.36814	12.58693	11.51784	10.60858	9.82932	9.15656	7.60910
36	25.99862	24.14516	22.48722	19.66461	17.37419	15.49825	12.65457	11.56682	10.64416	9.85524	9.17550	7.61661
37	26.48884	24.55625	22.83225	19.90828	17.54685	15.62099	12.71719	11.61176	10.67651	9.87859	9.19241	7.62314
38	26.96945	24.95732	23.16724	20.14258	17.71129	15.73678	12.77518	11.65299	10.70592	9.89963	9.20751	7.62882
39	27.44064	25.34860	23.49246	20.36786	17.86789	15.84602	12.82887	11.69082	10.73265	9.91859	9.22099	7.63375
40	27.90259	25.73034	23.80822	20.58448	18.01704	15.94907	12.87858	11.72552	10.75697	9.93567	9.23303	7.63805

COMPANY INDEX

SUBJECT INDEX